Fodor's 2002

Great Britain

S0-BNF-583

Fodor's Travel Publications • New York, Toronto, London, Sydney, Auckland
www.fodors.com

CONTENTS

Destination Great Britain 5
Great Itineraries 26
Fodor's Choice 30

1 LONDON 33
Exploring London 38
CLOSE-UP *Just Remember to Address Her as "Your Majesty"* 46
CLOSE-UP *Shakespeare Lives! Rebirth of the Globe Theatre* 70
Dining 80
Lodging 94
Nightlife and the Arts 104
Outdoor Activities and Sports 110
Shopping 111
London A to Z 120

2 THE SOUTHEAST 126
Canterbury to Dover 132
Along the South Coast: Rye to Glyndebourne 140
Brighton to East Grinstead 145
Masterpieces and Moats: From Tunbridge Wells to Finchcocks 156
CLOSE-UP *"Doing the Statelies": Visiting the Treasure Houses of England* 159
Southeast A to Z 164

3 THE SOUTH 167
From Winchester to Southampton 174
CLOSE-UP *In Search of Jane Austen* 179
Isle of Wight 183
Salisbury, Stonehenge, and the New Forest 186
Far from the Madding Crowd: Bournemouth to Lyme Regis 196
The South A to Z 204

4 THE WEST COUNTRY 207
King Arthur Country: From Bristol to Tintagel 214
The Cornwall Coast: On the Road to Plymouth 224
Dartmoor, Torbay, and Exeter 236
The West Country A to Z 246

5 THE CHANNEL ISLANDS 249
Channel Islands A to Z 263

6 THE THAMES VALLEY 266
Royal Berkshire: Windsor and Environs 272
"Wind in the Willows" Country: To and From Henley 279
Oxford 283
On the Road to Blenheim Palace 290
Thames Valley A to Z 295

7 SHAKESPEARE COUNTRY 298
Stratford-upon-Avon 303
In and Around Shakespeare Country 311
Shakespeare Country A to Z 319

8 THE HEART OF ENGLAND 321
Bath and Environs 326
The Cotswolds 334
CLOSE-UP *And the Most Beautiful Place in the Cotswolds is . . .* 347
Gloucester, Berkeley, and the Forest of Dean 348
The Heart of England A to Z 353

9 THE WELSH BORDERS 357
Birmingham 362
From Worcester to Dudley 369

Skirting the "Black Country":
From Shrewsbury to Chester 378
Welsh Borders A to Z 385

10 WALES 388
North Wales: In the Realm
of Snowdonia 393
Mid-Wales: The Historic Heartland 405
South Wales: From Cardiff to
Cardigan 412
Wales A to Z 422

11 LANCASHIRE AND
THE PEAKS 426
Manchester 430
Liverpool 441
The Peak District: On the Road to
Chatsworth and Haddon Hall 449
Lancashire and the Peaks A to Z 455

12 THE LAKE DISTRICT 460
The Southern Lakes 466
Penrith and the Northern Lakes 476
Lake District A to Z 482

13 EAST ANGLIA 486
Cambridge 492
From Ely to Bury St. Edmunds 502
Norwich to North Norfolk 508
Colchester and the
Aldeburgh Coast 515
Beyond the Fens: Lincoln, Boston,
and Stamford 521
East Anglia A to Z 526

14 YORKSHIRE 529
West Yorkshire and Brontë Country 533
The Yorkshire Dales 542
York 547
York Environs 554
The North Yorkshire Coast 557
The North York Moors 563
Yorkshire A to Z 566
CLOSE-UP Revisiting Brideshead: Calling
on Castle Howard 567

15 THE NORTHEAST 571
Durham and Its Environs 575
Hadrian's Wall Country 585
The Far Northeast Coast 591
The Northeast A to Z 595

16 SCOTLAND: EDINBURGH TO
THE HIGHLANDS 598
Edinburgh 605
Glasgow 621
The Borders: Sir Walter Scott
Country 630
Aberdeen and Royal Deeside 635
Inverness and Loch Ness 642
Scotland A to Z 645

17 BACKGROUND AND
ESSENTIALS 651
Portraits of Great Britain 652
Books and Videos 663
Chronology 666
Map of Great Britain 670
Smart Travel Tips A to Z 672

INDEX 705

MAPS

LONDON 40–41
London Postal Districts 42
London Dining 82–83
London Lodging 96–97
London Shopping 112–113

THE SOUTHEAST
130–131
Canterbury 133
Brighton 147

THE SOUTH 172–173
Winchester 175
Salisbury 187

THE WEST COUNTRY
210–211
Plymouth 235

THE CHANNEL
ISLANDS 251
St. Helier 254
St. Peter Port 259

THE THAMES
VALLEY 270–271
Windsor Castle 273
Oxford 284

SHAKESPEARE
COUNTRY 302
Stratford-upon-Avon 304

THE HEART OF
ENGLAND
Bath Environs 327
Bath 328
The Cotswold Hills 336
The Forest of Dean 349

THE WELSH
BORDERS 360
Birmingham 363
Shrewsbury 379

WALES 394–395
Aberystwyth 409
Cardiff 413

LANCASHIRE AND
THE PEAKS 430
Manchester 432
Liverpool 443

THE LAKE DISTRICT
464–465

EAST ANGLIA 490–491
Cambridge 493
Norwich 510
Lincolnshire 522

YORKSHIRE 534–535
York 550

THE NORTHEAST 574
Durham 576

SCOTLAND
The Scottish Borders 603
Glasgow Environs 604
Edinburgh 607
Glasgow 624
Royal Deeside 636
Inverness and Environs 643

GREAT BRITAIN 670–671

Circled letters in text correspond to letters on the photographs. For more information on the sights pictured, turn
to the indicated page number Ⓐ⟩ on each photograph.

DESTINATION
GREAT BRITAIN

An afternoon at York's historic Middlethorpe Hall reveals Britain at its most appealing. The house is so stately it must be a mirage, headily perfumed by flowers. A spot of sun emerges, fleetingly, and you half expect to encounter a character out of English literature. The experience is all the finer because you know that wherever you find yourself on this island, you may come upon some other charming grace note just around the next bend. That may be an enchanted castle or a village whose clocks seem to have stopped two centuries ago, a brooding moor or a glittering loch rimmed by craggy peaks, a half-timbered Tudor house out of a postcard or a long-distance footpath where you can tramp for miles with a view of the sea. Little wonder the atlas marks this realm as *Great* Britain.

LONDON

The city of Ⓐ**Big Ben** is one of the most vibrant places on the planet, thanks to outrageous restaurants created by superstar chefs and stylish boutiques like ©**Jigsaw** on New Bond Street. Yet despite the buzz, Europe's largest metropolis remains the bastion of just about everything the British traditionally hold most dear. Have tea at the Savoy, stroll through Kensington Gardens or Hyde Park, ogle the jewels in the Tower of London, or explore the British Museum. As you get to know this fascinating city, the national character begins to reveal itself. Treasure troves like Kensington Palace and Ⓓ**Apsley House,** once home to the Duke of Wellington, exhibit the national fondness for heroes— after all, this was the duke who defeated Napoléon at Waterloo and gave his name to

Ⓐ▷ 47

Ⓑ▷ 47

JIG Ⓒ▷ 117

Wellies, essential foot protection against English downpours. Landmarks like the Dickens House and the Globe Theatre, a replica of Shakespeare's original, recall the English way with words. At the ⒻSherlock Holmes pub, which is filled with memorabilia about the fictional detective, you can bend an elbow with other fans. And the fabled British reserve is on display in front of the Horse Guards, where members of

the ⒷMounted guard keep a stiff upper lip when standing still as statues through drizzle, as well as through the most reassuring—and longest running—show in town. This is not at a theater in the West End or even a performing arts venue such as ⒺRoyal Albert Hall. It's the pageant that unfurls nearly every day at Horse Guards, Whitehall, and outside Buckingham Palace: the Changing of the Guard. Probably the most-photographed shift change in the world, this time-honored ceremony proves that even as London's trends come and go, the essence of the city will endure.

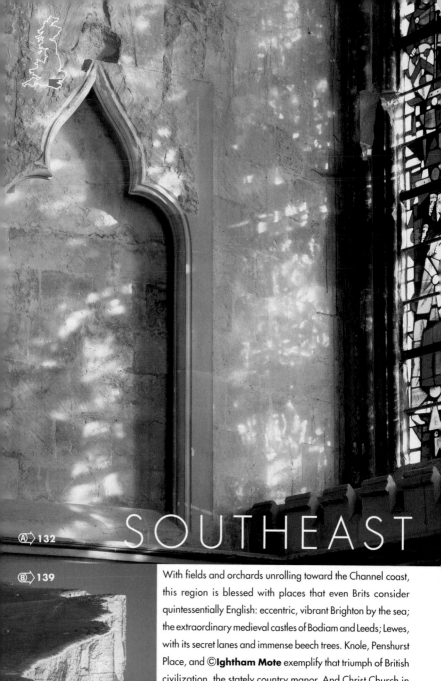

SOUTHEAST

Ⓐ 132

Ⓑ 139

With fields and orchards unrolling toward the Channel coast, this region is blessed with places that even Brits consider quintessentially English: eccentric, vibrant Brighton by the sea; the extraordinary medieval castles of Bodiam and Leeds; Lewes, with its secret lanes and immense beech trees. Knole, Penshurst Place, and Ⓒ**Ightham Mote** exemplify that triumph of British civilization, the stately country manor. And Christ Church in Ⓐ**Canterbury** is the most beloved of cathedrals, immortalized by Geoffrey Chaucer. Towering above the sea are the Ⓑ**White Cliffs of Dover,** cherished symbols of the realm.

Ⓒ 161

SOUTH

If Jane Austen's countryside "sweet to the eye and mind" seems familiar, it may be because so much of English history has been played out here. In prehistoric times, stone monuments such as Avebury and Ⓐ**Stonehenge** rose on the plains. Winchester was England's capital until the 11th century; its cathedral huge

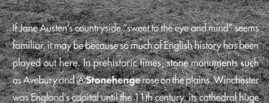

Ⓑⰻ191

Ⓒⰻ191

and imposing. Ⓑ**Stourhead** and other stately homes, such as Wilton House and Longleat House, evoke just the sort of "English culture, English verdure and English comfort" that Austen described so vividly in her novels. In the 19th century, Ⓒ**Shaftesbury** inspired another literary titan, Thomas Hardy. Yet even without this claim to fame, the South remains as sweet a corner of rural England as you're likely to encounter.

9

Leaving the beaten path is the way to explore Somerset, Devon, and Cornwall—unless that path is the cobbled causeway to the island-fortress near

Ⓐ 223

THE WEST COUNTRY

Penzance, ©**St. Michael's Mount.** Other rambles inevitably lead to ancient market towns, windswept beaches, and mellow villages like Boscastle and ®**Buckland-in-the-Moor** in boggy Dartmoor. And in King Arthur Country it's hard not to stumble upon structures linked to medieval legends—ruined Glastonbury Abbey and Ⓐ**Tintagel Castle** would be romantic even without their connection to the once and future king.

Ⓑ 236

© 229

THE CHANNEL ISLANDS

Ⓐ〉258

Ⓑ〉256

Jersey, Ⓐ**Guernsey,** and their out-islets, off the Brittany coast, reveal Britain with a Gallic slant—most islanders speak French and observe Norman customs. Even more exotically, these landfalls are endowed with an attribute that every British man, woman, and child craves—sunshine. Gardens flourish; witness the rare blooms at Jersey's Ⓒ**Eric Young Orchid Foundation.** Beach lovers fan out from St. Peter Port and St. Helier to explore the islands' sandy coves. Between VAT-free shopping in branches of England's major chain stores and naps on the spectacular white sands, you can take in the glittering sea-and-sky panoramas from clifftop footpaths or from Jersey's Ⓑ**Gorey Castle,** proud atop its granite rock.

Ⓒ〉256

Ⓐ 277

The rose-cloaked countryside that flanks this stretch of old father Thames has become something of a weekend destination for sophisticated Londoners. Rarefied social occasions persist here: the annual meeting at Ⓐ**Ascot,** the world's most famous horse race, and the Ⓓ**Henley Royal Regatta,** rowing's toniest

THE THAMES VALLEY

Ⓑ 283

competition and the occasion for an opulent lawn party that draws thousands. Since the 12th century, spired-and-turreted Ⓑ©**Oxford** has educated the nation's elite. Lewis Carroll invented Alice along Oxford's River Cherwell. The Duke of Marlborough's Blenheim Palace and Ⓔ**Windsor,** the largest inhabited castle in England and home to eight successive royal houses, are both here. These great houses take the biscuit for splendor, and there are many others nearby; Diana, the late Princess of Wales, is buried at Althorp. But before you assume that these well-groomed riverbanks belong only to the titled and entitled, remember that Western Europe took its boldest step toward democracy here when King John signed the Magna Carta at Runnymede in 1215.

© 283

D 267

E 272

With its slow-moving river patrolled regally by swans, ⒶⒷ**Stratford-upon-Avon** would be lovely even without the omnipresent reminders of its famous son. But clearly the chief reason to visit this bustling town is to walk in the Bard's footsteps. This might entail strolling across the lawns and among the flower beds in Bancroft Gardens; touring Ⓒ**Shakespeare's Birthplace,** the half-timbered cottage where Master Will was born in an upstairs room; following a footpath beneath apple and hawthorn trees to Ⓔ**Anne Hathaway's Cottage**; or applauding the peerless

Ⓐ▷ 303

SHAKESPEARE COUNTRY

Ⓑ▷ 303

ⓒ ▷308

plays in performances at the Royal Shakespeare Theatre. When you move on you will find that the rest of Warwickshire puts on a pretty good show. This is a gentle countryside, a merry old England of thatch-roof cottages, sleepy villages, sun-dappled meadows, and stately country seats. Stratford shares the limelight with landmarks such as Baddesley Clinton and Ⓓ**Warwick Castle,** whose turrets, towers, and historic turbulence have earned it the moniker "medieval England in stone." Or visit Charlecote Park, home to the Fairfax-Lucy family for 500 years, and let the centuries roll back—Shakespeare reputedly poached some of the family deer back when. The back roads here do not accommodate tour buses, and impenetrable ivy often renders villages of time-worn stone nearly invisible. But for the TV antennae, the region's houses all look like parsonages out of a *Masterpiece Theater* saga. The prize goes to the Marquess of Northampton's legendary abode, Compton Wynyates. But all are worthy of more than passing admiration.

Ⓓ ▷313

Ⓔ ▷ 306

15

HEART OF
ENGLAND

In the sleepy hamlets of the Cotswolds, stone cottages, old coaching inns, and tile-roof farmsteads add up to England at its most delightfully rural. Bourton-on-the-Water and Chipping Campden are among the area's rich, well-tended towns, along with Lower Slaughter (one of the most idyllic villages imaginable, despite its sinister name). But to judge from the traffic, everyone goes to Ⓓ**Broadway,** notable for its close-clipped

Ⓑ〉343

Ⓒ〉326

lawns and historic inns. The town of Stow-on-the-Wold is home to fine antiques shops such as David Rosa's Ⓑ**Country Life Antiques.** But don't come expecting bargains: after all, these heavenly tracts are as refined as they are pastoral. Royals and poets have long sojourned nearby in ⒶⒸ**Bath,** sipping waters that tasted, as Dickens told us, of "warm flat irons." England's best-planned town, Bath is dotted with Regency terraces and Georgian villas, and it continues to evoke all that was most wonderful in 18th-century England.

Ⓓ〉340

A 385

THE WELSH BORDERS

B 378

Before England relinquishes her turf to Wales, she lays on an extra measure of charm, as if to persuade travelers to linger. Some of England's loveliest countryside rises and drops over the hills and valleys of Shropshire, Herefordshire, and Cheshire. Everywhere are well-kept farms, surrounded by meadows and drystone walls. Civilization does intrude, but in enticing ways. Brooding castles loom over the landscape. Ballet, orchestral music, and theater flourish in Birmingham; it also has the Birmingham Museum and Art Gallery, full of Victorian masterworks. Worcester has its proud cathedral. And half-timbered "magpie" buildings line elegant avenues in Ludlow. ⒶLittle Moreton Hall is the most atmospheric of these country houses, but there are others in Tudor England's bold black-and-white style in historic ©Chester. Don't forget to visit medieval ⒷShrewsbury for a bit of time travel that might include a session in the abbey's scriptorium.

© 383

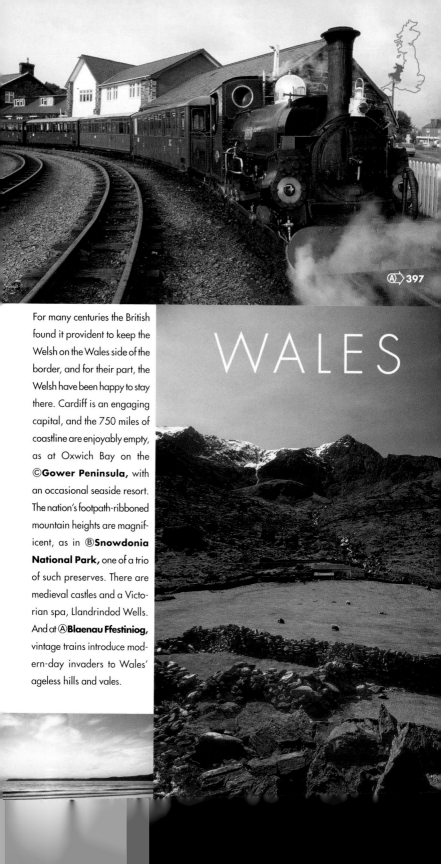

WALES

For many centuries the British found it provident to keep the Welsh on the Wales side of the border, and for their part, the Welsh have been happy to stay there. Cardiff is an engaging capital, and the 750 miles of coastline are enjoyably empty, as at Oxwich Bay on the Ⓒ**Gower Peninsula,** with an occasional seaside resort. The nation's footpath-ribboned mountain heights are magnificent, as in Ⓑ**Snowdonia National Park,** one of a trio of such preserves. There are medieval castles and a Victorian spa, Llandrindod Wells. And at Ⓐ**Blaenau Ffestiniog,** vintage trains introduce modern-day invaders to Wales' ageless hills and vales.

No one's going to argue about who lately put this part of England on the map—one of the region's landmarks is 20 Forthlin Road, Paul McCartney's house in Ⓐ**Liverpool.** But the Fab Four can't take all the credit. The scions of the Industrial Revolution propelled the region and Britain to the forefront of the 19th century. Even earlier, the dukes of Devonshire constructed ⒷⒸ**Chatsworth House,** one of the most sumptuous country seats in the land, complete with the River Wye flowing down from the nearby Peak District.

LANCASHIRE

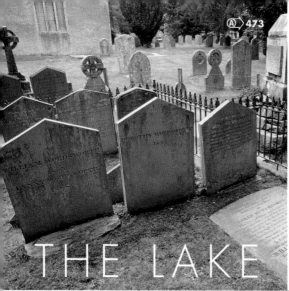

Ⓐ 473

THE LAKE
DISTRICT

Ⓑ 468

You can visit the grave of William Wordsworth in Ⓐ**Grasmere,** but to pay true homage to the poet, go out for a ramble, preferably "lonely as a cloud"—although that's not so easy in the region of craggy hills, wild moorland, and silvery lakes that inspired the Romantic poet and other literati from Samuel Coleridge to Beatrix Potter. Some 250 days of rain a year ensure that such noted spots as Ⓒ**Keswick,** on the shores of Derwentwater, are always pleasingly verdant. Likewise, the weather doesn't put a damper on an afternoon's sail across Ⓑ**Windermere.** After a stay here you may be inspired to pen your own ode to tranquillity.

Ⓒ 479

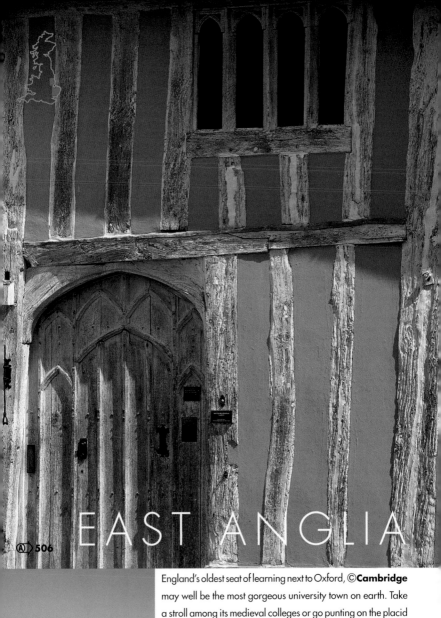

EAST ANGLIA

Ⓐ▷ 506

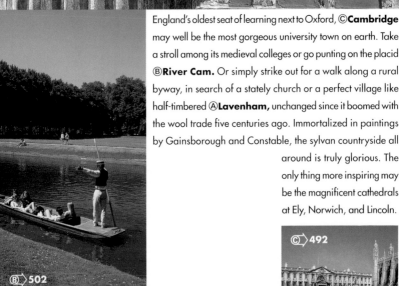

England's oldest seat of learning next to Oxford, ©**Cambridge** may well be the most gorgeous university town on earth. Take a stroll among its medieval colleges or go punting on the placid Ⓑ**River Cam.** Or simply strike out for a walk along a rural byway, in search of a stately church or a perfect village like half-timbered Ⓐ**Lavenham,** unchanged since it boomed with the wool trade five centuries ago. Immortalized in paintings by Gainsborough and Constable, the sylvan countryside all around is truly glorious. The only thing more inspiring may be the magnificent cathedrals at Ely, Norwich, and Lincoln.

Ⓑ▷ 502

©▷ 492

YORKSHIRE

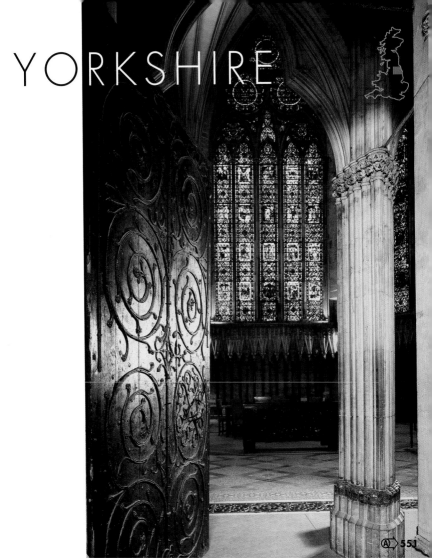

Ⓐ›551

Ⓑ›540

This expansive region makes an indelible impression. Poets have immortalized its ruined monasteries, and hamlets like Hutton-le-Hole are almost too pretty to be real. Castle Howard is the grandest country house of all, provoking the comment that its pheasants live better here than dukes elsewhere. The Yorkshire Moors around Ⓑ**Haworth**—wild and heather-covered—are as haunting as any a *Wuthering Heights* reader could hope for, and York is home to both the nation's biggest Gothic cathedral, Ⓐ**York Minster,** and the Ⓒ**National Railway Museum.** In Yorkshire, history beckons around every corner.

Ⓒ›551

NORTHEAST

Ⓐ 585

Ⓑ 594

The gateway to Scotland, this remote corner of England is the climax to all that is grand and wild in the nation's footpath-crossed northerly reaches. For centuries, Northeasterners struggled mightily to keep outsiders out. Barbarian attacks from the north were repelled by mammoth fortifications such as Ⓐ**Hadrian's Wall**— the Roman Empire's formidable northernmost boundary. On the stark Northumberland coastline towering castles such as Bamburgh held marauders at bay; the one at Ⓑ**Lindisfarne,** also known as Holy Island, sheltered one of England's earliest Christian communities as well. With its stone bulk silhouetted against the sky, the island seems to hurl defiance at the restless North Sea waves. Elaborate Alnwick Castle, resplendent inside, grew up around a Norman keep. And handsome Ⓒ**Durham Cathedral,** the stone centerpiece of one of England's most memorable medieval cities, was described as "Half church of God, half castle 'gainst the Scot." Both inland and by the sea, the landscape is generously blessed with wide-open space—a precious commodity on this densely populated isle.

Ⓒ 576

Ⓐ 605

The British see the Scots as a race apart, a stubborn and thrifty breed who toss the caber rather than play cricket, don skirts regardless of gender, and value bracing competitions like

SCOTLAND

the Ⓑ**Braemar Highland Gathering** over the Ascot races. Self-respecting Scots are pleased to accept the compliment. Meanwhile, anyone venturing into this tradition-rich land can't help but admire bustling Victorian-era Glasgow, not to mention refined Ⓐ**Edinburgh,** whose looming castle, dignified homes, and civilized ways set the standard for urbanity. Beyond the cities, scenic splendor prevails: purple moors, salmon-filled streams, rolling highlands, heathery slopes, and shimmering lakes such as Ⓒ**Loch Ness.** Baronial castles preside over the Highland hills. Traveling the countryside you'll be unpredictably accompanied by sunshine and showers. Don't complain: they produce the magical rainbows and mists that inspired Scotland's makers of legend.

Ⓑ 640

Ⓒ 644

GREAT ITINERARIES

Not so very long ago, for some a trip to Britain meant London, period: the Crown Jewels in the Tower of London, neighborhood Bobbies, the Elgin Marbles in the British Museum, red double-decker buses. Not any more. Now, London is the jumping-off point. Today's travelers want to see what inspired Wordsworth in the Lake District, gawk at the grandeur of Blenheim Palace, catch tomorrow's divas trilling at the Glyndebourne Opera Festival, and track Heathcliff's shadow roaming the Yorkshire moors. The following tours distill an entire kingdom into manageable measures, picking out the essential sights that you might otherwise kick yourself for missing.

Ⓐ 291

Highlights of Britain
14 days

It's no wonder that many visitors see Great Britain as a giant patchwork quilt thickly studded with must-see sights. This roundup introduces you to the best of them. After two days doing the town in London, head out to Windsor.

WINDSOR
1 day. Windsor Castle is the main reason to be here, resplendent in its finery, but a respite for the riches within is found in its tranquil Great Park. If you want to live like a duke for a day, head up the valley to Lord Astor's Clive-den, the Thames Valley's most spectacular hotel.
☞ *Royal Berkshire in Chapter 6*

SALISBURY
1 day. Visible for miles around, Salisbury Cathedral's soaring spire is one of the quintessential images of rural England, immortalized in paint by John Constable (you can still find the exact spot the artist set up his easel on the Town Path). Pay an afternoon call on either awe-inspiring ©Stonehenge or Stourhead, the finest garden of England's Neoclassical era.
☞ *Salisbury, Stonehenge, and the New Forest in Chapter 3*

BATH AND THE COTSWOLDS
2 days. Once upon a time Bath was *the* place to be, and this posh city has never forgotten it. The popularity is understandable, as Bath is an immaculately preserved gem of Georgian architecture. The key spots to see are the Royal Crescent, the Circus, the Pump Room, immortalized in Jane Austen's *Persuasion*. The next day head via car or guided-tour bus to the Cotswolds, whose storybook villages will tempt you to stay forever. Antique-shop in Broadway, visit historic Snowshill Manor, then feed the ducks at the brook in Lower Slaughter.
☞ *Bath and Environs and The Cotswolds in Chapter 8*

OXFORD
1 day. The "dreaming spires" of Oxford's weathered old buildings bear witness to the transience of countless generations of students. Tour the town's largest quad at Christ Church College, then don't miss the short trip to Ⓐ Blenheim Palace, England's grandest house.
☞ *Oxford and On the Road to Blenheim Palace in Chapter 6*

STRATFORD-UPON-AVON
1 day. If you don't chime with the Bard, skip this stop, because this is Shakespeare's town, end of story; if you dig, then you won't be disappointed. See Shakespeare's Birthplace and Ⓑ Anne

Ⓑ 306

Hathaway's Cottage, and catch a once-in-a-lifetime performance at the Royal Shakespeare Theatre.
☞ *Stratford-upon-Avon in Chapter 7*

WORCESTER
2 days. On the banks of the River Severn, Worcester Cathedral is a majestic apparition and offers one of the finest chantry chapels in the country. The town's 15th-century Commandery brings alive the days of England's Civil War. Spend your second day here roaming the spa towns of the Malvern Hills, then head north to see the half-timbered "magpie" houses of Shrewsbury and Chester.
☞ *From Worcester to Dudley and Skirting the "Black Country" in Chapter 9*

THE LAKE DISTRICT
2 days. In the area surrounding Windermere and Oxenholme (near Kendal), you get your chance to expose yourself to the English elements and do some real walking. Check out the local Wordsworth industry at Dove Cottage and Grasmere, where you can pay your respects to the Wordsworth family's graves, then bring your sketch pad on a cruise on Ⓓ Windermere.
☞ *The Southern Lakes in Chapter 12*

YORK
2 days. The principal city of northern England since Roman times, York is crammed with 15th- and 16th-century buildings in varying degrees of sag, but medieval-era York Minster and the Shambles are the musts. Save half a day for

visiting Castle Howard, where eye-popping grandeur is the keynote.
☞ *York and The North York Moors in Chapter 14*

LINCOLN AND CAMBRIDGE

2 days. Heading south, make a lunchtime halt at Lincoln, whose stunning Cathedral of St. Mary demands a slow wander. Bed down in Cambridge for your last stop. After touring King's College Chapel, leave an hour or two to hone your punting skills on the River Cam before heading back to London.
☞ *Beyond the Fens and Cambridge in Chapter 13*

By Public Transportation
For Windsor, take a train from either London's Waterloo or Paddington station. For

Salisbury, head back to London's Clapham Junction to catch a train on the Portsmouth line. Trains leave twice hourly from Salisbury to Bath, itself connected by hourly trains to Oxford. From Oxford there are direct trains to Stratford-upon-Avon, or opt for more frequent Stagecoach bus service. For Worcester change trains at Oxford or Birmingham's New Street station, which is the place to catch trains to Windermere and Oxenholme. Take a train via either station to York (changes required). From York to Lincoln transfer at Doncaster or Retford. For Cambridge change at Doncaster or Newark and again at Peterborough. Trains leave Cambridge for London frequently.

The Literary Trail
12 days

After the Beatles, perhaps the greatest contribution that Britain has made to Western culture has been its literary achievements. The legacy of a thousand years of literature has insinuated itself into every aspect of life. You'll have glimpsed many of these landscapes as romantic backdrops in the movies.

LONDON

2 days. The author most associated with London is Charles Dickens, and Dickens House, where he wrote *Oliver Twist* and *Nicholas Nickleby*, sits appropriately in literary Bloomsbury. Dr. Johnson's House lies a short walk south of here, and Shakespeare beckons across the Thames in Southwark at the reconstruction of the Bard's Globe Theatre.
☞ *Exploring London in Chapter 1*

© 193

27

WINCHESTER AND CHAWTON

1 day. Stop in the lovely old town of Winchester; Jane Austen is buried in its Ⓔcathedral. Sixteen miles northeast lies Chawton and Jane Austen's House, where the atmosphere still reverberates with the tinkle of teacups lofted by the likes of Emma and the dashing Mr. Darcy.
☞ *From Winchester to Southampton in Chapter 3*

Ⓔ 174

DORCHESTER AND LYME REGIS

2 days. Thomas Hardy made this region into *Far from the Madding Crowd* country. The town of Dorchester was the 19th-century author's Casterbridge. Dorset County Museum has a re-creation of his study, and Hardy walking tours lead to Hardy's Cottage at Higher Bockhampton. To the west is Lyme Regis, seaside setting of John Fowles's *The French Lieutenant's Woman*.
☞ *Far from the Madding Crowd in Chapter 3*

BATH

1 day. Head north to honey-toned Bath, identified with a host of Georgian-era literati, chief among them Jane Austen, who set *Northanger Abbey* and *Persuasion* here. Look into guided theme walks and visit Holburne Museum, where genteel Jane promenaded in the gardens.
☞ *Bath and Environs in Chapter 8*

STRATFORD-UPON-AVON

2 days. Scholars rub shoulders with sightseers here. Everyone visits Shakespeare's

Birthplace, though you may feel closer to him at his simple tomb in Holy Trinity Church. Escape the tour buses by exploring Master Will's country haunts, from Henley-in-Arden to ⒽWarwick Castle.
☞ *Stratford-upon-Avon and In and Around Shakespeare Country in Chapter 7*

THE LAKE DISTRICT

2 days. The countryside around Keswick and Windermere is the cradle of English Romanticism: its mountains and lakes attracted Wordsworth and other inspired men of letters. Visit the poet's home, ⒻDove Cottage in Grasmere, then young William's school in Hawkshead, and his and Dorothy's birthplace at Cockermouth. Coniston, the home of John Ruskin, is in Brantwood, near Hawkshead.
☞ *The Southern Lakes and Penrith and the Northern Lakes in Chapter 12*

HAWORTH

2 days. No one who has read a page of the Brontë canon can miss this literary shrine. Sadly that adds up to quite a few million people. Still the Brontë Parsonage Museum casts a spell, as do the paths to the moors and the Brontë Waterfall. Overnight here and head back to London the next day.
☞ *West Yorkshire and Brontë Country in Chapter 14*

By Public Transportation
Take the train from Waterloo station to Winchester. For Dorchester change trains at Southampton. To reach Bath from Dorchester change at Yeovil. For Stratford change at Bristol and Birmingham. Catch connections for Keswick or Windermere at Birmingham's New Street Station. From the Lake District to reach Haworth take a train for Keighley from Windermere or Oxenholme, changing at Lancaster, sometimes at Leeds. From Keighley there are frequent Keighley and District buses, which also head to Bradford, from which frequent trains depart for London.

Ⓔ 473

A Stately Homes Grand Tour
9 days

Though occasionally changing hands and even dynasties, England's stately houses as a rule have retained the priceless furniture, and—sometimes—the wallpaper of generations past. These bastions of privilege often overwhelm you with admiration for some of the finest architecture and landscape gardening in the country.

SALISBURY

2 days. Base yourself in this graceful Wiltshire town for trips to a trio of superb stately homes. Wilton House was designed by Inigo Jones around 1647. Its classically proportioned Double Cube Room features a gigantic Van Dyck family portrait. On the western edge of Wiltshire, Palladian Stourhead is most loved for its parkland. Nearby Longleat House is an Italian Renaissance structure complete with safari park.
☞ *Salisbury, Stonehenge, and the New Forest in Chapter 3*

OXFORD

2 days. Blenheim Palace, home of the dukes of Marlborough and birthplace of Winston Churchill, is one of the most ornate Baroque concoctions anywhere. Nine miles west of Oxford is Stanton Harcourt, dwarfed in comparison, and Kelmscott Manor, a famed Arts & Crafts landmark is nearby. To the south is Mapledurham House, model for Toad Hall.
☞ *"Wind in the Willows" Country and On the Road to Blenheim Palace in Chapter 6*

BROADWAY

2 days. Stay in this lovely Cotswold town to explore Sudeley Castle, home of

Glasgow

Plymouth

Henry VIII's last wife. Stanway House, a short drive away, is a Jacobean manor perfectly in keeping with its setting, and nearby Snowshill Manor is a sequence of serendipities. Farther west, Owlpen Manor is a Cotswold classic.
☞ *The Cotswolds in Chapter 8*

BAKEWELL

2 days. Within hailing distance are two of England's most fabulous historic homes: one of them, Chatsworth House, displays the art treasures of the dukes of Devonshire. Medieval in

style, nearby 15th-century Haddon Hall is among the most English of great houses.
☞ *The Peak District in Chapter 11*

YORK

1 day. Doing the tedious crawl up the M1 motorway is worthwhile so that you can see Yorkshire's spectacular ⒼCastle Howard. Several miles away are Harewood House, which has a cornucopia of Chippendale furniture, and Studley Royal, with its exquisite water gardens. Overnight in York and head back to London the next morning.
☞ *West Yorkshire and Brontë Country, York Environs, and The North York Moors in Chapter 14*

By Public Transportation

This tour often leads to backwaters and byways, so public transport can be sketchy. Buses can get you close to many stately homes, but a taxi is sometimes required for the last leg of the journey. From London's Waterloo Station take a train to Salisbury, then a bus to Wilton House or Warminster, for Longleat; for Stourhead, continue on the train to Gillingham. From Salisbury, change at Bath or Basingstoke for Oxford, then catch a bus to Blenheim, Stanton Harcourt, and, for Kelmscott Manor, Faringdon. Take a train from Oxford to Moreton-in-Marsh for Broadway, then walk to Snowshill Manor; for Sudeley Castle, take a bus from Broadway to Winchcombe, then walk. Take a train back to Oxford and then up to Manchester for the connection to Buxton, then a bus to Bakewell. Take a train from Manchester to York, then a bus to Castle Howard; take a train to Leeds, then a bus over to Harewood House; for Studley Royal, take a train to Harrowgate, then a bus to Ripon. Express trains connect York with London.

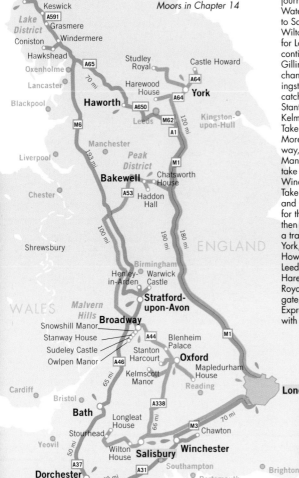

 © 565

Ⓗ 313

FRANCE

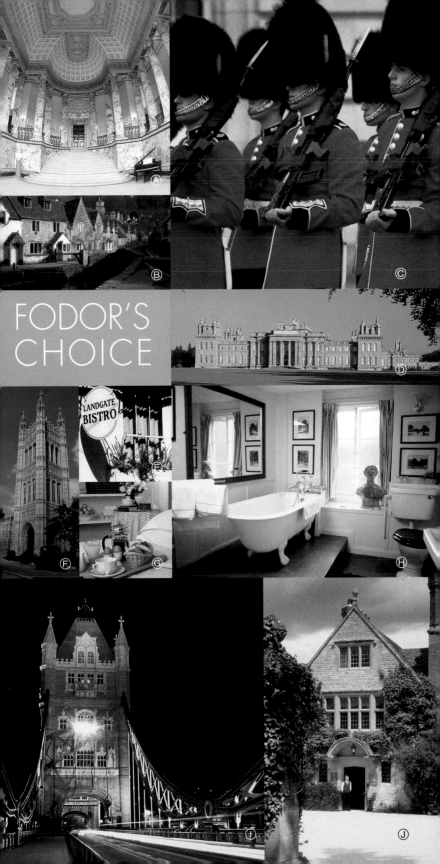

FODOR'S
CHOICE

Even with so many special places in Great Britain, Fodor's writers and editors have their favorites. Here are a few that stand out.

QUINTESSENTIAL ENGLAND

Ⓒ **Changing of the Guard, London.** Adding a dash of red to the gloomiest of London days, the colorful regiments of guards march with regal pomp as the band plays (they have been known to cut loose to Billy Joel when Her Majesty is away). ☞ p. 47

Henley Royal Regatta, Thames Valley. The boat races stop twice a day—for luncheon and 4 o'clock tea—at this elegant July event, regarded by some as the last bastion of Edwardian England. ☞ p. 267

Ⓕ **Houses of Parliament, Thames-side, London.** This storybook view is headlined by Victoria Tower and Big Ben, which looks almost as magical as when Walt Disney used it as a perch for Peter and the children in *Peter Pan.* ☞ p. 47

A ramble around Windermere, Lake District. Have your colored-pencil kit handy to capture the sublime scenery that once inspired Wordsworth and the great Romantic poets. ☞ p. 468

Shakespeare at Stratford-upon-Avon, Shakespeare Country. Seeing the Bard performed in his hometown at the Royal Shakespeare Theatre is one of the most unforgettable theatrical experiences in the world. ☞ p. 303

Ⓘ **Tower Bridge at night, London.** A dramatically floodlighted Tower Bridge confronts you as you come out of the Design Museum on a winter's night. Have your camera handy. ☞ p. 62

PICTURE-PERFECT VILLAGES AND STATELY HOUSES

Ⓓ **Blenheim Palace, Thames Valley.** Magnificent is the adjective to describe this 18th-century house, seat of the dukes of Marlborough. ☞ p. 291

Ⓑ **Castle Combe, Bath Environs.** Once a stand-in Puddleby-on-the-Marsh in the Rex Harrison film *Doctor Dolittle*, this village has a toylike, once-upon-a-time magic. ☞ p. 333

Castle Howard, Yorkshire. The masterpiece of English Baroque architecture, this birthday cake of a house was used to memorable effect as Lord Marchmain's residence in TV's *Brideshead Revisited.* ☞ p. 565

Haddon Hall, Lancashire and the Peaks. A medieval book illumination come to life, this castellated 15th-century manor bristles with slate roofs and towers and is surrounded by famous rose gardens. ☞ p. 452

Ⓐ **Holkham Hall, East Anglia.** A 60-ft-tall marble entryway and salons filled with old masters distinguish this splendid Palladian palace. ☞ p. 513

Lower Slaughter, Cotswolds. One of the Cotswold's "water villages," this is built around Slaughter Brook, home to a gaggle of geese, who can often be seen paddling under the footbridges. ☞ p. 344

Portmeirion, Wales. This fantasy-Italianate village, complete with town hall and hotel, is un-Welsh but very charming. ☞ p. 398

DINING

La Tante Claire. Pierre Koffmann may be London's best chef, and he is practicing his seemingly effortless art at the Berkeley Hotel. The service is impeccable and the French wine list impressive, but food is the point. ££££ ☞ p. 88

Ⓙ **Le Manoir aux Quat' Saisons, Great Milton, Thames Valley.** Owner-chef Raymond Blanc's 15th-century manor house has held its position as one of Britain's most patrician restaurants for years. ££££ ☞ p. 294

Miller Howe, Windermere, Lake District. At this small Edwardian hotel you find some of the best food in England, served with idyllic

views across Windermere. ££££ ☞ p. 470

Oak Room, London. Expect grand style at this creation of superstar chef Marco Pierre White—foie gras, caviar, and truffles—and truly adventurous preparations. ££££ ☞ p. 89

Rules, London. London's answer to Maxim's in Paris has entertained everyone from Dickens to the Duke of Windsor in its sublimely beautiful Regency salons. £££ ☞ p. 86

Ⓔ **Landgate Bistro, Rye, Southeast.** All the fish from nearby waters are excellent at this lively, bustling establishment. ££ ☞ p. 141

LODGING

Cliveden, Thames Valley. Want to live like Lord Astor for a night? He once called this mansion home, and today lucky guests enjoy his palatial parlors and breathtaking river parterres. ££££ ☞ p. 279

Covent Garden Hotel, London. Relentlessly stylish, this vintage-1880 abode now shimmers with painted silks, 19th-century oils, and off-duty celebrities. ££££ ☞ p. 95

Middlethorpe Hall, York, Yorkshire. This handsome, superbly restored 18th-century mansion looks like a Gainsborough painting come to life. ££££ ☞ p. 553

Owlpen Manor, Cotswolds, Heart of England. Incomparably romantic, this hotel occupies a tiny, sequestered Stuart-period hamlet that is the quintessence of all things Cotswold. ££££ ☞ p. 347

Ⓖ **Queensberry Hotel, Bath, Heart of England.** This intimate hotel near the Circus is in three 1772 town houses built for the marquis of Queensberry. Beau Nash would feel right at home. £££–££££ ☞ p. 332

Ⓗ **Hazlitt's, London.** Disarmingly friendly and full of personality, the hotel is loved for its 19th-century charm. £££ ☞ p. 98

1 LONDON

If London contained only its famous landmarks—the Tower of London, Big Ben, Parliament, Buckingham Palace—it would still rank as one of the world's top destinations. But London is so much more. It is a bevy of British bobbies, an ocean of black umbrellas, and an unconquered continuance of more than 2,000 years of history. A city that loves to be explored, London beckons with great museums, royal pageantry, and history-steeped houses. Take in a performance at Shakespeare's Globe or track Jack the Ripper's shadows in Whitechapel. East End, West End, you'll find London is a dickens of a place.

Updated by
Catherine
Belonogoff,
Jacqueline
Brown, Roland
Chambers,
Julius Honnor,
Alex Wijeratna

LONDON IS AN ANCIENT CITY whose history greets you at every turn. To gain a sense of its continuity, stand on Waterloo Bridge at the hour of sunset. To the east, the great globe of St. Paul's Cathedral glows golden in the fading sunlight as it has since the 17th century, still majestic amid the modern towers of glass and steel that hem it in. To the west stand the mock-medieval ramparts of Westminster, home to the "Mother of Parliaments," which has met here or hereabouts since the 1250s. Past them both snakes the swift, dark Thames, following the same course as when it flowed past the first Roman settlement nearly 2,000 years ago.

For much of its history, innumerable epigrams and observations have been coined about London by enthusiasts and detractors. The great 18th-century author and wit Samuel Johnson said that a man who is tired of London is tired of life. Oliver Wendell Holmes said, "No person can be said to know London. The most that anyone can claim is that he knows something of it." In short, the capital of Great Britain is simply one of the most interesting cities on earth. There is no other place like it in its agglomeration of architectural sins and sudden intervention of almost rural sights, in its medley of styles, in its mixture of the green loveliness of parks and the modern gleam of neon. Thankfully, the old London of Queen Anne and Georgian architecture can still be discovered under the hasty routine of later additions.

Discovering London takes a bit of work, however. Modern-day London still largely reflects its medieval layout, a willfully difficult tangle of streets. This swirl of spaghetti will be totally confusing to anyone brought up on the rigidity of a grid system. Even Londoners, most of whom own a dog-eared copy of the indispensable A–Z street finder (these books come under different names), get lost in their own city. But London's bewildering street patterns will be a plus for anyone who likes to get lost in atmosphere. London is a walker's city and will repay every moment you spend exploring on foot. If you want to penetrate beyond the crust of popular knowledge, you are well advised not only to visit St. Paul's Cathedral and the Tower, but also to set aside some time for random wandering. Walk in the city's backstreets and mews, around Park Lane and Kensington. Pass up Buckingham Palace for Kensington Palace, beautifully situated in regal gardens. Take in the National Gallery, but don't forget London's "time machine" museums, such as the 19th-century homes of Lord Frederic Leighton and Sir John Soane. Abandon the city's standard-issue chain stores to discover the gentlemen's outfitters of St. James's. In such ways can you best visualize the shape or, rather, the various shapes of Old London, a curious city that engulfed its own past for the sake of modernity but still lives and breathes the air of history.

Today, that sense of modernity is stronger than ever. Swinging-again London is still, as *Vanity Fair* proclaimed, "the coolest, hottest city in the world." Millennium fever left its trophies on the capital, including a panoply of new buildings and impressively revamped museums. A sound economy has helped the city's art, style, fashion, and dining scenes make headlines around the world. London's chefs have become superstars. Its fashion designers have conquered Paris, avant-garde artists have caused waves at the august Royal Academy of Arts, the city's raging after-hours scene is packed with music mavens ready to catch the Next Big Thing, and the theater continues its tradition of radical, shocking productions, which barely seem to turn most hairs. Even Shakespeare entered the millennium: the Bard's reconstructed Globe Theatre—the fabled "Wooden O"—is going swimmingly on the banks of the Thames just 200 yards from where it stood in the 16th century; when the troupe here presented *Two Gentlemen of Verona*, cast members sported Ray-Bans and sneakers.

On the other hand, although the outward shapes may alter and the inner spirit may be warmer—Princess Diana's 1997 funeral was far removed from the conventional picture of a staid city of people who don't display their emotions—the base-rocks of London's character and tradition remain the same. Deep down, Britons have a sense of the continuity of history. Even in the modern metropolis, some things rarely change. The British bobby is alive and well. The tall, red, double-decker buses still lumber from stop to stop, although their aesthetic match at street level, the glossy red telephone booth, is slowly disappearing. And, of course, teatime is still a hallowed part of the day, with, if you search hard enough, toasted crumpets honeycombed with sweet butter. Then, of course, there's that greatest living link with the past—the Royal Family. Don't let the tag of "typical tourist" stop you from enjoying the pageantry of the Windsors, one of the greatest free shows in the world. Line up for the Changing of the Guard and poke into the Royal Mews for a look at the Coronation Coach, which will be polished brilliantly for the Queen's Golden Jubilee state occasions in 2002.

The London you might discover some enthusiastic recommendations from this guide, but be prepared to be taken by surprise as well. The best that a great city has to offer often comes in unexpected ways. Armed with energy and curiosity, you can find, to quote Dr. Johnson again, "in London all that life can afford."

New and Noteworthy

Post-millennium building frenzy has abated only slightly as museums and galleries strive to become more high-tech and visitor-friendly. Many national collections have extended opening hours and free admission for kids. Every museum, in fact, has been part of this recent whirlwind of activity in which classicism spearheaded by innovation is the byword: the glittering Great Court of the British Museum; the technological gizmos at the staid British Library; the state-of-the-art Tate Modern (with a new look at the old Tate, or Tate Britain) at the futuristic Bankside Power Station; the new face of the National Portrait Gallery; and the scintillating space-age Earth Galleries at the Natural History Museum. Thanks to these attractions, swinging-again London has staked its claim as Europe's most future-forward spot.

Culturally, the city is making a bid to catch up with its overseas rivals in terms of modern art, and the word here is that big is beautiful— opened in 2000, **Tate Modern** houses the huge number of works of art formerly hidden from public view because of lack of space. Londoners on their way to the Tate Modern on the South Bank, the Docklands developments, and ancient Greenwich have new tube stations on the ultra-modern Jubilee Line, plus extra services on the time-honored mode of transport called Old Father Thames. Also on the south side of the Thames is the **British Airways London Eye,** which opened in 2000; the public is still lining up to see the unrivaled views of London from this observation wheel. Beside the London Eye is the new **Waterloo Millennium Pier,** with boat service to the Millennium Dome Pier. The **Millennium Bridge,** purely for pedestrians, opened in June 2000 to great fanfare and promptly shut after a wobbly start. With new stabilizers in place, it was scheduled to reopen in fall 2001.

The **British Museum** shows the Elgin Marbles (still here, despite the wanted notice out on them by the Greek government) in a grand but up-to-date interactive display in the Parthenon Galleries. The crowning attraction is the awesome Great Court. The British Galleries at the **Victoria & Albert Museum** were set to open in late 2001; with amazing detail and masses of historical objects, the galleries tell the story of the last 400 years in Britain from art to design to day-to-day life. The revamped **Tate Britain** also opened new exhibition galleries for its fine collection of British art in fall 2001. New to the scene is the **Museum in Docklands,** set to open in mid-2002, which will provide a history of the area.

The architectural grandeur of **Somerset House,** including its classical courtyard, old Navy Board rooms, and Royal Barge by the old river gateway, are free for all to see, along with the view from the riverside terrace. Also here are the Gilbert Collection of jewel-encrusted decorative pieces and the Hermitage Rooms, which provide a rare chance to see treasures from the Hermitage Museum in St. Petersburg.

In 2002, the Queen's **Golden Jubilee** year will see much pomp and pageantry, and at Buckingham Palace there is extra celebration for the spring 2002 completion of the new entrance and expansion of the **Queen's Gallery.** The Royal Collection of old masterpieces will have twice the exhibition space and a micro gallery for perusing more of the unhung collection on screen.

Pleasures and Pastimes

Dining

London now ranks among the world's top dining scenes. A new generation of chefs has precipitated a fresh approach to food preparation, which you could call London-style although most refer to it as Modern British. Everyone reads the many pages devoted to food and restaurant reviews in newspapers and magazines, and everyone dines out to the point where London has become the most significant foodies' town in Europe. The days are long gone when British cuisine was best known for shepherd's pie—ubiquitously available in pubs—and fish-and-chips. As it turns out, there's a new return to British favorites, with old standbys like bangers and mash getting nouvelle treatments with such modish garnishes as sausages of wild boar and potato puree with pesto. This thriving dining scene rests on a solid foundation of ethnic cuisines. Thousands of Indian restaurants have long ensured that Londoners view access to a tasty tandoori as a birthright. Chinese—Cantonese, primarily—restaurants in London's tiny Chinatown and beyond have been around a long time, as have Greek tavernas, and there are even more Italian restaurants than Indian. Now add Thai, Malaysian, Spanish, and Japanese cuisines to those easily found in England's capital. After all this, traditional British food, lately revived from a certain death, appears as one more exotic cuisine in the pantheon. If, in fact, you're out for traditional English food, but with a stylish twist, head to London's hot new "gastro-pubs."

As for cost, the democratization of restaurants does not necessarily mean smaller checks, and London is still not an inexpensive city. Damage-control methods include making lunch your main meal—many top places feature good-value lunch menus—taking advantage of fixed-price menus, and ordering a pair of appetizers instead of an entrée, to which few places object.

The Performing Arts

There isn't *a* single London "arts scene"—there's an infinite variety of them. As long as there are audiences for Feydeau revivals, drag queens, teenage rock bands, hit musicals, body-painted dancers, and improvised stand-up comedy, someone will stage them in London. Admission prices are not always bargain-basement, but when you consider how much a London hotel room costs, the city's arts are a bargain.

MUSIC

London is home to four world-class orchestras. The London Symphony Orchestra is in residence at the Barbican Centre, whereas the London Philharmonic lives in the South Bank Arts Complex at the Royal Festival Hall, one of the finest concert halls in Europe. Between the Barbican and South Bank, there are concert performances almost every night of the year. The Barbican also presents chamber music concerts with such celebrated orchestras as the City of London Sinfonia. The Royal Albert Hall during the Promenade Concert season—July through September—is a pleasure. Also look for the lunchtime concerts held throughout the city in either smaller concert halls, arts-center foyers, or churches; they usually cost less than £5 or are free.

THEATER

From Shakespeare to the umpteenth year of *Les Misérables* (or "The Glums," as it's affectionately known), London's West End has the cream of the city's theater offerings. But there's much more to see in London than the offerings of Theatreland and the national companies: of the 100 or so legitimate theaters operating in the capital, only about half are officially "West End," and the remainder fall under the blanket title of "Fringe," which encompasses everything from off-the-wall "physical theater" to premieres of new plays and revivals of old ones.

Shakespeare, of course, supplies the backbone to the theatrical life of the city. On the London stage, the plays have survived being turned into musicals (from Purcell to rock); they have made the reputations of generations of famous actors (and broken not a few); they have seen women playing Hamlet and men playing Rosalind. Though the Bard of Bards remains a headliner around town, the London theater scene is amazingly varied. From a West End *Oliver* revival to an East End feminist staging of *Ben-Hur,* London remains a theatergoer's town.

OPERA AND BALLET

For decades, London's leading troupes, the Royal Opera and the Royal Ballet, have shared grandiose quarters at the Royal Opera House in Covent Garden—a fact that cut down on the number of opera and ballet performances that could be mounted in a season. Fortunately, the grand Opera House reopened in 1999 after a major two-year renovation, with quite literally—as anyone who has sat through a performance on a hot, humid night will testify—enough breathing space for public and performers.

The Pub Experience

Londoners could no more live without their "local" than they could forgo dinner. The pub—or public house, to give it its full title—is ingrained in the British psyche as social center, refuge, second home. Pub culture—revolving around pints, pool, darts, and sports—is still male-dominated; however, as a result of the gentrification trend that was launched in the late '80s by the major breweries (which own most pubs), transforming many ancient smoke- and spittle-stained dives into fantasy Edwardian drawing rooms, women have been entering their welcoming doors in unstoppable numbers. More recently, the trend has been toward the bar, identified by its cocktail list, creative paintwork, bare floorboards and chrome fittings, and to the gastro-pub, where a good kitchen fuels the relaxed ambience. When doing a London pub crawl, remember that arcane licensing laws forbid the serving of alcohol after 11 PM (10:30 on Sunday; there are different rules for restaurants)—a circumstance you see in action at 10 minutes to 11, when the "last orders" bell triggers a stampede to the bar.

EXPLORING LONDON

London grew from a wooden bridge built over the Thames in the year AD 43 to its current 600 square mi and 7 million souls in haphazard fashion, meandering from its two official centers: Westminster, seat of government and royalty, and the City, site of finance and commerce. However, London's *un*official centers multiply and mutate year after year, and it would be a shame to stop only at the postcard views. Life is not lived in monuments, as the patrician patrons of the great Georgian architects understood when they commissioned the city's elegant squares and town houses. Westminster Abbey's original vegetable patch (or convent garden), which became the site of London's first square, Covent Garden, is now an unmissable stop on any agenda.

If the great, green parks are, as in Lord Chatham's phrase, "the lungs of London," then the River Thames is its backbone. The South Bank section absorbs the Southwark stews of Shakespeare's day and the reconstruction of his original Globe Theatre, the concert hall from the '50s Festival of Britain, the arts complex from the '70s, and—farther downstream—the gorgeous 17th- and 18th-century symmetry of Greenwich, where the world's time is measured.

Numbers in the text correspond to numbers in the margin and on the London map.

Great Itineraries

In a city with as many richly stocked museums and marvels as London, you risk seeing half of everything and all of nothing. One could easily spend two solid weeks exploring the many layers of the city, but if time is limited you'll need to plan carefully. The following suggested itineraries will help your visit be exciting and efficient.

IF YOU HAVE 1 DAY

Touring the largest city in England in the space of a single day sounds like an impossible goal, but it can actually—almost—be done in a single sunrise-to-sunset span. Think London 101. Begin at postcard London, the Houses of Parliament, best viewed from Westminster Bridge. If you're lucky, you'll hear Big Ben chiming. Move on to centuries-old Westminster Abbey—if and when Prince Charles becomes king, this is where his coronation will be staged—then tube it from the Westminster stop to Charing Cross (if you want to catch a glimpse of Her Majesty's two mounted sentries at Horse Guards Parade, bus it up Whitehall) to arrive at Trafalgar Square for your photo op with Nelson's Column and hundreds of pigeons. Take in the treasures of the National Gallery, which rank with the collections of the Louvre and the Uffizi. History buffs might opt instead for a flip-book-fast tour of the adjacent National Portrait Gallery, heavy on the likes of England's heroes and literateurs. Break for lunch in the Brasserie of the National Gallery, then take a short taxi trip over to a sight dear to your heart: for connoisseurs, this might be the Wallace Collection or the Tate Britain; for time travelers, the home of the Duke of Wellington or Sir John Soane's Museum; for kids, the London Dungeon or Madame Tussaud's. For a mid-afternoon session, choose between two royal monuments. First choice: heading west from Trafalgar Square, taxi through the impressive Admiralty Arch down the Mall to Buckingham Palace. During summer, when the State Rooms are open to the public, their full pomp can be ogled. Theatreland awaits palace trekkers with a hit West End musical—a refreshing finale to the day. Second choice: eastward (take the tube to the Tower Hill stop) lies the Tower of London, home to the Beefeaters, the Crown Jewels, and the six resident ravens. At dusk, after leaving the Tower, head across the way to the East End for a guaranteed spine chiller, a Jack the Ripper guided walking tour. Of course, if you have more than one day to spend, many of these sights would merit an extended visit—an entire afternoon, for example, could easily be spent at the National Gallery or the Tower.

IF YOU HAVE 3 DAYS

A breakneck first day in London has been outlined above. On your second day you can slow down a bit, so you can afford to begin at the beginning of mankind's search for enlightenment and art: the legendary British Museum, resting place of such wonders as the Rosetta Stone, the Elgin Marbles, and the Lindow Man. If the idea of traipsing through "mankind's attic" doesn't grab you—the number of Londoners who have never been to the British Museum is vast—head for that amazing fun house, Sir John Soane's Museum, a time machine whose interiors will transport you to Regency-era England. Here in Bloomsbury other treats beckon: Pollock's Toy Museum the Charles Dickens House. For an early lunch, tube it from Russell Square to Tottenham Court Road in Soho, for dim sum in Chinatown, or the menu du jour at a cute French bistro. Next, for a dose of magisterial grandeur, hop back on the tube to arrive at the St. Paul's stop and St. Paul's Cathedral. Walk off lunch by strolling south through Blackfriars—a district full of crooked streets, historic courtyards, and minuscule cul-de-sacs—to the Thames River. After downing a pint at the Black Friar (possibly London's most ornately decorated 19th-century pub), cross Blackfriars Bridge to Southwark's riverside embankment for a splendid view of St. Paul's dome. A stone's throw away is the rebuilt Shakespeare's Globe Theatre. If you're not catching a performance at the Globe (held only in warm-weather months), tour the museum beneath the theater. Keep heading eastward along the river, cross Southwark Bridge, then tube it from the Mansion House stop to Covent Garden. Dine at one of the area's chic restaurants, then watch the colorfully costumed street performers called buskers or attend a gala evening (book ahead) at the Royal Opera House.

Start your third day with Buckingham Palace's Changing of the Guard, held April–July at 11:30 daily, August–March at the same hour on alternate days. Warm up for this ceremony by viewing the superb treasures in the Queen's Gallery—Her Majesty's greatest paintings are here—and the nearby Royal Mews. If the state rooms of the palace are closed to viewing when you're in town, head through Green Park to Apsley House, the 18th-century mansion of the Duke of Wellington. Wander up Park Lane into ritzy Mayfair and stroll past Grosvenor Square and Oxford Street to Manchester Square and the Wallace Collection, whose gilded interiors are stuffed with 18th-century art. For serious retail therapy, return south, then east to scout three great shopping destinations: Bond Street for world-class glitz, Regent Street for savvy sophistication, and Carnaby Street for some rocker-style street gear. For an evening highlight, pick a play of your choice.

IF YOU HAVE 7 DAYS

Each section of London provides distinct clues to the city's past. In your first three days, you've made a start on piecing together the story of this great, crowded, endlessly fascinating city. Now you're ready to build on that foundation. Kick off day four at the South Kensington museums, a district planned by the Victorians to induce gallery gout and museum feet: the Victoria & Albert, the Natural History Museum, and the Science Museum. Art lovers will want to explore the first, while budding Einsteins will run for either of the latter. All three cultural palaces could easily consume an entire day, so pick one to do it justice. Then head over to Knightsbridge to mercantile-and-fashion giants Harrods

London

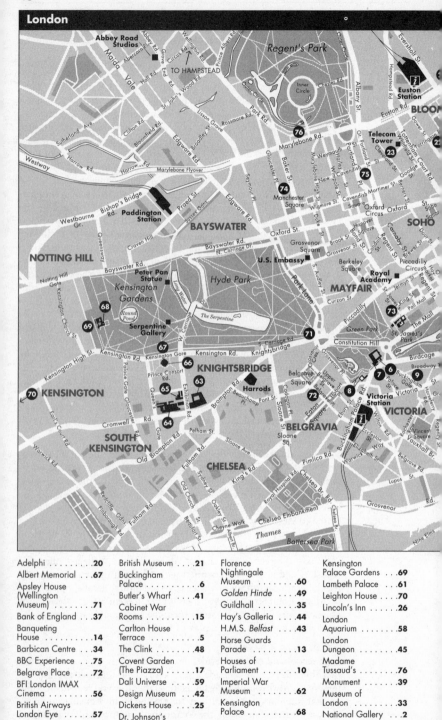

Adelphi **20**

Albert Memorial . . .**67**

Apsley House
(Wellington
Museum) **71**

Bank of England . . .**37**

Banqueting
House **14**

Barbican Centre . . .**34**

BBC Experience . . .**75**

Belgrave Place **72**

BFI London IMAX
Cinema **56**

British Airways
London Eye **57**

British Library **24**

British Museum **21**

Buckingham
Palace **6**

Butler's Wharf **41**

Cabinet War
Rooms **15**

Carlton House
Terrace **5**

The Clink **48**

Covent Garden
(The Piazza) **17**

Dalí Universe **59**

Design Museum . . .**42**

Dickens House **25**

Dr. Johnson's
House **29**

Florence
Nightingale
Museum **60**

Golden Hinde **49**

Guildhall **35**

Hay's Galleria **44**

H.M.S. *Belfast* . . .**43**

Horse Guards
Parade **13**

Houses of
Parliament **10**

Imperial War
Museum **62**

Kensington
Palace **68**

Kensington
Palace Gardens . . .**69**

Lambeth Palace . . .**61**

Leighton House **70**

Lincoln's Inn **26**

London
Aquarium **58**

London
Dungeon **45**

Madame
Tussaud's **76**

Monument **39**

Museum of
London **33**

National Gallery . . .**2**

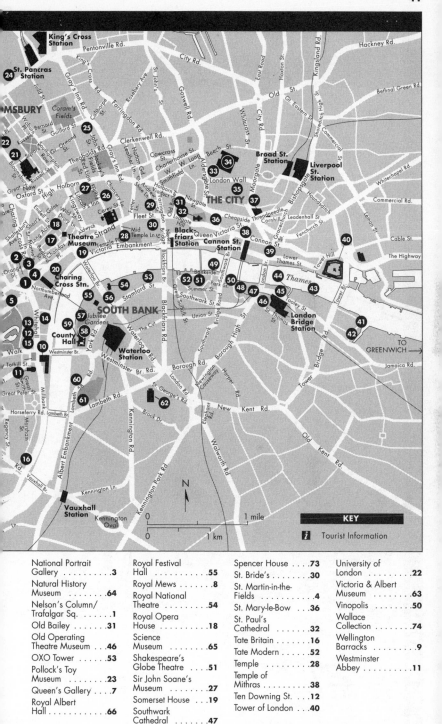

King's Cross Station

St. Pancras Station

MSBURY

Coram's Fields

Clerkenwell Rd.

Broad St. Station

Liverpool St. Station

THE CITY

London Wall

Theatre Museum

Fleet St.

Black-friars Station

Charing Cross Stn.

Cannon St. Station

Temple

SOUTH BANK

Jubilee Gardens

County Hall

Waterloo Station

London Bridge Station

TO GREENWICH →

Vauxhall Station

Kennington Oval

N

0 .... 1 mile
0 .... 1 km

KEY

🛈 Tourist Information

National Portrait
Gallery **3**

Natural History
Museum **64**

Nelson's Column/
Trafalgar Sq. . . . **1**

Old Bailey **31**

Old Operating
Theatre Museum . . **46**

OXO Tower **53**

Pollock's Toy
Museum **23**

Queen's Gallery . . . **7**

Royal Albert
Hall **66**

Royal Festival
Hall **55**

Royal Mews **8**

Royal National
Theatre **54**

Royal Opera
House **18**

Science
Museum **65**

Shakespeare's
Globe Theatre . . **51**

Sir John Soane's
Museum **27**

Somerset House . . **19**

Southwark
Cathedral **47**

Spencer House **73**

St. Bride's **30**

St. Martin-in-the-
Fields **4**

St. Mary-le-Bow . . **36**

St. Paul's
Cathedral **32**

Tate Britain **16**

Tate Modern **52**

Temple **28**

Temple of
Mithras **38**

Ten Downing St. . . **12**

Tower of London . . **40**

University of
London **22**

Victoria & Albert
Museum **63**

Vinopolis **50**

Wallace
Collection **74**

Wellington
Barracks **9**

Westminster
Abbey **11**

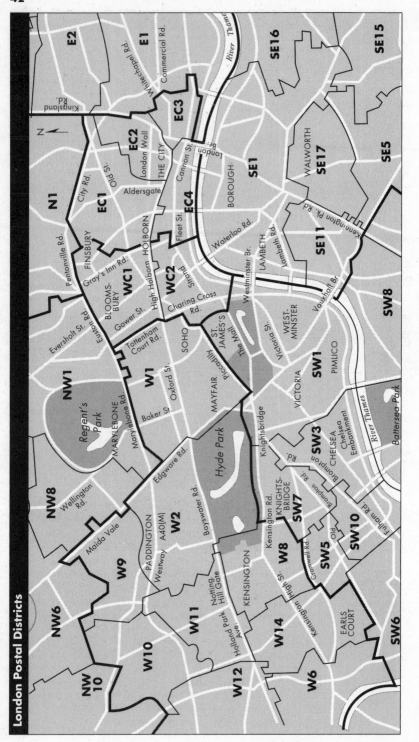

or Harvey Nichols. Move on to Kensington Gardens, where almost every-one throws a kiss to the famous statue of *Peter Pan,* and to Kensing-ton Palace, home to royals from Queen Anne to today's Windsors, where the state rooms are open to view year-round. Along the way, let your-self venture into the area's winding lanes and well-kept squares.

Day five dawns at the City—London's ancient core. Built up around St. Paul's, the area has numerous attractions, including Dr. Johnson's House, t he Museum of London, and several Christopher Wren churches. After lunch, serious folk will want to tube westward over to Holborn (Chancery Lane, Temple stops) to visit the historic Inns of Court and the Temple, the historic foundations of legal London. Farther along lies that storybook icon, Tower Bridge, which you must cross to reach the South Bank, where the London Dungeon awaits—this medieval wax-works show is devoted to the more gory aspects of British history.

On day six, leave the city behind for pleasures along the Thames, at Greenwich or the storied palace and gardens of Hampton Court—don't even *consider* attempting both.

Begin your last day by taking the tube to the Knightsbridge stop and heading south for an early morning stroll through Belgravia; few tourists venture here, but it's London at its most Edwardian. Head over to the cavalcade of emporiums of Sloane Street and Sloane Square and enjoy some high-style shopping. Chelsea, along King's Road, is where much of London comes to shop and stroll. Relax over lunch at a King's Road eatery, then bus over to Millbank to take in the Tate Britain's collec-tion of paintings by J. M. W. Turner, the Romantic-period artist who painted the most beautiful sunsets of any century. As dusk settles, head over to the South Bank Arts Complex, where you might finish up your visit with a play in the Olivier Theatre or a concert in the Queen Eliz-abeth Hall. Don't fret if the performances are entirely booked—Lon-don itself is the most wonderful free show in all the world.

Westminster and Royal London

Westminster and Royal London might be called "London for Begin-ners." If you went no farther than these few acres, you would have seen many of the famous sights, from the Houses of Parliament, Big Ben, Westminster Abbey, and Buckingham Palace, to two of the world's greatest art collections, housed in the National and Tate Britain gal-leries. You can truly call this area Royal London, since it is neatly bounded by the triangle of streets that make up the route that the Queen usually takes when journeying from Buckingham Palace to Westmin-ster Abbey or to the Houses of Parliament on state occasions. The three points on this royal triangle are Trafalgar Square, Westminster, and Buck-ingham Palace. Naturally, in an area that regularly sees the pomp and pageantry of royal occasions, the streets are wide and the vistas long. St. James's Park lies at the heart of the triangle, which has a feeling of timeless dignity—flower beds bursting with color, long avenues of trees framing classically proportioned buildings, constant glimpses of pinnacles and towers over the treetops, the distant *bong!* of Big Ben counting off the hours. This is concentrated sightseeing, so pace your-self. Remember that for a large part of the year, much of Royal Lon-don is floodlighted at night, adding to the theatricality of the experience.

A Good Walk

Trafalgar Square is the obvious place to start. It is the geographical core of London, by dint of a plaque on the corner of the Strand and Charing Cross Road from which distances on U.K. signposts are mea-sured. After taking in the instantly identifiable **Nelson's Column** ① in the center (read about the area on a plaque marking its 150th anniversary), head for the **National Gallery** ② on the north side, Britain's greatest trove of masterpieces. Detour around the corner to see the **National Portrait Gallery** ③—a parade of the famous that can be very rewarding to anyone interested in what makes the British tick. East of the National Gallery, still on Trafalgar Square, see the much-loved church of **St. Martin-in-the-Fields** ④. Then, stepping through grand Admiralty Arch down on the southwest corner, enter the royal pink road, the Mall, with St. James's Park running along the south side. On your right is the Institute of Contemporary Art, known as the ICA, housed in the great Regency architect John Nash's **Carlton House Terrace** ⑤. At the foot of the Mall is one of London's most famous sights, **Buckingham Palace** ⑥, home, of course, to the monarch of the land, with the **Queen's Gallery** ⑦—showing some of Her Majesty's vast art collection—and the **Royal Mews** ⑧ nearby. Turning left and left again, almost doubling back, follow the southern perimeter of St. James's Park around Birdcage Walk, passing the headquarters of the Queen's foot guard, the **Wellington Barracks** ⑨, on your right. Cross Horse Guards Road at the eastern edge of the park, walk down Great George Street, and across Parliament Square, and you come to another of the great sights of London, the **Houses of Parliament** ⑩. A mock-medieval extravaganza designed by two celebrated Victorian-era architects, down to the last detail (Gothic umbrella stands), it was built along the Thames and includes the famous Clock Tower, known as Big Ben after the nickname of the bell that chimes the hour. A clockwise turn around the square brings you to yet another major landmark, historic **Westminster Abbey** ⑪. Complete the circuit and head north up Whitehall, where you'll see a simple monolith in the middle of the street—the Cenotaph, designed by Edwin Lutyens in 1920 in commemoration of the 1918 Armistice. The gated alley there on your left leads to **Ten Downing Street** ⑫, where England's modest "White House" stands. Soon after that you pass **Horse Guards Parade** ⑬, setting for the Queen's birthday celebration, Trooping the Colour, with the perfect classical Inigo Jones **Banqueting House** ⑭, scene of Charles I's execution, opposite. The hub of the execution of Sir Winston's war is back down toward Westminster on the left, deep in Foreign Office government buildings, in the **Cabinet War Rooms** ⑮. If it's art you're mad about, skip the last three sights and head directly down Millbank to the **Tate Britain** ⑯— the most famous museum for British painting and sculpture.

TIMING

You could finish this walk of roughly 3 mi in just over an hour or spend a week's vacation on this route alone. Allow as much time as you can for the two great museums—the National Gallery requires *at least* two hours; the National Portrait Gallery can be whizzed round in less than one. Westminster Abbey can take a half day—especially in summer, when lines are long. In summer, you can get inside Buckingham Palace, too, a half-day's operation increased to a whole day if you see the Royal Mews or the Queen's Gallery. If the Changing of the Guard is a priority, make sure you time this walk correctly.

Sights to See

⑭ **Banqueting House.** Commissioned by James I, Inigo Jones (1573–1652), one of England's great architects, created this banqueting hall in 1619–22 out of an old remnant of the Tudor Palace of Whitehall. Influenced by Andrea Palladio's work, which he saw during a sojourn in Tuscany, Jones remade the palace with Palladian sophistication and purity. James I's son, Charles I, enhanced the interior by employing the Flemish painter Peter Paul Rubens to glorify his father all over the ceiling. As it turned out, these allegorical paintings, depicting a wise monarch being received into heaven, were the last thing Charles saw before he was beheaded on a scaffold outside in 1649. ⊠ *Whitehall, SW1,* ☎ *020/7930–4179,* WEB *www.hrp.org.uk.* ⊒ *£3.60, includes audio guide.* ⊙ *Mon.–Sat. 10–5; closed on short notice for banquets, so call first. Tube: Westminster, Embankment, Charing Cross.*

❻ Buckingham Palace. Supreme among the symbols of London, indeed of Britain generally and of the Royal Family, Buckingham Palace tops many must-see lists—although the building itself is no masterpiece and has housed the monarch only since Victoria (1819–1901) moved here from Kensington Palace on her accession in 1837. Its great gray bulk sums up the imperious splendor of so much of the city: stately, magnificent, and ponderous. In 1824 the palace was substantially rebuilt by John Nash, that tireless architect, for George IV, that tireless spendthrift. Compared to other great London residences, it is a Johnny-come-lately affair: the Portland stone facade dates from only 1913, and the interior was renovated and redecorated only after World War II bombs damaged it. It contains some 600 rooms, including the State Ballroom and, of course, the Throne Room. These State Rooms are where much of the business of royalty is played out—investitures, state banquets, receptions. The royal apartments are in the north wing; when the Queen is in, the royal standard is raised. The State Rooms can be toured from August to early October, when the Royal Family is away. The **Changing of the Guard**—which, with all the pomp and ceremony monarchists and children adore, remains one of London's best free shows—culminates in front of the palace. Marching to live music, the **Queen's guards** proceed up the Mall from St. James's Palace to Buckingham Palace. Shortly afterward, the new guard approaches from Wellington Barracks via Birdcage Walk. Once the old and new guards are in the forecourt, the old guard symbolically hands over the keys to the palace. The ceremony takes place daily at 11:30 AM April–July, and on alternating days August–March, but the guards sometimes cancel due to bad weather; check the signs in the forecourt or phone. Arrive by 10:30 AM for a decent view of all the panoply. Be sure to prebook tour reservations of the palace with a credit card by phone. ⊠ *Buckingham Palace Rd., SW1,* ☎ *020/7839–1377; 020/7799–2331 for 24-hr information; 020/7321–2233 credit-card reservations (50p booking charge),* WEB *www.royal.gov.uk.* ⊒ *£11.* ⊙ *Early Aug.–early Oct. (confirm dates, which are subject to Queen's mandate), daily 9:30–4:15. Tube: St. James's Park, Victoria.*

❶❺ Cabinet War Rooms. It was from this small maze of 17 bomb-proof underground rooms—in back of the hulking Foreign Office—that Britain's World War II fortunes were directed. During air raids, the Cabinet met here, and the Cabinet Room is still arranged as if a meeting were about to convene. In the Map Room, the Allied campaign is charted. The Prime Minister's Room holds the desk from which Winston Churchill made his morale-boosting broadcasts, and the Telephone Room has his hot line to FDR. ⊠ *Clive Steps, King Charles St., SW1,* ☎ *020/7930–6961,* WEB *www.iwm.org.uk.* ⊒ *£4.80.* ⊙ *Apr.–Sept., daily 9:30–5:15; Oct.–Mar., daily 10–5:15. Tube: Westminster.*

❺ Carlton House Terrace. A glorious example of Regency architect John Nash's genius, Carlton House Terrace was built between 1812 and 1830, under the patronage of George IV (Prince Regent until George III's death in 1820). Nash was responsible for a series of West End developments, of which these white-stucco facades and massive Corinthian columns may be the most imposing. Today, No. 12 houses the **Institute of Contemporary Art,** one of Britain's leading modern-art centers. ⊠ *The Mall, W1. Tube: Charing Cross.*

JUST REMEMBER TO ADDRESS HER AS "YOUR MAJESTY"

YOU'VE SEEN BIG BEN, the Tower, and Westminster Abbey. But somehow you feel something is missing: a close encounter with Britain's most famous attraction—Her actual Majesty. True, you've toured Buckingham Palace, but the Windsors are notorious for never standing at a window (the London *Times* once suggested that the palace mount a mechanical procession of royal figures to parade in and out of the palace, on the hour, in cuckoo-clock fashion), and the odds are that you won't bump into Elizabeth II on the tube. But at a wide variety of royal events, you can catch a glimpse of her, along with other Windsor personages. Fairs and fetes, polo matches and horse races galore—her date book is crammed with such events. On one of them—who knows?—you might even meet her on a royal walk-about.

The Queen and the RF in fact, attend some 400 functions a year, and if you want to know what she and the rest of the Royal Family are doing on any given date, turn to the *Court Circular* printed in the major London dailies. You might catch Prince Charles launching a ship or the Queen at a hospital's ribbon-cutting ceremony. But most visitors want to see the Royals in all their dazzling pomp and circumstance. For this, the best bet is the second Saturday in June, when the Trooping the Colour is usually held to celebrate the Queen's official birthday. This spectacular parade begins when she leaves Buckingham Palace in her carriage and rides down the Mall to arrive at Horse Guards Parade at 11 AM exactly. (Well, occasionally the clock has been timed to strike as she arrives and not vice versa.) If you wish to obtain one of the 7,000 seats (no more than two per request, distributed by ballot), enclose a letter and stamped, self-addressed envelope or International Reply Coupon—January to February 28 only—to Ticket Office, Headquarters Household Division, Horse Guards, London SW1A 2AX, ☎ 020/7414-2479. Of course, you can also just line up along the Mall with your binoculars.

Another time you can catch the Queen in all her regalia is when she and the Duke of Edinburgh ride in state to Westminster to open the Houses of Parliament. The famous gilded coach, which became such an icon of fairy-tale glamor at Elizabeth II's coronation parades from Buckingham Palace to Parliament, is escorted by the brilliantly uniformed Household Cavalry—on a clear day, it is to be hoped, for this ceremony takes place in late October or early November, depending on the exigencies of Parliament. As the Queen enters the Houses, the air shakes with the booming of heavy guns, and all London knows that the democratic processes that have so long protected England from oppression have once again been renewed with all their age-old ceremony. But perhaps the nicest time to see the Queen is during Royal Ascot, held at the race track near Windsor Castle—just a short train ride out of London—usually during the third week of June (Tuesday to Friday). After several races, the Queen invariably walks down to the paddock on a special path, greeting race goers as she proceeds. U.S. citizens wishing a seat in the Royal Enclosure—fashion note: the big party hats come out on Ladies Day, normally the Thursday of the meet—should apply to the American Embassy, 24 Grosvenor Square, London W1, before the end of March (note: you must be sponsored by two guests who have attended Ascot at least seven times before!). If you're lucky enough to meet the Queen, you'll be in for a treat—contrary to her stodgy public persona, she's actually a great wit. Should you miss seeing the Queen, you can seek comfort at www.royal.gov.uk, the official Web site of the British monarchy.

⓭ Horse Guards Parade. Horse Guards Parade is now notable mainly for the annual **Trooping the Colour** ceremony, in which the Queen takes the Royal Salute, her official birthday gift, on the second Saturday in June. (Like Paddington Bear, the Queen has two birthdays; her real one is on April 21.) There's pageantry galore, with marching bands and the occasional guardsman fainting clean away in his weighty busby (those furry hats). Covering the vast expanse of the square that faces Horse Guards Road, opposite St. James's Park, at one end and Whitehall at the other, the ceremony is televised. You can see it from the Mall, but you have to get there very early in the morning for any kind of decent view. You can also attend the queenless rehearsals on the preceding two Saturdays. At the Whitehall facade of Horse Guards, the **mounted guard** provides what may be London's most frequently exercised photo op during the daily ceremony—complete with military music and much stamping of boots—when the old guards are replaced with the new. ⊠ *Whitehall, SW1.* ۞ *Queen's mounted guard ceremony: Mon.–Sat. 11 AM, Sun. 10 AM. Tube: Westminster.*

★ **⓾ Houses of Parliament.** Seat of Great Britain's government, the Houses of Parliament are, arguably, the city's most famous and photogenic sight. Facing them you see, from left to right, Big Ben—keeping watch on the corner—the Houses of Parliament themselves, Westminster Hall (the oldest part of the complex), and the Victoria Tower. The most romantic view of the complex is from the opposite, south side of the river, a vista especially dramatic at night when the spires, pinnacles, and towers of the great building are floodlighted green and gold. After a catastrophic fire in 1834, these buildings arose, designed in a delightful mock-medieval style by two Victorian-era architects: Sir Charles Barry and Augustus Pugin. The Palace of Westminster, as the complex is still properly called, was established by Edward the Confessor in the 11th century. It has served as the seat of English administrative power, on and off, ever since. Now virtually the symbol of London, the 1858 **Clock Tower** designed by Pugin contains the bell known as **Big Ben** that chimes the hour (and the quarters); weighing a mighty 13 tons, the bell takes its name from Sir Benjamin Hall, the far-from-slim Westminster building works commissioner. For many, the sound of Big Ben's chimes is a link with the heart and soul of the commonwealth. At the other end of Parliament is the freshly cleaned, 336-ft-high **Victoria Tower.** The rest of the complex was scrubbed down some years ago, revealing honey stone under the dowdy, smog-blackened facades. There are two Houses, the Lords and the Commons. The Visitors' Galleries of the House of Commons affords a view of the best free show in London, staged in the world's most renowned ego chamber (if you want to take it in during its liveliest hour, Prime Minister's Question Time, you'll need to book tickets in advance). The **Lord Chancellor's Residence** within the Palace of Westminster has been renovated spectacularly; be sure to have your name placed in advance on the waiting list for the twice-weekly tours. Note that lines for the House of Commons are always long, so try to come early. You can apply in advance for the special "line of route" tour—open only to overseas visitors—by writing to the **Parliamentary Education Unit** (⊠ House of Commons Information Office, House of Commons, London, SW1A 2TT) at least a month in advance of your visit. ⊠ *St. Stephen's Entrance, St. Margaret St., SW1,* ☎ *020/7219–3000; 020/7219–4272 (Commons information); 020/7219–3107 (Lords information); 020/7219–2184 (Lord Chancellor's Residence),* WEB *www.parliament.uk.* ☞ *Free.* ۞ *Commons Mon.–Thurs. 2:30–10, Fri. 9:30–3 (although not every Fri.); Lords Mon.–Thurs. 2:30–10; Lord Chancellor's Residence Tues. and Thurs. Closed Easter wk, July–Oct., and 3 wks in Dec. Tube: Westminster.*

Institute of Contemporary Art. A handsome Regency building at No. 12 Carlton Terrace houses the ICA, one of Britain's leading modern-art centers. It has provided a stage for the avant-garde in theater, dance, visual art, and music since it was established in 1947. The ICAfé offers good hot dishes, salads, quiches, and desserts. The bar upstairs has a picture window overlooking the Mall. ⊠ *The Mall, W1,* ☎ *020/7930–3647,* WEB *www.ica.org.uk.* 🎫 *£1.50 weekdays, £2.50 weekends, additional charge for specific events.* ☉ *Daily noon–9:30, later for some events. Tube: Charing Cross.*

★ ❷ **National Gallery.** Jan Van Eyck's *Arnolfini Marriage,* Leonardo da Vinci's *Virgin and Child,* Velázquez's *Rokeby Venus,* Constable's *Hay Wain* . . . you get the picture. There are approximately 2,200 other paintings in this museum, many of them instantly recognizable and among the most treasured works of art anywhere. The museum's low, gray, colonnaded, Neoclassic facade fills the north side of Trafalgar Square. The collection ranges from painters of the Italian Renaissance and earlier—housed in the 1991 Sainsbury Wing, designed by the U.S. architect Robert Venturi—through the Flemish and Dutch masters, the Spanish school, and of course the English tradition, including Hogarth, Gainsborough, Stubbs, and Constable.

The collection is really too overwhelming to absorb in a single viewing. The **Micro Gallery,** a computer information center in the Sainsbury Wing, might be the place to start. You can access in-depth information on any work here, choose your favorites, and print out a free personal tour map that marks the paintings you most want to see. Rounding out the top-10 list (the first four lead off above) are Uccello's *Battle of San Romano* (children love its knights on horseback), Bellini's *Doge Leonardo Loredan* (notice the snail-shell buttons), Botticelli's *Venus and Mars,* Caravaggio's *Supper at Emmaus* (almost cinematically lit), Turner's *Fighting Téméeáire* (one of the artist's greatest sunsets), and Seurat's *Bathers at Asnières.* Note that free admission encourages repeat visits: although you may plan to see just the top of the top, the National Gallery, like so many first-rate collections, reveals more gems the more one explores. For a great time-out and fashionable lunch, head for the Brasserie in the Sainsbury Wing. ⊠ *Trafalgar Sq., WC2,* ☎ *020/ 7747–2885,* WEB *www.nationalgallery.org.uk.* 🎫 *Free; charge for special exhibitions.* ☉ *Daily 10–6; June–Aug., Wed. until 9, Sainsbury Wing until 10; 1-hr guided tour starts at Sainsbury Wing weekdays 11:30 and 2:30, Sat. 2 and 3:30. Tube: Charing Cross, Leicester Sq.*

★ ❸ **National Portrait Gallery.** An idiosyncratic collection that presents a potted history of Britain through its people, past and present, this museum is an essential visit for all history and literaturebuffs. It holds the largest cache of portraits in the world, and a superb architectural face-lift in 2000 doubled (and brightened) its exhibition space. As an art collection the museum is eccentric, since the subject, not the artist, is the point. Highlights range from Holbein to Hockney. Many of the faces are obscure and will be just as unknown to English visitors, because the portraits outlasted their sitters' fame—not so surprising when the portraitists are such greats as Reynolds, Gainsborough, Lawrence, and Romney. But the annotation is comprehensive, the chronological layout is easy to negotiate, with the oldest at the top—and there's a separate research center for those who get hooked on particular personages. Don't miss the Victorian and early 20th-century portrait galleries. ⊠ *St. Martin's Pl., WC2,* ☎ *020/7312–2463 recorded information,* WEB *www.npg.org.uk.* 🎫 *Free.* ☉ *Mon.–Wed., Sat.–Sun. 10–6, Thurs.–Fri. 10–9. Tube: Charing Cross, Leicester Sq.*

❶ Nelson's Column. Centerpiece of Trafalgar Square, this famed landmark is topped with E. H. Baily's 1843 statue of Admiral Lord Horatio Nelson, who keeps watch from his 145-ft-high granite perch. The bas-reliefs depicting scenes of Nelson's life, installed around the base, were cast from cannons he captured. The four majestic lions, designed by the Victorian painter Sir Edwin Landseer, were added in 1867. The calling cards of generations of picturesque pigeons have been a corrosive problem for the statue; this may have been finally solved by the addition of a gel coating to the statue. ⊠ *Trafalgar Sq., WC2. Tube: Charing Cross, Leicester Sq.*

❼ Queen's Gallery. Housed in a former chapel at the south side of **Buckingham Palace,** this gallery with much of the greatest art the Queen owns is scheduled to reopen in spring 2002 after a renovation, expansion, and technological update, to coincide with the Queen's Golden Jubilee. A Standing Gallery displays a selection of paintings, and the Graphic Art Gallery exhibits drawings and watercolors; the original main gallery shows changing exhibitions including fine furniture, porcelain, and decorative arts. As only a part of the collection is hung at any one time, in the micro gallery you can view other works in the Queen's vast art collection on screen. ⊠ *Buckingham Palace Rd., SW1,* ☎ *020/7799–2331,* WEB *www.royal.gov.uk.* ⊠ *Call to check price.* ⊙ *Tues.–Sat. 9:30–4:30, Sun. 2–4:30. Tube: St. James's Park, Victoria.*

☝ ❽ Royal Mews. Unmissable children's entertainment, this museum is the home of Her Majesty's Coronation Coach. Standing nearly next door to the Queen's Gallery, the Royal Mews were designed by Regency-era architect John Nash. Mews were falcons' quarters (the name comes from their "mewing," or feather-shedding), but horses gradually eclipsed birds of prey. Now some of the royal beasts live here alongside the bejeweled glass and golden coaches they draw on state occasions. ⊠ *Buckingham Palace Rd., SW1,* ☎ *020/7839–1377,* WEB *www.royal. gov.uk.* ⊠ *£4.60.* ⊙ *Oct.–July, Mon.–Thurs. noon–4; Aug.–Sept., Mon.–Thurs. 10:30–4:30; last admission 30 mins before closing. Call to confirm hours before visiting; the Royal Mews often closes for holidays or for royal events. Tube: St. James's Park, Victoria.*

St. James's Park. London's smallest, most ornamental park and the oldest of its royal ones, St. James's Park makes a spectacular frame for the towers of Westminster and Victoria—especially at night, when the illuminated fountains play and the skyline beyond the trees looks like a floating fairyland. Its present shape more or less reflects what John Nash designed under George IV, turning the canal into a graceful lake (cemented in at a depth of 4 ft in 1855) and generally naturalizing the gardens. More than 17 species of birds—including swans that belong to the Queen—congregate on Duck Island at the east end of the lake. On summer days, the deck chairs (which you must pay to use) are often crammed with office lunchers being serenaded by music from the bandstands. Along the northern side of the park, you'll find the grand thoroughfare known as **the Mall**—best seen on those days when the Queen is hosting her garden parties and it is thronged with guests on their way to Buckingham Palace. *Tube: St. James's Park, Victoria.*

❹ St. Martin-in-the-Fields. One of Britain's best-loved churches, St. Martin's was completed in 1726; James Gibbs's classical temple-with-spire design became a familiar pattern followed for churches in early colonial America. The church is also a haven for music lovers, since the internationally known Academy of St. Martin-in-the-Fields was founded here, and a popular program of lunchtime and evening concerts (often free) continues today. The church's fusty interior has a wonderful atmosphere for music making—but the wooden benches can make it hard to give your undivided attention to the music. The **London Brass-Rubbing Centre,** where you can make your own souvenir knight from replica tomb brasses, with metallic waxes, paper, and instructions provided for about £5, is in the crypt, along with a café and bookshop. ⊠ *Trafalgar Sq.,* ☎ *020/7930–0089; 020/7839–8362,* WEB *www. stmartin-in-the-fields.org.* ☉ *Church daily 8–8; crypt Mon.–Sat. 10–8, Sun. noon–6; box office Mon.–Wed. 10–6, Thurs.–Sat. 10–7, or online; credit-card bookings for evening concerts (charge 50p). Tube: Charing Cross, Leicester Sq.*

★ **⑯** **Tate Britain.** The gallery previously known as the Tate was given a new name and direction in 2000, after its offspring, Tate Modern, opened across the river. As the name proclaims, the Tate Britain, which overlooks the Thames about a 20-minute walk from the Houses of Parliament, focuses on great British artists from the 16th century to the present day. It's a brilliant celebration, done in a new way: the galleries, organized around themes (Family and Society, Literature and Fantasy, and Home and Abroad) display key works from different eras alongside one another. Noteworthy works include those by Hogarth, Gainsborough, Reynolds, and Stubbs from the 18th century, and by Constable, Blake, and the Pre-Raphaelite painters from the 19th. Also from the 19th century is the J. M. W. Turner Bequest, housed magnificently in the James Stirling–designed **Clore Gallery,** the largest collection of work by this leading British romantic artist. New main- and ground-floor galleries opened in fall 2001 provide additional space for the collections. ⊠ *Millbank, SW1,* ☎ *020/7887–8000,* WEB *www.tate.org.uk.* 🎟 *Free; special exhibitions £3–£7.* ☉ *Daily 10–5:50. Tube: Pimlico.*

⑫ **Ten Downing Street.** The British version of the White House occupies three unassuming 18th-century houses. No. 10 has been the official residence of the prime minister since 1732. The cabinet office, hub of the British system of government, is on the ground floor; the prime minister's private apartment is on the top floor. The chancellor of the exchequer traditionally occupies No. 11. Downing Street is cordoned off, but you should be able to catch a glimpse of it from Whitehall. *Whitehall, SW1. Tube: Westminster.*

Trafalgar Square. Permanently alive with people—Londoners and tourists alike—and pigeons and roaring traffic, Trafalgar Square remains London's "living room." Great events, such as royal weddings, elections, and sporting triumphs, will always see the crowds gathering in the city's most famous square. It is a commanding open space—originally built to reflect the width and breadth of an empire that once reached to the farthest corners of the globe—containing a bevy of must-see attractions, including **Nelson's Column** and the **National Gallery.** Today, street performers enhance the square's intermittent atmosphere of celebration, which is strongest in December, first when the lights on the gigantic Christmas tree are turned on, and then—less festively—when thousands gather to see in the New Year. ⊠ *Trafalgar Sq., SW1. Tube: Charing Cross.*

⑨ **Wellington Barracks.** These are the headquarters of the Queen's five regiments of foot guards, who protect the sovereign and patrol her palace dressed in tunics of gold-purled scarlet and tall busbies of black bearskin. If you want to learn more about the guards, you can visit the **Guards Museum;** the entrance is next to the Guards Chapel. ⊠ *Wellington Barracks, Birdcage Walk, SW1,* ☎ *020/7930–4466 Ext. 3428.* 🎟 *£2.* ☉ *Daily 10–4. Tube: St. James's Park.*

★ **⑪** **Westminster Abbey.** Nearly all of Britain's monarchs have been crowned here since the coronation of William the Conqueror on Christmas

Day 1066—and most are buried here, too. The majestic main nave is packed with atmosphere, crowds, and memories, as it has witnessed many splendid coronation ceremonies, royal weddings, and more recently, the funeral of Diana, Princess of Wales. Other than the mysterious gloom of the vast interior, the first thing that strikes most people is the proliferation of statues, tombs, and commemorative tablets: in parts, the building seems more like a stonemason's yard than a place of worship. But it is in its latter capacity that this landmark truly comes into its own. Although attending a service is not something to undertake purely for sightseeing reasons, it provides a glimpse of the abbey in its full majesty, accompanied by music from the Westminster choristers and the organ that Henry Purcell once played.

The present abbey is a largely 13th- and 14th-century rebuilding of the 11th-century church founded by Edward the Confessor, with one notable addition being the 18th-century twin towers over the west entrance, completed by Sir Christopher Wren. Entering by the north door, what you see first on your left are the extravagant 18th-century monuments of statesmen in the north transept, as well as the north-transept chapels. Look up to your right to see the painted-glass rose window, the largest of its kind. At many points the view of the abbey is crowded by the many statues and screens; to your right is the 19th- (and part 13th-) century choir screen, while to the left is the sacrarium, containing the medieval kings' tombs that screen the **Chapel of St. Edward** (due to its ancient fragility, the shrine is closed off). Continuing to the foot of the Henry VII Chapel steps, you can still see the hot seat of power, the **Coronation Chair,** which has been graced by nearly every royal posterior. Then proceed into one of the architectural glories of Britain, **Henry VII Chapel,** passing the huge white marble tomb of Elizabeth I, buried with her half-sister, "Bloody" Mary I. All around are magnificent sculptures of saints, philosophers, and kings, with wild mermaids and monsters carved on the choir-stall misericords (undersides), and exquisite fan vaulting above (binoculars will help you spot the statues high on the walls)—the last riot of medieval design in England and one of the miracles of Western architecture.

Continue to **Poets' Corner;** in 1400 Geoffrey Chaucer became the first poet to be buried here. There are also memorials to William Shakespeare, William Blake, and Charles Dickens (who is also buried here). Exit the abbey by a door from the south transept. Outside the west front is an archway into the quiet, green **Dean's Yard** and the entrance to the **Cloisters.** (If time allows, visit the **Chapter House;** for a small fee you can see the stunning octagonal room, adorned with 14th-century frescoes, where the King's Council met between 1257 and 1547. The **Abbey Museum** is in the Undercroft, which survives from Edward the Confessor's original church; the museum includes a collection of effigies made from the death masks and actual clothing of Charles II and Admiral Lord Nelson, among other fascinating relics. The **Pyx Chamber** contains the abbey's treasure.

As you return to the abbey, look again at the truly awe-inspiring nave. Pause finally for the poignant **Tomb of the Unknown Warrior,** an anonymous World War I martyr who lies buried here in memory of the soldiers fallen in both world wars.

Arrive early if possible, but you should still be prepared to wait in line with the many other visitors to tour the abbey. Note that photography is not permitted. ✉ *Broad Sanctuary, SW1,* ☎ *020/7222–5152,* WEB *www. westminster-abbey.org.* ✉ *Abbey £6; Museum, Pyx Chamber treasury, and Chapter House £2.50, £1 with a ticket to the abbey.* ☉ *Mon.–Sat. 9–3:45 (last admission Sat. 1:45). Undercroft Museum, Pyx Chamber treasury, and Chapter House daily 10:30–4. Abbey closed weekdays and Sunday to visitors during services. Tube: Westminster.*

Soho and Covent Garden

A quadrilateral bounded by Regent Street, Coventry and Cranbourn streets, Charing Cross Road, and the eastern half of Oxford Street encloses Soho, the most fun part of the West End. This appellation, unlike the New York City neighborhood's similar one, is not an abbreviation of anything, but a blast from the past—derived from the shouts of "Soho!" that royal huntsmen in Whitehall Palace's parklands were once heard to cry. One of Charles II's illegitimate sons, the Duke of Monmouth, was an early resident, his dubious pedigree setting the tone for the future: for many years Soho was London's strip show–peep show–clip joint–sex shop–brothel center. The mid-'80s brought legislation that granted expensive licenses to a few such establishments and closed down the rest. Today, Soho remains the address for many wonderful ethnic restaurants, including those of London's Chinatown.

Best known as Eliza Doolittle's stomping grounds in Shaw's *Pygmalion* and Lerner and Loewe's *My Fair Lady,* the former Covent Garden Market became the Piazza in 1980, and it still functions as the center of a neighborhood—one that has always been alluded to as "colorful." It was originally the "convent garden" belonging to the Abbey of St. Peter at Westminster (later Westminster Abbey). Centuries of magnificence and misery, vice and mayhem, and more recent periods of art–literary bohemia followed, until it became the vegetable supplier of London when its market building went up in the 1830s, followed by the Flower Market in 1870. When the produce moved out to the bigger, better Nine Elms Market in Vauxhall in 1974, the (now defunct) Greater London Council stepped in with a rehabilitation scheme, and a new neighborhood was born.

A Good Walk

Soho, being small, is easy to explore, although it's also easy to mistake one narrow, crowded street for another. Enter from the northwest corner, Oxford Circus, and head south for about 200 yards down Regent Street, turn left onto Great Marlborough Street, and head to the top of **Carnaby Street.** Turn right off Broadwick Street onto Berwick (pronounced *ber*-rick) Street, famed as central London's best fruit and vegetable market. Then step through tiny Walker's Court, cross Brewer and Wardour streets, and you'll have arrived at Soho's hip hangout, Old Compton Street. From here, Wardour, Dean, Frith, and Greek streets lead north, all of them bursting with restaurants and clubs. Either of the latter two leads north to charming Soho Square—it has a storybook Tudor cottage just made for a picnic setting—but for lunch, head one block south instead, to Shaftesbury Avenue, heart of Theatreland, across which you'll find Chinatown's main drag, Gerrard Street. Below Gerrard Street is **Leicester Square,** and running along its west side is Charing Cross Road, a bibliophile's dream. You'll find some of the best of the specialty bookshops in little Cecil Court, running east just before Trafalgar Square. During your Soho sojourn, take any excuse to visit either of the neighborhood's wonderful rival patisseries: the old-style French Maison Bertaux at 8 Greek Street or the busy Italian-run but French-accented Pâtisserie Valerie at 44 Old Compton Street. Both serve divine cakes, croissants, and éclairs and offer a perfect time-out.

The easiest way to find **Covent Garden (The Piazza)** ⑰ is to walk down Cranbourn Street, next to Leicester Square tube, then down Long Acre, and turn right at James Street. Near here are St. Paul's—the actors' church—and the **Theatre Museum,** as well as shops and cafés. (If your aim is to shop, Neal Street, Floral Street, the streets around Seven Dials, and the Thomas Neal's mall all repay exploration.) At the northwest corner of the Piazza is the **Royal Opera House** ⑱. A detour down Wellington Street to The Strand brings you to **Somerset House** ⑲ and the Impressionist-stocked **Courtauld Institute of Art.** Follow the Strand west to the **Adelphi** ⑳, cross the Victoria Embankment Gardens to the river, and by sticking to the embankment walk, you'll pass Waterloo Bridge, where (weather permitting) you can catch some of London's finest views, toward the City and Westminster around the Thames bend.

TIMING

The distance covered here is around 5 mi, if you include the lengthy walk down the Strand and riverside stroll back. Skip that, and it's barely a couple of miles, but you will almost certainly get lost, because the streets in Covent Garden and Soho are winding and chaotic. You can whiz round both neighborhoods in an hour, but if the area appeals at all, you'll want all day—for shopping, lunch, the Theatre Museum, and the treasures of Somerset House. You might start at Leicester Square at 2 PM, when the Half Price Theatre Booth opens, pick up tickets for later, and walk, shop, and eat in between.

Sights to See

⑳ **Adelphi.** Near the triangular-handkerchief Victoria Embankment Gardens, this regal riverfront row of houses was the work of all four of the brothers Adam (John, Robert, James, and William: hence the name, from the Greek *adelphoi,* meaning "brothers"), London's noted 18th-century Scottish architects. The best mansion is 7 Adam Street. ⊠ *The Strand, WC2. Tube: Charing Cross, Temple.*

Carnaby Street. The '60s synonym for swinging London fell into a postparty depression, re-emerging sometime during the '80s as the main drag of a public-relations invention called West Soho. Blank stares would greet anyone asking directions to such a place, but it is geographically logical, and the tangle of streets—Foubert's Place, Broadwick Street, Marshall Street—do cohere, at least, in type of merchandise (youth accessories, mostly, with a smattering of designer boutiques). ⊠ *Carnaby St., W1. Tube: Oxford Circus.*

Courtauld Institute of Art. In 1998 this collection was moved to a setting worthy of its fame: a grand 18th-century classical mansion, **Somerset House.** Founded in 1931 by the textile maven Samuel Courtauld, it is London's finest impressionist and postimpressionist collection (Manet's *Bar at the Folies-Bergère* is the star), with bonus Baroque works thrown in. Other historic parts of Somerset House can be enjoyed for free. ⊠ *The Strand, WC2,* ☎ *020/7848–2526,* WEB *www.courtauld.ac.uk.* ☞ *£4. Free Mon. noon–6; combined ticket to Gilbert Collection and Courtauld £7.* ☉ *Mon.–Sat. 10–6, Sun. noon–6 (last admission 5:15). Tube: Covent Garden, Holborn, Temple (closed Sun.).*

⑰ **Covent Garden (The Piazza).** The original "convent garden" produced fruits and vegetables for the 13th-century Abbey of St. Peter at Westminster. In 1630, the duke of Bedford, having become owner, commissioned Inigo Jones to lay out a square, with St. Paul's Church (designed by Jones and known as the actors' church) at one end. The fruit, flower, and vegetable market established in the 1700s flourished until 1974, when it was moved south of the Thames. Since then, the area has been transformed into the Piazza, a mostly higher-class shopping mall that has a couple of cafés and some knickknack stores that are good for gifts. Open-air entertainers perform under the portico of St. Paul's Church, where George Bernard Shaw set the first scene of

Pygmalion (reshaped as the musical *My Fair Lady*). ⊠ *Covent Garden, WC2. Tube: Covent Garden.*

Leicester Square. This is the big magnet for nightlife lovers. Looking at the neon of the major movie houses, the fast-food outlets, and the disco entrances, you'd never guess the square—it's pronounced *les*-ter— was laid out around 1630. The Odeon, on the east side, is the venue for all the Royal Film Performances, and the movie theme is continued by a jaunty little statue of Charlie Chaplin in the opposite corner. Shakespeare sulks in the middle, chin on hand, clearly wishing he were somewhere else. One landmark certainly worth visiting is the **Society of London Theatre (SOLT) ticket kiosk,** on the southwest corner, which sells half-price tickets for many of that evening's performances. ⊠ *Leicester Sq., WC2. Tube: Covent Garden.*

🔞 **Royal Opera House.** The fabled home of the Royal Ballet and Britain's finest opera company reopened in 1999, after mammoth renovations that brought this 19th-century treasure right into the 21st century. Here, in days of yore, Joan Sutherland brought down the house as Lucia di Lammermoor, and Rudolf Nureyev and Margot Fonteyn became the greatest ballet duo of all time. London's premier opera venue was designed in 1858 by E. M. Barry, son of Sir Charles, the House of Commons architect. Without doubt, the glass and steel Floral Hall (used previously for storing scenery) is the most wonderful jaw-dropping feature, and you can wander in and drink in the atmosphere during the day, when there may be free lunchtime concerts and events. You can also visit the Amphitheatre Bar and Piazza concourse, which give a splendid panorama across the city. The whole feeling is of a grand opening up of a formerly elite institution. Behind the scenes, conditions for the two companies have been drastically improved—the Royal Ballet has a real home with state-of-the-art rehearsal rooms, and practice rooms for the musicians. The aim is for Londoners to pack the house and not repeat the performances of 1763, 1792, and 1809, when riots broke out as the cost of rebuilding inflated the price of admission. ⊠ *Bow St., WC2,* ☎ *020/7240–1200 or 020/7304–4000,* WEB *www.royaloperahouse. org. Tube: Covent Garden.*

🔞 **Somerset House.** This grand 18th-century pile, constructed during the reign of George III, was designed to house government offices, principally those of the Navy; these gracious rooms are on view for free, including the Seamen's Waiting Hall and the Nelson Stair. The rooms are on the south side of the building, by the river, while the **Courtauld Institute of Art** occupies most of the north building, facing the busy Strand. Cafés and a river terrace adjoin the property, and a stone-and-glass footbridge leads across the river. In the vaults of the house is **The Gilbert Collection**, a museum of intricate works of silver, gold snuff boxes, and Italian mosaics. The **The Hermitage Rooms** contain permanent exhibition space for some of the treasures from the State Hermitage Museum in Russia. ⊠ *The Strand, WC2,* ☎ *020/7845–4600; 020/7240–4080 Gilbert Collection; 020/7845–4630 Hermitage,* WEB *www.somerset-house.org.uk.* 🎫 *Somerset House free; Gilbert Collection £4 (combined ticket to Gilbert and Courtauld Institute of Art £7); Hermitage Rooms £6.* 🕐 *Mon.–Sat. 10–6, Sun. noon–6 (last admission 5:15). Tube: Charing Cross.*

🔄 **Theatre Museum.** The museum aims to re-create the excitement of theater. There are usually programs allowing children to get in a mess with makeup or have a giant dressing-up session. Permanent exhibits attempt a history of the English stage, with artifacts from those of the 16th century to Mick Jagger's jumpsuit, and tens of thousands of theater playbills and sections on such topics as Hamlet-through-the-ages and pantomime.

⊠ *7 Russell St., WC2,* ☎ *020/7836–7891,* 〚WEB〛 *www.theatremuseum.org.* 🖼 *£4.50.* ⊙ *Tues.–Sun. 10–6. Tube: Covent Garden.*

Bloomsbury and Legal London

The character of an area of London can change visibly from one street to the next. Nowhere is this so clear as in the contrast between fun-loving Soho and intellectual Bloomsbury, a mere 100 yards to the northeast, or between arty, trendy Covent Garden and—on the other side of Kingsway—sober Holborn. Both Bloomsbury and Holborn are almost purely residential and should be seen by day. The first district is best known for its famous flowering of literary-arty bohemia, personified by the clique known as the Bloomsbury Group during the first three decades of the 20th century, and for the British Museum and the University of London, which dominate it now. The second sounds as exciting as, say, a center for accountants or dentists, but don't be put off—filled with magnificently ancient buildings, it's more interesting and beautiful than you might suppose.

Most people head here to find the ghosts of all those great Bloomsbury figures such as Virginia Woolf, E. M. Forster, Vanessa Bell, and Lytton Strachey. Ghosts of their literary salons soon lead into the time-warp territory of interlocking alleys, gardens and cobbled courts, town houses and halls where London's legal profession grew up. The Great Fire of 1666 razed most of the city but spared the buildings of legal London, and the whole neighborhood—known as Holborn—oozes history. Leading landmarks here are the Inns of Court, where the country's top solicitors and barristers have had their chambers for centuries.

A Good Walk

From Russell Square tube station, walk south down Southampton Row, and west on Great Russell Street, passing Bloomsbury Square on the left, en route to London's biggest and most important collection of antiquities, the **British Museum** ㉑. Leaving this via the back exit leads you to Montague Place; then head left to Malet Street to reach the **University of London** ㉒. For a delightful detour, head west toward the Goodge Street tube stop on Tottenham Court Road to Scala Street to find the Victorian-era wonders of **Pollock's Toy Museum** ㉓. Back at the university, head north on Gordon Street to busy Euston Road and east toward St. Pancras and the bold new **British Library** ㉔. But if time is short, head south through the university, veering left down Guilford Street past Coram's Fields, then right to Doughty Street and the **Dickens House** ㉕. Two streets west, parallel to Doughty Street, is charming Lamb's Conduit Street (whose pretty pub, the Lamb, Dickens inevitably frequented). At the bottom of Lamb's Conduit Street you reach Theobalds Road, where you enter the first of the Inns of Court, Gray's Inn, emerging from here onto High Holborn (pronounced *hoe*-bun)—the noisy main route from the City to the West End and Westminster—and Hatton Garden, running north from Holborn Circus and still the center of London's diamond and jewelry trade. Pass another ghost of former trading, Staple Inn, and turn left down tiny Great Turnstile Row to reach **Lincoln's Inn** ㉖. Cross to the north side of Lincoln's Inn Fields to **Sir John Soane's Museum** ㉗. Head south and cross the Strand to **Temple** ㉘, and pass through the elaborate stone arch to Middle Temple Lane, which you follow to the Thames.

TIMING

This is a substantial walk of 3 to 4 mi, and it has two distinct halves. The first half, around Bloomsbury, is not so interesting on the surface, but it features the British Museum, where you could spend two hours—or two days. The Dickens House is also worth a stop. The second half, legal London, is a real walker's walk, with most of the highlights in the architecture and atmosphere. The exception is Sir John Soane's Museum. The walk alone can be done comfortably in two hours.

Sights to See

㉔ British Library. Since 1759, the British Library had been housed in the British Museum on Gordon Square—but space ran out long ago, necessitating this grand new edifice, a few blocks north of the British Museum, between Euston and St. Pancras stations. The great exodus of 18 million volumes is now complete, and the library's treasures are on view to the general public: the Magna Carta, Gutenberg Bible, Jane Austen's writings, Shakespeare's First Folio, and musical manuscripts by Handel and Sir Paul McCartney are on show in the John Ritblat Gallery. The library's amphitheater has a series of free concerts. ✉ *96 Euston Rd., NW1,* ☎ *020/7412–7332,* WEB *www.bl.uk.* ✆ *Free.* ☺ *Weekdays 9:30–6 (Tues. 9:30–8); Sat. 9:30–5; Sun. 11–5. Tube: Euston or King's Cross.*

★ ☕ **㉑ British Museum.** With a facade like a great temple, this celebrated treasure house, filled with plunder of incalculable value and beauty from around the globe, occupies a ponderously dignified Greco-Victorian building that makes a suitably grand impression. Inside you'll find some of the greatest relics of humankind: the Elgin Marbles, the Rosetta Stone—everything, it seems, but the Ark of the Covenant. The museum has shaken off its ponderous dust as galleries open and sections are updated, particularly with the addition of collections from the now-closed Museum of Mankind, including those in the impressive **Sainsbury African Galleries,** opened in 2001. The focal point is the **Great Court,** a brilliant techno-classical design with a vast glass roof, which highlights and reveals the museum's most well-kept secret—an inner courtyard—for the first time in 150 years. The revered **Reading Room** has also been carefully restored. New galleries and exhibit space will celebrate the museum's 250th birthday in 2003. Beyond the new frontage, there are 2½ mi of floor space inside, split into nearly 100 galleries—so arm yourself with a free floor plan directly as you go in, or they'll have to send out search parties to rescue you.

The collection began in 1753 and grew quickly, thanks to enthusiastic kleptomaniacs during the Napoleonic Wars—most notoriously the seventh earl of Elgin, who lifted marbles from the Parthenon and Erechtheum while on a Greek vacation between 1801 and 1804. Here follows a highly edited résumé (in order of encounter) of the British Museum's greatest hits: close to the entrance hall, in the south end of Room 25, is the **Rosetta Stone,** found in 1799, and carved in 196 BC with a decree of Ptolemy V in Egyptian hieroglyphics, demotic, and Greek. It was this multilingual inscription that provided the French Egyptologist Jean-François Champollion with the key to deciphering hieroglyphics. Maybe the **Elgin Marbles** ought to be back in Greece, but since they are here—and they are, after all, among the most graceful and heartbreakingly beautiful sculptures on earth—make a beeline for them in Room 8, west of the entrance in the Parthenon Galleries, which also include the remains of the Parthenon frieze that girdled the cella of Athena's temple on the Acropolis, carved around 440 BC. Also in the West Wing is one of the Seven Wonders of the Ancient World—in fragment form, unfortunately—in Room 12: the **Mausoleum of Halikarnassos.**

Upstairs are some of the most popular galleries, especially beloved by children: Rooms 62–63 where the **Egyptian Mummies** live. The Roxie Walker Galleries display even more relics from the Egyptian Land of the Dead. Nearby are the glittering 4th-century Mildenhall Treasure and the equally splendid 8th-century Sutton Hoo Treasure. A more pro-saic exhibit is that of Pete Marsh, sentimentally named by the ar-chaeologists who unearthed the Lindow Man from a Cheshire peat marsh; poor Pete was ritually slain, probably as a human sacrifice.

The Chase Manhattan Gallery of **North America**, opened in 1999, has one of the largest collections of native culture outside the North American continent, going back to the earliest hunters 10,000 years ago. The **Korean Gallery**, opened in late 2000, showcases the royal gold crown of Silla (5th–6th centuries), on loan from the National Museum of Korea. ⊠ *Great Russell St., WC1,* ☎ *020/7636–1555,* WEB *www. thebritishmuseum.ac.uk.* ⛱ *Free (suggested donation of £2). Guided tours: check at the information desk.* ⊙ *Mon.–Sat. 10–5, Sun. noon– 6. Tube: Tottenham Court Rd., Holborn, Russell Sq.*

㉕ Dickens House. This is the only one of the many London houses Charles Dickens (1812–70) inhabited that's still standing, and it would have had a real claim to his fame in any case, since he wrote *Oliver Twist* and *Nicholas Nickleby* and finished *The Pickwick Papers* here between 1837 and 1839. The house looks exactly as it would have in Dickens's day, complete with first editions, letters, and tall clerk's desk, plus a treat for Lionel Bart fans—his score of *Oliver!* ⊠ *48 Doughty St.,* ☎ *020/7405–2127,* WEB *www.dickensmuseum.com.* ⛱ *£4.* ⊙ *Mon.–Sat. 10–5. Tube: Chancery La., Russell Sq.*

㉖ Lincoln's Inn. One of the oldest, best preserved, and most comely of the Inns of Court, Lincoln's Inn offers plenty to see—from the Chancery Lane Tudor brick gatehouse to the wide-open, tree-lined, atmospheric Lincoln's Inn Fields and the 15th-century Chapel remodeled by Inigo Jones in 1620. The wisteria-clad New Square is London's only com-plete 17th-century square. ⊠ *Chancery La., WC2,* ☎ *020/7405–1393.* ⛱ *Free.* ⊙ *Gardens weekdays 7–7; chapel weekdays noon–2:30; pub-lic may also attend Sun. service at 11:30 in chapel during legal terms. Tube: Chancery La.*

㉓ Pollock's Toy Museum. Historians tell us that the Victorians invented the concept of childhood, and no better proof can be offered than this magical place, a treasure trove of a small museum in a 19th-century town house. Most of the objects are dolls, dollhouses, teddy bears, folk toys—and those bedazzling mementos of Victorian childhood, Pollock's famed cardboard cutout miniature theaters, all red velvet and gold trim, with movable scenery and figurines. Happily, Pollock's still sells these theaters, a souvenir that will drive both children and connoisseurs mad with joy. ⊠ *1 Scala St., W1,* ☎ *020/7636–3452,* WEB *www.tao2000.net/ pollocks.* ⛱ *£3.* ⊙ *Mon.–Sat. 10–5. Tube: Goodge St.*

★ ㉗ Sir John Soane's Museum. Guaranteed to raise a smile from the most blasé and footsore traveler, this collection hardly deserves the burden of its dry name. Sir John, architect of the Bank of England, who lived here from 1790 to 1831, created one of London's most idiosyncratic and fascinating houses. Everywhere mirrors and colors play tricks with light and space, and split-level floors worthy of a fairground fun house disorient you. In a basement chamber sits the vast 1300 BC sar-cophagus of Seti I, lit by a skylight two stories above. ⊠ *13 Lincoln's Inn Fields, WC2,* ☎ *020/7405–2107,* WEB *www.soane.org.* ⛱ *Free.* ⊙ *Tues.–Sat. 10–5; also 6–9 on 1st Tues. of every month. Tube: Holborn.*

㉘ Temple. This is the collective name for **Inner Temple** and **Middle Tem-ple,** and its entrance, the exact point of entry into the City, is marked by a young (1880) bronze griffin, the **Temple Bar Memorial.** In the buildings opposite is an elaborate stone arch through which you pass into Middle Temple Lane, past a row of 17th-century timber-frame houses, and on into Fountain Court. If the Elizabethan **Middle Temple Hall** is open, don't miss its hammer-beam roof—among the finest in the land. There's no admission charge, but a tip should be given to the porter. ⊠ *2 Plowden Bldgs., Middle Temple La.,* ☎ *020/7427–4800.* ⊘ *Weekdays 10–11:30 and (when not in use) 3–4. Tube: Temple.*

㉒ **University of London.** A relatively youthful instit ution that grew out of the need for a nondenominational center for higher education, the University of London was founded by Dissenters in 1826, with its first examinations held 12 years later. Jews and Roman Catholics were not the only people admitted for the first time to an English university—women were, too, although they had to wait until 1878 to sit for a degree. ⊠ *Russell Sq., WC1,* 🕸 *www.lon.ac.uk. Tube: Russell Sq.*

The City

When people in London tell you that they work in the City, they aren't being vague. They're using the British equivalent of Wall Street. The City extends eastward from Temple Bar to the Tower of London, and north from the Thames to Chiswell Street. Despite its small size (it's known as the Square Mile), this area is the financial engine of Britain and one of the world's leading centers of trade. The City, however, is more than just London's Wall Street: it is also home to two of the city's most notable sights, the Tower of London and St. Paul's, one of the world's greatest cathedrals—truly, a case of the money changers encompassing the temple. The pedestrian-only Millennium Bridge, set to reopen in fall 2001, connects the area with the South Bank.

Twice, the City has been nearly wiped off the face of the earth. The Great Fire of 1666 necessitated a total reconstruction, in which Sir Christopher Wren had a big hand, contributing not only his masterpiece, St. Paul's Cathedral, but 49 additional parish churches. The second wave of destruction was dealt by the German bombers of World War II. The ruins were rebuilt, but slowly, and with no overall plan, leaving the City a patchwork of the old and the new, the interesting and the flagrantly awful. Since a mere 8,000 or so people call it home, the financial center of Britain is deserted on weekends, with restaurants shuttered and streets forlorn and windswept.

A Good Walk

Begin at the gateway to the City, the Temple Bar of the Temple district, a bronze griffin on the Strand opposite the Royal Courts of Justice. Walk east to Fleet Street and turn left on Bolt Court to Gough Square, and **Dr. Johnson's House** ㉙, passing Ye Olde Cheshire Cheese on Wine Office Court en route back to Fleet Street and the journalists' church, **St. Bride's** ㉚. At the end of Fleet Street, cross Ludgate Circus to Ludgate Hill to reach **Old Bailey** ㉛ and the Central Criminal Courts. Continuing along Ludgate Hill, you reach **St. Paul's Cathedral** ㉜, Wren's masterpiece. The spirits of those who used to feed the pigeons on its steps—remember the old lady from Walt Disney's *Mary Poppins*?—seem to hover nearby.

Retrace your steps to Newgate Street to reach London's meat market, Smithfield—where, for centuries, livestock was sold. From Smithfield Market, cross Aldersgate Street and take the right fork to London Wall, named for the Roman rampart that stood along it, with a remaining section of 2nd- to 4th-century wall at St. Alphege Garden. There's another bit outside the **Museum of London** ㉝, behind which is the important arts mecca of gray concrete, the **Barbican Centre** ㉞. Back on London Wall, turn south onto Coleman Street, then right onto Masons Avenue to reach Basinghall Street and the **Guildhall** ㉟, then follow Milk Street south to Cheapside. Here is another symbolic center of London, the church of **St. Mary-le-Bow** ㊱.

Walk to the east end of Cheapside, where seven roads meet, and you will be facing the **Bank of England** ㊲. Turn your back on the bank and there's the Lord Mayor's Palladian-style abode, the Mansion House, with Wren's St. Stephen Walbrook church—considered his finest effort by architectural historians—behind it, and the Royal Exchange in between Threadneedle Street and Cornhill. Now head down Queen Victoria Street, where you'll pass the remains of the Roman **Temple of Mithras** ㊳, then, after a sharp left turn onto Cannon Street, you'll come upon the **Monument** ㊴, Wren's memorial to the Great Fire of London. Just south of there is London Bridge. Turn left onto Lower Thames Street, for just under a mile's walk—passing Billingsgate, London's principal fish market for 900 years, until 1982, and the Custom House, built early in the last century—to the **Tower of London** ㊵, which may be the single most unmissable of London's sights. Children of all ages will be enchanted by that Thames icon, the **Tower Bridge.**

TIMING

This is a marathon. Unless you want to be walking all day, without a chance to do justice to London's most famous sights, the Tower of London and St. Paul's Cathedral—not to mention the Museum of London, Tower Bridge, and the Barbican Centre—you should consider splitting the walk into segments. Conversely, if you're not planning to go inside, this walk makes for a great day out, with lots of surprising vistas, river views, and history. The City is a wasteland on weekends and after dark, so choose your time.

Sights to See

㊲ **Bank of England.** Known familiarly for the past couple of centuries as "the Old Lady of Threadneedle Street," the bank has been central to the British economy since 1694. Sir John Soane designed the Neoclassical hulk in 1788, wrapping it in windowless walls (which are all that survive of his building) to project a facade of unshakable stability. This and other facets of the bank's history are traced in the Bank of England Museum, just around the corner. ✉ *Museum, Bartholomew La., EC4,* ☎ *020/7601–5545,* WEB *www.bankofengland.co.uk.* 🎫 *Free.* ⊙ *Weekdays 10–5. Tube: Bank, Monument.*

㉞ **Barbican Centre.** An enormous concrete maze Londoners love to hate, the Barbican is home to the London Symphony Orchestra and its auditorium, the Guildhall School of Music and Drama, the **Barbican Art Gallery** (for touring exhibitions), two cinemas, and a convention center. In 2001 the Royal Shakespeare Company (RSC), which had made the Barbican its London base, announced plans to present plays around the West End, beginning in mid-2002, though it still planned to use the Barbican as well. Londoners have come to accept the place, if not exactly love it, because of its contents. ✉ *Silk St., EC2,* ☎ *020/7638–8891; 020/7628–3351 RSC backstage tour,* WEB *www.barbican.org.uk.* 🎫 *Barbican Centre free, gallery £5.* ⊙ *Barbican Centre Mon.–Sat. 9 AM–11 PM, Sun. noon–11; gallery Mon.–Sat. 10–7:30, Sun. noon–7:30. Tube: Moorgate, Barbican.*

㉙ **Dr. Johnson's House.** Samuel Johnson lived here between 1746 and 1759, while in the worst of health, compiling his famous *Dictionary of the English Language* in the attic. Like Dickens, he lived all over town, but, like Dickens's House, this is the only one of Johnson's abodes remaining today. The 17th-century house is a shrine to the man possibly more attached to London than anyone else has ever been, and it includes a first edition of his dictionary among the Johnson-and-

Boswell mementos. After your visit, repair around the corner in Wine Office Court to the Ye Olde Cheshire Cheese pub, once Johnson and Boswell's favorite watering hole. ✉ *17 Gough Sq., EC4,* ☎ *020/7353–3745.* 💷 *£4.* ⊘ *May–Sept., Mon.–Sat. 11–5:30; Oct.–Apr., Mon.–Sat. 11–5. Tube: Blackfriars, Chancery La.*

❸❺ **Guildhall.** In the symbolic nerve center of the City, the Corporation of London ceremonially elects and installs its Lord Mayor as it has done for 800 years. The Guildhall was built in 1411, and although it failed to escape either the 1666 or 1940 flames, its core survived. The fabulous hall is a psychedelic patchwork of coats of arms and banners of the City Livery Companies. Also here is the Worshipful Company of Clockmakers Collection in the Guildhall Library, with more than 600 timepieces; to the right of Guildhall Yard is the **Guildhall Art Gallery,** the corporation's collection of London scenes and portraits of royals and statesmen. ✉ *Gresham St., EC2,* ☎ *020/7606–3030; 020/7332–1632 gallery; 020/7332–3700 recorded information,* WEB *www.cityoflondon. gov.uk.* 💷 *Free; gallery £2.50.* ⊘ *Mon.–Sat. 9:30–5; Clockmakers Collection weekdays 9:30–4:45; gallery Mon.–Sat. 10–5, Sun. noon–4. Print Room and bookshop closed Sat. Tube: St. Paul's, Moorgate, Bank, Mansion House.*

OFF THE BEATEN PATH

JACK THE RIPPER'S LONDON – *Cor blimey, guv'nor, Jack the Ripper woz here!* Several organizations offer tours of "Jack's London"—the (still) mean streets of the East End, the working-class neighborhood directly to the east of the City. Here, in 1888, the Whitechapel murders traumatized Victorian London. At the haunting hour, tour groups head out to Bucks Row and other notorious scenes of the crime. **Original London Walks** (☎ 020/7624–3978) offers frequent tours leaving at 7 PM from the Tower Hill tube stop. The **Jack the Ripper Mystery Walk** (☎ 020/ 8558–9446) departs at 8 PM from the Aldgate tube stop Wednesday and Sunday; Friday 7 PM. Even with a large tour group, this can be a spooky and unforgettable experience.

Lloyd's of London. Architect Richard Rogers's (of Paris Pompidou Centre fame) fantastical steel-and-glass medium-rise of six towers around a vast atrium, with his trademark inside-out ventilation shafts, stairwells, and gantries, may be the most exciting recent structure erected in London. This fabulous fun house of a building, which houses the world-famous insurance agency, is best seen at night, when cobalt and lime spotlights make it leap out of the deeply boring gray skyline. ✉ *1 Lime St., EC3,* ☎ *020/7623–7100. Tube: Bank, Monument, Liverpool St., Aldgate.*

Millennium Bridge. This pedestrian-only bridge of aluminum and steel, designed by Norman Foster and sculptor Anthony Caro, opened in 2000. A stabilization problem led to its closing, but at press time it was scheduled to reopen by fall 2001. The bridge connects the City—St. Paul's Cathedral area—with the Tate Modern art gallery. On the South Bank side, the bridge marks the middle of the **Millennium Mile,** a walkway taking in a clutch of popular sights. The city views from the bridge are breathtaking, with perhaps the best-ever view of St. Paul's Cathedral. ✉ *Peters Hill or Bankside, EC4 or SE1,* ☎ *020/7403–8299. Tube: Mansion House, Blackfriars, or Southwark.*

❸❾ **Monument.** Commemorating the "dreadful visitation" of the Great Fire of 1666, this is the world's tallest isolated stone column—the work of Wren. The viewing gallery is 311 steps up. ✉ *Monument St., EC3,* ☎ *020/7626–2717.* 💷 *£1.50; combination ticket with Tower Bridge £6.75.* ⊘ *Daily 10–5:40 (hrs subject to change; phone before visiting). Tube: Monument.*

☺ ㉝ **Museum of London.** Anyone with the least interest in how this city evolved will adore this museum, especially its reconstructions and dioramas of the Great Fire (flickering flames! sound effects!), a 1940s air-raid shelter, a Georgian prison cell, and a Victorian street complete with stocked shops. Come right up to date in the "London Now" gallery. "World City," opening in December 2001, examines London from 1789 to 1914, one of the city's most interesting periods. ✉ *London Wall, EC2,* ☎ *020/7600–0807,* WEB *www.museumoflondon.org.uk.* ⌧ *£5, free 4:30–5:50.* ☉ *Mon.–Sat. 10–5:50, Sun. noon–5:50. Tube: Barbican.*

㉛ **Old Bailey.** The present-day Central Criminal Court is where legendary Newgate Prison stood from the 12th century right until the beginning of the 20th century. Dickens visited Newgate several times—Fagin ended up in the Condemned Hold here in *Oliver Twist.* Ask the doorman which current trial is likely to prove juicy, if you're that kind of ghoul—you may catch the conviction of the next Crippen or Christie (England's most notorious wife murderers, both tried here). There are some restrictions on entry (cameras and children under 14 are not allowed); call the information line first. ✉ *Newgate St., EC4,* ☎ *020/7248–3277.* ☉ *Public Gallery weekdays 9:30–1 and 2–4:30 (line forms at Newgate St. entrance). Tube: Blackfriars.*

㉚ **St. Bride's.** One of the first of Wren's city churches, St. Bride's was also one of those bomb-damaged in World War II, reconsecrated only in 1960 after a 17-year-long restoration. From afar, study its extraordinary steeple. Its uniquely tiered shape gave rise, legend has it, to the traditional wedding cake. ✉ *Fleet St., EC4,* ☎ *020/7353–1301.* ⌧ *Free.* ☉ *Weekdays 8–5, Sat. 9–5, Sun. between services at 11 and 6:30. Tube: Chancery La.*

㊱ **St. Mary-le-Bow.** Wren's 1673 church has one of the most famous sets of bells around—a Londoner must be born within the sound of Bow Bells to claim to be a true cockney. The origin of that idea was probably the curfew rung on the Bow Bells during the 14th century, even though "cockney" came to mean Londoner three centuries later, and then it was an insult. The Bow in the name comes from the bow-shape arches in the Norman crypt. In the crypt is The Place Below, a handy spot for great soups and quiches. Packed during weekday lunchtimes, it's also open for breakfast. ✉ *Cheapside, EC2.* ☉ *Mon.–Thurs. 6:30–5:45, Fri. 6:30–4, weekends special services only. Tube: Mansion House.*

★ ㉜ **St. Paul's Cathedral.** The symbolic heart of London, St. Paul's will take your breath away. The dome—the world's third largest—will already be familiar, since you see it peeping through on the skyline from many an angle. The structure is, of course, Sir Christopher Wren's masterpiece, completed in 1710 after 35 years of building, then, much later, miraculously spared (mostly) by World War II bombs. Wren's first plan, known as the New Model, did not make it past the drawing board. The second, known as the Great Model, got as far as the 20-ft oak rendering you can see here today before it also was rejected, whereupon Wren is said to have burst into tears. The third, however, was accepted, with the fortunate coda that the architect be allowed to make changes as he saw fit. Without that, there would be no dome, since the approved design had featured a steeple.

When you enter and see the dome from the inside, you may find that it seems smaller than you expected. You aren't imagining things; it *is* smaller, and 60 ft lower than the lead-covered outer dome. Beneath the lantern is Wren's famous epitaph, which his son composed and had set into the pavement, and which reads succinctly: *Lector, si monumentum requiris, circumspice*—"Reader, if you seek his monument, look around you." The epitaph also appears on Wren's memorial in the Crypt. Up 259 spiral steps is the **Whispering Gallery,** an acoustic phenomenon; you whisper something to the wall on one side, and a second later it transmits clearly to the other side, 107 ft away. Ascend farther to the **Stone Gallery,** which encircles the outside of the dome and has a spectacular panorama of London.

The poet John Donne, who had been dean of St. Paul's for his final 10 years (he died in 1631), lies in the south choir aisle. The vivacious choir-stall carvings nearby are the work of Grinling Gibbons, as are the organ's, which Wren designed and Handel played. Behind the high altar, you'll find the **American Memorial Chapel,** dedicated in 1958 to the 28,000 GIs stationed here who lost their lives in World War II. Among the famous whose remains lie in the **Crypt** are the Duke of Wellington and Admiral Lord Nelson. The Crypt also has a gift shop and a café. ✉ *St. Paul's Churchyard, EC4,* ☎ *020/7236–4128,* WEB *www.stpauls.co.uk.* 🎫 *£5.* ⏲ *Cathedral Mon.–Sat. 8:30–4 (closed occasionally for special services); ambulatory, crypt, and galleries Mon.–Sat. 9:30–4:15. Tube: St. Paul's.*

38 **Temple of Mithras.** Unearthed on a building site in 1954 and taken, at first, for an early Christian church, this was a minor place of pilgrimage in the Roman City. In fact, worshipers here favored Christ's chief rival, Mithras, the Persian god of light, during the 3rd and 4th centuries. You can see the foundations of the temple on this site. ✉ *Temple Court, Queen Victoria St., EC4. Tube: Bank.*

Tower Bridge. Despite its venerable, nay, medieval, appearance, this is a Victorian youngster that celebrated its centenary in June 1994. Constructed of steel, then clothed in Portland stone, it was styled in the Gothic persuasion to complement the Tower of London next door and is famous for its enormous bascules, the "arms," which open to allow large ships through, which is a rare occurrence these days. The bridge's 100th-birthday gift was a new exhibition, one of London's most imaginative. You are conducted in the company of "Harry Stoner," an animatronic bridge construction worker worthy of Disneyland, back in time to witness the birth of the Thames's last downstream bridge. Be sure to hang on to your ticket and follow the signs to the Engine Rooms for part two, where the original steam-driven hydraulic engines gleam, and a cute rococo theater is the setting for an Edwardian music-hall production of the bridge's story. ☎ *020/7403–3761,* WEB *www.towerbridge.org.uk.* 🎫 *£6.25; combination ticket with the Monument £6.75.* ⏲ *Apr.–Oct., daily 10–6:30; Nov.–Mar., daily 9:30–6 (last entry 1¼ hrs before closing). Tube: Tower Hill.*

★ 40 **Tower of London.** Nowhere else does London's history come to life so vividly as in thisminicity of melodramatic towers stuffed to bursting with heraldry and treasure, the intimate details of lords and dukes and princes and sovereigns etched in the walls (literally, in some places), and quite a few pints of royal blood spilled on the stones. You can save time and avoid lines by buying a ticket in advance from any Underground stop; arriving early (before 11) can also help at busy times. Moving walkways within the prize exhibit, the Crown Jewels, hasten progress there at the busiest times.

The Tower holds the royal gems because it's still one of the royal palaces, although no monarch since Henry VII has called it home. It has also housed the Royal Mint, the Public Records, the Royal Menagerie (which formed the basis of London Zoo), and the Royal Observatory, although its most renowned and titillating function has been, of course, as a jail and place of torture and execution.

A person was mighty privileged to be beheaded in the peace and seclusion of **Tower Green** instead of before the mob at Tower Hill. In fact, only seven people were ever important enough—among them Anne Boleyn and Catherine Howard, wives two and five of Henry VIII's six; Elizabeth I's friend Robert Devereux, Earl of Essex; and the nine-days' queen, Lady Jane Grey, age 17. In 1998 the executioner's block, with its pathetic forehead-size dent, and his axe, along with the equally famous rack and the more obscure "scavenger's daughter" (which pressed a body nearly to death), plus assorted thumbscrews, "iron maidens," and so forth, took up temporary residence in the Royal Armouries in Leeds, Yorkshire; eventually, they will return to the Royal Armouries collection of the Tower of London. Until then, fans of this horrifying niche of heavy metal might want to pay a call on the London Dungeon attraction, just across the Thames.

Free tours depart every half hour or so from the Middle Tower. They are conducted by the 39 Yeoman Warders, better known as "Beefeaters"—ex-servicemen dressed in resplendent navy-and-red (scarlet-and-gold on special occasions) Tudor outfits. Beefeaters have been guarding the Tower since Henry VII appointed them in 1485. One of them, the Yeoman Ravenmaster, is responsible for making life comfortable for the Tower ravens—an important duty, because if Hardey, George, Hugine, Mumin, Cedric, Odin, Thor (who talks), and Gwylem were to desert the Tower, goes the legend, the kingdom would fall. Today, the Tower takes no chances: the ravens' wings are clipped.

In prime position stands the oldest part of the Tower and the most conspicuous of its buildings, the **White Tower.** This central keep was begun in 1078 by William the Conqueror; Henry III (1207–72) had it whitewashed, which is where the name comes from. The spiral staircase is the only way up, and here you'll find the **Royal Armouries,** with a collection of arms and armor. Most of the interior of the White Tower has been altered over the centuries, but the **Chapel of St. John the Evangelist,** downstairs from the armories, is a pure example of 11th-century Norman style—very rare, very simple, and very beautiful. Across the moat, **Traitors' Gate** lies to the right. Immediately opposite Traitors' Gate is the former Garden Tower, better known since about 1570 as the **Bloody Tower.** Its name comes from one of the most famous unsolved murders in history, the saga of the "little princes in the Tower." In 1483 the uncrowned boy king, Edward V, and his brother Richard were left here by their uncle, Richard of Gloucester, after the death of their father, Edward I. They were never seen again, Gloucester was crowned Richard III, and in 1674 two little skeletons were found under the stairs to the White Tower. The obvious conclusions have always been drawn—and were, in fact, even before the skeletons were discovered. The **New Armouries** have been renovated into a restaurant, a welcome addition for visitors.

The most dazzling and famous exhibits here are, of course, the **Crown Jewels,** housed in the **Jewel House, Waterloo Block.** You get so close to the fabled gems you feel you could polish them (if it weren't for the wafers of bulletproof glass), and they are enhanced by laser lighting, which nearly hurts the eyes with sparkle. Before you meet them in person, you are given a film preview with scenes from Elizabeth's 1953 coronation. Security is as fiendish as you'd expect, since the jewels—even though they would be impossible for thieves to sell—are *so* priceless that they're not insured. However, they are polished every January by the crown jewelers. A brief résumé of the top jewels: finest of all is the Royal Sceptre, containing the earth's largest cut diamond, the 530-carat Star of Africa. This is also known as Cullinan I, having been cut from the South African Cullinan, which weighed 20 ounces when dug up from a De Beers mine at the beginning of the century. Another chip off the block, Cullinan II, lives on the Imperial State Crown that Prince Charles is due to wear at his coronation—the same one that Elizabeth II wore in her coronation procession; it was made for Victoria's coronation in 1838. The other most famous gem is the Koh-i-noor, or "Mountain of Light," which adorns the Queen Mother's crown. When Victoria was presented with this gift horse in 1850, she looked it in the mouth, found it lacking in glitter, and had it chopped down to almost half its weight.

The little chapel of **St. Peter ad Vincula** can be visited only as part of a Yeoman Warder tour. The second church on the site, it conceals the remains of some 2,000 people executed at the Tower, Anne Boleyn and Catherine Howard among them.

One of the more evocative towers is **Beauchamp Tower,** built west of Tower Green by Edward I (1272–1307). It was soon designated as a jail for the higher class of miscreant, including Lady Jane Grey, who is thought to have added her Latin graffiti to the many inscriptions carved by prisoners that you can see here. Allow at least three hours to explore the Tower, and don't forget to stroll along the battlements before you leave; from them, you get a wonderful overview of the whole Tower of London. ⊠ *H. M. Tower of London, Tower Hill, EC3N,* ☎ *020/7709–0765; 020/7680–9004 recorded information,* WEB *www. hrp.org.uk.* 🖃 *£11.* ☉ *Mar.–Oct., Mon.–Sat. 9–5, Sun. 10–5; Nov.– Feb., Tues.–Sat. 9–4, Sun.–Mon. 10–4 (the Tower closes 1 hr after last admission time. All internal buildings close 30 mins after last admission). Yeoman Warder guided tours leave daily from Middle Tower (subject to weather and availability), at no charge, about every 30 mins until 3:30 Mar.–Oct., 2:30 Nov.–Feb. For tickets to Ceremony of the Keys (the locking of the main gates, nightly at 10), write well in advance to ⊠ The Resident Governor and Keeper of the Jewel House, Queen's House, H. M. Tower of London, EC3. Give your name, the dates you wish to attend (including alternative dates), and number of people (up to 7), and enclose an SASE. Tube: Tower Hill.*

The South Bank

That old North London quip about needing a passport to cross the Thames is no longer heard on Londoners' lips. Tourists, too, rarely frequented the area unless they were departing from Waterloo Station. Today new attractions draw even the most ardent northerners across the great divide. Tate Modern, the new branch of the Tate Gallery, is the star attraction, installed in a 1930s power station. At the South Bank Centre, the world's largest observation wheel, officially called the British Airways London Eye, gives you a flight over the city. Even from a great height, the South Bank—which occupies the riverside stretch between Waterloo Bridge and Hungerford Bridge—isn't beautiful, but this area of theaters and museums has Culture w ith an emphatic capital C. Starting with the 1976 construction of the South Bank Centre, developers and local authorities have expanded the South Bank's potential farther east, turning this once-neglected district into London's most happening new neighborhood. The '80s brought renovations and innovations such as Gabriel's Wharf, London Bridge City, Hay's Galleria, and Butler's Wharf. In the '90s came the reconstruction of Shakespeare's Globe, the OXO Tower, and the London Aquarium.

It is fitting that so much of London's artistic life should once again be centered on the South Bank—back in the days of Ye Olde London Towne, Southwark was the location for the theaters, taverns, and cock-fight-

HOW TO USE THIS GUIDE

Great trips begin with great planning, and this guide makes planning easy. It's packed with everything you need—insider advice on hotels and restaurants, cool tools, practical tips, essential maps, and much more.

COOL TOOLS

Fodor's Choice Top picks are marked throughout with a star.

Great Itineraries These tours, planned by Fodor's experts, give you the skinny on what you can see and do in the time you have.

Smart Travel Tips A to Z This special section is packed with important contacts and advice on everything from how to get around to what to pack.

Good Walks You won't miss a thing if you follow the numbered bullets on our maps.

Need a Break? Looking for a quick bite to eat or a spot to rest? These sure bets are along the way.

Off the Beaten Path Some lesser-known sights are worth a detour. We've marked those you should make time for.

POST-IT® FLAGS

Dog-ear no more!

"Post-it" is a registered trademark of 3M.

ICONS AND SYMBOLS

Watch for these symbols throughout:

★   Our special recommendations

✕   Restaurant

🏠   Lodging establishment

✕🏠   Lodging establishment whose restaurant warrants a special trip

🐣   Good for kids

☞   Sends you to another section of the guide for more information

✉   Address

☎   Telephone number

FAX   Fax number

WEB   Web site

🎫   Admission price

🕐   Opening hours

$-$$$$ Lodging and dining price categories, keyed to strategically sited price charts. Check the index for locations.

①❶   Numbers in white and black circles on the maps, in the margins, and within tours correspond to one another.

ON THE WEB

Continue your planning with these useful tools found at **www.fodors.com**, the Web's best source for travel information.

"Rich with resources." —*New York Times*

"Navigation is a cinch." —*Forbes* "Best of the Web" list

"Put together by people bursting with know-how."
                             —*Sunday Times* (London)

Create a Miniguide Pinpoint hotels, restaurants, and attractions that have what you want at the price you want to pay.

Rants and Raves Find out what readers say about Fodor's picks—or write your own reviews of hotels and restaurants you've just visited.

Travel Talk Post your questions and get answers from fellow travelers, or share your own experiences.

On-Line Booking Find the best prices on airline tickets, rental cars, cruises, or vacations, and book them on the spot.

About our Books Learn about other Fodor's guides to your destination and many others.

Expert Advice and Trip Ideas From what to tip to how to take great photos, from the national parks to Nepal, Fodors.com has suggestions that'll make your trip a breeze. Log on and get informed and inspired.

Smart Resources Check the weather in your destination or convert your currency. Learn the local language or link to the latest event listings. Or consult hundreds of detailed maps—all in one place.

ing arenas that served as after-hours entertainment. The Globe Theatre, in which Shakespeare acted and held shares, was one of several established here. In truth the Globe was as likely to stage bearbaiting as Shakespeare, but today, at the reconstructed "Wooden O," you can see only the latter. Be sure to take a walk along Bankside—the embankment along the Thames from Southwark to Blackfriars Bridge—and ride in British Airways London Eye for vistas of London's skyline.

A Good Walk

Start scenically at the south end of Tower Bridge, finding the steps on the east (left) side, which descend to the start of a pedestrians-only street, Shad Thames. Now turn your back on the bridge and follow this quaint path between cliffs of the good-as-new warehouses, which now constitute **Butler's Wharf** ㊶, but were once the dangerous shadowlands where Dickens killed off Bill Sikes in *Oliver Twist.* See the foodies' center, the Gastrodrome, and the **Design Museum** ㊷; then just before you get back to Tower Bridge, turn away from the river along Horsleydown Lane, follow Tooley Street, and take the right turn at Morgan Lane to **HMS *Belfast*** ㊸, or continue to **Hay's Galleria** ㊹ with the **London Dungeon** ㊺ beyond. Next, turn left onto Joiner Street underneath the arches of London's first (1836) railway, then right onto St. Thomas Street, where you'll find the **Old Operating Theatre Museum** ㊻, with **Southwark Cathedral** ㊼ across Borough High Street, and another of the South Bank's recent office developments, St. Mary Overy's Dock, down Cathedral Street. See the west wall, with rose window outline, of Winchester House, palace of the bishops of Winchester until 1626, built into it, and **The Clink** ㊽ next door. Also near St. Mary Overy Dock is a replica of Sir Francis Drake's ship the ***Golden Hinde*** ㊾. To imbibe some wine along with all the culture, stop at **Vinopolis** ㊿, celebrating wine. Just west of Southwark Bridge is New Globe Walk, where the reconstruction of **Shakespeare's Globe Theatre** (51) stands. Then you will reach Bankside Power Station, now the **Tate Modern** (52).

Ahead lies the fifth bridge (counting the Millennium Bridge for pedestrians) on this walk, Blackfriars Bridge, which you pass beneath to join the street called Upper Ground, spending some time in the Coin Street Community Builders' fast-emerging neighborhood, which features the **OXO Tower** (53) and Gabriel's Wharf, a marketplace of shops and cafés. Farther along Upper Ground, you reach the **South Bank Centre,** with the **Royal National Theatre** (54) first, followed by the **Museum of the Moving Image (MOMI),** closed until 2003, and the **Royal Festival Hall** (55). The **BFI London IMAX Cinema** (56) sits just down Waterloo Road behind the MOMI and the Hayward Gallery. Carry on round the curve of the river and you come to the Jubilee Gardens with the magnificent **British Airways London Eye** (57). Look to the opposite bank for the postcard vista of the Houses of Parliament. Just after the London Eye, you reach the former County Hall, now the **London Aquarium** (58) and the surrealist museum, **Dalí Universe** (59). Farther along the river, beyond the **Florence Nightingale Museum** (60), **Lambeth Palace** (61)—for 800 years the London base of the archbishop of Canterbury, top man in the Church of England—stands by Lambeth Bridge. A little farther east along Lambeth Road you will reach the **Imperial War Museum** (62).

TIMING

On a fine day, this 2- to 3-mi walk makes for a very scenic wander, since you're following the south bank of the Thames nearly all the way. Fabulous views across to the north bank include everything from St. Paul's to the Houses of Parliament, and you pass—under, over, or around—no fewer than eight bridges. Allow a full day to see the sights. The Tate Modern, the Imperial War Museum, Shakespeare's Globe, the Design Museum, and the Aquarium each could take more than an hour (depending on your interests), but the London Dungeon doesn't take long, unless you have kids in tow. The other museums on this route are compact enough to squeeze together en route to your main event. And that's the nicest thing to do with this walk: to have theater tickets waiting at the end. Remember, though, that the theaters stay dark on Sundays. Dinner or a riverside drink at the OXO Tower Brasserie, Gastrodome, or the People's Palace is another idea for a big finish. Public transportation is thin here, so pick a day when you're feeling energetic; there are few shortcuts.

Sights to See

56 BFI London IMAX Cinema. With the largest screen in London—it's the height of five doubledecker buses and wide enough to fill your eye—you're guaranteed an eyeful of technological and celluloid innovation. Choose from 2-D or 3-D films, generally on educational topics from archaeology to natural science. ⊠ *Waterloo Bridge at Stamford St., SE1,* ☎ *020/7902–1234,* WEB *www.bfi.org.uk.* 🎫 *£6.40.* ☉ *Sun.–Thurs. noon–8:45, Fri.–Sat. noon–10. Tube: Waterloo, Exit 5.*

57 British Airways London Eye. If you want a pigeon's-eye view of London, this is the place to get it. The highest observation wheel in the world, at 500 ft, towers over the South Bank from the Jubilee Gardens next to County Hall. For 25 minutes, passengers hover over the city in a slow-motion flight. You can book by phone or on-line, or buy tickets in advance at the Eye itself; it's very popular. ⊠ *Jubilee Gardens, SE1,* ☎ *0870/500–0600 advance booking 4 or more days in advance,* WEB *www.british-airways.com/londoneye.* 🎫 *£9.* ☉ *Apr.–Oct., daily 9–sunset; Nov.–Mar., daily 10–6. Tube: Embankment, Waterloo.*

41 Butler's Wharf. An '80s development that is maturing gracefully, this wharf is full of deluxe loft-style warehouse conversions and swanky new buildings housing restaurants and galleries. People flock here thanks partly to London's saint of the stomach, Sir Terence Conran (also responsible for high-profile central London restaurants Bibendum, Mezzo, and Quaglino's). He gave it his Gastrodome of four restaurants, a vintner's, a deli, and a bakery. ⊠ *SE1. Tube: London Bridge or Tower Hill, then walk over bridge.*

48 The Clink. Giving rise to the term "the clink," which still refers to a jail, this institution was originally the prison attached to Winchester House, palace of the bishops of Winchester until 1626. It was one of the first prisons to detain women, most of whom were called "Winchester Geese"—a euphemism meaning prostitutes. The world's oldest profession was endemic in Southwark; a museum traces the history of prostitution here and shows what the Clink was like in its 16th-century prime. ⊠ *1 Clink St., SE1,* ☎ *020/7403–6515,* WEB *www.clink.co.uk.* 🎫 *£4.* ☉ *Daily 10–6. Tube: London Bridge.*

59 Dalí Universe. Neatly arranged into three areas, "Sensuality and Femininity," "Religion and Mythology," and "Dreams and Fantasy," the museum reflects the eclectic work of surrealist artist Salvador Dalí (1904–89), from sculpture to painting to drawings. ⊠ *County Hall, Riverside Bldg., Westminster Bridge Rd., SE1,* ☎ *020/7620–2420,* WEB *www.daliuniverse.com.* 🎫 *£8.50.* ☉ *Daily 10–5:30. Tube: Waterloo, Westminster.*

42 Design Museum. Opened in 1989, this was the first museum in the world to elevate everyday design to the status of art, presenting designs in their social and cultural context. The top floor traces the evolution of mass-produced goods. Check out the very good Blueprint Café, with its own river terrace. ⊠ *28 Shad Thames, SE1,* ☎ *020/7403–6933,*

WEB *www.designmuseum.org.* ⊠ *£5.50.* ⊙ *Weekdays 11:30–5:50, weekends 10:30–5:50. Tube: London Bridge, Bermondsey.*

60 **Florence Nightingale Museum.** Here you can learn all about that most famous of health care reformers, "The Lady with the Lamp." On view are fascinating reconstructions of the barracks ward at Scutari (Turkey), where she tended soldiers during the Crimean War (1854–56) and earned her nickname, and a Victorian East End slum cottage, to show what she did to improve living conditions among the poor. The museum is in **St. Thomas's Hospital.** ⊠ *2 Lambeth Palace Rd., SE1,* ☎ *020/7620–0374,* WEB *www.florence-nightingale.co.uk.* ⊠ *£4.80.* ⊙ *Daily 10–4. Tube: Waterloo or Westminster, then walk over the bridge.*

49 *Golden Hinde.* Sir Francis Drake circumnavigated the globe in this little galleon, or one just like it anyway. This exact replica finished *its* 23-year, round-the-world voyage—much of it spent along American coasts, both Pacific and Atlantic—and has settled here to continue its educational mission. ⊠ *St. Mary Overy's Dock, Cathedral St., SE1,* ☎ *020/7403–0123,* WEB *www.goldenhinde.co.uk.* ⊠ *£2.50.* ⊙ *Daily 9:30–5:30. Tube: London Bridge.*

44 **Hay's Galleria.** Once known as "London's larder" because of the edibles sold here, it was reborn in 1987 as a Covent Garden–esque parade of bars and restaurants, offices, and shops, all weatherproofed by an arched glass atrium roof supported by tall iron columns. Inevitably, jugglers, string quartets, and crafts stalls abound. ⊠ *2 Battlebridge La., SE1,* ☎ *020/7940–7770,* WEB *www.haysgalleria.co.uk.* ⊙ *Varies from shop to shop. Tube: London Bridge.*

☺ **43** **HMS** *Belfast.* At 656 ft, this is one of the largest and most powerful cruisers the Royal Navy has ever had. It played a role in the D-Day landings off Normandy. There's an outpost of the **Imperial War Museum** on board. ⊠ *Morgan's La., Tooley St., SE1,* ☎ *020/7940–6434,* WEB *www.iwm.org.uk.* ⊠ *£5.* ⊙ *Mid-Mar.–Oct., daily 10–6, Nov.–mid-Mar., daily 10–4:15. Tube: London Bridge.*

62 **Imperial War Museum.** Housed in an elegantly colonnaded 19th-century building that was once the home of the infamous insane asylum called Bedlam, this museum of 20th-century warfare does not glorify bloodshed but attempts to evoke what it was like to live through the two world wars. Of course, there is hardware—a Battle of Britain Spitfire, a German V2 rocket—but there's an equal amount of war art (John Singer Sargent to Henry Moore). One very affecting exhibit is *The Blitz Experience,* a 10-minute taste of an air raid in a street of acrid smoke with sirens blaring and searchlights glaring. There's also a Holocaust exhibition. ⊠ *Lambeth Rd., SE1,* ☎ *020/7416–5320,* WEB *www.iwm. org.uk.* ⊠ *£5.50.* ⊙ *Daily 10–6. Tube: Lambeth North.*

61 **Lambeth Palace.** The London residence of the archbishop of Canterbury, the senior archbishop of the Church of England since the 13th century, is closed to the public, but you can admire the fine Tudor gatehouse. *Lambeth Palace Rd., SE1,* WEB *www.archbishopofcanterbury. org/lambeth.htm. Tube: Waterloo.*

☺ **58** **London Aquarium.** County Hall was the original name of this curved, colonnaded Neoclassical hulk, which took 46 years (1912–58; two world wars interfered) to build. It was home to London's local government, the Greater London Council, until it disbanded in 1986. After a £25 million injection, a three-level aquarium was installed, full of sharks and stingrays, educational exhibits, and piscine sights previously unseen on these shores. ⊠ *County Hall, Westminster Bridge Rd., SE1,* ☎ *020/7967–8000,* WEB *www.londonaquarium.co.uk.* ⊠ *£8.50.* ⊙

Daily 10–6; last admission at 5. Tube: Waterloo, or Westminster and walk over the bridge.

45 London Dungeon. Did you ever wonder what a disembowelment actually looks like? See it here. Preteens seem to adore this place, which, although the city's most grisly, gruesome museum, is among London's top tourist attractions and usually has long lines. Inside, realistic waxwork people are subjected in graphic detail to all the historic horrors that you hear about at the Tower of London. Tableaux depict bloody historic moments—like Anne Boleyn's decapitation—alongside the torture and ritual slaughter of more anonymous victims, all to a sound track of screaming and agonized moaning. London's times of deepest terror, which were the Great Fire and the Great Plague, are brought to life, too, and a whole section is devoted to Jack the Ripper. ⊠ *28– 34 Tooley St., SE1,* ☎ *020/7403–7221.* ⊠ *£9.50.* ☉ *Apr.–Sept., daily 10–5:30; Oct.–Mar., daily 10–4:30. Tube: London Bridge.*

Museum of the Moving Image (MOMI). MOMI is closed until 2003 for major refurbishment. During 2002, the museum has a touring exhibition at the Science Museum in South Kensington. Some exhibits are also in the foyer of the BFI London IMAX Cinema. The adjacent **National Film Theatre** (NFT) is also being renovated. For details on British Film Institute activities, phone the events line at ☎ 0870/240– 4050. ⊠ *South Bank Centre, SE1,* ☎ *020/7401–2636,* WEB *www.bfi.org. Museum closed until 2003. Tube: Waterloo.*

46 Old Operating Theatre Museum. One of England's oldest hospitals stood here from the 12th century until the railway forced it to move in 1862. Today, its operating theater has been restored into an exhibition of early 19th-century medical practices: the operating table onto which the gagged and blindfolded patients were roped, the box of sawdust underneath for catching their blood, the knives, pliers, and handsaws the surgeons wielded, and—this was a theater-in-the-round—the spectators' seats. ⊠ *9A St. Thomas St.,* ☎ *020/7955–4791,* WEB *www.thegarret.org.uk.* ⊠ *£3.25.* ☉ *Daily 10:30–5:30. Tube: London Bridge.*

53 OXO Tower. Long a London landmark to the cognoscenti, this wonderful Art Deco tower has graduated from its former incarnations as power-generating station and warehouse into a vibrant community of artists' and designers' workshops, a pair of restaurants, and cafés, as well as five floors of the best low-income housing in the city, via a £20 million scheme by Coin Street Community Builders. A rooftop viewing gallery adjacent to the well-regarded OXO Tower Restaurant and Brasserie provides the best river vista in town, and there's a performance area on the first floor. ⊠ *Bargehouse St., SE1,* ☎ *020/7401– 3610.* ⊠ *Free.* ☉ *Studios and shops Tues.–Sun. 11–6. Tube: Black- friars or Waterloo.*

55 Royal Festival Hall. The largest auditorium of the South Bank Centre, this hall has superb acoustics and a 3,000-plus capacity. It's the oldest of the riverside blocks, raised as the centerpiece of the 1951 Festival of Britain, a postwar morale-boosting exercise. The London Philharmonic resides here; symphony orchestras from around the world like to visit; and choral works, ballet, serious jazz and pop, and even film with live accompaniment are also staged. There's a good, independently run restaurant, the People's Palace, and a very good bookstore. The next building you come to also contains two concert halls, the **Queen Elizabeth Hall** and the **Purcell Room.** ⊠ *South Bank Centre, Belvedere Rd., SE1,* ☎ *020/7960–4242,* WEB *www.rfh.org.uk. Tube: Waterloo.*

❺❹ Royal National Theatre. Londoners generally felt the same way about Sir Denys Lasdun's stolid function-dictates-form building when it opened in 1976 as they would a decade later about the far nastier Barbican. But the interior of the Royal National Theatre—still abbreviated colloquially to the pre-royal warrant "NT"—makes up for its exterior. Three auditoriums—the Olivier, named after Sir Laurence, first artistic director of the National Theatre Company; the Lyttleton; and the Cottesloe—host an ever-changing array of presentations. The NT attracts many of the nation's top actors (Sir Anthony Hopkins, for one, does time here) in addition to launching stars and star productions. ✉ *South Bank, SE1,* ☎ *020/7452–3000 box office,* 🌐 *www.nationaltheatre. org.uk.* ✉ *Tour £3.50.* ☉ *1-hr backstage tours Mon.–Sat. at 10:15, 12:30, and 5:30. Tube: Waterloo.*

★ **❺❶ Shakespeare's Globe Theatre.** More than three decades ago, American Sam Wanamaker—then an aspiring actor—pulled up in Southwark in a cab and was amazed to find that the fabled Shakespeare's Globe Theatre didn't actually exist. Worse: a tiny plaque was the only sign on the former site of the world's most legendary theater. So appalled had he been that London lacked a center for the study and worship of the Bard of Bards, Wanamaker worked ceaselessly until his death in 1993 to raise funds for a full-scale reconstruction of the theater. The dream was realized in 1997 when an exact replica of Shakespeare's openroof Globe Playhouse (built in 1599; incinerated in 1613) was completed, using authentic Elizabethan materials and craft techniques and the first thatched roof in London since the Great Fire. A second, indoor theater is built to a design of the 17th-century architect Inigo Jones. The whole complex stands 200 yards from the original Globe, the famous "Wooden O." Today, a repertory season of four Shakespeare plays is presented during the summer, usually mid-May to late September in natural light (and sometimes rain), to 1,000 people on wooden benches in the "bays," plus 500 "groundlings," standing on a carpet of filbert shells and clinker, just as they did nearly four centuries ago. For any theater buff, this stunning project is a must. Although the main theater is open only for performances during the summer season, it can be viewed year-round (unless a performance is scheduled; check in advance). The **New Shakespeare's Globe Exhibition,** touted as the largest ever to focus on Shakespeare, his work, and his contemporaries, is in the Underglobe, beneath the Globe site. ✉ *New Globe Walk, Bankside, SE1,* ☎ *020/7902–1500; 020/7401–9919 box office,* 🌐 *www. shakespeares-globe.org.* ✉ *£6.* ☉ *Exhibition daily 9–4, plays May– Sept. (call for performance schedule). Tube: Mansion House, then walk across Southwark Bridge; Blackfriars, then walk across Blackfriars Bridge; or Southwark, then walk down to the river.*

South Bank Centre. On either side of Waterloo Bridge is London's chief arts center. Along Upper Ground is the **Royal National Theatre,** three auditoriums that are home to some of the finest theater in Britain. Underneath Waterloo Bridge are the **National Film Theatre** and the **Museum of the Moving Image** (**MOMI**) (both currently closed). Also here are the **Royal Festival Hall,** the **Queen Elizabeth Hall,** and the **Purcell Room,** three of London's finest venues for classical music. Finally, tucked away behind the concert halls is the **Hayward Gallery,** a venue for impressive, ever-changing art exhibitions. Along the wide paths of the complex you'll find distractions of every sort such as secondhand bookstalls, entertainers, and arrogant pigeons. ✉ *South Bank Centre,* ☎ *020/7401– 2636. Tube: Waterloo, Embankment.*

❹❼ Southwark Cathedral. This cathedral (pronounced *suth*-uck) is the second-oldest Gothic church in London, next to Westminster Abbey.

SHAKESPEARE LIVES!
REBIRTH OF THE GLOBE THEATRE

LIKE THE TRUE CHURCH, Britain's theater is founded on a rock—Shakespeare. Stratford-upon-Avon remains the primary shrine, but 1997 welcomed the opening of the cathedral—the Globe Theatre. More than three centuries ago, the Puritans closed the fabled "Wooden O," the open-air polygonal structure on London's South Bank, for which Shakespeare wrote *Hamlet, King Lear*, and *Julius Caesar*, among other peerless dramas. Now the most famous playhouse in the world has been re-created, down to its Norfolk-reed roof. For any Shakespeare lover, arriving for the first time at the new Globe is bound to be a near-religious experience. The theater was reconstructed just 200 yards from its original site—ground as holy to Shakespeare's followers as Bayreuth's is to Wagner-philes.

For sheer drama few things can top (well, maybe Kenneth Branagh's rendition of "To be or not to be") the memorable jolt of walking into the new Globe. Enter, and a Wellsian genie transports you back to Elizabethan England. You step past the entrance (remember, legend has it that Shakespeare got his start in theater by tending horse-and-carriages for theatergoers at entryways very similar to this) into a 45-ft-tall arena, made surprisingly intimate by three picturesque half-timbered galleries. Ahead of you is the "pit," or orchestra level, filling up with 500 standees—or "groundlings," to use the historic term—massed in front of the high stage. Soaring overhead is a twin-gabled stage canopy—the "heavens"—framed by trompe l'oeil marble columns and a "lords'" gallery, all fretted with gilded bosses, painted planets, and celestial stars (other than this backdrop and a few props, the Globe boasts no scenery—to quote Will, "The play's the thing"). Above you—if you are an "understander" in the pit—is the lowering London sky, which may at any time provide an authentic mid-performance drenching.

The new Globe is not a perfect time capsule. Occasionally, Juliet has to compete with the roar of jets above—"Romeo, O Romeo, wherefore ART THOU, ROMEO?" There are no longer ladies proffering oranges and stools, and in lieu of yesteryear's magpie hats are Ray-Bans and baseball caps—and we're not just talking about the audience, for the actors will be doing a fair share of modern-dress Shakespeare. The ground rules have also changed. Many performances begin in the afternoon, and although flood lighting is used to illuminate the theater at dusk, there are no spotlights. The audience, on view at all times, becomes as much a part of the theatrical proceedings as the actors on stage. Elizabethans loved to cheer and heckle, making theatergoing almost as blood-and-thunder an experience as a football match today. You've heard of the Super Bowl: this is the Shakespeare Bowl—so go ahead and boo Iago or hiss Macbeth. During a performance of *Two Gentlemen of Verona*, when the love-struck Julia asked for "a holy kiss" from the departing Proteus and he offered only a handshake, a voice in the crowd interjected, "Go on, give her a kiss!"

The Globe theater is but one facet of the entire complex, which includes the 300-seat Inigo Jones indoor theater, a restaurant, an audio-visual archive, an education center, a library, and the largest Shakespearean exhibition in the world, now installed, and open daily. The Globe presents four plays each season. Londoners have thought the whole project to be less theater than tourism, and it will be a while until they come flocking to the Globe as the rest of the world is. Happily, a visit to the exhibition includes a guided tour of the theater (unless a performance is scheduled; check in advance)—a perfect opportunity to try out your "Friends, Romans, Countrymen!"

Look for the gaudily renovated 1408 tomb of the poet John Gower, friend of Chaucer, and for the Harvard Chapel, named after John Harvard, founder of the United States college, who was baptized here in 1608. Another notable buried here is Edmund Shakespeare, brother of William. ✉ *Montague Close, SE1,* ☎ *020/7367–6700,* WEB *www. dswark.org.* 🖾 *Free.* ☉ *Daily 8–6. Tube: London Bridge.*

52 **Tate Modern.** This new branch of the Tate Gallery opened in 2000 in the huge Bankside Power Station, a dazzling venue for some of the Tate's treasures. Shuttered for decades, the station has glowered magnificently on its Thames-side site ever since it was built in the 1930s; it was handsomely renovated by Swiss architects Herzog and de Meuron. For decades, the old Millbank Gallery of the Tate Britain had been so overstuffed the curators had to resort to a revolving menu of paintings and sculpture. The power station (designed by the same man who created the famous red telephone box) and its 8½-acre site now house the surplus, running from classic works by Matisse, Picasso, Dalí, Moore, Bacon, and Warhol to the most-talked-about British artists of today. ✉ *25 Summer St., SE1,* ☎ *020/7887–8000,* WEB *www.tate.org.uk.* 🖾 *Free.* ☉ *Sun.– Thurs. 10–6, Fri.–Sat. 10–10. Tube: Blackfriars, Southwark.*

50 **Vinopolis.** The British are perhaps not the first nation you would expect to erect a monument to wine, but here it is—Vinopolis, City of Wine. Spread over two acres between the Globe Theatre and London Bridge, its arched vaults promise multimedia tours of the world's wine cultures, tastings, retail shops, an art gallery, restaurants, and a wine school. ✉ *1 Bank End St., SE1,* ☎ *0870/444–4777,* WEB *www.vinopolis.co.uk.* 🖾 *£11.50.* ☉ *Mon. 11–9, Tues.–Fri. 11–6, Sat. 11–8, Sun 11–6. Tube: London Bridge.*

Kensington, Knightsbridge, Mayfair, Belgravia, and Hyde Park

Even in these supposedly democratic days, you still sometimes hear people say that the *only* place to live in London is in the grand residential area of the Royal Borough of Kensington. True, the district is an endless cavalcade of streets lined with splendid, pillared houses redolent of wealth, but there are other fetching attractions here—some of the most fascinating museums in London, stylish squares, elegant antiques shops, and Kensington Palace, the former home of both Diana, Princess of Wales, and Queen Victoria, which put the district literally on the map back in the 17th century. To Kensington's east is one of the highest concentrations of important artifacts anywhere, the "museum mile" of South Kensington, with the rest of Kensington offering peaceful strolls, a noisy main street, and another palace. Kensington first became the *Royal* Borough of Kensington (and Chelsea) when William III, who suffered terribly from the Thames mists over Whitehall, decided in 1689 to buy Nottingham House in the rural village of Kensington so that he could breathe more easily. Courtiers and functionaries and society folk soon followed where the crowns led, and by the time Queen Anne was on the throne (1702–14), Kensington was overflowing. In a way, it still is, since most of its grand houses have been divided into apartments, or else are serving as foreign embassies.

Hyde Park and Kensington Gardens together form by far the biggest of central London's royal parks. It's probably been centuries since any major royal had a casual stroll here, but the parks remain the property of the Crown, and it was the Crown that saved them from being devoured by the city's late-18th-century growth spurt.

Around the borders of Hyde Park are several of London's poshest and most beautiful neighborhoods. To the south of the park and a short carriage ride from Buckingham Palace is the most splendidly aristo- cratic enclave to be found in London: Belgravia. Its stucco-white build- ings and grand squares—particularly Belgrave Square- –are Regency-era jewels. On the eastern border of Hyde Park is Mayfair, which gives Belgravia a run for its money as London's wealthiest district. Here are three mansions that will allow you to get a peek into the lifestyles of London's rich and famous—19th- and 20th-century versions: Apsley House, the home of the Duke of Wellington; Spencer House, home of Princess Diana's ancestors; and the Wallace Collection, a grand man- sion on Manchester Square stuffed with great art treasures.

A Good Walk

When you surface from the Knightsbridge tube station—one of Lon- don's deepest—you are immediately engulfed by the manic drivers, pro- fessional shoppers, and ladies-who-lunch who compose the local population. Walk west down Brompton Road, past **Harrods,** to the junc- tion of Cromwell Road and the pale, Italianate Brompton Oratory, which marks the beginning of museum territory. The **Victoria & Albert Mu- seum** ㊆, or V&A, is first, at the start of Cromwell Road, followed by the **Natural History Museum** ㊄ and the **Science Museum** ㊅ behind it. Turn left to continue north up Exhibition Road, a kind of unfinished cultural main drag that was Prince Albert's conception, toward the road after which British moviemakers named their fake blood, Kensington Gore, to reach the giant round Wedgwood china box of the **Royal Al- bert Hall** ㊅ and the brilliantly renovated **Albert Memorial** ㊆ opposite, on the edge of **Kensington Gardens.**

Walk northwest through the park to reach **Kensington Palace** ㊅. From here you can either head west to check out some of London's current sanctuaries of the rich and famous at **Kensington Palace Gardens** ㊅ or take an extra leg of the journey to see **Leighton House** ㊆. If opulent 19th-century interiors are not your cup of tea, head east instead to ex- plore Kensington Gardens further, including the Serpentine Gallery (which displays art), beside the lake of the same name. When you pass its bridge, you leave Kensington Gardens and enter **Hyde Park.** Walk to the southern perimeter and along the sand track called Rotten Row. It's still used by the Household Cavalry (the brigade that mounts the guard at the palace), who live at the Knightsbridge Barracks to the left. Then head toward the Hyde Park Corner exit of the park and discover glorious **Apsley House (Wellington Museum)** ㊆. If you decided to skip Hyde Park, tube it from Kensington High Street (and Leighton House) over to Hyde Park Corner to take in the Wellington Museum, then head south to see chic **Belgrave Place** ㊆ or north for some more palatial treats: several blocks northeast is **Spencer House** ㊆, and farther north through elegant Mayfair—custom-built for expansive strolling—is the **Wallace Collection** ㊆. For sights to delight children, keep heading northward to discover the sights around Regent's Park: the **BBC Experience** ㊆, **Madame Tussaud's** ㊆, and the **London Zoo.**

TIMING

This walk is at least 4 mi long, with an abundance of places to stop along the way; you'll need plenty of time and probably some money for taxis or the tube. The best way to approach these neighborhoods is to treat Knightsbridge shopping and the South Kensington museums as separate days out, although you may find the three vast museums too much to take in at once. The parks are best in the growing sea- sons and during fall, when the foliage is turning. On Sunday, the Hyde

Park and Kensington Gardens railings all along the Bayswater Road are hung with mediocre art, which may slow your progress; this is prime perambulation day for locals. Whatever your priorities, this is a long walk if you explore every corner, with the perimeter of the two parks alone covering 4 mi, and about half as far again around the remainder of the route. A jaunt from Belgrave Square up to the Apsley and Spencer houses (note that Spencer House is open Sundays only) and on to the Wallace Collection would add another 2 mi to this outing. You could cut out a lot of Hyde Park without missing out on essential sights, and walk the whole thing in a good five hours.

Sights to See

OFF THE
BEATEN PATH

ABBEY ROAD STUDIOS – Strawberry Fields Forever. Here, outside the legendary Abbey Road Studios, is the world's most famous zebra crossing. Immortalized on the Beatles's *Abbey Road* album of 1969, this footpath is a spot beloved to Beatlemaniacs and baby boomers. Adjacent to the traffic crossing, at No. 3 Abbey Road, are the studios where the Beatles recorded their entire output, from "Love Me Do" on, including *Sgt. Pepper's Lonely Hearts Club Band* (1967). To see this and other Fab Four sites, **Original London Walks** offers two Beatles tours: "The Beatles In-My-Life Walk" and "The Beatles Magical Mystery Tour" (☎ 020/7624–3978). Abbey Road is in the elegant neighborhood of St. John's Wood, a 10-minute ride on the Jubilee tube line from central London. After you exit, head southwest three blocks down Grove End Road. ⊠ *3 Abbey Rd., NW8,* WEB *www.abbeyroad.co.uk. Tube: St. John's Wood.*

67 **Albert Memorial.** This gleaming, neo-Gothic shrine to Prince Albert epitomizes the Victorian era. The 14-ft bronze statue of Albert looks as if it had been created yesterday, thanks to its fresh coat of gold leaf. Albert's grieving widow, Queen Victoria, had this elaborate confection erected on the spot where his Great Exhibition had stood a mere decade before his early death, from typhoid, in 1861. ⊠ *Kensington Gore, opposite Royal Albert Hall, Hyde Park. Tube: Knightsbridge.*

★ **71** **Apsley House (Wellington Museum).** Once known, quite simply, as Number 1, London, this was celebrated as the best address in town. Built by Robert Adam in the 1770s, the mansion was home to the celebrated conqueror of Napoléon, the Duke of Wellington, who lived here from the 1820s until his death in 1852. The great Waterloo Gallery—scene of legendary dinners—is a veritable orgy of opulence. Not to be missed, in every sense, is the gigantic Canova statue of a nude (but fig-leafed) Bonaparte in the entry stairwell. The current Duke of Wellington still lives here. ⊠ *149 Piccadilly,* ☎ *020/7499–5676.* ⊡ *£4.50.* ☼ *Tues.–Sun. 11–5. Tube: Hyde Park Corner.*

75 **BBC Experience.** For those who have been weaned on a steady diet of *Masterpiece Theatre* presentations, the BBC is the greatest television producer in the world. Its in-house museum includes an audiovisual show that traces the BBC's history, an interactive section—want to try your hand at commentating on a sports game, presenting a weather forecast, or making your own director's cut of a segment of *EastEnders?*—and, of course, a massive gift shop. You can purchase tickets at the door, or you can prebook a tour with a credit card. ⊠ *Broadcasting House, Portland Pl., W1,* ☎ *0870/603–0304,* WEB *www.bbc.co.uk/experience.* ⊡ *£7.50.* ☼ *Tues.–Sun. 10–4:30, Mon. 11–4:30. Tube: Oxford Circus.*

72 **Belgrave Place.** One of the main arteries of Belgravia—London's swankiest neighborhood—Belgrave Place is lined with grand, imposing Regency-era mansions, now mostly embassies. Walk down this street

toward Eaton Place to pass two of Belgravia's most beautiful mews—
Eaton Mews North and Eccleston Mews, both fronted by grand West-
minster-white rusticated entrances right out of a 19th-century engraving.
There are few other places where London is both so picturesque and
elegant. *Tube: Hyde Park Corner.*

☺ **Harrods.** Just in case you hadn't noticed it, this well-known shopping
mecca outlines its domed terra-cotta Edwardian bulk in thousands of
white lights at night. Owned by Mohamed Al Fayed, whose son Dodi
was killed in the 1997 car crash that also claimed Princess Diana's life,
the 15-acre store has world-class, frenetic sale weeks. Don't miss the
extravagant **Food Hall,** with its Art Nouveau tiling in the neighborhood of meat and poultry. This is the department in which to acquire
your green-and-gold-logo souvenir Harrods bag, since food prices are
competitive. ⊠ *87–135 Brompton Rd., SW1,* ☎ *020/7730–1234,* WEB
www.harrods.com. ⊘ *Mon.–Sat. 10–7. Tube: Knightsbridge.*

☺ **Hyde Park.** Along with the smaller St. James's and Green parks to the
east, Hyde Park started as Henry VIII's hunting grounds. Along its south
side runs **Rotten Row,** once Henry's royal path to the hunt—hence the
name, a corruption of *route du roi.* It is still used by the Household
Cavalry, who live at the **Knightsbridge Barracks**—a high-rise and a low,
ugly red block to the left. This brigade mounts the guard at the palace,
and you can see them leave to perform this duty, in full regalia, at about
10:30, or see the exhausted cavalry return about noon. Hyde Park is
wonderful for strolling, watching the locals, or just relaxing by the **Serpentine,** the long body of water near its southern border. On Sunday,
Speaker's Corner, in the park near Marble Arch, is an unmissable
spectacle of vehement, sometimes comical, and always entertaining or-
ators. ⊠ ☎ *020/7298–2100.* ⊘ *Daily 5–midnight. Tube: Hyde Park
Corner, Marble Arch, Lancaster Gate.*

☺ **Kensington Gardens.** More formal than neighboring Hyde Park, Kensington Gardens was first laid out as palace grounds. The paved Italian garden at the top of the Long Water, **The Fountains,** is a reminder
of this; although, of course, **Kensington Palace** itself is the main clue
to its royal status, with the early 19th-century Sunken Garden north
of it. Nearby is George Frampton's beloved 1912 *Peter Pan,* a bronze
of the boy who lived on an island in the Serpentine and never grew up,
and whose creator, J. M. Barrie, lived at 100 Bayswater Road, not 500
yards from here. The **Round Pond** is a magnet for model-boat enthusiasts and duck feeders. ⊘ *Daily dawn–dusk. Tube: Lancaster Gate,
Queensway.*

❻❽ **Kensington Palace.** The long and regal history of this palace has been
somewhat eclipsed by one of its most recent inhabitants: the late
Princess Diana. Of course, Kensington Palace was well known long before Diana. Kensington was put, socially speaking, on the map when
King William III, "much incommoded by the Smoak of the Coal Fires
of London," decided in the 17th century to vacate Whitehall and re-
locate to a new palace outside the center city in the village of Kensington. Royals have lived here since William and Mary—and some have
died here, too. In 1760, poor George II burst a blood vessel while on
the toilet. The **State Apartments,** where Victoria had her ultrastrict upbringing, depict the life of the Royal Family through the centuries. This
palace is an essential stop for royalty vultures, because it's the onl y
one where you may actually catch a glimpse of the real thing. Princess
Margaret, the Duke and Duchess of Gloucester, and Prince and Princess
Michael of Kent all have apartments here. The palace has found new
life in the shape of the **Royal Ceremonial Dress Collection.** Extending
back centuries, the collection shows an array of state and occasional

dresses, hats, and shoes worn by Britain's Royal Family. Diana-watchers will note the difference between the regal if dowdy garments of Her Majesty the Queen compared to the glittering, cutting-edge fashions of her late daughter-in-law. You can also repair to the palace's nearby **Orangery** for an elegant tea. ☒ *The Broad Walk, Kensington Gardens, W8,* ☎ *020/7937–9561,* WEB *www.hrp.org.uk.* ☞ *£9.50, including admission to dress collection.* ☉ *Daily 10–5. Tube: High Street Kensington.*

69 **Kensington Palace Gardens.** Immediately behind Kensington Palace is Kensington Palace Gardens (called Palace Green at the south end), a wide, leafy avenue of mid-19th-century mansions that used to be one of London's most elegant addresses. Today, it's largely Embassy Row, including those of Russia and Israel. *Tube: High Street Kensington.*

70 **Leighton House.** The exotic richness of late 19th-century aesthetic tastes is captured in this fascinating home, once the abode of Lord Frederic Leighton (1830–96)—painter, sculptor, president of the Royal Academy. The Arab Hall is lavishly lined with Persian tiles and pieced woodwork. The neighborhood was one of the principal artists' colonies of Victorian London. If you are interested in 19th-century domestic architecture, wander through the surrounding streets. ☒ *12 Holland Park Rd., W14,* ☎ *020/7602–3316,* WEB *www.rbkc.gov.uk.* ☞ *Free.* ☉ *Wed–Mon. 11–5:30. Tube: High Street Kensington.*

Linley Sambourne House. Stuffed with Victorian and Edwardian antiques, fabrics, and paintings, this 19th-century house was built and furnished in the 1870s. It was home to Edward Linley Sambourne, who for more than 30 years was the political cartoonist for the satirical magazine *Punch.* It's closed during 2002 for repairs. ☒ *18 Stafford Terr., W8,* ☎ *020/8944–1019,* WEB *www.rbkc.gov.uk.*

London Zoo. Opened in 1828 and now housing an extensive collection of animals from all over the world, this zoo has long been a local favorite. ☒ *Regent's Park, NW1,* ☎ *020/7722–3333,* WEB *www. londonzoo.co.uk.* ☞ *£9.* ☉ *Mar.–Oct., daily 10–5:30; Nov.–Feb., daily 10–4; pig feed daily 12:30, pelican feed daily 1; aquarium feed daily 2:30. Tube: Camden Town, then Bus 74.*

76 **Madame Tussaud's.** This is nothing more, nothing less, than the world's premier exhibition of lifelike waxwork models of celebrities. Madame T. learned her craft while making death masks of French Revolution victims and in 1835 set up her first show of the famous ones near this spot. You can see everyone from Shakespeare to Benny Hill here, but top billing still goes to the murderers in the Chamber of Horrors, who stare glassy-eyed at you—one from the electric chair, one next to the tin bath where he dissolved several wives in quicklime. Just next door is the London Planetarium, which offers a special combo ticket with Tussaud's. Beat the crowds by calling in advance for timed entry tickets. ☒ *Marylebone Rd., NW1,* ☎ *020/7935–6861; 0870/400–3000 advance tickets,* WEB *www.madame-tussauds.com.* ☞ *£11.95; joint ticket with planetarium £14.45.* ☉ *Sept.–June, weekdays 10–5:30, weekends 9:30–5:30; July–Aug., daily 9:30–5:30. Tube: Baker St.*

64 **Natural History Museum.** When you want to heed the call of the wild, discover this fun place—enter to find Dinosaurs on the left and the Ecology Gallery on the right. Both these exhibits (the former with life-size moving dinosaurs, the latter complete with moonlit "rain forest") make essential viewing in a large museum that has overhauled itself creatively. Don't miss the ambitious Earth Galleries or the Creepy Crawlies Gallery, which features a nightmarish super-enlarged scorpion, yet ends up making tarantulas seem cute. ☒ *Cromwell Rd., SW7,* ☎ *020/7942–5000,*

WEB *www.nhm.ac.uk.* ✉ *£9; free as of Dec. 2001.* ☉ *Mon.–Sat. 10–5:50, Sun. 11–5:50. Tube: South Kensington.*

Notting Hill. Currently the best place to wear sunglasses, smoke Gauloises, and contemplate the latest issue of *Wallpaper,* "the Hill" now ranks as London's coolest neighborhood (for this week, at least). Centered around the Portobello Road antiques market, this district is bordered on the west by Lansdowne Crescent—address to the Hill's poshest 19th-century terraced row houses—and to the east by Chepstow Road, with Notting Hill Gate and Westbourne Grove Road marking the southern and northern boundaries. In between, Rastafarians rub elbows with wealthy young British types (a.k.a. "Trustafarians"), and residents like fashion designer Rifat Ozbek, CNN's Christiane Amanpour, and historian Lady Antonia Fraser can be spotted at the chic shops on Westbourne Grove and the lively cafés on Kensington Park Road. No historic sites here, so just wander the streets to shop or savor the flavor. *Tube: Notting Hill Gate, Ladbroke Grove.*

66 Royal Albert Hall. This famous theater was made possible by the Victorian public, who donated funds for the domed, circular 8,000-seat auditorium. The Albert Hall is best known and best loved for its annual July through September Henry Wood Promenade Concerts (the "Proms"), with bargain-price standing (or promenading, or sitting-on-the-floor) tickets sold on the night of the world-class classical concerts. ✉ *Kensington Gore,* ☎ *020/7589–4185,* WEB *www.alberthall.co.uk.* ✉ *Admission varies according to event. Tube: South Kensington.*

65 Science Museum. Up-to-date, hands-on exhibits make this museum enormously popular. Highlights include the Launch Pad gallery, the Computing Then and Now show, *Puffing Billy,* the oldest train in the world, and the actual *Apollo 10* capsule. A new attraction is the spectacular **Wellcome Wing,** devoted to contemporary science, medicine, and technology, which also includes a 450-seat IMAX cinema. ✉ *Exhibition Rd., SW7,* ☎ *020/7942–4000,* WEB *www.sciencemuseum.org.uk.* ✉ *£7.95; free as of Dec. 2001.* ☉ *Daily 10–6. Tube: South Kensington.*

★ 73 Spencer House. Ancestral abode of the Spencers, the family who gave us Princess Diana, this great mansion is perhaps the finest example of 18th-century elegance on a domestic scale, extant in London. Superlatively restored by Lord Rothschild, the house was built in 1766 for the first earl Spencer, heir to the first duchess of Marlborough. James "Athenian" Stuart decorated the gilded State Rooms, including the Painted Room, the first completely Neoclassical room in Europe. The most ostentatious part of the house is the florid bow window of the Palm Room: covered with stucco palm trees, it conjures up both ancient Palmyra and modern Miami Beach. Children under 10 are not admitted. ✉ *27 St. James's Pl., SW1,* ☎ *020/7499–8620,* WEB *www. spencerhouse.co.uk.* ✉ *£6.* ☉ *Feb.–July and Sept.–Dec., Sun. 10:30– 5:30; 1-hr guided tour leaves approx. every 25 mins (tickets on sale Sun. at 10:30). Tube: Green Park.*

★ 63 Victoria & Albert Museum. Recognizable by the copy of Victoria's Imperial Crown it wears on the lantern above the central cupola, this museum is always referred to as the V&A. It is a huge museum, showcasing the decorative arts of all disciplines, all periods, all nationalities, and all tastes, and it is a wonderful, generous place in which to get lost. The collections are *so* all-encompassing that confusion is a hazard. One minute you're gazing on the Jacobean oak 12-ft-square four-poster Great Bed of Ware (one of the V&A's most prized possessions, given that Shakespeare immortalized it in *Twelfth Night*), and the next, you're in the 20th-century end of the equally celebrated Dress Collection, coveting a Jean Muir frock you can actually buy at nearby Harrods. Prince Albert was responsible for the genesis of this permanent version of the 1851 Great Exhibition, and Victoria laid its foundation stone in her final public London appearance in 1899. The British Galleries, opened in late 2001, showcase 400 years of British art and design from 1500 to 1900, with displays such as George Gilbert Scott's model of the Albert Memorial and the first English fork ever made (1632). On Wednesdays, the Late View salons lure the trendy with lectures and a wine bar. To rest your overstimulated eyes, head for the brick-walled V&A café; its Sunday Jazz Brunch is fast becoming a London institution. ☒ *Cromwell Rd.,* ☏ *020/7942–2000,* 🕸 *www.vam.ac.uk.* 🎟 *£5; free as of late Nov. 2001.* ☉ *Daily 10–5:45; Wed. Late View 6:30–9:30, last Fri. of the month 6–10. Tube: South Kensington.*

★ ⓴ **Wallace Collection.** Assembled by four generations of marquesses of Hertford, the Wallace Collection is important, exciting, undervisited—and free. As at the Frick Collection in New York, the setting here, Hertford House, is part of the show, a fine late-18th-century mansion. It was the eccentric fourth marquess who really built the collection, snapping up Bouchers, Fragonards, Watteaus, and Lancrets for a song after the French Revolution rendered this art dangerously unfashionable. A highlight is Fragonard's *The Swing,* which conjures up the 18th-century's let-them-eat-cake frivolity better than any other painting. Don't forget to smile back at Frans Hals's *Laughing Cavalier* in the Big Gallery. ☒ *Hertford House, Manchester Sq., W1,* ☏ *020/7935–0687,* 🕸 *www.the-wallace-collection.org.uk.* 🎟 *Free.* ☉ *Mon.–Sat. 10–5, Sun. 2–5. Tube: Bond, Baker St.*

Up and Down the Thames

Downstream—meaning seaward, or east—from central London, Greenwich has such riches, especially if the maritime theme (strong in an island nation) is your thing, that you should allow a very full day to see them. Meanwhile, upstream, the royal palaces and grand houses that dot the area were built not as town houses but as country residences with easy access to London by river; Hampton Court Palace is the best and biggest of all.

Greenwich
8 mi east of central London.

Home to the now-closed Millennium Dome, Greenwich makes an ideal day out from central London, thanks to its historic and maritime attractions. Sir Christopher Wren's Royal Naval College and Inigo Jones's Queen's House reach architectural heights; the Old Royal Observatory measures time for our entire planet; and the Greenwich Meridian divides the world in two. You can stand astride it with one foot in either hemisphere. The National Maritime Museum and the proud clipper ship *Cutty Sark* will appeal to seafaring types, and landlubbers can stroll the green acres of parkland that surround the buildings, the quaint 19th-century houses, and the weekend crafts and antiques markets.

Once, Greenwich was thought of as remote by Londoners, with only the river as a direct route. With new transport links in the form of the Docklands Light Railway (DLR) and the tube's Jubilee Line, getting here is both easy and inexpensive. The quickest route to maritime Greenwich is the tube to Canary Wharf and the Docklands Light Rail to the *Cutty Sark* stop. However, river connections to Greenwich (you can choose to take the tube and DLR one-way and a ferry the other) make the journey memorable in itself. On the way, the boat glides past famous London sights and the ever-changing Docklands, and there's always a cockney navigator enhancing the views with wise-guy commentary. **Ferries** from central London to Greenwich take 30–55 minutes and leave from various piers: from Charing Cross and Tower piers (☎ 020/7987–1185), from Westminster Pier (☎ 020/7930–4097), and from the Thames Barrier Pier (☎ 020/8305–0300).

🜚 *Cutty Sark.* This romantic tea clipper was built in 1869, one of fleets and fleets of similar wooden tall-masted clippers that during the 19th century plied the seven seas, trading in exotic commodities—tea, in this case. The *Cutty Sark,* the last to survive, was also the fastest, sailing the China–London route in 1871 in only 107 days. Now the photogenic vessel lies in dry dock, a museum of one kind of seafaring life—and not a comfortable kind for the 28-strong crew, as you'll see. The collection of figureheads is amusing, too. ⊠ *King William Walk, SE10,* ☎ *020/8858–3445,* WEB *www.cuttysark.org.uk.* 🎟 *£3.50.* ☉ *Daily 10–5; last admission 4:30. DLR: Cutty Sark.*

★ 🜚 **National Maritime Museum.** One of Greenwich's outstanding attractions contains everything to do with the British at sea, in the form of paintings, models, maps, globes, sextants, uniforms (including the one Nelson died in at Trafalgar, complete with bloodstained bullet hole), and—best of all—actual boats, including an ornately gilded royal barge. New exhibitions, such as the excellent interactive All Hands gallery for kids, and an immense glazed roof that creates an indoor courtyard have revitalized this museum. Don't miss the Nelson galleries. ⊠ *Romney Rd., SE10,* ☎ *020/8858–4422,* WEB *www.nmm.ac.uk.* 🎟 *£6; £10.50, including Queen's House and Old Royal Observatory.* ☉ *Mon.–Sat. 10–6, Sun. noon–6. DLR: Cutty Sark.*

Old Royal Observatory. Founded in 1675 by Charles II, this observatory (now a museum) was designed the same year by Christopher Wren for John Flamsteed, the first Astronomer Royal. The red ball you see on its roof has been there only since 1833. It drops every day at 1 PM, and you can set your watch by it, as the sailors on the Thames always have. Everyone comes here to be photographed astride the **Prime Meridian,** a brass line laid on the cobblestones at zero degrees longitude, one side being the eastern, one the western, hemisphere. An excellent exhibition documents the search for a way to measure longitude (described in Dava Sobel's book *Longitude*); John Harrison's maritime clocks H1 through H4, created to help calculate longitude (H4 succeeded) are here, in working order. ⊠ *Greenwich Park, SE10,* ☎ *020/ 8858–4422,* WEB *www.rog.nmm.ac.uk.* 🎟 *£4.80; £10.50, including Queen's House and National Maritime Museum.* ☉ *Daily 10–5, last admission 4:30. DLR: Cutty Sark.*

★ **Queen's House.** The queen for whom Inigo Jones began designing the house in 1616 was James I's Anne of Denmark, but she died three years later, and it was Charles I's French wife, Henrietta Maria, who inherited the building when it was completed in 1635. This is Britain's first Classical building to use the lessons of Italian Renaissance architecture, and is of enormous importance in the history of English architecture. The Great Hall is a perfect cube, exactly 40 ft in all three directions, and it is decorated with paintings of the Muses, the Virtues, and the Liberal Arts. ⊠ *Romney Rd., SE10,* ☎ *020/8858–4422,* WEB *www.nmm.ac.uk.* 🎟 *£1; £10.50, including National Maritime Museum and Old Royal Observatory.* ☉ *Daily 10–5, last admission 4:30. DLR: Cutty Sark.*

Royal Naval College. Begun by Christopher Wren in 1694 as a home for ancient mariners, it became a school for young ones in 1873; today the University of Greenwich uses it for classes. You'll notice how the two main blocks part to reveal the Queen's House behind the central lawns, one of England's most famous architectural set pieces. Wren, with the help of his assistant, Nicholas Hawksmoor, was at pains to preserve the river vista from the house, and there are few more majestic views in London than the awe-inspiring symmetry he achieved. The Painted Hall and the College Chapel are the two outstanding interiors on view here. ⊠ *King William Walk, SE10,* ☎ *020/8269–4747.* 🖾 *Free; £5 for admission to the Painted Hall and the College Chapel.* ⊙ *Mon.–Sat. 10–5; Sun. 12:30–5.*

Hampton Court Palace

★ *20 mi southwest of central London.*

On a loop of the Thames lies Hampton Court, one of London's oldest royal palaces and more like a small town in size; it requires a day of your time to do it justice. The magnificent Tudor brick house was begun in 1514 by Cardinal Wolsey, the ambitious and worldly lord chancellor (roughly, prime minister) of England and archbishop of York. He wanted it to be the best palace in the land, and he succeeded so effectively that Henry VIII grew deeply envious, whereupon Wolsey felt obliged to give Hampton Court to the king. Henry moved in during 1525, adding a great hall and chapel, and proceeded to live much of his astonishing life here. Later, during the reign of William and Mary, the palace was much expanded by Sir Christopher Wren. The site beside the slow-moving Thames is perfect. The palace itself, steeped in history, hung with priceless paintings, full of echoing cobbled courtyards and cavernous Tudor kitchens complete with deer pies and cooking pots—not to mention the ghost of Catherine Howard, who is still aboard, screaming her innocence (of adultery) to an unheeding Henry VIII—is set in a fantastic array of ornamental gardens, lakes, and ponds. Best of all is the celebrated maze; it was planted in 1714 and is truly fiendish. Six themed routes, including Henry VIII's State Apartments and the King's (William III's) Apartments help you plan your visit; special guides in period costume add to the fun. Trains run frequently from London Waterloo to Hampton Court Station, with the trip taking about 30 minutes. The palace is a five-minute walk from the station. ⊠ *East Molesey,* ☎ *020/8781–9500,* WEB *www.hrp.org.uk.* 🖾 *Apartments and maze £10.50, maze alone £2.30, grounds free.* ⊙ *State apartments Apr.–Oct., Tues.–Sun. 9:30–6, Mon. 10:15–6; Nov.–Mar., Tues.–Sun. 9:30–4:30, Mon. 10:15–4:30; grounds daily 7 AM–dusk. British Rail: Hampton Court Station from Waterloo. Tube: Richmond, then bus R68.*

Kew Gardens

★ *6 mi southwest of central London.*

Kew Gardens, or more formally the Royal Botanic Gardens at Kew, is the headquarters of the country's leading botanical institute as well as a spectacular public garden of 300 acres and more than 60,000 species of plants. The highlights of a visit are the two great 19th-century greenhouses filled with tropical plants, many of which have been there as long as their housing. The ultramodern Princess of Wales Conservatory opened in 1987. Two 18th-century royal ladies, Queen Caroline and Princess Augusta, were responsible for the garden's founding. Kew Palace, on the grounds, was home to George III for much of his life. ⊠ *Kew Rd., Richmond,* ☎ *020/8940–1171,* WEB *www.kew.org.* 🖾 *£6.50.* ⊙ *Gardens Apr.–Oct., weekdays 10–6, weekends 9:30–7:30; greenhouses Apr.–Oct., daily 9:30–5:30; Nov.–Mar., daily 10–4. Tube: Kew Gardens.*

DINING

No longer would Somerset Maugham be justified in saying, "If you want to eat well in England, have breakfast three times a day." London is in the midst of a restaurant revolution and its dining scene is one of the hottest around; even Lord Lloyd Webber, composer of *Cats* and *Phantom of the Opera,* has taken on a second career as dining critic. The city has fallen head-over-heels in love with its restaurants—all 9,000 of them—from its vast, glamorous eateries to its tiny neighborhood joints, from pubs where young foodniks find their feet to swank trendsetters where celebrity chefs launch their ego flights.

This restaurant renaissance is due to a talented bunch of entrepreneurs and chefs: Sir Terence Conran, Marco Pierre White, Jean-Christophe Novelli, Oliver Peyton, and Mogens Tholstrup lead the list. Read all about them, and many others, when you get here, which you can easily do by picking up any newspaper. To keep up with the onslaught, newspapers have about 15 restaurant reviewers apiece. Luckily, London also does a good job of catering to people more interested in satisfying theirappetites without breaking the bank than in following the latest food fashions. The listings here strike a balance between these extremes and include hip-and-happening places, neighborhood spots, ethnic alternatives, and old favorites. Ethnic restaurants have always been a good bet here, especially the thousands of Indian restaurants, since Londoners see a good curry as their birthright.

London is not an inexpensive dining city, although you will often find set-price menus at lunchtime, bringing even the finest establishments within reach. Prix-fixe dinners are beginning to proliferate, too. Few places these days mind if you order a second appetizer instead of an entrée. The law obliges all British restaurants to display their prices, including VAT (sales tax) outside, but watch for hidden extras such as bread and vegetables charged separately, and service. Most restaurants add 10%–15% automatically to the check, or else stamp SERVICE NOT INCLUDED along the bottom, in which case you should add the 10%–15% yourself. Beware of paying twice for service—restaurateurs have been known to add service, then leave the total on the credit-card slip blank, hoping for more.

A final caveat: many restaurants are closed on Sunday, especially for dinner; the same is true on public holidays. Over the Christmas period, the London restaurant community all but shuts down—only hotels will be prepared to feed you. When in doubt, call ahead.

CATEGORY	COST*
££££	over £22
£££	£16–£22
££	£9–£15
£	under £9

per person for a main course at dinner

Bloomsbury

ENGLISH

£ ✗ **Truckles of Pied Bull Yard.** Wine bars were the hits of '70s London, although hardly any survive to tell the tale. This one's fantastic for a post–British Museum glass of something, and they purportedly serve the cheapest glass of bubbly here. The old English ham salad has gone upscale, and southern European foods (goat-cheese sandwiches on chewy *ciabatta* bread) are more often than not on the menu. The nicest area is the courtyard with tables galore in summer. ⊠ *Off Bury Pl.,*

WC1, ☎ 020/7404–5338. AE, DC, MC, V. Closed Sun. No dinner Sat. Tube: Holborn.

FRENCH

££–£££ ✗ **Chez Gérard.** One of a small chain of steak-frites restaurants, this one has expanded its utterly Gallic menu to include more for non–red meat eaters. Steak, served with shoestring fries and béarnaise sauce, remains the reason to visit. ⊠ 8 Charlotte St., W1, ☎ 020/7636–4975. AE, DC, MC, V. Tube: Goodge St.

SEAFOOD

£ ✗ **North Sea Fish Restaurant.** This is the place for the British national dish of fish-and-chips—battered and deep-fried whitefish with thick fries shaken with salt and vinegar. It's a bit tricky to find: three blocks south of St. Pancras station, down Judd Street. Only freshly caught fish is served, and you can order it grilled, although that would defeat the purpose. You can take out or eat in. ⊠ 7–8 Leigh St., WC1, ☎ 020/ 7387–5892. AE, DC, MC, V. Closed Sun. Tube: Russell Sq.

Chelsea

AMERICAN/CASUAL

££ ✗ **PJ's Grill.** The decor here evokes the Polo Joe lifestyle, with wooden floors and stained glass, a vast, slowly revolving propeller from a 1940s Vickers–Viny flying boat, and polo memorabilia. A menu of all-American staples should please all but vegetarians. ⊠ 52 Fulham Rd., SW3, ☎ 020/7581–0025. AE, DC, MC, V. Tube: South Kensington.

ANGLO-INDIAN

££ ✗ **Chutney Mary.** London's stalwart Indian restaurant provides a fantasy version of the British Raj, all giant wicker armchairs and palms. Dishes such as masala roast lamb (practically a whole leg, marinated and spiced) and Malabar chicken curry (with coconut, red chile, and cinnamon) alternate with the more familiar North Indian dishes such as *dum ka murgh* (chicken, poppy seed, green chili, and onion). The best choices are the dishes re-created from the kitchens of Indian chefs cooking for English palates back in the old Raj days. ⊠ 535 King's Rd., SW10, ☎ 020/7351–3113. Reservations essential. AE, DC, MC, V. Tube: Fulham Broadway.

CONTEMPORARY

££–£££ ✗ **Bluebird.** Here's another Sir Terence Conran "gastrodome"—food market, florist, fruit stand, butcher, kitchen shop, and café-restaurant, all housed in a snappy King's Road former garage. The place is pale blue and white, very light, and not in the least cozy. The menu has more than a nod in the Asia-Pacific direction: you might try steamed mussels with coriander and lime; and then warm chocolate cake and espresso ice cream. Go for the visual excitement—Conran's chefs tend to promise more than they deliver. ⊠ 350 King's Rd., SW3, ☎ 020/ 7559–1000. Reservations essential. AE, DC, MC, V. Tube: Sloane Sq.

ENGLISH

£ ✗ **Chelsea Kitchen.** Always crowded, this place is fine for hot, filling, and inexpensive pub-style food, including steak and mushroom pies or traditional Cornish pasties (turnovers) with carrots and runner beans. ⊠ 98 King's Rd., SW3, ☎ 020/7589–1330. No credit card. Tube: Sloane Sq.

FRENCH

££££ ✗ **Gordon Ramsay.** A table here has been London's toughest reserva-
★ tion to score for almost as long as it's been open, because Gordon Ramsay, considered London's greatest chef, has diners gasping in awe.

London Dining

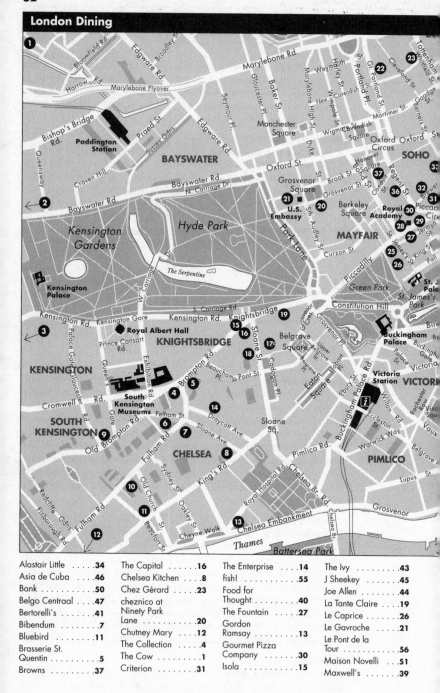

Alastair Little **34**

Asia de Cuba **46**

Bank **50**

Belgo Centraal **47**

Bertorelli's **41**

Bibendum **7**

Bluebird **11**

Brasserie St.
Quentin **5**

Browns **37**

The Capital **16**

Chelsea Kitchen . . . **8**

Chez Gérard . . . **23**

cheznico at
Ninety Park
Lane **20**

Chutney Mary . . . **12**

The Collection **4**

The Cow **1**

Criterion **31**

The Enterprise . . . **14**

fish! **55**

Food for
Thought **40**

The Fountain **27**

Gordon
Ramsay **13**

Gourmet Pizza
Company **30**

Isola **15**

The Ivy **43**

J Sheekey **45**

Joe Allen **44**

La Tante Claire . . . **19**

Le Caprice **26**

Le Gavroche **21**

Le Pont de la
Tour **56**

Maison Novelli . . **51**

Maxwell's **39**

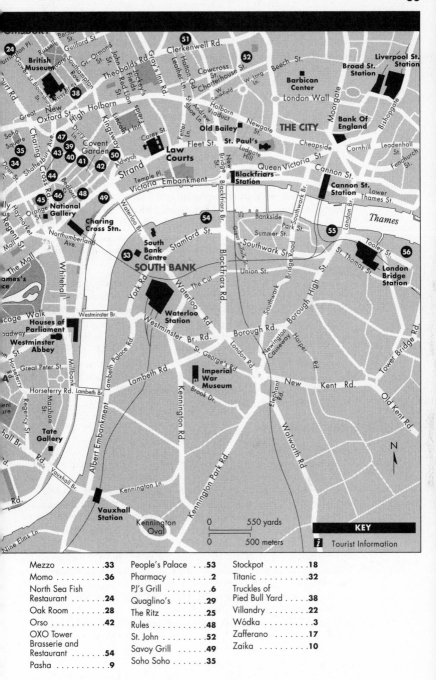

Mezzo **33**

Momo **36**

North Sea Fish
Restaurant **24**

Oak Room **28**

Orso **42**

OXO Tower
Brasserie and
Restaurant **54**

Pasha **9**

People's Palace . . . **53**

Pharmacy **2**

PJ's Grill **6**

Quaglino's **29**

The Ritz **25**

Rules **48**

St. John **52**

Savoy Grill **49**

Soho Soho **35**

Stockpot **18**

Titanic **32**

Truckles of
Pied Bull Yard **38**

Villandry **22**

Wódka **3**

Zafferano **17**

Zaika **10**

Ramsay whips up a storm with white beans, girolles, foie gras, scallops, and truffles, and by the time you read this he will probably have won another 5 awards. Reserve months ahead; go for lunch (£30 set menu) if the set-price dinner menus seem too steep. ⊠ *68–69 Royal Hospital Rd., SW3,* ☎ *020/7352–4441. Reservations essential. AE, DC, MC, V. Closed weekends. Tube: Sloane Sq.*

INDIAN

££ ✗ **Zaika.** Zaika has zoomed in from nowhere to become one of London's finest Indian restaurants. The chef-owner, Vineet Bhatia, mixes age-old flavors with modern sensibilities and is pushing the boundaries of Indian cuisine. The restaurant itself is dark (muds and browns), refined, sensual, and subtle. Indian artifacts hide in holes in the wall. You can't top the signature starter of *dhungar machli tikka* (tandoor home-smoked salmon with drips of mustard and dill), nor can you better the poached scallops in coconut milk drizzled with chili oil and served with masala mashed potato. Sign off with cheeky chocolate samosas ("choco-mosas") and Indian ice cream. ⊠ *257–259 Fulham Rd., SW3,* ☎ *020/ 7351–7823. Reservations essential. AE, MC, V. Tube: South Kensington.*

MEDITERRANEAN

££ ✗ **The Collection.** Enter the former Katharine Hamnett shop through the spotlighted tunnel over the glass drawbridge to find a vast warehouse setting. Adorned with industrial wooden beams and steel cables, a huge bar, and a suspended gallery, it seems more dance club than eatery. Around you is the local ab-fab crowd gawking at the neighboring tables, or hoping director-*doré* Mogens Tholstrup will table-hop to theirs, while they pick at Med food seasoned with Japanese and Thai flavors (seared tuna with sesame, soy, and shiitake mushrooms; sea bream with cilantro). ⊠ *264 Brompton Rd.,* ☎ *020/7225–1212. AE, DC, MC, V. Tube: South Kensington.*

City and South Bank

CONTEMPORARY

££–£££ ✗ **Maison Novelli.** Jean-Christophe Novelli is one of the heroes of the
★   modern British movement, and his restaurant has drawn foodies from the day it opened in up-and-buzzing Clerkenwell, near stylish Islington. These days, gladly, Novelli has downsized and is back running the kitchen after almost burning out, expanding his empire across London and sharing his cooking secrets in the *Times.* Favorites include glazed goat cheese, celeriac, and mozzarella terrine; roast fillet of beef; Beaufort cheese, garlic, and tomatoes; and the famed pig's trotter stuffed "following the mood of the day." You can also come by an elegant sea bass with chorizo or truffle oil, or pan-fried halibut with mussel sauce. ⊠ *29–31 Clerkenwell Green, EC1,* ☎ *020/7251–6606. Reservations essential. AE, DC, MC, V. Tube: Farringdon.*

££–£££ ✗ **OXO Tower Brasserie and Restaurant.** How delightful it is for London to get a room with a view—and *such* a view. On the eighth floor of the OXO Tower Wharf building near the South Bank Centre is this elegant space, run by the same people who put the chic Fifth Floor at Harvey Nichols on the map. It features Euro-Asia food with the latest trendy ingredients (acorn-fed black pig charcuterie with tomato and pear chutney; Dover sole with sea urchin butter). The ceiling slats turn and change from white to midnight blue, but who on earth notices, with the new London Eye wheel and St. Paul's dazzling you across the water? The Brasserie is slightly less expensive than the restaurant, but both have great river views. For food with a view, the terrace tables in summertime are probably the best places in London. ⊠ *Barge House St., Southbank, SE1,* ☎ *020/7803–3888. AE, DC, MC, V. Tube: Waterloo.*

££ ✕ **St. John.** This former smokehouse (pork, not cigars), converted by erstwhile architect owner-chef Fergus Henderson has soaring white walls, schoolroom lamps, stone floors, iron railings, and plain wooden chairs. Entrées (roast lamb and parsnip, smoked haddock and fennel, deviled crab) are hearty and unadorned, but usually taste great. Service is efficiently friendly. ✉ *26 St. John St., EC1,* ☎ *020/7251–0848. Reservations essential. AE, DC, MC, V. Closed Sun. Tube: Farringdon.*

ENGLISH

££ ✕ **People's Palace.** Thank goodness for this place—now you can have a civilized meal during your South Bank arts encounter. With menus by trendy chef Gary Rhodes, it has remarkably low prices considering it has the greatest river view in town (apart from OXO). There are occasional mistakes here, but the more British the dish, the more reliable it proves—roast beef, potted duck, Cornish crab and red pepper, marmalade sponge, and pecan and banana pudding are good choices. ✉ *Royal Festival Hall, Level 3, South Bank, SE1,* ☎ *020/7928–9999. AE, DC, MC, V. Tube: Waterloo.*

FRENCH

££ ✕ **Le Pont de la Tour.** Sir Terence Conran's place across the river, over-
★ looking the bridge that gives it its name, comes into its own in summer, when the outside tables are heaven. Inside are a vintner and baker and deli, a seafood bar, a brasserie, and this '30s diner-style restaurant, smart as the captain's table. Fish and seafood (lobster salad, sea bream with herb risotto) and meat and game (Denham-estate venison with parsnip and bitter chocolate sauce, Gressingham duck with orange and thyme) feature heavily—vegetarians are out of luck. Prune and Armagnac tart or nut fondant could finish a glamorous, and expensive, meal. ✉ *36D Shad Thames, Butler's Wharf, SE1,* ☎ *020/7403–8403. Reservations essential. AE, DC, MC, V. Tube: Tower Hill.*

SEAFOOD

££ ✕ **fish!** One of the sensations to hit the London scene, this remarkable diner—sleek and modern—sits in the shadow of Southwark Cathedral looking like the glass-covered innards of a giant whale. The fish at fish! is excellent, and politically correct. The langoustine are creel-caught, the salmon organic, and the scallops landed by divers. There are always at least eight types of fish on the menu, from swordfish to brill, skate, and turbot. The splish-splosh in-and-out formula has struck a chord; six more fish! are coming on-stream. ✉ *Cathedral St., SE1,* ☎ *020/7234–3333. AE, DC, MC, V. Tube: London Bridge.*

Covent Garden

AMERICAN

££ ✕ **Joe Allen.** Long hours (thespians flock here after the curtain falls in Theatreland) and a welcoming, if loud, brick-wall interior mean New York Joe's London branch is still swinging after more than two decades. The fun, contemporary menu helps: barbecued ribs with black-eyed peas and London's only available corn muffins, roast monkfish with sun-dried-tomato salsa, egg dishes, and huge salads, too. ✉ *13 Exeter St., WC2,* ☎ *020/7836–0651. Reservations essential. AE, MC, V. Tube: Covent Garden.*

£ ✕ **Maxwell's.** London's first-ever burger joint, now more than a quarter-century old, cloned itself and then grew up. Here's the result, a happy place under the Royal Opera House serving the kind of food you may be homesick for: quesadillas, Buffalo chicken wings, barbecued ribs, Cajun chicken, chef's salad, and a burger to die for. ✉ *8–9 James St., WC2,* ☎ *020/7836–0303. AE, DC, MC, V. Tube: Covent Garden.*

BELGIAN

££   ✗ **Belgo Centraal.** The wackiest dining concept in town started with a bistro in Camden, and was so adored it was cloned uptown in a big basement space you have to enter by elevator. Have mussels and fries in vast quantities, served with 101 Belgian beers (fruit-flavored, Trappist-brewed, white, or light) by people dressed as monks in a hall like a refectory in a Martian monastery. The luxury index is low, but so is the check. ⊠ *50 Earlham St., WC2,* ☎ *020/7813–2233. AE, DC, MC, V. Tube: Covent Garden.*

CONTEMPORARY

£££   ✗ **The Ivy.** This seems to be everybody's favorite restaurant—every-
★   body who works in the media or the arts, that is. In a Deco dining room with blinding white tablecloths, and Hodgkins and Paolozzis on the walls, the celebrated and the wannabes eat Caesar salad, roast grouse, Thai baked sea bass, braised oxtail, and rice pudding with Armagnac prunes, or sticky toffee pudding. Try the weekday three-course lunch for £15.50. ⊠ *1 West St., WC2,* ☎ *020/7836–4751. Reservations essential. AE, DC, MC, V. Tube: Covent Garden.*

££   ✗ **Bank.** City and fashionable folk flock to this vast eatery with its spec-
★   tacular chandelier and equally exciting menu. Seared mullet, paillard of pheasant with creamed cabbage, spinach and puy lentils, and mousses, brûlées, and nursery puds are just small examples of the fast-changing world palette, with a Mod-Brit touch. Although not a steal pricewise, the dishes rarely fail to please. ⊠ *1 Kingsway, WC2,* ☎ *020/7397–9797. Reservations essential. AE, DC, MC, V. Tube: Holborn.*

CONTINENTAL

£££   ✗ **Savoy Grill.** The grill continues in the first rank of power-dining lo-cations. Politicians, newspaper barons, and tycoons like the comforting food and impeccably discreet and attentive service in the low-key, yew-panel salon. On the menu, an omelet Arnold Bennett (with cheese and smoked haddock) is perennial, as is beef Wellington and roast saddle of lamb. Diners can also get their dancing shoes on at the weekly "Stompin' at the Savoy" events. ⊠ *The Strand, WC2,* ☎ *020/7836–4343. Reservations essential. Jacket and tie. AE, DC, MC, V. Closed Sun. No lunch Sat. Tube: Covent Garden.*

ENGLISH

£££   ✗ **Rules.** Come, escape from the 21st century. More than 200 years
★   old, this London institution has welcomed everyone from Dickens to Charlie Chaplin to Lillie Langtry and the Prince of Wales. The menu is historic and good—try its fabled steak-and-kidney-and-mushroom pudding—but the decor is even more delicious. With plush red banquettes and lacquered yellow walls, which are festively adorned with oil paintings and hundreds of engravings, this is probably the most handsome dining salon in London. Rules is more than a little touristy, but that's because it's so quaint. ⊠ *35 Maiden La., WC2,* ☎ *020/7836–5314. Reservations essential. AE, DC, MC, V. Tube: Covent Garden.*

ITALIAN

££   ✗ **Orso.** The Italian sister of Joe Allen, this basement restaurant has the same snappy staff and a glitzy clientele of showbiz types and hacks. The Tuscan-style menu changes every day but always includes excellent pizza and pasta dishes. Food here, much like the place itself, is never boring. Orsino, at 119 Portland Road in W11, is a stylish offshoot, serving much the same fare. ⊠ *27 Wellington St., WC2,* ☎ *020/7240–5269. Reservations essential. AE, MC, V. Tube: Covent Garden.*

£–££ ✗ **Bertorelli's.** Right across from the stage door of the Royal Opera House, Bertorelli's is quietly chic, the food tempting and just innovative enough: sea bass with walnut pesto or monkfish ragout with fennel, wonder beans, Swiss Chard, and lime butter are typical dishes. Even more decorous and delicious is the branch at 19–23 Charlotte Street. ✉ *44A Floral St., WC2, ☎ 020/7836–3969. AE, DC, MC, V. Closed Sun. Tube: Covent Garden.*

PAN-ASIAN

£££ ✗ **Asia de Cuba.** Maybe it's ironic, but it takes an American, Ian Schrager, and his Philippe Starck–designed hotel to bring Cool Britannia to its apogee. Asia de Cuba, the lead restaurant at Schrager's St. Martins Lane Hotel, is sexy and loud; the Calvin Klein–clad waiters bop and sit by your side. The food is fusion, and you're supposed to share. The Thai beef salad with Asian greens and roasted coconut is delicious, as is the lobster Mai Tai with rum and red curry. Ian Schrager is right: hotels (and their restaurants) are the new disco. ✉ *St. Martins Lane Hotel, 45 St. Martins La., WC2, ☎ 020/7300–5588. AE, DC, MC, V. Tube: Leicester Sq.*

SEAFOOD

££–£££ ✗ **J Sheekey.** J Sheekey completes the golden hat trick from the team behind Le Caprice and The Ivy. Now a top-line destination, it's where the stars go as an alternative to the Ivy. Sleek, discreet, and clublike, in the heart of Theatreland, this revived former fish restaurant is once again a seafood haven. The walls are crammed with photos of old-school talent: Peter O'Toole, Noel Coward, Laurence Olivier, Peter Sellers. The decor charms: cracked glazed tiles, lava-rock bar tops, oak paneling. Sample the wonderful jellied eels, pickled herrings, Dover sole, and fish pie. Try the weekend set lunch for £13.50. ✉ *28–32 St. Martin's Ct., WC2, ☎ 020/7240–2565. AE, DC, MC, V. Tube: Leicester Sq.*

VEGETARIAN

£ ✗ **Food for Thought.** This simple basement restaurant (no liquor license) seats only 50 and is popular, so you'll almost always find a line of people down the stairs. The menu—stir-fries, casseroles, salads, and desserts—changes every day, and each dish is freshly made; there's no microwave. ✉ *31 Neal St., WC2, ☎ 020/7836–0239. Reservations not accepted. No credit cards. Closed 1 wk in Dec. Tube: Covent Garden.*

Kensington and Notting Hill Gate

CONTEMPORARY

££–£££ ✗ **Bibendum.** This converted Michelin showroom, adorned with Art
★   Deco decorations and brilliant stained glass, remains one of London's dining showplaces. Chef Matthew Harris aspires to simple but perfect Euro-Brit dishes: herring with sour cream, risottos, steak aupoivre, or sea bass with salsa verde. Here, too, are brains and tripe as they ought to be cooked. The £28 set-price menu at lunchtime is money well spent. ✉ *Michelin House, 81 Fulham Rd., SW3, ☎ 020/7581–5817. Reservations essential. AE, DC, MC, V. Tube: South Kensington.*

££–£££ ✗ **Pharmacy.** The Pharmacy is one of those trendy places where the bar is larger than the restaurant. In this case, the bar seats 120 and is shaped like a gigantic aspirin. Yes, this spot looks like its namesake, and even the menu looks fab—but then, Damien Hirst, artist extraordinaire, was involved in setting up the place. The menu highlights comfort food and ranges from carpaccio of whitefish with ginger and sesame to roast Dorset lamb with puy lentils and suckling pig with baked quince. If you can't snag a table, just have fun at the bar and order the drink called "Blood Transfusion." ✉ *150 Notting Hill Gate, W11, ☎ 020/7221–2442. AE, DC, MC, V. Tube: Notting Hill Gate.*

££ ✗ **The Cow.** Oh, no, not *another* Conran. This place belongs to Tom, son of Sir Terence, although it's a million miles from Quag's and Mezzo. A tiny and chic gastro-pub, it comprises a faux-Dublin back-room bar serving up oysters, salmon fish cakes, and baked brill; upstairs, a serious chef whips up Tuscan–British specialties; skate poached in minestrone is one temptation. Notting Hillbillies and other stylish folk adore the house special, a half-dozen Irish rock oysters with a pint of Guinness. ⊠ *89 Westbourne Park Rd., W2,* ☎ *020/7221–5400. Reservations essential. AE, MC, V. Tube: Westbourne Park.*

MOROCCAN

££ ✗ **Pasha.** Not quite a taste of old Tangiers, Pasha delivers modern Morocco and due east in a very à la mode manner. Waiters in traditional dress drift between piles of silken cushions and flickering candlelight to bring delicacies such as *pastilla* (pie) of chicken and stylish cross-cuisine desserts (brûlée with Turkish Delight). ⊠ *1 Gloucester Rd., SW7,* ☎ *020/7589–7969. Reservations essential. AE, DC, MC, V. Tube: Gloucester Rd.*

POLISH

££ ✗ **Wódka.** This smart, modern Polish restaurant serves the smartest, most modern Polish food around. It's popular with elegant locals plus a sprinkling of celebs and often has the atmosphere of a dinner party. With your smoked salmon, herring, caviar, eggplant blinis, or venison sausages, order a carafe of the purest vodka in town; it's encased in a block of ice and hand-flavored with rowanberries. ⊠ *12 St. Albans Grove, W8,* ☎ *020/7937–6513. Reservations essential. AE, DC, MC, V. No lunch weekends. Tube: High Street Kensington.*

Knightsbridge

CONTEMPORARY

£–££ ✗ **The Enterprise.** One of the new breed of gastro-pubs, this hot spot near Harrods and Brompton Cross is filled with decorative types who complement the decor: paisley-stripe wallpaper, Edwardian side tables covered with baskets and farmhouse fruit, vintage books piled up in the windows, fresh flowers on the tables. The menu isn't overly pretty— seared tuna and char-grilled asparagus, timbale of aubergine, salmon with artichoke hearts—but the ambience certainly is. ⊠ *35 Walton St., SW3,* ☎ *020/7584–3148. AE, MC, V. Tube: South Kensington.*

CONTINENTAL

£ ✗ **Stockpot.** You'll find speedy service at this chain of large, jolly restaurants, often packed to the brim with young people and shoppers. The food is sometimes unstartling but filling and wholesome: try the Lancashire hot pot, for example, and the apple crumble. ⊠ *6 Basil St., SW3,* ☎ *020/7589–8627. No credit cards. Tube: Knightsbridge;* ⊠ *38 Panton St., off Leicester Sq., SW1,* ☎ *020/7839–5142;* ⊠ *273 King's Rd., Chelsea, SW3,* ☎ *020/7823–3175.*

FRENCH

££££ ✗ **The Capital.** This elegant, clublike dining room has a grown-up atmosphere and formal service. Chef Eric Chavot pursues traditional French cooking, and most of his creations never fail to astonish. His fine dishes include saddle of rabbit with sweet onion pastille and thyme *jus* or sea bass with Alsace bacon and fried calamari. Desserts follow the same exciting route. Set-price menus at lunch (£24) make it more affordable. ⊠ *22–24 Basil St., SW3,* ☎ *020/7589–5171. Reservations essential. Jacket and tie. AE, DC, MC, V. Tube: Knightsbridge.*

££££ ✗ **La Tante Claire.** One of the best restaurants in London successfully
★   upped its sticks, pots, and pans and moved to the Berkeley Hotel. Chef Pierre Koffmann still reigns over the kitchen, so you can expect the same brilliant standards of haute cuisine. From the *carte,* you might choose langoustine tails with citrus *jus* and celeriac mousse, oxtail with truffle sauce on foie gras, or Koffmann's signature dish of pigs' feet sweetbreads and wild mushrooms. The set lunch menu (£28) is a bargain.

Lunch reservations must be made three to four days in advance, dinner reservations three to four weeks in advance. ⊠ *Berkeley Hotel, Wilton Pl., SW1,* ☎ *020/7823–2003. Reservations essential. Jacket and tie. AE, DC, MC, V. Closed Sun. No lunch Sat. Tube: Knightsbridge.*

££–£££ ✕ **Brasserie St. Quentin.** A very popular slice of Paris, this spot is frequented by French expatriates and locals alike. Every inch of the Gallic menu is explored—quiche, escargots, cassoulet, lemon tart—in the bourgeois provincial comfort so many London bistro chains try for yet fail to achieve. ⊠ *243 Brompton Rd., SW3,* ☎ *020/7589–8005. AE, DC, MC, V. Tube: South Kensington.*

ITALIAN

££££ ✕ **Zafferano.** Princess Margaret, Eric Clapton, Joan Collins (she asked
★ that the lights be turned down), and any number of other Cartier-brooch-wearing neighborhood Belgravians have flocked to this place, which, since 1995, has been London's best exponent of *cucina nuova*. The fireworks are in the kitchen, not in the brick-wall-and-saffron-hued decor, but *what* fireworks: on the set menus you may find pheasant with rosemary and black truffle, venison medallions with mash and roast cod, lentils and parsley sauce. The desserts are also *delizioso,* especially the Sardinian pecorino pastries served with undersweetened vanilla ice cream and the panettone bread-and-butter pudding. Be sure to book early. ⊠ *15 Lowndes St., SW1,* ☎ *020/7235–5800. Reservations essential. AE, DC, MC, V. Tube: Knightsbridge.*

£££ ✕ **Isola.** Isola guns for the title of coolest restaurant in London, so don't be surprised to see Joseph Fiennes mooching in a corner. The brainchild of Oliver Peyton (Atlantic Bar & Grill, Mash), Isola is grown-up osteria and Italian fine dining cooked by a Frenchman, Bruno Loubet. Upstairs is banquette-and-booth power dining; downstairs is more larky and glam—diners sit at off-white leather "compromise sofas" amid the sparkle of chrome and mirrors. Head for the *zuppa di fagiano e farro* (pheasant soup with cabbage and faro) and the *faraona al forno* (wood-roasted guinea fowl with liver and mascarpone). ⊠ *145 Knightbridge, SW1,* ☎ *020/7838–1044. Reservations essential. AE, DC, MC, V. Tube: Knightsbridge.*

Mayfair

ENGLISH

£–££ ✕ **Browns.** Unpretentious, crowd-pleasing, child-friendly English food is delivered here at the former establishment of the bespoke tailors Messrs. Cooling and Wells, now converted to Edwardian style by the group behind the very successful regional Browns eateries (the Oxford and Cambridge ones are student standbys). The classic steak-and-Guinness pie is still on the menu, but king prawns, lamb shanks, roasted peppers, salads, and pastas now predominate. ⊠ *47 Maddox St., W1,* ☎ *020/7491–4565. AE, DC, MC, V. Tube: Oxford Circus.*

FRENCH

££££ ✕ **Le Gavroche.** Albert Roux's son, Michel, retains many of his father's "capital C" Classical dishes and has added his own style to this place, once considered London's finest restaurant. Much of the food is still fabulous—the lobster *tagine* is a wonder—but the decor of the basement dining room is, some would say, generic: brown-green walls, dullish modern oil paintings, and potted plants. The set lunch is relatively affordable at £38.50. ⊠ *43 Upper Brook St., W1,* ☎ *020/7408–0881 or 020/7499–1826. Reservations essential. Jacket and tie. AE, DC, MC, V. Closed weekends and 10 days in Dec. Tube: Marble Arch.*

££££ ✕ **Oak Room.** Marco Pierre White used to enjoy Jagger-like fame from
★ his TV appearances and gossip-column reports. Sadly, he has stopped

cooking and now concentrates on building his substantial restaurant empire. Still, his charges are superbly trained here, and the restaurant has one of London's most spectacular settings—all Belle Epoque soaring ceilings and gilded bits, and palms and paintings. ⌧ *Le Meridien, 21 Piccadilly, W1,* ☎ *020/7437–0202. Reservations essential. Jacket and tie. AE, DC, MC, V. Tube: Piccadilly Circus.*

£££ ✕ **cheznico at Ninety Park Lane.** Those with refined palates and deep pockets would be well advised not to miss Nico Ladenis's exquisite cuisine, served in this suitably hushed and plush Louis XV dining room next to the Grosvenor House Hotel. Autodidact Nico is one of the world's great chefs, and he's famous for knowing it. The menu is stately with heavenly light touches. There's no salt on the table—ask for some at your peril. It's all more affordable in daylight, with fixed-price lunch menus from £25 for three courses. ⌧ *90 Park La., W1,* ☎ *020/7409– 1290. Reservations essential. Jacket and tie. AE, DC, MC, V. Closed Sun. No lunch Sat. Tube: Marble Arch.*

££ ✕ **Criterion.** This palatial neo-Byzantine mirrored marble hall, which first opened in 1874, is heavy on the awe factor, and Marco Pierre White's team scores highly. He doesn't cook here, but some of his well-known dishes, including ballotine of salmon with herbs and *fromage blanc,* appear on the vast menu. The glamor of the soaring golden ceiling, peacock-blue theater-size drapes, oil paintings, and attentive Gallic service adds up to an elegant night out. ⌧ *Piccadilly Circus, W1,* ☎ *020/ 7930–0488. AE, DC, MC, V. Tube: Piccadilly Circus.*

PIZZA

£–££ ✕ **Gourmet Pizza Company.** Fine pies with wacky toppings are served up at this California-style über-pizzeria. ⌧ *7–9 Swallow St., SW1,* ☎ *020/7734–5182. AE, MC, V. Tube: Piccadilly Circus.*

St. James's

CONTEMPORARY

£££ ✕ **Quaglino's.** Sir Terence Conran's original huge restaurant, "Quags," is *the* out-of-towners' post-theater or celebration destination, whereas Londoners like its late hours. The gigantic sunken restaurant boasts a glamorous staircase, "Crustacea Altar," large bar, and live jazz music. The food is fashionably pan-European with some Asian trimmings. Desserts come from somewhere between the Paris bistro and the English nursery: raspberry *sablé* (a delicate, crumbly cookie), crème pudding with butterscotch sauce, and wine from the Old World and the New, some bottles at modest prices. ⌧ *16 Bury St., SW1,* ☎ *020/7930– 6767. Reservations essential. AE, DC, MC, V. Tube: Green Park.*

££–£££ ✕ **Le Caprice.** Secreted in a small street behind the Ritz, Le Caprice may
★   command the deepest loyalty of any restaurant in London because it gets everything right: the glamorous, glossy black Eva Jiricna interior; the perfect pitch of the informal but respectful service; the food, halfway between Euro-peasant and fashion plate. This food—crispy duck and watercress salad, seared scallops with bacon and sorrel, risotto *nero* (with squid), grilled rabbit with black olive polenta, and divine desserts, too—has no business being so good, because the other reason everyone comes here is that everyone else does, which leads to the best people-watching in town (apart from at its sister restaurant, the Ivy. ⌧ *Arlington House, Arlington St., SW1,* ☎ *020/7629–2239. Reservations essential. AE, DC, MC, V. Tube: Green Park.*

CONTINENTAL

££££ ✕ **The Ritz.** Constantly accused of being London's prettiest dining room, this Belle Epoque palace of marble, gilt, and trompe l'oeil would moisten even Marie Antoinette's eye; add the view over Green Park and the Ritz's secret sunken garden, and it seems beside the point to eat. But the British-French cuisine stands up to the visual onslaught with costly morsels (foie gras, lobster, truffles, caviar, etc.), super-rich, all served with a flourish. Englishness is wrested from Louis XVI by a daily roast "from the trolley." A three-course fixed-price lunch at £35 and a four-course dinner at £51 make the check more bearable, but wine is pricey. A Friday and Saturday dinner dance sweetly maintains a dying tradition. ✉ *150 Piccadilly, W1,* ☎ *020/7493–8181. Reservations essential. Jacket and tie. AE, DC, MC, V. Tube: Green Park.*

ENGLISH

£–£££   ✕ **The Fountain.** At the back of Fortnum & Mason is this old-fash-
★   ioned restaurant, as frumpy and popular as a boarding-school matron, serving delicious light meals, toasted snacks, and ice cream sodas. During the day, go for the Welsh rarebit or Fortnum's steak-and-ale pie; in the evening, a no-frills rump steak is a typical option. It's just the place for afternoon tea and ice cream sundaes after the Royal Academy or Bond Street shopping, and for pretheater meals. ✉ *181 Piccadilly, W1,* ☎ *020/7734–8040. AE, DC, MC, V. Closed Sun. Tube: Green Park.*

NORTH AFRICAN

££   ✕ **Momo.** Momo is one of the hottest tickets in town. Algerian-born Mourad Mazouz—Momo to his friends—has stormed London with his kasbah-like Moroccan-inspired North African restaurant, set in a cul-de-sac behind Regent Street. Eating here is a real experience. The seats are low and spaced close together, and there's a DJ and often live music. North African music troupes sometimes work their way among the diners. Downstairs is the members-only Kemia Bar, and next door is Mô—a Moroccan tearoom, open to all. The restaurant menu, which is based on *pastilla* (a pie-like dish made of phyllo dough), *tagine* (a Moroccan stew), and couscous, doesn't quite match the excitement of the place. ✉ *25 Heddon St., W1,* ☎ *020/7434–4040. Reservations essential. AE, DC, MC, V. Tube: Piccadilly Circus.*

Soho

CONTEMPORARY

£££   ✕ **Alastair Little.** Little is one of London's most original, and most imitated chefs, drawing inspiration from practically everywhere (Thailand, Japan, Scandinavia, France, but chiefly Italy) and sometimes bringing it off brilliantly. His restaurant is stark and sparse so all attention focuses on the menu, which changes not once but twice daily to take advantage of the best ingredients. Look out also for his smaller, cheaper version with the same name near Ladbroke Grove tube station. ✉ *49 Frith St., W1,* ☎ *020/7734–5183. AE, DC, MC, V. Closed Sun. No lunch Sat. Tube: Leicester Sq.*

££–£££   ✕ **Titanic.** London's Titanic initially rode high on the crest of a media wave, yet Marco Pierre White, the noted chef who opened this—the splashiest in the tide of trend-driven dining spots—claims it was not inspired by the blockbuster film. But like the movie, this place has pulled in the crowds, plus a clientele of the young, loud, and fashionable (Peter O'Toole, the marquess of Londonderry). Decor is Art Deco ocean liner, dinner is fun and casual, ranging from fish and chips to squid ink risotto to sticky toffee pudding, and prices are lower than you'd expect for this corner of town. ✉ *81 Brewer St., W1,* ☎ *020/7437–1912. Reservations essential. AE, DC, MC, V. Tube: Piccadilly Circus.*

ECLECTIC

££   ✕ **Mezzo.** Sir Terence Conran's gargantuan 480-seater is funky, and the young office and evening crowd likes to hang out here. Downstairs is the restaurant proper, with its huge glass-walled show kitchen, its

Allen Jones murals, its grand piano and dance floor, and its contemporary menu of seafood, rabbit, and chocolate and ginger truffle tart. Upstairs, the lounge overlooks a canteen-style operation called Mezzonine that serves Southeast Asian fare. A late-night café-patisserie-newsstand is next door. ⊠ *100 Wardour St., W1,* ☎ *020/7314–4000. AE, DC, MC, V. Tube: Leicester Sq.*

FRENCH

££–£££   ✗ **Villandry.** Heaven for food lovers, Villandry occupies a food hall ideal for the food-obsessed. French pâtés, Continental cheeses, fruit tarts, biscuits, and breads galore are for sale. If you must indulge but can't wait to take a bite, a tearoom café, a bar, and a fashionable dining room are places in which to enjoy some exquisite offerings; breakfast, lunch, and dinner are served daily. ⊠ *170 Great Portland St., W1,* ☎ *020/ 7631–3131. AE, DC, MC, V. Tube: Great Portland St.*

MEDITERRANEAN

££   ✗ **Soho Soho.** The ground floor is a lively café-bar with a (no reservations) rotisserie, and upstairs is a more formal and expensive restaurant. Inspiration comes from Provence, both in the olive-oil cooking style and the decor, with its murals, primary colors, and pale ocher terracotta floor tiles. The rotisserie serves omelets, salads, charcuterie, and cheeses, plus a handful of such bistro dishes as suckling pig with Provençal potatoes, fillet of silver mullet, and vanilla custard tart and berry compote. Or you can stay in the café-bar and have just a Kir or a beer. ⊠ *11–13 Frith St., W1,* ☎ *020/7494–3491. Reservations essential. AE, DC, MC, V. Tube: Leicester Sq.*

Pubs

London's pubs include some of the most gorgeous and historic interiors in the city. An integral part of the British way of life, public houses dispense beer "on tap" and usually a basic, inexpensive menu of sandwiches, quiche, and salads, and other snacks at lunchtime. But you don't go to a "local" for just pub grub. Rather, pubs are the best place to get to meet the locals in their habitat. Sit at a table if you want privacy; better, help prop up the bar, where no introductions are needed, and watch that legendary British reserve fade away.

Gastro-pub fever is still sweeping London. At many places, char-grills are being installed in the kitchen out back, and up front the faded wallpapers and the dear ole Mums are being replaced by abstract paintings and food mavens galore (the best of these new luxe pubs are reviewed above). Some of the following also feature nouveau pub grub, but whether you have Moroccan chicken or the usually dismal ploughman's special, you'll want to order a pint. Note that American-style beer is called "lager" in Britain, whereas the real British brew is "bitters" (usually served warm). You can order up your choice in two sizes—pints or half pints. If this is your first taste of British beer, order a half. Some London pubs also sell "real ale," which is less gassy than bitters and, many would argue, has a better flavor. Remember that many pubs stop serving alcoholic beverages at 11 PM.

✗ **Black Friar.** A step from Blackfriars tube, this stunning pub has an Arts-and-Crafts interior that is entertainingly, satirically ecclesiastical, with inlaid mother-of-pearl, wood carvings, stained glass, and marble pillars all over the place. In spite of the finely lettered temperance tracts on view just below the reliefs of monks, fairies, and friars, there's a nice group of beers on tap from independent brewers. ⊠ *174 Queen Victoria St., EC4,* ☎ *020/7236–5474. Tube: Blackfriars.*

✗ **Dove Inn.** Read the list of famous ex-regulars, from Charles II and Nell Gwynn (mere rumor, but a likely one) to Ernest Hemingway, as you queue for a beer at this very popular, very comely 16th-century riverside pub by Hammersmith Bridge. If it's *too* full, stroll upstream to the Old Ship or the Blue Anchor. ⊠ *19 Upper Mall, W6,* ☎ *020/ 8748–5405. Tube: Hammersmith.*

✕ **George Inn.** Sitting in a courtyard where Shakespeare's plays were once performed, the present building dates from the late 17th century and is central London's last remaining galleried inn. Dickens was a regular: the Southwark district inn is featured in *Little Dorrit.* ⊠ *77 Borough High St., SE1,* ☎ *020/7407–2056. Tube: London Bridge.*

✕ **Lamb and Flag.** This 17th-century pub was once known as "The Bucket of Blood," because the upstairs room was used as a ring for bare-knuckle boxing. Now, it's a trendy, friendly, and entirely bloodless pub, serving food (at lunchtime only) and real ale. It's on the edge of Covent Garden, off Garrick Street. ⊠ *33 Rose St., WC2,* ☎ *020/ 7497–9504. Tube: Covent Garden.*

✕ **Mayflower.** This atmospheric 17th-century riverside inn in the Rotherhithe district has exposed beams and a terrace. The inn is licensed to sell American postage stamps. ⊠ *117 Rotherhithe St., SE16,* ☎ *020/ 7237–4088. Tube: Rotherhithe.*

✕ **Museum Tavern.** Across the street from the British Museum, this gloriously Victorian pub makes an ideal resting place after the rigors of the culture trail. With lots of fancy glass—etched mirrors and stained-glass panels—gilded pillars, and carvings, the heavily restored hostelry once helped Karl Marx to unwind after a hard day in the library. He could have spent his capital on any one of six beers available on tap. ⊠ *49 Great Russell St., WC1,* ☎ *020/7242–8987. Tube: Tottenham Court Road.*

✕ **Sherlock Holmes.** This Westminster district pub used to be known as the Northumberland Arms. It figures in Arthur Conan Doyle's *The Hound of the Baskervilles,* and you can see the hound's head and plaster casts of its huge paws among other Holmes memorabilia in the bar. ⊠ *10 Northumberland St., WC2,* ☎ *020/7930–2644. Tube: Charing Cross.*

✕ **Ye Olde Cheshire Cheese.** Yes, it is a tourist trap, but this most historic of all London pubs (it dates from 1667) deserves a visit anyway, for its sawdust-covered floors, low wood-beam ceilings, and the 14th-century crypt of a Whitefriars' monastery under the cellar bar. This City pub was the most regular of Dr. Johnson's and Dickens's *many* locals. ⊠ *145 Fleet St., EC4,* ☎ *020/7353–6170. Tube: Chancery Lane.*

Afternoon Tea

In the grandest places, teatime is still a ritual, so be prepared for a dress code: Claridge's, the Ritz, and the Savoy all require jacket and tie.

✕ **Brown's Hotel.** Famous for its teas, this hotel lounge does rest on its laurels somewhat, with a packaged aura and nobody around but fellow tourists. For £20 you get sandwiches, a scone with cream and jam, tart, fruitcake, and shortbread. Champagne tea is £28. ⊠ *33 Albermarle St., W1,* ☎ *020/7518–4108. Tea served daily 3–6. Tube: Green Park.*

✕ **Claridge's.** This is the real McCoy, with liveried footmen proffering sandwiches, a scone, and superior pastries (£19 or £22) in the palatial yet genteel foyer, to the tune of the resident "Hungarian orchestra" (actually a string quartet). ⊠ *Brook St., W1,* ☎ *020/7629–8860. Tea served daily 3–5:30. Tube: Bond Street.*

✕ **Fortnum & Mason's.** Upstairs at the Queen's grocers, three set teas are ceremoniously offered: standard afternoon tea (sandwiches, scone, cakes, £17.50), old-fashioned high tea (the traditional nursery meal, adding something more robust and savory, £19.50), and champagne tea (£23). ⊠ *St. James's Restaurant, 4th floor, 181 Piccadilly, W1,* ☎

020/7734–8040. *AE, DC, MC, V.* ☺ *Tea served Mon.–Sat. 3–5:15. Tube: Green Park.*

✕ **Harrods.** The Georgian Restaurant at the ridiculously well-known department store has an afternoon tea that'll give you a sugar rush for a week. ⊠ *Brompton Rd., SW3,* ☎ *020/7730–1234. Tea served Mon.–Sat. 3:15–5:15. Tube: Knightsbridge.*

✕ **The Ritz.** The Ritz's stagey Palm Court offers tiered cake stands, silver pots, a harpist, and Louis XVI chaises, plus a great deal of Rococo gilt and glitz, all for £27. Reservations are booked months in advance for weekends. ⊠ *150 Piccadilly, W1,* ☎ *020/7493–8181. Tea served daily 2–6. Tube: Green Park.*

✕ **Savoy.** The glamorous Thames-side hotel does one of the most pleasant teas (£21.50 or £26). Its triple-tier cake stands packed with goodies, its tailcoated waiters thrillingly polite. ⊠ *The Strand, WC2,* ☎ *020/7836–4343. Tea served daily 3–5:30. Tube: Charing Cross.*

LODGING

Staying at one of London's grand-dame hotels is the next best thing to—some say better than—being a guest at the palace. Royally resplendent decors abound and armies of extra-solicitous staff are stuck in the pampering mode: the Windsors should have it so good. But even in more affordable choices, classic British style brings you a taste of home, with tea-makers and Queen Mum pastel wallpapers. Still not cozy enough? Borrow some door keys, and be a bed-and-breakfast guest. Happily, there is no dearth of options where friendliness outdistances luxe.

London is an expensive city to stay in, and in the ££££ category, you can often pay considerably more than £230 per room. In any event, you should confirm *exactly* what your room costs before checking in. British hotels are obliged by law to display a price chart at the reception desk; study it carefully. In January and February you'll often find reduced rates, and large hotels with a business clientele have frequent weekend packages. The usual practice these days in all but the cheaper hotels is for quoted prices to cover room alone; breakfast, whether Continental or "full English," costs extra. VAT (Value Added Tax—sales tax) follows the same rule, with the most expensive hotels excluding a hefty 17.5%, whereas middle-of-the-range and budget places include it in the initial quote. Be sure to reserve, as special events can fill hotel rooms suddenly.

If you do manage to arrive in the capital without a room, the **London Tourist Board Information Centres** at Heathrow and Victoria Station Forecourt can help (☎ 0839/123435; calls cost 49p per minute). The **Visitorcall** service (☎ 0891/505487; calls cost 49p per minute) provides general advice. The **LTB Bookings Hotline** (☎ 020/7932–2020), open weekdays 9:30–5:30, handles prepaid credit-card bookings (MC, V).

CATEGORY	COST*
££££	over £230
£££	£160–£230
££	£100–£160
£	under £100

All prices are for a standard double room for two people, including VAT.

Bayswater and Notting Hill Gate

££　🏠 **Abbey Court.** This elegant little hotel is more like a private home, albeit one with a resident designer. It's in a gracious Victorian mansion in a quiet street off Notting Hill Gate. Inside, the era of Victoria is reflected in deep-red wallpapers (downstairs), Murano glass and gilt-framed mirrors, framed prints, mahogany, and antiques. Bathrooms look the part but are entirely modern in gray Italian marble, with brass fittings and whirlpool baths. There's 24-hour room service instead of a restaurant (there are plenty around here, though), and you can relax in the sitting room or the conservatory. ⊠ *20 Pembridge Gardens, W2 4DU,* ☎ *020/7221–7518,* FAX *020/7792–0858,* WEB *www.abbeycourthotel. co.uk. 22 rooms. Room service, breakfast room. AE, DC, MC, V. Tube: Notting Hill.*

££ ☐ **Commodore.** This peaceful hotel of three converted Victorians in
★ the leafy square known as Lancaster Gate has some amazing rooms for the price—as superior to the regular ones (which usually go to tour groups) as Harrods is to Kmart, but priced the same. Three of these are large split-levels, with sleeping galleries; all rooms have tea- and coffeemakers, hair dryers, and TVs with pay movies. Number 11 is a duplex, entered through a mirrored door. This place is increasingly popular, so book ahead. ⊠ *50 Lancaster Gate, W2 3NA,* ☎ *020/7402– 5291,* FAX *020/7262–1088,* WEB *www.commodore-hotel.com. 90 rooms. Bar, business services. AE, MC, V. Tube: Lancaster Gate.*

££ ☐ **London Elizabeth Hotel.** This family-owned gem is only steps from Hyde Park and the Lancaster Gate tube (and from rows of depressing, cheap hotels). The foyer and lounge are crammed with chintz drapery, and little chandeliers. With their palest blue-striped walls, wooden picture rails, and Welsh wool bedspreads, or pink cabbage-rose prints and mahogany furniture, the rooms do vary in size, but they all have TVs, direct-dial phones, and hair dryers, and they're serviced by a charming Anglo-Irish staff. ⊠ *Lancaster Terr., W2 3PF,* ☎ *020/7402–6641,* FAX *020/722 4–8900,* WEB *www.londonelizabethhotel.co.uk. 55 rooms. Restaurant, bar. AE, DC, MC, V. Tube: Lancaster Gate.*

£ ☐ **Columbia.** The public rooms in these five joined-up Victorians are as big as museum halls. The clean, high-ceiling rooms, some of which are very large (three to four beds) and have park views and balconies, also offer TVs, hair dryers, tea- and coffeemakers, and direct-dial phones. Decor tends to teak veneer, khaki-beige-brown color schemes, and avocado bathroom suites, but you can't expect Regency Revival at these prices. ⊠ *95–99 Lancaster Gate, W2 3NS,* ☎ *020/7402–0021,* FAX *020/7706–4691,* WEB *www.columbiahotel.co.uk. 103 rooms. Restaurant, bar, meeting rooms. AE, MC, V. Tube: Lancaster Gate.*

Bloomsbury, Holborn, Soho, and the City

££££ ☐ **Covent Garden Hotel.** Relentlessly chic and extra-stylish, this is an-
★ other Tim and Kit Kemp extravaganza—a former 1880s vintage hospital in the midst of the artsy Covent Garden district, now the London home-away-from-home for a mélange of off-duty celebrities, actors, and style mavens. Theatrically baronial, fashionably Victorian, the public rooms will keep even the most picky atmosphere-hunter happy. Guest rooms are *World of Interiors* chic, each showcasing matching-but-mixed couturier fabrics to stunning effect. Antique-style desks are vast, beds are gargantuan, and modern bathrooms feature they-*have*-thought-of-everything heated mirrors (steam doesn't stick). ⊠ *10 Monmouth St., WC2H 9HB,* ☎ *020/7806–1000,* FAX *020/7806–1100,* WEB *www. firmdale.com. 55 rooms, 3 suites. Restaurant, minibars, gym, laundry service. AE, MC, V. Tube: Covent Garden.*

££££ ☐ **Myhotel.** A hotel where tipping is discouraged and where guests brief the management on their likes and dislikes? Where a public room is dedicated to inner karma? Yes, here it is, the work of owner Andrew Thrasyvoulou and the frighteningly omniscient Sir Terence Conran with the help of a Feng Shui designer to check the building for negative energy. Myhotel, Conran's first hotel venture, is evidently aimed at the

Abbey Court 1
Abbey House 3
Beaufort 14
Berkeley 17
Blakes 12
Brown's 27
Claridge's 26
Columbia 7
Commodore 5
Connaught 25
Covent Garden
Hotel 34
The Diplomat 18
The Dorchester 22
Dorset Square
Hotel 15
Dukes 28
Durrants 24
Eden Plaza 10
Edward Lear 16
The Gallery 12
The Generator 36
The Gore 8
The Halkin 21
Hazlitt's 31
Hotel 167 9
Le Meridien
Grosvenor House . . .23
London County Hall
Travel Inn Capital . . .41
London Elizabeth 6
London Tower
Bridge Travel Inn
Capital 40
Melita House 20
Morgan 32
Myhotel 33
The Pelham 13
Posthouse Kensington . .4
The Ritz 29
The Rookery 38
The Savoy 39
The Sloane 19
St. Ermin's Hotel 30
St. Margaret's 37
Thistle Bloomsbury . . .35
Vicarage 2

London Lodging

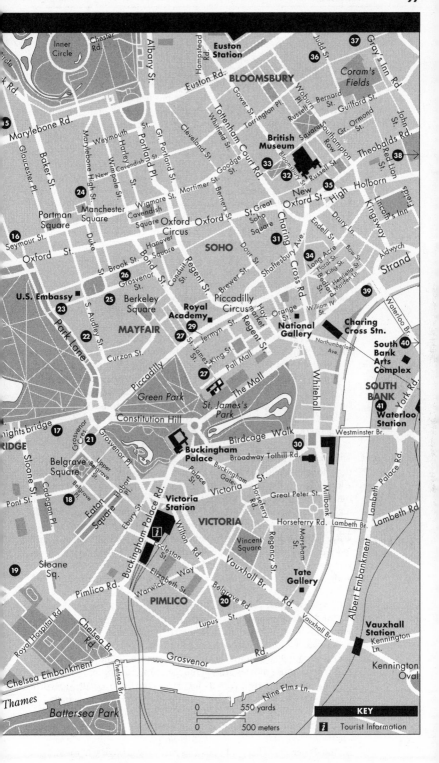

Inner Circle

Chester Rd.

Albany St.

Euston Station

Judd St.

Gray's Inn Rd.

Euston Rd.

BLOOMSBURY

Coram's Fields

Marylebone Rd.

Gower St.

Torrington Pl.

Woburn

Russell

Bernard St.

Guilford St.

Gloucester Pl.

Baker St.

Marylebone High St.

Weymouth St.

Portland Pl.

Gt. Portland St.

Cleveland St.

Whitfield St.

Tottenham Court Rd.

Goodge St.

Russell Square

Southampton Row

Gr. Ormond St.

John St.

Theobalds Rd.

Red Lion St.

New Cavendish St.

Wimpole St.

Harley St.

British Museum

Bloomsbury

Russell St.

High Holborn

Portman Square

Manchester Square

Wigmore St.

Cavendish Square

Mortimer St.

Berners St.

St.

Great

Soho Square

New Oxford St.

Charing Cross Rd.

Drury Ln.

Endell St.

Lincoln's Inn

Kingsway

Lincoln's Inn Fields

Seymour St.

Oxford St.

Duke St.

Oxford Circus

Oxford St.

SOHO

Dour St.

Shaftesbury Ave.

Long Acre

Floral St.

Bow St.

King St.

Henrietta St.

Maiden Ln.

Strand

Aldwych

Brook St.

Bond St.

Hanover Square

Regent St.

Brewer St.

Conduit St.

Grosvenor St.

U.S. Embassy

S. Audley St.

Berkeley Square

Royal Academy

Piccadilly Circus

Haymarket

Regent St.

Orange St.

William IV St.

Northumberland Ave.

Charing Cross Stn.

South Bank Arts Complex

Waterloo Br.

MAYFAIR

Jermyn St.

St. James's St.

King St.

National Gallery

Whitehall

York Rd.

SOUTH BANK

Curzon St.

Park Lane

Pall Mall

The Mall

Waterloo Station

KNIGHTSBRIDGE

Piccadilly

Green Park

St. James's Park

Westminster Br.

Birdcage Walk

Broadway

Tothill Rd.

Grosvenor Cres.

Constitution Hill

Buckingham Palace

Grosvenor Pl.

Upper Belgrave St.

Belgrave

Belgrave Square

Eaton Square

Hobart Pl.

Buckingham Gate

Palace St.

Victoria St.

Horseferry Rd.

Great Peter St.

Lambeth Palace Rd.

Lambeth Rd.

Sloane St.

Codogan Pl.

Pont St.

Ebury St.

Buckingham Palace Rd.

Eccleston St.

Wilton Rd.

Victoria Station

Victoria St.

VICTORIA

Marsham St.

Regency St.

Horseferry Rd.

Lambeth Br.

Millbank

Albert Embankment

Sloane Sq.

Elizabeth St.

Warwick St.

Way

Vincent Square

Tate Gallery

Pimlico Rd.

Royal Hospital Rd.

Chelsea Br. Rd.

PIMLICO

Belgrave Rd.

Lupus St.

Vauxhall Station

Kennington Ln.

Kennington Oval

Grosvenor

Rd.

Vauxhall Br.

Nine Elms Ln.

Chelsea Embankment

Chelsea Br.

Thames

Battersea Park

0   550 yards

0   500 meters

KEY

ℹ️ Tourist Information

young, hip (and well-heeled) traveler who expects his or her hotel to be an experience in itself. It's within easy walking distance of the British Museum, Soho, Covent Garden, and the West End. ✉ *11–13 Bayley St., Bedford Sq., WC1 B3HD,* ☎ *020/7667–6000,* 𝖥𝖠𝖷 *020/7667–6001,* 𝖶𝖤𝖡 *www.myhotels.co.uk. 76 rooms. Bar, gym, library, business services. AE, DC, MC, V. Tube: Tottenham Court Rd.*

££££   🏠 **The Rookery.** From the bijoux-size but beautiful rooms in this little hotel you see some of the most ancient parts of London. Set in the City district, the Rookery is just a step away from the Jerusalem Tavern, where it is said the Knights of St. John left to fight the Crusades. From the magnificent Rook's Nest (the hotel's tower is a complete duplex suite) you can see both St. Paul's and the Old Bailey, London's famous criminal court. If you look closely, some of Dickens's characters still seem to linger around this district, if they haven't been ousted by the fashionable and wealthy young crowd now busy colonizing the area. Each double has an antique four-poster bed and period pictures, with all the modern appliances tastefully hidden away. ✉ *Peter's La., Cowcross St., EC1M 6DS,* ☎ *020/7336–0931,* 𝖥𝖠𝖷 *020/7336–0932. 33 rooms. Bar, business services. AE, MC, V. Tube: Farringdon.*

££££   🏠 **The Savoy.** This historic, grand, late-Victorian hotel is beloved by
★   wielders of international influence, now as ever. Its celebrated Grill has the premier power-lunch tables, and it poured one of Europe's first martinis in its equally famous American Bar—haunted by Hemingway, Fitzgerald, Gershwin, et al. The spacious, elegant, bright, and comfortable rooms are furnished with antiques and serviced by valets. A room facing the Thames costs extra, but the view now includes the London Eye observation wheel. Bathrooms have original fittings, with sunflower-size showerheads. Although the Savoy is as grand as they come, the air is tinged with a certain theatrical naughtiness (due in part to the on-premises theater), which goes down well with Hollywood types. ✉ *Strand, WC2R 0EU,* ☎ *020/7836–4343,* 𝖥𝖠𝖷 *020/7240–6040,* 𝖶𝖤𝖡 *www.savoy-group.co.uk. 224 rooms. 3 restaurants, 2 bars, indoor pool, hair salon, health club. AE, DC, MC, V. Tube: Aldwych.*

£££   🏠 **Hazlitt's.** The solo Soho hotel is in three connected early 18th-cen-
★   tury houses, one of which was the last home of essayist William Hazlitt (1778–1830). It's a disarmingly friendly place, full of personality, but devoid of elevators, owing to its status as a listed historic building. Robust antiques are everywhere, assorted prints crowd every wall, plants and stone sculptures appear in odd corners, and every room has a Victorian claw-foot tub in its bathroom. There are tiny sitting rooms, wooden staircases, and more restaurants within strolling distance than you could patronize in a year. Book way ahead—this is the London address of media people, literary types, and antiques dealers. ✉ *6 Frith St., W1V 5TZ,* ☎ *020/7434–1771,* 𝖥𝖠𝖷 *020/7439–1524. 23 rooms. AE, DC, MC, V. Tube: Piccadilly.*

£££   🏠 **Thistle Bloomsbury.** On the main street, steps from the British Museum, this is one Edwardian-style hotel that really does feel sweetly old-fashioned, avoiding shabbiness or stuffiness. This former temperance house has English country-house decor, with tea- and coffeemakers, and free in-house movies among the facilities. The rooms in the turret on the southwest corner, with their curved, six-window wall, are worth requesting; executive rooms have four-posters and whirlpool baths. ✉ *Bloomsbury Way, WC1A 2SD,* ☎ *020/7242–5881,* 𝖥𝖠𝖷 *020/7831–0225,* 𝖶𝖤𝖡 *www.thistlehotels.com. 138 rooms. Restaurant, bar, meeting rooms. AE, DC, MC, V. Tube: Holborn.*

£   🏠 **The Generator.** This youth hostel is easily the grooviest in town, with a friendly, funky vibe and vibrant decor—blue neon and brushed steel downstairs, and upstairs dorm rooms painted in bright blue and orange. Talking Heads, the Internet café, provides handy maps and leaflets, plus a chance to get online. The Generator Bar has cheap drinks, and the Fuel Stop cafeteria provides inexpensive meals. Rooms, designed on a prison-cell theme complete with bunk beds and dim views, are simple but clean; prices drop very low for the ones with multiple beds in them. October to March are bargain-rate months, too. ⊠ *MacNaghten House, Compton Pl., WC1H 9SD,* ☎ *020/7388–7666,* FAX *020/7388–7644,* WEB *www.the-generator.co.uk. 217 rooms without bath. Restaurant, bar. MC, V. Tube: Russell Sq.*

£ 🏨 **London Tower Bridge Travel Inn Capital.** The name may not be snappy, but the price certainly is—practically unbeatable, especially for families. Not exactly central, this 1999 hotel is based in the Tower Hill area, which has good tube connections. Despite having been around for centuries, this is now one of London's most up-and-coming neighborhoods. If a bargain and a different look at London are what you want—or the Tower of London is one of your main destinations—save your pennies and stay here. ⊠ *Tower Bridge Rd., SE1,* ☎ *020/7940–3700,* FAX *020/7940–3719,* WEB *www.travelinn.co.uk. 196 rooms. Restaurant, bar. AE, MC, V. Tube: Tower Bridge.*

£ 🏨 **The Morgan.** This is a Georgian row-house hotel, family run with
★ charm and panache. Rooms are small and functionally furnished yet cheerful overall, with phones and TVs. The five newish apartments are particularly pleasing: three times the size of normal rooms (and an extra £15 per night), complete with kitchens and private phone lines. The tiny, paneled breakfast room is straight out of an 18th-century doll's house. The back rooms overlook the British Museum. ⊠ *24 Bloomsbury St., WC1B 3QJ,* ☎ *020/7636–3735,* FAX *020/7636–3045. 15 rooms, 5 apartments. MC, V. Tube: Tottenham Court Rd., Russell Sq.*

£ 🏨 **St. Margaret's.** A popular hotel near the British Museum, St. Margaret's offers well-lit rooms with high ceilings, telephones, and TVs in a Georgian-era building. The Italian family that runs the hotel is sure to welcome you by name if you stay long enough. Note that prices are higher for one-night stays. Back rooms have a garden view. ⊠ *26 Bedford Pl., WC1B 5JL,* ☎ *020/7636–4277,* FAX *020/7323–3066. 64 rooms, 12 with bath. No credit cards. Tube: Russell Sq., Holborn.*

Kensington

££££ 🏨 **Blakes.** This has to be the most exotic hotel in town, the work of Lady Weinberg, a.k.a. Anouska Hempel, '70s style goddess. A sober, dark-green Victorian exterior belies the arty mix of Biedermeier, bamboo, four-poster beds, and Oriental screens inside, with rooms bedecked in anything from black moiré silk to dove gray or top-to-toe blush pink. Guests tend to be music or movie mavens. ⊠ *33 Roland Gardens, SW7 3PF,* ☎ *020/7370–6701,* FAX *020/7373–0442. 52 rooms. Restaurant. AE, DC, MC, V. EP. Tube: South Kensington.*

£££–££££ 🏨 **The Gore.** Just down the road from the Albert Hall, this very friendly hotel is run by the same people who run Hazlitt's and has a similarly eclectic selection of prints, etchings, and antiques. The lobby looks like a set from a Luchino Visconti film. Upstairs are spectacular follylike rooms. Room 101 is a Tudor fantasy with minstrel gallery, stained glass, and four-poster bed. Room 211, done in over-the-top Hollywood style, has a tiled mural of Greek goddesses in the bathroom. The hotel gets a fun, chic, partying crowd. ⊠ *189 Queen's Gate, SW7 5EX,* ☎ *020/7584–6601,* FAX *020/7589–8127,* WEB *www.gorehotel.com. 54 rooms. Restaurant. AE, DC, MC, V. Tube: Gloucester Rd.*

££ 🏨 **The Gallery.** This hotel is a stone's throw from the Natural History Museum, the shops of South Kensington and Chelsea, and the once racy but now merely trendy King's Road. It has lush carpets, cozy fires, and sturdy furniture, and guest rooms are a good size with solid, comfortable beds. The bathrooms have London's ubiquitous polished granite. Included in the price is a full English breakfast, which will make lunching something of a challenge. ⊠ *10 Queensberry Pl., SW7 2E8,* ☎ *020/7915–0000,* FAX *020/7915–4400,* WEB *www.eeh.co.uk. 36 rooms. Breakfast room. AE, DC, MC, V. Tube: South Kensington.*

££ 🔲 **Posthouse Kensington.** This large, utilitarian hotel feels like a smaller one and offers extras you wouldn't expect for the reasonable rate and convenient location in a quiet lane off Kensington High Street. The main attraction is the health club, with an 18-m pool. Standard rooms are on the small side, with plain chain-hotel built-in furnishings. Some executive rooms are twice the size and are a particularly good value. ⊠ *Wrights La., W8 5SP,* ☎ *020/7937–8170 or 0870/400–9000,* FAX *020/ 7937–8289,* WEB *www.posthouse-hotels.co.uk. 543 rooms. 3 restaurants, 2 bars, indoor pool, health club, squash, baby-sitting. AE, DC, MC, V. Tube: High Street Kensington.*

£   🔲 **Abbey House.** It's been voted "Best Value, Best Quality B&B in Lon-
★   don" in several surveys, so you'll have to book well in advance for the doubles here. The place occupies a pretty, white-stucco 1860 Victorian town house, once home to a bishop and an MP before World War II, and overlooks a garden square. Rooms are spacious and have color TVs and washbasins, but every room shares a bath with another. An English breakfast is included in the rates, and a cuppa (cup of tea) is complimentary. ⊠ *11 Vicarage Gate, W8,* ☎ *020/7727–2594,* WEB *www. abbeyhousekensington.com. 16 rooms without bath. No credit cards. Tube: High Street Kensington.*

£   🔲 **Eden Plaza.** It isn't very idyllic at all, but it is across the street from the Natural History Museum in swanky South Kensington. The reasonably priced rooms are extremely compact—there's about one foot of space around the bed, and the walls have been painted in bright neon colors. Despite their small size, the rooms do have a closet, mirror, satellite TV, tea/coffeemaker, and a hair dryer cleverly concealed. ⊠ *68– 69 Queensgate, SW7 5JT,* ☎ *020/7370–6111,* FAX *020/7370–0932. 62 rooms. Bar. AE, MC, V. Tube: Gloucester Rd.*

£   🔲 **Hotel 167.** Just a two-minute walk from the V&A is this white-stucco Victorian corner house. Rooms are pleasantly decorated in muted tones and have pine furniture; each has cable TV and minibar. The hallways and stairwells have seen better days. ⊠ *167 Old Brompton Rd., SW5 0AN,* ☎ *020/7373–0672,* FAX *020/7373–3360,* WEB *www.hotel167.com. 18 rooms. Breakfast room. AE, DC, MC, V. Tube: Gloucester Rd.*

£   🔲 **Vicarage.** Spend the cash you save here in the surrounding Kensington antiques shops. This has long been a budget favorite—family-owned, set on a leaf-shaded street just off Kensington Church Street, the Vicarage is in a large white Victorian house. The decor is sweetly anachronistic, full of heavy, dark-stained wood furniture, and brass pendant lights, and there's a little conservatory. Many of the bedrooms have TVs. All in all, this still remains a charmer, but it's beginning to fray around the edges. ⊠ *10 Vicarage Gate, W8 4AG,* ☎ *020/7229– 4030,* WEB *www.londonvicaragehotel.com. 19 rooms, 2 with bath. No credit cards. Tube: High Street Kensington.*

Knightsbridge, Chelsea, and Belgravia

££££ 🔲 **Berkeley.** A remarkable mixture of the old and new, the Berkeley stars a splendid penthouse swimming pool that opens to the sky when the weather's good. The bedrooms tend to be serious and opulent, with swags of William Morris prints, or are plain and masculine with little balconies overlooking the street. All have sitting areas and big, tiled bathrooms with bidets. La Tante Claire, one of London's finest restaurants, is designed on a camellia theme, the flower that was the favorite of French fashion guru Coco Chanel. The other restaurant is Vong, the fabulous Thai–French hybrid cloned from New York. ✉ *Wilton Pl., SW1X 7RL,* ☎ *020/7235–6000,* FAX *020/7235–4330,* WEB *www.savoy-group.co.uk. 160 rooms. 2 restaurants, pool, hair salon, health club, cinema. AE, DC, MC, V. Tube: Knightsbridge.*

££££ 🏠 **The Halkin.** This luxurious little place is so contemporary you worry it will be outdated in a couple of years and they'll have to redo the whole thing. Milanese designers were responsible for the clean-cut white marble lobby, and the gray-on-gray bedrooms that light up when you insert your electronic key and contain every high-tech toy you never knew you needed. It might be like living in the Design Museum, except that this place employs some of the friendliest people around—who look pretty good in their Armani uniforms. ✉ *5 Halkin St., SW1X 7DJ,* ☎ *020/7333–1000,* FAX *020/7333–1100,* WEB *www.halkin. co.uk. 41 rooms. Restaurant, business services. AE, DC, MC, V. Tube: Hyde Park Corner.*

£££–££££ 🏠 **Beaufort.** You can practically hear the jingle of Harrods' cash reg-
★ isters from a room here. Actually, "hotel" is a misnomer for this elegant pair of Victorian houses. There's a sitting room instead of reception; guests have a front door key, the run of the drinks cabinet, and even their own phone number. The high-ceiling, generously proportioned rooms are decorated in muted, sophisticated shades to suit the muted, sophisticated atmosphere—but don't worry, you're encouraged by the incredibly sweet staff to feel at home. ✉ *33 Beaufort Gardens, SW3 1PP,* ☎ *020/7584–5252,* FAX *020/7589–2834,* WEB *www.thebeaufort. co.uk. 28 rooms. AE, DC, MC, V. Tube: Knightsbridge.*

£££–££££ 🏠 **The Pelham.** The second of Tim and Kit Kemp's gorgeous hotels
★ opened in 1989 and is run along exactly the same lines as the Dorset Square, except that this one looks less town than country. There's 18th-century pine paneling in the drawing room—one of the more magnificently handsome hotel salons in the city—flowers galore, quite a bit of glazed chintz, and the odd four-poster and bedroom fireplace. The Pelham stands opposite the South Kensington tube stop, by the big museums, and close to the shops of Knightsbridge. ✉ *15 Cromwell Pl., SW7 2LA,* ☎ *020/7589–8288,* FAX *020/7584–8444,* WEB *www.firmdale. com. 50 rooms. Restaurant. AE, MC, V. Tube: South Kensington.*

£££–££££ 🏠 **The Sloane.** The tiny Sloane is the only hotel we know of in which you can lie in your canopy bed, pick up the phone, and buy the bed—and the phone, too, and the tasty antiques all around you. Nothing so tacky as a price tag besmirches the gorgeous decor; instead, the sweet, young Euro staff harbors a book of price lists at the desk. There's an aerie of a secret roof terrace where meals are served, with upholstered garden furniture and a panorama over Chelsea. ✉ *29 Draycott Pl., SW3 2SH,* ☎ *020/7581–5757,* FAX *020/7584–1348,* WEB *www.premierhotels. com. 12 rooms. AE, DC, MC, V. Tube: Sloane Sq.*

££–£££ 🏠 **The Diplomat.** From its elegant exterior, this hotel looks like a Cecil Beaton stage set: a Wedgwood-white "palazzo" terrace house built by the 19th-century architect Thomas Cubitt, flatiron-shape, and often decked out with hanging flowerpots of geraniums, it is the very picture of Belgravia chic. Inside, the tiny reception area gives way to a vintage elevator and a circular staircase lighted by a Regency-era chandelier and topped by a winter-garden dome. Rooms are pleasantly decorated. In the heart of Belgravia's 19th-century mansions and mews, the hotel is a small hoof away from the tube stop. ✉ *2 Chesham St., SW1X 3DT,* ☎ *020/7235–1544,* FAX *020/7259–6153. 27 rooms. Business services. AE, DC, MC, V. Tube: Sloane Sq., Knightsbridge.*

£ 🏠 **London County Hall Travel Inn Capital.** This lacks a river view (it's at the back of the grand former seat of local government), but you get an incredible value, with the standard facilities of the cookie-cutter rooms of this chain: TV, tea–coffeemaker, and—best of all for families on a budget—fold-out beds that let you accommodate two kids at no extra charge. *That's* a bargain. ⊠ *Belvedere Rd., SE1 7PB,* ☎ *020/7902–1600 (central reservation line),* 𝔽𝔸𝕏 *020/7902–1619,* 𝕎𝔼𝔹 *www.travelinn.co.uk. 312 rooms. Restaurant. AE, DC, MC, V. Tube: Westminster.*

£ 🏨 **Melita House Hotel.** Run by the Gabriele family for 30 years, this small hotel is a short walk from Buckingham Palace and St. James's Park. It isn't fairyland, but the rooms have refrigerators, hair dryers, safes, and direct phone lines. A full English breakfast is included in the rate. ⊠ *35 Charlwood St., SW1V 2DU,* ☎ *020/7828–0471,* 𝔽𝔸𝕏 *020/ 7932–0988,* 𝕎𝔼𝔹 *www.melita.co.uk. 22 rooms. Breakfast room. AE, MC, V. Tube: Victoria.*

Marylebone

££ 🏨 **Dorset Square Hotel.** This pair of Regency town houses belongs to the welcome new breed of small, luxurious, privately run hotels. The creation of architect–interior designer husband-and-wife team, Tim and Kit Kemp, this is *House Beautiful* come to life, from marble and mahogany bathrooms to antique lace counterpanes, and the staff bends over backward to accommodate your wishes. For on-the-town jaunts, there's even a vintage Bentley available. ⊠ *39–40 Dorset Sq., NW1 6QN,* ☎ *020/7723–7874,* 𝔽𝔸𝕏 *020/7724–3328,* 𝕎𝔼𝔹 *www.firmdale.com. 38 rooms. Restaurant, bar. AE, MC, V. Tube: Baker St.*

££ 🏨 **Durrants.** A hotel since the late-18th century, Durrants occupies a quiet corner almost next to the Wallace Collection, a stone's throw from Oxford Street and the smaller, posher shops of Marylebone High Street. It's a good value for the area, and if you like ye wood-paneled, leather-armchaired, dark-red-pattern-carpeted style of olde Englishness, this will suit you. ⊠ *George St., W1H 6BH,* ☎ *020/7935–8131,* 𝔽𝔸𝕏 *020/7487–3510. 92 rooms, 85 with bath. Restaurant, bar. AE, MC, V. Tube: Bond St.*

Mayfair, St. James's, and Victoria

££££ 🏨 **Brown's.** Founded in 1837 by Lord Byron's "gentleman's gentleman," James Brown, this Victorian country hotel in central Mayfair occupies 11 Georgian houses and is frequented by many Anglophilic Americans—a habit that was established by the two Roosevelts (Teddy while on honeymoon). Bedrooms feature thick carpets, soft armchairs, sweeping drapes, brass chandeliers, and moiré or brocade wallpapers, as well as air-conditioning. The public rooms retain their cozy oak-panel, chintz-laden, grandfather-clock-ticking-in-the-parlor ambience. ⊠ *34 Albemarle St., W1X 4BT,* ☎ *020/7493–6020,* 𝔽𝔸𝕏 *020/7493–9381,* 𝕎𝔼𝔹 *www.brownshotel.com. 118 rooms. Restaurant, bar, gym. AE, DC, MC, V. Tube: Green Park.*

££££ 🏨 **Claridge's.** A hotel legend (founded in 1812), Claridge's has one of
★ the world's classiest guest lists. The liveried staff is friendly and not in the least condescending, and the rooms are never less than luxurious. Have a drink in the foyer lounge with its Hungarian mini-orchestra, or retreat to the reading room for perfect quiet, interrupted only by the sound of pages turning. The bedrooms are spacious, as are the bathrooms. Beds are handmade and supremely comfortable—the King of Morocco once brought his own, couldn't sleep, and ended up ordering 30 from Claridge's to take home. ⊠ *Brook St., W1A 2JQ,* ☎ *020/7629–8860 or 800/223–6800,* 𝔽𝔸𝕏 *020/7499–2210,* 𝕎𝔼𝔹 *www.savoy-group.co.uk. 200 rooms. Restaurant, bar, hair salon, health club. AE, DC, MC, V. Tube: Bond St.*

££££ 🏨 **Connaught.** Make reservations well in advance for this *very* exclu-
★ sive small hotel just off Grosvenor Square—the most understated of

any of London's grand hostelries, and the London home-away-from-home for guests who inherited the Connaught habit from their great-grandfathers. The bar and lounges have the air of an ambassadorial residence, an impression reinforced by the imposing oak staircase and dignified staff. Each bedroom has a foyer, antique furniture (if you don't like the desk, they'll change it), and fresh flowers. If you value privacy, discretion, and the kind of luxury that eschews labels, then this is the hotel for you. ⊠ *Carlos Pl., W1Y 6AL,* ☎ *020/7499–7070,* FAX *020/7495–3262,* WEB *www.savoy-group.co.uk. 90 rooms. Restaurant, bar. AE, DC, MC, V. Tube: Bond St.*

££££   **The Dorchester.** A London institution, the Dorchester appears on
★   every "World's Best" list. The glamor level is off the scale: 1,500 square yards of gold leaf, 1,000 of marble, and 2,000 of hand-tufted carpet gild this lily, and bedrooms feature Irish linen sheets on canopied beds; brocades and velvets; Italian marble and etched-glass bathrooms with Floris toiletry goodies; and cable TV. Afternoon tea, drinking, lounging, and posing are all accomplished in the catwalk-shape Promenade lounge, where you may spot one of the film-star types who will stay nowhere else. Probably no other hotel this opulent manages to be this charming. ⊠ *Park La., W1A 2HJ,* ☎ *020/7629–8888,* FAX *020/7409–0114,* WEB *www.dorchesterhotel.com. 195 rooms, 53 suites. 2 restaurants, bar, health club, nightclub, business services, meeting rooms. AE, DC, MC, V. Tube: Marble Arch.*

££££   **Dukes.** This small, exclusive, Edwardian-style hotel is centrally lo-
★   cated, yet is possibly London's quietest hotel, secreted in its own discreet cul-de-sac. It's filled with squashy sofas, oils of assorted dukes, and muted, rich colors, and offers guest rooms decorated inpatrician, antiques-spattered style, plus the best in personal service (they greet you by name every time). ⊠ *35 St. James's Pl., SW1A 1NY,* ☎ *020/7491–4840,* FAX *020/7493–1264,* WEB *www.dukeshotel.co.uk. 80 rooms. Restaurant, bar, health club. AE, DC, MC, V. Tube: Green Park.*

££££   **Le Meridien Grosvenor House.** "The old lady of Park Lane" is not the kind of place that encourages hushed whispers or that frowns on outré outfits, despite the marble floors and wood-panel "library," open fires, oil paintings, and fine antiques. The hotel health club is one of the best around, thanks to its good-size pool. Bedrooms are spacious, and most of the marble bathrooms have natural light. ⊠ *Park La., W1A 3AA,* ☎ *020/7499–6363,* FAX *020/7493–3341,* WEB *www. grosvenorhouse.co.uk. 380 rooms, 70 suites, 136 apartments. 2 restaurants, bar, indoor pool, health club. AE, DC, MC, V. Tube: Marble Arch.*

££££   **The Ritz.** The name implies the kind of luxury associated with thick swagged curtains, handwoven carpets, the smell of cigars, polish, and fresh lilies; it signifies a magical Edwardian opulence. Although the hotel was not itself in recent decades, a 1995 renovation by the Barclay brothers made it a by-word for blue-chip luxury once more. The only thing that has been lost is a certain vein of moneyed naughtiness that someone like F. Scott Fitzgerald, at least, would have banked on. ⊠ *150 Piccadilly, W1J 9BR,* ☎ *020/7493–8181,* FAX *020/7493–2687,* WEB *www.theritzhotel.co.uk. 133 rooms. Restaurant, bar, gym, hair salon, meeting rooms. AE, DC, MC, V. Tube: Piccadilly Circus.*

£££   **St. Ermin's Hotel.** Smack-dab in the middle of Westminster, this hotel is just a short stroll from Westminster Abbey and minutes from Buckingham Palace and the Houses of Parliament. An Edwardian anomaly in the shadow of modern skyscrapers, the hotel is set on a tiny cul-de-sac courtyard fronted with beasts-rampant gates. The lobby is an extravaganza of Victorian Baroque: all cake-frosting stucco work in shades of baby blue and creamy white. The Cloisters restaurant has one of the most magnificent (and overlooked) dining decors in London: a 19th-century Jacobean-style salon. Guest rooms are tastefully decorated; some have snug dimensions, but are all the cozier for it. ⊠ *Caxton St., SW1H 0QW,* ☎ *020/7222–7888,* ℻ *020/7222–6914. 290 rooms, 8 suites. Restaurant, bar, minibars, laundry service. AE, DC, MC, V. Tube: St. James's Park.*

£ 🖬 **Edward Lear.** This family-run guest house, just a minute's walk from Oxford Street, is in a Georgian town house that was formerly the home of the master of nonsense verse, Edward Lear. The location is the biggest selling point for this place, as rooms tend to be small and the decor outdated. There are no hotel-type facilities, although if you want a jacket pressed you're welcome to borrow the iron. The management is very proud of the English breakfasts—it uses the same butcher as the Queen. ⊠ *28–30 Seymour St., W1H 5WD,* ☎ *020/7402–5401,* ℻ *020/7706–3766,* 🕸 *www.edlear.com. 31 rooms, 4 with bath. Breakfast room. MC, V. Tube: Marble Arch.*

NIGHTLIFE AND THE ARTS

Nightlife

Nighttime London has rejuvenated itself, with a tangible new spirit of fun abroad on the streets, and new hangouts opening at an unprecedented rate. Whatever your pleasure, there's somewhere to go. London's clubs are famously hip, hot, and happening. Music is everywhere. Cabaret and comedy remain favorite ways to wind down. Many places accept credit cards, but call ahead to check or bring some cash. All you need remember when you hit the town at night is that regular bars (those without special extended licenses) stop serving alcohol at 11 PM (10:30 on Sunday), and the tubes stop around midnight.

Bars

The American Bar. Festooned with a chin-dropping array of collegiate ties, bric-a-brac, and antique toys, this is one of London's most sensational funhouse interiors. Even if you're not feeling homesick for the other side of the pond, be sure to check out this dazzler. *Stafford Hotel, 16–18 St. James's Pl., SW1A,* ☎ *020/7493–0111.* ⊙ *Weekdays 11:30 AM–midnight, Sat. 11:30 AM–3 PM and 5:30–midnight, Sun. noon–2:30 PM and 6:30–10:30. Tube: Green Park.*

The Atlantic Bar and Grill. This vast, glamorous, wood-floored basement caused a revolution when, in early 1994, it became the first central London bar to be granted a late-late alcohol license. Although there are now others, it's still popular, so that the only way to get a table on a weekend night is to book it for dinner. Luckily the food's fine. ⊠ *20 Glasshouse St., W1,* ☎ *020/7734–4888.* ⊙ *Mon.–Sat. noon–3 AM, Sun. 6 PM–10:30 PM. Tube: Piccadilly Circus.*

Beach Blanket Babylon. In Notting Hill, close to Portobello Market, this always-packed singles bar is distinguishable by its fanciful decor, like a fairy-tale grotto or a medieval dungeon, visited by the gargoyles of Notre Dame. ⊠ *45 Ledbury Rd., W11,* ☎ *020/7229–2907.* ⊙ *Daily noon–11. Tube: Notting Hill Gate.*

Cadogan Hotel Bar. One step beyond the door here and you're back in the Edwardian era. You half expect Lillie Langtry, the famed actress and mistress of King Edward VII, to waltz in the door, but then she used to live upstairs. If you feel like toasting Oscar Wilde with his favorite drink, a Hock and Seltzer, you'd better do it elsewhere—poor Oscar was arrested in this very bar that fateful day. ⊠ *Cadogan Hotel, Sloane St., SW1,* ☎ *020/7235–7141.* ⊙ *Daily 11–11. Tube: Sloane Sq.*

The Library. The comfortable, self-consciously "period" bar at the swanky Lanesborough Hotel harbors a collection of ancient cognacs, made in years when something important happened. Don't ask for a brandy Alexander. ⊠ *1 Lanesborough Pl., Hyde Park Corner, SW1,* ☎ *020/7259–5599.* ◷ *Mon.–Sat. 11–11, Sun. noon–10:30. Tube: Hyde Park Corner.*

Cabaret

Comedy Store. This is the improv factory where the United Kingdom's funniest stand-ups cut their teeth. The name performers and new talent you'll see may be strangers to you, but you're guaranteed to laugh. ⊠ *Haymarket House, 1A Oxendon St., SW1,* ☎ *020/7344–4444 or 020/7344–0234.* ▭ *£12–£15.* ◷ *Shows Tues.–Thurs. and Sun. at 8, Fri.–Sat. at 8 and midnight. Tube: Piccadilly Circus.*

Dance Clubs

Camden Palace. It would be difficult to find a facial wrinkle in this huge place, even if you could see through the laser lights. Try to find your way around the three floors of bars. There's live music on indie-rock Tuesday, anthemic house every Friday, and harder-edged house on Saturday. ⊠ *1A Camden High St., NW1,* ☎ *020/7387–0428.* ▭ *£5–£20.* ◷ *Tues.–Thurs. 10 PM–2 AM, Fri.–Sat. 10 PM–6 AM. Tube: Mornington Crescent, Camden Town.*

The End. After five years, one of London's best clubs got even better in 2001 when they knocked through to the adjoining bar and created a cool space with three dance floors, four bars, and a lounge area. In essence, The End is a club run by clubbers (noted DJ Mr. C owns the joint), and the air-conditioning is a bonus. Expect big names, such as Carl Cox and Fatboy, on weekends. ⊠ *16A West Central St., WC1,* ☎ *020/7419–9199.* ▭ *£5–£15.* ◷ *Mon., Wed.–Thurs. 9 PM–3:30 AM, Fri. and Sat. 10 PM–6 AM. Tube: Tottenham Court Rd.*

Notting Hill Arts Club. In one of London's trendiest neighborhoods, this is an innovative club-bar with a high-profile reputation. Saturdays showcase Outcaste, devoted to Asian underground music; other nights include Brazilian Love Affair or French house beats. Radio 4 is an indie disco that attracts rock stars like Liam Gallagher and Courtney Love; it's run by Oasis's former label boss. Art exhibitions are sometimes held here, too. ⊠ *21 Notting Hill Gate, W11,* ☎ *020/7460–4459.* ▭ *£3–£5.* ◷ *Mon.–Wed. 6 PM–1 AM, Sat. 6 PM–2 AM, Sun. 4 PM–1 AM. Tube: Notting Hill Gate.*

Jazz

Jazz Café. This palace of high-tech cool in a converted bank in bohemian Camden remains an essential hangout both for fans of the mainstream end of the repertoire and younger crossover performers. It's way north, but steps from Camden Town tube station. ⊠ *3–5 Parkway, NW1,* ☎ *020/7916–6060.* ▭ *£6–£20.* ◷ *Mon.–Thurs. 7 PM–1 AM, Fri.–Sat. 7 PM–2 AM, Sun. 7 PM–midnight. Tube: Camden Town.*

Pizza Express. It may seem strange, since Pizza Express is the capital's best-loved chain of pizza houses, but this is one of London's principal jazz venues, with music every night except Monday in the basement restaurant. The subterranean interior is darkly lighted, the lineups (often featuring visiting U.S. performers) are interesting, and the Italian-style thin-crust pizzas are great. Eight other branches also have live music; check the listings for details. ⊠ *10 Dean St., W1,* ☎ *020/7437–9595 or 020/7439–8722.* ▭ *£8–£20.* ◷ *From 11:30 AM for food; music 9 PM–midnight. Tube: Tottenham Court Rd.*

Ronnie Scott's. Since opening in the '60s, this legendary Soho jazz club has attracted all the big names. It's usually packed and hot, the food isn't great, and service is slow—the staff can't move through the crowds, either—but the atmosphere can't be beat, and it's probably still London's best, even since the sad departure of its eponymous founder and saxophonist. Reservations recommended. ⊠ *47 Frith St.,*

W1, ☎ 020/7439–0747. 🖃 *£15–£20 nonmembers, £5–£9 members, annual membership £50.* ⊘ *Mon.–Sat. 8:30 PM–3 AM, Sun. 7:30 PM–11:30 PM. Tube: Leicester Sq.*

Rock

The Astoria. Very central and quite hip, this place holds 2,000 people and hosts the hottest bands. Shows can start very early, as the building is often cleared immediately following gigs for club events. Check listings or call for open hours. ✉ *157 Charing Cross Rd., W1,* ☎ *020/7434–9592.* 🖃 *£8–£15. Tube: Tottenham Court Rd.*

The Forum. This ex-ballroom with balcony and dance floor packs in the customers, and it consistently attracts the best medium-to-big-name performers, too. ✉ *9–17 Highgate Rd., NW5,* ☎ *020/7344–0044.* 🖃 *£10–£15.* ⊘ *Most nights 7–11. Tube: Kentish Town.*

The Arts

London's nightlife scene is populated by here-today-gone-tomorrow boîtes and clubs. In contrast, London's arts scenes have entertainment options that, by and large, remain forever sparkling. At the top of anyone's must-do list, of course, are the Broadway-style shows presented at the West End theaters, the gala nights offered by the Royal Opera and Ballet, and the best performances of the Bard given by the Royal Shakespeare Company and at Shakespeare's Globe Theatre.

To find out what's showing during your stay, the weekly magazine *Time Out* (it comes out every Wednesday) is an invaluable resource. The *Evening Standard,* especially the Thursday edition, also carries listings, as do the "quality" Sunday papers and the Saturday *Independent, Guardian,* and *Times.* You'll find leaflets and flyers in most cinema and theater foyers, and you can pick up the free bimonthly *London Theatre Guide* leaflet from most hotels and tourist information centers.

Ballet

The freshly renovated Royal Opera House is the traditional home of the world-famous **Royal Ballet** (✉ Bow St., Covent Garden, WC2, ☎ 020/7304–4000). As well as traditional favorites like *The Nutcracker,* the company presents works by various international choreographers. Bookings should be made well in advance.

The **City Ballet of London** performs at the Peacock Theatre (✉ Portugal St., WC2, ☎ 020/7314–8800). **The Place** (✉ 17 Duke's Rd., WC1, ☎ 020/7387–0031) is indeed the place for contemporary and avant-garde dance. The **Sadler's Wells Theatre** (✉ Rosebery Ave., EC1, ☎ 020/7863–8000) hosts various other ballet companies and regional and international modern dance troupes.

Concerts

Ticket prices for symphony concerts range from £5 to £45. International guest appearances usually mean higher prices; reserve well in advance for such performances. Those without reservations might go to the hall half an hour before the performance for a chance at returns. Between the Barbican and South Bank, there are concert performances every night of the year.

The London Symphony Orchestra is in residence at the **Barbican Centre** (✉ Barbican, EC2, ☎ 020/7638–8891 or 020/7638–4141), and the Philharmonia and the Royal Philharmonic also perform here. The **South Bank Centre** (✉ South Bank, SE1, ☎ 020/7960–4242), which includes the Royal Festival Hall, Queen Elizabeth Hall, and the Purcell Room, is a major venue. The Barbican also features chamber music concerts with such smaller orchestras as the City of London Sinfonia.

To experience a great British institution, try the **Royal Albert Hall** during the "Proms" concerts (July–September, ☎ 020/7589–8212). Unfortunately, demand for tickets is so high that you must enter a lottery. For regular "proms," tickets run £3–£30; special "promenade" (standing) tickets usually cost half the price of normal tickets and are available at the hall on the night of the concert. Note, too, that the concerts have begun to be jumbo-screen broadcast in Hyde Park, but even here a seat on the grass requires a paid ticket. In summer, don't miss the outdoor concerts by the lake at elegant **Kenwood House** (Hampstead Heath, ☎ 020/7973–3427)—usually held every Saturday from mid-June to early September. **Holland Park** (☎ 020/7602–7856) is the setting for summer concerts.

Numerous lunchtime concerts take place across London in smaller concert halls and churches. They feature string quartets, vocalists, jazz ensembles, and gospel choirs. **St. Martin-in-the-Fields** (✉ Trafalgar Sq., WC2, ☎ 020/7839–1930) is a very popular location for lunchtime concerts. Performances usually begin about 1 PM and last an hour. **St. John's** (✉ Smith Sq., SW1, ☎ 020/7222–1061) has a good program of lunchtime and evening concerts.

Movies

Despite the video invasion, West End movies still thrive. The largest major first-run houses are found in the Leicester Square–Piccadilly Circus area, where tickets average £8. Monday and matinees are usually half price; lines are also shorter.

Opera

The Royal Opera presides over the main venue for opera in London, the fabled Royal Opera House (✉ Covent Garden, WC2E 9DD, ☎ 020/7304–4000), which ranks with the Metropolitan Opera House in New York—in every way, except, surprisingly, expense. Long castigated in Britain for its outrageous ticket prices, the Opera House pledged to lower its ticket prices in 1999. Indeed, now the doors really are open to the masses, since the cheapest tickets are just £2 (for a ballet matinee), although prices escalate to £150 for a top-price opera. Conditions of purchase vary—call for information. There are performances year-round, but some periods are reserved for visiting companies.

English-language productions are staged at the Coliseum (✉ St. Martin's La., WC2N 4ES, ☎ 020/7632–8300), home of the **English National Opera Company.** Prices here range from £8 for standing room to about £55 for the best seats, and productions are often innovative.

Theater

One of the experiences the city has to offer is great theater. London's theater scene consists, broadly, of the state-subsidized companies, the Royal National Theatre and the Royal Shakespeare Company; the commercial West End, equivalent to Broadway; and the Fringe—small, experimental companies. Another category could be added: known in the weekly listings magazine *Time Out* as Off-West End, these are shows staged at the longer-established fringe theaters.

The Royal National Theatre Company performs at one of London's main arts complexes, the Royal National Theatre. During 2001, the Royal Shakespeare Company announced plans to change the company's structure and to mount plays in the West End rather than only at the Barbican Centre, another of the city's primary arts venues. Both companies mount consistently excellent productions and are usually a safe option for anyone having trouble choosing which play to see. From mid-May through mid-September you can see the Bard served up in at the open-air reconstruction of Shakespeare's Globe Theatre in South-wark, across the Thames from St. Paul's Cathedral.

Shakespeare under the stars is performed by the New Shakespeare Company from the last week of May to the third week in September at the **Regent's Park Open-Air Theatre** (✉ Regent's Park Inner Circle, ☎ 020/7486–2431). Two Shakespeare plays are presented every season, along with a modern musical, from Monday to Saturday at 8 PM, and on Wednesday, Thursday, and Saturday at 2 PM.

Most theaters have a matinee twice a week (Wednesday or Thursday, and Saturday) and nightly performances at 7:30 or 8, except Sunday. Prices vary: expect to pay from £10 for an upper balcony seat to at least £25 for the stalls (orchestra) or dress circle. Reserve tickets at the box office, over the phone by credit card (numbers in the phone book or newspaper marked "cc" are for credit-card reservations), or (for a couple of pounds) through ticket agents such as **First Call** (☎ 020/7420–0000). You can also get tickets through **Ticketmaster** (☎ 020/7344–0055; 800/775–2525 in the U.S.). Half-price, same-day tickets are sold for cash only (subject to availability) from the **Society of London Theatres (SOLT)** kiosk on the southwest corner of Leicester Square, open Monday–Saturday, 2–6:30, Sunday noon–3, and from noon on matinee days; there's a £2 service charge. There is always a long line. The "half-price" tickets here are often the orchestra seats. If you wish to snag a cheaper, balcony seat, try the theater box office.

THEATER DIRECTORY

Most of London's theaters are in the neighborhood nicknamed Theatreland, around the Strand and Shaftesbury Avenue. For further information about theatrical events in London, contact the **Society of London Theatres** (✉ 32 Rose St., London WC2 E9E5, ☎ 020/7557–6700, WEB www.officiallondontheatre.co.uk).

Of the 100 or so legitimate theaters in the capital, about half are officially West End; the others go under the blanket title of Fringe. Much like New York's off- and off-off-Broadway, Fringe theater encompasses everything from first runs of new plays to revivals of old ones. Fringe tickets are always considerably less expensive than tickets for West End productions. The following is a list of West End theaters:

Adelphi. ✉ *Strand, WC2E 7NA,* ☎ *020/7344–0055. Tube: Charing Cross.*

Albery. ✉ *St. Martin's La., WC2N 4AH,* ☎ *020/7369–1740. Tube: Leicester Sq.*

Aldwych. ✉ *Aldwych, WC2B 4DF,* ☎ *020/7416–6003. Tube: Covent Garden.*

Apollo. ✉ *Shaftesbury Ave., W1V 7HD,* ☎ *020/7494–5070. Tube: Piccadilly Circus.*

Apollo Victoria. ✉ *Wilton Rd., SW1V ILL,* ☎ *020/7416–6054. Tube: Victoria.*

Arts Theatre. ✉ *6–7 Great Newport St., WC2H 7JB,* ☎ *020/7836–2132. Tube: Leicester Sq.*

Barbican Centre. ✉ *Barbican, EC2Y 8DS,* ☎ *020/7638–8891. Tube: Moorgate.*

Cambridge. ✉ *Earlham St., WCA 9HH,* ☎ *020/7494–5081 or 020/7494–5080. Tube: Covent Garden.*

Comedy. ✉ *Panton St., SW1Y 4DN,* ☎ *020/7369–1741 or 020/7369–1731. Tube: Piccadilly Circus.*

Dominion. ✉ *Tottenham Court Rd., W1 0AG,* ☎ *020/7656–1888. Tube: Tottenham Court Rd.*

Donmar Warehouse. ✉ *41 Earlham St., WC2H 9LD,* ☎ *020/7369–1732. Tube: Covent Garden.*

Drury Lane (Theatre Royal). ☒ *Catherine St., WC2B 5JF,* ☎ *020/ 7494–5060. Tube: Covent Garden.*

Duchess. ☒ *Catherine St., WC2B 5LA,* ☎ *020/7494–5076. Tube: Covent Garden.*

Fortune. ☒ *Russell St., WC2B 5HH,* ☎ *020/7836–2238. Tube: Covent Garden.*

Garrick. ☒ *Charing Cross Rd., WC2H 0HH,* ☎ *020/7494–5085. Tube: Leicester Sq.*

Gielgud. ☒ *Shaftesbury Ave., W1V 8AR,* ☎ *020/7494–5065. Tube: Piccadilly Circus.*

Globe (Shakespeare's Globe). ☒ *New Globe Walk, Bankside, SE1,* ☎ *020/7401–9919. Tube: Mansion House, then walk across Southwark Bridge, or Blackfriars, then walk across Blackfriars Bridge.*

Haymarket Theatre Royal. ☒ *Haymarket, SW1Y 4HT,* ☎ *020/7930– 8800. Tube: Piccadilly Circus.*

Her Majesty's. ☒ *Haymarket, SW1Y 4QR,* ☎ *020/7494–5050. Tube: Piccadilly Circus.*

London Palladium. ☒ *8 Argyll St., W1V 1AD,* ☎ *020/7494–5020. Tube: Oxford Circus.*

Lyceum. ☒ *Wellington St., WC2,* ☎ *020/7656–1803. Tube: Charing Cross.*

Lyric. ☒ *Shaftesbury Ave., W1V 7HA,* ☎ *020/7494–5045. Tube: Piccadilly Circus.*

Lyric Hammersmith. ☒ *King St., W6 0QL,* ☎ *020/8741–2311. Tube: Hammersmith.*

Mermaid. ☒ *Puddle Dock, EC4 3DB,* ☎ *020/7236–1919. Tube: Blackfriars.*

New London. ☒ *Drury La., WC2B 5PW,* ☎ *020/7405–0072. Tube: Covent Garden.*

Old Vic. ☒ *Waterloo Rd., SE1 8NB,* ☎ *020/7928–7616. Tube: Waterloo.*

Palace. ☒ *Shaftesbury Ave., W1V 8AY,* ☎ *020/7434–0909. Tube: Leicester Sq.*

Phoenix. ☒ *Charing Cross Rd., WC2H 0JP,* ☎ *020/7369–1733. Tube: Leicester Sq.*

Piccadilly. ☒ *Denman St., W1V 8DY,* ☎ *020/7369–1734. Tube: Piccadilly Circus.*

Players. ☒ *The Arches, Villiers St., WC2N 6NQ,* ☎ *020/7839–1134 or 020/7976–1307. Tube: Charing Cross.*

Playhouse. ☒ *Northumberland Ave., WC2N 6NN,* ☎ *020/7839– 4401. Tube: Embankment.*

Prince Edward. ☒ *Old Compton St., W1V 6HS,* ☎ *020/7447–5400. Tube: Leicester Sq.*

Prince of Wales. ☒ *31 Coventry St., W1V 8AS,* ☎ *020/7839–5987. Tube: Leicester Sq.*

Queens. ☒ *51 Shaftesbury Ave., W1V 8AS,* ☎ *020/7494–5040. Tube: Leicester Sq.*

Regent's Park Open-Air Theatre. ☒ *Inner Circle, Regent's Park, NW1,* ☎ *020/7486–2431. Tube: Baker St., Regent's Park.*

Royal Court Downstairs at the Duke of York's. ☒ *St. Martin's La., WC2,* ☎ *020/7565–5000. Tube: Leicester Sq.*

Royal Court Upstairs at the Ambassadors. ☒ *West St., WC2,* ☎ *020/ 7565–5000. Tube: Leicester Sq.*

Royal National Theatre (Cottesloe, Lyttelton, and Olivier). ☒ *South Bank Arts Complex, SE1 9PX,* ☎ *020/7452–3000. Tube: Waterloo.*

Savoy. ☒ *Strand, WC2R 0ET,* ☎ *020/7836–8888. Tube: Charing Cross.*

Shaftesbury. ☒ *Shaftesbury Ave., WC2H 8DP,* ☎ *020/7379–5399. Tube: Holborn.*

St. Martin's. ⊠ *West St., WC2H 9NH,* ☎ *020/7836–1443. Tube: Leicester Sq.*

Strand. ⊠ *Aldwych, WC2B 5LD,* ☎ *020/7930–8800. Tube: Covent Garden.*

Vaudeville. ⊠ *Strand, WC2R 0NH,* ☎ *020/7836–9987. Tube: Charing Cross.*

Victoria Palace. ⊠ *Victoria St., SW1E 5EA,* ☎ *020/7834–1317. Tube: Victoria.*

Whitehall. ⊠ *14 Whitehall, SW1A 2DY,* ☎ *020/7369–1735 or 020/ 7344–4444. Tube: Charing Cross.*

Wyndhams. ⊠ *Charing Cross Rd., WC2H 0DA,* ☎ *020/7369–1736. Tube: Leicester Sq.*

OUTDOOR ACTIVITIES AND SPORTS

Spectator Sports

Cricket

Lord's (⊠ St. John's Wood, NW8, ☎ 020/7432–1066) has been hallowed turf for worshipers of England's summer game since 1811. Five-day international Test Matches are played here, but tickets are hard to procure. One-day internationals and top-class county matches can usually be seen by lining up on the day of the match.

Football

Three British football (soccer in the U.S.) clubs competing in the **Premier League** and FA Cup are particularly popular: Arsenal (⊠ Avenell Rd., Highbury, N5, ☎ 020/7413–3366), Chelsea (⊠ Stamford Bridge, Fulham Rd., SW6, ☎ 020/7386–7789), and Tottenham Hotspur (⊠ White Hart La., 748 High Rd., N17, ☎ 0870/840–2468). More than likely you won't see a hint of the infamous hooliganism, but will be quite carried away by the electric atmosphere only a vast football crowd can generate.

Running

The **Flora London Marathon** (☎ 020/7620–4117) starts at 9:30 AM on a Sunday in April, with some 30,000 athletes running from Blackheath or Greenwich to Westminster Bridge or the Mall. Entry forms for the following year are available between August and October.

Tennis

The **Wimbledon Lawn Tennis Championships** is, of course, one of the top four Grand Slam events of the tennis year. To enter the lottery for show-court tickets, send a self-addressed stamped envelope between October and December to All England Lawn Tennis & Croquet Club (⊠ Box 98, Church Rd., Wimbledon SW19 5AE, ☎ 020/8946–2244), and hope. Alternatively, during the last-week-of-June, first-week-of-July tournament, tickets collected from early departing spectators are resold (profits go to charity). These can provide grandstand seats with plenty to see; play continues until dusk. You can also line up (start as early as possible) for tickets for the outside courts. The London Tourist Board's **Wimbledon Information Line** (☎ 0839/123417; calls cost 49p per minute) has up-to-date information.

Participant Sports and Fitness

For information on London's sports clubs and facilities, call **Sportsline** (☎ 020/7222–8000) weekdays 10–6.

Gyms

As you'd expect from the Y, **Central YMCA** ⊠ 112 Great Russell St., WC1, ☎ 020/7637–8131) has every facility and sport, including a great

25-m pool and a well-equipped gym. Weekly membership is £37.50; "one-day taster" £15.

At **Jubilee Hall** (✉ 30 The Piazza, Covent Garden, WC2, ☎ 020/7379–0008), the day rate is £6.90, monthly £51. This is a very crowded but happening and super-well-equipped central gym.

The trendy yoga school **Life Centre** (✉ 15 Edge St., W8, ☎ 020/7221–4602) in the heart of Notting Hill specializes in the energetic Ashtanga Vinyasa yoga technique. Classes cost £8–£10.

Running

Green Park and St. James's Park are convenient to the Piccadilly hotels. It's about 2 mi around both. Hyde Park and Kensington Gardens together supply a 4-mi perimeter route, or you can do a 2½-mi run in Hyde Park if you start at Hyde Park Corner or Marble Arch and encircle the Serpentine. Near the Park Lane hotels, Regent's Park has the Outer Circle loop, measuring about 2½ mi. **London Hash House Harriers** (☎ 020/8995–7879) organizes noncompetitive hour-long runs (£1) around interesting parts of town, with loops and checkpoints built in.

Swimming

Ironmonger Row (✉ Ironmonger Row, EC1, ☎ 020/7253–4011), a 33- by 12-yard city pool, is in a '30s complex that includes a Turkish bath. **Oasis** (✉ 32 Endell St., WC2, ☎ 020/7831–1804) is just that, with a heated outdoor pool, open year-round, right in Covent Garden, and a 30- by 10-yard pool indoors.

SHOPPING

Napoléon must have known what he was talking about when he called Britain a nation of shopkeepers. The finest emporiums are in London, still. You can shop like royalty at Her Majesty's glove maker, discover an uncommon Toby jug in a Kensington antiques shop, or find a leather-bound edition of *Wuthering Heights* on Charing Cross Road. If you have a yen to keep up with the Windsors, head for stores proclaiming they are "By Appointment" to H. M. the Queen—or to the Queen Mother, Prince Philip, or the Prince of Wales. The fashion-forward crowd favors places like Harvey Nichols or Browns of South Molton Street (a label hunter's heaven), whereas the most ardent fashion victims will shoot to Notting Hill, London's prime fashion location. If you have only limited time, zoom in on one or two of the West End's grand department stores, such as Harrods or Marks & Spencer, where you'll find enough booty for your entire gift list. Below is a brief introduction to the major shopping areas.

CHELSEA

Chelsea centers on King's Road, once synonymous with ultrafashion; it still harbors some designer boutiques, plus antiques and home furnishings stores.

COVENT GARDEN

This something-for-everyone neighborhood has chain clothing stores and top designers, stalls selling crafts, and shops selling gifts of every type—bikes, kites, tea, herbs, beads, hats, you name it.

KENSINGTON

Kensington's main drag, Kensington High Street, houses some small, classy shops, with some larger stores at the eastern end. Try Kensington Church Street for expensive antiques, plus a little fashion.

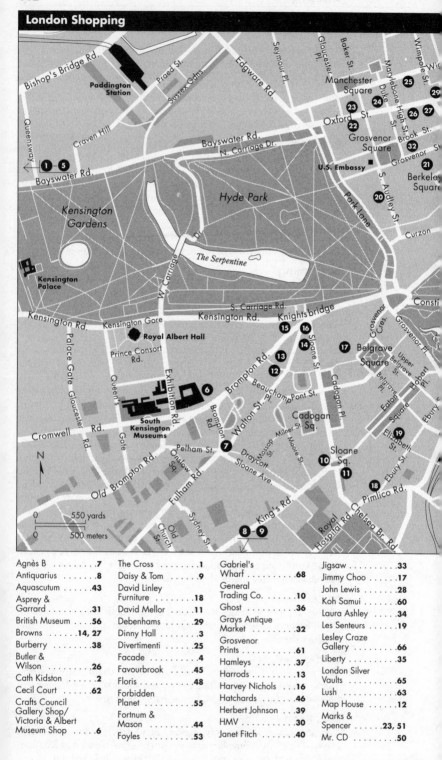

Agnès B **7**

Antiquarius **8**

Aquascutum **43**

Asprey &
Garrard **31**

British Museum **56**

Browns **14, 27**

Burberry **38**

Butler &
Wilson **26**

Cath Kidston **2**

Cecil Court **62**

Crafts Council
Gallery Shop/
Victoria & Albert
Museum Shop **6**

The Cross **1**

Daisy & Tom **9**

David Linley
Furniture **18**

David Mellor **11**

Debenhams **29**

Dinny Hall **3**

Divertimenti **25**

Facade **4**

Favourbrook **45**

Floris **48**

Forbidden
Planet **55**

Fortnum &
Mason **44**

Foyles **53**

Gabriel's
Wharf **68**

General
Trading Co. **10**

Ghost **36**

Grays Antique
Market **32**

Grosvenor
Prints **61**

Hamleys **37**

Harrods **13**

Harvey Nichols **16**

Hatchards **46**

Herbert Johnson . . .**39**

HMV **30**

Janet Fitch **40**

Jigsaw **33**

Jimmy Choo **17**

John Lewis **28**

Koh Samui **60**

Laura Ashley **34**

Les Senteurs **19**

Lesley Craze
Gallery **66**

Liberty **35**

London Silver
Vaults **65**

Lush **63**

Map House **12**

Marks &
Spencer **23, 51**

Mr. CD **50**

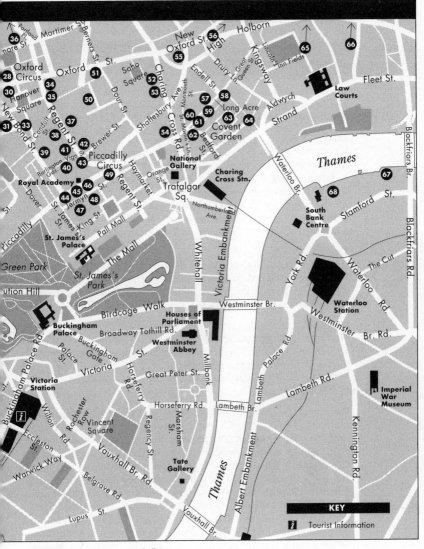

OXO Tower **67**
Ozwald
Boateng **41**
Paul Smith **59**
Penhaligon's **64**
Scotch House **15**
Selfridges **24**
Stanfords **58**
Summerhill
& Bishop **5**
Tea House **57**
Thomas Goode . . .**20**
Tower Records **49**

Turnbull &
Asser **47**
Virgin
Megastore **22**
Vivienne
Westwood **21**
Waterstone's **52**
Zara **42**
Zwemmer **54**

KNIGHTSBRIDGE

Knightsbridge, east of Kensington, has Harrods, of course, but also Harvey Nichols, the top clothes stop, and many expensive designers' boutiques along Sloane Street, Walton Street, and Beauchamp Place.

MAYFAIR

In Mayfair are the two Bond streets, Old and New, with desirable dress designers, jewelers, and fine art. South Molton Street has high-price, high-style fashion—especially at Browns—and the tailors of Savile Row are of worldwide repute.

NOTTING HILL

Go westward from the famous Portobello Road market and explore the Ledbury Road–Westbourne Grove axis, Clarendon Cross, and Kensington Park Road for an eclectic mix of antiques and up-to-the-minute must-haves for body and lifestyle. Toward the more bohemian foot of Portobello are Ladbroke Grove and Golborne Road, where, in among the tatty stores, Portuguese cafés, and patisseries, you can bag a bargain.

REGENT STREET

At right angles to Oxford Street is Regent Street, with possibly London's most pleasant department store, Liberty, plus Hamleys, the capital's toy mecca. Shops around once-famous Carnaby Street stock designer youth paraphernalia and 57 varieties of the T-shirt.

ST. JAMES'S

Here the English gentleman buys everything but the suit (which is from Savile Row): handmade hats, shirts and shoes, silver shaving kits, and hip flasks. Nothing in this neighborhood is cheap, in any sense.

Department Stores

Debenhams (⊠ 334–348 Oxford St., W1, ☎ 020/7408–4444, Tube: Oxford Circus) has moved up the fashion stakes with the pretty, affordable, Jasper Conran collection for women. Other creations—for men, too—by in-house designers are desirable. Kelly Hoppen, top interiors creator, has stylish housewares here. **Harrods** (⊠ 87 Brompton Rd., SW1, ☎ 020/7730–1234, Tube: Knightsbridge), one of the world's most famous department stores, can be forgiven its immodest motto, *Omnia, omnibus, ubique* ("everything, for everyone, everywhere"), since it has more than 230 well-stocked departments. The food halls are stunning—so are the crowds, especially during the post-Christmas sales, which usually run during the last three weeks of January. **Harvey Nichols** (⊠ 109 Knightsbridge, SW1, ☎ 020/7235–5000, Tube: Knightsbridge) is famed for five floors of ultimate fashion; every label any chic well-bred London lady covets is here. There's also a home furnishings department. It's also known for its restaurant, Fifth Floor. **John Lewis** (⊠ 278 Oxford St., SW1, ☎ 020/7629–7711, Tube: Oxford Circus) claims as its motto, "Never knowingly undersold." This is a traditional English department store, with a good selection of dress fabrics and curtain and upholstery materials. **Liberty** (⊠ 200 Regent St., SW1, ☎ 020/7734–1234, Tube: Oxford Circus), full of nooks and crannies, is like a dream of an Eastern bazaar realized as a Western store. Famous principally for its fabrics, it also carries Asian goods, menswear, womenswear, fragrances, soaps, and accessories. **Selfridges** (⊠ 400 Oxford St., SW1, ☎ 020/7629–1234, Tube: Bond Street), London's mammoth version of Macy's, includes a food hall, a theater ticket counter, and a Thomas Cook travel agency. Miss Selfridge (also on Oxford Street, east of Oxford Circus, and other branches) is its outpost for trendy, affordable young women's clothes.

Specialty Stores

Antiques

Antiquarius (⊠ 131–145 King's Rd., SW3, ☎ 020/7351–5353, Tube: Sloane Sq.), near the Sloane Square end of King's Road, is an indoor antiques market with more than 200 stalls offering collectibles, including things that won't bust your baggage allowance: Art Deco brooches, meerschaum pipes, silver salt cellars. It's closed Sunday. **Facade** (⊠ 196 Westbourne Grove, W11, ☎ 020/7727–2159, Tube: Notting Hill Gate) has one of the largest eclectic collections of French and Italian chandeliers, sconces, and table lamps. Most of them aren't wired and polished, and this is reflected in the reasonable prices. It's closed Sunday and Monday. **Grays Antique Market** (⊠ 58 Davies St., W1, ☎ 020/7629–7034, Tube: Bond St.) assembles dealers specializing in everything from Sheffield plates to Chippendale furniture. Bargains are not impossible, and proper pedigrees are guaranteed. It's closed Saturday (except December) and Sunday. **London Silver Vaults** (⊠ 53–64 Chancery La., WC2, ☎ 020/7242–3844, Tube: Chancery Lane) has 36 dealers specializing in antique silver and jewelry.

Books, CDs, and Records

Charing Cross Road is London's "booksville," with a couple dozen antiquarian booksellers, and many new bookshops, too. The nearest tube to most of the following is Tottenham Court Road; exceptions are listed.

Cecil Court, off Charing Cross Road, is a pedestrian-only lane filled with specialty bookstores. **Bell, Book and Radmall** (⊠ 4 Cecil Ct., WC2, ☎ 020/7240–2161) offers quality antiquarian tomes and specializes in modern first editions. **Marchpane** (⊠ 16 Cecil Ct., WC2, ☎ 020/7836–8661) stocks a fine selection of rare and antique illustrated children's books. **Dance Books** (⊠ 15 Cecil Ct., WC2, ☎ 020/7836–2314) has—yes—dance books, including how-to ballet books. **Pleasures of Past Times** (⊠ 11 Cecil Ct., WC2, ☎ 020/7836–1142) indulges the collective nostalgia for Victoriana in their stock of modern and old books.

Forbidden Planet (⊠ 71 New Oxford St., WC1, ☎ 020/7836–4179) is the place for sci-fi, fantasy, horror, and comic books. **Foyles** (⊠ 113–119 Charing Cross Rd., WC2, ☎ 020/7437–5660) is especially large—so vast it can be confusing, but it is the place to find almost anything. **Hatchards** (⊠ 187 Piccadilly, W1, ☎ 020/7439–9921, Tube: Piccadilly Circus) has not only a huge stock but also a well-informed staff. **Stanfords** (⊠ 12–14 Long Acre, WC2, ☎ 020/7836–1321, Tube: Covent Garden) is the place for travel books and, especially, maps. **Waterstone's** (⊠ 121–125 Charing Cross Rd., WC2, ☎ 020/7434–4291) is part of an admirable, and expanding, chain with long hours and a program of author readings and signings. **Zwemmer** (⊠ 24 Litchfield St., WC2, ☎ 020/7240–4158), just off Charing Cross Road, is for art books.

London created the great music megastores that have taken over the globe. These three stock most, if not all, of your CD, record, and video needs—but don't forget to check out the many independents for a more eclectic selection. **HMV** (⊠ 150 Oxford St., W1, ☎ 020/7631–3423) has branches everywhere, but make a special trip to the HMV (did you know this stands for His Majesty's Voice?) flagship store for the widest selection. There are lots of autograph sessions and free shows, too. **Mr CD** (⊠ 80 Berwick St., W1, ☎ 020/7439–1097, Tube: Oxford Circus) stocks a wide selection for all possible tastes in a tiny shop where you must delve to find the bargains. **Tower Records** (⊠ 1 Piccadilly Circus, W1, ☎ 020/7439–2500, Tube: Piccadilly Circus) has specialty departments that are some of the best in London. **Virgin Megastore** (⊠

14–16 Oxford St., W1, ☎ 020/7631–1234, Tube: Tottenham Court Rd.) is Richard Branson's pride and joy (although his New York City store is even bigger). It's nice to have it all under one roof—music of all kinds, books, magazines, computer games.

China and Glass

David Mellor (✉ 4 Sloane Sq., SW1, ☎ 020/7730–4259, Tube: Sloane Square) has practical Dartington crystal along with more unique porcelain and pottery pieces by British craftspeople. **Divertimenti** (✉ 45–47 Wigmore St., W1, ☎ 020/7935–0689, Tube: Oxford Circus) specializes in beautiful kitchenware, French pottery from Provence, and culinary gifts such as spoons made from polished horn. **Summerhill & Bishop** (✉ 100 Portland Rd., W11, ☎ 020/7221–4566, Tube: Notting Hill Gate) is a little piece of French country kitchen, supplying French embroidered linen, Portuguese and Tuscan stoneware, and designer culinary ware. **Thomas Goode** (✉ 19 S. Audley St., W1, ☎ 020/7499–2823, Tube: Bond Street) has vast ranges of formal china and lead crystal, including English Wedgwood and Minton, and is one of the world's top shops.

Clothing

Aquascutum (✉ 100 Regent St., W1, ☎ 020/7675–9050, Tube: Piccadilly Circus) is known for its classic raincoats but also stocks the garments to wear underneath, for both men and women. Style keeps up with the times but is firmly on the safe side, making this a good bet for solvent professionals with an anti-fashion-victim attitude. **Burberry** (✉ 165 Regent St., W1, ☎ 020/7734–4060; ✉ 18–22 The Haymarket, SW1, ☎ 020/7730–3343, Tube: Piccadilly Circus) tries to evoke an English Heritage ambience, with mahogany closets and stacks of merchandise adorned with the trademark "Burberry Check" tartan—scarves, umbrellas, even shortbread tins, and of course, those famous raincoat linings. **Daisy & Tom** (✉ 181–183 King's Rd., SW3, ☎ 020/7352–5000, Tube: Sloane Square) is for cool kids and smart parents. On one floor are high-fashion junior clothes (Kenzo, IKKS, and Polo), shoes aplenty (for newborns to 10-year-olds), a bookshop, and a soda fountain café. **Marks & Spencer** (✉ 458 Oxford St., W1, ☎ 020/7935–7954, Tube: Marble Arch; ✉ 173 Oxford St., ☎ 020/7437–7722, Tube: Tottenham Court Road, Oxford Circus) is a major chain of stores that's an integral part of the British way of life—sturdy practical clothes, good materials, and workmanship. Dukes to dustmen buy their underwear here. The **Scotch House** (✉ 2 Brompton Rd., SW1, ☎ 020/7581–2151, Tube: Knightsbridge) is the place to buy kilts, tartan scarves, and argyle socks without going to Edinburgh. It's also well stocked with cashmere and accessories.

MENSWEAR

Favourbrook (✉ 18 Piccadilly Arcade, W1, ☎ 020/7491–2337, Tube: Piccadilly Circus) tailors exquisite, handmade vests and jackets, ties and cummerbunds. You can order your own *Four Weddings and a Funeral* outfit. **Herbert Johnson** (✉ 54 St. James's St., W1, ☎ 020/7408–1174, Tube: Bond Street Piccadilly Circus) is one of a handful of gentleman's hatters who still know how to construct deerstalkers, bowlers, flat caps, and panamas—all the classic headgear, and Ascot-worthy hats for women, too. **Ozwald Boateng** (✉ 9 Vigo St., W1, ☎ 020/7734–6868, Tube: Piccadilly Circus) is one of the new breed of bespoke tailors not on Savile Row but on the fringe. His made-to-measure suits are sought after by rock luminaries for their shock-color linings as well as great classic cuts. **Paul Smith** (✉ 40–44 Floral St., WC2, ☎ 020/7379–7133, Tube: Covent Garden) is your man if you don't want to look outlandish but you're bored with plain pants and sober jackets.

Sir Paul McCartney is a famous customer. **Turnbull & Asser** (✉ 71–72 Jermyn St., W1, ☎ 020/7808–3000, Tube: Piccadilly Circus) is *the* custom shirtmaker. Unfortunately, the first order must be for a minimum of six shirts, from about £100 each. There's a range of less expensive, still exquisite ready-to-wear shirts, too.

WOMENSWEAR

Agnès B (✉ 111 Fulham Rd., SW3, ☎ 020/7225–3477, Tube: South Kensington) has oh-so-pretty, timeless, understated French clothing. Prices are mid-range and worthy for the quality. There are branches in Marylebone High Street (W1) andHeath Street, Hampstead (NW3); Floral Street (WC2) has elegant men's suits. **Browns** (✉ 23–27 S. Molton St., W1, ☎ 020/7491–7833, Tube: Bond Street; ✉ 6C Sloane St., SW1, ☎ 020/7493–4232, Tube: Knightsbridge) was the first notable store to populate the South Molton Street pedestrian mall, and it seems to sprout offshoots every time you visit. Well-established designers (Donna Karan, Romeo Gigli, Jasper Conran) rub shoulder pads here with younger, funkier names (Dries Van Noten, Jean Paul Gaultier, Hussein Chalayan). Its July and January sales are famed. **Cath Kidston** (✉ 8 Clarendon Cross, W11, ☎ 020/7221–4000, Tube: Notting Hill Gate) translates charming, fresh ginghams and flower-sprig cotton prints into nightclothes, bed linens, and bath wear. There are also cozy handknit sweaters, skirts in flouncy wools, and a children's wear line in the same nostalgic vein. **Ghost** (✉ 36 Ledbury Rd., W11, ☎ 020/7229–1057, Tube: Notting Hill Gate) presents up-to-the-minute offerings such as willowy dresses and skirts in silks, velvets, and viscose, which sculpts into wonderful crinkly textures. Little cardigans in silky weaves are popular, as are the pretty puff-sleeved blouses. It's also at 14 Hinde Street (W1). **Jigsaw** (✉ 126–127 New Bond St., W1, ☎ 020/7491–4484, Tube: Bond Street) is popular for its separates, which don't sacrifice quality for fashion, are reasonably priced, and suit women in their twenties to forties. **Jimmy Choo** (✉ 20 Motcomb St., SW1, ☎ 020/7235–6008, Tube: Knightsbridge) is the name on every supermodel's and fashion editor's feet. His exquisite, elegant shoes are fantasy itself, but nothing is under £100.

Koh Samui (✉ 65 Monmouth St., WC2, ☎ 020/7240–4280, Tube: Covent Garden) stocks the clothing of around 40 hot young designers. Discover the next fashion wave before *Vogue* gets there. **Laura Ashley** (✉ 256–258 Regent St., W1, ☎ 020/7437–9760, Tube: Oxford Circus, and other branches) offers designs from the firm founded by the late high priestess of English traditional. **Vivienne Westwood** (✉ 6 Davies St., W1, ☎ 020/7629–3757, Tube: Bond Street) is one of the top British designers. Her Pompadour-punk ball gowns, Lady Hamilton vest coats, and foppish getups still represent the apex of high-style British couture, and her boutique is as intoxicatingly glamorous as her creations. **Zara** (✉ 118 Regent St., W1, ☎ 020/7534–9500, Tube: Piccadilly Circus) has swept across Europe and the East; the style is young and snappy, and the prices are low. However, don't expect durability—these are fun fashion pieces, plus accessories including beady bags and wacky shoes. Menswear and a terrific line for kids are here, too.

Crafts

The Crafts Council Gallery Shop/Victoria & Albert Museum Shop (✉ Cromwell Rd., SW7, ☎ 020/7589–5070, Tube: South Kensington) is where you will find a microcosm of the wide range of British craftspeople's work—jewelry, glass, ceramics, toys. **David Linley Furniture** (✉ 60 Pimlico Rd., SW1, ☎ 020/7730–7300, Tube: Sloane Square) is the outpost for Viscount Linley—the only gentleman in the kingdom who can call the Queen "Auntie" and, more important, one of the finest furniture designers of today. The large pieces are suitably expensive, but small desk accessories and objets d'art are also available. At the **Lesley Craze Gallery** (⌧ 33–35 Clerkenwell Green, EC1, ☎ 020/7608–0393, Tube: Farringdon), in a newly fashionable area, carries exquisite jewelry by some 100 young British designers. The adjacent Craze 2 and C2+ specialize in nonprecious metals and sumptuous scarves and textiles. **OXO Tower** (⌧ Bargehouse St., SE1, ☎ 020/7401–2255, Tube: Southwark) holds shops and studios, open Tuesday–Sunday 11–6, that are a mecca for handmade goods. **Gabriel's Wharf** (⌧ Upper Ground, SE1, ☎ 020/7401–2255, Tube: Southwark) is a collection of craftspeople in a brightly painted village, who sell porcelain, jewelry, mirrors, clothes, toys, and more.

Gifts

The **British Museum** (⌧ Great Russell St., WC1, ☎ 020/7323–8175, Tube: Tottenham Court Road) has stacks of Egyptiana such as cute scarabs in ceramic. You can also buy your own ancient pottery pieces. The wide-ranging bookshop on the ground floor is a mine of information. **The Cross** (⌧ 141 Portland Rd., W11, ☎ 020/7727–6760, Tube: Notting Hill Gate) is a thoughtful, ultrachic shop with something to suit everyone. This place is big with the high-style crowd, thanks to its ambience (bleached-beach house), its hedonistic, beautiful things (silk scarves, brocade bags, jeweled butterflies by Jade Jagger), and its location—bang in the middle of trendy Portobello-cum–Holland Park. **Floris** (⌧ 89 Jermyn St., W1, ☎ 020/7930–2885, Tube: Piccadilly Circus) is one of the most beautiful shops in London, with 19th-century glass and Spanish mahogany showcases filled with swan's-down powder puffs, cut-glass bottles, and faux tortoiseshell combs. **Fortnum & Mason** (⌧ 181 Piccadilly, W1, ☎ 020/7734–8040, Tube: Piccadilly Circus), the Queen's grocer, is, paradoxically, the most egalitarian of gift stores, with plenty of irresistibly packaged luxury foods, stamped with the gold "By Appointment" crest, for less than £5. Try the teas, preserves, tins of pâté, or turtle soup. **General Trading Company** (⌧ 144 Sloane St., SW1, ☎ 020/7730–0411, Tube: Sloane Square) "does" just about every upper-class wedding gift list, but caters also to slimmer pockets with its merchandise shipped from far shores (as the name suggests) but moored securely to English taste. **Hamleys** (⌧ 188–196 Regent St., W1, ☎ 020/7494–2000, Tube: Oxford Circus) has six floors of toys and games for children and adults.

Les Senteurs (⌧ 71 Elizabeth St., SW1, ☎ 020/7730–2322, Tube: Sloane Square) is an intimate, unglossy gem of a perfumery run by a French family and sells little-known yet timeless fragrances, such as "Creed," worn by Eugenie, wife of Emperor Napoléon III. **Lush** (⌧ 7 The Piazza Court, Covent Garden, WC2, ☎ 020/7240–4570, Tube: Covent Garden) is crammed with fresh, very wacky, handmade cosmetics. Don't leave London without a supply of Tisty Tosty Ballastics—heart-shape bath bombs. **Penhaligon's** (⌧ 41 Wellington St., WC2, ☎ 020/7836–2150, Tube: Covent Garden), established by William Penhaligon, court barber to Queen Victoria, was parfumier to Lord Rothschild and Winston Churchill. The **Tea House** (⌧ 15A Neal St., WC2, ☎ 020/7240–7539, Tube: Covent Garden) purveys everything to do with the British national drink; you can dispatch your entire gift list here with "teaphernalia"—strainers, trivets, infusers, and such.

Jewelry

Asprey & Garrard (⌧ 167 New Bond St., W1, ☎ 020/7493–6767, Tube: Bond Street) has been described as the "classiest and most luxurious shop in the world," offering a range of exquisite jewelry and gifts, both antique and modern. **Butler & Wilson** (✉ 20 S. Molton St., W1, ☎ 020/7409–2955, Tube: Bond Street) has irresistible costume jewelry displayed against dramatic black, and is especially strong on diamanté, jet, and French gilt. **Dinny Hall** (✉ 200 Westbourne Grove, W11, ☎ 020/7792–3913, Tube: Notting Hill Gate) has a collection of simple designs in gold and silver, including dainty gold and diamond earrings or chokers with delicate curls. There is another branch in Fulham Road. **Janet Fitch** (✉ 37A Neal St., WC2, ☎ 020/7240–6332, Tube: Covent Garden), frequently featured in the glossy fashion pages, showcases contemporary British designers. From cuff links to tiaras, at a great price range, you'll find a bauble or two to tempt you. Other branches are at 25A Old Compton Street and King's Road.

Prints
Grosvenor Prints (✉ 28 Shelton St., WC2, ☎ 020/7836–1979, Tube: Covent Garden) sells antiquarian prints, with an emphasis on views and architecture of London—and dogs. The **Map House** (✉ 54 Beauchamp Pl., SW3, ☎ 020/7589–4325, Tube: Knightsbridge) has antique maps costing from a few pounds to several thousand, and excellent reproductions of maps and prints, especially of botanical subjects and cityscapes.

Street Markets

Bermondsey is the market the dealers frequent for small antiques, which gives you an idea of its scope. The real bargains start going at 5 AM, but there'll be a few left if you arrive later. Take Bus 15 or 25 to Aldgate, then Bus 42 over Tower Bridge to Bermondsey Square; or take the tube to London Bridge and walk. ✉ *Tower Bridge Rd., SE1.* ☉ *Fri. 5 AM–noon. Tube: London Bridge.*

Camden Passage, in Islington, is hugged by curio stores and is dripping with jewelry, silverware, and myriad other antiques. Saturday and Wednesday are when the stalls go up; the rest of the week, only the stores are open. Bus 19 or 38 or the tube to the Angel stop will get you there. ✉ *Off Upper St., Islington, N1.* ☉ *Wed. and Sat. 8:30–3. Tube: Angel.*

Portobello Market, London's most famous market, still wins the prize for the all-round best. There are 1,500 antiques dealers here, so bargains are still possible. Nearer Notting Hill Gate, prices and quality are highest; the middle is where locals buy fruit and vegetables and hang out in trendy restaurants. Under the Westway elevated highway there's a great flea market, and more bric-a-brac and bargains appear as you walk toward Golborne Road. Take Bus 52 or the tube here. ✉ *Portobello Rd., W11.* ☉ *Fruit and vegetables Mon.–Wed. and Fri. 8–5, Thurs. 8–1; antiques Fri. 8–3; both food market and antiques Sat. 6–5. Tube: Ladbroke Grove, Notting Hill Gate.*

Spitalfields, an old 3-acre indoor fruit market near Petticoat Lane, has turned into Trendsville, in the form of creative crafts and design shops. It's also home to food and clothes stalls, cafés, and performance and sports areas. On Sunday the place really comes alive, with stalls selling beautiful paper lampshades, antique clothing, handmade rugs, and cookware. The resident stores have more lovely things for body and home (particularly Redhouse). For refreshment, you can eat anything from Spanish tapas to Thai. ✉ *Brushfield St., E1.* ☉ *Organic market Fri. and Sun. 10–5; general market weekdays 11–3, Sun. 10–5. Tube: Liverpool St., Aldgate, or Aldgate East.*

LONDON A TO Z

To research prices, get advice from other travelers, and book travel arrangements, visit www.fodors.com.

ADDRESSES

Central London and its surrounding districts are divided into 32 boroughs—33, counting the City of London. More useful for finding your way around, however, are the subdivisions of London into postal districts. The first one or two letters give the location: N means north, NW means northwest, etc. You won't find W2 next to W3, but the general rule is that the lower numbers, such as W1 or SW1, are closest to the city center. Abbreviated (for general location) or full (for mailing information) postal codes are given for many listings in this chapter.

AIR TRAVEL TO AND FROM LONDON

For information, *see* Air Travel *in* Smart Travel Tips A to Z.

AIRPORTS AND TRANSFERS

For information about Heathrow, Gatwick, and Stansted airports, *see* Airports *in* Smart Travel Tips A to Z. Airport Travel Line has information on transfers between Heathrow and Gatwick airports and into London by bus. However, you may just be directed to some of the numbers listed below.

From Heathrow, the least-expensive route into London is by train, via the Piccadilly line of the Underground. Trains on the tube run every four to eight minutes from all four terminals; the 50-minute trip costs £3.50 one-way and connects with London's extensive tube system. The quickest way into London is the Heathrow Express, which takes just 15 minutes to and from Paddington Station (in the city center and a main hub on the Underground). One-way tickets cost £12 for standard–express class (£22 round-trip). Daily service departs every 15 minutes, from 5:10 AM to 11:40 PM.

Bus service to London is available from the Heathrow Central Bus Station. Airbus A2 costs £7 one-way and £12 round-trip; travel time is about one hour. Buses leave for King's Cross and Euston, with stops at Marble Arch and Russell Square, every 30 minutes 6 AM–9:30 PM, but can be tedious as there are more than a dozen stops en route. National Express leaves every 30 minutes to Victoria Coach Station: cost is £7 one-way, from 5:40 AM to 9:30 PM.

From Gatwick, the fast, nonstop Gatwick Express train leaves for Victoria Station every 15 minutes 5:20 AM–midnight, then hourly 1:35 AM–5:20 AM. The 30-minute trip costs £10.20 one-way, £20.40 round-trip. A frequent local train also runs all night. By bus, the Jetlink 777 service, run by National Express, leaves hourly from Gatwick South Terminal Coach Station to Victoria Coach Station. The trip takes about 90 minutes, from 4:15 AM–9:15 PM, and costs £7 one-way. Stops include Marble Arch, Hyde Park Corner, Baker Street, Finchley Road, and Hendon Central, but there are sometimes delays.

Stansted serves mainly European destinations. The Stansted Skytrain to Liverpool Street Station runs every half hour and costs £12 one-way, £22 round-trip; travel time is about 50 minutes. Jetlink 777, by National Express, runs cheaper hourly bus services to Victoria Coach Station from 12:30 AM to 11:30 PM; the cost is £8 one-way, £10 round-trip, and travel time is about 1 hour 40 minutes.

If you are thinking of taking a taxi from Heathrow and Gatwick, remember that they can get caught in traffic; the trip from Heathrow, for

example, can take more than an hour and costs £30–£40. From Gatwick, the taxi fare is at least £50. Add a tip of 10 to 15% to the basic fare.
➤ TAXIS AND SHUTTLES: **Airbus A2** (☎ 0870/574–7777). **Airport Travel Line** (☎ 0870/574–7777). **Gatwick Express** (☎ 0870/530–1530). **Heathrow Express** (☎ 0845/600–1515). **National Express** (☎ 0870/580–8080, WEB www.gobycoach.com). **Stansted Skytrain** (☎ 0845/748–4950).

BUS TRAVEL TO AND FROM LONDON

Buses, or "coaches" as long-distance services are known, operate mainly from London's Victoria Coach Station to more than 1,200 major towns and cities. Buses are about half as expensive as the train, but trips can take twice as long. For information, *see* Bus Travel *in* Smart Travel Tips A to Z.

BUS TRAVEL WITHIN LONDON

In central London, buses are traditionally bright red double- and single-deckers, although there are now many privately owned buses of different colors. Not all buses run the full length of their route at all times; check with the driver or conductor. On some buses you pay the conductor after finding a seat; on others you pay the driver upon boarding. Bus stops are clearly indicated; the main stops have a red LT symbol on a plain white background. When the word REQUEST is written across the sign, you must flag the bus down. Buses are a good way to see the town, but don't take one if you are in a hurry. Single fares start at 70p for short hops.

London is divided into six concentric zones for both bus and tube fares: the more zones you cross, the higher the fare. However, for buses only, short single fares in the city center (Zone One) are 70p; then for travel through any number of outer zones, just add an extra £1.20. Regular single-journey or round-trip One-Day Travelcards (£3.80–£4.50) allow unrestricted travel on bus and tube after 9:30 AM and all day on weekends and national holidays (except on N-prefixed Night Buses). Other options are Weekend Travelcards, for the two days of the weekend and on any two consecutive days during public holidays (£5.70–£6.70); Family Travelcards, which are one-day tickets for one or two adults with one to four children (£3–£3.60 with one child, additional children cost 60p each); or the Carnet, a book of 10 single tickets valid for central Zone 1 (£10) to use anytime over a year. Visitor Travelcards are similar to the One-Day Travelcards but with the bonus of a booklet of money-off vouchers to major attractions (available only in the United States, for three, four, and seven days). Visitor Travelcards are available from Rail Europe.

Traveling without a valid ticket makes you liable for an on-the-spot fine (£10 at press time), so always pay your fare before you travel. For more information, there are London Transport Travel Information Centres at the following tube stations: Euston, Hammersmith, King's Cross, Oxford Circus, Piccadilly Circus, St. James's Park, Victoria, and Heathrow (in Terminals 1, 2, and 4); open 7:15 AM–10 PM, with Terminal 4's TIC closing at 3 PM, or call London Transport.

Night Buses can prove helpful when traveling in London from 11 PM to 5 AM—these buses add the prefix "N" to their route numbers and don't run as frequently and don't operate on quite as many routes as day buses. You'll probably have to transfer at one of the Night Bus nexuses: Victoria, Westminster, and either Piccadilly Circus or Trafalgar Square. For safety reasons, avoid sitting alone on the top deck of a Night Bus.

➤ BUS INFORMATION: **London Transport** (☎ 020/7222–1234, WEB www. londontransport.co.uk). **Rail Europe** (⊠ 226 Westchester Ave., White Plains, NY 10604, ☎ 888/274–8724, WEB www.raileurope.com).

CAR TRAVEL

The major approach roads to London are motorways (six-lane highways; look for an "M" followed by a number) or "A" roads; the latter may be "dual carriageways" (divided highways), or two-lane highways. Motorways (from Heathrow, M4; from Gatwick, M23 to M25, then M3; Stansted, M11) are usually the faster option for getting in and out of town, although rush-hour traffic is horrendous. Stay tuned to local radio stations for regular traffic updates.

The simple advice about driving in London is: don't. Because the city grew as a series of villages, there was never a central street plan, and the result is a chaotic winding mass, made no easier by the one-way street systems. If you must drive in London, remember to drive on the left, and stick to the speed limit (30 mph on most city streets).

DISCOUNTS AND DEALS

The London Pass, a smart card, offers entry to more than 60 top attractions such as museums, art galleries, tours on boats, buses, and guided walks. It also includes restaurant discounts and free travel in London on the tube and buses. You can buy the pass in one-, two-, three-, or six-day options for £22, £39, £49, or £79 for an adult. Children (5–14 years, under 5s go free) pay £14, £24, £30, or £42 for the same durations. You will most likely recoup your card payment if you visit two major attractions. London Pass is available by phone, online, or from the Britain Visitor Centre and Tourist Information Centre branches.
➤ INFORMATION: **London Pass** (☎ 0870/242–9988, WEB www.londonpass. com).

EMBASSIES

For information, *see* Embassies *in* Smart Travel Tips A to Z.

EMERGENCIES

For hospitals in different areas of London that provide free 24-hour accident and emergency facilities, the following are listed: in the west of London, Charing Cross Hospital; in the city center is University College Hospital; to the north of the center is the Royal Free Hospital; and on the south bank of the city center is St. Thomas's Hospital. Bliss Chemist is open daily 9 AM–midnight.
➤ EMERGENCY SERVICES: **Ambulance, fire, police** (☎ 999).
➤ HOSPITALS: **Charing Cross Hospital** (⊠ Fulham Palace Rd., W6, ☎ 020/8846–1234). **Royal Free Hospital** (⊠ Pond St., Hampstead, NW3, ☎ 020/7794–0500). **St. Thomas's Hospital** (⊠ Lambeth Palace Rd., SE1, ☎ 020/7928–9292). **University College Hospital** (⊠ Grafton Way, WC1, ☎ 020/7387–9300).
➤ LATE-NIGHT PHARMACIES: **Bliss Chemist** (⊠ 5 Marble Arch, W1 ☎ 020/7723–6116; ⊠ 50 Willesden La., WC2, ☎ 020/7624–8000).

LODGING

Bed-and-breakfasts (rooms in private homes) or apartment rentals may be an economical choice for your stay. A number of agencies offer rooms and apartments in different neighborhoods. In some cases you can check out many of the properties online before you book. Of the firms listed below, the Bulldog Club and Uptown Reservations offer tonier accommodations; London B&B also represents some fancier homes; Primrose Hill B&B is committed to affordable lodgings.

➤ RESERVATION SERVICES: **Bulldog Club** (✉ 14 Dewhurst Rd., W14 0ET, ☎ 020/7371–3202, FAX 020/7371–2015, WEB www.bulldogclub.com). **London B&B** (✉ Box 124859, San Diego, CA 92112, ☎ 800/872–2632, WEB www.londonbandb.com). **Primrose Hill B&B** (✉ *14 Edis St., NW1 8LG, ☎ 020/7722–6869).* **Uptown Reservations** (✉ 50 Christchurch St., SW3 4AR, ☎ 020/7351–3445, FAX 020/7351–9383).

TAXIS

Hotels and main tourist areas have taxi ranks; you can also hail taxis on the street. If the yellow FOR HIRE sign is lighted on top, the taxi is available. But drivers often cruise at night with their signs unlighted to avoid unsavory characters, so if you see an unlighted cab, keep your hand up and you might be lucky. Fares start at £1.40 and increase by units of 20p per 281 yards or 55.5 seconds until the fare exceeds £8.60. After that, it's 20p for each 188 yards or 37 seconds. Surcharges are added after 8 PM and on weekends and public holidays. Over Christmas and New Year's Eve, the surcharge rises to £2—and there's 40p extra for each additional passenger. Note that fares are usually raised in April of each year. Tips are extra, usually 10%–15% per ride.

TOURS

BOAT TOURS

During summer, narrow boats and barges cruise London's two canals, the Grand Union and Regent's Canal. Most vessels operate on the latter, which runs between Little Venice in the west (the nearest tube is Warwick Avenue on the Bakerloo Line) and Camden Lock (about 200 yards north of Camden Town tube station). Jason's Trip operates one-way and round-trip narrow-boat cruises on this route. The London Waterbus Company operates this route year-round with a stop at London Zoo: trips run daily April–October and weekends only November–March. Canal Cruises offers three or four cruises daily March–October on the *Jenny Wren* and all year on the cruising restaurant *My Fair Lady.*

Boats also cruise the Thames throughout the year. Most leave from Westminster Pier, Charing Cross Pier, and Tower Pier. Downstream routes go to the Tower of London, Greenwich, and the Thames Barrier; upstream destinations include Kew, Richmond, and Hampton Court. Depending on the destination, river trips may last from 30 minutes to four hours. For trips downriver from Charing Cross to Greenwich Pier and historic Greenwich, call Catamaran Cruisers or Westminster Passenger Boat Services (which runs the same route from Westminster Pier). Thames Cruises goes to Greenwich and onward to the Thames Barrier. Westminster Passenger Service Upriver runs through summer to Kew and Hampton Court from Westminster Pier. A Sail and Rail ticket combines the modern wonders of Canary Wharf and Docklands development by Docklands Light Railway with the historic riverside by boat. Tickets are available year-round from Westminster Pier or Tower Gateway. London River Services should be able to give information on all companies.

➤ FEES AND SCHEDULES: **Canal Cruises** (☎ 020/7485–4433). **Catamaran Cruisers** (☎ 020/7839–3572). **Jason's Trip** (☎ 020/7286–3428). **London River Services** (☎ 020/7941–2400). **London Waterbus Company** (☎ 020/7482–2660). **Sail and Rail Passes** (☎ 020/7363–9700). **Thames Cruises** (☎ 020/7930–3373). **Westminster Passenger Boat Services** (☎ 020/7930–4097). **Westminster Passenger Service Upriver** (☎ 020/7930–2062).

BUS TOURS

Guided sightseeing tours provide a good introduction to the city from double-decker buses, which are open-topped in summer. Tours run daily and depart from Haymarket, Baker Street, Grosvenor Gardens, Marble Arch, and Victoria. You may board or alight at any of about 21 stops to view the sights, and then get back on the next bus. Tickets (£12) may be bought from the driver, several companies run tours. London Pride has informative staff on easily recognizable double-decker buses. The Original London Sightseeing Tour also offers frequent daily tours, departing from 8:30 AM from Baker Street (Madame Tussaud's), Marble Arch (Speakers' Corner), Piccadilly (Haymarket), or Victoria (Victoria Street) around every 12 minutes (less often outside peak summer season). The Big Bus Company runs a similar operation with a Red and Blue tour. The Red is a two-hour tour with 18 stops, and the Blue, one hour with 13. Both start from Marble Arch, Speakers' Corner. Evan Evans offers good bus tours that also visit major sights just outside the city. Another reputable agency that operates bus tours is Frames Rickards.

Green Line, Evan Evans, and Frames Rickards all offer day excursions by bus to places within easy reach of London, such as Hampton Court, Oxford, Stratford, and Bath.
➤ FEES AND SCHEDULES: **Evan Evans** (☎ 020/8332–2222). **Frames Rickards** (☎ 020/7837–3111). **Green Line** (☎ 020/8668–7261). **London Pride** (☎ 020/7520–2050). **Original London Sightseeing Tour** (☎ 020/8877–1722). **The Big Bus Company** (☎ 020/8944–7810).

PRIVATE GUIDES
Black Taxi Tour of London is a personal tour by cab direct from your hotel. The price is per cab, so the fare can be shared among as many as five people.
➤ CONTACTS: **Black Taxi Tour of London** (☎ 020/7289–4371).

WALKING TOURS
One of the best ways to get to know London is on foot, and there are many guided walking tours from which to choose. Original London Walks has theme tours devoted to the Beatles, Sherlock Holmes, Dickens, Jack the Ripper—you name it. For a more historical accent, check the tours from Historical Walks. Peruse the leaflets at a London Tourist Information Centre for special-interest walks. You can tailor your own walking tour of the city with a Blue Badge guide.
➤ FEES AND SCHEDULES: **Blue Badge** (☎ 020/7495–5504). **Historical Walks** (☎ 020/8668–4019). **Original London Walks** (☎ 020/7624–3978, WEB eee.walk.com).

TRAIN TRAVEL
London has 15 major train stations, each serving a different area of the country, all accessible by Underground or bus. The once-national British Rail is now several private companies, but there is a central rail information number.
➤ TRAIN INFORMATION: **National Rail Inquiries** (☎ 0845/748–4950, WEB www.railtrack.co.uk).

TRAVEL AGENCIES
➤ LOCAL AGENT REFERRALS: **American Express** (✉ 6 Haymarket, WC2, ☎ 020/7930–4411; ✉ 89 Mount St., W1, ☎ 020/7499–4436). **Thomas Cook** (✉ 1 Marble Arch, W1, ☎ 020/7530–7100; ✉ 184 Kensington High St., W8, ☎ 020/7707–2300; and other branches).

UNDERGROUND TUBE TRAVEL
Some lines have branches (Central, District, Northern, Metropolitan, and Piccadilly), so be sure to note which branch is needed for your particular destination. Electronic platform signs tell you the final stop and route of the next train and how many minutes you'll have to wait for

the train to arrive. There are two recent developments: Jubilee Line has a state-of-the-art extension, opened on the eve of the millennium, connecting Canary Wharf to the Millennium Dome. The zippy Docklands Light Railway runs through the modern Docklands with a new extension to the *Cutty Sark* and maritime Greenwich.

FARES AND SCHEDULES

For information, including discount passes, *see* Bus Travel Within London, *above.*

VISITOR INFORMATION

The main London Tourist Information Centre at Victoria Station Forecourt is open in summer, Monday–Saturday 8–7 and Sunday 8–5; winter, Monday–Saturday 8–6 and Sunday 8:30–4; also at Heathrow Airport (Terminals 1, 2, and 3). Britain Visitor Centre, open weekdays 9–6:30, weekends 10–4, provides details about travel, accommodations, and entertainment for the whole of Britain, but you need to visit the center in person to get information. Visitorcall is the London Tourist Board's 24-hour phone service—it's a premium-rate (60p per minute at all times) recorded information line, with different numbers for theater, events, museums, sports, getting around, etc. The city also has a helpful official Internet site with links to other sites.

➤ TOURIST INFORMATION: **Britain Visitor Centre** (⌧ 1 Regent St., Piccadilly Circus, SW1Y 4NX, ☎ no phone). **London Tourist Information Centre** (⌧ Victoria Station Forecourt, ☎ no phone). **London's official Internet site** (WEB www.londontown.com). **Visitorcall** (☎ 09068/ 123400.

2 THE SOUTHEAST

CANTERBURY, DOVER, BRIGHTON, TUNBRIDGE WELLS

Everyone stands to win in the Southeast. Among the prizes here you'll find Kent—the "Garden of England"—as well as major icons, such as Canterbury Cathedral, the white cliffs of Dover, and the Royal Pavilion at Brighton. Everywhere there are storybook villages grown drowsy with age. Here, too, are some of the finest stately treasure houses: Knole, Hever Castle, Penshurst Place, and Sissinghurst. So idyllic have these visions become to us by now that when viewed from afar, they look like old master paintings resting on easels.

Updated by
Robert
Andrews

I N AN ERA WHEN IT HAS BECOME FASHIONABLE to have everything as small as possible, from radios to cameras, the Southeast will inevitably have great appeal. People visiting England and this region for the first time take away an impression of rural perfection in miniature, for the portrait shows a landscape of small-scale features and pleasant hills; from the air, the tiny fields, neatly hedged, form a patchwork quilt. On the ground, once away from the fast motorways and commuter tract housing, the Southeast, including Surrey, Kent, and Sussex, East and West, reveals some of England's loveliest countryside, where gentle, rolling hills and woodlands are punctuated with hundreds of small farms and sleepy villages rooted in history and with cathedral cities waiting to be explored. Rivers wind down to a coast that is alternately sweeping chalk cliff and seaside resort.

Although it is one of the most densely populated areas of Britain because of its proximity to London, the Southeast is home to Kent, the famous "Garden of England." Here, fields of hops and acre upon acre of orchards burst into a mass of pink and white blossoms in spring and stretch away into the distance. Here, too, are ancient Canterbury, site of the mother cathedral of England, and Dover, whose chalky white cliffs and brooding castle have become veritable symbols of Britain.

A series of famous seaside towns and resorts is strung along the coasts of Sussex and Kent, the most famous being that picturesque combination of carnival and culture, Brighton, site of 19th-century England's own Xanadu, the Royal Pavilion. Except for the unaccountable moods that mark English weather countrywide, this resort area proves the wisdom of the traditional watchwords: "South for Sunshine." In addition, the coast is home to the busy ports of Newhaven, Folkestone, Dover, and Ramsgate, which have served for centuries as gateways to continental Europe. The Channel Tunnel, linking Britain to France by rail, now runs from near Folkestone.

Indeed, because the English Channel is at its narrowest here, a great deal of British history has been forged in the Southeast. The Romans landed in this area and stayed to rule Britain for four centuries. So did the Saxons—Sussex means "the land of the South Saxons." William ("the Conqueror") of Normandy defeated the Saxons at a battle near Hastings in 1066. Canterbury has been the seat of the Primate of All England, the Archbishop of Canterbury, since Pope Gregory the Great dispatched St. Augustine to convert the heathen hordes of Britain in 597. And long before any of these invaders, the ancient Britons blazed trails that formed the routes for today's modern highways.

Pleasures and Pastimes

Dining
Around the coast, seafood, with much of it locally caught, is a specialty. If you're in a seaside town, look for that great British staple, fish-and-chips. Perhaps "look" isn't the word— just follow your nose. You'll also discover local dishes such as Sussex smokies (smoked mackerel) and some of the most succulent oysters in Britain. In the larger towns, trendy restaurants tend (as ever) to spring up for a time and then disappear. This is an area in which to experiment.

CATEGORY	COST*
££££	over £22
£££	£16–£22
££	£9–£15
£	under £9

*per person for a main course at dinner

Lodging

All around this coast, resort towns stretch along beaches, their hotels standing cheek by jowl. Of the smaller hotels and guest houses only a few remain open year-round, as most do business only from mid-April to September or October. Note that some hotels feature all-inclusive rates for a week's stay, which is cheaper than taking room and meals by the day. Of course, prices rise in July and August, when the seaside resorts can get solidly booked, especially Brighton, which is a popular conference center. It is always worth asking if there are special deals.

CATEGORY	COST*
££££	over £150
£££	£100–£150
££	£60–£100
£	under £60

*All prices are for two people sharing a standard double room, including service, breakfast, and VAT.

Stately Homes

Britain has a rich heritage of stately homes scattered all over the nation, but this region has one of the greatest concentrations. To select the superlatives: Chartwell was home and is permanent memorial to Sir Winston Churchill; Hever Castle was the abode of Henry VIII's second wife, Anne Boleyn, and was restored in this century by William Waldorf Astor; Ightham Mote is perhaps the most enchanting medieval house in all Europe; Knole is one of the largest houses in Europe—more a town than a residence, it's built around seven romantic courtyards; Leeds Castle, pretty as a picture, stands in the middle of a lake; Penshurst Place, dating from 1340, was once home to poet Sir Philip Sidney, whose direct descendants still live there; and Sissinghurst Castle Garden was made world-famous through the dedication and horticultural vision of renowned author Vita Sackville-West.

Walking

The Southeast is characterized by long sweeps of chalky downland—open, rolling terrain used mainly for pasture. Ardent walkers can explore both the North Downs Way (141 mi) and the South Downs Way (106 mi), following ancient paths along the tops of the downs. Both trails give you wide views over the countryside. The North Downs Way follows in part the ancient Pilgrims' Way to Canterbury. The South Downs Way crosses the chalk landscape of Sussex Downs, with parts of the route going through deep woodland. You can easily do short sections of both trails. Along the way, there are plenty of towns and villages, mostly just off the main trail, with old inns offering refreshment and/or accommodations. The two routes are joined (north–south) by the 30-mi Downs Link. One way of seeing the Kent coast is to follow the Saxon Shore Way, 143 mi from Gravesend to Rye, passing many historical sites, including four Roman forts. Guides to all these walks are available from the Southeast England Tourist Board.

Exploring the Southeast

The Southeast can be divided into four sections. The eastern part of the region takes in the cathedral town of Canterbury, in the heart of

Kent, as well as Dover, England's "Continental gateway," to the south. Another area is the coast, from pretty Rye in the east to Lewes on the west, including historic seaside towns along the way. A third area begins in the coastal resort of Brighton and takes in Chichester, in West Sussex, and then swings north into Surrey, taking in Guildford and East Grinstead. The fourth region takes in the spa town of Royal Tunbridge Wells and western Kent, with its rich collection of stately homes, castles, and historic landmarks.

Many of the towns can easily be reached by public transportation from London for a day trip. Local buses, trains, and occasionally even steam trains provide regular service to most major sights. If you're especially interested in stately homes or quiet villages, it's wiser to rent a car.

Numbers in the text correspond to numbers in the margin and on the Southeast, Canterbury, and Brighton maps.

Great Itineraries

Although the Southeast is a relatively compact region, it is densely packed with points of interest. Most of the essential sights are contained in and around the towns, whereas the rustic attractions such as castles, country homes, and gardens invite a more leisurely appreciation. Note that your own transport is essential for some. You could spend several weeks here and still have more to see, but if you have only three days, confine your travels to one or two specific areas. A visit of seven days or so will allow you to explore a number of highlights as well as some of the Southeast's better-kept secrets.

IF YOU HAVE 3 DAYS

You could opt for the glories of historic ☷ **Canterbury** ①–⑬ as a first choice. Stay one night here, making the cathedral your priority stop, and spend any extra time meandering through the old streets, taking in the city's secondary sights. For your next two nights, pencil in ☷ **Brighton** ㉚–㊲, whose Royal Pavilion is a must on any itinerary. Keeping Brighton as your base, you could spend a third day exploring **Lewes** ㉙, with its castle in a commanding position over the town and an impressive collection of Tudor timber-frame buildings scattered along its steep lanes. Or, if you're lucky enough, you might attend a performance at the nearby Glyndebourne Opera House.

IF YOU HAVE 7 DAYS

On your way east, you could spend half a day at the dockyards at Chatham and the castle and cathedral at neighboring **Rochester** ㊽, both of which should be a great hit with children. Spend your first two nights at ☷ **Canterbury** ①–⑬, which you can explore in the morning, reserving the afternoon for a foray to the coast, tracing it down from **Broadstairs** ⑱, with its Dickensian associations, to **Dover** ㉒. On your third morning, head back west, veering south near Maidstone for **Leeds Castle** ㊾, whose lovely grounds vie for your attention with the treasures within. Farther south, the gardens of **Sissinghurst Castle and Garden** ㊼ are likely to convert even those who have never lifted a trowel. Overnight in pretty ☷ **Rye** ㉓, take in nearby **Winchelsea** ㉔ the next day; then continue west to the site of the Battle of Hastings at **Battle** ㉖, where one of the most momentous events in English history is marked by the remains of an abbey founded by William the Conqueror. **Hastings** ㉕ is a typical south-coast town, but Herstmonceux, 12 mi farther west, has beautiful **Herstmonceux Castle** ㉗. From here, head to ☷ **Brighton** ㉚–㊲, which deserves a two-night stay. After a morning of ambling around the promenades of this bustling seaside town and shopping in the Lanes and North Laine area, visit nearby **Lewes** ㉙, where some advance planning may get you seats at the Glyndebourne Opera for an evening treat.

The Southeast

GREAT BRITAIN

Thames

Hampstead

LONDON

Windsor

Hounslow
Heathrow Airport

Richmond

Woolwich

Thames

Egham

Staines

Merton

Sydenham

Sidcup

Dartfor

Bromley

Beckenham

Leatherhead

Great Bookham

Westerham

Knole   A25

A227

46

52

53

Clandon Park

Box Hill

A246

M25

Chartwell

54

Guildford

45

A25

A2

Ightham Mote

44

47

Dorking

B2027

A31

Hever Castle

Tonb

A248

Reigate

M23

Penshurst Place

51

50

B2176

NORTH DOWNS

Farnham

SURREY

Penshurst

A26

Hartfield

49

A3

Gatwick Airport

A264

Royal Tunbridge Wells

A267

Milford

A287

Crawley

East Grinstead

48

B2026

A264

A24

Haslemere

A286

Horsham

A264

Wadhurs

A22

THE

A283

Wisborough Green

Cuckfield

A26

Midhurst   A272

WEST

Haywards Heath

Uckfield

A265

SOUTH

Petworth House

39

SUSSEX

Burgess Hill

Ouse

EAST

A286

A285

Singleton

43

A283

Storrington

A23

SUSSEX

DOWNS

A284

A281

Lewes

Hers

Sculpture at Goodwood

42

Rodmell

A27

29

Glyndebourne

Castl

Fishbourne Roman Palace

38

Arundel

A27

Hove

Wilmington

28

A27

41

40

Chichester

A259

Worthing

A259

Eastbourne

Bognor Regis

A259

Brighton

30 — 37

English Channel

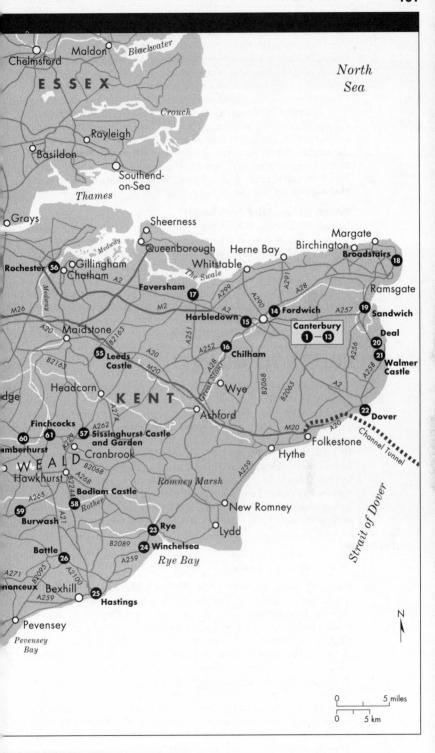

North
Sea

Chelmsford
Maldon
Blackwater

E S S E X

Crouch

Rayleigh

Basildon

Southend-
on-Sea

Thames

Grays

Sheerness

Margate
Birchington
Broadstairs 18

Queenborough
Herne Bay

Medway
Whitstable
The Swale
Ramsgate

Rochester 56
Gillingham
Chatham A2

Faversham 17
A299
A291
A28

M26
M2
A2
A290
Fordwich A257 19 Sandwich
Harbledown 15 14
Canterbury
1 — 13
Deal 20

Maidstone A20
B2163
A251
A252
Chilham 16
A256
Walmer 21
Castle
A258

55 Leeds
Castle
A20
M20
Great Stour
Wye
B2068
B2065
A2
22 Dover

Headcorn
K E N T
A274
Ashford
M20
A20
Channel Tunnel

dge

Finchcocks 61 57 Sissinghurst Castle
and Garden
A262
A229
Folkestone
Hythe

60
mberhurst
Cranbrook
B2068
A259

W E A L D
Hawkhurst
A268
A265
B2244
Bodiam Castle 58
Rother
Romney Marsh

New Romney

59 Burwash
A21

Rye 23
Lydd

Battle
26
B2089
24 Winchelsea
Rye Bay
A259

nonceux
Bexhill
A271
B2095
A2100
A259
25 Hastings

Pevensey

*Pevensey
Bay*

Strait of Dover

N

0   5 miles
0   5 km

Proceeding west along the coast on your sixth morning, take in **Arundel** ㊳ and **Chichester** ㊵, either of which would make a wonderful place for your sixth night: Arundel is dominated by Arundel Castle, whereas Chichester has a Norman cathedral in town and an impressive Roman villa outside. For your last day, you can opt to travel north and toward London, which will bring you through **Guildford** ㊹, a commuter town with some good 18th-century remnants and, east of here, a graceful Italianate palace, **Clandon Park** ㊺. An alternative is to drive northeast back into Kent, where you can choose among the magnificent historic houses around **Royal Tunbridge Wells** ㊾. Some of the most stirring are the medieval manor house **Penshurst Place** ㊿; **Hever Castle** (51), associated with two famous families, the Boleyns of the Tudor era and the Astors of our own; beautiful **Ightham Mote** (54); and **Chartwell** (52), home of Sir Winston Churchill for more than 40 years.

When to Tour the Southeast

Because the counties of Kent, Surrey, and Sussex offer some of the most scenic landscape in southern England, lovers of the open air will want to get their fill of the many outdoor attractions here. And because most of the privately owned castles and mansions are open only between April and September or October, it's best to tour the Southeast in the spring, summer, or early fall. Failing that, however, the great parks surrounding the stately houses are often open all year. In Canterbury and in the seaside towns, you would do well to avoid August, Sunday, and national holidays if you don't like crowds.

CANTERBURY TO DOVER

The ancient city of Canterbury, worldwide seat of the Church of England, shrine of Thomas à Becket, and a place immortalized in Geoffrey Chaucer's *Canterbury Tales,* is a prime historic center. Even in prehistoric times, this part of England was relatively well settled. Saxon settlers, Norman conquerors, and the folk who lived here in more settled late-medieval times all left their mark—most notably in the city's magnificent cathedral, the Mother Church of England. There are endless excursions to be made through the varying countryside between Canterbury and Dover. Here, the Kentish landscape ravishes the eye in the spring with apple blossoms. It is a county of orchards, market gardens, and the typical round, red-roof oasthouses, used for drying hops.

Canterbury

56 mi southeast of London.

For many people, Geoffrey Chaucer's *The Canterbury Tales,* about a pilgrimage to Canterbury Cathedral, brings back memories of senior-class English. Judging from the tales, however, Canterbury was as much a tailgate party for people on horses as a spiritual center. These pilgrims fought their way across the rolling terrain of Kent to this spot on the banks of the River Stour to visit the shrine of the martyr Thomas à Becket, making this southeastern town one of the most visited in England (if not Europe). Once the Iron Age capital of the kingdom of Kent, currently headquarters of the Anglican Church, Canterbury still has a lively atmosphere, a fact that has impressed visitors since 1388, when Master Chaucer wrote his stories. Today, most pilgrims come in search of picture-perfect moments rather than spiritual enlightenment, and magnificently medieval Canterbury obliges: it was one of the first cities in Britain to "pedestrianize" its center, bringing a measure of tranquillity to its streets. Nevertheless, to see it at its best, walk around early, before the tourist buses arrive, or wait until after they depart.

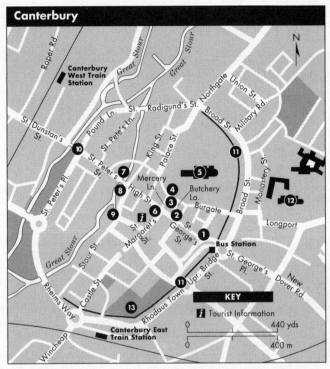

Buttermarket . .**3**

Canterbury
Cathedral **5**

Canterbury
Heritage
Museum **9**

Canterbury
Roman
Museum **2**

The Canterbury
Tales
Exhibition **6**

Christchurch
Gate **4**

Dane John
Mound **13**

Eastbridge
Hospital of St.
Thomas **8**

Medieval
city walls . . .**11**

St. Augustine's
Abbey **12**

St. George's
Church **1**

Weavers'
Houses **7**

West Gate
Museum **10**

Canterbury is bisected by a road running northwest, beside which lie all the major tourist sites. This road begins as St. George's Street, then becomes High Street, and finally turns into St. Peter's Street. On St. George's Street a lone church tower marks the site of **St. George's Church**—the rest of the building was destroyed in World War II— where playwright Christopher Marlowe was baptized in 1564. The **Canterbury Roman Museum,** including its colorful mosaic Roman pavement and a hypocaust (the Roman version of central heating), is below ground, at the level of the Roman town. Displays and computer-generated reconstructions of Roman buildings and the marketplace help to re-create the ancient atmosphere. ⊠ *Butchery La.,* ☎ *01227/785575,* ⓦⒺⒷ *www.canterbury-museum.co.uk.* 🖭 *£2.40.* ⊘ *June–Oct., Mon.– Sat. 10–5, Sun. 1:30–5; Nov.–May, Mon.–Sat. 10–5; last entry at 4. Closed last wk Dec.*

Mercery Lane, with its medieval-style cottages and massive, overhanging timber roofs, runs right off High Street and ends in the tiny **Buttermarket,** an old market square where dairy products were sold. The immense **Christchurch Gate,** built in 1517, leads into the cathedral close.

★ ❺ **Canterbury Cathedral,** the focal point of the city, was the first of England's great Norman cathedrals. Nucleus of worldwide Anglicanism, the Cathedral Church of Christ Canterbury (its formal name) is a living textbook of medieval architecture. The building was begun in 1070, demolished, begun anew in 1096, and then systematically expanded over the next three centuries. When the original choir section burned to the ground in 1174, it was replaced by a new one, designed in the Gothic style, with tall, pointed arches. The North Choir aisle holds two newly restored Bible windows, which show Jesus in the Temple, the three kings asleep, and Lot's wife turned to a pillar of salt; the windows are among the earliest parts of the cathedral, and only 33 of the original 208 survive.

The cathedral was only a century old, and still relatively small in size, when Thomas à Becket, the archbishop of Canterbury, was murdered here in 1170. Becket, an uncompromising defender of ecclesiastical interests, had angered his friend Henry II, who was heard to exclaim, "Who will rid me of this troublesome priest?" Thinking they were carrying out the king's wishes, four knights burst in on Becket in one of the side chapels and killed him. Two years later Becket was canonized, and Henry II's subsequent submission to the authority of the Church and his penitence helped establish the cathedral as the undisputed center of English Christianity.

Becket's tomb, destroyed by Henry VIII in 1538 as part of his campaign to reduce the power of the Church and confiscate its treasures, was one of the most extravagant shrines in Christendom. It was placed in **Trinity Chapel**, where you can still see a series of 13th-century stained-glass windows illustrating Becket's miracles. So hallowed was this spot that in 1376, Edward, the Black Prince, warrior son of Edward III and a national hero, was buried near it. The actual site of Becket's murder is down a flight of steps just to the left of the nave. In the corner, a second flight of steps leads down to the enormous Norman undercroft, or vaulted cellarage, built in the early 12th century. Its roof is supported by a row of squat pillars whose capitals dance with fantastic animals and strange monsters.

If time permits, be sure to explore the **Cloisters** and other small monastic buildings to the north of the cathedral. The 12th-century octagonal water tower is still part of the cathedral's water supply. The Norman staircase in the Northwest corner of the Green Court is a unique example of the domestic architecture of the times (1167). As you pass through the great gatehouse back into the city, look up at the sculpted heads of two young figures: Prince Arthur, elder brother of Henry VIII, and the young Catherine of Aragon, to whom he was betrothed. After Arthur's death, Catherine married Henry. Her failure to produce a male heir after 25 years of marriage led to Henry's decision to divorce her, creating an irrevocable breach with the Catholic Church, and altering the course of English history. ✉ *Cathedral Precincts,* ☎ *01227/762862,* WEB *www.canterbury-cathedral.org.* ✉ *Precincts free, cathedral £3, free for services.* ☺ *Precincts daily 7 AM–9 PM; cathedral weekdays 9–5:30, Sat. 9–2:30, Sun. 12:30–2:30 and 4:30–5:30 (open all day Sun. for worship). Restricted access during services.*

❻ To help bring Canterbury's rich history alive, spend some time at the vivid exhibition called **The Canterbury Tales,** a dramatization of 14th-century English life in an unused church down High Street, near the cathedral. First you'll "meet" Chaucer's pilgrims at the Tabard Inn near London; next you'll come to tableaus illustrating five tales. Then, passing through a reconstruction of the city gate, you can enter the marketplace. Don't be surprised if one of the figures comes to life: an actor dressed in period costume often performs a charade as part of the scene. ✉ *St. Margaret's St.,* ☎ *01227/479227,* WEB *www.heritageattractions. co.uk.* ✉ *£5.90.* ☺ *Mar.–June and Sept.–Oct., daily 9:30–5:30; July–Aug., daily 9–5:30; Nov.–Dec., Sun.–Fri. 10–4:30, Sat. 9:30–5:30.*

❼ A lopsided group of half-timber buildings, the **Weavers' Houses** were built in the 16th century and occupied by Huguenot weavers who settled in Canterbury after fleeing from religious persecution in France. The houses are just past where St. Peter Street crosses a branch of the

⑧ River Stour. The 12th-century **Eastbridge Hospital of St. Thomas** (which would now be called a hostel) lodged poor pilgrims who came to pray at the tomb of Thomas à Becket. The refectory, the chapel, and the crypt are open to the public. ✉ *25 High St.,* ☎ *01227/471688.* 🎫 *£1.* ☉ *Mon.–Sat. 10–5; last admission 30 mins before closing.*

⑨ The medieval Poor Priests' Hospital is now the site of the comprehensive and popular **Canterbury Heritage Museum,** whose exhibits provide an excellent overview of the city's history and architecture from Roman times to World War II. Visit early in the day to avoid the crowds. The building is on a street leading off High Street, an extension of St. Peter's Street. ✉ *20 Stour St.,* ☎ *01227/452747,* WEB *www.canterbury-museum. co.uk.* 🎫 *£2.40.* ☉ *June–Oct., Mon.–Sat. 10:30–5, Sun. 1:30–5; Nov.– May, Mon.–Sat. 10:30–5. Last entry at 4. Closed last wk Dec.*

🖑 ⑩ The only survivor of the city's seven gatehouses, at one end of St. Peter's Street (an extension of High Street), contains the **West Gate Museum.** Inside are medieval bric-a-brac and armaments used by the city guard, as well as more contemporary weaponry. The building became a jail in the 14th century, and you can see prison cells. Climb to the roof to catch a panoramic view of the city spires before walking along the landscaped riverside gardens. ☎ *01227/452747,* WEB *www.canterbury-museum. co.uk.* 🎫 *£1.* ☉ *Mon.–Sat. 11–12:30 and 1:30–3:30.*

⑪ One of the essential Canterbury experiences is to follow the circuit of the mainly 13th- and 14th-century **medieval city walls,** built on the line of the original Roman walls. Those to the east survive intact, towering some 20 ft high and offering a panoramic view of the town. You can access these from a number of places, including Castle Street and

⑫ Broad Street. **St. Augustine's Abbey,** one of the oldest monastic sites in the country, is where Augustine, England's first Christian missionary, was buried in 597. The abbey was later seized by Henry VIII, who destroyed some of the buildings and converted others into a royal manor for his fourth wife, Anne of Cleves. An interactive audio tour vividly puts the whole thing into context. ✉ *Longport,* ☎ *01227/767345,* WEB *www.english-heritage.org.uk.* 🎫 *£2.60.* ☉ *Apr.–Sept., daily 10–6; Oct., daily 10–5; Nov.–Mar., daily 10–4.*

⑬ The **Dane John Mound,** just opposite the Canterbury East train station, was originally part of the city defenses.

Dining and Lodging

£–££ ✕ **Weavers.** In the Old Weavers House, one of the Weavers' Houses on the River Stour, this popular restaurant in the center of town is an ideal place to feast on Tudor atmosphere as well as generous portions. The menu includes traditional English, seafood, and pasta dishes, and a good selection of wines. ✉ *1 St. Peter's St.,* ☎ *01227/464660. AE, MC, V.*

££–£££ ✕🖃 **County Hotel.** This traditional English hotel was first licensed in the year of the Spanish Armada, 1588. A refurbishment has added all the modern comforts without destroying the historic atmosphere. A number of specialty bedrooms are done in a Tudor, Georgian, or Colonial style; some have four-poster beds. The bar and tea rooms are pleasantly traditional, and the formal Sully's Restaurant is known for traditional English dining. ✉ *High St., CT1 2RX,* ☎ *01227/766266,* FAX *01227/451512,* WEB *www.macdonaldhotels.co.uk. 73 rooms. Restaurant, bar, coffee shop. AE, DC, MC, V.*

££–£££ ✕🖃 **Falstaff Hotel.** This old coaching inn sits right outside Westgate. Some of the beamed and oak-furnished rooms overlook the River Stour, and four-posters are available for added romance. Classic English fare at the restaurant includes pan-fried salmon, roast leg of lamb, and medallions of pork. The central location is a big plus: reserve well in advance. ⊠ *8 St. Dunstan's St., CT2 8AF,* ☎ *01227/462138,* FAX *01227/463525,* WEB *www.corushotels.com. 48 rooms. Restaurant, bar. AE, DC, MC, V.*

£–££   🔟 **Pointers.** This comfortable Georgian hotel is within easy walking distance of the cathedral and city center. From its prominent position Pointers looks down to the Westgate; extra window glazing ensures peace and quiet despite the location on a busy road. The O'Briens provide a warm and friendly welcome. ⊠ *1 London Rd., CT2 8LR,* ☎ *01227/456846,* FAX *01227/452786,* WEB *www.cantweb.co.uk/pointers. 12 rooms. Dining room, bar. AE, DC, MC, V. Closed Dec. 20–mid-Jan.*

£   🔟 **Slatters.** Although the site has been occupied since Roman times, this city-center hotel offers plenty of 20th-century comfort and fully equipped guest rooms. Tudor beams and a medieval wall also form part of the hotel. ⊠ *St. Margaret's St., CT1 2DR,* ☎ *01227/463271,* FAX *01227/764117. 29 rooms. AE, DC, MC, V.*

Nightlife and the Arts

Canterbury has a two-week **mixed-arts festival** every October (☎ 01227/452853). The **Gulbenkian Theatre** (⊠ Giles La., ☎ 01227/769075), at the University of Kent, mounts a full range of plays, particularly experimental works. The **Marlowe** (⊠ St. Margaret's St., ☎ 01227/787787), named after the Elizabethan playwright, who was born in Canterbury, is a venue for touring drama and opera companies.

Shopping

The **National Trust Shop** (⊠ 24 Burgate, ☎ 01227/457120) stocks the National Trust line of household items, ideal for gifts.

Fordwich

⑭ *1½ mi east of Canterbury.*

The village of Fordwich was originally the river port for Canterbury, where the Caen stone quarried in Normandy and shipped across the Channel to be used in the construction of the cathedral was brought ashore. Don't miss England's smallest town hall, with stocks and ducking stool outside.

Harbledown

⑮ *1 mi west of Canterbury.*

Along the old Roman road to London (now A2) lies Harbledown; once a separate village, it is now part of Canterbury. The main sight here is the cluster of pretty almshouses, built in the 11th century to house the poor. Harbledown was customarily the spot from which pilgrims caught their first glimpse of Canterbury Cathedral.

Chilham

⑯ *5 mi southwest of Canterbury.*

From the hilltop village of Chilham, midway between Canterbury and Ashford on the A252 (off the A28), energetic visitors can walk the last few miles of the traditional Pilgrim's Way back to Canterbury. The Chilham village square is filled with textbook examples of English rural architecture with gabled windows beneath undulating roofs. The church dates from the 14th century.

Dining

£ ✕ **White Horse.** A 16th-century inn shadowed by Chilham's church, the White Horse has a pleasant beer garden and provides lunchtime and evening meals superior to the usual pub grub. You might try the salmon creole or the smokey fisherman's pie. There's a log fire in winter. ⊠ *The Square,* ☎ *01227/730355. MC, V.*

Faversham

⑰ *9 mi west of Canterbury, 11 mi northwest of Chilham.*

In Roman times, Faversham was a thriving seaport. Today the port is hidden from sight, and you could pass through this pretty market town without knowing it was there. Still, Faversham is a must for those in search of Ye Quaint Olde Englande: the town center, with its Tudor houses grouped around the 1574 guildhall and covered market, looks like a perfect stage set.

Dining and Lodging

££££ ✕ **Read's.** The glorious food in this restaurant just outside Faver-
★ sham, mainly modern British, is the work of chef-proprietor David Pitchford. Presented in elegant surroundings, his cuisine tempts the serious eater with its audacious spin on old favorites. The changing menu includes a selection of prix-fixe meals, including cheese soufflé served with provençale vegetables; for dessert, don't miss the scrumptious "chocoholics anonymous." The extensive wine list contains some unusual bottles. This is an excellent spot for lunch, when there's a set-price menu from £18.50. Six spacious rooms in Georgian style are available if you want to overnight here; the 3½ acres of gardens are an added plus. ⊠ *Canterbury Rd., Painters Forstal (2¼ mi southwest of Faversham off A2),* ☎ *01795/535344. AE, DC, MC, V. Closed Sun. and Mon.*

£ ✕ **Sun Inn.** The flagship of the Shepherde Neame Brewery chain, established in Faversham in the 17th century, this pub is even older, dating to the 1500s. The inn follows the local tradition of hanging up hops in September; they are not only decorative but also add a distinctive fragrance. ⊠ *West St.,* ☎ *01795/535098. MC, V. No dinner.*

££ ✕🏠 **White Horse Inn.** Outside Faversham on the old London-to-Dover
★ road (now A2), this 15th-century coaching inn retains much of its traditional character, although it has been comfortably modernized. There's a friendly bar and an excellent restaurant, with daily specials. The back rooms are the quietest. ⊠ *The Street, Boughton ME13 9AX,* ☎ *01227/751343,* ℻ *01227/751090. 13 rooms. Restaurant, bar. AE, MC, V.*

En Route Taking A299 from Faversham leads you east through the seaside towns of Whitstable and Herne Bay, after which you make a small detour onto the A28 to Margate and Broadstairs. The **Powell-Cotton Museum,** 2 mi west of Margate on the A28, focuses on the work of Major Powell-Cotton, a Victorian explorer, ethnographer, and big game hunter. The exotic animal dioramas, as pioneered by the Major in 1896, form the centerpiece of the exhibition, but you can also peruse other artifacts of ethnographic interest. The museum is at **Quex House,** a fine Regency mansion surrounded by 250 acres of park, woodland, and lovely gardens, worth a visit in its own right. ⊠ *Park La., Birchington,* ☎ *01843/842168.* ☜ *£3.50.* ☉ *Apr.–Oct., Tues.–Thurs. and Sun., museum 11–5, house 2:30–5; Mar. and Nov.–Dec., Sun. 11–4.*

Broadstairs

⑱ *25 mi east of Faversham, 17 mi east of Canterbury.*

Like the other towns on this stretch of coast, Broadstairs was once the playground of vacationing Londoners. Charles Dickens spent many summers here (1837–51) and wrote glowingly of its bracing freshness. One of Dickens's favorite abodes in the town was **Bleak House,** perched on a cliff overlooking Viking Bay, where he wrote much of *David Copperfield* and drafted *Bleak House,* after which the house was later renamed. His study and other rooms here have been preserved, and there are also rooms dedicated to local history, including one on the wrecks at nearby Goodwin Sands, and a Smuggling Cellar with contrabanders' exhibits. ⌧ *Fort Rd.,* ☎ *01843/862224.* ⌸ *£3.* ☽ *Feb.– mid-Dec., daily 10–6.*

The **Dickens House Museum** was the setting Dickens imagined as the home of Betsy Trotwood, David Copperfield's aunt. There's a reconstruction of her room, and local prints and photographs commemorate Dickens's association with Broadstairs. ⌧ *2 Victoria Parade,* ☎ *01843/ 862853.* ⌸ *£1.50.* ☽ *Apr.–mid-Oct., daily 2–5.*

Nightlife and the Arts

Each year in June, Broadstairs holds a **Dickens Festival** (☎ *01843/ 865265*), lasting about a week, with readings, people in Dickensian costume, a Dickensian cricket match, and Victorian vaudeville, among other entertainments. Aficionados of the author are also drawn to another Dickens festival in Rochester.

Sandwich

⑲ *11 mi south of Broadstairs, 12 mi east of Canterbury.*

The coast near Canterbury holds three of the ancient **Cinque Ports** (pronounced *sink ports*), a confederacy of ports along the southeast seaboard whose heyday lasted from the 12th through the 14th centuries. These towns, originally five in number (hence *cinque,* from the Norman French), are rich in history and atmosphere and are generally less crowded than the other resorts of Kent's northeast coast.

In Saxon times, Sandwich, the most important of the Cinque Ports, stood in a sheltered bay, and in the Middle Ages prospered and later became England's chief naval base. From 1500 the port began to silt up, however, and the town is now 2 mi inland. The 16th-century checkerboard barbican (gatehouse) by the toll bridge is one of many medieval and Tudor buildings. The other Cinque Ports were Dover, Hythe, Romney, and Hastings.

Deal

⑳ *7 mi south of Sandwich, 8 mi northeast of Dover.*

The large seaside town of Deal is famous in history books as the place where Caesar's legions landed in 55 BC, and it was from here that William Penn set sail in 1682 on his first journey to the American colony he founded, Pennsylvania.

Deal Castle, erected in 1540 and intricately built to the shape of a Tudor rose, is the largest of the coastal defenses built by Henry VIII. Its gloomy passages and unrelentingly austere walls are surrounded by a moat. The castle museum has a range of exhibits of prehistoric, Roman, and Saxon Britain. ⌧ *Victoria Rd.,* ☎ *01304/372762,* WEB *www. english-heritage.org.uk.* ⌸ *£3.10.* ☽ *Apr.–Sept., daily 10–6; Oct., daily 10–5; Nov.–Mar., Wed.–Sun. 10–4.*

Walmer Castle

㉑ *7 mi northeast of Dover, 1 mi south of Deal.*

Walmer Castle, one of Henry VIII's fortifications, was converted in 1730 into the official residence of the Lord Warden of the Cinque Ports, and it now has the atmosphere of a cozy country house. Among the famous Lord Wardens were William Pitt the Younger; the Duke of Wellington, hero of the Battle of Waterloo, who lived here from 1829 until his death here in 1852 (there's a small museum of Wellington memorabilia); and Sir Winston Churchill. The present Lord Warden is the Queen Mother; her drawing and dining rooms are open to the public. After you have seen the castle chambers, take a stroll in the gardens. The moat has been converted to a grassy walk flanked by flower beds. ✉ *A258,* ☎ *01304/364288,* WEB *www.english-heritage.org.uk.* 🎫 *£4.80.* ☉ *Apr.–Sept., daily 10–6; Oct., daily 10–5; Nov. and Mar., Wed.–Sun. 10–4; Jan. and Feb. weekends only 10–4.*

Dover

㉒ *7 mi south of Walmer Castle, 78 mi east of London.*

One of the busiest passenger ports in the world, Dover has for centuries been Britain's gateway to Europe. Its chalk **White Cliffs** are a famous and inspirational sight. Many visitors find the town disappointing; the savage bombardments of World War II and the shortsightedness of postwar developers have left their scars on the city center. Roman legacies include a lighthouse, adjoining a stout Anglo-Saxon church. The **Roman Painted House,** believed to have been a hotel, includes some well-preserved wall paintings, along with the remnants of an ingenious heating system. ✉ *New St.,* ☎ *01304/203279.* 🎫 *£2.* ☉ *Apr.–Sept., Tues.–Sun. 10–5.*

★ ☾ The spectacular **Dover Castle,** towering high above the ramparts of the White Cliffs, was one of the mightiest medieval castles in Western Europe and served as an important strategic center over the centuries. Most of the castle, including the keep, dates back to Norman times. It was begun by Henry II in 1181 but incorporates additions from almost every succeeding century. There's a lot to see here besides the castle rooms: exhibitions include the Siege of 1216, the Princess of Wales Regimental Museum, and Castle Fit for a King. You can also explore the Secret Wartime Tunnels, a medieval underground tunnel system that was used as a World War II command center. ✉ *Castle Rd.,* ☎ *01304/211067,* WEB *www.english-heritage.org.uk.* 🎫 *£7.* ☉ *Apr.–Sept., daily 10–6; Oct., daily 10–5; Nov.–Mar., daily 10–4.*

Now part of Dover's town hall, the ancient **Maison Dieu** was founded in 1203 as a hostel for pilgrims traveling to Canterbury. The hall houses a collection of flags and armor, and the stained-glass windows tell the story of Dover through the ages. ✉ *Biggin St.,* ☎ *01304/201200.* 🎫 *Free.* ☉ *By appointment only.*

Beneath the town hall, the Victorian cells of **Old Town Gaol** evoke the misery endured by convicted felons. The reconstructed courtroom and exercise yard are enhanced by audiovisual gadgetry. ✉ *Biggin St.,* ☎ *01304/202723.* 🎫 *£3.50.* ☉ *June–Sept., Tues.–Sat. 10–4:30, Sun. 2–4:30; Oct.–May, Wed.–Sat. 10–4:30, Sun. 2–4:30.*

Lodging

£ 🏠 **Number One Guest House.** This popular guest house is a great bargain. A corner terrace home built in the early 19th century, it's cozy and friendly, decorated with mural wallpapers and porcelain collections. The walled garden has a view of the castle, and the owners give advice on local sightseeing. ⊠ *1 Castle St., CT16 1QH,* ☎ *01304/ 202007,* FAX *01304/214078,* WEB *www.number1guesthouse.co.uk. 4 rooms. No credit cards.*

ALONG THE SOUTH COAST: RYE TO GLYNDEBOURNE

From Dover, the coast road winds west through Folkestone, a genteel resort, a small port, and Channel Tunnel terminal, across Romney Marsh, reclaimed from the sea and famous for its sheep and, at one time, its ruthless smugglers, to the delightful town of Rye. The region along the coast is noted for pretty Winchelsea, the history-rich sites of Hastings and Herstmonceux, and the famous Glyndebourne Opera House festival, based outside Lewes, a town celebrated for its architectural heritage. The area is partly serviced by one of the three steam railroads in the Southeast: the Romney, Hythe, and Dymchurch Railway, a main-line service that uses locomotives one-third normal size.

Rye

★ ㉓ *68 mi southeast of London, 34 mi southwest of Dover.*

With cobbled streets and timbered dwellings, pretty Rye remains an artist's dream, dotted with such historic buildings as the Mermaid Inn as well as the secret places that made it a smuggler's strategic retreat. In fact, today the former port of Rye lies nearly 2 mi inland. **Rye Castle Museum,** housed in rooms below the castle, displays watercolors and exhibits of local history, including an 18th-century fire engine. A topographical map of Romney Marsh, shows the changes in sea level. ⊠ *3 East St.,* ☎ *01797/226728,* WEB *www.rye.org.uk.* ☞ *Museum only £1.90, £2.90 including Ypres Tower.* ⊙ *Apr.–Oct., Thurs.–Mon. 10:30–1 and 2–5; last admission 30 mins before closing.*

On an elevation behind Church Square, **Ypres Tower** was built as part of the town's fortifications in 1249 and later used as a prison. The stone chambers now hold a motley exhibition of local items, including police truncheons, smuggling bric-a-brac, and shipbuilding mementos. ⊠ *Gungarden,* ☎ *01797/226728.* ☞ *£1.90, £2.90 including Rye Castle.* ⊙ *Apr.–Oct., Thurs.–Mon. 10:30–1 and 2–5; Nov.–Mar., weekends 10:30–3:30; last admission 30 mins before closing.*

Sharing the Rye Heritage Centre with the tourist information office, the **Rye Town Model** is a huge scale model of the town, incorporating an imaginative sound-and-light show with a historic bent. The tourist office provides a good audio guided tour of the town. The building is at the bottom of Mermaid Street. ⊠ *Strand Quay,* ☎ *01797/226696.* ☞ *£2.* ⊙ *Mar.–Oct., daily 9–5:30; Nov.–Feb., daily 10–4.*

Lamb House, an early Georgian structure, has been home to several well-known writers. The most famous was the novelist Henry James, who lived here from 1898 to 1916. A later resident was E. F. Benson, author of the delightfully witty *Lucia* novels (written in the 1920s and 1930s, with a number set in a town based on Rye) and one-time mayor of Rye. The ground-floor rooms contain some of James's furniture and personal belongings. There's also a pretty walled garden. ⊠ *West St.,* ☎ *01892/890651,* WEB *www.nationaltrust.org.uk.* ☞ *£2.60.* ⊙ *Apr.– Oct., Wed. and Sat. 2–6; last admission 5:30.*

A wonderfully nostalgic tour of the exhibits at the **Rye Treasury of Mechanical Music** treats you to tunes from music boxes and barrel organs to a 1920s dance organ. ⊠ *20 Cinque Ports St.,* ☎ *01797/223345.* 📧 *£3.* ⊘ *Mar.–Oct., daily 10–5; Nov.–Feb., Wed.–Mon. 11–4.*

Dining and Lodging

££ ✕ **Landgate Bistro.** Although definitely a bistro, with plenty of bustle,
★ the Landgate is serious about its food. Try the scallops and monkfish in an orange and vermouth sauce—all the local fish is excellent—and the compote of quince with a lemon sauce. The restaurant, in an old, small building in keeping with Rye's atmosphere, attracts a steady local clientele. A fixed-price menu (about £16) is available Tuesday through Thursday. ⊠ *5–6 Landgate,* ☎ *01797/222829. AE, DC, MC, V. Closed Sun., Mon., and last wk Dec., 1st wk Jan. No lunch.*

£££–££££ ✕🖭 **The Mermaid.** This classic half-timber inn has served this ancient town for nearly six centuries; it was once the headquarters of one of the notorious smuggling gangs that ruled Romney Marsh. Sloping floors, oak beams, low ceilings, and a huge open hearth in the bar testify to its age. Five rooms have four-poster beds. Even if you're not staying at the inn, the main restaurant allows you to drink in the period decor while choosing from an extensive English menu. An adjacent bar serves pub meals, and in summer, the Tudor Tearoom offers a lovely cuppa. But be warned, the Mermaid is *very* popular, and you will need to book well ahead. ⊠ *Mermaid St., TN31 7EY,* ☎ *01797/223065,* 𝔽𝔸𝕏 *01797/225069. 31 rooms. Restaurant, bar. AE, DC, MC, V.*

££ 🖭 **Jeake's House.** The cozy bedrooms in this lovely 1689 house are furnished with antiques; many of the rooms have views over the town. Breakfast is served in a former chapel. Like all accommodations in Rye, Jeake's House needs to be booked well in advance. ⊠ *Mermaid St., TN31 7ET,* ☎ *01797/222828,* 𝔽𝔸𝕏 *01797/222623,* 𝕎𝔼𝔹 *www. jeakeshouse.com. 12 rooms, 10 with bath. Bar. MC, V.*

Winchelsea

㉔ *2 mi southwest of Rye, 71 mi southeast of London.*

Like Rye, Winchelsea is perched atop its own small hill amid farmland and tiny villages. One of the prettiest places to visit in the region, it has many attractive houses, some with clapboards, and a splendid (though damaged) church built in the 14th century with Caen stone from Normandy. The town was built on a grid system devised in 1283, after the sea destroyed an earlier settlement at the foot of the hill, then receded, leaving the town high and dry. Some of the original town gates still stand.

Dining and Lodging

£–££ ✕🖭 **The New Inn.** This 18th-century hostelry is an excellent place to stop for a pub lunch or a bed for the night. The quiet, refurbished rooms have pleasant views, and the bar serves up scrumptious roasts and cask ales, along with a log fire. ⊠ *German St.,* ☎ *01797/226252. 6 rooms. MC, V.*

Hastings

㉕ *9 mi southwest of Winchelsea, 68 mi southeast of London.*

Hastings, famous as the base for the invasion led by William, Duke of Normandy, in 1066, is now a large, slightly run-down seaside resort. A visit to the old town provides an interesting overview of 900 years of English maritime history. Below the East Cliff, the tall wooden **Net Shops,** called "deezes," unique to the town, are still used for drying fishermen's nets. The 250-ft **Hastings Embroidery,** housed in the White Rock Theatre opposite the pier, was made in 1966 to mark the battle's 900th anniversary. Twenty-seven panels depict 81 great events in

British history. ⊠ *White Rock,* ☎ *01424/781010.* ⌸ *£2.* ☉ *Daily 11–4 (last admission at 3:30).*

You can take the West Hill Cliff Railway from George Street precinct to the Norman **Hastings Castle,** built by William the Conqueror in 1069. All that remains are fragments of the fortifications, some ancient walls, and a number of gloomy dungeons. Nevertheless, it is worth a visit for the excellent view it provides of the chalky cliffs, the coast, and the town below. The "1066 Story" tells the story of the Norman invasion using audiovisual technology. ⊠ *West Hill,* ☎ *01424/781112.* ⌸ *£3.20.* ☉ *Apr.–Sept., daily 10–5:30 (10–6 in Aug.); Oct.–Mar., daily 11–4; last admission 30 mins before closing.*

Ⓒ Kids and adults will enjoy the waxworks and exhibits at the **Smuggler's Adventure,** housed in a labyrinth of caves and passages a five- or 10-minute walk above Hastings Castle. *St. Clement Caves,* ☎ *01424/422964,* WEB *www.smugglersadventure.co.uk.* ⌸ *£5.25.* ☉ *Apr.–Sept. 10–6; Oct.–Mar., daily 10–5; last admission 30 mins before closing.*

Dining and Lodging

££££–££££ ✗ **Rösers.** This seafront restaurant, which has dark walls with booths for dining, takes food very seriously. The chef-proprietor, Gerald Röser, is German, although his cuisine is mainly French. Try the local game in season, the pike soufflé, and the prize-winning caramelized lime cream in bitter orange sauce. The wine list is terrific. A moderate fixed-price menu is available. ⊠ *64 Eversfield Pl., St. Leonards,* ☎ *01424/712218. AE, DC, MC, V. Closed Sun., Mon., last 2 wks June, and 1st 2 wks Jan. No lunch Sat.*

£ ⊞ **Eagle House.** Its own attractive garden surrounds this guest house in a large, detached Victorian building. In St. Leonards, the western section of Hastings, the lodging is within easy reach of the town center. The rooms are spacious and comfortable, and the dining room uses fresh produce from local farms. ⊠ *12 Pevensey Rd., St. Leonards TN38 0JZ,* ☎ *01424/430535,* FAX *01424/437771,* WEB *www.eaglehousehotel.com. 18 rooms. Restaurant. AE, DC, MC, V.*

Battle

㉖ *7 mi northwest of Hastings, 61 mi southeast of London.*

Battle is the actual site of the crucial Battle of Hastings, at which, on October 14, 1066, King Harold's Anglo-Saxon army was trounced by the more disciplined forces of William of Normandy. Harold was killed, and the Norman state was established with the coronation of William I—also known as William the Conqueror—in Westminster Abbey in London on Christmas Day.

The ruins of **Battle Abbey,** the great Benedictine abbey William the Conqueror erected after his victory, are worth the trip. The high altar stood on the spot where Harold II was killed, now marked by a memorial stone. The abbey was destroyed in 1539 during Henry VIII's dissolution of the monasteries, but you can take the mile-long Battlefield Walk around the edge of the battlefield and see the remains of many of the domestic buildings. The **Abbot's House** (closed to the public) is now a girls' school. ⊠ *High St.,* ☎ *01424/773792,* WEB *www.english-heritage.org.uk.* ⌸ *£4.30.* ☉ *Apr.–Sept., daily 10–6; Oct., daily 10–5; Nov.–Mar., daily 10–4.*

Dining and Lodging

££££–££££ ✗⊞ **Netherfield Place.** This spacious and quiet hotel, in a Georgian manor half a mile north of Battle, sits on 30 acres of beautiful park and gardens. The large bedrooms are comfortably furnished, with plenty of cozy armchairs, and have well-equipped bathrooms (towels are especially thick). The paneled restaurant looks out at the gardens and has a sensible fixed-price menus. Try the salmon and sole terrine, the Sussex lamb, local venison, and the home-grown vegetables. ✉ *Netherfield Rd., Netherfield, TN33 9PP,* ☎ *01424/774455,* FAX *01424/ 774024,* WEB *www.netherfieldplace.demon.co.uk. 14 rooms. Restaurant, tennis court, croquet. AE, DC, MC, V. Closed last week Dec. and 1st week Jan.*

££–£££   ✗🖽 **Powder Mills Hotel.** This Georgian country house, close to Battle Abbey and adjoining the 1066 battlefield, was once used to make gunpowder, although there is little to remind you of this volatile activity amid the 150 acres of calm parkland. Among the lavishly furnished bedrooms in country-house style are one used by the duke of Wellington and another supposedly haunted by a "lady in white." The conservatory-style Orangery Restaurant makes a pleasant stop for lunch. In summer you can eat alfresco; there's a fixed-price menu at dinner. The food, especially the seafood, is superb; try the roasted Sussex pork fillet or the breast of pheasant. Bar snacks are also available. ✉ *Powdermill La., TN33 0SP,* ☎ *01424/775511,* FAX *01424/774540,* WEB *www.powdermills.co.uk. 35 rooms. Restaurant, pool, fishing. AE, DC, MC, V.*

Herstmonceux Castle

㉗ *11 mi southwest of Battle, 61 mi southeast of London.*

Back in the Edwardian era, formidable Herstmonceux was famous the world over as the quintessential image of the romantic English castle. Surrounded by a moat and built of rose-color brick and limestone crenellations, it looked like the veritable abode of Sleeping Beauty. In 1911, rich connoisseurs so completely renovated the structure, the magic nearly evaporated. That noted, Herstmonceux is still a fabled name for castle lovers (the house, however, is of the fortified square-shaped variety, not the multi-turreted species). Sir Roger Fiennes, ancestor of actor Ralph Fiennes, originally built it in 1444. Now an International Study Centre owned by Queen's University of Canada, the castle is open for guided tours only. There are no deluxe salons, but the interior still has some fine Elizabethan-era staircases and ceilings. ✉ *Hailsham,* ☎ *01323/834444,* WEB *www.herstmonceux-castle.com.* 🎫 *Castle tours £2.50; grounds £4.00.* ☉ *Mid-Apr.–Sept., daily 10–6; Oct., daily 10– 5 (last entry 1 hr before closing). Tours by appointment.*

Dining

£££   ✗ **The Sundial.** This old Sussex farmhouse is the setting for a popular restaurant that chef Vincent Rongier and his wife, Mary, have taken over. The menu is extensive, with some imaginative combinations, and vegetables are fresh and expertly cooked. Try the sea bass in lobster sauce or the lamb in a rosemary cream sauce. ✉ *Gardner St., Herstmonceux,* ☎ *01323/832217. AE, DC, MC, V. Closed Mon. No dinner Sun.*

Wilmington

㉘ *9 mi southwest of Herstmonceux Castle, 7 mi west of Pevensey on A27.*

Pretty Wilmington has a famous landmark. High on the downs to the south of the village (signposted off the A27) a giant white figure, 226 ft tall, known as the **Long Man of Wilmington,** is carved into the chalk; he has a club in each hand. His age is a subject of great debate, but some researchers think he might have originated in Roman times.

🔄 **Drusilla's Park** is one of the best small zoos in England, with gardens, a miniature railroad, and an adventure playground. You can play miniature golf for a small extra charge, too. The zoo is 1½ mi west of Wilmington on the A27, in the picturesque Cuckmere Valley. Alfriston itself is a lovely old town worth a stop. ⊠ *Alfriston,* ☎ *01323/ 870234,* WEB *www.drusillas.co.uk.* 🎫 *Apr.–Oct. £7.60, Nov.–Mar. £5.25.* ⊘ *Apr.–Oct., daily 10–6; Nov.–Mar., daily 10:30–5 (last admission 1 hr before closing).*

Lewes

★ ㉙ *10 mi northwest of Wilmington, 8 mi northeast of Brighton, 54 mi south of London.*

The town nearest to the celebrated Glyndebourne Opera House, Lewes is so rich in architectural history that the Council for British Archaeology has named it one of the 50 most important English towns. Lewes is a place to walk in rather than drive in to appreciate its picturesque jumble of building styles and materials—flint, stone, brick, tile—and the secret lanes (called twittens) behind the castle with their huge beeches. Here and there you'll find smart antiques shops and second-hand-book dealers. **High Street** is lined with buildings of all ages, styles, and descriptions, including a timber-frame house once occupied by Thomas Paine (1737–1809), author of *Rights of Man.*

Lewes is one of the few towns left in England that still celebrates in high-style Guy Fawkes Night (November 5), the anniversary of Fawkes's attempt to blow up the Houses of Parliament in 1605. It's rather like an autumnal Mardi Gras, with costumed processions and flaming tar barrels rolled down High Street.

A few miles from Lewes are two sites of interest to fans of the Bloomsbury Group, an influential collection of friends who were writers, artists, and critics in the earlier part of the 20th century: the homes of Virginia and Leonard Woolf and Vanessa Bell.

High above the valley of the River Ouse stand the majestic ruins of **Lewes Castle,** begun in 1100. For a panoramic view of the surrounding region, climb the keep. Inside the castle is the **Barbican House Museum,** where you can see the Town Model, a re-creation of Lewes in the 19th century. ⊠ *169 High St.,* ☎ *01273/405730,* WEB *www.sussexpast.co.uk.* 🎫 *£4, or £5.50 with Anne of Cleves House.* ⊘ *Mon.– Sat. 10–5:30 or dusk if earlier, Sun. 11–5:30 or dusk if earlier (last admission 30 mins before closing).*

The 16th-century **Anne of Cleves House,** a fragile timber-frame building, holds a notable collection of Sussex ironwork and other items of local interest such as Sussex pottery. A famous painting of the local Guy Fawkes procession is also here. The house was part of Anne of Cleves's divorce settlement from Henry VIII, but she did not live here. To get to the house, walk down steep, cobbled Keere Street, past lovely Grange Gardens, to Southover High Street. ⊠ *52 Southover High St.,* ☎ *01273/474610,* WEB *www.sussexpast.co.uk.* 🎫 *£2.60, or £5.50 with Lewes Castle.* ⊘ *Mar.–Oct., Mon.–Sat. 10–5, Sun. noon–5; Nov.– Dec., Tues.–Sat. 10–5, Sun. noon–5; Jan.–Feb., Tues., Thurs., Sat. 10– 5; last admission at 4.*

Of interest to serious Bloomsbury fans, **Monk's House** was home to novelist Virginia Woolf and her husband, Leonard Woolf, who purchased it in 1919; Leonard lived here until his death in 1969. Rooms in the small cottage include Virginia's study, where she wrote a number of her books, and her bedroom. Artists Vanessa Bell (Virginia's sister) and Duncan Grant had a hand in the house's decoration. ⊠ C7, *off A27, Rodmell (3 mi south of Lewes),* ☎ *01892/890651,* WEB *www. nationaltrust.org.* ☜ *£2.60.* ☉ *Apr.–Oct., Wed. and Sat. 2–5:30.*

Art and daily life mixed at **Charleston,** the farmhouse Vanessa Bell bought in 1916 and decorated with Duncan Grant (who resided here until 1978), painting not only the walls but also the doors and furniture. The house became a creative refuge for writers and artists of the Bloomsbury Group and holds ceramics and textiles of the Omega Workshop—in which Bell and Grant participated—and paintings by Picasso and Renoir as well as Bell and Grant. The house is seen on a guided tour, except on Sunday. ⊠ *Off A27, Firle (7 mi east of Lewes),* ☎ *01323/811265,* WEB *www.charleston.org.uk.* ☜ *£5.50.* ☉ *May–June and Sept.–Oct., Wed.– Sun 2–6; July–Aug., Wed.–Sat. 11:30–6, Sun. 2–6; last entry at 5.*

Dining and Lodging

£–££ ✗ **Tortellini.** This is a simple, stylish restaurant serving authentic Italian dishes. In the evening, it usually winds up bustling and crowded. ⊠ *197 High St.,* ☎ *01273/487766. AE, DC, MC, V.*

££££ ✗▥ **Horsted Place.** A few minutes' drive from Glyndebourne, and 6 mi
★ north of Lewes, this special hotel on 1,100 acres once belonged to Prince Philip's treasurer and has frequently accommodated members of the Royal Family. Built in 1850 and full of Gothic Revival elements by Augustus Pugin, the house is beautifully furnished in country-house style and has such features as a magnificent Victorian staircase and a Gothic library with a secret door that leads to a hidden courtyard. The dining room, also Gothic, offers superb haute cuisine (try the roasted guinea fowl). Three guest rooms are in detached cottages on the golf course. ⊠ *Little Horsted (2½ mi south of Uckfield, 6 mi north of Lewes), TN22 5TS,* ☎ *01825/750581,* FAX *01825/750459,* WEB *www.horstedplace.co.uk. 15 rooms, 5 suites. Restaurant, indoor pool, golf privileges, tennis court, croquet. AE, DC, MC, V.*

££££ ▥ **Shelleys.** An elegant 17th-century building in a town of attractive architecture, this hotel on the hilly main road is a traditional overnight stop for visitors to the opera at Glyndebourne. It's furnished with antiques, and the garden is a joy. The hotel maintains a reputation for old-fashioned, friendly service. ⊠ *High St., BN7 1XS,* ☎ *01273/472361,* FAX *01273/483152. 19 rooms. Restaurant, bar. AE, DC, MC, V.*

Nightlife and the Arts

Glyndebourne Opera House (⊠ Glyndebourne, near Lewes, ☎ 01273/ 812321, WEB www.glyndebourne.com) is one of the world's leading opera houses. Nestled beneath the Downs, Glyndebourne combines first-class productions, in a state-of-the-art auditorium, with a beautiful setting. Seats are *very* expensive (£18–£138) and often difficult to acquire, but they're worth every cent to aficionados, some of whom wear evening dress and bring a hamper for a picnic in the gardens during the long dinner interval. The main season generally runs from the end of May to the end of August. The Glyndebourne Touring Company performs here in October, when seats are cheaper and slightly easier to obtain.

BRIGHTON TO EAST GRINSTEAD

The self-proclaimed belle of the coast, Brighton is an upbeat, friendly old-new sprawl. It started as a tiny fishing village called Brighthelmstone, with no claim to fame until a certain Dr. Russell sent his patients there for its dry, bracing, crystal-clear air. The Prince Regent, later George IV, went, discovered sea bathing, and for nearly 200 years, the place prospered—deservedly so, for few British resorts have ever catered so well as Brighton to its appreciative patronage from London and the world over. Today, the city is a lively mixture of carnival and culture, and it contains one of the must-sees of Britain—the fantastic palace known as the Royal Pavilion. Built mainly by John Nash in a mock-Oriental manner, with domes and pinnacles abounding, the Royal Pavilion has never failed to shock and delight in equal measure. After taking in this Regency-era wonder, and after the children have had their fill of Brighton's amusement parks, the area beckons with other great residences, including Arundel Castle, Petworth House, and Polesden Lacey. Along the way, you'll discover the largest Roman villa in Britain, the bustling city of Guildford, and Chichester, whose cathedral is a poem in stone.

Brighton

9 mi southwest of Lewes, 54 mi south of London.

Ever since the Prince Regent first visited in 1783, Brighton has been England's most exciting seaside city, and today it's as vibrant, eccentric, and cosmopolitan as ever. A rich cultural mix—Regency architecture, pleasure pier, specialty shops, sidewalk cafés, lively arts, and, of course, the exotic Royal Pavilion—makes the city truly unique. In decades gone by, it became known for its tarnished allure, its faded glamor. Happily, a young, bustling spirit has given a face-lift to this ever-popular destination, which was given a further boost by being granted city status in 2000, in amalgamation with neighboring Hove, as genteel a resort as Brighton is a-buzz. In keeping with Brighton's offbeat image, the bid to be a city was delivered to the Home Office by bicycle.

The city owes its modern fame and fortune to the supposed healing attributes of seawater. In 1750 physician Richard Russell published a book recommending seawater treatment for glandular diseases. The fashionable world flocked to Brighton to take Dr. Russell's "cure," and sea bathing became a popular pastime.

The next windfall for the town was the arrival of the Prince of Wales (later George IV), who acted as Prince Regent from 1811 to 1820 during the madness of his father, George III. "Prinny," as he was called, created the Royal Pavilion, a pleasure palace that attracted London society. The influx of visitors triggered a wave of villa building. Fortunately, this was one of the most creative periods in the history of English architecture, and the elegant terraces of Regency houses are today among the town's greatest attractions. The coming of the railroad set the seal on Brighton's popularity: one of the most luxurious trains in the country, the Pullman *Brighton Belle,* brought Londoners to the coast within an hour. They expected to find the same comforts they had in London, and Brighton obliged, which explains the town's remarkable range of restaurants, hotels, and pubs. Horse racing was, and still is, another strong attraction.

Although fast rail service to London has made Brighton an important base for commuters, the town has unashamedly set out to be a pleasure resort. In the 1840s, Brighton featured the very first example of that peculiarly British institution, the amusement pier. The restored **③⓪ Brighton Pier** follows the great tradition. The original mechanical amusements, including the celebrated flip-card device, "What the Butler Saw," are now protected as exhibits in the town museum, but you can still admire the pier's handsome ironwork. As for the damaged West Pier, an extensive renovation program is being planned, which, by 2005, will restore it to its former glory, complete with museum, performance area, and restaurants.

Brighton Museum and Art Gallery **33**

Brighton Pier **30**

British Engineerium . **36**

The Lanes **34**

Preston Manor **37**

Royal Pavilion **32**

The Steine **31**

Volk's Electric Railway **35**

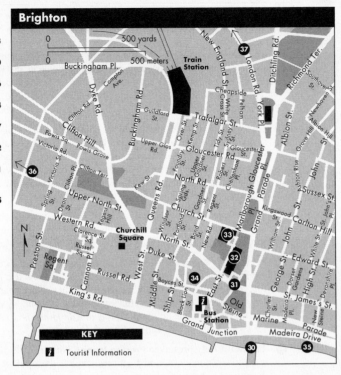

Brighton

KEY

_i_ Tourist Information

③① The heart of Brighton is the **Steine** (pronounced steen), a large open area close to the seafront. This was a river mouth until the Prince of Wales had it drained in 1793. One of the houses here was the home of Mrs. Maria Fitzherbert, later the prince's wife. The most remarkable building on the Steine, perhaps in all Britain, is unquestionably

★ ③② the Prince of Wales's extravagant fairy-tale palace, the **Royal Pavilion.** First planned as a simple seaside villa and built in the fashionable classical style of 1787, the Pavilion was rebuilt between 1815 and 1822 for the Prince Regent, who favored an exotic, Indian-inspired design with Chinese interiors. When Queen Victoria came to the throne in 1837, she so disapproved of the palace that she stripped it of its furniture and planned to demolish it. Fortunately, Brighton Council bought it from her, and it is now recognized as unique in all Europe. After a lengthy process of restoration, the Pavilion looks much as it did in its Regency heyday. The interior is filled with quantities of superb period furniture and ornaments, some given or lent by the present Royal Family. The two great set pieces are the **Music Room,** styled in the form of an Oriental pavilion, and the **Banqueting Room,** with its enormous flying-dragon "gasolier," or gaslight chandelier, a revolutionary new invention in the early 19th century. Also remarkable are the kitchens, whose ceilings are supported by palm-tree columns. The upstairs bedrooms contain a selection of cruel caricatures of the Prince Regent, most produced during his lifetime. The gardens, too, have been restored to Regency splendor, following John Nash's design of 1826. For an elegant time-out, repair to one of the Pavilion's upstairs bedrooms, where a tearoom offers a variety of snacks and light meals. ✉ _Old Steine,_ ☎ _01273/290900,_ WEB _www.royalpavilion.brighton.co.uk._ ⚐ _£5.20._ ☉ _Oct.–May, daily 10–5:30 (last admission); June–Sept., daily 10–6:30 (last admission 30 mins before closing)._

㉝ The grounds of the Royal Pavilion contain the **Brighton Museum and Art Gallery,** whose buildings were designed as a stable block for the prince's horses. The museum has especially interesting Art Nouveau and Art Deco collections. Look out for Salvador Dali's famous sofa in the shape of Mae West's lips, and have a pause at the Balcony Café for its bird's-eye view over the 20th Century Art and Design Gallery. The museum underwent a major refurbishment in 2001. ⊠ *Church St.,* ☎ *01273/290900.* ◻ *Free.* ☉ *Call ahead for opening times.*

㉞ Just west of the Old Steine lies **the Lanes,** a maze of alleys and passageways that were once home to legions of fishermen and their families and is now filled with restaurants, boutiques, and antiques shops. Vehicular traffic is barred from the area, so you may wander at will. The heart of the Lanes is Market Street and Square, lined with fish and seafood restaurants.

㉟ **Volk's Electric Railway** (☎ 01273/292718), built by inventor Magnus Volk in 1883, was the first public electric railroad in Britain; mid-April through September you can take the 1¼-mi trip along Marine Parade.

㊱ In Hove, the **British Engineerium** is a beautifully restored Victorian pumping station housing hundreds of steam engines, electric motors, motorcycles, and interactive children's exhibits. Note that boilers are only lighted and engines set in full steam on the first Sunday of the month, and on major public holidays. ⊠ *Nevill Rd., Hove,* ☎ *01273/559583.* ◻ *£4.* ☉ *Daily 10–5. Closed last wk Dec.*

㊲ The beautifully preserved **Preston Manor,** with its collection of paintings, silver, porcelain, and furniture, evokes the opulence of Edwardian times. There are charming bedrooms and a nursery in the attic, and you can also tour the servants' quarters and wander through the extensive grounds. The house is north of the town center, on the main London road. ⊠ *Preston Park,* ☎ *01273/292770.* ◻ *£3.20.* ☉ *Mon. 1–5, Tues.–Sat. 10–5, Sun. 2–5.*

Dining and Lodging

£–£££   **✕ English's Oyster Bar.** Buried in the Lanes, this is one of the few old-
★   fashioned seafood havens left in England. It has been a restaurant for more than 150 years and a family business for more than 50. You can eat succulent oysters and other seafood dishes at the counter or have a table in the restaurant section. It's well priced and ideal for a relaxing lunch after antiques hunting. ⊠ *29–31 East St.,* ☎ *01273/327980. AE, DC, MC, V.*

££   **✕ Terre à Terre.** This inspiring vegetarian restaurant is popular, so come early for a light lunch or a more sophisticated evening meal. The saffron rice parcels, Kiev Niçoise with caper butter, and eclectic choice of salads—try roquefort and radicchio topped with prickly pear—should satisfy most palates. ⊠ *71 East St.,* ☎ *01273/729051. AE, DC, MC, V. No lunch Mon.*

£–££   **✕ Donatello.** This popular Italian restaurant in the Lanes has exposed brick walls and pine decor, and is bright with plants and checked cloths. The food is standard Italian, with an emphasis on pizzas. Donatello is a brother eatery to Pinocchio's, close to the Theatre Royal. ⊠ *3 Brighton Pl.,* ☎ *01273/775477. AE, DC, MC, V.*

££££   **✕🏨 Brighton Thistle Hotel.** This modern, four-story hotel, a little east of the Grand Hotel, is built around a huge atrium and is a popular choice of conference delegates. With views to the sea, it's well designed and offers top facilities. The restaurant, La Noblesse, serves delicious fare such as smoked haddock with a saffron cheese sauce, wild mushroom and red wine risotto, and roast saddle of lamb, with not-too-expensive fixed menus. ⊠ *King's Rd., BN1 2GS,* ☎ *01273/206700,* **FAX**

01273/820692, WEB *www.thistlehotels.com. 208 rooms. Restaurant, indoor pool, sauna, gym. AE, DC, MC, V.*

££££ 🏨 **Grand Hotel.** This classic old hotel overlooks the seafront. The refurbished decor, especially in the public rooms, is of the spectacular chandelier-and-marble variety; the comfortable bedrooms are done in traditional style. ✉ *King's Rd., BN1 2FW,* ☎ *01273/321188,* FAX *01273/202694,* WEB *www.grandbrighton.co.uk. 200 rooms. Restaurant, indoor pool, sauna, gym, parking (fee). AE, DC, MC, V.*

£££ 🏨 **Granville Hotel.** Opposite the West Pier on hotel row, to the west of the Grand, this hotel has been converted from three grand residences facing the sea. Bedrooms are beautifully decorated and themed, and include the pink-and-white Brighton Rock and the art deco Noel Coward rooms. Trogs, the restaurant, caters to vegetarians and uses free-range and organic products. ✉ *124 King's Rd., BN1 2FA,* ☎ *01273/ 326302,* FAX *01273/728294,* WEB *www.granvillehotel.co.uk. 24 rooms. Restaurant, bar, coffee shop. AE, DC, MC, V.*

££ 🏨 **Adelaide Hotel.** Quiet informality, comfort and a sympathetic restoration are the hallmarks of this elegant Georgian town-house hotel. Try to book the Regency Room, which has a magnificent four-poster bed and luxurious bathroom. ✉ *51 Regency Sq., BN1 2FF,* ☎ *01273/205286,* FAX *01273/220904. 12 rooms. AE, MC, V.*

££ 🏨 **The Dove.** Washes of light, modern prints on the walls, and an uncluttered feel are the keynotes of this Regency house. There is one luxuriously large room with a balcony and a sea view, and three others have a sideways sea view from their bow windows. There's no elevator, and the stairs to the attic rooms are steep. Breakfasts are generous. ✉ *18 Regency Sq., BN1 2FG,* ☎ *01273/779222,* FAX *01273/ 746912. 9 rooms. AE, MC, V.*

Nightlife and the Arts

NIGHTLIFE

Live music is played most nights, and on weekends a lively club scene pulls in the crowds from across the Southeast. The **Zap Club** is Brighton's most well-established club (✉ 188–193 King's Road Arches, ☎ 01273/ 821588), but there are several others on the seafront between the two piers. East of Brighton Pier, try the trendy **Escape Club** (✉ 10 Marine Parade, ☎ 01273/606906).

THE ARTS

The **Brighton Festival** (☎ 01273/706771, WEB www.brighton-festival.org.uk), one of England's biggest arts festivals, is held every May. More than 600 events in just three weeks cover drama, music—from classical to rock—dance, visual arts, and literature at various venues throughout the city.

Brighton has several theaters. **The Dome** (☎ 01273/709709), beside the Royal Pavilion, was converted into an auditorium from the Prince Regent's stables in the 1930s. It stages pantomime and classical and pop concerts. The **Theatre Royal** (✉ New Rd., ☎ 01273/328488), close to the Royal Pavilion, is a very attractive Regency building with a period gem of an auditorium. It's a favorite venue for shows either on their way to or fresh from London's West End. The **Gardner Arts Centre** (☎ 01273/685861), on the campus of Sussex University, a few miles northeast of town at Falmer, presents plays, concerts, and cabaret.

The **Cinematheque** (✉ 9–10 Middle St., ☎ 01273/384300) screens art-house fare. The **Duke of York's Cinema** (☎ 01273/626261) on Preston Circus, a 10-minute walk north of the main train station, is one city option for art-house movies.

Shopping

The main shopping area to head for is **the Lanes,** especially for antiques or jewelry. It also has clothing boutiques, coffee shops, and pubs. Across North Street from the Lanes lies the **North Laine,** a network of narrow streets full of weird and wonderful little stores, less glossy than those in the Lanes, but fun, funky, and exotic.

Betjeman & Barton (✉ 10 Dukes La., ☎ 01273/329402) sells a variety of teas and teapots, with tea tastings to help you decide what to buy. **Colin Page** (✉ 36 Duke St., at the western edge of the Lanes, ☎ 01273/325954) is a book collector's dream, with a wealth of antiquarian and secondhand books at all prices. The **Pavilion Shop** (✉ 4–5 Pavilion Bldgs., ☎ 01273/290900), next door to the Royal Pavilion, carries well-designed souvenirs of Regency Brighton and has high-quality fabrics, wallpapers, and ceramics based on material in the Pavilion itself. The delightfully old-fashioned **Pecksniff's Bespoke Perfumery** (✉ 45–46 Meeting House La., ☎ 01273/723292) will mix and match ingredients to suit your wishes, from drawerfuls of scents and fragrances.

Arundel

❸❽   *23 mi west of Brighton, 60 mi south of London.*

The little hilltop town of Arundel is dominated by its great castle, the much-restored home of the dukes of Norfolk for more than 700 years, and an imposing neo-Gothic Roman Catholic cathedral—the duke is Britain's leading Catholic peer. The town itself is full of interesting old buildings, well worth a stroll.

Begun in the 11th century, **Arundel Castle** suffered destruction during the Civil War and was later remodeled during the 18th century and the Victorian era; still, it's rich with the history of the Fitzalan and Howard families and also with treasures such as paintings by Van Dyck, Gainsborough, and Reynolds. The keep, rising from its conical mound, is as old as the original castle, whereas the barbican (gatehouse) and the Barons' Hall date from the 13th century. The interior of the castle was reconstructed in the then-fashionable Gothic style of the 19th century. Among the treasures on view are the rosary beads and prayer book used by Mary, Queen of Scots, in preparing for her execution. The spacious grounds are open to the public, and there's a restaurant. The ceremonial entrance to Arundel Castle is at the top of High Street, but you enter at the bottom, close to the parking lot. ✉ *Mill Rd.,* ☎ *01903/882173,* WEB *www.arundel.castle.org.* ✇ *£7.50.* ✆ *Apr.–Oct., Sun.–Fri. noon–5 (gates close at 4).*

Dining and Lodging

£–££   ✗ **Black Rabbit.** A renovated 18th-century pub, the Black Rabbit is a find, and you must persevere along Mill Road in order to find it. Its location by the River Arun, with views of the castle and the bird sanctuary, makes it ideal for a summer lunch. The good English bar food is reasonably priced. ✉ *Mill Rd.,* ☎ *01903/882828. AE, DC, MC, V.*

£££   ▣ **Hilton Avisford Park.** This converted Georgian house is set on 89 acres of parkland, 3 mi west of Arundel off the A27 on B2132. It began as the home of an admiral and was a private school before its conversion into a hotel in the 1970s. Rooms have been carefully refurbished in traditional style, with close attention to detail; most have good views. ✉ *Yapton La., Walberton BN18 0LS,* ☎ *01243/551215,* FAX *01243/ 552485,* WEB *www.arundel.hilton.com. 139 rooms. Restaurant, indoor-outdoor pool, sauna, 18-hole golf course, 2 tennis courts, croquet, gum, squash, helipad. AE, DC, MC, V.*

£££   🏨 **Norfolk Arms Hotel.** Like the cathedral and the castle in Arundel, this 18th-century coaching inn was built by one of the dukes of Norfolk. The main body of the hotel is traditional in appearance, with narrow passages and cozy little rooms. There's an annex with modern rooms in the courtyard block. ✉ *22 High St., BN18 9AD,* ☎ *01903/882101,* FAX *01903/884275,* WEB *www.forestdale.com. 34 rooms. Restaurant. AE, DC, MC, V.*

Nightlife and the Arts

The **Arundel Festival** (☎ 01903/883690) presents drama productions and classical concerts in and around the castle grounds for a week in August/September.

Petworth House

★ ㉟ *12 mi northwest of Arundel, 54 mi south of London.*

Petworth House, one of the National Trust's greatest treasures, stands in a picturesque patch of Sussex. Try to approach through the charming village of Wisborough Green, northeast of the house. A 13th-century chapel is all that remains of the original manor house, and most of the present building was constructed between 1688 and 1696; a 700-acre deer park was added later by the celebrated landscape architect Capability Brown (1716–83). The house holds a distinguished collection of English paintings, including works by Gainsborough, Reynolds, Van Dyck, and J. M. W. Turner, the great proponent of Romanticism, who immortalized Petworth's sumptuous interiors in some of his most evocative watercolors. Other treasures include Greek and Roman sculpture and Grinling Gibbons wood carvings. Six rooms in the servants' quarters, including the old kitchen, are open to the public, and light lunches are served in the Servants Block. Explore the town of Petworth, too, a jewel studded with old, narrow streets and timbered houses. You can access the house off A272 and A283 (car parks). ☎ *01798/342207,* WEB *www.nationaltrust.org.uk.* ✍ *House £6; gardens only £1.50; park free.* ☉ *House Apr.–June and Sept.–Oct., Sat.–Wed. 1–5:30; July–Aug., Fri.–Wed. 1–5:30; last admission 5. Gardens Apr.–June and Sept.–Oct., Sat.–Wed. noon–6; July–Aug., Fri.–Wed. noon–6. Park daily 8–dusk.*

Chichester

㊵ *15 mi south of Petworth House, 66 mi southwest of London.*

The capital city of West Sussex, Chichester, was founded by the Romans on the low-lying plains between the wooded South Downs and the sea. Although it has its own large cathedral and all the trappings of a commercial city, Chichester is not much bigger than many of the towns around it. The city walls and major streets follow the original Roman plan; the intersection of the four principal streets is marked by a cross dated 1501.

Chichester's Norman **cathedral,** near the corner of West and South streets, stands on Roman foundations. Inside, a glass panel reveals Roman mosaics uncovered during restoration. Other treasures include wonderful, moving Saxon limestone reliefs of *The Raising of Lazarus* and *Christ Arriving in Bethany,* both in the choir area, and some outstanding pieces of contemporary work, notably a stained-glass window by Marc Chagall, a colorful tapestry by John Piper, and a painting by Graham Sutherland. ✉ *West St.,* ☎ *01243/782595.* ✍ *Donation requested.* ☉ *Easter–Sept., daily 7:30–7; Oct.–Easter, daily 7:30–5.*

Today Chichester is mainly Georgian, with countless 18th-century houses. One of the best is **Pallant House,** built in 1712 as a wine merchant's mansion. At that time, its state-of-the-art design showed the latest in complicated brickwork and superb wood carving. The rooms have been faithfully restored and furnished with appropriate antiques and porcelains. The **Pallant House Gallery** showcases a small but important collection of mainly modern British art, as well as touring exhibitions. Admission includes entry to the **Hans Fiebusch Studio**, nearby in St. Martin's Square, which houses an exact re-creation of the St. John's Wood (London) studio of this exiled German artist (1898–1998) who was the last member of the so-called Degenerate Art Group. ⊠ 9 N. Pallant, ☎ 01243/774557, WEB www.pallant.co.uk. 🖂 £4. ⊙ Tues.–Sat. 10–5, Sun. 12:30–5.

Dining and Lodging

££££   ✗ **Comme Ça.** This attractively converted pub is about a five-minute walk across the park from the Festival Theatre, making it a very good spot for a meal before a performance. Bunches of dried hops, suspended from the ceiling, and antique children's toys decorate the dining room. The owner, Michel Navet, is French, and his chef cooks authentic French dishes; simpler fare is served in the bar at much lower prices, and there is a fixed-price lunchtime menu for around £15. ⊠ 67 Broyle Rd., ☎ 01243/788724. AE, DC, MC, V. Closed Mon. No dinner Sun.

£   ✗ **Shepherds.** This relaxed tearoom is ideal for a morning coffee, light lunch, or afternoon break while seeing Chichester. Most of its tables are in a modernized conservatory at the rear. There are six kinds of rarebit on the menu, including Hawaiian with pineapple, and oodles of fattening home-baked foods, as well as a renowned assortment of first-rate teas. Smoking is not permitted. Credit cards are accepted only for bills over £10. ⊠ 35 Little London, ☎ 01243/774761. MC, V. Closed Sun. No dinner.

£££   🏨 **Ship Hotel.** Staying in this hotel is something of an architectural experience. Built in 1790, it was originally the home of Admiral Sir George Murray, one of Admiral Nelson's right-hand men. Outstanding features are the classic Adam staircase and colonnade. The hotel is carefully being restored to its 18th-century elegance. It's close to the Festival Theatre. ⊠ North St., PO19 1NH, ☎ 01243/778000, FAX 01243/788000, WEB www.shiphotel.com. 36 rooms. Restaurant, bar. AE, DC, MC, V.

Nightlife and the Arts

The **Festival Theatre** (☎ 01243/781312, WEB www.cft.org.uk) presents classics and modern plays from May through September and is a venue for touring companies the rest of the year. Built in 1962, it has an international reputation and can be the evening focus for a relaxed day out of London.

Fishbourne Roman Palace

㊶   ½ mi west of Chichester, 66 mi southwest of London,

Fishbourne Roman Palace is the largest and grandest Roman villa in Britain. Many of its 100 rooms are lavishly decorated with intricate mosaics and painted walls. Sophisticated bathing and heating systems remain, and the Roman garden, the only known example extant in northern Europe, is laid out in the style of the 1st century AD. A museum displays artifacts from the site and provides a history of the building. ⊠ Salthill Rd., Fishbourne, ☎ 01243/785859, WEB sussexpast.co.uk. 🖂 £4.40. ⊙ Mar.–July and Sept.–Oct., daily 10–5; Aug., daily 10–6; Nov.–mid-Dec., daily 10–4; mid-Dec.–mid-Feb., weekends 10–4; mid-Feb.–end Feb., daily 10–4.

Sculpture at Goodwood

42 *63 mi southwest of London, 3 mi north of Chichester.*

Twenty acres of woodland provide a natural setting for this collection of contemporary British sculpture, specially commissioned by the Hat Hill Sculpture Foundation. A third of the exhibits change annually, and the pieces are sited to maximize their impact, connected by walks through glades and green fields. The park is signposted on the right off A286. ⊠ *Hat Hill Copse, Goodwood,* ☎ *01243/538449,* WEB *www. sculpture.org.uk.* ⊠ *£10.* ☉ *Mar.–Oct, Thurs.–Sat. 10:30–4:30.*

Singleton

43 *5 mi north of Chichester, 59 mi south of London.*

Singleton, a secluded village, is home to an open-air museum. The **Weald and Downland Open Air Museum** gives sanctuary to endangered historical buildings. Among the 45 structures on 50 acres of wooded meadows are a cluster of medieval houses, a working water mill, a Tudor market hall, and an ancient blacksmith's shop. The building styles on display span more than 400 years. A Conservation Centre, set to open early in 2002, will exhibit artifacts and provide storage space. ⊠ *Singleton,* ☎ *01243/811348,* WEB *www.wealddown.co.uk.* ⊠ *£6.* ☉ *Mar.– Oct., daily 10:30–6; Nov.–Feb., Wed. and weekends 10:30–4 (last admission 1 hr before closing).*

Guildford

44 *30 mi north of Singleton, 28 mi southwest of London, 35 mi north of Chichester.*

Guildford, the largest town in Surrey and the county's capital, is an important commuter town, but it has managed to retain a faint 18th-century air. No other English town can claim such a brilliant succession of royal visits, from Alfred the Great down to the present queen. The steep High Street is lined with gabled merchants' houses, now home to upscale fashion and household shops, and preserves a pleasant, provincial appearance. **The Royal Grammar School,** at the top end of High Street, contains one of Britain's three surviving chained libraries (books were so precious during the Middle Ages, they were literally chained to prevent theft); this one dates from the 16th century and now holds the principal's study. The school was founded in 1507. ⊠ *Upper High St.,* ☎ *01483/539880.* ☉ *By appointment only.*

You won't be able to miss the massive Tudor facade of the ancient **Hospital of the Blessed Trinity.** It was founded in 1619 as almshouses (a function it still performs, as it is a senior-citizens' home) by George Abbot, Archbishop of Canterbury. Abbot, one of the translators of the King James Bible, was born in Guildford. ⊠ *High St.,* ☎ *01483/562670.* ☉ *Chapel and common room by appointment.*

The **Guildford Museum,** in the old castle building, has interesting exhibits on local history and archaeology, along with memorabilia of Charles Dodgson, better known as Lewis Carroll, the author of *Alice in Wonderland.* Dodgson spent his last years in a house on nearby Castle Hill, dying there with his sisters at his side. He was buried in the Mount Cemetery, up the hill on High Street. **Castle Arch,** which is all that remains of the entrance of the old castle, displays a slot for a portcullis. Beyond the arch lie the remains of the castle. ⊠ *Quarry St.,* ☎ *01483/444750,* WEB *www.guildfordborough.co.uk.* ⊠ *Free.* ☉ *Mon.–Sat. 11–5.*

Guildford Cathedral, looming on its hilltop across the River Wey, is only the second Anglican cathedral to be built on a new site since Henry VIII's Reformation of the 1500s. It was consecrated in 1961. The red-brick exterior is severely simple, whereas the interior, with its stone and plaster, looks bright and cool. The Refectory Restaurant is open for light refreshments from 9:30 AM to 4:30 PM. ✉ *Stag Hill,* ☎ *01483/ 565287,* WEB *www.guildford-cathedral.org.* ☜ *Donation accepted.*

Dining and Lodging

£   ✕ **The Jolly Farmer.** This riverside pub has a conservatory and terraced garden alongside the River Wey, a few minutes from the Yvonne Arnaud Theatre (just past the boatyard). The standard pub meals include ploughman's lunch and baked pastas. ✉ *Millbrook,* ☎ *01483/538779. AE, MC, V.*

£   ✕ **Rumwong.** The elegant waitresses at this Thai restaurant wear their
★   traditional long-skirted costumes, so at busy times the dining room looks like a swirling flower garden. On the incredibly long menu, the Thai name of each dish is given with a clear English description. Try the fisherman's soup, a spicy mass of delicious saltwater fish in a clear broth, or *yam pla muek,* a hot salad with squid. ✉ *16–18 London Rd.,* ☎ *01483/536092. MC, V. Closed Mon. and 2 wks in Aug.*

£££–££££   ✕🏠 **The Angel.** This is the last of the old coaching inns for which Guild-
★   ford was famous. The courtyard, where coaches and horses clattered to a stop, is still open to the sky, and light lunches are served here in summer. The hotel is at least 400 years old and is even said to have a ghost. Individually designed guest rooms have attractive fabrics, reproduction antiques, and marble-lined bathrooms; 10 are in a modern annex. The hotel has a salon with a fireplace and minstrel's gallery. An excellent restaurant (fixed-price menu at dinner) in the medieval stone cellar swims with atmosphere; among the modern British choices are red mullet soup and breast of Barbary duck. ✉ *91 High St., GU1 3DP,* ☎ *01483/564555,* FAX *01483/533770,* WEB *www.slh.com. 21 rooms. Restaurant, coffee shop. AE, DC, MC, V.*

Nightlife and the Arts

The **Yvonne Arnaud Theatre** (✉ Milbrook, ☎ 01483/440000, WEB www.yvonne-arnaud.co.uk) is an unusual horseshoe-shape building on an island in the River Wey. It frequently previews West End productions and also has a restaurant.

Clandon Park

🔵 *3 mi east of Guildford, 29 mi southwest of London.*

The grand **Clandon Park** was built in the 1730s by Venetian architect Giacomo Leoni in the graceful Palladian style. The park was landscaped by Capability Brown. The real glory of the mansion is its interior, especially the magnificent two-story Marble Hall. There's a fine collection of 18th-century furniture, needlework, and porcelain; a regimental museum on the grounds is full of weapons and medals. The gardens, too, are of interest, with a parterre, grotto, and sunken garden. ✉ *A247, West Clandon,* ☎ *01483/222482,* WEB *www.nationaltrust.org.uk.* ☜ *£5.* ☉ *Apr.–Oct., Tues.–Thurs., Sun., 11–5; last admission 30 mins before closing; gardens open daily 11–5.*

Great Bookham

🔵 *8 mi northeast of Guildford, 25 mi southwest of London.*

Great Bookham has some fine old buildings at its core, including a 12th-century church, one of the most complete medieval buildings extant in Surrey. The most absorbing of Great Bookham's historic attractions is **Polesden Lacey,** a handsome Regency mansion built in 1824 by Thomas Cubitt on the site of one owned by the famed 18th-century playwright Richard Brinsley Sheridan. From 1906 to 1942, it was the home of Edwardian society hostess Mrs. Ronald Greville, who remodeled it substantially. Her many famous guests included Edward VII. Elizabeth, now the Queen Mother, and her husband, the Duke of York (later George VI), stayed here for part of their honeymoon. Polesden Lacey contains beautiful collections of furniture, paintings, porcelain, and silver. In summer, open-air theatrical performances are given on the grounds. Refreshments are available in the stableyard restaurant. ☎ 01372/458203, WEB *www.nationaltrust.org.uk.* ✉ *House £3, grounds £4.* ⊙ *House Apr.–Oct., Wed.–Sun. 1–5; grounds daily 11–6 or dusk.*

En Route As you start making your way southeast to Royal Tunbridge Wells via Dorking (about 28 mi), you'll pass under the shadow of **Box Hill** (✉ A24, ☎ 01306/885502, WEB www.nationaltrust.org.uk), the setting of the famous picnic in Jane Austen's *Emma.* It's a favorite spot for walking excursions, with lovely views of the South Downs. At the bottom of Box Hill, the Burford Bridge Hotel was where Keats wrote the last chapters of *Endymion* (and Admiral Nelson stayed there when traveling down to Portsmouth, and on to fame and death at Trafalgar).

Dorking

⓲ *6 mi southeast of Great Bookham, 29 mi south of London.*

The southeasterly route to Royal Tunbridge Wells leads to the busy commuter town of Dorking, a pleasant neighborhood that has inspired the pens of many writers. The cemetery holds the remains of the writer George Meredith (1828–1909) after he was refused burial in Westminster Abbey, and its wide High Street houses the White Horse Inn, or "The Marquis o' Granby," as Dickens dubbed it for his *Pickwick Papers.*

Dining and Lodging

££££ ✗ **Partners and Sons.** Behind the genuine 16th-century, half-timber facade a comfortable, air-conditioned restaurant offers a modern English menu with Mediterranean influences. Fresh local produce is used, and the local lamb dishes are recommended. There's a fixed-price menu at dinner. ✉ *2–4 West St.,* ☎ *01306/882826. Reservations essential. AE, DC, MC, V. Closed Sun., Mon.*

££–£££ ▥ **White Horse.** This inn provides a taste of both ancient and modern. The foundations of the hotel probably go back to the 13th century, whereas the interior is mostly 18th century. A winding staircase leads to older-style rooms, and the Garden Block has more modern rooms. The older rooms have a bit more character but most look out onto the High Street, so many people prefer the slightly larger and quieter but blander rooms in the Garden Block. Rates are considerably lower during the week. ✉ *High St., RH4 1BE,* ☎ *01306/881138,* FAX *01306/887241. 69 rooms. Restaurant. AE, DC, MC, V.*

East Grinstead

⓳ *15 mi southeast of Dorking, 32 mi south of London.*

The small country town of East Grinstead claims the longest continuous run of 14th-century timber-frame buildings in the country. Six miles to the east is the village of Hartfield, where A. A. Milne wrote his Winnie the Pooh stories in the 1920s.

Tours of **Saint Hill Manor,** 2 mi southwest of town, concentrate on the five families who have occupied the house since its construction in 1795. Some rooms have elegant English oak and Canadian pinewood paneling, and several show touches contributed by such former residents as the Maharajah of Jaipur (black marble pillars) and the archaeologist Edgar March Crookshank (a mosque door). The house was for many years the home of L. Ron Hubbard (1911–86), science fiction writer and founder of the Church of Scientology. He left his 530 published works on display in the library. Pride of place must go to the 100-ft Monkey Mural, in which the nephew of Winston Churchill, John Spencer Churchill, depicted famous personalities (including his uncle) as monkeys. ⊠ *Off A22,* ☎ *01342/326711.* ☞ *Free.* ☉ *Daily; tours at 2, 3, 4, and 5.*

A small family country house dating from the 1890s, **Standen** typifies the Arts and Crafts movement. Designed by the influential architect Philip Webb (1831–1913), it contains a wealth of William Morris carpets, wallpapers and fabrics, and even the original electric light fittings. It's 2 mi south of East Grinstead. ⊠ *Off B2110,* ☎ *01342/323029,* WEB *www.nationaltrust.org.uk.* ☞ *House and garden £5.50; garden only £3.* ☉ *House Apr.–early Nov., Wed.–Sun. 12:30–4:30. Garden Apr.– early Nov., Wed.–Sun. 11–6; early Nov.–mid Dec., Fri.–Sun. 11–3.*

At **Nymans Garden,** exotic plants collected by the gardener Ludwig Messel mingle with more homely varieties. Spring is the best time to appreciate the prolific rhododendrons and the rare Himalayan magnolias in the romantic walled garden; in summer it's the turn of the roses. The garden is 10 mi southwest of East Grinstead. ⊠ *B2114, Handcross,* ☎ *01444/400321,* WEB *www.nationaltrust.org.uk.* ☞ *£6.* ☉ *Mar.–Oct., Wed.–Sun. 11–6 or dusk; Nov.–Feb., weekends 11–4.*

Dining and Lodging

££££ ✕🏠 **Gravetye Manor.** This lovely Elizabethan stone mansion, built in 1598, stands on a hilltop site in 1,000 acres of grounds landscaped by William Robinson (1838–1935), an advocate of the natural rather than the formal garden. Restored with oak paneling and ornamental plaster ceilings, it represents the epitome of the luxurious English country house hotel. The superb restaurant (fixed-price menu; reservations essential) favors seafood and has an excellent wine list. ⊠ *East Grinstead RH19 4LJ (5 mi south of East Grinstead, signposted off B2110),* ☎ *01342/810567,* FAX *01342/810080,* WEB *www.gravetyemanor.co.uk. 18 rooms. Restaurant, bar, lake, croquet, fishing. MC, V.*

MASTERPIECES AND MOATS: TUNBRIDGE WELLS TO FINCHCOCKS

One of England's greatest attractions is its many magnificent stately homes and castles. For people who love great treasure houses, there are almost endless opportunities in Great Britain, but for those with limited vacation time, the dismaying fact is that the greatness is thinly spread, with many houses scattered across the country. Within a 15-mi radius of Tunbridge Wells, however, lies a remarkable array of historic homes, castles, and monuments: Penshurst Place, Hever Castle, Chartwell, Knole, Ightham Mote, Leeds Castle, Sissinghurst Castle Gardens, Bodiam Castle, Rudyard Kipling's Batemans, and Finchcocks.

Royal Tunbridge Wells

❹❾ *13 mi east of East Grinstead, 39 mi southeast of London.*

Humorists have always referred to this city as unbelievably straitlaced (officially known as Royal Tunbridge Wells), but locals ignore the prefix "royal," which was added only in 1909, during the reign of Edward VII. Tunbridge Wells owes its prosperity to the 17th- and 18th-century passion for spas and mineral baths, initially as medicinal treatments and later as social gathering places. In 1606, a spring of chalybeate (mineral) water was discovered here, drawing legions of royal visitors. It's still possible to drink the waters when a "dipper" (the traditional water dispenser) is in attendance, from Easter through September. Tunbridge Wells reached its zenith in the mid-18th century, when Richard "Beau" Nash presided over its social life. Today it's a pleasant town and home to many London commuters. The buildings at the lower end of High Street are mostly 18th-century, but as the street climbs the hill north, changing its name to Mount Pleasant Road, the buildings become more modern.

A good place to begin a visit is at the **Pantiles,** a famous promenade with colonnaded shops near the spring on one side of town, which derives its odd name from the Dutch "pan tiles" that originally paved the area. Now bordered on two sides by busy main roads, the Pantiles remains an elegant, tranquil oasis. The **Church of King Charles the Martyr,** across the road from the Pantiles, dates from 1678, when it was dedicated to Charles I, who was executed by Parliament in 1649. Its plain exterior belies its splendid interior; take special note of the beautifully plastered Baroque ceiling. A network of alleyways behind the church leads north back to High Street.

Tunbridge Wells Museum and Art Gallery, at the northern end of Mount Pleasant Road, houses a fascinating jumble of local artifacts, prehistoric relics, and Victorian toys, as well as a permanent exhibition of interesting Tunbridge Ware pieces: small, wooden items intricately inlaid with tiny pieces of differently colored woods. ⊠ *Civic Centre, Mount Pleasant Rd.,* ☎ *01892/526121,* WEB *www.tunbridgewells.gov.uk.* ➡ *Free.* ⊙ *Mon.–Sat. 9:30–5.*

OFF THE
BEATEN PATH

ALL SAINTS CHURCH — A modest building holds one of the glories of 20th-century church art. The church is awash with the luminous yellows and blues of 12 superb windows by Marc Chagall (1887–1985), commissioned as a tribute by the family of a young girl who was drowned in a sailing accident in 1963. The church is 4 mi north of Royal Tunbridge Wells; turn off A26 before Tonbridge and continue a mile or so east along B2017. ⊠ *B2017, Tudeley,* ☎ *0870/744–1456.* ➡ *Free.* ⊙ *Daily 9–6 or dusk.*

Dining and Lodging

££–£££
★

✕ **Thackeray's House.** Food lovers flock to this mid-17th-century house, once the home of Victorian novelist William Makepeace Thackeray (he wrote *Tunbridge Toys* here). The chef-owner, Bruce Wass, tolerates none but the freshest ingredients and cooks everything with great flair and imagination. Specialties include mini-bouillabaisse, Hereford duck in many guises, and a famous chocolate Armagnac loaf with coffee sauce. Below the main restaurant there's a friendly little bistro, Downstairs at Thackeray's, with food every bit as good as that upstairs, but less expensive (entrance in the courtyard). ⊠ *85 London Rd.,* ☎ *01892/511921. MC, V. Closed Mon. and last wk Dec. No dinner Sun. Bistro closed Sun.–Mon.*

£–££

✕ **Sankey's Selections.** This eatery includes a basement wine bar and a lively upstairs restaurant. The wine bar has inexpensive food, and the restaurant specializes in wonderfully fresh fish. The *soupe de poissons* is excellent, and there are good British cheeses. ⊠ *39 Mount Ephraim,* ☎ *01892/511422. AE, DC, MC, V. Closed Sun.*

£

✕ **The Hogshead and Compasses.** This spacious, well-kept pub claims to be the oldest in town. As well as offering a notable range of "real ales," the pub serves tasty homemade food at lunchtime, from salads and wraps to all-day breakfasts. In winter you can snuggle up to the cozy open fires. The pub lies on a tiny, steep lane off High Street. ✉ *Little Mount Sion,* ☎ *01892/530744. MC, V.*

£££–££££   🏠 **Spa Hotel.** Carefully chosen furnishings and details help give this Georgian mansion of 1766 the atmosphere of a country house, although guest rooms are thoughtfully equipped with many modern extras. This hotel is run by the Goring family, who also own the noted Goring Hotel in London. Its extensive grounds give superb views across the town and into the Weald of Kent. The traditional English fare of the Chandelier Restaurant is very popular with locals. ✉ *Mount Ephraim, TN4 8XJ,* ☎ *01892/520331,* FAX *01892/510575,* WEB *www.spa-hotel.co.uk. 71 rooms. Restaurant, indoor pool, hair salon, sauna, tennis court, gym, croquet. AE, DC, MC, V.*

££   🏠 **Old Parsonage.** This very comfortable, friendly guest house, 2 mi south of Tunbridge Wells via the A267, stands at the top of a quiet lane beside the village church. Built in 1820, the Georgian manor has a country-house feel to it, with lovely antique furniture, including two four-posters, and a big conservatory for afternoon tea. The lodging stands amid three acres of grounds. Two pubs and a restaurant lie within a short walk from the house. ✉ *Church La., Frant TN3 9DX,* ☎ FAX *01892/ 750773,* WEB *www.theoldparsonagehotel.co.uk. 3 rooms. MC, V.*

Outdoor Activities and Sports

The nine-hole golf course at **Langton Road** (☎ 01892/523034) welcomes visitors (members only on weekends).

Penshurst Place

★ 🔵50   *7 mi northwest of Tunbridge Wells, 33 mi southeast of London.*

At the center of the hamlet of Penshurst lies one of England's finest medieval manor houses, Penshurst Place, hidden behind tall trees and a walled garden. Although retaining its Baron's Hall, dating from the 14th century, the house is mainly Elizabethan, with additions from later periods. It has been in the Sidney family since 1552, bringing it a particular richness. The most famous Sidney is the Elizabethan poet, Sir Philip, author of *Arcadia.* The **Baron's Hall,** topped in 1341 with a timber roof, is the oldest and one of the grandest to survive from the early Middle Ages. Family portraits, furniture, tapestries, and armor help tell the story of the house. The grounds include a 10-acre walled Tudor garden; there's a toy museum and a garden restaurant. Although Penshurst is basically an appendage of the "Great House," the village is a delightful destination. It centers around Leicester Square, which has late-15th-century half-timber structures adorned with soaring brick chimneys. A low-beam passageway gives access to the churchyard—all in all, a vision right out of Ye Merrie Olde Englande. ✉ *Off B2188 (from Tunbridge Wells follow A26 and B2176),* ☎ *01892/870307,* WEB *www.penshurstplace.com.* 🎫 *House and grounds £6; grounds only £4.50.* ☉ *House Mar., weekends noon–5; Apr.–Oct., daily noon–5. Grounds daily 10:30–6. Last admission 30 mins before closing.*

Dining and Lodging

£–££   ✕ **Spotted Dog.** This pub first opened its doors in 1520; today, it tempts you with an inglenook fireplace, heavy beams, imaginative food, and a splendid view of Penshurst Place. ✉ *Smarts Hill,* ☎ *01892/ 870253. AE, MC, V.*

££–£££   🏠 **Rose and Crown.** Originally a 16th-century inn, this hotel on the main street in Tonbridge (5 mi east of Penshurst, 5 mi north of Tunbridge Wells) has a distinctive portico, added later. Inside, low-beam ceilings and Jacobean woodwork make the bar and the restaurant snug and inviting. Guest rooms in the main building are traditionally furnished,

"DOING THE STATELIES": VISITING THE TREASURE HOUSES OF ENGLAND

CURIOSITY AS TO HOW the other half lives is undoubtedly one of the most deep-seated traits of human nature, and it's extremely pleasing to know you can satisfy your healthy desire to snoop through the great array of Kent's stately homes for the payment of a very small amount of conscience money. The fact that you will see some of the greatest of the world's treasures at the same time is a bonus.

Even the most highly developed sense of curiosity isn't enough to explain why millions of people have surged on to England's stately home trail. They have been urged to move by a great deal of exposure—the houses all over the country touched by Royal Family upheavals, such as Althorp, the ancestral home of Princess Diana, and the Mountbatten home, Broadlands; the numerous television serials, which have brought new fame to such spectacular houses as Castle Howard and Blenheim Palace; the continuing spate of historical movies shot on location, including the numerous versions of Jane Austen's novels (Lyme Park played a starring role in *Pride and Prejudice*), *The Madness of King George* (the spectacular interiors of Wilton House dazzled here), *Sense and Sensibility* (partly shot at Saltram), or the over-the-top style of Charles II on view in *Restoration*. Today, thousands follow in the footsteps of Elizabeth Bennet and the Gardiners who paid a call on Mr. Darcy's regal Pemberley, one of the more fetching episodes penned by Miss Austen. Here, in Kent, Penshurst Place and Knole are still the homes of the aristocratic families who built them more than half a millennium ago.

The reason for the pressing need for the owners of stately homes to throw them open is simply that they need the ready money. Spiritually rewarding as it must be to own vast tracts of countryside, paintings by Rembrandt and Gainsborough, a house designed by one of the Adam brothers and furnished by Chippendale, and tapestries by the mile and porcelain by the ton—it is all a dead loss as far as cash flow (and death duties) are concerned.

What you get for your entrance fee differs enormously from one house to another. In some houses you are left completely free to wander at will, soaking up the atmosphere. In some you are organized into groups that then proceed through the house like bands of prisoners behind enemy lines. Occasionally you may find that your mentor is a member of the family, who will gleefully relate stories of uncles, aunts, and cousins back to the Crusades. Those are often the most memorable experiences.

Four facts should be kept in mind when touring the treasure houses of England. Depending on your itinerary, you may be able to save money by purchasing a special pass or joining an organization such as the National Trust (☞ Discounts and Deals in Smart Travel Tips A to Z). Many houses are unreachable except by car. Hours are always subject to change, so it's always best to call the day before and inquire: at times, people arrive standing on the doorstep staring at a bolted door. Also, most houses are open only in the warm-weather seasons, from April to October. However, some of these houses have celebrated parks—Blenheim Palace and Chatsworth come to mind—that are utter delights and are open through much of the year. Everyone has a top-10 list—Knole, Longleat, Woburn, and so on—but don't forget lesser-known Neoclassical abodes and those wonderful mock-medieval Victorian piles, such as Castle Drogo in Devon, designed for Sir Julius Drewe, the founder of a chain of grocery stores. There is something keenly appropriate about the fact that the last great castle built in Britain was created for a shopkeeper. Napoléon would have approved.

whereas rooms in the newer annex are more modern in style; all are attractive and cozy. ⊠ *125 High St., Tonbridge TN9 1DD,* ☎ *01732/ 357966,* FAX *01732/357194. 50 rooms. Restaurant, bar. AE, MC, V.*

Hever Castle

★ ⑤ *30 mi southeast of London, 10 mi northwest of Tunbridge Wells, 3 mi west of Penshurst.*

For some, 13th-century Hever fits the stereotype of what a castle should look like, all turrets and battlements, the whole encircled by a water lily–bound moat; for others, it's a bit too squat in structure (and perhaps too renovated). Its main attraction is its past association with the ill-fated Anne Boleyn, second wife of Henry VIII and mother of Elizabeth I. It was here that she was courted and won by Henry, who had her beheaded in 1536. He later gave Hever to his fourth wife, Anne of Cleves. The castle was acquired in 1903 by American millionaire William Waldorf Astor, who built an entire Tudor village to house his staff (now a hotel for corporate functions) and had the stunning gardens laid out, with Italian and Tudor plantings, a yew maze, and topiary walks. ⊠ *Off B2026 (near Edenbridge),* ☎ *01732/865224,* WEB *www.hevercastle.co.uk.* ⊠ *Castle and grounds £7.80; grounds only £6.10.* ☉ *Castle Apr.–Oct., daily noon–6; Mar. and Nov., daily noon– 4. Grounds Apr.–Oct., daily 11–6; Mar. and Nov., daily 11–4. Last admission 1 hr before closing.*

Chartwell

⑤ *9 mi north of Hever Castle, 12 mi northwest of Tunbridge Wells, 28 mi southeast of London.*

Chartwell was Sir Winston Churchill's home from 1924 until his death in 1965. The Victorian house was acquired by the National Trust and has been decorated to appear as it did in Churchill's lifetime, even down to a half-smoked cigar in an ashtray. In the garden you can see a wall he built himself. ⊠ *Off B2026 (near Westerham),* ☎ *01732/866368,* WEB *www.nationaltrust.org.uk.* ⊠ *House £5.60; garden and studio £2.80.* ☉ *Apr.–June and Sept.–Oct., Wed.–Sun. 11–5; July–Aug., Tues.–Sun., 11–5; last admission 45 mins before closing.*

Knole

★ ⑤ *27 mi southeast of London, 11 mi north of Tunbridge Wells, 8 mi east of Chartwell.*

The town of Sevenoaks in Kent lies in London's commuter belt, a world away from the baronial air of its premier attraction, Knole, the grand home of the Sackville family since the 16th century. Begun in the 15th century and enlarged and embellished in 1603 by Thomas Sackville, Knole, with its vast complex of courtyards and buildings, resembles a small town, and, in fact, you'll need most of an afternoon to explore it thoroughly. The house is noted for its collection of tapestries, embroidered furnishings, and the most famous set of 17th-century silver furniture to survive. Most of the salons are in the pre-Baroque mode, rather dark and armorial. Paintings on display include a series of portraits by 18th-century artists Thomas Gainsborough and Sir Joshua Reynolds. The magnificently florid staircase was a novelty in its Elizabethan heyday. The noted writer Vita Sackville-West grew up at Knole and set her novel *The Edwardians,* a witty account of life among the gilded set, here. Encompassed by a 1,000-acre deer park, the house lies in the center of Sevenoaks, opposite St. Nicholas Church. To get there from Chartwell, drive north to Westerham, then pick up A25 and head east for 8 mi. ⊠

When you pack your MCI Calling Card, it's like packing your loved ones along too.

Your MCI Calling Card is the easy way to stay in touch when you travel. Use it to call to and from over 125 countries. Plus, every time you call, you can earn frequent flier miles. So wherever your travels take you, call home with your MCI Calling Card. It's even easy to get one. Just visit **www.mci.com/worldphone**.

EASY TO CALL WORLDWIDE

1. Just enter the WorldPhone® access number of the country you're calling from.
2. Enter or give the operator your MCI Calling Card number.
3. Enter or give the number you're calling.

Aruba ✛	800-888-8
Bahamas ✛	1-800-888-8000

Barbados ✛	1-800-888-8000
Bermuda ✛	1-800-888-8000
British Virgin Islands ✛	1-800-888-8000
Canada	1-800-888-8000
Mexico	01-800-021-8000
Puerto Rico	1-800-888-8000
United States	1-800-888-8000
U.S. Virgin Islands	1-800-888-8000

✛ Limited availability.

EARN FREQUENT FLIER MILES

SEE THE WORLD
IN FULL COLOR

Fodor's Exploring Guides bring all the great sights vividly to life with hundreds of photographs, fascinating historical background, and colorful anecdotes. Detailed maps and practical information keep you headed in the right direction.

Pair a **Fodor's** Exploring Guide with your trusted Gold Guide for a complete planning package.

Off A225, ☎ *01732/450608,* WEB *www.nationaltrust.org.uk.* ✉ *£5, grounds £1.* ☉ *Apr.–Oct., Wed.–Sat. noon–4 (last admission at 3:30), Sun. 11–5 (last admission at 4); gardens May–Sept., 1st Wed. of each month 11–4 (last admission at 3).*

Ightham Mote

★ **54** *7 mi southeast of Knole, 10 mi north of Royal Tunbridge Wells, 31 mi southeast of London.*

Finding Ightham Mote requires careful navigation, but it's worth the effort to see a vision right out of the Middle Ages. This outstanding example of a small manor house is entered by crossing a stone bridge over one of the dreamiest moats in England—the absolute quintessence of medieval romanticism. This moat, however, does not relate to the "mote" in the name, which refers to the role of the house as a meeting place, or "moot." Ightham (pronounced *i*-tem) Mote's magical exterior has changed little since it was built in the 14th century, but within you'll find it does encompass styles of several periods, Tudor to Victorian. The Great Hall is an antiquarian's delight, both comfy and grand. Be sure to see the magnificent Tudor chapel, drawing room, and billiards room in the North West quarter. Ongoing restoration may mean that parts of Ightham Mote are closed to the public at times. To reach the house from Sevenoaks, follow A25 east to A227 (8 mi) and follow the signs. ✉ *Off A227, Ivy Hatch, Sevenoaks,* ☎ *01732/810378,* WEB *www.nationaltrust.org.uk.* ✉ *£5.* ☉ *Apr.–Oct., Mon., Wed.–Fri., and Sun. 11–5:30 (last admission 1 hr before closing).*

Leeds Castle

★ **55** *12 mi east of Ightham Mote, 19 mi northwest of Royal Tunbridge Wells, 40 mi southeast of London.*

The bubbling River Medway runs through Maidstone, Kent's county seat, with its backdrop of chalky downs. Nearby, the fairy-tale stronghold of Leeds Castle commands two small islands on a peaceful lake. Dating back to the 9th century and rebuilt by the Normans in 1119, Leeds (not to be confused with Leeds in the North of England) became a favorite home of many English queens. Henry VIII liked it so much he had it converted from a fortress into a grand palace. The house (much restored) offers a fine collection of paintings and furniture, plus an unusual dog-collar museum. Other attractions include a maze and grotto, an aviary, and woodland gardens. To get to Maidstone from Ightham Mote, go north on the A227, then east on the A20. ✉ *A20 (5 mi east of Maidstone),* ☎ *0870/600–8880,* WEB *www.leeds-castle.co.uk.* ✉ *Castle and grounds £10; grounds only £8.50.* ☉ *Mar.–Oct., daily 10–5; Nov.–Feb., daily 10–3. Castle closed Sat. on last weekend in June and 1st weekend in July.*

Rochester

56 *12 mi north of Leeds Castle, 28 mi southeast of London.*

Kent is Charles Dickens country and all Dickens aficionados will want to head to Rochester, the place outside of London most closely associated with the great author. He lived for many years at Gad's Hill Place, just outside of town. You can find out all about Dickens and his connections with the town at the **Charles Dickens Centre,** with displays featuring life-size models of scenes from the author's books that can amuse and horrify you at the same time (parents be warned). Opposite the center, look out for the abode of Uncle Pumblechook in *Great Expectations,* one of the many buildings in High Street still "full of gables with old beams and timbers," as Dickens described it. ⊠ *Eastgate House, High St.,* ☎ *01634/844176.* ☜ *£3.50.* ⊙ *Daily 10–5:30; last admission 4:45.*

Rochester Castle is one of the finest surviving examples of Norman military architecture. The keep, built in the 1100s and partly based on the Roman city wall, is 125 ft high, the tallest in England. ⊠ *Boley Hill,* ☎ *01634/402276,* WEB *www.english-heritage.org.uk.* ☜ *£3.70.* ⊙ *Apr.–Sept., daily 10–6; Oct., daily 10–5; Nov.–Mar., daily 10–4; last admission 30 mins before closing.*

The first English bishop was ordained in a small cathedral on the site of the **Rochester Cathedral** in AD 604 by Augustine of Canterbury. The present cathedral, England's second-oldest, is rather a jumble of architectural styles. Work was started in 1077 by the Norman Bishop Gundulph, who also built the castle. The elaborate Norman west front is striking. ⊠ *Boley Hill,* ☎ *01634/401301.* ☜ *Donation requested.* ⊙ *Daily 8:30–5:30.*

The 47 retired ships at the **World Naval Base,** across the River Medway in Chatham, constitute the world's most complete Georgian–early Victorian dockyard. Some 400 naval ships were built here over as many years, as shown by the sights, sounds, and smells of the "Wooden Walls" exhibit. There's a guided tour of the submarine HMS *Ocelot,* the last warship to be built for the Royal Navy at Chatham. ⊠ *Historic Dockyard, Chatham,* ☎ *01634/823800.* ☜ *£8.50.* ⊙ *Apr.–Oct., daily 10–6 (last admission 2 hrs before closing in summer); Nov., Feb.–Mar., Wed., Sat., and Sun. 10–4.*

Nightlife and the Arts

A **Dickens festival** (☎ 01634/306000 for details) is held in Rochester in late May or early June, at which thousands of people in period dress attend enactments of scenes from the author's novels. Another important Dickens festival takes place in Broadstairs (40 mi east).

Sissinghurst Castle and Garden

★ ⑤⑦ *22 mi south of Rochester, 53 mi southeast of London.*

One of the most famous gardens in the world, Sissinghurst is deep in the Kentish countryside around the remains of a moated Tudor castle. Unpretentiously beautiful, quintessentially English, the gardens were laid out in the 1930s around the remains of a former wing of the castle by the writer Vita Sackville-West (one of the Sackvilles of Knole) and her husband, the diplomat Harold Nicolson. The grounds are at their best in June and July, when the roses are in bloom. The gardens are informal in style; the White Garden, with its white flowers and silver-gray foliage, is a classic, and the herb garden and cottage garden show Sackville-West's knowledge of plants. Children may feel restricted in the gardens, and strollers are not allowed. Wheelchair access is limited. From Leeds Castle, make your way south on B2163 and A274 through Headcorn, then follow signs. ⊠ *A262, Cranbrook,* ☎ *01580/710701,* WEB *www.nationaltrust.org.uk.* ☜ *£6.50.* ⊙ *Apr.–mid-Oct., Tues.–Fri. 1–6:30, weekends 10–6:30; last admission 1 hr before closing. Admission often restricted due to limited space; a timed ticket system may be in effect, usually May–July.*

Dining and Lodging

£ ✕ **Claris's Tea Shop.** Claris's, near Sissinghurst Castle, serves traditional English teas in a 15th-century setting and displays attractive English crafts items. There's a pretty garden for summer teas. ⊠ *3 High St., Biddenden,* ☎ *01580/291025. No credit cards. Closed Mon.*

££££ ✕🏨 **Kennel Holt Hotel.** This is a quiet hotel in a redbrick Elizabethan
★   manor house surrounded by beautiful, well-kept gardens. You are treated
      like a guest in a private house; the library is well stocked with books for
      a rainy day. The restaurant offers three- and four-course set-price menus,
      with dishes such as salmon with cream, tomato, herb, and cucumber sauce,
      or guinea fowl and foie gras with wild mushroom sauce. Antiques and
      flowers grace the restaurant as well as the rest of the hotel. The hotel is
      3 mi from Goudhurst, off A262. ✉ *Goudhurst Rd., Cranbrook TN17
      2PT,* ☎ *01580/712032,* 🖷 *01580/715495,* 🌐 *www.kennelholt.co.uk.
      10 rooms. Restaurant, croquet, library. MC, V. Restaurant closed Mon.;
      no Sun. lunch Apr.–Oct.; hotel closed last 2 wks Jan.*

En Route As you leave Sissinghurst, continue south along A229 through
      Hawkhurst, a little village that was once the headquarters of a noto-
      rious and ruthless gang of smugglers. Turn left onto the B2244 and
      left at the Curlew pub to arrive in the tiny Sussex village of Bodiam.

Bodiam Castle

★ ⑤⑧ *9 mi south of Cranbrook, 15 mi southeast of Royal Tunbridge Wells,
      57 mi southeast of London.*

      Immortalized in 1,001 travel posters, Bodiam Castle is Britain's most
      picturesque medieval stronghold, and nonetheless so for being virtu-
      ally a shell. Built in 1385 to withstand a threatened French invasion,
      it was "slighted" (partly demolished) during the English Civil War of
      1642–46 and has been uninhabited ever since. Nevertheless, you can
      still climb some of the towers. Surrounded by a lovely moat, this pho-
      togenic castle seems designed for the viewfinders of today's video cam-
      eras. ✉ *Off B2244, Bodiam,* ☎ *01580/830436,* 🌐 *www.nationaltrust.
      org.uk.* 🎫 *£3.70.* ☉ *Mid-Feb.–Oct., daily 10–6 or dusk; Nov.–mid-
      Feb., weekends 10–4 or dusk; last admission 1 hr before closing.*

Burwash

⑤⑨ *10 mi west of Bodiam, 14 mi south of Tunbridge Wells, 58 mi south-
      east of London.*

      Burwash, a pretty Sussex village, is known for its association with writer
      Rudyard Kipling. Close by, between Burwash Common and the River
      Dudwell, is the setting for *Puck of Pook's Hill,* one of Kipling's well-
      known children's books. To get to Burwash, turn west from Hawkhurst
      onto A265.

      Kipling lived from 1902 to 1936 at **Bateman's,** a beautiful 17th-cen-
      tury house off the main road a half mile south of the village. It was built
      for a prominent ironmaster when Sussex was the center of England's
      iron industry. Kipling's study looks exactly as it did when he lived here,
      and in the garden a water mill still grinds flour (most Saturdays in sum-
      mer at 2 PM); it's thought to be one of the oldest working water tur-
      bines. ✉ *Off A265,* ☎ *01435/882302,* 🌐 *www.nationaltrust.org.uk.*
      🎫 *£5 (£2.50 during Mar.).* ☉ *Mar., weekends 11–4; Apr.–Oct., Sat.–
      Wed. house 11–5, grounds 11–5:30.*

Lamberhurst

⑥⓪ *11 mi north of Burwash, 7 mi east of Tunbridge Wells, 46 mi south-
      east of London.*

      Set among the orchards on the Kent-Sussex border, this village once
      rang to the sound of hammers, as the center of the local iron-smelting
      industry; it was responsible for most of the gates and railings of St.
      Paul's Cathedral in London. The long village street passes over the River

Teise and has some handsome old buildings. One of England's noted vineyards, **Lamberhurst Vineyard,** lies (signposted) outside the village. Until the mid-1990s, grape growing in England was a rich man's hobby. Today it's an important rural industry, and the wines produced here are world-renowned. There's a restaurant as well as a shop in the style of a Tuscan villa. ⊠ *Ridge Farm, off A21,* ☎ *01892/890412.* 🖃 *Free, guided tours £4.50.* ۞ *Weekdays 9–5:30, weekends 10–5:30. Closed last wk Dec.*

Outdoor Activities and Sports

Bewl Water takes advantage of its location at one of England's largest reservoirs, providing a range of aquatic sports. There's also an adventure playground, and bicycles can be rented. You pay a small parking fee. ⊠ *Off B2099,* ☎ *01892/890661.* ۞ *Open daily 10–sunset.*

Finchcocks

❻1 *2 mi east of Lamberhurst, 10 mi east of Tunbridge Wells, 48 mi southeast of London.*

A visit to Finchcocks, an elegant Georgian mansion between Lamberhurst and Goudhurst, is a must for music lovers. It contains the **Finchcocks Living Museum of Music,** a magnificent collection of nearly 100 historic keyboard instruments, which are played whenever the house is open. (Demonstration recitals are included in the admission fee.) A festival is held on September weekends. ⊠ *Off A262, Goudhurst,* ☎ *01580/211702,* WEB *www.finchcocks.co.uk.* 🖃 *£6.50.* ۞ *Mid-Apr.–July and Sept., Sun. 2–6; Aug., Wed.–Thurs. and Sun. 2–6; private visits by arrangement Apr.–Oct.*

Dining and Lodging

£–££ ✕🖃 **Star and Eagle.** This traditional village inn has been serving pints and offering hospitality since 1600. The place has exposed beams and open brick fireplaces, and some rooms overlook the village graveyard. Rooms come in all sizes: one of them (No. 5) has a huge four-poster, although others have better views. Snacks and full meals are available in the popular bar downstairs. The extensive menu lists Spanish, Mexican, and Italian dishes but is probably best for English treats such as beef Wellington, smoked salmon pancakes, baked oysters, and steak pie. ⊠ *High St., Goudhurst TN17 1AL,* ☎ *01580/211512,* FAX *01580/ 211416. 10 rooms. Restaurant, bar. MC, V.*

SOUTHEAST A TO Z

To research prices, get advice from other travelers, and book travel arrangements, visit www.fodors.com.

AIRPORTS

Gatwick Airport, 27 mi south of London, has direct flights from many U.S. cities and is more convenient for this region than Heathrow. The terminal for the British Rail line is in the airport buildings, and there are connections to all the major towns in the region.

➤ AIRPORT INFORMATION: **Gatwick Airport** (⊠ M23, Junction 9, Crawley, ☎ 01293/535353, WEB www.baa.co.uk).

BUS TRAVEL

National Express serves the region from London's Victoria Coach Station. Trips to Brighton and Canterbury take less than two hours; to Chichester, about three hours. For regional bus transport inquiries, contact the number listed below. Maps and timetables are available at bus depots, train stations, local libraries, and tourist information centers.

➤ Bus Information: **National Express** (☎ 0870/580–8080, WEB www.gobycoach.com). **Regional bus information** (☎ 0870/608–2608).

CAR RENTAL
➤ Local Agencies: **Avis** (✉ 6A Brighton Marina, Brighton, ☎ 01273/673738; ✉ Eastern Docks, Dover, ☎ 01304/206265). **Hertz** (✉ 47 Trafalgar St., Brighton, ☎ 01273/738227; ✉ c/o Total Garage, Broad Oak Rd., Canterbury, ☎ 01227/470864; ✉ 173–177 Snargate St., Dover, ☎ 01304/207303; ✉ Guildford Railway Station, Station Approach, Guildford, ☎ 01483/536677).

CAR TRAVEL
Major routes radiating outward from London to the Southeast are, from west to east: M23/A23 to Brighton (52 mi); A21, passing by Tunbridge Wells to Hastings (65 mi); A20/M20 to Folkestone; and A2/M2 via Canterbury (56 mi) to Dover (71 mi).

A good link route for traveling through the region, from Hampshire across the border into Sussex and Kent, is A272 (which becomes A265). It runs through the Weald (uplands), which separates the North Downs from the more inviting South Downs. Although smaller, less busy roads forge deeper into the downs, even the main roads take you through lovely countryside and villages. The main route east from the downs to the Channel ports and resorts of Kent is A27. To get to Romney Marsh (just across the Sussex border in Kent), take A259 from Rye. Be warned that more traffic tickets are issued per traffic warden in Brighton than anywhere else in the country.

EMERGENCIES
➤ Contacts: **Ambulance, fire, police** (☎ 999). **Royal Sussex County Hospital** (✉ Eastern Rd., Brighton, ☎ 01273/696955). **Canterbury Hospital** (✉ Ethelbert Rd., Canterbury, ☎ 01227/766877).

TOURS
BUS TOURS
Guide Friday has a go-as-you-please bus tour of Brighton lasting at least an hour. It operates April–September, costing £6.50.
➤ Fees and Schedules: **Guide Friday** (☎ 01273/540893, WEB www.guide-friday.com).

PRIVATE GUIDES
The Southeast England Tourist Board can arrange private tours with qualified Blue Badge guides. The Guild of Guides provides guides who have a specialized knowledge of Canterbury and the surrounding area.
➤ Fees and Schedules: **Guild of Guides** (☎ 01227/459779). **Southeast England Tourist Board** (☎ 01892/540766).

TRAIN TRAVEL
Connex South Eastern and Connex South Central serve the area from London's Victoria and Charing Cross (for all areas) and Waterloo (for the west). From London, the trip to Brighton takes about one hour by the fast train, and to Dover, about two hours. South West Trains runs service to Guildford. For local and regional information, call National Rail Enquiries.

The line running west from Dover passes through Ashford, where you can change trains for Hastings and Eastbourne. There are connections from Eastbourne for Lewes, and from Brighton for Chichester. For local and regional information, call National Rail Enquiries.

CUTTING COSTS
A "Network" card costing £20, valid throughout the southern and south-eastern regions for a year, entitles you and three companions to one-third off many fares.

FARES AND SCHEDULES
➤ TRAIN INFORMATION: **National Rail Enquiries** (☎ 08457/484950, WEB www.railtrack.co.uk).

TRAVEL AGENCIES
There are other Thomas Cook offices in Dover, Eastbourne, Folkestone, Guildford, Hastings, Hove, Maidstone, Ramsgate, and Sevenoaks.
➤ LOCAL AGENT REFERRALS: **American Express** (✉ 82 North St., Brighton, ☎ 01273/712905). **Thomas Cook** (✉ 58 North St., Brighton, ☎ 01273/367700; ✉ 9 High St., Canterbury, ☎ 01227/597800; ✉ 109 Mount Pleasant Rd., Royal Tunbridge Wells, ☎ 01892/791500).

VISITOR INFORMATION
The Southeast England Tourist Board will send you a useful illustrated booklet, *Hundreds of Places to Visit* (£2.95), and can give you information on tours and excursions. The office is open Monday to Thursday 9–5:30, Friday 9–5. Local tourist information centers (TICs) are normally open Monday–Saturday 9:30–5:30, but hours vary seasonally; offices are listed below by town.
➤ TOURIST INFORMATION: **Southeast England Tourist Board** (✉ The Old Brewhouse, 1 Warwick Park, Royal Tunbridge Wells TN2 5TU, ☎ 01892/540766, FAX 01892/511008, WEB www.southeastengland.uk.com). **Arundel** (✉ 61 High St., BN18 9AJ, ☎ 01903/882268, WEB www.sussex-by-the-sea.co.uk). **Brighton** (✉ 10 Bartholomew Sq., BN1 1JS, ☎ 0906/711–2255, WEB www.visitbrighton.com). **Canterbury** (✉ 34 St. Margaret's St., CT1 2TG, ☎ 01227/766567, WEB www.canterbury.co.uk). **Chichester** (✉ 29A South St., PO19 1AH, ☎ 01243/775888). **Dover** (✉ Townwall St., CT16 1JR, ☎ 01304/205108). **Guildford** (✉ 14 Tunsgate, GU1 3QT, ☎ 01483/444333, WEB www.guildfordborough.co.uk). **Hastings** (✉ Town Hall, Queens Rd. and, in summer only, 2 The Stade, TN34 1TL, ☎ 01424/781111). **Lewes** (✉ 187 High St., BN7 2DE, ☎ 01273/483448). **Maidstone** (✉ The Gatehouse, Palace Gardens, Mill St., ME15 6YE, ☎ 01622/602169, WEB www.digitalmaidstone.co.uk). **Royal Tunbridge Wells** (✉ The Old Fish Market, The Pantiles, TN2 5TN, ☎ 01892/515675, WEB www.tunbridgewells.gov.uk/tourism). **Rye** (✉ The Heritage Centre, Strand Quay, TN31 7AY, ☎ 01797/226696).

3 THE SOUTH

WINCHESTER, SALISBURY, STONEHENGE

The South of England is perfect for time travelers. In just a long weekend you can go from the silent monoliths of prehistoric Stonehenge to the fanciful curlicues of Victorian Salisbury. History has highlights by the hundreds here—Winchester Cathedral, Wilton House, and Beaulieu Abbey are just a few places that bear witness to the past. And like a library, the South is tailor-made for browsing, thanks to its many literary landmarks. Make a pilgrimage to Jane Austen's home or travel to Dorset—Thomas Hardy country—to get far from the madding crowd.

Updated by
Robert
Andrews

T HE SOUTH, MADE UP OF HAMPSHIRE (Hants), Dorset, and Wiltshire counties, holds a wide range of attractions, and not a few
quiet pleasures. Two important cathedrals, Winchester and Salisbury (pronounced *sawls*-bree), are here, as well as stately homes—
Longleat, Stourhead, and Wilton House, among them—attractive
market towns, and literally hundreds of haunting prehistoric remains,
two of which, Avebury and Stonehenge, should not be missed. These,
of course, are but the tourist-brochure superlatives. Sooner or later, however, anyone spending time in these parts should rent a bike (preferably one of those black clunkers that look so at home in English
villages) and set out to discover the back-roads villages—much favored
by those who migrate here from every corner of the country in search
of upward mobility—*not* found in those brochures. After a drink in
the village pub and a look at the cricket game on the village green, take
a break at a strawberry farm where you can lie on straw strewn between the rows and gorge yourself on sun-warmed berries, or collapse
in a grassy field that has "nap time" written all over it. *This* is what
summer in England is all about.

Hampshire has been called the Cinderella County because for many it
is just a county to be crossed in the feverish holiday migration from London to the familiar cliffs and coves of Devon and Cornwall in the west.
To many others, Hampshire means the last sight of England from departing steamers, or a first solid acquaintance with her on stepping ashore
at Southampton. The county may seem but the gateway to England,
through which to pass hurriedly. Nothing could be further from the truth,
for the sandwich shire is a seventh heaven for the perceptive visitor.

One of the area's many historical highlights was when Alfred the
Great, teaching religion and letters, made Winchester the capital of 9th-
century England and helped lay plans for Britain's first navy, sowing
the seeds of its Commonwealth. This well-preserved market town is
dominated by its cathedral, an imposing edifice dotted with the Gothic
tombs of 15th-century bishops, who lie peacefully behind grillwork,
their marble hands crossed for eternity. Winchester is a good center
from which to visit quiet villages where so many of England's once great
personages, from Florence Nightingale to Lord Mountbatten, lived or
died. Jane Austen and her works are enduringly popular, and thanks
to a '90s spate of filmed versions of her classic novels, her home at Chawton has become a favored pilgrimage spot. But everywhere, the un-
scheming hand of time has scattered pretty villages over Hampshire.
Many of them have cottages grouped around a green, as seems fitting
in a proper English village.

Moving beyond the gentle, gardenlike features of Hampshire, you can
explore the somewhat harsher terrain of Salisbury Plain. Two monuments, millennia apart, stand sentinel over the plain. One is the 404-
ft stone spire of Salisbury Cathedral, immortalized in oil by John
Constable, which dominates the entire Salisbury valley. Not far away
is the most imposing and dramatic prehistoric structure in Europe: Stonehenge. The many theories about its construction and purpose only add
to its attraction, which endures despite the hordes of visitors.

There are numerous other districts to explore, each with its own pleasures, and many with literary or historical associations. Turn your sights
to the Dorset heathlands, the countryside explored in the novels of
Thomas Hardy. This district is spanned by rolling grass-covered chalk
hills—the Downs—wooded valleys and meadows through which course

meandering rivers. Along the coastline you'll find Lyme Regis, where the tides and currents strike fear into the hearts of sailors, and Cowes on the Isle of Wight—Queen Victoria's favorite getaway place—which welcomes high-flyers who enter their yachts in the famous regattas.

The South has been quietly central to England's history for well over 4,000 years, occupied successively by prehistoric man, the Celts, the Romans, the Saxons, and the modern British. History continues to be made here, right up to the modern era. On D-Day, forces sailed for Normandy from ports along this coast; nearly 40 years later, they set out to recover the Falklands.

Pleasures and Pastimes

Dining

Fertile soil, well-stocked rivers, and a long coastline ensure excellent farm produce and a plentiful stock of fish throughout the South. Try fresh-grilled river trout or sea bass poached in brine, or dine like a king on the New Forest's renowned venison.

CATEGORY	COST*
££££	over £22
£££	£16–£22
££	£9–£15
£	under £9

per person for a main course at dinner

Literary Shrines

Among this region's proudest claims is its connection with Thomas Hardy (1840–1928), one of England's most celebrated novelists. If you have a chance to read some of Hardy's novels before visiting Dorset—immortalized by Hardy as his part-fact, part-fiction county of Wessex—you'll already have a feeling for it, and indeed, you'll recognize some places immediately from his descriptions. The tranquil countryside surrounding Dorchester, in particular, is lovingly described in *Far from the Madding Crowd,* and Casterbridge, in *The Mayor of Casterbridge,* stands for Dorchester itself. You can actually walk the farm track where Tess of the d'Urbervilles's pony fell or share the timeless vista of the Blackmore Vale that the tragic heroine so loved. Any pilgrimage to Hardy's Wessex begins at the author's birthplace in Higher Bockhampton, 3 mi east of Dorchester. Here, in a lovely thatched cottage, Hardy penned the story of Bathsheba Everdene. Salisbury makes an appearance as "Melchester" in *Jude the Obscure.* Walk in the footsteps of Jude Fawley by climbing Shaftesbury—"Shaston"—and its steeply picturesque Gold Hill. Today, many of these sights seem frozen in time, and Hardy's spirit is ever present. In addition to Hardy landmarks, Jane Austen sites and shrines abound in the South of England.

Lodging

Modern hotel chains are well represented, and in rural areas there are elegant country-house hotels, traditional coaching inns, and modest guest houses. Note that some seaside hotels do not accept one-night bookings in the summer.

CATEGORY	COST*
££££	over £150
£££	£100–£150
££	£60–£100
£	under £60

All prices are for two people sharing a standard double room, including service, breakfast, and VAT.

Markets

Open-air markets are almost daily events. For a complete list, ask the Southern Tourist Board. Among the best are Salisbury's traditional city market (Tuesday and Saturday), Kingsland Market in Southampton for bric-a-brac (Thursday), and a general country market (Wednesday) at Ringwood, near Bournemouth.

Exploring the South

The South of England ranges from the broad plains of Wiltshire, including the Marlborough Downs, the Vale of Pewsey, and the great Salisbury Plain, to the gaudy bucket-and-spade resorts of the coast, and the sedate retirement homes of the Isle of Wight. The wide-open, wind-blown feel of the inland county of Wiltshire offers a sharp contrast both to the tame, sequestered villages of Hampshire and Dorset, and the self-important bustle of Southampton and Portsmouth. On the whole, you will not want to spend much time in these two ports; instead, spend your nights in the more compelling cities of Salisbury and Winchester.

This good-size area can be divided into a number of self-contained destinations for touring, each with its own distinctive character. The cathedral city of Winchester makes a useful base for visiting a handful of villages within easy reach, before you move on to the historic ports of Southampton and Portsmouth, each of which has its appeal—although most of their historic architecture was blown away in World War II. You can end your tour on the Isle of Wight. The city of Salisbury, with its own lovely cathedral, is another major starting point. The obvious draw outside town is Stonehenge, one of Britain's most popular tourist attractions, and within reach of an equally interesting prehistoric monument, Avebury. From there, you can swing south to the cultivated woodlands of the New Forest. The southern coast of Dorset is another major area, with a couple of popular holiday resorts, Bournemouth and Weymouth, and a string of ancient sites: Corfe Castle, Maiden Castle, and Cerne Abbas. Lyme Regis, on the Devon border at the center of the wide arc of Lyme Bay, is a favorite holiday destination in this area.

Numbers in the text correspond to numbers in the margin and on the South, Winchester, and Salisbury maps.

Great Itineraries

You could spend weeks exploring the South, but you can take in the flavor of the area in seven days or less. On a three-day visit, you can see the highlights of Winchester and Salisbury, plus Stonehenge and a stately home or two. In five days you can cover the same ground but also add sights from Portsmouth to Corfe Castle, Dorchester, and Cerne Abbas in Dorset. A week-long visit allows time to see a number of areas and sights off the beaten path—to see Avebury in addition to Stonehenge, for example—and to explore the New Forest or relax by the shore a bit.

IF YOU HAVE 3 DAYS

With limited time, you will want to combine the most sights with the least amount of traveling. If you are coming from London or southeast England, ☒ **Winchester** ①–⑧ will be your first stop, a quiet, solid town, conducive to walking about, with the great cathedral at its heart. Art historians remark on how the cathedral presents a sturdy, chunky appearance in keeping with its Norman construction, so that its Gothic lightness within is even more breathtaking. Other historic sites include the Great Hall and Winchester College, one of the country's noted "public" schools. Spend a night here, then move across to another cathedral city, 🔛 **Salisbury** ㉒–㉙. Surely few cathedrals have a more beautiful setting than this town—worth a two-night stay to take in the city sights and **Stonehenge** ㊱, an easy ride out of town. Even closer to Salisbury are magnificent **Wilton House** ㉚ and its gardens, which you can see on your way to visiting the village of **Shaftesbury** ㉛, and two more country estates, **Stourhead** ㉜ and **Longleat House** ㉝. The former holds—many believe—the most beautiful garden in England; the latter marries an African game park with a famous Elizabethan house.

IF YOU HAVE 5 DAYS

A longer stay in the South will give you greater freedom to explore some of the region's lower-key but no less enjoyable sights. After a day touring 🔛 **Winchester** ①–⑧ and nearby **Chawton** ⑩, indelibly associated with Jane Austen, return to overnight in the cathedral city. The next morning, head for the south coast and **Portsmouth** ⑫ to take in its notable historic ships and the Royal Naval Museum. Spend the next two nights in 🔛 **Salisbury** ㉒–㉙ to discover the city and the marvels surrounding it, including **Wilton House** ㉚ and **Stonehenge** ㊱. Head south again to **Wimborne Minster** ㊶, a town dwarfed by the twin towers of its great church. If you have time, head farther south to see **Corfe Castle** ㊸, whose jagged ruins cast an eerie spell over the village at its foot. Spend your last two days in the area around 🔛 **Dorchester** ㊹, a must for fans of Thomas Hardy, although even without this literary connection it would be a captivating town, with the excavations of a Roman villa and an amphitheater just outside. Also nearby is the grassy site of **Maiden Castle** ㊻, a bare but still powerfully evocative spot that is one of the South's chief prehistoric settlements. North of town, the chalk giant at **Cerne Abbas** ㊺ provides more links with the distant past.

IF YOU HAVE 7 DAYS

More time will enable you to tread farther off the beaten track and pursue a more adventurous itinerary. Spend your first day and night in 🔛 **Winchester** ①–⑧, then head down to Portsmouth to take a ferry across to **Cowes** ⑮, the most noted town on the Isle of Wight, a favorite island haven for both Queen Victoria and Charles Dickens. The former vacationed at Osborne House, an Italianate villa, whereas one of her forebears, Charles I, was the unwilling guest of the Parliamentary army during his incarceration in **Carisbrooke Castle** ㉑. Overnight in nearby 🔛 **Ryde** ⑯. Leave the Isle of Wight from Cowes, disembarking at **Southampton** ⑬, not a particularly noteworthy place but home to a couple of absorbing museums as well as the Pilgrim Fathers' Memorial. North of town, the village of **Romsey** ⑭ is an attractive spot, with the lovely 18th-century mansion of Broadlands lying just outside. From here, you are well placed to spend two nights in 🔛 **Salisbury** ㉒–㉙ to take in the city and the attractions around it, as far north as the stone circles of **Avebury** ㉞ and the nearby town of **Marlborough** ㉟, said to be the burial place of Merlin. If you have already toured this area, you might swoop down instead to the leafy New Forest; **Lyndhurst** ㊲ is a useful gateway. It's an excellent place to take a breather and some exercise, including riding. Heading westward, stop in at 🔛 **Bournemouth** ㊵, containing the Shelley Rooms and the grave of his wife Mary, author of *Frankenstein*. If the seaside frivolity doesn't grab you, carry on as far as **Corfe Castle** ㊸. Farther west is the genteel resort of **Weymouth** ㊼, where you can dine on fish by the harborside. South of Weymouth lies the **Isle of Portland** ㊽, which together with Chesil Beach will provide both beach fun and interest to anyone intrigued by geological phenomena. 🔛 **Dorchester** ㊹ and **Maiden Castle** ㊻ lie just north of here, and a few miles west, **Abbotsbury** ㊾ contains a famous 600-year-old swannery. Farther along Lyme Bay, the small port of

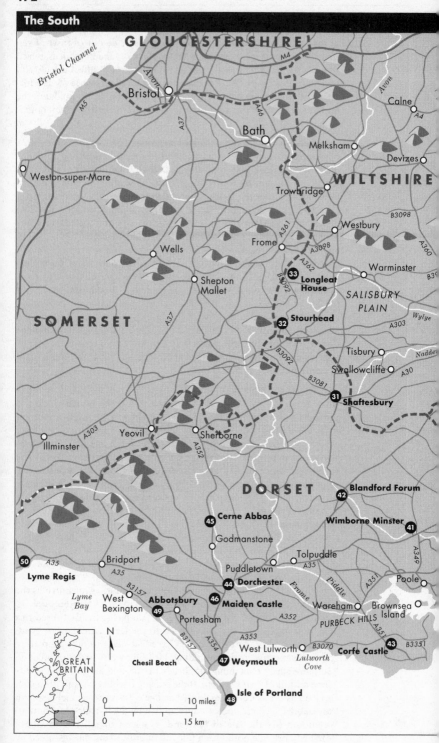

GLOUCESTERSHIRE

Bristol Channel

M4

Avon

Bristol

M5

A37

A46

Bath

Melksham

Calne

A4

Weston-super-Mare

Devizes

Avon

WILTSHIRE

Trowbridge

Westbury

B3098

A360

A361

Frome

A3098

A362

Warminster

B3

Wells

A3092

33 Longleat House

32 Stourhead

SALISBURY PLAIN

Shepton Mallet

A37

Wylye

A303

Tisbury

Swallowcliffe

A30

Nadder

SOMERSET

B3092

B3081

Yeovil

Sherborne

31 Shaftesbury

Illminster

A303

A352

DORSET

42 Blandford Forum

45 Cerne Abbas

Wimborne Minster

41

Godmanstone

A349

50

A35

Bridport

Puddletown

Tolpuddle

A35

Frome

Poole

Lyme Regis

Lyme Bay

West Bexington

B3157

Abbotsbury

44 Dorchester

Puddle

A351

Wareham

Brownsea Island

49

Portesham

46 Maiden Castle

A352

PURBECK HILLS

A351

GREAT BRITAIN

N

B3157

A354

A353

West Lulworth

B3070

43 Corfe Castle

B3351

Chesil Beach

47 Weymouth

Lulworth Cove

0   10 miles

0   15 km

48 Isle of Portland

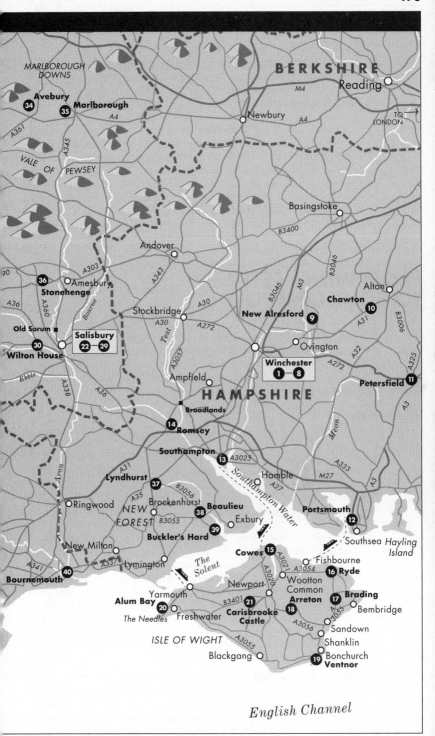

MARLBOROUGH
DOWNS

BERKSHIRE

Reading

34 Avebury
35 Marlborough

A4

Newbury

A4

TO
LONDON

A361

A345

VALE OF
PEWSEY

Basingstoke

B3400

Andover

A303

A343

A30

M3

B3046

B3046

Alton

Chawton

10

36
Stonehenge

Amesbury

Stockbridge

A30

A272

New Alresford **9**

A31

B3006

A36

A360

Old Sarum

30

Salisbury

22 — **29**

Wilton House

A338

A36

Ebble

Bourne

Test

A3057

Ampfield

Ovington

A32

A325

Winchester

1 — **8**

A272

Petersfield **11**

A3

HAMPSHIRE

Broadlands

Meon

14 Romsey

Southampton

13 *A3025*

Hamble

M27

A333

A3

Lyndhurst

37

A35

B3056

Brockenhurst

NEW
FOREST

B3055

A31

Ringwood

38 Beaulieu

Exbury

Southampton Water

A27

Portsmouth

12

A341

New Milton

Buckler's Hard **39**

Cowes **15**

Lymington

40

Bournemouth

A337

The
Solent

A3021

Southsea *Hayling
Island*

Fishbourne

A3054

16 Ryde

Yarmouth

Newport

Wootton
Common

Alum Bay **20**

Freshwater

The Needles

B3401

21

Carisbrooke
Castle

A3020

Arreton

18

17 Brading

Bembridge

A3055

Sandown

A3056

ISLE OF WIGHT

A3055

Blackgang

Shanklin

19 Bonchurch
Ventnor

English Channel

Lyme Regis ⑩ will appeal to fans of both John Fowles and Meryl Streep: it is where *The French Lieutenant's Woman* was set and filmed.

When to Tour the South

Make sure you don't see the great cathedrals of Salisbury and Winchester on a Sunday, when your visit will be restricted, or during services, when it won't be overly appreciated. Places such as Stonehenge and Longleat House attract plenty of visitors at all times; bypass such sights on weekends or public holidays. In summer, the coastal resorts of Bournemouth and Weymouth are crowded with day-trippers and longer-stay tourists, so your movement may be hampered by the crowds; it may also be difficult to find suitable accommodations. The Isle of Wight, too, gets its fair share of visitors, and you may have to wait longer for the ferries. Some of the smaller, less frequented stops should always be reasonably free of the crush. Choose these lower-profile attractions when the going gets tough. Otherwise, this is one area of the country you are relatively free to visit at any time of year. Fall in the New Forest is spectacular, although you should take waterproof boots for the puddles.

FROM WINCHESTER TO SOUTHAMPTON

From the lovely cathedral city of Winchester, 70 mi southwest of London, you can meander southward to the coast, stopping at the bustling ports of Southampton and Portsmouth to explore their maritime heritage. From either of these you can strike out for the restful shores of the Isle of Wight, vacation home to Queen Victoria and thousands of modern-day Britons.

Winchester

70 mi southwest of London, 14 mi north of Southampton.

Winchester is among the most historic of English cities, and as you walk its graceful streets, a sense of the past envelops you. Although it is now merely the county seat of Hampshire, for more than four centuries Winchester served as England's capital. Here, in AD 827, Egbert was crowned first king of England, and his successor, Alfred the Great, held court until his death in 899. In late Saxon times the town became the home of the finest school of calligraphy and manuscript illumination in Europe. After the Norman Conquest in 1066, William I ("the Conqueror") had himself crowned in London, but took the precaution of repeating the ceremony in Winchester. William also commissioned the local monastery to produce the Domesday Book, a record of the general census taken in England in 1085. The city remained the center of ecclesiastical, commercial, and political power until the 13th century. Winchester's power has long vanished, and some fast-food outlets and retail chains have moved onto pretty High Street, but the city has still preserved much of its past glory.

★ ❶   **Winchester Cathedral,** begun in 1079 and consecrated in 1093, is the city's greatest monument. Its tower, transepts, and crypt, and the inside core of the great nave, reveal some of the world's best surviving examples of Norman architecture. Other features, such as the arcades, the presbytery (behind the choir, holding the high altar), and the windows, are Gothic alterations carried out between the 12th and 14th centuries. The remodeling of the nave in the Perpendicular style was not completed until the 15th century. Little of the original stained glass has survived, thanks to Cromwell's Puritan troops, who ransacked the

City Mill 7
City
Museum 6
Close 2
Great Hall . . .5
King's Gate/
St. Swithun's
Church 3
St. Giles's
Hill 8
Winchester
Cathedral . . .1
Winchester
College 4

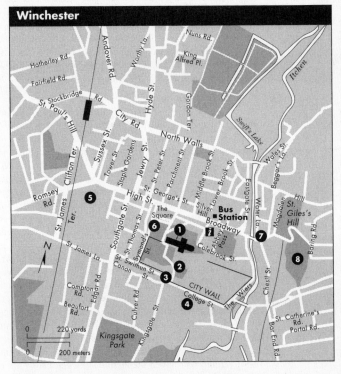

Winchester

cathedral in the 17th century during the English Civil War. The church's library holds an illuminated 12th-century copy of the Winchester Bible.

Among the many well-known people buried in the cathedral are William the Conqueror's son, William II ("Rufus"), mysteriously murdered in the New Forest in 1100; Izaak Walton (1593–1683), author of *The Compleat Angler,* whose memorial window in Silkestede's Chapel was paid for by "the fishermen of England and America"; and Jane Austen, whose memorial window can be seen in the north aisle of the nave. Try to be here during Evensong (usually at 5:30 PM), to hear the ancient stone resound to heavenly choral music. In summer free tours take place on the hour and in winter at 11 AM and 2 PM. Near the west (main) entrance is a visitor center with a gift shop and restaurant. ⊠ *The Close, Cathedral Precincts,* ☎ *01962/857225,* WEB *www.winchester-cathedral. org.uk.* 🖾 *£3.50 donation requested.* ⊗ *Daily 9–4:30.*

❷ The **Close,** behind the cathedral, is an area containing neat lawns and
❸ the Deanery, Dome Alley, and Cheyney Court. **King's Gate,** on St. Swithun St. on the south side of the Close, was built in the 13th century and is one of two gates remaining from the original city wall. **St. Swithun's Church** is built over the ancient King's Gate. The saint himself is interred in the cathedral; it is said that it rained for 40 days when his body was transferred there from the churchyard, giving rise to the legend that rain on St. Swithun's Day (July 15) means another 40 days of wet weather. Nearby, at 8 College Street, is the house where Jane Austen died on July 18, 1817, three days after writing a comic poem about the legend of St. Swithun's Day (copies are usually available in the cathedral).

❹ **Winchester College,** one of England's oldest "public" (i.e., private) schools, was founded in 1382 by Bishop William of Wykeham, who has his own chapel in Winchester Cathedral. The school chapel is notable for its delicately vaulted ceiling. Among the original buildings still in use is Chamber Court, center of college life for six centuries. Notice the "scholars"—students holding academic scholarships—clad in their traditional gowns. ⊠ *College St.,* ☎ *01962/621209.* 🎫 *£1.50.* ☉ *Mon.–Sat. 10–1 and 2–5, Sun. 2–5; 1-hr tours Mon.–Sat. at 10, 11, noon, 2:15, 3:15, Sun. at 2:15 and 3:15, no tour at 10 Sept.–May.*

❺ The historic **Great Hall,** a few blocks west of the cathedral, is all that remains of the city's Norman castle. The English Parliament met here for the first time in 1246; Sir Walter Raleigh was tried for conspiracy against King James I and condemned to death here in 1603 (although he wasn't beheaded until 1618); and Dame Alice Lisle was sentenced here by the infamous Judge George Jeffreys to be burned at the stake for sheltering fugitives, following Monmouth's Rebellion in 1685. (King James II, in a rare act of mercy, commuted her sentence to beheading.) The floor of the Great Hall is dominated by a huge and gaudy sculpture of Victoria, carved by Sir Alfred Gilbert (responsible for *Eros* in Piccadilly Circus) to mark the Queen's Golden Jubilee in 1887, and deposited here for lack of anywhere else in town large enough to hold it. But the greatest relic hangs on the Hall's west wall, the object fondly known as King Arthur's Round Table, which has places for 24 knights and a portrait of Arthur bearing a remarkable resemblance to King Henry VIII. In fact, the table dates no further back than the 13th century and was repainted by order of Henry on the occasion of a visit by the Holy Roman Emperor Charles V; the real Arthur was probably a Celtic cavalry general who held off the invading Saxons following the fall of the Roman Empire in the 5th or 6th century AD. The Tudor monarchs revived the Arthurian legend for political purposes. Allow some time to view the adjoining exhibition on the history of the castle and Great Hall, and you can also take a brief wander in Queen Eleanor's Medieval Garden—a re-creation of a noblewoman's shady retreat. ⊠ *Castle Hill,* ☎ *01962/846476.* 🎫 *Free.* ☉ *Mar.–Oct., daily 10–5; Nov.–Feb., weekdays 10–5, weekends 10–4.*

❻ Across from the cathedral, the **City Museum** interprets Winchester's past through displays of Celtic pottery, Roman mosaics, Saxon coins, and reconstructed life-size Victorian shop fronts. ⊠ *The Square,* ☎ *01962/848269,* WEB *www.winchester.gov.uk/heritage.* 🎫 *Free.* ☉ *Apr.– Oct., Mon.–Sat. 10–5, Sun. noon–5; Nov.–Mar., Tues.–Sat. 10–4, Sun. noon–4.*

❼ The **City Mill** is a working 18th-century water mill, complete with small island garden. You'll find it at the east end of High Street; part of the premises is a National Trust gift shop open year-round, and part is used as a youth hostel. Call ahead for milling days. ⊠ *Bridge St.,* ☎ *01962/870057,* WEB *www.winchestercitymill.co.uk.* 🎫 *£2.* ☉ *Mar., weekends 11–4:30; Apr.–June and Sept.–Oct., Wed.–Sun. 11–4:30; July and Aug., daily 11–4.30.*

❽ To top off a tour of Winchester, you can climb **St. Giles's Hill** for a panoramic view of the city. A walk down High Street and Broadway will bring you to the hill.

Dining and Lodging

£–££   ✕ **Nine the Square.** This modern restaurant makes the most of its prime position opposite the cathedral. The menu, which the downstairs wine bar shares with the more sedate dining area upstairs, changes regularly, but may include roast Gressingham duck and other game in season; a selection of homemade pastas and vegetarian dishes is always available. ⊠ *9 Great Minster St., The Square,* ☎ *01962/864004. AE, DC, MC, V. Closed Sun.*

£ ✗ **The Royal Oak.** Try a half pint of draft bitters or dry cider at this traditional pub, which claims to have Britain's oldest bar (it has a Saxon wall). It also has two no-smoking bars—a British rarity—in the cellar and on the upper level. Bar meals are served daily until 9 PM. ⊠ *Royal Oak Passage, off High St.,* ☎ *01962/842701. MC, V.*

££–£££ ✗⊞ **Hotel du Vin.** Rooms in this elegant redbrick Georgian town house are richly furnished, with Oriental rugs enhancing the polished wooden floors. Egyptian cotton bed linens, huge baths, and power showers make for a luxurious stay. As you would expect from the name, you'll find a large and eclectic selection of wines in the stylish bistro, where you can sup on traditional fare such as calf's liver with bacon and braised lamb with swede mash. Call ahead to arrange a private wine-tasting session. In summer food is served in the walled garden. ⊠ *Southgate St., S023 9EF,* ☎ *01962/841414,* FAX *01962/842458,* WEB *www.hotelduvin.com. 23 rooms. Restaurant, bar, minibars. AE, DC, MC, V.*

££–£££ ✗⊞ **Winchester Royal.** Formerly a bishop's house and then a Benedictine convent, this classy hotel has an attractive walled garden and beautifully furnished bedrooms. It is within easy reach of the cathedral but lies on a quiet side street. Some rooms are in a recent extension, but the older rooms have more atmosphere. You can have an excellent lunch in the bar or a fuller, fixed-price meal in the conservatory restaurant. ⊠ *St. Peter St., S023 8BS,* ☎ *01962/840840,* FAX *01962/841582,* WEB *www. marstonhotels.com. 75 rooms. Restaurant, bar. AE, DC, MC, V.*

££ ✗⊞ **Wykeham Arms.** This old inn is centrally located, close to the cathedral and the college. The bars, warmed by log fires in winter, are happily cluttered with everything from old sports equipment to pewter mugs, and the handsomely furnished bedrooms (some in the modern annex) also reflect the proprietor's eclectic tastes. The restaurant, whose French and English dishes are set off by a good wine list, is very popular with locals, so call ahead. ⊠ *75 Kingsgate St., SO23 9PE,* ☎ *01962/ 853834,* FAX *01962/854411. 13 rooms. Restaurant, 2 bars, sauna. AE, DC, MC, V.*

££££ ⊞ **Lainston House.** Dating from 1668, this elegant country-house hotel is set in a 63-acre park, its discreet seclusion an obvious attraction for such eminent guests as Margaret Thatcher, who stayed here to write her memoirs. Inside, public rooms are adorned with cedar and oak paneling and other restored 17th-century features. All rooms are attractively furnished in a traditional style, but try for the ground-floor Garden or Chapel Suites, which have access to the gardens. Additional rooms, some with four-posters and whirlpool baths, are in a nicely converted stable wing. ⊠ *Sparsholt (off B3049, 2½ mi northwest of Winchester), SO21 2LT,* ☎ *01962/863588,* FAX *01962/776672,* WEB *www. exclusivehotels.co.uk. 41 rooms. Restaurant, putting green, tennis court, croquet, helipad. AE, DC, MC, V.*

Shopping

A complete list of local antiques stores is available from the **Winchester Tourist Information Centre** (⊠ The Guildhall, Broadway, ☎ 01962/ 840500). The **Antiques Market** (⊠ King's Walk, ☎ 01962/862277) sells crafts and gift items, as well as antiques. **P&G Wells** (⊠ 11 College St., ☎ 01962/852016), the oldest bookshop in town, stocks a range of new titles and also has a small selection of secondhand books in an annex in nearby Kingsgate Street.

New Alresford

➒ *8 mi northeast of Winchester, by A31 and B3046.*

New Alresford (pronounced *awls*-ford) has a pleasant village green crossed by a stream and some Georgian houses and antiques shops. The village is the starting point of the **Watercress Line,** a 10-mi railroad reserved for steam locomotives. The line (named for the watercress beds formerly in the area) takes you on a nostalgic tour through reminders of 19th-century England. ⊠ *Railway Station,* ☎ *01962/733810,* WEB *www. watercressline.co.uk.* 🖼 *£9.* ⊘ *Feb.–Oct., weekends and national holidays, with daily departures May–early Sept.; call for details.*

Chawton

⑩ *8 mi east of New Alresford.*

Jane Austen lived the last eight years of her life in the village of Chawton (she moved to Winchester only during her final illness), and the site now draws literary pilgrims. Here, in an unassuming redbrick house, Austen revised *Sense and Sensibility,* created *Pride and Prejudice,* and worked on *Emma, Persuasion,* and *Mansfield Park.* Now a museum,
★ the rooms of **Jane Austen's House** retain the atmosphere of restricted gentility suitable to the unmarried daughter of a clergyman. In the left-hand parlor, Jane would play her piano every morning, then repair to her mahogany writing desk in the family sitting room—leaving her sister Cassandra to do the household chores ("I find composition impossible with my head full of joints of mutton and doses of rhubarb," Jane wrote). In the 18th century, the house was much closer to a bustling thoroughfare, and one traveler reported that a window view proved that the Misses Austen were "looking very comfortable at breakfast." Jane was famous for working unperturbed through any and all interruptions, but one protection against the outside world was the famous door that creaked, whose hinges she asked might remain unattended to because they gave her warning that someone was coming. ⊠ *Signed off the A31/ A32 roundabout,* ☎ *01420/83262,* WEB *www.janeaustenmuseum.org.uk.* 🖼 *£3.* ⊘ *Mar.–Dec., daily 11–4:30; Jan.–Feb., weekends 11–4:30.*

Petersfield

⑪ *10 mi south of Chawton, along B3006 and A325.*

The Georgian market town of Petersfield is set in a wide valley between wooded hills and open downs. **Queen Elizabeth Country Park** has 1,400 acres of chalk hills and shady beeches with scenic hiking trails. You can climb to the top of Butser Hill (888 ft) to take in a splendid view of the coast. ⊠ *A3 (4 mi south of town),* ☎ *023/9259–5040.* 🖼 *Free; car park £1, £1.50 Sun..* ⊘ *Park open 24 hrs; visitor center (including café and shop) Apr.–Oct., daily 10–5:30; Nov.–March, weekends 10–dusk.*

Portsmouth

⑫ *15 mi south of Petersfield, 77 mi southwest of London.*

The city of Portsmouth has been England's naval capital and principal port of departure for centuries. Plenty of ferries still leave here for the Continent and the Isle of Wight. The harbor covers about 7 square mi, incorporating the world's first dry dock (built in 1495) and extensive defenses. The city is not particularly scenic but it possesses England's richest collection of maritime memorabilia, including the Royal Naval Museum and some well-preserved warships.

Portchester Castle, built as a Roman fort more than 1,600 years ago, contains the most complete set of Roman walls in northern Europe. In the 12th century a castle (now in ruins) was built inside the impressive fortifications. The keep's central tower affords a sweeping view of the harbor and coastline. ⊠ *Off A27, near Fareham,* ☎ *023/9237–8291,*

IN SEARCH OF JANE AUSTEN

A tour of "Jane Austen country" in the lovely South of England invariably leads to or enhances the experience of reading her novels, and today, thanks to the 1990s film adaptations of *Sense and Sensibility, Emma, Persuasion,* and *Pride and Prejudice,* the great author has captured a whole new audience eager to peer into the decorous 18th- and early 19th-century world of Austen's circle. By visiting one or two main locales—such as Chawton and Winchester—it is possible to imagine hearing the tinkle of teacups raised by the likes of Elinor Dashwood, Emma Woodhouse, and the bold and dashing Mr. Darcy. Serious Janeites will want to retrace the complete itinerary of her life—starting out in the hamlet of Steventon, southwest of Basingstoke, where she spent the first 25 years of her life, then moving on to Bath, Southampton, Chawton, and Winchester.

It is easy to see the self-contained world that is Jane Austen country—a pleasant landscape filled with intimately scaled villages, gently rolling downland, and tree-canopied paths—as a perfectly civilized stage on which her characters organized visits to stately homes, mid-afternoon strawberry parties, and husband-hunting expeditions. As Austen herself described this terrain in *Emma,* "It has a sweet view—sweet to the eye and the mind. English verdure, English culture, English comfort, seen under a sun bright, without being oppressive." Entering that world, you'll find its heart is not Bath, nor London, nor Winchester, but the tiny Hampshire village of Chawton. Here at a former bailiff's cottage on her brother's estate, Austen produced three of her greatest novels, writing at the minute, pedestaled table still standing in the dining parlor. Her 6-mi-a-day walks often took her to Chawton Manor—her brother's regal Jacobean mansion, now being transformed into a center for the study of women's literature—or to nearby Lyards Farm, where her favorite niece, Anna Lefroy (thought to be the model for Emma Woodhouse, with "a disposition to think a little too well of herself") came to live in 1815. She would use a little donkey cart, still at the cottage, to shop in nearby Alton. A bit farther away is Great Bookham—closely identified with the "Highbury" of *Emma,* and nearby lies Box Hill (to the east of A24 between Leatherhead and Dorking), the probable inspiration for the locale of the famous walking expedition that left Miss Woodhouse in tears.

Heading southwest from Chawton, take A31 for about 15 mi to Winchester, where you can visit Austen's austere grave within the city cathedral; then take in No. 8 College Street, where her losing battle with Addison's disease ended with her death on July 18, 1817. Heading 90 mi southwest, take A31 to Dorchester (where several scenes from the Gwyneth Paltrow version of *Emma* were filmed), then take A35 to Lyme Regis, the lovely 18th-century seaside resort where Austen spent the summers of 1804–05. Here, at the Cobb, the famous stone jetty that juts into Lyme Bay, Louisa Musgrove suffers her terrible accident when she jumps off the steps known as Granny's Teeth—a turning point in Chapter 12 of *Persuasion.* Northwest of Winchester by some 60 mi is Bath, the elegant setting that served as the backdrop for many of Austen's razor-sharp observations on the social order of the day. The city holds the Jane Austen Centre, which explores the relationship between Bath and the writer.

"It is the only place for happiness," Austen once said of the county of Kent, some 150 mi to the east of Chawton. "Everybody is rich there." Here, Godmersham Park, another of her brother's estates (located off the A28 between Canterbury and Ashford), offered her an escape to the countryside, where baronets lived "in unrepentant idleness." The magnificent redbrick mansion is privately owned, but you can take a nearby public footpath to pass the little Grecian Temple where she completed *Sense and Sensibility*; views of the Palladian house from this spot may have inspired her visions of Pemberley and Mansfield Park. No matter if you search for Jane Austen country in Hampshire or Kent, you can revisit it again and again in its home base: English literature.

WEB *www.english-heritage.org.uk.* ✉ *£2.70.* ⊙ *Apr.–Sept., daily 10– 6; Oct., daily 10–5; Nov.–Mar., daily 10–4.*

★ The city's most impressive attraction is the **Flagship Portsmouth,** which includes an unrivaled collection of historic ships and the comprehensive Royal Naval Museum. The youngest ship, HMS *Warrior 1860,* was England's first iron-clad battleship. Admiral Lord Horatio Nelson's flagship, **HMS** *Victory,* has been painstakingly restored to appear as she did at the battle at Trafalgar (1805). You can inspect the cramped gun decks, visit the cabin where Nelson entertained his officers, and stand on the spot where he was mortally wounded by a French sniper. The *Mary Rose,* former flagship of the Tudor navy, which capsized and sank in the harbor in 1545, was raised in 1982 in a much-publicized exercise in marine archaeology. Described at the time as "the flower of all the ships that ever sailed," the *Mary Rose* is now housed in a specially constructed enclosure, where her timbers are continuously sprayed with water to prevent them from drying out and breaking up. Exhibits in the intriguing *Mary Rose* Museum hold artifacts from the ship. The **Royal Naval Museum** has a fine collection of painted figureheads, exhibits about Nelson and the battle of Trafalgar, and galleries of paintings and mementos recalling different periods of naval history from King Alfred to the present. **Action Stations** gives you insight into the modern navy through a swashbuckling movie and tests your sea legs with interactive tasks such as piloting boats through gales. ✉ *Historic Dockyard, Portsmouth Naval Base,* ☎ *023/9286–1512,* WEB *www.flagship.org.uk.* ✉ *All-inclusive tickets £12.50; Mary Rose £6; HMS Victory £6.50, which includes Royal Naval Museum; Royal Naval Museum only, £3.50.* ⊙ *Mar.–Oct., daily 10–6 (last admission 4:30); Nov.–Feb., daily 10–5 (last admission 4).*

In the popular **D-Day Museum,** in nearby Southsea, exhibits vividly reconstruct the many stages of planning and the communications and logistics involved in the D-Day landings, as well as the actual invasion on June 6, 1944. The centerpiece of the museum is the Overlord Embroidery ("Overlord" was the code name for the invasion), a 272-ft tapestry with 34 panels illustrating the history of World War II, from the Battle of Britain in 1940 to D-Day and the first days of the liberation. ✉ *Clarence Esplanade, Southsea,* ☎ *023/9282–7261.* ✉ *£4.75.* ⊙ *Apr.–Oct., daily 10–5 (last admission 4:30).*

Dining and Lodging

£££–££££ ✗ **Bistro Montparnasse.** Modern paintings on terra-cotta walls lend a contemporary atmosphere to this bustling restaurant. Among the dishes on the fixed-price menu are pan-fried sea bass, salmon and king prawns with a vermouth and saffron sauce, and such delicious desserts as a hot chocolate and brandy pudding. ✉ *103 Palmerston Rd., Southsea,* ☎ *023/9281–6754. MC, V. Closed Sun.–Mon.*

£–££ ⚏ **Westfield Hall.** Portsmouth is well supplied with chain offerings, but
★ here's a pleasant smaller establishment with personal service and character. Located close to the water in the resort of Southsea, Westfield Hall occupies two converted early 20th-century houses, one of them set aside for nonsmokers. Rooms (seven of which are on the ground floor) have large bay windows, and all have satellite TV. Dinner is available. ✉ *65 Festing Rd. (off Eastern Parade), PO4 0NQ,* ☎ *023/9282– 6971,* FAX *023/9287–0200. 27 rooms. Dining room. AE, DC, MC, V.*

Southampton

❶ *21 mi northwest of Portsmouth, 25 mi southwest of Salisbury, 79 mi southwest of London.*

Seafaring Saxons and Romans used Southampton's harbor, Southampton Water, as a commercial trading port for centuries, and the city thrived, becoming one of England's wealthiest. But Plymouth eventually supplanted it, and Southampton has been going downhill ever since. Still, as the home port of Henry V's fleet bound for Agincourt, the *Mayflower,* the *Queen Mary,* and the ill-fated *Titanic,* along with countless other great ocean liners of the 20th century, Southampton has one of the richest maritime traditions in England. Much of the city center is shoddy, having been hastily rebuilt after World War II. But bits and pieces of the city's history—spared from Nazi bombs—occasionally peek out from between modern buildings. Fortunately, the Old Town still retains its medieval air, and considerable parts of Southampton's castellated walls remain. Other attractions in town include a good art gallery, extensive parks, and a couple of superb museums.

Incorporated in the town walls are a variety of old buildings, including **God's House Tower,** originally a gunpowder factory and now a good regional archaeology museum. ⊠ *Winkle St.,* ☎ *023/8063–5904.* 🎫 *Free.* ☉ *Tues.–Fri. 10–noon and 1–5, Sat. 10–noon and 1–4, Sun. 2–5.*

Mayflower Park and the Pilgrim Fathers' Memorial on Western Esplanade commemorate the sailing of the *Mayflower* from Southampton to the New World on August 15, 1620. (The ship was forced to stop in Plymouth for repairs.) John Alden, the hero of Longfellow's poem *The Courtship of Miles Standish,* was a native of Southampton.

The **Southampton Maritime Museum** brings together models, mementos, and items of furniture from the age of the great clippers and cruise ships, including a wealth of memorabilia relating to the *Titanic*—footage, photos, crew lists, etc. Boat buffs will relish plenty of other vital statistics dealing with the history of commercial shipping. ⊠ *Bugle St.,* ☎ *023/8022–3941.* 🎫 *Free.* ☉ *Tues.–Fri. 10–noon and 1–5, Sat. 10–noon and 1–4, Sun. 2–5.*

One of the largest Tudor constructions still standing in Southampton is the **Tudor House Museum,** a 15th-century customs-controller's house. The Great Hall is the most impressive of the creaky-floored rooms, with a gallery and grand fireplace. Other rooms contain a miscellany of items from the city's past, and there is a re-created Victorian kitchen and Tudor garden. ⊠ *St. Michael's Sq.,* ☎ *023/8033–2513.* 🎫 *Free.* ☉ *Tues.–Fri. 10–noon and 1–5, Sat. 10–noon and 1–4, Sun. 2–5.*

Dining and Lodging

£–££ ✕ **La Brasserie.** This is a busy spot at lunchtime, popular with the business community, although it quiets down in the evening. The decor is straightforward and ungimmicky, and the atmosphere is as traditionally French as the menu. ⊠ *33–34 Oxford St.,* ☎ *023/8063–5043. AE, DC, MC, V. Closed Sun. No lunch Sat.*

£–££ ✕ **Langley's.** Mirrors and posters from the days of Southampton's steamship era adorn the walls of this busy bistro in a good central location near the docks. Ceiling fans keep things cool in summer, while such dishes as Breton fish soup and baked chicken breast with Parma ham and mozzarella show European influences alongside more native fare. ⊠ *10–11 Bedford Pl.,* ☎ *023/8022–4551. AE, MC, V. Closed Sun. No lunch Sat.*

££ 🏠 **Dolphin Hotel.** Originally a Georgian coaching inn—although there's been an inn of some sort on this site for seven centuries—the Dolphin has seen past visitors such as Queen Victoria, Lord Nelson, and Jane Austen. It offers stylish accommodations in the form of cozily old-fashioned rooms. The lounge is wood-paneled, and the Thackeray Restaurant and Nelson Bar offer good meals and bar snacks, respectively. ⊠ *35 High St., SO14 2HN,* ☎ *023/8033–9955,* FAX *023/8033–3650,* WEB *www.corushotels.com. 73 rooms. Restaurant, bar, lounge. AE, DC, MC, V.*

Nightlife and the Arts

The refurbished **Mayflower Theatre** (⊠ Commercial Rd., ☎ 023/8071–1811) is among the larger theaters outside London, and everyone from the Royal Shakespeare Company to Black Sabbath and Sting have packed the house. The **Nuffield Theatre** (☎ 023/8067–1771), on the Southampton University campus, has its own repertory company and also hosts national touring groups, which perform some pre–West End productions.

Romsey

⑭   *10 mi northwest of Southampton.*

This small town on the River Test has an authentic Norman abbey church and, in the marketplace, an iron bracket said to have been used to hang two of Cromwell's soldiers. The flint and stone house nearby, known as King John's Hunting Box, dates from the 13th century. Florence Nightingale lies under a simple stone in East Wellow churchyard in Romsey, near her former house at Embley Park.

Broadlands, outside Romsey, was the home of the late Lord Mountbatten (1900–79), uncle of Queen Elizabeth II, and is undoubtedly the grandest house in Hampshire. The 18th-century Palladian mansion, with gardens laid out by Capability Brown and wide lawns sweeping down to the banks of the River Test, abounds with ornate plaster moldings and paintings of British and Continental royalty. Personal mementos trace Lord Mountbatten's distinguished career in the navy and in India. In 1947 the Queen and the Duke of Edinburgh spent their honeymoon here, and the Prince and Princess of Wales spent a few days here after their wedding in 1981. ⊠ *Off A3057,* ☎ *01794/505010,* WEB *www.broadlands.net.* 🖾 *£5.95.* ☉ *Mid-June–early Sept., daily noon–5:30; last admission at 4.*

Dining and Lodging

£££   ✗ **Old Manor House.** This is one of those restaurants that is inseparable from its owner-chef, in this case Mauro Bregoli. The decor is typical of the area, with oak beams and huge fireplaces, and the Italian-influenced food is rich and flavorsome. Specialties include quenelle of pike, duck breast with apples, hare, suckling pig, and venison. The wine list is exceptionally good. There is a worthwhile fixed-price menu at lunch. ⊠ *21 Palmerston St.,* ☎ *01794/517353. AE, DC, MC, V. Closed Mon. No dinner Sun.*

£££   ⊡ **Potters Heron Hotel.** An ideal place to stay if you're visiting Broad-
★   lands, this hotel has a modern addition besides the original thatched building. Choose an old or new room to suit your taste; many have balconies. Dine in the oak-beamed Potters Pub or the Garden restaurant. ⊠ *Ampfield SO51 9ZF (3 mi east of Romsey),* ☎ *023/8026–6611,* FAX *023/8025–1359,* WEB *www.corushotels.com. 54 rooms. Restaurant, pub, sauna. AE, DC, MC, V.*

Outdoor Activities and Sports

The hilly parkland cradling the par 69, 5,767-yard golf course of the **Dunwood Manor Country Club** (⊠ Danes Rd., Awbridge, near Romsey, ☎ 01794/340549) includes five ponds.

ISLE OF WIGHT

The Isle of Wight (pronounced white) has a very special atmosphere, quite distinct from that of the mainland: it is essentially Victorian. Although the island was known to the Romans and the ill-fated Stuarts, it was Queen Victoria who put it on the map by choosing it for the site of Osborne House. She lived here as much as she could, and ultimately she died here. Clearly she must have created a great vogue, because most of the domestic architecture is Victorian. The islanders are fiercely chauvinistic; like Tennyson, once an inhabitant of the island until he was driven away by tourist harassment, they are somewhat resentful of vacationers. But every season the day-trippers arrive—thanks to the ferries, hovercraft, and hydrofoils that connect the Isle of Wight with Southampton, Portsmouth, Southsea, and Lymington. People are drawn to this 23-mi-long island by its holiday resorts—Ryde, Bembridge, Ventnor, Freshwater (stay away from tacky Sandown and Shanklin)—its rich vegetation, narrow lanes, thatched cottages, curving bays, sandy beaches, walking paths, and fabulous ocean air, which, to quote Tennyson, is "worth six pence a pint." All is not sea and sails. There is splendid motoring to be done in the interior of the island in such places as Brading Down, Ashley Down, and Mersely Down and the occasional country house to visit, none more spectacular than Queen Vicky's own Osborne House.

Cowes

⑮ *11 mi northwest of Ryde.*

If you embark from Southampton, your ferry will cross the Solent channel and dock at Cowes (pronounced cows), a magic name in the sailing world and internationally known for the "Cowes Week" annual yachting festival, held in July or August. Fifty years ago, the Cowes Regatta was a supreme event, attended by Imperial Majesties and Serene Highnesses from all over the world; the fantastically green lawns of the Royal Yacht Squadron were crowded with the world's most famous figures. Although elegance is a thing of the past, the Cowes Regatta is still an important event in yachting circles and is occasionally attended by that venerable royal seaman, the Duke of Edinburgh. At the north end of High Street, on the Parade, a tablet commemorates the 1633 sailing from Cowes of two ships carrying the first English settlers of the state of Maryland.

Queen Victoria built **Osborne House,** which was designed by Prince Albert after a villa in the stodgiest Italian Renaissance style. For anyone drawn to the domestic side of history, Osborne is enormously interesting. The queen spent much of her time here in seclusion after Albert's death in 1861, mourning her loss. Here one sees the engineer manqué in Prince Albert and his clever innovations—even central heating—and evidence of Victoria's desperate attempts to give her children a normal but disciplined upbringing. A carriage ride will take you to the Swiss Cottage, a superior version of a playhouse, especially built for the children. The state rooms, perfect for antiques lovers, have scarcely been altered since her death here in 1901. The house and grounds were used as a location for the 1998 movie *Mrs. Brown,* with Dame Judi Dench and Billy Connolly. ⊠ *Off A3021, 1 mi southeast of Cowes,* ☎ *01983/200022,* WEB *www.english-heritage.org.uk.* ⌨ *House and grounds £7.20, grounds only £3.80.* ☉ *Apr.–Oct., daily 10–5 (last admission to house at 4); phone for prebooked guided tours in winter.*

Lodging

££–£££   🏨 **New Holmwood Hotel.** This Best Western hotel occupies an unrivaled location above the Esplanade—ideal for watching yachters in the Solent. The three lounges include one allowing an open fire on winter evenings and one for nonsmokers. The sheltered sun terrace and pool take full advantage of fine weather. Book well in advance in summer, as the hotel fills up quickly. ✉ *Queens Rd., Egypt Point, PO31 8BW,* ☎ *01983/292508,* FAX *01983/295020,* WEB *www.newholmwoodhotel. co.uk. 26 rooms. Restaurant, bar, lounge, pool, meeting room. AE, DC, MC, V.*

Ryde

⑯   *11 mi southeast of Cowes.*

The town of Ryde has long been one of the Isle of Wight's most popular summer resorts, with a variety of family attractions. Following the construction of Ryde Pier in 1814, elegant (and occasionally ostentatious) town houses sprang up along the seafront and on the slopes behind, commanding fine views of the harbor. In addition to its long, sandy beach, Ryde has a large boating lake (rowboats and pedal boats can be rented) and children's playgrounds. To get here from Cowes, leave on A3021, then follow the signs on A3054.

Many of the birds will eat from your hand at **Flamingo Park,** a waterfowl reserve 2½ mi east of Ryde. Penguins, macaws, and cockatoos are also kept here, and feeding times are accompanied by informative talks. ✉ *Springvale, Seaview,* ☎ *01983/612153.* 🎫 *£5.25.* ☉ *Apr.–Sept., daily 10–5 (last admission 4); Oct., daily 10:30–4 (last admission 3:15).*

Dining and Lodging

££–£££   ✕🏨 **Seaview Hotel.** Set in the heart of a harbor village just outside Ryde, this smart hotel has a strong maritime flavor and comfortable, well-equipped bedrooms. The main attractions, however, are the restaurants (smoking and no-smoking), which specialize in fresh island produce. Try the hot crab ramekin (baked with cream and tarragon with a cheese topping) to start, and lobster, sea bass, or crab for a main course. This is the spot to try grilled plaice, a British flat fish with tender white flesh. The desserts are a revelation: Floating Islands (poached meringues) are a must. For an extra fee, guests have access to the nearby Isle of Wight Sports Club. ✉ *High St., Seaview PO34 5EX,* ☎ *01983/612711,* FAX *01983/613729,* WEB *www.seaviewhotel. co.uk. 16 rooms. 2 restaurants, 2 bars. AE, DC, MC, V.*

££–£££   🏨 **Biskra Beach Hotel.** Its location off the Esplanade means that this spacious Victorian hotel has a low noise level. A beach theme prevails throughout; natural colors and stylish rattan and wooden furniture give the hotel a colonial flavor. There are excellent views over the Solent from the upper bedrooms as well as from the garden terrace. ✉ *17 St. Thomas St., PO33 2DL,* ☎ *01983/567913,* FAX *01983/616976. 14 rooms. Restaurant, bar. AE, DC, MC, V.*

££   🏨 **Priory Bay Hotel.** This hotel, whose origins date back to medieval times, has been sympathetically developed in country house style. Lawns and woodlands on the 70-acre estate, as well as a private beach, help make for a pampered sojourn. Public rooms are furnished with antiques, and guest rooms are light and airy. ✉ *Priory Dr., Seaview PO34 5BU,* ☎ *01983/613146,* FAX *01983/616539,* WEB *www.priorybay.co.uk. 16 rooms, 9 suites. Restaurant, bar, pool, 9-hole golf course, tennis court, beach. AE, DC, MC, V.*

Brading

17 *3 mi south of Ryde on A3055.*

In Brading, St. Mary's Church, dating from Norman times, holds monuments to the local Olgander family. Next to the Old Town Hall stands the 16th-century rectory, said to be the oldest inhabited dwelling on the island; it now holds a wax museum.

The remains of the substantial 3rd-century **Brading Roman Villa,** a mile south of Brading, retain splendid mosaic floors and a well-preserved heating system. ✉ *Off A3055,* ☎ *01983/406223,* WEB *www.brading.co.uk.* 🖾 *£3.* ⊙ *Apr.–Oct., daily 9:30–5 (last admission 4:30).*

Arreton

18 *5 mi west of Brading, 6 mi southwest of Ryde.*

Arreton Village Old Barns, a group of restored farm buildings in the medieval village of Arreton, were once part of the local manor. A crafts shop sells items in wood, wool, clay, metal, and other materials, made elsewhere on the island. There are lavender gardens as well as a bistro and bar with regular live music. ☎ *01983/528353.* 🖾 *Free.* ⊙ *Crafts shop Apr.–Oct., daily 10–5; Nov.–Mar., daily 11–5.*

Ventnor

19 *7 mi southeast of Arreton, 11 mi south of Ryde.*

The south coast resorts are the sunniest and most sheltered on the Isle of Wight. Ventnor itself rises from such a steep slope that the ground floors of some of its houses are level with the roofs of those across the road. The **Ventnor Botanic Gardens,** laid out over 22 acres, contain more than 3,500 species of trees, plants, and shrubs; there's also an excellent restaurant, the Garden. ✉ *Undercliff Dr.,* ☎ *01983/855397,* WEB *www.botanic.co.uk.* 🖾 *Free.* ⊙ *Daily 10–5.*

Outdoor Activities and Sports

James Braid, who designed the famous Gleneagles golf course in Scotland, helped create the challenging par 70, 5,804-yard, heathland **Shanklin and Sandown** (✉ The Fairway, Sandown, ☎ 01983/403170) golf course.

En Route Taking the coast road from Ventnor to the Needles, you will come across the fantasy theme park **Blackgang Chine,** built in a deep chine (cleft in the cliffs) overlooking a former smugglers' landing place. There's a film about the history of the area, as well as Dinosaurland, Smugglersland, Cowboytown, Water Force (a large water slide), and other attractions for ages 3–12. You can spend a couple of hours here. ✉ *A3055, Ventnor,* ☎ *01983/730330,* WEB *www.blackgangchine.com.* 🖾 *£5.95.* ⊙ *Late Mar.–early June and mid-Sept.–Oct., daily 10–5:30; early June–mid-Sept., daily 10–10.*

Alum Bay and the Needles

20 *19 mi northwest of Ventnor, 18 mi southwest of Cowes.*

At the western tip of the Isle of Wight is the island's most famous natural landmark, the **Needles,** a long line of jagged chalk stacks jutting out of the sea like monstrous teeth, with a lighthouse at the end. It's part of the Needles Pleasure Park, which has various attractions, mostly for kids. Adjacent is **Alum Bay,** which you can access from the Needles by chairlift. Here you can catch a good view of the multicolor sand in the cliff strata or take a boat to view the lighthouse.

At **Alum Bay Glass** you can buy souvenirs or just watch the glassblowing and jewelry crafting. There are regular tours, talks, and demonstrations in summer. ☎ *01983/753473.* 🏷 *80p.* ⊙ *Daily 10–4.*

Dimbola Lodge is the former home of Julia Margaret Cameron (1815–79), the eminent Victorian portrait photographer and friend of Lord Tennyson. The building houses a gallery including more than 60 examples of her work, as well as a bookshop and café. ⊠ *Terrace La., Freshwater Bay,* ☎ *01983/756814.* 🏷 *Gallery £2.50.* ⊙ *Tues.–Sun. and national holidays 10–5.*

Lodging

£££   🏨 **Farringford Hotel.** Once the splendid home of the Victorian poet laureate Alfred, Lord Tennyson, this is now an unpretentious hotel. The 18th-century house is set on 33 acres of grounds; outbuildings contain 28 suites and cottages with kitchens, as well as standard bedrooms. ⊠ *Bedbury La., Freshwater PO40 9PE, near Alum Bay,* ☎ *01983/ 752500,* FAX *01983/756515,* WEB *www.farringford.co.uk. 15 rooms, 23 suites, 5 apartments, 4 cottage rooms. Restaurant, pool, 9-hole golf course, tennis court, croquet. AE, DC, MC, V.*

Outdoor Activities and Sports

Overlooking the bay, the par 68/69, 5,725-yard **Freshwater Bay Golf Club** (⊠ Southdown Rd., Freshwater Bay, ☎ 01983/752955) is on land owned by the National Trust.

Carisbrooke Castle

★ ㉑   *14 mi east of Alum Bay, 1¼ mi southwest of Newport, 5 mi south of Cowes.*

Standing above the village of Carisbrooke, this castle built by the Normans but enlarged in Elizabethan times had its moment of historical glory when King Charles I was imprisoned here during the English Civil War. Note the small window in the north curtain wall through which he tried unsuccessfully to escape. A museum holds items from his incarceration. You can stroll along the battlements to watch the donkey wheel, where a team of donkeys draws water from a deep well. The castle is a short distance outside the Isle of Wight's modern-day capital, Newport. ⊠ *Off B3401,* ☎ *01983/522107,* WEB *www.english-heritage.org.uk.* 🏷 *£4.50.* ⊙ *Apr.–Sept., daily 10–6; Oct., daily 10–5; Nov.– Mar., daily 10–4.*

SALISBURY, STONEHENGE, AND THE NEW FOREST

This roster of famous sights kicks off in the attractive city of Salisbury, renowned for its glorious cathedral, then loops west around Salisbury Plain, up to Avebury, and back to Stonehenge. From Stonehenge you can dip south into Hampshire, to the wild, scenic expanse of the New Forest, ancient hunting preserve of William the Conqueror. Your own transportation is essential to see anything beyond Salisbury.

Salisbury

25 mi northwest of Southampton, 55 mi southeast of Bristol, 90 mi southwest of London.

Although Salisbury is a historic city, and its old stone shops and houses grew up in the shadow of the great church, the city did not become important until the 13th century, when the seat of the diocese was transferred here from Old Sarum, the original settlement 2 mi to the north,

High Street
Gate **24**

Long
Bridge **28**

Market
Square **26**

Mompesson
House **23**

Old Mill **29**

Poultry
Cross **25**

St. Thomas's
Church **27**

Salisbury
Cathedral . . . **22**

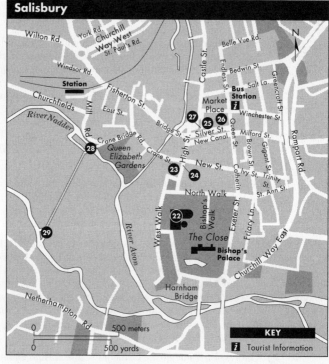

Salisbury

(Map labels: Wilton Rd., York Rd., Churchill Way West, St. Paul's Rd., Windsor Rd., Station, Fisherton St., Churchfields, River Nadder, East St., Mill Rd., Crane Bridge Rd., Bridge St., High St., Crane St., Queen Elizabeth Gardens, Castle St., Endless St., Bedwin St., Belle Vue Rd., Salt La., Greencroft St., Market Place, Bus Station, Winchester St., Silver St., New Canal, Queen St., Milford St., Brown St., Gigant St., Rampart Rd., New St., Catherine St., Ivy St., Trinity St., St. Ann St., Exeter St., Friary Ln., Churchill Way East, North Walk, West Walk, River Avon, Bishop's Walk, The Close, Bishop's Palace, Harnham Bridge, Netherhampton Rd.)

0 — 500 meters
0 — 500 yards

KEY
🛈 Tourist Information

of which only ruins remain today. In the 19th century, novelist Anthony Trollope based his tales of ecclesiastical life, notably *Barchester Towers,* on life here, although his fictional city of Barchester is really an amalgam of Salisbury and Winchester. Today, the city remains reasonably scaled, dotted with places of historic interest. The local tourist office organizes walks—of differing lengths for varying staminas—to lead you to the treasures.

★ ㉒ Salisbury continues to be dominated by the towering **Salisbury Cathedral,** a soaring hymn in stone. It is unique among cathedrals in that it was conceived and built as a whole, in the amazingly short span of only 38 years (1220–58). The spire, added in 1320, is the tallest in England and a miraculous feat of medieval engineering—even though the point, 404 ft above the ground, is 2½ ft off vertical. For a fictional, keenly imaginative reconstruction of the drama underlying such an achievement, read William Golding's novel *The Spire.* Anyone with a taste for the technical achievement of the Middle Ages will be fascinated by the excellent model of the cathedral in the north transept, the "arm" of the church to your left as you look at the altar. It shows the building about 20 years into construction, and makes very clear the ambition of Salisbury's medieval builders. For all their sophistication, the height and immense weight of their great spire have always posed structural problems. In the late 17th century Sir Christopher Wren was summoned from London to strengthen the spire, and in the mid-19th century Sir George Gilbert Scott, a leading Victorian Gothicist, undertook a major program of restoration on it. At the same time he began a clearing out of the interior, in the process getting rid of some less-than-sympathetic 18th-century alterations. For all that, the interior still seems spartan and a little gloomy, but check out the remarkable lancet windows and sculpted tombs of crusaders and other medieval heroes. The clock in the north aisle—probably the oldest working mechanism in Europe, if not the world—was made in 1386. You can join a free 45-minute tour of the church leaving two or more times a day, and there are also tours to the roof and spire at least once a day. The spacious **cloisters** are the largest in England, and the octagonal **Chapter House** contains a marvelous 13th-century frieze showing scenes from the Old Testament. In the chapter house you can also see one of the four original copies of the **Magna Carta,** the charter of rights the English barons forced King John to accept in 1215; it was sent here for safekeeping in the 13th century. ⊠ *Cathedral Close,* ☎ *01722/555120,* WEB *www.salisburycathedral.org.uk.* 🎟 *Cathedral £3.50 donation, roof tour £3, Chapter House free.* ☉ *Cathedral June–Aug., daily 7:15 AM–8:15 PM; Sept.–May, daily 7–6:15. Chapter House June–Aug., daily 9:30–7:45; Sept.–May, daily 9:30–5:30.*

Salisbury's **Cathedral Close** forms probably the finest backdrop of any British cathedral, with its smooth lawns and splendid examples of architecture of all ages (except modern) creating a harmonious background. Some of the historic houses are open to the public.

㉓ **Mompesson House,** on the north side of Cathedral Close, dates from 1701 and can justifiably be called one of the most appealing Queen Anne houses in Britain. There are no treasures per se, but some fine original paneling and plasterwork, as well as a fascinating collection of 18th-century drinking glasses, and an attractive walled garden where tea and refreshments are served. ⊠ *The Close,* ☎ *01722/ 335659,* WEB *www.nationaltrust.org.uk.* 🎟 *£3.90.* ☉ *Apr.–Oct., Sat.– Wed. noon–5:30 (last admission at 5).*

㉔ On the north side of the Cathedral Close is **High Street Gate,** one of the four castellated stone gateways built to separate the close from the rest of the city. Passing through it, you enter into the heart of the modern town. One of Salisbury's best-known landmarks, the hexagonal
㉕ **Poultry Cross** (⊠ Silver St.), is the last remaining of the four original
㉖ market crosses, and dealers still set up their stalls beside it. **Market Square** is site of one of southern England's most popular markets, held on Tuesday and Saturday. Permission to hold an annual fair here was granted in 1221, and that right is still exercised for three days every October. A narrow side street links Poultry Cross to Market Square.

㉗ **St. Thomas's Church** contains a rare medieval doom painting. One of the few left in the country, this depiction of Judgment Day is the best preserved and most complete. Created around 1470 and covering the whole of the chancel arch, it would have served to instill the fear of hell and damnation into the congregation. It's best seen on a spring or summer evening when the light through the west window illuminates the details. ⊠ *Silver St.,* ☎ *01722/322537.* 🎟 *Free.* ☉ *Apr.–Oct., Mon.–Sat. 9:30– 6, Sun. noon–6; Nov.–Mar., Mon.–Sat. 9:30–3:30, Sun. noon–6.*

㉘ For a classic view of Salisbury, head to the **Long Bridge** and the town path. From High Street walk west to Mill Road, which leads you across Queen Elizabeth Gardens. Cross the bridge and continue on the town path; along here you can locate the very spot that John Constable set down his easel to create that 19th-century icon *Salisbury Cathedral,* now hung in the Constable Room of London's National Gallery. Reached via a 20-minute walk southwest of the town center along the town path,
㉙ the **Old Mill** (⊠ Town Path, West Harnham), dating from the 12th century, makes a pleasant destination. It is now a restaurant and coffee shop under the same management as the Old Mill Hotel next door.

Massive earthwork ramparts in a bare sweep of Wiltshire countryside are all that remain of the impressive Iron Age hill fort of **Old Sarum,** which was successively taken over by Romans, Saxons, and Normans.

The site was still fortified in Tudor times, though the population had mostly decamped in the 13th century for the more amenable site of New Sarum, or Salisbury. You can clamber over the huge banks and ditches and take in the bracing views over the chalk downland. ⊠ *Off A345 (2 mi north of Salisbury),* ☎ *01722/335398,* WEB *www.english-heritage. org.uk.* ⊡ *£2.* ☉ *Apr.–June and Sept., daily 10–6; July–Aug., daily 9– 6; Oct., daily 10–5; Nov.–Mar., daily 10–4.*

Dining and Lodging

££–£££   ✕ **LXIX.** A stone's throw from the cathedral, this small restaurant is a much-needed addition to the city's restaurant scene. Its cool, modern, elegant style does not compromise its convivial, relaxed atmosphere. Dishes such as smoked river eel and calves' liver with sage butter are presented with care and with an eye to design. ⊠ *69 New St.,* ☎ *01722/ 340000. AE, DC, MC, V. Closed Sun. and last wk in Dec., first wk in Jan. No lunch Sat.*

£–££   ✕ **Harper's.** This is a popular second-floor restaurant overlooking Market Place. The cuisine mingles English and French dishes, and specialties include fillet of salmon and New Forest venison. There are good-value early bird lunches and dinners. ⊠ *7 Ox Row,* ☎ *01722/333118. AE, DC, MC, V. No dinner Sun. and no lunch Sun. Oct.–May.*

£–££   ✕ **Haunch of Venison.** Opposite the Poultry Cross, this place has been going strong for more than six centuries, and it brims with period details, such as the mummified arm of an 18th-century card player still clutching his cards that was found in 1903 by workmen. The wood-paneled restaurant has an open fire and antique, leather-covered settees; Angus steaks and venison are typical main courses. A noisy but comfortable bar, with timbered walls and black-and-white tile floors, offers simpler fare. You can choose among more than 100 malt whiskeys. ⊠ *1 Minster St.,* ☎ *01722/322024. AE, MC, V. No dinner Sun. in winter, usually Oct.–Easter.*

£££   ✕⊡ **Grasmere House.** A large late-Victorian edifice (1896), this red-brick lodging has fine views over the river to the cathedral. The 1½ acres of garden include a ha-ha (ask at reception), and the comfortable bedrooms are named after local worthies (a saint, a canon, and so on); 16 are in an extension. The restaurant, in a conservatory, provides peaceful country views. Fresh local ingredients and dishes such as roast lamb with an herb crust are on the menu. ⊠ *70 Harnham Rd., SP2 8JN,* ☎ *01722/338388,* FAX *01722/333710,* WEB *www.grasmerehotel.com. 20 rooms. Restaurant, bar. AE, DC, MC, V.*

£££   ✕⊡ **Howard's House.** If you're after complete tranquillity, head for this early 17th-century dower house 10 mi from Salisbury, set on 2 acres of grounds. French windows lead from the tidy lawns into the restaurant, which serves sophisticated contemporary fare and features home-grown produce. You'll also find a soothing atmosphere in the bedrooms, which are decorated in subtle colors. ⊠ *Teffont Evias, Salisbury, SP3 5RJ,* ☎ *01722/716392,* FAX *01722/716820,* WEB *www.howardshousehotel.com. 9 rooms. Restaurant. AE, DC, MC, V.*

£££   ✕⊡ **Red Lion Hotel.** A former coaching inn—parts of the building date from 1220—this hotel is now in the Best Western consortium. It's packed with old clocks and other relics from its long past, and has a choice of comfortable rooms in either modern or antique style. The restaurant (reservations essential) serves mainly modern British fare including pan-fried lamb with roasted fig and Angus beef fillet on a toasted crouton. The Red Lion is centrally located and an ideal base for exploring the city on foot. ⊠ *Milford St., SP1 2AN,* ☎ *01722/323334,* FAX *01722/325756,* WEB *www.the-redlion.co.uk. 53 rooms. Restaurant. AE, DC, MC, V.*

£–££   🖫 **Cricket Field House Hotel.** As the name suggests this modernized game-keeper's cottage overlooks a cricket ground, allowing you to puzzle over the intricacies of the game at leisure. Some rooms are in the main house and others in the pavilion annex, but all are comfortable and individually furnished. It's on the main A36 road, a couple of miles west of Salisbury's center. ✉ *Wilton Rd., SP2 7NS,* ☎ FAX *01722/322595,* WEB *www.cricketfieldhousehotel.com. 14 rooms. MC, V.*

Nightlife and the Arts

The **Salisbury Festival** (☎ 01722/323888, WEB www.salisburyfestival.co.uk), held in May and June, has excellent classical concerts, recitals, plays, and outdoor events.

The **Salisbury Playhouse** (✉ Malthouse La., ☎ 01722/320333) presents high-caliber drama all year and is the main venue for the Salisbury Festival.

Outdoor Activities and Sports

Hayball's Cycle Shop (✉ 26–30 Winchester St., ☎ 01722/411378) rents a variety of bikes for about £9 per day or £45 per week, £25 cash deposit.

Shopping

Trevan's Old Books (✉ 30 Catherine St., ☎ 01722/325818) stocks a wide range of tax-free secondhand books, including some rare first editions. **Watsons** (✉ 8–9 Queen St., ☎ 01722/320311) is worth visiting for its buildings dating from 1306 and 1425, with their original windows, a carved oak mantelpiece, and other period features. The company specializes in Aynsley and Wedgwood bone china, Waterford and Dartington glass, Royal Doulton, and a wide range of fine ornaments.

Wilton House

★ ㉚ *4 mi west of Salisbury.*

Five rivers—the Avon, the Bourne, the Nadder, the Wylye, and the Ebble—wind slowly from Salisbury into the rich heart of Wiltshire. Following the valley of the Nadder will lead you to the ancient town of Wilton, from which the county takes its name. A traditional market is held here every Thursday, but the main attraction is Wilton House and Gardens, home of the 17th earl of Pembroke. The original Tudor house burned down in 1647; the present mansion replacing it was designed by Inigo Jones, Ben Jonson's stage designer and the architect of London's Banqueting House. In fine weather, the lordly expanse of sweeping lawns that surrounds the house, bisected by the River Avon and dotted with towering oaks and a gracious Palladian bridge, is a quintessential English scene. The house contains one of the most extravagantly beautiful rooms in the history of interior decoration, the aptly named Double Cube Room. The name refers to its simple proportions, evidence of Jones's classically inspired belief that beauty in architecture derives from the harmony and balance. The room's headliner is the spectacular, Cinerama-size Van Dyck portrait of the Pembroke family. Adorned with gilded William Kent furniture, the Double Cube was where Eisenhower prepared some of his plans for the Normandy invasion; it has been used in numerous period films, including *Lady Caroline Lamb* and Emma Thompson's adaptation of *Sense and Sensibility.* Other delights include superb old master paintings, an exhibition of 7,000 toy soldiers, the "Wareham Bears" (200 dressed teddy bears), and, on a higher note, some great old master paintings. ✉ *Off A30,* ☎ *01722/746729,* WEB *www.wiltonhouse.com.* 🖭 *House and grounds £7.25, grounds only £3.75.* ☉ *Mid-Apr.–Oct., daily 10:30–5:30 (last admission 4:30).*

Shaftesbury

③① *18 mi west of Wilton, 22 mi west of Salisbury.*

The charming village of Shaftesbury—the model for the town of Shaston in Thomas Hardy's *Jude the Obscure*—lies just inside the Dorset county border. From the top of **Gold Hill,** a steep, relentlessly picturesque street lined with cottages, you can catch a sweeping view of the surrounding countryside. Although Gold Hill itself is something of a tourist cliché (it has even appeared in TV commercials), it is still well worth visiting.

Stourhead

★ **③②** *9 mi northwest of Shaftesbury, 30 mi west of Salisbury.*

Close to the village of Stourton lies one of Wiltshire's most breathtaking sights—Stourhead, a country-house-and-garden combination that has few parallels for beauty anywhere in Europe. Most of Stourhead was built between 1721 and 1725 by "Henry the Magnificent," a wealthy banker by the name of Henry Hoare. Many of the rooms contain Chinese and French porcelain, and there is furniture by Chippendale. The elegant library and floridly colored picture gallery were both built for the cultural development of this exceedingly civilized family. Still, the house must take second place to its adjacent gardens, the most celebrated example of the English 18th-century taste for "natural" landscaping. Temples, grottoes, and bridges have been skillfully placed among colorful shrubs, trees, and flowers to make the grounds look like a three-dimensional oil painting. A walk around the lake (1½ mi) reveals changing vistas that conjure up the 17th-century landscapes of Claude and Poussin. The best time to visit is early summer, when the massive banks of rhododendrons are in full bloom, but it is beautiful at any time of year. You can get a fine view of the estate from Alfred's Tower, a 1772 folly. During the summer, there are occasional concerts, sometimes accompanied by fireworks and gondoliers on the lake. There is a small restaurant and inn near the entrance to the grounds. From London by train, get off at Gillingham and take a 5-minute cab ride to Stourton (cabs will take several travelers on one trip). ⊠ *Stourton, near Mere (follow B3081 to B3092 from Shaftesbury),* ☎ *01747/841152,* WEB *www.nationaltrust.org.uk.* ☐ *House and gardens £8.50, house only £4.80, gardens only £4.80 (Mar.–Oct.) or £3.70 (Nov.–Feb.).* ☺ *House Apr.–Oct., Sat.–Wed. noon–5:30 or dusk (last admission 30 mins before closing); gardens daily 9–7 or sunset.*

Lodging and Dining

££ ✕☷ **Spread Eagle Inn.** You can't live at Stourhead, but this hostelry
★ at the gates to the landscaped park is the next best thing. When renovated by the National Trust, the inn was nearly gutted, so guest rooms are more country home than formal manor in appearance—discreetly understated, they are elegant nonetheless (although sadly, they face the courtyard and not the park). A gracious ground-floor restaurant has a bar menu with sandwiches, steak and kidney pie, and curries, or a dinner menu with mussels, ravioli, and meat and vegetarian dishes. But this inn really comes into its own once you step outside the door—and you find yourself steps away from England's 10 most gorgeous acres. ⊠ *Stourton, near Mere BA12 6QE,* ☎ *01747/840587,* FAX *01747/ 840954. 5 rooms. Restaurant, bar. AE, MC, V.*

Longleat House

★ ☾ **③③** *6 mi north of Stourhead, 19 mi south of Bath, 27 mi northwest of Salisbury.*

Longleat House, home of the marquess of Bath, is one of southern England's most famous private estates. The blocklike Italian Renaissance building was completed in 1580 (for just over £8,000, an astronomical sum at the time) and contains outstanding tapestries, paintings, porcelain, and furniture, as well as notable period features of its own, such as the Victorian kitchens, the Elizabethan minstrels' gallery, and the great hall with its massive wooden beams. Giant antlers of the extinct Irish elk decorate the walls. In 1966, the grounds of Longleat became Britain's first safari park, with giraffes, zebras, rhinos, and lions all on view. Longleat also has dollhouses, a butterfly garden, a private railroad, the world's longest hedge maze, and an adventure castle, all of which make it extremely popular, particularly in summer and during school vacations—don't expect to have the place to yourself. ⊠ *Off A362, Warminster,* ☎ *01985/844400,* WEB *www.longleat.co.uk.* ⊠ *All-inclusive £14, house only £7, safari park £7.* ⊘ *House Apr.–Oct., daily 10–5:30; Nov.–Dec., daily 11–4, guided tours only; safari park Apr.–Oct., weekdays 10–4, weekends and school vacations 10–5.*

Dining and Lodging

££££ ✕⊡ **Bishopstrow House.** It's not often that you'll find a Georgian
  ★   house converted into a luxurious hotel that combines whirlpool baths with antiques and fine carpets. There are attractive public areas, an airy conservatory, and peaceful rooms overlooking either the grounds (27 acres) or an interior courtyard. The Mulberry restaurant offers imaginatively prepared meals (fixed-price menus) and has appealing views of the gardens. Bishopstrow House is 1½ mi out of town. ⊠ *Boreham Rd., Warminster BA12 9HH,* ☎ *01985/212312,* FAX *01985/216769. 32 rooms. Restaurant, indoor-outdoor pool, hair salon, sauna, golf privileges, tennis court, croquet, gym, fishing, helipad. AE, DC, MC, V.*

En Route Four miles west of Avebury, on A4, is **Cherhill Down,** a prominent hill carved with a vivid white horse and topped with a towering obelisk. This is one of a number of hillside etchings in Wiltshire, but unlike the others, this one isn't an ancient symbol—it was put there in 1780 to indicate the highest point of the downs between London and Bath. It's well worth the half hour climb to the top for the views. (The best view of the horse is from A4, on the approach from Calne.)

Avebury

 ㉞ *25 mi northeast of Longleat, 27 mi east of Bath, 34 mi north of Salisbury.*

 ★ The **Avebury Stone Circles** are one of England's most evocative prehistoric monuments—not so famous as Stonehenge, but all the more powerful for their lack of commercial exploitation. The main site consists of a wide, circular ditch and bank, about 1,400 ft across and well over half a mile around; it actually surrounds part of the village of Avebury. The perimeter is broken by entrances at roughly the four points of the compass, and inside stand the remains of three stone circles. The largest one originally had 98 stones, although only 27 remain. Many of the stones on the site were destroyed centuries ago, especially in the 17th century, when they were the target of religious fanaticism. The first stones at Avebury predate those at Stonehenge by at least 200 years, but here they have been much less revered, to the extent that many were pillaged to build the thatched cottages you see flanking the fields. You can walk around the circles at any time; in terms of atmosphere, early morning and early evening are recommended. ⊠ *1 mi north of A4,* ☎ *no telephone,* WEB *www.english-heritage.org.uk.* ⊠ *Free.* ⊘ *Daily.*

Finds from the Avebury area are displayed near the stones in the **Alexander Keiller Museum,** where charts, photos, and models put the site into context. Recent revelations suggest that the archaeologist Keiller, responsible for the excavation of Avebury in the 1930s, may have adapted the site's layout more in the interests of presentation than authenticity. *1 mi north of A4,* ☎ *01672/539250,* WEB *www.english-heritage.org.uk.* ✉ *£2.* ☉ *Apr.–Oct., daily 10–6; Nov.–Mar., daily 10–4.*

The Avebury monument lies at the end of the **Kennett Stone Avenue,** a sort of prehistoric processional way leading to Avebury. The stones of the avenue were spaced 80 ft apart, but only the half mile nearest the main monument survives intact. The lost ones are marked with concrete.

Dining

£   ✕ **Waggon and Horses.** This spot just beside the traffic circle linking A4 and A361 serves an excellent sandwich lunch beside a blazing fire. The thatch-roof pub is built of stones taken from the Avebury site. ✉ *Beckhampton,* ☎ *01672/539418. AE, MC, V.*

En Route   The entire Avebury area is crowded with relics of the prehistoric age. Be sure to stop off at the **West Kennett Long Barrow,** a chambered tomb dating from about 3250 BC, 1 mi east of Avebury on A4. As you turn right at the traffic circle onto A4, **Silbury Hill** rises up on your right. This man-made mound, 130 ft high, dates from about 2500 BC. Excavations over 200 years have provided no clue as to its original purpose, but the generally accepted notion is that it was a massive burial chamber.

Marlborough

㉟   *7 mi east of Avebury, 28 mi north of Salisbury.*

The attractive town of Marlborough developed as an important staging post on the old London–Bath stagecoach route. Today it is better known for its unusually wide main street, its elegant Georgian houses—these replaced the medieval town center, which was destroyed in a great fire in 1653—and its celebrated public school. The grounds of the school, on the west side of town, enclose a small, man-made hill called Castle Mound, or Maerl's Barrow, which gave the town its name. This was said to be the grave of Merlin, King Arthur's court wizard, but it is clearly much older than the period when the historic Arthur may have lived.

Lodging

££–£££   🏠 **Ivy House.** This Georgian house right on the attractive, colonnaded High Street makes an excellent touring base. The bedrooms are comfortably furnished, with small modern bathrooms attached. Those in the Vines annex fall into the lower price category. There is a courtyard bistro for relaxed meals, and a more formal restaurant with views overlooking the terrace. ✉ *43 High St., SN8 1HJ,* ☎ *01672/515333,* FAX *01672/515338. 36 rooms. 2 restaurants, meeting room. AE, MC, V.*

Outdoor Activities and Sports

The **Marlborough Golf Club** (✉ The Common, ☎ 01672/512147), with a par 72, 6,491-yard course, has spectacular views down the Og Valley.

Stonehenge

★ **㊱**   *21 mi south of Marlborough, 8 mi north of Salisbury.*

One of England's most visited and most puzzling monuments, Stonehenge is dwarfed by its lonely isolation on the wide sweep of Salisbury Plain. Sadly, the great circle of stones has been enclosed by barriers to control both the relentless throngs of tourists and, during the summer solstice, crowds of New Age druids who embark on an annual struggle with the police to celebrate, in the monument's imposing shadows, an obscure pagan festival. But if you visit in the early morning, when the crowds have not yet arrived, or in the evening, when the sky is heavy with scudding clouds, you can experience Stonehenge as it once was: a magical, mystical, awe-inspiring place.

Stonehenge was begun about 3000 BC, enlarged between 2100 and 1900 BC, and altered yet again by 150 BC. It has been excavated and rear-ranged several times over the centuries. The medieval term "Stonehenge" means "hanging stones." Many of the huge stones that ringed the center were brought here from great distances. The original 80 bluestones (dolerite), which made up the two internal circles, were transported from the Preseli mountains, near Fishguard on the Atlantic coast of Wales, presumably by raft over sea and river. Next they were dragged on rollers across country—a total journey of 130 mi as the crow flies, but closer to 240 by the practical route. The labor involved in quarrying, transporting, and carving these stones is astonishing, all the more so when you realize that it was accomplished at about the same time that the major pyramids of Egypt were built.

If some of the mysteries concerning the site have been solved, we still do not know why Stonehenge was undertaken in the first place. It is fairly certain that it was a religious site, and that worship here involved the cycles of the sun; the alignment of the stones to point to sunrise at midsummer and sunset in midwinter makes this clear. For some historians, one thing is certain: the Druids had nothing to do with the construction. The monument had already been in existence for nearly 2,000 years by the time they appeared. Most historians feel that Stonehenge may have been a kind of neolithic computer, with a sophisticated astronomical purpose—an observatory of sorts.

You can't get very close to the monoliths, and then only along one section of the site, so it's a good idea to bring a pair of binoculars to help make out the details more clearly. It pays to hike all about the site, near and far, to get that magical Kodak shot. If you're a romantic, needless to say, you'll want to view Stonehenge at dawn or dusk, or by a full moon. The visitors' amenities at Stonehenge are rather squalid, but there are plans to improve them. Visitors from Marlborough should join A345 south for Stonehenge, turning west onto A303 at Amesbury. The monument stands near the junction with A344. ✉ *Junction of A303 and A344/ A360, near Amesbury,* ☎ *01980/624715,* WEB *www.english-heritage. org.uk.* 🎫 *£4.20.* ☉ *June–Aug., daily 9–7; mid-Mar.–May and Sept.– mid-Oct., daily 9:30–6; mid-Oct.–late Oct., daily 9:30–5; end Oct.–mid-Mar., daily 9:30–4.*

Lyndhurst

🟠 *26 mi southeast of Stonehenge, 18 mi southeast of Salisbury, 9 mi west of Southampton.*

Lyndhurst is famous as the capital of the New Forest. To explore the depths of this natural wonder, take A35 out of Lyndhurst (the road continues southwest to Bournemouth). To get here from Stonehenge, head south along A360 to Salisbury, then follow A36, B3079, and continue along A337 another 4 mi or so. Lewis Carroll's *Wonderland* fans should note that Alice Hargreaves (*née* Liddell) is buried in the **churchyard at Lyndhurst.**

The **New Forest** (WEB www.thenewforest.co.uk) consists of 145 square mi of mainly open, unfenced countryside interspersed with dense woodland, a natural haven for herds of free-roaming deer, cattle, and hardy New Forest ponies. The forest was "new" in 1079, when William the Conqueror cleared the area of farms and villages and turned it into his private hunting grounds. Although some favorite spots can get crowded in summer, there are ample parking lots, picnic areas, and campgrounds. Miles of walking trails crisscross the region.

Outdoor Activities and Sports

GOLF

Right in the middle of the New Forest, the par 69, 5,772-yard **New Forest Golf Course** (⊠ Southampton Rd., ☎ 023/8028–2752) even has New Forest ponies grazing on it.

HORSEBACK RIDING

The New Forest was custom-built for riding and there's no better way to enjoy it than on horseback. The **New Park Manor Stables** (⊠ New Park, Brockenhurst, ☎ 01590/623919; from £9 for 30 mins) gives full instruction. You can arrange a ride at the **Forest Park Riding Stables** (⊠ Rhinefield Rd., Brockenhurst, ☎ 01590/623429; from £16 for 1 hr).

WALKING

The **New Forest** is more domesticated than, for example, the Forest of Dean, and the walks it provides are not much more than easy strolls. For one such walk (about 4 mi), start from Lyndhurst and head directly south for Brockenhurst, a commuter village. You will pass through woods, pastureland, and leafy river valleys—you may even see some New Forest ponies.

Beaulieu

38 *7 mi southeast of Lyndhurst.*

The unspoiled village of Beaulieu (pronounced *byoo*-lee) has three major attractions in one. **Beaulieu** includes a ruined abbey, a stately home, and an automobile museum. **Beaulieu Abbey** was originally established by King John in 1204 for the Cistercian monks, who gave their new home its name, which means "beautiful place" in French. It was badly damaged during the reign of Henry VIII, leaving only the cloister, the doorway, the gatehouse, and two buildings, one of which today contains a well-planned exhibition re-creating daily life in the monastery. The gatehouse has been incorporated into **Palace House,** home of the Montagu family since 1538. In this stately home you can see drawing rooms, dining halls, and a number of very fine family portraits. The present Lord Montagu is noted for his work in establishing the **National Motor Museum,** which traces the development of motor transport from 1895 to the present, with more than 200 classic cars, buses, and motorcycles. Museum attractions include a monorail, audiovisual presentations, and a trip in a 1912 London bus (weekends only in winter). ⊠ *Off B3056,* ☎ *01590/612123,* WEB *www.beaulieu.co.uk.* ⊠ *Palace House, Abbey, and Motor Museum £9.95.* ⊙ *May–Sept., daily 10–6; Oct.–Apr., daily 10–5; last admission 40 mins before closing.*

Buckler's Hard

39 *2 mi south of Beaulieu.*

Among local places of interest around Beaulieu is Buckler's Hard, an almost perfectly restored 18th-century hamlet of 24 brick cottages, leading down to an old shipyard on the River Beaulieu.

The fascinating **Maritime Museum** tells the story of Lord Nelson's favorite ship, HMS *Agamemnon,* which was built here of New Forest oak. Exhibits trace the shipbuilding history of the town, and you can view a variety of model ships. ☎ *01590/616203.* ⊠ *£4.50.* ⊙ *Apr.–Sept., daily 10–6; Oct.–Mar., daily 10–5.*

En Route From Beaulieu, take any of the minor roads leading west through wide-open heathland to Lymington and pick up A337 for the popular seaside resort of Bournemouth, a journey of about 18 mi.

FAR FROM THE MADDING CROWD: BOURNEMOUTH TO LYME REGIS

"I am convinced that it is better for a writer to know a little bit of the world remarkably well than to know a great part of the world remarkably little," wrote Thomas Hardy, the immortal author of *Far from the Madding Crowd* and other classic Victorian-era novels. His "little bit" was the county of Dorset, the setting for most of his books and, today, a green and hilly area that is largely unspoiled. A visit to one of the last remaining corners of old, rural England follows the Dorset coastline, immortalized by Hardy and, more recently, by John Fowles. Places of historic interest such as Maiden Castle and the chalk-cut giant of Cerne Abbas are interspersed with the seaside resorts of Bournemouth and Weymouth, although you may find the quieter towns of Lyme Regis and the smaller picturesque villages scattered along the route closer to your ideal of rural England. Chief glory of the county is Dorchester, an ancient agricultural center with a host of historical and literary associations, and worth a prolonged visit.

Bournemouth

🔸 *30 mi southwest of Southampton, 30 mi south of Salisbury, 30 mi east of Dorchester.*

Bournemouth was founded in 1810 by Lewis Tregonwell, an ex-army officer who had taken a liking to the area when stationed there some years before. He settled near what is now The Square and planted the first pine trees in the steep little valleys—or chines—cutting through the cliffs to the famous Bournemouth sands. The scent of fir trees was said to be healing for consumption (tuberculosis) sufferers, and the town grew steadily. The Square and the beach are linked by gardens laid out with flowering trees and lawns. This is an excellent spot to relax and listen to stirring music wafting from the Pine Walk bandstand. Regular musical programs take place at the Pavilion and at the Winter Gardens (home of the Bournemouth Symphony Orchestra) nearby.

Taking the zig-zag paths through the leafy public gardens, you can descend to the seafront, where Bournemouth Pier juts into the Channel from the pristine sandy beach. The waters here are said to be some of southern England's cleanest, but if you're not tempted to have a paddle, you can always saunter along the wide promenade behind the beach to soak up the atmosphere.

Concerts and shows are staged at the **Bournemouth International Centre** (⊠ Exeter Rd., ☎ 01202/456400), which includes a selection of restaurants and bars, and a swimming pool. For an old-fashioned tea, try the **Cumberland Hotel** (⊠ E. Overcliffe Dr., ☎ 01202/290722), which serves outdoors in summer.

On the corner of Hilton Road stands **St. Peter's** parish church, easily recognizable by its 200-ft-high tower and spire. Lewis Tregonwell is buried in the churchyard. Here, too, you will notice the elaborate tombstone of Mary Shelley, author of *Frankenstein* and wife of the great Romantic poet Percy Bysshe Shelley, whose heart is buried with her.

Admirers of Shelley will want to visit the **Shelley Rooms** in Boscombe (on the west side of Bournemouth), with its collection of Shelley memorabilia. The Casa Magni house was the home of Shelley's son, Sir Percy Shelley (1819–89). ⊠ *Boscombe Manor, Beechwood Ave.,* ☎ *01202/ 303571.* ⊡ *Free.* ☉ *Tues.–Sun. 2–5.*

The **Russell-Cotes Art Gallery and Museum,** a late Victorian mansion perched on top of East Cliff, overflows with Victorian paintings and miniatures, cases of butterflies, and treasures from the Far East, including an exquisite suit of Japanese armor. A major refurbishment in 2000 restored the museum to its appearance in Russell-Cotes's day. The main entrance, the East Cliff Hall, is now a picture gallery, and the gardens have been re-landscaped. ⊠ *East Cliff,* ☎ *01202/451800,* WEB *www.russell-cotes.bournemouth.gov.uk.* ⊡ *Free.* ☉ *Tues.–Sun. 10–5.*

Dining and Lodging

££–£££ ✕ **Farthings.** Although centrally located within minutes of the seafront, this restaurant in a former coach house has the sequestered air of a country retreat. Its four dining areas—one in a conservatory—are tastefully arrayed around an elegant garden. The dishes, embracing both classic and modern, are also refined: pot-roasted salmon on saffron noodles, Dover sole poached in champagne, or roast pheasant à l'anglaise. In fine weather, tables are placed on the terrace. ⊠ *5–7 Grove Rd.,* ☎ *01202/558660. AE, DC, MC, V. Closed Mon. No dinner Sun.*

££££ ✕🖪 **Chewton Glen.** Once the home of Captain Frederick Marryat, au-
★ thor of *The Children of the New Forest* and many naval adventure novels, this 18th-century country house is now a deluxe hotel, among the most expensive in Britain, set on extensive grounds 12 mi east of Bournemouth. All the rooms are sumptuously furnished, with an eye to the minutest detail. Many diners consider its restaurant, the Marryat Room, and the cooking of its chef, Pierre Chevillard, worthy of a pilgrimage. With a genuinely helpful and friendly staff, Chewton Glen deserves its fine reputation. ⊠ *Christchurch Rd., New Milton BH25 6QS,* ☎ *01425/275341,* FAX *01425/27231,* WEB *www.chewtonglen.com. 60 rooms. Restaurant, indoor-outdoor pool, 9-hole golf course, 4 tennis courts, croquet, gym, helipad. AE, DC, MC, V.*

££–£££ ✕🖪 **Langtry Manor Hotel.** Edward VII built this house for his mistress Lillie Langtry in 1877, and it still preserves its Edwardian atmosphere, even in the newer annex. Individually named rooms continue the theme. In the restaurant (fixed-price menu), lacy tablecloths, real silver cutlery, and other details set off the dishes, which are mainly British with French trimmings and include Lillie's Special—meringue in the shape of a swan. There's an Edwardian banquet every Saturday. ⊠ *26 Derby Rd., East Cliff BH1 3QB,* ☎ *01202/553887,* FAX *01202/290115,* WEB *www. langtrymanor.com. 29 rooms. Restaurant. AE, DC, MC, V.*

£ 🖪 **San Remo.** This well-built Victorian hotel is near the sea and the town center, in a residential part of town. Cheerfully patterned wallpapers decorate the bedrooms, all of which have good amenities but no telephone. Dinner is available for guests only at 6 PM (bring your own wine). ⊠ *7 Durley Rd., West Cliff, BH2 5JQ,* ☎ *01202/290558. 18 rooms, 14 with bath. Dining room. No credit cards. Closed mid-Oct.–mid-Apr.*

Nightlife and the Arts

Bournemouth holds a **Music Festival** (☎ 0906/802–0234) June–July, with choirs, brass bands, and orchestras, some from overseas.

Wimborne Minster

㊶ *7 mi northwest of Bournemouth.*

The impressive twin-towered minster of this quiet market town makes it seem like a miniature cathedral city. To get here from Bournemouth, follow the signs northwest on A341.

Set on the main square in a Tudor building with a garden, the **Priest's House Museum** includes rooms furnished in various period styles and a Victorian kitchen. It also has Roman and Iron Age exhibits, including a cryptic, three-faced Celtic stone head. ⊠ *23 High St.,* ☎ *01202/ 882533.* ⬚ *£2.40.* ⊙ *June–Sept., Mon.–Sat. 10:30–5, Sun. 2–5; Oct.– Apr., Mon.–Sat. 10:30–5.*

Kingston Lacy, a grand 17th-century house built for the Bankes family (who had lived in Corfe Castle), was altered in the 19th century by Sir Charles Barry, co-architect of the Houses of Parliament in London. The building holds a choice picture collection with works by Titian, Rubens, Van Dyck, and Velásquez, as well as the fabulous Spanish Room, lined with gilded leather and topped with an ornate Venetian ceiling. There is also a fine collection of Egyptian artifacts. Parkland with walking paths surrounds the house and gardens. ⊠ *B3082 (1½ mi northwest of Wimborne Minster),* ☎ *01202/883402,* ⟦WEB⟧ *www.nationaltrust. org.uk.* ⬚ *£6.50; park and garden £3.* ⊙ *House Apr.–Oct., Wed.–Sun. noon–5:30. Garden and park Feb.–Mar., weekends 11–4; Apr.–Oct., daily 11–6; Nov.–Dec., Fri.–Sun. 11–4.*

Dining

££ ✕ **Primizia.** This popular bistro serves a range of Continental dishes with French and Italian influences; try fillet of beef Wellington with a Madeira jus, with crème brûlée for dessert. ⊠ *26 Westborough,* ☎ *01202/883518. MC, V. Closed Sun.–Mon.*

Blandford Forum

㊷ *11 mi northwest of Wimborne Minster.*

Endowed with perhaps the handsomest Georgian town center in the southwest, this market town of brick and stone on the River Stour was Thomas Hardy's "Shottesford Forum." The Church of St. Peter and St. Paul, with an imposing cupola and dating from 1739, is worth a detour on its own.

Corfe Castle

★ ㊸ *20 mi south of Blandford Forum, 15 mi south of Poole, 6 mi south of Wareham.*

The spectacular ruins of Dorset's Corfe Castle overlook the pretty village of Corfe. The castle site guards a gap in the surrounding range of hills and has been fortified from very early times. The present ruins are of the castle built between 1105, when the great central keep was erected, and the 1270s, when the outer walls and towers were built. It owes its ramshackle state to Cromwell's soldiers, who blew the castle up in 1646 during the Civil War after Lady Bankes led its defense during a long siege. This is one of the most impressive ruins in Britain and will stir the imagination of all history buffs. ⊠ *A351,* ☎ *01929/ 481294,* ⟦WEB⟧ *www.nationaltrust.org.uk.* ⬚ *£4.20.* ⊙ *Mar., daily 10– 5; Apr.–Oct., daily 10–6; Nov.–Feb., daily 10–4.*

OFF THE
BEATEN PATH

CLOUDS HILL – A tiny, spartan, brick and tile cottage served as the retreat of T. E. Lawrence (Lawrence of Arabia) before he was killed in a motorcycle accident on the road from Bovington in 1935. It's still very much as he left it, with photos and other memorabilia from the Middle East. It's particularly atmospheric on a gloomy day, as there's no electric light. ⊠ *Wareham, 8 mi northwest of town, off B3390,* ☎ *01929/ 405616,* ⟦WEB⟧ *www.nationaltrust.org.uk.* ⬚ *£2.60.* ⊙ *Apr.–Oct., Wed.–Fri., Sun., and national holidays noon–5 or dusk.*

Dining and Lodging

£ ✕ **The Fox.** An age-old pub, the Fox has a fine view of Corfe Castle from its flower garden. There's an ancient well in the lounge bar and more timeworn stonework in an alcove, as well as a pre-1300 fireplace. Sandwiches, soups, and pies are cheerfully doled out from the bar, but things can get uncomfortably congested in summer. ⌂ *West St.,* ☎ *01929/480449. MC, V.*

£ ⌂ **Castle Inn.** This thatched hotel, 10 mi west of Corfe and just five minutes' walk from the sea, has a flagstone bar and other 15th-century features. The good restaurant has an à la carte menu for evening meals and Sunday lunch, as well as an extensive bar menu. The bedrooms are plain but comfortable, and there is a lovely rose garden to sit in and satisfying walks to take nearby. ⌂ *Main Rd., West Lulworth BH20 5RN,* ☎ *01929/400311,* FAX *01929/400415. 15 rooms, 12 with bath. Restaurant, bar. AE, DC, MC, V.*

Dorchester

44 *21 mi west of Corfe on A351 and A352, 30 mi west of Bournemouth, 43 mi southwest of Salisbury.*

In many ways Dorchester, the Casterbridge of Hardy's novel *The Mayor of Casterbridge,* is a traditional southern country town. The town owes much of its fame to its connection with Thomas Hardy, whose bronze statue looks westward from a bank on Colliton Walk. Born in a cottage in the hamlet of Higher Bockhampton, about 3 mi northeast of Dorchester, Hardy attended school in the town and was apprentice to an architect here.

Roman history and artifacts abound in Dorchester. The town was laid out by the Romans about AD 70, and if you walk along Bowling Alley Walk, West Walk, and Colliton Walk, you will have followed the approximate line of the original Roman town walls. On the north side of Colliton Park lies an excavated Roman villa with a marvelously preserved mosaic floor.

Dorchester is also associated with Monmouth's Rebellion of 1685, when Charles II's illegitimate son, the Duke of Monmouth, led a rising against his unpopular uncle, James II. The rising was ruthlessly put down, and the chief justice, Lord Jeffreys, was dispatched from London to try the rebels and sympathizers for treason. A swearing, bullying drunkard, Jeffreys was the prototypical hanging judge, and memories of his mass executions lingered for centuries throughout the South. The gruesome outcome led to the trials being called the Bloody Assizes. Jeffreys's courtroom in Dorchester was in what is now the Antelope Hotel on South Street.

To appreciate the town's character, visit the local Wednesday market in the **Market Square,** where you can find Dorset delicacies such as Blue Vinney cheese (which some connoisseurs prefer to Blue Stilton), and various handcrafted items. Things, of course, have changed a bit since the days when, to quote Hardy, "Bees and butterflies in the cornfields at the top of the town, who desired to get to the meads at the bottom, took no circuitous route, but flew straight down High Street . . ."

The **Dorset County Museum** holds a range of ancient Celtic and Roman remains, but is better known for possessing a large collection of Hardy memorabilia. ⌂ *High West St.,* ☎ *01305/262735.* ⌂ *£3.50.* ☼ *May–Oct., daily 10–5; Nov.–Apr., Mon.–Sat. 10–5.*

The small thatch and cob **Hardy's Cottage,** where the writer was born in 1840, was built by his grandfather and is little altered since that time. From here Hardy would make his daily 6-mi walk to school in Dorchester. Among other things, you can see the desk at which the author completed *Far from the Madding Crowd.* ✉ *Higher Bockhampton, ½ mi south of Blandford Rd. (A35),* ☎ *01305/262366,* WEB *www.nationaltrust.org.uk.* ￼ *£2.60.* ☉ *Apr.–Nov., Sun.–Thurs. 11–5 or dusk.*

Max Gate was the home of Hardy from 1885 until his death in 1928. An architect by profession, Hardy designed and supervised the building of the house, in which the dining room and the light and airy drawing room are now open. He wrote much of his poetry here and many of his novels, including *Tess of the d'Urbervilles* and *The Mayor of Casterbridge.* ✉ *Allington Ave., 1 mi east of Dorchester on A352,* ☎ *01305/262538.* ￼ *£2.30.* ☉ *Apr.–Sept., Mon., Wed., Sun. 2–5.*

The **Maumbury Rings** (✉ Maumbury Rd.), the remains of a Roman amphitheater on the edge of town, are one of Dorchester's most interesting sights. The site was later used as a place of execution. (Hardy's *Mayor of Casterbridge* contains a vivid evocation of the Rings.) As late as 1706, a girl was burned at the stake here.

The popular **Dinosaur Museum** has life-size models, interactive displays, and a hands-on Discovery Gallery. ✉ *Icen Way, off High East St.,* ☎ *01305/269880,* WEB *www.dinosaur-museum.org.uk.* ￼ *£4.50.* ☉ *Apr.–Oct., daily 9:30–5:30; Nov.–Mar., daily 10–4:30.*

It's hardly what you might expect from a small county town, but the **Tutankhamun Exhibition** re-creates the young pharaoh's tomb and treasures in all its glory, complemented by the smell of ointments and cedarwood oil. ✉ *High West St.,* ☎ *01305/269571,* WEB *www. tutankhamun-exhibition.co.uk.* ￼ *£4.50.* ☉ *Apr.–Oct., daily 9:30–5:30; Nov.–Mar., weekdays 9:30–5:30, Sat. 10–5, Sun 10–4:30.*

Athelhampton House and Gardens, 5 mi east of Dorchester, is one of the glories of the English Middle Ages. Thomas Hardy called this place Athelhall in some of his writings, referring to the legendary King Aethelstan, who had a palace on this site. In the 15th century the current house was built, complete with Great Hall and King's Room. There are also 10 acres of impressive landscaped gardens. ✉ *A35 (1 mi east of Puddletown),* ☎ *01305/848363,* WEB *www.athelhampton.co.uk.* ￼ *£5.50, gardens only £3.95.* ☉ *Mar.–Oct., Sun.–Fri. 10:30–5; Nov.–Feb., Sun. 10:30–5.*

Dining and Lodging

£   ✕ **Potter In.** This is just the place for a range of teas and coffees and deliciously caloric cakes and pastries, as well as homemade savory dishes. It is on two floors of a 17th-century cottage, where local crafts are also sold. In summer you can eat outside in the pleasant garden. ✉ *19 Durngate St.,* ☎ *01305/260312. No credit cards. Closed Sun.*

££ ✕▦ **Yalbury Cottage.** A thatch roof and inglenook fireplaces enhance
★   the traditional ambience here, just 2½ mi east of Dorchester, which puts it close to Hardy's cottage. The three-course fixed-price menu, featuring modern British and Continental dishes, might include herb-crusted rack of lamb (with tomato and basil jus), or pan-fried fillet of brill. There are also comfortable bedrooms available in a discreet extension overlooking gardens or adjacent fields. ✉ *Lower Bockhampton DT2 8PZ,* ☎ *01305/262382,* FAX *01305/266412. 8 rooms. Restaurant. MC, V. Closed Jan. No lunch.*

££ 🏠 **Casterbridge Hotel.** This Georgian building (1790) reflects its age,
★ with period furniture and old-world elegance. It is small but full of character. The guest rooms are each individually and impeccably furnished,
and those in the modern annex are slightly larger. The husband-and-
wife team who own and run the hotel are a congenial pair. ✉ *49 High
East St., DT1 1HU,* ☎ *01305/264043,* FAX *01305/260884,* WEB *www.
casterbridgehotel.co.uk. 14 rooms. Bar. AE, DC, MC, V.*

Outdoor Activities and Sports

From April through October the Thomas Hardy Society (✉ Box 1438,
Dorchester DT1 1YH, ☎ FAX 01305/25150) organizes **walks** that follow in the steps of the novels. The walks, which take the most part of
a day, are accompanied by readings and discussions.

Cerne Abbas

45 *6 mi north of Dorchester.*

The village of Cerne Abbas, worth a short exploration on foot, has
some appealing Tudor houses on the road beside the church. Nearby
you can also see the original village stocks. Tenth-century **Cerne Abbey**
is now a ruin, with little left to see except its old gateway, although
the nearby Abbey House is still in use.

Cerne Abbas's main claim to fame is the colossal and unblushingly pri-
apic **figure of a giant,** cut in chalk on a hillside overlooking the village.
The 180-ft-long giant with a huge club bears a striking resemblance to
Hercules, although he probably originated as a tribal fertility symbol
long before the Romans. His outlines are formed by 2-ft-wide trenches.
The present giant is thought to have been carved in the chalk about AD
1200, but he could well be based on a very much older figure.

Lodging

£ 🏠 **Lamperts Cottage.** Here's an idyllic thatch-roof B&B about 2 mi southwest of Cerne Abbas. It has a stream in front and back, so you have
to cross a little bridge to reach it. In summer the cottage is covered with
roses. The house, dating from the 16th century, is very comfortable although small; the rooms share two baths. The interior has exposed beams
and fireplaces. ✉ *Dorchester Rd., Sydling St. Nicholas, Cerne Abbas
DT2 9NU,* ☎ *01300/341659,* FAX *01300/341699. 3 rooms without bath.
MC, V.*

Maiden Castle

★ **46** *2 mi southwest of Dorchester.*

After Stonehenge, Maiden Castle (✉ A354) is the most important
pre-Roman archaeological site in England. It is not really a castle at
all, but an enormous, complex hill fort of stone and earth, built by England's mysterious prehistoric inhabitants. Many centuries later it was
a Celtic stronghold. In AD 43, the invading Romans, under the general
(later emperor) Vespasian, stormed it. To experience an uncanny silence and sense of mystery, climb Maiden Castle early in the day (access to it is unrestricted), when other visitors are unlikely to be stirring.
Finds from the site are on display in the Dorset County Museum in
Dorchester.

Weymouth

47 *8 mi south of Dorchester.*

Dorset's main coastal resort, Weymouth, is known for its wide, safe, sandy beaches and its royal connections. King George III took up sea bathing here for his health in 1789, setting a trend among the wealthy and fashionable people of the day. They left Weymouth with many fine period buildings, including the Georgian row houses lining the esplanade. Striking historical details clamor for attention. A wall on Maiden Street, for example, still holds a cannonball that was embedded in it during the Civil War. Nearby, a column commemorates the launching of the United States forces from Weymouth on D-Day, June 6, 1944.

Dining and Lodging

££–£££ ✗ **Perry's.** A fairly basic restaurant right by the harbor, Perry's serves simple dishes of the best local seafood. Try the lobster, crab, or mussels in white wine and shallots. The meat dishes, such as roast rack of lamb, are tasty, too. ⊠ *The Harbourside, 4 Trinity Rd.,* ☎ *01305/ 785799. AE, MC, V. No lunch Mon., Sat.; no dinner Sun. Sept.–June.*

£ ✗ **Old Rooms.** A fisherman's pub full of character and low beams, this popular choice has great views over the harbor. The long menu includes pastas, curries, and meat pies. There's a separate dining area, or you can mix with the locals at the bar. ⊠ *Trinity Rd.,* ☎ *01305/771130. MC, V.*

££ ⌂ **Streamside Hotel.** Quiet and cozy, this hotel on the outskirts of town
★ is a stone's throw from the beach. Rooms are comfortable, and there are spectacular gardens. The restaurant specializes in English cooking, steaks, smoked salmon, and other fish in season. ⊠ *29 Preston Rd., Overcombe DT3 6PX,* ☎ *01305/833121,* FAX *01305/832043. 11 rooms. Restaurant. MC, V.*

Isle of Portland

48 *4 mi south of Weymouth.*

A 5-mi-long peninsula jutting south from Weymouth leads to the Isle of Portland, well known for its limestone. The peninsula is the eastern end of the unique geological curiosity known as **Chesil Beach**—a 200-yard-wide, 30-ft-high bank of pebbles that decrease in size from east to west. The beach extends for 18 mi. A powerful undertow makes swimming dangerous, and tombstones in local churchyards attest to the many shipwrecks the beach has caused.

Abbotsbury

49 *10 mi northwest of Weymouth.*

The attractive village of Abbotsbury is at the western end of Chesil Beach. A lagoon outside the village serves as the **Abbotsbury Swannery,** a famous breeding place for swans. Introduced by Benedictine monks as a source of meat in winter, the swans have remained for centuries, building new nests every year in the soft, moist pampas grass. ⊠ *New Barn Rd.,* ☎ *01305/871684.* 🖾 *£5.20.* ☾ *Mid-Mar.–Oct., daily 10–6 (last admission 5).*

On the hills above Abbotsbury stands the **Hardy Monument**—dedicated not to the novelist but to Sir Thomas Masterman Hardy, Lord Nelson's flag captain at Trafalgar, to whom Nelson's dying words, "Kiss me, Hardy," were addressed. The monument is without much charm, but the surrounding view more than makes up for it. In clear weather you can scan the whole coastline between the Isle of Wight and Start Point in Devon. ⊠ *Black Down, Portesham,* ☎ *01202/882493,* 🖳 *www.nationaltrust.org.uk.* 🖺 *£1.* ☉ *Apr.–Sept., weekends 11–5. Subject to closure in bad weather.*

Dining and Lodging

£££ ✕🖫 **Manor Hotel.** The pedigree of this comfortable hotel and restaurant goes back more than 700 years—note its flagstone floors, oak paneling, and beamed ceilings. Among the English and French dishes in which the Manor specializes are seafood and game; the fixed-price menu changes daily. Some rooms have sea views, and Chesil Beach is a couple of minutes' walk away. Self-catering facilities are also available. ⊠ *Beach Rd., West Bexington DT2 9DF (3 mi west of Abbotsbury),* ☎ *01308/897785,* 🖷 *01308/897035. 13 rooms. Restaurant, playground. AE, DC, MC, V.*

Lyme Regis

㊿ *19 mi west of Abbotsbury.*

"A very strange stranger it must be, who does not see the charms of the immediate environs of Lyme, to make him wish to know it better," wrote Jane Austen in *Persuasion.* Judging from the summer crowds, most people appear to be not at all strange. The ancient, scenic town of Lyme Regis and the so-called Fossil Coast are highlights of southwest Dorset. The crumbling seaside cliffs in this area are especially fossil rich. In 1810, a local child named Mary Anning dug out a complete ichthyosaur here (it is on display in London's Natural History Museum). You may prefer to browse in the Fossil Shop in Lyme Regis.

Lyme Regis is famous for its curving stone breakwater, **The Cobb,** built by King Edward I in the 13th century to improve the harbor. It was here that the duke of Monmouth landed in 1685 in his ill-fated attempt to overthrow his uncle, James II. The Cobb figures prominently in the movie *The French Lieutenant's Woman,* based on John Fowles's novel, as well as the film version of Jane Austen's *Persuasion.* Fowles is Lyme's most famous current resident.

Dining and Lodging

££–£££ ✕🖫 **Alexandra.** A short walk from the Cobb in a high, panoramic location, the Alexandra is a genteel haven with an old-fashioned air. Informal lunches and teas are served in a sunny conservatory that overlooks an expanse of lawn. The formal restaurant has a good wine list to complement the four-course dinners, with entrées such as roast duck in a soy and ginger sauce, grilled salmon, and monkfish in a red vermouth sauce. Guest rooms are attractively furnished in pastels, and most have sea views. ⊠ *Pound St., DT7 3HZ,* ☎ *01297/442010,* 🖷 *01297/443229,* 🖳 *www.hotelalexandra.co.uk. 27 rooms. Restaurant, bar. AE, DC, MC, V. Closed Jan.*

Outdoor Activities and Sports

The 72-mi **Dorset Coast Path** runs east from Lyme Regis to Poole, bypassing Weymouth. It takes you by the characteristic quiet bays, shingle beaches, and low chalk cliffs of the coast. Some highlights are Golden Cap, the highest point on the South Coast; the Swannery at Abbotsbury; Chesil Beach; and Lulworth Cove (between Weymouth and Corfe Castle). As with most walks in Britain, the route is dotted with villages and isolated pubs for meals; there are also many rural B&Bs.

THE SOUTH A TO Z

To research prices, get advice from other travelers, and book travel arrangements, visit www.fodors.com.

AIRPORTS

The small international airport at Southampton is useful for flights to the Channel Islands and some European destinations.

➤ AIRPORT INFORMATION: **Southampton International Airport** (☎ 023/8062–0021).

BOAT AND FERRY TRAVEL

Wightlink operates a car-ferry service between the mainland and the Isle of Wight. The crossing takes about 30 minutes from Lymington to Yarmouth; 40 minutes from Southsea (Portsmouth) to Fishbourne. It also operates catamaran service between Portsmouth and Ryde (15 minutes). Red Funnel runs a car-ferry and hydrofoil service between Southampton and Cowes. Hovertravel has a hovercraft shuttle between Southsea and Ryde (10 minutes).

FARES AND SCHEDULES

➤ BOAT AND FERRY INFORMATION: **Hovertravel** (☎ 01983/811000 or 023/9281–1000, WEB www.hovertravel.co.uk). **Red Funnel** (☎ 023/8033–4010, WEB www.redfunnel.co.uk). **Wightlink** (☎ 0870/582–7744, WEB www.wightlink.co.uk).

BUS TRAVEL

National Express buses at London's Victoria Coach Station on Buckingham Palace Road depart hourly for Bournemouth (2½ hours) and every two hours for Southampton (2½ hours), Portsmouth (2½ hours), and Winchester (2 hours). There are three buses daily to Salisbury (2¾ hours). Solent Blue and Stagecoach Hampshire Bus operate a comprehensive service in the Southampton, New Forest, Winchester, and Bournemouth areas. Southern Vectis covers the Isle of Wight.

CUTTING COSTS

Wilts (Wiltshire) & Dorset Bus Co. offers both one-day "Explorer" and seven-day "Busabout" tickets; in summer, it also conducts "Explorer Special" open-top tours around Bournemouth. Also ask about the "Rover" tickets offered by Solent Blue and Southern Vectis.

FARES AND SCHEDULES

➤ BUS INFORMATION: **National Express** (☎ 0870/580–8080, WEB www.gobycoach.com). **Solent Blue** (☎ 023/8061–8233). **Stagecoach Hampshire Bus** (☎ 01256/464501). **Southern Vectis** (☎ 01983/827005). **Wilts (Wiltshire) & Dorset Bus Co.** (☎ 01722/336855).

CAR RENTAL

➤ LOCAL AGENCIES: **Avis** (⊠ 33–39 Southcote Rd., Bournemouth, ☎ 01202/296942). **Budget Rent a Car** (⊠ Brunel Rd., Churchfields Industrial Estate, Salisbury, ☎ 01722/336444). **Enterprise Rent-a-Car** (⊠ Train Station, Winchester, ☎ 01962/844022). **Esplanade** (⊠ 9–11 George St., Ryde, ☎ 01983/562322). **Europcar** (⊠ c/o Ibis Hotel, West Quay Rd., Southampton, ☎ 023/8033–2973). **Hertz** (⊠ Hinton Rd., Bournemouth, ☎ 01202/291231; ⊠ 1 Queensway, Southampton, ☎ 023/8063–8437).

CAR TRAVEL

The South is linked to London and other major cities by a well-developed road network, which includes M3 to Winchester (59 mi) and Southampton (77 mi); A3 to Portsmouth (70 mi); and M27 along the coast, from the New Forest and Southampton to Portsmouth. For Salisbury, take M3 to A303, then A30. A31 and A35 connect Bournemouth to Dorchester and the rest of Dorset.

ROAD CONDITIONS

Driving is very easy in this area. In northeast Hampshire and in many parts of neighboring Wiltshire there are lanes overhung by trees and lined with thatched cottages and Georgian houses. Often these lanes begin near the exits of main highways. Salisbury Plain has long, straight roads surrounded by endless vistas; the problem here is staying within the speed limit.

EMERGENCIES

➤ CONTACTS: **Ambulance, fire, police** (☎ 999). **Queen Alexandra Hospital** (✉ Southwick Hill Rd., Cosham, Portsmouth, ☎ 023/9228–6000). **St. Mary's Hospital** (✉ Newport, Isle of Wight, ☎ 01983/524081). **Southampton General Hospital** (✉ Tremona Rd., Southampton, ☎ 023/8079–6220).

TOURS

Guide Friday has a daily Stonehenge tour from Salisbury May through September costing £13.50, which includes admission to the monument, but check for availability. A.S. Tours arranges day tours of Stonehenge, Avebury, and Winchester year-round in six- or eight-seater minibuses. Salisbury City Guides run a program of daily summer (weekends in winter) walks in Salisbury starting at 11.

The Southern Tourist Board and Wessexplore can reserve qualified Blue Badge guides who will arrange to meet you anywhere in the region for private tours of different lengths and themes.

➤ TOUR INFORMATION: **A.S.Tours** (☎ 01980/862931). **Guide Friday** (☎ 01789/294466). **Salisbury City Guides** (☎ 01980/623463, WEB www.salisburycityguides.co.uk). **Southern Tourist Board** (☎ 023/8062–5400, WEB www.gosouth.co.uk). **Wessexplore** (☎ 01722/326304, WEB www.dmac.co.uk/wessexplore).

TRAIN TRAVEL

South West Trains serves the South from London's Waterloo Station. Travel times average an hour to Winchester, 1¼ hours to Southampton, two hours to Bournemouth, and 2½ hours to Weymouth. Salisbury takes an hour and 40 minutes, and Portsmouth about two hours. There is at least one fast train every hour on all these routes. For local information throughout the region, contact National Rail Enquiries.

CUTTING COSTS

A "Network" card, valid throughout the South and Southeast for a year, entitles you to one-third off particular fares.

FARES AND SCHEDULES

➤ TRAIN INFORMATION: **National Rail Enquiries** (☎ 08457/484950, WEB www.railtrack.co.uk). **South West Trains** (☎ 08457/484950, WEB www.railtrack.co.uk).

TRAVEL AGENCIES

➤ LOCAL AGENT REFERRALS: **American Express** (✉ 99 Above Bar, Southampton, ☎ 0870/600–1060). **Thomas Cook** (✉ 7 Richmond Hill, Bournemouth, ☎ 01202/452800; ✉ 9 Palmerston Rd., Southsea, ☎ 023/9230–2100; ✉ 18 Queen St., Salisbury, ☎ 01722/313500; ✉ 30 High St., Winchester, ☎ 01962/743100).

VISITOR INFORMATION

The Southern Tourist Board is open Monday–Thursday 8:30–5, Friday 8:30–4:30. Local tourist information centers are normally open Monday–Saturday 9:30–5:30.

➤ TOURIST INFORMATION: **Southern Tourist Board** (✉ 40 Chamberlayne Rd., Eastleigh S050 5JH, ☎ 023/8062–5400, FAX 023/8062–0010, WEB www.gosouth.co.uk). **Bournemouth** (✉ Westover Rd., near the bandstand, BH1 2BU, ☎ 0906/802–0234 [calls cost 50p per min]). **Dorchester** (✉ 11 Antelope Walk, DT1 1BE, ☎ 01305/267992, WEB www.westdorset.com). **Lyndhurst** (✉ High St., S043 7NY, ☎ 01590/689000). **Marlborough** (✉ Car Park, George La., SN8 1EE, ☎ 01672/513989). **Portsmouth** (✉ The Hard, PO1 3QJ, ☎ 023/9282–6722, WEB www.portsmouthharbour.co.uk; ✉ Clarence Esplanade, Southsea [mid-Apr.–Oct.], Portsmouth, ☎ 023/9283–2464). **Ryde** (✉ 81 Union St., PO33 2LW, ☎ 01983/813813). **Salisbury** (✉ Fish Row, off Market Sq., SP1 1EJ, ☎ 01722/334956, WEB www.salisbury.gov.uk/tourism). **Southampton** (✉ 9 Civic Centre, SO14 7YP, ☎ 023/8022–1106, WEB www.southampton.gov.uk/tourism). **Winchester** (✉ The Guildhall, Broadway, SO23 9LJ, ☎ 01962/840500, WEB www.winchester.com).

4 THE WEST COUNTRY

SOMERSET, DEVON, CORNWALL

Half the fun of exploring the West Country
is in letting yourself get lost. On your way
down to Land's End, every zig and zag
of the road reveals rugged moorlands—
The Hound of the Baskervilles was set
here—lush river valleys, and festive coastal
resorts. Explore the mist-wreathed sights
of King Arthur Country and then head for
enchanting Clovelly, precipitously perched
above a tiny harbor. Whatever your
itinerary, be sure to allow yourself to stray
from the main roads—it would be a great
pity not to.

Updated by
Robert
Andrews

T HE SOUTHWEST OF ENGLAND can be one of the most relaxing regions to visit. The secret of exploring this area is to ignore the main highways and just follow the signposts through the leafy, narrow country roads that lead through miles of buttercup meadows and cider apple orchards to countless mellow villages of stone and thatch and heathery heights overlooking the sea. The village names alone are music to the ears: there's Tintinhull, Midsomer Norton, Huish Episcopi, and Bower Hinton—just to name a few of the hamlets that *haven't* been covered below.

Somerset, Devon, and Cornwall are the three counties that make up the long southern peninsula known as the West Country. Each has its own distinct flavor, and each also comes with a regionalism that borders on patriotism. Somerset is noted for its rolling green countryside; Devon's wild and dramatic moors—bare, boggy upland heath dominated by heathers and gorse, with a scattering of trees—contrast with the restfulness of its many sandy beaches and coves; and Cornwall has managed to retain a touch of its old insularity, despite the annual invasion of thousands of people lured by the ocean or the English Channel. Natives don't mind the water's very doubtful temperature, but foreigners, many of them pampered by the warm waves of the Mediterranean, are not so eager to brave the elements. The sea—even in Cornwall, where it seems to be warmer than anywhere else in the British Isles—is not to be enjoyed in a sensuous way: it is a bracing experience that sometimes leaves you shivering and breathless.

Many travelers head first for King Arthur Country. Although King Arthur's name is linked with more than 150 places in Britain, no area claims stronger ties than the West Country. According to tradition, Arthur was born at Tintagel Castle in Cornwall and later lived at Camelot (said to be Cadbury Castle, in Somerset).

Bristol is where you'll come across the first unmistakable burrs of the western brogue. A historic port retaining a strong maritime flavor, its graceful Georgian architecture and dramatic gorge are a backdrop to what has recently become one of Britain's most dynamic cities. You might want to weave south through the lovely Chew Valley on your way to the cathedral city of Wells, in Somerset. This mellow county is characterized by rolling green countryside—best seen in a cloak of summer heat when its orchards give ample shade, its bees are humming, and its old stone houses and inns welcome you with a breath of coolness. Abutting the north coast are the Quantock and Mendip hills, and the stark, heather-covered expanse of Exmoor, the setting for R. D. Blackmore's historical romance, *Lorna Doone.*

Devon, farther west, is famed for its wild moorland—especially Dartmoor, fictional home of Sir Arthur Conan Doyle's "Hound of the Baskervilles," and actual home to wild ponies and an assortment of strange tors—rocky outcroppings eroded into weird shapes. Devon's large coastal towns are as interesting for their cultural and historical appeal—many were smugglers' havens—as for their scenic beauty. Some propagandists of east Devon speak of the "red cliffs" of Devon in contrast to the more famous "white cliffs of Dover." Parts of south Devon, on the other hand, are more reminiscent of some balmy Mediterranean shore—hence its soubriquet, the English Riviera. The best times to visit Devon are late summer and early fall, during the end-of-summer festivals, especially popular in the small towns of eastern Dartmoor.

Cornwall, England's southernmost county, has a mild climate, and here you are never more than 20 mi from the sea. Until relatively recently, the county regarded itself as separate from the rest of Britain. Its Atlantic coast is lined with high, jagged cliffs—the dangerous and dramatic settings that Daphne du Maurier often waxed eloquent about—and indeed poses a menace to passing ships. The south coast, Janus-like, is filled with sunny beaches, delightful coves, and popular resorts.

Pleasures and Pastimes

Dining

Lamb, venison, and, in Devon and Cornwall, seafood are favored in West Country restaurants, which have improved markedly in recent years, notably the outposts of Rick Stein's empire in Padstow. Somerset is the home of Britain's most famous cheese—the ubiquitous Cheddar, from the Mendip Hills village. If you are lucky enough to taste real farmhouse Cheddar, made in the traditional "truckle," you may find it hard to return to processed cheese. The calorie-conscious should beware of Devon's cream teas, which traditionally consist of a pot of tea, homemade scones, and lots of thickened clotted cream and strawberry jam (clotted, or specially thickened cream, is a regional specialty and is sometimes called "Devonshire cream"). Cornwall's specialty is the pasty, a pastry shell filled with chopped meat, onions, and potatoes. The pasty was devised as a handy way for miners to carry their dinner to work; today's versions are rather pale versions of the original. Scrumpy, a homemade dry cider, is refreshing but carries a kick. English wine, similar to German wine, is made in Somerset, and in Cornwall you can find a variant of age-old mead made from local honey.

CATEGORY	COST*
££££	over £22
£££	£16–£22
££	£9–£15
£	under £9

*per person for a main course at dinner

Lodging

Accommodations in the West Country range from national hotel chains, represented in all the region's principal centers, to ubiquitous bed-and-breakfast places. Many farmhouses also rent out rooms, offering tranquillity in a rural setting, yet these lodgings are often difficult to reach without a car.

CATEGORY	COST*
££££	over £150
£££	£100–£150
££	£60–£100
£	under £60

*All prices are for two people sharing a standard double room, including service, breakfast, and VAT.

Walking

A wonderful 10-mi walk is a cliff-top hike along the coast from Hartland Quay, near Clovelly, down to Lower Sharpnose Point, just above Bude. The coast below Bude is also ideal for walking, especially the section around Tintagel. Long walks in the bleak, unpeopled region of Dartmoor, although fascinating, are only appropriate for the most experienced walkers. The areas around Widgery Cross, Becky Falls, and the Bovey Valley, and—for the truly energetic and adventurous—the tors south of Okehampton, in Dartmoor, are all worth considering. A much shorter walk, but no less spectacular, is along the Lydford Gorge. If you are interested in "theme" walks, note the Saints Way, a 30-mi walk between Padstow and the Camel Estuary on Cornwall's

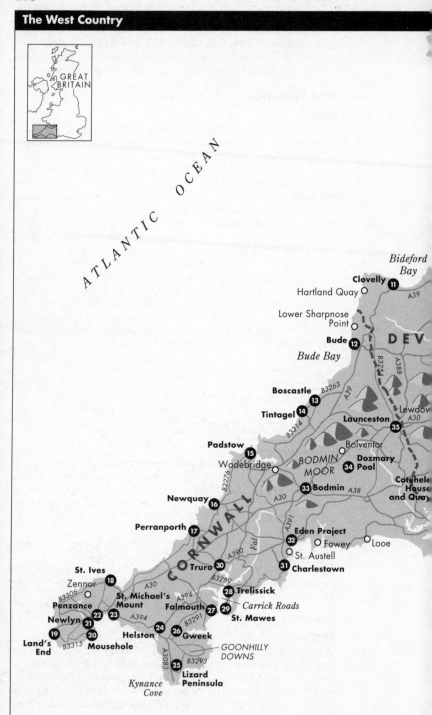

GREAT
BRITAIN

ATLANTIC OCEAN

*Bideford
Bay*

Clovelly 11

Hartland Quay O

Lower Sharpnose
Point O

Bude 12

Bude Bay

D E V

Boscastle B3263
13

Tintagel 14
B3314

Launceston

Lewdow
A30

35

Padstow
15

Wadebridge O

Bolventor O

**BODMIN
MOOR**

**Dozmary
Pool**

34

Cotehele
House
and Quay

Bodmin A38
33

B3276

A30

A39

Newquay
16

C O R N W A L L

A391

Eden Project

32 O **Fowey**

O **Looe**

Perranporth 17

A390

Fal

31 **Charlestown**

O **St. Austell**

Truro 30

B3289

St. Ives
18

A30

Zennor O

Trelissick
28

B3306

**St. Michael's
Mount**

A394

Falmouth
27

Penzance

A394

29

Carrick Roads

Newlyn 22 23

21

St. Mawes

B3291

**Land's
End** 19 20

24 26

Helston

Gweek

25

B3315 **Mousehole**

A3083

*GOONHILLY
DOWNS*

B3293

*Kynance
Cove*

**Lizard
Peninsula**

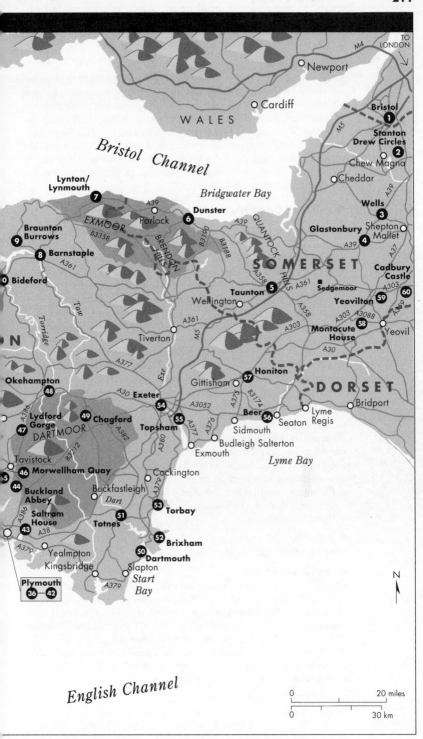

TO LONDON

M4

○ Newport

○ Cardiff

WALES

Bristol
①

Stanton
Drew Circles
②

○ Chew Magna

○ Cheddar

M5

Bristol Channel

Bridgwater Bay

Wells
③

Shepton ○
Mallet

Glastonbury
④

A39

A37

Lynton/
Lynmouth
⑦

EXMOOR

○ Porlock

Dunster
⑥

A39

B3190

B3188

QUANTOCK HILLS

SOMERSET

A39

■ Sedgemoor

Cadbury
Castle

Yeovilton
⑤⑨   **⑥⓪**

A303

A3088

Braunton
Burrows
⑨

B3356

BRENDON HILLS

Barnstaple
⑧

A361

⓪ Bideford

Taw

A358

A358

Taunton
⑤

A361

○ Wellington

Montacute
House
⑤⑧

A303

Yeovil ○

A30

N (torridge)

Tiverton ○

M5

Exe

A361

Okehampton
⑧

Honiton
⑤⑦

DORSET

A30

Gittisham ○

Exeter
⑤④

A3052

A375

B3174

Bridport ○

Chagford
⑨

A382

Topsham
⑤⑤

A376

A377

Beer
⑤⑥

Seaton ○

Lyme ○
Regis

Lydford
Gorge
⑦

DARTMOOR

B3212

Sidmouth ○

Budleigh Salterton ○

Exmouth ○

Lyme Bay

⑤ Tavistock
⑥ Morwellham Quay

A386

⑤

⑭

Buckland
Abbey

Dart

Buckfastleigh ○

A381

A379

Cockington ○

Saltram
House
④③

A38

Totnes
⑤①

Torbay
⑤③

A386

A379

○ Yealmpton

Kingsbridge ○

Slapton ○

Dartmouth
⑤⓪

Brixham
⑤②

A379

Start
Bay

Plymouth
㊱ — ㊷

N ↑

English Channel

0		20 miles
0		30 km

north coast to Fowey on the south coast. Britain's longest National Trail, the South West Coast Path, runs for 630 mi from Minehead (Somerset) to South Haven Point, near Poole (Dorset).

Water Sports

Looe, on the south coast of Cornwall, is known for shark fishing, and boats can be rented for shark or mackerel fishing from most harbors along the south coast. This is also a good sailing area, with plenty of safe harbors, marinas, and deep-water channels, mainly at Falmouth, Plymouth Sound, and Torbay. Its beaches have long made the West Country one of Britain's main family vacation destinations. At many of the major resorts, flags show the limits of safe swimming. There can be strong undertows, especially on the northern coast, where the region's best surfing beaches are found.

Exploring the West Country

A circular tour of the West Country covers a large territory, from the bustling city of Bristol in Somerset, two hours outside London, to the remote and rocky headlands of Devon and Cornwall. Unless you confine yourself to a few choice towns—for example, Exeter, Penzance, and Plymouth—you will be at a huge disadvantage without your own transport. The main arteries of the region are the M5 motorway, ending at Exeter; A30, which burrows through the center of Devon and Cornwall all the way to Land's End; and A38, which loops south of Dartmoor to take in Plymouth. Beyond Plymouth, there are few main roads, which results in heavy traffic in summer. Take minor roads whenever possible, if only to see the real West Country, which should be appreciated at a leisurely pace. Rail travelers can make use of a fast service connecting Exeter, Plymouth, and Penzance, and there is also a good network of coach services.

Stark contrasts abound in this peninsula, and the farther west you travel, the more the sea becomes an overwhelming presence. On the whole, the northern coast is more rugged, the cliffs dropping dramatically to tiny coves and beaches, whereas the south coast shelters many more resorts and much wider expanses of sand. The crowds are usually found in the south, but there are also plenty of more remote inlets and estuaries along this southern littoral, and you do not need to go far to find a degree of seclusion.

Numbers in the text correspond to numbers in the margin and on the West Country and Plymouth maps.

Great Itineraries

The West Country requires some time to explore. Three days will provide only a sadly limited view of what Somerset and Devon have to offer, and you should rein in your wanderlust to avoid excessive traveling at the expense of exploring. In five days you can visit Somerset and Devon and get a good sense of their variety. Even a week would not do justice to this dense region, but it would certainly give you a chance to push on into Cornwall, where you will get a more balanced idea of what the West Country has to offer.

IF YOU HAVE 3 DAYS

Start off from the gateway to the West, **Bristol** ①, where you should make a point of crossing the Avon Gorge, before heading down the motorway to spend the best part of a day and your first night in 🖬 **Exeter** ㊴. The cathedral here commands the most attention, but the city has plenty more to offer, not least the quayside, home to fine period architecture and lively pubs. The next morning, follow A30 back east, along the coast to the fishing village of **Beer** ㊱ before heading inland to **Honiton** ⑤, a handsome Georgian town renowned for its lace industry; an eponymous pattern has been a lace-collector's delight for several centuries. Spend your second overnight in ⊞ **Glastonbury** ④, a small town awash in Arthurian and early Christian myth. Explore the Abbey here in the morning—run up to the Tor if you're feeling energetic—before making the short hop to the tiny city of **Wells** ③. The cathedral here is very different from Exeter's but is equally grand.

IF YOU HAVE 5 DAYS

Spend your first morning in **Bristol** ①, moving on to ⊞ **Wells** ③ for your first night's stop. Visit **Glastonbury** ④ the next day, before meeting up with the M5 to take you on to ⊞ **Exeter** ⑤④ for your second night. After exploring the city, drive southwest to **Plymouth** ③⑥–④②, which offers a wide range of attractions despite its modest appearance. Arguably the most impressive of these is Plymouth Hoe itself, a spectacular platform overlooking Plymouth Sound, where you can look down on a timeless scene of sailing craft set against the mighty backdrop of the Atlantic. Don't miss the Mayflower Steps, or the old Barbican area, a nucleus of shops, restaurants, and bobbing boats. Then leave the city behind to explore **Dartmoor,** one of England's last wildernesses. Specific targets on or around Dartmoor include Castle Drogo, an impressive 20th-century version of a medieval castle, near **Chagford** ④⑨; **Lydford Gorge** ④⑦, a secluded corridor of torrents and gushing waterfalls; and **Buckland Abbey** ④④, former home of Sir Francis Drake. Spend your third overnight in ⊞ **Dartmouth** ⑤⓪. The next day you could enjoy the sea air here and in the nearby "Riviera" region of **Torbay** ⑤③. Your fourth night could be east of Exeter in ⊞ **Honiton** ⑤⑦, well placed to make stops the next day at the exquisite Elizabethan **Montacute House** ⑤⑧ and the lonely **Cadbury Castle** ⑥⓪, one of the supposed sites of Camelot and a fitting place to wind up your West Country tour.

IF YOU HAVE 7 DAYS

Once out of **Bristol** ①, first up is a tour of the northern coast of Somerset and Devon, making stops at **Dunster** ⑥, site of a turreted and battlemented castle, and the twin towns of **Lynton** and **Lynmouth** ⑦, in a narrow cleft once likened to a fragment of Switzerland, but thankfully outliving the hype. Any of these would make a good place to break for lunch, before continuing on to the lovely cliff-top village of ⊞ **Clovelly** ⑪, which will be your first overnight stay. The second day, continue into Cornwall to take in **Tintagel** ⑭, which, with or without the Arthurian associations, presents a dramatic sight perched on its black rock above the swirling waves. Enjoy a refined seafood lunch in **Padstow** ⑮ and make a stop in **Newquay** ⑯ if you want to sample the more down-to-earth fish-and-chips atmosphere and generous beaches of this typical seaside resort. Pull into ⊞ **St. Ives** ⑱ for your second night; the town has a great deal to offer in the way of art and a good selection of hotels and restaurants. After taking in St. Ives the third day, set out for the very tip of the peninsula, **Land's End** ⑲, which is worth exploring on foot. Head for your next overnight, ⊞ **Penzance** ㉒. Nearby, the island fortress of **St. Michael's Mount** ㉓ is clearly visible and demands a closer inspection. Now make a brief sortie into the **Lizard Peninsula** ㉕, basing yourself in the resort of ⊞ **Falmouth** ㉗, which offers a range of accommodations as well as a brace of castles—the imposing Pendennis and its sibling across the estuary, **St. Mawes** ㉙. On your fifth day, begin by exploring seaside **Charlestown** ㉛, leaving the main part of the day for the eye-popping plant collection of the **Eden Project** ㉜, outside St. Austell. End the day in ⊞ **Plymouth** ③⑥–④②. After exploring the city in the morning, track north to Dartmoor, making a stop at Castle Drogo, near **Chagford** ④⑨; spend your sixth night in ⊞ **Exeter** ⑤④. Once you've soaked up the sights of this historic city, head up the M5, swinging east to see the majestic ruins of ⊞ **Glastonbury** ④ and the cathedral at nearby **Wells** ③.

When to Tour the West Country

Come July and August, the roads leading into the West Country are choked with traffic. Somehow the region seems able to absorb all the "grockles," or tourists, although the chances of finding a remote oasis of peace and quiet are severely curtailed. The beaches heave with sun-seekers, and the resort towns are either bubbling with zest or unbearably tacky, depending on your point of view. If you can't avoid visiting during the holiday season, your best option would be to find a secluded hotel and to make brief excursions from there. Otherwise, try to time your visit to coincide with the beginning or end of the summer. The West Country enjoys more hours of sunshine than most other parts of Britain, so you can take your chances with the weather. Fall and spring are good times to escape the crowds, although most people find the sea too cold for swimming and there is often a strong ocean breeze. Most properties not open all year open for Easter and close in late September or October. Those that remain open have reduced hours. Winter has its own special appeal, when the Atlantic waves crash dramatically against the coast, and the austere Cornish cliffs are at their most spectacular.

KING ARTHUR COUNTRY: FROM BRISTOL TO TINTAGEL

Exploring King Arthur Country means wending your way between documented history and the world of myth. Starting out from Bristol, your journey takes you south to the cathedral city of Wells and continues on via Glastonbury, possibly the Avalon of Arthurian legend. Taunton, to the west, is the capital of cider country and was the focus of fierce skirmishes during the English Civil War. Proceed west along the Somerset coast into Devon, skirting Exmoor and tracing the northern shore via Clovelly and Bude, and end at the cliff-top ruins of Tintagel Castle in Cornwall, the legendary birthplace of Arthur.

Bristol

❶ *120 mi west of London, 46 mi south of Birmingham, 13 mi northwest of Bath.*

A treasure of great historic interest, Bristol can be called the "birthplace of America" with some confidence, for it was from the old city docks of Bristol that John Cabot and his son Sebastian sailed in 1497 to touch down on the North American mainland, which he claimed for the English crown. Furthermore, Bristol was the home of William Penn, developer of Pennsylvania, and a haven for John Wesley, whose Methodist movement played such a significant role in Georgia's history. The city had been a major center since medieval times, but it was in the 17th and 18th centuries that it became an important port for the North American trade. Now that the city's industries no longer rely on the docks, the historic harbor along the River Avon has been largely given over to pleasure craft. The quayside offers arts and entertainment complexes, movie theaters, museums, stores, pubs, and restaurants; and carnivals, speedboat races, and regattas are held here in summer.

On view in the harbor stands the **SS *Great Britain,*** the first iron ship to cross the Atlantic. Built by the great English engineer Isambard Kingdom Brunel in 1843, it remained in service until the end of the century, first on the North American route and then on the Australian. ✉

Gas Ferry Rd., ☎ *0117/926–0680.* 🎫 *£6.25.* ⊙ *Apr.–Oct., daily 10–5:30; Nov.–Mar., daily 10–4:30.*

Bristol is the home of the **Church of St. Mary Redcliffe** (a five-minute walk from Temple Meads train station toward the docks), called "the fairest in England" by Queen Elizabeth I. It has rib vaulting and dates from the 1300s, and was built by Bristol merchants who wanted a place in which to pray for the safe (and profitable) voyages of their ships. A chapel holds the arms and armor of Sir William Penn, father of the founder of Pennsylvania. ⊠ *Redcliffe Way,* ☎ *0117/929–1487.* ⊙ *Daily 8:30–5:30.*

Among the Dissenters from the Church of England who found a home in Bristol were John Wesley and Charles Wesley. In 1739 they built the **New Room** here, a meeting place that became the first Methodist chapel; its austere simplicity contrasts sharply both with Anglican churches and with the modern shopping center hemming it in. The rooms upstairs contain mementos of the early Methodists and material relating to their proselytizing work in Georgia. Call ahead to combine your visit with a tour of **Charles Wesley's House** (a 10-minute walk away), a well-restored Georgian town house where the Wesleys lived while in Bristol. ⊠ *Broadmead,* ☎ *0117/926–4740.* 🎫 *Free; tours £2.80.* ⊙ *Mon.–Sat. and national holidays 10–4.*

🔄 **@ Bristol,** in the rebuilt Harbourside area, has three science- and nature-themed attractions with innovative exhibits. Explore@Bristol gives you the "hands-on, minds-on" experience of science, and at Wildscreen@Bristol you can find interactive natural history exhibits and walk through a rain forest teeming with exotic birds and butterflies. You can also view a film, generally science related, at the region's only giant-screen IMAX cinema. The open spaces linking the sites act as a venue for live performances and multimedia activities, with shops, cafés, and restaurants nearby. ⊠ *Deanery Rd., Harbourside,* ☎ *0117/909–2000,* WEB *www.at-bristol.org.uk.* 🎫 *£6.50 for 1 attraction, £11 for 2 attractions, £15.50 for 3 attractions.* ⊙ *Daily 10–6.*

In the Georgian suburb of Clifton—a sort of Bath in miniature—you can take in that monument to Victorian engineering, the 702-ft-long **Clifton Suspension Bridge** (⊠ Suspension Bridge Rd., Clifton), which spans the Avon Gorge. It was started in 1829 by Isambard Brunel and was not completed until after his death in 1864. The **Clifton Suspension Bridge Visitor Centre** (⊠ Bridge House, Sion Pl., ☎ 0117/974–4664, WEB www.clifton-suspension-bridge.org.uk), opposite the city end of the bridge, has a small exhibition with plenty of illuminating background on the bridge and its construction. A large model of Brunel's winning design illustrates how the engineering works.

🔄 The **Bristol Zoo Gardens,** near the Clifton Suspension Bridge, is one of the country's most famous zoos. Here, more than 300 animal species live in 12 acres of landscaped gardens; the Seal and Penguin Coasts, with spectacular underwater viewing, are rival attractions for Gorilla Island, Bug World, Twilight World, and the walk-through aviary. ⊠ *Clifton Down,* ☎ *0117/973–8951,* WEB *www.bristolzoo.org.uk.* 🎫 *£8.40.* ⊙ *June–Aug., daily 9–5:30; Sept.–May, daily 9–4:30.*

Dining and Lodging

For a spectacular overture to your West Country excursion, you might book a night at historic Thornbury Castle, just 12 mi north of Bristol in Thornbury (☞ Berkeley Castle *in* Chapter 8).

£££ ✗ **Markwicks.** This restaurant, in busy downtown Bristol, inhabits a basement that was once a safety deposit chamber. Black-and-white marble floors and iron grille doors retain the vaultlike atmosphere. The food is excellent; try the fish soup, or the local turbot and sea bass. The fixed-price menus, changed daily, are a good value. ⊠ *43 Corn St.,* ☎ *0117/926–2658. AE, DC, MC, V. Closed Sun., 1 wk at Christmas and Easter, and last 2 wks in Aug. No lunch Sat.*

££   ✗ **Bell's Diner.** Although it's a Bristol institution, this bistro is rather hidden—take A38 (Stokes Croft) north, then turn right on Ashley Road and immediately left at Picton Street, which will lead you to York Road. Bell's is in a converted corner shop and has Bristol prints on its pale gray walls, polished wooden floors, and an open fire. The inventive Mediterranean menu changes regularly, with particular attention paid to light dishes and toothsome desserts. ⊠ *1 York Rd., Montpelier,* ☎ *0117/924–0357. MC, V. Closed Sun. and Dec. 24–30. No lunch Sat. and Mon.*

£££   ✗🖬 **Hotel du Vin.** This hip Anglo-French chain, which also runs hotels in Winchester, Birmingham, and Tunbridge Wells, has established an ambitious outlet in the Sugar House—the collective name of six former sugar-refining warehouses—close to the rejuvenated docklands and the city center. The rooms are in contemporary style, retaining many of the original industrial features, and each is sponsored by a wine house. The restaurant's wine list is as extensive as you might expect—visit the cellar for a private tasting session—and the menu entices with modern but robust French flavors. *Narrow Lewin Mead, BS1 2NU,* ☎ *0117/ 925–5577,* FAX *0117/925–1199,* WEB *www.hotelduvin.com. 35 rooms 5 suites. Restaurant, billiards. AE, DC, MC, V.*

££–£££   🖬 **Redwood Lodge Hotel.** Primarily a business hotel and health center, this is a handy stopover for anyone touring by car—it's just off A4, close to the Clifton Suspension Bridge. Modern and attractively furnished, it has a number of amenities, including 16 acres of pleasant woodland surroundings. Weekend rates are an especially good value. ⊠ *Beggar Bush La., Failand, BS8 3TG,* ☎ *01275/393901,* FAX *01275/ 392104. 112 rooms. Restaurant, brasserie, indoor–outdoor pool, tennis court, gym, squash, cinema. AE, DC, MC, V.*

££   🖬 **Naseby House Hotel.** This Victorian hotel is on a tree-lined street in the heart of elegant Clifton, not far from Bristol's major sights. The comfortable bedrooms have TVs and tea- and coffeemakers; the plushest and most expensive is the one in the basement, which has a fourposter bed and a French window overlooking the garden. The sitting room is filled with period bric-a-brac, and the breakfast room is also impressive. ⊠ *105 Pembroke Rd., BS8 3EF,* ☎ FAX *0117/973–7859. 14 rooms, 13 with bath. Breakfast room. MC, V.*

Nightlife and the Arts

The **Bristol Old Vic** (⊠ King St., ☎ 0117/987–7877), the oldest working theater in the country, dates to 1766. Performances, ranging from classic productions to new works, are staged in three theaters: the Theatre Royal, the New Vic Studio, and the Basement Theatre.

Outdoor Activities and Sports

The Badminton Horse Trials are held annually during four days in May at the Duke of Beaufort's magnificent estate in **Badminton** (☎ 01454/ 218272), 12 mi northeast of Bristol.

En Route   The area south of Bristol is notable for its scenery and walks, its picturesque villages, and its ancient stone circles. Take A38 (follow signs for airport), then B3130 and B3114 to the villages of Chew Magna and Chew Stoke. At Chew Magna note the gargoyles on the ancient church. Continue on to Chew Valley Lake, a reservoir in a drowned valley surrounded by woods, which shelter 240 species of birds.

Stanton Drew Circles

❷ *6 mi south of Bristol, 10 mi west of Bath.*

Just east of the village of Stanton Drew are the Stanton Drew Circles, where three rings, two avenues of standing stones, and a burial chamber make up one of the grandest and most mysterious monuments in the country, dating from 3000 to 2000 BC. Excavations beneath the circles in 1997 revealed evidence of an older site, from around 3000 BC, consisting of a wood henge, or timber circle. Its great size suggests that it was once as important as Stonehenge for its ceremonial functions, although there is little of great visual impact now. The site lies in a field reached through a farmyard—you'll need suitable shoes to visit it. The stones stand on private land but are supervised by English Heritage. Access is given at any reasonable time, and a small admission may be requested. To get here from Chew Magna, turn east on B3130. ⊠ *B3130,* ☎ *0117/975–0700,* WEB *www.english-heritage.org.uk.*

Wells

❸ *22 mi south of Bristol, 20 mi southwest of Bath, 132 mi west of London.*

Wells, England's smallest cathedral city, lies at the foot of the Mendip Hills. Although it feels more like a quiet country town than a city, Wells is home to one of the great masterpieces of Gothic architecture, its great cathedral—the first to be built in the Early English style. The city's name refers to the underground streams that bubble up into St. Andrew's Well within the grounds of the Bishop's Palace. Spring water has run through High Street since the 15th century. The ancient marketplace in the city center is surrounded by 17th-century buildings. William Penn was arrested here in 1695 for preaching without a license at the Crown hotel. Wells has market days on Wednesday and Saturday.

★ The great west towers of the medieval **Cathedral Church of St. Andrew** can be seen for miles. This is the oldest surviving English Gothic church, dating from the 12th century. The cathedral derives its beauty from the perfect harmony of all of its parts, the glowing colors of its original stained-glass windows, and its peaceful setting among stately trees and majestic lawns. To appreciate the elaborate west front facade, approach the building on foot from the cathedral green, accessible from Market Place through a great medieval gate called "penniless porch" (named after the beggars who once waited here to collect alms from worshipers). The cathedral's west front is twice as wide as it is high, and is adorned with some 300 statues. Vast inverted arches were added in 1338 to stop the central tower from sinking to one side. The cathedral also has a rare medieval clock, consisting of the seated figure of a man called Jack Blandiver, who strikes a bell on the quarter hour while mounted knights circle in mock battle. Near the clock is the entrance to the Chapter House—a small wooden door opening onto a great sweep of stairs worn down on one side by the tread of pilgrims over the centuries. Free guided tours begin at the information desk. ⊠ *Cathedral Green,* ☎ *01749/674483.* 🖃 *£4 suggested donation.* ☉ *Apr.–June and Sept., Mon.–Sat. 9:30–7, Sun. 12:30–2:30; July–Aug., Mon.–Sat. 9:30–8:30, Sun. 12:30–2:30; Oct.–Mar., Mon.–Sat. 9:30–6:15, Sun. 12:30–2:30. Open longer on Sun. for services.*

The Bishop's Eye gate leading from Market Place takes you to the magnificent moat-ringed **Bishop's Palace,** which still contains most of the original 12th- and 13th-century residence. You can also see the ruins of a late 13th-century great hall, which lost its roof in the 16th century because Edward VI needed to use the lead it contained. The palace is surrounded by a moat that is home to swans. ⊠ *Market Pl.,* ☎ *01749/ 678691.* 🎫 *£3.* ⊙ *Apr.–July and Sept.–Oct., Tues.–Fri. and national holidays 10:30–6, Sun. 2–6; Aug., daily 10:30–6 (may close some days in Aug.).*

To the north of the cathedral, the cobbled **Vicar's Close** is one of Europe's oldest streets. It has terraces of handsome 14th-century houses with strange, tall chimneys, and a tiny medieval chapel that is still in use.

OFF THE
BEATEN PATH

WOOKEY HOLE – Signs in Wells's town center direct you 2 mi north to a complex of limestone caves in the Mendip Hills that may have been the home of Iron Age people. Here, according to ancient legend, the Witch of Wookey turned to stone. In addition to a museum, there is an underground lake and several chambers to explore, plus a working paper mill and a display of Madame Tussaud's early waxwork collection dating from the 1830s. ☎ *01749/672243.* 🎫 *£7.30.* ⊙ *Apr.–Oct., daily 10–5; Nov.–Mar., daily 10:30–4:30.*

Dining and Lodging

£££ ✕ **Ritcher's.** You can choose between eating downstairs or in the plant-filled loft upstairs in this bistro, where you can get good-value two- or three-course fixed-price meals. Among the dishes on the daily-changing menus are pan-fried duck breast, Chinese-style leg of pork, and (occasionally) guinea fowl. ⊠ *5 Sadler St.,* ☎ *01749/679085. MC, V.*

££ ✕🏠 **Ancient Gate House.** The guest rooms of this centrally located restaurant run by Italian Franco Rossi and his two sons make this a convenient base. The premises are old and full of character, and six rooms have four-poster beds, but in other respects the facilities are completely up-to-date. The restaurant, Rugantino, specializes in Italian dishes made largely from local produce, and there is also a traditional English menu. There's an especially good-value set-price menu at lunchtime. ⊠ *20 Sadler St., BA5 2SE,* ☎ *01749/672029,* ℻ *01749/670319,* 🖳 *www.ancientgatehouse.co.uk. 9 rooms, 7 with bath. Restaurant. AE, DC, MC, V.*

££ ✕🏠 **The Crown.** This hotel has been a landmark in Wells since the Middle Ages; William Penn was arrested here in 1695 for illegal preaching. There is a period atmosphere to the place, and four of the rooms have four-poster beds. The staff is particularly helpful. The Penn Bar and Eating House serves salads and such hot dishes as steak-and-kidney pie, or you can eat in the more comfortable French bistro, Anton's. ⊠ *Market Pl., BA5 2RP,* ☎ *01749/673457,* ℻ *01749/679792,* 🖳 *www.crownatwells.co.uk. 15 rooms. Restaurant, bar. AE, MC, V.*

££ ✕🏠 **Swan Hotel.** The Swan, a former coaching inn built in the 15th century, faces the cathedral. Nine rooms have four-poster beds, and on cold days you can relax in front of a log fire in one of the lounges. The restaurant serves traditional English roasts and fish dishes and displays costumes owned by the great Victorian actor Sir Henry Irving. ⊠ *11 Sadler St., BA5 2RX,* ☎ *01749/836300,* ℻ *01749/836301,* 🖳 *www.Bhere.co.uk. 35 rooms. Restaurant. AE, DC, MC, V.*

Glastonbury

★ ❹ *5 mi southwest of Wells, 27 mi south of Bristol, 27 mi southwest of Bath.*

A town steeped in history, myth, and legend, Glastonbury lies in the lee of Glastonbury Tor, a grassy hill rising 520 ft above the Somerset Levels. In legend, Glastonbury is identified with Avalon, the paradise into which King Arthur was reborn after his death. It is also said to be the burial place of Arthur and Guinevere, his queen. And according to Christian tradition, it was to Glastonbury, the first Christian settlement in England, that Joseph of Arimathea brought the Holy Grail, the chalice used by Christ at the Last Supper.

At the foot of **Glastonbury Tor** is **Chalice Well,** the legendary burial place of the Grail. It's a stiff climb up the tor, but you'll be rewarded by the fabulous view across the Vale of Avalon. At the top stands a ruined tower, all that remains of **St. Michael's Church,** which collapsed after a landslide in 1271. With all these marvels, it's little wonder that thousands of New Age aficionados descend on this town every summer, to mix the Christian with the Druidic and to search for Jesus, Arthur, Guinevere—and even Elvis.

The ruins of the great **Glastonbury Abbey,** in the center of town, are on the site where, according to legend, Joseph of Arimathea built a church in the 1st century. A monastery had certainly been erected here by the 9th century, and the site drew many pilgrims. The ruins are those of the abbey completed in 1524 and destroyed in 1539, during Henry VIII's dissolution of the monasteries. ⊠ *Magdalene St.,* ☎ *01458/832267,* WEB *www.glastonburyabbey.com.* 🖻 *£3.* ☉ *Feb., daily 10–5; Mar., daily 9:30–5:30; Apr.–May and Sept., daily 9:30–6; June–Aug., daily 9–6; Oct., daily 9:30–5; Nov., daily 9:30–4:30; Dec.–Jan., daily 10–4:30.*

Ⓒ The **Somerset Rural Life Museum** is housed in an impressive 14th-century tithe barn, named the Abbey Barn. More than 90 ft in length, it once stored the one-tenth portion of the town's produce that was owed to the church. Exhibits (some in a Victorian farmhouse) illustrate the world of 19th-century farming. Events especially designed for children take place most weekends during school holidays. ⊠ *Chilkwell St.,* ☎ *01458/831197,* WEB *www.somerset.gov.uk/museums.* 🖻 *£2.50.* ☉ *Apr.–Oct., Tues.–Fri. 10–5, weekends 2–6; Nov.–Mar., Tues.–Sat. 10–3.*

Held annually a few miles away in Pilton, the **Glastonbury Festival** (☎ 01749/890470 or pick up an issue of *New Musical Express* for the complete lineup) is the biggest and perhaps the best rock festival in England. For three days over the last weekend in June, it hosts hundreds of bands—basically a mix of established and up-and-coming, with a few big names from the past thrown in—on five stages. Festival tickets are steep—£85—but include entertainment, a camping pitch, and service facilities.

Lodging

££ 🏨 **George and Pilgrims Hotel.** Pilgrims en route to Glastonbury Abbey stayed here in the 15th century. Today the hotel is equipped with all the modern comforts, but retains its flagstone floors, wooden beams, and antique furniture; three rooms have four-poster beds. ⊠ *1 High St., BA6 9DP,* ☎ *01458/831146,* FAX *01458/832252. 13 rooms. Restaurant, bar. AE, DC, MC, V.*

Shopping

Glastonbury's market day is Tuesday. **Morlands Factory Shop** (⊠ 2 mi southwest of Glastonbury on A39, ☎ 01458/835042) is one of several good outlets for sheepskin products in Somerset sheep country, selling coats, slippers, and rugs.

En Route West of Glastonbury, take A39 and A361 toward Taunton to cross the Somerset Levels, marshes that were drained by open ditches (known as rhines) for peat digging, an industry that is now heavily restricted. The broad, marshy expanse of **Sedgemoor** is where, in 1685, the Duke of Monmouth's troops were routed by those of his uncle James II in the last battle fought on English soil; a flagstaff and memorial stones indicate the site. R. D. Blackmore's novel *Lorna Doone*, published in 1869, is set during Monmouth's Rebellion.

Taunton

❺ *22 mi southwest of Glastonbury, 50 mi southwest of Bristol, 18 mi northeast of Exeter.*

Somerset's principal town lies in the heart of the cider-making country. Two of the loveliest examples of Somerset's famous pinnacled and battlemented churches, St. James and St. Mary Magdalene, overlook the county cricket ground in the center of town. Besides cricket, Taunton is most celebrated for its cider. The town lies in the fertile Vale of Taunton, in the heart of the cider-making country. As you might expect, cider rather than beer is the traditional beverage in these parts, and can be far more potent. In the fall, some cider mills open their doors to visitors. If you're interested, visit **Sheppys,** a local farm and cider museum. The grounds, which include orchards and a fish pond, are always open for picnickers, and there's a café (summer only) and farm shop. ✉ *Three Bridges, Bradford-on-Tone (on A38 west of Taunton),* ☎ *01823/461233.* 🎫 *Museum £1.75; guided tour (2½ hrs) £4.25.* ☉ *Mon.–Sat. 8:30–6; mid-Apr.–Dec. 25, also Sun. noon–2.*

Dining and Lodging

£   ✕ **Brettons.** This small, casual spot serves both light lunches, such as pastas and curries, and more substantial meals, including saddle of lamb and baked monkfish. It's a 10-minute walk from the center of town. ✉ *49 East Reach,* ☎ *01823/256688. MC, V. Closed Sun. No lunch Sat., Mon.*

£££   ✕🏠 **The Castle.** The battlements and towers of this 300-year-old build-
★   ing will leave you in no doubt as to why this hotel, considered to be among England's finest, has the name it does. The facade is covered by a huge, 150-year-old wisteria, magnificent when in flower from April to June. Bedrooms are individually decorated, and garden suites have separate dressing rooms. In the hotel's restaurant, which has daily-changing, fixed-price menus, the haute cuisine ranges from braised shoulder of lamb with thyme and garlic to elaborate desserts such as baked egg custard tart with nutmeg ice cream. The cheese selection includes many English varieties, and is served with homegrown prunes. ✉ *Castle Green, TA1 1NF,* ☎ *01823/272671,* 📠 *01823/336066,* 🌐 *www.the-castle-hotel. com. 39 rooms, 5 suites. Restaurant, brasserie. AE, DC, MC, V.*

En Route   North of Taunton you will see the outlines of the **Quantock** and **Brendon hills.** The eastern Quantocks are covered with beech trees and are home to herds of handsome red deer. Climb to the top of the hills for a spectacular view of the Vale of Taunton Deane and, to the north, the Bristol Channel.

Dunster

❻ *21 mi northwest of Taunton, 43 mi north of Exeter.*

Lying between the Somerset coast and the edge of Exmoor National Park, Dunster is a picture-book village with a broad main street. The eight-sided yarn-market building on High Steet dates from 1589. The village is dominated by **Dunster Castle,** a 13th-century fortress remodeled in 1868–72. Acres of scenic parkland surround the building, which has fine plaster ceilings and a magnificent 17th-century staircase. Note that there is a steep climb up to the castle from the parking lot. ✉ *Off A39,* ☎ *01643/823004,* 🌐 *www.nationaltrust.org.uk.* 🎫 *£6, gardens only £3.* ☉ *Castle Apr.–Sept., Sat.–Wed. 11–5; Oct., Sat.–Wed. 11–4. Gardens Apr.–Sept., daily 10–5; Oct.–Mar., daily 11–4.*

En Route Heading west, the coast road A39 mounts Porlock Hill, an incline so steep that signs encourage drivers to "keep going." The views across Exmoor and north to the Bristol Channel and Wales are worth it. Buried at the bottom of a valley, with the slopes of Exmoor all about, the town of **Porlock** lies near the fabled Doone Country, setting for R. D. Blackmore's swashbuckling saga *Lorna Doone*. Porlock had already achieved a small place in literary history after Coleridge declared it was a "man from Porlock" who interrupted his opium trance while the poet was composing "Kubla Khan."

Lynton and Lynmouth

❼ *19 mi west of Dunster, 60 mi northwest of Exeter.*

This pretty pair of Devonshire villages is separated by a steep hill and linked by a water-powered cliff railway. Lynmouth, a fishing village, is at the bottom, crouching below 1,000-ft cliffs at the mouths of the East and West Lynne rivers. To 19th-century visitors, the place evoked an Alpine scene. The grand landscape of Exmoor lies all about, with undemanding walks possible to Watersmeet or the Valley of the Rocks, two local beauty spots.

Dining and Lodging

£££ ✗🏠 **Rising Sun.** On Bristol Channel, this atmospheric hotel with oak
★ paneling and creaking floorboards was once a 14th-century inn and a row of thatched cottages. It has great views over Lynmouth, especially from the terraced garden out back. The rooms are decorated in the latest-design print fabrics and furnished in pine or older pieces. If you want more privacy, ask for the detached cottage in the garden (also available for weekly rental), one of two places in Lynmouth claiming to be where the poet Shelley spent his honeymoon. The traditional restaurant specializes in local cuisine, including such dishes as roasted lamb shank on a celeriac puree and roast breast of guinea fowl. ✉ *Harbourside, Lynmouth EX35 6EQ,* ☎ *01598/753223,* 🆃🆇 *01598/753480,* 🆆🅴🅱 *www.risingsunlynmouth.co.uk. 16 rooms, 1 cottage. Restaurant, fishing. AE, DC, MC, V.*

££ 🏠 **Shelley's Hotel.** The second of Lynmouth's two hotels that claim to be Percy Bysshe Shelley's honeymoon haunt, this does not have such a fine location as the Rising Sun, but is more spacious and modern inside. Bright rooms have big windows and good views, and the staff are cheerful and helpful. Shelley and his sixteen-year-old bride, Harriet Westbrook, apparently left without paying their bill—although the poet later mailed £20 of the £30 owed. During his nine-week sojourn in Lynmouth, Shelley found time to write his polemical *Queen Mab*. ✉ *8 Watersmeet Rd., Lynmouth EX35 6EP,* ☎ *01598/753219,* 🆃🆇 *01598/753751,* 🆆🅴🅱 *www.shelleyshotel.co.uk. 11 rooms. Restaurant, bar. MC, V.*

Barnstaple

❽ *21 mi southwest of Lynton, 42 mi northwest of Exeter.*

Barnstaple, on the banks of the River Taw, is northern Devon's largest town. Its bustling center retains its traditional role as the region's principal market. West of Barnstaple, along the Taw estuary, lie desolate stretches of sand dunes offering long vistas of marram grass and sea.

Off the crowded High Street, you can catch the colorful scene at the **Pannier Market,** where crafts are traded on Monday and Thursday, antiques on Wednesday, and general goods and local produce on Tuesday, Friday, and Saturday. **Butchers' Row,** opposite the Pannier Market, holds 33 mainly identical butcher's shops. The 14th-century **St. Anne's**

Chapel, between High Street and Boutport Street, was converted into a grammar school in 1549, and later numbered among its pupils John Gay (1685–1732), author of *The Beggar's Opera*.

Dining and Lodging

££ ✕🖫 **Royal and Fortescue Hotel.** Edward VII, who stayed here when he was Prince of Wales, gave this Victorian hotel the royal part of its name. It is set by the river in the center of town, although the functionally furnished rooms have no view to speak of. There's a choice of dining: either in the excellent bistro, 62 The Bank, or in the self-service Lord Fortescue's. Room rates do not include breakfast. ✉ *Boutport St., EX31 1HG,* ☎ *01271/342289,* 𝖥𝖠𝖷 *01271/340102,* 𝖶𝖤𝖡 *www.royalfortescue.co.uk. 51 rooms. 2 restaurants. AE, DC, MC, V.*

Braunton Burrows

❾ *18 mi southwest of Lynton.*

Braunton Burrows, on the north side of the Taw estuary, is a National Nature Reserve, with miles of trails running through the dunes. This spot has some first-class bird-watching, especially in winter. The reserve warden can put people in touch with organized walks. ✉ *Off B3231 (2 mi west of Braunton),* ☎ *01271/812552 for warden.*

Bideford

❿ *8 mi southwest of Barnstaple by A39, 49 mi northwest of Exeter.*

Broad Bideford Bay is fed by the confluence of the rivers Taw and Torridge. Bideford lies on the Torridge, which you can cross either by the 14th-century 24-arch bridge or by the more modern structure to reach the scenic hillside sheltering the town's elegant houses. At one time they were all painted white, and Bideford is still sometimes called the "little white town." The area was a mainstay of 16th-century shipbuilding; the trusty vessels of Sir Francis Drake were built here. From the Norman era until the 18th century, the port was the property of the Grenville family, whose most celebrated scion was Sir Richard Grenville (c.1541–91), commander of the seven ships that carried the first settlers to Virginia, and later a key player in the defeat of the Spanish Armada.

Clovelly

⓫ *12 mi west of Bideford, 60 mi northwest of Exeter.*

Clovelly always seems to have the sun shining on its stepped and cobbled streets. A village of quaint atmosphere and picturesque beauty, it can be compared with villages in the south of France, such as St. Tropez. (Alas, it can also be as overrun with day-trippers as that Provence pleasure spot). Perched precariously among cliffs, a steep, cobbled road—tumbling down at such an angle that it is closed to cars—leads to the toylike harbor. The climb back has been likened to the struggles of Sisyphus, but, happily, a Land Rover service (in summer) will take you to and from the parking lot at the top. You pay £3.50 to park and use the visitor center; this is the only way to enter the village.

Dining and Lodging

£££ ✕🖫 **Red Lion Hotel.** One of only two hotels in this coastal village, the Red Lion is an 18th-century inn set right on the harbor. All rooms have sea views and are well equipped, although you have to put up with uneven floors, tiny windows, and restricted space. The climb up through Clovelly is perilously steep, but hotel guests can bring cars via a back road to and from the Red Lion. There are harbor views from the smart restaurant (fixed-price menu at dinner; lunch served July through

September only), which specializes in seafood such as grilled plaice with creamed herb potato; meat dishes might include roasted honey duck. You can have snacks in either of the two bars. ⊠ *The Quay, EX39 5TF,* ☎ *01237/431237,* 𝖥𝖠𝖷 *01237/431044. 11 rooms. Restaurant, 2 bars. AE, MC, V.*

Bude

⑫ *15 mi south of Clovelly.*

Just across the Cornish border, the popular Victorian seaside town of Bude is known for its long sandy beaches. But beware: in summer, the town and beaches are overrun with tourists.

Boscastle

⑬ *15 mi southwest of Bude.*

In tranquil Boscastle, some of the stone and slate cottages at the foot of the steep valley date from the 1300s. The town is centered around a little harbor, set snug within towering cliffs. Nearby, 2 mi up the valley of the Valency, is St. Juliot's, the "Endelstow" referred to in Thomas Hardy's *A Pair of Blue Eyes*—the young author was involved with the restoration of this church while he was working as an architect.

Lodding

£–££ ⊡ **The Old Rectory.** Hardy stayed here while restoring St. Juliot's, and it is here that he first met his wife-to-be, Emma, the rector's sister-in-law. The house, set on 3 acres of grounds, has been in the same family for five generations, and has been updated mainly in Victorian style. You can sleep in the Rector's Room, Emma's Room (with four-poster bed and original "thunder box"), or in Mr. Hardy's Room. Organic produce from the walled kitchen garden is served at breakfast, and Hardy-related workshops are available. The house is signposted off B3263 from Boscastle. ⊠ *St. Juliot, Boscastle, PL35 0BT,* ☎ *01840/250225,* 𝖶𝖤𝖡 *www.stjuliot.fsnet.co.uk. 3 rooms, 1 with bath. Croquet. MC, V. Closed Dec.–Feb.*

Tintagel

⑭ *5 mi southwest of Boscastle.*

The romance of Arthurian legend thrives around Tintagel's ruined castle on the coast. Ever since the somewhat unreliable 12th-century chronicler Geoffrey of Monmouth identified Tintagel as the home of Arthur, son of Uther Pendragon and Ygrayne, the site has been revered by devotees of the legend cycle. The historical Arthur is likely to have been a Christian Celtic chieftain battling against the heathen Saxons in the 6th century. Today the village itself has more than its share of tourist junk—including Excaliburgers.

The **Old Post Office,** a 14th-century stone manor house with smoke-blackened beams, has been restored to its appearance during Victorian times. ⊠ *3–4 Tintagel Centre,* ☎ *01840/770024,* 𝖶𝖤𝖡 *www.nationaltrust.org.uk.* 🕮 *£2.30.* ☉ *Apr.–Sept., daily 11–5:30; Oct., daily 11–4.*

★ All that is left of the ruined cliff-top **Tintagel Castle,** legendary birthplace of King Arthur, is the outline of its walls, moats, and towers, but it only requires a bit of imagination to conjure up a picture of Sir Lancelot and Sir Galahad riding out in search of the Holy Grail over the narrow causeway above the seething breakers. Archaeological evidence, however, suggests that the castle dates from much later—about 1150, when it was the stronghold of the earls of Cornwall, and the site may have been occupied by the Romans. The earliest identified remains at the castle are of Celtic (5th-century) origin, and these may have some connection with the legendary Arthur. But legends aside, nothing can detract from the castle ruins, dramatically set off by the wild, windswept Cornish coast, on an island connected by a narrow isthmus. (There are also traces of a Celtic monastery here.) Paths lead down to the pebble beach, to a cavern known as **Merlin's Cave.** Exploring Tintagel Castle involves some arduous climbing up and down steep steps, but even on a summer's day, when people swarm over the battlements and a westerly Atlantic wind seems always to be sweeping through Tintagel, you cannot help being awed by the proximity of the distant past. ⊠ *Castle Rd. (½ mi west of village),* ☎ *01840/770328,* ᵂᴱᴮ *www.english-heritage.org.uk.* ᴤ *£3.* ⊙ *Mid-July–Aug., daily 10–7; Apr.–mid-July and Sept., daily 10–6; Oct., daily 10–5; Nov.–Mar., daily 10–4.*

Displays in the **Arthurian Centre** provide background to the story of King Arthur. Highlights include Arthur's Stone, dated to 540 BC, and a lovely woodland walk to the site of Arthur's "last battle." There is also a gift shop and tea garden. The center is 5 mi southeast of Tintagel Castle, on the edge of Bodmin Moor. ⊠ *Slaughterbridge, Camelford,* ☎ *01840/ 212450.* ᴤ *£1.75.* ⊙ *Mid-Feb.–Dec., daily 10–6.*

Lodging

££   🏠 **Trebrea Lodge.** All rooms in this lovely Georgian manor house are furnished with antiques, and west-facing bedrooms have glorious sunsets over the sea. The oak-paneled dining room (dinner only; nonguests should reserve ahead) prepares meals from spankingly fresh local ingredients, or you can relax in front of a fire in the cozy snug (the only room where smoking is allowed). The house is a mile from Tintagel on the Trenale road. ⊠ *Trenale, Tintagel PL34 0HR,* ☎ *01840/770410,* ꜰᴀˣ *01840/770092. 7 rooms. Restaurant. AE, MC, V. Closed Jan.*

THE CORNWALL COAST: ON THE ROAD TO PLYMOUTH

This excursion covers the whole of Cornwall, first traveling southwest from Tintagel along the north Cornish coast to Land's End, the westernmost tip of Britain, known for its savage land- and seascapes and panoramic views. From Land's End, turn northeast, stopping in the popular seaside resort of Penzance, the harbor city of Falmouth, and a string of pretty Cornish fishing villages. Next set off across the boggy, heath-covered expanse of Bodmin Moor, and then turn south to Plymouth, Devon's largest city, whose present-day dockyards recall a rich, centuries-old naval tradition.

Padstow

🅑   *15 mi southwest of Tintagel.*

At the mouth of the Camel River, this small fishing port has attracted considerable attention as a center of culinary excellence, largely due to Rick Stein's dining establishment. However, Padstow is worth visiting even if you're not turned on by seafood. Its lively harbor is clamorous with the shrieks of gulls, a string of fine beaches lies within a short ride—including some choice strands highly prized by surfers—and there are two scenic walking routes: the Saints Way across the peninsula to Fowey, and the Camel Trail, a footpath and cycling path that follows the river as far as Bodmin Moor.

Dining

££££ ✕ **The Seafood Restaurant.** Celebrity chef Rick Stein has reigned in Pad-
★ stow since 1975, making it an essential stop on any foodie's itinerary.
The restaurant, just across from where the lobster boats and trawlers
unload their catch, has built its reputation on its combination of the
freshest fish and high culinary artistry. The fixed-price dinners are the
best option, and may include scallops with ginger, soy, and sesame, or
brill with poached oysters and chives. Meat is also on the menu, and
desserts are worth a visit—look for the panna cotta with baked plums.
If you can't get a table here, Stein has two other places in town, St.
Petroc's Bistro (⊠ 4 New St., ☎ 01841/532700) and Rick Stein's
Café (⊠ 10 Middle St., ☎ 01841/532700), both consistently good; the
latter has a Rick Stein delicatessen next door. All three restaurants also
provide tasteful lodgings. ⊠ *Riverside,* ☎ *01841/532700. Reservations
essential. AE, DC, MC, V. Closed 1 wk around Christmas.*

Outdoor Activities and Sports

BICYCLING

Bikes of all shapes and sizes can be rented at **Brinham's** (⊠ South Quay,
☎ 01841/532594).

WALKING

The **Saints Way,** a 30-mi path between Padstow and the Camel Estuary on Cornwall's north coast to Fowey on the south coast, follows a
Bronze Age trading route, later used by Celtic pilgrims to cross the peninsula. Several relics of such times can be seen along the way. Contact
the Cornwall Tourist Board for information.

Newquay

16 *14 mi southwest of Padstow, 30 mi southwest of Tintagel.*

The principal resort on the north Cornwall coast, Newquay is a fairly
large town established in 1439. It was once the center of the trade in
pilchards (a small herringlike fish), and on the headland you can still
see a little white hut where a lookout known as a "huer" watched for
pilchard schools and directed the boats to the fishing grounds. Newquay
has become the country's surfing capital, and the wide beaches can be
uncomfortably packed in summer with the young California-dream-
ing devotees.

Perranporth

17 *8 mi south of Newquay, 13 mi northwest of Truro.*

Past the sandy shores of Perran Bay, Perranporth, one of Cornwall's
most popular seaside spots, is extremely crowded in high season. The
swells off this 3-mi stretch of beach attract swarms of surfers, too. The
best times to visit are the beginning and end of the summer. Enjoy the
enchanting coastal walks along the dunes and cliffs.

St. Ives

18 *20 mi southwest of Perranporth on A30, 10 mi north of Penzance.*

James McNeill Whistler came here to paint his landscapes, Daphne du
Maurier and Virginia Woolf to write their novels. Today, sand, sun,
and world-class art continue to attract thousands of stylish vacationers to the fishing village of St. Ives, named after St. Ia, a 5th-century
female Irish missionary said to have arrived on a floating leaf. The town
has long played host to a well-established artists' colony, and there are
plenty of craftspeople, too. St. Ives is often crowded with day-trippers,
so it's best to park outside the town.

Dame Barbara Hepworth (1903–75), who pioneered abstract sculpture in England, lived here for 26 years. Her house and garden, now the **Barbara Hepworth Museum and Sculpture Garden,** is run by London's prominent Tate Gallery. ⊠ *Trewyn Studio, Barnoon Hill,* ☎ *01736/796226.* ▣ *£3.75, combined ticket with Tate Gallery St. Ives £6.50.* ۞ *Sept.–June, Tues.– Sun. and national holidays 10:30–5:30; July–Aug., daily 10:30–5:30.*

★ The spectacular **Tate Gallery St. Ives** houses the work of artists who lived and worked in St. Ives, mostly from 1925 to 1975, drawn from the rich collection of the Tate in London. It occupies a lavish modernist building—a fantasia of seaside deco-period architecture with a panoramic view of turquoise rippling ocean. The four-story gallery, set at the base of a cliff fronted by Porthmeor Beach, may be the only art museum in the world with a special storage space for visitors' surfboards. The rooftop café is excellent. ⊠ *Porthmeor Beach,* ☎ *01736/796226,* ᴡᴇʙ *www.tate.org.uk.* ▣ *£3.95, combined ticket with Barbara Hepworth Museum and Sculpture Garden £6.50.* ۞ *Sept.–June, Tues.–Sun. and national holidays 10:30–5:30; July–Aug., daily 10:30–5:30.*

At the **St. Ives Society of Artists Gallery,** local artists display selections of their current work for sale in the Old Mariners' Church. The Crypt is hired out for private exhibitions. ⊠ *Norway Sq.,* ☎ *01736/795582.* ▣ *25p.* ۞ *Mid-Mar.–Oct., daily 10–4:30.*

Dining and Lodging

££ ✕ **The Blue Fish.** This small, simple restaurant in the heart of St. Ives is a handy spot for seafood. Try the monkfish wrapped in Parma ham with scallops and a spinach mash, or seared tuna steak with a spicy sauce. Paella, pastas, and meat dishes round out the menu. There's a terrace for lunching in fine weather. ⊠ *Norway La.,* ☎ *01736/794204. AE, DC, MC, V. No lunch Mon.–Thurs. Oct.–Apr.*

£–££ ✕ **The Sloop Inn.** One of Cornwall's oldest pubs, the harborfront Sloop Inn was built in 1312. Pub lunches and evening meals are available in the wood-beam rooms, where you can also see the work of local artists. ⊠ *The Wharf,* ☎ *01736/796584. MC, V.*

£££ ✕▣ **Garrack Hotel.** A family-run, ivy-clad hotel with panoramic sea
★   views from its hilltop location, the Garrack offers a relaxed, undemanding atmosphere. Courteous staff are always on hand to provide local information. Some rooms are furnished in traditional style; others are more modern. The restaurant is one of the best in the region. Lobster is a house specialty, sauteed and tossed in pasta or served cold with a mixed-leaf salad. The contemporary English menu features locally sourced fish, such as grilled fillet of turbot, and Cornish lamb. Breads are made in-house, and the wine list includes Cornish vineyards. ⊠ *Burthallan La., TR26 3AA,* ☎ *01736/796199,* ꜰᴀx *01736/798955,* ᴡᴇʙ *www.garrack.com. 18 rooms. Restaurant, indoor pool, sauna, gym. AE, DC, MC, V.*

En Route   The B3306 coastal road southwest from St. Ives is a winding route passing through some of Cornwall's starkest yet most beautiful countryside. Barren hills crisscrossed by low stone walls drop abruptly to granite cliffs and wide bays. Evidence of the ancient tin-mining industry— the remains of smokestacks and pumping houses—is everywhere. Near the village of Pendeen, the historic **Geevor Tin Mine** is an early 20th-century mine that by the 1930s was the only mine left in the St. Just district. At its peak Geevor employed 400 men, but in October 1985, the collapse of the world tin market wiped Cornwall from the mining map. Surface and underground tours are conducted from March through October at what is now a fascinating mining heritage center; make sure you have suitably sturdy footwear. A museum, shop, and

café are on the site. ✉ B3306, ☎ 01736/788662. 🎫 £5.50; £2 Nov.–
Feb. ☉ Apr.–Oct., Sun.–Fri. and Sat. before bank holiday Mon. 10–
5; Nov.–Feb. (museum and shop only), Sun.–Fri. and Sat. before bank
holiday Mon. 10–4.

Land's End

★ ⑲ *10 mi southwest of St. Ives, 10 mi west of Penzance.*

The coastal road, B3306, ends at the western tip of Britain at what is,
quite literally, Land's End. The sea crashes against its rocks and lashes
ships battling their way around it. Approach it from one of the coastal
footpaths for the best panoramic view. Over the years, sightseers have
caused some erosion of the paths, but new ones are constantly being
built, and Cornish "hedges" (granite walls covered with turf) have been
planted to prevent future erosion. The scenic grandeur of Land's End
remains undiminished, although the point draws crowds of people from
all over the world. A glitzy theme park, the **Land's End Experience** (☎
0870/458–0099), runs a poor second to nature.

Nightlife and the Arts

The open-air **Minack Theatre,** perched high above a wedge of sandy
beach at Porthcurno, 3 mi southeast of Land's End, was the inspiration of local benefactress Rowena Cade, who began its construction
in the 1930s for amateur productions. The slope of the cliff forms a
natural amphitheater, with bench seats on the terraces and the sea as
a magnificent backdrop. Plays from classic dramas to modern comedies are performed afternoons and evenings in summer. An exhibition
center recounts the theater's creation. ✉ *Off B3315,* ☎ *01736/810181.*
🎫 *Exhibition center £2.50; performances £5.50–£6.50.* ☉ *Apr.–Sept.,
daily 9:30–5:30; Oct.–Mar., daily 10–4. Closed during matinée, currently May–Sept., Wed. and Fri. at 2.*

Outdoor Activities and Sports

Cornwall was often the mariner's last sighting of England on departing this country and his first on returning. But many ships foundered
on the rocky coastline, resulting in an estimated 3,600 shipwrecks lit-
tering the seabed. The area around Land's End has some of the best
diving in Europe, and the convergence of the Atlantic and the Gulf Stream
results in impressive visibility and unusual subtropical marine life. **Ly-
onesse Scuba Dive Centre** offers courses and guided dives for begin-
ners and experts. ✉ *Trewellard Industrial Estate, Pendeen,* ☎ *01736/
787773 or 07974/012037.*

Mousehole

⑳ *7 mi east of Land's End, 3 mi south of Penzance.*

On B3315 between Land's End and Penzance, Mousehole (pronounced
mow-zel), is worth a stop—and plenty of people do stop—to see this
archetypal Cornish fishing village of tiny stone cottages. It was the home
of Dolly Pentreath, supposedly the last native Cornish speaker, who
died in 1777.

Newlyn

㉑ *2 mi north of Mousehole.*

Newlyn has long been the county's most important fishing port and
became the magnet for a popular artists' colony at the end of the 19th
century. Few of the appealing fishermen's cottages that first attracted
artists to the area remain. To see the works of the Newlyn School, drop
into the Penlee House Gallery in Penzance.

Penzance

❷ *1½ mi north of Newlyn, 10 mi south of St. Ives.*

The popular seaside resort of Penzance offers spectacular views over Mount's Bay. Because of the town's isolated position, it has always been open to attack from the sea. During the 16th century, Spanish raiders destroyed most of the original town, and the majority of old buildings date from as late as the 18th century. The main street is called Market Jew Street, a folk mistranslation of the Cornish expression "Marghas Yow," which means "Thursday Market." Look for Market House, constructed in 1837, an impressive, domed granite building that is now a bank.

One of the prettiest streets in Penzance is **Chapel Street,** formerly the main street. It winds down from Market House to the harbor, its predominantly Georgian and Regency houses suddenly giving way to the extraordinary **Egyptian House,** whose facade is an evocation of ancient Egypt. Built around 1830 as a geological museum, today it houses holiday apartments. Across Chapel Street is the 17th-century **Union Hotel,** where in 1805 the death of Lord Nelson and the victory of Trafalgar were first announced from the minstrels' gallery in the assembly rooms. Near the Union Hotel on Chapel Street is one of the few remnants of old Penzance, the **Turk's Head,** an inn said to date from the 13th century.

The **Maritime Museum** simulates the lower decks of a four-deck man-of-war and exhibits items salvaged from shipwrecks off the Cornish coast. ✉ *19 Chapel St.,* ☎ *01736/368890.* 🎫 *£2.* ☉ *Mid-Apr.–Oct., Mon.–Sat. 10:30–4:30.*

The small collection at the **Penlee House Gallery and Museum,** in the gracious setting of a Victorian house and park, focuses on paintings by members of the so-called Newlyn School from about 1880 to 1930. These works evoke the life of the inhabitants of Newlyn, mostly fisher folk. There are also decorative arts, costume, and photography exhibits. The museum covers 6,000 years of history in West Cornwall. A café and a gift shop are on the ground floor. ✉ *Penlee Park,* ☎ *01736/ 363625,* WEB *www.penleehouse.org.uk.* 🎫 *£2, Sat. free.* ☉ *May–Sept., Mon.–Sat. 10–5; Oct.–Apr., Mon.–Sat. 10:30–4:30.*

Dining and Lodging

£££   ✕ **Harris's.** Tucked away off Market Jew Street, Harris's is a rare outpost of quality cuisine in Penzance. Two small rooms provide an elegant refuge for the travel-weary, although the decor may be a shade overpowering. Seafood is the main event, whatever the boats bring in: crab Florentine, grilled on a bed of spinach with cheese sauce, is usually available. Meat dishes might include medallions of Scottish venison with wild mushrooms. ✉ *46 New St.,* ☎ *01736/364408. AE, MC, V. Closed Sun., also Mon. Nov.–May, and 4 wks Nov.–Mar.*

£–££   ✕ **Admiral Benbow Inn.** One of the most famous inns in Penzance, the
★   15th-century Admiral Benbow was once a smugglers' pub (look for the armed smuggler on the roof) and is filled with seafaring memorabilia, a brass cannon, model ships, ropes, and figureheads. In the restaurant area, which is kitted out to resemble a ship's galley, you can dine on seafood dishes or a simple steak-and-Guinness pie. ✉ *46 Chapel St.,* ☎ *01736/363448. MC, V.*

£££–££££   ✕🏨 **Abbey Hotel and Restaurant.** Owned by former model/icon Jean
★   Shrimpton and her husband, this small, 17th-century hotel has a marvelous homey feel. The drawing room is filled with books, and many rooms are furnished with antiques; there is also a comfortable small apartment. The attractive restaurant has a short but intriguing menu,

with seafood gratin, Barbary duck, and homemade ice cream. ⊠ *Abbey St., TR18 4AR,* ☎ *01736/366906,* FAX *01736/351163. 6 rooms, 1 apartment. AE, MC, V.*

£ 🔟 **Camilla House.** The comfortably furnished Camilla stands on a road parallel to the Promenade, close to the harbor. The front rooms have sea views, and the top room is coziest. The owners are agents for the ferry line and can help with trips to the Isles of Scilly. There is a strict no-smoking policy in guest rooms. ⊠ *12 Regent Terr., TR18 4DW,* ☎ FAX *01736/363771,* WEB *www.camillahouse-hotel.co.uk. 8 rooms, 4 with bath. MC, V.*

St. Michael's Mount

★ ㉓ *3 mi east of Penzance on A394.*

Rising out of Mount's Bay just off the coast, the spectacular granite and slate island of St. Michael's Mount is one of Cornwall's greatest natural attractions. A 14th-century castle perched at the highest point— 200 ft above the sea—was built on the site of a Benedictine chapel founded by Edward the Confessor. In its time, it has been a church, a fortress, and a private residence. The buildings around the base of the rock range from medieval to Victorian, but appear harmonious. The Mount is surrounded by fascinating gardens, in which a great variety of plants flourish in microclimates—snow can lie briefly on one part, and it can be 70°F in another. To get there, follow the causeway—just as you can to its "sister" of the same name in France—or, when the tide is in during the summer, take the ferry. If you have to wait for the ferry, there is a convenient restaurant at the harbor, but the island also has a café and restaurant. Wear stout shoes for your visit to this site, which is unsuitable for anyone with mobility problems. ⊠ *Marazion,* ☎ *01736/710507,* WEB *www.nationaltrust.org.uk.* ⊡ *£4.50; £1 for ferry each way.* ☉ *Apr.–June and Sept.–Oct., weekdays 10:30–5:30 (last admission 4:45); July–Aug., daily 10:30–5:30 (last admission 4:45); Nov.–Mar., phone for hrs.*

Helston

㉔ *13 mi east of Marazion, 14 mi east of Penzance, 18 mi southwest of Truro.*

The attractive Georgian town of Helston is most famous for its annual "Furry Dance," which takes place on Floral Day, May 8 (unless the date is a Sunday or Monday, in which case it takes place on the previous Saturday). The whole town is decked with flowers, and dancers weave their way in and out of the houses along a 3-mi route.

🅒 **Flambards Theme Park** has an aircraft collection, a re-creation of a wartime street during the Blitz, and a reconstructed Victorian village. ⊠ *Off A394, 2 mi from Helston,* ☎ *01326/573404; information line 01326/564093.* ⊡ *£9.50.* ☉ *Mid-Apr.–mid-July and Sept.–Oct., daily 10:30–5; mid-July–Aug., daily 10–6. Possibly closed Mon. and Fri. in May, Sept., and Oct. (check first).*

Dining and Lodging

££–£££ ✕🔟 **Nansloe Manor.** Although near Helston's center, this peaceful manor house gives the impression of being deep in the country, with its attractive ½-mi driveway and 4 acres of grounds. The public areas and guest rooms are done in country-house style, with upholstered furniture and print fabrics. There are good half-board rates for longer stays. The four-course fixed-price menu in the dining room is wide-ranging and changes daily: fish is top choice. Full lunches are available only on Saturday, and light snacks are available the rest of the week. ✉ *Meneage Rd., TR13 0SB,* ☎ *01326/574691,* ℻ *01326/564680,* 🖳 *www.nansloe-manor.co.uk. 7 rooms. Restaurant, lounge. MC, V.*

Lizard Peninsula

★ ㉕ *10 mi south of Helston.*

The Lizard Peninsula is the southernmost point on mainland Britain and is an officially designated Area of Outstanding Natural Beauty. The huge, eerily rotating dish antennae of the Goonhilly Satellite Communications Earth Station are visible from the road as it crosses Goonhilly Downs, the backbone of the peninsula. A path, close to the tip of the peninsula, plunges down 200-ft cliffs to the tiny **Kynance Cove**, with its handful of pint-sized islands. The sands here are reachable only in the 2½ hours before and after low tide. The Lizard's cliffs are made of greenish serpentine rock, interspersed with granite; local souvenirs are carved out of the stone.

Gweek

㉖ *2 mi east of Helston.*

The fishing village of Gweek is at the head of the River Helford. The **Seal Sanctuary,** a conservation area, shelters sick and injured seals brought in from all over the country. Try to be here for feeding time, which occurs at least four times a day; call the information line for precise times. ☎ *01326/221361, 01326/221874 for information line.* 🖭 *£6.50.* ☉ *Daily from 9 AM; call for closing times, usually about 2 hrs before sunset.*

Falmouth

㉗ *7 mi northeast of Gweek, 12 mi south of Truro.*

The bustle hubbub of this busy resort town's fishing harbor, yachting center, and commercial port only adds to its charm. In the 18th century, Falmouth was a mail-boat port, and in Flushing, a village across the inlet, are the slate-covered houses built by prosperous mail-boat captains. A ferry service now links the two towns. On Custom House Quay, off Arwenack Street, is the King's Pipe, an oven in which seized contraband was burned.

At the end of the peninsula stands the formidable **Pendennis Castle,** built by Henry VIII in the 1540s and later improved by his daughter Elizabeth I. You can explore the different defenses developed over the centuries. The castle has sweeping views over the English Channel and across the water known as Carrick Roads to St. Mawes Castle on the Roseland Peninsula, designed as a companion fortress to guard the roads. ✉ *Pendennis Head,* ☎ *01326/316594,* 🖳 *www.english-heritage.org.uk.* 🖭 *£3.80.* ☉ *Apr.–Sept., daily 10–6; Oct., daily 10–5; Nov.–Mar., daily 10–4.*

Dining and Lodging

££ ✕ **Pandora Inn.** Four miles north of Falmouth, this thatched pub, with both a patio and a moored pontoon for summer dining, is a great discovery. The ambience derives from maritime memorabilia and fresh flowers, and you can eat in the bar or in the candlelit restaurant. The menu highlight is fresh seafood—try the creamy crab thermidor; other choices depend on the catch of the day. ✉ *Restronguet Creek, Mylor Bridge,* ☎ *01326/372678. MC, V. No lunch in restaurant.*

££ ✕ **Seafood Bar.** The window of this restaurant on the quay is a fish
★ tank, and beyond it is the very best seafood. Try thick crab soup, locally caught lemon sole, or, in summer, turbot cooked with cider, apples, and cream. ⊠ *Quay St.,* ☎ *01326/315129. MC, V. Closed Sun.
Oct.–June, Mon. Oct.–Easter. No lunch.*

££ 🏨 **St. Michael's Hotel.** At this seaside hotel in a long, low, white building overlooking Falmouth Bay, the gardens sweep down to the sea. The
staff is extremely friendly, and the place is especially recommended for
families. ⊠ *Stracey Rd., TR11 4NB,* ☎ *01326/312707,* ℻ *01326/
211772. 65 rooms. Restaurant, bar, indoor pool, hot tub, sauna, gym.
AE, DC, MC, V.*

£ 🏨 **Gyllyngvase House Hotel.** This hotel is centrally located near the
seafront. The bedrooms are a bit small but pleasantly furnished, and
there is a garden at the back. Evening meals are available for guests
on request. ⊠ *Gyllyngvase Rd., TR11 4GH,* ☎ *01326/312956,* ℻
01326/316166. 15 rooms, 12 with bath. AE, DC, MC, V.

Trelissick

28 *6 mi north of Falmouth on B3289.*

At Trelissick, the **King Harry Ferry,** a chain-drawn car ferry, runs to
the scenically splendid Roseland Peninsula three times hourly every day
(☎ 01872/862312 for last crossings). From its decks you can see up
and down the Fal, a deep, narrow river with steep, wooded banks. The
river's great depth provides mooring for old ships waiting to be sold;
these mammoth shapes lend a surreal touch to the riverscape.

★ Taking the King Harry Ferry, you can visit **St. Just in Roseland,** one of
the most beautiful spots in the West Country. This tiny hamlet made
up of stone cottage terraces and a 13th-century church is set within a
subtropical garden, often abloom with magnolias and rhododendrons
on a summer's day. Here, beneath a moss-covered, tiled roof, is a
spring, from which water has been used for centuries to baptize babies in the church font. St. Just is 9 mi south of Truro.

St. Mawes

29 *16 mi east of Falmouth (by road), 1½ mi east by sea, 11 mi south of
Truro by ferry.*

At the tip of the Roseland Peninsula is the pretty, quiet village of St.
Mawes. The well-preserved Tudor-era **St. Mawes Castle,** outside the
village, has a cloverleaf shape that makes it seemingly impregnable, yet
during the Civil War, its Royalist commander surrendered without firing a shot. (In contrast, Pendennis Castle held out at the time for 23
weeks before submitting to the siege.) ☎ 01326/270526, 🌐 *www.en-
glish-heritage.org.uk.* 🎟 *£2.70.* ☼ *Apr.–Sept., daily 10–6; Oct., daily
10–5; Nov.–Mar., Wed.–Sun. 10–1 and 2–4.*

En Route The shortest route from St. Mawes to Truro is via the ferry. The longer
way swings in a circle on A3078 for 19 mi through attractive countryside, where subtropical shrubs and flowers thrive, past the town of
Portloe (and its cozy hotel) and the 123-ft church tower in the village
of Probus, flaunting its gargoyles and pierced stonework.

Truro

30 *12 mi north of Falmouth, 13 mi southwest of Charlestown.*

Truro is a compact, elegant Georgian city, nestled in a crook at the head
of the River Truro. Although Bodmin is the county seat, Truro is Cornwall's only real city. For an overview of Truro's Georgian house fronts,

take a stroll down Lemon Street. The 18th-century facades along this steep, broad street are of pale stone—unusual for Cornwall, where granite is predominant. Like Lemon Street, Walsingham Place is a typical Georgian street—a curving, flower-lined pedestrian oasis.

The **Cathedral Church of St. Mary**—the first cathedral built in England after the completion of St. Paul's in London in the early 1700s—dominates the city. Although comparatively modern (built 1880–1910), it evokes the feeling of a medieval church, with an impressive exterior in early English Gothic style. The interior is filled with relics from the 16th-century parish church that originally stood on this site, part of which has been incorporated in a side chapel. In front of the west porch there is an open, cobbled area called High Cross, and the city's main shopping streets fan out from here. ⊠ *14 St. Mary's St.,* ☎ *01872/276782.* ⛳ *£2 suggested donation.* ☉ *Mon.–Sat. 9–5, Sun. noon–5 (open longer hrs for services and evensong).*

The **Royal Cornwall Museum,** in a striking Georgian building, offers old-master drawings, a sampling of Cornish art and archaeology, an extensive collection of minerals, and a café and shop. ⊠ *River St.,* ☎ *01872/272205,* WEB *www.royalcornwallmuseum.org.uk.* ⛳ *£3.* ☉ *Mon.–Sat. 10–5.*

Dining and Lodging

£££   ✕⌂ **Alverton Manor.** This was once a bishop's house, then a convent, and it is now an up-to-date hotel-restaurant, both efficient and atmospheric. The former chapel is used as an unusual conference room. Guest rooms are large, with French cherrywood furniture. Quiet elegance is the keynote of the public rooms, and in the Terrace restaurant, standards are kept high with the use of the best local produce in traditional and modern English recipes. ⊠ *Tregolls Rd., TR1 1ZQ,* ☎ *01872/276633,* ℻ *01872/222989. 33 rooms. Restaurant. AE, DC, MC, V. Closed 10 days at Christmas.*

Charlestown

❸❶ *15 mi east of Truro.*

This port was built by a local merchant in 1791 to export the huge reserves of china clay from St. Austell, 1 mi to the north. Charlestown was one of the ports from which 19th-century emigrants left for North America. It has managed to avoid overdevelopment since its heyday in the early 1800s, preserving its charming Georgian harbor, which is often used as a set for period film and television productions.

Lodging

£   ⌂ **T'Gallants.** This refurbished Georgian house directly behind the harbor takes its name from top gallant, one of the sails of a square-rigged sailing ship. Ask for a south-facing room to enjoy the tranquil morning view. The garden at the front is ideal for afternoon tea or an evening drink. ⊠ *6 Charlestown Rd., Charlestown, St. Austell, PL25 3NJ,* ☎ *01726/70203. 8 rooms. MC, V.*

Eden Project

★ ❸❷ *3 mi northeast of Charlestown.*

Spectacularly set in a former china clay pit, the Eden Project, a "living theater of plants and people," presents the world's major plant systems in microcosm. Its mission is to encourage sustainability as well as to show the sheer beauty of the natural plant world, and the venture generally lives up to the publicity it received at its opening in spring 2001. The crater contains more than 70,000 plants—many belonging to rare or endangered species—from three climate zones, two of them housed in the largest conservatories in the country. The emphasis is on conservation and ecology, yet without the slightest hint of moralizing. There's a Land Train (free) for the footsore, and well-informed guides provide information. An entertaining exhibition in the visitor center gives you the lowdown on the entire project. To avoid the biggest crowds, you may want to visit later in the afternoon. ✉ *Bodelva, St. Austell (signposted off the A30, A390, and A391),* ☎ *01726/222900,* WEB *www. edenproject.com.* 🎫 *£9.50.* ☉ *Daily 10–6; last admission at 5.*

Bodmin

③③ *14 mi north of Charlestown.*

Bodmin was the only Cornish town recorded in the 11th-century *Domesday Book,* William the Conqueror's census. During World War I, both the *Domesday Book* and the Crown Jewels were sent to Bodmin Prison for safekeeping. From the Gilbert Memorial on Beacon Hill, you can see both of Cornwall's coasts.

One of Cornwall's greatest country piles, **Lanhydrock,** former home of the powerful Robartes family, was originally constructed in the 17th century but was totally rebuilt after a fire in 1881. The granite exterior remains true to its original form, however, and the long picture gallery in the north wing, with its barrel-vaulted plaster ceiling depicting 24 biblical scenes, also survived the devastation. A small museum in the north wing shows photographs and letters relating to the family, whose spectacular wealth is best illustrated in the kitchen, built in the style of a college hall with clerestory windows. Nine hundred acres of wooded parkland border the River Fowey, and in spring the gardens present an exquisite ensemble of magnolias, azaleas, and rhododendrons. ✉ *3 mi southeast of Bofmin, signposted off A30, A38, and B3268,* ☎ *01208/73320,* WEB *www.nationaltrust.org.uk.* 🎫 *House and grounds £6.80; grounds £3.70.* ☉ *Apr.–Sept., Tues.–Sun. 11–5:30; Oct., Tues.–Sun. 11–5.*

Dozmary Pool

③④ *10 mi northeast of Bodmin.*

For a taste of Arthurian legend, follow A30 northeast out of Bodmin across the boggy, heather-clad granite plateau of Bodmin Moor, and turn right at Bolventor to get to Dozmary Pool. A lake of considerable size rather than a pool, it was here that King Arthur's legendary magic sword, Excalibur, was supposedly returned to the Lady of the Lake after Arthur's final battle.

Dining and Lodging

£–££ ✕🛏 **Jamaica Inn.** This inn near the center of Bodmin Moor, just off A30, was made famous by Daphne du Maurier's novel of the same name. Originally a farmstead, it is now Cornwall's best-known pub, and it incorporates a reproduction of du Maurier's study, an entertaining museum of curiosities, and a smuggler's museum, all worth a look. The inn makes a good base for excursions onto the moor, and three of the comfortable bedrooms here have four-poster beds. ✉ *Bolventor, PL15 7TS,* ☎ *01566/86250,* FAX *01566/86177. 6 rooms. Restaurant, pub.*

Launceston

③⑤ *25 mi northwest of Plymouth.*

Cornwall's ancient capital, Launceston (pronounced *larn-*ston), on the eastern side of Bodmin Moor, retains parts of its medieval walls, including the South Gate. For a full view of the surrounding country-side, you can climb up to the ruins of 14th-century **Launceston Castle.** ☎ *01566/772365,* WEB *www.english-heritage.org.uk.* ☞ *£1.90.* ☉ *Apr.–Sept., daily 10–6; Oct., daily 10–5; Nov.–Mar., Fri.–Sun. 10–1 and 2–4.*

Dining and Lodging

££££–££££   ✕🏠 **Lewtrenchard Manor.** This spacious 1620 manor house, on the northwestern edge of Dartmoor, is filled with paneled rooms, stone fire-places, and ornate leaded windows. Some bedrooms have antique four-poster beds. The restaurant (fixed-price menu at dinner), with its big log fire and family portraits, serves good, fresh fish, caught an hour away. ⊠ *Lewdown, between Launceston and Okehampton, EX20 4PN,* ☎ *01566/783256,* FAX *01566/783332. 9 rooms. Restaurant, fishing, helipad. AE, DC, MC, V.*

Plymouth

48 mi southwest of Exeter, 124 mi southwest of Bristol, 240 mi south-west of London.

Devon's largest city has long been linked with England's commercial and maritime history. Much of the city center was destroyed by air raids in World War II and has been rebuilt in an uninspiring style, but there 36 are worthwhile sights. From the **Hoe,** a wide, grassy esplanade with crisscrossing walkways high above the city, you will find a magnifi-cent view of the many inlets, bays, and harbors that make up Plymouth 37 Sound. An excellent vista of the city is provided atop **Smeaton's Tower,** 38 along the Hoe. The huge **Royal Citadel** (☎ 01752/775841), at the end of the Hoe, was built by Charles II in 1666 and still operates as a mil-itary center. There are daily guided tours May through September last-ing about 1¼ hours, at 2:30 (☞ £3).

The **Barbican,** east of the Royal Citadel, is the oldest surviving section 39 of Plymouth. Here, Tudor houses and warehouses rise from a maze of narrow streets leading down to the fishing docks and harbor. Many of these buildings have become antiques shops, art shops, and bookstores. 40 By the harbor you can visit the **Mayflower Steps,** where the Pilgrims embarked in 1620; the **Mayflower Stone** marks the exact spot.

Near the Barbican, just off the Royal Parade, the largely 18th-century 41 **Merchant's House** has a museum of local history. ⊠ *33 St. Andrew's St.,* ☎ *01752/304774.* ☞ *£1.50.* ☉ *Apr.–Sept., Tues.–Fri. 10–1 and 2–5:30, Sat. 10–1 and 2–5.*

☺ ★ 42   The excellent **National Marine Aquarium,** on a central harborside site, presents aqueous environments from freshwater stream to seawater wave tank and huge "shark theater." Not to be missed are the extensive col-lection of sea horses, part of an important breeding program, and shark-feeding time, which takes place three times a week. There is a café alongside the aquarium. ⊠ *Rope Walk, Coxside, Plymouth,* ☎ *01752/ 600301,* WEB *www.national-aquarium.co.uk.* ☞ *£6.50.* ☉ *Apr.–Oct., daily 10–6; Nov.–Mar., daily 10–4; last entry 1 hr before closing.*

Pleasure boats travel up the River Tamar, giving you a view of sights such as the Hoe and the historic Royal Naval Dockyard. **Plymouth Boat Cruises Ltd.** (⊠ 8 Anderton Rise, Millbrook, Torpoint, ☎ 01752/ 822797) runs 1-hr trips that leave every 30 minutes in peak season from Phoenix Wharf and the Mayflower Steps; the cost is £4.50. **Tamar Cruis-ing** (⊠ Cremyll Quay, Cremyll, Torpoint, ☎ 01752/822105) has hour-long trips for £4.50; in peak season, boats leave every 30 minutes from Phoenix Wharf and the Mayflower Steps.

Barbican . . .**39**

Hoe **36**

Mayflower
Stone and
Steps **40**

Merchant's
House **41**

National
Marine
Aquarium . .**42**

Royal
Citadel **38**

Smeaton's
Tower **37**

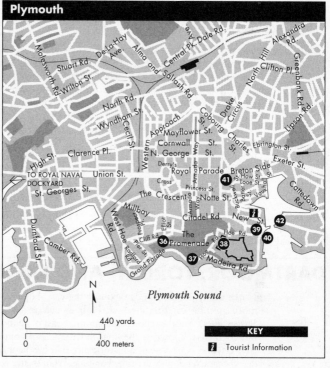

Dining and Lodging

££££ ✕ **Chez Nous.** This French—*très* French—restaurant is worth search-
★ ing for among the rows of stores in the shopping precinct. Fresh local
fish is served, and the atmosphere is pleasant and relaxed. The fixed-
price menu, chalked up on the blackboard, is quite pricey, but it usually repays the splurge with interest. ⊠ *13 Frankfort Gate,* ☎ *01752/
266793. AE, DC, MC, V. Closed Sun.–Mon. and 1st 3 wks in Feb. and
Sept. No lunch Sat.*

££–£££ ✕ **Piermaster's.** Fresh fish landed at nearby piers is the specialty
here. The decor is basic seafront, with a tiled floor and wooden tables. ⊠ *33 Southside St., Barbican,* ☎ *01752/229345. AE, DC, MC,
V. Closed Sun.*

££–£££ ☷ **Copthorne Hotel.** This efficient modern hotel downtown delivers the
expected comforts and amenities. Its Burlington Restaurant has been
given an Edwardian look, and there is also a brasserie. Weekend rates
are considerably lower than during the week. ⊠ *Armada Way, PL1
1AR,* ☎ *01752/224161,* ℻ *01752/670688,* ꟼꟾꟼ *www.stay.with-us.com.
135 rooms. Restaurant, bar, brasserie, indoor pool, steam room, gym.
AE, DC, MC, V.*

£ ☷ **Bowling Green Hotel.** This refurbished Victorian house overlooks
Sir Francis Drake's bowling green on Plymouth Hoe. It's in a central
location for shopping and sightseeing. ⊠ *9–10 Osborne Pl., Lockyer
St., PL1 2PU,* ☎ *01752/209090,* ℻ *01752/209092. 12 rooms. AE,
DC, MC, V.*

Nightlife and the Arts

Plymouth's **Theatre Royal** (⊠ Royal Parade, ☎ 01752/267222) offers
ballet, musicals, and plays by some of Britain's best companies.

Saltram House

★ ⓱ *3½ mi east of Plymouth city center.*

One of Plymouth's most outstanding attractions requires a short excursion from the center: Saltram House is a lovely 18th-century home built around the remains of a late Tudor mansion. It has one of the grandest neoclassical rooms in Britain, a vast salon designed by the great Robert Adam and adorned with paintings by Sir Joshua Reynolds, first president of the Royal Academy of Arts, who was born nearby in 1723. The house is set in a beautiful garden, with rare trees and shrubs. (Saltram House was used in the 1995 film *Sense and Sensibility*.) There is a restaurant in the house and a cafeteria in the Coach House. ✉ *Plympton,* ☎ *01752/ 333500,* WEB *www.nationaltrust.org.uk.* 🎫 *£6, garden £3.* ⊙ *House Apr.– Sept., Sun.–Thurs. noon–5; Oct., Sun.–Thurs. noon–4. Garden Feb.– Mar., weekends 11–4; Apr.–Oct., Sun.–Thurs. 10:30–5:30.*

En Route   From Plymouth, you have a choice of routes northeast to Exeter. If rugged, desolate, moorland scenery appeals to you, take A386 and B3212 northeast across Dartmoor.

DARTMOOR, TORBAY, AND EXETER

North of Plymouth, you can explore the vast, boggy reaches of Dartmoor (setting for the Sherlock Holmes classic *The Hound of the Baskervilles*). Another choice is to continue east of Plymouth along Start Bay to Torbay, known as the English Riviera. Both options end in Exeter, Devon's county seat, a historic city that has kept some of its medieval character despite wartime bombing. From Exeter you can meander south to Exmouth, then turn northeast to Yeovil in Somerset, reentering King Arthur country at Cadbury Castle, the legendary Camelot.

Dartmoor

13 mi west of Exeter.

Even on a summer's day the scarred and brooding hills of this sprawling national park appear a likely haunt for such monsters as the Hound of the Baskervilles. Sir Arthur Conan Doyle set his Sherlock Holmes thriller in this landscape. Sometimes the wet, peaty wasteland vanishes in rain and mist, although in very clear weather you can see as far north as Exmoor. Much of northern Dartmoor consists of open heath and moorland, unspoiled by roads—wonderful walking and horseback-riding territory but an easy place to lose your bearings. Dartmoor's earliest inhabitants left behind stone monuments, burial mounds, and hut circles, which make it easy to imagine prehistoric man roaming these bogs and pastures. Scattered along the borders of this vast reserve—one-third of which is owned by Prince Charles—are several villages that can make useful bases for hiking excursions: **Okehampton** is a main gateway to the reserve. Other scenic spots include **Buckland-in-the-Moor,** a charming hamlet with thatched-roof cottages, **Widecombe-in-the-Moor,** whose lovely church is known as the "Cathedral of the Moor," and **Grimspound,** the Bronze Age site featured in Conan Doyle's tale. Most of Dartmoor's towns and villages are connected by Transmoor Link buses. There are a number of information centers in the park; contact the park authority. ✉ *Dartmoor National Park Authority, Parke, Haytor Rd., Bovey Tracey, Newton Abbot, Devon TQ13 9JQ,* ☎ *01626/ 832093,* WEB *www.dartmoor-npa.gov.uk.*

Buckland Abbey

★ ⓸ *8 mi north of Plymouth.*

This 13th-century Cistercian monastery became the home of Sir Francis Drake in 1581. Today it is filled with mementos of Drake and the Spanish Armada. The abbey has a licensed restaurant. From Tavistock, take A386 south to Crapstone, then west. ✉ *Yelverton,* ☎ *01822/853607,* WEB *www.nationaltrust.org.uk.* 🎫 *£4.60, grounds only £2.40.* ☉ *Apr.–Oct., Fri.–Wed. 10:30–5:30; Nov.–Dec. and mid-Feb.–Mar., weekends 2–5; last admission 45 mins before closing.*

OFF THE
BEATEN PATH

GARDEN HOUSE – Horticulturists should not miss this rich naturalistic garden. Terraced around the remains of a 16th-century vicarage, this spot developed since 1945 is vivid with wisterias cascading over ancient brick walls, along with azaleas, roses, and innumerable other flowering plants, many of them rare. The garden is a mile northwest of Buckland Abbey and is signposted off the A386. ✉ *Buckland Monachorum, near Yelverton,* ☎ *01822/854769,* WEB *www.thegardenhouse.org.uk.* 🎫 *£4.* ☉ *Mar.–Oct., daily 10:30–5.*

Cotehele House and Quay

⓺ *4 mi east of Buckland Abbey, 15 mi north of Plymouth.*

This was formerly a busy port on the River Tamar, but it is now usually visited for the late-medieval manor house, whose facade is a vision from the pages of Prince Valiant. Complete with original furniture, tapestries and armor, impressive gardens, a restored mill, and a quay museum, the complex is now run by the National Trust. A limited number of visitors are allowed per day, so arrive early and be prepared to wait. Choose a bright day, as there is no electric light in the rooms. There are also shops, an arts and crafts gallery, a restaurant, and a tearoom. ✉ *St. Dominick (north of Saltash, signposted off A390),* ☎ *01579/352739,* WEB *www.nationaltrust.org.uk.* 🎫 *£6.20, gardens and mill only £3.40.* ☉ *House Apr.–Sept., Sat.–Thurs. 11–5; Oct., Sat.–Thurs. 11–4. Mill Apr.–June and Sept., Sat.–Thurs. 1–5:30; July–Aug., daily 1–6; Oct., Sat.–Thurs., 1–4; Nov., Sat.–Thurs., 1–4:30. Gardens daily 10:30–dusk.*

Morwellham Quay

⓻ *2 mi east of Cotehele House and Quay, 5 mi southwest of Tavistock, 18 mi north of Plymouth.*

Morwellham Quay was England's main copper-exporting port in the 19th century, and it has been restored as a working museum, with quay workers and coachmen in costume, and a copper mine open to visitors. The museum is off the Gunnislake-to-Tavistock road. ☎ *01822/832766; 01822/833808 (recorded information),* WEB *www.morwellham-quay.co.uk.* 🎫 *Easter–Oct. £8.90, Nov.–Easter £5.* ☉ *Easter–Oct., daily 10–5:30; Nov.–Easter, daily 10–4; last admission 2 hrs before closing.*

Dining and Lodging

£££–££££
★

✕🛏 **Horn of Plenty.** A "restaurant with rooms" is the way this establishment in a Georgian house describes itself. From the restaurant, there are magnificent views across the wooded, rhododendron-filled Tamar Valley. The fixed-price menu is changed monthly, and Peter Gorton's cooking is mainly classic French with some imaginative seafood recipes, such as the sea bass in shellfish broth with fresh fennel. A converted coach house next to the house contains nine modern guest rooms, and a suite suitable for families is in the main building. ⊠ *Gulworthy (3 mi west of Tavistock on A390), PL19 8JD,* ☎ FAX *01822/832528,* WEB *www.thehornofplenty.co.uk. 9 rooms, 1 suite. Restaurant. AE, MC, V. Restaurant closed Mon. lunch.*

Lydford Gorge

★ ❹⑦   *12 mi north of Morwellham Quay, 7 mi north of Tavistock, 9 mi east of Launceston, 24 mi north of Plymouth.*

The River Lyd has carved a spectacular chasm through the rock at Lydford Gorge. Two paths follow the gorge past gurgling whirlpools and waterfalls with names such as the Devil's Cauldron and the White Lady. Sturdy footwear is recommended. The walk can be quite arduous, although it can still get congested during busy periods. To drive here from Launceston, continue east along A30, following the signs. ⊠ *Off A386, Lydford,* ☎ *01822/820441 or 01822/820320,* WEB *www.nationaltrust. org.uk.* ⊡ *£3.60.* ◷ *Apr.–Sept., daily 10–5:30; Oct., daily 10–4; Nov.– Mar., daily 10:30–3 (walk restricted to main waterfall).*

Lodging

££   🏠 **Castle Inn.** This 16th-century inn lies midway between Okehampton and Tavistock next to Lydford Castle. It has a rosy brick facade framed by rose trellises and is the heart of the village of Lydford, mainly because of its popular restaurant, known for game dishes and curries. Period furniture adorns the public rooms, and some guest rooms are fitted out with Victorian-era antiques. ⊠ *Lydford, 1 mi off A386, EX20 4BH,* ☎ *01822/820241,* FAX *01822/820454. 9 rooms. Restaurant. MC, V.*

Outdoor Activities and Sports

Lydford has one of the most popular Dartmoor riding facilities, the **Lydford House Riding Stables** (⊠ Lydford House Hotel, ☎ 01822/ 820321).

Okehampton

❹⑧   *8 mi northeast of Lydford Gorge, 28 mi north of Plymouth, 23 mi west of Exeter.*

At the confluence of the rivers East and West Okement, this town is a good base from which to explore North Dartmoor. It has numerous pubs and cottage tearooms, and a helpful tourist office (☎ 01837/53020). On the river banks a mile southwest of the town center, the jagged ruins of the Norman **Okehampton Castle** occupy a verdant site, with a picnic area and lovely woodland walks. ☎ *01837/52844,* WEB *www. english-heritage.org.uk.* ⊡ *£2.50.* ◷ *Apr.–Sept., daily 10–6; Oct., daily 10–5.*

The **Museum of Dartmoor Life** includes interactive models, a working waterwheel, and photos of traditional farming methods, spread over three floors. ⊠ *3 West St.,* ☎ *01837/52295.* ⊡ *£2.* ◷ *Easter–May and Oct., Mon.–Sat. 10–5; June–Sept., daily 10–5; Nov.–Easter, weekdays 10–4.*

Outdoor Activities and Sports

Skaigh Stables Farm (⊠ Skaigh La., Higher Sticklepath, near Okehampton, ☎ 01837/840917) is used by many Dartmoor natives.

Chagford

❹⑨   *9 mi southeast of Okehampton, 30 mi northeast of Plymouth.*

Chagford was once a tin-weighing station and an area of fierce fighting between the Roundheads and the Cavaliers in the Civil War. A Roundhead was hanged in front of one of the pubs on the village square. The town makes a convenient base from which to explore North Dartmoor.

The intriguing **Castle Drogo,** in Drewsteignton across A282, seems to be a medieval castle, complete with battlements, but it was built between 1910 and 1930. Designed by Sir Edwin Lutyens for Julius Drewe, a wealthy grocer, it's only half finished (funds ran out). The half that's built resembles a magisterial vision out of the Dark Ages. Take the A30 Exeter–Okehampton road to reach the castle, which is 4 mi northeast of Chagford and 6 mi south of A30. ☎ 01647/433306, WEB *www.nationaltrust.org.uk.* ✉ *£5.60, grounds only £2.80.* ☉ *Castle: Mar., Wed.–Sun. call for times; Apr.–Oct., Sat.–Thurs. 11–5:30. Grounds daily 10:30–dusk.*

Dining and Lodging

££££ ✗ ▥ **Gidleigh Park.** One of the most elegant hotels and restaurants in
★ England, Gidleigh Park is set within its own little universe of landscaped gardens and croquet lawns, surrounded by one of the most ferocious wildernesses left in Britain. Once you pass 20 signposts, you espy a sign that says KEEP HEART, and, finally, you arrive at the long, black-and-white 1930s Tudor-style residence. Inside, decor is fairly generic country-house hotel, the staff wears Laura Ashley, and the extremely expensive restaurant, under the direction of chef Michael Caines, has been showered with culinary awards. You'll see why when you sample a raviolo (crimped pasta parcel) of langoustine with zucchini tagliatelle or the roast sea bass with fennel puree and red wine sauce. ✉ *Gidleigh Rd., TQ13 8HH,* ☎ *01647/432367,* FAX *01647/432574,* WEB *www.gidleigh.com. 14 rooms, 1 estate cottage. Restaurant, putting green, tennis court, croquet. AE, DC, MC, V.*

£££ ▥ **Easton Court.** Discerning travelers such as C. P. Snow, Margaret Mead, John Steinbeck, and Evelyn Waugh—who completed *Brideshead Revisited* here—made this their Dartmoor home-away-from-home. It occupies a pretty (when the ivy allows you to see it) Tudor thatched-roof manse, complete with cozy inglenooks, timbered beams, and flower garden. There is also a charming restaurant on the premises. Ask about special discounts for stays of more than one night. ✉ *Easton Cross, TQ13 8JL,* ☎ *01647/433469,* FAX *01647/433654. 8 rooms. Restaurant. MC, V. Closed Jan.*

Dartmouth

50 *35 mi east of Plymouth, 35 mi south of Exeter.*

Dartmouth was an important port in the Middle Ages and is today a favorite haunt of yacht owners. Traces of its past include the old houses in Bayard's Cove near Lower Ferry, the 16th-century covered Butterwalk, and the two castles guarding the entrance to the River Dart. The town is dominated by the Royal Naval College, built in 1905.

Dining and Lodging

££–£££ ✗ **Carved Angel.** On the quay, this restaurant with views of the harbor has a long-standing reputation as one of Britain's finest eateries.
★ Its offerings embrace international cuisine and fresh local products, such as River Dart salmon and samphire, a seashore plant used in fish dishes. ✉ *2 S. Embankment,* ☎ *01803/832465. MC, V. No dinner Sun., no lunch Mon.*

££ ✗ **Carved Angel Café.** This extension of the Carved Angel provides a good opportunity to sample some of the parent's culinary experience without paying lavishly for it. In fact, the fare is much more modest, consisting of traditional daytime snacks such as bangers and mash; there's a fixed-price menu at dinner. The kitchen turns out delicious soups, and desserts are also worth leaving room for. Kids are made to feel especially welcome. ⊠ *7 Foss St.,* ☎ *01803/834842. AE, DC, MC, V. Closed Sun. No dinner Sun.–Wed.*

££–£££   🏠 **Royal Castle Hotel.** This hotel has truly earned the name "Royal"— several monarchs have slept here. Part of Dartmouth's historic waterfront (and consequently a continual hub of activity), it was built in the 17th century, reputedly of timber from wrecks of the Spanish Armada. There are traditional fireplaces and beamed ceilings, and six rooms have four-poster beds. Rooms with river views cost about 30% more. ⊠ *11 The Quay, TQ6 9PS,* ☎ *01803/833033,* 𝖥𝖠𝖷 *01803/835445,* 𝖶𝖤𝖡 *www. royalcastle.co.uk. 25 rooms. Restaurant, 2 bars. AE, MC, V.*

En Route   Two **ferries** cross the river at Dartmouth; in summer, to avoid long waiting lines, you may want to try the inland route via A3122 and A381 to Totnes.

Totnes

🟡 *9 mi northwest of Dartmouth, 28 mi southwest of Exeter.*

This busy market town preserves an atmosphere of the past, particularly on summer Tuesdays and Saturdays, when most of the shopkeepers dress in Elizabethan costume. Its historic buildings include a guildhall and St. Mary's Church. You can climb up the hill in town to the ruins of **Totnes Castle**—a typical Norman motte and bailey design—for a wonderful view of Totnes and the River Dart. ☎ *01803/864406,* 𝖶𝖤𝖡 *www. english-heritage.org.uk.* 🎟 *£1.60.* ☼ *Apr.–Sept., daily 10–6; Oct., daily 10–5; Nov.–Mar., Wed.–Sun. 10–1 and 2–4.*

☾ Steam trains of the **South Devon Railway** run through 7 wooded mi of the Dart Valley between Totnes and Buckfastleigh, on the edge of Dartmoor. ⊠ *Littlehempston, near Totnes,* ☎ *01364/642338.* 🎟 *£6.50 round-trip.* ☼ *Easter and mid-May–early Oct., daily; call for winter times, including specials at Christmas and New Year's.*

Lodging

££   🏠 **Cott Inn.** The exterior of this inn has remained almost completely unchanged since 1320. It is a long, low, thatched building with flagstone floors, thick ceiling beams, and open fireplaces. Good English rustic meals are available from the restaurant. ⊠ *Dartington (2 mi west of Totnes on A385) TQ9 6HE,* ☎ *01803/863777,* 𝖥𝖠𝖷 *01803/866629. 6 rooms. Restaurant. AE, MC, V.*

Shopping

Near Dartington Hall (2 mi north of Totnes) is a collection of stores selling world-famous Dartington lead crystal as well as shoes, woolens, farm foods, kitchenware, pottery, and other Devon wares. **Dartington Trading Centre** (⊠ Shinners Bridge, 2 mi west of Totnes, ☎ 01803/ 864171), a collection of shops and two restaurants inside the old Dartington Cider Press, markets handmade crafts from Devon and elsewhere, including clothes, glassware, and kitchenware. The farm shop sells fudge, ice cream, and cider, as well as local produce.

Brixham

🟡 *10 mi southeast of Totnes by A385 and A3022.*

Brixham, at the southern point of Tor Bay, has kept much of its original charm, partly because it is still an active fishing village. Much of the catch is dispatched straight to restaurants as far away as London. Sample a portion of the local fish-and-chips on the quayside, where there is a (surprisingly petite) full-scale replica of the vessel on which Sir Francis Drake circumnavigated the world.

Torbay

53 *5 mi north of Brixham via A3022, 23 mi south of Exeter.*

As the most important resort area in South Devon, Torbay envisions itself as the center of the "English Riviera." Since 1968, the towns of Paignton and Torquay (pronounced tor-*kee*) have been amalgamated under the common moniker of Torbay. Torquay is the supposed site of the hotel in the popular British television show *Fawlty Towers*—and the town has much of the same: modern hotels, luxury villas, and apartments that climb the hillsides above the harbor. Palm trees and other semitropical plants flourish in the seafront gardens. The sea is a clear and intense blue, and the whole place in summer has that unmistakable air of what was once called "Continental." To sun and bathe, head for Anstey's Cove, a favorite spot for scuba divers, with more beaches farther along at neighboring Babbacombe.

★ Just outside Torbay lies the most Devonish hamlet in England, the old-world show village of **Cockington**, which has thatched cottages, a 14th-century Old Forge, and the square-towered Church of St. George and St. Mary, all surrounded in springtime by daffodils. Repair to the Old Mill for a café lunch or head to Drum Inn, designed by Sir Edwin Lutyens to be an archetypal pub. At the top of the hill sits Higher Lodge, whose second story rests on tree trunks. Finally, on the outskirts of the village lies Cockington Court—a grand estate with shops and an eatery. Although the whole has more than a touch of the faux about it—cottages that do not sell anything even put up signs to this effect—who can resist this dreamy dollop of Devon?

Dining and Lodging

£££ ✗ **Remy's.** Torquay's oldest-established French restaurant is known for delightful, straightforward traditional French cooking. Scallops with wild mushrooms and shallots, and guinea fowl with Roquefort cheese and spinach are typical choices on the fixed-price menu. The wine list has a selection of good Alsatian vintages. ✉ *3 Croft Rd.,* ☎ *01803/ 292359. MC, V. Closed Sun.–Mon. No lunch.*

££–£££ ✗ **Capers.** A spot for anyone who likes enthusiasm along with the food,
★ this small, select restaurant goes in for serious cooking. Local fish ranks high on the menu, accompanied by vegetables and herbs grown by the chef. Try the turbot with lime and ginger and the crispy duck salad, or the monkfish with green peppercorns. ✉ *7 Lisburne Sq.,* ☎ *01803/ 291177. AE, MC, V. Closed Sun. and 1 wk mid-Aug. No lunch.*

££££ 🏨 **The Imperial.** This is arguably Devon's most luxurious hotel, perched
★ above the sea, overlooking Torbay. The gardens surrounding the hotel, which dates to 1866, are magnificent, and the interior is . . . well, imperial, with chandeliers, marble floors, and the general air of a bygone world. Most bedrooms are large and very comfortable, and some have seaward-facing balconies. The staff is attentive. ✉ *Park Hill Rd., TQ1 2DG,* ☎ *01803/294301,* 🅵🅰🆇 *01803/298293,* 🆆🅴🅱 *www. paramount-hotels.co.uk. 153 rooms, 17 suites. 2 restaurants, indoor-outdoor pool, beauty salon, sauna, tennis court, health club, squash. AE, DC, MC, V.*

£ 🏨 **Fairmount House Hotel.** Near the village of Cockington, on the edge of Torquay, this Victorian hotel has a pretty garden and a restaurant that favors fresh home-grown and local produce. The Victorian Conservatory Bar opens onto the garden. Guest rooms are solidly furnished, and one has a four-poster bed. ✉ *Herbert Rd., Chelston, TQ2 6RW,* ☎ 🅵🅰🆇 *01803/605446. 8 rooms. Restaurant, bar. MC, V.*

Exeter

 23 mi north of Torbay, 48 mi northeast of Plymouth, 85 mi southwest of Bristol, 205 mi southwest of London.

Devon's county seat, Exeter, has been the capital of the region since the Romans established a fortress here 2,000 years ago. Little evidence of the Roman occupation exists, apart from the great city walls. Although it was heavily bombed in 1942, Exeter retains much of its medieval character, as well as examples of the gracious architecture of the 18th and 19th centuries.

At the heart of Exeter, the great Gothic **Cathedral of St. Peter** was begun in 1275 and completed almost a century later. The twin towers are even older survivors of an earlier Norman cathedral. The 300-ft stretch of unbroken Gothic vaulting, rising from a forest of ribbed columns, is the longest in the world. Myriad statues, tombs, and memorial plaques adorn the interior. In the minstrels' gallery, high up on the left of the nave, stands a group of carved figures singing and playing musical instruments, including bagpipes. The cathedral is surrounded by a charming **Close**, a green, pleasant space for relaxing on a sunny day. Don't miss the 400-year-old door to No. 10, the bishop of Crediton's house, ornately carved with angels' and lions' heads. ⊠ *Cathedral Close,* ☎ *01392/214219,* WEB *www.exeter-cathedral.org.uk.* ☞ *£2.50 donation.* ☉ *Sun.–Fri. 7:30–6:30, Sat. 7:30–5.*

With its black-and-white half-timber facade bearing the coat of arms of Elizabeth I, **Mol's Coffee House** (now a store), on the corner of Cathedral Close, is redolent of bygone times. It is said that Sir Francis Drake met his admirals here to plan strategy against the Spanish Armada in 1588. Opposite Exeter's cathedral, the **Royal Clarence Hotel** was built in 1769 and was the first inn in England to be described as a "hotel"— a designation applied by an enterprising French manager. It is named after the duchess of Clarence, who stayed here in 1827 on her way to visit her husband, the future William IV.

The **Guildhall,** just behind the Close, is the oldest municipal building in the country. The present hall dates from 1330, although a guildhall has been on this site since at least 1160. Its timber-braced roof is one of the earliest in England, dating from about 1460. ⊠ *High St.,* ☎ *01392/ 265500.* ☞ *Free.* ☉ *Weekdays 10:30–1 and 2–4, Sat. 10–noon, unless in use for a civic function.*

Devon's fine **Royal Albert Memorial Museum** houses natural-history displays, a superb collection of Exeter silverware, and the work of some West Country artists. There is also an excellent international gallery and a fine archaeological section. ⊠ *Queen St.,* ☎ *01392/265858.* ☞ *Free.* ☉ *Mon.–Sat. 10–5.*

The **Rougemont Gardens,** off Queen Street and behind the Royal Albert Memorial Museum, were first laid out at the end of the 18th century. The land was once part of the defensive ditch of Rougemont Castle, built in 1068 by decree of William the Conqueror. Here you will find the original Norman gatehouse and the remains of the Roman city wall, the latter forming part of the ancient castle's outer wall; nothing else remains.

Exeter's historic waterfront on the banks of the River Exe was once the center of the city's medieval wool industry, whose prosperity is attested by **The Custom House,** built in 1682 on The Quay. Flanked by Victorian warehouses, it's the earliest surviving brick building in the city. The **Quay House,** a late-17th-century stone warehouse, now houses a Heritage Centre with documents on the maritime history of

the city and an audiovisual display. ⊠ *The Quay,* ☎ *01392/265213.*
☞ *Free.* ⊙ *Mid-Apr.–Oct., daily 10–5.*

OFF THE BEATEN PATH	**POWDERHAM CASTLE –** Seat of the earls of Devon, Powderham is a no-table stately house, famed for its staircase hall, a soaring fantasia of white stuccowork on a dazzling turquoise background, constructed in 1739–69. Other sumptuous rooms, adorned with family portraits by Kneller and Reynolds, were used in the Merchant–Ivory film *Remains of the Day*. In the surrounding deer park is a tower built in 1400 by Sir Philip Courtenay, ancestor of the present owners. A restaurant serves traditional English fare, made from local produce, and there's also a farm shop and plant center. ⊠ *A379, Kenton (8 mi south of Exeter),* ☎ *01626/890243,* 🌐 *www.powderham.co.uk.* ☞ *£5.85.* ⊙ *Apr.–Oct., Sun.–Fri. 10–5:30.*

Dining and Lodging

££–£££ **✕ St. Olaves.** Part of St. Olaves Court Hotel, set in a Georgian house
★ with a walled garden, this restaurant is one of the finest dining spots
of the West Country. The bar overlooks the lovely garden. There are
fixed-price menus; try the escalopes of salmon, or for dessert, the
brioche bread-and-butter-pudding with apricot and sultana coulis. ⊠
Mary Arches St., ☎ *01392/217736. AE, DC, MC, V.*

£–££ **✕ Ship Inn.** If you feel like lifting a tankard of stout in the very rooms
where Sir Francis Drake and Sir Walter Raleigh enjoyed their ale, this
is the place. Drake, in fact, once wrote, "Next to mine own shippe, I
do most love that old 'Shippe' in Exon, a tavern in Fyssh Street, as the
people call it, or as the clergie will have it, St. Martin's Lane." The pub
dishes out casual bar fare, whereas the upstairs restaurant offers the
usual grilled lemon sole and other English dishes. ⊠ *St. Martin's La.,*
☎ *01392/272040. MC, V. No dinner upstairs restaurant except Apr.–
Sept., Tues.–Thurs.*

£ **✕ Hansons.** While you explore Exeter's Close, stop in at this spot, ideal
for lunch, coffee, snacks, or one of Devon's famous cream teas (served
with jam, scones, and clotted cream). ⊠ *1 Cathedral Close,* ☎ *01392/
276913. AE, DC, MC, V. Closed Sun. No dinner.*

£££ **✕🏨 Royal Clarence Hotel.** This historic hotel is wonderfully situated
within the Cathedral Close. It has a branch of the ultra-chic Michael
Caines (of Gidleigh Park fame) restaurants, with fine contemporary
fare, and has been made a great deal more attractive by redecoration.
Many rooms have oak paneling—those with a view of the cathedral
cost an extra £10. ⊠ *Cathedral Yard, EX1 1HB,* ☎ *01392/319955,*
🖷 *01392/439423. 56 rooms. Restaurant, 2 bars. AE, DC, MC, V.*

££ **✕🏨 White Hart.** It is said that Oliver Cromwell stabled his horses here,
and guests have been welcomed since the 15th century. Through the
lovely cobbled entrance, the main building has all the trappings of a
period inn—beams, stone walls, a central courtyard—but there are also
fully modern bedrooms in a new wing. The hotel has a restaurant, a
wine bar, and a more casual ale-and-port house. Ask about good-
value weekend terms for a minimum of two nights. ⊠ *66 South St.,*
EX1 1EE, ☎ *01392/279897,* 🖷 *01392/250159. 57 rooms. 2 restaurants, 2 bars. AE, DC, MC, V.*

Nightlife and the Arts

Among the best known of the West Country's festivals is the **Exeter
Festival** (☎ 01392/213161), a mixture of musical and theater events
held in July. At the **Northcott Theatre** (⊠ Stocker Rd., ☎ 01392/
493493) you can often see plays performed by some of the best London companies.

Shopping

Until 1882 Exeter was the silver-assay office for the entire West Country, and it is still possible to find Exeter silver, particularly spoons, in some antiques and silverware stores. The earliest example of Exeter silver (now a museum piece) dates from 1218, and Victorian pieces are still sold. The Exeter assay mark is three castles. **William Bruford** (⊠ 17 The Guildhall Centre, Queen St., ☎ 01392/254901) sells interesting antique jewelry and silver. Exeter has a **daily market** on Sidwell Street.

Topsham

⑤⑤ *4 mi southeast of Exeter on B3182.*

The town of Topsham is full of narrow streets and hidden courtyards. Once a bustling port, it is rich in 18th-century houses and inns. Occupying a 17th-century Dutch-style merchant's house beside the river, with period-furnished rooms, the **Topsham Museum** houses an eclectic collection, displaying everything from local history and wildlife to memorabilia belonging to Vivien Leigh. ⊠ *25 The Strand,* ☎ *01392/873244.* ☞ *£1.50.* ☉ *Easter–Oct., Mon., Wed., and weekends 2–5.*

★ **A la Ronde,** 5 mi south of Topsham, is one of the most unusual houses in England. A 16-sided, nearly circular house, it was built in 1798 and inspired by the Church of San Vitale in Ravenna, Italy. Among the 18th- and 19th-century curiosities here is an elaborate display of feathers and shells. ⊠ *Summer La., on A376 near Exmouth,* ☎ *01395/265514,* WEB *www.nationaltrust.org.uk.* ☞ *£3.40.* ☉ *Apr.–Oct., Sun.–Thurs. 11–5:30.*

En Route The Devon coast from Exmouth to the Dorset border 26 mi to the east has been designated an Area of Outstanding Natural Beauty. The reddish, grass-topped cliffs of the region are punctuated by quiet seaside resorts such as Budleigh Salterton, Sidmouth, and Seaton.

Beer

⑤⑥ *22 mi east of Topsham, 26 mi east of Exeter, 33 mi south of Taunton.*

Beer, just outside Seaton, was once a favorite smugglers' haunt, and this fishing village has remained fairly unchanged. It was also the source of the white stone used to build Exeter Cathedral. **Beer Quarry Caves,** one of the main quarries that provided the stone for Devon's churches, can still be visited. Regular tours guide you around the underground network, and there is a small exhibition. ⊠ *Quarry La.,* ☎ *01297/680282.* ☞ *£4.25.* ☉ *Easter–Sept., daily 10–6; Oct., daily 11–5; last admission 1 hr before closing.*

Honiton

⑤⑦ *10 mi northwest of Beer on A3052/A375, 19 mi south of Taunton.*

Handsome Georgian houses line Honiton's long High Street. Modern storefronts have intruded, but the original facades have been preserved at second-floor level. For 300 years the town was known for lace-making, and the industry was revived when Queen Victoria selected the fabric for her wedding veil in 1840.

After viewing the splendid collection of lace at **Allhallows Museum,** it's worth delving into the specialty shops where prized early examples of the Honiton patterns and new lace are sold. ⊠ *High St.,* ☎ *01404/44966,* WEB *www.cyberlink.co.uk/allhallows.* ☞ *£2.* ☉ *Apr.–Sept., weekdays 10–5, Sat. 10–1:30; Oct., Sat. 10–1:30.*

Dining and Lodging

£–££   ✕ **Dominoes.** For a satisfying lunch, try this wine bar, extravagantly decorated with murals, cherubs, and other Parisian frippery, where you can get everything from nachos to rack of lamb. Evening meals are also available. ⊠ *178 High St.,* ☎ *01404/47707. MC, V.*

£££–££££   ⛺ **Combe House Hotel.** Rolling parkland surrounds this Elizabethan manor house. From the imposing entrance hall, with its huge, open fireplace, to the individually decorated bedrooms—all large and one with a four-poster bed—the emphasis is on country-house style and modern comfort. A 1½-mi stretch of the River Otter is available for fishing, and the village of Gittisham is charming. ⊠ *Gittisham, near Honiton, EX14 0AD,* ☎ *01404/540400,* FAX *01404/46004,* WEB *www.thishotel.com. 13 rooms, 2 suites. Restaurant, fishing, meeting rooms. AE, DC, MC, V.*

£   ⛺ **New Dolphin Hotel.** The age of this former coaching inn shows in the sloping floors, but every room has modern comforts. It's in the town center. ⊠ *High St., EX14 1LS,* ☎ *01404/42377,* FAX *01404/47662. 10 rooms. Restaurant, bar. MC, V.*

Montacute House

★ ⑤⑧   *30 mi northeast of Honiton on A30 and A303, 30 mi southeast of Taunton, 44 mi south of Bristol, 21 mi northwest of Dorchester.*

This part of Somerset is famous for its golden limestone, used in the construction of local villages and mansions. An outstanding example is Montacute House, built in the late 16th century. The house has a 189-ft gallery brimming with Elizabethan and Jacobean portraits, most on loan from the National Portrait Gallery, as well as a good collection of textiles. Pick a bright day to visit: some rooms do not have electric light. ⊠ *A3088, Yeovil (turn right off A303 at Stoke sub Hamdon),* ☎ *01935/823289,* WEB *www.nationaltrust.org.uk.* ⊠ *£6; garden and park only £3.30 Apr.–Oct., £2 Nov.–Mar.* ☉ *House Apr.–Oct., Wed.–Mon. noon–5:30. Garden and park Apr.–Oct., Wed.–Mon. 11–5:30 or dusk; Nov.–Mar., Wed.–Sun. 11:30–4.*

Dining and Lodging

££   ✕⛺ **King's Arms.** Built of the same warm, golden stone as nearby Montacute House, this 16th-century inn has charming decor. Much of the interior incorporates the local stone, harmoniously integrated with details such as an engraved archway rescued from Coventry Cathedral (bombed in World War II). Guest rooms are quite modern, however. Meals range from bar snacks to a full à la carte selection in the fine Abbey Room; there's a huge range of dishes but the fare is mostly British, from steak and kidney pie to roast pheasant. ⊠ *Bishopston, Montacute TA15 6UU,* ☎ *01935/822513,* FAX *01935/826549. 15 rooms. 2 restaurants. AE, MC, V.*

Yeovilton

⑤⑨   *7 mi north of Yeovil.*

The present reasserts itself in the village of Yeovilton, which is home to a Royal Naval Air Station. The **Fleet Air Arm Museum** has more than 50 historic aircraft on display, among them the Concorde 002. The spectacular "Carrier" display includes a simulated helicopter ride over the ocean to an aircraft carrier and a unique re-creation of the flight deck of a working carrier, complete with 12 actual planes from the 1960s and 1970s. ⊠ *Royal Naval Air Station Yeovilton,* ☎ *01935/840565,* WEB *www.fleetairarm.com.* ⊠ *£7.* ☉ *Apr.–Oct., daily 10–5:30; Nov.–Mar., daily 10–4:30.*

Cadbury Castle

⑥⓪ *7 mi northeast of Yeovilton, 17 mi south of Wells.*

Cadbury Castle (⊠ off A303) is said to be the site of Camelot—one among several contenders for the honor. Glastonbury Tor, rising dramatically in the distance across the plain, adds to the atmosphere of Arthurian romance. There is even a legend that every seven years the hillside opens and Arthur and his followers ride forth to water their horses at nearby Sutton Montis. Cadbury Castle is, in fact, an Iron Age fort (circa 650 BC), with grass-covered, earthen ramparts forming a green wall 300 ft above the surrounding fields.

THE WEST COUNTRY A TO Z

To research prices, get advice from other travelers, and book travel arrangements, visit www.fodors.com.

AIRPORTS
Bristol International Airport, a few miles southwest of the city on the A38, has flights to and from destinations in Britain and Europe. Plymouth has a small airport 3 mi from town. Exeter International Airport is 5 mi east of Exeter, 2 mi from the M5 motorway.

➤ AIRPORT INFORMATION: **Bristol International Airport** (⊠ Bridgwater Rd., ☎ 01275/474444, 〔WEB〕 www.bristolairport.co.uk). **Exeter International Airport** (⊠ M5, Junction 29, ☎ 01392/367433, 〔WEB〕 www .eclipse.co.uk/exeterair). **Plymouth City Airport** (⊠ Plymbridge Rd., ☎ 01752/209500).

BUS TRAVEL
National Express buses leave London's Victoria Coach Station for Bristol (2½ hours), Exeter (3¾ hours), Plymouth (4¾ hours), and Penzance (about 8 hours).

The bus company Stagecoach Devon covers mainly South Devon. First Red Bus runs most of the services in North Devon. First Western National operates a regular service in Plymouth and throughout Cornwall. Truronian operates in West Cornwall. Ask any of these companies about 1-, 3-, and 7-day Explorer passes good for unlimited travel.

FARES AND SCHEDULES
➤ BUS INFORMATION: **First Red Bus** (☎ 01271/345444, 〔WEB〕 www.first-westernnational.co.uk). **First Western National** (☎ 01752/222666, 〔WEB〕 www.firstwesternnational.co.uk). **National Express** (☎ 0990/808080, 〔WEB〕 www.gobycoach.com). **Stagecoach Devon** (☎ 01392/427711). **Truronian** (☎ 01872/273453, 〔WEB〕 www.truronian.co.uk).

CAR RENTAL
➤ LOCAL AGENCIES: **Avis** (⊠ 29 Marsh Green Rd., Marsh Barton Trading Estate, Exeter, ☎ 01392/259713; ⊠ 20 Commercial Rd., Coxside, Plymouth, ☎ 01752/221550; ⊠ Tregolls Rd., Truro, ☎ 01872/262226). **Europcar** (⊠ 30 Valley Rd., Plympton, Plymouth, ☎ 01752/344782). **Hertz** (⊠ Sutton Rd., Coxside, Plymouth, ☎ 01752/207207).

CAR TRAVEL
The fastest way from London to the West Country is via the M4 and M5 motorways, bypassing Bristol (115 mi) and heading south to Exeter, in Devon (172 mi). The main roads heading west are A30—which leads all the way to Land's End at the tip of Cornwall—A39 (near the northern shore of the peninsula), and A38 (near the southern shore of the peninsula).

ROAD CONDITIONS

Driving can be tricky, especially as you travel farther west. Most small roads are twisting country lanes flanked by high stone walls and thick hedges, which severely restrict visibility.

EMERGENCIES

➤ CONTACTS: **Ambulance, fire, police** (☎ 999). **Royal Devon and Exeter Hospital** (✉ Barrack Rd., Exeter, ☎ 01392/411611). **Derriford Hospital** (✉ Derriford, Plymouth, ☎ 01752/792511). **Royal Cornwall Hospital (Treliske)** (✉ A390, Higher Town, Truro, ☎ 01872/250000).

NATIONAL PARKS

➤ CONTACTS: **Dartmoor National Park Authority** (✉ Parke, Haytor Rd., Bovey Tracey, Newton Abbot TQ13 9JQ, ☎ 01626/832093, WEB www.dartmoor-npa.gov.uk). **Exmoor National Park Authority** (✉ Exmoor House, Dulverton TA22 9HL, ☎ 01398/323665, WEB www.exmoor-nationalpark.gov.uk).

OUTDOORS AND SPORTS

WALKING

For information about walking in Dartmoor or Exmoor, contact the National Parks Authority. The South West Coast Path Association has information about the 630-mi-long coastal path.

➤ CONTACTS: **South West Coast Path Association** (✉ Windlestraw, Penquit, Ermington, PL21 0LU, ☎ 01752/896237, WEB www.swcp.org.uk).

TOURS

South West Tourism and local tourist information centers have lists of qualified guides. Blue Badge Tour Services offers walking tours around Plymouth's old town and can arrange tours throughout Devon and Cornwall.

➤ FEES AND SCHEDULES: **Blue Badge Tour Services** (✉ 18 Margaret Park, Plymouth, ☎ FAX 01752/775841, ☎ 01752/266496). **South West Tourism** (☎ 0870/442–0830).

TRAIN TRAVEL

First Great Western and South West Trains serve the region from London's Paddington and Waterloo stations; contact National Rail Inquiries for details. Average travel time to Exeter is 2½ hours; to Plymouth, 3½ hours; and to Penzance, about 5½ hours.

CUTTING COSTS

Regional Rail Rover tickets are available for seven days' unlimited travel throughout the West Country, and there are localized Rovers covering Devon or Cornwall.

FARES AND SCHEDULES

➤ TRAIN INFORMATION: **National Rail Inquiries** (☎ 0845/748–4950, WEB www.railtrack.co.uk).

TRAVEL AGENCIES

➤ LOCAL AGENT REFERRALS: **American Express** (✉ 139 Armada Way, Plymouth, ☎ 01752/502706). **Thomas Cook** (✉ c/o HSBC Bank, 38 High St., Exeter, ☎ 01392/425712; ✉ 9 Old Town St., Plymouth, ☎ 01752/612600).

VISITOR INFORMATION

Local tourist information centers are usually open Monday–Saturday 9:30–5:30, and are listed after the regional and park offices below by town.

➤ TOURIST INFORMATION: **South West Tourism** (✉ Woodwater Park, Exeter EX2 5WT, ☎ 0870/442–0830, FAX 0870/442–0840, WEB www.

westcountrynow.com). **Cornwall Tourist Board** (✉ Pydar House, Pydar St., Truro TR1 1EA, ☎ 01872/274057, 𝐅𝐀𝐗 01872/322919, 𝐖𝐄𝐁 www.cornwalltouristboard.co.uk). **Devon Tourist Information Service** (✉ Box 55, Barnstaple EX32 8YR, ☎ 0870/608–5531, 𝐖𝐄𝐁 www. devon-cc.gov.uk). **Somerset Visitor Centre** (✉ Sedgemoor Service Station, M5 Southbound, ☎ 01934/750833, 𝐅𝐀𝐗 01934/750755, 𝐖𝐄𝐁 www. somerset.gov.uk/tourism).

Bristol (✉ The Annexe, Wildscreen Walk, Harbourside, ☎ 0117/926–0767; written inquiries ✉ Bristol Tourism and Conference Bureau, St. Nicholas St., BS1 1UE; 𝐖𝐄𝐁 www.visitbristol.co.uk). **Exeter** (✉ Civic Centre, Paris St., EX1 1JJ, ☎ 01392/265700, 𝐖𝐄𝐁 www.exeter.gov.uk). **Falmouth** (✉ 28 Killigrew St., TR11 3PN, ☎ 01326/312300, 𝐖𝐄𝐁 www. falmouth-sw-cornwall.co.uk). **Penzance** (✉ Station Approach, TR18 2NF, ☎ 01736/362207; 𝐖𝐄𝐁 www.west-cornwall-tourism.co.uk). **Plymouth** (✉ Island House, 9 The Barbican, PL1 2LS, ☎ 01752/304849, 𝐖𝐄𝐁 www.plymouth.gov.uk). **St. Ives** (✉ The Guildhall, Street-an-Pol, TR26 2DS, ☎ 01736/796297, 𝐖𝐄𝐁 www.west-cornwall-tourism.co.uk). **Truro** (✉ City Hall, Boscawen St., TR1 2NE, ☎ 01872/274555, 𝐖𝐄𝐁 www. truro.gov.uk). **Wells** (✉ Town Hall, Market Pl., BA5 2RB, ☎ 01749/ 672552).

5 THE CHANNEL ISLANDS

GUERNSEY, JERSEY

Blessed with more than 2,000 hours of sunshine every year, the Channel Islands remain a favorite getaway for the British and visitors alike. Jersey and Guernsey lie just off the coast of Brittany, so this is England with a French twist. Pleasures await—pretty fishing harbors, princely villas (don't miss Victor Hugo's historic house in St. Peter Port), and sublimely tasty crab creole. Later, perhaps after a walk along the ocean cliffs, everyone winds up the white-sand beaches, soaking up all that sun.

Updated by
Robert
Andrews

T HE CHANNEL ISLANDS became part of the British Isles when their ruler, Duke William of Normandy, or William the Conqueror, seized the English throne in 1066. The connection with the British royal house has lasted ever since, with very few breaks, but the Channel Islands claim no allegiance to the Parliament in Westminster—only to the monarch. They are self-ruling, with a Common Law based on the Norman code of law, which differs from the legal system followed in the rest of Britain. The islands do not impose VAT (which means that shopping is 17.5% cheaper), and they issue their own currency and stamps.

The islands served as the background for struggles between Royalists and Roundheads in the 17th-century Civil War. In 1781, the French made an unsuccessful attempt to invade, but since 1066, the islands have only been seriously invaded once: the Germans occupied them from 1940 to 1945, incorporating them into their great Western defense system, the "Atlantic Wall." All over the islands there is still evidence of the German fortifications, which were built by thousands of slave laborers who used 613,000 cubic meters of reinforced concrete. The coasts bristled with gun emplacements, and the rocky landscape was honeycombed with tunnels to get supplies to hospitals and to ammunition magazines. The islands became total fortresses. In fact, when the Allies overran Europe in 1944, they circumvented the islands, leaving their elaborate defenses untouched.

The most popular island is Jersey (44½ square mi), because of its mild climate, magnificent beaches, and well-run hotels and restaurants. Second to Jersey, both in size and popularity, is Guernsey (24½ square mi), which has 2,000 hours of sunshine a year and runs at a more relaxed pace. The islands are bordered by magnificent cliffs that provide superb walking trails—very tough on the leg muscles—with great views both seaward and inland. The landscapes of both Jersey and Guernsey are crowded with prosperous-looking, neat houses, threaded together by an interminable network of winding lanes. For this reason the islands are difficult to explore by car, even if you are adept at map reading. But both islands have excellent bus services, which provide a cheap, worry-free means of sightseeing and a way to avoid traffic snarls, particularly in summer.

Pleasures and Pastimes

Dining

The gustatory specialty of the Channel Islands is seafood in all its delectable glory. Crab and lobster dishes are on many menus, but don't overlook the daily catch from the tiny harbors or the mollusk called Jersey Ormer or sea ear (appropriately named). When you tire of seafood, the locally bred lamb is also superb, and thick cream slathers the desserts.

CATEGORY	COST*
££££	over £22
£££	£16–£22
££	£9–£15
£	under £9

*per person for a main course at dinner

Lodging

Jersey is chock-full of hotels, guest houses, and bed-and-breakfasts, all organized and regulated by the Jersey Hospitality Association. You can also get a comprehensive listing from the Jersey or Guernsey tourist boards. Many places offer half board (meaning breakfast and dinner

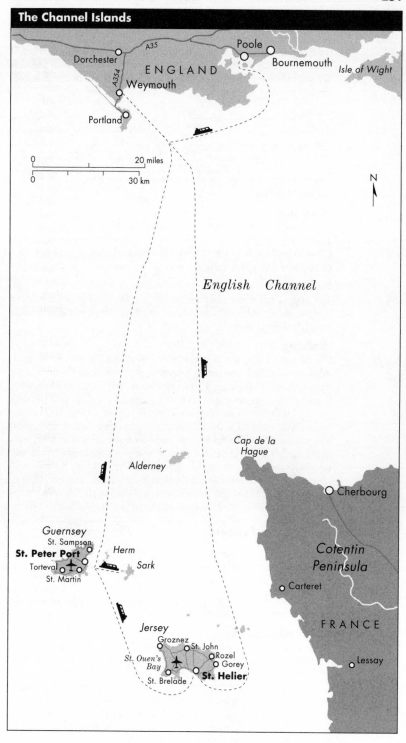

The Channel Islands

are included in the lodging price) at a savings. Outlying parts of Jersey are more low-key when compared with the razzmatazz of St. Helier. Guernsey is Jersey writ small—more relaxed, with hotels to match; these are regulated by the Guernsey Hotel and Tourist Association. If you want to stay on the islands of Alderney or Sark, plan well ahead—accommodations are few and transport to the isles can be complicated. There's no VAT on lodging.

CATEGORY	COST*
££££	over £150
£££	£100–£150
££	£60–£100
£	under £60

All prices are for two people sharing a standard double room, including service and breakfast.

Shopping

It's a pleasant surprise that the Channel Islands don't add the usual 17.5% VAT to prices. St. Helier and St. Peter Port are full of shops selling everything from cosmetics to liquor, and the towns have branches of all the major chain stores.

Swimming

The unpolluted water and magnificent beaches are a major attraction of these islands. Although the tides can be fierce, most popular beaches have lifeguards on duty.

Walking

On all the islands the best routes for walking are along the well-marked coast trails. On Jersey's north coast, walk from Grosnez in the west to Rozel in the east. Part of this route will take you along 300-ft-high cliffs. On Guernsey, the coastal trail runs for almost 30 mi, with views as sensational as those on Jersey. If you are feeling particularly robust, you can tackle the full length of these paths all at once, or, if you just want a comfortable stroll, head for any section that takes your fancy. Simply hop a bus to the point where you want to start, and pick up a bus whenever you feel like giving up. The best time to walk is in spring and early summer, when the wildflowers are at their riotous best. Be careful in the fall—the paths can be muddy and treacherous. Maps and guides to the cliff walks are available at the islands' tourist offices.

Exploring the Channel Islands

Any visit to the two main islands of Jersey and Guernsey will begin in the capital cities of St. Helier and St. Peter Port, respectively; most attractions are here or close by.

Numbers in the text correspond to numbers in the margin and on the St. Helier and the St. Peter Port maps.

Great Itineraries

Because of their relative remoteness from the English mainland, the Channel Islands need to be savored over several days. Put away your clocks and calendars, and dedicate yourself to settling into the kinder and gentler pace of life here. Unless you fly, you will spend the best part of a day in reaching the islands, and another day to unwind. If you come by sea, consider a night crossing, to make the most of your waking hours. You might choose to disembark at one of the main islands and return from the other one. Jersey and Guernsey are each well worth visiting, but if your time is limited, confine yourself to just one.

Spend two days in ⊞ **St. Helier,** main town of **Jersey.** Get your bearings by climbing up to **Fort Regent** ①, then stroll through the town's
streets and along the seafront, perhaps walking out to **Elizabeth
Castle** ⑦, the 16th-century stronghold lying on an island in St. Aubin's
Bay. Spend an afternoon at the absorbing **Jersey Museum** ④. On your
second day, you can see something more of the island: a morning
would be enough to visit the world-famous **Durrell Wildlife Conservation
Trust,** and the afternoon could be spent seeing **Gorey Castle,** on the island's eastern side. End the day with a meal in the village of Gorey.
Your last day should be devoted to a day trip to **Guernsey.** Arrive mid-
morning for a walk around **St. Peter Port,** taking in **Castle Cornet** ⑨,
the elegant **Hauteville House** ⑩, where Victor Hugo lived, and the delightfully idiosyncratic **Les Vauxbelets Chapel** ⑭. In the afternoon,
rent a car or bicycle to see some of the rest of Guernsey, especially **Sausmarez Manor** ⑫ and one of the relics of the German occupation, for
example, the **German Military Underground Hospital** ⑬. Take the ferry
(or plane) back to Jersey.

Three days on Jersey will allow you to take in the pleasures of ⊞ **St.
Helier,** including the attractions mentioned in the three-day itinerary,
and leave you time to explore farther afield in town and elsewhere on
the island. Make sure you take in the **Island Fortress–Occupation Museum** ⑤, which recaptures the experience of living under the German
jackboot. The **Glass Church** at Millbrook makes an easy excursion, perhaps en route to the **Battle of Flowers Museum,** outside St. Ouen. The
theme of flowers is a prominent one on Jersey, and it can be pursued
further at the **Eric Young Orchid Foundation.** Nearby, the **Durrell Wildlife
Conservation Trust** shouldn't be missed. Spend your fourth day and night
on ⊞ **Guernsey,** where **Castle Cornet** ⑨ and **Hauteville House** ⑩ are must-
sees in **St. Peter Port.** Outside town, **Sausmarez Manor** ⑫ and the
meticulous reconstructions of the **German Military Underground Hospital** ⑬ provide plenty of interest. From Guernsey, there are regular ferries to the tiny isle of ⊞ **Sark,** 45 minutes from Guernsey, where you
could spend your last night if you don't need to return to Jersey or
Guernsey. Sark can be toured on foot, by bicycle, or with a horse and
cart. A day would be enough to absorb its pace, although you'll find
it hard to leave—just don't expect bright lights or ready-made entertainment.

When to Tour the Channel Islands

The Channel Islands show their best face under a blue sky. Since they
can claim more sunshine than any other part of the British Isles, they're
a good bet at any time of year outside the depths of winter, when fierce
storms can put a damper on your trip. From April through September
is best if you want to enjoy the beaches; note, too, that many of the
best attractions close after October.

Jersey

St. Helier, Jersey's capital, is a lovely vacation center, full of hotels, good
swimming spots, and quaint streets. Nearby are secluded coves, difficult to access but a delight to explore, rugged rocks, and photo-wor-
thy scenery. You'll soon appreciate why the French call Jersey "La Reine
de la Manche"—Queen of the Channel. Not only is the climate soothing and the surroundings lush, but the atmosphere of Continental-cum-
Gallic know-how appeals to all visitors.

Elizabeth
Castle 7
Fort
Regent 1
Island
Fortress–
Occupation
Museum 5
Jersey Maritime
Museum and
Occupation
Tapestry 6
Jersey
Museum 4
Parish
Church 3
Royal
Square 2

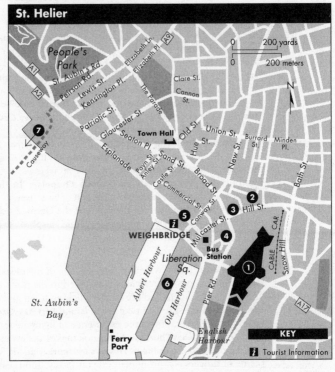

St. Helier

❶ In St. Helier, start out at **Fort Regent**—the panoramic view will give
you an idea of the town's layout. The fort, high on a rock, was built
between 1806 and 1811 as a defense against Napoleon's army (although
the measure was never put to the test). During World War II, German
antiaircraft guns were sited in the fort. In 1958 the British government
sold the fortification to the State of Jersey, which in 1967 turned it into
a vast leisure complex, with a terraced swimming pool, concert hall,
squash courts, a good-size amusement park, restaurants, bars, and cafés.
Near Pier Rd., ☎ *01534/500200.* ✐ *Free; fees for individual facilities.* ⊙ *Weekdays 9 AM–10 PM, weekends 9–6.*

❷ Now shaded by chestnut trees, **Royal Square** (behind Hill Street in the
center of town) was once the site of executions and the town pillory.
Witchcraft and its punishment were constant elements in Jersey life for
most of the 16th and 17th centuries, with interminable trials held all
over the island. The States offices, the **Royal Court,** and the **States Cham-**
❸ **ber** (Jersey's parliament) surround the square. The **parish church** of St.
Helier, on the west side of Royal Square, is the latest in the 900-year-
long series of churches that have stood here.

❹ The **Jersey Museum,** in a lovely building completed in 1817 for the
merchant and shipbuilder Philippe Nicolle, contains some fascinating
collections that illuminate Jersey's past: works by local artists; re-creations of Victorian rooms; and memorabilia of Lillie Langtry (1853–
1929), the beautiful mistress of Edward VII. "The Jersey Lily" was born
on the island and is buried in St. Saviour's churchyard. The museum,
next to the bus station off Liberation Square, has won awards for its
design and user-friendliness, centered on its facilities geared toward people with disabilities, moms and tots, and foreign-language visitors. ⊠
The Weighbridge, ☎ *01534/633300,* WEB *www.jerseyheritagetrust.org.*
✐ *£3.70, special discount tickets for any 3 of Jersey's 6 principal mu-*

seums (including Elizabeth Castle and Gorey Castle) £8.40. ☉ *Apr.–
Oct., daily 10–5; Nov.–Mar., daily 10–4.*

A few steps away from Liberation Square, the busy center of St. He-
❺ lier's harbor life, the **Island Fortress–Occupation Museum** has an extensive display of World War II propaganda relating to Germany's
presence on the island. ✉ *9 Esplanade,* ☎ *01534/734306.* ☜ *£3.* ☉
*Apr., daily 9:30–6; May–Sept., daily 9:30 AM–10:30 PM; Oct., daily 9:30–
6:30; Nov.–Mar., daily 10–4.*

🖐 ❻ A Victorian warehouse adjacent to Liberation Square holds the **Jersey
Maritime Museum and Occupation Tapestry** including the museum's
imaginative exhibits, such as a 9-ft high Voyages Globe detailing voyages made from Jersey, and modern interpretations of nautical myths
and legends. Children can sail model boats in a wave tank, while
adults may prefer watching the restoration of historic boats in the workshop. The same site displays the **Occupation Tapestry,** a huge collective undertaking to commemorate the 50th anniversary of the islands'
liberation from Nazi occupation. The tapestry consists of 12 panels,
each embroidered by the people of one of Jersey's parishes, and each
focusing on a particular theme of the experience of occupation and liberation. ✉ *New North Quay,* ☎ *01534/811043,* ⟦WEB⟧ *www.jerseyher-
itagetrust.org.* ☜ *Museum £4, tapestry £2.* ☉ *Apr.–Oct., daily 10–5;
Nov.–Mar., daily 10–4.*

West along the **Esplanade,** yachts from all over the world berth at the
Albert Harbour Marina. You can take short or long cruises from here,
including an evening cocktail trip down the coast or a weekend jaunt
❼ to Brittany. Across St. Helier's main harbor is **Elizabeth Castle,** with a
military museum and historical exhibits that interpret its role as a fortification since its beginnings in the 16th century. The castle is on an
island joined to the Esplanade by a causeway that begins opposite the
Grand Hotel, by **People's Park.** You can cross the causeway between
high tides, but listen for the bell rung from the castle's gatehouse a half
hour before the sea covers the stones; the water can rise until it's 15
ft deep. When the causeway is not usable, an amphibious craft takes
visitors across. The little island was a holy isle beginning in the 6th
century with the arrival of Helier, the missionary son of a Belgian war-
lord. Legend places his cell on the headland beyond the castle, still called
Hermitage Rock. Near the castle's entrance, in former barracks, is a
military museum housing an exhibition that tells the building's story.
In the granite Governor's House in the heart of the complex, there are
waxwork tableaus of events in the castle's long history, notably the meeting of Sir Philippe de Carteret and Charles II, who took refuge here
during the Civil War in 1646. Allow several hours for a visit. ✉ *St.
Aubin's Bay,* ☎ *01534/723971,* ⟦WEB⟧ *www.jerseyheritagetrust.org.* ☜
*£3.70, special discount tickets for any 3 of Jersey's 6 principal muse-
ums (including Jersey Museum and Gorey Castle) £8.40.* ☉ *Apr.–
Oct., daily 9:30–6 (last admission 5).*

The following Jersey highlights are arranged clockwise, starting just
west of the capital.

St. Matthew's Church, known as the **Glass Church,** is a Victorian
chapel restored in 1934 as a memorial to Sir Jesse Boot (1850–1931),
a millionaire pharmacist known throughout Britain for his drugstore
chain, Boots. The fashionable Parisian glass sculptor, René Lalique
(1860–1945), transformed the interior with artisanal glass. He embellished the church with fluid applications of Art Deco glass forms;
the front appears to be supported by a cluster of icicles, and the glass
cross, pillars, and altar rail all scintillate with refracted light. The

church is in Millbrook, about 1½ mi from Elizabeth Castle. ⊠ *St. Aubin's Rd., Millbrook, St. Lawrence,* ☎ *01534/502864.* ☜ *Free.* ☉ *Apr.–Nov., weekdays 9–6 (or dusk), Sun. 1–6.*

The **Battle of Flowers Museum** is devoted to the parade of flowers, a summer festival taking place in August, which has been held annually (except during wartime) since 1902. Originally, the floral decorations were torn from the floats for use as "ammunition" in the "battle," but now they survive longer, some to become exhibits in this museum (with materials such as dyed hare's tail and marram grass instead of flowers). A lakeside tearoom beside the museum is open May through September. The museum, reached from St. Aubin's Bay via A12 (Grand Route de St. Ouen), is in the northwest corner of the island, 5 mi northwest of St. Helier and 1 mi west of St. Ouen. ⊠ *La Robeline, Mont des Corvées, St. Ouen,* ☎ *01534/482408.* ☜ *£2.75.* ☉ *Mid-Mar.–Oct., daily 10–5.*

The **Jersey Flower Centre** in the north of the island (off B23), 3 mi northwest of St. Helier and 2 mi east of St. Ouen, has magnificent displays of carnations grown under glass on the grounds of an old farmhouse. You can also wander among wildflowers and exotic birds, including a flock of greater flamingos. ⊠ *Retreat Farm, St. Lawrence,* ☎ *01534/ 865665.* ☜ *£3.75.* ☉ *Apr.–Oct., daily 9:30–5:30.*

★ ✺ Even those who hold no brief with zoos will enjoy the country setting and educational programs that are an intrinsic part of the **Durrell Wildlife Conservation Trust,** based 3 mi north of St. Helier and 4 mi east of St. Ouen. The trust was started in 1963 by the celebrated wildlife writer Gerald Durrell, who chose the 25 acres of Augres Manor as a center for breeding and conserving endangered species, including gorillas, orangutans, lemurs, and marmosets, together with many kinds of birds and reptiles. There are talks, videos, and displays as well as the Dodo Restaurant, named after a bird Durrell was one century too late to save. The zoo lies a half mile inland from Bouley Bay, in the northeast corner of the island. ⊠ *Les Augres Manor, Trinity,* ☎ *01534/ 860000,* WEB *www.jersey.co.uk/jwpt.* ☜ *£8.* ☉ *Daily 9:30–6 (or dusk).*

One of the world's finest collections of orchids can be seen at the **Eric Young Orchid Foundation,** 2 mi north of St. Helier. Four big greenhouses re-create the particular environments needed for specific orchid groups, and there's a viewing gallery over the growing area. The buildings were being renovated in 2001; check times before you visit. ⊠ *Victoria Village, Trinity,* ☎ *01534/861963.* ☜ *£2.50.* ☉ *Wed.–Fri. 10–4.*

★ For centuries Jersey's chief fortress, **Gorey Castle,** otherwise named **Mont Orgueil** (Mount Pride), rises massive and square-cut on its granite rock above the busy harbor, 4 mi northeast of St. Helier and 3 mi east of Victoria Village. It was built in the 14th century as a series of concentric defenses, pierced by five gateways. There are also waxwork tableaus of historic events. An extensive restoration project will be in progress until 2004, but the castle will remain open. ☎ *01534/853292,* WEB *www.jerseyheritagetrust.org.* ☜ *£3.70, special discount tickets for any 3 of Jersey's 6 principal museums (including Jersey Museum and Elizabeth Castle) £8.40.* ☉ *Apr.–Oct., daily 10–6; Nov.–mid-Feb., Fri.–Mon. 10–4; mid-Feb.–Mar., daily 10–4 (last admission 1 hr before closing).*

Dining and Lodging

££££–££££ ✕ **Victoria's.** The Grand Hotel's restaurant is *the* place to go for dinner and dancing. The decor is firmly Victorian. There's a long menu, but the critics' choice is the salmon, or the lamb with wild mushroom and olive stuffing. The set-price menus are a good-value, too. ⊠ *Pier-*

son Rd., St. Helier, ☎ 01534/722301. *Jacket and tie. AE, DC, MC. No lunch Sat., no dinner Sun.*

££–££££   ✕ **Jersey Pottery.** This restaurant is part of the Jersey Pottery complex and likes to boast that Queen Elizabeth II lunched here when visiting her dukedom. The restaurant, in an attractive conservatory, offers great seafood, but since it's very popular and often full, the cafeteria is a fair alternative. ✉ *Gorey Village, Grouville,* ☎ *01534/851119. AE, DC, MC, V. Closed Mon. No dinner.*

££   ✕ **Village Bistro.** You'll find plenty to tempt you from the extensive fish menu as you sit amid the uplifting sun and sea colors of blue and yellow, surrounded by decorative suns, moons, and stars. A creamy risotto of smoked haddock, prawn, saffron, and spinach is one choice. Meat-eaters are also well served by such dishes as Navarin of Lamb (braised, with parsnip mash, root vegetables, and a beetroot jus), and pan-fried rib-eye steak. ✉ *Gorey Village, Grouville,* ☎ *01534/853429. MC, V. Closed Mon. No lunch Tues.*

££££   ✕⌑ **Hotel l'Horizon.** L'Horizon is one of Jersey's luxury hotels, with wonderful views over St. Brelade's Bay. Although the hotel is big for the island, it manages to maintain a bright, upbeat feeling, with large, comfortable bedrooms and plenty of places to relax in comfort. There are three restaurants—the Crystal Room, the Grill, and the Brasserie. The first two are traditionally elegant, whereas the Brasserie is more relaxed and is near the pool and exercise area. In the more formal restaurants, some good options are the quail salad, roast saddle of lamb, or any of the wonderful seafood dishes. If you don't want to dine, you can always drop by for a special tea in one of the lounges. ✉ *St. Brelade's Bay, St. Brelade JE3 8EF,* ☎ *01534/743101,* ℻ *01534/746269,* ⩃⩁ *www.hotellhorizon.com. 107 rooms. 3 restaurants, pool, sauna, spa, steam room. AE, DC, MC, V.*

££££   ✕⌑ **Longueville Manor.** The Manor, one of Britain's few members of
★   the Relais & Châteaux group, is set on lovely grounds and has the polished look of age combined with elegance plus comfort, derived from a long-established, caring proprietorship. Antiques abound, the bedrooms are supremely comfortable, and the bathrooms are luxurious. The cuisine in the paneled dining room is inventive, modern, and English, with vegetables coming in for special treatment. Try the chicken with foie gras in red wine sauce or the lasagna of roast pumpkin. Besides the à la carte menu, there's a taste of Jersey menu (£42) and a gourmet menu (£70). ✉ *Longueville, St. Saviour JE2 7NF,* ☎ *01534/ 725501,* ℻ *01534/731613,* ⩃⩁ *www.longuevillemanor.com. 32 rooms. Restaurant, pool, tennis court. AE, DC, MC, V.*

£££–££££   ✕⌑ **Château la Chaire.** Spacious and dignified, this mansion is hidden on a cul-de-sac just above Rozel Harbour. All the bedrooms are luxurious and sunny; some of the bathrooms have whirlpool tubs. The property is opulent, and the restaurant is a good place to try Jersey's excellent fresh fish in a variety of elegant preparations. From June through September a minimum two-night stay is required, and only half- or full-board is available. ✉ *Rozel Valley, St. Martin JE3 6AJ,* ☎ *01534/ 863354,* ℻ *01534/865137,* ⩃⩁ *www.hatton-hotels.co.uk. 14 rooms. Restaurant. AE, DC, MC, V.*

££   ✕⌑ **Old Court House Inn.** This is an ancient inn—the core of the building is about 500 years old—with a few rooms, a bistro, two atmospheric lunchtime bars, and a fine restaurant. Rooms overlook the harbor; the best view is from the penthouse. In summer you can dine alfresco on grilled oysters, crab salad, and Jersey plaice, all featured on the big menu. ✉ *The Bulwarks, St. Aubin's Harbour JE3 8AB,* ☎ *01534/746433,* ℻ *01534/745103. 9 rooms. Restaurant, 3 bars. AE, DC, MC, V.*

Nightlife and the Arts

The **Jersey Arts Centre** (✉ Phillips St., St. Helier, ☎ 01534/700444) presents films and has concerts and art exhibitions.

The **Battle of Flowers** (☎ 01534/639000), a parade of flowers, is held on the second Thursday in August. Jersey has an international **Jazz Festival** (☎ 01534/700444) at the beginning of April in St. Helier. For a week in mid-May, the island hosts the **Jersey International Food Festival,** when Jersey chefs along with colleagues from overseas demonstrate their culinary skills.

Outdoor Activities and Sports

BICYCLING

You can rent bikes from **Zebra Hire** (✉ 8–9 The Esplanade, St. Helier, ☎ 01534/736556); the company also runs tours for cyclists of different levels. **Jersey Cycletours** (✉ 2 La Hougue Mauger, St. Mary, ☎ 01534/482898) rents bikes and can organize theme tours with routes for all skills and endurance levels.

DIVING

To dive in Jersey, contact **Watersports** (✉ First Tower, St. Helier, ☎ FAX 01534/732813) or the **Diving Centre** (✉ Bouley Bay, ☎ 01534/861817).

GOLF

Jersey has two 18-hole courses, both of which can be used by any visitor who is affiliated with a golf club back home and can provide proof of handicap. These are **La Moye** (✉ St. Brelade, ☎ 01534/743401) and **Royal Jersey Golf Club** (✉ Grouville, ☎ 01534/854416).

SAILBOARDING AND SURFING

Surfing is great at St. Ouen's Bay, and windsurfing is popular at St. Aubin's Bay and St. Brelade's Bay. You can rent equipment from **Atlantic Waves** (✉ Le Port, St. Ouen's Bay, ☎ 01534/865492).

SWIMMING

St. Ouen's Bay, on the west side of the island, and Royal Bay of Grouville, on the east, have excellent fine-sand beaches and safe water.

Shopping

In St. Helier pedestrian malls on Queen Street and King Street have classic shops selling international brands, and smaller boutiques line roads like Bath Street, New Street, and Halkett Place. Two major markets are the Central Market and Indoor Market, also in this area.

Jersey Pearl (✉ La Route des Issues, St. John, ☎ 01534/862137) exhibits the largest collection of pearl jewelry on the island, and you can watch artisans crafting new pearl pieces; Jersey Pearl also has four retail outlets in different parts of the island (Jersey Airport; Gorey Pier; 11 Halkett St.; and 75 King St., St. Helier). The **Jersey Pottery Shop** (✉ 1 Bond St., St. Helier, ☎ 01534/725115) has a selection of wonderful pottery. You can buy pottery directly from the source at the **Jersey Pottery** (✉ Gorey Village, Grouville, ☎ 01534/851119), where there's also a good restaurant and brasserie. Jersey sweaters are famous the world over and can be purchased at **Jersey Woollen Mills** (✉ La Grande Route des Mielles, St. Ouen, ☎ 01534/481342), where the garments are produced using pure oiled wool.

Guernsey

About 16,000 people, just over one third of the population of Guernsey, live in **St. Peter Port,** which has prospered over the centuries from the harbor around which it climbs. Guernsey is well placed for trade—legal

Beau Sejour
Centre 11

Castle
Cornet 9

German
Military
Underground
Hospital . . .13

Hauteville
House 10

Les Vauxbelets
Chapel 14

Parish
Church of
St. Peter 8

Sausmarez
Manor 12

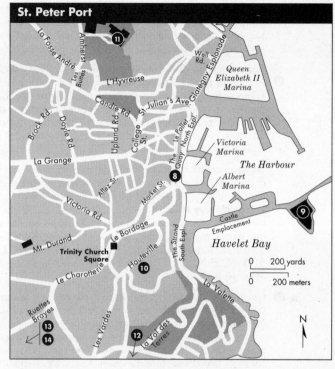

St. Peter Port

or illegal—between France and England. In the 18th and 19th centuries St. Peter Port was a haven for privateers who preyed on merchantmen. Victor Hugo furnished his house, Hauteville, with some of the looted pieces flooding the Guernsey market. In a modern version of its privateering past, St. Peter Port is now home to many tax exiles, who have luxurious houses on the town's outskirts. The heart of the old town, around the harbor, is usually jammed with traffic, but a walk along the quaint streets in the old quarter will provide at least a morning's entertainment. You might start at Trinity Church Square.

8 The **parish church of St. Peter,** right beside the Quay, dates at least to the days of William the Conqueror, although the oldest part of the present building is from the 12th century. Events through the centuries have played havoc with it, not least an air raid in 1944.

★ **9** The southern arm of St. Peter Port's harbor, Castle Emplacement, leads out to **Castle Cornet,** a magnificent spot where you can get a bird's-eye view of St. Peter Port and an 8-mi-away glimpse of France. The castle was built early in the 13th century and contains several small museums, including the **Royal Guernsey Militia Museum,** the **Armoury,** and the **Main Guard Museum,** whose collection ranges from model ships to relics from the German occupation to island art. There's a cafeteria. ☎ 01481/726518, WEB *www.museum.guernsey.net/castle. htm.* 🎟 *£5.* ☉ *Apr.–Oct., daily 10–5.*

★ **10** You can climb up from Castle Pier to Hauteville (High Town) to reach **Hauteville House,** once the home of writer Victor Hugo (1802–85). For 18 years he was a political exile on Guernsey; in 1856 he bought this house. It is now owned by the City of Paris and is a completely French enclave, filled with lovely old furniture and tapestries. From the top floor the author could see across to his beloved France and also into the house of his mistress, Juliette Drouet. ☒ *38 Rue de Hauteville,* ☎

01481/721911, WEB *www.mairie-paris.fr.* ⊡ *£4.* ⊙ *Apr.–June and Sept., Mon.–Sat. 10–noon and 2–4:45 (last entry); July–Aug., Mon.– Sat. 10–5. Guided tours only, every 15 minutes, limited to 15 people; early arrival recommended.*

Just north of St. Peter Port's town center, inland from the North Beach
⑪ Marina, is the **Beau Sejour Centre,** a multipurpose sports and entertainment complex. Equipped with an indoor heated pool, squash, badminton, and tennis courts, a cinema-theater, a cafeteria, and a bar, this
is the perfect place to visit on a rainy day. ⊠ *Amherst,* ☎ *01481/727211.*
⊡ *50p; separate fees for use of individual facilities.* ⊙ *Daily 8 AM–
midnight, but check for pool schedule and other activities.*

Hidden beneath the rocks south of the center of St. Peter Port lies one
of the underground networks of tunnels built on Guernsey by the German occupying forces and their slave labor. Now it's home to **La
Valette Military Museum,** a complex that focuses on Guernsey's military history dating back to the Victorian island militia. It holds various World War II exhibits, including the indomitable German truck
used in the film *Indiana Jones and the Last Crusade.* ⊠ *La Valette,* ☎
01481/722300. ⊡ *£2.75.* ⊙ *Apr.–Oct., daily 10–5; Nov.–Mar., Thurs.–
Mon. 10–5.*

★ ⑫ Guernsey's only stately home open to the public is **Sausmarez Manor**
(not to be confused with Sausmarez Park, northwest of St. Peter Port).
Although there was once a Norman house here, the present building,
a solid, plain structure, dates from the 18th century, when it was built
at the behest of the first governor of New York. It has been called the
country's finest example of the Queen Anne colonial style of architecture
and is set among gardens; the most important is the Woodland Garden, full of tropical plants. A 200-piece sculpture trail, a 9-hole pitch-
and-putt course, a children's farm animal area, playgrounds, and a tea
garden by the lake complete the picture. Within, tapestries and family portraits are on display. The manor, 2 mi south of St. Peter Port,
has a notable collection of dollhouses, as well as changing exhibitions.
⊠ *St. Martin,* ☎ *01481/235571,* WEB *www.guernsey.org/sausmarez.* ⊡
£4.90, extra charge for some attractions. ⊙ *Apr.–Oct., daily 10–5; guided
tours Apr.–May and Sept.–Oct., Mon.–Thurs. at 10:30, 11:30; June–
Aug., Mon.–Thurs. at 10:30, 11:30, 2.*

⑬ The **German Military Underground Hospital,** 3 mi southwest of St.
Peter Port, is one of the main relics attesting to the German occupation
on Guernsey. These grim catacombs were built by slave labor, and
many workers who died on the job are entombed in the concrete. ⊠
La Vassalerie Rd., St. Andrew's, ☎ *01481/239100.* ⊡ *£2.75.* ⊙ *Mid-
Mar.–mid-Nov., 9:30–4:30; mid-Nov.–mid-Dec., Sun. and Thurs. afternoons only.*

One of England's most delightful buildings and one of the smallest
★ ⑭ churches in the world, **Les Vauxbelets Chapel** is a folk art masterpiece
made of cement completely studded with seashells, kitchenware, china,
and bits of broken crockery (even old teapot lids). This dollhouse
Chartres is barely tall enough for most people to stand up in and has
a maximum congregation of eight. The ornate shrine of the "pretty little valleys" was built by Brother Deodat between 1914 and 1923, but
the current chapel was actually the friar's third attempt: the first version was pulled down by himself, and the second had to go when the
corpulent Catholic Bishop of Portsmouth was unable to squeeze himself in when he came to bless it. The chapel is now part of the Roman
Catholic College of Les Vauxbelets; the church is consecrated, although services are extremely rare. ⊠ *Bouillon Rd.,* ☎ *01481/236479*

(11 AM–noon only). ☒ *Free; donation welcome.* ☉ *Weekdays 9–6 (or dusk), Sat. 9–1, Sun. for worship only.*

The Nazi presence on Guernsey is remembered at the **German Occupation Museum,** 4 mi southwest of St. Peter Port. The museum includes a reconstruction of a street during the occupation and access to German fortifications, as well as numerous tableaux and videos. ☒ *Forest (near the airport),* ☎ *01481/238205.* ☒ *£2.75.* ☉ *Apr.–Oct., daily 10–5; Nov.–Mar., Tues.– Sun. 10–1.*

Dining and Lodging

££ ✕ **Absolute End.** This quietly elegant little restaurant in a neat, white
★   building facing the sea is about a mile north along the coast from the center of St. Peter Port. Since 1987, the chef has been Antonio Folni, whose emphasis is on fresh seafood—if you linger nearby in the morning, you may spot the procession of fishermen bringing in their day's catch. Home-smoked fish and shellfish are very tasty starters; also try the salmon coulibiac. There is a good-value set-price lunch menu for £12.50. ☒ *Longstore, St. George's Esplanade, St. Peter Port,* ☎ *01481/ 723822. AE, MC, V. Closed Sun. and Jan.*

££ ✕ **L'Atlantique Hotel.** The sunset views over the bay are exceptionally fine in this excellent hotel restaurant. It specializes in local and seasonal products, with an à la carte menu that changes monthly. However, you'll always find seafood strongly featured; wash it down with a wine from the extensive and well-chosen list. ☒ *Perelle Bay, St. Saviour,* ☎ *01481/264056. DC, MC, V.*

££ ✕ **La Nautique.** Gunter Botzenhardt, former chef of La Frégate, owns this restaurant where fresh fish are prominent on the menu. The accent also falls on the desserts, the owner's specialty; try the Austrian nut pudding with walnut ice cream and vanilla sauce. La Nautique claims one of the best wine cellars on the Channel Islands. ☒ *The Quay Steps, St. Peter Port,* ☎ *01481/721714. AE, MC, V. Closed Sun.*

££–£££ ✕⊞ **La Frégate.** This small 17th-century manor house has been carefully converted into a hotel. Its setting in colorful gardens on a quiet hillside overlooking the harbor makes it an excellent choice for a restful sojourn. The bedrooms, some with balconies, are comfortable and sizable and the staff attentive. The restaurant, with big windows overlooking the town, serves top-notch cuisine, especially seafood dishes. ☒ *Les Côtils, St. Peter Port GY1 1UT,* ☎ *01481/724624,* ℻ *01481/ 720443,* 🕸 *www.lafregate.guernsey.net. 13 rooms. Restaurant. AE, DC, MC, V.*

££ ⊞ **Imperial Hotel.** Here is a simple hotel that's very popular for family vacations. The bedrooms, decorated with sturdy furnishings, are uncluttered, and some have views of the sandy beaches of Rocquaine Bay. There are two bars, and one of them, the Portlet Bar, is a popular haunt of locals. ☒ *Torteval GY8 0PS,* ☎ *01481/264044,* ℻ *01481/ 266139,* 🕸 *www.imperialinguernsey.com. 17 rooms. Restaurant, 2 bars. MC, V.*

Nightlife and the Arts

Guernsey has an Eisteddfod (a traditional music festival) during February, a Battle of Flowers at the end of August, and a Film and Video Festival in mid-September. Contact the tourist board for the latest dates.

Outdoor Activities and Sports

BICYCLING

On Guernsey, you can rent bikes from **Quay Cycle Hire** (☒ New Jetty, White Rock, St. Peter Port, ☎ 01481/714146), which delivers and collects bikes anywhere on the island, **Rent-a-bike** (☒ The Bridge, St. Sampson's, ☎ 01481/249311), and **Cycleworld** (☒ Camp du Roi Crossroads, Vale, ☎ 01481/258917).

DIVING

To rent and buy diving equipment and to arrange lessons in Guernsey, contact **Dive Guernsey** (⊠ Castle Emplacement, St. Peter Port, ☎ 01481/714525).

GOLF

The 18-hole **Royal Guernsey** (⊠ L'Ancresse, Vale, ☎ 01481/45070) has wonderful views of the beach and sea. To play here visitors must produce handicap certificates, and they can't play on Sunday or on Thursday and Saturday afternoons.

SAILBOARDING AND SURFING

A good place to try the surf is Vazon Bay. For rentals and equipment, contact **Nauti-Fun** (⊠ L'Islet Crossroads, St. Sampson's, ☎ 01481/246690) or **Sail or Surf** (⊠ 24 Commercial Arcade, St. Peter Port, ☎ 01481/712621).

SWIMMING

Guernsey's beaches are one of its chief attractions. Try Vazon Bay, on the northwest coast, which has a section reserved for surfers; Petit Port, in the lee of Jerbourg Point, great for sunbathing but at the bottom of a 296-step descent; and L'Ancresse Bay, to the north, where the water is shallow.

Shopping

The main shopping district in St. Peter Port, not as glitzy as St. Helier's, begins in Le Pollet, near Queen Elizabeth Marina. The mostly pedestrian area is a network of lanes with specialty shops—particularly jewelers. This is a great place to buy a watch. For antiques and women's fashions, head for the old quarter and Mill Street, Mansell Square, and Trinity Square. **Moulin Houet Pottery** (⊠ Moulin Houet Bay, St. Martin, ☎ 01481/237201) is a good source for sturdy, attractive pottery.

Sark

Sark, 7 mi east of Guernsey, is the odd man out of the Channel Islands. Turning its back on the 21st century, it has banned the automobile, allowing only horse- or tractor-drawn carriages, and even planes are prohibited from flying overhead unless special permission is granted. The tranquil island is in two sections; the smaller part, Little Sark, is joined to the main island by a narrow neck of land whose vertiginous drop is 260 ft. Boat or carriage rides, walking, biking, and swimming are some of the low-key ways to unwind here.

Dining and Lodging

£££   ✕▥ **Stocks Island Hotel.** For a relaxed lunch—and what else would you expect on Sark?—try the restaurant here. Lunchtime fare in the Courtyard Bistro or in the Smuggler's Bar, a converted wine cellar, might be quiche or the local lobster and crab, and Stocks' cakes and pastries also rank high on the menu. The Cider Press Restaurant serves more formal meals: the fillet of sea bass is memorable. If you feel like staying over, there are guest rooms. ⊠ *Sark GY9 0SD,* ☎ *01481/832001,* FAX *01481/832130,* WEB *www.stocks-sark.com. 24 rooms, 20 with bath. Restaurant. AE, DC, MC, V. Closed last wk Dec.*

Outdoor Activities and Sports

On Sark, both **Avenue Cycle Hire** (⊠ The Avenue, ☎ 01481/832102) and **A–B Cycles** (☎ 01481/832844) rent bikes. **Isle of Sark Carriage and Cycle Hire** (☎ 01481/832262) also offers guided tours by horse and carriage.

CHANNEL ISLANDS A TO Z

To research prices, get advice from other travelers, and book travel arrangements, visit www.fodors.com.

AIR TRAVEL

Jersey is well served by flights from both mainland Britain and the Continent. Flying time from London is one hour, from Manchester 90 minutes, from Plymouth 70 minutes. The London–Jersey round-trip fare starts from about £70. There are regular daily flights all summer between Jersey and Guernsey, and fewer flights in winter. You can also fly to the islands from France.

CARRIERS

There are direct flights to Jersey from Birmingham (British European), Bristol (British Airways), Edinburgh (British Airways), East Midlands (British Midland), Exeter (British European), Gatwick (British Airways, British European), Glasgow (British European), Leeds–Bradford (British Midland), Manchester (British Airways), Newcastle (British Airways), Plymouth (British Airways), and Southampton (British European). Guernsey Airport is served by Aurigny Air Services, British Airways, British European, and British Midland. There are regular air departures to the island of Alderney from Jersey, Guernsey, and the mainland, also run by Aurigny Air Services.

➤ AIRLINES AND CONTACTS: **Aurigny Air Services** (☎ 01481/822886, WEB www.aurigny.com). **British Airways** (☎ 0845/773–3377, WEB www.britishairways.com). **British European** (☎ 0870/567–6676, WEB www.british-european.com). **British Midland** (☎ 0870/607–0555, WEB www.britishmidland.com). **Channel Island Travel Service** (☎ 01534/746181, WEB www.guernseytravel.com).

AIRPORTS

➤ AIRPORT INFORMATION: **Jersey Airport** (✉ St. Peter, ☎ 01534/490999). **States of Guernsey Airport** (✉ La Villiaze, Forest, ☎ 01481/237766).

BOAT AND FERRY TRAVEL

Larger ferries travel between Jersey and Guernsey; those from the British mainland stop at both islands going and returning. You can sail to Jersey or Guernsey year-round from Weymouth and Portsmouth and in summer from Poole. Condor Ltd. has a daily catamaran service (five times a week in winter). Most boats stop at Guernsey first. The average time from Weymouth and Poole is 2¼ hours to Guernsey, 1 hour more to Jersey. From Portsmouth, the average time is 6½ hours to Guernsey and 10 hours to Jersey. An average fare runs from £80 for a five-day round-trip for a foot passenger (£90 in summer) to £254 for a car with two passengers (£302 in summer).

Fast hydrofoils skim around all the islands. Sark can be reached from Guernsey in about 45 minutes by Isle of Sark Shipping and in the same amount of time from Jersey by Emeraude (April through September only). Herm can be reached from Guernsey in 20 minutes by Trident Charter Co., which operates all year. There is no scheduled boat service to the island of Alderney, although operators do run sporadic excursions in summer. Condor runs a foot-passenger catamaran service from Jersey and Guernsey to St. Malo, France, from April through October.

FARES AND SCHEDULES

➤ BOAT AND FERRY INFORMATION: **Condor Ferries** (☎ 0845/345–2000, WEB www.condorferries.co.uk). **Emeraude** (Apr.–Sept., ☎ 01534/766566, WEB www.emeraude.co.uk). **Isle of Sark Shipping** (☎ 01481/

724059, WEB www.sarkshipping.guernsey.net). **Trident Charter Co.** (☎ 01481/721379).

BUS TRAVEL

Jersey and Guernsey have excellent services, including regular buses to and from both airports and all over both islands. Jersey Motor Transport Co. and on Guernsey, Island Coachways, have reasonably priced Rover tickets, which provide unlimited travel over a short period of time.

FARES AND SCHEDULES

➤ BUS INFORMATION: **Island Coachways** (✉ Les Banques, St. Peter Port, Guernsey, ☎ 01481/720210). **Jersey Motor Transport Co.** (✉ Central Bus Station, Weighbridge, St. Helier, Jersey, ☎ 01534/721201).

CAR RENTAL

➤ LOCAL AGENCIES: **Avis** (✉ Les Caches, St. Martin, Guernsey, ☎ 01481/235266; Rue Cappelain, St. Peter Port, Jersey, ☎ 01534/519100). **Europcar** (✉ Arrivals Hall, Jersey Airport, St. Peter Port, Jersey, ☎ 0800/801495; 0800/378548 after 5 PM). **Hertz** (✉ Jackson's Garage, Airport Forecourt, Guernsey, ☎ 01481/237638; Alares House, Jersey Airport, Jersey, ☎ 01534/745621). **Harlequin Hire Cars** (✉ Les Caches, St. Martin, Guernsey, ☎ 01481/239511).

CAR TRAVEL

You can ship your car by ferry from mainland Britain at fairly low rates or rent a car, but the islands are small and easily explored by local bus. The traffic, especially on Jersey, can be regularly snarled up, particularly in high season; taking a bus or walking are good alternatives.

RULES OF THE ROAD

Driving is on the left, and the speed limit is 40 mph on Jersey; 35 on Guernsey and Alderney; cars are not permitted on Sark.

EMERGENCIES

➤ CONTACTS: **Ambulance, fire police** (☎ 112 or 999). **General Hospital** (✉ St. Helier, Jersey, ☎ 01534/622000). **Princess Elizabeth Hospital** (✉ Le Vauquiedor, St. Andrews, Guernsey, ☎ 01481/725241)

LODGING

➤ CONTACTS: **Guernsey Hotel and Tourist Association** (✉ Suite 3, 16 Glategny Esplanade, St. Peter Port, Guernsey GY1 1WN, ☎ 01481/713583, FAX 01481/715882, WEB www.ghata.guernsey.net). **Jersey Hospitality Association** (✉ La Rue le Mesurier, St. Helier, Jersey JE2 4YE, ☎ 01534/721421, FAX 01534/722496).

MONEY MATTERS

CURRENCY

Although the islands use pounds and pence, both have their own version, with specially printed bills. This currency is *not* legal tender elsewhere in the United Kingdom, although you are able to use U.K. currency on the islands.

CURRENCY EXCHANGE

Financial wheeling and dealing is big business here, and you'll find *bureaux de change* at banks, travel agencies, the main post offices, airports, and the main harbors. Note that only local stamps may be used to post letters.

TOURS

BOAT TOURS

South Coast Cruises runs guided motor boat excursions from St. Helier along Jersey's south coast. Dolphin Cruises on Jersey operates one- to three-hour catamaran trips. For longer tours, including weekend trips to Brittany, contact Jersey Cruising School and Yacht Charters, which arranges boat charters either with or without a skipper.

➤ FEES AND SCHEDULES: **Dolphin Cruises** (⊠ Gorey Pier, Gorey, Jersey, ☎ 01534/858647). **Jersey Cruising School and Yacht Charters** (⊠ St. Helier, Jersey, ☎ 01534/888100, FAX 01534/888088). **South Coast Cruises** (⊠ Albert Quay, St. Helier, Jersey, ☎ 01534/732466).

BUS TOURS

All-day, morning, afternoon, and evening coach tours of Jersey are run by Tantivy Blue Coach Tours, and, in reconditioned 1930s buses, by Classic Coach Company. In Guernsey, from April through October, Island Coachways arranges bus tours, or you can go on one of the walking tours starting from the tourist office.

➤ FEES AND SCHEDULES: **Classic Coach Company** (⊠ c/o Town Park Hotel, Pierson Rd., St. Helier, Jersey JE2 3PD, ☎ 01534/505888). **Island Coachways** (⊠ Les Banques, St. Peter Port, Guernsey, ☎ 01481/720210). **Tantivy Blue Coach Tours** (⊠ 70–72 Columberie, St. Helier, Jersey JE2 4QA, ☎ 01534/722584).

TRAVEL AGENCIES

➤ LOCAL AGENT REFERRALS: **Bellingham Travel** (⊠ 33 Queen St., St. Helier, Jersey, ☎ 01534/727575; 41 Commercial Arcade, St. Peter Port, Guernsey, ☎ 01481/726333). **Channel Islands Travel Service** (⊠ Room 222, Guernsey Airport, Forest, Guernsey, ☎ 01481/235471). **Marshall's Travel** (⊠ 1 Quennevais Precinct, St. Brelade, Jersey, ☎ 01534/741278). **Thomas Cook** (⊠ 14 Charing Cross, St. Helier, Jersey, ☎ 01534/506900; 22 Le Pollet, St. Peter Port, Guernsey, ☎ 01481/724111).

VISITOR INFORMATION

In London, you can obtain information on the islands at the Jersey Tourism Office. On the islands, various tourist offices provide information on local attractions and events.

➤ TOURIST INFORMATION: **Guernsey Tourist Board** (⊠ North Esplanade, St. Peter Port GY1 3AN, ☎ 01481/723552, FAX 01481/714951, WEB gtonline.net/business/tourism/htdocs). **Jersey Tourism Department** (⊠ Liberation Sq., St. Helier JE1 1BB, ☎ 01534/500777; 01534/500888 for accommodations, FAX 01534/500808). **Jersey Tourism Office** (⊠ 7 Lower Grosvenor Pl., London SW1W 0EN, ☎ 020/7630–8787, FAX 020/7630–0747, WEB www.jtourism.com). **Sark Tourist Information Office** (⊠ Harbour Hill, ☎ 01481/832345, FAX 01481/832483, WEB www.sark-tourism.com).

6 THE THAMES VALLEY

WINDSOR, HENLEY-ON-THAMES, OXFORD, BLENHEIM PALACE

Triumphant in landscape and history, this "second coastline" of England bred many of the traditions that lie at the heart of British culture. Windsor has housed the monarchy since William the Conqueror, while Eton and Oxford have educated more who's whos than perhaps any other institutions. In summer, leisure-class recreational pursuits abound, with polo matches, Royal Ascot, and the Henley Royal Regatta. Champagne or Pimm's, and the right hat, are still de rigueur.

T HE RIVER GLIDETH AT HIS OWN SWEET WILL was how Wordsworth described the Thames in "Upon Westminster Bridge." Like many another great river, it creates the illusion of flowing not only through the prosperous countryside of Berkshire and Oxfordshire, but through long centuries of history, too. The past seems to rise from its swiftly moving waters like an intangible mist. In London, where it is a broad, oily stream, the Thames speeds almost silently past great buildings, menacingly impressive. Higher upstream it is a busy part of the living landscape, flooding meadows in spring and fall and rippling past places holding significance not just for England but also the world. Runnymede is one of these. Here, on a riverside greensward, the Magna Carta was signed, a crucial step in the Western world's progress toward democracy.

Updated by Benjamin Morse

Nearby rises the medieval bulk of Windsor Castle, home to eight successive royal houses. Anyone who wants to understand the mystique of the British monarchy should visit Windsor, where a fraction of the present Queen's vast wealth is on display in surroundings of heraldic splendor. Farther upstream lies Oxford, where generations of the ruling elite have been educated. In the bustling city, with industrial development on its outskirts, the colleges maintain their scholarly, nearly medieval, calm amid modern traffic's clamorous rush. The less you are guided in such a place, the better. The main thing is to explore at your own pace, absorbing the sense of history and the graces of myriad quadrangles, spires, bridges, and college lawns. Close by Oxford are the storybook village of Woodstock and Blenheim Palace, one of the grandest houses in all the land.

Along the River Thames, scattered throughout the unfolding landscape of trees, meadows, and rolling hills, are numerous small villages and larger towns, some spoiled by ill-considered modern building, many still sleepily preserving their ancient charm. The railroads and superhighways carrying heavy traffic between London, the West Country, and the Midlands have turned much of this area into commuter territory, but you can easily depart from these beaten tracks to discover timeless villages whose landscapes are kept green by the river and its tributaries. The stretches of the Thames near Marlow, Henley, Bray, and Sonning-on-Thames are havens for relaxation. There are rowing clubs and piers all over that part of the river, excellent lawns, and well-built cottages and villas. This is the Thames's shopwindow, and anyone who comes to London in summer and has some time to spare would be well advised to spend it touring the Thames Valley.

Pleasures and Pastimes

Henley Royal Regatta
During the cusp of June and July Henley hosts rowing's most elegant race, the Henley Royal Regatta. Its riverbanks become one gigantic, opulent lawn party as 500,000 visitors, including members of the Royal Family, descend en masse during the week. Dozens of Jaguars and Rolls-Royces disgorge favored guests at the invitation-only Stewards' Enclosure, while everywhere, English oarsmen appear in short-brimmed school caps, straw boaters, and eye-catching rowing jackets with color-coded piping signifying the college or club that aided their rowing careers. Each day, the racing pauses twice—at noon for luncheon and at 4 PM for tea (more likely a bottle of Pimm's "champers"— champagne—and some Kent strawberries with fresh Henley cream). If you're lucky enough to get a spot near the finish line, you'll swear you're back in Edwardian England: winning crews traditionally cheer the losers with a chorus of three "hip, hip, hoorays!"

Dining

Londoners weekend here, and where they go, Cordon Bleu restaurants follow. Ascot, Henley, and Woodstock claim some of Britain's best tables—beginning with Le Manoir aux Quat' Saisons in Great Milton (whose eight-course *menu gourmand* is the perfect topper to an afternoon spent enjoying *le style Rothschild* at nearby Waddesdon Manor) and continuing on with the Oak Leaf in Oakley Court near Windsor and the jewel-like Feathers in Woodstock. Of course simple pub food, as well as classic French cuisine, can be enjoyed in waterside settings at many restaurants beside the Thames. Even in towns away from the river, well-heeled commuters and Oxford professors support top-flight establishments. On weekends it's advisable to make reservations.

CATEGORY	COST*
££££	over £22
£££	£16–£22
££	£9–£15
£	under £9

per person for a main course at dinner

Hiking and Walking

For long-distance walkers, the Oxfordshire Way runs 65 mi from Henley-on-Thames to Bourton-on-the-Water, on the eastern edge of the Cotswolds. A 13-mi ramble starts in Henley, runs north through the Hambleden Valley, takes in Stonor Park, and returns to Henley via the Assendons, Lower and Middle. For a less arduous walk, try the trails through the beech woods at Burnham Beeches.

The Thames Valley is a good area for gentle walking; it is not too hilly, and it is dotted with handy eateries, especially pubs—many of them beside the river—and plenty of easily accessible, comfortable lodgings. Most of the Thames Valley walks include busy traffic areas. One walk that is almost completely free of traffic is the Thames Path, a 180-mi route following the river from the London flood barrier to its source near Kemble, in the Cotswolds. The path follows towpaths from the outskirts of London, through Windsor, to Oxford and Lechlade. There is also good public transportation in the region, so you can easily start and stop anywhere along the route.

Lodging

From converted country houses to refurbished Elizabethan inns, the region's accommodations are rich in history and distinctive in charm. Many hotels cultivate traditional gardens and retain a sense of the past with impressive collections of antiques, while others have embraced the future with fully modern amenities. Some establishments may include a service charge, or it may be added to your bill; ask in advance.

CATEGORY	COST*
££££	over £150
£££	£100–£150
££	£60–£100
£	under £60

All prices are for two people sharing a standard double room, including breakfast and VAT.

Exploring the Thames Valley

An exploration of the Thames Valley can begin in the lively town of Windsor, favorite home-away-from-home of Britain's Royal Family. From there you can follow the river to Henley, site of the famous regatta, and then make a counterclockwise sweep west to Wallingford—the countryside immortalized by *The Wind in the Willows*. You can then head north to Oxford, and end with a visit to some of the region's stately homes and palaces. The area also abounds with tiny villages hidden from the major highways. Turn off from time to time to see if that tiny hamlet, deep in the trees, is as attractive as its name sounds.

Numbers in the text correspond to numbers in the margin and on the Thames Valley and Oxford maps.

Great Itineraries

With your own transport, you could see all the places outlined below on day trips from London, but to get the most out of the region, it's worth searching out that perfect riverside inn or High Street hotel and settling in for a night—or more. Evenings in Windsor or Oxford will allow you to take in some world-class theater, and to make the most out of the mornings for touring the surrounding countryside. The area offers the greatest pleasure to those willing to leave the main roads to explore the smaller centers; the Thames itself is best appreciated by locking the car and setting off on foot along the towpath that runs alongside much of the river.

It would require a bulky volume—and a month-long tour—to describe the Thames Valley in all its aspects, for the Thames, like the Seine, the Rhine, and the Danube, is a river rich with history. Three days will give you a taste of Windsor, a few towns, Blenheim Palace, and Oxford; five days allows you to spend more time in Oxford and to explore additional villages and the area's many stately homes.

IF YOU HAVE 3 DAYS

Begin at ☷ **Windsor** ①, where royalty is the predominant note, and spend a morning visiting the castle, leaving part of the day for Eton College and Windsor Great Park. The next day, follow the river upstream, taking in the grandeur of the great Astor estate at **Cliveden** ⑤ and the charming village of **Marlow** ⑥, where the pubs offer decent snacks for lunch. Head toward **Henley** ⑦, where the Thames forms a harmonious dialogue with the medieval buildings alongside, and easy and tranquil walks beckon upstream or down. Reserve the last morning for ☷ **Oxford** ⑬– ㉕, whose scholastic air does not dampen the aesthetic and gastronomic pleasures on tap, with an afternoon visit to nearby **Woodstock** ㉖—a lovely English village—and **Blenheim Palace** ㉗, birthplace of Winston Churchill and one of the most spectacular houses in England.

IF YOU HAVE 5 DAYS

A longer sojourn will allow you to unearth the rustic charms of the region, including all the hamlets strung along the Thames. Make your base at ☷ **Windsor** ① for your first night. From there you can take excursions to **Ascot** ④, for some of England's finest horse racing, and, to the north, **Cliveden** ⑤. For your second night, consider staying in ☷ **Henley** ⑦, from which it is an easy trip to two aristocratic mansions— **Mapledurham House** ⑨ and **Stonor Park** ⑩, and a cluster of picturesque Thameside villages, such as **Ewelme** ⑪, **Sonning-on-Thames** ⑧, **Dorchester-on-Thames** ㉙, and **Wallingford** ⑫. Reserve the third day and night for the medieval wonders of ☷ **Oxford** ⑬–㉕, then head on your fourth day to the nearby 18th-century village of ☷ **Woodstock** ㉖, site of magisterial **Blenheim Palace** ㉗ and, in fact, some lovely hotels. For the final day, swing eastward to the town of **Great Milton** ㉝ for perhaps the grandest luncheon of your English trip, at Le Manoir aux Quat' Saisons, then pay a call on one or two of a trio of stately homes: **Waddesdon Manor** ㉞, **Woburn Abbey** ㉟, or **Althorp** ㊱.

The Thames Valley

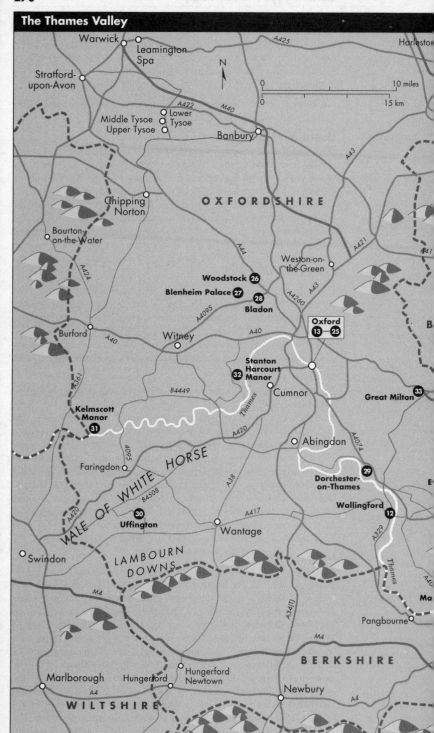

N

0   10 miles

0   15 km

Warwick

Leamington Spa

Harleston

Stratford-upon-Avon

A425

M40

A422

Middle Tysoe
Upper Tysoe
Lower Tysoe

Banbury

A43

OXFORDSHIRE

Chipping Norton

Bourton-on-the-Water

A424

A44

Weston-on-the-Green

A421

A41

Woodstock 26

Blenheim Palace 27

Bladon 28

A4095

A43

A4260

Burford

A40

A361

Witney

A40

Oxford 13 – 25

Stanton Harcourt Manor 32

Cumnor

Great Milton 33

B4449

Thames

Kelmscott Manor 31

A420

Abingdon

A4074

Dorchester-on-Thames 29

4095

Faringdon

VALE OF WHITE HORSE

A38

Wallingford 12

A420

B4508

A417

Uffington 30

Wantage

A329

Thames

Swindon

LAMBOURN DOWNS

M4

A34(T)

Ma

Pangbourne

M4

BERKSHIRE

Marlborough

Hungerford

Hungerford Newtown

Newbury

A4

A4

WILTSHIRE

Harlestone

36 Althorp

Great
Brington   Northampton   A428

Castle
Ashby

10 miles

15 km

A509

M1

A5   Milton
Keynes

**35 Woburn
Abbey**

Leighton
Buzzard

A41(T)

Dunstable

34 Waddesdon
Manor

Aylesbury

B U C K I N G H A M S H I R E   A41(T)

Amersham

Great Milton 33

A40

M40

Watford

C H I L T E R N

Rickmansworth

High Wycombe

Beaconsfield

**Ewelme
11**

12

**Stonor
Park
10**

A4130

B480

Nuffield

**Marlow
A4155 6**

Cookham

**Cliveden
5**

*Burnam
Beeches*

H I L L S

B416

rd

**9 Mapledurham
House**

A4074

A329

B481

Henley 7

Sonning
Common

A4155

A423

Hurley

A404

Thames

A4094

Maidenhead

Burnham

TO LONDON →

M4

Thames

8

Caversham

A4

M4

**Eton
2**

1   **Windsor**

Slough

Sonning-on-Thames

Reading

A329

gbourne

Wokingham

A332

4   **Ascot**

*Windsor
Great
Park*

Shinfield

M4

Runnymede

3

Heathrow
Airport ✈

Staines

A308

Thames

M3

R E

GREAT
BRITAIN

When to Tour the Thames Valley

Although the countryside around the Thames can be alluring year-round, the depths of winter may not be the time most conducive to appreciating its special beauty—nor are rain and chill winds the best accompaniments to soaking up the charms of such places as Windsor and Oxford. Moreover, many of the aristocratic country houses are closed between October and Easter. High summer can see droves of visitors in these places; avoid the months of August and September if you can, if only to escape long lines at attractions. Spring and autumn reveal the countryside at its best, and you can usually venture outdoors during these seasons without too much discomfort. Remember that Eton and the Oxford colleges are much more restricted during term time, and avoid any driving in the London area during the rush hour, which starts an hour or two earlier on Friday.

ROYAL BERKSHIRE: WINDSOR AND ENVIRONS

Windsor

❶ *21 mi west of London.*

Only a small part of old Windsor—the settlement that grew up around the town's famous castle in the Middle Ages—has survived. Windsor Town is not what it used to be in the time of Sir John Falstaff and the *Merry Wives of Windsor,* when it was famous for its inns, of which, in 1650, it boasted about 70. Today, there are only a handful left, and the beer is not so strong and the wit not so rapier-sharp. The presence of droves of visitors can be overwhelming at times, but seekers of romantic history will enjoy tiny Church Lane and Queen Charlotte Street, both narrow and cobbled, opposite the castle entrance. The venerable buildings of Windsor Town now house antiques shops and restaurants.

★ It was no mistake that **Windsor Castle,** the longtime home to England's monarchs, was built to be visible for miles around, a monumental symbol of authority. From William the Conqueror to Queen Victoria, the kings and rulers of England added towers and wings to the brooding structure, and it is today the largest inhabited castle in the world. Yet despite the multiplicity of hands that have gone into its design, the palace has managed to emerge with a unity of style and character. Easily accessible from London, the castle and its surrounding town make for a rewarding day trip.

The most impressive view of Windsor Castle is from the A332 road, on the southern approach to the town. Although there have been settlements here from time immemorial, including a Roman villa, the present castle was begun by William the Conqueror in the 11th century and modified and extended by Edward III in the mid-1300s. One of Edward's largest contributions was the enormous and distinctive round tower. Finally, between 1824 and 1837, George IV transformed what was still essentially a medieval castle into the fortified royal palace you see today. In all, work on the castle spread over more than eight centuries, with most kings and queens of England demonstrating their undying attachment to it. In fact, Windsor is the only royal residence that has been in continuous use by the Royal Family since the Middle Ages.

It is from the North Terrace that entry is gained into the State Apartments, which can be visited by the public when the Queen is not in residence. (The State Apartments are sometimes closed when the Queen

Windsor Castle

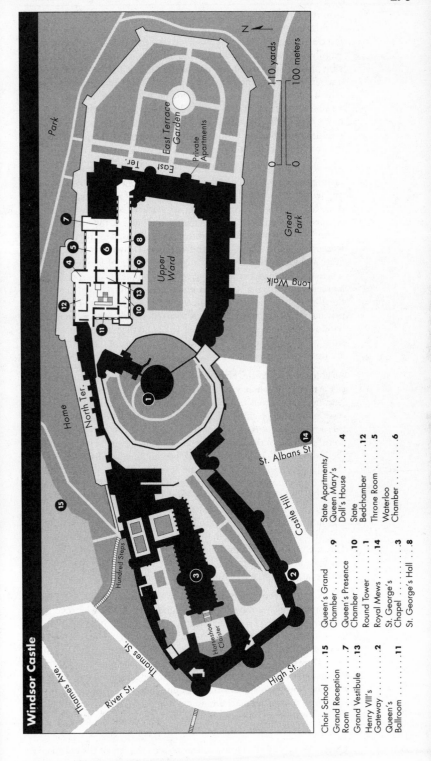

Park

East Terrace Garden

Private Apartments

East Ter.

Great Park

Long Walk

Upper Ward

Home

North Ter.

St. Albans St.

Castle Hill

Hundred Steps

Horseshoe Cloister

Thames Ave.

River St.

Thames St.

High St.

N

0   110 yards

0   100 meters

Choir School **15**
Grand Reception
Room **7**
Grand Vestibule . . .**13**
Henry VIII's
Gateway **2**
Queen's
Ballroom **11**

Queen's Grand
Chamber **9**
Queen's Presence
Chamber **10**
Round Tower **1**
Royal Mews **14**
St. George's
Chapel **3**
St. George's Hall . . .**8**

State Apartments/
Queen Mary's
Doll's House **4**
State
Bedchamber **12**
Throne Room **5**
Waterloo
Chamber **6**

is in residence; call ahead to check.) The Queen, in fact, uses the castle far more than did any of her predecessors. It has become, over the last decade, a sort of country weekend residence, which allows the Royal Family a few days of relaxation and informality away, as much as possible, from the glare of the public eye. To see the royal abode come magnificently alive, check out the Windsor Castle **Changing of the Guard,** which takes place at 11 AM daily or on odd-numbered days. It's advisable to confirm (☎ 01753/868286) the exact schedule of the ceremony. When the Queen is in town, the guard and a regimental band parade through town to the castle gate; when Her Majesty is away, a drum-and-fife band takes over.

The devastating fire of November 1992, which started in the Queen's private chapel, gutted some of the State Apartments. Miraculously, hardly any works of art were lost. In fact, fragments of a 17th-century mural, done for Charles II by Antonio Verrio, surfaced during the renovation. Reopened to the public in 1997 with grand fanfare, the castle has never looked more impressive. Phenomenal repair work restored the **Grand Reception Room,** the **Green and Crimson Drawing Rooms,** and the **State and Octagonal Dining Rooms.** The ceiling of St. George's Hall, where the Queen gives state banquets, was completely destroyed—today, a green oak roof, the largest hammer-beam roof to have been built in the 20th century, looms magnificently over the 600-year-old hall. The private chapel of the Royal Family was redesigned, with a stained-glass window commemorating the fire of 1992 and the restoration work that subsequently took place. All restored rooms, except the private chapel, are open to the public.

As you enter the castle, **Henry VIII's gateway** leads uphill into the wide castle precincts, where visitors are free to wander. Directly opposite the entrance is the exquisite **St. George's Chapel.** The seemingly endless succession of arches on either side creates an impression of dignity that makes this a most appropriate site for the Queen to invest new knights at the colorful Order of the Garter ceremonies held in June. Here lie some of the most famous kings of England, beginning with Henry VI, and including Charles I, Henry VIII (Jane Seymour is the only one of his six wives buried here), and many others. One of the noblest buildings in England, the chapel was built in the 15th- and 16th-century Perpendicular style and has elegant stained-glass windows, a high, vaulted ceiling, and intricately carved choir stalls. The heraldic banners of the Knights of the Garter hang in the choir, giving it a richly medieval look. The ceremony in which the knights are installed as members of the order has been held here with much pageantry for more than five centuries. Note that St. George's Chapel is closed to the public on Sunday.

The **North Terrace** provides especially good views across the Thames to Eton College, perhaps the most famous of Britain's exclusive "public" boys' schools. From the terrace, you enter the **State Apartments,** containing priceless furniture, including a magnificent Louis XVI bed; Gobelin tapestries; and paintings by Canaletto, Rubens, Van Dyck, Holbein, Dürer, and del Sarto. The high points of the tour are the **Throne Room** and the **Waterloo Chamber,** where Sir Thomas Lawrence's portraits of Napoléon's victorious foes line the walls. You can also see a collection of arms and armor, much of it exotic, and an exhibition on the restoration of Windsor Castle and The Gallery. Some of these rooms may be closed to the public at any given time.

Queen Mary's Doll's House, on display to the left of the entrance to the State Apartments, is a perfect miniature Georgian palace-within-a-palace, created in 1923. Electric lights work, the doors all have keys, the elevators are practical, and there is running water. There is even a library of Lilliputian-size books especially written by famous authors of the 1920s. Just outside the castle, on St. Albans Street, is the **Royal Mews**, where the royal horses are kept, with carriages, coaches, and splendid crimson and gold harnesses. ☎ *01753/868286; 01753/831118 for recorded information,* WEB *www.royalresidences.com.* 🎟 *£10.50 for the Precincts, the State Apartments, the Gallery, St. George's Chapel, the Albert Memorial Chapel, and the Doll's House.* ⊙ *Mar.–Oct., Mon.–Sat. 10–5:30 (last admission at 4), Sun. 8:30–6:30; Nov.–Feb., daily 10–4 (last admission at 3).*

Windsor Great Park, the remains of an ancient royal hunting forest, stretches for some 8 mi (about 5,000 acres) south of Windsor Castle and invites exploration. Much of it is open to the public and can be seen by car or on foot, including its geographical focal points, the romantic and spectacular 3-mi **Long Walk**, designed by Charles II to join castle and park, and **Virginia Water**, a 2-mi-long lake. The park contains the realm of Frogmore, which was one of Queen Victoria's most treasured residences and is still used by Elizabeth II and her family members as a retreat. On rare occasions, however, the public is invited to **Frogmore House** (☎ 01753/868286, 🎟 house £3.50, gardens and mausoleum £2.50, ⊙ May, selected days only [check by phone, 10–6]; Aug., selected days only [check by phone, 11–4]). Nearby is holy ground for the Windsor family: the **Royal Mausoleum at Frogmore,** where two famous royal couples are buried: inside, Victoria and Albert; outside, the Duke and Duchess of Windsor. This is open only a few days a year, in May and August, with prebooked guided tours also possible on selected weekdays August–October. The main horticultural delight of Windsor Great Park is the **Savill Garden** (✉ Wick La., Englefield Green, Egham, ☎ 01753/860222. 🎟 £3–£5. ⊙ Apr.–Oct., daily 10–6; Nov.–Mar., daily 10–4), which contains a huge variety of trees and shrubs.

☺ Parents of young children can relax with the kids at **Legoland,** an extensive theme park 2 mi outside Windsor, designed along the lines of the original in Copenhagen and dedicated to the versatile Lego building brick. There are a plethora of ingenious models small and large, as well as rides and interactive activities. A lakeside picnic area, 150 acres of parkland, and restaurants allow you to make a day of it. ✉ *Winkfield Rd.,* ☎ *0990/040404,* WEB *www.legoland.co.uk.* 🎟 *£18.* ⊙ *Sept.–Jan. and Mar.–June, daily 10–6; July–Aug. daily 10–8.*

Dining and Lodging

Most of Windsor's restaurants are uninspiring, so if you're not opting for a special meal at one of the choices below, head across the river to Eton.

£   ✕ **Nell Gwynne's House.** Once the home of one of Charles II's mistresses, this tea house serves satisfying omelets and salads at affordable prices. It's halfway down the road opposite the castle exit, so Charles didn't have far to travel and neither will you. ✉ *6 Church St.,* ☎ *01753/ 850929. AE, DC, MC, V.*

££££   ✕🏠 **Oakley Court.** A romantic getaway, this Victorian-era mock castle stands on picture-perfect grounds beside the Thames, 3 mi west of Windsor. Its bristling towers and spires have been used in several films (including the *Rocky Horror Picture Show*); note, however, that half the rooms are in a modern annex. At the excellent Oak Leaf Restaurant, serving French and English fare, Prince Charles has been known to enjoy the fillet of beef with Stilton mousse. ✉ *Windsor Rd., Water Oakley, Windsor SL4 5UR,* ☎ *01753/609988,* FAX *01628/637011. 115 rooms. Restaurant, indoor pool, sauna, putting green, croquet, gym, billiards, helipad. AE, DC, MC, V.*

££££ ✕⊡ **Sir Christopher Wren's House Hotel.** A private mansion built by
the famous architect in 1676, this is an impressively sober house, its
brick facade adorned with a white classical doorway and elegant sash
windows. Inside, the entrance hall is 17th-century grand, and rooms
are tastefully appointed and lined with rich wood paneling. The riverside terrace is ideal for tea; Stroks Restaurant has a fixed-price dinner
menu of Continental fare. ⊠ *Thames St., SL4 1PX,* ☎ *01753/861354,*
FAX *01753/860172,* WEB *www.wrensgroup.com. 70 rooms. Restaurant,
bar, café, health club, meeting rooms. AE, DC, MC, V.*

££££ ✕⊡ **Stoke Park Club.** On a 350-acre estate 4 mi southwest of Windsor, Stoke Park can make Windsor Castle, off in the distance, seem almost humble in comparison. Architect James Wyatt perfected this
version of neoclassical grandeur when he built the house for the Penn
family in 1791. The world-renowned golf course was the setting for
James Bond's victory round in the movie *Goldfinger.* A spa and indoor
recreation center, set to open mid-2002, will add further luxury. Elegant bedrooms are individually decorated with antiques, paintings, and
original prints. The Brasserie serves traditional English cuisine, including rosemary-glazed lamb and haddock fishcakes. ⊠ *Park Rd., Stoke
Poges SL2 4PG,* ☎ *01753/717171,* FAX *01753/717181,* WEB
*www.stokeparkclub.com. 20 rooms. Restaurant, 2 bars, 27-hole golf
course, 9 tennis courts, croquet, fishing, meeting rooms. AE, MC, V.*

Nightlife and the Arts

Windsor's **Theatre Royal** (⊠ Thames St., ☎ 01753/853888), where productions have been staged for nearly 200 years, is one of Britain's leading provincial theaters. It puts on a range of plays and musicals throughout
the year, including a pantomime for the six weeks following Christmas.

Concerts of all kinds, poetry readings, and children's events are highlights of the two-week **Windsor Festival** (☎ 020/8883–8740), usually
held in early September or October, with events occasionally taking
place in the castle itself.

Outdoor Activities and Sports

Bikes and in-line skates can be rented at **Windsor Cycle Hire** (⊠ Alexandra Gardens, Alma Rd., ☎ 0468/452531).

Shopping

Most Windsor stores are open on Sunday, particularly those selling antiques along Peascod Street, High Street, and King Edward Court. The
Windsor Royal Station shopping center (Central Train Station, ☎
0800/923–0017) includes Jaeger, Pied-a-Terre, and an outpost of the
quintessential London department store, Liberty's. **Past Times** (⊠ 126
Peascod St., ☎ 01753/867762) sells souvenirs from England's past and
displays them according to era, simplifying your search for the perfect
Edwardian tea cup. The **Edinburgh Woollen Mill** (⊠ 10 Castle Hill, ☎
01753/855151) has a large range of Scottish knitwear, tartans, and
tweeds, particularly for women.

Eton

② *23 mi west of London, linked by a footbridge across the Thames to
Windsor.*

Some observers may find it almost symbolic that almost opposite
Windsor Castle—which embodies the continuity of the royal tradition—
a school was established that for centuries has been responsible for the
upbringing of many future leaders of the country. This, of course, is
Eton. With its single main street leading from the river to the famous
school, the town itself, with its old-fashioned charm, is a much quieter place than Windsor.

★ The splendid redbrick, Tudor-style buildings of **Eton College,** founded in 1440 by King Henry VI, border the north end of High Street; drivers are warned of "Boys Crossing." During the college semesters, the schoolboys are a distinctive sight, dressed in their pinstripe trousers, swallow-tailed coats, and stiff collars (top hats have not been worn by the boys since the '40s), but don't let the dapper duds fool you. Some of the more mischievous Etonians have been known to fill visitors' heads with fantastic stories regarding the supposedly mythic origins of their alma mater.

The Gothic **Chapel** rivals St. George's at Windsor in both size and magnificence, and is both impressively austere and intimate at one and the same time. Beyond the cloisters are the school's playing fields where, according to the Duke of Wellington, the Battle of Waterloo was really won, since so many of his officers had learned discipline in their school days there. The **Museum of Eton Life** has displays on the school's history, and there are guided tours of the school and chapel. ⊠ *Main Entrance Brewhouse Yard,* ☎ *01753/671177,* WEB *www.etoncollege.com.* ⌁ *£2.80; £4 with tour.* ☉ *During term, daily 2–4:30; out of term, daily 10:30–4:30; guided tours Mar.–Oct., daily at 2:15 and 3:15.*

Dining

££–£££ ✕ **The Cockpit.** Cockfighting once took place in the courtyard of this 500-year-old oak-beamed inn. Now a restaurant with an emphasis on Italian cuisine, its specialties include fresh fish. ⊠ *47–49 High St.,* ☎ *01753/860944. AE, DC, MC, V. Closed Mon. No lunch Tues.*

££–£££ ✕ **Gilbey's.** Just over the bridge from Windsor, this restaurant sits at the center of Eton's Antiques Row and now serves a fine menu of English fare that changes every two months. ⊠ *82 High St.,* ☎ *01753/ 854921. AE, DC, MC, V.*

Shopping

Eton has a reputation for excellent, if pricey, antiques shops, most of them along High Street. **Turk's Head Antiques** (⊠ 98 High St., ☎ 01753/ 863939) specializes in jewelry, silver, and Victoriana.

Runnymede

★ ❸ *5 mi southeast of Windsor on A308.*

A giant step in the history of democracy was taken at Runnymede, outside Egham. On what was an island in the Thames (but which now, with the silting up of the channel, is part of a meadow on the river's south side), King John, under his baron's compulsion, signed the Magna Carta in 1215, affirming the individual's right to justice and liberty. On the wooded hillside, in a meadow given to the United States by Queen Elizabeth in 1965, stands a **memorial to President John F. Kennedy.** Nearby is another memorial, a classical temple in style, erected by the American Bar Association for the 750th anniversary of the signing. There is no visitor center at Runnymede, just informational plaques and a parking lot.

Ascot

❹ *10 mi southwest of Runnymede, 8 mi southwest of Windsor, 28 mi southwest from London.*

The town of Ascot (pronounced *as*-cut) has for centuries been famous for horse racing and for style. Queen Anne chose to have a racecourse here, and the first race meeting took place in 1711. Every third week of June (Tuesday–Friday), the titled and the gentry watch the world's finest thoroughbreds pound the turf during the **Royal Meeting,** or

Royal Ascot, at **Ascot Racecourse,** though eyes are not always on the track. The impressive show of millinery for which the Royal Meeting is known was immortalized in Cecil Beaton's Ascot sequence in *My Fair Lady,* in which black and white silk roses, osprey feathers, and a lorgnette held high transformed Eliza Doolittle into Milady. Today more than a quarter of a million race goers continue to bet, sip champagne, and be seen. Thursday is the most popular day for the Gold Cup, a race inaugurated in 1807, but each day offers top-class racing and people-watching opportunities. The Racecourse is divided into several enclosures, the Royal Enclosure being the most famous and the most snooty. Entrance to the Royal Enclosure is limited to those who have applied in advance, and new members must be sponsored by two existing Royal Enclosure badge holders. Morning dress—meaning tail coats, top hats, and striped pants—must be worn by gentlemen whereas hats are de rigueur for the ladies in the Royal Enclosure. But all is not lost, even if you can't persuade the Queen to invite your party into her patch. The two main public enclosures, the Grandstand and the Silver Ring, have great views and all the fun of the chase for less cash and much less snobbery. Budget travelers can even try for the Course Enclosure, which costs £2 a head for entry. With around 100 bars and four large catering facilities, no one wants for food or drink.

The Royal Meeting may be the most chichi and the best known, but racing goes on year-round (except March) at England's largest racecourse. Diamond Day, the fourth Saturday in July, or the Ascot Festival, the last Saturday and Sunday in September, may be a little more low-key, but the racing remains some of the best in the world. During most of the year the Royal Enclosure becomes the Members' Enclosure and seats are readily bookable, although it is advised to phone ahead. Advance booking is advised for Royal Ascot (tickets are usually sold out months before) and other major race meets—make general inquiries to the Sales Office, Ascot. For admission to the **Royal Enclosure,** write to ✉ Her Majesty's Representative, Ascot Office, St. James's Palace, London SW1 (☎ 0171/930–9882).

Ascot is easily accessible from London: trains leave Waterloo on the half hour (trip time takes as long) and buses depart from Victoria Coach Station. ✉ *Ascot Racecourse, A329, Ascot, Berkshire SL5 7JN,* ☎ *01344/622211 (racecourse); 01344/876876 (credit card hot line),* WEB *www.ascot-authority.co.uk.* ✉ *Royal Enclosure £63; Grandstand £46; Silver Ring £10; Course Enclosure £2; reserved grandstand seats for Diamond Day and the Ascot Festival £5; all other race days general admission £2, with special enclosures £6–£60.*

Lodging

££££   🏨 **Berystede Country House Hotel.** A leafy driveway curves around to reveal the architectural excesses of this Victorian-era hotel. With turrets and half-timbering, it is a magnificent neo-Gothic fantasy landed in traditional British countryside. Inside, every square inch pays homage to the horsey culture of Ascot, with horse and jockey prints lining the walls. Most of the rooms are pleasantly standard; a few are nothing short of extraordinary. If your winnings or losings on the racecourse are grand enough, one of the turret suites will see you celebrate—or commiserate, if things go the other way—in plenty of style. ✉ *Bagshot Rd., Sunninghill, Ascot, Berkshire SL5 9JH,* ☎ *01344/623311,* FAX *01344/872301. 90 rooms, 4 suites. Restaurant, bar, pool, croquet. AE, DC, MC, V.*

Cliveden

❺   *8 mi northwest of Windsor, 16 mi north of Ascot, 26 mi west of London.*

Deemed by Queen Victoria a "bijou of taste," this magnificent country mansion has for more than 300 years lived up to its Georgian heritage as a bastion of aesthetic delights. The house, set in woods high above the River Thames, was rebuilt for the Duke of Sutherland by Sir Charles Barry in 1861; it was made famous by the Astors, who purchased it in 1893. In the 1920s and '30s it was the setting for the Cliveden Set, the strongly conservative (not to say fascist) salon presided over by Nancy Astor, who—though she was an American—was the first woman to sit in Parliament, in 1919. The house now belongs to the National Trust, which has leased it for use as a *very* exclusive hotel. The public can visit the spectacular grounds and formal gardens that run down to bluffs overlooking the Thames, as well as three rooms in the west wing of the house. ⊠ *Taplow, near Maidenhead,* ☎ *01628/ 605069,* WEB *www.clivedenhouse.co.uk.* ✆ *Grounds £4.50; house £1 extra.* ☉ *Grounds Mar.–Oct., daily 11–6; Nov.–Dec., daily 11–4; house Mar.–Oct., Thurs. and Sun. 3–6; restaurant in the Orangery Apr.– Oct., Wed.–Sun. 11–5; Nov.–mid-Dec., weekends 11–4.*

Dining and Lodging

££££   X🖬 **Cliveden.** One of the grandest hotels in Britain—and one of the
★   most expensive—provides sophisticated luxury at its best. If you've ever wondered what it would feel like to be an Edwardian grandee, try a stay here. The 376 acres of gardens and parkland include wonderful river views and walks. Cliveden's interior is opulent, featuring Sargent's portrait of Nancy Astor in the Great Hall; suits of armor; a library; a richly paneled staircase; fine historic portraits; and room after room with beautifully molded plaster ceilings. Bedrooms are named after the famous people who once stayed here. Among the three restaurants is the well-regarded Waldo's, known for sophisticated contemporary British and French cuisine. ⊠ *Taplow, near Maidenhead, SL6 0JF,* ☎ *01628/668561,* FAX *01628/661837,* WEB *www.clivedenhouse.co.uk.* 38 *rooms. 3 restaurants, indoor-outdoor pool, spa, 3 tennis courts, horseback riding, squash, boating. AE, DC, MC, V.*

"WIND IN THE WILLOWS" COUNTRY: TO AND FROM HENLEY

"Believe me, my young friend, there is nothing—absolutely nothing— half so much worth doing as simply messing about in boats. Simply messing." You'll probably agree with Water Rat's opinion, voiced in Kenneth Grahame's classic 1908 children's book *The Wind in the Willows,* if you do some of your own "messing about" on this stretch of the Thames Valley, from Marlow to Wallingford. Boat-borne or by foot, you'll find here some of the most delightfully wooded scenery in the region. On each bank are fine wooded hills, with spacious houses, greenhouses, flower beds, and clean lawns that stretch down to the water's edge. It was to Pangbourne, along this stretch of the river, that Grahame retired to write his beloved book. His illustrator, E. H. Shepard, used the great house at Mapledurham as the model for Toad Hall, and an elaborate Victorian boathouse, not far from Pangbourne, was immortalized in pen and ink as Rat's House. Many travelers enjoy a stay Thameside here because of the famed Henley Royal Regatta.

Marlow

❻   *7 mi west of Cliveden, 15 mi northwest of Windsor.*

Just inside the Buckinghamshire border, Marlow overflows with Thameside charm and is often overwhelmed by tourism on summer weekends. Take particular note of its unusual suspension bridge, which William

Tierney Clark built in the 1830s. Marlow has a number of striking old buildings, particularly the stylish, privately owned Georgian houses along Peter and West streets. In 1817, the Romantic poet Percy Bysshe Shelley stayed with friends at 67 West Street and then bought **Albion House** on the same street. His second wife, Mary, completed her Gothic novel *Frankenstein* here. **Marlow Place,** on Station Road, dates from 1721 and has been lived in by several princes of Wales.

Henley

❼ *7 mi southwest of Marlow on A4155, 8 mi north of Reading, and 36 mi west of central London.*

Forget about Henley's origins as a medieval merchants' port. The town's identity manifests itself in one word: rowing. Indeed, Henley Royal Regatta, held in early July (the dates for 2002 are July 3–7) each year on a long, straight stretch of the River Thames, has made the charming little riverside town—set in a broad valley between gentle hillsides just off A423—famous throughout the world. Competition in this event is between the best amateur oarsmen from all over the world. Henley during Regatta Week is one of the high points of the social summer, rating with Royal Ascot and Wimbledon as a sports event and a fashionable outing in one. Needless to say, for this time, book a room months in advance.

Townspeople launched the Henley Regatta in 1839, initiating the Grand Challenge Cup, the most famous of its many trophies. After 1851, when Prince Albert, Queen Victoria's consort, became its patron, it was known as the Royal Regatta. Oarsmen compete in crews of eight, four, or two, or as single scullers. For many of the spectators, however, the social side of the event is far more important. Elderly oarsmen wear brightly colored blazers and straw boater hats; businesspeople entertain wealthy clients, and everyone admires the ladies' fashions.

Swan-Upping, a traditional event that dates back 800 years, takes places in the third week of July. Most of the swans on the Thames are owned by the Queen. Swan-markers in Thames skiffs start from Sunbury-on-Thames, catching the new cygnets and marking their beaks to establish ownership. The Queen's Swan Keeper, dressed in scarlet livery, presides over this colorful ceremony, complete with festive banners.

Henley's historic buildings, including one of Britain's oldest theaters, the Kenton, are all within a few minutes' walk. Half-timber Georgian cottages and inns abound. The mellow brick **Red Lion** hotel (⊠ Hart St., ☎ 01491/572161), beside the bridge, has been the town's focal point for nearly 500 years. Kings, dukes, and writers have stayed here, including Charles I and James Boswell. The Duke of Marlborough used the hotel as a base during the building of Blenheim Palace.

The 16th-century "checkerboard" tower of **St. Mary's Church** overlooks Henley's bridge on Hart Street. If the church's rector is about, ask permission to climb to the top to take in the superb views up and down the river. The adjacent **Chantry House,** built in 1420, is one of England's few remaining merchant houses. Converted into a school for impoverished boys in 1604, it is an unspoiled example of the rare timber-frame design, with upper floors jutting out. ⊠ Hart St., ☎ 01491/577062. ☞ Free. ☉ Church services or by appointment.

The handsome **River & Rowing Museum** focuses not just on the history and sport of rowing but on the Thames and the town itself. One gallery interprets the Thames and its surroundings as the river flows from its source to the ocean; another explores Henley's history and the regatta. Galleries devoted to rowing display models and actual boats, from Greek triremes to lifeboats to sleek modern rowing boats. David Chipperfield's striking building, combining traditional oak and modern steel, takes full advantage of its riverside setting. ⌧ *Mill Meadows,* ☎ *01491/415600,* WEB *www.rrm.co.uk.* ⌧ *£4.95.* ☉ *Easter–Sept., weekdays 10–6, weekends 10:30–6; Oct.–Easter, weekdays 10–5, weekends 10:30–5.*

Dining and Lodging

£–££   ✗ **Little Angel Inn.** This building just over Henley bridge dates from the 17th century and houses a traditional alehouse, an elegant conservatory restaurant, and a less expensive brasserie that overlooks Henley Cricket Club. The pub at the front serves a luxe bar menu. In summer there is alfresco dining in the garden, where there are occasional barbecues. Daily specials may include fish and duck. ⌧ *Remenham La. (¼ mi from Henley on A4130),* ☎ *01491/574165. AE, DC, MC, V. No dinner Sun. in winter.*

£££–££££   ✗⊞ **Stonor Arms.** Four miles north of Henley lies one of the showpiece restaurants of the Thames region. Dating from the 18th century, the hotel draws many to its popular formal dining salon, also called the Stonor Arms. The sophisticated menu ranges from venison in white bean sauce to fillet of beef and celeriac. A sister restaurant, Blades, has two glass conservatories and a slightly less expensive menu. Rooms are comfortable and antiques-bedecked, if somewhat cramped. ⌧ *B480, off A4130, Stonor RG9 6HE,* ☎ *01491/638345,* FAX *01491/638863,* WEB *www.stonor-arms.co.uk. 10 rooms. 2 restaurants. AE, MC, V.*

£££   ✗⊞ **Red Lion.** This ivy-draped, redbrick, 16th-century hotel overlooks the river and the town bridge. During its 400-year history, guests have included King Charles I and Dr. Samuel Johnson, the 18th-century critic, poet, and lexicographer. Rooms are furnished with antiques, and some have river views. An oak-beamed brasserie has an all-day menu offering everything from a cappuccino to a three-course meal of contemporary fare. ⌧ *Hart St., RG9 2AR,* ☎ *01491/572161,* FAX *01491/410039,* WEB *www.redlionhenley.co.uk. 26 rooms. Restaurant, bar, meeting rooms. AE, MC, V.*

££   ✗⊞ **Little White Hart.** There aren't many better views of the boat races than those from the balcony rooms of this Victorian version of a riverside retreat. Topped by three imposing gables, the hotel is reminiscent of a chalet. Refurbishment has made the ground floor and guest rooms more spacious, while traditional furnishings maintain their historic charm. A brasserie and an adjacent pub serve affordable food and locally brewed ales. ⌧ *Riverside RG9 2LJ,* ☎ *01491/574145,* FAX *01491/ 411772. 23 rooms. Restaurant. AE, MC, V.*

Nightlife and the Arts

Henley Festival (⌧ Henley Festival, 14 Friday St., Henley RG9 1AH, ☎ 01491/843400, FAX 01491/575509) takes place each July, during the week following the regatta. All kinds of open-air concerts and events are staged during this popular summer event.

Outdoor Activities and Sports

GOLF

At **Badgemore Park** (⌧ Henley-on-Thames, ☎ 01491/573667), a parkland 18-hole course, visitors are welcome on weekdays, and on weekends by arrangement.

ROWING

Henley Royal Regatta (☎ 01491/572153, WEB www.hrr.co.uk), the famous international amateur rowing competition, takes place over five days at the beginning of July each year. Large tents go up, especially along both sides of the unique straight stretch of river here known as

Henley Reach (1 mi, 550 yards), and every surrounding field becomes a parking lot. The most prestigious place for spectators is the Stewards' Enclosure, but admission here is by invitation only and, however hot, men must wear jackets and ties—ladies in slacks are refused entry. For guest badges for the exclusive enclosure, write to ⊠ Secretary, Henley Royal Regatta, Henley-on-Thames, Oxfordshire RG9 2LY, ☎ 01491/572153. Fortunately, there is plenty of space on the public towpath from which to watch the early stages of the races.

En Route   Across the river, on the eastern side, follow the towpath north along the shady banks to **Temple Island,** a tiny, privately owned island with trailing willows and a solitary house. This is where the regatta races start. On the south side of the town bridge, a riverside promenade passes **Mill Meadows,** where there are gardens and a picnic area. Along both stretches, the river is alive with boats of every shape and size, from luxury "gin palace" cabin cruisers to tiny rowboats.

Sonning-on-Thames

❽ *5 mi south of Henley, 4 mi northeast of Reading.*

It is plausible that Sonning's reputation as the prettiest village on the Thames goes back as far as its Saxon bishops. Its 18th-century bridge spanning the Thames, the Georgian-fronted houses, the ancient mill mentioned in the *Domesday Book,* and the black, white, and yellow cottages make it an all-too-perfect Thameside village.

Dining and Lodging

£££   ×🖫 **Great House.** A former 16th-century inn, this hotel has a long history as an overnight spot for boaters, and the half mile of docks that starts at the hotel's bank allows it to continue that tradition. The best rooms come with tasteful chintz and wood-paneling and lie in the original Great House, a redbrick building standing apart from the main hotel. In an effort to fill the void left by the closing of L'Ortolan, the inn's own restaurant has upped its standards and serves an impressive and hearty international menu. ⊠ *Thames St., RG4 0UT,* ☎ *0118/969–2277,* FAX *0118/944–1296. 41 rooms. Restaurant, bar, dock. AE, DC, MC, V.*

Mapledurham House

★ ❾ *5 mi west of Sonning-on-Thames, 10 mi southwest of Henley.*

The section of the river from Caversham to Mapledurham inspired Kenneth Grahame's 1908 children's book, *The Wind in the Willows,* which began as a bedtime story for Grahame's son Alastair while the Grahames were living at Pangbourne. Some of E. F. Shepherd's charming illustrations are of specific sites along the river—none more fabled than this redbrick Elizabethan mansion, bristling with tall chimneys, mullioned windows, and battlements, which became the inspiration for Shepherd's vision of Toad Hall. Mapledurham is still home to the Eyston family, and so has kept a warm, friendly atmosphere along with family portraits, magnificent oak staircases, and Tudor plasterwork ceilings. Here you can see a 15th-century water mill—the last working grain mill on the Thames. The estate also has 11 self-catering cottages (some more than 300 years old) available for rent, for £215–£505 a week. On summer weekends, the house can be reached in true *Wind-in-the-Willows* fashion by a **Thames River Cruises** (☎ *0118/948–1088*) boat from Caversham Promenade in Reading. The boat leaves at 2 PM, and travel time is about 45 minutes. ⊠ *Mapledurham, near Reading,* ☎ *0118/972–3350,* WEB *www.mapledurham.co.uk.* ⌧ *House and mill £5; house only £4; grounds and mill £3.* ⊙ *Easter–Sept., weekends only 2:30–5.*

Stonor Park

⑩ *5 mi northwest of Henley on A4130/B480, 10 mi north of Mapledurham House.*

Home to the Catholic Stonor family for more than 800 years, this ancestral estate is lost in the network of leafy country lanes on the fringes of the Chiltern Hills. A medieval mansion with a Georgian facade, it stands in a wooded deer park. Mass has been celebrated in its tiny chapel since the Middle Ages, and there is an exhibition of the life and work of the Jesuit Edmund Campion, who took shelter here in 1581 before his martyrdom. ✉ *Stonor*, ☎ *01491/638587*, WEB *www.stonor.com.* ✉ *£4; gardens and chapel only £2.20.* ⊘ *Apr.–Sept., but hrs are very restricted and subject to change, so check locally.*

Ewelme

★ ⑪ *6 mi northwest of Stonor Park, 10 mi northwest of Henley off A4130.*

One of England's prettiest and most unspoiled villages lies near the town of Benson, in Oxfordshire. Its picture-book almshouses, church, and school—one of the oldest in Britain—huddle close together, as they did more than 500 years ago. The church shelters the carved alabaster tomb of Alice, duchess of Suffolk, the granddaughter of England's greatest medieval poet, Geoffrey Chaucer. Jerome K. Jerome, author of the humorous book *Three Men in a Boat,* describing a 19th-century Thameside vacation, is also buried here.

Wallingford

⑫ *2 mi west of Ewelme, 13 mi southeast of Oxford on A4074.*

The busy marketplace of this typical riverside market town is bordered by a town hall, built in 1670, and an Italianate corn exchange, now a theater and cinema. Market day is Friday.

OXFORD

Arguably the most famous university in the world, Oxford has been a center of learning since the 12th century, with only the Sorbonne preceding it. To get the city placed in your mind's eye, say the phrase "dreaming spires" (the words are Matthew Arnold's) over and over, as all tour guides do, and think *Brideshead Revisited,* Sebastian Flyte, and Evelyn Waugh. Save for the modern storefronts, the city stands as it has for hundreds of years, in part because Adolf Hitler had designs on making it his European capital and so spared it from bombings. Whereas most university libraries add modern annexes to house growing volumes of books, Oxford took its Bodleian underground to preserve appearances. When arriving, try to stop on one of the low hills that surround the city and look at the skyline. Stretched out in front of you is the home of erudition and scholarship, where students are still required to take their exams in "sub fusc" attire (cap, gown, and white bowtie). Despite the appearance of a town trapped in yesteryear, industry plays a vital role in Oxford's economy, and you'll find plenty of traffic and even suburban sprawl. Oxford, 55 mi northwest of London, is home to two major industrial complexes: the Rover car factory and the Pressed Steel works, and so the proverbial rivalry between "town and gown" continues to play itself out.

Exploring Oxford

Newcomers are surprised to learn that Oxford University is not one unified campus, but a collection of many colleges and buildings, new

Oxford

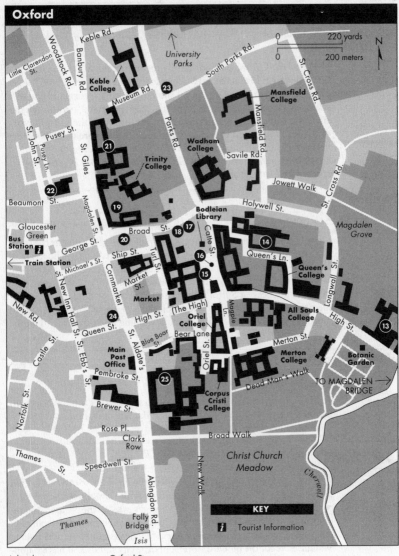

University Parks

Keble Rd.

Keble College

Museum Rd.

Banbury Rd.

Woodstock Rd.

Little Clarendon St.

South Parks Rd.

St. Cross Rd.

0   220 yards
0   200 meters

N

Mansfield College

Pusey St.

St. John St.

St. Giles

Parks Rd.

Mansfield Rd.

21

Trinity College

Wadham College

Savile Rd.

Jowett Walk

22

Beaumont St.

19

Magdalen St.

Magdalen Grove

Gloucester Green

Bus Station

Broad St.

20

Bodleian Library

18 **17**

Catte St.

Holywell St.

14

Queen's Ln.

Train Station

George St.

Ship St.

16

15

Queen's College

Longwall St.

St. Michael's St.

Turl St.

Cornmarket

Market St.

Market

(The High)

Oriel College

All Souls College

High St.

13

New Inn Hall St.

New Rd.

Castle St.

24

Queen St.

St. Aldate's

Blue Boar

Bear Lane

Oriel St.

Magpie

Merton St.

Merton College

Botanic Garden

St. Ebbe's St.

Main Post Office

Pembroke St.

25

Corpus Cristi College

Dead Man's Walk

TO MAGDALEN BRIDGE

Norfolk St.

Brewer St.

Rose Pl.

Clarks Row

Broad Walk

Thames St.

Speedwell St.

Abingdon Rd.

New Walk

Christ Church Meadow

Cherwell

Thames

Folly Bridge

Isis

KEY

i Tourist Information

Ashmolean Museum	**22**	Oxford Story Exhibition	**20**
Balliol College	**19**	Radcliffe Camera	**16**
Carfax Tower	**24**	Sheldonian Theatre	**17**
Christ Church College	**25**	St. John's College	**21**
Magdalen College	**13**	University Church	**15**
Museum of the History of Science	**18**	University Museum	**23**
New College	**14**		

as well as old, scattered across the city. All together there are 40 different colleges where undergraduates live and study. Most of the college grounds and magnificent dining halls and chapels are open to visitors, though the opening times (displayed at the entrance lodges) vary greatly. Some colleges are open only in the afternoons during university semesters, when the undergraduates are in residence; access is often restricted to the chapels and dining rooms (called halls) and sometimes the libraries, too, and you are politely requested to refrain from picnicking in the quadrangles. All are closed during exams, usually from mid-April to late June, when the May Balls are held. By far the best way to gain access is to join a walking tour led by an official Blue Badge guide. These two-hour tours leave up to five times daily from the Tourist Information Centre. As you walk through this scholastic wonderland, try to spot as many Gothic gargoyles as you can; after all, this *was* the home turf of Alice and Lewis Carroll.

The St. Clement's car park before the roundabout that leads to Magdalen Bridge is one of the only places with public parking, so pay the price if making a day-trip.

A Good Walk

The most picturesque approach to the town is from the east, over Magdalen (pronounced *maud*-lin) Bridge. After crossing the bridge, turn left off gently curving High Street for a sojourn through the Botanic Garden and Christ Church Meadow (think Sebastian Flyte toasting Charles Ryder in *Brideshead Revisited*) or turn right into **Magdalen College** ⑬. Its quadrangle is a quiet area enclosed by ancient vaulted cloisters covered with wisteria—although it was probably never *that* quiet when alumni Oscar Wilde and Dudley Moore were present. For a punt up the River Cherwell, head for Magdalen Tower. Almost halfway up High Street, turn right onto Queen's Lane and take in the extensive gardens and notorious row of gargoyles at **New College** ⑭. A little farther up High Street turn right at the 14th-century tower of the **University Church** (St. Mary's) ⑮ and behold the gilded gates of All Souls College and the magnificent 17th-century dome of the **Radcliffe Camera** ⑯. The Bridge of Sighs and Bodleian Library lie straight ahead, and left at Broad Street brings you to Christopher Wren's **Sheldonian Theatre** ⑰. Step past its iron gates and those fabulous megabusts of the Roman emperors to check out the schedule for evening concerts here. Next door to the Sheldonian is the **Museum of the History of Science** ⑱, the original site of the Ashmolean, the oldest public museum in Britain. Book lovers will want to cross the street to Blackwell's before heading down St. Giles to see **Balliol College** ⑲. You can view the scorch marks of Bloody Mary's martyrs, who were burned alive here in the 16th century.

If you have time, go back to Broad Street and stop in at the **Oxford Story Exhibition** ⑳, an imaginative presentation of 800 years of Oxford life. You may want to continue north along St. Giles to a possible lunch stop, the famed Eagle and Child pub, where J. R. R. Tolkien often met his friends, the "Inklings." Next, check out either the lovely gardens of **St. John's College** ㉑ or the **Ashmolean** ㉒, Oxford's finest art and archaeology museum, on Beaumont Street. After viewing Oliver Cromwell's death mask you may be up for a spot of tea—just across the way, dip into the Randolph, the town's finest hotel, for a reviving cuppa and to view the enchanting Victorian Gothic interior. If you're a history buff, head over to the **University Museum** ㉓ on Parks Road. Late afternoon should lure you south, down Cornmarket, passing **Carfax Tower** ㉔, Oxford's preeminent lookout point, to St. Aldate's and **Christ Church College** ㉕, Oxford's snobbiest college, with its vast Tom Quad, 800-year-old chapel, medieval dining hall, and scholarly Picture Gallery.

TIMING

You can walk this route in 1½ hours, but it's easy to spend a full day here if you visit each of the key museums for an hour and take more time to absorb the scene by exploring the colleges. One note: if you're arriving at the train station for an Oxford day outing, you might wish to start at the Ashmolean Museum above and work your way backward.

Sights to See

② **Ashmolean Museum.** Britain's oldest public museum, the Ashmolean has among its priceless collections (all university owned) many Egyptian, Greek, and Roman artifacts uncovered during archaeological expeditions conducted by the university. Michelangelo drawings, the Alfred jewels, and a Chinese gallery are among the highlights. ⊠ *Beaumont St.,* ☎ *01865/278000,* WEB *www.ashmol.ox.ac.uk.* 🖃 *Free.* ☉ *Tues.–Sat. 10–5, Sun. 2–5.*

⑲ **Balliol College.** Broad Street leads westward to St. Giles, and at the corner is Balliol (1263). The wooden doors between its inner and outer quadrangles still bear scorch marks from 1555 and 1556, when during the reign of Mary ("Bloody Mary"), Bishops Latimer and Ridley and Archbishop Cranmer were burned alive on huge pyres in Broad Street for their Protestant beliefs. A cross on the roadway marks the spot. The three men are also commemorated by the **Martyrs' Memorial** at St. Giles and Beaumont Street. ⊠ *Broad St.,* WEB *www.balliol.ox.ac.uk.* ☉ *Daily 2–5.*

㉔ **Carfax Tower.** Passing through Carfax, where four roads meet, you will see this tower, all that is left of **St. Martin's Church,** where Shakespeare once stood as godfather for William Davenant, who himself became a playwright. Every 15 minutes, little mechanical "quarter boys" mark the passage of time on the tower front. For a small fee, you can climb up the dark stairwell for a good view of the town center. ⊠ *Corner of Carfax and Cornmarket.*

㉕ **Christ Church College.** Built in 1546, Christ Church is referred to by its members as "The House." This is the site of Oxford's largest quadrangle, "Tom Quad," named after the huge bell (6¼ tons) that hangs in the gate tower. The vaulted, 800-year-old chapel in one corner has been Oxford's cathedral since the time of Henry VIII. The college's medieval dining hall contains portraits of many famous alumni, including John Wesley, William Penn, and 13 of Britain's prime ministers. Lewis Carroll was a teacher of mathematics here for many years; a shop opposite the meadows on St. Aldate's sells Alice paraphernalia. ⊠ *St. Aldate's,* WEB *www.chch.ox.ac.uk.* 🖃 *£3.* ☉ *Mon.–Sat. 9:30–4:30, Sun. 2–4:30.*

Christ Church Picture Gallery. In Canterbury Quadrangle, this connoisseur's delight exhibits works by the Italian masters as well as Hals, Rubens, and Van Dyck. Drawings in the 2,000-strong collection are shown on a changing basis. ⊠ *Oriel Sq.,* ☎ *01865/276172.* 🖃 *£1.* ☉ *Mon.–Sat. 10:30–1 and 2–4:30, Sun. 2–4:30 (later in summer).*

★ ⑬ **Magdalen College.** Founded in 1458, with an impressive main quadrangle and a supremely monastic air, Magdalen is one of the richest and most impressive of Oxford's colleges. A walk around the Deer Park and along Addison's Walk is a good way to appreciate the place, although it may cause you to envy members of the college who have the privilege of living here. They have included such diverse people as Cardinal Wolsey, Edward Gibbon, and Oscar Wilde. ⊠ *High St.,* WEB *www.magd.ox.ac.uk.* 🖃 *Summer £2, winter free.* ☉ *Daily 2–6.*

⑱ **Museum of the History of Science.** The Ashmolean, Britain's oldest public museum, was originally housed in this 1638 building, which now holds centuries of scientific and mathematical instruments from astrolabes to quadrants to medical equipment. You can descend to the restored 18th-century chemical laboratory in the basement. The museum reopened its doors in mid-2001 after a massive renovation. ⊠ *Broad St.,* ☏ *01865/ 277280,* WEB *www.mhs.ox.ac.uk.* ⊠ *Free.* ⊙ *Tues.–Sat. noon–4; call for additional hrs.*

🄬 **New College.** Founded in 1379, New College has extensive gardens, partly enclosed by the medieval city wall, and a notorious row of gargoyles. Famous alumni include actor Hugh Grant and Richard Mason, who published his international best-seller, *The Drowning People,* only months after first "coming up" to Oxford. ⊠ *Holywell St.,* WEB *www.new.ox.ac.uk.*

🄴 **Oxford Story Exhibition.** Set in a converted warehouse, this imaginative presentation makes 800 years of Oxford life come alive with models, sounds, and smells. You ride through the exhibition in small cars shaped like medieval students' desks. ⊠ *6 Broad St.,* ☏ *01865/790055.* ⊠ *£5.70.* ⊙ *Daily 10–4:30, with seasonal variations.*

★ 🄶 **Radcliffe Camera and Bodleian Library.** The most spectacular building in Oxford has one of the largest domes in Britain. Built in 1737–1749 by James Gibbs, it is the Italian Baroque style transplanted to Oxfordshire. The Camera contains part of the **Bodleian Library**'s collection, which was begun in 1602 and has grown to more than 6 million volumes. While visitors are not allowed in the Camera, the general public may stop into another part of the Bodleian, the Divinity School, a superbly vaulted room dating back to 1462. (Note: for an even more beautiful scholarly library, medieval in vintage, check out the library at Merton College on Merton Street.) ⊠ *Broad St.,* ☏ *01865/277224 for information on tour,* WEB *www.bodley.ox.ac.uk.* ⊠ *£3.50, extended tour £7.* ⊙ *Tours Mar.–Oct., weekdays 10:30, 11:30, 2, 3 and Sat. 10:30, 11:30; Nov.–Feb., weekdays 2, 3 and Sat. 10:30, 11:30. Closed for degree ceremonies. Children under 14 not admitted.*

🄷 **Sheldonian Theatre.** This fabulously ornate theater is where the impressive graduation ceremonies are held, conducted almost entirely in Latin. Built in 1663, it was the first building designed by Sir Christopher Wren when he served as professor of astronomy. Semicircular, the theater has pillars, balconies, and an elaborately painted ceiling. Outside, stone pillars are topped by the massive stone heads of 18 Roman emperors, sculpted in the 1970s to replace the originals that had been rendered featureless by air pollution. ⊠ *Broad St.,* ☏ *01865/277299.* ⊠ *£1.50.* ⊙ *Mon.–Sat. 10–12:30 and 2–4:30; mid-Nov.–Feb., closes at 3:30. Closed for 10 days at Christmas and Easter; also closed for degree ceremonies and events. Call ahead to check.*

🄵 **St. John's College.** For a quiet pause, step inside St. John's (1555) to see its huge gardens, among the city's loveliest. Across St. Giles is the Eagle and Child pub, with its narrow interior leading to a conservatory and small terrace—this was the meeting place of J. R. R. Tolkien and his friends, the "Inklings." ⊠ *St. Giles.* ⊙ *Daily 1 PM–dusk.*

★ **Trout Inn.** More than a century ago, Lewis Carroll took three children on a Thames river picnic. "We rowed up to Godstow, and had tea beside a haystack," he told a friend of his at Christ Church College; "I told them the fairy tale of Alice's adventures in Wonderland." There are no more haystacks around, but today, you can stop at the creeper-covered, historic, and still excellent Thameside pub on the northern edge of Oxford (2 mi north of the city center). Its interior, fitted out with old sporting prints and engravings of Oxford, is remarkable in itself. Of course, there's a corner devoted to Carroll, and a Morse bar with Morse memorabilia, as the inspector (of book and TV fame) often drank here, and his novelist creator still does. ✉ *195 Godstow Rd.,* ☎ *01865/302071.*

⓯ University Church. From the top of the 14th-century tower of St. Mary the Virgin, you can see a panoramic view of the city's skyline with nearly every architectural style since the 11th century. The interior is crowded with 700 years' worth of funeral monuments, including one belonging to Amy Robsart, the wife of Dudley, Elizabeth I's favorite. One pillar marks the site of Thomas Cranmer's unfortunate trial under Bloody Mary for his marital machinations on behalf of Henry VIII. The Convocation House, a part of the church accessible from Radcliffe Square, serves generous portions—cafeteria style—under the room in which OxFam was founded. ✉ *High St.,* ☎ *01865/279111.* ▨ *Tower £1.50.* ☉ *Tower daily 9–5 (until 4:30 in winter).*

㉓ University Museum. Across the street from the Rhodes House, in which hangs a portrait of former president Bill Clinton, this massive Victorian Gothic structure houses one of the world's most eclectic natural history collections. Among the myriad exhibits here are local dinosaur remains and the head and left foot of a dodo bird. ✉ *Parks Rd.,* ☎ *01865/272950.* ▨ *Free.* ☉ *Daily noon–5.*

Dining and Lodging

££££   ✕ **Le Petit Blanc.** Raymond Blanc's brasserie, a more hip cousin of Le
 ★   Manoir aux Quat' Saisons in Great Milton, is the finest place to eat in Oxford and sophisticated by any connoisseur's standards. The changing menu always lists innovative, visually stunning adaptations of bourgeois fare, sometimes with Mediterranean or Asian influences. Try the herb pancakes with mushrooms, gruyère, and ham or the chargrilled rib-eye steak with frites. The 10-minute walk north of the city center to the Terence Conran–designed space and the dent you might put on your credit card are worth it. ✉ *71–72 Walton St.,* ☎ *01865/ 510999. AE, DC, MC, V.*

£££   ✕ **Cherwell Boathouse.** About a mile north of town, this is an ideal spot for a meal along the riverside; you can rent punts here, too. The fixed-price menus change weekly but may include local pheasant with red cabbage and garlic jus or three fillets of fish with lobster sauce. It's a very friendly spot, so be prepared to linger. ✉ *Bardwell Rd. (off Banbury Rd.),* ☎ *01865/552746. AE, DC, MC, V. Closed Mon. No dinner Sun.*

£££   ✕ **Restaurant Elizabeth.** These small, elegant dining rooms, across from Christ Church College, impress upon you their history as a 16th-century bishop's palace. Salmon rolls, roast lamb, duck à l'orange, and crème brûlée are among the Spanish chef's specialties. ✉ *82 St. Aldate's,* ☎ *01865/242230. AE, DC, MC, V. Closed Mon.*

££–£££   ✕ **Gee's.** With its glass and steel framework, this former florist's shop
 ★   has a quintessential English conservatory setting. The constantly changing menu highlights French and English dishes with seasonal variations, and the place is popular with both town and gown. It's just north of the town center. ✉ *61 Banbury Rd.,* ☎ *01865/553540. AE, MC, V.*

£–££   ✕ **Café Joe's.** For some of the best eggs Benedict in the valley, cross the Magdalen Bridge out of town, take the center fork, and pass its takeout sibling, Espresso Joe, on the left. Here students "living out" sip lattes and read newspapers in comfortable style. Some typical lunch and dinner choices are goat cheese salad, grilled chicken with couscous, and penne with wild mushrooms. ✉ *21 Cowley Rd.,* ☎ *01865/201120. MC, V.*

££££   ✕▥ **Old Bank Hotel.** This hotel opened its doors in 1999 and has earned a reputation for bringing some style to the city. From the sleek lobby, set subtly back from the High Street, to the subdued designer decor, the former Barclay's Bank has a cosmopolitan air—disrupted only by the occasional lapse in service. Oxford's most centrally located hotel also holds the Quod Bar and Grill, a contemporary restaurant that has become a local favorite. ⊠ *92–94 High St., OX1 4BN,* ☎ *01865/ 799599,* FAX *01865/799598,* WEB *www.oxford-hotels-restaurants.co.uk. 43 rooms. Restaurant, bar, lounge. AE, DC, MC, V.*

££££   🏩 **Old Parsonage.** This gabled country-house hotel in a building dat-
★   ing to 1660 is a dignified, romantic escape from the surrounding city center. Dark wood paneling in the lobby and tasteful chintz patterns in the rooms are far from trendy, but expeditious room service and memorable meals by an open fire keep people coming back. ⊠ *1 Banbury Rd., OX2 6NN,* ☎ *01865/310210,* FAX *01865/311262,* WEB *www.s-h-systems.co.uk/hotels/oldparson.html. 30 rooms. Restaurant. AE, DC, MC, V.*

££££   🏩 **The Randolph.** A 19th-century neo-Gothic landmark in its own right, the hotel faces both the Ashmolean and the Martyrs' Memorial. If their parents are feeling generous, undergraduates are treated to tea in the Fellows Bar or dinner in the Spires Restaurant. Scenes from PBS's Inspector Morse *Mystery* series and the film *Shadowlands* were shot here. Floorboards in this historic hotel can be *too* historic; in some rooms, squeaky ceilings can lead to sleepless nights. ⊠ *Beaumont St., OX1 2LN,* ☎ *01865/247481 or 0870/400–8200,* FAX *01865/791678. 119 rooms. Restaurant, bar. AE, DC, MC, V.*

£   🏩 **Nanford Guest House.** A practical answer to Oxford's stiff hotel rates is this modest but convenient guest house. Busy patterns in the bedrooms can border on kitsch, but earnest hosts, free parking, and the mere five-minute walk to the High Street make this a viable option. ⊠ *Iffley Rd., OX4 1EJ,* ☎ FAX *01865/244743. 60 rooms. No credit cards.*

Nightlife and the Arts

Festivals and Music

Music at Oxford (☎ 01865/798600) is a highly acclaimed series of weekend classical concerts performed mid-September–June in such illustrious surroundings as Christ Church Cathedral and Sir Christopher Wren's Sheldonian Theatre. Postmodern design has endowed the **Jacqueline Du Pre Music Building** (⊠ St. Hilda's College, ☎ 01865/ 798600 for information) with the best acoustics in the city, and attendance at a recital here is a way to track rising talent. **Oxford Coffee Concerts** is a program of chamber concerts performed on Sunday at the Holywell Music Room on Holywell Street. String quartets, piano trios, and soloists present a variety of baroque and classical pieces in this venerable 1748 hall. Tickets are reasonably priced and are available from the Oxford Playhouse (⊠ Beaumont St., ☎ 01865/ 798600). During the summer, **Blenheim Palace** (☎ 01993/811091) in Woodstock is occasionally the venue for classical concerts, sometimes combined with fireworks displays.

Theaters

During term time, undergraduate productions are often given in the colleges or local halls. In summer there are usually some outdoor performances in ancient quadrangles or college gardens. Look for announcement posters.

The Apollo (⊠ George St., ☎ 0870/606–3500) is Oxford's main theater. It stages a varied program of plays, opera, ballet, pantomime, and concerts, and it is the recognized second home of the Welsh National Opera and the Glyndebourne Touring Opera. The **Oxford Playhouse** (⊠ Beaumont St., ☎ 01865/798600) is a serious theater presenting classical and modern drama productions appropriate for a university city.

Outdoor Activities and Sports

Bicycling

Bikes can be rented in Oxford at **Bike Zone** (⊠ Market St., ☎ 01865/728877).

Punting

You may wish, like many an Oxford student, to spend a summer afternoon punting, while dangling your champagne bottle in the water to keep it cool. Punts—shallow-bottomed boats that are poled slowly up the river—can be rented in several places.

From mid-March through mid-October, **Cherwell Boathouse** (⊠ Bardwell Rd., ☎ 01865/515978), a punt station and restaurant a mile north of the heart of town, will loan you a boat and, if you wish, someone to punt it. Rentals are £8–£10 per hour. At the foot of **Magdalen Bridge** on High Street you can rent a punt for £10 an hour, plus a £25 refundable deposit.

Spectator Sports

At the end of May, during **Oxford's Eights Week,** men and women from the university's colleges compete to be "Head of the River." Because the river is too narrow and twisting for eights to race side-by-side, the boats set off, 13 at a time, one behind another. Each boat tries to catch and bump the one in front. Spectators can watch all the way.

Oxford University Cricket Club competes against leading county teams and, each summer, the major foreign team visiting Britain. In the middle of the sprawling University Parks—worthy of a walk in and of itself—the club's playing field is one of the loveliest in England.

Shopping

Small shops line High Street, Cornmarket, and Queen Street, while the Clarendon and Westgate centers, which lead off them, have branches of several nationally known stores. **Blackwell's** (⊠ Broad St., ☎ 01865/792792) has one of the world's widest selections of books and has been family owned and run since 1879. For a cheap sandwich and a leisurely browse, try the **Covered Market** (⊠ off High St.), where the smell of pastries follows you from cobbler to jeweler to cheese monger. The **Oxford Gallery** (⊠ 23 High St., ☎ 01865/242731) carries limited editions of traditional cityscapes as well as more contemporary British crafts. **Shepherd & Woodward** (⊠ 109 High St., ☎ 01865/249491) is a traditional tailor specializing in university gowns, ties, and scarves. Specialty stores like the **Tea House** (⊠ Golden Cross, ☎ 01865/728838) are gathered around Golden Cross, a cobbled courtyard off of Cornmarket. The **University of Oxford Shop** (⊠ 106 High St., ☎ 01865/247414), run by the university, is the seller of authorized clothing, ceramics, and tea towels, all emblazoned with university crests.

ON THE ROAD TO BLENHEIM PALACE

The River Thames takes on a new graciousness as it flows along the borders of Oxfordshire for 71 mi; each league it increases in size and importance. Three tributaries swell the river as it passes through the landscape: the Windrush, the Evenlode, and the Cherwell. Tucked among the hills and dales are one of England's most impressive stately homes, the best country restaurant, one of its most Edenic villages, and the last Rothschild estate. Little wonder that for chic Londoners, this is instant countryside, with every blade manicured with charm.

Woodstock

★ ㉖ *8 mi northwest of Oxford on A44.*

Handsome 17th- and 18th-century houses line the trim streets of Woodstock, which sits at the edge of the Cotswalds and was the birthplace of the Black Prince, Edward III's ill-fated son. It is, however, best known for bordering the grounds of the grand **Blenheim Palace**. In summer Woodstock's ancient streets are clogged with tour buses, and the lofty halls of Blenheim echo with the clamor of voices from all parts of the world. On a quiet fall or spring afternoon, however, the village is a sublime experience: a mellowed 18th-century church and town hall mark the central square, while along its back streets you'll find flower-bedecked houses and quiet lanes right out of a 19th-century etching. A public bus route runs (usually every half hour) from Oxford to Woodstock, making it a good overnight alternative to Oxford.

Dining and Lodging

££££ ✕⌂ **The Bear.** This is an archetypal English coaching inn, with Tudoresque
★ wood paneling, beamed ceilings, wattle-and-daub walls, and dancing fireplaces in winter. The guest rooms, overlooking either a quiet churchyard or the town square, have enough carved oak to please anyone in search of period atmosphere, while the duplex suites would make a Stuart king feel at home, thanks to their timbered loft-balconies and gargantuan four-posters. Legend has it that the Bear is where Richard Burton finally popped the question to Elizabeth Taylor. The restaurant is a bit large for true elegance, but it's just the sort of place to order a top-flight hot Stilton soufflé. The staff is terribly friendly—even if your first name isn't Earl. ⊠ *Park St., OX20 1SZ,* ☎ *08704/008202,* 🅵🅰🆇 *01993/813380. 51 rooms, 3 suites. Restaurant, bar. AE, DC, MC, V.*

£££–££££ ✕⌂ **The Feathers.** Possibly one of the most stylish small hotels out-
★ side London, this place attracts honeymooners and film stars alike. The roast wood pigeon, grilled turbot, and honey roasted duckling are worth the restaurant's hefty prices. Upstairs, cozy guest rooms fill a 17th-century building that has been thoughtfully restored. One side of the hotel is near a busy intersection, so ask for a quiet room. ⊠ *Market St., OX20 1SX,* ☎ *01993/812291,* 🅵🅰🆇 *01993/813158,* 🆆🅴🅱 *www.feathers.co.uk. 22 rooms. Restaurant. AE, DC, MC, V.*

££ ⌂ **Blenheim Guest House and Tea Rooms.** The Cinderella of all British
★ hotels, this place stands in one of the most magical corners in England—the quiet village cul-de-sac that leads to the back gates of Blenheim Palace. It's a small guest house, three stories tall, with its facade still bearing a Victorian-era banner that states "Views and Postcards of Blenheim," and a storefront tearoom. The unassuming guest rooms have modern furnishings, but the Marlborough room is unique—after all, its bathroom offers a view of Blenheim. ⊠ *17 Park St., OX20 1SJ,* ☎ *01993/813814,* 🅵🅰🆇 *01993/813810,* 🆆🅴🅱 *www.theblenheim.com. 6 rooms. MC, V.*

Blenheim Palace

★ ㉗ *8 mi northwest of Oxford via A44 to A4095.*

So grandiose is Blenheim's masonry and so breathtaking are its articulations of splendor, some have pondered why it hasn't been named a wonder of the world. Built by Sir John Vanbrugh in the early 1700s, Blenheim was given by Queen Anne and the nation to General John Churchill, first duke of Marlborough. The exterior is mind-boggling, with its huge columns, enormous pediments, and upturned obelisks, all exemplars of English Baroque. Inside, lavishness abounds in monumental extremes. The Red Drawing Room—on whose walls hang the incomparable sittings of the 4th and 9th dukes and their families painted by Sir Joshua Reynolds and John Singer Sargent, respectively—could possibly be the most richly opulent room in England. In most rooms, great family portraits look down at sumptuous furniture and immense pieces of silver. For some, however, the most memorable room is the small, low-ceiling chamber where Winston Churchill (his father was the younger brother of the then-duke) was born in 1874.

Sir Winston once wrote that the unique beauty of Blenheim lay in its perfect adaptation of an English parkland to an Italian palace. Indeed the grounds, the work of Capability Brown, 18th-century England's most gifted landscape gardener, are arguably the best example of the "cunningly natural" park in the country. Brown declared that his object at Blenheim was to "make the Thames look like a small stream compared with the winding Danube." At points he almost succeeds—the scale of these grounds must be seen to be believed. Stick around for dusk, when enormous flocks of sheep are let loose to become living mowers for the magnificent lawns. Tucked away here is the little summerhouse where Winston Churchill proposed to his future wife, Clementine. A short detour to the neighboring hamlet of Bladon will lead you to the grave of the great man. Leave Blenheim by the back gates, which will deposit you in lovely Woodstock. ⊠ *Woodstock,* ☎ *01993/811091,* WEB *www.blenheimpalace.com.* 🎟 *Palace £9.50.* ☉ *Palace mid-Mar.–Oct., daily 10:30–4:45; park daily 9–4:45; special events, fairs, and concerts throughout year.*

Bladon

②⑧ *2 mi southeast of Woodstock on A4095; 6 mi north of Oxford.*

A small, tree-lined churchyard holds the burial place of Sir Winston Churchill, his grave the more impressive for its simplicity.

Dorchester-on-Thames

②⑨ *7 mi southeast of Abingdon, 9 mi southeast of Oxford.*

An important center in Saxon times, when it was the seat of a bishopric, Dorchester deserves a visit chiefly for its ancient abbey. With a main street that was once a leg of the Roman road to Silchester, Dorchester's charm now lies in its timber houses, thatched cottages, and ancient inns. Crossing the Thames at Day's Lock and turning left at Little Wittenham takes you on a pleasant walk past the remains of the village's Iron Age settlements.

In addition to secluded cloisters and gardens, **Dorchester Abbey** has a spacious church (1170), with traceried medieval windows and a lead baptismal font. The east window was restored in 1966 by the American Friends of the Abbey in memory of Sir Winston Churchill. The abbey is a popular concert venue. ⊠ *Off the A4074,* WEB *www.dorchester-abbey.org.uk.* 🎟 *Free.* ☉ *Summer, daily 8:30–7, winter 8:30–dusk, except during services.*

Lodging

££   🏨 **George Hotel.** Overlooking Dorchester Abbey, this 500-year-old hotel was built as a coaching inn—there's still an old coach parked outside—and it retains whitewashed walls, exposed beams, and log fires. Each room has an individual style and two have four-poster beds. ⊠ *25 High St., OX10 7HH,* ☎ *01865/340404,* FAX *01865/341620. 18 rooms. Restaurant. AE, MC, V.*

Uffington and the Vale of the White Horse

③⓪ *15 mi west of Dorchester-on-Thames, 18 mi southwest of Oxford, 9 mi northeast of Swindon.*

Stretching up into the foothills of the Berkshire Downs between Swindon and Oxford is a wide, fertile plain known as the Vale of the White Horse. To reach it from Oxford, follow A420, then B4508 to the village of Uffington. Here, cut into the chalk hillside, is the huge **figure of a white horse,** one of the most important of Britain's prehistoric sites. Until recently, some historians believed that it might have been carved to commemorate King Alfred's victory over the Danes in 871, while others dated it back to the Iron Age, around 750 BC. More current research suggests that it is at least 1,000 years older, created at the beginning of the second millennium BC. Nearby **Dragon Hill** is equally mysterious. An unlikely legend suggests that St. George slew his dragon there. Uffington was the home of Tom Brown, fictional hero of the Victorian classic *Tom Brown's School Days.* The novel's author, Thomas Hughes, was born in Uffington in 1822.

Kelmscott Manor

③① *7 mi northwest of Uffington, 20 mi southwest of Oxford.*

From its seemingly innocuous medieval exterior, it is hard to believe that Kelmscott Manor was, in its Victorian day, a site of social and domestic unrest. Here, artist, writer, and socialist William Morris (1834–1896) launched his anti-industrial arts and crafts movement. And it was here that his wife Jane openly cohabited with her lover Dante Gabriel Rossetti (1828–1882), Morris's business partner. The surrounding landscape was an obvious source of Morris's inspiration: some nearby tree clusters look as if they grew straight out of one of his textile designs, whereas, of course, the reverse is true. The house is now owned by Oxford University and is a unique monument to the "Brotherhood." Morris died at Kelmscott and is buried in the local churchyard. ⊠ *Off A417, Kelmscott, Lechlade,* ☎ *01367/252486,* WEB *www.kelmscottmanor.co.uk.* ⊞ *£7.* ⊙ *Apr.–Sept., Wed. 11–1 and 2–5, 3rd Sat. of each month 2–5.*

Stanton Harcourt Manor

③② *11 mi northeast of Kelmscott Manor, 9 mi southwest of Oxford.*

Reached through twisting lanes, Stanton Harcourt Manor lies among streams, small lakes, and woods. It was here, in 1718, that Alexander Pope translated Homer's *Iliad.* The manor—stuffed with silver, pictures, and antique furniture—is worth a visit apart from this association; it has a complete medieval kitchen and 12 acres of gardens. ⊠ *Stanton Harcourt,* ☎ *01865/881928,* WEB *www.stantonharcourt.net.* ⊞ *House and garden £5; garden £3.* ⊙ *Easter–Sept., every other Thurs. and Sun., and bank holiday Mon.; check locally for opening times.*

Dining

£–££ ✕ **Bear and Ragged Staff.** This 16th-century inn—the name comes from
★ the medieval insignia of the Warwick family—has long been a popular haunt of Oxford town and gown. The food is traditional British, with such fare as roast duck and venison. The inn is 3 mi east of Stanton Harcourt and 4½ mi southwest of Oxford via A420. ⊠ *28 Appleton Rd., Cumnor,* ☎ *01865/862329. AE, MC, V.*

Great Milton

㉝ *7 mi southeast of Oxford.*

With attractive thatched cottages built of local stone and a single street about a mile long with wide grass verges, this is another stop on the literary pilgrim's route, for the poet John Milton, author of *Paradise Lost* (1667), was married in the local church. The church also has an unusual collection of old musical instruments. The town is also a haunt of culinary pilgrims.

Dining and Lodging

££££ ✕▥ **Le Manoir aux Quat' Saisons.** Standards run high at this 15th-
★ century manor house, which now has one of England's finest kitchens (complete with cooking school) and a distinctive choice of individually decorated rooms ranging from rococo fantasy to chic chinoiserie to Lalique and lacquer. Chef Raymond Blanc's epicurean touch is evident at every turn. Spare yourself the trouble of deciding among the innovative French creations and simply treat yourself to the *Menu Gourmand*—8 courses of haute cuisine for £89. ✉ *Church Rd., OX44 7PD,* ☎ *01844/278881,* ℻ *01844/278847,* 🌐 *www.manoir.com. 32 rooms. Restaurant, tennis court. AE, DC, MC, V.*

Waddesdon Manor

㉞ *20 mi east of Oxford.*

Many of the regal residences built by the Rothschild family throughout Europe are gone now, but Waddesdon Manor remains in all its splendor. A vision of the 19th century at its most sumptuous, it was built in 1880–1889 by G. H. Destailleur for Baron Ferdinand de Rothschild in the style of a French chateau. Furnished with Savonnerie carpets, Sèvres porcelain, furniture made by Riesener for Marie Antoinette, and numerous paintings by Rubens, Watteau, Gainsborough, and Reynolds, the mansion underwent a top-to-bottom renovation, thanks to Lord Rothschild, current head of the English branch of the family. There is a pleasant restaurant in the house and a summerhouse café on the grounds. ✉ *Waddesdon, on the A41 near Aylesbury,* ☎ *01296/653226,* 🌐 *www.waddesdon.org.uk.* 🎟 *£10, grounds £3.* ☉ *House Apr.–Oct., Wed.–Sun. and bank holiday Mon. 11–4; gardens Mar.–late Dec., Wed.–Sun. and bank holiday Mon. 10–5.*

Woburn Abbey

★ **㉟** *10 mi northeast of Waddesdon.*

Still the ancestral residence of the Duke of Bedford, Woburn Abbey houses countless Grand Tour treasures and Old Master paintings, including 20 Canalettos, which practically wallpaper the crimson dining salon—one of the most sumptuous rooms in England. Works by Gainsborough and Reynolds are also notable. The Palladian mansion contains a number of etchings by Queen Victoria, who left them behind when she stayed here. Nine species of deer roam the grounds, where an antiques center and small restaurant add to the list of attractions. (The very popular **Woburn Safari Park**, a very popular drive-through experience that takes you past a number of endangered African species, is entered separately.) To get to Woburn from London, head north on M1; to get there from Oxford, head for Milton Keynes, the nearest large town to the house, on A5. ✉ *Woburn,* ☎ *01525/290666,* 🌐 *www.woburnabbey.co.uk.* 🎟 *House and deer park £7.50; safari £12.50.* ☉ *Late Mar.–early Nov., Mon.–Sat. 11–4, Sun. 11–5.*

Althorp

36 *27 mi northwest of Woburn Abbey.*

Deep in the heart of Northamptonshire—one of the loveliest of English counties—sits Althorp, the ancestral home of the Spencers, the family of Diana, Princess of Wales. Here, set on a tiny island within the estate park, is Diana's final resting place. Back in 1765 Horace Walpole described the setting as "one of those enchanted scenes which a thousand circumstances of history and art endear to a pensive spectator." As it turns out, Princess Diana and her siblings found the house ugly and melancholy, calling it "Deadlock Hall," as it sits in the middle of a plain without many trees. What the house does have are room after room of Van Dycks, Reynoldses, and Rubens, all portraits of the Spencers going back 500 years, and an entry hall that Nikolaus Pevsner called "the noblest Georgian room in the country." To these attractions, Earl Spencer has opened a visitor center devoted to Diana. Tickets must be booked in advance; you can do this on the Web site, too. Althorp is 5 mi northwest of Northampton, on the Rugby Road leading from Northampton. Northampton (☎ 01604/622677 for the **tourist office**) has both a bus and a train station. On the west side of the estate park is Great Brington, the neighboring village where the Spencer family crypt can be found in the church of St. Mary the Virgin. ⊠ *Off the A428, Northampton,* ☎ *01604/770107 (house); 01604/592020 (advance tickets),* WEB *www.althorp.com.* ☞ *£9.50.* ☉ *July–Aug., daily 9–5.*

THAMES VALLEY A TO Z

To research prices, get advice from other travelers, and book travel arrangements, visit www.fodors.com.

BUS TRAVEL

Traveling by bus continues to be the preferred method of transportation to the Thames Valley. Oxford's bus companies depart every 12 minutes (24 hours a day) from Victoria, Marble Arch, and Notting Hill in London, offer shuttle service to Gatwick and Heathrow every half-hour, and—at £9.50 for round-trip service—are considerably cheaper than the train.

The Oxford Bus Company and other local bus services, such as Stagecoach, link the towns between Oxford and Henley with services to Heathrow Airport and London. Reading Buses also accesses Oxford and Reading to the airports, while First Beeline of Bracknell serves the smaller towns of Berkshire.

CUTTING COSTS

The Oxford Bus Company offers a one-day ticket and a seven-day "Freedom" ticket, for unlimited bus travel within Oxford.

FARES AND SCHEDULES

➤ BUS INFORMATION: **First Beeline** (☎ 01344/424938, WEB www.firstbeeline.co.uk). **Oxford Bus Company** (☎ 01865/785400, WEB www.oxfordbus.co.uk). **Reading Buses** (☎ 0118/959–4000). **Stagecoach Oxford Tube** (☎ 01865/772250, WEB www.stagecoach-oxford.co.uk).

CAR RENTAL

➤ LOCAL AGENCIES: **A. A. Clark Self-Drive** (⊠ 72–74 Arthur Rd., Windsor, ☎ 01753/800600). **Europcar Interrent** (⊠ BP Petrol Station, Hartford Motors, Seacourt Tower, Botley, 4 mi north of Oxford, ☎ 01865/246373). **Hertz** (⊠ City Motors Ltd., Wolvercote Roundabout, Woodstock Rd., Oxford, ☎ 01865/319972).

CAR TRAVEL

The M4 and M40 radiate west from London, bringing Oxford (55 mi) and Reading (42 mi) within an hour's drive, except in rush hour. Although the roads are good, this wealthy section of the commuter belt has surprisingly heavy traffic, even on the smaller roads. Parking in town can be a problem, too, so allow plenty of time.

EMERGENCIES

The John Radcliffe Hospital is accessible by Bus 13 from Carfax Tower in Oxford or from the A40.

➤ CONTACTS: **Ambulance, fire, police** (☎ 999). **John Radcliffe Hospital** (⌗ Marston Ferry Rd., Oxford, ☎ 01865/741166).

OUTDOORS AND SPORTS

The Countryside Commission has been charting and preserving Thames paths for years and offers publications about them—write the Countryside Commission Postal Sales for a brochure. The Rambler's Association also publishes an excellent book, *The Thames Path,* by David Sharp (£12.99), which includes information and detailed maps of the whole length of the river, from Greenwich to Gloucestershire.

➤ WALKING: **Countryside Commission** (⌗ John Dower House, Crescent Pl., Cheltenham, ☎ 01242/521381, WEB www.countryside.gov.uk; postal address, ⌗ Box 124, Walgrave, Northampton NN6 9TL, or call ☎ 01604/781848). **Rambler's Association** (⌗ 1 Wandsworth Rd., London SW8 2XX, ☎ 0207/339–8500, WEB www.ramblers.org.uk).

TOURS

BOAT TOURS

The ideal way to see the Thames region is from the water; summertime trips range from 30 minutes to all day. Hobbs and Sons covers the Henley Reach and also rents boats from Station Road, Henley-on-Thames. Salter Brothers runs daily steamer cruises, mid-May to mid-September from Windsor, Oxford, Abingdon, Henley, Marlow, and Reading. Thames River Cruises conducts outings from Caversham Bridge, Reading, Easter–September. French Brothers operates river trips from the Promenade, Windsor, and from Runnymede, as far as Hampton Court.

➤ FEES AND SCHEDULES: **French Brothers** (⌗ The Promenade, Windsor, ☎ 01753/851900). **Hobbs and Sons** (⌗ Henley-on-Thames, ☎ 01491/572035). **Salter Brothers** (⌗ Folly Bridge, Oxford, ☎ 01865/243421). **Thames River Cruises** (⌗ Caversham Bridge, Reading, ☎ 0118/948–1088).

BUS TOURS

Guide Friday runs guided, open-bus tours, mid-March–November, of Windsor, £7, and Oxford, £8.50.

➤ FEES AND SCHEDULES: **Guide Friday** (☎ 01865/790522, WEB www.guide-friday.com).

WALKING TOURS

Themed walking tours, including the "William Morris Tour" and "Ghost Tour," leave several times daily from outside Oxford's tourist office in Gloucester Green (£4.50). Call for details.

➤ FEES AND SCHEDULES: **Oxford Tourist Office** (The Old School, Gloucester Green, ☎ 01865/726871, WEB www.oxford.gov.uk).

TRAIN TRAVEL

Trains to Oxford (1¼ hrs) and the region depart from London's Paddington station. Because of the problems that have increased since privatization, you should confirm that everything is on time before arriving at the station—especially since train service in the southwest is the busiest in all of Britain. For timetables, call the National Rail.

➤ TRAIN INFORMATION: **National Rail** (☎ 0845/748–4950, WEB www.nationalrail.co.uk).

TRAVEL AGENCIES

➤ LOCAL AGENT REFERRALS: **Thomas Cook** (✉ 5 Queen St., Oxford, ☎ 01865/447000; King Edward Ct., Windsor, ☎ 01753/851966).

VISITOR INFORMATION

➤ TOURIST INFORMATION: **Henley** (✉ Town Hall, ☎ 01491/578034). **Marlow** (✉ 31 High St., ☎ 01628/483597, WEB www.marlowtown.co.uk). **Oxford** (✉ The Old School, Gloucester Green, Oxford, ☎ 01865/726871, WEB www.oxford.gov.uk). **Oxford University** (WEB www.ox.ac.uk). **Windsor** (✉ 24 High St., Windsor, ☎ 01753/743900, WEB www.windsor.gov.uk). **Woodstock** (✉ Park St., Oxfordshire Museum, ☎ 01993/813276).

7 SHAKESPEARE COUNTRY

STRATFORD-UPON-AVON AND ENVIRONS

Much ado about nothing? Far from it. Even if you know little about William Shakespeare, one flourish through his home territory will leave you referring to him familiarly as the Bard. Stratford-upon-Avon is where Shakespeare grew up before he went on to fame in London. But aside from the landmarks in town, nearby attractions, including Warwick, Baddesley Clinton, and Kenilworth Castle, are integral parts of the classic English countryside. On a summer's day, maybe after a matinee at the Royal Shakespeare Theatre, you can stroll by the River Avon and simply beguile the time.

Updated by
Benjamin
Morse

SYNONYMOUS AS IT IS WITH SHAKESPEARE, Stratford-upon-Avon has overshadowed other villages in the region with its popularity. But it was an important market town and malt-making center for more than 300 years before the Bard came along, and its environs do not seem to mind the association with the Shakespeare juggernaut. Stratford itself has taken immense care to preserve its ancient buildings, making it in many ways a perfect specimen of a four-centuries-old provincial town. Stratford is also home to the Royal Shakespeare Theatre, where thespians continue to pay their finest tribute to the Bard. Although for these reasons Stratford is the region's highlight, it is not nearly the whole story. Warwickshire—the ancient county of which Stratford is the southern nexus—is a land of sleepy villages, thatched-roof cottages, and solitary farmhouses. It was the birthplace of the image of Britain that has been spread around the world by the works of Shakespeare. This is, quintessentially, the realm of the yeoman, the wooded land of Arden, the home of the prosperous tradesman and the wealthy merchant, the region where landowners still pasture deer as they have done for the last 900 years, and the county of peace and prosperity that is the fire in the heart of "this precious stone set in a silver sea."

Beautiful, but not conspicuous in its beauty, "leafy Warwick's" landscape is studded with a rich selection of historic sites. Three of England's most memorable abodes are here: the home of Anne Hathaway, Shakespeare's wife; Charlecote, a grand Elizabethan manor house and park, where, legend has it, Shakespeare was caught poaching deer; and Baddesley Clinton, probably the most perfect example of late medieval domestic architecture in England. Other treasure houses are here: Ragley Hall, Coughton Court, and Broughton Castle, brimming with splendid art treasures, would be worth viewing even if they were empty, as they represent some of the greatest examples of English architecture. Also near Stratford is "medieval England in stone"—Warwick Castle, which, with its magnificent machicolations and picturesque parapets, provides a glimpse into England's turbulent history. Little wonder Henry James once wrote that Warwickshire "is the core and center of the English world."

The core and center of Warwickshire is, of course, Stratford. The town's historic monuments, as well as charting Shakespeare's achievements, give a thrilling insight into life in the England of late medieval, Tudor, and Elizabethan times. Pride of place goes to the five properties administered by the Shakespeare Birthplace Trust: Shakespeare's Henley Street birthplace, the New Place/Nash's House site, Hall's Croft, Anne Hathaway's Cottage, and Mary Arden's House. These not only give us a picture of Shakespeare as writer and man of wealth, status, and property but also help trace the social pattern of Shakespeare's family, following its rise from quite humble beginnings to a position of eminence through the generations.

The price you pay for absorbing these scenes and treading the streets once frequented by Shakespeare is the press of the thousands of others who also come to pay their respects, and the sometimes ruthless commercialization. But most people find it's worth it, especially if you attend a stage production by the Royal Shakespeare Company, whose mastery of the dramatic arts have never been affected by the hype of the heritage industry. If the hustle and bustle become too much, just take a hint from Mr. William Shakespeare, Gentleman, who, it should be noted, was a country lad, and well versed in the high roads and byways of his native Midland countryside. He often turned his back on the town and followed the Avon as it wended its sleepy way through meadows and small villages. Today you, too, can discover the country that surrounds the Bard's hometown and wander through a landscape seemingly untouched by the brasher aspects of modern life.

Pleasures and Pastimes

Dining

Although Stratford has little in the way of high-class dining establishments, the town is peppered with reasonably priced bistros and unpretentious restaurants offering a broad, international cuisine. For fancier fare, find one of the better hotels, whose kitchens have drawn some of the foremost chefs from London and beyond. Warwick and Kenilworth have their share of excellent eateries, ideal for a midday lunch or a more substantial evening meal, and the countryside has many atmospheric old pubs in which meals are prepared to a fine standard.

CATEGORY	COST*
££££	over £22
£££	£16–£22
££	£9–£15
£	under £9

*per person for a main course at dinner

Lodging

As you might expect, Stratford holds the highest concentration of lodgings in the area, from B&Bs to hotels. Here you can find accommodations to fit every pocket, and for the most part, they are well maintained. The best establishments are the older, centrally located ones, often with fine period architecture; most are owned by national chains. Because the town is *so* popular with theater-going visitors, be sure to book ahead whenever possible. Most hotels offer discounted two- and three-day packages. Outside town, there are some top-notch country hotels, where discreet but attentive service is guaranteed—at very fancy prices. At the other end of the scale, almost every village has a gnarled old inn with rooms available at very reasonable rates.

CATEGORY	COST*
££££	over £150
£££	£100–£150
££	£60–£100
£	under £60

*All prices are for two people sharing a standard double room, including breakfast and VAT.

Shakespearean Theater

One of the main reasons that so many people want to visit Stratford is the Royal Shakespeare Theatre, home of the Royal Shakespeare Company (RSC), arguably the finest repertory troupe in the world and long the backbone of the theatrical life of the country. (The company also mounts its productions in London and around the country, but seeing a play in Stratford is a favored experience.) The RSC's annual season begins in November and ends during October; usually, five Shakespearean plays are offered. Shakespeare's plays, of course, have proved as nearly indestructible as anything crafted by man. The theaters where his plays have been performed have been less so: London's Globe burned down in 1613, and the current Stratford auditorium is the replacement for two former playhouses. The current theater, designed by Elizabeth Scott, was built in 1932 and was quickly dubbed a "factory for Shakespeare" because of its modern utilitarian aspect. No matter: "The play's the thing." Here, the Bard's plays have made the reputations of generations of actors (and broken not a few), have been staged as archaeological reconstructions and science fiction, and have seen women playing Hamlet and men playing Rosalind. However Shakespeare's plays are reshaped by directors and actors, they continue to reveal new facets of some eternal truth about humanity.

Shopping

Stratford has more than its fair share of tourist junk, often dressed up to appeal to day-tripping souvenir hunters. That said, there are some good-quality items to be found, generally in the established shops specializing in silver, jewelry, and china. For bargains, check out the Friday market. Beware of antiques dealers, however, who are, for the most part, "cunning past man's thought." You will find lower prices in Warwick and in the villages scattered around the area, but even here genuine bargains are rare.

Walking

This part of England has glorious, gentle countryside, with many of the local historic houses surrounded by parkland with scenic walks. Even Stratford can be the base for easy walks along the River Avon or the canal. The Stratford-upon-Avon Canal is bordered by a towpath that provides a chance to escape the throng. Pick up a leaflet on the Avon Valley walk from the town's tourist office.

Exploring Shakespeare Country

Stratford-upon-Avon is neighbor to a number of villages that have legends connected with the Bard, as well as the beautiful architecture dating from his time. Complementing these humble hamlets, and often in the midst of them, is an impressive gathering of country houses open to the public, each of which requires a good half day to explore and is easily reachable from Stratford. To the north lie two magnificent castles, Warwick and Kenilworth. Warwick has much more to offer besides its castle, and it is worth a protracted jaunt.

Numbers in the text correspond to numbers in the margin and on the Shakespeare Country and Stratford-upon-Avon maps.

Great Itineraries

Stratford-upon-Avon will be the lead destination for most travelers. As a small city, it's ideal for day visits or as a convenient base from which to brush up on your Shakespeare by exploring the Bard's home turf. If you can manage only a day excursion here, arrive early and confine your visit to two or three of the main Shakespeare Trust properties, a couple of other town sights, a pub lunch, and a walk along the river, capped off by a stroll out of town to the splendid cottage of Anne Hathaway. Unless you're planning to venture beyond Stratford, you can rely on public transport from London or other major cities. Outside Stratford, public transportation gets tricky. To see most of the sights outside the town, a car is best. If you're just focusing on a few places, inquire at the stately houses or regional tourist offices about taxis and back-road bus services.

A couple of nights in Shakespeare's home city would allow you to gather the gist of the place without testing too severely your tolerance for crowds. More time—four days is sufficient—would mean you could use the town as a base to acquaint yourself with the rural delights of the countryside.

IF YOU HAVE 2 DAYS

 Stratford-upon-Avon ①–⑨ deserves at least a full day and a drama-packed night—that is, if you wish to catch a performance of the Bard's works at the Royal Shakespeare Theatre on the banks of the Avon.

Shakespeare Country

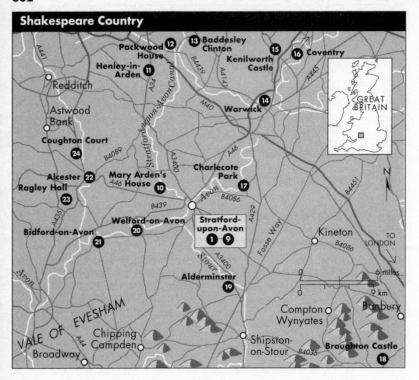

Among the attractions, five historic properties are must-sees: three are in town—**Shakespeare's Birthplace** ① and the Shakespeare Centre, on Henley Street, home of the Shakespeare Birthplace Trust, the **Nash's House and New Place** ③ property, and **Hall's Croft** ⑥—whereas the others, **Anne Hathaway's Cottage** ⑦ and **Mary Arden's House** ⑩, are just a few minutes out of town. (If you want to spend both days in Stratford and wish to enjoy these attractions and many other sights in a more leisurely manner, follow the self-guiding Town Heritage Trail or the black-and-gold signposts that direct you to the historic landmarks.) After your Stratford sojourn, spend the next day touring selected sights in Shakespeare Country, including the mansions of **Baddesley Clinton** ⑬ and **Charlecote Park** ⑰. In between, take in some of the minor villages in the vicinity, ideal for a spot of lunch or a riverside stroll. Spend your second night back in Stratford or in one of the inns along the rural way.

IF YOU HAVE 4 DAYS

After two days spent touring the august abodes of ▣ **Stratford-upon-Avon** ①–⑨ and the Shakespeare-linked attractions of the immediate vicinity—including **Henley-in-Arden** ⑪, the setting for *As You Like It*—you will be ready for a complete change of scene. In your remaining time, dedicate a couple of mornings to visiting two or three of the stately houses within easy driving distance of the town. On the way, plan your route along minor roads to take in some of the off-the-beaten-track hamlets seemingly suspended in time. Nearest of these, and fetchingly picturesque, is **Welford-on-Avon** ⑳, hugging the river as it loops west out from Stratford. A couple of miles farther west is **Bidford-on-Avon** ㉑, "drunken Bidford" as portrayed in the doggerel attributed to Shakespeare. A short distance north, the village of **Alcester** ㉒ beckons, a charming one-horse town on either side of which lie two of the area's most notable country houses, the Palladian **Ragley Hall** ㉓ and the Elizabethan **Coughton Court** ㉔, both surrounded by acres of inviting parkland. After spending your first night based in Stratford, plan for your second in ▦ **Warwick** ⑭, devoting the next morning to exploring the town's medieval castle. Other lower-key attractions are worth an hour or two, especially if you're traveling with kids. If castles are your thing, you should also make time to see **Kenilworth Castle** ⑮, a short drive north, whose red sandstone ruins are redolent of royal pageantry. South of Stratford, ▦ **Alderminster** ⑲, the largest of another cluster of villages well worth driving through, makes a suitable night stop and is en route to **Broughton Castle** ⑱.

When to Tour Shakespeare Country

Schedule your tour here, if possible, to avoid weekends and school holidays, and time your visits to the main Shakespeare shrines for the early morning, to see them at their least frenetic. One of the high points of Stratford's calendar is the Shakespeare Birthday Celebrations, usually on the weekend nearest to April 23. If you choose to visit during this time, hotel reservations throughout the area should be made as early as possible. Warwick Castle, too, usually brims with visitors, and you should plan to beat the rush. Elsewhere, you can be more flexible, although some country properties also fill up quickly on weekends. A number of these close for the winter.

STRATFORD-UPON-AVON

"Famous people do seem to have a habit of being born in pretty places—Mozart in Salzburg, Wordsworth in the Lake District, Hardy in Dorset, the Brontës in Yorkshire," begins Susan Hill's 1987 travel book (now out of print), *Shakespeare Country*. "It all helps to establish them as focuses for visitors, but those visitors would still come, simply to enjoy the charms of the locality. And Stratford's charms are very evident." Under the swarming busloads of visitors, Strat-forde—to use the old Saxon name, which means "a ford over a river"—has hung on to its original character as an English market town on the banks of the slow-flowing River Avon. It is close to Birmingham, which lies 37 mi to the northwest and London, 102 mi to the southeast.

Still, it is Shakespeare who counts. Born in a half-timber, early 16th-century building in the center of Stratford on April 23, 1564, Shakespeare was buried in Holy Trinity Church after he had died (on his 52nd birthday) in a more imposing house at New Place. Although he spent much of his life in London as a leading figure of the theater, the world still associates him with "Shakespeare's Avon." Here, in the years between his birth and 1587, he played as a young lad, attended the local grammar school, and married Anne Hathaway; here he returned to the town a man of prosperity. Today, you can see his birthplace on Henley Street; his burial place in Holy Trinity Church; Anne Hathaway's cottage; his mother's home at Wilmcote; New Place and the neighboring Nash's House, home of Shakespeare's granddaughter; and Hall's Croft, home of the Stratford physician who married the Bard's daughter. Whether or not their connections to Shakespeare are historically valid, these sites reveal Elizabethan England at its loveliest.

Then, of course, there is the theater, a sturdy, brick-built structure opened in 1932 and home of the Royal Shakespeare Company. Make the Royal Shakespeare Theatre your real reason for visiting Stratford: productions here are unrivaled. Anyone who considers attending a Shakespeare play a duty—rather than a pleasure—will delightfully admit they were wrong. Believers will need no persuading.

Stratford-upon-Avon is a fascinating town, so take Antonio's advice (*Twelfth Night*, Act 3, scene 3) and "beguile the time, and feed your knowl-

304

Anne
Hathaway's
Cottage 7

Guild
Chapel 4

Guildhall 5

Hall's Croft . .6

Harvard
House 2

Holy Trinity
Church 8

Nash's House
and New
Place 3

Royal
Shakespeare
Theatre 9

Shakespeare's
Birthplace . . .1

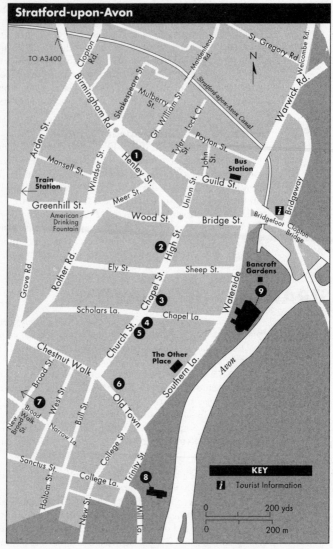

edge with viewing the town." By the 16th century, it was already a prosperous market town with thriving guilds and industries. Its characteristic half-timber houses from this era have been preserved over the centuries, and they are set off by the charm of later architecture, such as the elegant Georgian storefronts on Bridge Street, with their 18th-century porticoes and arched doorways. By 1769, the town's literary preeminence was confirmed by a three-day festival commemorating Shakespeare, attended and supported by the great actor David Garrick. Since then, Stratford's flame has been shining ever more brightly, yet the town is far from being a museum piece or a tourist trap. Although full of souvenir shops—every back lane seems to have been converted into a shopping mall—Stratford isn't overly strident in its search for a quick buck.

Exploring Stratford-upon-Avon

The town is easily manageable for a walking tour. Most sights are grouped around Henley Street (off the roundabout as you come in on the A3400 Birmingham road), High Street, and Waterside, which skirts the public gardens through which the River Avon flows. Bridge Street and parallel Sheep Street are Stratford's main thoroughfares, and site of most of the banks, shops, and eating places. The town's tourist office lies at Bridgefoot, between the canal and the river, next to Clopton Bridge—"a sumptuous new bridge and large of stone" built in the 15th century by Sir Hugh Clopton, once Lord Mayor of London and one of Stratford's richest (and most philanthropic) residents.

The main places of Shakespearean interest are run by the **Shakespeare Birthplace Trust**: Anne Hathaway's Cottage, Hall's Croft, Mary Arden's House, Nash's House, Shakespeare's Birthplace. They all have similar opening times, and you can buy a combination ticket to the five properties or pay separate entry fees if you want to visit only one or two. ☎ 01789/204016, WEB www.shakespeare.org.uk, www.stratford-upon-avon.co.uk. ✉ Joint ticket £12.

A Good Walk

To begin at the beginning, pay your respects at **Shakespeare's Birthplace** ① on Henley Street. Elizabethan antiques and theater memorabilia are on view. Be sure to photograph the exquisite garden out back. Right next door is the Shakespeare Centre, which has an impressive library. Then head east down Henley Street to the old city center. Take High Street to the right, passing several of Stratford's half-timber buildings, the most magnificent of which is **Harvard House** ②, with beautiful twin gables and a hanging iron sign; at the nearby corner of Sheep Street is a stone bust of the Bard mounted on the north front of the Town Hall. Where High Street becomes Chapel Street, one block down on the left, is the timber-and-daub **Nash's House and New Place** ③, home of the Bard's granddaughter. After viewing the table inlaid with wood from the legendary mulberry tree, count the varieties of roses in the elegant Elizabethan knot gardens of New Place next door. On Chapel Street is the Shakespeare Hotel—its five gables make one of the longest Elizabethan facades extant—with its elegant David Garrick restaurant. Continue south, and where Chapel Street becomes Church Street are several buildings, seen on the left, that were old when Shakespeare was young: the **Guild Chapel** ④ and the timbered **almshouses** (notice the high chimneys that carried sparks safely above the once thatched roofs), and the **Guildhall** ⑤, with Shakespeare's school. A left turn at the end of Church Street leads to Old Town and to **Hall's Croft** ⑥, an impressive Tudor residence associated with the poet's daughter. Detour now, taking the footpath from Evesham Place 1 mi northwest to the country hamlet of Shottery and **Anne Hathaway's Cottage** ⑦. After viewing this stunningly romantic house, stroll back to the **Holy Trinity Church** ⑧, by the banks of the Avon. Here is Shakespeare's tomb *and* the north aisle font where he was christened. Twilight—and your performance at the **Royal Shakespeare Theatre** ⑨—may be approaching now, so head over to Southern Lane. Opt for dinner at the theater restaurant or toast the Bard at the nearby Black Swan—with an evening aperitif in its river garden.

TIMING

If you don't tour the sites themselves, this walk takes about three hours, including the walk to Anne Hathaway's Cottage. A more thorough exploration, with an hour for lunch, could last six or seven hours.

Sights to See

Almshouses. Immediately beyond the Guildhall on Church Street lies a delightful row of timber-and-daub almshouses. These were built to accommodate the poor by the Guild of the Holy Cross in the early 15th century and still serve as housing for pensioners.

★ ❼ **Anne Hathaway's Cottage.** The most perfectly picturesque of the Shakespeare Trust properties, set on the western outskirts of Stratford, was the family home of the woman Shakespeare married in 1582, in what was evidently a shotgun wedding (she was seven or eight years his senior and may well have been pregnant). The "cottage," actually a substantial farmhouse, has latticed windows and a grand thatch roof; inside, there is period furniture, including the "second best bed" left by Shakespeare to his wife. Set in a garden (now planted with herbs and flowers mentioned in the Bard's plays), the cottage is one of the loveliest spots in Shakespeare Country. Although you can catch a bus from Stratford, the best way to get here is to walk (there are two main footpaths, one via Greenhill Street by the railroad bridge, the other leaving from Holy Trinity Church up Old Town and Chestnut Walk), especially in late spring when the apple trees are in blossom. ⊠ *Cottage La., Shottery.* ☎ *£5; Shakespeare Trust joint ticket £12.* ⓒ *Mid-Mar.–mid-Oct., Mon.–Sat. 9–5, Sun. 9:30–5; mid-Oct.–mid-Mar., Mon.–Sat. 9:30–4, Sun. 10–4; last entry 30 mins before closing.*

Bancroft Gardens. Between the Royal Shakespeare Theatre and Clopton Bridge lie these well-tended expanses of lawns and flower beds. The swans gliding gracefully along the river are permanent residents, coexisting with the pleasure craft plying the waters of the river and the nearby canal. The centerpiece of the gardens (incidentally, Bancroft is not a proper name but refers to the "croft on the banks") is the Gower Memorial statue, designed in 1888 by Lord Gower, and adorned with bronze figures of Hamlet, Lady Macbeth, Falstaff, and Prince Hal—symbols of philosophy, tragedy, comedy, and history, respectively.

ⓒ **Butterfly Farm.** An escape for children or anyone needing a break from the Bard, the Butterfly Farm houses Europe's largest display of butterflies, a mock rain forest, and the Goliath Bird-Eater—the world's largest species of spider. The farm is a two-minute walk past the Bridgefoot footbridge. ⊠ *Swan's Nest La.,* ☎ *01789/299288,* ⓦⓔⓑ *www.butterflyfarm.co.uk.* ☎ *£3.95.* ⓒ *Daily 10–dusk.*

❹ **Guild Chapel.** This chapel on the corner of Chapel Lane and Church Street is the noble centerpiece of Stratford's Guild buildings, including the Guildhall, the Grammar School, and the almshouses—all structures well known to Shakespeare. The ancient structure was rebuilt in the late Perpendicular style in the first half of the 15th century, thanks to the largesse of Hugh Clopton. The otherwise plain interior includes fragments of a remarkable medieval fresco of the Last Judgment. The chapel is presently used for occasional functions, and the bell, also given by Sir Hugh, still rings with the peal that once told Shakespeare the time of day. ⊠ *Chapel La.,* ☎ *01789/293351.* ☎ *Free.* ⓒ *Daily 9–5.*

❺ **Guildhall.** Dating to 1416–1418, the Guildhall is occupied by **King Edward's Grammar School,** which Shakespeare probably attended as a boy and which is still used as a school. On the first floor is the Guildhall proper: it was here that traveling acting companies came to perform, and many historians believe that it was after seeing the troupe known as the Earl of Leicester's Men in 1587 that Shakespeare got the acting bug and set off for London. Upstairs is the classroom in which the Bard is reputed to have learned "little Latin and less Greek." A brass plate at its far end records the traditional position of Master Will's seat. The conjunction of church and school here may have an echo in *Twelfth Night* (Act 3, scene 2): "Cross-gartered? Most villainously; like a pedant that keeps a school i' the church." Today, the classroom is still used by students, so visits may be made by prior arrangement only, during after-school hours or vacation time. Contact the tourist information office to schedule a visit. ⊠ *Church St.*

❻ Hall's Croft. One of the finest surviving Tudor town houses, this impressive residence has a delightful walled garden. Tradition has it that Hall's Croft was the home of Shakespeare's elder daughter Susanna and her husband, Dr. John Hall, whose dispensary is on view along with the other rooms, all containing Jacobean (early 17th-century) furniture of heavy oak. ⊠ *Old Town.* 🖾 *£3.50; Shakespeare Trust joint ticket £12.* ☉ *Mid-Mar.–mid-Oct., Mon.–Sat. 9:30–5, Sun. 10–5; mid-Oct.–mid-Mar., Mon.–Sat. 10–4, Sun. 10:30–4; last entry 30 mins before closing.*

❷ Harvard House. This is the grand and glorious half-timber 16th-century home of Catherine Rogers, mother of the John Harvard who founded Harvard University in 1636. There is little to see inside, as the house is virtually unfurnished, but the twin-gabled facade, dating from about 1600, is one of the glories of Stratford. Note the exterior beams carved with fleurs-de-lis in high relief, the sculpted human faces on the corbels, and the hewn bear and ragged staff (motifs of the Warwick earls) on the bracket heads. ⊠ *High St.* ☉ *May–Sept. Contact the Shakespeare Centre (next to the Shakespeare Birthplace) for hrs.*

❽ Holy Trinity Church. The fabled burial place of William Shakespeare, the 13th-century Holy Trinity Church sits along the banks of the Avon, with an avenue of lime trees framing its entrance. Shakespeare's final resting place is in the chancel, rebuilt in 1465–1491 in the late Perpendicular style. He was buried here, incidentally, not because he was a famed poet but because he was a lay-rector of Stratford, owning a portion of the township tithes. Here, on the north wall of the sanctuary over the altar steps, you'll find the famous marble bust created by Gerard Jansen in 1623; along with the Droeshout engraving in the First Folio, this is one of the only two contemporary portraits of the Bard. Rigidly stylized in the Elizabethan mode, the bust offers a more human, even humorous, perspective when viewed from the side. Also in the chancel are the graves of Shakespeare's wife, Anne; his daughter Susanna; his son-in-law, John Hall; and his granddaughter's husband, Thomas Nash. Nearby, the Parish Register is displayed, containing both Shakespeare's baptismal entry (1564) and his burial notice (1616). Just outside the church, the Avon "with gentle murmur glides" past the embankment. ⊠ *Trinity St.* 🖾 *Small fee for chancel.* ☉ *Mar.–Oct., Mon.–Sat. 8:30–6, Sun. 2–5; Nov.–Feb., Mon.–Sat. 8:30–4, Sun. 2–5.*

❸ Nash's House and New Place. This is the home of the Thomas Nash who married Shakespeare's last direct descendant, his granddaughter Elizabeth Hall. The heavily restored house has been furnished in 17th-century style, and it also contains a local museum. In the gardens (where there's an intricately laid-out Elizabethan knot garden) are the foundations of **New Place,** the house in which Shakespeare died in 1616. Built in 1483 "of brike and tymber" for a Lord Mayor of London, it was Stratford's grandest piece of real estate when Shakespeare bought it in 1597 for £60; tragically, it was torn down in 1759. The man responsible for this, Reverend Francis Gastrell, had already shown his ire at the hordes of sightseers by cutting down a mulberry tree said to have been planted by Shakespeare himself. The townspeople were in such an uproar at Gastrell's vandalism that they stoned his house. Today you can see what is claimed to be a descendant of the mulberry tree in the middle of the lawn. If Nash's House is closed, you can get a good view of the garden (which may be more interesting than the house itself) from the adjoining **Shakespeare Memorial Garden,** entered from Chapel Lane. ⊠ *Chapel St.* 🖾 *£3.50, Shakespeare Trust joint ticket £12.* ☉ *Mid-Mar.–mid-Oct., Mon.–Sat. 9:30–5, Sun. 10–5; mid-Oct.–mid-Mar., Mon.–Sat. 10–4, Sun. 10:30–4; last entry 30 mins before closing.*

❾ Royal Shakespeare Theatre. The beloved Stratford home of the Royal Shakespeare Company (RSC) is set amid lovely gardens along the River Avon. Throughout the year some of the finest productions in the world of the Bard's peerless plays are presented here. The theater has existed since 1879, established by Charles Edward Flower, a brewer, although the original building burned down in 1926. Six years later the present building was inaugurated, according to a design by Elizabeth Scott, cousin of the more famous Sir Giles Gilbert Scott, architect of Liverpool's Anglican Cathedral. Many people criticize the modern appearance of the building, calling it "a factory for Shakespeare." At the rear is the **Swan Theatre,** created in the only part of the Victorian theater to survive a fire in the 1930s. The theater follows the lines of Shakespeare's original Globe and is one of the most exciting performing spaces in Britain. Beside the Swan is an art gallery, where you can see theater-related exhibitions and portraits and depictions of scenes from the plays. You might also consider taking a tour of the entire theater complex, but book well in advance. Farther down Southern Lane toward Holy Trinity Church is **The Other Place,** a modern auditorium for experimental productions. ✉ *Waterside,* ☎ *01789/403403 for box office; 01789/296655 for information; 01789/412602 for tours,* WEB *www.rsc.org.uk.* ✆ *Tours £4, gallery £1.50.* ☉ *Tours weekdays (except matinee days) 1:30 and 5:30; matinee days 5:30 and after show; tours Sun. noon, 1, 2, and 3. No tours when shows are being prepared. Exhibition Mon.–Sat. 9:30–6:30, Sun. noon–4:30.*

❶ Shakespeare's Birthplace. A half-timber house typical of its time, the Bard's birthplace has been much altered and restored since Shakespeare lived here but remains a much-visited shrine. Shakespeare's ambitious father, John, left farming to set up as a glove maker in Stratford, first renting this house. Inside, an auction notice describes the property as it was when it was offered for sale in 1847. Until then, the house had been maintained in a somewhat ramshackle state by two widowed ladies, but with the approach of the tercentennial of the Bard's birth, and in response to a rumor that the building was to be purchased by P. T. Barnum and shipped across the Atlantic, the city shelled out £3,000 for the relic, whereupon it was tidied up and made the main attraction for the stream of Shakespeare devotees that was steadily growing into a torrent. Half the house has been furnished to reflect Elizabethan domestic life; the other half contains an exhibition illustrating Shakespeare's professional life and work. In the upstairs room thought to have been where the Bard was born, you can see the signatures of pilgrims of earlier epochs cut into the windowpanes, including those of Sir Walter Scott and Thomas Carlyle. The **Shakespeare Centre,** just to the west of Shakespeare's Birthplace, is the home of the Shakespeare Birthplace Trust. Scholars head here for the library; visitors will find information and an exhibition about the Bard. ✉ *Henley St.* ✆ *Shakespeare's Birthplace only £5.50, Town Heritage Trail ticket (includes 3 town properties) £7, Shakespeare Trust joint ticket £12.* ☉ *Mid-Mar.–mid-Oct., Mon.–Sat. 9–5, Sun. 9:30–5; mid-Oct.–mid-Mar., Mon.–Sat. 9:30–4, Sun. 10–4; last entry 30 mins before closing.*

☾ Teddy Bear Museum. If the young children with you are suffering from a surfeit of Shakespeareana, they'll find this museum a good diversion. The collection contains hundreds of the furry things in all shapes and sizes from around the world. ✉ *19 Greenhill St.,* ☎ *01789/293160,* WEB *www.theteddybearmuseum.com.* ✆ *£2.25, family ticket £5.95.* ☉ *Jan.–Feb., daily 9:30–5; Mar.–Dec., daily 9:30–6.*

Dining

££££ ✕ **Box Tree Restaurant.** Overlooking the River Avon and its resident
★ swans, this attractive spot is handily located in the Royal Shakespeare
Theatre itself and has some of the best food in town. You can dine here
either before or after a play, but it's worth a meal even if you're not
attending a performance. Specialties on the fixed-price menu have an
Italian slant and include wild boar casserole, breast of duck, and vegetarian pasta dishes. ⊠ *Waterside,* ☎ *01789/293226. Reservations essential. AE, MC, V. Closed when theater is closed.*

££ ✕ **Vintner Wine Bar.** This bar/restaurant just up the hill from the theater serves imaginative food from a menu that changes daily. The
shoulder of lamb ranks among the favorite main courses, and a wide
selection of tapas is also popular. Try to arrive early, especially if you
hope to dine before curtain time; the restaurant can get crowded with
out-of-town visitors. ⊠ *5 Sheep St.,* ☎ *01789/297259. AE, MC, V.*

£–££ ✕ **Black Swan.** Known locally as the Dirty Duck, one of Stratford's
most celebrated pubs has attracted actors since Garrick's days. It has
a little veranda overlooking the theaters and the river. Along with a
pint of lager, you can sample English grill specialties, as well as braised
oxtail and honey-roasted duck, plus an assortment of bar meals. ⊠
Southern La., ☎ *01789/297312. AE, MC, V. No dinner Sun.*

£–££ ✕ **The Opposition.** Close to the theater, this restaurant, set in a converted 16th-century building on Stratford's main dining street, offers
pre- and post-theater meals. The American and Continental dishes on
the menu are popular with the locals. Try the smoked haddock or, among
the vegetarian options, the mushrooms and asparagus served in a
cream sauce. ⊠ *13 Sheep St.,* ☎ *01789/269980. MC, V.*

£–££ ✕ **Slug and Lettuce.** Don't let the name put you off—this pine-paneled
pub serves excellent meals and is highly favored by pub aficionados
nationwide. Long-standing favorites are chicken breast baked in avocado and garlic, and monkfish wrapped in bacon or venison sausages.
⊠ *38 Guild St.,* ☎ *01789/299700. AE, MC, V.*

£ ✕ **River Terrace.** The meals and snacks at this informal cafeteria in the
theater are crowd-pleasers. Typical dishes include lasagna, shepherd's
pie, salads, sandwiches, and cakes, with wine and beer available. ⊠
Royal Shakespeare Theatre, Waterside, ☎ *01789/293226. Reservations
not accepted. No credit cards. Closed when theater is closed.*

Lodging

££££ 🛏 **Shakespeare Hotel.** Minutes from the theater and right in the heart
of Stratford near the Guildhall, this half-timber Elizabethan town
house, originally built in the 1400s, is a vision right out of *The Merry
Wives of Windsor.* It has five gables and one of the longest black-and-
white half-timber fronts in England. The interiors have been comfortably modernized, and public rooms are adorned with Shakespeareana
and old playbills. Upstairs, rooms are named after the Bard's characters and leading thespians, and some are adorned with hewn timbers
carved with rose-and-thistle patterns. ⊠ *Chapel St., CV37 6ER,* ☎
08704/008182, FAX *01789/415411,* WEB *www.heritage-hotels.com. 74
rooms. Restaurant. AE, DC, MC, V.*

£££–££££ 🛏 **Alveston Manor.** Across the river from the Royal Shakespeare Theatre, this redbrick Elizabethan manor house hosted, on its lawns, the
first production of *A Midsummer Night's Dream.* Ask for a room with
a four-poster bed in the Manor or Queen Anne wings. ⊠ *Clopton Bridge,
CV37 7HP,* ☎ *08704/008181,* FAX *01789/414095,* WEB *www.heritage-
hotels.com. 114 rooms. Restaurant. AE, DC, MC, V.*

£££–££££ 🛏 **Thistle Stratford-Upon-Avon.** Three 18th-century town houses have
been converted into a centrally located hotel, right at the water's edge

and directly opposite the Swan Theatre. The best rooms are enhanced by beam ceilings, period furniture, and views over the river. The elegant Bard's restaurant serves good English and Continental fare, and the lounge bar and terrace are amenable places to relax. ⊠ *44 Waterside, CV37 6BA,* ☎ *01789/294949,* FAX *01789/415874,* WEB *www.stratford-upon-avon.co.uk/arden.htm. 63 rooms. Restaurant, bar. AE, DC, MC, V.*

£££   🏨 **Falcon County Hotel.** Licensed as an alehouse since 1640, this black-and-white timber-frame hotel still has the atmosphere of a friendly inn. The heavily beamed rooms in the older part are small and quaint; those in the modern extension are in standard international style. You can enjoy a refreshment in the Merlin Lounge, a pretty retreat with wattle-and-daub decor. In the Oak Bar, wood panels salvaged from New Place, the Bard's last home, accent the impressive setting. ⊠ *Chapel St., CV37 6HA,* ☎ *01789/279953,* FAX *01789/414260,* WEB *www.corushotels.com. 84 rooms. Restaurant, 2 bars. AE, DC, MC, V.*

£££   🏨 **Stratford Victoria.** Although the Victoria may lack the authentic feel of the older hotels, its up-to-date facilities are making it a Stratford standard. The well-equipped rooms are not the tiny boxes travelers to the United Kingdom learn to dread, but are large and airy. After your short walk back from the town center, you might want to try the whirlpool tub. ⊠ *Arden St., CV37 6QQ,* ☎ *01789/271000,* FAX *01789/271001,* WEB *www.stratford-upon-avon.co.uk/victoria.htm. 102 rooms. Restaurant, bar, hot tub, gym. AE, DC, MC, V.*

££   🏨 **Caterham House.** This comfortable old building dating from 1830
★ is in the center of town, within an easy walk of the theater. You may spot an actor or two among the guests. Bedrooms are individually decorated in early 19th-century style, with brass beds and antique furnishings; the public rooms, too, show discriminating taste at work. ⊠ *58 Rother St., CV37 6LT,* ☎ *01789/267309,* FAX *01789/414836. 10 rooms. Bar. DC, MC, V.*

£   🏨 **Penryn House.** Traditional English prints and furnishings plus some simple modern pieces decorate this charming budget choice. It's an easy walk from the city center, Anne Hathaway's Cottage, and the rail station. ⊠ *126 Alcester Rd., CV37 9DP,* ☎ *01789/293718,* FAX *01789/266077,* WEB *www.stratford-upon-avon.co.uk/penryn.htm. 8 rooms, 6 with bath. AE, DC, MC, V.*

£   🏨 **Victoria Spa Lodge.** This grand B&B lies just outside town, within view of the canal. Draped with clematis, the historic building dates from 1837; you can see Queen Victoria's coat of arms in two of its gables. Victoria herself stayed here before ascending the throne. The lounge-breakfast room and spacious guest rooms are a pleasure, tastefully decorated with dark wood or plain white furnishings. ⊠ *Bishopton La., Bishopton CV37 9QY,* ☎ *01789/267985,* FAX *01789/204728,* WEB *www.stratford-upon-avon.co.uk/victoriaspa.htm. 7 rooms. Breakfast room. MC, V.*

Nightlife and the Arts

Festivals

The **Stratford-upon-Avon Shakespeare Birthday Celebrations** (⊠ Shakespeare Centre, Henley St., Stratford-upon-Avon CV37 6QW, ☎ 01789/204016) take place on and around the weekend closest to April 23 (unless Easter occurs around that date). The events, spread over four days, include a formal reception, lectures, free concerts, processions, and a special performance of one of the plays. For tickets for the three-course birthday luncheon in the marquee on the Avon Paddock, write the Shakespeare Birthday Celebrations Secretary at the address above, call ☎ 01789/415536, or check WEB www.shakespeare.org.uk.

Dating from medieval times, the **Mop Fair** is a local delight, taking place on or around October 12, traditionally the time when farmworkers, laborers, and apprentices from the surrounding area came to seek work. It still attracts entertainers and fairground amusements and includes a formal ceremony attended by local dignitaries, the whole in essence little changed from the past.

Theater

The **Royal Shakespeare Theatre** (✉ Stratford-upon-Avon CV37 6BB, ☎ 01789/403403 for box office; 01789/296655 for general information) usually puts on five of Shakespeare's plays in a season lasting from November into October. In September and October, visiting companies often perform a variety of opera, ballet, and musicals. Prices usually range from £7 to £45. Book ahead, as seats go fast, but "day of performance" (two per person to personal callers only) and returned tickets are often available. You can also book tickets from London with Ticketmaster (☎ 0870/534–4444, WEB www.ticketmaster.co.uk), operating 24 hours a day. In the Swan Theatre at the rear, plays by Shakespeare contemporaries, such as Christopher Marlowe and Ben Jonson, are staged. In The Other Place, some of the RSC's most adventurous work is performed.

Outdoor Activities and Sports

Avon Cruises (✉ The Boatyard, Swan's Nest Lane, ☎ 01789/267073) rents boats and provides half-hour river excursions and some longer trips by arrangement. Contact **Bancroft Cruises** (✉ The Boatyard, Clopton Bridge, ☎ 01789/269669) for half-hourly excursions on the river. Hour-long trips farther afield can also be scheduled. You can rent a boat by the hour or day.

Shopping

Stratford-upon-Avon has a bustling shopping district, and there's an open market every Friday in the Market Place at Greenhill and Meer Streets. The **Antique Market** (✉ Ely St.) is 50 stalls of jewelry, silver, linens, porcelain, and memorabilia. **B&W Thornton** (✉ 23 Henley St., ☎ 01789/269405), just above Shakespeare's Birthplace, has an extensive range of exclusive Moorcroft pottery ware and glass. **Robert Vaughan** (✉ 20 Chapel St., ☎ 01789/205312) is the best of Stratford's many secondhand bookshops. **Once a Tree** (✉ 8 Bard's Walk, ☎ 01789/297790) is thoroughly "green," selling items crafted from sustainable wood sources—animals, bowls, and dozens of imaginative articles. **Waterstone's** (✉ 18 High St., ☎ 01789/414418), part of the popular chain, is a prime general bookstore.

IN AND AROUND SHAKESPEARE COUNTRY

Although that section of Warwickshire known as Shakespeare Country is, in reality, no more than a continuation of that familiar Midlands scene of green fields, slow-moving, mirrorlike rivers, quiet villages, and time-burnished old halls, castles, and churches, it becomes an area apart through its role as the homeland of England's greatest dramatist. Shakespeare, although born in what was then the smallish town of Stratford, was essentially a country lad at heart, and his knowledge of nature and rural lore that is evident in his plays. So as you venture to the sights below, keep an eye out for—as immortalized in *Cymbeline*—that cowslip blossom growing wild.

Mary Arden's House

❿ *3 mi northwest of Stratford.*

The hamlet of Wilmcote holds the fifth Shakespeare Birthplace Trust property—Mary Arden's House—the family home of Shakespeare's mother. This bucolic site attracted a flurry of attention in 2000 because the Tudor farmhouse, considered for years to have been the home of Shakespeare's mother (and so named), was proved to have been the home of Adam Palmer instead. The farmhouse has been renamed Palmer's Farm. However, it was also shown that Mary Arden lived on a house on Glebe Farm, which adjoins the farmhouse and is run by the Trust; this farm has now assumed the name Mary Arden's House. The Tudor farmhouse and farm form the **Shakespeare Countryside Museum,** with crafts exhibits, a café, and a garden of trees mentioned in the plays. The museum is home to rare breeds of poultry, longhorn cows, and Cotswold sheep, and there are special events and demonstrations of farming techniques as practiced during the last 400 years. You can get to Wilmcote on a regular bus from Stratford; by train Monday–Saturday only; or on a Guide Friday tour, unless, of course, you opt for the traditional means—on foot. ⊠ *Off A3400,* ☎ *01789/293455 for information on special events,* WEB *www.shakespeare.org.uk.* ⊠ *£5.50; Shakespeare Trust joint ticket £12.* ☉ *Mid-Mar.–mid-Oct., Mon.–Sat. 9:30–5, Sun. 10–5; mid-Oct.–mid-Mar., Mon.–Sat. 10–4, Sun. 10:30–4; last entry 30 mins before closing.*

En Route   From Wilmcote, continue west for 1½ mi on minor roads to reach **Aston Cantlow.** The church here was where Shakespeare's parents, Mary Arden and John Shakespeare, were wed.

Henley-in-Arden

⓫ *8 mi northwest of Stratford.*

A brief drive out of Stratford on the A3400 will take you under the Stratford-upon-Avon Canal aqueduct to picturesque Henley-in-Arden, whose wide main street forms an architectural pageant of attractive buildings of various periods. You are now in the area of what was once the Forest of Arden, where Shakespeare set one of his greatest comedies, *As You Like It.* Among the buildings to look out for are the former Guildhall, dating from the 15th century, and the White Swan pub, built in the early 1600s. By that time, the town had already seen a good many historical ups and downs: associated with the influential de Montfort family, it was razed following the defeat of Simon de Montfort by the future Edward I in the battle of Evesham, in 1265.

Packwood House

⓬ *12 mi north of Stratford-upon-Avon, 5 mi north of Henley-in-Arden.*

Packwood House draws garden enthusiasts to its re-created 17th-century gardens, highlighted by a remarkable topiary Tudor garden, in which yew trees depict Christ's Sermon on the Mount. The house itself combines redbrick and half-timbering, and its tall chimneys are another Tudor characteristic. The interiors are a 20th-century version of Tudor architecture, but there are good collections of period furniture and textiles. To get here from Henley-in-Arden, follow A3400 north another 4 or 5 mi, turn right, just before Hockley Heath, onto B4439, and follow the signs 2 mi farther along a back road. ⊠ *Near Hockley Heath,* ☎ *01564/782024,* WEB *www.nationaltrust.org.uk.* ⊠ *£4.60.* ☉ *Apr.–Oct., Wed.–Sun. and national holiday Mon. noon–4:30.*

Baddesley Clinton

★ **⑬** *2 mi east of Packwood House, 15 mi north of Stratford-upon-Avon.*

"As you approach Baddesley Clinton Hall, it stands before you as the perfect late medieval manor house. The entrance side of grey stone, the small, creeper-clad Queen Anne brick bridge across the moat, the gateway with a porch higher than the roof and embattled—it could not be better." So wrote the eminent architectural historian Sir Nikolaus Pevsner, and the house actually lives up to this fervent praise. Set off a winding back road, the moated manor still retains its great fireplaces, 17th-century paneling, and priest holes (secret chambers for Roman Catholic priests, who were persecuted at various times throughout the 16th and 17th centuries). Stables and barns around the manor have been renovated; one contains a café, an idyllic spot for tea and cakes. ✉ *Rising La., off A4141, near Chadwick End (7½ mi northwest of Warwick),* ☎ *01564/783294,* WEB *www.nationaltrust.org.uk.* 🎫 *£5.60, grounds only £2.80.* ☉ *Mar.–Apr. and Oct., Wed.–Sun. and national holiday Mon. 1:30–5; May–Sept., Wed.–Sun. noon–4:30; restaurant, National Trust store, and grounds open at noon.*

Warwick

⑭ *4 mi south of Kenilworth on A46, 9 mi northeast of Stratford-upon-Avon.*

Most famous for Warwick Castle—that vision out of the feudal ages—Warwick (pronounced *wa*-rick) is an interesting architectural mixture of Georgian redbrick and Elizabethan half-timbering. Although much of the town center has been spoiled by unattractive postwar development, look for the 15th-century **Lord Leycester Hospital,** which has been ★ a home—offering "hospitality"—for old soldiers since the Earl of Leicester dedicated it to that purpose in 1571. The half-timber complex, built on a terrace overlooking a vista of the distant Cotswold hills, includes a tiny chapel devoted to St. James. Within the complex is a magnificently picturesque courtyard, complete with a wattle-and-daub balcony. The 500-year-old gardens have been restored and reopened to the public. ✉ *High St.,* ☎ *01926/491422.* 🎫 *£2.95.* ☉ *Apr.–Sept., Tues.–Sun. 10–5; Oct.–Mar., Tues.–Sun. 10–4.*

Crowded with gilded, carved, and painted tombs, the **Beauchamp Chapel** of the **Collegiate Church of St. Mary** is the very essence of late medieval and Tudor chivalry—although it was built (1443–1464) to honor the somewhat less than chivalrous Richard Beauchamp, who consigned Joan of Arc to the flames. Brightly colored bosses, fan tracery, and flying ribs distinguish the chapel, which holds many monuments to the Beauchamps (several of whom became Earl of Warwick), including Richard Beauchamp's effigy in bronze—a great example of the metalworker's art—and the alabaster table tomb of Thomas Beauchamp and his wife. Robert Dudley, Earl of Leicester, adviser and favorite of Elizabeth I, is also buried here. Don't miss the little memorial for Cecily Puckering, who died in 1626, age 13, inscribed "I sleep secure; Christ's my King." ✉ *Church St., Old Sq.,* ☎ *01926/403940.* 🎫 *Free.* ☉ *Apr.–Sept., daily 10–6; Oct.–Mar., daily 10–4.*

★ The city's chief attraction is **Warwick Castle,** the finest medieval castle in England, built on a cliff overlooking the Avon. "The fairest monument of ancient and chivalrous splendor which yet remains uninjured by time," to use the words of Sir Walter Scott, the castle is marked by two soaring towers, the 147-ft-high Caesar's Tower, built in 1356, and the 128-ft-high Guy's Tower, built in 1380. The towers bristle with battlements, and their irregular form was designed to allow defenders to shoot from numerous points. The castle's most powerful commander was Richard Neville, Earl of Warwick, known during the Wars of the Roses as "the Kingmaker." He was killed in battle near London in 1471 by Edward IV, whom he had just deposed in favor of Henry VI. Warwick Castle's monumental walls now enclose one of the best collections of medieval armor and weapons in Europe, as well as historic furnishings and paintings by Rubens, Van Dyck, and other Old Masters. Twelve rooms are devoted to an imaginative Madame Tussaud's wax exhibition, "A Royal Weekend Party—1898." Another exhibit displays the sights and sounds of a great medieval household as it prepares for an important battle. The year chosen is 1471, when the Earl of Warwick was killed. Below the castle, along the Avon, strutting peacocks patrol 60 acres of grounds elegantly landscaped by Capability Brown in the 18th century. A restaurant in the cellars serves lunch. Head to the bridge across the river to get the best vista of the castle. ☎ 01926/ 495421, WEB www.warwick-castle.co.uk. ☜ £9.25 (July–Aug. £9.95). ☉ Apr.–Oct., daily 10–6; Nov.–Mar., daily 10–5.

The historic half-timber Oken's House, near the castle entrance, is home to the **Warwickshire Doll Museum,** housing a large collection of antique dolls, toys, and games. ⊠ Oken's House, Castle St., ☎ 01926/ 495546. ☜ £1.50. ☉ Easter–Sept., Mon.–Sat. 10–5, Sun. 1–5; Oct.– Easter, Sat. 10–dusk.

Kids as well as adults will appreciate **St. John's House,** a Jacobean building on the site of a medieval hospital and now surrounded by beautiful gardens. The interior displays period costumes and scenes of domestic life, as well as a Victorian schoolroom. ⊠ Smith St., ☎ 01926/410410. ☜ Free. ☉ Tues.–Sat. 10–12:30 and 1:30–5:30, also Sun. in summer 2:30–5.

Dining and Lodging

£–££   ✕ **Fanshawe's.** Cheerful prints and vases of flowers decorate this friendly, centrally located restaurant on the market square. The menu is wide-ranging—you can have simple open-face sandwiches if you just want a light lunch, or try the Wellington lamb with spinach and mushroom stuffing or the cod with chervil butter. Game is offered in season. ⊠ 22 Market Pl., ☎ 01926/410590. AE, MC, V. No dinner Sun., no lunch Mon. Closed 1 wk mid-Apr. and 2nd wk Oct.

££   ✕▥ **Tudor House Inn.** Here is a simple hotel of genuine character. The Tudor House dates from 1472, having survived the great Warwick fire of 1694 because it was on the road to Stratford, beyond the West Gate, placing it outside the devastated medieval town center. The rooms are beamed and basic, and the floors creak satisfactorily. The great hall, with its cavernous fireplace and gallery, is the restaurant, which offers up hearty portions of inexpensive food including homemade soups. ⊠ 90–92 West St., CV34 6AW, ☎ 01926/495447, FAX 01926/492948. 11 rooms, 6 with bath. Restaurant, bar. AE, DC, MC, V.

Kenilworth Castle

⓯ 5 mi north of Warwick.

The great, red ruins of Kenilworth Castle loom over the rather nondescript village of Kenilworth. Founded in 1120, this castle remained one of the most formidable fortresses in England until it was finally dismantled by Oliver Cromwell after the Civil War in the mid-17th century. Still intact are its keep (central tower) with 20-ft-thick walls; its great hall; and its curtain walls (low outer walls forming the castle's first line of defense). Here the Earl of Leicester, one of Queen Elizabeth I's favorites, entertained her four times, most notably in 1575 with

19 days of sumptuous feasting and revelry. ⊠ *Off A452, Kenilworth,* ☎ *01926/852078.* 🎫 *£3.10.* ☉ *Apr.–Sept., daily 10–6; Oct., daily 10–5; Nov.–Mar., daily 10–4.*

Dining

£££–££££   ✕ **Restaurant Bosquet.** This attractive restaurant serves set menus cooked by the French *patron,* with regularly changing à la carte selections. Try the veal or venison with wild mushrooms. The desserts are mouthwatering. It is mainly a dinner spot, although lunch is available by prior reservation. ⊠ *97A Warwick Rd.,* ☎ *01926/852463. AE, MC, V. Closed Sun., 3 wks in Aug., last wk Dec. No dinner Mon.*

£–££   ✕ **Clarendon Arms.** This pub is a good spot for lunch after a visit to the castle. Fine home-cooked food is offered at the small bar downstairs, and a larger, slightly pricier restaurant upstairs serves complete meals. ⊠ *44 Castle Hill,* ☎ *01926/852017. AE, DC, MC, V.*

Coventry

16   *7 mi northeast of Warwick, 16 mi northeast of Stratford-upon-Avon.*

Coventry thrived in medieval times as a center for the cloth and dyeing industries; in the 19th century it became an industrial powerhouse, though its fortunes have fallen today. The Germans bombed the city with devastating thoroughness in 1940, and many people decry the postwar industrial architecture, with the notable exception of the rebuilt cathedral. Coventry is where a naked Lady Godiva allegedly rode through the strees to protest high taxes and where the first British automobiles were manufactured.

★   The modern bulk of **Coventry Cathedral,** designed by Sir Basil Spence and dedicated in 1962, stands beside the ruins of the blitzed St. Michael's, a powerful symbol of rebirth and reconciliation. Outside the sandstone building is Sir Jacob Epstein's *St. Michael Defeating the Devil;* inside are a number of modern artworks, including Graham Sutherland's stunning 70-ft-high tapestry, *Christ in Glory.* The undercroft holds a visitor center that includes a film about the cathedral and a charred cross wired together from timbers from the bombed cathedral. ⊠ *Priory Row,* ☎ *024/7622–7597,* WEB *www.coventrycathedral.org .* 🎫 *Cathedral free; visitor center £2.* ☉ *Daily 9:30–4:30, services permitting.*

Charlecote Park

17   *13 mi south of Coventry, 6 mi south of Warwick.*

This celebrated house in the village of Hampton Lucy was built in 1572 by Sir Thomas Lucy to entertain the new Queen Elizabeth (the house even takes the form of the letter "E"). According to tradition, Shakespeare was caught poaching deer here soon after his marriage and was forced to flee to London. Years later he is supposed to have retaliated by portraying Sir Thomas Lucy, in *Henry IV Part 2* and the *Merry Wives of Windsor,* as the foolish Justice Shallow. Some historians doubt the reference, but the Bard does mention the "dozen white luces"—which figure in the Lucy coat of arms—as well as having Shallow tax Falstaff with killing his deer, and breaking his fences. The brick house has an early Victorian interior after its extensive renovation in the neo-Elizabethan style by the Lucy family. Its Tudor gatehouse is unchanged since Shakespeare's day. The deer park, with its emerald lawns, was landscaped by Capability Brown. From Warwick, take A429 south 4 or 5 mi, and then turn right onto B4086. ⊠ *Hampton Lucy,* ☎ *01789/470277,* WEB *www.nationaltrust.org.uk.* 🎫 *£5.60, grounds only £3.* ☉ *Apr.–June and Sept.–Oct., Fri.–Tues. noon–5 (house), 11–6 (grounds); July–Aug., Fri.–Wed. noon–5 (house), 11–6 (grounds).*

Lodging

£££ ⌂ **Charlecote Pheasant.** Farm buildings have been converted into a pleasant, country-house hotel across from Charlecote Park (follow B4086 east out of Stratford for about 4 mi). The fine, 17th-century red brick has been matched in the modern wing, and all rooms have tasteful chintz and sober wooden furniture. Aspiring sleuths may want to book during a murder-mystery weekend. ⊠ *Charlecote CV35 9EW,* ☎ *01789/ 279954,* 𝖥𝖠𝖷 *01789/470222,* 𝖶𝖤𝖡 *www.corushotels.com. 67 rooms. Restaurant, bar, pool, tennis court, billiards. AE, DC, MC, V.*

Broughton Castle

⑱ *14 mi southeast of Charlecote Park, 18 mi southeast of Stratford-upon-Avon.*

Once owned by the great chancellor and patron William of Wykeham, this moated mansion passed to Lord and Lady Saye and Sele in 1451 and has been occupied by their family ever since. Parts of the building date back to around 1300, though it was remodeled in Tudor times. The exterior is magnificent, and the inside is rich with period atmosphere, with fireplaces, plasterwork, and exquisite furniture. High points are the Great Chamber, the Chapel, and a fine collection of Chinese wallpapers. ⊠ *Broughton,* ☎ *01295/262624,* 𝖶𝖤𝖡 *www.broughton-castle.demon.co.uk.* ◩ *£4.50.* ◷ *Late-May–mid-Sept., Wed. and Sun. 2–5, also Thurs. in July and Aug., and national holidays Sun. and Mon. 2–5.*

OFF THE
BEATEN PATH

COMPTON WYNYATES – Although not open to the public, Compton Wynyates is worth an excursion to view the house from the hills that surround its tiny valley. A perfect example of Tudor domestic architecture, it was built between 1480 and 1520 by the noted Warwickshire family that takes its name from the little village of Compton (Wynyates refers to the vineyards that once surrounded the house). The house, notable for its timber roof and radiant rose hue, was constructed from bricks dismantled from a castle given to the family by Henry VIII (who, in fact, stayed here). Compton Wynyates is 11 mi southeast of Stratford, near the village of Upper Tysoe, but is best reached by turning north from the village of Brailes off the Shipston–Banbury B4035. Today it is the private residence of the Marquess of Northampton and should only be viewed from the surrounding hillside roads—just as well, since the house looks best from a distance, framed by its miniature lake and topiaries.

Alderminster

⑲ *5 mi south of Stratford-upon-Avon on A3400.*

Alderminster is one of the most interesting of the so-called "Stour villages"—those places so characteristic of Shakespeare Country, strung along the winding route of the River Stour south of Stratford. The main street holds an unusual row of old stone cottages, and the church has a tower dating from the 13th century and a Norman nave. Although the interior of the church has been much restored, it is worth a peek for the carved faces between the arches and the old altar stone.

Close by, **Preston-on-Stour** has an unspoiled air and contains a church with lots of stained glass donated by James West, a civil servant of the 18th century who is also buried in the church. West was responsible for building the Gothic manor house Alscott Park, a half mile northeast of the village. Its broad grounds are open just two days a year, in June and July (contact Stratford's tourist office for precise dates), although the house remains out of bounds.

Other Stour villages include Clifford Chambers, Newbold-on-Stour, Honington, Shipston-on-Stour, and Tredington. Honington is one of the most fetching, set around a village green, with a lovely five-arched bridge crossing the river. Shipston, the largest of the group, is an old sheep-market town, its handsome batch of Georgian houses formerly owned by wealthy wool merchants. Tredington is an exquisite nutshell of a village, with an old stone church.

Dining and Lodging

££££ ✕🏨 **Ettington Park Hotel.** This marvelously restored, huge Victorian Gothic house makes an ideal spot to stay if you want to see the plays at Stratford but don't want to cope with the crowds. It stands on 40 acres of grounds—which contain a ruined church—and looks across river meadows haunted by herons. Individual settings include four-poster rooms, a Shakespeare suite, and the tented Kingmaker Chamber. The restaurant (fixed-price menu) has extremely good food, imaginatively cooked. ⊠ *Alderminster CV37 8BU,* ☎ *01789/450123,* FAX *01789/ 450472,* WEB *www.arcadianhotels.co.uk. 48 rooms. Restaurant, indoor pool, sauna, spa, 2 tennis courts, health club, fishing. AE, DC, MC, V.*

£ ✕🏨 **The Horseshoe.** One of a good concentration of historic inns in the village, the Horseshoe is timbered outside, with a friendly open fire within. Ales and good coffee are available, and there are plain guest rooms and a restaurant. ⊠ *6 Church St., Shipston-on-Stour,* ☎ *01608/ 661225,* FAX *01608/663762. 4 rooms. Restaurant. MC, V.*

Welford-on-Avon

20 *4 mi southwest of Stratford-upon-Avon.*

Welford is most famous for its May Day revelry, when Morris dancers perform their obscure rites around the maypole on the green. Park up in the village, which lies on a loop of the River Avon off B439, and take a walk over the old bridge. Nearby Boat Lane is festooned with timber and whitewashed thatched cottages. Welford also boasts what is said to be the oldest lych-gate in the county, leading to the church. Close by the church, which is partly Norman, stands Cleavers, an attractive brick-built Georgian house worth the stroll.

Dining

£ ✕ **The Bell Inn.** This quiet spot has a flagstone public bar with an open fire, and a conservatory and garden in which to enjoy the generous casual food. ⊠ *Binston Rd.,* ☎ *01789/750353. MC, V.*

Bidford-on-Avon

21 *3 mi southwest of Welford-on Avon, 7 mi southwest of Stratford-upon-Avon.*

The village of Bidford-on-Avon was immortalized in a piece of doggerel popularly ascribed to Shakespeare in his youth:

Piping Pebworth, dancing Marston
Haunted Hillborough, hungry Grafton
Dodging Exhall, Papist Wixford
Beggarly Broom and drunken Bidford.

The lines were supposedly composed after a drinking bout in Bidford's Falcon Inn—no longer a pub but still to be seen, featuring mullioned windows in a Cotswold-stone front. The verse lists the places known as the "Shakespeare Villages," all worth passing through. Bidford is one of the most compelling: it has a main street with 15th- and 16th-century houses and a medieval bridge with eight irregular arches. In

1922 an Anglo-Saxon burial ground containing 200 warriors and their families was unearthed near the church of St. Lawrence.

The other villages mentioned in the verse are worth sniffing out. All are within the triangle formed by A435, A46, and B439 and are close enough to walk to along the tiny roads.

Alcester

㉒ *4 mi north of Bidford-on-Avon, 8 mi west of Stratford-upon-Avon.*

The small market town of Alcester (pronounced *al*-ster) holds a picturesque cluster of ancient roofs and timber-frame Tudor houses. Search out the narrow **Butter Street,** off High Street, site of the 17th-century Churchill House, and, on Malt Mill Lane (off Church Street), the **Old Malt House,** dating from 1500.

Dining and Lodging

££–£££   ✕🏠 **Arrow Mill.** This inn, housed in a former mill, has an ambience that is articulated by heavy beams and flagstones. The rooms—in warm autumn colors—are individually decorated with pine furnishings. There is still a mill wheel in the restaurant, which serves a hearty country menu. ⊠ *Arrow St., B49 5NL,* ☎ *01789/762419,* ℻ *01789/765170. 18 rooms. AE, DC, MC, V. Restaurant closed last wk Dec., 1st wk Jan.*

Ragley Hall

㉓ *2 mi southwest of Alcester.*

A Palladian-style mansion, Ragley Hall was begun in 1680 and worked on by some of the country's most outstanding architects. Inside is a panoply of treasures and architectural features as well as magnificent views of the parkland originally laid out by Capability Brown in the 1750s. The Great Hall has fine baroque plasterwork, and there are portraits by Joshua Reynolds and various Dutch masters, among others, as well as some striking 20th-century murals. This is the ancestral home of the Marquesses of Hertford, the third of whom figured in Thackeray's *Vanity Fair,* and the fourth of whom collected many of the treasures in London's Wallace Collection. ⊠ *Off A435 and A46,* ☎ *01789/762090.* 🎟 *House £5, garden £4.* ⊙ *House Apr.–Oct., Thurs., Fri., Sun., 12:30–5, Sat. 11–3:30; park Apr.–Sept., Thurs.–Sun. 10–6.*

Coughton Court

㉔ *2 mi north of Alcester.*

Coughton Court is a grand Elizabethan manor house that is home to the Catholic Throckmorton family, as it has been since 1409. The impressive gatehouse is the centerpiece of a half-timber courtyard, and it contains a grand fan-vaulted ceiling and various memorabilia, including the dress worn by Mary, Queen of Scots, at her execution. There are children's clothes and Gunpowder Plot exhibitions, and you can wander in the formal gardens and alongside a river and lake. ⊠ *A435,* ☎ *01789/400777,* ᵂᴱᴮ *www.coughtoncourt.co.uk.* 🎟 *House and gardens £6.95, grounds only £5.10.* ⊙ *House mid-Mar.–Apr. and Oct., weekends 11:30–5; May–June and Sept., Sat.–Wed. 11:30–5; July–Aug., Fri.–Wed. 11:30–5. Grounds same days as house, 11–5:30.*

SHAKESPEARE COUNTRY A TO Z

To research prices, get advice from other travelers, and book travel arrangements, visit www.fodors.com.

BUS TRAVEL

National Express serves the region from London's Victoria Coach Station with eight buses daily to the Stratford region. Flights Coach Travel Ltd. of Birmingham operates "Flightlink" service from London's Heathrow and Gatwick airports to Coventry and Warwick, while Stagecoach serves local routes throughout the Stratford, Birmingham, and Coventry areas.

FARES AND SCHEDULES
➤ BUS INFORMATION: **Flights Coach Travel Ltd. of Birmingham** (☎ 0870/575–7747). **National Express** (☎ 0870/580–8080, WEB www.gobycoach.com). **Stagecoach Midland Red (South) Ltd. and Stagecoach Stratford Blue** (☎ 01788/535555, WEB www.stagecoach.co.uk).

CAR RENTAL

➤ LOCAL AGENCIES: **Hertz** (✉ Rail Station, Stratford-upon-Avon, ☎ 01789/298827). **Listers** (✉ Western Rd., Stratford-upon-Avon, ☎ 01789/294477, WEB www.listersgroup.co.uk).

CAR TRAVEL

Stratford lies about 100 mi northwest of London; take M40 to Junction 15. The city is 37 mi southeast of Birmingham by the A435 and A46 or by the M40 to Junction 15. Main roads provide easy access between towns, but one pleasure of this rural area is exploring the smaller "B" roads, which lead deep into the countryside.

EMERGENCIES

Saint Michael's Hospital in Warwick is off of Cape Road, easily accessible from the A46 and A425, while the Stratford-upon-Avon Hospital is on Arden Street, easily walkable from the tourist attractions.
➤ CONTACTS: **Ambulance, fire, police** (☎ 999). **Saint Michael's Hospital** (✉ St. Michael's Rd., Warwick, ☎ 01926/496241 or 01926/406789). **Stratford-upon-Avon Hospital** (✉ Arden St., Stratford-upon-Avon, ☎ 01926/495321).

TOURS

The Heart of England Tourist Board can arrange a variety of tours throughout the region. Guide Friday runs guided tours of Stratford, for £8, and Warwick, for £16. Since Guide Friday's charges don't include admissions to the Stratford sights—most are within walking distance—some people find the tour unnecessary.
➤ FEES AND SCHEDULES: **Guide Friday** (☎ 01789/294466, WEB www.guide-friday.com). **Heart of England Tourist Board** (☎ 01905/763436).

TRAIN TRAVEL

Try to catch the direct train each morning from London's Paddington Station, or you'll be doomed to at least one change, at Leamington Spa. There are two direct trains back from Stratford each afternoon, and the journey time is up to three hours. On winter Sundays there are bus connections from Leamington Spa or Warwick when the Stratford train station is closed. The fastest route is by train *and* bus using the "Shakespeare Connection Road & Rail Link" from Euston Station to Coventry then a Guide Friday bus.

The "Shakespeare Connection" trip takes two hours, and there are four departures weekdays—the three that would allow you to catch an evening performance in Stratford are at 9:15 AM, 10:45 AM, and 4:55 PM; Saturday departures are at 9:05 AM, 10:35 AM, and 5:05 PM; the Sunday departure is at 9:45 AM. Returns to London usually depart at about 11:15 PM. Schedules are subject to change, so it's best to phone to confirm times. Note that a seven-day "Heart of England Rover" ticket is valid for unlimited travel within the region.

FARES AND SCHEDULES
➤ TRAIN INFORMATION: **National Rail Inquiries** (☎ 0845/748–4950, WEB www.nationalrail.co.uk). **Guide Friday** (☎ 01789/294466, WEB www.guidefriday.com).

TRAVEL AGENCIES
➤ LOCAL AGENT REFERRALS: **American Express** (✉ c/o Tourist Information Centre, Bridgefoot, Stratford-upon-Avon, ☎ 01789/415856). **Thomas Cook** (✉ c/o Midland Bank, 13 Chapel St., Stratford-upon-Avon, ☎ 01789/294688.

VISITOR INFORMATION
Local tourist information centers are normally open Monday–Saturday 9:30–5:30, but times vary according to season.
➤ TOURIST INFORMATION: **Heart of England Tourist Board** (✉ Woodside, Larkhill, Worcester WR5 2EF, ☎ 01905/763436, FAX 01905/763450, WEB www.visitheartofengland.com). **Stratford-upon-Avon** (✉ Bridgefoot, ☎ 01789/293127, WEB www.stratford-upon-avon.co.uk). **Warwick** (✉ The Court House, Jury St., ☎ 01926/492212, WEB www.warwick-uk.co.uk).

8 THE HEART OF ENGLAND

BATH, THE COTSWOLDS, GLOUCESTER, THE FOREST OF DEAN

Visiting the Cotswold region can be likened to stepping inside a 19th-century English pastoral novel. Nowhere else in Britain are the hedges so perfectly clipped, the churches so ivy clad, the villages so charmingly quaint. Here, hidden in sheltered valleys, you'll find fabled abodes—Sudeley Castle, Stanway House, and Snowshill Manor among them. Not far away is 18th-century Bath, a handsome city of Georgian splendor. Be sure to amble about its elegant Assembly Rooms—you'll be following in the footsteps of Jane Austen.

Updated by
Robert
Andrews

T HE HEART OF ENGLAND is a term coined by the tourist powers-that-be to designate the heart of *tourist* England, so immensely popular are its attractions. Here it means the county of Gloucestershire, in west-central England, with slices of neighboring Oxfordshire, Worcestershire, and Somerset. Together they make up a sweep of land stretching from Shakespeare Country in the north down through Bath to the Bristol Channel in the south. Bath, among the most alluring small cities in Europe, offers up "18th-century England in all its urban glory," to use a phrase of writer Nigel Nicolson. Northward, beyond Regency-era Cheltenham—like Bath, a spa town adorned with remarkably elegant architecture—the Cotswolds are a region that conjure up "olde Englande" at its most blissfully rural. Urban Gloucester and the ancient Forest of Dean are the western edge of the area.

Bath rightly boasts of being the best-planned town in England. Although the city was founded by the Romans when they discovered here the only true hot springs in England, its popularity during the 17th and 18th centuries ensured its aesthetic immortality. Bath's fashionable period luckily coincided with one of Britain's most elegant architectural eras, producing a quite remarkable urban phenomenon—money available to create virtually an entire town of stylish buildings. Today's city fathers have been wise enough to make sure that Bath is kept spruce and welcoming. Its present prosperity keeps the streets overflowing with flowers in the summer and is channeled into cleaning and painting the city center, making it a joy to explore. Gainsborough, Lord Nelson, and Queen Victoria traveled here to sip the waters, which Dickens described as tasting like "warm flatirons," but most of today's travelers are here to walk in the footsteps of Jane Austen and opt for tea and clotted cream and strawberries in one of the town's elegant eateries.

North of Bath are the Cotswolds—a region that more than one writer has called the very soul of England. Is it the sun, or the soil? The pretty-as-a-picture villages? The mellow, centuries-old, stone-built cottages festooned with honeysuckle? Whatever the reason, this idyllic region remains a vision of rural England. Here are time-defying churches, sleepy hamlets, and ancient farmsteads so sequestered that they seem to offer everyone the thrill of personal "discovery." Of course, the Cotswolds can hardly claim to be undiscovered, but, happily, its poetic appeal has a way of surviving the tour groups who pierce its timeless tranquillity. More than ever, people come here to taste fully the glories of the old English village—its thatched roofs, low-ceiling rooms, and gardens meticulously built on a gentle slope; its old-world atmosphere is as thick as honey, and equally as sweet.

Pleasures and Pastimes

Dining

Even in the old days, when critics would joke about British cuisine ("if you can call it that"), few people carped about the abundance of superb regional produce available in restaurants. Here, in the heart of England, chefs have never had a problem with a fresh food supply: excellent produce, salmon from the Rivers Severn and Wye, local lamb, venison from the Forest of Dean, and pheasant, partridge, quail, and grouse in season. Now more than ever, this region is dotted with good restaurants, thanks to a steady flow of fine chefs seeking to cater to wealthy locals and waves of demanding tourists.

CATEGORY	COST*
££££	over £22
£££	£16–£22
££	£9–£15
£	under £9

per person for a main course at dinner

Lodging

While staying at a Cotswold inn, in the village of Banbury during the spring of 1776, the immortal Dr. Johnson spoke his noted panegyric on English hostelries: "There is no private house in which people can enjoy themselves so well as at a capital tavern." Today the hotels of this region still please myriad travelers, and they are among Britain's most highly rated—ranging from bed-and-breakfasts in village homes and farmhouses to luxurious country-house hotels. Because the region is so popular, book ahead whenever possible. You should also brace yourself for very fancy prices. Most hotels offer two- and three-day packages. Keep in mind when booking reservations that hotels can front on heavily trafficked roads; ask for quiet rooms.

CATEGORY	COST*
££££	over £150
£££	£100–£150
££	£60–£100
£	under £60

All prices are for two people sharing a standard double room, including service, breakfast, and VAT.

Shopping

The antiques shops here are, it is sometimes whispered, "temporary" storerooms for the great families of the region; filled with tole-ware, treen, faience fire-dogs, toby jugs, and silhouettes, plus lovely country furniture, Edwardiana, and ravishing 17th- to 19th-century furniture. The center of antiquing, with more than 30 dealers, is Stow-on-the-Wold. Other towns that have a number of antiques shops are Burford, Cirencester, Tetbury, and Moreton-in-Marsh. Unfortunately, the Cotswolds—once the happiest of hunting grounds for antiques lovers—now offer very few of those "anything in this tray for £5" shops. For information about dealers and special events, contact the Cotswold Antique Dealers' Association. As across England, many towns in this region have market days: head for Moreton-in-Marsh on Tuesday, Tetbury on Wednesday, and Cirencester on Friday and Saturday.

Walking

This part of England offers glorious, gentle countryside, with many short walks in the areas around the historic towns of the region. The local tourist information centers often have route maps for themed walks. If you want to branch out on your own, but not get lost, track the rivers on which many towns are built. They usually have towpaths running alongside that are easy to follow and scenically rewarding. However, they wind a lot, and you may find yourself walking for much longer than you had intended. The scenic Cotswold Way runs through parts of the country you will never see from a car window, stretching about 100 mi between Bath and Chipping Campden. The path traces the ridge marking the edge of the Cotswolds and the Severn Valley and affords incomparable views. The Forest of Dean is quite special for walking; it's densely wooded, with interesting villages and monastic ruins to view. Many of its public footpaths are signposted, as are most of the Forestry Commission trails. You'll find easy walks out of Newland, around New Fancy (great view) and Mallards Pike Lake, and a slightly longer one (three hours), which takes in Wench Ford, Danby Lodge, and Blackpool Bridge. There are picnic grounds, good car parking, and, hidden away, old pubs where you can wet your whistle.

Exploring the Heart of England

The region's major points of interest—the elegant city of Bath, the Cotswold Hills, and the Gloucester-Cheltenham axis—are a good way to organize your exploration of the area. Bath, which can also be easily visited on a day out from London, makes an elegant center from which to travel westward to Bristol, the Severn Estuary, and prehistoric sites, this time in the Chew Valley. The Cotswold Hills cover some of southern England's most beautiful terrain, with which the characteristic stone cottages found throughout the area are in perfect harmony. Some villages have become overrun by coach parties and antiques shops, but at least they have for the most part retained their historic appearance, and can still be fun. To the west of the Cotswolds lie Gloucester and Cheltenham, almost twin towns; beyond them, between the River Severn and the border of Wales, is the Forest of Dean. The road from Gloucester to Bath takes you by the evocative castle at Berkeley.

Numbers in the text correspond to numbers in the margin and on the Bath Environs, Bath, the Cotswold Hills, and the Forest of Dean maps.

Great Itineraries

You can get a taste of Bath and the Cotswolds in three days, and a week-long visit will give you plenty of time to wander this relatively small region. Bath makes a useful place from where to start or finish, not far off the M4 motorway on the A46. The cities of Gloucester and Cheltenham also hold many attractions. Once outside the towns, you'll discover that the Cotswold Hills should be relished on a slow schedule, to allow you time to smell the roses, as well as the pink saffron and moon-daisies.

Driving down the scenic roads of the Cotswold Hills can be one of the real joys of a British vacation. However, even without your own transportation, a Cotswold circuit can be undertaken—easily, by using the excellent guided bus tours in the area, or, more adventurously, using public transportation (this requires planning as some buses stop at certain Cotswold villages only twice a week). A car can be an encumbrance in urban Bath, Cheltenham, and Gloucester; garage your car or leave it at your hotel and forego the stress of finding parking spaces and negotiating one-way streets.

IF YOU HAVE 3 DAYS

A day in ⊠ **Bath** ①–⑨ will enable you to tour the Roman Baths, followed by a whirl round the Abbey. In the afternoon, stroll along the river or canal, drop in on the collection of ceramics and silverware in the Holburne Museum, then cross town to the Royal Crescent for an early evening promenade. Spend the night here, heading out early for **Cheltenham** ⑫, whose Regency architecture and fashionable shops will occupy a morning's amble. After lunch, drive northeast on the minor B4632 through **Winchcombe** ⑬, near which lie the majestic grounds of historic **Sudeley Castle** ⑭ and **Stanway House** ⑮. Lunch in **Broadway** ⑰ will allow you to sample its sugary charms, or you might prefer to press on to that Cotswold showpiece, ⊠ **Chipping Campden** ⑱. Now head south on the A429 through the classic Cotswold villages of **Moreton-in-Marsh** ⑳ and **Stow-on-the-Wold** ㉑, where cottage pubs are sandwiched between antiques shops. Nearby, don't miss the smaller places such as ⊠ **Lower and Upper Slaughter** ㉓. For your final afternoon, head westward on A436 to **Gloucester** ㉜, whose restored docks hold the National Waterways Museum.

IF YOU HAVE 7 DAYS

Two days in ⊞ **Bath** ①–⑨ will give you time to explore that treasure chest of Georgian elegance, along with browsing its antiques shops and taking in an evening at the Theatre Royal. Outside Bath, make sure you see **Castle Combe** ⑩, "the prettiest village in England," or **Lacock** ⑪. On your third day, head north to swank ⊞ **Cheltenham** ⑫ and walk its Regency-era terraces and promenades. Overnight there, then start out on a circuit that takes in the best of the Cotswold villages and countryside; Cheltenham's tourist office has useful information. Driving north out of Cheltenham, take a look at **Winchcombe** ⑬, then explore the majestic grounds of **Sudeley Castle** ⑭ and **Stanway House** ⑮. A little farther north, the manor house of **Snowshill Manor** ⑯ is set in an unspoiled village and contains an amazing collection of curios. The popular Cotswold center of **Broadway** ⑰—whose charms are in inverse proportion to the number of other visitors there at the same time— lies a couple of miles farther, on A44.

Spend your fourth night in that Cotswold showpiece, ⊞ **Chipping Campden** ⑱, from which it is an easy drive to the rare shrubs and "garden rooms" of **Hidcote Manor Gardens** ⑲, where you'll need several hours to absorb the splendor of this creation. From here, head southward, through a pair of irresistible Cotswold villages, **Moreton-in-Marsh** ⑳ and **Stow-on-the-Wold** ㉑, both deserving a leisurely wander. You can stretch your legs in a ramble around the ancient Rollright Stones, a few miles to the east, for an abrupt change of timeframe. South of Stow, kids may enjoy the museum attractions of **Bourton-on-the-Water** ㉒ and **Northleach** ㉔, while **Chedworth Roman Villa** ㉗ is an evocative reminder of the area's importance in Roman times—nearby **Cirencester** ㉘ was Corinium, an important provincial capital. The chances are that you will already have seen the ideal rural retreat for your fifth night, perhaps in the wilds around ⊞ **Lower and Upper Slaughter** ㉓. In the morning, an outing eastward might take in idyllic **Bibury** ㉖ and the wool town of **Burford** ㉕. Driving west from Cirencester on A417, make your farewells to the Cotswolds in the model village of **Owlpen** ㉚, immaculate **Painswick,** and the market town of **Tetbury** ㉛.

⊞ **Gloucester** ㉜ presents an urban contrast to the rustic tone of your last few days. Spend your final day either south of here, exploring the medieval atmosphere of **Berkeley Castle** ㊳ and the celebrated **Slimbridge Wildfowl Trust** ㊲, or else east, toward the Wye Valley and Wales, to take a gentle hike through the Forest of Dean with an overnight in ⊞ **Coleford** ㊱. The Dean Heritage Center at Soudley makes a good introduction to this ancient woodland, but be sure to put on your walking shoes and explore. If you have children along, the nearby Clearwell Caves can be special fun.

When to Tour the Heart of England

This area contains some of the most popular destinations in the country, and you would do well to avoid weekends in the busier areas of the Cotswold Hills. During the week, you will hardly see a soul. Bath is particularly congested in summer, when students flock to the language schools here. On the other hand, Gloucester and Cheltenham are workday places that can effortlessly absorb the visiting coach tours and be seen comfortably at any time. Note that the private properties of Hidcote Manor, Snowshill Manor, and Sudeley Castle close in winter. Hidcote Manor Gardens is at its best in spring and fall.

BATH AND ENVIRONS

Anyone who listens to the local speech of Bath will note the inflections that herald the beginning of England's West Country. Yet the city retains an inescapable element of the Heart of England: Bath itself is at the bottom edge of the Cotswold Hills, and the Georgian architecture and mellow stone so prominent here are reminders of the stone mansions and cottages of the Cotswolds. In the hinterland of the county of Somerset, the gentle, green countryside harbors country pubs.

Bath

★ *13 mi southeast of Bristol, 115 mi west of London.*

"I really believe I shall always be talking of Bath . . . I do like it so very much. Oh! who can ever be tired of Bath," wrote Jane Austen in *Northanger Abbey* and, today, thousands of visitors heartily agree with the great 19th-century author. One of the delights of staying in Bath is being surrounded by the magnificent 18th-century architecture, a lasting reminder of the elegant world described by Austen. Bath suffered slightly from World War II bombing and even more from urban renewal, but the damage was halted before it could ruin the Georgian elegance of the city. This doesn't mean that Bath is a museum. It is lively and interesting, offering dining and shopping, excellent art galleries, and theater, music, and other performances throughout the year. The Romans first put Bath on the map in the 1st century, when they built a temple here, in honor of the goddess Minerva, and a sophisticated network of baths to make full use of the mineral springs that gush from the earth at a constant temperature of 116°F (46.5°C).

Much later, 18th-century People of Quality took the city to heart, and Bath became the most fashionable spa in Britain. The architect John Wood (1704–1754) created a harmonious city, building beautiful terraces, crescents, and villas of the same local stone used by the Romans. Wood was a dedicated antiquarian and an architect obsessed: he envisioned Bath as a city destined for almost mythic greatness along the lines of Winchester and Glastonbury, and his choice of the dignified Palladian style and his use of decorative motifs from local legends and nearby stone circles reflected his beliefs. Assembly rooms, theaters, and pleasure gardens were all built to entertain the rich and titled, when they weren't busy attending the parties of Beau Nash (the city's Master of Ceremonies and chief social organizer) and having their portraits painted by Gainsborough.

Today, Bath's big news is the Bath Spa Project, a major spa that will be built in the heart of the city. People will once again be able to bathe in the mineral waters, and many other therapeutic and aesthetic treatments will be available. The spa, set to open in fall 2002, will incorporate a number of historic buildings such as the Cross Bath and Hot Bath.

A Good Walk

Start in the traffic-free Abbey Churchyard, at the heart of Bath, and the **Roman Baths Museum** ①, to see the impressive remains of the bath complex. The lively piazza is dominated by the **Abbey** ②, whose facade—itself packed with detail—invites further investigations within. Off Abbey Churchyard, where buskers (strolling musicians) of all kinds perform, are tiny alleys leading to little squares of stores, galleries, and eating places. Walk up Stall and Union streets toward Milsom Street, and you'll find numerous alleyways with fascinating small shops. Work your way east to Bridge Street and the graceful, Italianate **Pulteney Bridge** ③, a shop-lined masterpiece over the River Avon.

Bath Environs

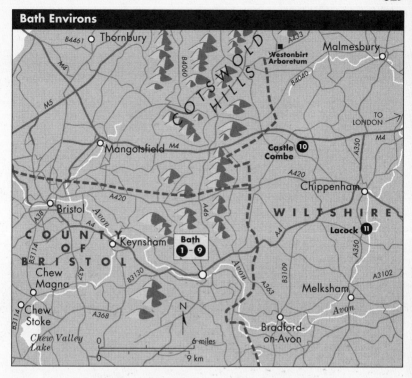

South of here, the Grand Parade looks out over flower-filled gardens. Stroll over the bridge to Great Pulteney Street, a broad thoroughfare that leads to the **Holburne Museum** ④, Bath's finest collection of crafted objets. Cross back over the bridge, and head up Broad Street and its extension, Lansdown Road. Turn left into Bennett Street, site of the Neoclassical **Museum of Costume and Assembly Rooms** ⑤. The Assembly Rooms were once the 18th-century hub of elegant society. The Museum of Costume provides an amusing overview of some of the weird and wonderful apparel our forebears wore. From here, it's a short hop to the **Jane Austen Centre** ⑥, on a street where the author lived in the early 1800s. Continuing north, you will reach **The Circus** ⑦, an architectural tour de force compared by some to an inverted Colosseum. The two John Woods—father and son—were responsible for this, and Wood *fils* was also creator of Bath's most dazzling terrace, the Royal Crescent, a graceful arc embracing a swath of green lawns at one end of Brock Street. Once you've feasted your eyes on this vista, you might take in **Number 1 Royal Crescent** ⑧, a perfectly preserved example of Georgian domestic architecture. Return to the Circus, and walk south down Gay Street, which will bring you past dignified **Queen Square,** with its obelisk, to **Theatre Royal** ⑨, one of the country's most impressive dramatic venues. Wander east from here back to the Abbey, where tea shops, including Sally Lunn's, offer relief to tired limbs.

TIMING

Allow a full day to see everything, with frequent tea stops; you should save two hours for the Roman Baths Museum. If you're planning some retail therapy, keep in mind that on Sunday many shops close. Bath Abbey is more difficult to visit on Sunday, too. The walk itself takes only about 1½ hours, but in summer your progress will be hampered by the sheer volume of sightseers.

Abbey 2

The Circus . . .7

Holburne
Museum and
Crafts Study
Centre 4

Jane Austen
Centre 6

Museum of
Costume/
Assembly
Rooms 5

Number 1
Royal
Crescent . . .8

Pulteney
Bridge 3

Roman Baths
Museum/
Pump Room . .1

Theatre
Royal 9

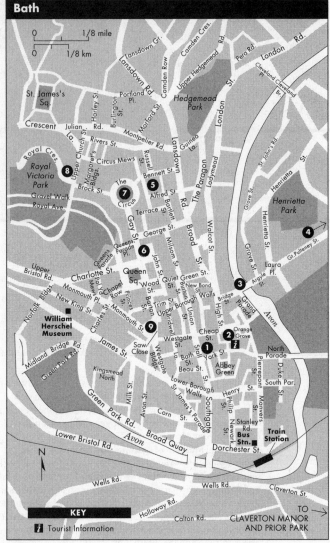

Bath

Sights to See

② Abbey. Dominating Bath's center, and dating from the 15th century, the edifice has a splendid west front, with carved figures of angels ascending ladders on either side. Notice, too, the miter, olive tree, and crown motif, a play on the name of the present building's founder, Bishop Oliver King. The Abbey was built in the Perpendicular (English late-Gothic) style on the site of a Saxon abbey, and it has superb, fan-vaulted ceilings in the nave. Visit the **Heritage Vaults,** accessible from outside the building (the entrance is in the Abbey's south wall, off Abbey Church Yard), to see an audiovisual presentation of the history of the Abbey and a reconstruction of the Norman cathedral that preceded it. ⊠ *Abbey Churchyard,* ☎ *01225/422462,* WEB *www.bathabbey.org.* ⊠ *Abbey: £2 donation; Heritage Vaults £2.* ◷ *Abbey Apr.–Sept., Mon.–Sat. 9–6; Oct.–Mar., Mon.–Sat. 9–4:30; open Sun. 1:15–2:30 and 4:30–5:30 and for 6 services. Heritage Vaults Mon.–Sat. 10–4.*

American Museum and Gardens. The first museum of American decorative arts to be established outside the United States is housed in a Greek

Revival (19th-century) mansion in a truly majestic setting southeast of the city. The objects displayed are from 17th-century New England to the 19th-century South; galleries are devoted to folk art and Native American culture, and quilts are always on display. The fine parkland includes a replica of George Washington's garden. ⊠ *Warminster Rd. (A36), Claverton Down, 2½ mi southeast of Bath,* ☎ *01225/460503.* ⊠ *Museum, grounds, and galleries £5.50, grounds and galleries £3.* ⊙ *Late Mar.–early Nov., Tues.–Sun. 2–5, also Mon. in Aug. 2–5, and national holiday and preceding Sun. 11–5.*

★ **❼ The Circus.** Influenced by nearby stone circles as well as round Roman temples, John Wood broke loose from convention in his design for the masterful Circus, a full circle of curving, perfectly proportioned Georgian houses broken only three times for intersecting streets. Notice the acorns atop the houses; Wood nurtured the myth that Prince Bladud founded Bath, ostensibly with the help of an errant pig rooting for acorns (this is one of a number of variations of Bladud's story), and the architect adopted the acorn motif in a number of places. A round garden fills the center of the Circus.

❹ Holburne Museum. This elegant 18th-century building houses a small but superb collection of 17th- and 18th-century decorative arts, ceramics, and silverware. Highlights include paintings by Gainsborough (*The Byam Family,* on indefinite loan) and Stubbs (his exquisite portrait, *Reverend Carter Thelwall and Family*), and Rachmaninov's Steinway piano. It also holds temporary exhibitions on historical themes. As the Sydney Hotel, the house was once one of the pivots of Bath's high society, who came to perambulate in the pleasure gardens that still lie behind. One of the visitors was Jane Austen, whose main Bath residence was No. 4 Sydney Place, a brief stroll across the road from the museum. ⊠ *Great Pulteney St.,* ☎ *01225/466669,* ⓦⒺⒷ *www.bath.ac.uk/holburne.* ⊠ *£3.50.* ⊙ *Mid-Feb.–mid-Dec., Tues.–Sat. 10–5, Sun. 2:30–5:30.*

❻ Jane Austen Centre. In 1805, Jane Austen lived a few doors up from this cozy Georgian house, one of several addresses she had in Bath at different times. The Centre shows the influence of the city through her writings. If you haven't had time to read *Northanger Abbey* and *Persuasion,* both set in the city, the displays here will give you a pictorial introduction, while the digitally enlarged panorama of Bath in 1800 by Robert Havell helps to put it all in context. Jane Austen walking tours leave from the Abbey Churchyard at 11 AM daily from May through September and on weekends from October through April. ⊠ *40 Gay St.,* ⓦⒺⒷ *www.janeausten.co.uk,* ☎ ⒻⒶⓍ *01225/443000.* ⊠ *£4.* ⊙ *Mon.–Sat. 10–5:30, Sun. 10:30–5:30.*

★ **❺ Museum of Costume and Assembly Rooms.** In its role as the **Assembly Rooms**, this classical-style building was the leading center for social life in 18th-century Bath, with an ever-changing schedule of dress balls, concerts, and choral nights. Jane Austen came here often, and it was here, in the Ballroom, that Catherine Morland had her first, disappointing encounter with Bath's beau monde in *Northanger Abbey*; the Octagon Room became the setting for an important encounter between Anne Elliot and Captain Wentworth in *Persuasion*. Built by the younger John Wood in 1771, the building was badly damaged by bombing in 1942, but was subsequently and faithfully restored. Today, the Assembly Rooms house the entertaining **Museum of Costume**, displaying, in lavish settings, costumes from Beau Nash's day up to the present. Throughout the year, concerts of Vivaldi, Bach, and other classical composers are given in the Ballroom, just as they were in bygone days. ⊠ *Bennett St.,* ☎ *01225/477789,* ⓦⒺⒷ *www.museumofcostume.co.uk.* ⊠ *£4.20, combined ticket with Roman Baths £9.50.* ⊙ *Daily 10–5.*

★ ❽ **Number 1 Royal Crescent.** The majestic arc of the Royal Crescent, much used as a location for period films, is the crowning glory of Palladian architecture in Bath. The work of John Wood the Younger, these 30 houses fronted by 114 columns were laid out between 1767 and 1774. A house in the center is now the elegant Royal Crescent Hotel. On the corner of Brock Street and the Royal Crescent, Number 1 Royal Crescent has been turned into a museum and furnished as it might have been at the turn of the 19th century. The museum crystallizes a view of the English class system—upstairs all is gentility and elegance, while downstairs is a fascinating kitchen museum. ☎ *01225/428126,* WEB *www. bath-preservation-trust.org.uk.* ⌑ *£4.* ☉ *Mid-Feb.–Oct., Tues.–Sun. 10:30–5; Nov., Tues.–Sun. 10:30–4.*

Prior Park. A vision to warm Jane Austen's heart, Bath's grandest house lies a mile or so southeast of the center, with splendid views over the Georgian townscape. Built by John Wood in around 1738, it was the home of local philanthropist Ralph Allen (1693–1764), whose guests included such contemporary luminaries as Pope, Fielding, and Richardson. Today, it is a Roman Catholic school and the house is only visible from the outside, but you may wander through the beautiful grounds, designed by Capability Brown and embellished with a Palladian bridge and lake; tours are occasionally given. Note that there is no parking lot here or in the vicinity: unless you relish the uphill trudge, take a taxi to get here, or use the frequent bus service (Nos. 2 or 4 from the center). ⊠ *Ralph Allen Dr.,* ☎ *01225/833422.* ⌑ *£4.* ☉ *Apr.–Sept., Wed.–Mon. 11–5:30; Oct.–Nov., Wed.–Mon. noon–dusk; Dec.–Jan., Fri.–Sun. noon–dusk.*

❸ **Pulteney Bridge.** One of the most famous landmarks of the city, the 18th-century span, inspired by Florence's Ponte Vecchio, is the only work of Robert Adam in the city and is unique in all Britain because it's lined with shops.

Queen Square. Houses and the Francis Hotel surround the garden in the center of this peaceful, intimate square. An obelisk designed by John Wood and financed by Beau Nash celebrates the 1738 visit of Frederick, Prince of Wales.

★ ❶ **Roman Baths Museum.** The hot springs are what has drawn people here since prehistoric times, so it's most appropriate to begin an exploration of the city at this excellent museum, which occupies the site of the ancient city's temple complex and primary "watering hole." Here, the patrician elite would gather to immerse themselves, drink the mineral waters, and socialize. With the departure of the Romans, the baths fell into disuse, but when the practice again became fashionable, the site was reopened, and the magnificent Georgian building now standing was erected at the end of the 18th century. Almost the entire Roman bath complex has now been excavated (the East Baths opened in 2001), and informative Acoustiguide handsets allow you to tour the site at your own pace. The museum displays numerous relics of the temple once dedicated to Sulis Minerva. Exhibits include a mustachioed, Celtic-influenced Gorgon's head and fragments of colorful curses invoked by the old Romans against some of their neighbors. The **Great Bath** is now roofless, and the statuary and pillars belong to the 19th century, but there is much remaining from the original complex, and the steaming, somewhat murky waters are undeniably evocative. On August evenings, you can take part in torchlighted tours of the baths.

Adjacent to the Roman bath complex is the famed **Pump Room**, built in 1792–1796, a favored rendezvous place for 18th-century Bath society, where lords and ladies liked to check on the new arrivals to the city. Here Catherine Morland and Mrs. Allen "paraded up and down for an hour, looking at everybody and speaking to no one," to quote from Jane Austen's *Northanger Abbey*. Today, you can have a bite to eat on the premises—or you can simply, for a small fee, taste the fairly vile mineral water. ⊠ *Abbey Churchyard,* ☎ *01225/477785,* WEB *www. romanbaths.co.uk.* 🎫 *Pump Room free, Roman Baths £7.50, combined ticket with Costume Museum £9.50.* ☉ *Apr.–Sept., daily 9–6 (and Aug. 8 PM–10 PM); Oct.–Mar., daily 9:30–5.*

❾ Theatre Royal. George Dance the younger designed this magnificent auditorium, which opened in 1805 and was restored in 1982—a vision in damson plush, raspberry-striped silk, and gold grisaille. Next door to the Theatre Royal, the former home of Richard "Beau" Nash—the dictator of fashion for mid-18th-century society in Bath—and his mistress Juliana Popjoy, is now a restaurant called Popjoy's. ⊠ *Saw Close,* ☎ *01225/448844,* WEB *www.theatreroyal.org.uk.*

William Herschel Museum. In this modest Bath town house, using a handmade telescope of his own devising, William Herschel (1738–1822) identified the planet Uranus, and the house is now a small museum devoted to his studies and discoveries. You can see examples of his telescopes, the workshop where he cast his speculum metal mirrors, musical instruments of his time (Herschel originally came to Bath from his native Hannover as a musician, and was organist at Bath's Octagon Chapel), and the tiny garden where the discovery of Uranus was made. A Star Vault (a miniplanetarium) re-creates the night sky and takes you on a virtual trip through the solar system. ⊠ *19 New King St.,* ☎ *01225/ 311342,* WEB *www.bath-preservation-trust.org.uk.* 🎫 *£3.50.* ☉ *Mar.– Oct., daily 2–5; Nov.–Feb., weekends 2–5.*

Dining and Lodging

£££ ✕ **Popjoy's Restaurant.** Named for the mistress of Beau Nash, the restau-
★ rant provides an elegant setting for a fine, English-style, after-theater dinner. You have the choice of dining on the ground floor or in the lovely Georgian drawing room upstairs. There is an unmistakable French flavor to the dishes, such as pan-fried noisette of lamb with caramelized garlic and shallots, though there are plenty of international touches, too. The fixed-price lunch and pre-theater menus are especially good values. ⊠ *Beau Nash House, Saw Close,* ☎ *01225/460494. AE, DC, MC, V. Closed Sun.*

££–£££ ✕ **Pump Room.** The 18th-century Pump Room, next to the Roman Baths Museum, serves morning coffee, lunches, and afternoon tea, often to music by a string trio. Soup and a filled baguette are one lunch choice, along with chicken and lamb meals; do save room for the English cheese board and homemade Bath biscuits. The Terrace Restaurant has views over the Baths and is also open for evening meals during the Bath Festival, and in August and December (there's a fixed-price menu for dinner, and reservations are essential). Be prepared to wait in line for a table during the day. ⊠ *Abbey Churchyard,* ☎ *01225/444477. AE, MC, V. No dinner.*

££–£££ ✕ **Rascals.** Tucked away close to the Circus, this is a good spot for a meal on a sightseeing day. In the elegant first-floor restaurant you can choose the set menu or the daily specials. You might try the garlicky English field mushrooms for a starter, follow with the pan-fried fillet of sea bass with spinach, and have the bread and butter pudding made with raisins soaked in spirits as a finale. ⊠ *4 Saville Row,* ☎ *01225/ 330201. MC, V.*

££ ✕ **Number Five.** An ideal spot for a light lunch, this airy bistro, with its plants, framed posters, and cane-back chairs, is just over the Pulteney Bridge from the center of town. The menu changes daily but includes tasty homemade soups and such dishes as roast quail on wild rice and char-grilled loin of lamb. You can bring your own bottle of wine on Monday and Tuesday. There is no smoking in the restaurant. ⊠ *5 Argyle St.,* ☏ *01225/444499. AE, DC, MC, V. Closed Sun. No lunch Mon.*

£–££ ✕ **Sally Lunn's.** This popular spot near the Abbey occupies the oldest house in Bath, dating to 1482, and is famous for the Sally Lunn bun (served here since 1680), actually a light, semi-sweet bread. You can choose from more than 40 sweet and savory toppings to accompany your bun, or turn it into a full-scale meal with such dishes as trencher pork in apple and cider. Daytime diners can view the small kitchen museum in the cellar (free). ⊠ *4 North Parade Passage,* ☏ *01225/461634, MC, V. No dinner Jan. and Mon. late Dec. and Feb.–Mar.*

££££ ✕🏠 **Royal Crescent Hotel.** Part of the Royal Crescent, this lavishly con-
★ verted house is an architectural treasure. The furnishings are consistent with the building's period elegance, and if some of the bedrooms are on the small side, there are ample luxuries to compensate. The hotel's Pimpernel's restaurant has won consistent praise, and a Palladian villa in the garden provides extra rooms. ⊠ *16 Royal Crescent, BA1 2LS,* ☏ *01225/823333,* FAX *01225/339401,* WEB *www.royalcrescent.co.uk. 25 rooms, 19 suites. Restaurant. AE, DC, MC, V.*

£££–££££ ✕🏠 **Queensberry Hotel.** This intimate, elegant hotel, in a residential
★ street near the Circus, is in three 1772 town houses built by the architect John Wood for the Marquis of Queensberry. Renovations have preserved the Regency stucco ceilings and cornices and original marble tiling on the fireplaces, and each room is decorated in pastels and flower prints. Downstairs, the Olive Tree restaurant serves English and Mediterranean dishes. ⊠ *Russell St., BA1 2QF,* ☏ *01225/447928,* FAX *01225/446065,* WEB *www.bathqueensberry.com. 29 rooms. Restaurant, bar. MC, V. Closed Dec. 24–30.*

££££ 🏠 **Bath Spa Hotel.** Its location on 7 acres of well-kept grounds (complete with grotto) gives this splendid hotel of golden glowing stone a feeling of seclusion, although you're just a 10-minute walk from the heart of bustling Bath. Public areas, including a sitting room and a lobby with a fireplace, are traditional in feeling, as you'd expect in a converted Georgian mansion; many rooms are in wings matching the style of the original building. Guest rooms are modern and neutral in hue, with pampering touches in the large marble bathrooms. ⊠ *Sydney Rd., BA2 6JF,* ☏ *0870/400–8222,* FAX *01225/444006,* WEB *www.bathspahotel.com. 97 rooms, 5 suites. 2 restaurants, indoor pool, sauna, spa, tennis court, croquet, gym, baby-sitting, meeting rooms. AE, DC, MC, V.*

££–£££ 🏠 **Paradise House.** Don't be put off by the 10-minute uphill walk from the center of Bath—you'll be rewarded by a wonderful prospect of the city from the upper stories of this Georgian guest house. Cheerfully decorated in cool pastels, it has open fires in winter and a lush, secluded garden for the spring and summer. Rooms 3 and 5 have the best views. ⊠ *88 Holloway, BA2 4PX,* ☏ *01225/317723,* FAX *01225/482005,* WEB *www.paradise-house.co.uk. 11 rooms. AE, DC, MC, V. Closed last wk in Dec.*

££ 🏠 **Cranleigh.** Standing in a quiet location on the hill high above the city, Cranleigh has wonderful views over Bath from the back of the house. Rooms are richly decorated, and extensive breakfasts are served in the dining room, which looks out on the garden. Smoking is not permitted. ⊠ *159 Newbridge Hill, BA1 3PX,* ☏ *01225/310197,* FAX *01225/423143,* WEB *www.bath.org/hotel/cran.htm. 8 rooms. MC, V.*

Nightlife and the Arts

FESTIVALS
The **Bath International Music Festival** (⊠ Bath Festival Box Office, 2 Church St., Bath BA1 1NL, ☏ 01225/463362, WEB www.bathfesti-

vals.org.uk) is held for two weeks in May and June. Concerts (classical, jazz, and world music), dance performances, and exhibitions are staged in and around Bath, many in the Assembly Rooms and Abbey.

THEATER

The **Theatre Royal** (⊠ Box Office, Saw Close, Bath BA1 1ET, ☎ 01225/448844), a lovely Regency playhouse, has a year-round program that often includes pre- or post-London tours. You have to reserve for the best seats well in advance, but you can line up for same-day standby seats or standing room. Check the location of your seats—sight lines can be poor.

Shopping

Bath's excellent shopping district centers on Stall and Union streets (modern stores) and Milsom Street (traditional stores). Leading off these main streets are fascinating alleyways and passages lined with galleries and a wealth of antiques shops. **Bartlett Street Antique Centre** (⊠ Bartlett St.) has more than 160 showcases selling every kind of antique imaginable, including vintage clothing, linens, and furniture. The **Bath Antiques Market** (⊠ Paragon Antiques, 3 Bladud Buildings, The Paragon, ☎ 01225/463715), open Wednesday 6:30 AM–3 PM, is a wonderful place to browse; 50 dealers have stalls here, and there's also a restaurant. **Beaux Arts Ceramics** (⊠ 12–13 York St., ☎ 01225/464850) carries the work of prominent potters and holds eight solo exhibitions a year. **Margaret's Buildings** (⊠ Halfway between the Circus and Royal Crescent) is a lane with several secondhand and antiquarian bookshops.

Castle Combe

★ ⑩ *12 mi northeast of Bath, 5 mi northwest of Chippenham.*

This Wiltshire village had lived a sleepy existence until 1962, when it was voted the Prettiest Village in England—without any of its inhabitants knowing that it had even been a contender. The village's magic is that it is so toylike, so delightfully all-of-a-piece: you can see almost the whole town at one glance from any one position. It consists of little more than a brook, a pack bridge, a street—which is called the Street—of simple stone cottages, a market cross from the 13th century, and the Perpendicular-style church of St. Andrew. The grandest house in the village (actually, on its outskirts) is the Upper Manor House, built in the 15th century by Sir John Fastolf, chosen to be Dr. Dolittle's house in the 1967 Rex Harrison film, and now the Manor House Hotel.

Dining and Lodging

£££–££££ ✕🆃 **Manor House Hotel.** Outside the village, the manor house is a ba-
★ ronial swirl of solid chimney stacks, carvings, and columns, partly 14th-century, though as a manor it dates back to the Normans. Inside, a stone frieze depicts characters from Shakespeare's Falstaff plays, to commemorate the fact that Sir John Fastolf, thought to be the playwright's model for the character, was once lord of this manor. The bedrooms are comfortably furnished, with lavish bathrooms; some rooms are in mews cottages. There are log fires in the public rooms and antiques everywhere. The Bybrook restaurant serves imaginative contemporary cuisine—try the loin of lamb rolled in herbs with tarragon mash and garlic cream. Outside is a landscaped 23-acre park. ⊠ *Castle Combe SN14 7HR,* ☎ *01249/782206,* FAX *01249/782159,* WEB *www. exclusivehotels.co.uk. 45 rooms. Restaurant, pool, 18-hole golf course, tennis court, helipad. AE, DC, MC, V.*

Lacock

🔟 *3 mi south of Chippenham, 8 mi southeast of Castle Combe.*

This lovely Wiltshire village is the victim of its own charm, its unspoiled gabled and stone-tiled cottages drawing coach parties aplenty. Left to its own devices, however, Lacock slips back into its profound slumber, the mellow stone and brick buildings little changed in 500 years. There are a few antiques shops, the handsome wool church of St. Cyriac, a 14th-century tithe barn, and a scattering of pubs that serve bar meals in atmospheric surroundings.

At Lacock's center, the **Abbey** was founded in the 13th century and closed down during the dissolution of the monasteries in 1539, when its new owner, Sir William Sharington, demolished the church and converted the cloisters, sacristy, chapter house, and monastic quarters into a private dwelling. The last of his descendants, Mathilda Talbot, donated the property as well as Lacock itself to the National Trust in the 1940s. The most notable family member was William Henry Fox Talbot (1800–77), who developed the first photographic negative here, showing an oriel window. You can see this and other results of his experiments in the 1830s at the **Museum of Photography**, in a 16th-century barn at the Abbey gates. The Abbey's grounds are also worth a wander, with a Victorian woodland garden and an 18th-century summer house. ✉ *Just east of A350,* ☎ *01249/730227,* WEB *www.nationaltrust.org.uk.* 🎟 *Abbey, museum, and garden £6; Abbey and garden £4.80; garden and museum £3.80; museum only (Nov.–Mar.) £2.30.* 🕐 *Abbey Apr.–Oct., Wed.–Mon. 1–5:30. Museum and garden Apr.–Oct., daily 11–5:30; Nov.–Mar. (museum only), weekends 11–4.*

THE COTSWOLDS

The Thames rises among the limestone Cotswold Hills, and a more delightful cradle could not be imagined for that historic river. The Cotswolds are among the best-preserved rural districts of England, and their quiet but touching grays and ambers are truly unsurpassed. A great deal has been written about the area's pretty towns, which age has mellowed rather than withered, and perhaps, on closer inspection, there is little difference in the architecture of the individual villages from that of villages in other regions in England. Rather, it is in the character of their surroundings: the valleys are deep and rolling and cozy hamlets appear to drip in foliage from high church tower to garden gate. Beyond the village limits, you'll often find the "high wild hills and rough uneven ways" that Shakespeare wrote about.

In this region, beauty is not just skin deep: over the centuries, quarries of honey-color stone have yielded building blocks for many Cotswold houses and churches and have transformed little towns into realms of gold. Nowhere else in Britain does that superb combination of church tower and gabled manor house shine so brightly, nowhere else are the hedges so perfectly clipped, nor the churchyards so peaceful.

There is an elusive spirit about the Cotswolds, so make Bourton-on-the-Water, or Chipping Campden, or Stow-on-the-Wold your headquarters for a few days, and wander aimlessly for a while, going through this valley and along that byroad, all the time absorbing something of the Cotswold atmosphere. Then ask yourself what it is all about. Its secret seems shared by two things—sheep and stone. And if such a combination sounds strange, perhaps some further explanation is necessary. These were once the great sheep-rearing areas of England, and during the peak of prosperity in the Middle Ages, Cotswold wool was in demand the world over. This made the Cotswold merchants rich, but many gave back to the Cotswolds by restoring old churches (the famous "wool churches" of the region) or building rows of almshouses, of limestone now seasoned to a glorious golden-gray.

Begin with Cheltenham—a gateway to the Cotswolds, but slightly outside the boundaries—then move on to the beauty spots in and around Winchcombe; next are Stanway House, Sudeley Castle, and Snowshill Manor, the three most impressive houses of the region; the oversold village of Broadway, which has many rivals for beauty hereabouts; Chipping Campden—the Cotswold cognoscenti's favorite; Hidcote Manor, one of the most spectacular gardens in England; then circle back south, down through Moreton-in-Marsh, Stow-on-the-Wold, Upper and Lower Slaughter, Bourton-on-the-Water; and end with Bibury, Tetbury, and Owlpen. But this is definitely a region where it pays to wander off the beaten track to take a look at that village among the trees. Many sequestered nooks and villages snuggled deep into dells can, in fact, be rendered magically invisible by impenetrable coverings of ivy. Like four-leaf clovers, their discovery must come serendipitously.

Cheltenham

🟊 *50 mi north of Bath, 13 mi east of Gloucester, 50 mi south of Birmingham, 99 mi west of London.*

Although Cheltenham has managed to acquire a reputation as the snootiest place in England, its renown for architectural distinction is well deserved. It rivals Bath in its Georgian elegance, with wide, tree-lined streets and graceful villas, and, like Bath, the town owes part of its fame to mineral springs. By 1740 Cheltenham's first spa was built, and the town became in vogue with a visit from George III and Queen Charlotte in 1788, quickly becoming a capital consecrated to gaiety, idleness, and enjoyment: the "merriest sick resort on earth," as one scribe put it. "A polka, parson-worshipping place"—in the words of resident Lord Tennyson—Cheltenham gained its reputation for snobbishness when stiff-collared Raj majordomos returned from India to find that the town's springs—the only purely natural alkaline waters in England—were the most effective cure for their "tropical ailments."

If you visit in spring or summer—take either M4 and M5 north from Bath, or M5 south from Birmingham, turning east on A40 to reach Cheltenham—you'll see the town's handsome buildings enhanced by a profusion of flower gardens. The flowers cover even traffic circles, while the elegantly laid-out avenues, crescents, and terraces, with their characteristic row houses, balconies, and iron railings, make Cheltenham an outstanding example of the Regency style. Great Regency architectural set pieces—Lansdowne Terrace, Pittville Spa, Sherborne Walk, the Lower Assembly Rooms, among them—were built solely to adorn the town. The Rotunda building at the top of Montpellier Walk—now a bank—contains the spa's original "pump room," i.e., the room in which the mineral waters were on draft, built in 1826. More than 30 statues, like the caryatids on the Acropolis in Athens, adorn the storefronts of Montpellier Walk. Wander past Imperial Square, with its intricate ironwork balconies, past the ornate Neptune's Fountain, and along the elegant Promenade. Parts of the town may look like something out of a Gilbert and Sullivan stage set, but, today Cheltenham is the site of two of England's most progressive arts festivals—the Cheltenham Festival of Literature and the town's music festival—as well as an annual jazz fest.

The Cotswold Hills

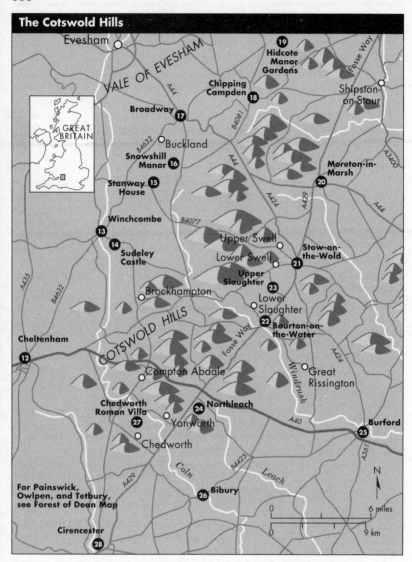

GREAT BRITAIN

Evesham

VALE OF EVESHAM

Hidcote Manor Gardens ⑲

Chipping Campden ⑱

Shipston-on-Stour

Broadway ⑰

Buckland

Snowshill Manor ⑯

Moreton-in-Marsh

Stanway House ⑮

⑳

Winchcombe

Upper Swell

Lower Swell

Stow-on-the-Wold ㉑

⑬

⑭

Sudeley Castle

Upper Slaughter ㉓

Brockhampton

Lower Slaughter

COTSWOLD HILLS

Bourton-on-the-Water ㉒

Cheltenham

⑫

Compton Abdale

Great Rissington

Fosse Way

Windrush

Chedworth Roman Villa ㉗

Northleach ㉔

Yanworth

Chedworth

Burford ㉕

For Painswick, Owlpen, and Tetbury, see Forest of Dean Map

Coln

Bibury ㉖

Leach

N

Cirencester ㉘

0 — 6 miles
0 — 9 km

The grandest of the spa buildings remaining in town, the **Pittville Pump Room** is set amid parkland, a 20-minute walk from the town center. The classic Regency structure was built in the late 1820s and still offers its musty mineral waters to be sampled by the strong of stomach. ⊠ *East Approach Dr., Pittville,* ☎ *01242/523852.* 🎟 *Free.* ☉ *May–Sept., Wed.–Mon. 10–4:30; Oct.–Apr., Wed.–Mon. 11–4.*

Dining and Lodging

££££–££££ ✕ **Le Champignon Sauvage.** The menu here is not long, but it's perfectly balanced, and the contemporary cooking is superb. Indulge your palate with the deceptively simple dishes such as roast lamb or braised beef, followed for dessert by mango with Thai-spiced cream, served with mulled red wine. There's a wide range of cheese as well. Fixed-price menus at lunch and dinner help keep the cost down. ⊠ *24 Suffolk Rd.,* ☎ *01242/573449. AE, DC, MC, V. Closed Sun., Mon., 2 wks in summer and 10 days in Dec.*

££–£££ ✕ **The Daffodil.** The heyday of 1930s elegance has been preserved in this former cinema. Admire the Art Deco trappings as you sip an aperitif in the Circle Bar, then sweep down the staircase to watch the chefs at work "on stage." The restaurant offers either brasserie cuisine or more traditional dishes such as local pheasant braised in apple and cider. A plate of bite-size samples relieves you of the task of making decisions among the various mouthwatering desserts. ✉ *18–20 Suffolk Parade,* ☎ *01242/700055. AE, DC, MC, V.*

£–££ ✕ **Montpellier Wine Bar.** An ideal place for a light snack or a fuller evening meal, this informal wine bar in Cheltenham's fashionable shopping district serves pies, quiches, and medallions of monkfish, at reasonable prices. Get in early for fast service. ✉ *Bayshill Lodge, Montpellier St.,* ☎ *01242/527774. AE, MC, V.*

££££ ✕🏨 **Queen's Hotel.** Overlooking Imperial Gardens from the center of The Promenade, this classic Regency building has welcomed visitors to Cheltenham since 1838. The hotel's decor is very British, and every bedroom is individually designed. There's a taste of France, however, in one of the hotel's two restaurants, Le Petit Blanc, an offshoot of renowned chef Raymond Blanc's Manoir aux Quat' Saisons in Great Milton. It's a great place to sample French provincial cooking. ✉ *The Promenade, GL50 1NN,* ☎ *0870/4008107; restaurant 01242/266800,* FAX *01242/224145,* WEB *www.forte-hotels.co. 79 rooms. 2 restaurants. AE, DC, MC, V.*

££ 🏨 **Lypiatt House.** This splendid Victorian house—only a short walk
★ from central Cheltenham—is an excellent B&B with attentive service from the friendly husband-and-wife owners. The bedrooms are individually decorated and have chic bathrooms. There's a small dining room and a conservatory bar. Young children are not accommodated. ✉ *Lypiatt Rd., GL50 2QW,* ☎ *01242/224994,* FAX *01242/224996,* WEB *www.lypiatt.co.uk. 10 rooms. Bar. AE, MC, V.*

££ 🏨 **Hotel Kandinsky.** A fashionably cool style that doesn't stint on the comfort factor makes a stay in this Georgian hotel a memorable experience at a sensible price. Colorful rugs, huge potted plants, and antiques in the clubby public rooms are offset by modern teak designer furniture in the bedrooms. A 1950s-style nightclub attached. ✉ *Bayshill Rd., GL50 3AS,* ☎ *01242/527788,* FAX *01242/226412,* WEB *www. hotelkandinsky.com. 48 rooms. Restaurant, bar, nightclub. AE, DC, MC, V.*

£–££ 🏨 **Georgian House.** Dating back to 1807, this is one of the earliest terraced houses in Cheltenham, and all its Georgian features are intact. Rooms are stylishly furnished with antiques, and the management is obliging. It's only a few minutes from the center of town. ✉ *77 Montpellier Terrace, GL50 1XA,* ☎ *01242/515577,* FAX *01242/545929. 3 rooms. MC, V.*

Nightlife and the Arts

For information on festivals, contact the **Festival Office** (✉ Town Hall, Imperial Sq., Cheltenham GL50 1QA, ☎ 01242/227979, WEB www.cheltenhamfestivals.co.uk). Cheltenham's famous annual **International Festival of Music,** during the first two weeks of July, highlights new compositions, often conducted by the composers, together with classical repertory pieces. The **International Jazz Festival,** held the last weekend of April, attracts noted jazz musicians. The town's **Festival of Literature** in October brings together world-renowned authors, actors, and critics.

Outdoor Activities and Sports

Important steeplechase races take place at **Cheltenham** racecourse (☎ 01242/513014); the National Hunt Festival in mid-March is crowned by the Gold Cup awards on the last day.

Shopping

A stroll along elegant Montpellier Walk and then along the flower-bedecked Promenade will bring you to a range of quality stores. Behind the Promenade is the Regent Arcade, a modern shopping area with a wide variety of stores, dominated by a bubble-blowing Wishing Fish Clock, designed by Kit Williams. A market is held every Sunday at the racecourse, there's another general market every Thursday morning off Lower High Street, and there's an indoor antiques market Monday–Saturday at 54 Suffolk Road.

Cavendish House (⊠ 32–48 The Promenade, ☎ 01242/521300) is a high-quality department store. **Hoopers** (⊠ 33 The Promenade, ☎ 01242/527505) sells select clothes, handbags, and leather goods. **H. W. Keil** (⊠ 129 The Promenade, ☎ 01242/522509) has 17th- and 18th-century antiques in a huge Regency house. **Martin** (⊠ 19 The Promenade, ☎ 01242/522821) carries a good stock of modern jewelry. **Scott Cooper** (⊠ 52 The Promenade, ☎ 01242/522580) is worth a visit for its antique jewelry, silver, and china.

Winchcombe

⑬ *7 mi northeast of Cheltenham.*

It's hard to believe that the sleepy village of Winchcombe was once the capital of the Anglo-Saxon kingdom of Mercia. There are some attractive half-timber and stone houses, a clutch of nice old inns serving food, and a typical Cotswold wool church, the Perpendicular-style St. Peter's, carved with an outlandish array of almost 40 gargoyles. If you're keen to exercise your lungs, you can walk a bracing 2 mi out of Winchcombe on the Cotswold Way to the hilltop site of **Belas Knap,** a neolithic long barrow, or submerged burial chamber. There's not much to see of the

★ site itself, but you'll be hiking next to and through the **Humblebee Wood**—one of the most enchanting natural domains in England, with terrific views stretching over to Sudeley Castle. If you have a car, be sure to take the scenic Humblebee Wood road down to the villages of Sevenhampton and Brockhampton.

A mile outside Winchcombe, at Greet, you can board a steam-hauled train of the **Gloucester Warwickshire Railway,** which chugs its way along a 6-mi stretch at the foot of the Cotswolds. ☎ *01242/621405.* ⊠ *£7 one-way.* ☉ *Mid-Mar.–Oct., weekends 11–5, daily during school holidays and some dates in Dec.*

Sudeley Castle

★ **⑭** *1 mi southeast of Winchcombe, 9 mi northeast of Cheltenham.*

One of the grand showpieces of the Cotswolds, Sudeley Castle was the home and burial place of Catherine Parr (1512–1548), Henry VIII's sixth and last wife (who outlived him by one year). Here, Catherine undertook, in her later years, the education of the ill-fated Lady Jane Grey and the future queen, Princess Elizabeth—Sudeley, for good reason, has been called a woman's castle. The term "castle," however, is misleading, for Sudeley appears more like a grand Tudor-era palace. Today its peaceful air belies its turbulent history. During the 17th century, Charles I took refuge here, causing Oliver Cromwell's army to besiege the castle, leaving it in ruins until the Dent-Brocklehurst family stepped in with a 19th-century renovation. The romantic grounds include the Queen's Garden, with its spectacular roses; a Tudor knot garden; a carp pond; and varied settings for outdoor Shakespeare performances, concerts, and other events in summer. ⊠ *Off the B4632, Winchcombe,* ☎ *01242/604357,* WEB *www.stratford.co.uk/sudeley.* ⊠

£6.20; gardens and exhibitions only, £4.70. ☉ Castle: Apr.–late-Oct.,
daily 11–5; gardens, grounds, plant center, and shop: early Mar.–late-
Oct., daily 10:30–5:30.

Lodging

££££ 🏠 **Sudeley Castle Cottages.** These stone houses are on the grounds of
Sudeley Castle. Some converted from estate buildings, others recently
built in sympathetic style, they ring the estate and range in size from
cottage to full-size detached house; the smallest can take two guests,
the largest five. Rooms are beautifully decorated, with a mixture of
period and locally crafted furniture in keeping with the theme of the
cottage. From May through September, accommodations are available
on a weekly basis only; in winter they can be booked for two-night
stays. ⊠ Sudeley Castle, Winchcombe GL54 5JD, ☎ 01242/602308,
FAX 01242/602959, marketing@sudeley.org.uk; or Blakes Country Cottages, ☎ 01282/445555. 14 cottage houses.

Stanway House

★ ⑮ 5 mi northeast of Sudeley Castle, 11 mi northeast of Cheltenham.

Dominating the small village of Stanway, the perfect Cotswold manor,
Stanway House, dates from the Jacobean era and is constructed in glowing limestone. Its triple-gabled gatehouse is a Cotswold landmark and
has been featured in many a TV series, such as The Buccaneers. The
house's Great Hall is noted for its towering windows. Divided by mullions and transoms into 60 panes, these windows are "so mellowed by
time"—to quote Lady Cynthia Asquith (a former chatelaine)—"that
whenever the sun shines through their amber and green glass, the effect is of a vast honeycomb." They illuminate a 22-ft shuffleboard table
from 1620 and an 18th-century bouncing exercise machine. The other
well-worn rooms are adorned with family portraits, tattered tapestries,
vintage armchairs, and Lord Neidpath himself, the current owner. On
the grounds is a cricket pavilion built by J. M. Barrie, author of Peter
Pan, who leased the house during summers. To get to Stanway, take
B4632 north of Winchcombe, turning right at B4077. ⊠ Stanway, ☎
01386/584469. 🎟 £3. ☉ Aug.–Sept., Tues., Thurs. 2–5 (other times
by appt. only for groups of at least 20).

Snowshill Manor

★ ✋ ⑯ 4 mi northeast of Sudeley Castle, 3 mi south of Broadway, 13 mi
northeast of Cheltenham.

Snowshill is one of the most sequestered and unspoiled of all Cotswold
villages, although its appearance as the home of Bridget's parents in
the film version of Bridget Jones's Diary may draw more admirers.
Snuggled beneath Oat Hill, with little room for any expansion, the
hamlet is centered around a historic burial ground, the 19th-century
St. Barnabas Church, and Snowshill Manor, a splendid 17th-century
house that is overflowing with the collections of Charles Paget Wade,
gathered between 1919 and 1956. Over the door of the house is his
family motto, Nequid pereat ("Let nothing perish"). The rooms here
are bursting with Tibetan scrolls, spinners' tools, ship models, Persian lamps, and bric-a-brac. The Green Room is devoted to 26 suits
of Japanese Samurai armor. Children love it. Outside, an imaginative
Cotswold terraced garden provides an exquisite frame for the house.
⊠ Snowshill, off the A44, ☎ 01386/852410, WEB www.ntrustsevern.
org.uk. 🎟 £6; grounds only, £3. ☉ Apr.–Oct., Wed.–Sun. noon–5,
also Mon. in July and Aug; grounds open 11–5:30 Apr.–Sept.; last admission 30 mins before closing.

Broadway

⑰ *3 mi north of Snowshill Manor, 17 mi northeast of Cheltenham.*

The Cotswold town to end all Cotswold towns, Broadway has become a mecca for day-trippers. William Morris first discovered the delights of this village, and J. M. Barrie, Vaughan Williams, and Edward Elgar soon followed. Today some people tend to avoid Broadway in summer, when it is clogged with cars and buses. Named for its handsome, wide main street, the village is home to the renowned Lygon Arms and has numerous antiques shops, tea parlors, and boutiques, which now that a highway bypass relieves the village of express traffic, can be visited in relative quiet. Step off onto Broadway's back roads and alleys and you'll find serenity, along with any number of honey-colored houses and pretty gardens.

The attractions of **Broadway Tower Country Park,** on the outskirts of town, include a tower, an 18th-century "folly" built by the sixth Earl of Coventry. From the top you can see more than 13 counties in a breathtaking vista. Nature trails, picnic grounds with barbecue grills, an adventure playground, and rare animals and birds are surrounded by peaceful countryside. ⊠ *Off A44,* ☎ *01386/852390.* 🎫 *Apr.–Oct. £4; Nov.–Mar. £3.* ☉ *Apr.–Oct., daily 10:30–5; Nov.–Mar. (tower only) weekends 11–3.*

Dining and Lodging

££££ ✕🏨 **Buckland Manor.** As an alternative to the razzmatazz of Broad-
★   way, try this exceptional hotel 2 mi away in Buckland—an idyllic little Cotswold hamlet—just off B4632. Parts of the building date from Jacobean times, and there are pleasant old pictures and fine antiques everywhere. The garden is lovely and peaceful. Fine contemporary fare is served in the baronial and expensive restaurant (jacket and tie required). ⊠ *Buckland WR12 7LY,* ☎ *01386/852626,* ℻ *01386/853557,* ⓦⓔⓑ *www.bucklandmanor.com. 13 rooms. Restaurant, pool, tennis court, croquet. AE, DC, MC, V.*

££££ ✕🏨 **Dormy House Hotel.** Guest rooms here overlook the Vale of Eve-
★   sham from high on the Cotswolds ridge, one of the region's most celebrated vistas. This luxurious country-house hotel has been converted from a 17th-century Cotswolds farmhouse. Bedrooms are individually furnished, some with four-poster beds. The restaurant, noted in the region, has a superlative wine list and serves fine contemporary fare such as lemon sole with salmon and chive mousse. ⊠ *Willersey Hill (2 mi north from Broadway), WR12 7LF,* ☎ *01386/852711,* ℻ *01386/ 858636,* ⓦⓔⓑ *www.dormyhouse.co.uk. 49 rooms. Restaurant, café, sauna, steam room, putting green, croquet, gym. AE, DC, MC, V.*

££££ ✕🏨 **Lygon Arms.** Here you'll find modern luxury combined with old-world charm—the Lygon has been in business since 1532 and is now part of the Savoy Hotels group. Multigabled, with mullioned windows, it has a facade from 1620; inside, there are antiques-bedecked parlors, baronial fireplaces, 18th-century paneling, and rooms that once sheltered Charles I and Oliver Cromwell. The Great Hall dining room specializes in creative adaptations of traditional dishes and even has a minstrel's gallery. If you're daunted by the period feel, there are also more modern and less expensive bedrooms. Although the Lygon Arms is on the main street, it has 3 acres of formal gardens to relax in, or you can just seek refuge in the spa. ⊠ *High St., WR12 7DU,* ☎ *01386/ 852255,* ℻ *01386/858611,* ⓦⓔⓑ *savoy-group.co.uk. 65 rooms. Restaurant, bar, brasserie, indoor pool, sauna, spa, tennis court, billiards, helipad. AE, DC, MC, V.*

Chipping Campden

18 *4 mi east of Broadway, 18 mi northeast of Cheltenham.*

Undoubtedly one of the most beautiful towns in the heart of England, Chipping Campden is the Cotswolds in a microcosm—it has St. James, the region's most impressive church, frozen-in-time streets, a silk mill once the center of the Guild of Handcrafts, and charming (and untouristy) shops. It also has one of the most seductive settings of the area, which will unfold before you as you travel on B4081 through sublimely lovely English countryside to happen upon the town tucked in a slight valley.

The soaring pinnacled tower of **St. James** (⊠ Church St.), a prime example of a Cotswold wool church (rebuilt in the 15th century), announces the town from a distance and is worth stepping inside for its lofty nave. It recalls the old saying, due to the vast numbers of houses of worship in the Cotswolds, "As sure as God's in Gloucestershire." Nearby, on Church Street, is an important row of almshouses dating from King James I's reign. The broad High Street follows a picturesque curve and is lined with attractive houses and shops. In the center, on Market Street, is the **Market Hall,** a gabled Jacobean structure built by Sir Baptiste Hycks in 1627 "for the sale of local produce."

The **Silk Mill** was taken over by the Guild of Handcrafts in 1902, when arts-and-crafts evangelist C. R. Ashbee (1863–1942) brought 150 acolytes here from London, including 50 guildsmen, to revive and practice such skills as cabinetmaking and bookbinding. The operation folded in 1920, but the building has been refurbished to house crafts workshops, including a silversmith, sculptor, and printmaker. ⊠ *Sheep St.* ☉ *Weekdays 9–5, Sat. 9–1.*

Dining and Lodging

££££ ✕⌂ **Charingworth Manor.** Views of the Cotswold countryside are limitless from this 14th-century manor-house hotel a short distance outside town. Each room is named for previous owners or local villages and is individually done in English floral fabrics, with antique and period furniture. Rooms in the old manor have the best views and original oak beams. As a guest, T. S. Eliot used to enjoy walking its 50 acres of grounds. The restaurant (fixed-price menu), with its low-beamed ceilings, is charming though on the expensive side; for hotel guests, dinner is included in the price. ⊠ *Charingworth GL55 6NS, 3 mi east of Chipping Campden,* ☎ *01386/593555,* FAX *01386/593353,* WEB *www.englishrosehotels.com. 23 rooms, 3 suites. Restaurant, indoor pool, sauna, steam room, tennis court, croquet, billiards. AE, DC, MC, V.*

£££ ⌂ **Noel Arms Hotel.** In the heart of Chipping Campden, the Noel Arms was built for foreign wool traders in the 14th century and is the oldest inn in town. It retains its period atmosphere with exposed beams and stonework, even though it has been enlarged. The individually decorated bedrooms—some dating back to the 14th century—offer every modern comfort. ⊠ *High St., GL55 6AT,* ☎ *01386/840317,* FAX *01386/841136,* WEB *www.cotswold-inns-hotels.co.uk. 26 rooms. Restaurant, bar. AE, DC, MC, V.*

Hidcote Manor Gardens

★ **19** *4 mi northeast of Chipping Campden, 9 mi south of Stratford-upon-Avon.*

Laid out around a Cotswold manor house, Hidcote Manor Gardens is arguably the most interesting and attractive large garden in Britain; it can also be terribly overcrowded at the height of the season. The garden was created in 1907 by a horticulturist from the United States, Major

Lawrence Johnstone. Johnstone was not just an imaginative gardener but a widely traveled plantsman as well, who brought back specimens from all over the world. The formal part of the garden is arranged in "rooms" without roofs, separated by hedges, often with fine topiary work and walls. The White Garden was probably the forerunner of the popular white gardens at Sissinghurst and Glyndebourne. ✉ *Hidcote Bartrim,* ☎ *01386/438333,* WEB *www.ntrustsevern.org.uk.* 🎟 *£5.70.* ⊙ *Apr.–Sept., Mon., Wed., Thurs., and weekends 10:30–6:30, also Tues. June–July; Oct., Mon., Wed., Thurs., and weekends 10:30–5:30; last admission 1 hr before closing.*

Hidcote Manor Gardens borders on the hamlet of **Hidcote Bartrim,** set in another storybook Cotswold dell. A handful of thatched stone houses, a duck pond, and a well make up the center of this fetching cul-de-sac; less than a mile away is the equally idyllic hamlet of Hidcote Boyce, which has a 17th-century manor house, Hidcote House.

Moreton-in-Marsh

㉑ *13 mi south of Hidcote Manor Gardens, 18 mi northeast of Cheltenham, 5 mi north of Stow-on-the-Wold.*

In Moreton-in-Marsh, the houses have been built not around a central square but along a street wide enough to accommodate a market (every Tuesday). The village has fine views across the hills. A town landmark is St. David's Church, which has a lovely tower of honey-gold ashlar. The town also possesses one of the last remaining curfew towers, dated 1633; curfew dates back to the time of the Norman Conquest, when a bell was rung to "cover-fire" for the night against any invaders. From Chipping Campden, take B4081 south, then A44 south and east to reach Moreton-in-Marsh.

Sezincote, outside Moreton-in-Marsh, off the Stow-to-Broadway road, is an exotic garden almost fit for a Scheherazade. Created in the early 19th century, the estate was the vision of Sir Charles Cockerell, who made a fortune in the East India Company. Asian aquatic gardens, a Hindu temple folly, and an Indian-style bridge have charmed visitors ever since the Prince Regent came to the estate in 1807 (and was promptly inspired to create that Xanadu of Brighton, the Royal Pavilion). ✉ *Off A424,* ☎ *01386/700444.* 🎟 *House and grounds £5; grounds £3.50.* ⊙ *House: May–July and Sept., Thurs.–Fri. 2:30–6; grounds Jan.–Nov., Thurs.–Fri. 2–6 or dusk.*

A reminder of the obscure civilizations of prehistoric Britain can be seen about 8 mi east of Moreton, where the **Rollright Stones** occupy a high position on the Wolds off A3400. This stone circle has none of the grandeur of Stonehenge and Avebury but is almost as important. Legend gives the stone groups, dating from before 1500 BC, the names of the King's Men and the Whispering Knights.

Stow-on-the-Wold

㉒ *5 mi south of Moreton-in-Marsh, 15 mi east of Cheltenham.*

At 800 ft, Stow is the highest, as well as the largest, town in the Cotswolds—"Stow-on-the-Wold, where the wind blows cold" is the age-old saying. Built around a wide square, Stow's imposing golden stone houses have been discreetly converted into a good number of quality antiques stores. The Square, as it is known, has a fascinating history. In the 18th century, Daniel Defoe wrote that more than 20,000 sheep could be sold here on a busy day; such was the press of livestock that sheep "runs," known as Tures, were used to control the sheep, and these narrow streets still run off the main square. Also look for St. Edward's Church and the Kings Arms Old Posting House, its wide entrance still seeming to wait for the stagecoaches that once stopped here on their way to Cheltenham. As well as being a lure for the antiques hunter, Stow is a convenient base: eight main Cotswolds roads intersect here but all—happily—bypass the town center.

Dining and Lodging

£–££   ✗ **Queen's Head.** An excellent stopping-off spot for a pub lunch, the Queen's Head has a courtyard out back, perfect for a summer afternoon. The bench in front, under a climbing rose, makes a relaxing spot for imbibing outdoor refreshment. ⊠ *The Square,* ☎ *01451/830563. MC, V. No dinner Sun.*

£££   🏨 **Fosse Manor.** This lovely manor-house hotel, just out of town (1 mi south on A429), has a reputation for solid comfort and service. Golf and riding are available nearby. ⊠ *Fosse Way, GL54 1JX,* ☎ *01451/ 830354,* FAX *01451/832486,* WEB *www.bestwestern.co.uk. 21 rooms. Restaurant, bar, gym. AE, DC, MC, V.*

££   🏨 **Stow Lodge Hotel.** Set well back from the main square in its own quiet gardens, the lodge is a typical Cotswold manor house; its large, open fireplaces provide added warmth in winter. The hotel is no-smoking. ⊠ *The Square, GL54 1AB,* ☎ *01451/830485,* FAX *01451/831671,* WEB *www.stowlodge.com. 21 rooms. Restaurant, bar. DC, MC, V. Closed 5 wks Jan.–Feb.*

Shopping

Stow-on-the-Wold is the leading center for antiques stores in the Cotswolds, with more than 30 dealers centered around The Square, Sheep Street, and Church Street. The elegant premises of **Country Life Antiques** (⊠ The Square, ☎ 01451/831564) glow with the copper plate and brassware collections of proprietor David Rosa. A visit to **Huntington Antiques** (⊠ The Old Forge, Church St., ☎ 01451/830842) is like a step back into the 16th and 17th centuries, with a stock replete with refectory tables, carved wooded reliefs, and Renaissance furniture in a period setting. **Roger Lamb Antiques** (⊠ The Square, ☎ 01451/831371) specializes in objets d'art and small pieces of furniture from the Georgian and Regency periods, with Regency "faux bamboo," tea caddies, and antique needlework the particular fortes. **Woolcomber House** (⊠ Sheep St., ☎ 01451/830662) has fine old English furniture, portrait and landscape paintings, and garden statuary and ornaments.

Bourton-on-the-Water

22 *12 mi northeast of Cheltenham, 4 mi southwest of Stow-on-the-Wold.*

Bourton-on-the-Water, off A429 on the eastern edge of the Cotswold Hills, is deservedly famous as a classic Cotswold village. The little River Windrush runs through Bourton, crossed by low stone bridges. This village makes a good touring base, but in summer, as in Broadway and Chipping Campden, it's overcrowded with tourists. A stroll through Bourton takes you past Cotswold cottages, many now converted to little stores and coffee shops.

☻ An old mill, now the **Cotswold Motor Museum and Toy Collection,** holds more than 30 vintage motor vehicles and a collection of old advertising signs (supposedly the largest in Europe), as well as two caravans (trailers) from the 1920s, ancient bicycles, and a trove of children's toys. ⊠ *Sherborne St.,* ☎ *01451/821255.* 🎟 *£2.25.* ☉ *Mar.–Oct., daily 10–6.*

☻ The **Model Railway Exhibition** displays more than 40 British and Continental trains running on 400 square ft of scenic layout. There are plenty of trains, models, and toys to buy in the shop. ⊠ *Box Bush, High St.,*

☎ *01451/820686.* ✉ *£1.75.* ☉ *Apr.–Sept., daily 11–5:30; Oct.–Mar., weekends only, 11–5.*

An outdoor working replica of Bourton village, the **Model Village** was built in 1937 to a scale of one-ninth. ✉ *Old New Inn,* ☎ *01451/820467.* ✉ *£2.50.* ☉ *Apr.–Oct., daily 9–5:45; Nov.–Mar., daily 10–3:45.*

Lodging

££   🏠 **Coombe House.** An attractive garden fronts this modern Cotswold stone guest house a few steps from the center of the village. Rooms are immaculately kept, and the first floor has a balcony where you can enjoy a drink when the weather permits. This is a no-smoking establishment, and breakfasts are as organic as possible. ✉ *Rissington Rd., GL54 2DT,* ☎ *01451/821966,* FAX *01451/810477,* WEB *www.coombe-housecotswolds.co.uk. 6 rooms. DC, MC, V. Closed Nov.–Mar.*

Shopping

The **Cotswold Perfumery** carries a wide range of perfumes, which are manufactured here. While deciding what to buy, visit the Exhibition of Perfumery and the Perfumed Garden. Perfume bottles and jewelry are also on sale. ✉ *Victoria St.,* ☎ *01451/820698.* ✉ *Exhibition £1.75.* ☉ *Mon.–Sat. 9:30–5, Sun. 10:30–5.*

Lower and Upper Slaughter

★ ㉓   *2 mi north of Bourton-on-the-Water, 15 mi east of Cheltenham.*

For a quieter, more typical Cotswolds atmosphere, go to villages with the evocative names Lower Slaughter and Upper Slaughter (the names have nothing to do with mass murder, but come from the Saxon word *sloh,* which means "a marshy place"). Lower Slaughter is one of the "water villages," with Slaughter Brook running down the center road of the town. Little stone footbridges ford the brook, while the town's resident gaggle of geese can often be seen paddling their merry way through the sparkling water. Connecting the two Slaughters is Warden's Way, a mile-long pathway, beginning in Upper Slaughter at the town center parking lot. Along the way, you'll pass neat stone houses, the greenest of meadows, the most immemorial of trees, and a noted mill. Warden's Way continues south to Bourton-on-the-Water. Lower and Upper Swell are two other quiet towns to explore in the area.

Dining and Lodging

££££ ✕🏠 **Lords of the Manor Hotel.** A characteristic 17th-century Cotswolds manor house, "the Lords" is set among rolling fields threaded by a fishing stream. It offers comfort and a warm welcome in a quintessential Cotswolds village. Refurbishment has created additional bedrooms in a converted granary and barn, now more modern than those in the main house. Country-house chintz and antiques set the style throughout, including the acclaimed restaurant, which features a creative British-French menu. ✉ *Upper Slaughter GL54 2JD,* ☎ *01451/820243,* FAX *01451/820696,* WEB *www.lordsofthemanor.com. 27 rooms. Restaurant, fishing. AE, DC, MC, V.*

££££ ✕🏠 **Washbourne Court.** This fine 17th-century building stands amid 4 acres of grounds beside the River Wye. The interior has flagstone floors, beams, and open fires. The bedrooms in the main building have a deliberately country feel to them, while rooms in the converted barn and cottages are more modern. The food in the restaurant (fixed-price menu) is traditional English. ✉ *Lower Slaughter GL54 2HS,* ☎ *01451/822143,* FAX *01451/821045,* WEB *www.washbournecourt.co.uk. 27 rooms, 4 suites. Restaurant, tennis court. AE, DC, MC, V.*

Northleach

㉔ *7 mi southwest of Lower and Upper Slaughter, 14 mi southeast of Cheltenham.*

By the 13th century, Northleach was one of the richest Cotswold towns, thanks to the wool trade. Proof remains in the form of the magnificent church of St. Peter and St. Paul, dating from the 15th century. It is one of the Cotswold's most notable wool churches and within is a collection of memorial brasses, all bearing the likenesses of leading medieval woolmen.

Keith Harding's World of Mechanical Music displays a diverting collection of pianolas, music boxes, and other mechanical instruments from times past, which you can hear played. ⊠ *The Oak House, High St.,* ☎ *01451/860181.* ⌂ *£5.* ☉ *Daily 10–6, last tour at 5.*

In a renovated 18th-century prison, the **Cotswold Heritage Centre** comprises the Lloyd-Baker collection of agricultural history. Items include antique wagons and tools, and there is an exhibition of the area's social history. ⊠ *Fosse Way,* ☎ *01451/860715.* ⌂ *£2.50.* ☉ *Apr.–Oct., Mon.–Sat. 10–5, Sun. 2–5.*

Burford

㉕ *9 mi east of Northleach, 18 mi north of Swindon, 18 mi west of Oxford.*

Burford's broad main street leads steeply down to a narrow bridge across the River Windrush. The village has many historic inns, as it was a stagecoach stop for centuries. The **Golden Pheasant Hotel** (⊠ High St., ☎ 01993/823223) is the perfect spot for afternoon tea in the lounge while relaxing in a deep, velvet armchair; in winter, there's a lovely log fire.

Dining and Lodging

££££–££££   ✕🏠 **Bay Tree.** The atmospheric Bay Tree, set away from Burford's bustle, is in a 16th-century stone house, visited in its prime by both Elizabeth I and James I. Try for a room in the main house. The restaurant overlooks the rose and herb garden and serves mainly English dishes, stressing healthful eating. ⊠ *Sheep St., OX18 4LW,* ☎ *01993/822791,* ‹FAX› *01993/823008,* ‹WEB› *www.cotswold-inns-hotels.co.uk. 21 rooms. Restaurant. AE, DC, MC, V.*

Bibury

㉖ *10 mi southwest of Burford, 6 mi northeast of Cirencester, 15 mi north of Swindon.*

The tiny town of Bibury, on the B4425, occupies an idyllic setting beside the little River Coln; it was famed Arts and Crafts artist William Morris's choice for Britain's most beautiful village. Fine old cottages, a river meadow, the church of St. Mary's, and **Arlington Row**—a picturesque stone group of 17th-century weavers' cottages—are some of the delights here. On a site recorded in the Domesday Book stands **Arlington Mill,** a huge 17th-century working corn mill that contains examples of agricultural implements and machinery from the Victorian era, as well as country exhibits. ☎ *01285/740368.* ⌂ *£2.* ☉ *Apr.–Oct., daily 10–6; Nov.–Mar., daily 10–5:30.*

Chedworth Roman Villa

★ **㉗** *6 mi northwest of Bibury, 9 mi north of Cirencester, 10 mi southeast of Cheltenham.*

In a wooded valley on the eastern fringe of the Cotswolds, Chedworth Roman Villa is one of the best-preserved Roman villas in England. Thirty-two rooms, including two complete bath suites, have been identified. The visitor center and museum give a picture of Roman life in Britain. From Bibury, go across A429 to Yanworth and Chedworth, where you will pick up the signs. The villa is also signposted from A40. ⊠ *Yanworth,* ☎ *01242/890256,* WEB *www.ntrustsevern.org.uk.* ☜ *£3.70.* ☉ *Apr.–Oct., Tues.–Sun. and national holidays 10–5:30; Mar. and Oct.–mid-Nov., Tues.–Sun. 10–4.*

Cirencester

㉘ *9 mi south of Chedworth, 14 mi southeast of Cheltenham.*

Cirencester has been a major hub of the Cotswolds since Roman times, when it was called Corinium and lay at the intersection of the Fosse Way and the Ermin Way (today A429 and A417). Today this lovely old market town preserves a fine array of mellow stone buildings—take a stroll down Dollar Street to see the bowfront stores—and the magnificent Gothic parish church, St. John the Baptist. The **Corinium Museum** has an outstanding collection of Roman artifacts, including mosaic pavements, as well as full-scale reconstructions of local Roman interiors. ⊠ *Park St.,* ☎ *01285/655611.* ☜ *£2.50.* ☉ *Mon.–Sat. 10–5, Sun. 2–5.*

Barnsley House Gardens is home to Rosemary Verey, one of the world's foremost gardeners. She and her family live here in a Cotswold stone mansion, surrounded by her exquisite gardens, her world-famous potager, a neo-Gothic folly, and a garden shop where you can pick up one of her 18 books. It's best in early summer when the laburnum walk and herbaceous borders are in full bloom. ⊠ *The Close, Barnsley GL7 5EE, 4 mi north of Cirencester on the B4425,* ☎ *01285/740561,* WEB *www.barnsleyhouse.com.* ☜ *£3.75; personal tour by Rosemary Verey £100, other guides (including her son Charles) £50.* ☉ *Feb.–Dec., Mon. and Wed.– Sat. 10–5:30.*

Shopping

Every Monday and Friday Cirencester's central **Market Place** is packed with stalls selling a motley range of goods, mainly household items but some local produce and craft work, too. On Market Place, the **Corn Hall** is the venue for a Friday antiques market, and a crafts market on Saturday (unless it's the fifth Saturday in the month).

Painswick

㉙ *16 mi northwest of Cirencester, 8 mi southwest of Cheltenham, 5 mi south of Gloucester.*

This old Cotswold wool town has become a chocolate-box picture of quaintness, attracting plenty of day-trippers and coach parties. But come during the week and you can discover the genuine charm of the place in relative tranquility. The huddled gray stone houses and inns date from as early as the 14th century and include a notable group from the Georgian era. The churchyard is renowned for its 99 yew trees (legend has it that the devil prevents the 100th from growing) planted in 1792. Painswick's annual "Clypping Ceremony," occurring on the first Sunday after September 19, has nothing to do with topiary—the name derives from the Anglo-Saxon word, "clyppan" meaning "encircle." Children with garlands make a ring round the church, while traditional hymns are sung. Another good time to be here would be for the town's Victorian Market Day in early July: contact Cheltenham's tourist office for precise dates.

AND THE MOST BEAUTIFUL PLACE IN THE COTSWOLDS IS . . .

THERE ARE SOME magical spots that capture—like the phenomenon of experiencing the ocean in a single drop of water—the essence of an entire world. Owlpen's drop of water transmutes all there is to know about rural England into one enchanting package. Like a British version of Brigadoon, it lies hidden away, known only to a select few. "Owlpen in Gloucestershire—Ah, what a dream is there!" rhapsodized Vita Sackville-West in 1941. Later, Prince Charles, who ought to know—his Highgrove manor is just a few miles away—called it "the epitome of the English village." The secret was out.

This fairy-tale Cotswold hamlet centers around a picturesque church, a Tudor manor house, and cottages, all set against an equally picturesque mountainside. The seignorial bearing of the Tudor-era manor house is softened by a graceful grouping of pearl-gray stone cottages, tithe barns, garden buildings, and grist mills. What makes the village (population: 35) the Cotswolds' Shangri-la is that it has remained uniquely unspoiled by the modern world, and for this its guardian mountain must be thanked. Owlpen not only lies deep in archetypal English countryside but deep in history as well; it was first settled in Saxon days as Olla's Pen (meaning valley). The triple-gabled stone manor house (called Owlpen Manor) was built between 1450 and 1720, its south elevation asymmetrical, yet "illogically satisfactory" in its appeal, according to the noted architectural historian James Lees-Milne. The house's medieval embrasures and 17th-century gables were restored decades ago by local Arts and Crafts–period artisans, who also created some of the furnishings found within. Inside are oak chests fashioned by William Morris, family portraits, Georgian doorcases, painted cloths from the Tudor and Stuart eras, and Queen Margaret's Room, said to be haunted by the spirit of Queen Margaret of Anjou, wife of Henry VI, who visited here during the War of the Roses. The garden is hardly changed from the days of Queen Anne; its great yew "ballroom" was the everlasting envy of gardening greats, such as the renowned Gertrude Jekyll. Today, the house and garden are open to the public from April through September, daily except Monday (unless it's a national-holiday Monday), 2–5. The restaurant, the Cyder Press, is open from noon. Admission charges are £4.50 for the house and grounds, or £2.50 for the grounds only.

But—imagine—all this can be your very own home-away-from-home. Several of Owlpen's cottages have been converted into luxurious guest accommodations, including a studio flat in the Tithe Barn; Summerfield Cottage, overlooking a murmuring brook; a gorgeous Cotswold-stone farmhouse nestled deep in the woods; and a dollhouse-size Stuart-era garden building (prices start from £80 for a weekend break per person, while a weekly rent in a larger accommodation ranges from £215 to £780 for a double room). Nicholas Mander—descendant of Sir Geoffrey and Lady Mander, the noted Pre-Raphaelite art patrons—and his family oversee this tiny kingdom. A storybook village, a sequestered forest—with a story or two to tell—and meadows full of getaway space and privacy: these three elements come together unforgettably at Owlpen to form the ultimate Cotswold hamlet. Singularly romantic, this could well rank as the loveliest place in England. To get to Owlpen from Painswick, head south on A415 to Stroud, then head west on A419. Turn south on B4066 to Uley and the Owlpen Manor signpost. Owlpen Manor is near Dursley, GL11 5BZ (☎ 01453/860261, FAX 01453/860819, sales@owlpen.com).

The **Painswick Rococo Garden** is a unique survivor from the brief but flamboyant Rococo period of English garden design (1720–1760). After 50 years in its original form, the garden became overgrown with woodland, and its central section became a vegetable plot. Then, beginning in 1984, after the rediscovery of a 1748 painting of the garden by Thomas Robins, the garden was restored. Now you can stroll and view the garden's original architectural wonders. There is also a restaurant and a gift shop. ✉ *B4073, ½ mi north of town,* ☎ *01452/ 813204.* 🎫 *£3.30.* ⊙ *Mid-Jan.–Nov., Wed.–Sun. 11–5 (daily July–Aug.).*

From Painswick, you can head north to the historic city of Gloucester or south to Tetbury. South of Painswick, don't miss the beauty spot of
★ ㉚ **Owlpen** —an off-the-beaten-track hamlet that is a fitting Cotswold coda.

Dining and Lodging

£££ ✕🏨 **Cardynham House.** The Cotswolds are really about the art of liv-
★ ing, and at this 16th-century former wool merchant's house this is literally the case. The stylish retreat, which retains its beamed ceilings, Jacobean staircase, and Elizabethan fireplace, has four-poster beds in many rooms and themed rooms such as Medieval Garden, Dovecote, or Arabian Nights. Downstairs, in the March Hare dining room, a grand English breakfast is served to guests; at night, the kitchen creates delicious Thai food (fixed-price menu). ✉ *The Cross, Painswick GL6 6XX,* ☎ *01452/814006; 01452/813452 restaurant,* FAX *01452/812321,* WEB *www.cardynham.co.uk. 9 rooms. Restaurant, lounge. MC, V.*

Tetbury

㉛ *12 mi south of Painswick, 6 mi southeast of Owlpen, 8 mi southwest of Cirencester.*

With Prince Charles and Princess Anne both nearby neighbors, Tetbury claims right royal connections. Indeed, the soaring spire of the church that presides over this charming small Elizabethan market town is within the sight of the Prince of Wales from his home at Highgrove House. At the center of the village, Market Square has the eye-catching white-painted stone **Market House,** dating from 1655 and built up on rows of Tuscan pillars. The antiques market is held here on Wednesday. The **Church of St. Mary** is in 18th-century Gothic style and has a spacious galleried interior with pews.

Tall gate piers and spreading trees frame the family-owned **Chavenage,** a gray Cotswold stone Elizabethan manor house. You can see the room, full of fine tapestries, where Cromwell lodged during the Civil War, and a fine main hall with minstrels' gallery. ✉ *2 mi northwest of Tetbury between B4104 and A4135,* ☎ *01666/502329.* 🎫 *£4.* ⊙ *May–Sept., Thurs., Sun., and national holidays 2–5.*

The 600-acre **Westonbirt Arboretum** is home to one of the most extensive collections of trees and shrubs in Europe. The best times to come for color are in late spring when the rhododendrons are blooming and in the fall when the maples come into their own. ✉ *3 mi southwest of Tetbury off A433,* ☎ *01666/880220.* 🎫 *£4.50.* ⊙ *Daily 10–8 or dusk.*

GLOUCESTER, BERKELEY, AND THE FOREST OF DEAN

West of the Cotswolds a rather urbanized axis connects Gloucester with Cheltenham. Despite their proximity, on either side of the M5 motorway, the towns have a very different feel; the down-to-earth Gloucester, built around docks connected to the River Severn, contrasts with the gentrified spa town of Cheltenham. North of Gloucester lies the riverside

The Forest of Dean

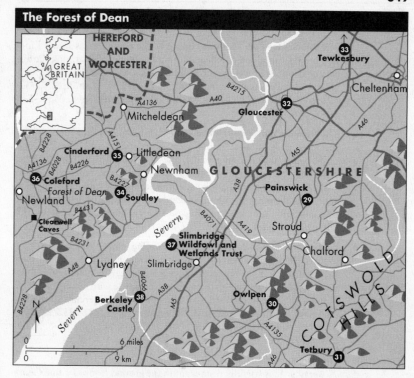

GREAT BRITAIN

HEREFORD AND WORCESTER

Tewkesbury ③③

Cheltenham

B4215

A40

A4136

Mitcheldean

Gloucester ③②

A46

GLOUCESTERSHIRE

M5

Cinderford ③⑤ Littledean

Newnham

A38

Painswick

②⑨

③⑥ Coleford

Forest of Dean ③④ Soudley

Newland

Stroud

Clearwell Caves

Severn

Slimbridge Wildfowl and Wetlands Trust ③⑦

Chalford

COTSWOLD HILLS

Lydney

Slimbridge

A38

M5

Owlpen ③⓪

Berkeley Castle ③⑧

Severn

A4135

Tetbury ③①

A46

0 — 6 miles
0 — 9 km

N

town of Tewkesbury with its imposing abbey, while to the south, easily accessible from M5, stands stern, battlemented Berkeley Castle. Southwest of Gloucester, the low-lying Forest of Dean, once a private hunting ground of kings, is now a recreation area for the general public, with some of the most extensive and beautiful woodlands in the country.

Gloucester

③② *13 mi southwest of Cheltenham, 56 mi south of Birmingham, 105 mi west of London.*

Although much of the ancient heritage of this county seat has been lost to nondescript modern stores and offices, Gloucester still has a number of worthwhile sites, most notably its cathedral. The historic **Gloucester Docks**, a short walk from the cathedral along the canal, still function but now cater mainly to pleasure craft. The vast Victorian warehouses have been restored, and new shops and cafés added, bringing the area back to life. One warehouse is now the Antique Centre, and others hold good museums.

★ The magnificent **Gloucester Cathedral,** originally a Norman abbey church, was consecrated in 1100, and its exterior soars in elegant lines. The interior has largely been spared the sterilizing attentions of modern architects. Reflecting a mishmash of periods, the cathedral mirrors perfectly the slow growth of ecclesiastical taste and the development of the Perpendicular style. The interior is almost completely Norman, with the massive pillars of the nave left untouched since their completion. The fan-vaulted roof of the cloisters is the finest in Europe, and the cloisters enclose a peaceful garden. A permanent exhibition of the history of the cathedral is in the Whispering Gallery, and tours are available April–October. ⌧ *Westgate St.,* ☎ *01452/528095,* WEB *www.gloucestercathedral.uk.com.* ✉ *Requested donation £3; ad-*

mission £1 to *Whispering Gallery.* ⊘ *Daily 8–6, except during services and special events.*

The **Gloucester Folk Museum,** opposite the cathedral, is housed in a row of fine Tudor and Jacobean half-timber houses. Illustrating the history of Gloucester and the surrounding areas, the museum includes exhibits on local crafts and domestic life. ⊠ *99–103 Westgate St.,* ☎ *01452/526467.* 🔄 *£2.* ⊘ *Oct.–June, Mon.–Sat. 10–5; July–Sept., Mon.–Sat. 10–5, Sun. 10–4.*

The **National Waterways Museum** holds examples of canal houseboats, including gaily painted "canal ware"—ornaments and utensils found on barges. Exhibits interpret the role of canals in the 18th and 19th centuries, and you can try your hand at steering a narrow boat at one of the many interactive displays. Tours around the Gloucester Docks, starting at the museum, are conducted every Sunday in August at 2:30. ⊠ *Llanthony Warehouse, Gloucester Docks,* ☎ *01452/318054,* WEB *www.nwm.org.uk.* 🔄 *£4.95.* ⊘ *Daily 10–5.*

At the **Museum of Advertising and Packaging,** you can view the Robert Opie Collection, a reflection of British consumer history over the past hundred years. It's an entertaining, higgledy-piggledy collection, showing such oddities as the "Nasti" toilet roll complete with picture of Hitler. Sipping your tea in the café, you can view old commercials shown on television. ⊠ *Albert Warehouse, Gloucester Docks,* ☎ *01452/302309,* WEB *www.themuseum.co.uk.* 🔄 *£3.50.* ⊘ *Mar.–Oct., daily 10–6; Nov.–Feb., Tues.–Sun. 10–5.*

Dining and Lodging

£–££   ✕ **Berry's.** This friendly restaurant in the ground floor of a fine Georgian house is an enjoyable spot for lunch. It offers commendable home cooking using local produce, with such dishes as pork steaks with Stilton and port wine sauce. ⊠ *117–119 Southgate St., Near the Gloucester Docks,* ☎ *01452/520894. DC, MC, V. Closed Mon. No dinner Sun.*

£   ✕ **The New Inn.** You'll find this rambling coaching inn a few steps down from the Cross—the historic heart of the old city where Northgate, Westgate, Southgate, and Eastgate streets meet. The place is steeped in atmosphere, not least its galleried courtyard, overgrown with creepers. Hearty meals are served throughout the day, either from the carvery or grills menu. ⊠ *16 Northgate St.,* ☎ *01452/522177. MC, V.*

££   🏨 **Hatherly Manor.** Standing on 37 acres of grounds 2 mi north of Gloucester, this renovated 17th-century house is fairly quiet unless a conference is going on—which happens frequently. There's a four-poster honeymoon suite. ⊠ *Down Hatherly La., GL2 9QA,* ☎ *01452/730217,* FAX *01452/731032,* WEB *www.hotel-selection.co.uk. 50 rooms. Restaurant, gym, croquet, helipad. AE, DC, MC, V.*

Outdoor Activities and Sports

From the pier outside the National Waterways Museum, you can take a brief tour of the Gloucester Docks, lasting 45 minutes, or longer all-day cruises, heading north as far as Tewkesbury or south to the Severn Estuary at Sharpness. Tours take place between Easter and October: contact the **National Waterways Museum** (☎ 01452/318054) for dates and prices.

Shopping

The locals say it's best to look in Cheltenham and buy in Gloucester, where prices are lower. The **Antique Centre** (☎ 01452/529716) offers some good buys, in a five-floor Victorian warehouse at Gloucester Docks. The **Beatrix Potter Gift Shop** (⊠ College Ct., ☎ 01452/422856), next to the Cathedral Gate, is the house of the tailor in Potter's story *The Tailor of Gloucester.* It also has a small museum.

Tewkesbury

③ *12 mi northeast of Gloucester.*

Tewkesbury is an ancient town of black-and-white half-timber buildings, as well as some fine Georgian ones, on the River Avon. From here, you can take a cruise up the river in the *Avon Belle*. The stonework in the Norman **Tewkesbury Abbey** has much in common with that of Gloucester Cathedral, but this church was built in the Romanesque (12th-century) and Decorated Gothic (14th-century) styles. Its exterior makes an impressive sight, with the largest Norman tower in the world and the impressive 65-ft-high arch of the west front. The beautifully kept interior is graced with 14 stout Norman pillars and often has massive flower displays along the nave. ⊠ *Church St.,* ☎ *01684/850959.* 🖃 *Requested donation £2.* ☉ *Daily 7:30–5:30.*

Lodging

£££–££££ 🏨 **Royal Hop Pole.** One of the most famous old English inns, the half-timber Hop Pole is mentioned in Charles Dickens's *Pickwick Papers*. The rooms at the rear have wood beams and views of the pretty gardens running down to the river, where there is private mooring for boats. ⊠ *Church St., GL20 5RT,* ☎ *01684/293236,* 📠 *01684/296680,* 🌐 *www.regalhotels.co.uk. 29 rooms. Restaurant, bar, lounge. AE, DC, MC, V.*

£££ 🏨 **Tewkesbury Park Hotel, Golf and Country Club.** Just outside town (1¼ mi south on A38), this former Victorian mansion set on 176 acres is the ideal stopover point for the athletically inclined. There's almost every sports facility, plus the wonderful countryside. The hotel also caters to a flourishing conference trade. ⊠ *Lincoln Green La., GL20 7DN,* ☎ *01684/295405,* 📠 *01684/292386,* 🌐 *www.corushotels.co.uk. 78 rooms. Restaurant, coffee shop, indoor pool, sauna, golf privileges, tennis court, gym, squash. AE, DC, MC, V.*

Soudley

③ *27 mi southwest of Tewkesbury, 15 mi west of Gloucester.*

★ The ancient **Forest of Dean** (🌐 www.fweb.org.uk/dean) covers much of the valley between the Rivers Severn and Wye. Although the primordial forest has long since been cut down and replanted, the landscape here remains one of strange beauty, hiding in its folds and under its hills deposits of iron, silver, and coal that have been mined for thousands of years.

Of the original royal forest established in 1016 by King Canute, 27,000 acres are preserved by the Forestry Commission. It's still an important source of timber, but parking lots and picnic grounds have been created and eight nature trails marked. Soudley has a museum that provides a useful introduction to the forest. For a driving tour of the forest, head to Littledean, where SCENIC DRIVE signs direct you through the best of the forest. To get to Littledean from Soudley, backtrack north on B4227, and turn east on A4151.

The **Dean Heritage Centre,** based in a restored mill building in a wooded valley on the forest's eastern edge, tells the history of the forest, with reconstructions of a mine and a miner's cottage, a waterwheel, and a "beam engine" (a primitive steam engine used to pump water from flooded coal mines). Within the grounds is a tiny farm, home to a resident pig as well as natural-history exhibitions. Craftspeople work in the outbuildings. ⊠ *Soudley, on B4227, near Cinderford,* ☎ *01594/822170,* 🌐 *www.fweb.org.uk/dean.* 🖃 *£3.50.* ☉ *Oct.–Mar., daily 11–4; Apr.–Sept., daily 10–6.*

Cinderford

㉟ *1 mi west of Littledean, 14 mi southwest of Gloucester.*

In Cinderford, a hiking trail links sculptures, commissioned by the Forestry Commission, around **Speech House,** the medieval verderer's court in the forest's center, and now a restaurant and inn. The verderer was responsible for the enforcement of the forest laws. It was usually a capital offense to kill game or cut wood without authorization.

Dining and Lodging

££ ✕🏨 **Speech House.** Dating from 1676, this former royal hunting lodge retains its satisfyingly creaky floors and low-beamed ceilings. Two of the rooms have 7-ft-square four-poster beds. The wood-paneled Verderer's Court still functions four times a year, but fortunately miscreants no longer find themselves hanging from the gibbet that used to stand outside. For the rest of the year, the courtroom functions as a restaurant (fixed-price menu), which serves such country platters as guinea-fowl and pheasant. While the postal address for Speech House is the town of Coleford, it is located outside the village of Cinderford. ✉ *Coleford GL16 7EL,* ☎ *01594/822607,* FAX *01594/823658,* WEB *www.thespeechhouse.co.uk. 32 rooms. Restaurant, café, spa, golf privileges. AE, DC, MC, V.*

Coleford

㊱ *4 mi west of Cinderford, 10 mi south of Ross-on-Wye.*

The **tourist information center** (☎ 01594/812388) at Coleford (drive west from Cinderford on A4151, and then west again on B4226 and B4028) has details of picnic grounds, nature and sculpture trails, and tours of the forest. The area is a maze of weathered and moss-covered rocks, huge ferns, and ancient yew trees—a shady haven on a summer's day.

A visit to the workings in the spectacular **Clearwell Caves** provides insight into the region's mining for iron and coal, which went on continuously from Roman times to 1945. Ochre (for paint pigments) is still mined here today. ✉ *Clearwell Caves, near Coleford (off B4228),* ☎ *01594/832535,* WEB *www.clearwellcaves.com.* 🎫 *£3.50.* ☾ *Mar.–Oct., daily 10–5; Nov.–Feb., weekends and school holidays 10–5; Dec., Christmas workshops (£4), weekends 10–5.*

Dining and Lodging

££ ✕ **Wyndham Arms.** This may be a modest, old-world village inn, but
★ its restaurant offers sophisticated cuisine. Try the local wild salmon, guinea fowl, or one of the excellent steaks, followed by sherry trifle or chocolate and walnut fudge cake. ✉ *Clearwell, Near Coleford,* ☎ *01594/833666. MC, V.*

££ ✕🏨 **Tudor Farmhouse.** Despite its name, parts of this converted farmhouse actually date to the 13th century. Polished oak staircases, mullioned windows, and a huge stone fireplace in the lounge imbue the place with antique calm. There are four-poster beds in two of the bedrooms, and the fine restaurant serves good-quality fare using solely seasonal ingredients. ✉ *Clearwell, near Coleford, GL16 8JS,* ☎ *01594/833046,* FAX *01594/837093,* WEB *www.tudorfarmhousehotel.co.uk. 11 rooms. Restaurant. AE, DC, MC, V.*

Slimbridge Wildfowl and Wetlands Trust

㊲ *12 mi southwest of Gloucester, 20 mi northeast of Bristol.*

The Slimbridge Wildfowl and Wetlands Trust, occupying a 73-acre site on the banks of the River Severn, encompasses rich marshland that harbors Britain's largest collection of wildfowl. Thousands of swans, ducks, and geese come to winter here; in spring and early summer, you can see the resulting cygnets, ducklings, and goslings. Trails with blinds (called hides in Britain) thread the preserve. The flashy visitor center has an observation tower, cinema, gift shop, and restaurant. There's also a gallery of wildlife art with changing exhibitions. The preserve is outside the village of Slimbridge (head west and across the little swing bridge over the Sharpness Canal) ☎ 01453/890333, WEB *www.wwt. org.uk.* ⬜ *£6.* ☉ *Daily 9:30–5, until 4 in winter.*

Berkeley Castle

★ ❸⓭   *4 mi southwest of Slimbridge, 17 mi southwest of Gloucester, 21 mi north of Bristol.*

Berkeley Castle, in the sleepy little village of Berkeley (pronounced barkley), is perfectly preserved down to its medieval turrets. It was the setting for the gruesome murder of King Edward II in 1327—the cell where it occurred can still be seen. He was deposed by his French consort, Queen Isabella, and her paramour, the Earl of Mortimer. They then connived at his imprisonment and subsequent death. The castle was begun in 1153 by Roger De Berkeley, a Norman knight, and has remained in the family ever since. The state apartments here are full of magnificent furniture, tapestries, and pictures. The surrounding meadows, now the setting for pleasant Elizabethan gardens, were once flooded to make a formidable moat. ✉ *Off the A38,* ☎ *01453/810332.* ⬜ *£5.50.* ☉ *Apr.–May, Tues.–Sun. 2–5; June and Sept., Tues.–Sat. 11–5, Sun. 2–5; July–Aug., Mon.–Sat. 11–5, Sun. 2–5; Oct., Sun. 2–4:30; national holidays 11–5.*

Dining and Lodging

£££–££££   ✕🏨 **Thornbury Castle.** An impressive castle-hotel, Thornbury has
★   everything a genuine 16th-century Tudor castle needs: huge fireplaces, antiques, paintings, and mullioned windows, to say nothing of an extensive garden. There's also plenty of history: Henry VIII, Anne Boleyn and Mary Tudor spent time here. The standards of comfort and luxury are famous, and people come from all over to eat in the restaurant, where they can sample such sophisticated fare as fillet of venison with red cabbage and truffle sauce. Note that there is no elevator. ✉ *Castle St., Thornbury BS35 1HH (12 mi north of Bristol, off A38),* ☎ *01454/281182,* FAX *01454/416188. 21 rooms. Restaurant, archery, croquet. AE, DC, MC, V. Closed 1st wk of Jan.*

££   🏨 **Drakestone House.** This lovely, reasonably priced Cotswold Arts-and-Crafts house 3 mi east of Berkeley has wooden floors and beamed and plasterwork ceilings that are complemented with fine antiques and period furniture. It is a no-smoking establishment. ✉ *Stinchcombe, Dursley GL11 6AS,* ☎ FAX *01453/542140. 3 rooms. No credit cards.*

THE HEART OF ENGLAND A TO Z

To research prices, get advice from other travelers, and book travel arrangements, visit www.fodors.com.

BIKE AND MOPED TRAVEL

The Gloucester Tourist Office has a full range of cycle touring route maps for the Cotswold region.

BUS TRAVEL

National Express serves the region from London's Victoria Coach Station. First Badgerline covers the area around Bath. Stagecoach,

Castleways, and Pulhams operate in the Gloucestershire and Cotswolds region. For all bus inquiries, call Gloucester's coach station.

Various bus routes to major Cotswold destinations are as follows (when not stated otherwise, routes are serviced by National Express buses and depart from London's Victoria Coach Station). Bourton-on-the-Water: take Pulhams Bus Company buses from Cheltenham or Stow-on-the-Wold. Broadway: four Castleways coaches serve the town daily (Monday–Saturday from Cheltenham). Burford: Swanbrook buses leave four times every weekday from Cheltenham; from London, change at Oxford. Cheltenham: buses leave London 10 times daily. Cirencester: Buses leave once daily from London. Moreton-in-Marsh: buses depart 10 times daily from London. Painswick: 12 Stagecoach buses run daily from Cheltenham. Stow-on-the-Wold: Pulhams Bus Company buses run from Moreton-in-Marsh.

FARES AND SCHEDULES

➤ BUS INFORMATION: **Castleways** (☎ 01242/602949). **First Badgerline** (☎ 01225/464446, WEB www.firstbadgerline.co.uk). **Gloucester Coach Station** (☎ 01452/527516). **National Express** (☎ 0870/580–8080, WEB www.gobycoach.com). **Pulhams** (☎ 01451/820369). **Stagecoach** (☎ 01453/5763421). **Transport queries in Gloucestershire** (☎ 01452/425543).

CAR RENTAL

➤ LOCAL AGENCIES: **Avis** (⊠ Unit 4B, Bath Riverside Business Park, Lower Bristol Rd., Bath, ☎ 01225/446680; Unit 7, Chancel Close Trading Estate, Eastern Ave., Gloucester, ☎ 01452/380356). **Budget Rent-a-Car** (⊠ Prestbury Rd., Cheltenham, ☎ 01242/235222). **Ford Rentacar** (⊠ Hayden Rd., off Tewkesbury Rd., Cheltenham, ☎ 01242/229937).

CAR TRAVEL

M4 is the principal route west from London to Bath and southern Gloucestershire. From exit 18, take A46 south to Bath. From exit 20, take M5 north to Gloucester (25 mi), Cheltenham, and Tewkesbury; and from exit 15 take A419 to A429 north to the Cotswolds. From London, you can also take M40 and A40 to the Cotswolds.

Parking in Bath is very restricted within the city, and visitors' cars—especially rental cars—are likely to be ticketed. If your car is towed, hundreds of pounds in fees may have to be paid to retrieve it. Public parking lots in the historic area fill up early; it's easier to park in the large lots on the outskirts of town, which provide shuttle service into the city center.

EMERGENCIES

➤ CONTACTS: **Ambulance, fire, police** (☎ 999). **Cheltenham General Hospital** (⊠ Sandford Rd., ☎ 01242/222222). **Gloucester Royal Hospital** (⊠ Great Western Rd., ☎ 01452/528555). **Royal United Hospital** (⊠ Combe Park, Bath, ☎ 01225/428331).

OUTDOORS AND SPORTS

For information on hiking the Cotswold Way, contact the Cotswold Way Office or various town tourist centers. For information on hiking in the Forest of Dean, contact the Forestry Commission.
➤ HIKING: **Cotswold Way Office** (⊠ Environment Department, Shire Hall, Gloucester GL1 2TH, ☎ 01452/425637, WEB www.cotswold-way.co.uk). **Forestry Commission** (⊠ Bank House, Bank St., Coleford GL16 8BA, ☎ 01594/833057).

SHOPPING

For information about dealers and special events, contact the Cotswold Antique Dealers' Association.

➤ INFORMATION: **Cotswold Antique Dealers' Association** (✉ Broad-well House, Sheep St., Stow-on-the-Wold, GL54 1JS, ☎ 01451/830053).

TOURS

Based in Oxford, Cotswold Roaming is a stylish outfit offering tours of the Cotswolds and excursions to Bath and Castle Combe in small vehicles. There are two separate full-day tours of the Cotswolds: the North Cotswold tour includes Bourton-on-the-Water, Upper and Lower Slaughter, Chipping Campden, Sudeley Castle, and Stow-on-the-Wold. The South Cotswold tour takes in Cirencester, Painswick, and other towns, including Owlpen. Half-day tours are also offered. The pickup point is next to the Playhouse Theatre in Beaumont Street, Oxford.

Gloucester Civic Trust organizes tours of the city and docks by appointment. Contact Gloucester's tourist office for details.

Guide Friday runs guided tours of Bath year-round and, from Strat-ford-upon-Avon, into the Cotswolds from Easter through October, in open-top single- and double-decker buses.

➤ FEES AND SCHEDULES: **Cotswold Roaming** (☎ 01865/308300, WEB www.oxfordcity.co.uk/cotswold-roaming). **Gloucester Tourist Office** (☎ 01452/421188). **Guide Friday** (in Stratford, ☎ 01789/294466; in Bath, ☎ 01225/444102, WEB www.guidefriday.com).

TRAIN TRAVEL

Great Western, Wales and West, Virgin, Central, and Thames Trains all serve the region from London's Paddington Station, or, less frequently, from Euston. Travel time from Paddington to Bath is about 90 minutes. Most trains to Cheltenham (2 hrs) and Gloucester (1 hr 45 mins) involve a change at Swindon. A three-day or seven-day "Heart of England Rover" ticket is valid for unlimited travel within the region.

To reach central Cotswold destinations by train, here are some pointers. Broadway: train to Moreton-in-Marsh or Evesham, then bus or taxi locally to reach the town. Burford: train to Oxford, then buses from the Taylor Institute there. Cirencester: train from London to Kemble (4 mi away). Bourton-on-the-Water, Chipping Campden, and Stow-on-the-Wold: train to Moreton-in-Marsh, then local bus lines (some lines have minimal schedules). Moreton-in-Marsh is serviced by train from London daily. Contact local tourist offices for details.

FARES AND SCHEDULES

➤ TRAIN INFORMATION: **Rail inquiries** (☎ 08457/484950, WEB www.rail-track.co.uk).

TRAVEL AGENCIES

➤ LOCAL AGENT REFERRALS: **American Express** (✉ 5 Bridge St., Bath, ☎ 01225/444747). **Thomas Cook** (✉ 20 New Bond St., Bath, ☎ 01225/492000; 159 High St., Cheltenham, ☎ 01242/847900; 24 Eastgate St., Gloucester, ☎ 01452/368000).

VISITOR INFORMATION

The Heart of England Tourist Board is open Monday–Thursday 9–5:30, Friday 9–5. The West Country Tourist Board has information on Bath. Local tourist information centers are normally open Monday–Saturday 9:30–5:30, but times vary according to season. Note that Cirencester's Web site serves the whole of the Cotswolds.

➤ TOURIST INFORMATION: **Heart of England Tourist Board** (✉ Larkhill, Worcester, WR5 2EZ, ☎ 01905/763436, FAX 01905/763450, WEB www.visitheartofengland.com). **Bath** (✉ Abbey Chambers, Abbey Church Yard, BA1 1LY, ☎ 01225/477101, www.visitbath.co.uk; West Country Tourist Board, Woodwater Park, Exeter EX2 5WT, ☎ 0870/4420830, FAX 0870/4420840, WEB www.westcountrynow.com). **Broad-**

way (✉ 1 Cotswold Court, WR12 7AA, ☎ 01386/852937). **Burford** (✉ The Brewery, Sheep St., OX18 4LP, ☎ 01993/823558). **Cheltenham** (✉ 77 Promenade, GL50 1PP, ☎ 01242/522878, WEB www. visitcheltenham.gov.uk). **Chipping Campden** (✉ Rosary Court, High St., GL55 6AT, ☎ 01386/841206). **Cirencester** (✉ Corn Hall, Market Place, GL7 2NW, ☎ 01285/654180, WEB www.cotswold.gov.uk). **Gloucester Tourist Office** (✉ 28 Southgate St., GL1 2DP, ☎ 01452/ 421188, WEB www.visit-glos.org.uk). **Stow-on-the-Wold** (✉ Hollis House, The Square, GL54 1AF, ☎ 01451/831082). **Tetbury** (✉ 33 Church St., GL8 8JG, ☎ 01666/503552, WEB www.tetbury.org.uk).

9 THE WELSH BORDERS

BIRMINGHAM, WORCESTER, HEREFORD, SHREWSBURY, CHESTER

Not far from Birmingham—epicenter of England's industrial production—lies some of England's loveliest and most peaceful countryside. Here, behind high hedges and wooded hills, time seems to have stood still: brooding medieval castles, built by the English and Welsh, loom above the old towns, suggesting that today's air of sleepy tranquillity has not always been so. Often overlooked, this region remains rich in sights, none more delightful than the "magpie" black-and-white buildings of Shrewsbury and Chester.

ENGLAND'S BORDER with the principality of Wales stretches from the town of Chepstow on the Severn estuary in the south to the city of Chester in the north. Along this border, in the counties

Updated by
Robert
Andrews

of Herefordshire, Shropshire, and southern Cheshire, lies some of England's prettiest countryside, remote and tranquil. But today's rural peace belies a turbulent past. Relations between the English and the Welsh have seldom been easy, and from the earliest times the English have felt it necessary to keep the "troublesome" Welsh firmly on the other side of the border. A string of medieval castles bears witness to this history. Many are romantic ruins; some are brooding fortresses. Built to control the countryside and repel invaders, they still radiate a sense of mystery and menace.

For the last 500 years or so, the people of this border country have enjoyed a peaceful existence, with little to disturb the traditional patterns of country life. In the 18th century, however, one small corner of Shropshire heralded the tumultuous birth of the Industrial Revolution, for here, in a wooded stretch of the Severn Gorge, the first coke blast furnace was invented and the first iron bridge was erected (1779).

The ramifications of that technological leap led to the growth of Britain's second-largest city, Birmingham, the capital of the Midlands. Birmingham has thankfully transcended its reputation as one of the country's least attractive cities, and its active artistic life is drawing people who appreciate what remains of its historic civic architecture, some of the most fascinating to be found anywhere.

Herefordshire, in the south, is a county of rich, rolling countryside and river valleys, gradually opening out in the high hills and plateaus of Shropshire. North of the Shropshire hills, the gentler Cheshire plain stretches toward the great industrial cities of Liverpool and Manchester. This is dairy country, dotted with small villages and market towns, many rich in the 13th- and 14th-century black-and-white, half-timber buildings typical of northwestern England. These are the legacy of a forested countryside, where wood was easier to come by than stone. In the market towns of Chester and Shrewsbury, the more elaborately decorated half-timber buildings are monuments to wealth, dating mostly from the early Jacobean period at the beginning of the 17th century. Although it requires a trek off the beaten path, Little Moreton Hall, the greatest example of "magpie" buildings, remains one of the most sensationally atmospheric buildings in England.

Pleasures and Pastimes

Dining
Birmingham has splendid international restaurants but is probably most famous for its Asian eateries, the best of which are tucked away off the main roads. Outside the city, this is all rich farming country where, for centuries, the orchards have produced succulent fruit, especially apples. Hereford cider, for example, is popular because it tastes much sweeter than the cider brewed farther south in Devon. The meat and milk products, which come from the local black-and-white breed of cattle, are second to none. With this natural bounty, it is surprising that formal restaurants are few and far between in this rural area, and those that exist are mostly small. There has been a slight improvement, however, with a pocket of high-quality dining spots in the Ludlow area, providing an added incentive to visit this lovely town.

CATEGORY	COST*
££££	over £22
£££	£16–£22
££	£9–£15
£	under £9

*per person for a main course at dinner

Lodging

The Welsh Borders are full of ancient inns and venerable Regency-style houses converted into hotels. Although some of these can be pricey, bargains can be found. You may have to put up with asthmatic plumbing and creaking beams that masquerade as period atmosphere, but it's usually worth the savings. Birmingham's hotels, geared to the convention crowd, are mostly bland and impersonal, but smart. In these, you'll often find weekend rates up to 50% less than they would be during the week.

CATEGORY	COST*
££££	over £150
£££	£100–£150
££	£60–£100
£	under £60

*All prices are for two people sharing a standard double room, including service, breakfast, and VAT.

Walking

The Malvern Hills make for climbs and walks of varying length and difficulty. The best places to start are Great Malvern and Ledbury. The route designated the Elgar Way extends for 45 mi, but you don't need to traipse the entire run. Views across the countryside from the top of the hills are spectacular—the isolated hills rise up from the fairly flat plain, providing vistas for many miles around. The area around Ross-on-Wye has ideal walks with scenic river views.

Exploring the Welsh Borders

The main gateway to the region is bustling Birmingham, now one of the best places in England for the performing arts, having redeemed itself from its reputation as a post–World War II urban disaster zone. The city of Worcester is renowned for its proud cathedral and fine bone china. To the south and west, along the lovely Malvern Hills, lie the peaceful spa town of Great Malvern and the prosperous agricultural city of Hereford. Northward is Bewdley, terminus of the Severn Valley Railway, and beyond, the West Midlands—birthplace of modern British industry.

The handsome medieval city of Shrewsbury is near the wooded banks of the River Severn and a cluster of Ironbridge museums interpreting the region's industrial heritage. To the south lies Ludlow, an architectural jewel of a town; at the northwestern edge of the region lies the ancient city of Chester.

Numbers in the text correspond to numbers in the margin and on the Welsh Borders, Birmingham, and Shrewsbury maps.

Great Itineraries

Although the main towns of the Welsh Borders region—Worcester, Hereford, Shrewsbury, and Chester—distill the essence of the surrounding countryside, there's much in between that should not be neglected. It would be easy to base yourself in one of these towns and launch expeditions from there, but you might do better to lodge in some of the smaller centers, or in one of the remoter country inns, to absorb the full flavor of the borderlands.

The Welsh Borders

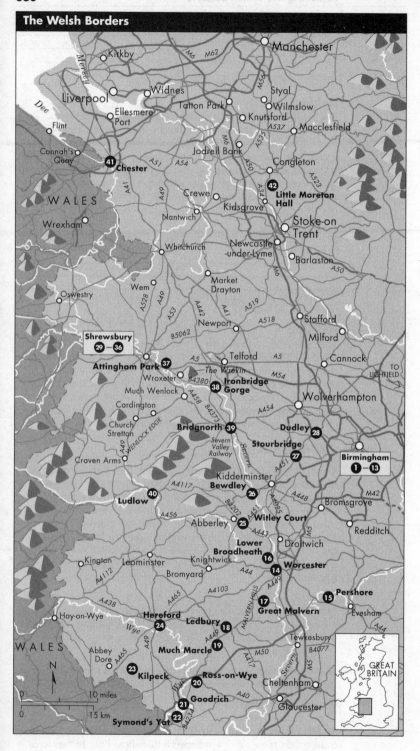

Manchester

Kirkby

Mersey

M62

M6

Liverpool

Widnes

Styal

Dee

Ellesmere
Port

Tatton Park

Wilmslow

Knutsford

Flint

M56

M6

A537

Macclesfield

Connah's
Quay

41 Chester

A51

Jodrell Bank

A54

A50

Congleton

A523

42 Little Moreton
Hall

WALES

Crewe

Kidsgrove

Stoke-on-
Trent

Wrexham

A41

A530

Nantwich

A34

Newcastle
-under-Lyme

Barlaston

A50

Whitchurch

A534

Wem

Market
Drayton

M6

Oswestry

A528

A49

A53

A442

A41

A519

Stafford

A518

Milford

Newport

B5062

A5

Telford

A5

Cannock

TO
LICHFIELD

Shrewsbury
29 – 36

Attingham Park **37**

Wroxeter

The Wrekin

B4380

M54

Much Wenlock

A458

B4373

38 Ironbridge
Gorge

A454

Wolverhampton

Cardington

Church
Stretton

WENLOCK EDGE

Bridgnorth **39**

Dudley **28**

Craven Arms

A49

Severn
Valley
Railway

Stourbridge

Severn

A451 **27**

Birmingham
1 – 13

Ludlow **40**

A4117

Kidderminster

Bewdley

A448

M42

Bromsgrove

A456

B4202

A451

A456

A449

26

A4095

Witley Court

Redditch

Abberley

25

A443

Droitwich

M5

Kington

A4112

Leominster

Knightwick

Lower
Broadheath
16

A44

14 Worcester

15 Pershore

Bromyard

A465

A4103

A449

Evesham

A44

Hay-on-Wye

A438

Hereford
24

Wye

Ledbury
18

MALVERN HILLS

17

Great Malvern

A49

A438

Abbey
Dore

A465

Much Marcle
19

Tewkesbury

M50

B4077

23 Kilpeck

WALES

N

Wye

20 **Ross-on-Wye**

A417

Severn

M5

Cheltenham

0   10 miles

21 Goodrich

B4234

A40

Gloucester

0   15 km

Symond's Yat **22**

GREAT
BRITAIN

In three days you can take in the highlights of a couple of major centers and visit some smaller, atmospheric towns. A week gives you a chance to explore Birmingham and several major towns, along with more scenic stops; if you can keep up the pace, these would include Chester.

IF YOU HAVE 3 DAYS

The city of ▦ **Worcester** ⑭ makes a convenient entry to the Welsh Borders. Spend your first night here, making sure you see the majestic cathedral and the Commandery, devoted exclusively to the 17th-century tussle between Cavaliers and Roundheads. Take a whirl 'round the famous Royal Worcester Porcelain Factory, where you can pick up some authentic souvenirs after admiring the rare porcelain in the attached museum. On your second day, take A443 northwest, making a stop at the evocative ruins of **Witley Court** ㉕, a good place for a picnic; alternatively, opt for a pub meal in the nearby village. Keep on the same road as far as **Ludlow** ㊵, stopping long enough to view its magnificent castle as well as the crowd of Tudor, Jacobean, and Georgian buildings that give the small town its unique aspect. On your final stretch, head south for ▦ **Hereford** ㉔, with another stout cathedral—Norman this time—and numerous reminders of the city's importance as a market town for the surrounding area. You can see most of the interesting sights here in a morning, leaving the afternoon free to explore **Ross-on-Wye** ⑳ and the nearby attractions of **Goodrich** ㉑, dramatically poised over the River Wye, and the beauty spot of **Symond's Yat** ㉒.

IF YOU HAVE 7 DAYS

Devote at least a day to ▦ **Birmingham** ①–⑬, in particular seeking out the Barber Institute of Fine Arts and the Birmingham Museum and Art Gallery. After an overnight stay, head south to Worcester and the Malvern Hills, dropping in along the way at Hellen's, a manor house dating from the 13th century; it's just outside **Much Marcle** ⑲. You could take a lunch break at the generously timbered village of **Ledbury** ⑱, before continuing on toward the Wye Valley, where the nearby ruins of the castle at **Goodrich** ㉑ and **Symond's Yat** ㉒ provide good excuses to stop traveling for a while and stretch your legs. A night in ▦ **Hereford** ㉔ will allow you to absorb the flavor of this old market town, before heading up to **Ludlow** ㊵ for a couple of hours' ramble around the castle and its surrounding streets. Spend the next two nights in ▦ **Worcester** ⑭, taking in the Malverns and, to the north, the quiet riverside town of **Bewdley** ㉖, with its fine array of Georgian architecture. From here you could take a trip on the Severn Valley Railway, whose old-style steam train affords opportunities to stroll around the banks of the Severn from the remote stations on the route. One of the main stops is **Bridgnorth** ㉟, occupying a sandstone ridge high above the Severn, and within a short distance of **Ironbridge Gorge** ㊳, a fascinating collection of sites that formed the crucible of the Industrial Revolution. You could stay here, or else visit it on a day's excursion from ▦ **Shrewsbury** ㉙–㊱. Outside this historic town lies **Attingham Park** ㊲, a mansion dating from 1785 with a deer park designed by Humphrey Repton. Your last overnight—entailing a sizable journey northward—could be spent in ▦ **Chester** ㊶, famous for its black-and-white "magpie" buildings and worthy of a full day's sightseeing. Black-and-white aficionados will want to make a special pilgrimage to that vision of Tudor England, **Little Moreton Hall** ㊷, just outside Congleton.

When to Tour the Welsh Borders

If you want to visit when most attractions are open and the countryside is most appealing, try to be here in the warmer weather between April and September. The official and fringe festivals take place at Malvern at the end of May, the open-air performances at Ludlow Castle at the end of June, and the Shrewsbury Festival in June and July. The Three Choirs Festival, rotating between Hereford, Gloucester, and Worcester, takes place in mid-August, for which you need to book as early as you can to guarantee the best seats. Most rural sights have limited opening hours in winter. Even in the towns, the majority of the attractions close at 5, which leaves several hours of dark and often chilly winter evenings to fill. Be on the road early to catch the best light. In the winter's favor are the creeping mists shrouding the valleys, and the warm hearths at inns and hotels.

BIRMINGHAM

Birmingham's appeal, thanks to heavy industry and German bombing during World War II, may be less than instantly evident, but there is satisfaction to be gained from discovering its treasures and the historic civic architecture that remains. The city's dynamic cultural life—the result of the museums, art galleries, theater, ballet, and symphony that thrive here—is a refreshing surprise.

The center of Britain's "second city" has undergone so many injudicious structural alterations in the postwar period that, as an official guidebook put it, "there is more of the future to be seen coming into being than there is of the past left to contemplate." Indeed, Birmingham has become something of a monument to late-20th-century civic architecture. Whether you agree that it's a *fitting* monument depends on your feelings toward the 20th century. Mercifully, city officials have, in the past few years, adopted a policy of humanizing the areas and buildings that their immediate predecessors did so much to ruin.

The city, which is 25 mi north of Stratford and 120 mi northwest of London, first flourished in the boom years of the 19th century's Industrial Revolution. Birmingham's inventive, hardworking citizens accumulated enormous wealth, and at one time the city had some of the finest Victorian buildings in the country (it still has some of the most ravishingly beautiful Pre-Raphaelite paintings, on view in the Birmingham Museum and Art Gallery). Sadly, postwar "planning" managed to destroy many 19th-century structures. Still, there are architectural treasures to be found, best reached on foot or by public transport, as negotiating the city's convoluted road network is best avoided. Much of Birmingham is now pedestrian-friendly, the downtown shopping area transformed into pedestrian arcades and buses-only streets. If you *are* driving, note that Birmingham's inner ring road twists right through the city center.

Birmingham, surprisingly, has more canals than Venice. It's at the center of a system of restored waterways built during the Industrial Revolution to connect inland factories to rivers and seaports—by 1840 the canals extended more than 4,000 mi throughout the British Isles. Contact any of the city's tourist offices for maps of walks along the towpaths and for details on canal barge cruises.

Exploring Birmingham

Most of Birmingham's sights form a tight-knit group and can be easily explored on foot, a pleasant walk in the mostly pedestrianized center, although you'll seldom be unaware of the roar of the city's traffic. If you're weary, you can also reach the Jewellery Quarter by public transport, which is the best means for arriving at the Barber Institute and Cadbury World, the only two city sites away from the center.

363

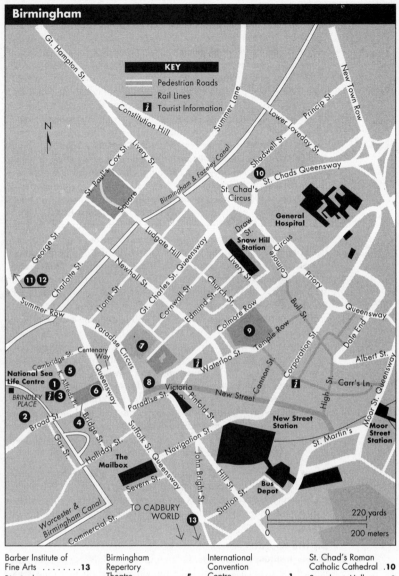

Birmingham

KEY
— Pedestrian Roads
— Rail Lines
i Tourist Information

Barber Institute of
Fine Arts **13**

Birmingham
Cathedral
(St. Philip's) **9**

Birmingham Museum
and Art Gallery **7**

Birmingham
Repertory
Theatre **5**

Centenary
Square **4**

Hall of Memory **6**

Ikon Gallery **2**

International
Convention
Centre **1**

Jewellery Quarter . . .**11**

Museum of the
Jewellery Quarter . .**12**

St. Chad's Roman
Catholic Cathedral .**10**

Symphony Hall **3**

Town Hall **8**

A Good Walk and Tour

Start from the **International Convention Centre** ①, where a tourist desk can equip you with information for your explorations. Cross the canal by the footbridge over to Brindley Place, full of shops and offices, all in interesting architectural styles. From the aptly named Water's Edge, cut across Central Square, with its fountains, to the ornate redbrick **Ikon Gallery** ②—a good coffee stop—to find out what's new in British contemporary art. Retracing your steps over the canal bridge and through the Convention Centre will bring you to **Symphony Hall** ③, whose plush wooden and chrome interior will be open to view if there's no rehearsal in progress. Entering **Centenary Square** ④, you'll be faced with **Birmingham Repertory Theatre** ⑤, and farther down the imposing **Hall of Memory** ⑥. Centenary Way leads through the shopping arcade past the library into Chamberlain Square, where the magnificent **Birmingham Museum and Art Gallery** ⑦ invites a couple of hours' lingering. South of the museum is the classical **Town Hall** ⑧, behind which Victoria Square spreads out, with its modern fountains and statues. From here, your route leaves the pedestrianized area and continues northeast through the bustle of Colmore Row and past the main tourist information center to the Georgian **Birmingham Cathedral** ⑨, distinguished by its concave tower. Continue north past Snow Hill train station to St. Chad's Circus, where the lofty twin towers of **St. Chad's Roman Catholic Cathedral** ⑩ rear incongruously above the busy intersection. Taking the metro from Snow Hill station the couple of stops to the **Jewellery Quarter** ⑪ will save you the 10-minute walk, but you'd miss some striking examples of redbrick and terra-cotta industrial architecture from the 19th century. The background to the neighborhood is given in the fascinating **Museum of the Jewellery Quarter** ⑫. After perusing this and the surrounding area, a short train ride or walk will take you back to the center. For the tour's grand finale, the **Barber Institute of Fine Arts** ⑬—one of the country's most absorbing collections of European art—you must drive or take a taxi or train (from New Street Station).

TIMING

Allow a full day to visit all the sights, which will give you time to linger in the Jewellery Quarter and browse the art museums; give yourself a half-day if you keep your walk to the very central part of the city. You may have to negotiate limited opening hours at some sights on Sunday, and the shops of the Jewellery Quarter are closed on that day.

Sights to See

★ ⑬ **Barber Institute of Fine Arts.** Belonging to the University of Birmingham, the museum has a small but astounding collection, including works by Bellini, Canaletto, Guardi, Poussin, Murillo, Gainsborough, Turner, Whistler, Renoir, Monet, and Van Gogh. ⊠ *Off Edgbaston Park Rd. near East Gate (take Cross City Line train from New St. Station south to University Station, or Bus 61, 62, 63, or 44 from city center),* ☏ *0121/414–7333,* WEB *www.barber.org.uk.* ⊡ *Free.* ☉ *Mon.–Sat. 10– 5, Sun. 2–5.*

⑨ **Birmingham Cathedral.** The early 18th-century cathedral of St. Philip stands a few blocks from the renovated Victoria Square. The gilded Georgian interior is elegant and has some lovely plasterwork. The windows behind the altar seem to glow with a garnet hue. They were designed by the Pre-Raphaelites' Edward Burne-Jones (1833–98) and executed by William Morris (1834–96). ⊠ *Colmore Row,* ☏ *0121/ 236–6323.* ☉ *Mon.–Fri. 7:30–6.30; Sat.–Sun. 9–4.30.*

★ ⑦ **Birmingham Museum and Art Gallery.** A vast, impressive place containing a magnificent collection of Victorian art, the museum is known internationally for its collection of works by the Pre-Raphaelites. All the big names are here, including William Holman Hunt, John Everett Millais, and Dante Gabriel Rossetti—reflecting the enormous wealth of 19th-century Birmingham and the aesthetic taste of its industrialists. There are also selections of contemporary art. ⊠ *Chamberlain Sq.,* ☎ *0121/303–2834,* WEB *www.bmag.org.uk.* ☞ *Free.* ☉ *Mon.–Thurs. and Sat. 10–5, Fri. 10:30–5, Sun. 12:30–5.*

❺ Birmingham Repertory Theatre. Set to one side of Centenary Square, the building houses one of England's oldest and most esteemed theater companies. The Birmingham Rep—as it's always called—has an excellent cafeteria/restaurant in its foyer, behind sweeping windows that allow for a great view over the square.

Cadbury World. The Quaker village of Bournville (4 mi south of the city center) is home to this museum devoted to—what else?—chocolate. Adjoining the factory, this model village was constructed for the factory workers by the philanthropic Cadbury brothers, who in 1879 moved the family business to this "factory in a garden" from the less than healthy conditions of the city. Today you can trace the history of the cocoa bean and the Cadbury dynasty, walking through a rain forest along the way. Chocoholics can watch (and smell) specialties being made in the factory, enjoy the free samples, then stock up afterward from the cut-price shop. The restaurant has specialty chocolate cakes as well as lunches. ⊠ *Off A38, Bournville (take train from New St. to Bournville Train Station),* ☎ *0121/451–4159,* WEB *www.cadburyworld. co.uk.* ☞ *£8.25.* ☉ *Mar.–Oct., daily 10–4 (reservations advised, and essential at busy times); times for rest of year vary.*

❹ Centenary Square. Just outside the International Convention Centre, the square is a sort of miniature complex for the performing arts. It's paved with bricks whose various shades form a pattern, like a Persian carpet, designed by artist Tess Jaray. The creamy figurative sculpture in the center of the square, *Forward,* represents the city's progressive outlook.

❻ Hall of Memory. The octagonal war memorial, across Centenary Square from the convention center, was built in the 1920s in remembrance of those who fell during World War I and, later, during World War II. Inside, there's a book containing their names and the poppies laid on Armistice Day. ⊠ *Centenary Sq.* ☞ *Free.* ☉ *Mon.–Sat. 10–4.*

❷ Ikon Gallery. This gallery, imaginatively converted from a Victorian Gothic–style school, is now the city's main venue for exhibitions of contemporary art from Britain and abroad. The bright and white interior is divided up into comparatively small display areas, making the shows easily digestible. ⊠ *1 Oozells Sq., Brindley Place,* ☎ *0121/248–0708,* WEB *www.ikon-gallery.co.uk.* ☞ *Free.* ☉ *Tues.–Sun. 11–6.*

❶ International Convention Centre. The main atrium of the high-tech convention center is dominated by a network of blue struts and gleaming air ducts, somewhat softened by indoor trees. There's a useful information center here, though the office at Colmore Row, near the cathedral, is more fully stocked. ⊠ *Broad St.* ☉ *Mon.–Thurs. 8:45–5, Fri. 8:45–4:45.*

⓫ Jewellery Quarter. For more than two centuries, jewelers have been working in the district of Hockley, northwest of the city center where there are more than 200 manufacturing jewelers and 50 silversmiths. The city has its own Assay Office, where 10 million items are hallmarked each year with the anchor symbol denoting Birmingham origin. The ornate green and gilded Chamberlain clock marks the center of the district. ⊠ *Hockley.*

OFF THE
BEATEN PATH

LICHFIELD CATHEDRAL – It's worth a detour (14 mi northeast of Birmingham on A38) to find Lichfield Cathedral, the only English cathedral with three spires. The present building dates mainly from the 12th and 13th centuries and has some fine 16th-century stained glass from the Cistercian Abbey of Herkenrode, near Liège, in Belgium. It stands on peaceful grounds surrounded by half-timber houses, and the town itself has a mix of buildings from different periods. ⊠ *Cathedral Close, Lichfield,* ☎ *01543/306100,* WEB *www.lichfield-cathedral.org.* ☞ *Free.* ☉ *Daily 7:30–5:45.*

⑫ **Museum of the Jewellery Quarter.** The museum is built around the workshops of Smith and Pepper, who operated here for more than 80 years until 1981; very little has changed since the early 1900s. The history of the neighborhood and the craft of the jeweler are explained on the guided tour, and you can watch jewelry-making in action. ⊠ *77–79 Vyse St.,* ☎ *0121/554–3598,* WEB *www.bmag.org.uk.* ☞ *£2.50.* ☉ *Weekdays 10–4, Sat. 11–5; last admission 1 hr before closing.*

☾ **National Sea Life Centre.** Even as far from the sea as you can get in Britain, this imaginatively landscaped aquarium allows a glimpse into Davey Jones's locker. There's an underwater tunnel for viewing sharks and stingrays in action, as well as other displays of oceanic and freshwater marine life. Children will gravitate to the touch pools and other interactive activities. ⊠ *The Water's Edge, Brindley Place,* ☎ *0121/643–6777,* WEB *www.sealife.co.uk.* ☞ *£8.* ☉ *Daily 10–5.*

⑩ **St. Chad's Roman Catholic Cathedral.** Dating from 1841, this redbrick pile was the first Roman Catholic cathedral to be built in England since the Reformation. It was designed by A. W. N. Pugin, leading architect of the Gothic revival, and basically consists of just one lofty room—the nave—divided by soaring slender pillars and decorated in red, blue, and gold. Many of the furnishings are 15th-century. ⊠ *Queensway,* ☎ *0121/236–2251.* ☞ *Free.* ☉ *Weekdays 8–6:30, Sat. 9–6, Sun. 8–12:30 and 3–6:30.*

❸ **Symphony Hall.** Attending a concert here is sufficient reason to visit Birmingham. The internationally recognized City of Birmingham Symphony Orchestra, which has won awards for its recordings under its former conductor Sir Simon Rattle (who still regularly guest conducts) has found a very welcome home here. Symphony Hall is housed in the same building as the International Convention Centre. ⊠ *Broad St.,* ☎ *0121/212–2555.*

❽ **Town Hall.** Surrounded by classical columns, the hall is a copy of the Temple of Castor and Pollux in Rome and took more than a decade (1832–46) to build. It used to be the home of the symphony orchestra—it heard the first performances of Mendelssohn's *Elijah* and Elgar's *Dream of Gerontius*—and it's now host to concerts and exhibitions, or at least will be when it reopens in 2003 after renovation. The statue of a woman in the prominent fountain outside has been affectionately dubbed by locals "the floozie in the Jacuzzi." ⊠ *Victoria Sq.*

Dining

££ ✕ **Le Petit Blanc.** The latest venture of noted chef Raymond Blanc (of Le Manoir aux Quat' Saisons, near Oxford), this brasserie provides a very contemporary ambience of gleaming metal, light wood, and plate glass for the French menu of regional dishes. The Roquefort soufflé with pear and walnut dressing should get you in the mood for starters, which you might follow up with roast cod with butter beans, fennel, and aioli. ⊠ *9 Brindley Pl.,* ☎ *0121/633–7333. AE, DC, MC, V.*

£–££ ✕ **Café Lazeez.** Set in the Mailbox development and overlooking water, this New Wave Indian restaurant blends the traditional with the contemporary taste for lighter, less oily dishes. Try the Peshawari naan bread as an accompaniment to fillets of salmon in a tomato and yogurt sauce, or herb breast of chicken. ⊠ *116 Wharfside St., The Mailbox,* ☎ *0121/643–7979. AE, DC, MC, V.*

£–££ ✕ **Shimla Pinks.** Some of Britain's finest Indian restaurants are to be found in Birmingham, and this is one of the most upbeat choices—the name refers to the "bright young things" of India's upper classes. Both decor and cooking are a mix of modern and traditional. Try the Assamese *jalfrezi*, tikka pieces of meat with coriander leaves and red peppers, or *rogan josh* made from fresh tomatoes, paprika, and chili. An abundant buffet is served on Sunday evenings. ⊠ *214 Broad St.,* ☎ *0121/633–0366. AE, DC, MC, V. No lunch.*

£–££ ✕ **Thai Edge.** The elegant, contemporary Oriental design will draw you into this restaurant, where you will be met with a graceful Thai welcome. Dishes such as *gang keow waan* (green curry cooked in coconut milk with eggplant, lime leaves, and basil) match up to the exotic feel of the place. You can eat all you want for £12.50 at the Sunday lunch buffet. ⊠ *7 Oozells Sq.,* ☎ *0121/643–3993. AE, DC, MC, V.*

£ ✕ **Henry's.** This very popular traditional Cantonese restaurant in the jewelry district is a haven for lunch during a shopping spree. The menu lists more than 180 dishes; there's also a good-value fixed-price menu and a Sunday buffet. ⊠ *27 St. Paul's Sq.,* ☎ *0121/200–1136. AE, DC, MC, V.*

Lodging

££££ ▨ **New Hall.** A tree-lined drive leads through 26 acres of gardens and
★ open land to this moated 12th-century manor-house-turned-country-hotel. The guest rooms, decorated in English country style with marble-tile baths, have expansive views overlooking the grounds. The public rooms have 16th-century oak-panel walls and Flemish glass, 18th-century chandeliers, and a stone fireplace from the 17th century. A formal restaurant is an elegant setting in which to indulge in chef David Lake's sophisticated English and French cuisine. ⊠ *Walmley Rd., Sutton Coldfield, Birmingham B76 1QX,* ☎ *0121/378–2442,* ℻ *0121/378–4637,* ⓦⓔⓑ *www.thistlehotels.com. 60 rooms. Restaurant, bar, 9-hole golf course, tennis court, croquet, meeting rooms. AE, DC, MC, V.*

££–££££ ▨ **Burlington Hotel.** This traditional hotel abounds in wood paneling, marble, and classical columns, and rooms are individually decorated in a conservative style with dark woods and print fabrics. At the sumptuous Berlioz restaurant, typical English dishes such as liver with swede and parsnip mash share menu space with classic French-influenced dishes. ⊠ *Burlington Arcade, 126 New St., B2 4JQ,* ☎ *0121/643–9191,* ℻ *0121/628–5005,* ⓦⓔⓑ *www.burlingtonhotel.com. 112 rooms. Restaurant, sauna, gym. AE, DC, MC, V.*

££–££££ ▨ **Copthorne Hotel.** Very centrally located, overlooking Centenary Square, the hotel is large and modern, but it aims for a traditional feel with leather armchairs and wood paneling in the public rooms. Bedrooms are smallish but comfortable. ⊠ *Paradise Circus, B3 3HJ,* ☎ *0121/200–2727,* ℻ *0121/200–1197,* ⓦⓔⓑ *www.mill-cop.com. 212 rooms. Restaurant, indoor pool, health club. AE, DC, MC, V.*

£££ ▨ **Birmingham Marriott Hotel.** Once a group of offices, this elegant building from the early part of the 20th century is now a luxuriously renovated hotel. The building has an interior rich with dark wood and chandeliers; the spacious bedrooms offer all the latest comforts. The Sir Edward Elgar formal restaurant (reservations essential) has a fixed-price menu that changes daily, while Langtry's Brasserie serves traditional British dishes in more casual surroundings. The health club is Egyptian-themed. ✉ *12 Hagley Rd., Five Ways B16 8SJ,* ☎ *0121/452–1144,* FAX *0121/456–3442,* WEB *www.marriott.com. 98 rooms. Restaurant, brasserie, pool, hair salon, health club. AE, DC, MC, V.*

£–££ 🏨 **Copperfield House Hotel.** In a quiet location (a few minutes' drive from Cadbury World) with secluded lawns, this Victorian, family-run hotel with simple, comfortable rooms is nevertheless convenient to the hustle and bustle of the center 2 mi away. The restaurant serves good English cooking, including delicious homemade desserts, and you can eat outdoors in summer. ✉ *60 Upland Rd., Selly Park, Birmingham B29 7JS,* ☎ *0121/472–8344,* FAX *0121/415–5655,* WEB *www.copperfieldhousehotel.co.uk. 14 rooms. Restaurant. AE, MC, V.*

Nightlife and the Arts

Nightlife

A nightly program of jazz runs at **Ronnie Scott's** (✉ 258 Broad St., ☎ 0121/643–4525), sister to the famous London club. The very plush Front Room, open to diners and drinkers, gives onto the intimate stage area.

Converted from a church, **The Bar** (✉ The Church, 55 Broad St., ☎ 0121/632–5501) has turned its attention from God to Mammon. It's a bar in the early evening and later plays commercial dance music for the over-21s. At **52° North** (✉ Arcadian, Hurst St., ☎ 0121/622–5250), the bar specializes in classic and contemporary cocktails and mixes up 14 different types of martinis.

The Arts

BALLET

The second company of the Royal Ballet, which used to be based at Sadler's Wells in London, has become the **Birmingham Royal Ballet** (✉ Hurst St., ☎ 0121/622–7486). It's based at the Hippodrome Theatre, which also hosts visiting companies, such as the Welsh National Opera.

CONCERTS

The distinguished **City of Birmingham Symphony Orchestra** (✉ International Convention Centre, Broad St., ☎ 0121/212–2555) performs regularly in Symphony Hall, also the venue for visiting artists.

THEATER

The **Alexandra Theatre** (✉ Station St., ☎ 0121/643–1231 welcomes touring companies on their way to or from London's West End. The **Birmingham Repertory Theatre** (✉ Centenary Sq., Broad St., ☎ 0121/236–4455), founded in 1913, is equally at home with modern or classical work. There's a restaurant on the ground floor.

Outdoor Activities and Sports

Boating

Birmingham has 34 miles of canals that provide a novel perspective on the city. You can take an hour ride on a canal barge from **Sherborne Wharf** (✉ Sherborne St., ☎ 0121/455–6163). Trips leave daily mid-April through October at 11:30, 1, 2:30, and 4, and on weekends throughout the rest of the year, departing from the International Convention Centre Quayside.

Cricket

To experience the vagaries of first-class cricket at one of the country's most hallowed venues, head for **Warwickshire County Cricket Club** (✉ County Ground, Edgbaston, ☎ 0121/446–4422). Tickets for test matches are sold out six months ahead, but those at county level are not so sought after.

Shopping

In the **Jewellery Quarter** (☎ 0121/554–3598) more than 100 shops sell and repair gold and silver handcrafted jewelry, clocks, and watches. The Museum of the Jewellery Quarter sells a selection of contemporary work and can give you information on individual artisans and retail outlets. **The Mailbox** (✉ 150 Wharfside St., ☎ 0121/643–4080), once a Royal Mail sorting office, is Birmingham's latest development, consisting of shops, hotels, and restaurants. It's home to designer outlets such as Armani, Christian Lacroix, and Prada. At **Highclere** (✉ City Plaza, 47 Cannon St., ☎ 0121/643–3393) you'll find quality leather goods and gifts.

FROM WORCESTER TO DUDLEY

In the arc of towns to the west of Birmingham and the cluster of places around the banks of the River Wye, history and tradition rub up against deepest rural England. The cathedral towns of Worcester and Hereford make great bases for soaking up the bucolic flavor of the Malverns and Elgar country, or to view the spectacular swing of the Wye at Symonds Yat. En route, there's a taste of Georgian architecture at Pershore and Bewdley, and reminders of the old industrial Midlands at Stourbridge and Dudley.

Worcester

🔞 *27 mi southwest of Birmingham, 118 mi northwest of London.*

Worcester (pronounced as in Bertie *Wooster*) sits on the River Severn in the center of Worcestershire. It's an ancient place proud of its history, and in particular, its nickname, "the Faithful City," bestowed on it for steadfast allegiance to the crown during the English Civil War. In that conflict between king and Parliament, two major battles were waged here. The second one, the decisive Battle of Worcester of 1651, resulted in the exile of the future Charles II. More recently the town's name has become synonymous with the fine bone china produced here. Despite unfortunate "modernization" in the 1960s, some of medieval Worcester remains. This ancient section forms a convenient and pleasant walking route around the great cathedral. Worcester's mainly pedestrianized High Street runs through the center of town, from the cathedral to Foregate Street train station.

★ There are few more quintessentially English sights than that of **Worcester Cathedral,** its towers overlooking the green expanse of the county cricket ground, and its majestic image reflected in the swift-flowing—and frequently flooding—waters of the River Severn. There has been a cathedral on this site since the year 680, and much of what remains dates from the 13th and 14th centuries. Notable exceptions are the Norman crypt (built in the 1080s), the largest in England, and the ambulatory, a cloister built around the east end. The most important tomb in the cathedral is that of King John (1167–1216), one of the country's least admired monarchs, who alienated his barons and subjects through bad administration and heavy taxation and in 1215 was forced to sign the Magna Carta, the great charter of liberty. The cathedral's most beautiful decoration is in the vaulted **chantry chapel of Prince Arthur,** Henry VII's elder son, whose body was brought to Worcester after his death at Ludlow in 1502. (Chantry chapels were endowed by the wealthy to enable priests to celebrate masses there for the souls of the deceased.) ✉ *College Yard at High St.,* ☎ *01905/28854.* 🖃 *Suggested donation £2.* ☉ *Daily 7:30–6.*

At the **Royal Worcester Porcelain Factory,** you can browse in the show-rooms or rummage in the "seconds" and "clearance" shops; especially good bargains can be had at the January and July sales. Tours of the factory take you through the process of making bone china figurines. The **Museum of Worcester Porcelain** houses a comprehensive collection of rare Worcester porcelain, representing work from the start of manufacturing in 1751 to the present. The factory lies south of Worcester Cathedral (follow Severn St.). ⊠ *Severn St.,* ☎ *01905/23221,* WEB *www.royal-worcester.co.uk.* 🎫 *£2.25 for visitor center, £5 for 1-hr tour of factory or £8 for tour, museum, and visitor center; prebooked 2-hr Connoisseur Tours £14.* ☉ *Mon.–Sat. 9–5:30, Sun. 11–5; tours week-days 10:30–2:30, Connoisseur Tours weekdays 10:15 and 1:15. Children under 11 not admitted on tours.*

The Commandery occupies a cluster of 15th-century half-timber build-ings that were originally built as a poorhouse and later became the head-quarters of the Royalist troops during the Battle of Worcester. Now an enthralling museum, it presents a colorful audiovisual presentation about the Civil War in the magnificent, oak-beam Great Hall. The mu-seum is across the road from the porcelain factory, minutes from the cathedral. The Commandery has a terrace tearoom. ⊠ *Sidbury,* ☎ *01905/361821.* 🎫 *£3.70.* ☉ *Mon.–Sat. 10–5, Sun. 1:30–5.*

The timber-frame **Museum of Local Life,** on a medieval street, focuses on Worcester's domestic and social history. You can see reconstructions of Victorian and Edwardian shops and homes, and there are changing exhibitions. ⊠ *Friar St.,* ☎ *01905/722349.* 🎫 *Free.* ☉ *Mon.–Wed. and Fri.–Sat. 10:30–5.*

Also the location of the tourist information office, the **Guildhall,** set back behind ornate iron railings, has an 18th-century facade with gilded statues of Queen Anne, Charles I, and Charles II, and a carv-ing of Cromwell's head pinned up by the ears, a savage addition by the Royalist citizens of Worcester. Inside, the walls of the Assembly Room are hung with an impressive collection of patrician portraits under a painted ceiling, which you can admire over tea and buns. ⊠ *High St.,* ☎ *01905/723471.* 🎫 *Free.* ☉ *Mon.–Sat. 9–5.*

Dining and Lodging

££££   ✕ **Brown's.** A former grain mill houses this light and airy riverside restau-
★   rant. The fixed-price menu and daily specialties include warm salad with breast of duck and croutons, and smoked haddock chowder with poached egg. ⊠ *24 Quay St.,* ☎ *01905/26263. AE, MC, V. Closed Mon. No lunch Sat., no dinner Sun.*

£££   ✕ **King's Restaurant.** The deluxe Fownes Hotel, a converted Victorian glove factory, now houses this classic English restaurant, where meals are served on Royal Worcester porcelain. The old-fashioned tone is coun-tered by a good selection of modern and exotic dishes, such as strips of pork with sesame and ginger. There's a fixed-price menu at dinner. ⊠ *Fownes Hotel, City Walls Rd.,* ☎ *01905/613151. AE, DC, MC, V.*

££   ✕ **King Charles II Restaurant.** Here you can dine in the black-and-white, half-timber house in which Charles II hid after the Battle of Worces-ter. It's now an oak-panel, silver-service restaurant with a very friendly atmosphere. Cuisine is mainly French and Italian, but there are also traditional English selections, such as beef Wellington, and such fresh fish dishes as Dover sole meunière. ⊠ *29 New St.,* ☎ *01905/22449. AE, DC, MC, V. Closed Sun.*

££   🏨 **Ye Old Talbot Hotel.** The Old Talbot was originally a courtroom be-longing to the cathedral, which stands close by. The hotel has been re-furbished, and there are modern extensions to the 16th-century core of the building. ✉ *Friar St., WR1 2NA,* ☎ *01905/23573,* FAX *01905/ 612760. 29 rooms. Restaurant. AE, DC, MC, V.*

£ 🔛 **Burgage House.** This traditional Georgian bed-and-breakfast, in a cobbled lane right next to the cathedral, offers a hearty welcome. Furnishings are authentic to the period, and there's a marvelous stone staircase dating from 1858, a century after the house was built, as well as an inglenook fireplace. Breakfast includes free-range hens' eggs. ✉ *4 College Precincts, WR1 2LG,* ☎ FAX *01905/25396. 4 rooms. No credit cards. Closed last wk Dec.*

Nightlife and the Arts

In 2002, from August 17 to 23, Worcester Cathedral takes its turn hosting the **Three Choirs Festival** (☎ 01905/616200, WEB www.3choirs.org). Besides full-scale classical choral works, there are plenty of fringe events and entertainments. **Huntingdon Hall** (✉ Crowngate, ☎ 01905/ 611427), a refurbished Methodist chapel founded in 1773, puts on a varied program of music and poetry recitals throughout the year. The original pews are—thankfully—now provided with cushions.

Outdoor Activities and Sports

BICYCLING

Bikes can be rented from **Peddlers** (✉ 46 Barbourne Rd., ☎ 01905/ 24238).

BOATING

There are plenty of opportunities in Worcester to rent boats or take short cruises on the Severn. **Bickerline River Trips** (✉ South Quay, near the cathedral, ☎ 01905/422499) has 45-minute excursions on a small passenger boat leaving several times daily April through October.

HORSE RACING

You can have a day at the races at **Worcester Racecourse** (✉ Pitchcroft, ☎ 08702/220–2772), picturesquely sited on the banks of the River Severn. Admission prices start at £5.

Shopping

All shoppers will first head for the emporium at the **Royal Worcester Porcelain Factory** (Severn St., ☎ 01905/23221), where, among other merchandise, you can buy "seconds." **Bygones** (✉ Dean's Way, ☎ 01905/25388; ✉ 55 Sidbury, ☎ 01905/23132) sells antiques, items of fine craftsmanship, and small gifts in silver, glass, and porcelain. **G. R. Pratley** (✉ The Shambles, ☎ 01905/22678) has tables piled high with fine china, such as Royal Worcester, Wedgwood, Spode.

Pershore

🔵 *8 mi southeast of Worcester.*

In the fruitful Vale of Evesham sits the the peaceful, unspoiled market town of Pershore. This is plum and asparagus country; trees are loaded down with blossom in spring, and May sees the asparagus harvest. The town's wide streets are flanked by impressive Georgian architecture with a variety of elegant facades.

The nave of **Pershore Abbey** did not survive the dissolution of the monasteries, but the beautiful chancel and crossing has been preserved. The choir has a rare "ploughshare" vault (so called because the curved panels resemble the blade of a ploughshare) with soaring ribs that culminate in 41 carved bosses; no two are the same. The fine lantern tower was opened up in the 1860s by the architect George Gilbert Scott to reveal the internal tracery. He replaced the old bellringing chamber with a suspended platform that seems to float in space.

✉ *Church Row,* ☎ *01386/552071,* WEB *www.pershoreabbey.fsnet.co.uk.* 🖅 *Free.* ⊙ *Daily 9–5.*

Dining and Lodging

££££ ✗ **Epicurean.** If you're here on a Friday, direct your steps toward this small, modern, and elegantly simple restaurant where star chef Patrick McDonald—when not cooking for royalty or troubleshooting other restaurants—has made his mark. You can choose between a contemporary British five- or six-course meal meticulously cooked and presented. It's usually necessary to book at least three weeks in advance. ✉ *76 High St.,* ☎ *01386/555576. Reservations essential. No credit cards. Closed Sat.–Thurs. and 2 wks Dec.–Jan. and 2 wks in Aug.*

Lower Broadheath

🟠 *10 mi northwest of Pershore, 2 mi west of Worcester.*

Southwest of Worcester lie the Malvern Hills, their long, low, purple profiles rising starkly from the surrounding plain. These were the hills that inspired much of the music of Sir Edward Elgar (1857–1934), as well as his remark that "there is music in the air, music all around us." The village of Lower Broadheath is on the B4204.

The **Elgar Birthplace Museum,** set in a peaceful little garden, is the tiny brick cottage in which the composer was born. It now exhibits photographs, musical scores, letters, and such. ✉ *Crown East La.,* ☎ *01905/ 333224,* WEB *www.elgar.org.* 🖅 *£3.50.* ⊙ *Mid-Jan.–Dec., daily 11–5.*

Great Malvern

🟠 *9 mi south of Lower Broadheath, 7 mi south of Worcester.*

Great Malvern, off the A449, is a Victorian spa town whose architecture has changed little since the mid-1800s. Exceptionally pure spring water is still bottled here and exported all over the world—the Queen never travels without a supply. Great Malvern is known today both as an educational center and as a great place for old folks' homes. The town also has a Winter Gardens complex with a theater, cinema, and gardens. The **Priory** dominates the steep streets downtown. This early Norman Benedictine abbey in Perpendicular style is decorated with vertical lines of airy tracery and fine 15th-century glass. ✉ *Entrance opposite church,* ☎ *01684/561020.* 🖅 *Free.* ⊙ *Easter–Sept., daily 9:30–6:30; Oct.–Easter, daily 9–4:30.*

Dining and Lodging

££££ ✗ **Croque en Bouche.** French, Italian, and Japanese dishes and a su-
★ perb handling of excellent local ingredients form the unlikely basis of the cuisine in this country restaurant. The chef-proprietor, Marion Jones, has earned a considerable reputation. Specialties include skate with mango basil salsa, wild boar with grilled vegetables and Oriental pesto, sushi, and roast guinea fowl with coriander. Delicious desserts and a dazzling wine list complete the evening's delights. Prices are significantly lower on Thursday. ✉ *221 Wells Rd., Malvern Wells,* ☎ *01684/ 565612. MC, V. Closed Sun.–Wed. No lunch.*

£££ ✗🖫 **Cottage in the Wood.** This hotel sits on shady grounds high up the side of the Malvern Hills with splendid views of the countryside. The furnishings are country-house comfortable; the rooms vary in size, and the ones with a view are equipped with binoculars. The restaurant has the best of the panorama through its tall windows. Food is English, with the accent on country fare, and there's a wide selection of more than 600 wines, including many local English ones. ✉

Holywell Rd., WR14 4LG, ☎ *01684/575859,* 𝖥𝖠𝖷 *01684/560662,* 𝖶𝖤𝖡 *www.cottageinthewood.co.uk. 20 rooms. Restaurant, bar. AE, MC, V.*

£ 🖻 **Sidney House.** In addition to its stunning views, this dignified Georgian hotel, run by a friendly husband-and-wife team, is also near the town center. The adequately sized bedrooms with television make this lodging a good bet for people traveling on a budget. On a clear afternoon you can gaze out over the Vale of Evesham to the Cotswolds. ⊠ *40 Worcester Rd., WR14 4AA,* ☎ *01684/574994. 8 rooms, 5 with bath. AE, DC, MC, V.*

Nightlife and the Arts

Malvern has historical connections with Sir Edward Elgar as well as with George Bernard Shaw, who premiered many of his plays here. Two festivals that run for two or three weeks from the end of May to early June keep up the cultural tone. The **Malvern Festival** (☎ 01684/892277 or 01684/892289) was originally devoted to the works of Elgar and Shaw, although now it also offers a wide variety of new music and new drama. The **Malvern Fringe Festival** (☎ 01684/891591 or 01684/892289) has an exceptional program of alternative events.

Ledbury

⑱ *10 mi southwest of Great Malvern on A449.*

Among the black-and-white half-timber buildings that make up the market town of Ledbury, take special note of two late-16th-century ones: the Feathers Hotel and the Talbot Inn. Almost hidden behind the 17th-century market house is a cobbled lane, crowded with medieval, half-timber buildings, leading to the church. The **Old Grammar School,** a heritage center housed in an old school, traces the history of local industries, with some displays on two literary celebrities linked to the area, John Masefield and Elizabeth Barrett Browning. ⊠ *Church La.,* ☎ *01531/636147.* 🖾 *Free.* ☉ *Mid-Apr.–Oct., daily 10:30–4:30.*

★ On the eastern outskirts of Ledbury is **Eastnor Castle,** a Victorian extravaganza that includes some magnificent neo-Gothic salons designed by 19th-century architect Augustus Pugin. Other grand rooms, all aswirl with lush tapestries, gilded paintings, Regency chandeliers, and Auntie's old armchairs have been restored to the height of *le style anglais* by the owners, the Hervey-Bathurst family, making Eastnor a must-do for lovers of English interior decoration. ⊠ *A438 Ledbury,* ☎ *01531/633160,* 𝖶𝖤𝖡 *www.eastnorcastle.com.* 🖾 *House £5, grounds £3.* ☉ *July–Aug., Sun.–Fri. 11–5; Apr.–June and Sept., Sun. 11–5.*

Dining and Lodging

£££ ✕🖻 **Feathers Hotel.** You can't miss the striking black-and-white facade of this central hostelry, which dates from the 16th century. The interior has a satisfyingly antique flavor, with creaking staircases and ancient floorboards, and some rooms have four-posters. The hop-bedecked Fuggles Brasserie (so named after a variety of hop) offers a range of starters and plenty of fresh fish, as well as lighter meals. If you're indulging, try the local pheasant with chestnuts and Madeira sauce. ⊠ *High St., HR8 1DS,* ☎ *01531/635266,* 𝖥𝖠𝖷 *01531/638955,* 𝖶𝖤𝖡 *www.feathers-ledbury.co.uk. 19 rooms. Restaurant, bar, indoor pool, health club. AE, DC, MC, V.*

Much Marcle

⑲ *4 mi southwest of Ledbury.*

Much Marcle is one of the English villages still holding the ancient annual ceremony of "wassailing"—beating the apple trees to make them fruitful in the coming year. The ritual takes place on Twelfth Night, January 6. There's also a beautiful 13th-century church here, richly endowed with effigies and tombs, notably one of Blanche, Lady Grandison. If you have a detailed map and plenty of time to spare, this is an area to wander around and discover tiny villages down sleepy lanes overhung by high hedges.

Just outside the village of Much Marcle lies the beautiful 17th-century mansion of **Hellen's,** still in singularly authentic and pristine condition (part of it from the 13th century). The gloom and dust are part of the atmosphere; the house is illuminated by candles, and central heating has been scorned. ⊠ ½ mi east of Much Marcle, ☎ 01531/660504. ⌨ £4. ⊙ Apr.–Sept., Wed. and weekends 2–5; tours on the hr (last tour at 4).

Ross-on-Wye

㉑ 6 mi southwest of Much Marcle.

Perched high above the River Wye, Ross-on-Wye seems oblivious to modern-day intrusions and remains at heart a small market town. Its steep streets come alive on Thursday and Saturday—market days—but they're always a happy hunting ground for antiques.

Lodging

££–£££ 🛏 **Chase Hotel.** This well-renovated Georgian-style country-house hotel is set on 11 acres. Rooms are simply and comfortably furnished in the main house, and more modern in the newer wing. ⊠ Gloucester Rd., HR9 5LH, ☎ 01989/763161, ℻ 01989/768330, 🌐 www.chasehotel.co.uk. 38 rooms. Restaurant. AE, DC, MC, V.

Goodrich

㉑ 3 mi south of Ross-on-Wye on B4234, 3 mi north of Symond's Yat on B4229.

The village of Goodrich is dominated by the ruins of a castle that is the English equivalent of a Rhineland schloss. Looming dramatically over the River Wye crossing at Kerne Bridge, **Goodrich Castle** from the south looks picturesque in its setting of green fields, but you quickly see its grimmer face when you stand on its battlements on the north side. Dating from the late 12th century, it's surrounded by a deep moat carved out of solid rock, from which its walls appear to soar upward. Built to repel Welsh raiders, Goodrich was destroyed in the 17th century during the Civil War. ⊠ Off A40, ☎ 01600/890538, 🌐 www.english-heritage.org.uk. ⌨ £3.60. ⊙ Apr.–Sept., daily 10–6; Oct., daily 10–5; Nov.–Mar., Wed.–Sun. 10–1 and 2–4.

Symond's Yat

㉒ 3 mi south of Goodrich, 6 mi south of Ross-on-Wye.

Outside the village of Symond's Yat ("gate"), the 473-ft-high Yat Rock commands superb views of the River Wye as it winds through a narrow gorge and swings around in a great 5-mi loop.

Kilpeck

㉓ 15 mi northwest of Goodrich, 7 mi southwest of Hereford.

Tucked away on a minor road off the A465, the tiny hamlet of Kilpeck is blessed with one of the best-preserved Norman churches in Britain. Much of the village, along with the remains of a castle and the church, is protected as a Scheduled Ancient Monument. The red sandstone **Kilpeck church,** completed in the mid-12th century, is lavishly decorated inside and out, with an order of sculpted carving exceptional for a country church. The carvings depict all manner of subjects, from rabbits to scenes so scandalously frank that they were removed by high-minded Victorians. (One or two ribald ones remain, however, so look carefully.) Don't miss the gargoyle rainwater spouts, either. ☎ 01981/ 570315. ☜ *Free.* ☉ *Daily 9–dusk.*

Hereford

24 *7 mi northeast of Kilpeck, 56 mi southwest of Birmingham, 31 mi northwest of Gloucester, 54 mi northeast of Cardiff.*

A busy country town, Hereford is the center of a wealthy agricultural area known for its cider, fruit, and cattle—the white-faced Hereford breed has spread across the world. It's also an important cathedral city, its massive Norman cathedral towering proudly over the River Wye. Before 1066, Hereford was the capital of the Anglo-Saxon kingdom of Mercia and, earlier still, the site of Roman, Celtic, and Iron Age settlements. Today, visitors come primarily to see the cathedral but quickly discover the charms of a town that has changed slowly but fairly unobtrusively with the passing centuries.

Built of local red sandstone with a massive central tower, **Hereford Cathedral** retains some fine 11th-century Norman carvings but suffered considerable "restoration" in the 19th century. Inside, its greatest glories include the 14th-century bishop's throne and some fine misericords (the elaborately carved undersides of choristers' seats). ✉ *Cathedral Close,* ☎ *01432/374200.* ☜ *suggested donation £2; tours £2.* ☉ *Mon.–Sat. 7:30–6:30, Sun. 8–4:30; daily tours at 11 and 2.*

★ The **Mappa Mundi and Chained Library Exhibition** are an extraordinary double attraction. The Mappa Mundi represents Hereford's own picture of the medieval world and shows the Earth as flat, with Jerusalem at its center. It's now thought that it was originally the central section of an altarpiece dating from 1290. The chained library contains some 1,500 chained books, among the most valuable volumes being an 8th-century copy of the Four Gospels. Chained libraries, in which the books were chained to cupboards to discourage theft, are extremely rare: they date from medieval times, when books were as precious as gold. ✉ *Cathedral Close,* ☎ *01432/374200.* ☜ *£4.* ☉ *Apr.–Oct., Mon.–Sat. 10–5, Sun. 11–4; Nov.–Mar., Mon.–Sat. 11–4; last admission 45 mins before closing.*

The half-timber **Old House** is a fine example of domestic Jacobean architecture, furnished in 17th-century style on three floors. You can see a kitchen and hall, among other rooms. ✉ *High Town,* ☎ *01432/ 260694.* ☜ *Free.* ☉ *Tues.–Sat. 10–5 (also Sun. 10–4, Apr.–Sept.).*

The 13th-century **All Saints Church,** on the west side of High Town, contains 300 chained books, as well as canopied stalls and fine misericords.

A farm cider house and a cooper's workshop have been re-created at the **Cider Museum,** where you can tour ancient cider cellars, complete with huge oak vats. Cider brandy (applejack) is made here, and the museum has its own brand for sale, along with other cider items. To reach the museum from All Saints Church, walk down the pedestrian Eign Gate, go through the pedestrian underpass, and down Eign Street, which continues as Whitecross Road. At the traffic lights, turn left onto Grimmer Road and bear right for the museum. ✉ *Pomona Pl. at Whitecross Rd.,* ☎ *01432/354207.* ☜ *£2.50.* ☉ *Apr.–Oct., daily 10–5:30; Nov.–Mar., Tues.–Sun. 11–3.*

Dining and Lodging

£　✕ **Orange Tree.** This refurbished, wood-panel pub is conveniently lo-
★　cated on King Street where it joins Bridge Street, near the cathedral. It's
a comfortable stopping place on a sightseeing day, with good, solid bar
food at lunchtime. ⊠ *16 King St.,* ☎ *01432/267698. No credit cards.*

££££　🏠 **Castle House.** All that's left of Hereford Castle is the moat, home
to dragonflies and families of wildfowl. Next to the moat, this Victorian hotel offers a welcoming ambience in a luxurious setting. The rooms
are all individually designed: the Cavalier Suite has French doors to
the garden, while the William & Mary Suite looks out over the moat.
⊠ *Castle St., HR1 2NW,* ☎ *01432/356321,* 🆑 *01432/365909,* 🌐
*www.castlehse.co.uk. 15 suites. Restaurant, bar, business services. AE,
DC, MC, V.*

£　🏠 **Hopbine Hotel.** The Hopbine is a mile from the center of town in
the direction of Leominster (pronounced "Lemster"), but it's worth
the jaunt. This Victorian guest house stands amid 2 acres of grounds.
Rooms are comfortable and quiet, and evening meals are available. You'll
appreciate the friendliness of this simple place. ⊠ *Roman Rd., HR1
1LE,* ☎ 🆑 *01432/268722. 13 rooms. MC, V.*

Shopping

Hereford has a different market each day—food, clothing, livestock—
on New Market Street.

At **Capuchin Yard** (⊠ Off 29 Church St.), you can find a wide variety
of crafts for sale, including handmade shoes and knitwear; other outlets sell books, posters, and watercolors. For quality foods, head for
the **Left Bank Village** (⊠ Bridge St., ☎ 01432/340200) development
and browse the delicatessen, patisserie, and wine shop.

Witley Court

㉕　*27 mi northeast of Hereford, 10 mi northwest of Worcester.*

The romantic shell of Witley Court will conjure up a haunting vision
of the Victorian heyday of the imposing stately home—a huge Italianate
pile—that stood here before being ravaged by fire in 1937. In contrast
to this ruin, the tiny baroque parish church is perfectly preserved.
Note its balustraded parapet, a small golden dome over its cupola, and,
inside, a ceiling painted by Bellucci, 10 colored windows, and the ornate case of an organ once used by Handel. The glorious gardens are
being restored, and the Poseidon and Flora fountains, when repaired,
should send their jets skyward "with the noise of an express train."
The house is little less than a mile outside Great Witley, ⊠ *A443,* ☎
01299/896636, 🌐 *www.english-heritage.org.uk.* 🎫 *£3.80.* ☼ *Apr.–
Sept., daily 10–6; Oct., daily 10–5; Nov.–Mar., Wed.–Sun. 10–4.*

Dining and Lodging

£££–££££　✕🏠 **Elms Hotel.** This luxurious, traditional country-house hotel, 16 mi
northeast of Worcester and near Great Witley, is in an ivy-clad Queen
Anne building surrounded by formal gardens. It was designed by
Gilbert White, a pupil of Sir Christopher Wren, and public rooms retain their ornate plasterwork. All the rooms in the former mansion are
individually and comfortably decorated and include antiques. The
restaurant, with its imaginative cooking and pleasant, family-dining
room ambience, is worth a visit on its own. ⊠ *Stockton Rd., Abberley WR6 6AT,* ☎ *01299/896666,* 🆑 *01299/896804,* 🌐 *www.slh.com.
16 rooms. Restaurant, tennis court, helipad. AE, DC, MC, V.*

Bewdley

26 *8 mi north of Great Witley, 14 mi north of Worcester, 3 mi west of Kidderminster.*

Bewdley is an exceptionally attractive Severn Valley town, with many tall, narrow-fronted Georgian buildings clustered around the river bridge. In what was the 18th-century butchers' market, the **Shambles,** there is now a museum of local history, trades, and crafts, with exhibitions and practical demonstrations of rope making and clay-pipe making. The nearby workshops are occupied by craftspeople, working in wood, glass, and felt. ⊠ *Load St.,* ☎ *01299/403573.* ▣ *£2.* ☉ *Mid-Apr.–Sept., daily 11–5; Oct., daily 10–4.*

Bewdley is the southern terminus of the **Severn Valley Railway,** a restored steam railroad running 16 mi north along the river to Bridgnorth. It stops at a handful of sleepy stations where time has apparently stood still since the age of steam. You can get off at any of these little stations, enjoy a picnic by the river, and walk to the next station to get a train back. ⊠ *Railway Station,* ☎ *01299/403816,* WEB *www.svr.co.uk.* ☉ *Mid-May–Sept., trains run daily; Oct.–mid-May, weekends only.*

Stourbridge

27 *8 mi northeast of Bewdley via A451, 11 mi west of Birmingham.*

Stourbridge is home to Britain's crystal glass industry, and although the industry is in decline, the exquisite glassware is still being produced. You'll find a number of shops offering "factory seconds" bargains.

Between mid-April and September, you can join the **Stourport Steamer Co.** (⊠ Riverside Walk, ☎ 01299/871177) for short river trips on weekends and national holidays, and for longer journeys as far as Worcester on Wednesday from the first week in July through September.

Shopping

The **Crystal and Glass Centre** (⊠ Churton House, Audnam, ☎ 01384/354400), a mile from Stourbridge on the A491 Wolverhampton road, stocks an international range of glassware as well as local products. There's a good selection of gifts on sale at the **Stuart Crystal Visitor Centre and Factory Shop** (⊠ High St., Wordsley, ☎ 01384/261777).

Dudley

28 *6 mi northeast of Stourbridge, 8 mi west of central Birmingham.*

It was in Dudley that coal was first used for smelting iron in the 17th century. The town subsequently gained the nickname of the capital of
★ the Black Country. The **Black Country Living Museum** was established to ensure that the area's industrial heritage is not forgotten. An entire industrial village has been reconstructed of disused buildings from around the region. There's a chain maker's house and workshop, with demonstrations of chain making; a druggist and general store, where costumed women describe life in a poor industrial community in the 19th century; a Methodist chapel; the Bottle & Glass pub, serving local ales and cheese rolls; Stables restaurant, serving such traditional delicacies as faggots and peas (a fried pork-liver dish); and a coal mine and wharf. You can also ride on a barge through a tunnel, where an audiovisual show portrays canal travel of yesteryear. ⊠ *Tipton Rd.,* ☎ *0121/557–9643,* WEB *www.bclm.co.uk.* ▣ *£7.95.* ☉ *Mar.–Oct., daily 10–5; Nov.–Feb., Wed.–Sun. 10–4.*

SKIRTING THE "BLACK COUNTRY": FROM SHREWSBURY TO CHESTER

The "peak" of this region—in terms of height—is the Wrekin, a hill geologists claim to be the oldest in the land. That may mean little to the average visitor. Far better to record that A. E. Housman and others have invested it with some of their poetic charm. To look around on its isolated summit is to gaze on a peaceful rural scene, quite different from most people's preconceptions of the industrial Midlands. The Wrekin has attracted renewed interest because of the enormous popularity of Ironbridge, several miles from the hill. Ironbridge has two identities, as a place as well as a thing. The thing itself is the first bridge to be made of iron, erected between 1777 and 1779. Now taken over by the Ironbridge Gorge Museum Trust, it's the centerpiece of a vast Industrial Revolution museum complex. The place is the 6-mi stretch of the Ironbridge Gorge, once an awesome scene of mining and charcoal burning, reeking with smoke and the stench of sulfur. The ironworking forges and the coal mining created the pollution that gave this region west of Birmingham its name—the Black Country—during the mid-19th century. The stretch has now been completely transformed into a scene of idyllic beauty, scars grassed over, woodland filling the gaps left by tree felling. Within easy reach of Ironbridge, rural Shropshire spreads invitingly, offering towns long famed as beauty spots, such as Bridgnorth and Ludlow. Around this area are two important cities of the Welsh Border region: Shrewsbury and Chester, both famous for their medieval heritage and their wealth of half-timber buildings.

Shrewsbury

47 mi northwest of Dudley, 55 mi north of Hereford, 46 mi south of Chester, 48 mi northwest of Birmingham, 150 mi northwest of London.

Shrewsbury (usually pronounced *shrose*-bury), the county seat of Shropshire, is within a great horseshoe loop of the Severn. One of England's most important medieval towns, it has a wealth of 16th-century half-timber buildings—many built by well-to-do wool merchants—plus elegant ones from later periods. Today, the town retains a romantic air (indeed, there are numerous bridal shops here, along with a number of churches), and it can be a lovely experience to stroll the Shrewsbury "shuts." These narrow alleys overhung with timbered gables lead off the central market square, which had originally been designed to be closed off at night to afford local residents greater protection. The town is especially proud of its flower displays, for which it has won many national awards; in summer, filled window boxes and hanging baskets are in vivid contrast to the black-and-white buildings.

Shrewsbury is an ideal town to see on foot, and indeed, traffic has been banned on some of the most historic streets. A good starting point for a walking tour is the small square between Fish Street and Butcher Row. These streets are little changed since medieval times, when some of them took their names from the principal trades carried on there, but Peacock Alley, Gullet Passage, and Grope Lane clearly got their names from
㉙ somewhere else. The stone spire of **St. Mary's** church (✉ off Castle St.), built around 1200, is one of the three tallest in England and merits a visit for its iron-framed stained glass, an indication of the proximity of the Ironbridge Gorge.

㉚ **St. Alkmund's** (✉ St. Alkmund's Pl.) is another prominent feature of the Shrewsbury skyline and is also worth seeing for its stained glass.

Ireland's
Mansion . . . **31**

Quarry
Park **33**

St.
Alkmund's . . **30**

St. Chad . . . **34**

St. Mary's . . **29**

Shrewsbury
Abbey **36**

Shrewsbury
Castle **35**

Shrewsbury
Museum
and Art
Gallery **32**

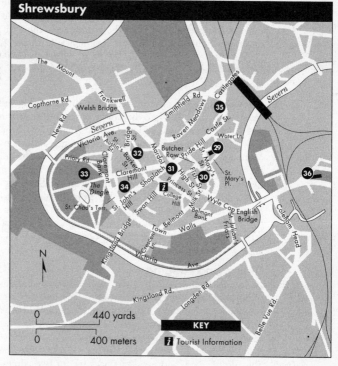

Shrewsbury

KEY

i Tourist Information

0   440 yards

0   400 meters

③① Near St. Mary's church, off Fish Street, it was built in 1795 on the site of a much earlier church. Bear Steps is a cluster of restored half-timber buildings that link Fish Street with Market Square. Here the most notable building is the massive **Ireland's Mansion,** built in 1575 with elaborate Jacobean timbering and richly decorated with quatrefoils.

③② A magnificent 16th-century timber-frame warehouse and brick and stone mansion built in 1618 form an eye-catching ensemble in the center of Shrewsbury. Today they house the **Shrewsbury Museum and Art Gallery,** containing clothing, Shropshire pottery and ceramics, Roman finds from Wroxeter, a reconstructed 17th-century bedroom with oak, holly, and walnut paneling and a four-poster bed, and other items of local history. ⊠ *Barker St.,* ☎ *01743/361196.* ⊠ *Free.* ⊙ *Apr.–Sept., Tues.–Sat. 10–5, Sun. 10–4; Oct.–Mar., Tues.–Sat 10–4.*

③③ Below Swan Hill you will see the manicured lawn of **Quarry Park** sloping down to the river. In a sheltered corner is the **Dingle,** a colorful garden offering changing floral displays throughout the year. To reach the park from the center of town, head for Welsh Bridge and stroll along the riverbank, or walk up Claremont Hill.

③④ On a hilltop setting west of the center, the church of **St. Chad,** designed by George Steuart, the architect of Attingham Park, is one of England's most original ecclesiastical buildings. Completed in 1792, the round Georgian church is surmounted by a tower, which is in turn square, octagonal, and circular—and finally topped by a dome. When being built, it provoked riots among the townfolk averse to its radical style and angry at the partial demolition of the city walls that the construction entailed. ⊠ *St. Chad's Terrace,* ☎ *01743/365478.* ⊠ *Free.* ⊙ *Apr.–Oct., daily 8–5; Nov.–Mar., daily 8–1.*

③⑤ Guarding the northern approaches to the town, **Shrewsbury Castle** rises up over the river at the bottom of Pride Hill. Originally Norman, it was dismantled during the Civil War and later rebuilt by Thomas Telford, the distinguished Scottish engineer who designed a host of notable buildings and bridges at the beginning of the 19th century. The castle now houses the **Shropshire Regimental Museum.** ⊠ *Shrewsbury Castle, Castle Gates,* ☎ *01743/358516.* 🎫 *£2.* ☉ *Apr.–Sept., Tues.– Sat. 10–5, Sun. 10–4; Oct.–Mar., Tues.–Sat. 10–4. Castle grounds daily 9–5.*

㊱ **Shrewsbury Abbey,** now unbecomingly surrounded by busy roads, was founded in 1083 and later became a powerful Benedictine monastery. The Abbey Church has survived various vicissitudes throughout its history, including the dissolution of the monasteries, and retains a good 14th-century west window above a Norman doorway. The abbey figures in the popular medieval whodunits by Ellis Peters that feature the detective Brother Cadfael; the novels provide an excellent idea of area life in the Middle Ages. To reach the abbey from the center of town, cross the river by the English Bridge. ⊠ *Abbey Church, Abbey Foregate,* ☎ *01743/232723,* 🕸 *www.virtual-shropshire.co.uk/shrewsbury-abbey.* 🎫 *£2 suggested donation.* ☉ *Apr.–Oct., daily 9:30–5:30; Nov.–Mar., daily 10:30–3.*

Dining and Lodging

££££ ✗ **Country Friends.** An attractive black-and-white building, 5 mi south of Shrewsbury by the A49, houses this light and airy restaurant overlooking a garden and pond. Specialties include halibut with olive and basil crust, venison with black currant sauce, and lamb noisettes roasted in mustard crust with mint hollandaise; there's a fixed-price menu at dinner. The restaurant also has a simple double bedroom available (dinner, bed, and breakfast package for two comes to £130). ⊠ *Dorrington,* ☎ *01743/718707. MC, V. Closed Sun., Mon., 2 wks mid-July, mid-wk in Oct.*

££ ✗ **Traitor's Gate.** Installed in a series of 13th-century vaulted brick cellars, this atmospheric restaurant serves reasonably priced meals with a Mediterranean flavor. Lunch choices include sandwiches on baguettes or ciabatta; at dinner some options are pastas and antipasto, baked salmon with lemon, and panfried venison. Close to the local castle, the Traitor's Gate gets its name from an incident in the Civil War, when a young Roundhead lieutenant ransacked the Cavalier-held fortress. He was later executed as a traitor. ⊠ *St. Mary's Water La. and Castle St.,* ☎ *01743/249152. AE, MC, V. Closed Sun. evening, Mon.*

££ 🏨 **Prince Rupert Hotel.** This black-and-white, half-timber inn in the historic city center was the headquarters of Prince Rupert, nephew of Charles I and the most famous Royalist general during the Civil War. It's now furnished in modern style, although four rooms have four-poster beds. ⊠ *Butcher Row, SY1 1UQ,* ☎ *01743/499955,* 📠 *01743/357306,* 🕸 *www.prince-rupert-hotel.co.uk. 69 rooms. 3 restaurants, spa, gym. AE, DC, MC, V.*

£ 🏨 **Sandford House.** This late-Georgian B&B, close to the river and the town center, is run by the hospitable Richards family. The bedrooms are clean and basic, but well furnished. There's an attractive rear garden. ⊠ *St. Julian Friars, SY1 1XL,* ☎ *01743/343829. 18 rooms. AE, MC, V.*

Nightlife and the Arts

During the **Shrewsbury International Music Festival** (⊠ Shrewsbury Festival Office, Box 264, Northwich, Cheshire CW8 1FB, ☎ 01606/872633) in June and July, the town vibrates to traditional and not-so-traditional music by groups from Europe and North America.

Shopping

The Parade, just behind St. Mary's church, is a shopping mall created from the former Royal Infirmary, built in 1830. It's one of the most appealing malls England has to offer, with attractive boutiques, posh apartments upstairs, a restaurant, and a terrace overlooking the river.

Attingham Park

37 *4 mi southeast of Shrewsbury.*

Built in 1785 by George Steuart (architect of the church of St. Chad in Shrewsbury) for the first Lord Berwick, this elegant stone mansion has a three-story portico, with a pediment carried on four tall columns. The building overlooks a sweep of parkland, including a deer park landscaped by Humphrey Repton (1752–1818). Inside the house, there's a fine picture gallery designed by John Nash (1752–1835), painted ceilings, delicate plasterwork, and a collection of 19th-century Neapolitan furniture. ⊠ *B4380, off A5, Atcham,* ☎ *01743/708162,* WEB *www. nationaltrust.org.uk.* 🖭 *£4.30, park and grounds only £2.* ☉ *Mid-Apr.– Oct., Fri.–Tues. 1:30–4:30; last admission 30 mins before closing; park and grounds Mar.–Oct., daily 9–8; Nov.–Feb., daily 9–5.*

En Route Continuing southeast on B4380, you will see, rising on the left, the **Wrekin,** a strange, conical extinct volcano. A few miles farther on you enter the wooded gorge of the River Severn.

Ironbridge Gorge

★ **38** *15 mi east of Shrewsbury, 28 mi northwest of Birmingham.*

Ironbridge Gorge is the name given to a group of villages south of Telford that were crucial in ushering in the Industrial Revolution. The Shropshire coalfields were of enormous importance to the development of the coke smelting process, which helped make producing anything in iron much easier. The fascinating history of the area is preserved and recounted at **Ironbridge Gorge Museum.** Spread over 6 square mi, it has nine component sections; there's no public transport between them, so you'll need your own vehicle. To appreciate all the major sights and perhaps take a stroll around the famous iron bridge, or go hunting for Coalport china in the stores clustered near it, you'll need at least a full day. The best starting point is the **Museum of the Gorge,** which has a good selection of literature and an audiovisual show on the gorge's history. In nearby Coalbrookdale, the **Museum of Iron** explains the production of iron and steel. You can see the original blast furnace built by Abraham Darby, who developed the original coke process in 1709. From here, drive the few miles along the river until the arches of the **Iron Bridge** come into view; it was designed by T. F. Pritchard, smelted by Darby, and erected between 1777 and 1779. An infinitely graceful arch spanning the River Severn, it can best be seen—and photographed or painted—from the towpath, a riverside walk edged with wildflowers and dense shrubs. The tollhouse on the far side houses an exhibition on the bridge's history and restoration.

A mile farther along the river is the old factory and the **Coalport China Museum** (the china is now made in Stoke-on-Trent). There are exhibits of some of the factory's most beautiful wares, and craftsmen give demonstrations. Above Coalport is **Blists Hill Victorian Town,** where you can see old mines, furnaces, and a wrought-iron works. But the main draw is the re-creation of the "town" itself, with its doctor's office, sweet-smelling bakery, grocer's, candlemaker's, sawmill, printing shop, and candy store. At the entrance you can change your money for specially minted old pennies, which you can use to make purchases from the shops. Shopkeepers, the bank manager, and the doctor's wife are on hand in period dress to give you advice or information. In summer there are regular craft demonstrations. ⊠ *Ironbridge Gorge Museum Trust, Ironbridge, B4380,*

Telford, ☎ *01952/433522,* WEB *www.ironbridge.org.uk.* ✉ *Ticket to all sights £10.* ⊙ *Apr.–Oct, daily 10–5; Nov.–Mar., daily 10–4.*

Dining and Lodging

£ ✕ **New Inn.** This Victorian building was moved from Walsall, 22 mi away, so that it could be part of the Blists Hill Victorian Town. It's a fully functioning pub, with gas lamps, sawdust on the floor, and traditional ales served from the cask. For an inexpensive meal, you can try a ploughman's lunch, a pasty from the antique-style bakery, or a pork pie from the butcher's store next door. ✉ *Blists Hill Victorian Town,* ☎ *01952/433522. No credit cards.*

£££ ✕🖼 **Clarion Hotel at Madeley Court, Telford.** This restored 16th-century stone manor house was once the home of Abraham Darby. The rooms are rich in antiques and period furnishings, although there are modern ones available as well. The Priory Restaurant has a warm, medieval atmosphere but serves contemporary British food. In the garden, you'll find a rare example of an Elizabethan stone cube sundial. ✉ *Castlefields Way, Madeley, Telford TF7 5DW,* ☎ *01952/680068,* FAX *01952/684275,* WEB *www.choicehotelseurope.com. 47 rooms. Restaurant, bar. AE, DC, M, V.*

£ 🖼 **Library House.** On the hillside near the Ironbridge museums, and only a few steps away from the bridge itself, this small guest house (at one point the village's library) has kept its attractive Victorian ambience while allowing for such modern-day luxuries as video players in all the bedrooms. You are welcomed with a glass of wine. Smoking is not permitted indoors. ✉ *11 Severn Bank, Ironbridge, Telford TF8 7AN,* ☎ *01952/432299,* FAX *01952/433967,* WEB *www.libraryhouse.com. 4 rooms. No credit cards. Closed last 3 wks in Jan.*

Bridgnorth

㊴ *9 mi south of Ironbridge, 22 mi southeast of Shrewsbury, 25 mi west of Birmingham.*

Perching perilously on a high sandstone ridge on the banks of the Severn, the pretty market town of Bridgnorth has two distinct parts, High Town and Low Town, connected by a winding road, flights of steep steps, and—best of all—a cliff railroad. Even the tower of the Norman castle seems to suffer from vertigo, having a 17° list (three times the angle of the Leaning Tower of Pisa). The Severn Valley Railway, which originates in Bewdley, terminates here.

Ludlow

★ ㊵ *29 mi south of Shrewsbury, 24 mi north of Hereford.*

Pretty Ludlow has medieval, Georgian, and Victorian buildings and a finer display of black-and-white buildings than even Shrewsbury itself. The center is dominated by the great Church of St. Lawrence on College Street, its extravagant size a testimony to the town's prosperous wool trade. Cross the River Teme and climb Whitcliff for the most spectacular view. The town is also notable for a cluster of fine restaurants.

The town is dwarfed by the massive, ruined, red sandstone **Ludlow Castle,** which dates from 1085 and was a vital stronghold for centuries. It was the seat of the Marcher Lords who ruled "the Marches," the local name for the border region. It was in this castle that John Milton wrote his verse drama *Comus,* and it is still privately owned by the earl of Powys. Follow the terraced walk around the castle for a lovely view. ✉ *Castle Sq.,* ☎ *01584/873355.* ✉ *£3.* ⊙ *Feb.–Mar. and Oct.– Dec., daily 10–4; Apr.–July and Sept., daily 10–5; Aug., daily 10–7; last admission 30 mins before closing.*

OFF THE
BEATEN PATH

STOKESAY CASTLE – Not a castle, but an immaculately preserved ensemble of leaning half-timber buildings, this 13th-century fortified manor house is arguably the finest of its kind in England. Inside, the original central fireplace takes pride of place, and outside the cottage-style gardens are a bewitching backdrop for the magnificent Jacobean timber-frame gatehouse. ⊠ *Craven Arms (Off the A49 Shrewsbury road, 7 mi northwest of Ludlow),* ☎ *01588/672544,* WEB *www.english-heritage. org.uk.* ☐ *£4.* ☼ *Apr.–Sept., daily 10–6; Oct., daily 10–5; Nov.–Mar., Wed.–Sun. 10–1 and 2–4.*

Dining and Lodging

££££ ✗ **The Merchant House.** Tucked away in the northern end of town, this black-and-white Jacobean building could easily be mistaken for a private terraced house. Service at the small restaurant is unfussy, and the daily changing set menu reflects the eclectic preferences of the chef, relying on organic products where possible. Typical dishes include saffron and artichoke risotto, and iced prune and Armagnac parfait. ⊠ *Lower Corve St.,* ☎ *01584/875438. MC, V. Closed Sun., Mon., 1 wk in late Dec., and 1 wk in spring. No lunch Tues.–Thurs.*

£££ ✗ 🏨 **Dinham Hall.** This hotel near Ludlow Castle is a converted merchant's town house dating from 1792. The owners have managed to combine the original historic elements in the house with modern comforts. The dining room serves imaginative dishes such as ravioli of lobster with mussel and basil sauce. ⊠ *Off Market Sq., SY8 1EJ,* ☎ *01584/876464,* FAX *01584/876019. 14 rooms. Restaurant, sauna. AE, DC, MC, V.*

£££ 🏨 **The Feathers.** Even if you're not staying here, you can't help but admire the extravagant half-timber facade of this building, described by the architectural historian Nicholas Pevsner as "that prodigy of timber-framed houses." The interior is equally impressive—dripping with ornate plaster ceilings, carved oak, paneling, beams, and creaking floors. Some guest rooms are furnished in modern style, but others preserve the antique look. ⊠ *The Bull Ring, SY8 1AA,* ☎ *01584/875261,* FAX *01584/876030. 40 rooms. Restaurant. AE, DC, MC, V.*

Nightlife and the Arts

In Shropshire, the **Ludlow Festival,** starting at the end of June, sums up much that is English: Shakespeare is performed in the open air against the romantic backdrop of the ruined castle to an audience armed with cushions, raincoats, lap robes, and picnic baskets—and not a few hip flasks. Telephone reservations are accepted starting in early May, or by mail from April. Details available from the Festival Box Office (⊠ Castle Sq., Ludlow, Shropshire SY8 1AY, ☎ 01584/872150).

Chester

④ *75 mi north of Ludlow, 46 mi north of Shrewsbury, 24 mi north of Hereford.*

Cheshire is mainly a land of well-kept farms, supporting their herds of cattle, but numerous places here are steeped in history. Villages contain many fine examples of the black-and-white "magpie" type of architecture more often associated with the Midlands—and every bit as attractive as anything to be found there.

The thriving center of the region is Chester, a city similar in some ways to Shrewsbury, though it has many more black-and-white half-timber buildings (some of which were built in Georgian and Victorian times), and its medieval walls are still standing. Chester has been a prominent city since the late 1st century AD, when the Roman Empire expanded northward to the banks of the River Dee. The original Roman town plan is still evident: the principal streets, Eastgate, Northgate, Watergate, and Bridge Street, lead out from the Cross—the site of the central area of the Roman fortress—to the four city gates. Since Roman times, seagoing vessels have sailed up the estuary of the Dee and anchored under the walls of Chester. The port enjoyed its most prosperous period during the 12th and 13th centuries.

History seems more tangible in Chester than in many other ancient cities. So much medieval architecture remains that the town center is quite compact, and modern buildings have not been allowed to intrude. A negative result of this perfection is that Chester has become a favorite bus-tour destination, with gift shops, noise, and crowds. It's also home to the popular Chester Zoo, the second largest in Britain.

★   Chester's unique **Rows** originated in the 12th and 13th centuries. Essentially, they are double rows of stores, one at street level, and the other on the second floor with galleries overlooking the street. The Rows line the junction of the four streets in the old town. They have medieval crypts below them, and some reveal Roman foundations.

The city **walls** are accessible from various points and provide splendid views of the city and its surroundings. The whole circuit is 2 mi, but if your time is short, climb the steps at Newgate and walk along toward Eastgate to see the great ornamental **Eastgate Clock**, erected to commemorate Queen Victoria's Diamond Jubilee in 1897. Lots of small shops by this part of the walls sell old books, old postcards, antiques, and jewelry. Where the **Bridge of Sighs** (named after the enclosed bridge in Venice that it closely resembles) crosses the canal, descend to street level and walk up Northgate Street into Market Square.

Tradition has it that a church of some sort stood on the site of what is now **Chester Cathedral** in Roman times, but records indicate construction around AD 900. The earliest work traceable today, mainly in the north transept, is that of the 11th-century Benedictine abbey. After Henry VIII dissolved the monasteries in the 16th century, the abbey church became the cathedral church of the new diocese of Chester. ⊠ *St. Werburgh St., Off Market Sq.,* ☎ *01244/324756,* WEB *www.chestercathedral.org.uk.* ◼ *Free.* ⊙ *Daily 7–6:30.*

Overlooking the River Dee, **Chester Castle** lost its moats and battlements at the end of the 18th century to make way for the classical-style civil and criminal courts, jail, and barracks. The castle houses the **Cheshire Military Museum**, exhibiting uniforms, memorabilia, and some fine silver. ⊠ *Castle St.,* ☎ *01244/327617.* ◼ *£1.* ⊙ *Daily 10–5.*

Dining and Lodging

£   ✕ **The Falcon.** A half-timber old pub, the Falcon is a handy spot for a wide range of lunch options, including Balti (Indian/Pakistani) and Cajun dishes, and seafood. ⊠ *Lower Bridge St.,* ☎ *01244/314555. MC, V.*

££££   ✕▥ **Chester Grosvenor Hotel.** This is a deluxe traditional hotel in a Tudor-style, downtown building; it's remarkable to find such quiet luxury and sumptuous comfort in a small country town. Rooms are plushly furnished, with plenty of amenities. The splendid Arkle Restaurant (named after a celebrated racehorse) has marble and stone walls, solid mahogany tables, and gleaming silver. The style here is *cuisine légère,* using little cream or butter, only natural ingredients, and sauces made by reduction rather than thickening. The wine cellar has more than 600 bins. ⊠ *Eastgate St., CH1 1LT,* ☎ *01244/324024,* FAX *01244/ 313246,* WEB *www.chestergrosvenor.co.uk. 85 rooms. Restaurant, brasserie, lounge, health club. AE, DC, MC, V.*

£££ ✕ 🏨 **Crabwall Manor.** This dramatic castellated, part-Tudor, part-neo-
★   Gothic mansion is set on 11 acres of farm and parkland. It has ele-
      gant, subtle furnishings in floral chintzes, a wonderful stone staircase,
      and extremely comfortable bedrooms. A luxurious fitness center has
      a 17-m (56-ft) swimming pool. The spacious restaurant offers Cordon
      Bleu cooking and is worth visiting—say, for lunch—while exploring
      the neighborhood. ✉ *A540, Parkgate Rd., Mollington CH1 6NE,* ☎
      01244/851666, 🅵🅰🆇 *01244/851400,* 🆆🅴🅱 *www.crabwall.com. 48 rooms.*
      Restaurant, indoor pool, spa, health club. AE, DC, MC, V.

££   ✕ 🏨 **Green Bough Hotel.** The Green Bough is in a large, late-Victorian
      house with a variety of antiques and bric-a-brac. Both the main build-
      ing and the annex contain roomy, comfortable bedrooms, fitted out
      in period style with iron and brass bedsteads and oak and mahogany
      furniture. The dining room offers an imaginative, reasonably priced
      menu that changes daily and includes vegetarian dishes. ✉ *60 Hoole
      Rd., CH2 3NL,* ☎ *01244/326241,* 🅵🅰🆇 *01244/326265. 20 rooms.*
      Restaurant. AE, DC, MC, V.

Nightlife and the Arts

The **Chester Mystery Plays** (for details, contact the tourist office or 🆆🅴🅱
www.chestermysteryplays.com), performed every five years, are the oldest and most complete of the English medieval mystery plays. The dramatized biblical stories are staged on the Cathedral Green. In 2002,
the cycle will take place June 29 through July 17.

Shopping

Chester has an **indoor market** in the Forum, near the Town Hall, every
day except Wednesday afternoon and Sunday. **Bookland** (✉ 12 Bridge
St., ☎ 01244/347323), in an ancient building with a converted 14th-
century crypt, has a wealth of travel and general-interest books.
Melodies Antique Galleries (✉ 32 City Rd., ☎ 01244/328968), on three
floors of an old Georgian building, sells a wide mix of fine furniture
and bric-a-brac.

Little Moreton Hall

④② *25 mi east of Chester, 4 mi south of Congleton.*

The epitome of "magpie" black-and-white half-timber buildings, this
house, in the words of Olive Cook's *The English Country House,* "ex-
aggerates and exalts the typical and humble medieval timber-framed
dwelling, making of it a bizarre, unforgettable phenomenon." Covered
with dazzling zigzags, crosses, and lozenge shapes crafted of timber and
daub, the house was built by the Moreton family between 1450 and
1580. Other features include a spectacular long gallery, Tudor-era wall
paintings, and a drunkenly reeling facade. Special events are held
throughout the year, including evening buffet suppers and concerts. To
get here from Chester, take the bus (PMT 77), or the train to the stations at Kidsgrove or Congleton (from either, it's a 3-mi taxi ride), or
drive by car via the A54 east to Congleton, then south along the A34.
✉ *A34, Congleton,* ☎ *01260/272018,* 🆆🅴🅱 *www.nationaltrust.org.uk.*
🎫 *£4.40.* ☉ *Late Mar.–early Nov., Wed.–Sun. 11:30–5; early Nov.–
Dec. 20, weekends noon–4.*

WELSH BORDERS A TO Z

*To research prices, get advice from other travelers, and book travel ar-
rangements, visit www.fodors.com.*

AIRPORTS

➤ AIRPORT INFORMATION: **Birmingham International Airport** (✉ A45, off Junction 6 of M42, ☎ 0121/767–7798 or 0121/767–7799, WEB www.bhx.co.uk).

BUS TRAVEL

National Express serves the region from London's Victoria Coach Station. Average travel time to Chester is five hours; to Hereford and Shrewsbury, four hours; and to Worcester, 3½ hours. Flightlink operates services from London's Heathrow and Gatwick airports to Birmingham.

National traveline fields all public transport inquires. You can also contact local companies individually. For information about bus services and Rover tickets for the Birmingham area, contact the Centro Hotline. For Worcester, Hereford and surrounding areas, contact First Midland Red. Call Crosville Bus Station for the Chester area.

FARES AND SCHEDULES

➤ BUS INFORMATION: **Centro Hotline** (☎ 0121/200–2700, WEB www. centro.org.uk). **Crosville Bus Station** (☎ 01244/381515). **First Midland Red** (☎ 01905/763888, WEB www.firstmidlandred.co.uk). **Flightlink** (☎ 0870/580–8080). **National Express** (☎ 0870/580–8080, WEB www. gobycoach.com). **National traveline** (☎ 0870/608–2608, WEB www. traveline.org.uk).

CAR RENTAL

➤ LOCAL AGENCIES: **Avis** (✉ 17 Horsefair, Birmingham, ☎ 0121/632–4361; ✉ 128 Brook St., Chester, ☎ 01244/311463). **Hertz** (✉ Auto Travel Ltd., Abley House, Trafford St., Chester, ☎ 01244/374705). **National Car Rental** (✉ 18–20 Bristol St., Birmingham, ☎ 0121/200–3010). **Otis** (✉ 14 Carden St., Worcester, ☎ 01905/24844). **Practical Car and Van Rental** (✉ 12–14 Catherine St., Hereford, ☎ 01432/278989, WEB www.practical.co.uk). **Sixt Kenning** (✉ 7 Hylton Rd., Worcester, ☎ 01905/748403).

CAR TRAVEL

To reach Birmingham (120 mi), Shrewsbury (150 mi), and Chester (180 mi) from London, take M40 and keep on it for M42, or else take M1/M6. M4/M5 from London takes you to Worcester in just under three hours. The prettier, more direct route (120 mi) on M40 via Oxford to A40 across the Cotswolds is actually slower because it's only partly motorway.

ROAD CONDITIONS

Driving can be difficult in the western reaches of this region—especially in the hills and valleys west of Hereford, where steep, twisting roads often narrow down into mere trackways. Winter travel along here can be particularly grueling.

EMERGENCIES

➤ CONTACTS: **Ambulance, fire, police** (☎ 999). **Birmingham Heartlands Hospital** (✉ Bordesley Green E, Birmingham, ☎ 0121/766–6611). **Countess of Chester Hospital** (✉ Liverpool Rd., Chester, ☎ 01244/365000).

OUTDOORS AND SPORTS

HIKING AND WALKING

For information on hiking the Malvern Hills, contact Malvern Tourist Office or Ross-on-Wye Tourist Office.

➤ CONTACTS: **Malvern Tourist Office** (✉ 21 Church St., WR14 2AA, ☎ 01684/892289). **Ross-on-Wye Tourist Office** (✉ Swan House, Edde Cross St., HR9 7BZ, ☎ 01989/562768).

TOURS

Local tourist offices can recommend day or half-day tours of the region and will have the names of registered Blue Badge guides. Quality Time Travel in Malvern offers chauffeur-driven tours, shopping trips, and evening travel to theaters and concerts. From June to September, Guide Friday operates tours of Birmingham in open-top buses.

➤ FEES AND SCHEDULES: **Guide Friday** (⊠ The Civic Hall, 14 Rother St., Stratford-upon-Avon, ☎ 01789/294466, WEB www.guidefriday.com). **Quality Time Travel** (⊠ Moel Bryn, 105 Fruitlands, Malvern WR14 4XB, ☎ 01684/566799, WEB www.qualitytimetravel.co.uk).

TRAIN TRAVEL

From London, Great Western and Thames Trains serve the region from Paddington station, and Virgin, Central, and Silverlink Trains leave from Euston (call National Rail Inquiries for all schedules and information). Average travel times are: Paddington to Hereford, three hours; to Worcester, 2¼ hours; Euston to Birmingham, 1¾ hour; Euston to Shrewsbury and Chester, with a change at Wolverhampton or Birmingham, three hours and 2½ hours, respectively. A direct local service links Hereford and Shrewsbury, with a change at Oswestry or Wrexham for Chester.

CUTTING COSTS

West Midlands Day Ranger tickets and three- and seven-day "Heart of England Rover" tickets allow unlimited travel.

FARES AND SCHEDULES

➤ TRAIN INFORMATION: **National Rail Inquiries** (☎ 08457/484950, WEB www.railtrack.co.uk).

TRAVEL AGENCIES

➤ LOCAL AGENT REFERRALS: **American Express** (⊠ Bank House, 8 Cherry St., Birmingham, ☎ 0121/644–5555; ⊠ 12 Watergate St., Chester, ☎ 0870/600–1060). **Thomas Cook** (⊠ 99 New St., Birmingham, ☎ 0121/255–2600; ⊠ 10 Bridge St., Chester, ☎ 01244/583500; ⊠ 4 St. Peter's St., Hereford, ☎ 01432/422500; ⊠ 36–37 Pride Hill, Shrewsbury, ☎ 01743/842000; ⊠ 26 High St., Worcester, ☎ 01905/871200).

VISITOR INFORMATION

The Heart of England Tourist Board is open Monday–Thursday 9–5:30, Friday 9–5. Local tourist information centers are usually open Monday–Saturday 9:30–5:30.

➤ TOURIST INFORMATION: **Heart of England Tourist Board** (⊠ Woodside, Larkhill Rd., Worcester WR5 2EZ, ☎ 01905/763436, FAX 01905/763450, WEB www.visitheartofengland.com). **Birmingham** (⊠ International Convention Centre, Broad St., B1 2EA, ☎ 0121/665–6116; ⊠ 130 Colmore Row, B3 3AP, ☎ 0121/6936300, WEB www.birmingham.org.uk). **Chester** (⊠ Town Hall, Northgate St., CH1 2HJ, ☎ 01244/402111, WEB www.chestergov.uk/tourism). **Hereford** (⊠ 1 King St., HR4 9BW, ☎ 01432/268430, WEB www.visitorlinks.com). **Herefordshire and Shropshire** (WEB www.herefordshire-shropshire.org.uk.) **Ludlow** (⊠ Castle St., SY8 1AS, ☎ 01584/875053, WEB www.ludlow.org.uk). **Ross-on-Wye** (⊠ Swan House, Edde Cross St., HR9 7BZ, ☎ 01989/562768, WEB www.visitorlinks.com). **Shrewsbury** (⊠ The Music Hall, The Square, SY1 1LH, ☎ 01743/281200, WEB www.shrewsburytourism.co.uk). **Worcester** (⊠ The Guildhall, High St., WR1 2EY, ☎ 01905/726311, WEB www.cityofworcester.gov.uk).

10 WALES

Lauded as the "Land of Castles," the ancient stronghold of Wales is one of Britain's best-kept secrets. Some people may still imagine it in terms of the coal mines of its past, but today Wales is evergreen and unspoiled. As conclusive proof of its scenic grandeur, it's home to three national parks, with Snowdonia the monarch of all it surveys. Other treasures await: the stately houses of Powis and Plas Newydd, steam-train rides through tree-clad chasms, the capital of Cardiff, and the glory of the Welsh language.

WALES, APART FROM BEING CALLED the Land of Song, is also a land of mountain and flood, where wild peaks challenge the sky and waterfalls thunder down steep, rocky chasms. Updated by Roger Thomas It is a land of gray-stone castles, ruined abbeys, male-voice choirs, and a handful of cities. Small pockets of the south and northeast were heavily industrialized, largely with mining and steelmaking in the 19th century, but long stretches of the coast and the mountainous interior remain areas of unmarred beauty. Small, self-contained Wales has three national parks (Snowdonia, the Brecon Beacons, and the Pembrokeshire Coast) and five official Areas of Outstanding Natural Beauty (the Wye Valley, Gower Peninsula, Llŷn Peninsula, Isle of Anglesey, and Clwydian Range), as well as large tracts of unspoiled moor and mountain in mid-Wales, the least traveled part of the country. Dotted over the entire country are riches of other sorts: medieval castles, seaside resorts, traditional market towns, the glorious Bodnant Garden, the dramatic Great Glass House at the National Botanic Garden, the stately houses of Powis and Plas Newydd, steam-powered train rides through Snowdonia and central Wales, and the cosmopolitan capital of Cardiff.

Wales suffers more than most destinations from the curse of the stereotype. Many visitors still perceive the country in terms of the 1941 film, *How Green Was My Valley,* in which Wales was depicted as an industrial cauldron filled with coal mines. The picture was not accurate then; it is certainly not accurate now—Wales has only one fully operational mine today. In any case, industrial activity has always been concentrated in a relatively small corner of southeast Wales, leaving the vast majority of the landscape untouched by modern development. In fact, one of the great glories of Wales is the drive through beautiful countryside from south to north without passing through any large towns. The same applies to the country's 750-mi coast, which consists mainly of sandy beaches, grassy headlands, cliffs, and estuaries.

The Welsh are a Celtic race. When, toward the middle of the first millennium AD, the Anglo-Saxons spread through Britain, they pushed the indigenous Celts farther back into their Welsh mountain strongholds. (In fact, "Wales" comes from the Saxon word "Weallas," which means "strangers," the name impertinently given by the new arrivals to the natives.) The Welsh, however, have always called themselves "Y Cymry," the companions. It was not until the fearsome English King Edward I (1272–1307) waged a brutal and determined campaign to conquer Wales that English supremacy was established. Welsh hopes were finally crushed with the death in battle of Llywelyn ap Gruffudd, last native prince of Wales, in 1282.

Without any violent battles or storming of castles, however, Wales has now achieved a measure of independence from its English neighbor. In 1999 a referendum was held in which a narrow majority of the Welsh people voted for partial devolution for the country. Elections were held in May 1999 and the Welsh Assembly was born. Unlike the Scottish Parliament that came into being on the same day, the Welsh Assembly has no law-making powers, but it does have wide-ranging administrative responsibilities and considerable control over Welsh affairs. The Assembly will eventually be housed in a new building on Cardiff Bay.

The Welsh language continues to flourish. Although spoken by only a fifth of the population, it has a high profile within the country. Welsh-language schools are popular, there is a dedicated Welsh TV channel, and all road signs are bilingual. It is ironic that, although in the 15th and 16th centuries the Tudor kings Henry VII and Henry VIII continued England's ruthless domination of the Welsh, principally by attempting to abolish the language, it was another Tudor monarch, Elizabeth I, who ensured its survival by authorizing a Welsh translation of the Bible in 1588. Today, many older people say they owe their knowledge of Welsh to the Bible. Welsh may look difficult to pronounce, but it is a totally phonetic language, and once the alphabet is learned, pronunciation is quite easy. Remember that "dd" is sounded like "th" in they, "f" sounds like "v" in save, and "ff" is the equivalent of the English "f" in forest. The tricky "ll" sound has no English equivalent; the closest match is the "cl" sound in close. Terms that crop up frequently are *bach* or *fach* (small), *craig* or *graig* (rock), *cwm* (valley), *dyffryn* (valley), *eglwys* (church), *glyn* (glen), *llyn* (lake), *mawr* or *fawr* (great, big), *mynydd* or *fynydd* (mountain, moorland), *pentre* (village, homestead), *plas* (hall, mansion), and *pont* or *bont* (bridge). However, there's no need to worry; everyone in Wales speaks English, too.

Pleasures and Pastimes

Castles

History addicts love Wales because it's well known as a "Land of Castles." The more than 400 fortresses provide an inexhaustible supply of inspiration. These ancient strongholds dot the landscape from south to north and range from romantic ruins to well-preserved fortresses still rising to their original imperious height. The great North Wales castles, such as Caernarfon, are nearly intact and particularly famous. But for many people, the lasting memory of Wales is the sight of weather-beaten ruins crowning hilltops or guarding mountain passes deep in the lush countryside.

Dining

The days when Wales was regarded as a gastronomic desert have ended, and today even country pubs are more interested in offering meals than serving pints of beer. Talented chefs have moved in, making the best use of Wales's bountiful natural resources. Succulent Welsh lamb is regarded as the best in the world, seafood is plentiful, and Welsh cheese-making is undergoing a revival. For traditionalists, there is the old favorite of Welsh lamb served with vegetables. Another traditional feast is *cawl,* a nourishing broth with vegetables and meat. The most unusual traditional delicacy is laverbread, made from seaweed and cooked to resemble a black pureed substance. It has a taste all its own and is usually eaten with bacon. More cosmopolitan palates can sample everything from French to Asian fare, especially in Cardiff. For a special treat, have dinner at one of Wales's country-house hotels—you don't have to be an overnight guest to enjoy the experience.

CATEGORY	COST*
££££	over £22
£££	£16–£22
££	£9–£15
£	under £9

per person for a main course at dinner

Lodging

A 19th-century dictum, "I sleeps where I dines," still holds true in Wales, where good hotels and good restaurants often go together. Conversion of buildings is the rage, and a number of castles, country mansions, and even small railway stations are being transformed into interesting hotels and restaurants. Traditional inns with low-beam ceilings, wood paneling, and cozy fireplaces remain Wales's pride, but they tend to be off the beaten track and you will need a car to make the most of them. The same goes for farmhouse accommodations. Of course,

Cardiff and Swansea have a number of large international hotels. For luxury, Wales has a good choice of country-house hotels. An added attraction is that prices are generally lower than they are for equivalent properties in the Cotswolds, Scotland, or southeast England. A service charge may be added to the room cost; ask if it's included.

CATEGORY	COST*
££££	over £150
£££	£100–£150
££	£60–£100
£	under £60

All prices are for two people sharing a standard double room, including breakfast and VAT.

Steam Railways

Wales is undoubtedly the best place in Britain for narrow-gauge steam railways, many of which wind through extraordinary landscapes. The Great Little Trains of Wales—narrow-gauge—operate during the spring, summer, and autumn months through the mountains of Snowdonia and central Wales (there are also a few lines in South Wales). The Ffestiniog Railway, which links two British Rail lines at the old slate town of Blaenau Ffestiniog and Porthmadog, climbs the mountainside around an ascending loop more reminiscent of the Andes than rural Britain. Tiny, copper-knobbed engines haul narrow carriages through deep cuttings and along rocky shelves above ancient oak woods through the heart of Snowdonia National Park. Other lines include the Talyllyn, following a deep valley from the coastal resort of Tywyn; the Vale of Rheidol Railway, from Aberystwyth to Devil's Bridge; the Welshpool and Llanfair Light Railway, between Welshpool and Llanfair Caereinion; the Welsh Highland Railway, from Porthmadog and Caernarfon; the Brecon Mountain Railway, from Merthyr Tydfil; the Llanberis Lake Railway, and Bala Lake Railway.

Snowdonia also has Britain's only alpine-style steam rack railway, the Snowdon Mountain Railway, where little sloping boiler engines on rack-and-pinion track push their trains 3,000 ft up from Llanberis to the summit of Snowdon.

Walking

An army of bipeds covers Wales every year, as this is a wonderful region for walking and hiking. There are long-distance paths to follow, such as the Pembrokeshire Coast Path (which runs all along the spectacular shores of southwest Wales), the south–north Offa's Dyke Path, based on the border between England and Wales established by King Offa in the 8th century, and the Glyndŵr Way, a 123-mi-long highland route that traverses Mid-Wales from the border town of Knighton via Machynlleth to Welshpool. In Wales's forested areas you will find signposted footpaths that are short and easy to follow. Enthusiasts might prefer the more challenging wide open spaces of the Brecon Beacons National Park or the rugged mountains of Snowdonia.

Exploring Wales

Wales has three main regions: south, mid, and north. The south is the most varied, for its boundaries include everything from Wales's capital city to unspoiled coastline, grassy mountains to wooded valleys. Mid-Wales is pure countryside, fringed on its western shores by the great arc of Cardigan Bay. North Wales is a mixture of high, rocky mountains, popular sandy beaches, and coastal hideaways.

Numbers in the text correspond to numbers in the margin and on the Wales, Aberystwyth, and Cardiff maps.

Great Itineraries

Do not be misled by Wales's relatively small size. Although less than 200 mi from south to north, the country is packed with scenic variety and a daunting range of places to visit. Many people make the mistake of thinking that they can see Wales in a day or so. In that time, you would only have the opportunity to scratch the surface of this fascinating place.

IF YOU HAVE 3 DAYS

Start off in **Cardiff** ㉖–㉝, Wales's capital city. You will want to spend at least a half day here before driving through the Brecon Beacons National Park to **Llandrindod Wells** ⑯, a Victorian spa town. On day two, drive via Rhayader and the Elan Valley, Wales's "Lake District," to **Aberystwyth** ⑰–㉑, then along the north coast of Cardigan Bay to **Porthmadog** ⑤ (handy accommodations are in nearby Harlech and Portmeirion). For your final day, drive via **Blaenau Ffestiniog** ④ through the Snowdonia National Park to **Betws-y-Coed** ⑥, and if you have the time, call into medieval **Conwy** ⑩ before leaving Wales via the A55 route to England.

IF YOU HAVE 9 DAYS

Travel to **Cardiff** ㉖–㉝ for a full day's visit and overnight stop, making sure that you have time to stop at the Museum of Welsh Life, at St. Fagans on the western outskirts of the city. On day two, drive via **Swansea** ㊲ to **Tenby** ㊴, a picturesque resort at the southern gateway to the Pembrokeshire Coast National Park. Day three is taken up by a tour of this wild and beautiful stretch of seashore. Drive to **St. David's** ㊶ in the far west to visit the cathedral built on a religious site founded by Wales's patron saint in the 6th century. If you have time, walk a stretch of the coast path before continuing on to **Fishguard** ㊷. Day four is taken up by more beautiful coastline on the way to **Cardigan** ㊸, then a tour along the lovely Vale of Teifi through Cilgerran to Drefach Felindre to explore the Museum of the Welsh Woolen Industry. From here, continue on to **Aberystwyth** ⑰–㉑. From Aberystwyth, drive along the Cardigan Bay coast via **Machynlleth** ㉒ to **Dolgellau** ㉕, then head inland through the southern section of the Snowdonia National Park to lakeside **Bala** ③.

There is more dramatic mountain scenery on day six on the way from Bala to **Blaenau Ffestiniog** ④, where you can visit the caverns that gave this town its past reputation as the "slate capital of North Wales." From here, follow the wooded Vale of Ffestiniog west to **Porthmadog** ⑤. Then continue northward to **Caernarfon** ⑧, home of one of Wales's most famous medieval castles. Day seven takes you across the Menai Strait by the road bridge near Bangor to the Isle of Anglesey and **Beaumaris** ⑨ for a brief visit, then back along the coast of mainland North Wales via medieval **Conwy** ⑩ to the handsome Victorian seaside resort of **Llandudno** ⑪ (on this leg, you may want to substitute the trip across to Anglesey with a short detour inland from Caernarfon to **Llanberis** ⑦ and the spectacular Llanberis Pass in the heart of Snowdonia). Borderland Wales is the theme of the next day, the route passing through **Denbigh** ⑫, **Ruthin** ⑬, **Llangollen** ②, **Chirk** ①, and **Welshpool** ㉕ on the way to **Llandrindod Wells** ⑯. On your last day, visit **Hay-on-Wye** ⑭, the borderland "town of books," then drive on through the mountains to **Brecon** ㊱ in the Brecon Beacons National Park. From here, follow the Vale of Usk through **Crickhowell** ㉟ and **Abergavenny** ㉞ before leaving Wales along the M4 motorway.

When to Tour Wales

The weather in Wales, as in the rest of Britain, is a lottery. It can be warm in the spring and cool in the summer, dry in May, and wet in

August. Come prepared for rain or shine. Generally speaking, southwest Wales enjoys a milder climate than elsewhere, thanks to the moderating effects of the sea. Spring and autumn are attractive times in Wales; note that spring can arrive very early in Pembrokeshire, while other parts of the country may still be in the grip of winter. These seasons can be surprisingly dry and sunny, and you will have the added advantage of quiet surroundings. That noted, crowds are rarely a problem, apart from the main tourist centers, for many parts of Wales remain peaceful even in the height of summer.

NORTH WALES: IN THE REALM OF SNOWDONIA

The north is the region where Wales masses all its savage splendor and fierce beauty. Dominating its southwestern corner is Snowdon, at 3,560 ft the highest mountain in England and Wales. It is impossible to describe the magnificence of the view on a clear day: to the northwest the Menai Strait, Anglesey, and beyond to the Irish Sea; to the south the mountains of Merionethshire, Harlech Castle, and the Cader Idris mountain range; and all around towering masses of wild and barren rock. If you ascend the peak by the Snowdon Mountain Railway from Llanberis, telephone from the terminus to ascertain whether Snowdon is free from mist, for you will lose much if you arrive when clouds, as often happens, encircle the monster's brow.

The peak gives its name to **Snowdonia National Park,** which extends southward all the way to Machynlleth in mid-Wales. The park consists of 840 square mi of rocky mountains, valleys clothed in oak woods, moorlands, lakes, and rivers, all with one thing in common: natural beauty, and, to a lesser extent, solitude. Increasingly, however, the park has become a popular climbing center and there are fears that Snowdon itself is becoming worn away by the boots of too many walkers. Along the sandy, north-facing coast, a string of seaside resorts has also been attracting visitors for well over a century. Llandudno, the dignified "Queen of the North Wales coast," was built in Victorian times as a seaside watering hole. If you prefer away-from-it-all seashore, there are two official Areas of Outstanding Beauty: the Isle of Anglesey (connected by bridge to mainland Wales), and the Llŷn Peninsula, dotted with quieter small resorts and coastal villages.

Chirk and the Ceiriog Valley

❶ *22 mi southwest of Chester.*

A favored first stop in Wales for travelers coming from England is Chirk, poised on the border between the two countries. It's a handy gateway to the Ceiriog Valley, a narrowing vale that penetrates the silent, green foothills of the lofty Berwyn Mountains. **Chirk Castle,** completed in its original form in 1310, is an impressive medieval fortress. Over the centuries it has evolved into a grand home, with interiors furnished in 16th- to 19th-century styles. The castle stands amid beautiful formal gardens and grounds. ⊠ *Off B4500,* ☎ *01691/777701,* WEB *www.nationaltrust.org.uk.* ⌿ *£5, garden £2.80.* ☉ *Castle Apr.–Oct., Wed.–Sun. noon–5; Garden Apr.–Oct., Wed.–Sun. 11–6.*

West of Chirk is the **Vale of Ceiriog,** nicknamed, and somewhat hyped, as Little Switzerland. Take B4500 west 6 mi through the picturesque valley to the village of Glyn Ceiriog, at the foothills of the remote Berwyn Mountains, an area that attracts pony trekkers, walkers, fishermen, and rough shooters.

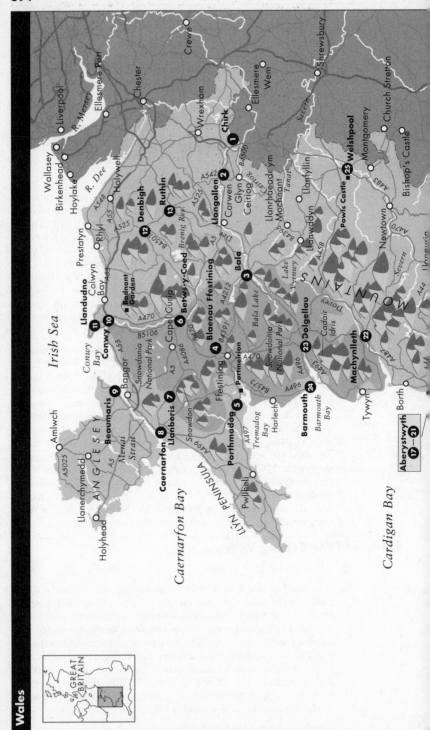

Wales

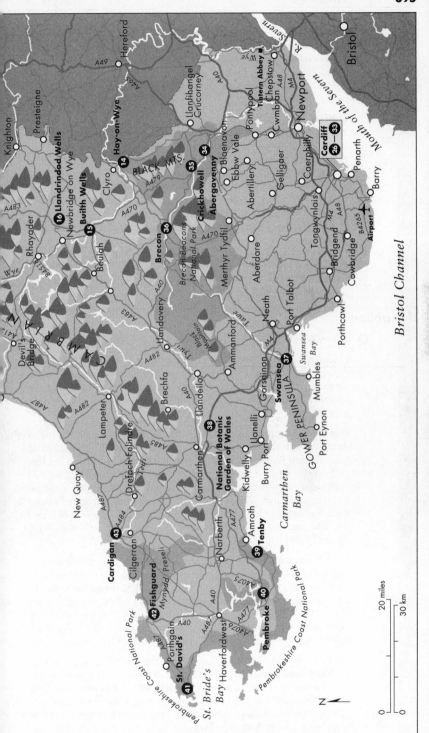

Bristol Channel

Mouth of the Severn

Severn R.

Bristol

Newport

Cardiff 26—33

Penarth

Barry

Airport

B4265

Bridgend

Cowbridge

Porthcawl

Tongwynlais

Caerphilly

Gelligaer

Abertillery

Ebbw Vale

Blaenavon

Abergavenny 34

Crickhowell 35

Hay-on-Wye 14

Llanfihangel Crucorney

Tintern Abbey

Chepstow

Cwmbran

Pontypool

Port Talbot

Neath

Aberdare

Merthyr Tydfil

Brecon 36

Brecon Beacons National Park

BLACK MTS.

Clyro

Builth Wells 15

Newbridge on Wye

Llandrindod Wells 16

Presteigne

Knighton

Hereford

Beulah

Rhayader

Devil's Bridge

CAMBRIAN

Llandovery

Brechfa

Llandeilo

Ammanford

Gorseinon

Swansea 37

Swansea Bay

Mumbles

Port Eynon

GOWER PENINSULA

Llanelli

Burry Port

Kidwelly

National Botanic Garden of Wales 38

Carmarthen

Drefach-Felindre

Lampeter

New Quay

Cardigan 43

Cilgerran

Mynydd Preseli

Fishguard 42

St. David's 41

Porthgain

Haverfordwest

Pembroke 40

Tenby 39

Amroth

Narberth

St. Bride's Bay

Carmarthen Bay

Pembrokeshire Coast National Park

20 miles

30 km

N

Pistyll Rhaeadr, the highest waterfall in Wales, has peat-brown water that thunders down a 290-ft double cascade. To get here, continue on B4500 southwest from Glyn Ceiriog, and then its unnumbered continuation, to reach Llanrhaeadr ym Mochnant, in the peaceful Tanat Valley. Here, in 1588, the Bible was translated into Welsh, thus ensuring the survival of the language. Turn northwest and go 4 mi up the road to the waterfall.

Dining and Lodging

££ ✕⌂ **Golden Pheasant.** Antiques and Victorian-style fabrics furnish this more than 200-year-old hotel, and the result is chinoiserie in the bar, horse prints and aspidistras in the lounge, draped curtains and parlor palms in the dining room, and no two bedrooms alike. The dining room's specialties include Ceiriog trout, pheasant, and game pie. ⊠ *Glyn Ceiriog, near Chirk, LL20 7BB,* ☎ *01691/718281,* FAX *01691/718479. 19 rooms. Restaurant. AE, DC, MC, V.*

£ ⌂ **Bron Heulog.** This guest house, a former Victorian doctor's surgery, has been lovingly restored with period decor. Breakfast is included, and the owners set an excellent table. Rooms have showers. ⊠ *Waterfall Rd. off B4396, Llanrhaeadr ym Mochnant SY100JX,* ☎ *01691/ 780521,* FAX *01691/780630,* WEB *www.kraines.enta.net. 3 rooms. No-smoking rooms. MC, V.*

Llangollen

❷ *5 mi northwest of Chirk, 23 mi southwest of Chester.*

Llangollen's setting in a deep valley carved by the River Dee gives it typically Welsh appeal. The bridge over the Dee, a 14th-century stone structure, is named in a traditional Welsh folk song as one of the "Seven Wonders of Wales." In July the International Musical Eisteddfod is held here.

Plas Newydd (not to be confused with the grand estate on the Isle of Anglesey with the same name) was the home from 1778 to 1828 of Lady Eleanor Butler and Sarah Ponsonby, the eccentric Ladies of Llangollen, who set up a then-scandalous single-sex household, collected curios and magnificent wood carvings, and made it into a tourist attraction even during their lifetimes. Among their celebrated guests were William Wordsworth, Sir Walter Scott, and the Duke of Wellington. The gardens are quite attractive. ⊠ *Hill St.,* ☎ *01978/861314,* FAX *01978/861906.* ☜ *£2.50.* ⊙ *Apr.–Oct., daily 10–5.*

From the **canal wharf** you can take a horse-drawn boat or a narrow boat (☎ 01978/860702) along the Llangollen Canal to the largest navigable aqueduct in the world at Pontcysyllte. The **Llangollen Railway,** a restored standard-gauge steam line, runs for a few miles along the scenic Dee Valley. The terminus is near the town's bridge. ☎ *01978/ 860979; 01978/860951 24-hr recorded information.* ☜ *£7.50 round-trip.* ⊙ *May–Nov., daily 10–5; Dec.–Apr., weekends (limited service).*

There are easy walks along the banks of the River Dee or along part of **Offa's Dyke Path.** The 168-mi-long path follows the line of an ancient earthen wall, still surviving in parts, which was built along the border with England in the 8th century by King Offa of Mercia (757–796) to keep out Welsh raiders. For a particularly scenic drive in this area, head for the Horseshoe Pass.

Lodging

£ ⌂ **Ty-Issa Farm.** Four miles from Llangollen and close to the Offa's Dyke Path, this cozy 17th-century farmhouse has scenic views of the lovely Ceiriog Valley. A full vegetarian breakfast is included, and evening meals can be arranged. You can try trout fishing for free. ⊠ *Off B4500, Pontfadog, Llangollen LL20 7AG,* ☎ *01691/718808,* FAX *01691/653278,* WEB *www.offas-dyke.co.uk/ty-issa-farm. 2 rooms. No-smoking rooms.*

Nightlife and the Arts

The six-day **International Musical Eisteddfod** (☎ 01978/860236, WEB www.international-eisteddfod.co.uk), held in early July, brings together amateur choirs and dancers, more than 12,000 participants in all, from all corners of the globe for a large, colorful arts festival. The tradition of the *eisteddfod,* held throughout Wales, goes back to the 12th century. Originally gatherings of bards, the *eisteddfodau* of today are more like competitions or festivals.

Bala

❸ *18 mi southwest of Llangollen.*

The staunchly Welsh town of Bala is a good base from which to explore the eastern and southern sections of Snowdonia National Park as well as the gentler landscapes of borderland Wales. It stands at the head of Llŷn Tegid (Bala Lake), at 4 mi long the largest natural lake in Wales. This is a good place for kayaking and windsurfing. A scenic **narrow-gauge railway** (☎ 01678/540666), one of the Great Little Trains of Wales, runs along the southern shore of Bala Lake.

★ To experience Wales at its wildest, you can drive over **Bwlch y Groes** (Pass of the Cross), the highest road in Wales, whose sweeping panoramas are breathtaking. To get here, take the narrow road south from Bala through Cwm Hirnant and over the mountain to Lake Vyrnwy. Turn right at the lake and drive for a mile on B4393 before heading west on the scenic mountain road.

Dining and Lodging

£££ ✕☱ **Lake Vyrnwy Hotel.** On 24,000 acres of lakeside grounds, this country mansion overlooking superb scenery offers the ultimate sporting holiday: you can fish, bird-watch, play tennis, or take long walks around the estate. Bicycles, sailboats, and quadbikes are also available. Rooms are quiet and comfortable and the restaurant is excellent. The contemporary cuisine (four-course prix-fixe menu only) makes good use of trout, pheasant, and duck from the estate and vegetables and fruit from the garden. ⊠ *Llanwddyn SY10 0LY,* ☎ *01691/870692,* FAX *01691/870259,* WEB *www.lakevyrnwy.com. 35 rooms. Restaurant, tennis court, boating, fishing, bicycles. AE, DC, MC, V.*

£–££ ☱ **Cyfie Farm.** This refurbished 17th-century farmhouse in a tranquil setting close to Lake Vyrnwy has luxurious rooms with all the sophistication of a top hotel. ⊠ *Llanfihangel-yng-Ngwynfa, near Llanfyllin, SY22 5JE,* ☎ FAX *01691/648451. 4 rooms. Lounge. No credit cards.*

Blaenau Ffestiniog

❹ *22 mi northwest of Bala, 10 mi southwest of Betws-y-Coed.*

The former "slate capital of North Wales"—most of the world's roofing tiles once came from here—still has commercial quarrying going on. The enterprises that attract all the attention nowadays, however, remain the old slate mines open to the public. The **Llechwedd Slate Caverns,** opened to the public in the 1970s and one of the first landmark sites to be based on Wales's industrial heritage, offers two trips: a tram ride through floodlighted tunnels where Victorian working conditions have been re-created, and a ride on Britain's deepest underground railway to a mine where you can walk by an eerie underground lake. There is also much to see on the surface of this popular site: a re-created Victorian village, old workshops, and slate-splitting demonstrations. ⊠ *Off A470,* ☎ *01766/830306,* WEB *www.llechwedd.co.uk.* 🎫 *Tour £7.25, surface free.* ⊙ *Mar.–Sept., daily 10–5:15; Oct.–Feb., daily 10–4:15.*

Porthmadog

⑤ *12 mi southwest of Blaenau Ffestiniog, 16 mi south of Caernarfon.*

At the gateway to Llŷn, an unspoiled peninsula of beaches, wildflowers, and country lanes, Porthmadog is a little seaside town, built as a harbor to export slate from Blaenau Ffestiniog. Its location, between Snowdonia and Llŷn, gives it a lively atmosphere in summer. There are good beaches nearby and a host of attractions in and around the town. From the east, Porthmadog is approached by a mile-long embankment known as the Cob (the small toll charge goes to charity).

★ The oldest of the Welsh narrow-gauge lines (founded in the early 19th century), the **Ffestiniog Railway** runs from a quayside terminus along The Cob, then through a lovely wooded vale into the mountains all the way to Blaenau Ffestiniog. ☎ *01766/512340.* 🎫 *£13.80 round-trip* ⊙ *Apr.–Nov., daily, plus limited winter service.*

★ One not-to-be-missed site in North Wales is a short trip east of Porthmadog over The Cob. **Portmeirion** is a tiny fantasy-Italianate village, said to be loosely modeled after Portofino, and built in 1926 by architect Clough Williams-Ellis (1883–1978), complete with hotel, restaurant, town hall, shops (selling pottery, gifts, and books), and cottages that are let to guests. He called it his "light-opera approach to architecture," and the result is pretty, though distinctly un-Welsh. Royalty, important political figures, famous artists, and other celebrities have stayed here. The atmosphere is genuinely inspirational. The cult '60s TV series *The Prisoner* was filmed here. ⊠ *Off A496* ☎ *01766/770228,* WEB *www.portmeirion.wales.com.* 🎫 *£4.50.* ⊙ *Daily 9:30–5:30.*

North of Porthmadog is **Tremadog,** a handsome village that was the birthplace of T. E. Lawrence (1888–1935), better known as Lawrence of Arabia. **Criccieth,** a few miles west of Porthmadog on A497, is a charming Victorian seaside resort whose headland is crowned by a medieval castle.

OFF THE BEATEN PATH

HARLECH CASTLE – What a wealth of legend, poetry, and song is conjured up by this famous 13th-century castle, which dominates the little coastal town 12 mi south of Porthmadog. The presence of its ruins, visible for miles and commanding wide views, is as dramatic as its history. The inspiring music of Ceiriog's song *Men of Harlech* typifies the heroic defense of this castle in 1468 by Dafydd ap Eynion, who, summoned to surrender, replied: "I held a castle in France until every old woman in Wales heard of it, and I will hold a castle in Wales until every old woman in France hears of it!" Later in the 15th century the Lancastrians survived an eight-year siege during the Wars of the Roses here, and it was the last Welsh stronghold to fall in the 17th-century Civil War. ⊠ *Off B4573,* ☎ *01766/780552.* 🎫 *£3.* ⊙ *Late Mar.–late Oct., daily 9:30–6:30; late Oct.–late Mar., Mon.–Sat. 9:30–4, Sun. 11–4.*

Dining and Lodging

£££–££££ ✕🏨 **Hotel Maes-y-Neuadd.** Eight acres of gardens and parkland are
★ a glorious setting for this hotel dating from the 14th century. It has walls of local granite, oak-beam ceilings, and an inglenook fireplace. The restaurant serves a three-course fixed-price menu of Welsh, En-

glish, and French specialties that makes good use of local ingredients, including vegetables grown on the property, fish, and cheeses. The hotel is 3½ mi northeast of Harlech via B4573. ✉ *Talsarnau, near Harlech, LL47 6YA,* ☎ *01766/780200 or 800/635–3602,* ℻ *01766/780211,* WEB *www.neuadd.com. 16 rooms. Restaurant. AE, DC, MC, V.*

£££–££££ ✕🖭 **Hotel Portmeirion.** This is one of the most elegant and unusual
★ places to stay in Wales. The mansion house that is now the hotel's main building was already here when Clough Williams-Ellis began to build his Italianate fantasy village around it. He restored its original Victorian splendor, preserved the library and the Mirror Room, and created the curved, colonnaded dining room. Accommodation is also available in cottages around the village, none more than a few minutes' walk from the main building. Castell Deudraeth, an imposing, castellated, 19th-century mansion on the grounds, has been beautifully restored with luxury suites. Local specialties are featured in the restaurant, which serves breakfast and has a three-course fixed-price dinner menu. ✉ *Off A496, Portmeirion LL48 6ET,* ☎ *01766/770228,* ℻ *01766/ 771331,* WEB *www.portmeirion.wales.com. 14 rooms in main hotel, 26 rooms in cottages, 11 suites in Castell Deudraeth. Restaurant, pool, tennis court. AE, DC, MC, V.*

££ ✕🖭 **Castle Cottage.** Close to Harlech's mighty castle, this cozy, friendly hotel is a charming "restaurant with rooms." The emphasis here is on the exceptional cuisine served by chef-proprietor Glyn Roberts, who makes the best possible use of fresh ingredients to create imaginative, beautifully presented contemporary dishes. There's a fixed-price dinner menu. The rooms, though small, are attractively appointed and decorated. This lodging is a wonderful little find, as well as an excellent all-round value. ✉ *Near B4573, Harlech LL46 2YL,* ☎ ℻ *01766/ 780479. 6 rooms, 4 with bath. Restaurant. AE, MC, V.*

Betws-y-Coed

❻ *25 mi northeast of Porthmadog, 19 mi south of Llandudno.*

The rivers Llugwy and Conwy meet at Betws-y-Coed, a popular tourist village set among wooded hills that have excellent views of Snowdonia. Busy in summer, the resort has a good selection of hotels and crafts shops. The chief landmark here is the ornate iron bridge (1815) over the Conwy, designed by Thomas Telford (1757–1834), while the magnificent Bodnant Garden south of the town of Conwy is a delightful excursion destination.

On the western (A5) approach to Betws-y-Coed are the **Swallow Falls** (small admission charge), a famous North Wales beauty spot where the River Llugwy tumbles down through a wooded chasm.

Dining and Lodging

£–£££ ✕ **Ty Gwyn.** After a browse through the small antiques shop next door, stop for a bite at the restaurant, which is under the same management. Inside the 17th-century building you'll find prints and chintz, old beams, and copper pans, and there's a nice view of the nearby Waterloo bridge. Try the king scallops and monkfish or the homemade pâté. ✉ *A5,* ☎ *01690/710383. MC, V.*

££ 🖭 **Pengwern Country House.** In Victorian times, this stone-and-slate country house on two acres of woodland was an artists' colony. It has been expertly restored to its former elegance, with polished slate floors and beamed bedrooms, and offers a warm welcome and good food (you can arrange arrange dinner here, too). The house is about a mile south of town. ✉ *A5, Allt Dinas LL24 OHF,* WEB *www.snowdoniaaccommodation.com,* ☎ ℻ *01690/710480. 3 rooms. Lounge, no-smoking rooms MC, V.*

Llanberis

❼ *17 mi west of Betws-y-Coed, 7 mi southeast of Caernarfon.*

Llanberis, like Betws-y-Coed, is a focal point for visitors to the Snowdonia National Park. The town stands beside twin lakes at the foot of the rocky **Llanberis Pass,** which cuts through the highest mountains in the park and is lined with slabs popular with rock climbers. There are hiking trails from the top of the pass, but the going can be rough for the inexperienced. Ask local advice before starting any ramble. At the Pen-y-Gwryd Hotel just beyond the summit of the pass, Lord Hunt and his team planned their successful ascent of Everest in 1953.

★ Llanberis has many attractions, but its most famous is the rack-and-pinion **Snowdon Mountain Railway,** with some of its track at a gradient of 1 in 5, which terminates within 70 ft of the 3,560-ft summit. Snowdon, *Yr Wyddfa* in Welsh, is the highest peak south of Scotland and is set within more than 800 square mi of national park. From May through September, weather permitting, trains go all the way to the summit; on a clear day, you can see as far as the Wicklow Mountains in Ireland, about 90 mi away. In 1998, the National Trust bought the mountain, ensuring its long-term protection. ☎ *01286/870223,* WEB *www.snowdonrailway.co.uk.* 🎫 *£16.60 maximum round-trip fare.* ☻ *Mar.–Oct., daily from 9 AM to late afternoon.*

On Lake Padern in the Padarn Country Park, the old Dinorwig slate quarry is now home to the **Welsh Slate Museum.** This living-history museum has quarry workshops and slate-splitting demonstrations. The narrow-gauge Llanberis Lake Railway runs from here. ⊠ *Dinorwig Quarry, A4086,* ☎ *01286/870630,* WEB *nmgw.ac.uk.* 🎫 *£3.50.* ☻ *Easter–Oct., daily 10–5; Nov.–Easter, Sun.–Fri. 10–4.*

Caernarfon

❽ *7 mi northwest of Llanberis, 26 mi southwest of Llandudno.*

The town of Caernarfon, which has a historic pedigree as a walled medieval settlement, has nothing to rival the considerable splendor of its castle and, in fact, is now overrun with tourist buses. Still, don't miss the garrison church of St. Mary, built into the city walls.

★ Standing like a warning finger, the grim majestic mass of **Caernarfon Castle,** "that most magnificent badge of our subjection," wrote Thomas Pennant (1726–1798), looms over the now peaceful waters of the River Seiont. Numerous bloody encounters were witnessed by these sullen walls, erected by Edward I in the 13th century as a symbol of his determination to subdue the Welsh. Begun in 1283, its towers, unlike those of Edward I's other castles, are polygonal and patterned with bands of different-colored stone. In 1284, the crafty monarch thought of an amazing scheme to steal the Welsh throne. Knowing that the proud Welsh chieftains would accept no foreign prince, he promised to designate a ruler who could speak no word of English. He sent his queen, Eleanor of Castile, who was expecting a child, posthaste to Caernarfon, and in this cold stone fortress the queen gave birth to a son. Edward presented the infant to the assembled chieftains as their prince "who spoke no English, had been born on Welsh soil, and whose first words would be spoken in Welsh." The ruse worked, and on that day was created the first prince of Wales of English lineage. This tradition still holds: in July 1969, Elizabeth II presented Prince Charles to the people of Wales as their prince from this castle. In the Queen's Tower, an intriguing museum charts the history of the local regiment, the Royal Welsh

Fusiliers. ⊠ *Castle Hill,* ☎ *01286/677617,* WEB *www.caernarfon.com.* ▣ *£4.20.* ◷ *Late Mar.–late Oct., daily 9:30–6:30; late Oct.–late Mar., Mon.–Sat. 9:30–4, Sun. 11–4.*

Outside Caernarfon is the extensive excavation site of the **Roman Fortress of Segontium,** a branch of the National Museums and Galleries of Wales. It contains material found on the site, one of Britain's most famous Roman forts. ⊠ *Beddgelert Rd. (A4085),* ☎ *01286/ 675625,* WEB *www.nmgw.ac.uk.* ▣ *£1.25.* ◷ *Mar.–Apr. and Oct., Mon.–Sat. 9:30–5:30, Sun. 2–5; May–Sept., Mon.–Sat. 9:30–6, Sun. 2–6; Nov.–Feb., Mon.–Sat. 9:30–4, Sun. 2–4.*

You can take a workshop tour and short trip on a coal-fired steam locomotive at the **Welsh Highland Railway/Rheilffordd Eryri,** a narrow-gauge line that operates on the route of an abandoned railway through the mountains. The terminus is on the quay near Caernarfon Castle. ⊠ *St. Helens Rd.,* ☎ *01766/514040.* ▣ *£7.60 round-trip.* ◷ *Feb.–Oct., daily 10–5:30.*

Dining and Lodging

££–£££ ✕🖭 **Ty'n Rhos.** This is an immaculate farmhouse with a difference: it
★ offers the highest standard of accommodation. It has a beautifully furnished lounge and dining room, with views across the fields to the Isle of Anglesey. The cooking is exceptional and innovative, based on the best fresh local ingredients. Try the homemade cheeses and yogurt and the Welsh breakfast, which includes locally gathered oysters. It is an ideal touring base, standing between Snowdonia and the sea, close to Caernarfon and Anglesey. ⊠ *Llanddeiniolen, near Caernarfon, LL55 3AE,* ☎ *01248/670489,* FAX *01248/670079,* WEB *www.tynrhos.co.uk. 11 rooms. Restaurant, lounge, croquet. AE, MC, V.*

Outdoor Activities and Sports

Caernarfon Airport operates Pleasure Flights in light aircraft over Snowdon, Anglesey, and Caernarfon; flights are 10–25 minutes. "Hands on" flying lessons are offered daily (1-hr lesson, £99). ⊠ *Dinas Dinlle Beach Rd.,* ☎ *01286/830800.* ▣ *£20–£65 per seat.* ◷ *Daily 9–5.*

Beaumaris

❾ *13 mi northeast of Caernarfon.*

Handsome Beaumaris is on the Isle of Anglesey, the largest island directly off the shore of Wales and England. It is linked to the mainland by the Britannia road and rail bridge and by Thomas Telford's remarkable chain suspension bridge, built in 1826 over the dividing Menai Strait. Though its name means "beautiful marsh," Beaumaris today is an elegant town of simple cottages, Georgian terraces, and bright shops. The nearest mainline train station is in Bangor, about 6 mi away on the mainland; a regular bus service operates between it and Beaumaris.

The town of Beaumaris dates from 1295, when Edward I commenced work on **Beaumaris Castle,** the last and largest link in an "iron ring" of fortifications around North Wales built to contain the Welsh. Guarding the western approach to the Menai Strait, the castle (now a World Heritage site) is solid and symmetrical, with arrow slits and a moat: a fine example of medieval defensive planning. ⊠ *Castle St.,* ☎ *01248/ 810361.* ▣ *£2.50.* ◷ *Late Mar.–late Oct., daily 9:30–6:30; late Oct.–late Mar., Mon.–Sat. 9:30–4, Sun. 11–4.*

Opposite Beaumaris Castle is the **courthouse** (☎ 01286/679090), built in 1614. A plaque depicts one view of the legal profession: two farmers pull a cow, one by the horns, one by the tail, while a lawyer sits in the middle milking. The **Museum and Memorabilia of Childhood** is an Aladdin's cave of music boxes, magic lanterns, trains, cars, toy soldiers, rocking horses, and mechanical savings banks. ⊠ *1 Castle St.,* ☎ *01248/712498,* WEB *www.nwi.co.uk/museumofchildhood.* ⊡ *£3.25.* ⊙ *Mar.–Oct., Mon.–Sat. 10:30–5, Sun. noon–5.*

On Castle Street, look for the **Tudor Rose,** a house dating from 1400 that's an excellent example of Tudor timberwork.

To discover the grim life of a Victorian prisoner, head to the old **gaol,** built in 1829 by Joseph Hansom (1803–1882), who was also the designer of the Hansom cab. ⊠ *Steeple La.,* ☎ *01286/679090.* ⊡ *£2.75* ⊙ *May–Sept., daily 11–5:30.*

The 14th-century **Church of St. Mary and St. Nicholas,** opposite the gaol in Steeple Lane, houses the stone coffin of Princess Joan, daughter of King John (1167–1216) and wife of Welsh leader Llewelyn the Great.

OFF THE BEATEN PATH

PLAS NEWYDD – The celebrated mansion of Plas Newydd on the Isle of Anglesey is worth a detour to see why some historians rate it the finest house in Wales. Built in the 18th century by James Wyatt (1747–1813) for the marquesses of Anglesey, it stands on the Menai Strait close to the Menai Bridge about 7 mi southwest of Beaumaris (don't confuse it with the Plas Newydd at Llangollen). In 1936–40 the society artist Rex Whistler (1905–44) painted the mural in the dining room here, his largest work and a great favorite of stately home buffs. A military museum commemorates the Battle of Waterloo, where the first marquess, Wellington's cavalry commander, lost his leg. The interior has some fine 18th-century Gothic Revival decorations, and the gardens have been restored to their original design. The views across the strait are magnificent. ⊠ *Off A4080, southwest of the Britannia Bridge, Llanfairpwll,* ☎ *01248/714795,* FAX *01248/713673.* ⊡ *£4.50.* ⊙ *Apr.–Oct., Sat.–Wed. noon–5; last admission ½ hr before closing.*

Nightlife and the Arts
The **Beaumaris Festival** (☎ 01248/811535) is held annually late May–early June. The whole town is used as a site, from the 14th-century parish church to the concert hall, with special concerts, dance performances, and plays.

Dining and Lodging

££   ✕▥ **Ye Olde Bull's Head.** Originally a coaching inn built in 1472, this place is small and charming. The oak-beam dining room, dating from 1617, serves contemporary specialties, including warm salad of pigeon breast with hazelnut oil, as well as local widgeon (wild duck), and it is also noted for its seafood. ⊠ *Castle St., LL58 8AP,* ☎ *01248/ 810329,* FAX *01248/811294,* WEB *www.bulldheadinn.co.uk. 15 rooms. Restaurant. AE, MC, V.*

£   ▥ **Llwydiarth Fawr.** It's worth seeking out this outstanding place in
★   the north central part of the Isle of Anglesey. Llwydiarth Fawr has exceptional farmhouse accommodations as well as being a convenient touring base for the island. It's a spacious, elegant Georgian house on an 850-acre cattle and sheep farm, with deluxe bedrooms and common areas with antiques and fireplaces. Owner Margaret Hughes welcomes guests warmly, serves good country cooking, and, in a nutshell, offers country living in style. ⊠ *Llanerchymedd LL71 8DF,* ☎ *01248/ 470321. 3 rooms. Dining room, lounge, fishing. No credit cards.*

Conwy

★ ⑩ *23 mi east of Beaumaris, 48 mi northwest of Chester.*

The still-authentic medieval town of Conwy grew up around its castle on the west bank of the River Conwy. The strong sense of period atmosphere is aided and abetted by a ring of ancient but extremely well-preserved walls that enclose the old town. You can walk along sections of the wall, which have impressive views across the huddled rooftops of the town to the castle and its estuary setting.

Conwy Castle, a mighty, many-turreted stronghold built between 1283 and 1287 by Edward I, can be approached on foot by a dramatic suspension bridge completed in 1825 and designed by the engineer Thomas Telford to blend in with the fortress's presence. The bridge toll-keeper's house has been restored as it was a century ago. Of all Edward's castles, Conwy preserves most convincingly the spirit of medieval times. ⊠ *Castle Sq.,* ☎ *01492/592358.* 🎫 *£3.60.* ⊘ *Mid-Mar.–mid-Oct., daily 9:30–6:30; mid-Oct.–mid-Mar., Mon.–Sat. 9:30–4, Sun. 11–4.*

What is said to be the **smallest house in Britain** (⊠ Lower Gate St.) is furnished in mid-Victorian Welsh style. The house, which is 6 ft wide and 10 ft high, was reputedly last occupied in 1900 by a fisherman who was more than 6 ft tall.

Plas Mawr, a jewel in the heart of Conwy, is the best-preserved Elizabethan town house in Britain. Built in 1576 by Robert Wynn (who later became both a Member of Parliament and Sheriff of Caernarvonshire), this richly decorated house with its ornamental plasterwork gives a unique insight into the lives of the Tudor gentry and their servants. ⊠ *High St.,* ☎ *01492/580167.* 🎫 *£4.* ⊘ *Apr.–Oct., Tues.–Sun. 10–6.*

Built in the 14th-century, **Aberconwy House** is the only surviving medieval merchant's house in Conwy. Each room in the restored building reflects different eras of its long history. ⊠ *Castle St.,* ☎ *01492/592246.* 🎫 *£2.* ⊘ *Apr.–Oct., Wed.–Mon. 11–5.*

★ With a reputation as the finest garden in Wales, **Bodnant Garden** remains a pilgrimage spot for horticulturists from around the world. Laid out in 1875, the 87 acres are particularly famed for their rhododendrons, camellias, magnolias, and a spectacular laburnam arch that in May forms a huge tunnel of golden blooms. This National Trust garden also has Italianate terraces, rock and rose gardens, and a pinetum, while the mountains of Snowdonia form a magnificent backdrop. The gardens are about 5 mi south of Conwy, in the lovely Vale of Conwy. ⊠ *Off A470, Tal-y-Cafn,* ☎ *01492/650460,* 🌐 *www.oxalis.co.uk/bodnant.htm.* 🎫 *£5.* ⊘ *Mid-Mar.–Oct., daily 10–5.*

Llandudno

⑪ *3 mi north of Conwy, 50 mi northwest of Chester.*

This charmingly old-fashioned North Wales seaside resort has a wealth of well-preserved Victorian architecture and an ornate pier. Unlike other resorts in Wales, and Britain as a whole, Llandudno preserves the genteel look of a bygone age. A wide promenade is lined with a huge selection of attractively painted hotels (Llandudno has the largest choice of lodging in Wales). The shopping streets behind also look the part, thanks to their original canopied walkways. Llandudno has little in the way of the garish amusement arcades that are nowadays such a feature of seaside resorts. Instead, it prefers to stick to its faithful cable car that climbs, San Francisco–style, to the summit of the Great Orme headland above the resort. There is also an aerial cable car to the top, and a large, dry ski slope and toboggan run.

Lovers of literature will delight in knowing that Llandudno was the summer home of the family of Dr. Liddell, the Oxford don and father of the immortal Alice, inspiration for Lewis Carroll's *Alice's Adventures in Wonderland*. The reference to the book's Walrus and the Carpenter may be based on two rocks on Llandudno's West Shore near the Liddell home, which Alice possibly described to Carroll. The Alice in Wonderland connection is reflected in the **Alice in Wonderland Centre,** where Alice's adventures are colorfully brought to life in enchanting displays of the best-known scenes from the book. ✉ *3–4 Trinity Sq.,* ☎ *01492/ 860082,* WEB *www.wonderland.co.uk.* ✍ *£3.25.* ☉ *Easter–Oct., daily 10–5; Nov.–Easter, Mon.–Sat. 10–5.*

The prehistoric **Great Orme Mines** are at the summit of the Great Orme (*orme* is a Norse word meaning sea monster), with its spectacular views of the coast and mountains of Snowdonia. Copper was first mined here during the Bronze Age, and you can tour the ancient underground workings to learn about the life of the miners. ✉ *Great Orme,* ☎ *01492/870447.* ✍ *£4.50.* ☉ *Feb.–Oct., daily 10–5.*

Dining and Lodging

££££   ✕▥ **Bodysgallen Hall.** Set inside wide, walled gardens 2 mi out of town,
★   the Hall is part 17th, part 18th century, full of antiques, comfortable chairs by cheery fires, pictures, and polished wood. The bedrooms (a few suites are available) combine elegance and practicality, and from some of them you'll see the mountains. The restaurant (three-course fixed-price menu at dinner) serves fine meals, using traditional ingredients in creative ways. The emphasis is on such local fare as lamb and smoked salmon. Prices are relatively low for the standard it offers. ✉ *Off A470, LL30 1RS,* ☎ *01492/584466,* FAX *01492/582519,* WEB *www.bodysgallen.com. 35 rooms. Restaurant, indoor pool, sauna, spa, tennis court, croquet, gym. AE, DC, MC, V.*

££–££££ ✕▥ **St. Tudno Hotel.** One of Britain's top seaside hotels sits on the seafront in Llandudno. From the outside, it blends unobtrusively with its neighbors, but inside are richly decorated and opulently furnished rooms. Service is first-class, and the contemporary cuisine, including dishes such as grilled goat cheese with Parma ham and saddle of hare with spicy cabbage, is accomplished. ✉ *Promenade, LL30 2LP,* ☎ *01492/874411,* FAX *01492/860407,* WEB *www.st-tudno.co.uk. 20 rooms. Restaurant, indoor pool. AE, DC, MC, V.*

£££   ✕▥ **The Old Rectory.** Michael and Wendy Vaughan look after their guests in their elegant Georgian home, which resembles a small country house furnished with Victorian antiques rather than a hotel. Another plus is the cooking—Wendy is recognized as one of Wales's top chefs. Nonguests can dine here but must reserve in advance. The Old Rectory overlooks the Conwy Estuary south of Llandudno, with magnificent views across lovely gardens to Conwy Castle and Snowdonia. ✉ *Off A470, Llansanffraidd Glan, Conwy LL28 5LF,* ☎ *01492/580611,* FAX *01492/584555,* WEB *www.oldrectorycountryhouse.co.uk. 6 rooms. Restaurant. MC, V.*

££   ▥ **Bryn Derwen Hotel.** Many hoteliers at British seaside resorts have not moved with the times to upgrade their accommodations and food. This immaculate Victorian hotel exemplifies how it should be done. There is great attention to detail, and fresh flowers and attractive period furnishings set the tone. The hotel offers truly excellent value. ✉ *34 Abbey Rd., LL30 2EE,* WEB *www.bryn-derwen-hotel.co.uk,* ☎ FAX *01492/876804. 9 rooms. Dining room, lounge, spa. MC, V.*

En Route Inland from Rhyl, **Bodelwyddan Castle,** off A55 between Abergele and St. Asaph, is a restored Victorian castle in spacious formal gardens, surrounded by lovely countryside. The Welsh home of the National Portrait Gallery in London, it exhibits Regency and Victorian portraits by the likes of Sargent, Lawrence, G. F. Watts, Rossetti, and Landseer. There are also hands-on galleries of Victorian amusements and inventions. ☏ *01745/584060.* ☞ *£4.50, grounds only £2.* ⊙ *Apr.–Oct., Sat.–Thurs. 11–5; Nov.–Mar., Tues.–Thurs. and weekends 11–4.*

Denbigh

⑫ *25 mi southeast of Llandudno.*

This market town (market day is Wednesday) was much admired by Dr. Samuel Johnson (1709–84), who stayed on Pentrefoelas Road at Gwaenynog Hall, where he designed two rooms. A walk along the riverbank at nearby Lawnt, a spot he loved, brings you to a monumental urn placed in his honor. Not that it pleased him: "It looks like an intention to bury me alive," thundered the great lexicographer.

Denbigh Castle, begun in 1282 as one of Edward I's ring of castles built to subdue the Welsh, is known as "the hollow crown" because it is not much more than a shell set on high ground, dominating the town. H. M. Stanley (1841–1904), the intrepid 19th-century journalist and explorer who found Dr. Livingstone in Africa, was born in a cottage below the castle. ☏ *029/2050–0200.* ☞ *£2.* ⊙ *Early Apr.–late Oct., weekdays 10–5:30, weekends 9:30–5:30.*

Ruthin

⑬ *8 mi southeast of Denbigh, 23 mi west of Chester.*

Ruthin is the capital of "Glyndŵr Country," where the Welsh hero Owain Glyndŵr (circa 1354–1416) lived and ruled. Architecturally, the town is full of interest, with many well-preserved buildings dating from the 16th through the 19th centuries. Ruthin also has elegant shops, good inns, and a crafts complex that displays the work of different craftspeople. Medieval-style banquets are held here regularly.

Lodging

£ 🏠 **Eyarth Old Railway Station.** This Victorian railway station near Ruthin ★ was converted in 1981 to an award-winning bed-and-breakfast. Bedrooms are spacious, with large windows looking out onto rural scenery. ⊠ *Off A525, Llanfair Dyffryn Clwyd LL15 2EE,* ☏ *01824/703643,* 🖷 *01824/707464. 6 rooms. Pool. MC, V.*

MID-WALES: THE HISTORIC HEARTLAND

If your idea of heaven is traditional market towns and country villages, small seaside resorts, quiet roads, and rolling landscapes filled with sheep farms, forests, and lakes, then heaven exists for you in mid-Wales, the green and rural heart of the country. As this is Wales's quietest holiday region, lodgings are scattered thinly across the landscape. Outside of one or two large centers, Aberystwyth and Llandrindod Wells, accommodations mainly tend toward country inns, small hotels, and farmhouses. This region also has some splendid country-house hotels, set within their own grounds in glorious locations. Although green is the predominant color here, you will notice distinct changes in the landscape as you travel through the region. The borderlands are gentle and undulating, rising to the west into high, wild mountains. Farther north, around Dolgellau, mountainous scenery becomes even more pronounced as you enter the southern section of the Snowdonia National Park. Mountains meet the sea along Cardigan Bay, a long coastline of headlands, peaceful sandy beaches, and beautiful estuaries that has long been a shelter from the crowd. In the 19th century, Tennyson, Darwin, Shelley, and Ruskin all came here to work and relax; today, thousands more come to delight in the numerous antiquarian bookstores of Hay-on-Wye.

Hay-on-Wye

★ **⑭** *57 mi north of Cardiff, 25 mi north of Abergavenny.*

This town on the border of Wales and England is dominated by its mostly ruined castle and its bookshops. Hay is a lively place, especially on Sunday, when the rest of central Wales seems to be closed down. In 1961 Richard Booth established a small secondhand and antiquarian bookshop here. Other booksellers soon got in on the act, and bookshops now fill several houses, a movie theater, shops, and a pub. At last count, there were about 25, all in a small town of only 1,500 inhabitants. The town is now the largest secondhand bookselling center in the world, where priceless 14th-century manuscripts rub spines with "job lots" selling for a few pounds. Hay also has a range of antiques and crafts centers. The town really buzzes in early summer when it hosts the International Festival of Literature, which attracts famous writers from all over the world.

Dining and Lodging

££ ✕🖾 **Old Black Lion.** A 17th-century coaching inn close to the center of Hay is ideal for a lunch break while you're ransacking the bookshops, or for an overnight stay. The low-beamed, atmospheric bar serves its own food, and the breakfasts are especially good. Its sophisticated country cooking with an international twist is well regarded. ⊠ *Lion St., HR3 5AD,* ☎ *01497/820841,* 🕸 *www.hay-on-wye.co.uk. 10 rooms. Restaurant, lounge. AE, MC, V.*

££ ✕🖾 **Three Cocks Hotel.** This historic hostelry with its cobbled forecourt has been beautifully restored by Michael and Marie-Jeanne Winstone. It stands on the western approach to Hay, about 6 mi from town. The contemporary cooking is superb, with a strong Continental influence. ⊠ *A438, Three Cocks LD3 0SL,* ☎ *01497/847215,* ℻ *01497/847339,* 🕸 *www.threecockshotel.com. 7 rooms. Restaurant. MC, V.*

Builth Wells

⑮ *20 mi northwest of Hay-on-Wye, 60 mi north of Cardiff.*

Builth Wells, a farming town and former spa on the banks of the River Wye, is the site of Wales's biggest rural gathering. The countryside around Builth and its neighbor, Llandrindod Wells, varies considerably. Some of the land is soft and rich, with rolling green hills and lush valleys, but close by are the wildernesses of Mynydd Eppynt and the foothills of the Cambrian Mountains, the lofty "backbone of Wales."

The annual **Royal Welsh Agricultural Show** (☎ 01982/553683), held in late July, is not only Wales's prime gathering of farming folk but also a colorful countryside jamboree that attracts huge crowds.

Dining and Lodging

£££ ✕🖾 **Lake Country House.** This is the place to go for total Victorian country elegance, and total tranquillity. Its 50 acres of sloping lawns and
★ lush rhododendrons contain a trout-filled lake that attracts anglers. Comfortable and quiet, the hotel has first-class service and excellent contemporary cuisine (fixed-price menu). The large rooms are tastefully furnished, and some have four-poster beds. The hotel is at Llangammarch Wells, another peaceful former spa town about 8 mi west of Builth. ⊠ *Llangammarch Wells LD4 4BS,* ☎ *01591/620202,* ℻ *01591/620457,* 🕸 *www.lakecountryhouse.co.uk. 19 rooms. Restaurant, bar,*

*9-hole golf course, putting green, tennis court, croquet, fishing, billiards.
AE, DC, MC, V.*

Llandrindod Wells

16 *7 mi north of Builth Wells, 67 mi north of Cardiff.*

Also known as Llandod, Llandrindod Wells is an old spa town that
preserves its original Victorian layout and look. It is architecturally fascinating, with an array of fussy turrets, cupolas, loggias, and balustrades,
and greenery everywhere. Llandrindod, on a branchline rail route and
with good bus service, is a useful base for exploring the region, and
the town itself is easily seen on foot. Cross over to South Crescent, passing the Glen Usk Hotel with its wrought-iron balustrade and the Victorian bandstand in the gardens opposite, and you soon reach Middleton
Street, another Victorian thoroughfare. From there, head to Rock Park
and the path that leads to the Pump Room. On the other side of town,
the lake, with its boathouse, café, and gift shop, is in a lovely setting:
wooded hills on one side and a broad common on the other.

The **Radnorshire Museum,** in Memorial Gardens, details the spa's development from Roman times and explains some of the Victorian
"cures" in gruesome detail. ☎ *01597/824513.* ⊡ *£1.50.* ⊙ *Apr.–Oct.,
Tues.–Sun. 10–1, 2–5; Nov.–Mar., Tues.–Fri. 10–1, 2–5, Sat. 10–1.*

The handsomely restored **Pump Room** (⊠ Rock Park Spa, ☎ 01597/
822997), where visitors would "take the waters," today serves tea and
refreshments and only one type of the many waters that used to be on
tap. It also plays a part during the town's **Victorian Festival** (☎ 01597/
823441), held in late August. Shop assistants, hotel staff, and anyone
else who cares to join in wear period costume and enjoy suitable "old-
style" entertainment.

Lodging

£ ⊞ **Guidfa House.** A stylish Georgian guest house run by friendly hosts
Tony and Anne Millan, Guidfa House provides comfortable accommodation and a welcoming atmosphere. The sitting room has a log fireplace. Homemade dinners (for guests only) are prepared by Cordon
Bleu–trained Anne from fresh local produce. All in all, this is an ideal
base from which to explore the countryside of mid-Wales. ⊠ *Cross-
gates, near Llandrindod Wells, LD1 6RF,* ☎ *01597/851241,* ℻ *01597/
851875,* ⧆ *www.guidfa-house.co.uk. 6 rooms. Dining room. MC, V.*

En Route From Llandrindod, take A4081/A470 to Rhayader, a good pony-
trekking center and gateway town for the **Elan Valley,** Wales's "Lake
District." This 7-mi chain of lakes, winding between gray-green hills,
was created in the 1890s by a system of dams to supply water to the
city of Birmingham, 73 mi to the east. From the Elan Valley, you can
follow the spectacular and narrow Cwmystwyth mountain road west
to **Devil's Bridge,** a famous (and popular) beauty spot with a number
of bridges over a raging river, before continuing on to Aberystwyth.

Aberystwyth

*41 mi northwest of Llandrindod Wells via A44, 118 mi northwest of
Cardiff.*

Aberystwyth makes the best of several worlds. Besides being a seaside
resort, it is a long-established university town, housing the magnificent National Library of Wales. It also has a little harbor and quite
clearly a life of its own. The town, attractively sited midway along Cardigan Bay, came to prominence as a Victorian watering hole thanks to
its curving beach set beneath a prominent headland. The resort is a

good gateway for exploring mid-Wales: there are few towns in Wales that present such a wide variety of scenery within their immediate neighborhood, here ranging from the extraordinary Devil's Bridge to the beautiful Rheidol Valley.

⑰ The modern **University of Wales, Aberystwyth,** on the hill above town, includes the National Library (housing Welsh and other Celtic literary works), an arts center with galleries, a theater, and a concert hall, all open to visitors. The original university, founded in the 19th century, stands on the seafront. ⊠ *National Library, off Penglais Rd.,* ☎ *01970/632800,* WEB *www.llgc.org.uk.* 🎫 *Free.* ☉ *Weekdays 9:30–6, Sat. 9:30–5.*

⑱ The **castle,** at the southern end of the bay near the New Promendate, was built in 1277 and rebuilt in 1282 by Edward I. It was one of several strongholds to fall, in 1404, to the Welsh leader Owain Glyndŵr. Today it is a romantic ruin on a headland separating the north shore from
⑲ the harbor shore. At the end of the promenade, **Constitution Hill** offers the energetic a zigzag cliff path–nature trail to the view from the top.

An enjoyable way to reach the summit of Constitution Hill is by the **Aberystwyth Cliff Railway,** the longest electric cliff railway in Britain. Opened in 1896 to great excitement, it has been refurbished without diminishing its Victorian look. ☎ *01970/617642.* 🎫 *£2.50 round-trip.* ☉ *Mid-Mar.–June and Oct., daily 10–5; July–Sept., daily 10–6.*

At the 430-ft summit of Constitution Hill is the **Great Aberystwyth Camera Obscura** (☎ *01970/617642*), a free modern version of a Victorian amusement: a massive 14-inch lens gives a bird's-eye view of more than 1,000 square mi of sea and scenery, including the whole of Cardigan Bay and 26 Welsh mountain peaks.

⑳ The excellent **Ceredigion Museum,** in a flamboyant 1905 Edwardian theater, displays a fine collection of folk history. Highlights include a reconstruction of a single-story, mud-walled, thatched Ceredigion cottage from 1850, exhibits from the museum's music hall past, and items illustrating the region's seafaring, leadmining, and farming history. ⊠ *Terrace Rd.,* ☎ *01970/633088.* 🎫 *Free.* ☉ *Mon.–Sat. 10–5.*

At Aberystwyth Station you can hop on the narrow-gauge steam-op-
㉑ erated **Vale of Rheidol Railway.** The railway terminus, an hour's ride away, is **Devil's Bridge,** where the rivers Rheidol and Mynach meet in a series of spectacular falls. Clamped between two rocky cliffs where a torrent of water pours unceasingly, this bridge well deserves the name it bears—*Pont y Gwr Drwg,* or Bridge of the Evil One. Legend has it that it was the devil himself who built it. There are actually three bridges, the oldest is all of 800 years old, and the walk down to the lowest bridge, "the devil's," is magnificent but strictly for the surefooted. ⊠ *Alexandra St.,* ☎ *01970/625819,* WEB *www.rheidolrailway.co.uk.* 🎫 *£11 round-trip.* ☉ *Apr.–Oct.; call for schedule.*

Dining and Lodging

£–££ ✕ **Gannets.** A simple, good-value bistro, Gannets specializes in locally supplied meat, fish, and game, which are transformed into hearty roasts and pies. Organically grown vegetables and a good French house wine are further draws for a university crowd. ⊠ *7 St. James's Sq.,* ☎ *01970/617164. MC, V. Closed Sun., Tues.*

£££ ✕🛏 **Conrah Country Hotel.** Part of the appeal of this country-house hotel is its air of seclusion, even though it's only a short drive south from Aberystwyth. The owners have decorated the house with traditional country furnishings and antiques, and fresh flowers fill each room. The restaurant is known for its good food and wines, with imaginative contemporary and traditional British cuisine making use of local

Castle **18**
Ceredigion
Museum . . . **20**
Constitution
Hill **19**
University of
Wales campus
sites (old and
new) **17**
Vale of
Rheidol
Railway . . . **21**

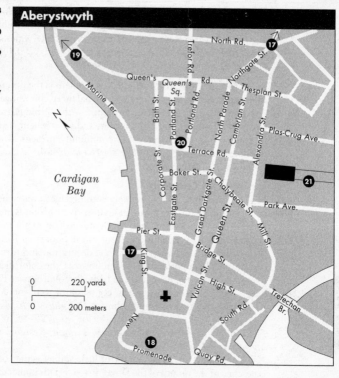

game, fish, and meat. There's a three-course prix-fixe menu at dinner. ⊠ *A487, Chancery, SY23 4DF,* ☎ *01970/617941,* FAX *01970/624546,* WEB *www.conrah.co.uk. 17 rooms. Restaurant, indoor pool, sauna, croquet. AE, DC, MC, V.*

££ ✕🖬 **Four Seasons.** This family-run hotel and restaurant in the town center has a relaxed atmosphere and friendly staff. The spacious rooms are simply and attractively decorated, while the restaurant serves excellent meals at reasonable prices, offering two- and three-course prix-fixe menus at dinner. ⊠ *50–54 Portland St., SY23 2DX,* ☎ *01970/ 612120,* FAX *01970/627458. 14 rooms. Restaurant. MC, V.*

Machynlleth

㉒ *18 mi northeast of Aberystwyth.*

Machynlleth, at the head of the beautiful Dovey Estuary, does not look like a typical Welsh country town. Its long and wide main street (Heol Maengwyn), lined with a mixed style of buildings, from sober gray stone to well-proportioned Georgian, creates an atypical sense of openness and space. Machynlleth's busiest day is Wednesday, when the main street is filled with the stalls of market traders.

At the **Owain Glyndŵr Centre,** a small exhibition celebrates Wales's last native leader, who established a Welsh parliament at Machynlleth in the early 15th century. ⊠ *End of Heol Maengwyn,* ☎ *01654/ 702827.* 🖾 *Free.* 🕙 *Easter–Oct., Mon.–Sat. 10–5.*

Housed in a cultural and performing arts center in a former chapel is the free **Y Tabernacl Museum of Modern Art** (⊠ Heol Penrallt, ☎ 01654/703355), a superb art gallery with permanent displays, including works by noted Welsh artist Kyffin Williams and temporary exhibitions highlighting contemporary artists.

Welsh history of an earlier time is the main theme at **Celtica,** an imaginative exhibition center in the large parkland behind the shops and pubs, where various interpretive displays re-create Wales's Celtic past. ☎ *01654/702702,* WEB *www.celtica.wales.com.* 💷 *£4.95.* ⊙ *Daily 10–6 (last entry to main exhibition 4:40).*

In the forested hills just north of Machynlleth is the unique **Centre for Alternative Technology,** where a water-balanced cliff railway transports you to a village of the future equipped with all things green: alternative energy sources, organic gardens, and an excellent vegetarian café. Interactive displays around the community present ideas about renewable resources. ⊠ *Off A487,* ☎ *01654/702400,* WEB *www.cat.org.uk.* 💷 *£6.75.* ⊙ *Daily 9–6.*

Dining and Lodging

££££–££££   ✕🖼 **Ynyshir Hall.** This supremely comfortable country-house hotel is
★ in a beautiful Georgian house in idyllic private grounds, near a wildlife reserve off A487, southwest of Machynlleth. The artistic talents of owners Joan and Rob Reen are evident in the bounty of Rob's paintings (he's an established artist) and in the decoration and furnishings. Antiques and Welsh pottery fill the public areas; the colorful guest rooms, named after artists, have antique beds. Personal service is paramount here, and the hotel is noted for its contemporary cuisine. A four-course fixed-price menu is offered at dinner. ⊠ *Eglwysfach, near Machynlleth, SY20 8TA,* ☎ *01654/781209 or 800/777–6536,* FAX *01654/ 781366,* WEB *www.ynyshir-hall.co.uk. 8 rooms. Restaurant, no-smoking rooms. AE, DC, MC, V.*

££   ✕🖼 **Penhelig Arms.** The delightful little sailing center of Aberdovey is perched at the mouth of the Dovey Estuary. This immaculate, friendly harborside inn has a terrace overlooking the harbor and bay, and most rooms have wonderful sea views. You can meet the locals in the wood-paneled Fisherman's Bar and dine in style at the fine restaurant (three-course fixed-price menu at dinner). The town is along the coast road running west from Machynlleth. ⊠ *A493, Aberdovey LL35 0LT,* ☎ *01654/767215,* FAX *016354/767690,* WEB *www.penheligarms.com. 14 rooms. Restaurant, bar. MC, V.*

Dolgellau

㉓ *16 mi north of Machynlleth, 34 mi north of Aberystwyth.*

Dolgellau (pronounced dol-*geth*-lee) is a solidly Welsh town with attractive dark buildings and handsome old coaching inns. It was the center of the Welsh gold trade in the 19th century, when high-quality gold was discovered locally. You can still try your luck and pan for gold in the Mawddach. A nugget of Dolgellau gold is used to make royal wedding rings. The town makes a good base for walks in the area.

The Dolgellau area has strong links with the Quaker movement and the Quakers' emigration to America. The **Museum of the Quakers,** in the town square, commemorates these associations. ☎ *01341/422888.* 💷 *Free.* ⊙ *Easter–Oct., daily 10–6; Nov.–Easter, Thurs.–Mon. 10–5.*

To the south of Dolgellau rises the menacing bulk of **Cader Idris** (2,927 ft); the name means "the Chair of Idris," though no one is completely sure just who Idris was, probably a warrior bard. It is said that anyone sleeping for a night in a certain part of the mountain will awaken either a poet or a madman, or not at all.

Barmouth

②④ *10 mi west of Dolgellau.*

Barmouth is one of the few places along the Welsh coast, and certainly along Cardigan Bay that can be described as a full-fledged seaside resort. On the northern mouth of the picturesque Mawddach Estuary, it has a 2-mi-long promenade, wide expanses of golden beach, and facilities for sea, river, and mountain lake fishing. Its splendid setting is best appreciated from the footpath beside the railway bridge across the mouth of the estuary. Even in the 19th century Barmouth was a popular holiday resort. Alfred Lord Tennyson wrote part of *In Memoriam* here and was inspired to write *Crossing the Bar* by the spectacle of the Mawddach rushing to meet the sea. Percy Bysshe and Mary Shelley stayed here in 1812; Charles Darwin worked on *The Origin of Species* and *The Descent of Man* in a house by the shore. Essayist and art critic John Ruskin was a frequent visitor and was trustee of the St. George's cottages built there by the Guild of St. George in 1871.

Lodging

££ 🏨 **Llwyndu Farmhouse.** This restored 17th-century, farmhouse, with
★ its inglenook fireplace, mullioned windows, exposed stone walls, and ancient beams, stands a mile or so north from Barmouth along the coast road. Its location on a hillside overlooking Cardigan Bay adds to the atmosphere. Accommodations are within the house or in the adjoining converted barn, and rooms have both modern conveniences and some of the charming quirks of age. ✉ *A496, Llanaber, near Barmouth, LL42 1RR,* ☎ *01341/280144,* FAX *01341/ 281236,* WEB *www.llwyndu-farmhouse.co.uk. 7 rooms. Dining room, lounge. MC, V.*

Welshpool

②⑤ *48 mi east of Barmouth, 19 mi west of Shrewsbury.*

The border town of Welshpool, "Trallwng" in Welsh, is famous as the home of Powis Castle, one of mid-Wales's greatest treasures, but it also has an appealing town center.

★ In continuous occupation since the 13th century, **Powis Castle,** is one of the most opulent residential castles in Britain. Its battlements rearing high on a hilltop, the castle is surrounded by splendid grounds and terraced gardens, and bounded by gigantic yew hedges, that fall steeply down to wide lawns and neat Elizabethan gardens. It contains many treasures: Greek vases, magnificent paintings by Gainsborough, Reynolds, and Romney, among others, superb furniture, including a 16th-century Italian table inlaid with marble, and, since 1987, the **Clive of India Museum,** with a fine collection of Indian art. The tearoom here is excellent. ☎ *01938/557018,* FAX *01938/554336,* WEB *www.nationaltrust.org.uk.* 🎫 *£7.50, gardens only £5.* ☉ *Apr.–June and Sept.–Oct., Wed.–Sun.; July–Aug., Tues.–Sun. Hrs: castle and museum 1–5, gardens 11–6; last admission ½ hr before closing.*

The excellent **Powysland Museum,** in a converted warehouse on the banks of the Montgomery canal, focuses on local history from the Stone Age to Victorian times. ✉ *Canal Wharf,* ☎ *01938/554656.* 🎫 *£1.* ☉ *May–Aug., Mon.–Tues., Thurs.–Fri. 11–1 and 2–5, weekends 10–1 and 2–5; Sept.–Apr., closed Sat.* AM *and Sun.*

SOUTH WALES: FROM CARDIFF TO CARDIGAN

The south is the most diverse of Wales's three regions. It covers not only the immediate region around Cardiff and the border of Wales and England, but also the southwest as far as the rugged coastline of Pembrokeshire. South Wales's scenic variety is reflected in the very different nature of its two national parks. The Brecon Beacons park, a short drive north of Cardiff, is an area of high, grassy mountains, lakes, and craggy limestone gorges. In contrast, the Pembrokeshire Coast National Park is recognized as one of Europe's finest stretches of coastal natural beauty, with mile after mile of spectacular sea cliffs, beaches, headlands, and coves. Other pieces of the complicated South Wales jigsaw include traditional farmlands, cosmopolitan urban areas, rolling border country, wooded vales, and the former industrial valleys where coal was mined in huge quantities during the 19th and early 20th centuries.

Cardiff

20 mi west of the Second Severn Bridge, which carries the M4 motorway across the Severn Estuary into Wales.

Financially, industrially, and commercially Cardiff is the most important city in Wales, but those attributes, some might point out, are not exactly exciting for tourists. Still, Cardiff is on the upswing, in part because of the presence of the Welsh Assembly. Once you get to know Wales's capital, there is a lot to delight the eye, including a handsome Civic Centre, magnificent parklands, and one of the most magical castles in the world. Even the docklands have become the focus of a massive plan to give the city a freshwater lake and 9 mi of new waterfront. Cardiff Bay Inner Harbor, with its promenades, shops, restaurants, and visitor attractions, is part of this ambitious development and is now the United Kingdom's fastest-growing tourist destination.

True to the Welsh tradition of vocal excellence, Cardiff is home of Britain's most adventurous opera company, the Welsh National Opera, which will move to a new home on the waterfront. Cardiff is also the sporting center of Wales, and this means the Welsh capital of rugby football. To hear crowds singing their support for the Welsh team is a stirring experience.

★ ㉖ Any exploration of Cardiff should begin at **Cardiff Castle** in Bute Park, one section of the city's hundreds of acres of parkland. The castle, on the edge of the shopping center, is an unusual "three-in-one" historic site, with Roman, Norman, and especially Victorian associations. Parts of the walls are Roman, the solid keep is Norman, and the whole complex was restored and transformed into an utter Victorian ego flight by the third Marquess of Bute. He employed William Burges (1827–81), an architect obsessed by the Gothic period, and Burges transformed the castle into an extravaganza of medieval color and detailed craftsmanship. It is the perfect expression of the anything-goes Victorian spirit, not to mention the vast fortune made by the marquess in Cardiff's booming docklands. ⊠ *Bute Park,* ☎ *029/2087–8100.* ▨ *Guided tour of castle £5.* ☉ *Mar.–Oct., daily 9:30–6; Nov.–Feb., daily 9:30–4:30; call for tour times.*

The **Civic Centre,** a well-designed complex of tree-lined avenues and Edwardian civic buildings with white Portland stone facades, is two blocks east of Cardiff Castle. A proud Welsh dragon sits atop the domed City Hall, and inside the building the Marble Hall contains statues of Welsh heroes including St. David, Henry Tudor, and Owain Glyndŵr (even

Cardiff Bay
Inner
Harbor **30**
Cardiff
Castle **26**
Castell
Coch **33**
Llandaff **31**
Millennium
Stadium **29**
Museum of
Welsh Life . **32**
National
Museum and
Gallery . . . **27**
St. David's
Centre **28**

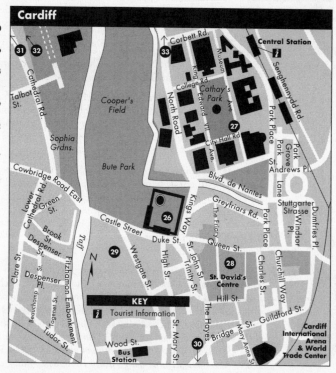

though he razed Cardiff to the ground in 1404). Neoclassical law courts and elegant University campus buildings are also here.

27 The **National Museum and Gallery,** next to the city hall in the Civic Centre, is a splendid museum that tells the story of Wales through its plants, rocks, archaeology, art, and industry. It also has a fine collection of modern European art, most notably a large selection of Impressionist and Postimpressionist works. Allow at least half a day here, and don't miss *La Parisienne* by Renoir. ⊠ *Cathays Park,* ☎ *029/ 2039–7951,* WEB *www.nmgw.ac.uk.* ☛ *£4.50.* ☉ *Tues.–Sun. 10–5.*

28 Around **St. David's Centre,** south of the Civic Centre, are the shopping and business areas of Cardiff. Here in a large, modern shopping mall is **St. David's Hall,** one of Europe's best concert halls, with outstanding acoustics, where people come for classical music, jazz, rock, ballet, and even snooker championships. Nearby is the **Cardiff International Arena,** a multipurpose center for exhibitions, concerts, and conferences.

29 The 72,000-seat **Millennium Stadium** has risen from the ashes of the famous Cardiff Arms Park, the spiritual home of Welsh rugby, and stands beside the River Taff. The stadium has a retractable roof that enables it to be used for concerts and special events throughout the year, as well as for rugby. On a one-hour tour you can walk the player's tunnel and see the Royal Box, dressing rooms, pitch, and broadcasting suite. ⊠ *Entrance Gate 3, Westgate St.,* ☎ *029/2082–2228.* ☛ *£5.* ☉ *Call for times.*

30 The revitalized **Cardiff Bay Inner Harbor,** in the old dockland 1 mi south of the city center, has appealing promenades, shops, restaurants, and panoramic bay views that make the area worth a visit. It also has a range of attractions including a science museum. The **Cardiff Bay Visitor Center,** a futuristic building known locally as "the Tube" (due to its distinctive shape), tells the story of the transformation of the bay area. Overlooking the bay is the lovely timber Norwegian seamen's church where Roald Dahl (noted author whose children's books include *Matilda* and *Charlie and the Chocolate Factory*) was baptized. It's now known as **The Norwegian Church Arts Centre** and houses performance space, a gallery, and a café.

Techniquest, Britain's leading Science Discovery Center, is on the waterfront and has 160 interactive exhibits, a planetarium, and science theater. ☒ *Stuart St., Cardiff Bay,* ☎ *029/2047–5475,* WEB *www.tquest.org.uk.* ☞ *£5.50.* ☼ *Weekdays 9:30–4:30, weekends 10:30–5.*

③① **Llandaff,** a suburb that retains its village atmosphere, is home to **Llandaff Cathedral,** which was completely renovated after serious bomb damage in World War II. The cathedral includes the work of a number of Pre-Raphaelites as well as the overwhelming *Christ in Majesty,* a 15-ft-tall aluminum by sculptor Jacob Epstein (1880–1959). To get here from Cardiff, cross the River Taff and follow Cathedral Road for about 2 mi.

★ ③② The 100 acres of parklands and gardens at the excellent open-air **Museum of Welsh Life** hold farmhouses, cottages, shops, a school, chapels, a castle, and terraced houses that celebrate Wales's rich rural culture and show the evolution of building styles. Special events highlight ancient rural festivals such as May Day, Harvest, and Christmas. The museum is accessible from Junction 33 on the M4. ☒ *St. Fagans,* ☎ *029/2057–3500,* WEB *www.nmgw.ac.uk/mwl/index.en.* ☞ *£4.50 Nov.–Mar., £5.50 Apr.–Oct.* ☼ *June–Aug., daily 10–6; Sept.–May, daily 10–5.*

★ ③③ **Castell Coch,** the Red Castle, is a structure so like a romantic, fairy-tale castle that few fail to be enchanted by it. The castle was built (on the site of a medieval stronghold) in the 1870s about the time that Ludwig II of Bavaria was creating his fantastic dream castles, and it might almost be one of them. Instead, the castle was another collaboration of the third Marquess of Bute and William Burges, builders of Cardiff Castle. Here Burges re-created everything—architecture, furnishings, carvings, murals—in a remarkable exercise in Victorian-Gothic whimsy. ☒ *A470, 4 mi north of Cardiff, Tongwynlais,* ☎ *029/2081–0101.* ☞ *£2.50.* ☼ *Late Mar.–late Oct., daily 9:30–6:30; late Oct.–late Mar., Mon.–Sat. 9:30–4, Sun. 11–4.*

The largest (with more than 30 acres of grounds) and one of the most impressive fortresses in Wales, **Caerphilly Castle** was remarkable at the time of its 13th-century Norman construction. The concentric fortification contained inner and outer defenses. Caerphilly is no longer on guard; some walls have toppled and others lean haphazardly. A substantial moat surrounds the castle, and exhibits trace its turbulent history. The castle is 7 mi north of Cardiff. ☒ *Access off A470/A468, Caerphilly,* ☎ *029/2088–3143.* ☞ *£2.50.* ☼ *Apr.–May and Oct., daily 9:30–5; June–Sept., daily 9:30–6; Nov.–Mar., Mon.–Sat. 9:30–4, Sun. 11–4.*

OFF THE
BEATEN PATH   **TINTERN ABBEY –** When Wordsworth penned "Lines Written a Few Miles Above Tintern Abbey," he had no idea of all the people who would flock to Tintern to gaze at the substantial ruins of the abbey. Remote and hauntingly beautiful as the site is, Tintern's appeal is diminished in summer because of crowds, so do try to visit early or late in the day to appreciate the complex stonework and tracery of the Gothic church. The abbey, 30 mi northeast of Cardiff, is set on the lovely River Wye. ☒ *A466, Tintern,* ☎ *01291/689251.* ☞ *£2.* ☼ *Late Mar.–late Oct., daily 9:30–6; late Oct.–late Mar., Mon.–Sat. 9:30–4, Sun. 11–4.*

Dining and Lodging

£££ ✕ **Le Gallois.** Its fresh modern decor and varied menu help make Le Gallois, located close to Sophia Gardens, one of the most popular restaurants in Cardiff. The cooking is European in style and makes use of the best of fresh local ingredients. Try the roast fillet of cod with mustard mash, spinach, and Penclawdd cockle gravy. A good-value fixed-price menu is available at lunch. ⊠ *8 Romilly Crescent,* ☎ *029/2034–1264. AE, MC, V. Closed Sun.–Mon.*

££–£££ ✕ **Le Cassoulet.** This is a genuine French restaurant, decorated in warm pastel shades and set in the maze of Victorian streets west of Cathedral Road. Try the very tasty fish soup as a starter, then the namesake dish, for a filling meal. ⊠ *5 Romilly Crescent,* ☎ *029/2022–1905. AE, DC, MC, V. Closed Sun.–Mon.*

£ ✕ **Celtic Cauldron.** Good-value lunches with a distinctive Welsh flavor, including traditional meat dishes and many vegetarian specialities, are the draw here. Try the Glamorgan sausages, an old Welsh recipe using leeks, cheese, eggs, herbs, and breadcrumbs, or a dish of cawl, a tasty meat stew with root vegetables. ⊠ *47–49 Castle Arcade,* ☎ *029/ 2038–7185. MC, V. No dinner.*

£ ✕ **Harry Ramsden's.** You can dine on the (reputedly) world's most famous fish and chips in a chandeliered, 200-seat dining room with wonderful views across Cardiff Bay. If you like live music with your meal, call ahead to ask for dates of opera and sing-along evenings. ⊠ *Landsea House, Stuart St.,* ☎ *029/2046–3334. MC, V.*

££££ 🏠 **St. David's Hotel and Spa.** Luxurious and expensive, this striking modern hotel is built along Cardiff's waterfront area. Every room has views over Cardiff Bay. You can indulge in a relaxing hydrotherapy spa treatment. ⊠ *Havannah St., CF1 6SD,* ☎ *029/2045–4045,* FAX *029/ 2048–7056,* WEB *www.rfhotels.com. 136 rooms. Restaurant, indoor pool, spa, gym, business services, meeting rooms. AE, DC, MC, V.*

£££ 🏠 **Cardiff Marriott.** The modern, high-rise Marriott (formerly the Holiday Inn) is a fair representative of Cardiff's new breed of hotels. It is practical, close to St. David's Hall and the shopping center, and has plenty of amenities. ⊠ *Mill La., CF1 1EZ,* ☎ *029/2039–9944,* FAX *029/ 2039–5578,* WEB *www.marriotthotels.com/cwldt. 182 rooms. Restaurant, coffee shop, indoor pool, sauna, gym. AE, DC, MC, V.*

£ 🏠 **Town House.** Cosmopolitan in style, this immaculate guest house
★ near the city center (shops and castle are a short walk away) is well known as the best B&B in Cardiff. The tall Victorian building with a richly decorated hallway has been tastefully refurbished. Bedrooms are neat and well equipped, and you can savor traditional British or American breakfasts in the beautifully appointed dining room. ⊠ *70 Cathedral Rd., CF1 9LL,* ☎ *029/2023–9399,* FAX *029/2022–3214,* WEB *www.thetownhousecardiff.co.uk. 9 rooms. MC, V.*

Nightlife and the Arts

NIGHTLIFE

There is a lively nighttime scene in Cardiff's clubs and pubs. **Clwb Ifor Bach** (⊠ Womanby St., ☎ 029/2023–2199) has a distinctive Welsh atmosphere and offers three floors of eclectic music from funk to folk to rock. Jazz fans will appreciate **Café Jazz** (⊠ 21 St. Mary St., ☎ 029/ 2038–7026), which has live jazz six nights a week and TV screens in the bar and restaurant so you can view the action on stage.

THE ARTS

The big theaters present a full program of entertainment, from drama to comedy, pop to the classics. The huge **Cardiff International Arena** (⊠ Mary Ann St., ☎ 029/2022–4488) stages performances from those artists who can draw huge crowds, from Welshman Tom Jones to Luciano Pavarotti. **St. David's Hall** (⊠ The Hayes, ☎ 029/2087–8444), a popular venue, hosts the Welsh Proms every July, attracting major international orchestras and soloists, and every two years is home to the prestigious Cardiff Singer of the World competition. It also stages rock, pop, jazz and folk events.

New Theatre (⊠ Park Place, ☎ 029/2087–8889) is a beautifully refurbished Edwardian playhouse that still attracts big names, including the Royal Shakespeare Company, the National Theatre, and the Northern Ballet.

Wales, as might be expected in a country where singing is a way of life, has one of Britain's four major opera companies, the **Welsh National Opera** (⊠ John St., CF1 4SP, ☎ 029/2046–4644, for performances). Its home base is scheduled to change from the New Theatre in the city center to a waterfront site by 2003, but the company spends most of its time touring Wales and England. The productions are often among the most exciting in Britain.

Shopping

Arcade shopping is a distinctive feature of Cardiff's city center. Canopied Victorian and Edwardian arcades, lined with specialty shops, weave in and out of the city's modern shopping complexes. A good place to buy antique jewelry, the **Cardiff Antiques Centre** (⊠ Royal Arcade, ☎ 029/2039–8891) is in an arcade dating from 1856. The **Welsh Lovespoon Gallery** (⊠ 10 Castle Arcade, ☎ 029/2023–1500) is a fine source for Welsh crafts. Cardiff's traditional **covered market** (⊠ The Hayes) sells a tempting variety of fresh foods beneath its Victorian glass canopy.

Abergavenny

❸❹ *28 mi north of Cardiff.*

The market town of Abergavenny, near Brecon Beacons National Park, is a popular base for walkers and hikers. The town's ruined **castle,** founded early in the 11th century, has a good local museum. The castle witnessed a tragic event at Christmas in 1176: the Norman knight William de Braose invited the neighboring Welsh chieftains to a feast and, in a crude attempt to gain control of the area, had them all slaughtered as they sat at dinner. Afterward, the Welsh attacked and virtually demolished the castle. Most of what now remains of the castle dates from the 13th and 14th centuries. The castle's 19th-century hunting lodge houses the **museum,** with exhibits ranging from the Iron Age to the present. The re-creation of a Victorian Welsh farmhouse kitchen is particularly appealing, with its old utensils and butter molds. ⊠ *Castle Museum, Castle St.,* ☎ *01873/854282.* 🎫 *£1.* ☉ *Mar.–Oct., Mon.–Sat. 11–1 and 2–5, Sun. 2–5; Nov.–Feb., Mon.–Sat. 11–1 and 2–4.*

West of Abergavenny lie the valleys—the Rhondda is the most famous—so well described by Richard Llewellyn in *How Green Was My Valley.* The slag heaps of the coal mines are green now, thanks to land reclamation schemes. The **Big Pit Mining Museum,** southwest of Abergavenny, provides a glimpse of what the area was like when mining was big business. Here, ex-miners take you underground on a tour of an authentic coal mine for a look at the hard life of the South Wales miner. You will also see the pithead baths and workshops. ⊠ *Blaenavon,* ☎ *01495/790311.* 🎫 *£5.75.* ☉ *Mar.–Nov., daily 9:30–5 (underground tours 10–3:30).*

Dining and Lodging

££ ✕🏨 **Llanwenarth House.** This beautifully restored 16th-century Welsh manor house with spacious bedrooms is set on tranquil grounds. The house's original features are enhanced by antiques, art, and period furniture. You can dine by candlelight on contemporary cuisine that makes excellent use of local ingredients; a fixed-price menu is offered. King Charles I is said to have kept horses and arms here during the Civil War (1642–51). Harnesses and armor from that period were discovered when an attic was opened up in the 1950s. ⊠ *Govilon, Abergavenny NP7 9SF,* ☎ *01873/830289,* FAX *01873/832199. 5 rooms. Restaurant. No credit cards.*

Crickhowell

35 *5 mi northwest of Abergavenny.*

Take A40 northwest out of Abergavenny and you'll pass Sugar Loaf mountain and Crickhowell, a pretty town on the banks of the River Usk with attractive little shops, an ancient bridge, and a ruined castle. **Tretower Court,** 2 mi from Crickhowell, is a splendid example of a fortified medieval manor house. Nearby, and part of the same site, is a ruined Norman castle. ⊠ *A479,* ☎ *01874/730279.* ⊡ *£2.50.* ☉ *Mar.–late Oct., daily 10–6.*

Dining and Lodging

£–£££ ✕🛏 **Bear Hotel.** This old coaching inn in the middle of the pretty little town of Crickhowell is full of character. The bar, decorated with memorabilia from the days when stagecoaches from London used to stop here, is popular with locals and visitors alike. A blazing log fire in winter adds to the atmosphere. Rooms are within the hotel itself or in the attractively converted stable yard under the arch; they vary widely, and the most luxurious have four-poster beds and antiques. The Bear is also noted for its contemporary cuisine—both the excellent-value bar food and the more formal restaurant offerings. ⊠ *A40, NP8 1BW,* ☎ *01873/810408,* FAX *01873/811696,* WEB *www.bear-hotel.co.uk. 36 rooms. Restaurant, bar. AE, MC, V.*

££ ✕🛏 **Ty Croeso Hotel.** A hillside setting with scenic views over the Usk Valley adds to the appeal of this friendly hotel (its name means "House of Welcome"). You'll find comfortable rooms, an inviting lounge with a log fire, and imaginative food with a Welsh emphasis. ⊠ *The Dardy, NP8 1PU,* WEB *www.wiz.to/tycroeso,* ☎ FAX *01873/810573. 8 rooms. Restaurant. AE, MC, V.*

Brecon

36 *19 mi northwest of Abergavenny, 41 mi north of Cardiff.*

Brecon is a historic market town of narrow passageways, handsome Georgian buildings, and pleasant riverside walks; it's also the gateway to the Brecon Beacons National Park. For the best atmosphere, time your visit to Brecon to coincide with market days (Tuesday and Friday). You may want to purchase a hand-carved wooden love spoon similar to those on display in the Brecknock Museum.

The town's cavernous **cathedral** with its heritage center is on the hill above the middle of town. In the colonnaded Shire Hall built in 1842 is the **Brecknock Museum** (☎ 01874/624121), with its superb collection of carved love spoons and its perfectly preserved 19th-century assize court. In rural Wales, the custom of giving a hand-carved wooden spoon to one's beloved dates from the mid-17th century. The **South Wales Borderers' Museum** (⊠ The Watton, off The Bulwark, ☎ 01874/613310) is a military museum with exhibits that span centuries of conflict. The Zulu Room recalls the regiment's defense of Rorke's Drift in the Anglo-Zulu war of 1879, an action dramatized in the 1964 film *Zulu* starring Michael Caine.

Each summer, the town plays host to **Brecon Jazz** (☎ 01874/625557), an international jazz festival that attracts top performers. The town has developed a small jazz museum, **Oriel Jazz gallery** (⊠ The Watton, ☎ 01874/625557), which through photographs and audiovisual material introduces the world of jazz and captures the spirit of the Brecon Jazz festival.

South of Brecon, the skyline fills with mountains, and wild, windswept uplands stretch to the horizon: this is the realm of Brecon Beacons National Park. Follow the signs for the **Brecon Beacons National Park Visitor Centre,** on Mynydd Illtyd, a high, grassy stretch of upland west of A470 near Libanus. The center, run by the Brecon Beacons National Park Authority, is an excellent source of information for attractions and activities within this 519-square-mi park of rolling hills and open moorlands, and it gives wonderful panoramic views across to Pen-y-fan, at 2,907 ft the highest peak in South Wales. If you plan to explore Wales's high country on foot, come well equipped, for mist and rain can quickly descend, and the Beacons' summits are exposed to high winds. ⊠ *Off A470, near Libanus, Brecon LD3 8ER,* ☎ *01874/ 623366,* WEB *www.breconbeacons.org.* ⊠ *Free; parking fee.* ◷ *Daily 9:30–5 (until 4:30 Nov.–Mar.).*

Dining and Lodging

££ ✕⊡ **Griffin Inn.** This village inn on the road to Builth is one of the oldest in the upper Wye Valley (said to date from 1467). The bedrooms are comfortably furnished, and the exposed stonework and old beams contribute to the historic character. The Griffin's hearty and traditional cuisine takes advantage of local salmon and beef. There's easy access to river and lake fishing, shooting, walking, and pony-trekking in the Brecon Beacons. ⊠ *A470, Llyswen, near Brecon, LD3 0UR,* ☎ *01874/ 754241,* FAX *01874/754592,* WEB *www.griffin-inn.co.uk. 7 rooms. Restaurant. AE, DC, MC, V.*

£   ⊡ **Cantre Selyf.** Spacious and exquisitely restored, this 17th-century town house with a large garden is close to the center of Brecon. It offers both welcoming hosts and innovative food (for guests only). The rooms have beamed ceilings, Georgian fireplaces, and cast-iron beds. ⊠ *5 Lion St., LD3 7AU,* ☎ *01874/622904,* FAX *01874/622315,* WEB *www.cantreselyf.co.uk. 3 rooms. Dining room. No credit cards.*

Shopping

Crickhowell Adventure Gear (⊠ Ship St., ☎ 01874/611586), which also has smaller shops in Crickhowell itself and Abergavenny, sells a good range of outdoor gear such as clothes and climbing equipment.

Swansea

🟢 *36 mi southwest of Brecon, 40 mi west of Cardiff.*

Swansea is Wales's second largest city and the birthplace of poet Dylan Thomas (1914–53). It marks the end of the industrial region of South Wales. Despite typically postwar, rather utilitarian and undistinguished architecture, the city has a number of appealing sights. The city was extensively bombed during World War II, and its old dockland has been transformed into the splendid **Maritime Quarter,** a modern marina with attractive housing and shops and a seafront that commands wonderful views across the sweep of Swansea Bay. The **Swansea Maritime and Industrial Museum,** beside the marina, tells the story of the city's growth and houses a fully operational wool mill. ☎ *01792/650351 or 01792/470371.* ⊠ *Free.* ◷ *Tues.–Sun. 10–4:45.*

The **Dylan Thomas Centre,** on the banks of the Tawe close to the Maritime Quarter, is the National Literature Centre for Wales. The center houses a permanent Dylan Thomas exhibition and hosts a variety of literary events including an annual Dylan Thomas Festival (usually last week in July and first two weeks of August). ⊠ *Somerset Pl.,* ☎ *01792/463980,* 𝖶𝖤𝖡 *www.dylanthomas.org.* ☉ *Tues.–Sun., 10:30–5.*

Swansea's modern shopping center is nothing special, but the **covered market,** part of Quadrant Shopping Centre, is not to be missed. It's the best fresh-foods market in Wales, where you can buy cockles from the Penclawdd beds on the nearby Gower Peninsula, and laverbread, that unique Welsh delicacy made from seaweed, which is usually served with bacon and eggs.

As if to make amends for the onetime desecration of so much natural beauty, and though the industrial scars have disappeared, the 14-mi-long **Gower Peninsula,** on the neck of which Swansea stands, has magnificent cliff scenery and unspoiled beaches. It's a designated Area of Outstanding Natural Beauty.

Dining and Lodging

££   ✕ **La Braseria.** This lively, welcoming spot has a Spanish bodega–style setting that includes flamenco music, oak barrels, and whitewashed walls. Some house specialties are sea bass in rock salt, roast suckling pig, and pheasant (in season). There's a good choice of 140 Spanish and French wines. ⊠ *28 Wind St.,* ☎ *01792/469683. AE, MC, V. Closed Sun.*

£££–££££   ✕🖼 **Fairyhill.** The western part of the lovely Gower Peninsula is home
★   to this 18th-century country house with a restful atmosphere, luxuriously furnished public rooms, spacious bedrooms, and 24 acres of wooded grounds. The hotel is known for its sophisticated contemporary cuisine (fixed-price menus are offered) and well-chosen wine list. Fairyhill is about 11 mi from Swansea. ⊠ *Off B4295, Reynoldston, near Swansea, SA3 1BS,* ☎ *01792/390139,* 𝖥𝖠𝖷 *01792/391358,* 𝖶𝖤𝖡 *www.fairyhill.net. 8 rooms. Restaurant, croquet. AE, MC, V.*

National Botanic Garden of Wales

❸❽   *20 mi northwest of Swansea, 60 mi northwest of Cardiff.*

The first modern botanic garden in Britain, built in 2000 as a Millennium Project, is dedicated to conservation and education. It is based at Middleton Park, an 18th-century, 568-acre estate with seven lakes, cascades, and water features. The garden's centerpiece is the spectacular Great Glass House, the largest single-span greenhouse in the world, whose design blends beautifully into the curving landforms of the Tywi valley. It houses an interior landscape, with a 40-ft-deep ravine, of 10,000 plants from all the Mediterranean climates of the world, and an interactive educational area called the Bioverse. The garden is signposted off the main road between Swansea and Carmarthen. ⊠ *Off the A48 or B4310, Llanarthne,* ☎ *01558/668768,* 𝖶𝖤𝖡 *www. gardenofwales.org.uk.* 🎫 *£6.50.* ☉ *Daily 9–dusk.*

Tenby

❸❾   *53 mi west of Swansea.*

Tenby is a picturesque seaside resort where pastel-color Georgian houses cluster around a harbor. Below the hotel-lined cliff top stretch two golden sandy beaches. Medieval Tenby's ancient town walls still stand, enclosing narrow streets and passageways full of shops, inns, and places to eat. From the harbor, you can take a boat trip to Caldey Island and visit the monastery, where monks make perfume.

The ruins of a castle stand on a headland overlooking the sea, close to the informative **Tenby Museum** (⊠ Castle Hill, ☎ 01834/842809), which recalls the town's maritime history and its growth as a fashionable resort. The late-15th-century **Tudor Merchant's House** (⊠ Quay Hill, ☎

01834/842279), in town, shows how a prosperous trader would have lived in the Tenby of old.

Lodging

£££ 🖫 **Penally Abbey Hotel.** Overlooking the sea close to town, this is a convenient and comfortable base for exploring Pembrokeshire. The dignified old house is full of character, and most bedrooms have four-poster beds. The host's lack of formality generates a relaxed atmosphere supported by first-class service. ✉ *Off A4139, Penally, near Tenby, SA70 7PY,* ☎ *01834/843033,* ꜰᴀˣ *01834/844714,* ᴡᴇʙ *www.penally-abbey.com. 12 rooms. Restaurant, indoor pool. AE, MC, V.*

Pembroke

❹⓿ *13 mi west of Tenby, 13 mi south of Haverfordwest.*

In Pembroke you are entering the heart of Pembrokeshire, one of the most curious regions of Wales. You may begin to doubt whether you are still in Wales, for all around are English names like Deeplake, New Hedges, and Rudbaxton. Natives more often than not don't seem to understand Welsh, and South Pembrokeshire is even known as "Little England beyond Wales." History is responsible. In the 11th century, this region was conquered by the English with the aid of the Normans, who intermarried and set about building castles.

One of the most magnificent Norman fortresses is Pembroke's **castle,** dating from 1190. Its walls remain stout, its gatehouse mighty, and the enormous cylindrical keep proved so impregnable to cannon fire in the Civil War that Cromwell's men had to starve out its Royalist defenders. It was the birthplace, in 1457, of Henry Tudor, who seized the throne of Britain as Henry VII in 1485, and whose son Henry VIII united Wales and England. ☎ *01646/681510.* 🎟 *£3.* ☉ *Apr.–Sept., daily 9:30–6; Oct. daily 10–5; Nov.–Feb. daily 10–4; Mar. daily 10–5.*

St. David's

❹❶ *16 mi northwest of Haverfordwest, 16 mi west of Fishguard.*

This place has been described as the holiest ground in Great Britain, for here, in the midst of a tiny village, is the Cathedral of St. David and the shrine of the patron saint of Wales, who founded a monastic community here in the 6th century.

The entire area around St. David's, steeped in sanctity and history, was a place of pilgrimage for many centuries, two journeys to St. David's equaling one to Rome. The savagely beautiful coastline here—Pembrokeshire at its unspoiled best—also gives St. David's a special atmosphere, one where you can almost recapture the feeling of those days nearly 1,500 years ago when this shrine was very nearly the solitary outpost of Christianity in the British Isles.

Unlike any other cathedral, the venerable 12th-century **Cathedral of St. David** (☎ 01437/720328, ᴡᴇʙ www.stdavidscathedral.org.uk) does not seek to dominate the surrounding countryside with its enormous mass, for it is set, quaintly enough, in a vast hollow. You must climb down 39 steps (called locally the Thirty-Nine Articles) to enter the cathedral, which also helped protect the church from Viking raiders by hiding it from the sea. From the outside, St. David's has a certain simple austerity that harmonizes well with the desolate, windswept countryside, but the rich interior more than compensates for this external severity: treasures include the fragile fan vaulting in Bishop Vaughan's Chapel, the intricate carving on the choir stalls, and the oaken roof over the nave. Across the brook are the substantial ruins of the medieval **Bishop's Palace,** which can be visited.

Dining and Lodging

££   ✕ **Harbour Lights.** The quality of its fresh local ingredients are the pride of this family-run shore restaurant tucked away on an attractive stretch of coast about 7 mi northeast of St. David's, at the tiny harbor of Porthgain. Seafood dishes are a specialty on the fixed-price three-course menu. The laverbread is handpicked, and the crabs are landed on the adjacent quayside. Pictures by local artists hang on the walls, and an adjoining gallery showcases more of their work. ✉ *Porthgain, Croesgoch SA62 5BW,* ☎ *01348/831549. MC, V.* ☺ *Call ahead in winter for hrs.*

£££–££££   ✕🏠 **Warpool Court Hotel.** Magical is the word for the location of this hotel set on a bluff above St. Non's Bay with its holy well and ruined chapel, overlooking one of Britain's most beautiful stretches of coastline. Many rooms have wonderful sea views. The building dates from the 1860s when it housed St. David's Cathedral Choir School. Now it is a well-equipped hotel that offers contemporary cuisine (four-course fixed-price menu at dinner) with fish as a specialty. Try the home-smoked salmon. ✉ *St. David's, SA62 6BN,* ☎ *01437/720300,* FAX *01437/ 720676,* WEB *www.stdavids.co.uk/warpoolcourt. 25 rooms. Restaurant, lounge, pool, sauna, tennis court, gym. AE, MC, V.*

Fishguard

㊷   *16 mi northeast of St. David's, 26 mi north of Pembroke.*

Fishguard is a town of three parts. The modern ferry terminal at Goodwick across the sheltered waters of Fishguard Bay sees activity throughout the year as boats sail to Rosslare across the Irish Sea. Fishguard's main town stands on high ground just south of Goodwick, separating the modern port from its picturesque old harbor in the lower town.

The 100-ft-long **Last Invasion Tapestry,** on display in a church hall, is modeled on the famous Bayeux Tapestry that celebrates the Norman invasion of 1066, but this work commemorates a far less successful assault. In 1797 a small French force, commanded by a U.S. citizen, landed near Fishguard. After some skirmishing the group was allegedly forced to surrender by local women. In 1997, 70 Fishguard women spent 40,000 hours stitching this impressive tapestry. ✉ *St. Mary's Church, Main St.,* ☎ *01348/874997.* 🎫 *£1.50.* ☺ *Apr.–Oct., Mon.– Sat. 10–5, Sun. 2–5; Nov.–Mar., Mon.–Sat. 11–4, Sun. 2–4.*

Cardigan and the Teifi Valley

㊸   *18 mi northeast of Fishguard.*

Cardigan is a charming little market town perched astride the Teifi on an ancient bridge, the scene of a never-allowed-to-be-forgotten victory by the Welsh over the Norman army in 1136. The town is near the mouth of the Teifi, a river that runs through a beautiful wooded valley dotted with traditional market towns and villages, as well as reminders of the area's once-flourishing woolen industry. Cardigan itself has an interesting history, for it was here, in the 12th century, that Wales's first eisteddfod, or folk festival, was held. The eisteddfod tradition, based on the Welsh language and culture, is still strong in Wales, and events large and small are held here (mainly in summer months).

Cilgerran, a village a few miles south of Cardigan, holds the dramatic ruins of 13th-century **Cilgerran Castle,** which stands above a deep wooded gorge where the River Teifi flows. ✉ *Off A478,* ☎ *01239/*

615136. ☞ £2. ⊙ Late Mar.–late Oct., daily 9:30–6:30; late Oct.–late Mar., Mon.–Sat. 9:30–4, Sun. 2–4.

OFF THE
BEATEN PATH

MUSEUM OF THE WELSH WOOLEN INDUSTRY – This museum in what was once the most important wool-producing area in Wales has working exhibits and displays that trace the evolution of the industry. There are also other crafts workshops and a working woolen mill. The museum is east of Cenarth a few miles past Newcastle Emlyn. ✉ *Off A484, Drefach Felindre,* ☎ *01559/370929,* 𝖶𝖤𝖡 *www.nmgw.ac.uk.* ☞ *£2.60.* ⊙ *Apr.– Sept., Mon.–Sat. 10–5; Oct.–Mar., weekdays 10–5.*

Lodging

££ 🖻 **Penbontbren Farm Hotel.** Set in peaceful countryside, the buildings of this hotel east of Cardigan began life as a farm. The one-time barns are now tastefully converted into cozy bedrooms, and a restaurant is just across the courtyard. ✉ *Off A487, Glynarthen SA44 6PE,* ☎ *01239/ 810248,* 𝖥𝖠𝖷 *01239/811129. 10 rooms. Restaurant. MC, V.*

WALES A TO Z

To research prices, get advice from other travelers, and book travel arrangements, visit www.fodors.com.

AIR TRAVEL

London's Heathrow and Gatwick airports, with their excellent door-to-door motorway links with Wales, are convenient gateways. Manchester Airport, which offers a wide range of international flights, is an excellent gateway for North Wales, with a journey time to the Welsh border, via M56, of under an hour. Wales International Airport near Cardiff has a number of direct international flights to European destinations and connecting services worldwide via Amsterdam.

AIRPORTS

➤ AIRPORT INFORMATION: **Manchester Airport** (✉ Near Junctions 5 and 6 of M56, ☎ 0161/489–3000, 𝖶𝖤𝖡 www.manchesterairport.co.uk). **Wales International Airport** (✉ A4226, Rhoose, ☎ 01446/711111, 𝖶𝖤𝖡 www.cial.co.uk).

BUS TRAVEL

Although the overall pattern is a little fragmented, most parts of Wales are accessible by bus. National Express serves Wales from London's Victoria Coach Station and also direct from London's Heathrow and Gatwick airports. Although primarily a carrier into Wales, National Express also has routes through Wales (from Cardiff farther west, for example, or along the North Wales coast). Average travel times from London to Wales are 3½ hours to Cardiff, 4 hours to Swansea, 5½ hours to Aberystwyth, and 4½ hours to Llandudno.

The main operators in South Wales are Cardiff Bus, Newport Transport, First Cymru, and Stagecoach Red and White. For details, contact the Wales Transport Information Line. Arriva Cymru operates in mid- and North Wales and offers unlimited-travel Day Rover and Weekly Rover tickets. It also has long-distance routes. The daily Traws Cambria cross-country service between Cardiff and Holyhead calls at Aberystwyth, Machynlleth, Dolgellau, Porthmadog, Caernarfon, and Bangor; the Wrexham to Barmouth service calls at Llangollen, Corwen, Bala, and Dolgellau.

FARES AND SCHEDULES

➤ BUS INFORMATION: **Arriva Cymru** (☎ 0870/6082608). **National Express** (☎ 0990/808080, 𝖶𝖤𝖡 www.gobycoach.com). **Traws Cambria** (☎ 0870/608–2608). **Wales Transport Information Line** (☎ 0870/6082608).

CAR RENTAL

➤ LOCAL AGENCIES: **Avis** (✉ 14–22 Tudor St., Cardiff, ☎ 029/2034–2111). **Budget Rent-a-Car** (✉ Penarth Rd., Cardiff, ☎ 029/2066–4499). **National Car Rental** (✉ 10 Dominions Way Industrial Estate, Newport Rd., Cardiff, ☎ 029/2049–6256). **Europcar** (✉ 1–11 Byron St., Cardiff, ☎ 029/2049–8978). **Hertz** (✉ 9 Central Sq., Cardiff, ☎ 029/2022–4548).

CAR TRAVEL

Take the M4 from London for Cardiff (151 mi), Swansea (190 mi), and South Wales. Aberystwyth (211 mi from London) and Llandrindod (204 mi) in mid-Wales are well-served by major roads. The A40 is also an important route through central and South Wales. From London, M1/M6 is the most direct route to North Wales. A55, the coast road from Chester on the English side of the border, goes through Bangor.

ROAD CONDITIONS

Distances in miles may not be great in Wales, but getting from place to place takes time because there are few major highways. The mountains mean that there is no single fast route from north to south, although A470 is good and scenic, and A487 does run along or near most of the coastline. The mountains also mean that many of the smaller roads are winding and difficult to maneuver, but the roads do have magnificent views of the surrounding landscape.

CONSULATES

➤ CANADA: (✉ Wales Airport Hotel, Port Rd., Rhoose, near Cardiff, ☎ 01446/719172).

DISCOUNTS AND DEALS

The Cadw/Welsh Historic Monuments Explorer Pass is good for unlimited admission to most of Wales's historic sites. The seven-day pass costs £15 (single adult), £25 (two adults), or £30 (family ticket); the three-day pass costs £9, £16, and £21, respectively. Passes are available at any site covered by the Cadw program.
➤ INFORMATION: **Cadw/Welsh Historic Monuments** (✉ Crown Building, Cathays Park, Cardiff CF1 3NQ, ☎ 029/2050–0200, WEB www.cadw.wales.gov.uk).

EMERGENCIES

➤ CONTACTS: **Ambulance, fire, police** (☎ 999). **Bronglais Hospital** (✉ Aberystwyth, ☎ 01970/623131). **Morriston Hospital** (✉ Heol Maes Eglwys, Cwm Rhydyceirw, Swansea, ☎ 01792/702222). **University Hospital of Wales** (✉ Heath Park, Cardiff, ☎ 029/2074–7747).

NATIONAL PARKS

➤ CONTACTS: **Brecon Beacons National Park** (✉ 7 Glamorgan St., Brecon LD3 7DP, ☎ 01874/624437, WEB www.breconbeacons.org.uk). **Pembrokeshire Coast National Park** (✉ Wynch La., Haverfordwest SA61 1PY, ☎ 01437/764636, WEB www.pembrokeshirecoast.org.uk). **Snowdonia National Park** (✉ Penrhyndeudraeth LL48 6LF, ☎ 01766/770274, WEB www.snowdonia.org.uk).

OUTDOORS AND SPORTS

Hiking and walking are the most popular outdoor activities in Wales, and a number of organizations can provide you with information.
➤ WALKING: **Offa's Dyke Centre** (✉ West St., Knighton LD7 1EN, ☎ 01547/528753, WEB www.offasdyke.demon.co.uk). **Ramblers' Association in Wales** (✉ Ty'r Cerddwyr, High St., Gresford, Wrexham LL12 8PT, ☎ 01978/855148, WEB www.ramblers.org.uk).

SIGHTSEEING GUIDES

If you are interested in having a personal guide, contact the Wales Official Tourist Guide Association through Derek Roberts. WOTGA only uses guides recognized by the Wales Tourist Board. It will put together tailor-made tours for you. You can book either a driver-guide or someone to accompany you as you drive.

➤ CONTACTS: **Wales Official Tourist Guide Association** (Derek Roberts, ✉ 1 Dodgson Close, Llandudno LL30 1AJ, ☎ 01492/878632).

TOURS

BUS TOURS

A good way to see Wales is by local tour bus; in summer there's a large choice of day and half-day excursions to most parts of the country. In major resorts and cities you should ask at a tourist information center or bus station for details.

TRAIN TRAVEL

From London's Paddington Station it's about two hours to Cardiff and three hours to Swansea on the fast InterCity rail service. Fast InterCity trains also run between London's Euston Station and North Wales. Average travel times are: from Euston, 3¾ hours to Llandudno in North Wales (some direct trains, otherwise change at Crewe), and about five hours to Aberystwyth in mid-Wales (changing at Birmingham).

The Regional Railways service covers South Wales, western Wales, central Wales, the Conwy Valley, and the North Wales coast on many scenic routes such as the Cambrian Coast Railway, running 70 mi between Aberystwyth and Pwllheli, and the Heart of Wales line, linking Swansea and Craven Arms, near Shrewsbury, 95 mi away.

A ride on one of Wales's many scenic steam railways, including the Great Little Trains of Wales and the Snowdon Mountain Railway, will give you lovely views of the countryside.

CUTTING COSTS

If you intend to use the Regional Railways network, ask about money-saving unlimited-travel tickets (such as Freedom of Wales Flexi Pass, North and Mid Wales Rover, and the South Wales Flexi Rover), which include the use of bus services. Wanderer tickets are also available from all participating railways for unlimited travel on the Great Little Trains of Wales: a four-day ticket is £35.

FARES AND SCHEDULES

➤ TRAIN INFORMATION: **Great Little Trains of Wales** (✉ c/o The Station, Llanfair Caereinion SY21 0SF, ☎ 01938/810441). **Regional Railways** (☎ 08457/484950). **Snowdon Mountain Railway** (✉ Llanberis, Caernarfon LL55 4TY, ☎ 01286/870223).

RESERVATIONS

➤ CONTACTS: **Flexipass information** (☎ 08457/125625, WEB www.travelwales-flexipass.co.uk). **Rail inquiries** (InterCity rail service, ☎ 08457/484950, WEB www.railtrack.co.uk).

TRAVEL AGENCIES

➤ LOCAL AGENT REFERRALS: **American Express** (✉ 3 Queen St., Cardiff, ☎ 029/2064–9304). **Thomas Cook** (✉ 16 Queen St., Cardiff, ☎ 029/2042–2500; 3 Union St., Swansea, ☎ 01792/332000).

VISITOR INFORMATION

Tourist information centers are normally open Monday through Saturday 10–5:30 and limited hours on Sunday, but vary by season.

➤ Tourist Information: **Wales Tourist Board** (✉ Box 1, Cardiff CF24 2XN, ☎ 029/2047–5226, WEB www.visitwales.com). **Aberystwyth** (✉ Terrace Rd., ☎ 01970/612125). **Betws-y-Coed** (✉ Royal Oak Stables, ☎ 01690/710426). **Caernarfon** (✉ Oriel Pendeitsh, opposite castle entrance, ☎ 01286/672232). **Cardiff** (national and city information, ✉ Wood St., Central Station, ☎ 029/2022–7281, WEB www.cardiffmarketing.co.uk). **Llandrindod Wells** (✉ Old Town Hall, ☎ 01597/822600). **Llandudno** (✉ Chapel St., ☎ 01492/876413). **Llanfair Pwllgwyngyll** (✉ Station Site, Isle of Anglesey, ☎ 01248/713177). **Llangollen** (✉ Town Hall, ☎ 01978/860828). **Machynlleth** (✉ Owain Glyndŵr Centre, ☎ 01654/702401). **Ruthin** (✉ Craft Centre, ☎ 01824/703992). **Swansea** (✉ Plymouth St., ☎ 01792/468321, WEB www.swansea.gov.uk). **Tenby** (✉ The Croft, ☎ 01834/842402). **Welshpool** (✉ Vicarage Garden, ☎ 01938/552043).

11 LANCASHIRE AND THE PEAKS

MANCHESTER, LIVERPOOL, AND THE PEAK DISTRICT

Birthplace of the boom and bravura of the Industrial Revolution, this region is dominated by the once powerful cities of Liverpool and Manchester. Here, fans of Victorian architecture and of John, Paul, George, and Ringo come to enjoy some of England's most interesting sights. (Even Sir Paul McCartney's childhood home is now a historic site.) Beyond, however, lies the emerald tranquillity of the Peak District and Derbyshire's Wye Valley—home to two of the most regal houses in the land, Haddon Hall and Chatsworth.

Updated by
Heather Elton
and Ed Glinert

FOR THOSE LOOKING FOR THE POSTCARD ENGLAND of little villages and churches, the northwest region of England might not be placed at the top of their sightseeing list. After all, the Industrial Revolution thrived nowhere more strongly than the major cities here, including Manchester and Liverpool. Manchester today is big and bustling, but 200 years of smokestack industry, which has only recently abated, have taken a toll on the east Lancashire landscape. Parts of the Merseyside area containing Liverpool still live up to its grimy image as an industrial port, and there are other parts of the countryside that lack scenic attraction. But inland, in Derbyshire (pronounced "Darbyshire"), lies the spectacular Peak District, a huge, unspoiled national park at the southern end of the Pennines range, where you'll find Victorian-era spas like Buxton, charming towns like Bakewell, and magnificent stately houses, such as Chatsworth and Haddon Hall.

The areas around Manchester and Liverpool are Britain's equivalent of the Rust Belt, a once-proud bastion of heavy industry and blue-collar values. These cities were the economic engines that propelled Britain in the 18th and 19th centuries. By the mid-18th century, the Lancashire cotton industry had become firmly established in Manchester and enjoyed a special relationship with the port of Liverpool, to the west. Here, at the massive docks, cotton was imported from the United States and sent to the Lancashire mills; the finished cotton goods were later returned to Liverpool for export to the rest of the world. Both cities suffered a marked decline during the second half of the 20th century, and today are trying to re-establish themselves as centers of musical and sporting excellence. Since 1962, the Manchester United, Everton, and Liverpool football (soccer in the United States) clubs have won everything worth winning in Britain and Europe, and Manchester has figured as an Olympic-site contender; in 2002 the city will host the Commonwealth Games. The Beatles launched the Merseysound of the '60s; contemporary Manchester groups often ride both British and U.S. airwaves. On the classical side of music, Manchester is also home to Britain's oldest leading orchestra, the Hallé (founded in 1857)—just one legacy of 19th-century industrialists' investments in culture.

The Peak District is a wilder part of England, a region of crags that rear violently out of the plain. The Pennines, a line of hills that begins in the Peak District and runs as far north as Scotland, are sometimes called the "backbone of England." This is a landscape of rocky outcrops and vaulting meadowland, where you'll see nothing for miles but sheep, drystone (unmortared) walls, and farms, interrupted—spectacularly—by 19th-century villages and treasure houses. The delight of the Peak District is being able to ramble for days in the wilderness but still enjoy civilization at its finest.

Pleasures and Pastimes

Beatlemania

For baby boomers in particular, Liverpool exerts a strange and powerful lure; it is, after all, the birthplace of the Beatles. John, Paul, George, and Pete Best (Ringo arrived a bit later) set up shop at the Cavern in 1961, and the Liverpool Sound soon conquered the world. Today, fans can follow in the footsteps of the Fab Four at the Beatles Story, an exhibition that draws the faithful to Liverpool's Albert Dock. Unfortunately, many city sites linked with John and Paul have been bulldozed, including Strawberry Field orphanage (the Victorian building was replaced several years ago by a modern structure). To properly celebrate the Beatles' enduring appeal, go to the annual Mathew

Street Festival, also known as Beatle Week, usually held the last week in August when what seems to be the entire city takes time out to dance, attend John and Yoko fancy-dress parties, and listen to any number of Beatle bands from around the world.

Dining

While this area may be short on native gustatorial delights, one local dish that has survived is the Bakewell pudding (*never* called "tart" in these regions, as its imitations are in other parts of England). Its recipe was allegedly discovered when a cook accidentally spilled a rich cake mixture over some jam tarts. Served with either custard or cream, the pudding is the joy of the pretty town of Bakewell. Manchester and Liverpool do have a complete selection of restaurants, from smart café-bars offering modern British and Continental fare to ethnic restaurants. In particular, Manchester has one of Britain's biggest Chinatowns, while locals also set great store in the 40-odd Asian restaurants along Wilmslow Road in the suburb of Rusholme, a mile south of the city center where you can savor Bangladeshi, Pakistani, and Indian food.

CATEGORY	COST*
££££	over £22
£££	£16–£22
££	£9–£15
£	under £9

*per person for a main course at dinner

Lodging

If your trip centers on the cities of the Northwest, you can base yourself in Manchester and make Liverpool a day trip. Manchester has a much better choice of accommodations, and although the larger city-center hotels rely on business guests during the week, they often offer reduced rates on weekends. There are also numerous smaller hotels and guest houses in the nearby suburbs, many just a short bus ride from downtown. The Manchester Visitor Centre operates a room-booking service; you can stop by in person to use it or reserve over the phone with a credit card for a fee.

The Peak District has a full complement of inns, B&Bs, and hotels, as well as a network of youth hostels. Local tourist offices have full details; reserve well in advance at Easter and in summer.

CATEGORY	COST*
££££	over £150
£££	£100–£150
££	£60–£100
£	under £60

*All prices are for two people sharing a standard double room, including service, breakfast, and VAT.

Exploring Lancashire and the Peak District

Manchester lies at the heart of a tangle of motorways in the northwest of England, about half an hour across the Pennines from Yorkshire. The city spreads west toward the coast and the mouth of the River Mersey, where Liverpool is still centered on its port. To the north, in Lancashire, the coast flattens out around the resort of Blackpool, undistinguished country for the most part though it includes miles of sandy beaches. But for the Northwest's most dramatic scenery—indeed, its only real geological feature of interest—you have to travel to the Peak District, a craggy national park less than an hour's drive southeast of Manchester.

England at its most grand and ducal is visible in the Derbyshire valley of the River Wye: majestic 18th-century Chatsworth is just about the most visited house in Britain. Haddon Hall is bare inside, but because it has an enchanting Tudor and Jacobean structure, it's widely regarded as the most romantic house in England.

Numbers in the text correspond to numbers in the margin and on the Lancashire and the Peaks, Manchester, and Liverpool maps.

Great Itineraries

Greater Manchester and Merseyside form one of the most built-up areas in Britain, but motorway access between the two is fast. One of the main towns of the Peak District, Buxton, could be visited on a day trip from Manchester if you wanted to base yourself in that city. But the Peaks require more than just a short drive around the principal sights, and a week's hiking tour of the Peak District could be constructed with no trouble at all.

If you have only a few days, you'll need to limit your exploration. You might stay in Manchester overnight and take in several of the area's stately homes the rest of the time. If you have a week, you can spend more time in the Peak District as well as explore Manchester and a bit of Liverpool.

IF YOU HAVE 3 DAYS

Base yourself in ⛴ **Manchester** ①–⑪ for your first night, which will give you a chance to see the central sights on your first day and catch a concert or a club that night. On the next day, journey to the lush green and peaceful calm of the Derbyshire Wye to visit two of England's most magnificent stately homes, **Haddon Hall** ㉖ and **Chatsworth House** ㉗, spending your second night in the nearby town of ⛴ **Bakewell** ㉕. If you're traveling when these two houses are closed for the season, call in at ⛴ **Liverpool** ⑫–㉓ instead for an overnight stay. Enjoy a lunch on the Albert Dock, then spend the afternoon in the museums and attractions of this dockside entertainment center.

IF YOU HAVE 7 DAYS

It's wisest to split your time between city and national park. Start in **Buxton** ㉔ for an afternoon's stroll and spend the night in the pretty town of ⛴ **Bakewell** ㉕. Visit **Haddon Hall** ㉖ and **Chatsworth House** ㉗, both among the top stately homes in Britain, returning to Bakewell for the night. On the morning of the third day, move on to **Matlock** ㉘ and its river, and take a cable-car ride to the Heights of Abraham, before aiming for **Castleton** ㉙ and its splendid caverns. If you want to do any walking around the isolated village of **Edale** ㉚, spend the third night back in ⛴ **Buxton** ㉔, making an early start on the day. After walking on the moors, you can take a short drive to ⛴ **Manchester** ①–⑪, where a two-night stay will let you see the best of that city, before moving on to enjoy your last night in ⛴ **Liverpool** ⑫–㉓.

When to Tour Lancashire and the Peak District

Manchester has a reputation as one of the wettest cities in Britain, and visiting in summer isn't any guarantee of fine weather. Nevertheless, the nature of many sights and cultural activities here and in Liverpool means that wet or cold weather shouldn't spoil a visit. Summer is the optimum time to see the Peak District, especially because early summer sees traditional festivities in many villages; the *only* time to see the great houses of the Derbyshire Wye valley—Chatsworth and Haddon Hall—is from Easter through September.

Lancashire and the Peaks

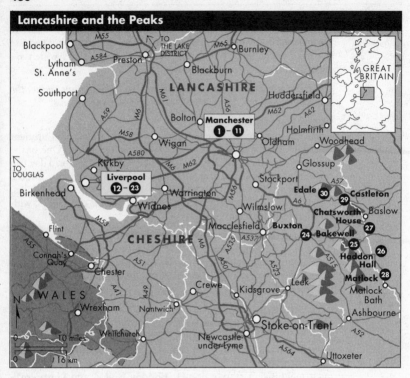

MANCHESTER

In the late 1980s Manchester began to clean up the grim industrial landscape of parts of the city. Although vestiges of this landscape remain, events as different as the severe damage to the city center caused by an IRA bomb in 1996 and the 2002 Commonwealth Games have fueled massive urban redevelopment. Canals have been tidied up and waterfront quays built, cotton mills have been converted into luxury loft apartments, and contemporary architecture has transformed the skyline. Bridgewater Hall and The Lowry, as well as the Imperial War Museum North scheduled to open in 2002, are examples of world-class cultural and sports facilities. Today the city center hums with the energy of cutting-edge popular music and the swank café-bar culture. Sure it still rains, but the rain-soaked streets are part of the city's charm, in a bleak northern kind of way.

For most of its history Manchester, Britain's third-largest city, has been a thriving and prosperous place. The Romans built a fort here in AD 79 and named it Mamucium. But the city that stands today—with the elegant Town Hall, Royal Exchange, Midland Hotel, the waterways, and railway—is a product of the Industrial Revolution. Its spectacular rise from a small town to the world's cotton capital (with the nickname Cottonopolis)in only 100 years began with the first steam-powered cotton mill, built in 1783. The rivers Irwell and Mersey were dredged and made navigable to ship coal to the factories. The world's first passenger railway opened in 1830, and construction of the Manchester Ship Canal in 1894 provided the infrastructure for Manchester to dominate the industrial world.

A few people acquired fabulous wealth, but factory hands worked under appalling conditions. Working-class discontent came to a head in 1819 in the Peterloo Massacre, when 11 workers were killed by soldiers at a protest meeting. The conditions under which factory hands worked were later recorded by Friedrich Engels (coauthor with Karl Marx of the *Communist Manifesto*), who managed a cotton mill in the city. More formal political opposition to the government emerged in the shape of the Chartist movement (which campaigned for universal suffrage) and the Anti-Corn Law League (which opposed trade tariffs), forerunners of the trade unions in the United Kingdom. From Victorian times until the 1960s, daily life for the average Mancunian was so oppressive that it bred the desire to escape, a yearning that still underpins popular culture in the city.

It's impossible to talk about Manchester without mentioning music and football. Out of poverty and unemployment came the brash sounds of punk and the indie record labels. The band New Order crossed the musical divide and produced a unique Mancunian sound that mixed live instruments with digital sound. The Haçienda Club marketed New Order to the world, and Manchester became the clubbing capital of England. Joy Division, Morrissey, Stone Roses, Happy Mondays, and Oasis rose to the top of the charts. The triumphant reign of Manchester United and its prince of tabloid fodder, footballer David Beckham, keep many eyes on Manchester.

Exploring Manchester

Manchester is compact enough that you can easily walk across the city center in 40 minutes and get to know your way around in a few days. The walk below starts at the Town Hall, winds through historic Castlefield, and continues back through the heart of the shopping district to Manchester Cathedral.

A Good Walk

Begin in Albert Square at the Albert Memorial, built in 1862 with a Gothic-style canopy and spire covering a statue of the Prince Consort. On the square, **Town Hall** ① is a French Gothic structure that reflects the economic power of 19th-century Manchester. Take the exit on to Lloyd Street, turn left, and walk to the end of the block. The Manchester Visitor Centre is on your right at the corner. Continue to your right, alongside the Town Hall Extension, to St. Peter's Square and the **Central Library** ②. Go inside and take a peek at the domed reading room, inspired by the Pantheon, on the first floor. The Edwardian building on the south side of St. Peter's Square is the Crowne Plaza Manchester—The Midland, originally a station hotel built in 1903.

Continue south on Lower Mosley Street to the **G-Mex** ③, a former train station. The original Victorian train shed has been reconfigured into an exhibition center. Cross Lower Mosley Street to arrive at the striking, contemporary Bridgewater Hall, home to the renowned Hallé Orchestra. From Bridgewater Hall, continue down Lower Mosley Street to Whitworth Street West. On the corner, to your left, is the legendary Haçienda Club–cum–luxury loft apartments. Turn right and you'll pass Deansgate Locks, a group of trendy bars, which is the gateway to Castlefield. Turn right on Deansgate and left onto Liverpool Road, and walk several blocks to **Castlefield Urban Heritage Park** ④, the site where Mamucium was founded and later the heart of Manchester's industrial boom. Pick up a brochure from the Castlefield Centre and walk the 45-minute Roman Trail; it begins outside the White Lion pub.

Liverpool Station, a passenger railway station, is now part of the sprawling **Museum of Science and Industry** ⑤, which explores the city's industrial heritage. The museum is across Liverpool Road from

Manchester

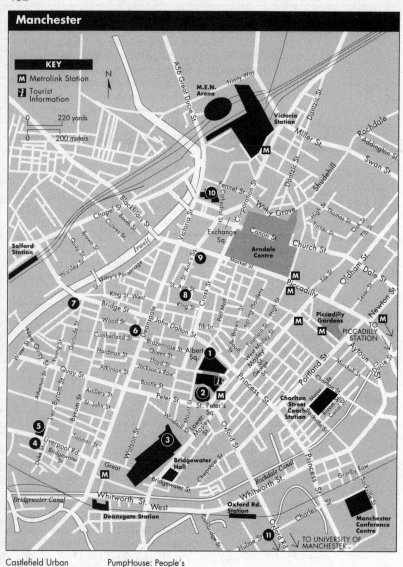

Castlefield Urban
Heritage Park **4**

Central Library **2**

G-Mex **3**

John Rylands
Library **6**

Manchester
Cathedral **10**

Museum of Science
and Industry **5**

PumpHouse: People's
History Museum **7**

Royal Exchange
Theatre **9**

St. Ann's Church **8**

Town Hall **1**

Whitworth Art
Gallery **11**

the Castlefield Centre. From the museum, walk north on Lower Byrom Street to Quay Street; the Opera House is on the corner. Turn right and walk up Quay Street to Deansgate. Turn left and continue five blocks until you reach **John Rylands Library** ⑥, a red neo-Gothic building on your left. Turn left in front of the library onto Wood Street and follow it to Bridge Street to visit the **PumpHouse: People's History Museum** ⑦ where you'll learn about Manchester's history from a worker's perspective. Turn right, outside the PumpHouse, and follow Bridge Street to Deansgate. Turn left on Deansgate and walk to Kendals department store. Cross Deansgate and walk along King Street. Turn left on Cross Street, and left again on St. Ann Street to proceed to **St. Ann's Church** ⑧, Manchester's oldest surviving classical building, with its impressive stained glass. Exit the church and walk north in a direct line through St. Ann's Square to the **Royal Exchange Theatre** ⑨, housed in the old cotton trade market.

From St. Ann's Square walk north in a straight line up Cathedral Street, between Marks & Spencer and Harvey Nichols, to Exchange Square in the heart of the city's Millennium Quarter. The Triangle, a contemporary shopping mall set in the historic facade of the Corn Exchange, is on your left, and the Printworks on your right. The Urbis, a landscaped park, is on Fennel Street. The walk reaches its conclusion at **Manchester Cathedral** ⑩, sitting majestically in the postmodern core of Manchester. If you want to spend some time exploring the **Whitworth Art Gallery** ⑪ at the University of Manchester, catch any bus with a number in the forties (except 47) on Oxford Road.

TIMING

Although you can complete the walk without stopping in about 45 minutes, you'll need to budget your time carefully at the various sites if you want to see everything in a day. Be sure to save three hours for Castlefield (two of these for the Museum of Science and Industry) and an hour for the PumpHouse. The Town Hall and the cathedral may occupy you for half an hour each.

Sights to See

❹ **Castlefield Urban Heritage Park.** Manchester's origins can be clearly seen in the district of Castlefield, site of an early Roman fort. It was later the center of the city's industrial boom, which resulted in the building of Britain's first modern canal in 1764 and the world's first railway station in 1830. What had become an urban wasteland has been beautifully restored into an urban park with pleasant canalside walks, landscaped open spaces, and refurbished warehouses. The 7-acre site contains the reconstructed gate to the Roman fort of Mamucium, the buildings of the **Museum of Science and Industry**, and several of the city's hippest bars and restaurants. Castlefield Centre has visitor information and offers tours. ⊠ *Castlefield Centre, 101 Liverpool Rd.,* ☎ *0161/834–4026,* WEB *www.castlefield.org.uk.* ▣ *Free.* ◷ *Weekdays 10–4, weekends noon–4.*

❷ **Central Library.** The city's main library was erected in 1930; its circular exterior, topped by a line of Doric columns and a massive Corinthian portico facing St. Peter's Square, is a major focus for Manchester's most prestigious civic quarter. The grand reading room is worth seeing; this was at one time the biggest municipal library in the world. The **Library Theatre** is part of the complex. ⊠ *St. Peter's Sq.,* ☎ *0161/234–1900,* WEB *www.manchester.gov.uk.* ◷ *Mon.–Thurs. 10–8, Fri.–Sat. 10–5.*

❸ **G-Mex.** The G-Mex is the old Central Station, built in 1879 as the railway terminus for goods shipped west of the city. The station shed has been reconfigured into an exhibition center that can handle everything from rock concerts to dog shows. The building is part of the Great Northern Development, a project that also includes the Manchester International Convention Centre with a multipurpose hall and an 800-seat theatre, and the massive industrial Great Northern Railway Company's Goods Warehouse, built in 1896. ⊠ *Lower Mosley St.,* ☎ *0161/834–2700,* WEB *www.g-mex.co.uk.* ☉ *Call for hours of events.*

Imperial War Museum North. Set to open in summer 2002, this stunning building by architect Daniel Libeskind will be worth a visit for the exterior alone. It will look like shards of an exploded globe, in which three of these fragments, symbolizing land, sea, and air, have come together to create the building. The displays document the way in which 20th-century wars have fragmented the world. A viewing platform will have superb vistas of Manchester. The museum is on the banks of the Manchester Ship Canal, across the footbridge from The Lowry. ⊠ *Trafford Wharf Rd., Salford Quays,* ☎ *0161/873–8598,* WEB *www.iwm.org.uk.*

❻ **John Rylands Library.** Now owned by the University of Manchester, this lovely Gothic Revival masterpiece designed by Alfred Waterhouse was built by Enriqueta Augustina Rylands as a memorial to her husband, a cotton magnate. Constructed of red sandstone in the 1890s, the library resembles a cathedral. A spectacular staircase leads to the reading room, with ornate plaster carvings, a soaring nave, and paneled reading alcoves. The library houses one of Britain's most important collections—priceless documents and charters, manuscripts dating from the dawn of Christianity, and fine bindings. There are always special exhibitions from the library's treasures. ⊠ *150 Deansgate,* ☎ *0161/834–5343,* WEB *rylibweb.man.ac.uk/.* 🎫 *Free; guided tours £1.* ☉ *Mon.–Sat. 10–5:30, Sun. 10–1; guided tours usually Wed. at noon.*

The Lowry. An impressive arts center in the heart of Manchester's waterways on Salford Quays, the Lowry occupies a spectacular building with a steel-gray exterior that reflects the light. L. S. Lowry was a local artist, and one of few who painted the industrial landscape. The center has galleries that showcase Lowry's and other contemporary artists' work from the region. The theater is Britain's largest outside London and presents an impressive lineup of international touring companies. ⊠ *Pier 8, Salford Quays,* ☎ *0161/876–2000,* WEB *www.thelowry.com.* 🎫 *Free; prices vary for theater tickets and exhibitions.* ☉ *Daily 9:30 until end of final performance.*

❿ **Manchester Cathedral.** The city's cathedral beside the River Irwell was originally the medieval parish church of the city but was elevated in status to a cathedral in 1847. Unusually proportioned, it's very broad for its length; the cathedral, part of which was built in the 15th century, is recognized as having the widest medieval nave in Britain. Inside is a wealth of attractive items: early 16th-century choir stalls with intriguing misericord seats; paintings of the Beatitudes by Carel Weight (1908–89); a sculpture by Eric Gill (1882–1919); a fine sculpted tomb brass of Warden Huntingdon, who died in 1458; and an octagonal chapter house from 1485. ⊠ *Victoria St.,* ☎ *0161/833–2220.* 🎫 *Free.* ☉ *Call for hrs.*

★ ☾ ❺ **Museum of Science and Industry.** The museum's five buildings, one of which is the world's oldest passenger rail station (1830), hold marvelous collections relating to the city's industrial past and present. You can walk through a reconstructed Victorian sewer and examine a huge collection of working steam mill engines. This section of town is filled with Industrial Revolution landmarks. Not far away, on Cooke Street, a certain Henry Royce built his first car in 1904, before he went into partnership with C. S. Rolls. ⊠ *Liverpool Rd., Castlefield,* ☎ *0161/832–1830,* WEB *www.msim.org.uk.* 🎫 *£6.50.* ☉ *Daily 10–5.*

⚓ ❼ **PumpHouse: People's History Museum.** Not everyone in 19th-century Manchester owned a cotton mill or made a fortune on the trading floor. You're reminded forcibly of this in one of Manchester's more thought-provoking museums, which recounts splendidly the struggles of working people in the city since the Industrial Revolution. The museum tells the story of the 1819 Peterloo Massacre and has an unrivaled collection of trade-union banners, tools, toys, utensils, and photographs, all illustrating the working lives and pastimes of the city's people. ✉ *Bridge St.,* ☎ *0161/839–6061,* WEB *www.nmlhweb.org.* 🎫 *£1; free on Fri.* ◷ *Tues.–Sun. 11–4:30.*

❾ **Royal Exchange Theatre.** Throughout its commercial heyday, this was the city's most important building—the cotton market—and it's the most recent of several buildings to hold the title. The existing structure was built with panache in 1874 to accommodate 7,000 traders. Severely damaged by the 1996 IRA bomb, the building has been refurbished and the giant glass-dome roof restored. Visit if only to see the lunar module–inspired Royal Exchange Theatre, to have a drink in the café, or to browse in the craft and clothes outlets in the arcade shopping center. ✉ *St Ann's Sq.* ☎ *0161/834–3731,* WEB *www.royalexchange.co.uk.*

❽ **St. Ann's Church.** Built in 1712 and sometimes wrongly attributed to Christopher Wren, St. Ann's is Manchester's oldest surviving classical building. The church building contains *The Descent from the Cross,* a painting by Annibale Carraci (1561–1609); after the 1996 IRA bomb exploded, the vicar resolutely remained in the church, lest the painting be looted. The 19th-century essayist Thomas De Quincey was baptized here. Guided tours are available if you call in advance. ✉ *St. Ann's Sq.,* ☎ *0161/834–0239.* ◷ *Daily 9:30–5.*

❶ **Town Hall.** Manchester's exuberant Town Hall, with its imposing 280-ft-tall clock tower, speaks volumes about the city's 19th-century sense of self-importance. It's a magnificent Victorian Gothic building (1867–76) designed by Alfred Waterhouse, with extensions added just before World War II. Over the main entrance is a statue of Roman general Agricola, who founded Mamucium in AD 79. Above him are Henry III and Elizabeth I and St. George, the patron saint of England. The Great Hall, with its soaring hammer-beam roof, is decorated with murals of the city's history, painted between 1852 and 1865 by the Pre-Raphaelite Ford Madox Brown. Guided tours, arranged through the tourist office (in the Town Hall Extension), can introduce you to the murals, but you can also ask at the front desk: if the rooms aren't being used for meetings, you'll be allowed to wander in. ✉ *Albert Sq., public entrance on Lloyd St.,* ☎ *0161/234–5000.* 🎫 *Free; guided tours £3.* ◷ *Daily 9–5; (not always open to public access); guided tours usually Wed. and Sat. at 2.*

⓫ **Whitworth Art Gallery.** This university-run art museum has a strong collection of British watercolors, old-master drawings, and Postimpressionist works. Captivating rooms full of textiles—Coptic and Peruvian fabrics, Spanish and Italian vestments, tribal rugs, and contemporary weaving—are just what you might expect in a city built on textile manufacture. There's a bistro and a good gift shop. ✉ *University of Manchester, Oxford Rd.,* ☎ *0161/275–7450,* WEB *www.whitworth.man.ac.uk.* 🎫 *Free.* ◷ *Mon.–Sat. 10–5, Sun. 2–5.*

Dining

££–££££ ✕ **Livebait.** An offshoot of the successful London-based restaurant serves fresh fish from around the world in an old building across from Albert Square. Tall windows, sage green walls, a black-and-white tile floor, and green banquettes create a comfortable setting. Among the many good choices are smoked haddock cakes with Asian vegetable salad, chargrilled tuna, and platters with Whitby crab, Nova Scotia lobster, langoustines, and Atlantic prawns. Dine early and you can take advantage of the fixed-price pre-theater menu. ⊠ *22 Lloyd St.,* ☎ *0161/817–4110. AE, MC, V.*

££–££££ ✕ **Pacific.** Designed around feng shui principles, this well-regarded split-level concept restaurant fuses old and new Asian culture. The lower floor is China, the upper Thailand; each has a separate kitchen and chef. China has a huge range of dim sum and à la carte dishes, with classic favorites as well as unusual Asian delicacies such as abalone in oyster sauce. Thailand has authentic regional cooking and ingredients. ⊠ *58–60 George St.,* ☎ *0161/228–6668. AE, MC, V.*

££–£££ ✕ **The Lincoln.** A refined contemporary restaurant with an innovative menu and exquisite food by chef Jem O'Sullivan attracts Manchester's most stylish crowd. Try the medium-rare beef fillet with foie gras and wild mushrooms, Moroccan roast lamb with mango and raisin chutney, or sautéed lamb kidneys with sweet potato, chorizo, and sage. This place never fails to impress. ⊠ *1 Lincoln Sq.,* ☎ *0161/834–9000. AE, MC, V.*

££–£££ ✕ **Market Restaurant.** At the edge of the Northern Quarter, this hid-
★   den treasure is a relaxing, unpretentious place that's serious about its cooking. The intimate room exudes personality, and each table has a unique antique china place setting. The menu favors sophisticated but earthy interpretations of British cuisine—cheese and parsnip roulade with sage and onion sauce, fillet of beef with celeriac puree, and venison, pork, and chestnut pie with port wine gravy. ⊠ *104 High St.,* ☎ *0161/834–3743. AE, DC, MC, V. Closed Sun.–Tues., 1 wk in Dec., and month of Aug.*

££–£££ ✕ **Simply Heathcote's.** Lancastrian chef Paul Heathcote earned his reputation as the "cook of the north" for his original, modern food, served in a smart atmosphere. A diverse clientele that includes pre-theater and football crowds packs the massive, minimalist dining room. Some signature dishes are the terrine of black pudding with ham hock and Lancashire cheese mustard dressing; chicken with sweet potato fondant, roasted salsify, and chestnuts and garlic; and the bread and butter pudding. ⊠ *Jackson's Row,* ☎ *0161/835–3536. AE, DC, MC, V.*

££–£££ ✕ **Yang Sing.** One of Manchester's best Chinese restaurants, this place is popular with Chinese families, which is always a good sign, but it is *so* popular that you must book ahead. The cooking is Cantonese, and there's a huge menu. The dim sum is legendary, and don't forget to ask about the daily specials—they're often listed only in Chinese on the menu. ⊠ *34 Princess St.,* ☎ *0161/236–2200. Reservations essential. AE, MC, V.*

£–££ ✕ **Le Petit Blanc.** Famed chef Raymond Blanc's upscale Manchester brasserie is faithful to its Parisian role models. Conversation buzzes in the relaxed yet elegant surroundings of the mostly white room, accented by exotic flowers in blue vases. The menu combines the best traditions of French bourgeois cuisine with a modern vision incorporating Asian and Mediterranean accents. Try the pumpkin soup, roast wild pigeon, and the caramel and Armagnac soufflé. ⊠ *55 King St.,* ☎ *0161/832–1000. AE, MC, V.*

£ ✕ **Atlas Bar & Cafe.** Tucked into a Victorian archway under Deansgate Station is an independently owned café that was one of the city's original smart bars. The industrial decor with wood-clad walls, wooden floor, giant glass windows, and a rear patio that overlooks the river and canal has great style—and devoted fans. The honest, uncomplicated food is Italian with a Mancunian twist. Try the Portobello mushroom lasagne, roast vegetables and couscous, sausages and mustard mash, or fish soup with pesto bruschetta. ⊠ *376 Deansgate,* ☎ *0161/834–2124. AE, MC, V.*

£   ✕ **Tampopo.** The flavors and aromas traditionally found at the bustling food stalls of Bangkok or Penang, or at the noodle vendors of Singapore or Tokyo, are delivered in Manchester in a friendly, modern, and efficient setting. At this busy spot, diners sit next to each other on benches at wooden tables. Specialties are noodle soups, pan-fried noodles, noodles in sauce, and rice dishes. Other choices are vegetarian yakatori and Malaysian red curry with chicken. ⊠ *16 Albert Sq.,* ☎ *0161/819–1966. AE, MC, V.*

£   ✕ **Tandoori Kitchen.** The menu of this Rusholme legend includes interesting Persian dishes alongside the usual curry offerings. It doesn't have a license, but you can bring your own drink. The takeaway next door caters to Manchester's nocturnal characters. ⊠ *131–133 Wilmslow Rd., Rusholme,* ☎ *0161/224–2329. AE, MC, V.*

Lodging

££££   🏨 **Crowne Plaza Manchester—The Midland.** The Edwardian splendor of the hotel's public rooms—including a grand lobby—evokes the days when the Midland was Manchester's station hotel. A traditional high tea is served in the lobby. Guest rooms are comfortable but unremarkable, with none of the Edwardian flair of the public rooms. Nico Central is a well-regarded, contemporary brasserie-style restaurant. ⊠ *Peter St., M60 2DS,* ☎ *0161/236–3333,* ℻ *0161/932–4100,* 🌐 *www.midlandcrowneplaza.co.uk. 303 rooms, 7 suites. 3 restaurants, 2 bars, lounge, in-room data ports, in-room VCRs, minibars, no-smoking rooms, indoor lap pool, hair salon, health club, sauna, business services, meeting rooms, airport shuttle. AE, DC, MC, V.*

££££   🏨 **The Lowry Hotel.** The luxurious Lowry has sumptuous bedrooms with neutral-tone, modern Italian styling and ergonomic design. This glass edifice on the banks of the River Irwell offers magnificent views and is part of the Chapel Wharf development. The deluxe Health and Fitness Centre has six treatment rooms and state-of-the-art equipment. The Lowry is minutes away from exclusive King Street shopping and smart café-bars across the landmark Trinity Bridge. ⊠ *97 Chapel St., Salford, M3 5DF,* ☎ *0161/833–4645,* ℻ *0161/833–4646,* 🌐 *www.rfhotels.com. 163 rooms, 1 suite. Restaurant, bar, in-room data ports, in-room VCRs, minibars, no-smoking floors, indoor lap pool, hair salon, health club, sauna, spa, steam room, business services, meeting rooms, airport shuttle. AE, DC, MC, V.*

£££–££££   🏨 **Le Meridien Victoria & Albert Hotel.** Built in an 1843 warehouse,
★   this comfortable, stylish hotel on the River Irwell has been lovingly restored down to the original brickwork, cast-iron pillars, and oak beams until it exudes authenticity and the charm of the Victorian age. Each room is subtly themed around various productions by Granada TV (*Coronation Street, Brideshead Revisited, Sherlock Holmes*), which has its headquarters across the street. Guests can use the facilities of a nearby health club. ⊠ *Water St., M3 4JQ,* ☎ *0161/832–1188 or 0870/400–8585,* ℻ *0161/834–2484,* 🌐 *www.lemeridien-hotels.com. 156 rooms. Restaurant, 2 bars, in-room data ports, minibars, no-smoking rooms, business services, meeting rooms. AE, DC, MC, V.*

£££   🏨 **Malmaison Hotel.** Stylish and chic, this is the kind of place that's popular with British Pop stars. The striking contemporary look, inside an Edwardian facade, includes good-size, individually designed rooms decorated in red, black, and cream with sumptuous beds and a CD player and library. Traditional French cuisine is the focus in the Malmaison Brasserie. The Malmaison is a few minutes' walk to Piccadilly Station, Chinatown, and Canal Street. ⊠ *Piccadilly, M1 3AQ,* ☎ *0161/278–1000,* ℻ *0161/278–1002,* 🌐 *www.malmaison.com. 167 rooms. Bar,* *brasserie, lounge, in-room data ports, minibars, no-smoking floors, gym, health club, sauna, spa, steam room, business services, meeting rooms. AE, DC, MC, V.*

££–£££ 🏨 **Etrop Grange.** A gracious Georgian mansion with a modern addition, this true gem takes you back in time, even though you're just minutes from the airport rather than out in the country. Fireplaces, chandeliers, flocked wallpaper, tapestry curtains, comfortable sofas, and antiques give a sense of luxurious warmth matched with excellent personal service. Some of the individually furnished bedrooms have four-poster beds and antique-style bathtubs. The Coach House Restaurant is known for exceptional British cuisine. ✉ *Thorley La., M90 4EG,* ☎ *0161/499–0500,* FAX *0161/499–0790,* WEB *www.corushotels.com/etropgrange. 64 rooms. Restaurant, bar, lounge, in-room data ports, in-room safes, no-smoking floor, room service, concierge, business services, meeting rooms, airport shuttle. AE, DC, MC, V.*

££–£££ 🏨 **Renaissance Manchester Hotel.** Behind the tower block facade is an airy, stylishly modern hotel. The Renaissance has the largest standard rooms in Manchester, some with great city views. Robbie's steak house offers certified Angus beef from Scotland and an excellent selection of single-malt Scotches. Guests have access to a nearby health club. The location at the end of Deansgate is within walking distance of the Printworks, the Royal Exchange Theatre, St. Ann's Square, King Street, and the M.E.N. Arena. ✉ *Blackfriars St., M3 2EQ,* ☎ *0161/835–2555,* FAX *0161/833–0731,* WEB *www.renaissancehotels.com/manbr. 196 rooms, 5 suites. Restaurant, bar, in-room data ports, no-smoking floor, sauna, steam room, night club, concierge, business services, meeting rooms. AE, DC, MC, V.*

££ 🏨 **Jurys Inn.** If you don't require room service, this outpost of the Irish-based chain is an excellent value. The sleek wooden lobby and contemporary design are light and attractive, and bedrooms are spacious. You can use the facilities of a nearby health club. The location is excellent, next to Bridgewater Hall and close to shopping on King Street and the thriving café-bar scene on Whitworth Street and Castlefield. ✉ *56 Great Bridgewater St., M1 5LE,* ☎ *0161/953–8888,* FAX *0161/953–9090,* WEB *www.jurysdoyle.com. 265 rooms. Restaurant, bar, lounge, in-room data ports, no-smoking floor, concierge, business services, meeting rooms. AE, DC, MC, V.*

£ 🏨 **Premier Lodge Manchester–City Centre G-Mex.** This new hotel with comfortable, inexpensive rooms may be the best deal in town. All rooms have a spacious desk area. The great location beside Bridgewater Hall and G-Mex is convenient to all shopping and clubbing. ✉ *7–11 Lower Mosley St., M2 3DW,* ☎ *0870/700–1476,* FAX *0870/700–1477,* WEB *www.premierlodge.com. 147 rooms. In-room data ports, no-smoking floor, no-smoking rooms, refrigerators, health club, business services, meeting rooms. AE, DC, MC, V.*

Nightlife and the Arts

For event listings, buy the fortnightly *City Life* magazine. The *Manchester Evening News* is a good source of information, especially the Friday "On the Go" section.

Nightlife

CAFÉ-BARS AND PUBS

Barça (✉ Catalan Sq., ☎ 0161/839–7099) is a hip Spanish bar-restaurant that has won architectural awards. The cavernous **Dukes 92** (✉ Castle St., Castlefield, ☎ 0161/839–8646) is named after the number of the lock on the Rochdale Canal by which it's situated. Still holding its own, **Dry Bar** (✉ 28–30 Oldham St., ☎ 0161/236–9840), the original café-bar in town, is a little faded at the edges but still full of young people drinking and dancing. **Revolution** (⊠ Whitworth St. W, ☎ 0161/839–7569) in trendy Deansgate Locks is a vodka bar.

The so-called **Gay Village** has a dozen stylish bars and cafés along the Rochdale Canal. Canal Street was made famous by the television series *Queer as Folk,* and the area is not only the heart of the gay scene but also the nightlife center for the young and trendy. **Manto** (⊠ 46 Canal St., ☎ 0161/236–2667), the original gay café-bar, still has a chic crowd hanging out in the split-level, post-industrial interior.

The Britons Protection (⊠ 50 Great Bridgewater St., ☎ 0161/236–5895) is a relaxed pub with stained glass and cozy back rooms, a Peterloo Massacre mural, quality cask ales, and more than 150 whiskies and bourbons. For the real thing, check out **Peveril of the Peak** (⊠ 127 Great Bridgewater St., ☎ 0161/236–6364), a Victorian pub with a tiled exterior, several tiny rooms, guest ales, and a crush of locals. **Sinclair's Oyster Bar** (⊠ 2 Cathedral Gates, ☎ 0161/834–0430) is a half-timber pub built in the 17th century. Try the real ales, fresh oysters, and local fare such as smoked haddock rarebit and beef and oyster pie.

DANCE CLUBS

Paradise Factory (⊠ 112–116 Princess St., ☎ 0161/228–2966) is a large, gay-friendly club on three floors that spins hard and uplifting house music. **Planet K** (⊠ 46–50 Oldham St., ☎ 0161/236–9497) hosts live music and big name DJs, dishing out everything from underground progressive house, funk, rap and electro, to R&B and U.K. garage. **Tiger Tiger** (⊠ 5–6 The Printworks, ☎ 0161/839–8080) is a huge bar with a 2,000 capacity arranged around seven loosely themed bars.

LIVE MUSIC

Band on the Wall (⊠ 25 Swan St., ☎ 0161/237–5554) is a cozy room with a formidable reputation for live music—from world fusion, to folk, jazz and rock—and club nights. **Manchester Apollo** (⊠ Stockport Rd., Ardwick Green, ☎ 0161/242–2560), an established concert venue, showcases diverse acts for all musical tastes. Major rock and pop stars appear at the **Manchester Evening News Arena** (⊠ 21 Hunts Bank, ☎ 0161/950–9000). **The Road House** (⊠ 8 Newton St., ☎ 0161/237–9789), an intimate live band venue, also hosts funk, hip hop, and drum 'n' bass nights.

The Arts

FESTIVALS

The city hosts annual events including the Manchester Festival (July–August). There will also be a program of cultural events to coincide with the 2002 Commonwealth Games. The **visitor information centre** (☎ 0161/234–3157 or 0161/234–3158) phone menu includes information on upcoming events.

FILM

The city's major center for cinema and the visual arts is **Cornerhouse** (⊠ 70 Oxford St., ☎ 0161/200–1500), a contemporary arts center with three movie screens plus galleries, bookshop, trendy bar, and café. **The Filmworks** (⊠ The Printworks, Exchange Sq., ☎ 0870/010–2030) is a state-of-the-art 20-screen complex with an IMAX 3-D screen.

THEATRE

Green Room (⊠ 54–56 Whitworth St. W, ☎ 0161/950–5900) is an alternative space for theater, poetry, dance, and performance art. **Library Theatre** (⊠ St Peter's Sq. ☎ 0161/236–7110) in the Central Library stages classical drama, Shakespeare, chamber musicals, and new work from local playwrights. **Royal Exchange Theatre** (⊠ St. Ann's Sq., ☎ 0161/833–9833) in the refurbished Royal Exchange building is the city's main venue for innovative contemporary theater.

Bridgewater Hall (✉ Lower Mosley St., ☎ 0161/907–9000) is home to Manchester's Hallé Orchestra and hosts both classical music and a varied light-entertainment program. **The Lowry** (✉ Pier 8, Salford Quays, ☎ 0161/876–2000) has two theaters and presents everything from musicals to dance and performance poetry. The **Opera House** (✉ Quay St., ☎ 0161/242–2524) is a venue for West End musicals, opera, and classical ballet. **Royal Northern College of Music** (✉ 124 Oxford Rd., ☎ 0161/274–2595) hosts classical and contemporary music concerts, jazz, and opera. The **Palace Theatre** (✉ Oxford St., ☎ 0161/242–2503) presents large touring shows of major plays, ballet, and opera.

Outdoor Activities and Sports

Participant Sports

Take a barge or follow the interpretive trail at **Castlefield Urban Heritage Park** Liverpool Rd., Castlefield, ☎ 0161/934–4026. You can stroll the 3 mi of landscaped walkways along the quays or relax in the restaurants, pubs, and cafés in **Salford Quays** (✉ Salford Quays, Salford, ☎ 0161/848–8601). Canoe, boat, windsurf, fish, or ride at the local nature reserve, **Chorlton Water Park** (✉ Maitland Ave., Barlow Moor Rd., Chorlton, ☎ 0161/881–5639), open between Easter and October.

Spectator Sports

In 2002 Manchester will host the XVII Commonwealth Games from July 25 to August 4. Athletes from 72 nations will participate. Existing games venues include the Manchester Evening News (M.E.N.) Arena (boxing and several other sports), Bolton Arena (badminton), Heaton Park (bowls), Salford Quays (triathlon), G-Mex Centre (gymnastics, judo, wrestling), Royal Northern College of Music (weightlifting), and the National Shooting Centre in Bisley. For **Commonwealth Games** information, call ☎ 0161/817–2002 or check WEB www.commonwealthgames.com. The main complex being built for the games, **Sportcity,** will have a 38,000-seat City of Manchester Stadium, which will house the opening and closing ceremonies as well as athletics events such as rugby.

The **Manchester Aquatics Centre** (✉ Oxford Rd., ☎ 0161/275–9450) is the only facility in the United Kingdom with two 50-meter pools, as well as separate diving and leisure pools. **Manchester Evening News Arena** (✉ 21 Hunts Bank, Victoria Station, ☎ 0161/950–5000) is Europe's largest multipurpose indoor sports arena and is home to the Manchester Giants basketball team and Manchester Storm ice hockey team. The **Manchester Velodrome** (✉ 1 Stuart St., Beswick, ☎ 0161/223–2244) is the home of British track cycling and hosts regular cycling, gymnastics, badminton, and basketball events.

Football (soccer in the United States) is *the* major passion in Manchester. Locals support the perennially unsuccessful local club, Manchester City, while glory-seekers come from afar to root for Manchester United, based in neighboring Trafford. Although matches for both clubs are usually sold out months in advance, touts are always ready to do business outside the grounds. **Manchester City** (✉ 21 Hunts Bank, Victoria Station, ☎ 0161/232–3000) plays at Maine Road, where tours are available by arrangement on non-match days. **Manchester United** (✉ Sir Matt Busby Way, ☎ 0161/868–8000) plays at Old Trafford.

You can take a trip to the Theatre of Dreams at the **Manchester United Museum and Tour** (☎ 0161/868–8631), which tells the history of the football club. The tour takes you behind the scenes, into the changing rooms and players' lounge, and down the tunnel to pitchside. It's open daily 9:30–4:30; admission is £4.50.

Shopping

Afflecks Palace (⊠ 52 Church St., ☎ 0161/834–2039) is a mecca for Mancunian youth and has four floors of bohemian glam, serious clubbing clothes, ethnic crafts and jewelry, army surplus, and innovative gift ideas. **Barton Arcade** (51–63 Deansgate, ☎ 0161/839–3172) has specialty shopping inside a lovely Victorian arcade. **Chinatown**—between Portland Street, Mosley Street, Princess Street, and Charlotte Street—has a Chinese supermarket, herbalists and doctors specializing in ancient Chinese medicines, and the Chinese Art Centre, which stocks books and magazines. A brand-new **Harvey Nichols,** currently under construction, will sell chic women's fashions on the site where the 1996 IRA bomb exploded.

The **Manchester Craft Centre** (⊠ 17 Oak St., ☎ 0161/832–4274), in a Victorian building, houses 16 workshop–cum–retail outlets where you can see craftspeople at work. The world's largest **Marks & Spencer** (⊠ 106 Market St., ☎ 0161/237–9888) department store offers its own brand of fashion and has an excellent food department. The Northern Quarter, especially **Oldham Street,** is littered with urban hip-hop and skater boutiques, fashionable bars, and indie music shops. The **Royal Exchange Shopping Centre and Arcade** (St. Ann's Sq., ☎ 0161/834–3731) has three floors of restaurants and specialty shops with antiques, Belgian chocolates, teddy bears, and more, inside the magnificent Cotton Exchange building. **The Triangle** (Millennium Quarter, ☎ 0161/834–8961), a stylish mall in the Victorian Corn Exchange, has more than 55 chain stores and independent designer shops. **Waterstone's** (⊠ 91 Deansgate, ☎ 0161/832–1332) bookshop organizes cultural events in addition to hosting regular events of its own.

LIVERPOOL

Lined with one of the most famous waterfronts in England, celebrated around the world as the birthplace of the Beatles, and still the place to catch that "Ferry 'Cross the Mersey," Liverpool has suffered acute decline over the past few decades. Authorities are pinning their hopes on relatively new developments such as the Tate Liverpool and the refurbishment of the adjacent Albert Dock historic area to reverse the city's fortunes.

Situated on the east bank of the Mersey River estuary, at the point where it merges with the Irish Sea, Liverpool developed from the 17th century through the slave trade. It became Britain's leading port for ferrying Africans to North America and for handling cargoes of sugar, tobacco, rum, and cotton, which began to dominate the local economy after the slave trade was abolished in 1807. Because of its close proximity to Ireland, the city was also the first port of call for those fleeing famine, poverty, and persecution in that country, and it was often the last British port of call for thousands of mostly Jewish refugees fleeing the pogroms in Eastern Europe.

Many of the best-known liner companies were based in Liverpool, including Cunard and White Star, whose best known vessel, the *Titanic,* was registered in Liverpool. The city was a dealt an economic blow in 1894 with the opening of the Manchester Ship Canal, which allowed traders to bypass Liverpool and head to Lancashire's other major city, 35 mi east. Liverpool's economy never recovered, and decline gradually set in. Wartime bombing in the 1940s devastated the city's infrastructure, and rebuilding was unsympathetic. The postwar growth of air travel curtailed the services of the ocean-going liners, and a few years later Britain's entry into the European Common Market saw more trade move from the west coast to the east.

As economic decline set in, Liverpool produced its most famous export—the Beatles. The group was one of hundreds that began copying the rock 'n' roll they heard from visiting American GIs and merchant seamen in the late 1950s, and one of many that played local venues such as the Cavern (demolished but since rebuilt nearby). All four Beatles were born in Liverpool, but the group's success dates from the time they left for London. Nevertheless, the city has milked the group's Liverpool connections for all they are worth, and there are a multitude of local attractions connected with the group.

Despite the roughness and shabbiness of parts of the city, a surprising number of people visit Liverpool to tour the Beatles sites, view the paintings in the renowned art galleries, and to learn about the city's industrial and maritime heritage at the impressive Albert Dock area.

Exploring Liverpool

Liverpool has a fairly compact center, and you can see many city highlights on foot. This walk includes some civic landmarks and museums, some key Beatles sights, and the renovated Albert Dock and its maritime heritage sights. Note that eight museums, including the Mersey Maritime Museum, are part of the National Museums and Galleries on Merseyside; a £3 pass gets you into all of them.

A Good Walk and Tour

Begin, as many visitors do, at Lime Street and **Lime Street Station** ⑫, home not just to the famous railway station but to the city's grandest Classical Revival building, **St. George's Hall** ⑬. To the north lies William Brown Street, a showcase boulevard of prestigious municipal buildings including the outstanding **Walker Art Gallery** ⑭.

A left turn at the end of William Brown Street leads into Whitechapel, a street of dowdy-looking stores. However, Nos. 12–14 were once the NEMS (North End Music Stores) record shop owned by Brian Epstein. In 1961, when a teenager asked for a record by Tony Sheridan and the Beat Brothers, Epstein couldn't find it in his catalogue. He discovered that the backing band was a local group, the Beatles. Epstein learned that the group was playing daily at a nearby dive club, the Cavern, so he made the short journey—as you can do now—down Whitechapel, turning right at Stanley Street and left onto **Mathew Street** to get to the Cavern at No. 10. The rest is, as they say, history.

The western end of Mathew Street leads into North John Street, and a right turn brings you out at Dale Street overlooked by the looming mass of the **Royal Liver Building** ⑮, part of Liverpool's famous waterfront skyline. Equally renowned is the palazzo-like Cunard Building to the south, once the Head Office for the world's most famous shipping company, the Cunard Steamship Company.

The wide Mersey estuary separating the city from the Wirral Peninsula is usually reached by the ferry, which leaves from the adjacent **Pier Head** ⑯. A riverside walk connects with the museum area that includes the **Merseyside Maritime Museum** ⑰ and **Albert Dock** ⑱, 19th-century brick warehouses that fell into disuse in the late 20th century but have been redeveloped into boutiques, restaurants, offices, and the northern branch of London's **Tate Liverpool** ⑲. The complex also in-

Albert
Dock **18**

Anglican
Cathedral . .**22**

The Beatles
Story **20**

Lime Street
Station **12**

Merseyside
Maritime
Museum **17**

Metropolitan
Cathedral
of Christ
the King **23**

Museum of
Liverpool
Life **21**

Pier
Head **16**

Royal Liver
Building **15**

St. George's
Hall **13**

Tate
Liverpool . . .**19**

Walker Art
Gallery **14**

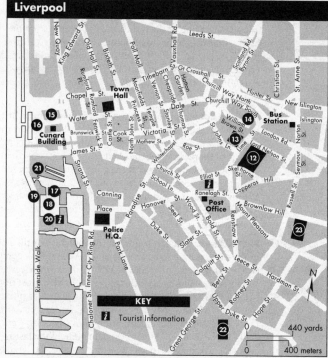

Liverpool

cludes **Beatles Story** ⑳, detailing the story of the city's best-known sons, and the **Museum of Liverpool Life** ㉑.

From Albert Dock it's a reasonably short walk back into the city center. For a longer walk that takes in the city's two cathedrals, head southeast along Duke Street and Upper Duke Street toward the Gothic-inspired **Anglican Cathedral** ㉒, the largest church in northern England. Hope Street, which runs along the eastern side of the cathedral, links the latter with its Catholic equivalent to the north, the modernistic **Metropolitan Cathedral of Christ the King** ㉓, and includes some romantic crumbling Georgian properties such as Gambier Terrace (John Lennon once lived at No. 3) and the College of Art where Lennon studied. From the Catholic cathedral, it's a five-minute walk northwest back to Lime Street Station.

TIMING

You can do this walk in an hour without stopping, but you'll need a full day if you want to visit all the museums and churches. Remember that 20 Forthlin Road, Paul McCartney's childhood home, is in Liverpool but lies outside the center city.

Sights to See

★ ⑱ **Albert Dock.** To understand the city's maritime past, head straight for the waterfront Albert Dock, 7 acres of restored warehouses built in 1846 and named after Queen Victoria's consort, Prince Albert. Albert Dock was used for storing silk, tea, and tobacco from the Far East but ultimately fell into decay and was closed in 1972. It was rescued by the Merseyside Development Corporation, and the fine colonnaded brick warehouse buildings were converted to what is now the country's largest heritage attraction, with museums (notably, the Merseyside Maritime Museum, Museum of Liverpool Life, Tate Liverpool, and the Beatles Story), shops, offices, and restaurants. As most amenities are indoors within the old warehouses it's an obvious choice if your visit coincides with one of the Northwest's rainy spells. When the weather allows, sit at one of the outdoor cafés overlooking the dock or take a boat trip through the docks and out onto the river to see the city as it was in its heyday. Albert Dock is part of the larger area known as **Liverpool's Historic Waterfront.** ⊠ *Tourist Information Centre, Atlantic Pavilion,* ☎ *0151/708–8854,* WEB *www.albertdock.com.* ☉ *Information center, daily 10–5.*

㉒ **Anglican Cathedral.** The largest church in northern Britain overlooks the city and the River Mersey. Built of local sandstone, the Gothic-style cathedral was begun in 1903 by architect Giles Gilbert Scott and was still not complete when he died in 1960; it was finally finished in 1978. Take a look around at the grand interior, view the exhibit of detailed Victorian embroidery, climb the 331-ft tower, and stop at the Visitor Centre. A refectory serves light meals and coffee. ⊠ *St. James's Rd.,* ☎ *0151/709–6271.* ☜ *£2 for tower.* ☉ *Daily 8–6, tower daily 11–4, refectory Mon.–Sat. 10–4, Sun. noon–5.*

⑳ **Beatles Story.** You can follow in the footsteps of the Fab Four at one of the more popular attractions in the Albert Dock complex. It has an entertaining series of scenes re-created from their career, as well as a John Lennon photographic exhibition. To visit most of the other Beatles sites, take city buses to the various points of interest or join the two-hour **Magical Mystery Tour,** which departs daily from Albert Dock at 2:20 PM. For information about Beatles Week, known officially as the Mathew Street Festival and held the last week in August, contact **Cavern City Tours** (☎ *0151/236–9091*). ⊠ *Britannia Vaults, Albert Dock,* ☎ *0151/709–1963,* WEB *www.albertdock.com.* ☜ *£6.95.* ☉ *Apr.–Sept., daily 10–6; Oct.–Mar., daily 10–5.*

⑫ **Lime Street Station.** Perhaps the most imposing expression of the city's former industrial might is this railway station, whose cast-iron train shed was the world's largest in the mid-19th century. The opening scene in the film *A Hard Day's Night,* which shows the Beatles on a railway station platform, supposedly Lime Street, was filmed in Marylebone Station, London. ⊠ *Lime St.*

Liverpool's Historic Waterfront. Liverpool's famous waterside sights include the Royal Liver and Cunard buildings, Pier Head (ferries leave for river trips), and the Albert Dock complex. The dock itself and some attractions are free; others require a separate admission fee or the purchase of a **Waterfront Pass,** which gets you into all the museums (Merseyside Maritime Museum, Museum of Liverpool Life, Tate Liverpool, Beatles Story) and offers a cruise across the River Mersey. There's free parking at the dock, while a shuttle bus runs here every 20 minutes from the Queen Square bus station, a couple of minutes' walk from Lime Street Station. ☎ *0151/708–8838.* ☜ *Waterfront Pass £9.99, boat trips only £2.50.* ☉ *Boat trip, departures every hr noon– 5; winter, weekends only.*

Mathew Street. It was at the Cavern on this street that Brian Epstein, who became the Beatles' manager, first heard the group in 1961. The Cavern had opened at No. 10 as a jazz venue in 1957 but had been taken over by beat groups, of whom the Beatles were clearly the most talented. Epstein became their manager a few months after first visiting the club, and within two years the group was the most talked-about phenomenon in music. The Cavern club fell on hard times in the early '70s and was demolished in 1973; it was later rebuilt a few yards from the original site. If you seek the Beatles knickknack of your dreams, check out the **Beatles Shop** (⊠ *31 Mathew St.,* ☎ *0151/236–8066*).

17 **Merseyside Maritime Museum.** Part of the Albert Dock complex, the museum tells the story of the port of Liverpool by way of models, paintings, and original boats and equipment spread across five floors. The same admission ticket also grants access to the **Transatlantic Slavery** and **Customs and Excise** exhibitions, the former being especially compelling on the human misery engendered by the slave trade. ⊠ *Albert Dock,* ☎ *0151/478–4499,* WEB *www.nmgm.org.uk.* *£3, including admission to Museum of Liverpool Life and Walker Art Gallery.* *Daily 10–5, last admission at 4.*

23 **Metropolitan Cathedral of Christ the King.** Consecrated in 1967, this Roman Catholic cathedral designed by Frederick Gibberd is a modernistic, funnel-like structure of concrete, stone, and mosaic, topped with a glass lantern; it's known as "Paddy's Wigwam" or the "Mersey Funnel." Long, narrow blue glass windows separate chapels, each with modern works of art. An earlier design by classically inspired architect Edwin Lutyens was abandoned when World War II began, but some of Lutyens's work can be seen in the crypt. ⊠ *Mount Pleasant,* ☎ *0151/709–9222,* WEB *www.liverpool-rc-cathedral.org.uk/.* *Donations welcome.* *Mon.–Sat. 8–6, Sun. 8–5.*

21 **Museum of Liverpool Life.** A somewhat offbeat look at Liverpool's history and culture can be viewed at this museum, housed in a former Boat Hall opposite the Albert Dock's Maritime Museum. There are special displays on Merseyside culture, focusing on matters as diverse as the city's changing trades following the decline of shipping, local sporting prowess, and arts and literature in Liverpool. This is the place to discover what it is that makes "Scousers" (as locals are known) tick. ⊠ *Albert Dock,* ☎ *0151/478–4080,* WEB *www.nmgm.org.uk.* *£3, including admission to Merseyside Maritime Museum and Walker Art Gallery.* *Daily 10–5, last admission at 4.*

16 **Pier Head.** Here you can take a ferry across the River Mersey from Pierhead to Birkenhead and back. The ferries leave regularly throughout the day and offer fine views of the city—a journey celebrated in "Ferry 'Cross the Mersey," Gerry and the Pacemakers' 1964 hit song. It was also from Pier Head that 9 million British, Irish, and European emigrants set sail between 1830 and 1930 for new lives in the United States, Canada, Australia, and Africa. ⊠ *Pier Head Ferry Terminal, Mersey Ferries,* ☎ *0151/ 630–1030.* *£1.80 round-trip 7:45–9:15 AM and 4:15–7:15 PM; £3.40 for cruises at other times.* *Ferries every 30–60 mins, 7:45 AM–7:15 PM.*

15 **Royal Liver Building.** Best seen from the ferry, the 322-ft-tall Royal Liver (pronounced "lie-ver") Building with its twin towers is topped by two 18-ft copper birds, purported to have given the city its name. The mythical Liver Birds are the town symbol, and local legend has it that if they fly away, Liverpool will cease to exist. For decades Liverpudlians looked to the Royal Liver Society for assistance—it was originally a burial club to which families paid contributions to ensure a decent send-off. ⊠ *Water St.*

13 **St. George's Hall.** Built between 1839 and 1847, St. George's Hall is among the country's finest Greek Revival buildings. When Queen Victoria visited Liverpool in 1851, she declared it "worthy of ancient Athens." Today, St. George's Hall serves as a home for music festivals and the Assize Courts. Exhibitions and concerts are held inside, and the public is allowed in for tours at other selected times in summer. The building is scheduled for major renovation in 2001 and 2002. ⊠ *Lime St.,* ☎ *0151/707–2391.*

19 **Tate Liverpool.** An offshoot of the London-based art gallery of the same name, the Liverpool building, a handsome conversion of existing Albert

Dock warehouses, was designed in the 1990s by the late James Stirling, one of Britain's leading late 20th-century architects. Changing exhibits of challenging modern art are displayed in superb galleries. The Tate also has an excellent shop selling art books, prints, and posters, as well as a children's art-play area and a fashionable dockside café-restaurant. ✉ *The Colonnades, Albert Dock,* ☎ *0151/709–0507,* WEB *www.tate.org.uk.* 🖙 *Free; charge for special exhibitions.* ☉ *Tues.–Sun. 10–5:50.*

20 Forthlin Road. The august National Trust (the overseers of such landmarks as Blenheim Palace) is responsible for the upkeep of the Merseyside home of the young Paul McCartney in the Liverpool suburb of Allerton. The mid-terraced 1950s council house, with its period-authentic windows, doors, and hedges, was occupied by the McCartney family from 1955 to 1963. A number of the Beatles' songs, including "Love Me Do" and "When I'm Sixty-Four," were written here. The house is viewable only on a special tour for which you must pre-book a seat on the minibus that connects the site with Albert Dock or Speke Hall (another Trust site, an impressive half-timber mansion also worth viewing). Call for tour departure times. ✉ *20 Forthlin Rd.,* ☎ *0151/ 486–4006,* WEB *www.spekehall.org.uk/beatles.htm.* 🖙 *£4.50.* ☉ *Aug.– Oct., Wed.–Sat.; Nov.–mid-Dec., Sat. only; 4–6 departures per day, reservations essential.*

★ ⑭ **Walker Art Gallery.** The Walker maintains its position as one of the best art collections outside London, with an excellent display of British art and some superb Italian and Flemish works. In particular, you'll find an unrivaled collection of paintings by 18th-century Liverpudlian equestrian artist George Stubbs, as well as paintings by J. M. W. Turner, John Constable, and Sir Edwin Henry Landseer, and representative work by the Pre-Raphaelites. Modern British artists are included, too—on display is one of David Hockney's typically Californian pool scenes. There are also engaging exhibits of glassware, china, silver, and furniture that once adorned the mansions of Liverpool's industrial barons. The Tea Room holds center stage in the airy museum lobby. Note: the gallery is closed for renovations and should reopen in February 2002. ✉ *William Brown St.,* ☎ *0151/478–4199,* WEB *www.nmgm.org.uk.* 🖙 *£3, including admission to Merseyside Maritime Museum and Museum of Liverpool Life.* ☉ *Mon.–Sat. 10–5, Sun. noon–5.*

Dining

£££ ✗ **Becher's Brook.** Modern British cooking in a stylish Georgian town
★ house keeps well-heeled locals coming back for more. Menus change seasonally, but solid British fare like oysters, cod, duck, beef, and game all appear regularly, softened by the addition of Mediterranean and Asian flourishes. The name, incidentally, is that of one of the jumps on the Grand National Aintree racecourse. ✉ *29a Hope St.,* ☎ *0151/707–0005. AE, DC, MC, V. Closed Sun. No lunch Sat.*

££ ✗ **Armadillo.** The fine Mediterranean cooking at this downtown restaurant in the Cavern Quarter includes classic dishes alongside trendy favorites. Starters may include lentil salad or eggplant and mozzarella combinations, and for an entrée try roast sea bass or a vegetarian dish such as chestnut cannelloni. ✉ *31 Mathew St.,* ☎ *0151/236–4123. AE, MC, V. Closed Sun., Mon., and Christmas wk. No lunch Sat.*

£–££ ✗ **Est Est Est.** This top budget choice in the Albert Dock complex is a lively spot for lunch. The restaurant makes good use of the old warehouse brickwork, though tables are a bit cramped. Still, the Italian menu is strong on appetizers, including a feast of antipasto and excellent crisp pizzas. ✉ *Unit 6, Edward Pavilion, Albert Dock,* ☎ *0151/708–6969. AE, DC, MC, V.*

£ ✕ **Taste.** The Tate Liverpool's café-bar is a real winner—dockside seats for those summer days, daytime sandwiches, soups, and salads, and an evening bistro menu of tapas, from stuffed eggplant to mushroom tortilla. ⊠ *The Colonnades, Albert Dock,* ☎ *0151/709–7097. MC, V.* ☾ *Café open daily 10–6, bistro Thurs.–Sat. dinner only.*

Lodging

£££–££££ ⊞ **Liverpool Marriott Hotel.** This 1998 city-center hotel is indicative of Liverpool's rise from the economic ashes. It's comfortable and modern, with well-appointed guest rooms. The unbeatable location is a minute from Lime Street Station and the Walker Art Gallery. ⊠ *Queen Sq., L1 1RH,* ☎ *0151/476–8000,* ℻ *0151/474–5000,* 🕸 *www.marriott.com. 146 rooms. Restaurant, bar, indoor pool, sauna, gym, business services. AE, DC, MC, V.*

£££ ⊞ **Liverpool Moat House.** Some may find this uncompromisingly modern hotel unattractive from the outside, but it lies in landscaped grounds right across from the River Mersey and Albert Dock, which means that much of what you've come to the city to see is right at your doorstep. Guest rooms are handsome and spacious, most with two large beds and fine bathrooms, and about half the rooms are nonsmoking. A good-size ground-floor pool aids relaxation after a day's sightseeing. ⊠ *Paradise St., L1 8JD,* ☎ *0151/471–9988,* ℻ *0151/709–2706. 244 rooms, 7 suites. 2 restaurants, bar, coffee shop, no-smoking rooms, room service, indoor pool, sauna, gym, business services. AE, DC, MC, V.*

££ ⊞ **Aachen Hotel.** The Aachen is in a historic building on Mount Pleasant that was owned in the mid-19th century by William Steers, a descendant of Thomas Steers who built the world's first dock, at Liverpool in 1709. Public areas and guest rooms are cheerfully furnished in traditional prints. The hotel sells special-event tickets for the city's two football clubs, and city tours, with themes such as the Beatles and Heritage, are available at a discount. ⊠ *89–91 Mount Pleasant, L3 5TB,* ☎ *0151/709–3477,* ℻ *0151/709–1126,* 🕸 *www.aachenhotel.co.uk. 17 rooms. Restaurant, bar. AE, DC, MC, V.*

££ ⊞ **Britannia Adelphi Hotel.** Liverpool's most famous hotel, a few yards from Lime Street Station, was built in 1876 and then rebuilt between 1912 and 1914 with money put up by the Midland Railway Company, which wanted a first-class hotel for wealthy passengers staying overnight before and after transatlantic trips. The Sefton Suite is a replica of the first-class smoking lounge on the *Titanic*. Today marble, dark wood, and fancy ceilings in public areas convey the grandeur of the past, though they may seem a bit kitschy. Guest rooms have modern amenities but a traditional feeling; some have whirlpool baths. ⊠ *Ranelagh Pl., L3 5UL,* ☎ *0151/708–8326,* ℻ *0151/708–8326,* 🕸 *www.britannia-hotels.co.uk. 402 rooms. 3 restaurants, 4 bars, indoor pool, hair salon, gym, squash, dance club, meeting rooms. AE, DC, MC, V.*

££ ⊞ **Royal Hotel.** Overlooking the Marine Gardens and the Mersey estuary, with views of the Wirral and North Wales in the distance, the Royal occupies an 1815 building that became the Royal Waterloo Hotel after the 1816 battle; the area around the hotel was also renamed. The hotel retains much of its original character, with its grand proportions, fireplaces, plasterwork, and maritime features. Rooms are traditionally decorated but have up-to-date amenities; some have four-poster beds and whirlpool baths. The hotel is a 10-minute drive from the city center. ⊠ *Marine Terr., Waterloo, L22 5PR,* ☎ *0151/928–2332,* ℻ *0151/949–0320,* 🕸 *www.liverpool-royalhotel.co.uk. 25 rooms. Restaurant, bar. AE, DC, MC, V.*

£ ⊞ **Liverpool Youth Hostel.** This hostel really should change its name, because it offers modest hotel standards for bargain prices. A few minutes' walk from Albert Dock in a specially designed building, the smart rooms (for two, four, or six people) are fully carpeted, with private bathrooms and heated towel rails. There's a licensed diner on the premises, and a full breakfast is included in the price. Book well in advance—especially to secure a twin-bedded room. ⊠ *Chalenor St., L1 8EE,* ☎ *0151/ 709–8888. 106 beds. Cafeteria, recreation room, coin laundry. MC, V.*

Nightlife and the Arts

Nightlife

Typical of the bars at the Albert Dock is **Blue** (⊠ Edward Pavilion, Albert Dock, ☎ 0151/709–7097), which attracts a funky young professional crowd to its late hours, bar and grill, and dockside seating. On the Beatles trail, many call into the **Cavern Club** (⊠ Mathew St., ☎ 0151/ 236–9091) without realizing that it's not the original spot—that was demolished years ago. For the sake of nostalgia, have a drink in the **Cavern Pub** (⊠ Mathew St., ☎ 0151/236–1957), in which are recorded the names of the groups and artists who played in the club between 1957 and 1973. The **Cream** nightclub (⊠ Wolstenholme Sq., ☎ 0151/709– 1693) is one of the hippest clubs in Britain. Nicest of the city-center pubs is the **Philharmonic** (⊠ 36 Hope St., ☎ 0151/709–1163) opposite the Philharmonic Hall, a Victorian-era extravaganza, outrageously decorated in colorful marble, with comfortable bar rooms and over-the-top rest rooms.

The Arts

The renowned Royal Liverpool Philharmonic Orchestra plays its concert season at **Philharmonic Hall** (⊠ Hope St., ☎ 0151/709–3789).

For experimental and British theatrical productions, check the program at the **Everyman Theatre** (⊠ 5–9 Hope St., ☎ 0151/709–4776). Major national and international ballet, opera, drama, and musical performances take place at the **Liverpool Empire** (⊠ Lime St., ☎ 0151/709– 1555). Liverpool hosts regular pop and rock concerts and stand-up comedy, and one of the most appealing venues is the Art Deco **Royal Court Theatre** (⊠ Roe St., ☎ 0151/709–4321).

Outdoor Activities and Sports

Football

Football (soccer in the United States) matches are played Saturday and, increasingly, Sunday and Monday. Ticket prices vary, but the cheapest seats start at about £16. The tourist offices can give you match schedules and directions to the grounds. **Liverpool,** English football's most successful club, plays at Anfield (☎ 0151/260–8680) 2 mi north of the city center. **Everton,** once a major force but now in a seemingly perpetual rebuilding phase, play at Goodison Park (☎ 0151/330–2300), about ½ mi north of Anfield.

Horse Racing

Britain's most famous horse race, the Grand National steeplechase, has been run at Liverpool's **Aintree Race Course** (⊠ Ormskirk Rd., ☎ 0151/ 523–2600) almost every year since 1839. The race is held every March or April, and even if you don't attend, you'll be able to see the race on TV. Admission on race days begins at £7. A Visitor Centre lets you sample the atmosphere of the race—or even ride it on the Grand National simulator.

Shopping

The **Stanley Dock Sunday Market** (⊠ Great Howard St. and Regent Rd.) is a historic affair, with 400 stalls operating each Sunday, selling bric-a-brac, clothes, and toys from 9 to 4.

The small lobby shop at the **Walker Art Gallery** (✉ William Brown St., ☎ 0151/478–4199) contains a high-quality selection of glassware, ceramics, and jewelry by local designers. The annual Merseycraft exhibition winners are on exclusive display in the shop every December.

THE PEAK DISTRICT: ON THE ROAD TO CHATSWORTH AND HADDON HALL

Heading southeast, away from the urban congestion of Manchester and Liverpool, it's not far to the southernmost contortions of the Pennine Hills. Here, sheltered in a great natural bowl, the spa town of Buxton, about an hour from Manchester, has a surprisingly mild climate, considering its altitude: at more than 1,000 ft, it's the second-highest town in England. Buxton makes a convenient base for exploring the 540 square mi of the Peak District, Britain's oldest—and, some say, most beautiful—national park. "Peak" is perhaps misleading; despite being a hilly area, it contains only long, flat-top rises that don't reach much higher than 2,000 ft. Yet touring around destinations such as Bakewell, Matlock, the grand estates of Chatsworth House and Haddon Hall, Castleton, and, finally, Edale, you'll often have to negotiate fairly perilous country roads, each of which repays the effort with enchanting views.

Outdoor activities are popular in the Peaks, particularly caving (or "potholing"), which entails underground exploration, and walking and hiking. Bring all-weather clothing and waterproof shoes.

Buxton

24 *25 mi southeast of Manchester.*

The Romans arrived in AD 79 and named Buxton *Aquae Arnemetiae,* loosely translated as "Waters of the Goddess of the Grove," suggesting they considered this Derbyshire hill town to be special. The mineral springs, which emerge from 3,500 to 5,000 ft below ground at a constant 82°F, were believed to cure a variety of ailments, and in the 18th century established the town as a popular spa, a minor rival to Bath. You can still drink water from the ancient St. Anne's Well, and it's also bottled and sold throughout Britain.

Buxton's spa days have left a legacy of 18th- and 19th-century buildings, parks, and open spaces that now give the town an air of faded grandeur. A good place to start exploring is the **Crescent** on the northwest side of the Slopes park (the town hall is on the opposite side); almost all out-of-town roads lead toward this central green. The three former hotels that make up the Georgian-era Crescent, with its arches, Doric colonnades, and 378 windows, were built in 1780 by John Carr for the fifth duke of Devonshire (of nearby Chatsworth House). The splendid ceiling of the former assembly room now looks down on the town's public library, while the thermal baths at the end of the Crescent house a shopping center. The Crescent buildings themselves are currently closed to the public (except the tourist information center, contained within), though renovations have cleaned the facade and it's hoped at some point to open other rooms to visitors.

The **Devonshire Royal Hospital,** behind the Crescent, also by John Carr, was originally a stable with room for 110 of the hotel guests' horses; it was converted into a hospital in 1859. The circular area for exercising horses was covered with a massive 156-ft-wide slate-color dome and incorporated into the hospital.

The **Buxton Museum** can give you a feeling for the town and its surroundings. Inside, there's a collection of Blue John stone, a semiprecious mineral found only in the Peak District. The museum also holds local archaeological finds, including a few pieces from Roman times, and there's a small art gallery, too. The museum is on the eastern side of the Slopes. ⊠ *Terrace Rd.,* ☎ *01298/24658.* ⊡ *£1.* ☉ *Tues.–Fri. 9:30–5:30, Sat. 9:30–5, Sun. (Apr.–Sept. only) 10:30–5.*

Pavilion Gardens (⊠ Pavilion Gardens, ☎ 01298/23114), with its ornate iron-and-glass roof, was originally a concert hall and ballroom. Erected in the 1870s, it's still a lively place, with a conservatory, several bars, a restaurant, and a cafeteria, set in 25 acres of well-kept Pavilion Gardens. It's adjacent to the Crescent and the Slopes on the west.

Buxton Opera House (⊠ Water St., ☎ 01298/72190), built in 1903, is one of the most architecturally exuberant structures in town. Its marble bulk, bedecked with carved cupids, is even more impressive inside— so impressive it may be worth buying a ticket to a concert. Otherwise, tours (£1) of the interior are conducted most Saturdays at 11 AM.

The Peak District's extraordinary geology is on show close to Buxton at **Poole's Cavern,** a large limestone cave far beneath the 100 wooded acres of Buxton Country Park. Named after a legendary 15th-century robber, the cave was inhabited in prehistoric times and contains, in addition to the standard stalactites and stalagmites, the source of the River Wye, which flows through Buxton. ⊠ *Green La.,* ☎ *01298/26978,* WEB *www.poolescavern.co.uk.* ⊡ *£4.50 including tour; Country Park and visitor center free.* ☉ *Mar.–Oct., daily 10–5.*

Lodging

£££   ⊞ **The Palace.** A Victorian hotel on a grand scale from the halcyon days
★   of the spa, the Palace is set on 5 acres overlooking the town center and surrounding hills. The smart rooms are traditional in style but equipped with satellite TV, tea–coffeemakers, and the other usual little comforts. What makes many of the rooms stand out are the wonderful views of Buxton. The room rate includes dinner. ⊠ *Palace Rd., SK17 6AG,* ☎ *01298/22001,* FAX *01298/72131,* WEB *www.paramount-hotels.co.uk. 122 rooms. Restaurant, bar, lobby lounge, pool, hair salon, sauna, gym, library. AE, DC, MC, V.*

££   ⊞ **Lakenham Guest House.** This large Victorian structure with a sweep-
★   ing garden has been converted into a comfortable guest house, with some attractive antique furniture. Potted plants proliferate and the Victorian-style bedrooms all have excellent views (the house overlooks Pavilion Gardens); rooms also have small refrigerators and satellite TV reception. ⊠ *11 Burlington Rd., SK17 9AL,* ☎ *01298/79209. 6 rooms, 5 with bath. No credit cards.*

££   ⊞ **Old Hall.** The building dates from the 16th century, and although everything else has been refurbished, Mary's Bower, in the oldest part of the hotel, still retains its original ceiling moldings; the name recalls Mary, Queen of Scots, who stayed here several times between 1573 and 1582. This friendly, central hotel overlooks the Opera House; some of the individually styled rooms have four-poster beds. ⊠ *The Square, SK17 6BD,* ☎ *01298/22841,* FAX *01298/72437,* WEB *www.oldhall-hotelbuxton.co.uk. 38 rooms. Restaurant, bar. AE, DC, MC, V.*

Nightlife and the Arts

Buxton Opera House (⊠ Water St., Buxton, ☎ 01298/72190) presents excellent theater, ballet, and jazz performances year-round; it also hosts an amateur drama festival in summer.

Buxton's renowned **Festival of Music and the Arts** (⊠ Festival Office, The Square, ☎ 01298/70395), held the second half of July and early

August each year, includes opera, drama, classical concerts, jazz, recitals, and lectures, many of them at the Buxton Opera House on Water Street.

Shopping

You'll find a wide variety of stores in Buxton, especially around Spring Gardens, the main shopping street. Stores in the **Cavendish Arcade** (⊠ The Crescent), on the site of the old thermal baths, sell a pleasing range of antiques, fashion, cosmetics, and leather-goods in stylish surroundings. **Ratcliffe's** (⊠ 7 Cavendish Circus, ☎ 01298/23993) specializes in fine silver cutlery. A local **market** is held in Buxton every Tuesday and Saturday.

En Route Heading southeast from Buxton on the A6, you'll pass through the spectacular valleys of Ashwood Dale, Wyedale, and Monsal Dale before reaching Bakewell.

Bakewell

❷ *12 mi southeast of Buxton.*

Narrow streets and houses built out of the local gray-brown stone and a location on the winding River Wye make Bakewell extremely appealing. A medieval bridge crosses the river in five graceful arches, while the great age of the town is indicated by the 9th-century Saxon cross that still stands outside the parish church. Unfortunately, ceaseless traffic through the streets takes the shine off—though there's respite down on the quiet riverside paths. For a self-guided stroll around town, pick up a map from the tourist office, where the town trail begins; the walk takes about an hour. The helpful office has a museum that explains the terrain of the Peak District, with samples of the limestone and grit stone that composes the landscape.

The only day the crowds are really substantial is on market day (Monday), attended by local farmers, while a similarly popular traditional agricultural show is held in the first week of August. Bakewell is also the source of Bakewell pudding, said to have been created inadvertently when, sometime in the 19th century, a cook at the town's Rutland Arms Hotel dropped some rich cake mixture over jam tarts. Every local bakery and tearoom claims an original recipe—it's easy to spend a gustatory afternoon tasting rival puddings.

As in other parts of the Peak District, the inhabitants of Bakewell still practice the early summer custom of "well-dressing," when certain wells or springs are elaborately decorated or "dressed" with flowers. Although the floral designs usually incorporate biblical themes, they are just a Christian veneer over an ancient pagan celebration of the water's life-giving powers. In Bakewell, the lively ceremony is the focus of several days of festivities in June.

Dining and Lodging

£ ✕ **The Old Original Bakewell Pudding Shop.** Given the plethora of local rivals, it takes a bold establishment to claim its Bakewell puddings as "original," but there's certainly nothing wrong with those served here, eaten hot with custard or cream. The oak-beam dining room also turns out commendable main courses of poached salmon, black pudding, or chicken, and it's open until 9 PM in summer. ⊠ *The Square,* ☎ *01629/812193. MC, V. 6 PM winter, 9 PM summer.*

££–£££ ✕🏠 **Fischer's.** It would be hard to discover a more relaxing and con-
★ venient base from which to visit Bakewell and Chatsworth House, both a few miles' drive away. The menu at this converted manor house, an excellent "restaurant with rooms" run by the Fischer family, represents

a range of Continental cuisines, with some fine local produce. Fish is a specialty, often served with fresh pastas and delicate sauces; duck, lamb, and game receive similar care. There's a bistro menu in Café Max, which offers food—including Continental breakfast and afternoon tea—at slightly lower prices. Guest rooms are pretty, with antique pine furniture—three larger rooms, classed as luxury, have a separate sitting area. Breakfast is not included. ⊠ *Baslow Hall, Calver Rd., Baslow DE45 1RR,* ☎ *01246/583259,* FAX *01246/583818. 6 rooms. Restaurant, bar, room service. AE, DC, MC, V. No lunch Sat. in restaurant; Sun. dinner for residents only.*

Shopping

ELF Gems (⊠ King St., ☎ 01629/814944) is a wonderful source for jewelry and items made out of the rare Blue John stone, which is mined only in the Peak District. Artisan Edward Fisher has a passion for the stone, and, because Blue John is so brittle, he covers his hand-crafted pieces with liquid crystal to protect them.

Haddon Hall

★ ㉖ *2 mi southeast of Bakewell.*

Stately house scholar Hugo Montgomery-Massingberd has called Haddon Hall "the *beau idéal* of the English country house," and once you see this storybook medieval manor set along the River Wye, you may agree that it's one of the most romantic houses in Britain. Unlike other trophy homes that are marble Palladian monuments to the Grand Tour, Haddon Hall remains quintessentially English in appearance. Bristling with crenellations and stepped roofs and landscaped with rose gardens, it seems like a medieval miniature come to life. Famed as the setting—apocryphal or not—for the elopement of Dorothy Vernon with Sir John Manners in the 16th century (the lord of the manor disapproved of his daughter's choice, so the young couple eloped one night during a banquet, and as elopement was unheard of by nobles then, this tale became a popular Victorian-era love story), the house conjures up the "When Knighthood Was in Flower" days as no other does. Constructed by generations of the Vernon family in the Middle Ages, Haddon Hall passed into the ownership of the dukes of Rutland. After they moved their county seat to nearby Belvoir Castle, time and history literally passed the house by for centuries. In the early 20th century, however, the 9th duke awoke this sleeping beauty of a castle through a superlative restoration. The wider world saw the hall to impressive effect in Franco Zeffirelli's 1996 film *Jane Eyre,* much of which was filmed on location in the neighborhood; part of the 1999 *Elizabeth,* starring Cate Blanchett, was also filmed here.

The house is virtually unfurnished but has some treasures, including an impressive selection of tapestries and a famous 1932 painting of Haddon Hall by Rex Whistler. This painting shows the 9th duke and his son gazing at the house from a nearby hillside vantage point. Dorothy and Sir John are buried side by side in Bakewell's parish church. ⊠ *A6,* ☎ *01629/812855,* WEB *www.haddonhall.co.uk.* ᴁ *£5.75; parking 50p.* ☾ *Apr.–Sept., daily 10:30–5; Oct., Mon.–Thurs. 10:30–4:30.*

Chatsworth House

★ ㉗ *6 mi north of Haddon Hall, 4 mi northeast of Bakewell.*

Glorious parkland leads to Chatsworth House, ancestral home of the dukes of Devonshire and one of England's greatest country houses. A vast expanse of parkland, grazed by deer and sheep, sets off the Palladian-style elegance of "the Palace of the Peak." Originally an Elizabethan house, Chatsworth was conceived on a grand, even monumental, scale. Unfortunately, it was altered by various dukes over several generations starting in 1686, and the house's architecture now has a decidedly hodgepodge look. Death duties have taken a heavy toll on the interior grandeur, with duke after duke forced to sell off treasures to keep the place going. The house is surrounded by woods, elaborate colorful gardens, greenhouses, rock gardens, and the most famous water cascade in the kingdom—all designed by two great landscape artists, Capability Brown and, later, Joseph Paxton, an engineer as well as a brilliant gardener. Perennially popular with children, the farmyard area has milking demonstrations at 3 PM, and an adventure playground. Plan on at least a half day to explore the grounds; avoid going on Sunday, when the place is very crowded. A brass band plays on Sunday afternoons in July and August.

Inside are intricate carvings, Van Dyck portraits, superb furniture, and a few fabulous rooms, including the Sculpture Gallery, the Library, and the Blue Drawing Room, where you can see two of the most famous portraits in Britain, Sir Joshua Reynolds's *Georgiana, Duchess of Devonshire, and Her Baby,* and John Singer Sargent's enormous *Acheson Sisters.* The magnificent condition of much of the furnishings and decorations is due to the current duchess's supervision of an ongoing program of repair and restoration. ⊠ *Bakewell, off the B6012,* ☎ *01246/582204,* WEB *www.chatsworth-house.co.uk.* ⌨ *House and gardens £7; gardens only £4; farmyard and adventure playground £3.50; parking £1.* ☉ *House, garden, farmyard, adventure playground: mid-Mar.–Oct., daily 11–4:30.*

Matlock

28 *8 mi south of Chatsworth, 8 mi southeast of Bakewell.*

In the heart of the Derbyshire Dales, Matlock and its near neighbor Matlock Bath are former spa towns compressed into a narrow gorge on the River Derwent. Some surviving Regency buildings in Matlock still testify to its former importance, although it's less impressive an ensemble than that presented by Buxton. The surroundings, however, are particularly beautiful. The **Matlock River Illuminations,** a flotilla of lighted boats shimmering after dark along the still waters of the river, takes place on weekends mid-August–mid-October.

At Matlock Bath, 2 mi south of Matlock, river and valley views unfold from the curving line of buildings that makes up the village. Aside from riverside strolls, the major attraction is the cable-car ride across the River Derwent that takes you to the bosky **Heights of Abraham Country Park and Caverns** on the crags above, with a visitor center and café. The all-inclusive ticket allows access into the 60-acre park, where there are woodland walks and nature trails, as well as entry to a cavern and a guided descent into an old lead mine, where 16th-century workers once toiled by candlelight. ⊠ *A6, Matlock Bath,* ☎ *01629/582365,* WEB *www.heights-of-abraham.co.uk.* ⌨ *£6.80.* ☉ *Cable car and visitor center Easter–Oct., daily 10–5, later in July–Aug.; also on winter weekends, call for details.*

Dining and Lodging

£££ ✗🏨 **Riber Hall.** This partly Elizabethan, partly Jacobean manor-house
★ hotel is a listed historic building, perched above the town and awash with romantic resonance. The half-timber bedrooms have been decorated with antiques, flowers, and four-poster beds, in keeping with the inn's origins; some baths have whirlpool tubs. The garden is particularly beautiful, and from the terrace it's easy to imagine you've stepped

back in time. The restaurant serves imaginative, seasonal dishes with superbly fresh ingredients, whose inspiration is drawn from modern French cuisine—expect plenty of flavor and careful presentation. There's a daily vegetarian menu. ⊠ *Off A615, DE4 5JU,* ☎ *01629/582795,* FAX *01629/580475,* WEB *www.riber-hall.co.uk. 14 rooms. Restaurant, lobby lounge, room service, tennis court. AE, DC, MC, V.*

Outdoor Activities and Sports

One of the major trails in the Peak District is the **High Peak Trail,** which runs for 17 mi from Cromford (south of Matlock Bath) to Dowlow, following the route of an old railway. For information, guidebooks, guide services, and maps, contact the Peak District National Park Office (☎ 01629/814321).

Castleton

🟢 *24 mi northwest of Matlock, 9 mi northeast of Buxton.*

The most famous manifestations of the peculiar geology of the Peak District are to be found around the attractive town of Castleton, in Hope Valley. The limestone caverns bring visitors from far and wide, which means that Castleton shows a certain commercialization and tends to be crowded in the peak season. The town has a long pedigree and was probably first established by Henry II in the mid-12th century. It was Henry II who in 1176 added the square tower to the Norman **Peveril Castle,** whose ruins occupy a dramatic crag above the town. The castle has superb views—from here you can clearly see a curving section of the medieval defensive earthworks still visible in the town center below. ⊠ *Market Pl., A1687,* ☎ *01433/620613,* WEB *www.english-heritage.org.uk.* 🎟 *£2.30.* ☉ *Apr.–Sept., daily 10–6; Oct., daily 10–5; Nov.–Mar., Wed.–Sun. 10–4.*

Peveril Castle is protected on its west side by a 230-ft-deep gorge formed by a collapsed cave. The entire town is riddled with such caves, and in the massive **Peak Cavern**—reputedly Derbyshire's largest natural cave—rope-making has been done on a great ropewalk for more than 400 years. You can also see the remains of a prehistoric village that has been excavated here. ☎ *01433/620285,* WEB *www.peakcavern.co.uk.* 🎟 *£5.* ☉ *Apr.–Oct., daily 10–5; Nov.–Mar., weekends 10–5; last tour at 4.*

The Castleton area has a number of caves and mines open to the public, including some former lead mines and Blue John mines (amethystine spar; the unusual name is a local corruption of the French *bleu-jaune*). The most exciting by far is **Speedwell Cavern,** where 105 slippery steps lead down to old lead-mine tunnels, blasted out by 19th-century miners. Here you transfer to a small boat for the claustrophobic ¼-mi chug through an illuminated access tunnel to the cavern itself. At this point you're 600 ft underground, in the deepest public-access cave in Britain, with views farther down to the so-called "Bottomless Pit," a water-filled cavern into which the miners used to dump their blasted limestone debris. Speedwell Cavern is at the bottom of Winnats Pass, 1 mi west of Castleton. ⊠ *Winnats Pass,* ☎ *01433/620512,* WEB *www.speedwellcavern.co.uk.* 🎟 *£5.50.* ☉ *Apr.–Oct., daily 9:30–5:30; Nov.–Mar., daily 10–5; last tour 45 min before closing.*

Lodging

£££ 🏨 **Ye Olde Nag's Head.** With a name like this it could only be a 17th-century coaching inn. The small, individually run hotel in the middle of Castleton is a little too chintzy-floral for its own good, but guest rooms (a few with four-posters) are certainly comfortable enough and some have views of the castle. Bar meals are adventurous; there's also dining in the more formal restaurant—at its best value when taken as

part of a weekend dinner, bed, and breakfast package. ⊠ *Cross St.,
S30 2WH,* ☎ *01433/620248,* FAX *01433/621604. 8 rooms. Restaurant,
bar. AE, DC, MC, V.*

£ ⌂ **Bargate Cottage.** This cottage dating to 1650, at the top of Market Place opposite the church, is one of Castleton's B&B treasures. Kindly owners scatter rag dolls and teddy bears with abandon, and the cutesy oak-beam rooms have been converted to incorporate shower cubicles, sinks, TVs, and tea–coffeemaking facilities. Breakfast is served communally downstairs, with the host very much in command, dispensing fried breakfasts, bonhomie, and hiking advice. ⊠ *Market Pl., S30 2WG,* ☎ *01433/620201,* FAX *01433/621739. 4 rooms. No credit cards.*

En Route   Heading northwest to Edale, the most spectacular route is over **Winnats Pass,** an eye-opening drive through a narrow, boulder-strewn valley. Beyond are the tops of Mam Tor (where there's a lookout point) and the hamlet of Barber Booth, after which you'll run into Edale.

Edale

❸⓿ *5 mi north of Castleton.*

At Edale, you're truly in the Peak District wilds. It's a sleepy, straggling village in the shadow of Mam Tor and Lose Hill and the moorlands of Kinder Scout (2,088 ft), set among some of the most breathtaking scenery in Derbyshire. Britain can show little wilder scenery than the sight of Kinder Scout, with its ragged edges of grit stone and its seemingly interminable leagues of heather and peat. Late summer brings a covering of reddish-purple as the heather flowers, but the time to really appreciate the somber beauties of Kinder and its neighbors is in late autumn or early winter, when the clouds hang low and every gully seems to accentuate the brooding spirit of the moor.

An extremely popular walking center, Edale is the starting point of the 250-mi **Pennine Way,** which crosses Kinder Scout in its early stages. If you plan to attempt this, seek local advice first, because bad weather can make the walk treacherous. However, there are several much shorter routes into the Edale valley, like the 8-mi route west to Hayfield, which will give you a taste of the dramatic local scenery.

The **Old Nag's Head** (☎ 01433/670291) at the top of the village has marked the official start of the Pennine Way since 1965. Call in at the Hiker's Bar, score a place by the fire, and tuck into hearty bar meals and warming hot toddies. In winter, whenever this pub is closed (two days a week), the Ramblers' Inn, at the other end of the village, is open.

In the village, the Edale **National Park Information Centre** has maps, guides, and information on all the walks in the area. There's limited accommodation in the village (all B&B style), but the information center can provide a list of possibilities, or point you toward the local youth hostel. ☎ *01433/670207,* WEB *www.peakdistrict.org.* ☉ *Daily 9–1 and 2–5:30; Nov.–Mar., closes at 5.*

LANCASHIRE AND THE PEAKS A TO Z

To research prices, get advice from other travelers, and book travel arrangements, visit www.fodors.com.

AIRPORTS

Manchester Airport, about 10 mi south of the city, is the third largest airport in the country. About 100 airlines serve 175 international and United Kingdom destinations. M56 north leads directly into Manchester via the A5103.

To reach the city center, take the Airport Rail Link that runs from the airport's train station to Piccadilly Railway Station. Trains run every six minutes early in the morning to late at night, seven days a week. Travel time is 25 minutes and the cost is £2.50 (£2.75 in peak hours, before 9:30 AM). There's also a bus service that leaves the airport every 15–30 minutes, 6 AM–10:45 PM, with reduced service after 7 PM. It costs £2 and takes almost an hour to reach Piccadilly Gardens Bus Station; for more information, call GMPTE. A taxi from the airport to Manchester city center costs approximately £12.

➤ AIRPORT INFORMATION: **Airport Rail Link** (☎ 0345/484950). **GMPTE information line** (☎ 0161/228–7811, WEB www.gmpte.gov.uk). **Manchester Airport** (✉ near Junctions 5 and 6 of M56, ☎ 0161/489–3000, WEB www.manairport.co.uk). **Piccadilly Station** (☎ 0345/484950).

BIKE TRAVEL

In an effort to get people out of their cars, special Peak District National Park Hire Centres rent bikes of all descriptions at reasonable rates. The service is restricted to weekends in winter and is popular in summer, so call ahead to reserve. Information is available directly from the centers. The most accessible centers are listed below, or contact any Peak District National Park Information Centre.

➤ BIKE RENTALS: **Peak District National Park Hire Centres** (✉ Hayfield, ☎ 01663/746222; ✉ Parsley Hay, ☎ 01298/84493; ✉ Middleton Top, ☎ 01629/823204; WEB www.peakdistrict.org).

BUS TRAVEL

National Express serves the region from London's Victoria Coach Station. Average travel time to Manchester or Liverpool is four hours. To reach Matlock, Bakewell, and Buxton you can take a bus from London to Derby and change to the TransPeak bus service, though you might find it more convenient to travel first to Manchester.

Chorlton Street Coach Station, a few hundred yards west of Piccadilly Train Station in Manchester's city center, is the main bus station for regional and long-distance buses. For general enquiries, call National Public Transport. Most local buses leave from Piccadilly Gardens Bus Station, the hub of the urban bus network. Timetables can be obtained from the Travel Shop in the row of shops flanking Piccadilly Gardens, but it's best to ask each bus driver about the fare. The Centreline Bus service transports passengers, free of charge, around the city center. It runs every 10 minutes from 7 AM to 6:30 PM Monday–Saturday.

In Liverpool, regional and long-distance National Express coaches use the Norton Street Coach Station Eastbound and cross-river buses depart from Queen Square Bus Station. Paradise Street Bus Station has southbound services.

Bus R1 runs directly to Buxton from Manchester's Chorlton Street Coach Station station every two hours during the day. In addition, the TransPeak service between Manchester and Derby calls at all major Peak District destinations, with departures every two hours from Manchester's Chorlton Street Bus Station. Wayfarer tickets are available for 24-hour weekdays (£6.75) or 48-hour weekends (£10.25). For local bus information in the Buxton and Peak District area, call Derbyshire Bus Line.

FARES AND SCHEDULES

For Manchester bus information, call the Greater Manchester Passenger Transport Executive (GMPTE) information line. For the latest timetable information for local bus, train, and ferry services in Liverpool, call the Mersey Travel Line, or visit one of the information centers located at Queen Square Bus Station, Pier Head, or Paradise Street Bus Station. The *Peak District Timetable* (75p) covers all local public transportation services and is available from tourist offices in the area.

➤ BUS INFORMATION: **Chorlton Street Coach Station** (✉ Chorlton and Bloom Sts., ☎ 0870/580–8080). **Derbyshire Bus Line** (☎ 01332/292200). **GMPTE information line** (☎ 0161/228–7811, WEB www.gmpte.gov.uk). **Mersey Travel Line** (☎ 0151/236–7676). **Metrolink** (☎ 0161/205–2000). **National Express** (☎ 0990/808080, WEB www.gobycoach.com). **National Public Transport** (☎ 0870/608–2608). **Norton Street Coach Station** (☎ 0870/580–8080).

CAR RENTAL

➤ LOCAL AGENCIES: **Avis** (✉ 1 Ducie St., Manchester, ☎ 0161/236–6716; 0161/436–2020 airport). **Budget Rent-a-Car** (✉ 660 Chester Rd., Old Trafford, ☎ 0161/877–5555; 0161/499–3042 airport). **Europcar** (✉ York St., Piccadilly Plaza, Manchester, ☎ 0161/832–4114; 0161/436–2200 airport). **Hertz** (✉ 31 Aytoun St., Manchester, ☎ 0161/236–2747; 0161/437–8208 airport).

CAR TRAVEL

To reach Manchester from London, take M1 north to M6, leaving M6 at exit 21a and joining M62 east, which becomes M602 as it enters Greater Manchester. M60 is the ring road around Manchester. Liverpool is reached by leaving M6 at the same junction, exit 21a, and following M62 west into the city. Travel time to Manchester or Liverpool is about 3–3½ hours. Expect heavy traffic out of London on weekends to all destinations in the Northwest; construction work also often slows progress on M6.

Driving from London to the Peak District, stay on the M1 until you reach exit 29, then head west via the A617/A619/A6 to Buxton. From Manchester, take the A6 southeast via Stockport to Buxton, about an hour's drive.

ROAD CONDITIONS

Roads within the region are generally very good, although traffic can get bogged down on M6. In both Manchester and Liverpool, you're advised to sightsee on foot—leave your car at your hotel to avoid parking problems in the city centers. In the Peak District, park in signposted parking lots whenever possible and expect heavy summer traffic. In winter keep an ear out for the weather forecast; moorland roads can quickly become impassable.

EMBASSIES AND CONSULATES

➤ AUSTRALIAN CONSULATE: (✉ Chatsworth House, Lever St., Manchester, ☎ 0161/228–1344).

EMERGENCIES

➤ EMERGENCY SERVICES: **Ambulance, fire, police** (☎ 999).
➤ HOSPITALS: **Royal Liverpool Hospital** (✉ Prescot St., Liverpool, ☎ 0151/706–2000). **Manchester Royal Infirmary & Royal Eye Hospital** (✉ Oxford Rd., ☎ 0161/276–1234).

NATIONAL PARK

The Peak District National Park head office is in Buxton. There are also regional offices.

➤ CONTACTS: **Peak District National Park** head office (✉ Baslow Rd., Bakewell, DE45 1AE, ☎ 01629/816200, WEB www.peakdistrict.org). **Bakewell** (☎ 01629/813227). **Buxton** (☎ 01298/25106). **Castleton** (☎ 01433/620679). **Edale** (☎ 01433/670207). **Matlock** (☎ 01629/583388). **Matlock Bath** (☎ 01629/55082).

TOURS

BOAT TOURS

City Centre Cruises offers tours on a barge traveling from Castlefield in Manchester city center to the renovated Salford Quays.

➤ FEES AND SCHEDULES: **City Centre Cruises** (☎ 0161/902–0222, WEB www.citycentrecruises.co.uk).

BUS TOURS

Cavern City Tours offers a Beatles Magical Mystery Tour of Liverpool, departing from Albert Dock daily at 2:20, with additional morning tours on Saturday in summer. The two-hour bus tour (£10) runs past John Lennon's childhood home, local schools attended by the Beatles, and other significant mop-top landmarks.

Tourist offices in Manchester and Liverpool can book visitors on short city coach tours that cover all the main sights.

➤ FEES AND SCHEDULES: **Cavern City Tours** (✉ Mathew St., Liverpool, ☎ 0151/236–9091).

WALKING TOURS

In Manchester, Blue Badge Guides has dozens of interesting tours, including the Ghost Pub Walk, Manchester's Victorian Underground, and daily one-hour walking tours of the city center. Tickets are also available at the Manchester Visitor Centre. Castlefield Guided Tour Service has one-hour tours of the Castlefield Urban Heritage Park, including the site of the original Roman fort and redevelopment projects.

The Liverpool Heritage Walk is a self-guided 7½-mi walk through Liverpool city center, following 75 metal markers that point out sights of historic and cultural interest. An accompanying guidebook is available from either of the Liverpool Tourist Information centers.

➤ FEES AND SCHEDULES: **Blue Badge Guides** (☎ 0161/440–0277 or 0161/969–5522 to book). **Castlefield Guided Tour Service** (☎ 0161/834–4026, WEB www.castlefield.org.uk). **Liverpool Tourist Information Centre** (✉ Queen Sq., ☎ 0906/680–6886; ✉ Atlantic Pavilion, Albert Dock). **Manchester Visitor Centre** (✉ Town Hall Extension, Lloyd St., ☎ 0161/234–3157, WEB www.manchester.gov.uk/visitorcentre).

TRAIN TRAVEL

Virgin Trains serves the region from London's Euston Station. Direct service to Manchester and Liverpool takes approximately 3 hours. To reach Buxton from London take the Manchester train and switch at Stockport.

There are trains between Manchester's Piccadilly Station and Liverpool's Lime Street every half hour during the day; the trip takes approximately 50 minutes. Local service—one train an hour—from Manchester to Buxton takes one hour. In all instances, call National Rail Inquiries for timetable information.

➤ TRAIN INFORMATION: **National Rail Inquiries** (☎ 08457/484950, WEB www.railtrack.co.uk). **Virgin Trains** (☎ 08457/222333, WEB www.virgintrains.co.uk).

TRAM TRAVEL

In Manchester, Metrolink electric tram service runs through the city center and out to the suburbs. The Eccles extension has convenient stops for the Lowry (Broadway) and for the Manchester United Stadium (Old Trafford). Trams run daily 7:30 AM–11:30 PM, Sunday until 10:30 PM. Buy tickets, which start at 80p, from the machines on the platforms.

➤ TRAM INFORMATION: **Metrolink** (☎ 0161/205–2000, WEB www.gmpte.gov.uk).

TRAVEL AGENCIES

➤ LOCAL AGENT REFERRALS: **American Express** (✉ 54 Lord St., Liverpool, ☎ 0151/708–9202; ✉ 10–12 St Mary's Gate, Manchester, ☎ 0161/833–0121). **Thomas Cook** (✉ 55 Lord St., Liverpool, ☎ 0151/236–1951; ✉ 23 Market St., Manchester, ☎ 0161/833–1110).

VISITOR INFORMATION

General information about the region is available from the North West Tourist Board or from the Manchester Visitor Centre. Local tourist information offices are listed below by town.

➤ TOURIST INFORMATION: **North West Tourist Board** (✉ Swan House, Swan Meadow Rd., Wigan Pier, Wigan WN3 5BB, ☎ 01942/821222, WEB www.visitnorthwest.com). **Peak District** (WEB www.peakdistrict-tourism.gov.uk). **Bakewell** (✉ Old Market Hall, Bridge St., DE4 1DS, ☎ 01629/813227). **Buxton** (✉ The Crescent, SK17 6BQ, ☎ 01298/25106). **Liverpool** (✉ Queen Sq., L1 1RG, ☎ 0906/680–6886; ✉ Atlantic Pavilion, Albert Dock, L1 1RG; WEB www.visitliverpool.com). **Manchester Visitor Centre** (✉ Town Hall Extension, Lloyd St., M60 2LA, ☎ 0161/234–3157, WEB www.manchester.gov.uk/visitorcentre; ✉ International Arrivals Hall, Manchester Airport Terminal 1, ☎ 0161/436–3344; ✉ International Arrivals Hall, Manchester Airport Terminal 2, ☎ 0161/489–6412). **Matlock** (✉ The Pavilion, Matlock Bath, DE4 3NR, ☎ 01629/55082).

12 THE LAKE DISTRICT

WINDERMERE, GRASMERE, KENDAL, KESWICK

"Let nature be your teacher . . ."
Wordsworth's ideal comes true in this fabled region of jagged mountains, waterfalls, wooded valleys, and stone-built villages. The Lake District is a contour map come to life, a stunning natural park beloved by outdoor enthusiasts. Some malicious statisticians allot to it about 250 rainy days a year, but when the sun breaks through and the surfaces of the lakes smile benignly, it is an away-from-it-all place to remember. Follow in the footsteps of Coleridge, De Quincey, Ruskin, and Wordsworth; everywhere you'll find specific locations that inspired some of their great poems and thoughts.

T HE POETS WORDSWORTH AND COLERIDGE, and other English men and women of letters, found the Lake District an inspiring setting for their work and fashion, and thousands of visitors have followed ever since. The Lake District, created in the 1950s as a national park from parts of the counties of Cumberland, Westmorland, and Lancashire, combines so much that is magnificent in mountain, lake, and dales that new and entrancing vistas open out at each corner of the road. No mountains in Britain are finer in outline or give a greater impression of majesty; deeper and bluer lakes can be found, but none that fit so readily into the surrounding scene.

Updated by Ed Glinert

Perhaps it is only natural that an area so blessed with natural beauty should have become linked with so many prominent figures in English literature. It may have all started on April 15, 1802, when William Wordsworth and his sister Dorothy were walking in the woods of Gowbarrow Park just above Aira Force, and Dorothy happened to remark that she had never seen "daffodils so beautiful." Two years later Wordsworth was inspired by his sister's words to write one of the best-known lyric poems in English, "I Wandered Lonely as a Cloud." In turn, many of the English romantic poets also came to the region and were inspired by its beauty. In addition to Wordsworth, other literary figures who made their homes in the region include Samuel Taylor Coleridge, Thomas De Quincey, Robert Southey, John Ruskin, Matthew Arnold, and later, Hugh Walpole, and the children's writers Arthur Ransome and Beatrix Potter, who set her beloved stories of Squirrel Nutkin and Mrs. Tiggy-Winkle in the hills and dales of this region.

The Lake District measures roughly 35 square mi and holds 16 major lakes and countless smaller stretches of water; it can be crossed by car in about an hour. Its mountains are not high by international standards—Scafell Pike, England's highest peak, is only 3,210 ft above sea level—but they are very tricky to climb, and the weather can be even more challenging. In spring, many of the higher summits remain snow-capped long after the weather below has turned mild. The Lake District can be one of Britain's most charming reservoirs of calm. Unfortunately, its calm is shattered in high season, when the district becomes far too popular for its own good. A little lakeside town, however appealing it may otherwise be, loses its charm when its narrow streets are clogged with cars and tour buses. Similarly, the walks and hiking trails that crisscross the region seem very much less inviting when you find yourself sharing them with a crowd that churns the grass into a quagmire. With a bit of effort and your own two feet, you will however be able to escape the crowds usually.

Some basic terminology will help you here: if someone gives you directions to walk along the "beck" to the "force" and then climb the "fell" to the "tarn," you've just been told to hike along the stream or river (beck) to the waterfall (force) before climbing the hill or mountain (fell) to reach the lake (tarn). Moreover, town or place names in the Lake District can also refer to the lake on which they stand. There's a Windermere village on the lake of that name, for example. And to confuse matters, locals would never say Lake Windermere but just Windermere, since "mere" means lake in Old English.

Off-season visits here can be a real treat. All those little inns and bed-and-breakfasts that turn away crowds in summer are desperate for business the rest of the year (and their rates drop accordingly). It's not an easy task to avail yourself of a succession of sunny days in the Lake

District, but when the sun descends upon this vast natural reserve, it is truly a place to remember.

Pleasures and Pastimes

Dining

The region of Cumbria, which encompasses the Lake District, is noted for its good country food. Dishes center on the local lamb, beef, game, and fish, especially salmon, and river and lake trout hooked from the district's freshwater streams and lakes. Cumberland sausage, a thick, meaty pork sausage, is another regional specialty. Look out, too, for locally baked bread, cake, pastries, gingerbread, and scones.

CATEGORY	COST*
££££	over £22
£££	£16–£22
££	£9–£15
£	under £9

per person for a main course at dinner

Festivals and Folk Sports

The Lake District hosts some of Britain's most unusual country festivals, featuring traditional music, sports, and entertainment. Major festivals are the Cockermouth and Keswick carnivals (June), Ambleside Rushbearing (August) and Sports (July), Grasmere Rushbearing (August) and Sports (August), and Kendal Folk Festival (August). Folk sports, often the highlights at these local shows, include Cumberland and Westmorland wrestling, a variety of traditional English wrestling in which the opponents must maintain a grip around each other's body. Fell (cross-country) running is also popular in these parts, with the peaks themselves often forming part of the race route. A calendar of events is available at tourist information centers.

Lodging

If the front hall has a row of muddy boots, you'll know you've made the right choice for a hostelry in the Lake District. The best of these hotels have a marvelous atmosphere where people eat hugely and loll about in front of roaring fires in the evenings, sharing an almost religious dedication to the mountains. You'll find everything from small country inns to grand lakeside hotels, though the mainstay of the region's accommodations is the local bed-and-breakfast. These range from the house on Main Street renting out one room to farmhouses with an entire wing to spare. Most country hotels and B&Bs gladly cater to hikers and climbers and can provide you with on-the-spot information and advice. There's also a great camaraderie among walkers in the Lake District's network of youth hostels, which are in fact open to anyone with a membership card from their home country's hostel association. Wherever you stay, be sure to book well in advance in summer. In winter many places close for a month or two.

CATEGORY	COST*
££££	over £150
£££	£100–£150
££	£60–£100
£	under £60

All prices are for two people sharing a standard double room, including service, breakfast, and VAT.

Walking

The Lake District is rugged and spectacular, and to see it at its best you must get out of the car and walk through at least part of the region. There's enough variation in the area to suit all tastes, from gentle rambles in the vicinity of the most popular towns and villages to full-scale hikes and climbs up some of England's most impressive peaks. Information boards are posted at parking lots throughout the region pointing out the possibilities. For tougher hikes, the famous Old Man of Coniston, the Langdale Pikes, Scafell Pike, Skiddaw, and Helvellyn are all accessible, though for these you'll need a certain amount of walking experience and a great deal of energy. The longest trail, the Cumbria Way (70 mi), crosses the whole of the Lake District, starting at the market town of Ulverston and finishing at Carlisle. Guidebooks to this and other lakeland walks are available in bookstores throughout the region.

For short, local walks it's always best to consult the tourist information centers: those at Ambleside, Cockermouth, Grasmere, Kendal, Keswick, and Windermere can provide maps and experienced advice. The other main sources of information are the various Lake District National Park information centers; the head office is at Brockhole, near Windermere. If you're sufficiently experienced and want to climb the higher and harder peaks, then you'll probably want to hook up with a climbing organization, of which there are several in the region.

Exploring the Lake District

The Lake District is in the northwest of England, north of the industrial belt along the River Mersey that stretches from Liverpool to Manchester, and south of the southwestern section of Scotland. The major gateway from the south is Kendal. From the north, the gateway is Penrith. Both are on the M6 motorway. The Lake District National Park breaks into two reasonably distinct sections. The southern lakes and valleys contain the most popular destinations in the entire park, incorporating the largest body of water, Windermere, as well as most of what are considered the quintessential lakeland towns and villages: Kendal, Bowness, Ambleside, Grasmere, Elterwater, Coniston, and Hawkshead. To the north, the landscape opens out across the bleaker fells to reveal challenging (and spectacular) walking country. Here, in the northern lakes, south of Keswick and Cockermouth, you have the best chance to get away from the crowds.

Numbers in the text correspond to numbers in the margin and on the Lake District map.

Great Itineraries

You could spend a lifetime tramping the hills, valleys, and fells of the Lake District, or, in three days, you could drive through the major towns and villages. The key is not to try to see or do too much in too short a time. Instead, you could pick one area—the southern lakes, for example—and spend some time walking, taking a boat out on the water, and relaxing at the inns. With five days, you would have the opportunity to stay the night in towns in both southern and northern lakeland. If you are traveling by public transportation (scarce at the best of times, much reduced in winter), many places will be off-limits.

IF YOU HAVE 3 DAYS
Although three days is scarcely adequate to tour the Lake District, if you must tour both south and north lakes together, start in **Kendal** ①. After you've looked around the market town, move on to ⊞ **Windermere and Bowness-on-Windermere** ②, where you spend the first night. You'll have time to take a boat trip on the lake that afternoon up to pretty **Ambleside** ④. Next day, cross Windermere by ferry, and drive through **Hawkshead** ⑨ and **Coniston** ⑧ to rural **Elterwater** ⑦, where you can have lunch in one of the fine walkers' inns thereabouts. The

The Lake District

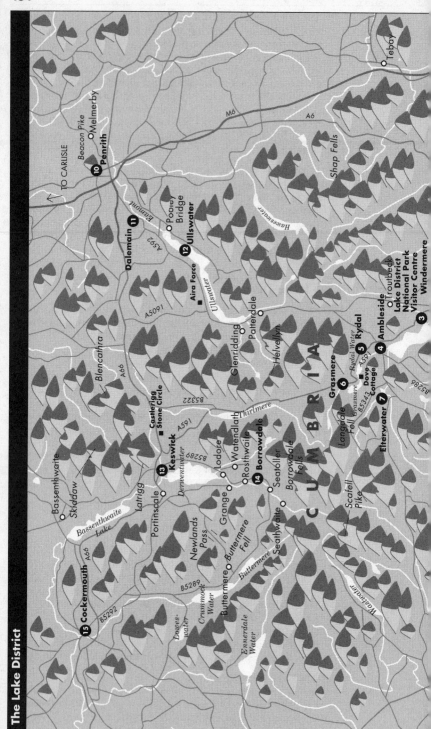

TO CARLISLE

Beacon Pike
Melmerby
Penrith **10**

Dalemain 11

A592 Eamont

Pooley **11** Bridge
Ullswater
12

Aira Force ■
A5091

Ullswater

Glenridding
Patterdale

Helvellyn

Haweswater

M6
A6

Shap Fells

Tebay

Troutbeck
Ambleside
Lake District
National Park
Visitor Centre
Windermere
3

Rydal **5**
B5343 **4**
Grasmere **6**
Rydal Water
A591
Dove Cottage
Grasmere
Longdale Fell
Elterwater **7**
B5286

Blencathra
A66

Skiddaw
Bassenthwaite

Latrigg

Castlerigg
Stone Circle ■
Keswick
13
Derwentwater
Lodore
Grange
Portinscale

Bassenthwaite
Lake

Newlands Pass

B5289
Buttermere
Buttermere
Fell
Crummock
Water

Cockermouth **13**

B5292

Loweswater

Dove-
dale

Ennerdale
Water

B5322
A591
Thirlmere
Watendlath
Rosthwaite
Borrowdale
14
Seatoller
Borrowdale
Fells
Seathwaite

Scafell
Pike

C U M B R I A

Wastwater

The Lake District

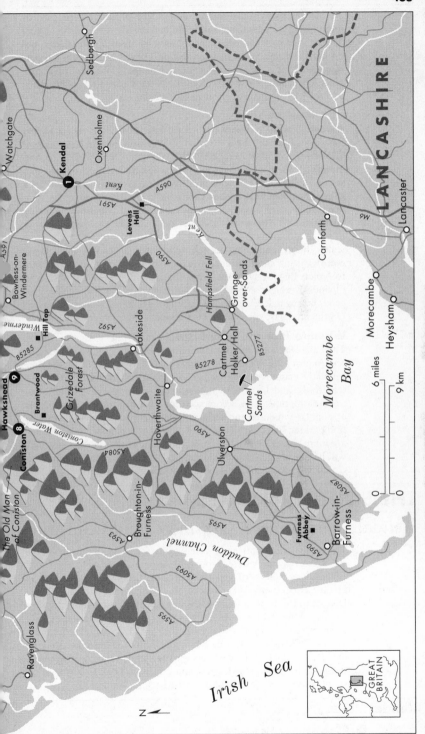

afternoon is spent in **Grasmere** ⑥ and nearby **Rydal** ⑤ touring the various destinations associated with William Wordsworth, such as Rydal Mount and Dove Cottage. Your second night is in 🎦 **Keswick** ⑬, and on the third day, you can loop around Derwentwater through **Borrowdale** ⑭ and isolated Seatoller to **Cockermouth** ⑮, Wordsworth's birthplace. From there it's an easy drive east to the market town of **Penrith** ⑩ and the M6 motorway (or north to Carlisle).

IF YOU HAVE 5 DAYS

Kendal ①, in the southern part of the Lake District, marks the starting point, followed by a drive to 🎦 **Windermere and Bowness-on-Windermere** ② and a cruise on the lake that afternoon up to **Ambleside** ④. The next morning you can mosey around the shops and museums in Bowness before venturing on to Brockhole and the **Lake District National Park Visitor Centre** ③. In the afternoon, cross Windermere by ferry, stopping in **Hawkshead** ⑨ and **Coniston** ⑧, before ending up at 🎦 **Elterwater** ⑦. This is a splendid place to spend the night in peaceful rural surroundings, and you can take in one of the local walks the next morning. Lunch and that night can be in 🎦 **Grasmere** ⑥, just a short distance away, giving you plenty of opportunity to explore that lovely village. From Grasmere, 🎦 **Keswick** ⑬ is the next obvious overnight stop, allowing you to make a day trip into the gorgeous Borrowdale Valley and perhaps take a boat trip on Derwentwater. On the final day, you can see **Cockermouth** ⑮ and **Penrith** ⑩.

When to Tour the Lake District

The Lake District is one of the rainiest areas in Britain, but June, July, and August hold the best guarantees of fine weather and are the time for all the major festivals. You will, however, be sharing the roads, hotels, trails, and lakes with thousands of other people. If you must travel at this time, book accommodations well in advance, turn up early at popular museums and attractions, and expect to have to work to find parking space. April and May, as well as September and October, are more clement visiting seasons. Later and earlier in the year, there will be more space and freedom, but you will find many attractions closed and snow on high ground, precluding any serious walking.

THE SOUTHERN LAKES

Kendal, Windermere, Grasmere, and Coniston

The southern lakes offer a diverse set of attractions, ranging from the small resort towns clustered around Windermere, England's largest lake, to hideaway valleys, rugged walking centers, and monuments rich in literary associations. What's more, this is the easiest part of the Lake District to reach, with Kendal, the largest town, just a short distance from the M6 motorway. An obvious route from Kendal takes in Windermere, the natural touring center for this whole area, before moving north through Ambleside and Rydal Water to Grasmere. Some of the loveliest of all lakeland scenery is to be found by then turning south, through Elterwater, Hawkshead, and Coniston. From Coniston, it's a simple drive south to the coast or east back to Windermere.

Kendal

❶ *70 mi north of Manchester.*

The natural southern gateway to the Lake District is the ancient town of Kendal. One of the most important textile centers in northern England before the Industrial Revolution, Kendal is an attractive place, cut through by the bubbling River Kent and with gray stone houses framed by the hills behind. So close are these hills that, with the aid of a walking guide picked up from the tourist information center, you can be astride the tops within an hour. Be sure to pack a slab of Kendal Mintcake, the renowned local peppermint candy, which all British walkers and climbers swear by to provide them with energy when the going gets tough. It's on sale in every gift shop in town.

In town, away from the busy main road, you'll discover quiet, narrow, winding streets known locally as "ginnels," and charming courtyards, many dating from medieval times. There's been a **market** (⊠ Market Pl. off Stricklandgate) held in Kendal since 1189. The old market hall has now been converted into an indoor shopping center, though outdoor stalls still do business here every Wednesday and Saturday.

One of the Lake District's finest museums is on the grounds of **Abbot Hall,** which was built as a private house in 1759. The **Museum of Lakeland Life and Industry,** in the former stable block, includes fascinating exhibits on blacksmithing, wheelwrighting, farming, weaving, printing, local architecture and interiors, and regional customs. A room is devoted to the curious life of Arthur Ransome (1884–1967), author of the *Swallows and Amazons* series of children's books, set in Coniston. In the main building is the **Art Gallery,** with works by Victorian artist and critic John Ruskin, who lived near Coniston, and by 18th-century portrait painter George Romney, who worked (and died) in Kendal. The gallery also holds a collection of watercolors of the region. There's a store, too, selling high-quality woven goods, tiles, ceramics, and glass, and there's an excellent café. Abbot Hall is on the River Kent, adjacent to the parish church. ⊠ *Kirkland,* ☎ *01539/722464,* WEB *www.abbothall.org.uk.* 🖃 *Museum and gallery £4, museum only £3.* ☉ *Apr.– Oct., daily 10:30–5; Nov.–Mar., daily 10:30–4.*

The **Kendal Museum** of natural history and archaeology was first founded in 1796, moving into a former wool warehouse in 1913. It details splendidly the flora and fauna of the Lake District, including displays on Alfred Wainwright, the region's most avid chronicler of countryside matters, who died in 1991. His multivolume, handwritten Lake District walking guides are famous the world over. You can find them in every local book and gift shop. The museum is at the northern end of town, close to the train station. ⊠ *Station Rd.,* ☎ *01539/721374,* WEB *www.kendalmuseum.org.uk.* 🖃 *£3, £1 additional for a combined ticket with Abbot Hall.* ☉ *Apr.–Oct., Mon.–Sat. 10:30–5; Nov.–Mar., Mon.–Sat. 10:30–4.*

OFF THE
BEATEN PATH

LEVENS HALL – This 16th-century house, built by James Bellingham, is famous for its topiary garden, laid out in 1694 and probably the most distinctive in the world. With yew and box hedges cut into amazing coronet and chess-piece-like shapes, it seems a hallucinatory vision from *Alice's Adventures in Wonderland.* The house itself is notable for its ornate plasterwork and oak paneling. Levens Hall is just 4 mi south of Kendal, and local buses run here from the town. ⊠ *Levens Park, Levens, Off the A6,* ☎ *015395/60321,* WEB *www.levenshall.co.uk.* 🖃 *House and gardens £6, gardens only £4.50.* ☉ *Apr.–mid-Oct., Sun.–Thurs. noon–5, gardens open at 10; last admission at 4:30.*

Dining and Lodging

££ ✗ **The Moon.** More like a bistro than a restaurant, the Moon has a good
★ local reputation, won with quality homemade dishes on a menu that changes at least monthly. There's always a strong selection of vegetarian dishes, and the cooking can be adventurous, using Mediterranean and Asian flourishes at times. ⊠ *129 Highgate,* ☎ *01539/729254. MC, V. Closed Mon. No lunch.*

£ ✕ **Waterside Café.** In summer, grab one of the outdoor picnic tables, order from the healthy whole-food vegetarian menu: soups, bakes, and stews are the mainstay. Eat overlooking the tranquil Kent. Dinner is sometimes served on Friday nights (call for details), although for the full lakeland experience, inquire about rooms in their inexpensive vegetarian guest house. ⊠ *Waterside,* ☎ *01539/729743. No credit cards. Closed Sun. in winter. No dinner.*

£ ✕⊞ **Punch Bowl Inn.** Hidden along a country road in the hamlet of Crosthwaite, 5 mi west of Kendal. The Punch Bowl, formerly a 16th-century coaching inn, delights with its inspired food and simply decorated bedrooms. In a series of cozy, oak-beam dining rooms, Modern British menus are delivered with panache: fresh fish, local lamb, warming soups, and rich desserts all hit the spot. There are just three rooms, each equipped with a four-poster bed. Make sure you book well in advance. ⊠ *Crosthwaite, near Kendal, LA8 8HR, off A5074,* ☎ *015395/ 682375,* FAX *015395/688755,* WEB *www.punchbowl.fsnet.co.uk. 3 rooms. Restaurant. MC, V.*

Nightlife and the Arts

The **Brewery Arts Centre,** a converted brewery, holds an art gallery, a theater, a theater workshop, and a cinema. It also has an excellent coffee bar, a real-ale bar, and a health-food café open for lunch. In November, the center holds the annual **Mountain Film Festival,** with productions aimed at climbers and walkers. ⊠ *Highgate,* ☎ *01539/725133.* ⊞ *Free, except for special exhibitions.* ☉ *Mon.–Sat. 9 AM–11 PM.*

Shopping

Kendal has its most interesting stores tucked away in the quiet lanes and courtyards around Market Place, Finkle Street, and Stramongate. **Henry Roberts Bookshop** (⊠ 7 Stramongate, ☎ 01539/720425), in Kendal's oldest house (a 16th-century cottage), has a superb selection of regional books. The **Kentdale Rambler** (⊠ 34 Market Pl., ☎ 01539/ 729188) is the best local store for walking boots and equipment, maps, and guides, including Wainwright's illustrated guides. Four miles north of Kendal along the A591, **Peter Hall & Son** (⊠ Danes Rd., Staveley, ☎ 01539/821633) is a woodcraft workshop selling ornamental bowls and other attractive gifts, all made from local woods.

Windermere and Bowness-on-Windermere

★ ❷ *10 mi northwest of Kendal.*

For a natural touring base for the southern half of the Lake District, you don't need to look much farther than Windermere. When the railroad was extended here from Kendal in 1847, local officials named the new station after the lake to cash in on Windermere's reputation, already well established thanks to Wordsworth and the romantic poets. The town flourished, despite being a mile or so from the water, and such was the lake's popularity as a Victorian resort that the development eventually spread to envelop the old lakeside village of Bowness-on-Windermere as well. Of the two settlements, Bowness is the more attractive, but they are so close it matters little where you stay. Bus 599, leaving every 20 minutes in summer (hourly the rest of the year) from outside Windermere train station, links the two.

The New Hall Inn, dating from 1612, is better known as the **Hole in t' Wall** (⊠ Fallbarrow Rd., Bowness-on-Windermere), an atmospheric pub complete with slate floors and a flagstone courtyard. Its most famous landlord was Thomas Longmire, a 19th-century Cumbrian wrestler who won no fewer than 174 championship belts. Charles Dickens stayed at the inn in 1857 and described Longmire as a "quiet-looking giant."

The **Windermere Steamboat Museum** exhibits a remarkable collection of steam- and motor-powered yachts and launches. The *Dolly*, built around 1850, is one of the two oldest mechanically powered boats in the world. She was raised from the bottom of Ullswater in 1962, having lain there for 70 years. Among the many vessels on view are also Beatrix Potter's rowing boat and Arthur Ransome's sailing dinghy. ⊠ *Rayrigg Rd., Bowness-on-Windermere,* ☎ *015394/45565,* WEB *www.steamboat.co.uk.* ☎ *£3.40.* ☉ *Mid-Mar.–Oct., daily 10–5.*

Children (and not a few adults) might appreciate **The World of Beatrix Potter,** a three-dimensional presentation of some of her most famous characters, alongside videos of her stories. There are Beatrix Potter souvenirs here, and a tearoom, though frankly there's less commercialism in Potter's former home close to Hawkshead at Hill Top. ⊠ *The Old Laundry, Crag Brow, Bowness-on-Windermere,* ☎ *015394/88444,* WEB *www.hop-skip-jump.com.* ☎ *£3.25.* ☉ *Easter–Sept., daily 10–5:30; Oct.–Easter, daily 10–4:30. Closed 2 wks in Jan.*

The restored **Blackwell,** one of Britain's most notable houses in the Arts and Crafts style, opened in summer 2001 as a public art gallery displaying metalwork, textiles, pottery, and fabrics of the Arts and Crafts movement. Exhibitions include works of different periods, including contemporary crafts, that embody Arts and Crafts ideals. The house, designed by H. M. Baillie Scott from 1897 to 1900, overlooks Windermere. The museum is being developed by Abbot Hall Art Gallery. ⊠ *B5360, Windermere,* ☎ *1539/722464,* WEB *www.blackwell.org.uk.* ☎ *£4.50.* ☉ *July–Oct., daily 10–5; Nov.–Dec., daily 10–4.*

There are no sights in Windermere or Bowness to compete with that of the lake itself. At 11 mi long, 1½ mi wide, and 200 ft deep, **Windermere** fills a rocky gorge between steep, thickly wooded hills. The waters here make for superb fishing, especially for char, a rare kind of reddish lake trout. In summer, the lake is alive with all kinds of boats, and a trip on the water, particularly the round-trip from Bowness to Ambleside or down to Lakeside, is a wonderful way to spend a few summer hours.

Although the lake's marinas and piers have some charm, you can bypass the busier stretches of shoreline (and in summer they can be packed solid) by walking beyond the boathouses. Here, from among the pine trees, is a fine view across the lake. The car ferry (which also carries pedestrians) crosses the water at this point to reach Far Sawrey and the road to Hawkshead; the crossing takes a few minutes. ☎ *Car ferry £2 cars, 40p foot passengers.* ☉ *Ferries every 20 mins Mon.–Sat. 6:50 AM–9:50 PM, Sun. 9:10 AM–9:50 PM; winter until 8:50 PM.*

If you take a boat to Lakeside, you can not only strike off on the vintage Lakeside & Haverthwaite Railway, but there's a happy hour or so to be spent at the excellent **Aquarium of the Lakes,** right on the quayside, with informative wildlife and waterside exhibits that culminate in an underwater tunnel walk along a re-created lake bed (watch out for the diving ducks). ⊠ *Lakeside, Newby Bridge,* ☎ *015394/30153,* WEB *www.aquariumofthelakes.co.uk.* ☎ *£5.50.* ☉ *Apr.–Oct., daily 9–6; Nov.–Mar., daily 9–5.*

OFF THE BEATEN PATH

ORREST HEAD – For a memorable view of Windermere—at the cost of a rigorous climb—follow signs near the Windermere Hotel (across from the train station) to Orrest Head. The signs will guide you to a rough, uphill track. Eventually you will see a stile on your right. Climb over it and continue up the path to a rocky little summit where you can sit on a bench and enjoy a breathtaking panorama of the mountains and lake. The walk back is only a mile but takes most people at least an hour.

Dining and Lodging

££ ✕ **Oregano.** Formerly the High Restaurant, this is the best spot in Windermere for informal French dining. The centrally located, candlelighted restaurant concentrates on high-quality meals with a classic basis but showing inventive flair: onion tart might come with Caesar salad, for example, while duck can be honey-glazed and enriched by soy and ginger. There's a good selection of cheeses, some very rich desserts, and a short but interesting wine list that covers the Americas as well as France. For the best value, choose from the fixed-price menu (£16.50). ⊠ *4 High St., Windermere,* ☎ *015394/44954. AE, DC, MC, V. Closed Sun. and 1 wk in Jan. No lunch.*

£–££ ✕ **Porthole Eating House.** This small restaurant, in an intimate 18th-★ century house in the center of Bowness, has an Italian menu that includes homemade pasta and excellent meat and fish dishes, including stuffed duck, fresh salmon, and (when available) Windermere char. Some nice touches are opera recordings played as you eat, good homemade bread, and petits fours served with coffee. In winter, a large open fire adds to the ambience. ⊠ *3 Ash St., Bowness-on-Windermere,* ☎ *015394/42793. AE, DC, MC, V. Closed Tues. and mid-Dec.–mid-Feb. No lunch Sat.*

££££ ✕🏠 **Miller Howe.** This small Edwardian hotel maintains an interna-★ tional reputation for comfort and cuisine. The bedrooms have exceptional individual style and views across Windermere to the Langdale Pikes. Every attention has been given to the interior, which includes fine antiques and paintings, a lake-view conservatory for afternoon tea, and a clubbable lounge, with fresh and dried flowers everywhere. The restaurant (reservations essential) is renowned for its experimental, almost theatrical take on British cuisine; every night is a new performance. Menus change seasonally, but there are always homemade breads, inventive vegetable accompaniments, and handcrafted *petit-fours.* ⊠ *Rayrigg Rd., Bowness-on-Windermere LA23 1EY,* ☎ *015394/42536,* 𝔽𝔸𝕏 *015394/45664,* 𝕎𝔼𝔹 *www.millerhowe.com. 13 rooms. Room rate includes dinner. Restaurant, lounge. AE, DC, MC, V. Closed Mon.*

£££–££££ ✕🏠 **Gilpin Lodge.** Hidden in 20 acres of grounds, a couple of miles out of town on the B5284 Kendal road, this is a peaceful kind of place in a house dating to 1901. The cozy public rooms are furnished with sofas and rugs, warmed by log fires, brightened by flowers, and scattered with books and magazines. Guest rooms are in the same welcoming style, with four-poster beds, pine and oak furniture, and floral fabrics. Five rooms have whirlpool tubs. Many people come for the food, whether a light lunch, afternoon tea, or more formal dinner, which leans strongly on local produce: smoked trout or haddock, homemade sausages, game, local lamb, and wild mushrooms are all regulars on the menu. Reservations are essential. ⊠ *Crook Rd., Bowness-on-Windermere LA23 3NE,* ☎ *015394/88818,* 𝔽𝔸𝕏 *015394/88058,* 𝕎𝔼𝔹 *www.gilpin-lodge.co.uk. 14 rooms. Restaurant. AE, DC, MC, V.*

£££–££££ 🏠 **Langdale Chase.** Built in the 19th century and tastefully refurbished, this estate, halfway between Windermere and Ambleside, has an atmosphere of grandeur evoked by the baronial entrance hall, Old Master paintings, and oak-panel lounge. But there's genuine comfort here, too, with a pleasing conservatory and terrace, and views of Lake Windermere from many of the rooms. Outside, five acres of landscaped gardens are ideal for a summer afternoon stroll. You can choose to include dinner in the rate. ⊠ *Ambleside Rd., Windermere LA23 1LW, near the A591,* ☎ *015394/32201,* 𝔽𝔸𝕏 *015394/32604,* 𝕎𝔼𝔹 *www.langdalechase.co.uk. 29 rooms, 7 in separate lodges. Restaurant, bar, lake, miniature golf, tennis court, croquet. AE, DC, MC, V.*

££ 🏠 **Mortal Man.** This converted 17th-century inn lies in an isolated valley 3 mi north of Windermere, well away from the bustle of the town. There are magnificent views all around and superb fell walking available right from the front door. Fitting the image of a lakeland inn, it has a log fire crackling away in winter and a cozy bar. Guest rooms are fairly simple but pleasantly decorated, and there's a relaxing atmosphere to the place. ⊠ *Troutbeck LA23 1PL,* ☎ *015394/33193,* ⨳ *015394/31261,* ⩗ *www.mortal-man-inns.co.uk. 12 rooms. Restaurant, bar. No credit cards. Closed mid-Nov.–mid-Feb.*

£ ⊡ **Brendan Chase.** This comfortable, well-maintained lodging is in the heart of Windermere's B&B land, on a side road not far from the train station but a mile or so from the lake. Some rooms do have distant water views. For the most comfort you'll want to book ahead for a room with private bath, but everyone gets a TV, tea- and coffeemaking facilities, and a full breakfast (English or vegetarian) that sets you up for the day. ⊠ *1–3 College Rd., Windermere LA23 1BU,* ☎ *015394/ 45638. 8 rooms, 3 with bath. No credit cards.*

Outdoor Activities and Sports

At **Windermere Lake Holidays Afloat** (⊠ Gilly's Landing, Glebe Rd., Bowness-on-Windermere, ☎ 015394/43415) you can rent every kind of boat, from small sailboats to large cabin cruisers.

Shopping

The best selection of shops is at the Bowness end of Windermere, on Lake Road and around Queen's Square: clothing stores, crafts shops, and souvenir stores of all kinds. The **Horn Shop** (⊠ Crag Brow, ☎ 015394/44519) is one of the last British firms to practice the craft of horn carving. Craftsmen make a remarkable variety of goods, including jewelry, utensils, mugs, and walking sticks with elaborately carved handles. At **Lakeland Jewellers** (⊠ Crag Brow, ☎ 015394/42992), the local experts set semiprecious stones in necklaces and brooches. The **Lakeland Sheepskin and Leather Centre** (⊠ Lake Rd., ☎ 015394/44466), which also has branches in Ambleside and Keswick, sells moderately priced leather and sheepskin goods.

Lake District National Park Visitor Centre

❸ *3 mi northwest of Windermere.*

A magnificent lakeside mansion with terraced gardens sloping down to the water houses the official Lake District National Park Visitor Centre at Brockhole. In addition to tourist information, the center has a fine range of exhibitions about the Lake District, including useful interpretative displays about the local ecology, flora, and fauna. The gardens are at their best in spring, when floods of daffodils cover the lawns and the azaleas burst into bloom. Park activities include lectures, guided walks, and demonstrations of fascinating, traditional lakeland crafts like dry-stone-wall building. There's also a well-stocked bookstore, where you can pick up hiking guides and maps, and a café-restaurant. ⊠ *A591, Ambleside Rd., near Windermere,* ☎ *015394/46601.* ⊿ *Free; parking £2.* ☉ *Easter–late Oct., daily 10–5.*

You can reach the Lake District National Park Visitor Centre by Bus 555/556 from the Windermere train station. It's also accessible by ferry from Ambleside; the service is operated by **Windermere Lake Cruises** (☎ 015394/43360).

Ambleside

❹ *4 mi north of Brockhole.*

Unlike Kendal and Windermere, Ambleside seems almost part of the hills and fells. Its buildings, mainly of local stone and many built in that local traditional style that forgoes the use of mortar in the outer walls, blend perfectly into their setting. The small town sits at the head of Windermere, making it a popular center for Lake District excursions. The town suffers terribly from tourist overcrowding in high season. Wednesday, when the local market takes place, is particularly busy. Nonetheless, there are many fine walks in the vicinity, such as local routes north to Rydal Mount or southeast over Wansfell to Troutbeck. Each walk will take up to a half day, there and back. Ferries from Bowness-on-Windermere dock at Ambleside's harbor, called Waterhead, where you can also rent rowboats for an hour or two.

★ **Bridge House,** a tiny and stunningly picturesque 17th-century cottage perched on an arched stone bridge, spans white-water Stock Ghyll. The building houses a National Trust shop and information center. ⊠ *Rydal Rd.,* ☎ *015394/35599.* ⌖ *Free.* ☉ *Easter–Nov., daily 10–5.*

Dining and Lodging

££   ✕ **Glass House.** This exciting conversion of an old water mill, adjacent to Adrian Sankey's Ambleside glassworks, switches from a café by day to a thoroughly modern restaurant by night. The bold, open-plan, plate-glass surroundings are matched by invention in the kitchen. Seasonally changing menus feature the fashionable styles of panfrying and char-grilling in many of its French- and Mediterranean-inspired dishes. Hip waiters keep the service moving briskly and foster an atmosphere a world away from many stuffy Lake District restaurants. ⊠ *Rydal Rd.,* ☎ *015394/32137. Reservations essential. MC, V.*

£   ☷ **3 Cambridge Villas.** Ambleside abounds in inexpensive B&Bs, but you'd be hard-pressed to find a more welcoming spot than this, a lofty Victorian house right in the center, with hosts who know a thing or two about local walks. As with all similar establishments, space is at a premium, but the rooms are charmingly decorated, there's a spacious lounge with plenty of books, and a good breakfast is offered. ⊠ *Church St., LA22 9DL,* ☎ *015394/32307. 8 rooms, 4 with bath. Lounge. No credit cards. Closed Dec.–Jan.*

Rydal

⑤   *1 mi northwest of Ambleside.*

The village of Rydal, on the small Rydal Water, is rich with Wordsworthian associations. One famous beauty spot associated with the poet is **Dora's Field,** below Rydal Mount next to the church of St. Mary's (where you can still see the poet's pew). Head here for a springtime show of daffodils, planted by the poet himself for the delight of his daughter. At nearby Rydal Hall, the grand estate hosts the Rydal Sheepdog Trials on the second Thursday after the first Monday in August every year.

If there's one poet associated with the Lake District, it is William Wordsworth (1770–1850), who made his home at **Rydal Mount** from 1813 until his death 37 years later. Wordsworth and his family moved to these grand surroundings when he was nearing the height of his career, and his descendants still live here, surrounded by his furniture and portraits. You'll see the study in which he worked and the 4½-acre garden, laid out by the poet himself, that gave him so much pleasure. Surrounding Rydal Mount and the areas around Dove Cottage and Grasmere are many footpaths and tracks once beloved by Wordsworth (his favorite can be found on the hill past White Moss Common and the River Rothay). Spend an hour or two walking them and you'll understand why the great poet composed most of his verse in the open air. ⊠ *A591,* ☎ *015394/33002.* ⌖ *£3.50.* ☉ *Mar.–Oct., daily 9:30–5; Nov.–Feb., Wed.–Mon. 10–4. Closed 3 wks in Jan.*

Grasmere

❻ *3 mi north of Rydal, 4 mi northwest of Ambleside.*

The heart of Wordsworth country, Grasmere is one of the most typical of lakeland villages, sited on a tiny, wood-fringed lake and made up of crooked lanes, where slate-built cottages house little shops, cafés, and galleries. Wordsworth lived on the town's outskirts for almost 50 years, walking the local hills with his numerous guests, who included the authors Ralph Waldo Emerson and Nathaniel Hawthorne. Wordsworth, his wife, Mary, his sister, Dorothy, and his daughter, Dora, are buried in the Grasmere churchyard. On the way out of the churchyard, be sure to stop at **The Gingerbread Shop,** in a tiny cottage by the gate—once the schoolhouse—where you can buy fine gingerbread made from a 150-year-old recipe. The most panoramic views of lake and village are from the south, from the bare slopes of **Loughrigg Terrace,** reached along a signposted track on the western side of the lake. It's under an hour's walk there, though your stroll can be extended by continuing around **Rydal Water,** passing Rydal Mount and Dove Cottage before returning to Grasmere, a 4-mi (3-hr) walk in total.

★ **Dove Cottage** was William Wordsworth's home from 1799 (he moved here when he was 19) until 1808. Wordsworth's sister, Dorothy, also spent time here, and mentions the cottage in her journals, which have proved invaluable for later biographies and studies of the poet. First opened to the public in 1891, this tiny house, formerly an inn, still contains much of his furniture and many personal belongings. This was one of the happiest of times for Wordsworth, and when he married, the poet brought his wife, Mary, to Dove Cottage. Here he nursed his good friend Coleridge back to health and good spirits. Coleridge had drafted his poem "Dejection" during his stay here. Here, too, of course, Wordsworth wrote some of his most famous works, including "Ode: Intimations of Immortality" and "The Prelude." Thomas De Quincey, best-known for his 1822 autobiographical masterpiece *Confessions of an Opium Eater,* rented the cottage intermittently from 1809 to 1833. Your ticket includes admission to the **Wordsworth Museum,** which documents the poet's life and the literary contributions made by Wordsworth and the Lake Poets. In front of display cases containing the poet's original manuscripts, headphone sets allow you to hear the poems read aloud. There's also a café and restaurant. ⊠ *A591, 1 mi south of Grasmere,* ☎ *015394/35544,* WEB *www.wordsworth.org.uk.* ✆ *£5.* ☉ *Mid-Feb.–mid-Jan., daily 9:30–5.*

Dining and Lodging

££££ ✕🏠 **White Moss House.** Relive those Wordsworthian memories with
★ a night at one of the poet's former properties, built in 1730 to overlook Rydal Water. Wordsworth later purchased the house for his son, and the Wordsworth family lived here until the 1930s. White Moss House is only a mile away from the more famous houses of Rydal Mount and Dove Cottage. The hosts, the Dixons, lavish attention on guests, who hike the hills and dales by day (or take advantage of free access to a nearby health club) to prepare for dinner in one of the Lake District's most renowned country-house restaurants. The menu changes daily, but the five courses of contemporary English cuisine always include an inventive soup, local meat and fish, and a fine selection of British cheeses; dinner is included in the room cost. ⊠ *A591, Rydal Water LA22 9SE,* ☎ *015394/35295,* FAX *015394/35516,* WEB *www.whitemoss.com. 7 rooms, 1 suite. Restaurant, lounge. MC, V. Closed Dec.–Feb.*

££ ✕🏠 **The Swan.** The handsome, flower-decked, 300-year-old Swan, a former coaching inn on the main road just outside Grasmere, was mentioned in Wordsworth's poem "The Waggoner"; Coleridge and Sir Walter Scott were guests here. Then, as now, the inn's watchword was comfort: a fire in the lounge grate, an oak-beamed restaurant serving lakeland specialties, and elegant guest rooms that combine space with fine views of the surrounding fells. Rooms at the rear, overlooking well-kept gardens, are quieter than those at the front. ☒ *A591, LA22 9RF,* ☎ *015394/35551,* ℻ *015394/35741. 36 rooms. Restaurant, bar. AE, DC, MC, V.*

£ 🏠 **Banerigg House.** You don't have to spend a fortune to find appealing lakeside lodgings in Grasmere. This early 20th-century family house, three-quarters of a mile south of the village, offers well-appointed, non-smoking rooms, most with lake views. It's walker-friendly, too, which means local advice from the owners, drying facilities for wet days, a roaring fire when needed, and a hearty breakfast. ☒ *Lake Rd., LA22 9PW,* ☎ *015394/35204. 7 rooms, 5 with bath. No credit cards.*

Elterwater

❼ *2½ mi south of Grasmere, 4 mi west of Ambleside.*

The delightful little village of Elterwater, at the eastern end of the Great Langdale Valley on the B5343, is a good stop in the Lake District for hikers. It's barely more than a cluster of houses around a village green, but from here a selection of excellent circular walks are possible. There are access points to the heights of Langdale Fell from various places along the main road; look for information boards at local parking places. Stroll up the river valley or embark on more energetic hikes to Stickle Tarn or to one of the peaks of the Langdale Pikes.

Dining and Lodging

£–££ ✕🏠 **Britannia Inn.** You'll sleep peacefully at the Britannia, a friendly, ★ family-owned inn in the heart of superb walking country. The inn itself has a fine, welcoming atmosphere, with quaint little rooms and outdoor seating, quickly taken up by resting ramblers. The hearty homemade English food is excellent and the beer is local, though there's wine by the glass or bottle if you prefer. Guest rooms are modern in style and perfectly reasonable for the price; the four across the road in the Maple Tree Corner annex are a few pounds cheaper, but you'll have to walk over to the inn for breakfast. ☒ *B5343, LA22 9HP,* ☎ *015394/37210,* ℻ *015394/37311,* 🌐 *www.britinn.co.uk. 13 rooms, 9 with bath. Restaurant, bar. MC, V.*

££ 🏠 **Old Dungeon Ghyll Hotel.** After a hard walk, there's no more comforting stop than the hiker's bar of this hotel, one of the most picturesque hostelries of the region. The stone floor and wooden beams echo to the clatter of hikers' boots, while the roaring range rapidly dries out wet walking gear. There's simple bar food served here, or you can eat and drink in the more formal, but still comfortable, resident's lounge and dining room; dinner, bed, and breakfast rates are a particularly good deal. Rooms are furnished in traditional lakeland style. ☒ *Great Langdale LA22 9JY,* ☎ ℻ *015394/37272,* 🌐 *www.odg.co.uk. 14 rooms, 4 with bath. Restaurant, bar, lounge. MC, V.*

Coniston

❽ *5 mi south of Elterwater.*

This small lake resort and boating center attracts climbers with the **Old Man of Coniston** (2,635 ft). Steep tracks lead up from the village. Follow the signs beyond the Sun inn, past an old mine to the peak, which you can reach in about two hours. Experienced hikers include the peak in a seven-hour circular walk from the village, also taking in the dramatic heights and ridges of Swirl How and Wetherlam.

Coniston Water, the lake on which Coniston stands, first came to prominence in the 1930s when Arthur Ransome made it the setting for *Swallows and Amazons,* his tale of childish derring-do. The lake is about 5 mi long, a tempting stretch that drew Donald Campbell here in 1959 to set a water speed record of 260 mph. He was killed when trying to beat it in 1967. His body was never recovered after his boat crashed, and a stone seat in the village commemorates him.

The **Ruskin Museum** holds manuscripts, personal items, and watercolors by John Ruskin that illuminate his thinking and influence. ⊠ *Yewdale Rd.,* ☎ *015394/41164,* WEB *www.coniston.org.uk.* 🖅 *£3.* ☉ *Easter–Oct., daily 10–5:30.*

★ **Brantwood,** on the eastern shore of Coniston Water, was the home of John Ruskin (1819–1900), the noted Victorian artist, writer, critic, and social reformer. It's a rambling white 18th-century house (with Victorian alterations) set on a 250-acre estate that perches on high ground above the lake. Here, alongside mementos like his mahogany desk and the bath chair he used in later life, is a collection of Ruskin's own paintings, drawings, and books. Also on display is much of the art—he was a great connoisseur—that he collected in his long life, not least a superb group of drawings by the noted landscape painter J. M. W. Turner (1775–1851), whom he championed. A video on Ruskin's life shows the lasting influence of his thoughts. The extensive grounds, complete with woodland walks, were laid out by Ruskin himself. It's an easy drive to Brantwood from Coniston, but it's much more agreeable to travel here by ferry across the lake. Services are with either the Coniston Launch or the *Gondola,* an enchanting 19th-century steam yacht. Both depart from Coniston Pier. ⊠ *Brantwood,* ☎ *015394/41396,* WEB *www.brantwood.org.uk.* 🖅 *£4, gardens only £2; combined ticket with ferry £7.* ☉ *House mid-Mar.–mid-Nov., daily 11–5:30; mid-Nov.–mid-Mar., Wed.–Sun. 11–4.*

Dining and Lodging

£–££ ✕ **Brantwood's Jumping Jenny's.** This brasserie and tearoom, named after Ruskin's beloved boat, offers Pre-Raphaelite–style decor, an open log fire, and mountain views as the setting for morning coffee, lunch, or afternoon tea. ⊠ *Brantwood,* ☎ *015394/41715. No credit cards. No dinner.*

££ ✕🏠 **Sun Hotel.** Hidden up a shady lane a few minutes out of Coniston center, the Sun combines the best of Victorian comfort with the age-old hospitality of a traditional lakeland inn. Guest rooms and restaurant are in the early 20th-century hotel, whose fell views, heavy drapes, open fires, and hanging watercolors paint a picture of relaxation; the attached, dark, wood-paneled, 16th-century inn fills up most nights with hikers and climbers. Meals in the restaurant are good-value British food but hold few surprises. It's as nice to eat in the inn, where pies are a specialty, or down a pint or two of the local beer. ⊠ *Coniston LA21 8HQ,* ☎ *015394/41248,* FAX *015394/41219. 11 rooms, 9 with bath. Restaurant, bar. MC, V.*

£ 🏠 **Shepherd's Villa Guest House.** This B&B in a stone country house stands on the edge of the village. From here, you can take in wonderful views of the lake and forested hills; packed lunches are available for hikers. The rooms are large and comfortable, and there's a garden for summer relaxing. ⊠ *Tilberthwaite Ave., Coniston LA21 8EE,* ☎ *015394/41337. 10 rooms, 5 with bath. MC, V.*

Outdoor Activities and Sports

Coniston Boating Centre (☎ 015394/41366) at the lake rents out launches, canoes, or traditional wooden rowboats, and there's a picnic area and café near the center.

Hawkshead

🄴 *3 mi east of Coniston.*

The village of Hawkshead has the usual lakeland complement of narrow, cobbled streets, whitewashed inns, and little bowfront stores. There's a good deal more to it than most local villages, however. The Hawkshead Courthouse, just outside town, was originally built by the monks of Furness Abbey in the 15th century. Hawkshead lay within the monastic domain and later derived much wealth from the wool trade, which flourished here in the 17th and 18th centuries. As a thriving market center, it could afford to maintain a school, **Hawkshead Grammar School,** at which William Wordsworth was a pupil from 1779 to 1787; he carved his name on a desk inside, now on display. A house in the village (Ann Tyson's House) claims the honor of providing the young William with lodgings. Not surprisingly, the twin draws of Wordsworth and Beatrix Potter—apart from her home, Hill Top, there's also a local Potter gallery—conspire to make Hawkshead hideously overcrowded throughout the year. In 2002, celebrations will mark the centenary of the publication of *The Tale of Peter Rabbit.*

Occupying rooms formerly used by Potter's lawyer husband, the **Beatrix Potter Gallery** has displays of the artist's book illustrations as well as information on her interests as a naturalist. Potter was also a conservationist and an early supporter of the National Trust. Admission is by time ticket. ✉ *Main St.,* ☎ *015394/36355.* 🎫 *£3.* ◷ *Apr.–Oct., Sun.,–Thurs. 10:30–4:30.*

🄲 **Hill Top** was the home of children's author and illustrator Beatrix Potter (1866–1943), most famous for her *Peter Rabbit* stories. The tiny house is a popular, and often crowded, spot; admission is controlled by timed tickets. Try to avoid visiting on summer weekends and during school vacations. The gardens and shop remain open on Thursday and Friday, when the house is closed. It lies 2 mi south of Hawkshead on the B5285, though you can also approach via the car ferry from Bowness-on-Windermere. ✉ *Near Sawrey,* ☎ *015394/36269,* 🕸 *www.nationaltrust.org.uk.* 🎫 *£4.* ◷ *Easter–Oct., Sat.–Wed. 11–5.*

Two miles northwest of the village (follow signs on B5285) is one of the Lake District's most celebrated beauty spots, **Tarn Hows,** a tree-lined lake that is considered one of the prettiest in the region. Scenic overlooks let you drink it all in, or you can take about an hour to putter along the paths. A free National Trust bus runs to the beauty spot from Hawkshead and Coniston (Sunday only, Easter–October).

Lodging

££   🛏 **Queen's Head.** One of the Lake District's prettiest villages also holds one of its quaintest inns—the black-and-white, timbered Queen's Head, with low, beamed ceilings, paneled walls, and cozy rooms that shout its 16th-century credentials. Guest rooms are comfortably furnished, though rather small and fussily decorated. All the real atmosphere is downstairs in the welcoming bar, in the paneled dining room serving local cuisine, or outside at tables fronting the sunny, traffic-free street. ✉ *Main St., LA22 0NS,* ☎ *015394/36271,* 📠 *015394/36722. 13 rooms, 11 with bath. Restaurant, bar. MC, V.*

PENRITH AND THE NORTHERN LAKES

The scenery of the northern Lakes is considerably more dramatic—some would say bleaker—than much of the landscape to the south. It's a change you'll notice on your way north from Kendal to Penrith. The easiest approach is a 30-mi drive that takes you through the wild and desolate Shap Fells. One of the most notorious moorland crossings in the country, the fells rise to a height of 1,304 ft. Even in summer it's a lonely place to be, and in winter snows the road can be dangerous. From Penrith, the road leads to Ullswater, possibly the grandest of all the lakes, and then there's a steady route west past Keswick, then south through the marvelous Borrowdale Valley and on to Cockermouth.

Penrith

10 *30 mi north of Kendal.*

The red-sandstone town of Penrith was the capital of the semi-independent kingdom of Cumbria in the 9th and 10th centuries. Later, Cumbria was part of the Scottish kingdom of Strathclyde; in the year 1070, it was incorporated into England. Even at this time, Penrith was a thriving market town (the market still takes place on Tuesday), and it continues to have a good variety of shops.

The tourist information center, in the Penrith Museum, has information about the historic "town trail" route, which takes you through narrow byways to the plague stone on King Street, where food was left for the plague-stricken, to a churchyard with 1,000-year-old "hogback" tombstones (stones carved as stylized "houses of the dead"), and finally to the ruins of Penrith Castle.

The evocative remains of the 14th-century redbrick **Penrith Castle** are set in its own little park. This was the first line of defense against the invading Scots. The ruins stand across from the town's train station. ✉ *Off Castlegate,* ☎ *No phone,* WEB *www.english-heritage.org.uk.* ✉ *Free.* ☉ *June–Sept., daily 7:30 AM–9 PM; Oct.–May, daily 7:30–4:30.*

The **Penrith Museum** occupies a 16th-century building that served as a school from 1670 to the 1970s. It now contains a fascinating exhibit of local historical artifacts as well as the local tourist information center. ✉ *Robinson's School, Middlegate,* ☎ *01768/212228.* ✉ *Free.* ☉ *Apr.–Sept., Mon.–Sat. 10–6, Sun. 1–6; Oct.–Mar., Mon.–Sat. 10–5.*

Lodging

££ 🏨 **The George.** This large, rambling coaching inn right in the center of Penrith has been hosting guests for more than 300 years. Stay overnight in one of the modernized rooms, all with private facilities, or just stop in for morning coffee or lunch. The lounges are full of wood paneling, antiques, copper and brass fixtures, old paintings, and comfortable chairs. ✉ *Devonshire St., CA11 7SH,* ☎ *01768/862696,* FAX *01768/868223. 30 rooms. Restaurant, bar, lobby lounge. MC, V.*

£–££ 🏨 **Queen's Head Inn.** One of two old inns in pleasant Askham, the Queen's Head is a friendly 17th-century building at the top of the village with big open fires, plenty of shining copper and brass, and pleasant old furniture. The pick of the rooms is the slightly more expensive Lowther Suite, with comfortable furnishings and its own sitting room. ✉ *Askham, 5 mi south of Penrith, CA10 2PF,* ☎ *01931/712225,* FAX *01931/712811. 4 rooms. Restaurant, bar. MC, V.*

Dalemain

11 *3 mi southwest of Penrith.*

Dalemain, a country house with a 12th-century peel (tower), was built to protect the occupants from raiding Scots. A medieval hall was added, as well as a number of extensions from the 16th through the 18th centuries, culminating in an imposing Georgian facade of local pink sandstone. The result is a delightful hodgepodge of architectural styles. Inside are a magnificent oak staircase, furniture dating from the mid-17th century, a Chinese drawing room, a 16th-century "fretwork room" with intricate plasterwork, a nursery complete with an elaborate 18th-century dollhouse, and many fine paintings, including masterpieces by Van Dyck. ⊠ *Off the A592,* ☎ *017684/86450.* 🖃 *£5, gardens only £3.* ⊙ *Apr.–Sept., Sun.–Thurs. 11:15–5.*

Ullswater

⑫ *3 mi southwest of Dalemain, 6 mi southwest of Penrith.*

Hemmed in by towering hills, Ullswater, the region's second-largest lake, has a spectacular setting that draws outdoor types. Some of the finest views are from the A592 as it sticks to the lake's western shore, through the adjacent hamlets of **Glenridding** and **Patterdale** at the southern end. Lakeside strolls, tea shops, and rowboat rental all help provide the usual lakeland experience here. Steamers leave Glenridding's pier for **Pooley Bridge**, offering a pleasant tour along the lake.

At **Aira Force** (⊠ off A592, 5 mi north of Patterdale), a spectacular series of waterfalls pound through a wooded ravine to feed into Ullswater. From the parking lot (parking fee charged), it's a 20-minute walk to the falls. Bring sturdy shoes in wet weather. Just above Aira Force in the woods of Gowbarrow Park is the spot where in 1802, William Wordsworth's sister Dorothy remarked that she had never seen "daffodils so beautiful . . . they tossed and reeled and danced and seemed as if they verily laughed with the wind that blew upon them." Two years later Wordsworth transformed his sister's words into one of the best-known lyric poems in English, "I Wandered Lonely as a Cloud." And two centuries later, National Park wardens have to patrol Gowbarrow Park in season to prevent tourists from picking the daffodils. There are precious few left, so be content with a photograph.

There's a telling reminder of the region's fundamental character in the brooding presence of **Helvellyn** (3,118 ft), one of the Lake District's most formidable mountains, which lies to the west of the lake's southern end. It's an arduous climb to the top, especially via the challenging ridge known as Striding Edge, and shouldn't be attempted in poor weather or by inexperienced hikers. Signposted paths to the peak run from the road between Glenridding and Patterdale and pass by **Red Tarn,** at 2,356 ft the highest Lake District tarn, which is a better target for anyone nervous of the heights.

Dining and Lodging

££££   ✕🏨 **Sharrow Bay.** Set between the lush green fields and the rugged crags
★   around Howtown, this luxurious country-house hotel commands a view of exceptional beauty. Sharrow Bay is celebrated for its restaurant; dishes on the fixed-price menu may include Aberdeen monkfish with borage cream and terrine of venison, duck, foie gras, and pistachio in Cumberland sauce. (Reservations are essential, but dinner is included in the room rate for guests.) Hotel decor is classic Lake Country, with salons filled with flocked wallpapers, oil paintings, and fringed lamp shades. The bedrooms, whether in the main house or three annexes, are extremely comfortable, although the rooms in Gatehouse and the Bank House (about 1½ mi away) are somewhat simpler. Stop by for the splendid afternoon tea. ⊠ *Howtown Rd., Pooley Bridge, CA10 2LZ,* ☎ *017684/86301,* 🅵🅰🅇 *017684/86349,* 🆆🅴🅱 *www.sharrow-bay.com. 28 rooms. Restaurant, lounge. MC, V. Closed Dec.–mid-Feb.*

Keswick

⓭ *14 mi west of Ullswater.*

The great lakeland mountains of Skiddaw and Blencathra brood over the gray slate houses of Keswick (pronounced kezzick), on the scenic shores of Derwentwater. Since many of the best hiking routes radiate from here, the town is more of a touring base than a tourist destination. People stroll the congested, narrow streets in boots and corduroy hiking trousers, and there are plenty of mountaineering shops in addition to hotels, guest houses, pubs, tea shops, and restaurants. Walkers may want to leave their cars behind, as parking is difficult in the higher valleys, and both the Derwentwater launches and the Borrowdale bus service between Keswick and Seatoller run frequently. The handsome 19th-century **Moot Hall** (⊠ Market Pl.) has served as both the Keswick town hall and the local prison. Now it houses the main **tourist information center** for the region.

At the **Keswick Museum and Art Gallery** in Fitz Park, exhibits include manuscripts by Wordsworth and other lakeland writers, a diorama of the Lake District, a local geological and natural-history collection, and an assortment of watercolor paintings. ⊠ *Station Rd.,* ☎ *017687/73263.* 🎟 *£1.* ⏰ *Easter–Oct., daily 10–4.*

★ To understand why **Derwentwater** is considered one of England's finest lakes, take a short walk from Keswick's town center to the lakeshore, and follow the **Friar's Crag** path, about a 15-minute level walk from the center. This pine-tree-fringed peninsula is a favorite vantage point, with its view over the lake, the surrounding ring of mountains, and many tiny wooded islands. Ahead you will see the crags that line the **Jaws of Borrowdale** and overhang a dramatic mountain ravine, the perfect setting for a romantic painting or poem. For the best lake views you should take a wooden-launch **cruise** around Derwentwater. Between late March and November, cruises set off every hour in each direction from a wooden dock at lakeshore. You can also rent a rowboat here. Landing stages around the lake provide access to some spectacular hiking trails, like the two-hour climb up Cat Bells and back, a celebrated lookout point on the western shore of Derwentwater.

The **Castlerigg Stone Circle** (⊠ off A66), 4 mi east of town, is in a brooding natural hollow called St. John's Vale, ringed by peaks and ranged by sheep, with the circle itself about 100 ft in diameter. The 38 stones are not large, but the setting makes them particularly impressive. The alignment of the 5,000-year-old circle suggests it may have been a calendar, but its origins remain a guessing game. A clearly marked route off the A66 leads to a 200-ft-long path through a pasture; you can visit the circle during daylight hours, no charge.

Dining and Lodging

£–££ ✕ **Loose Box Pizzeria.** The name refers to the fact that the building was formerly a horse stable. You'll find it at the back of the courtyard of the King's Arms pub. For satisfying budget food in the evening, the pizzas and pastas can't be beat. The house special is a toothsome spaghetti with tomato, garlic, chili, and shrimp. ⊠ *King's Arms Courtyard, Main St.,* ☎ *017687/72083. MC, V.*

£–££ ✕ **Luca's.** The River Greta runs beside this stylish Italian bistro-restaurant, which is somewhat isolated at the north end of town. There's a choice of pastas, such as the *linguine con peperoncino* (with olive oil, chili, and garlic), followed by classics like veal, steaks, shrimp, or fish. The daily specials are always worth inquiring about. ⊠ *Greta Bridge, High Hill,* ☎ *017687/74621. MC, V. Closed Mon. and Jan.–Feb.*

£   ✕ **Abraham's Tea Room.** George Fisher's outdoor store has its own welcoming tearoom, with good, honest Cumbrian home cooking—food as fuel for hikers. The tearoom is open shop hours only, usually Monday through Saturday 9–5:30. ✉ *2 Borrowdale Rd.,* ☎ *017687/72178. No credit cards.*

£   ✕ **Four in Hand.** This is a typical Cumbrian pub, once a stagecoach inn with a 19th-century paneled bar decorated with horse brasses and banknotes. The food is nothing fancy, but you can fill up on pub specials like steaks, meat pies, and Cumberland sausage. ✉ *Lake Rd.,* ☎ *017687/72069. No credit cards.*

£££–££££   ✕☰ **Keswick Country House Hotel.** Built to serve railroad travelers in
     ★   the 19th century, this hotel has all the grandeur and style of that age, with turrets, balconies, picture windows, and a lovely conservatory with cane chairs. Rooms with views lend it real Victorian class. The hotel sits in 4½ acres of private gardens in the center of Keswick; the elegant Lonsdale Restaurant overlooks the grounds. The room rate includes dinner, as well as breakfast, though you can opt for a stay without dinner if you wish. ✉ *Station Rd., CA12 4NQ,* ☎ *017687/72020,* 𝔽𝔸𝕏 *017687/71300,* 𝕎𝔼𝔹 *www.principalhotels.co.uk. 74 rooms. Restaurant, bar, putting green, croquet. AE, DC, MC, V.*

£–££   ✕☰ **Highfield Hotel.** Overlooking the lawns of Hope Park, just a few minutes' walk from lake or town, this small, family-run hotel shows remarkable character. A restoration job modernized all the guest rooms while preserving such features as its turret rooms and even a former attached chapel, now in use as a large four-poster bedroom. You'll be calmed by the crisp carpets, front-room balconies (with super valley views), and relaxing garden. Dinner, too, is a treat, with an inventive three-course menu that focuses on items like oak-smoked trout, cod wrapped in bacon, or a pigeon-breast salad. ✉ *The Heads, CA12 5ER,* ☎ *017687/72508. 19 rooms. Restaurant, bar. MC, V. Closed mid-Nov.–Jan.*

£   ☰ **Howe Keld.** Those in the know bypass the rows of identikit B&Bs in Keswick and head for Howe Keld for a bit of budget TLC. In a quiet part of town, the Fisher family goes about its business of putting guests at ease (there's tea or coffee on arrival) and making them comfortable in the pretty town house–hotel; rooms are nonsmoking. High-quality breakfasts are the big event, especially for vegetarians who do very well here with homemade buffet items, freshly baked bread, pancakes, or traditional Cumbrian fry-ups. Evening meals (on request) are a good value. ✉ *5–7 The Heads, CA12 5ES,* ☎ *017687/80378,* 𝕎𝔼𝔹 *www.howekeld.co.uk. 15 rooms, 14 with bath. Dining room. No credit cards. Closed Jan.*

Nightlife and the Arts

The **Keswick Jazz Festival** (☎ 01900/602122) is held each May; it consists of four days of music and events and is very popular. Reservations are taken before Christmas.

Outdoor Activities and Sports

FISHING

Local permits, for fishing in Derwentwater or Bassenthwaite, are available at **Field & Stream** (✉ 79 Main St., ☎ 017687/74396).

WATER SPORTS

Derwentwater Marina (✉ Portinscale, ☎ 017687/72912) offers boat rentals and instruction in canoeing, sailing, windsurfing, and rowing.

Shopping

Thanks to its size, Keswick is probably the most sophisticated shopping area in the Lake District. You will find a good choice of bookstores, crafts shops, and wool-clothing stores. Keswick's **market** is held Saturday. **George Fisher** (⊠ 2 Borrowdale Rd., ☎ 017687/72178) is famous for outdoor clothing: parkas, boots, skiwear, and many other kinds of sportswear. It also sells maps, and daily weather information is posted in the window. The **Viridian Gallery** (⊠ 13 St. John St., ☎ 017687/71328) is a local artists' co-op featuring the paintings, prints, and ceramics of a half-dozen Cumbrian artists.

En Route   The finest route from Keswick is the B5289 road south. This runs along the eastern edge of Derwentwater, past turnoffs to several natural attractions such as Ashness Bridge, the idyllic tarn of Watendlath, the Lodore Falls (best in wet weather), and the precariously balanced Bowder Stone before reaching the tiny village of **Grange,** a popular walking center at the head of Borrowdale, where there's a riverside café.

Borrowdale

🕙 *7 mi south of Keswick.*

South of Keswick and its lake lies the valley of Borrowdale, whose varied landscape of green valley floor and surrounding crags has long been considered one of the region's most magnificent treasures. **Rosthwaite,** a tranquil farming village, and **Seatoller,** the southernmost settlement, are the two main centers (and are accessible by bus from Keswick), though both are little more than a cluster of aged buildings surrounded by glorious countryside. Seatoller has a **Lake District National Park information center** (⊠ Dalehead Base, Seatoller Barn, ☎ 017687/77294), open Easter–November, daily 10–5.

The vaultingly steep **Borrowdale Fells** rise up dramatically behind Seatoller. Get out and walk whenever inspiration strikes, and in spring, keep an eye open and your camera ready for newborn lambs roaming the hillsides. England's highest mountain, the 3,210-ft **Scafell Pike** (pronounced scar-fell) is visible from Seatoller. The usual route up the mountain, for experienced walkers, is from the hamlet of Seathwaite, just a mile or so south of Seatoller.

Dining and Lodging

££–£££ ✕ **Yew Tree Restaurant.** Two 17th-century cottages make up this restaurant at the foot of Honister Pass. A low-beam ceiling, long, open fireplace, and excellent bar add to the intimate, gracious atmosphere. The appealing menu is based largely on local produce: panfried trout, marinated and smoked fish, venison, hare, eel, and salmon. ⊠ *Seatoller,* ☎ *017687/77634. MC, V. Closed Mon. and Jan.–mid-Feb.*

££–£££ ✕🏨 **Royal Oak Hotel.** Hikers really appreciate the comforts of the Royal Oak, whose firelit lounge and tiny nook of a residents' bar conspire to soothe away the day's aches. Rooms are trim, with good beds, though bathrooms are small; if you require a bath instead of a shower in your room, you must book ahead. Dinner (included in the rate), served promptly at 7, is a no-choice affair using local ingredients. An egg-and-bacon breakfast the next morning sends you on your way. ⊠ *Rosthwaite CA12 5XB,* ☎ *017687/77214. 15 rooms, 11 with bath. Restaurant, bar. MC, V. Closed 3 wks in Dec. and 2 wks in Jan.*

En Route   Beyond Seatoller, B5289 turns westward through **Honister Pass** (1,176 ft) and Buttermere Fell. It's a superb drive along one of the most dramatic of the region's roads, which is lined with huge boulders and at times channels through soaring rock canyons. The road sweeps down from the pass to the appealing lakeland village of Buttermere, sandwiched between two lakes at the foot of high, craggy fells.

Cockermouth

⑮ *14 mi northwest of Seatoller.*

Cockermouth, an attractive little town at the confluence of the Rivers
Derwent and Cocker, has a maze of narrow streets that are a delight to
wander, and a brisk market-town atmosphere. There's no public access
to the ruined 14th-century castle, but the outdoor market, held each Monday, still retains its traditions. An old bell is rung at the start of trading.
Cockermouth was the birthplace of William Wordsworth (and his sister Dorothy), whose childhood home, **Wordsworth House,** is a typical
18th-century North Country gentleman's home. Some of the poet's furniture and personal items are on display here, and you can explore the
garden he played in as a child. Incidentally, Wordsworth's father is
buried in the town churchyard, and in the church itself is a stained-glass
window in memory of the poet. ⊠ *Main St.,* ☎ *01900/824805,* WEB
www.nationaltrust.org.uk. ⚏ *£3.* ☼ *Apr.–June and Sept.–Oct., weekdays 11–5; July–Aug., Mon.–Sat. 11–5.*

♻ The **Cumberland Toy and Model Museum** has exhibits of mainly British
toys from 1900 to the present. Two buildings contain good model train
collections, the re-creation of a 1930s toy shop, and large collections
of dolls and dollhouses. There's a play area for younger children and
special exhibits throughout the year. ⊠ *Banks Ct. and Market Pl.,* ☎
01900/827606. ⚏ *£2.* ☼ *Feb.–Nov., daily 10–5.*

Dining and Lodging

£   ✕▥ **Kirkstile Inn.** This 16th-century inn stands 7 mi south of Cockermouth in lovely, quiet surroundings. Low, white, and slate-roofed,
this lodging has been welcoming travelers for almost 400 years. There's
a cozy pub downstairs, with a roaring fire in winter, and rooms upstairs, arranged along a long, oak-beam corridor. The rooms are all
simple, with rather garish floral carpets and creaky furniture, but
they're cool in summer and well-heated (if a little musty) in winter, and
the beds are supremely comfortable, just the thing after a day's walking. There's perfectly reasonable food on offer in the bar, and in summer you can eat outside in the garden, overlooking the river. The inn
is quite tricky to find, and you'd do best to phone for directions before setting off. ⊠ *Loweswater, Cockermouth CA13 ORU,* ☎ *01900/
85219. 10 rooms, 8 with bath. Bar, pub. MC, V.*

LAKE DISTRICT A TO Z

*To research prices, get advice from other travelers, and book travel ar-
rangements, visit www.fodors.com.*

AIRPORTS
➤ AIRPORT INFORMATION: **Manchester Airport** (⊠ near Junctions 5 and
6 of M56, ☎ 0161/489–3000, WEB www.manairport.co.uk).

BIKE TRAVEL
Several local operators rent out mountain bikes, an ideal, if calorie-
burning, way to see the Lake District countryside. The Cumbria Cycle
Way circles the county of Cumbria, while for local excursions guided
bike tours are often available, too, starting at about £25 per day. Con-
tact local tourist offices for details, or consult one of the following out-
fits for bike rental.
➤ BIKE RENTALS: **Grizedale Mountain Bikes** (⊠ Old Hall Car Park,
Grizedale Forest Park Centre, Hawkshead, ☎ 01229/860369). **Keswick
Mountain Bikes** (⊠ Southey Hill, ☎ 017687/75202). **Mountain Trad-**

ing (✉ Lake Rd., Bowness-on-Windermere, ☎ 015394/44786). **Windermere Cycles** (✉ 12 Main Rd., Windermere, ☎ 015394/47779).

BOAT AND FERRY TRAVEL

Keswick-on-Derwentwater Launch Company conducts cruises on vintage motor launches around Derwentwater, leaving from Keswick. Coniston Launch connects Coniston with Ruskin's home at Brantwood, offering hourly service for most of the year (though service is reduced in winter) on its wooden Ruskin and Ransome launches. Steam Yacht *Gondola* runs the National Trust's luxurious Victorian steam yacht between Coniston, Brantwood, and Park-a-Moor at the south end of Coniston Water, daily from Easter through October. Ullswater Navigation & Transit Company sends its oil-burning 19th-century steamers the length of Ullswater between Glenridding and Pooley Bridge. Service operates April through October.

Windermere Lake Cruises employs its handsome fleet of modern launches and vintage cruisers, the largest ships on the lake in regular service between Ambleside, Bowness, Brockhole, and Lakeside. Ticket prices vary, though a Freedom of the Lake ticket (£9.50) gives unlimited travel on any of the ferries for 24 hours.

FARES AND SCHEDULES

➤ BOAT AND FERRY INFORMATION: **Coniston Launch** (☎ 015394/36216). **Keswick-on-Derwentwater Launch Co.** (☎ 017687/72263). **Steam Yacht** *Gondola* (☎ 015394/41288). **Ullswater Navigation & Transit Co.** (☎ 01539/721626). **Windermere Lake Cruises** (☎ 015394/43360).

BUS TRAVEL

National Express serves the region from London's Victoria Coach Station and from Manchester's Chorlton Street Station. Average travel time to Kendal is just over seven hours from London; to Windermere, 7½ hours; and to Keswick, 8¼ hours. From Manchester there's one bus a day to Windermere (3½ hours) that stops in Ambleside, Grasmere, and Keswick. There's also direct bus service to the Lakes from Carlisle, Lancaster, and York.

Stagecoach Cumberland operates year-round throughout the Lake District and into north Lancashire. A one-day Explorer Ticket (£5.50) is available on the bus and valid on all routes. Services between main tourist centers are fairly frequent on weekdays, though service is much reduced on weekends and bank holidays. Don't count on being able to reach the more remote parts of the Lakes by bus. For off-the-beaten-track touring, you'll need a car, or strong legs.

CUTTING COSTS

The YHA Shuttle Bus operates a door-to-door service to eight of the most popular hostels in the Lakes (Easter through October only). Get on and off where you like for £2 a journey, or send your luggage ahead to the next hostel if you want to walk unencumbered.
➤ DISCOUNT PASSES: **YHA Shuttle Bus** (✉ Ambleside Youth Hostel, Waterhead, ☎ 015394/32304).

FARES AND SCHEDULES

➤ BUS INFORMATION: **National Express** (☎ 0870/580–8080, WEB www.gobycoach.com). **Stagecoach Cumberland** (☎ 01946/63222).

CAR RENTAL

➤ LOCAL AGENCIES: **Avis** (✉ Station Rd., Kendal, ☎ 01539/733582). **Keswick Motor Company** (✉ Lake Rd., Keswick, ☎ 017687/72064).

CAR TRAVEL

To reach the Lake District from London, take M1 north to M6, getting off either at exit 36 and joining A590/A591 west (around the Kendal bypass to Windermere) or at exit 40, joining A66 direct to Keswick and the northern lakes region. Travel time to Kendal is about four hours, to Keswick 5–6 hours. Expect heavy traffic out of London on weekends to all destinations in the Northwest; construction work also often slows progress on M6.

ROAD CONDITIONS

Roads within the region are generally very good, although many of the Lake District's minor routes and mountain passes can be both steep and narrow. Warning signs are normally posted if snow has made a road impassable; always listen to local weather forecasts in winter before setting out. In July and August and during the long public holiday weekends, expect heavy traffic. The Lake District has plenty of parking lots, which should be used to avoid blocking narrow lanes.

EMERGENCIES

➤ CONTACTS: **Ambulance, fire, police** (☎ 999). **Westmorland General Hospital** (✉ Burton Rd., Kendal, ☎ 01539/732288).

NATIONAL PARKS

The Lake District National Park head office is at Brockhole, near Windermere. There are also helpful regional national park centers.
➤ CONTACTS: **Lake District National Park Head Office** (☎ 015394/46601, WEB www.lake-district.gov.uk). **Bowness** (☎ 015394/42895). **Coniston** (☎ 015394/41533). **Grasmere** (☎ 015394/35245). **Hawkshead** (☎ 015394/36525). **Keswick** (☎ 017687/72645). **Pooley Bridge** (☎ 017684/86530). **Seatoller** (☎ 017687/77294). **Ullswater** (☎ 017684/82414). **Waterhead** (☎ 015394/32729).

TOURS

English Lakeland Ramblers organizes single-base and inn-to-inn guided tours of the Lake District from May through October. All meals and inn accommodations are included in packages. A lake steamer cruise and a ride on a narrow-gauge steam railroad line are all part of the adventure. Lakes Supertours offers full-day tours by coach and boat, with plenty of opportunities for getting out and strolling around.
➤ FEES AND SCHEDULES: **English Lakeland Ramblers** (✉ 18 Stuyvesant Oval, #1A, New York, NY 10009, ☎ 01229/587382; 212/505–1020 or 800/724–8801 in the U.S., WEB www.ramblers.com). **Lakes Supertours** (✉ 1 High St., Windermere, ☎ 015394/42751).

BUS TOURS

Mountain Goat Holidays provides special minibus sightseeing tours with skilled local guides. These are half- and full-day tours, which really get off the beaten track, departing from Bowness, Windermere, Ambleside, and Grasmere.
➤ FEES AND SCHEDULES: **Mountain Goat Holidays** (✉ Victoria St., Windermere, ☎ 015394/45161, WEB www.lake-district.gov.uk).

WALKING TOURS

The Lake District National Park office at Brockhole, near Windermere, has an advisory service that puts you in touch with members of the Blue Badge Guides, who are experts on the area. From Easter through October, they lead half-day or full-day walks. The Authority has 10 information offices throughout the district.
➤ FEES AND SCHEDULES: **Lake District National Park** (☎ 015394/46601, WEB www.lake-district.gov.uk).

TRAIN TRAVEL

InterCity West Coast serves the region from London's Euston Station. Take an InterCity train bound for Carlisle, Edinburgh, or Glasgow and change at Oxenholme for the branch line service to Kendal and Windermere. Average travel time to Windermere (including the change) is 4½ hours. If you're heading for Keswick, you can either take the train to Windermere and continue from there by Cumberland bus (Bus 555/556; 70 minutes) or stay on the main London–Carlisle train to Penrith Station (four hours), from which Cumberland buses (Bus X5) also run to Keswick (45 minutes). Direct trains from Manchester depart for Windermere five times daily (travel time two hours).

Train connections are good around the edges of the Lake District, especially on the Oxenholme–Kendal–Windermere line and the Furness and West Cumbria branch line from Lancaster to Grange-over-Sands, Ulverston, Barrow, and Ravenglass. However, these services aren't of much use for getting around the central lakeland region (where you'll really need to take the bus or drive), and they are reduced, or nonexistent, on Sunday.

The Lakeside & Haverthwaite Railway Company runs vintage steam trains between April and October on the 4-mi branch line between Lakeside and Haverthwaite along Lake Windermere's southern tip. Departures coincide with ferry arrivals from Windermere.

FARES AND SCHEDULES

➤ TRAIN INFORMATION: **InterCity West Coast** (☎ 0845/484950). **Lakeside & Haverthwaite Railway Co.** (☎ 015395/315945).

TRAVEL AGENCIES

➤ LOCAL AGENT REFERRALS: **Thomas Cook** (✉ 49 Stricklandgate, Kendal, ☎ 01539/724258).

VISITOR INFORMATION

Cumbria Tourist Board is open Monday–Thursday 9:30–5:30 and Friday 9:30–5.

➤ TOURIST INFORMATION: **Cumbria Tourist Board** (✉ Ashleigh, Holly Rd., Windermere, LA23 2AQ, ☎ 015394/44444, WEB www.cumbria-the-lake-district.co.uk). **Ambleside** (✉ Central Buildings, Market Cross, ☎ 015394/32582). **Cockermouth** (✉ The Town Hall, ☎ 01900/82263). **Coniston** (✉ Ruskin Ave., ☎ 015394/41533). **Grasmere** (✉ Red Bank Rd., ☎ 015394/35245). **Kendal** (✉ Town Hall, Highgate, ☎ 01539/725758). **Keswick** (✉ Moot Hall, Market Sq., ☎ 017687/72645). **Penrith** (✉ Penrith Museum, Middlegate, ☎ 01768/867466). **Ullswater** (✉ Main Car Park, Glenridding, ☎ 017684/82414). **Windermere** (✉ The Gateway Centre, Victoria St., ☎ 015394/46499).

13 EAST ANGLIA

CAMBRIDGE, BURY ST. EDMUNDS, NORWICH, LINCOLN

A quiet, eerie land, East Anglia is still the guardian of all that rural England holds dear. It delights with its tulip fields, flint churches, thatched-roof cottages, and, around the valley of the Stour, countryside scenes that inspired Constable. Outstanding are the majestic cathedrals of Ely, Norwich, and Lincoln, the stately houses of Holkham and fit-for-a-queen Sandringham, and the city of Cambridge—in parts, medieval, mesmerizing, and magnificent.

Updated by Ed Glinert

EAST ANGLIA IS ONE OF THOSE BEAUTIFUL English inconsistencies. No spectacular mountains or rivers disturb the storied, quiet land that is East Anglia—the guardian of all that rural England holds dear. Occupying an area of southeastern England that juts, knoblike, into the North Sea, its counties of Essex, Norfolk, Suffolk, Lincolnshire, and Cambridgeshire are a bit cut off from the central routes and pulse of Britain. People from London once called the region "silly Suffolk," and referred to the citizens of Norfolk county as "Norfolk Dumplings." In modern times, when life for many is busy and stressful, these terms strike an almost complimentary note.

But if this area is England's Vermont, it has also been home to some of the greatest thinkers, artists, and poets the country has produced. Milton, Bacon, Newton, Byron, Tennyson, and Thackeray received their education at Cambridge University, one of the world's top centers of learning and arguably the most gorgeous university town on Earth. Here, Oliver Cromwell groomed his Roundhead troops, and Tom Paine, the man who wrote "These are the times that try men's souls," developed his revolutionary ideas. Here, John Constable painted *The Hay Wain* along with luscious landscapes of the Stour Valley, and Thomas Gainsborough achieved eminence as England's most elegant portraitist. If East Anglia has remained rural to a large extent, its harvest of legendary minds has been just as impressive as its agricultural crops.

Despite its easy access from London, East Anglia (with the notable exception of Cambridge) remains relatively unfamiliar to visitors. It was a region of major importance in ancient times, as evidenced by the Roman settlements at Colchester and Lincoln; and during the medieval era, trade in wool with the Netherlands saw the East Anglian towns become strong and independent. But with the lack of main thoroughfares and canals, the industrial revolution mercifully passed East Anglia by.

As a result of being a historical backwater, the region is enormously rich in quiet villages, presided over by ancient churches, tiny settlements in the midst of otherwise deserted fenland, and manor houses surrounded by moats. Few parts of Britain can claim so many stately churches and half-timber houses. The towns are more like large villages; even the largest city, Norwich, has a population of only about 130,000.

For many people, the joy of East Anglia is its very separateness, its desolate landscapes, and isolated beaches. Of these, the fens of northern Cambridgeshire and the Broads of Norfolk are the most dramatic (or depressing, depending on your mood); the water in the marshes and dikes reflects the arching sky, whose cloudscapes are ever-changing, stretching toward seemingly infinite horizons. The sunsets here are to be treasured. The fens resemble areas of Holland directly across the North Sea, and, indeed, work on much of the drainage system here was carried out by Dutch engineers. In both Norfolk and Suffolk, the reed-bordered Broads make a gentle landscape of canals and lakes that are ideal for boating and are alive with birds and animals.

If you find such quiet, flat spaces dull, you need travel only a few miles to reach the bright lights: three of England's most splendid stately houses—Holkham Hall, Blickling, and Her Majesty's own Sandringham. There are incomparable cathedrals, at Ely and Lincoln particularly, and let's not forget the "finest flower of Gothic in Europe," the King's College Chapel in Cambridge. These are the superlatives of East Anglia. But half the attraction of the region lies in its subtle landscapes, where the beauties of rural England are seen at their enduring best: to rush in search of one or two highlights is to miss these qualities, which can be enjoyed only by leisurely journeys along the byways.

Pleasures and Pastimes

Biking and Hiking

There's a good reason why Cambridge instantly conjures up the image of the undergraduate hurtling along the streets on a bicycle with academic gown flowing behind. It's an ideal city to traverse by bike, and everyone seems to do so. The same could be said for the entire region. "Very flat, Norfolk," Noel Coward's remark, is something of an overstatement; nonetheless, many of the flat coastal areas of East Anglia, although sometimes windswept, are perfect for cycling, and a network of cycle routes and bike rental centers provide good means of getting around the towpaths and backwaters of the Norfolk Broads. East Anglia is also a walker's dream. The long-distance footpath known as the Peddar's Way follows the line of a pre-Roman road, running from near Thetford through heathland, pine forests, and arable fields, and on through rolling chalklands to the Norfolk coast near Hunstanton. The Norfolk Coastal Path then continues eastward along the coast, joining at Cromer with another delightfully varied path, the Weaver's Way, which passes through medieval weaving villages and deeply rural parts of the Norfolk Broads on its 56-mi route from Cromer to Great Yarmouth.

Dining

The word "Anglis" constantly appears as a prefix to brand names. Restaurant menus feature not only specialties of the area, such as duckling, oysters, Norfolk black turkey, hare, and partridge, but also offer various regional favorites. Samphire, sometimes called "poor man's asparagus," is a kind of (delicious) seaweed that grows in the salt marshes along the North Norfolk and Suffolk coasts. The long coastline also provides Cromer crabs and Yarmouth bloaters (a kind of smoked herring), whereas the Essex coast near Colchester has been producing oysters since Roman times. There's an equally venerable East Anglian tradition in wine-making. The Romans first introduced vines to Britain, and they took especially well to this region. Today there are more than 40 vineyards in East Anglia, most of which offer tours and tastings to visitors. If you want to try a bottle (dry whites are best), check wine lists in local restaurants.

CATEGORY	COST*
££££	over £22
£££	£16–£22
££	£9–£15
£	under £9

per person for main course at dinner

Lodging

The intimate nature of even East Anglia's larger towns has meant that there are few hotels with more than 100 rooms. As a result, even the biggest hostelries have a friendly atmosphere and offer personal service. In addition, few English regions have quite so many centuries-old, half-timber inns with rooms full of character, roaring fires, and cozy bars—it's worth going out of your way to stay in at least one during your visit. Cambridge has relatively few hotels downtown, and these tend to be rather overpriced: there simply isn't room for hotels among the numerous historic buildings, although there are many guest houses on the arterial roads and in the suburbs. These start at £15–£20 per person per night and can be booked through the tourist information center. It's always busy in Cambridge in summer, so reserve in advance.

CATEGORY	COST*
££££	over £150
£££	£100–£150
££	£60–£100
£	under £60

*All prices are for two people sharing a standard double room, including service, breakfast, and VAT.

Exploring East Anglia

For purposes of exploring, East Anglia can be divided into four main areas: the central area surrounding the ancient university city of Cambridge and including the attractive towns of inland Suffolk; to the northeast, the region's capital, Norwich, the waterways of Broadland, and the beaches and salt marshes of the North Norfolk coast; the southeast, including the ancient Roman town of Colchester and sweeping upward along the Suffolk Heritage Coast; and to the north, the fenland city of Ely with its magnificent cathedral rising out of the flatlands, with Peterborough, a much expanded commercial center, and Lincoln, landmarked by its tall, fluted, cathedral towers, lesser luminaries of the region. Farther north, the historic ports of King's Lynn and Boston, from where the Pilgrims made their first, unsuccessful, bid to sail to the New World, flank the shallow bay known as the Wash.

Numbers in the text correspond to numbers in the margin and on the East Anglia, Cambridge, Norwich, and Lincolnshire maps.

Great Itineraries

East Anglia has a reputation for being flat and featureless, which is mostly undeserved. Admittedly, much of the land is agricultural. But although the lowland marsh country in the west, the Fens, may yield more vegetables than it does tourist attractions, you'll certainly need more than a few days to soak up the medieval atmosphere of Norfolk, Suffolk, and the unspoiled coastal villages—including time to linger over a pint of locally brewed beer in one of the astonishing number of picturesque pubs. A stay of a week would enable you to explore some of the variety of East Anglia and allow you to match your step to its slow pace and follow some of the tiny country lanes to churches and vineyards. In three days, it's better to concentrate on one area, probably Cambridge and its surroundings, rather than try to cover the large distances separating major sights and towns.

IF YOU HAVE 3 DAYS

🖼 **Cambridge** is easy to visit from London—too easy, some say, to judge by the huge number of visitors year-round. It remains a great day trip from London and is also the best base from which to explore the rest of East Anglia in a three-day tour. Explore some of the ancient university buildings, stroll along the Backs, or punt down the River Cam to Grantchester. The next day, head for **Ely** ⑰, and spend a few hours exploring the medieval town and its majestic cathedral, before moving on to **Bury St. Edmunds** ㉒, an extremely attractive town with graceful Georgian streets. Spend the third day exploring the medieval Suffolk "wool towns" of **Sudbury** ⑲, **Long Melford** ⑳, and **Lavenham** ㉑, before returning to Cambridge.

IF YOU HAVE 7 DAYS

With a full week's time, you'll be able to linger a little and see more of the sights in and near the main town. Start, however, from 🖼 **Cambridge** and take in the medieval sights on your first day, spend the night, then head out to **Saffron Walden** ⑱ and northeast to overnight in 🖼 **Bury St. Edmunds** ㉒. Explore the town the next day, making time to

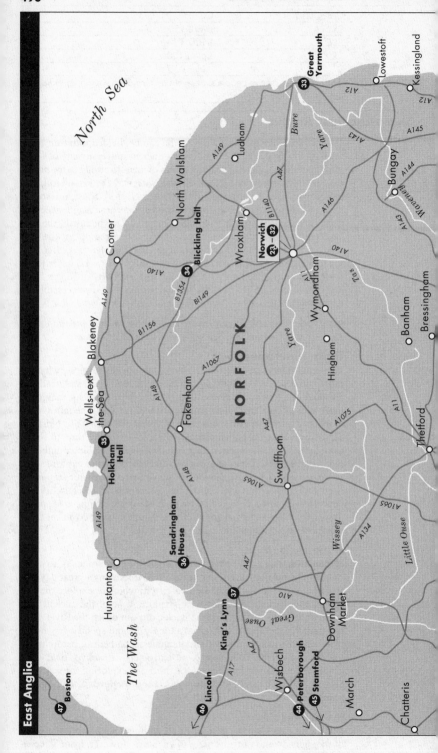

North Sea

Great Yarmouth 33

Lowestoft

Kessingland

A12

A12

A145

Bungay

A144

A143

Ludham

A149

Bure

Yare

A146

A47

Wroxham

B1140

Waveney

A143

North Walsham

Blickling Hall 34

Norwich 29 – 32

A11

A140

Cromer

A140

B1354

B1149

Wymondham

Tas

Banham

Bressingham

Blakeney

B1156

NORFOLK

Yare

Hingham

Wells-next-the-Sea

A149

A1067

Fakenham

A148

A47

A1075

A11

Thetford

Holkham Hall 35

Swaffham

A1065

A1065

A148

Little Ouse

Sandringham House 36

A149

Wissey

A134

Hunstanton

A47

Downham Market

A10

The Wash

King's Lynn 37

Great Ouse

A47

Lincoln

A17

A10

Wisbech

Peterborough 44

Stamford 45

March

46

44

Boston 47

Chatteris

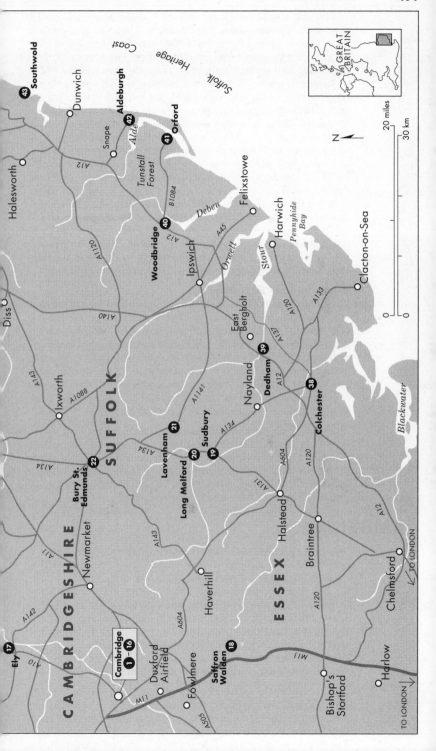

visit the charming Manor House Museum, and then head south through **Long Melford** ⑳, **Lavenham** ㉑ and **Sudbury** ⑲ (with a quick stopover to see Gainsborough's House) to ⊞ **Colchester** ㊳, the traditional base for exploring Constable Country. The next day, head for Constable's **Dedham** ㊴ (and perhaps lunch at Le Talbooth), then take the B1084 to **Orford** ㊶, a tiny village with a Norman church and castle and smokehouses, where traditional oak-wood methods of smoking fish are still used. After spending your fourth night in ⊞ **Aldeburgh** ㊷, head for **Southwold** ㊸, a charming seaside town where time seems to have stood still. Take the road via Bungay—notable for its crafts and antiques shops—to ⊞ **Norwich** to visit its cathedral and medieval alleys. After your fifth night spent in Norwich, the extensive journey northwest to ⊞ **Lincoln** ㊻, where you can spend your sixth night, takes you through flat Fenland. En route, you can visit **King's Lynn** ㊲ or detour northward toward the coast to visit one or two spectacular stately homes, including **Blickling Hall** ㉞, **Holkham Hall** ㉟, and **Sandringham House** ㊱. Lincoln is worthy of a day's exploration: on the way back to Cambridge the next day, opt to stop either at **Ely** ⑰, Fenland's "capital," to see its great cathedral, or at **Stamford** ㊺ to delight in Burghley House, an Elizabethan extravaganza.

When to Tour East Anglia

If you want to avoid crowds, stay away from Cambridge and the Norfolk Broads—the region's most popular tourist attractions—in late July and August. The May Bumps, intercollegiate boat races, are, confusingly, held the first week of June in Cambridge. During the "long vac," of course, Cambridge is empty of its many thousands of students, its life and soul. To see the city in full swing, visit October through June, although summer visitors won't miss out entirely because there's a range of enjoyable annual festivals, most notably the Strawberry Fair (mid-June), and the Folk Festival and Arts Festival (both July).

The world-famous Aldeburgh Festival of music and the arts, started in 1948 by Benjamin Britten, takes place in June, as does the archaic Dunmow Flitch Ceremony at Great Dunmow in Essex, where a side of bacon is awarded to a married couple who haven't quarreled for a year and a day. King's Lynn and Norwich both have renowned music and arts festivals, in July and October, respectively.

CAMBRIDGE

If you want to think about Cambridge, think Rupert Brooke, the short-lived World War I–era poet ("There is some corner of a foreign field/That is forever England"), a Cambridgeshire lad, who called his county "The shire for Men who Understand." Think Wordsworth and Thackeray, Byron and Tennyson, E. M. Forster and C. S. Lewis; and see *Chariots of Fire,* the film version of the true story of Harold Abrahams and Eric Liddell, two Cambridge graduates who shone in the 1924 Olympic Games. Exquisite King's College Chapel's equally exquisite-sounding choir defines the season for an entire nation, when the *Festival of Nine Lessons and Carols* is broadcast live on Christmas Eve.

With the spires of its university buildings framed by towering trees and expansive meadows, its medieval streets and passages enhanced by gardens and riverbanks, the city of Cambridge is among the loveliest in England. Situated on a bend of the River Cam, 54 mi north of London, and 63 mi southwest of Norwich, it's also one of the most ancient cities in Britain, its foundation lost in the mists of time, which is no cliché, for Cambridge is bedeviled by the mists that rise from the surrounding water meadows. Certainly the city predates the Roman

Cambridge

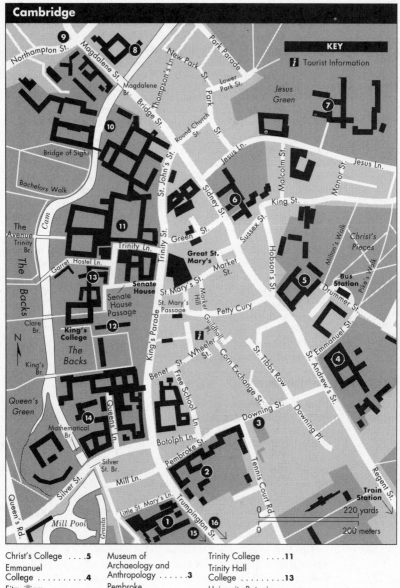

Christ's College **5**

Emmanuel
College **4**

Fitzwilliam
Museum **15**

Jesus College **7**

Kettle's Yard **9**

King's College
Chapel **12**

Magdalene
College **8**

Museum of
Archaeology and
Anthropology **3**

Pembroke
College **2**

Peterhouse
College **1**

Queens' College . . . **14**

St. John's
College **10**

Sidney Sussex
College **6**

Trinity College **11**

Trinity Hall
College **13**

University Botanic
Gardens **16**

occupation of Britain. There's similar confusion about when the university itself was founded. According to one version, Cambridge was founded by masters from Oxford who brought their pupils to Cambridge to escape the violence of Oxford's town–gown troubles. Another story attributes its founding to impoverished students from Oxford, who came in search of eels, no less—a cheap source of nourishment.

Keep in mind there is no recognizable campus here: "Where is the university?" is a question hard to answer—the scattered colleges *are* the university. The town reveals itself only slowly. It's filled with tiny gardens, ancient courtyards, imposing classic buildings, alleyways that lead past medieval churches, and wisteria-hung facades. Perhaps the best views are from the Backs, the green parkland that extends along the River Cam behind several colleges. Here you will feel the essential quality of Cambridge. Resulting in part from the larger size of the colleges, and partly from the lack of industrialization in the city center, this atmosphere of broad sweeping openness is just what distinguishes Cambridge from Oxford.

For centuries the University of Cambridge has been among the very greatest universities, rivaled in Britain only by Oxford; indeed, ever since the time of its most famous scientific alumnus, Sir Isaac Newton, it has outshone Oxford in the natural sciences. In recent years, the university has taken advantage of its scientific prestige, pooling its research facilities with various high-tech industries. As a result, the city is surrounded by IT companies, and has been dubbed "Silicon Fen" in comparison to California's Silicon Valley. The prosperity brought by hi-tech industries has done much to enliven the city center.

Exploring Cambridge

Each of the university's 25 oldest colleges is built around a series of courts, or quadrangles, whose velvety lawns are the envy of many an amateur gardener. Since students and fellows (faculty) live and work in these courts, access is sometimes restricted, especially during examination weeks (April, mid-June), and at *all* times you are politely requested to refrain from picnicking in the quadrangles! Visitors are not normally allowed into college buildings other than chapels, halls, and some libraries; some colleges levy an admission charge for certain buildings. The university's Web site, www.cam.ac.uk, has information about the colleges and other institutions associated with it. Public visiting hours vary from college to college depending on the time of year, and it's best to call ahead or to check first with the city tourist office. Some general guidelines for visiting hours, however, can be noted. Colleges close to visitors during the main exam time, late May to mid-June. Term-time (when classes are in session) means October to December, January to March, and April to June, whereas summer term, or vacations, runs from July to September. When the colleges are open, by far the best way to gain access without annoying anyone is to join a walking tour led by an official Blue Badge guide—in fact, many areas are off-limits unless you do. The two-hour tours leave up to five times daily from the city tourist office. The other traditional view of the colleges is gained from the relaxed confines of a punt—the flat-bottomed boats propelled by pole up and down the River Cam.

A Good Walk

Given the history all around you, it makes sense to start at **Peterhouse College** ①, the granddaddy of them all, founded by the bishop of Ely in 1281. One of the colleges closest to the train station, it lies on one side of Trumpington Street and stands across the way from **Pembroke College** ②—the "College of Poets," as graduates have included Spencer,

Cranshaw, and Gray—where you can gain a first glimpse of the 17th-century work of Christopher Wren in Cambridge, who helped design the college's chapel. From the Arts, head over to the Sciences. Walk up to Pembroke Street, turn right, and continue down Downing Street for the university's engaging **Museum of Archaeology and Anthropology** ③, on your right-hand side. At the end of Downing Street you're faced by **Emmanuel College** ④, and more of Wren's fine work. You then turn left up the busy shopping arteries of St. Andrew's Street and Sidney Street, passing the often overlooked **Christ's College** ⑤. To see the way that a college has grown over the centuries you could not do better than visit here. The Tudor main gateway, bearing a splendid coat of arms, leads into a fine courtyard, with the chapel framed by an ancient magnolia. The unfolding architecture leads you through, past a Fellows' building credited to Inigo Jones, to the spacious garden (once the haunt of Milton), and finally to a modern ziggurat-like confection. Onward, head to **Sidney Sussex College** ⑥—look for the famous portrait of Oliver Cromwell, who charged his painter to include "all these roughnesses, pimples, and warts," in the Hall here—before turning right down Jesus Lane for one of the prettiest of all colleges, **Jesus College** ⑦. Note the lovely Chapter House entrance, the chapel's Pre-Raphaelite stained glass, and the grounds.

Head farther north up Sidney Street and Bridge Street to Magdalene Bridge, where you're likely to get a first view of punts maneuvering their way along the River. By the river, quiet **Magdalene College** ⑧ flanks busy Magdalene Street—one of the glories of Cambridge is how quickly you can move from frantic, modern England to the seclusion of scholarly academe. A little farther north on the other side, a couple of museums beckon: the art displays in **Kettle's Yard** ⑨ and the city-related exhibits of the **Folk Museum.** Heading south, back into the city center, cross back over the river and down St. John's Street, past **St. John's** ⑩ and **Trinity** ⑪ colleges. Trinity is Sir Isaac Newton's college, and outside the Great Gate stands an apple tree said to be a descendant of the one whose falling apple caused Newton to formulate the laws of gravity. Ahead lies Cambridge's most famous sight, the soaring late-Gothic **King's College Chapel** ⑫. King's College itself faces King's Parade, where students bustle in and out of the coffee shops; you can take time out to climb the tower of **Great St. Mary's,** the university's main church, for a glorious city view. Behind King's, the city's Backs—its riverside gardens and meadows—make their presence felt at **Trinity Hall** ⑬ and **Queens'** ⑭ colleges, both of which will lure you off the beaten path for a while. Silver Street Bridge, by Queens', is another traditional spot to hire a chauffeured punt. For picture-perfect Cambridge, head back north along the riverbank to the Bridge of Sighs, modeled after its Venetian namesake, in St. John's. To complete the walking circuit, regain King's Parade and walk south, down to where it becomes Trumpington Street. Call in at the light, airy Church of Little St. Mary and pause at the monument to the Washington family on the wall to your left just inside the door. You will then pass Peterhouse, where you first started. Just beyond, the **Fitzwilliam** ⑮ is Cambridge's finest museum, with superb art and classical collections, and if this final attraction drains you, there's always the peaceful **University Botanic Gardens** ⑯ in which to recuperate, at least 10 minutes beyond, off Trumpington Street on Bateman Street. Ah, academia!

Sights to See

⑤ **Christ's College.** The gateway here bears the enormous coat of arms of its patroness, Lady Margaret Beaufort, mother of Henry VII, who established the institution in 1505; in the dining hall hang portraits of John Milton and Charles Darwin, two of the college's more famous students. Legend (now debunked) has it that Milton planted the mulberry tree in the Fellows' Garden at the behest of King James I, who was keen to encourage the silk industry. Admitted in 1625 at the age of 16, the great poet resided here in a first-floor room on the first stair on the north side of the first court. ✉ *St. Andrew's St.,* ☎ *01223/334900,* WEB *www.christs.cam.ac.uk.* ☉ *Apr.–Oct., daily 9:30–4:30; Nov.–Mar., daily 9:30–dusk. Gardens closed on weekends.*

❹ **Emmanuel College.** The master hand of architect Christopher Wren is evident throughout much of Cambridge, particularly at Emmanuel, built on the site of a Dominican Friary, where he designed the chapel and colonnade. In a stained-glass window in the Chapel, there's a likeness of John Harvard, founder of Harvard University, who studied here. The college, founded in 1584, was an early center of Puritan learning; a number of the Pilgrims were Emmanuel alumni, and they remembered their alma mater in naming Cambridge, Massachusetts. ✉ *St. Andrew's St.,* ☎ *01223/ 334200,* WEB *www.emma.cam.ac.uk.* ☉ *Daily 9–6, except exam time.*

★ ⑮ **Fitzwilliam Museum.** Housed in a classical-revival building renowned for its grand Corinthian portico, the Fitzwilliam, founded by the seventh Viscount Fitzwilliam of Merrion in 1816, has one of Britain's most outstanding collections of art (including paintings by John Constable, Gainsborough, the Pre-Raphaelites, and the French impressionists) and antiquities. The opulent interior displays its treasures to marvelous effect, with the Egyptian section in the lower gallery particularly noteworthy. Exhibits range from rare sculptures dating back to the Chinese Han dynasty of the 3rd century BC, inch-high figurines and burial goods to mummies, painted coffins, and stone inscriptions. In addition to its archaeological collections, the Fitzwilliam contains a large display of English Staffordshire and other pottery, as well as a fascinating room full of armor and muskets. The museum has a coffee bar and restaurant. ✉ *Trumpington St.,* ☎ *01223/332900,* WEB *www.fitz-museum.cam.ac.uk.* ☒ *Free, £3 donation requested.* ☉ *Tues.–Sat. 10–5, Sun. 2:15–5; guided tours Sun. at 2:30.*

Folk Museum. In a city where "gown" often dominates "town," the balance is redressed a little in this museum, adjacent to Kettle's Yard. In what was once the 16th-century White Horse Inn, Cambridgeshire's folk history is brought to life in rooms that display crafts, toys, trade utensils, paintings, and domestic paraphernalia in glorious profusion. ✉ *2–3 Castle St.,* ☎ *01223/355159,* WEB *www.folkmuseum.org.uk.* ☒ *£2.* ☉ *Tue.–Sat. 10:30–5, Sun. 2–5; closed Mon.*

Great St. Mary's. Known as the "university church," Great St. Mary's stands opposite the Senate House on King's Parade. Its origins are in the 11th century, although the present building dates from 1478. Celebrated archbishops who have preached here include Cranmer, Ridley, and Latimer. The main reason to visit today is to climb the tower, which, at 113 ft high, offers a superb view over the colleges and the colorful marketplace. ✉ *Market Hill,* ☎ *01223/350914.* ☒ *Tower £1.75.* ☉ *May–Sept., Mon.–Sat. 9–dusk; Oct.–Apr., Mon.–Sat. 9–4:15; open Sun. after services until 5 year-round.*

❼ **Jesus College.** Unique in Cambridge, the spacious grounds of Jesus College incorporate cloisters, a remnant of the nunnery of St. Radegund, which existed on the site before the college was founded in 1496. Lovely Cloister Court exudes a quiet medieval charm, an attribute evident in the adjacent chapel, which also belonged to the nunnery. Victorian restoration of the building includes some Pre-Raphaelite stained-glass windows and ceiling designs by William Morris. ✉ *Jesus La.,* ☎ *01223/ 339339,* WEB *www.jesus.cam.ac.uk.* ☉ *Daily 8–7, except exam period.*

⑨ Kettle's Yard. Originally a private house owned by a former curator of London's Tate Gallery, Kettle's Yard is home to a fine collection of 20th-century art, sculpture, furniture, and decorative arts, including works by Henry Moore, Barbara Hepworth, and Henri Gaudier-Brzeska. A separate gallery provides space for changing exhibitions of modern art and crafts, and weekly concerts (term time only) and lectures attract an eclectic mix of enthusiasts. ⊠ *Castle St.,* ☎ *01223/352124,* WEB *www.kettlesyard.co.uk.* 🖾 *Free.* ☉ *House Tues.–Sun. 2–4; gallery Tues.–Sat. 12:30–5, Sun. 2–5.*

★ ⑫ **King's College Chapel.** It seems almost invidious to single out just one building in Cambridge from the many that are masterpieces, but King's College Chapel is perhaps the supreme architectural work in the city. Based on Sainte Chapelle, the 13th-century private royal chapel in Paris, construction was overseen by Henry VI, the king after whom the college is named, toward the end of the 15th century. It was a crucial moment for the evolution of architecture in Britain, the last period before the classical architecture of the ancient Greeks and Romans, then being rediscovered by the Italians, began to make its influence felt in northern Europe. King's College Chapel is thus the final and, some would say, most glorious flowering of Perpendicular Gothic in Britain.

From the outside, the most prominent features are the expanses of glass, the massive flying buttresses, and the fingerlike spires that line the length of the building. Inside, the most obvious impression is of great space—the chapel has been described as "the noblest barn in Europe"—and of light flooding in from its huge windows. The brilliantly colored bosses (carved panels at the intersections of the roof ribs) are particularly intense, although hard to see without binoculars. An exhibition in the chantries, or side chapels, explains more about the chapel's construction. At the far end of the church, behind the altar, is an enormous and typically lively painting by Peter Paul Rubens of the *Adoration of the Magi,* originally painted for a convent in Louvain. Every Christmas Eve, a festival of carols sung by the chapel's famous choir is broadcast worldwide from here. Past students of King's College include the novelist E. M. Forster, the economist John Maynard Keynes, and the World War I poet Rupert Brooke. ⊠ *King's Parade,* ☎ *01223/331100 college; 01223/331447 chapel,* WEB *www.kings.cam.ac.uk.* 🖾 *Chapel £3.50.* ☉ *Oct.–June, weekdays 9:30–3:30, Sat. 9:30–3:15, Sun. 1:15–2:15; July–Sept., Mon.–Sat. 9:30–4:30, Sun. 1:15–2:15 and 5–5:30. Times subject to variation; phone in advance for complete information.*

⑧ **Magdalene College.** Across Magdalene (pronounced *maud*-lin) Bridge, a cast-iron 1820 structure, lies the only one of the older colleges to be sited across the river. Magdalene Street itself is narrow and traffic-heavy, but there's relative calm inside the pretty redbrick courts. It was a hostel for Benedictine monks for more than 100 years before the college was founded in 1542. In the second court, the college's Pepys Library—labeled *Bibliotecha Pepysiana*—contains the books and desk of the famed 17th-century diarist Samuel Pepys. ⊠ *Magdalene St.,* ☎ *01223/332100,* WEB *www.magd.cam.ac.uk.* 🖾 *Free.* ☉ *Library Apr.–Sept., Mon.–Sat. 11:30–12:30 and 2:30–3:30; Oct.–Mar., Mon.–Sat. 2:30–3:30.*

③ **Museum of Archaeology and Anthropology.** As befits a world-class institute of higher learning, Cambridge University maintains a series of fine museums in its research halls on Downing Street—the wonder is that they are not better known to visitors. Geological collections at the Sedgwick Museum and the exhibits at the Zoological Museum are typically extensive, but be sure to see the Museum of Archaeology and Anthropology, which has a superb collection of ethnographic objects brought back by early explorers, including members of Captain Cook's pioneering voyages to the Pacific. ⊠ *Downing St.,* ☎ *01223/333516.* 🖾 *Free.* ⊘ *Tues.–Sat., 2–4:30. Extended hrs Apr.–Oct.*

② **Pembroke College.** Established in 1347, Pembroke has some buildings dating from the 14th century in its first court. On the south side, Christopher Wren's chapel—his first major commission, completed in 1665—looks like a distinctly modern intrusion. You can walk through the college, around a delightful garden, and past the fellows' bowling green, whereas outside the library you can't miss the resplendent, toga-clad statue of William Pitt the Younger, perhaps the most precocious of the college's former members; he came up to university at age 15 and was appointed Prime Minister of Great Britain in 1783, when he was just 24. ⊠ *Trumpington St.,* ☎ *01223/338100,* WEB *www.pem.cam.ac.uk.* ⊘ *Daily 2–dusk, except in exam period.*

① **Peterhouse College.** Cambridge's oldest college, Peterhouse was founded in 1281 by the bishop of Ely. Parts of the dining hall date from 1290, although its most notable feature is the stained glass by William Morris and his contemporaries. The adjacent church of Little St. Mary's served as the college chapel until 1632, when the present late-Gothic chapel was built. ⊠ *Trumpington St.,* ☎ *01223/338200,* WEB *www.pet.cam.ac.uk.* ⊘ *Daily 9–5, except in exam period.*

⑭ **Queens' College.** One of the most eye-catching colleges is Queens' (1448), named after the respective consorts of Henry VI and Edward IV. It's tucked away on Queens' Lane, next to the wide lawns that lead down from King's to the Backs. The secluded "cloister court" looks untouched since its completion in the 1540s. Queens' distinctive masterpiece is the **Mathematical Bridge** (best seen from the Silver Street road bridge), an arched wooden structure that was originally held together without fastenings. The present bridge, dating from 1902, is securely bolted. If you're looking for a nice time-out, the Anchor, right by the Silver Street bridge, is a traditional riverside resting place. Have a drink overlooking the water and contemplate your next move, perhaps onto the river in a punt. ⊠ *Queens' La.,* ☎ *01223/335511,* WEB *www.quns.cam.ac.uk.* 🖾 *£1.* ⊘ *Apr.–Oct., daily 10–4:30; Nov.–Mar., daily 10–4, except exam time.*

⑩ **St. John's College.** The gateway to St. John's is guarded by two mythical beasts, "yales," holding up its coat of arms. Yales have the bodies of antelopes and heads of goats. St. John's is Cambridge's second-largest college, founded in 1511 by Henry VII's mother, Lady Margaret Beaufort. Its structures lie on two sites: from the main entrance walk to the left through the ancient courts—with their turrets, sculpted windows, and clock towers—to where a copy of the Bridge of Sighs in Venice reaches across the Cam to the mock-Gothic New Court (1825), whose white crenellations have earned it the nickname "the wedding cake." If you walk through until you reach the riverbank, you'll be able to stroll along the Backs and frame photographs of the elegant bridge (and less-than-elegant New Court buildings). ⊠ *St. John's St.,* ☎ *01223/338600,* WEB *www.joh.cam.ac.uk.* 🖾 *£1.75.* ⊘ *Apr.–Oct., daily 10–5:30, except exam time.*

⑥ **Sidney Sussex College.** Passing largely unnoticed on busy Sidney Street, Sidney Sussex is smaller than many colleges, yet it has interesting 17th- and 18th-century buildings, most of which were sadly given mock-Gothic "improvements" in 1832. Oliver Cromwell was a student here in 1616; the Hall contains his portrait, and his head has been buried here, in a secret location in the chapel, since 1960. ⊠ *Sidney St.,* ☎ *01223/ 338800,* WEB *www.sid.cam.ac.uk.* ⊘ *Daily 9–5, except exam time.*

⓫ **Trinity College.** Founded in 1546 by Henry VIII, Trinity replaced a 14th-century educational foundation. It's the largest college in either Cambridge or Oxford, with nearly 700 undergraduates, and many of its features match its size, not least its 17th-century "great court." Here is the massive and detailed gatehouse that holds a giant clock that strikes each hour with high and low notes. This was the original setting for the race around the quadrangle in the film *Chariots of Fire* (although the film itself was made elsewhere). The college's greatest masterpiece is Christopher Wren's magnificent library, colonnaded and seemingly constructed with as much light as stone, with woodcarving by the 17th century master Grinling Gibbons. Past alumni include Sir Isaac Newton, Lords Byron, Tennyson, Macaulay, and William Thackeray. Prince Charles was an undergraduate here in the late 1960s. ⊠ *St. John's St.,* ☎ *01223/338400,* WEB *www.trin.cam.ac.uk.* ⊠ *£1.75, Mar.–Nov.* ☉ *College daily 10–5, except exam time; library weekdays noon–2, Sat. in term time 10:30–12:30; hall and chapel also open to visitors: hrs vary.*

⓭ **Trinity Hall College.** The **Backs** are best appreciated from Trinity College's 14th-century neighbor, Trinity Hall, where you can sit on a wall by the river and watch students in punts manipulate their poles under the ancient ornamental bridges of Clare and King's. Access to the river is down Trinity Lane, off Trinity Street. The **Senate House** (⊠ King's Parade), which stands between Clare College and Trinity Hall, is one of the few strictly university buildings (not part of a particular college). A classical Palladian building of the 1720s, it's still used for graduation ceremonies and other university events. The building itself is closed to the public, but if the gate is open you're free to wander into the court and grounds. ⊠ *Trinity Hall, Trinity La.,* ☎ *01223/332500,* WEB *www.trinhall.cam.ac.uk.* ☉ *Daily 8–6, except exam time and summer term.*

⓰ **University Botanic Gardens.** These gardens were laid out in 1846 and contain, in addition to many rare specimens, a limestone rock garden. The gardens are a five-minute walk from the Fitzwilliam Museum, past lovely Brookside. ⊠ *Cory Lodge, Bateman St.,* ☎ *01223/336265.* ⊠ *Free, except weekends Nov.–Mar. (£1.50).* ☉ *Feb.–Oct., daily 10–5; Nov.–Jan., daily 10–4.*

OFF THE
BEATEN PATH

GRANTCHESTER – This pretty little village 2 mi up the river from the center of Cambridge is a delightful walk or bicycle ride along a path that follows the river through college-playing fields and the Grantchester Meadows. Grantchester takes its name from the River Granta, an earlier name for the Cam that runs through Cambridge, and was put on the map by its famous son, Rupert Brooke, whose very famous line "Stands the church clock at ten to three? And is there honey still for tea?" is from his poem, *The Old Vicarage, Grantchester,* in which he reinforced age-old rivalry between the village and the nearby city, railing against "Cambridge people rarely smile,/Being urban, squat and packed with guile." You can reach the village most enjoyably, if challengingly, by punt upstream along the Cam, or by walking along the signposted riverside path. On a sunny day, there's no better way of absorbing Cambridge's unique atmosphere—you feel as if you have all the time in the world.

Dining

£££   ✕ **Midsummer House.** A classy restaurant set beside the River Cam,
★   the gray-brick Midsummer House is particularly lovely in summer: it has a comfortable conservatory. Set menus for lunch and dinner offer a selection of robust yet sophisticated European and Mediterranean dishes. Choices might include tenderly cooked local lamb or the best

from the fish market, adorned with inventively presented vegetables. ⊠ *Midsummer Common,* ☎ *01223/369299. Reservations essential. AE, MC, V. Closed Mon. No lunch Sat., no dinner Sun.*

££ ✗ **Brown's.** This huge, airy, French American–style brasserie-diner is where Cambridge students take their parents when they're in town. Large fans still keep things cool in the pale-yellow dining room, while willing staff usher people from bar to table. The bountiful menu ranges from toasted tuna sandwiches, steak, mushroom, and Guinness pie, and house hamburgers, on up to venison or gigot of lamb. Check the daily specials, too: fresh fish and pasta are usually available. It's very busy on weekends, when you may have to wait in line. ⊠ *23 Trumpington St.,* ☎ *01223/461655. Reservations not accepted. AE, MC, V.*

££ ✗ **Three Horseshoes.** This is an early 19th-century thatched-cottage pub-restaurant with additional dining space in the conservatory. There's a tempting range of beautifully presented dishes, with the emphasis on modern British cuisine; for example, char-grilled meats or roast fish accompanied by those fashionable accoutrements, sun-dried tomatoes, polenta, and olives. It can get very busy, and waiting in line may be necessary. ⊠ *High St., Madingley (3 mi west of Cambridge, 10 mins by taxi),* ☎ *01954/210221. AE, DC, MC, V.*

££ ✗ **Twenty-Two.** An intimate dining room in a modest, Victorian house
★ ½ mi west of the center of Cambridge, the restaurant offers an extremely good-value fixed-price dinner. The menu changes monthly, and the kitchen rolls with the seasons, offering what are described as traditional English dishes with a "modern" approach alongside eclectic choices drawn from all quarters. Fish and game figure highly, but you're unlikely to be disappointed, whatever you choose. ⊠ *22 Chesterton Rd.,* ☎ *01223/351880. Reservations essential. AE, MC, V. Closed Sun.– Mon. and Christmas wk. Lunch by arrangement.*

£ ✗ **Copper Kettle.** Over the years, students have come to love this dowdy coffee shop, where they discuss work, life, and love over frothy coffees, sticky buns, and sandwiches. It's never going to win any gastronomic awards, but for a slice of real university life (and a fine view of King's College) it can't be beat. It closes at 5:30 PM. ⊠ *King's Parade,* ☎ *01223/365068. No credit cards. No dinner.*

£ ✗ **Eraina.** Crowded at the best of times, this cheap-and-cheerful Greek taverna is packed on Saturday nights (when no reservations are taken), seemingly with every student in town. The enormous menu ranges across Greek specialties, pizzas, salads, even curries, and everything comes in monster portions. If the food is, well, average, no one seems to mind— probably because the well-priced wine, good-natured service, and sheer buzz more than make up for it. ⊠ *2 Free School La., near Bene't St.,* ☎ *01223/368786. AE, MC, V.*

Lodging

££££ ⌂ **Garden Moat House Hotel.** Set among the colleges in 3 acres of pri-
★ vate grounds, this luxurious, modern hotel makes the most of its peaceful riverside location. Its gardens, lounge, bar, and conservatories all have river views, as do most of the rooms. If you want one, make it clear when you make your reservation, because some of the rooms at the rear of the L-shape hotel have less desirable views. The smart guest rooms have minibars, TVs, and fine bathrooms, and Club Moativation, a leisure center with indoor swimming pool, sauna, and steam room, reinvigorates tired limbs at the end of a grueling day's sightseeing. ⊠ *Granta Pl. and Mill La., CB2 1RT,* ☎ *01223/259988,* ℻ *01223/ 316605. 117 rooms. Restaurant, bar, room service, pool, sauna, steam room, health club. AE, DC, MC, V.*

£££–££££ ☐ **De Vere University Arms Hotel.** An elegant and sympathetically modernized 19th-century hotel, the De Vere is a top choice if you want to be in the city center. Space is at a premium in central Cambridge, and it shows here: the guest rooms are comfortable and well-appointed without being overly large. Many rooms also have views of Parker's Piece, the green backing the hotel, although you'll pay slightly more for these. The central lounge provides a comfortable place for afternoon tea, where you can sit by the fire enjoying a pot of Darjeeling and smoked salmon sandwiches. If you don't have a room with a view, then gaze out the windows of Parker's Bar, which also overlooks Parker's Piece. ✉ *Regent St., CB2 1AD,* ☎ *01223/351241,* FAX *01223/ 315256,* WEB *www.DeVere.com. 115 rooms. Restaurant, 2 bars, lounge, room service. AE, DC, MC, V.*

££–£££ ☐ **Arundel House Hotel.** This elegantly proportioned Victorian row hotel overlooks the River Cam, with Jesus Green in the background. The bedrooms are all furnished very comfortably with locally made mahogany furniture, and they come equipped with TV, and tea- and coffeemakers. Continental breakfast is included in the room rate, although a full breakfast is available for an extra charge. There are also meals and afternoon teas available in the Victorian-style conservatory, where rattan chairs, trailing plants, and patio garden add a certain cachet to the hotel. Ask about the hotel's special weekend rates, an excellent value. ✉ *53 Chesterton Rd., CB4 3AN,* ☎ *01223/367701,* FAX *01223/367721. 105 rooms. Restaurant, bar. AE, DC, MC, V. Closed Dec. 25–26.*

£ ☐ **Benson House.** Cambridge has few moderately priced accommodations, but this is one of the best of them. It's tastefully decorated, and located opposite the Fitzwilliam Museum, a 10-minute walk from the town center. ✉ *24 Huntingdon Rd., CB3 OHH,* ☎ *01223/311594. 9 rooms, 4 with bath. AE, MC, V.*

Nightlife and the Arts

Nightlife

The city's pubs provide the mainstay of Cambridge's nightlife, particularly when students are in town. First among equals is the **Eagle** (✉ Bene't St., ☎ 01223/505020), a 16th-century coaching inn with several separate bars and a cobbled courtyard that's lost none of its oldtime character—be warned that it's extremely busy on weekends. The **Free Press** (✉ Prospect Row, ☎ 01223/368337) is that rare beast, a nonsmoking pub, and all the better for it, attracting a fresh-faced student rowing clientele. For riverside views, honors go to the **Fort St. George** (✉ Midsummer Common, ☎ 01223/354327), a charming spot overlooking the university boathouses. The city's oldest pub is the **Pickerel** (✉ Magdalene St., ☎ 01223/355068), an ancient oak-beam hostelry attracting a younger student crowd.

The Arts

The **Cambridge Folk Festival** in late July, spread over the weekend at Cherry Hinton Hall, attracts major international folk singers and groups. Camping is available on the park grounds—reservations are essential. Details are available from the City Council Amenities and Recreation Department (☎ 01223/322640), or look in the local press.

Cambridge supports its own symphony orchestra, and regular musical events are held in many of the colleges, especially those with large chapels. Evensong at **King's College Chapel** is held Tuesday–Saturday at 5:30 PM, Sunday at 3:30 PM (☎ 01223/331447 for information). Concerts (classical and rock), opera, and ballet are held in Cambridge's beautifully restored **Corn Exchange** (✉ Wheeler St., ☎ 01223/357851).

The **ADC Theatre** (☎ 01223/504444) on Park Street hosts mainly student and fringe theater productions, including the famous Cambridge Footlights revue, training ground for much comic talent in the last 30 years. The city's main repertory theater, the **Arts Theatre** (✉ 6 St. Edward's Passage, ☎ 01223/5033333), built by economist John Maynard Keynes in 1936, supports a full program of theater, concerts, and events. It also has a good ground-floor bar and two restaurants, including the conservatory-style Roof Garden.

Outdoor Activities and Sports

Bicycling

Cambridge is the perfect city in which to rent a bike. **Geoff's Bike Hire** (✉ 65 Devonshire Rd., ☎ 01223/365629) is a short walk from the railroad station and charges from £7 per day and £15 per week, or £4.50 for up to three hours. Advance reservations are essential in July and August.

Punting

Punt rental is available at several places throughout the city, notably at Silver Street Bridge–Mill Lane, at Magdalene Bridge, and from outside the Rat and Parrot pub on Thompson's Lane on Jesus Green. Hourly rental costs about £8 (and requires a deposit of £40), although if you're not up to the challenge of steering yourself—by pole—along the **River Cam,** then chauffeured punting is also possible at most rental places. Around £5 per head is the usual rate for this, and your chauffeur will likely be a Cambridge student.

Shopping

Cambridge is a main shopping area for a wide region, and it has all the usual chain stores, many situated in the Grafton Centre and Lion's Yard shopping precincts. More interesting are the small specialty stores found among the colleges in the center of Cambridge, especially in and around Trinity Street, King's Parade, Rose Crescent, and Market Hill.

Bookshops are Cambridge's pride and joy. The **Cambridge University Press** bookshop (✉ 1 Trinity St., ☎ 01223/333333) stands on the oldest bookstore site in Britain, with books sold here since the 16th century. **Heffer's** (✉ 20 Trinity St., ☎ 01223/568568) is one of the world's biggest bookstores, with an enormous stock of books, many rare or imported. There's also a charming children's branch (✉ 30 Trinity St., ☎ 01223/568551). Cambridge is also known for its secondhand bookshops. Antiquarian books can be found at **G. David** (✉ 3 and 16 St. Edward's Passage, ☎ 01223/354619), tucked away near the Arts Theatre. The **Haunted Bookshop** (✉ 9 St. Edward's Passage, ☎ 01223/312913) offers a great selection of old, illustrated books and British classics. The **Bookshop** (✉ 24 Magdalene St., ☎ 01223/362457) is the best of Cambridge's secondhand bookshops.

FROM ELY TO BURY ST. EDMUNDS

This central area of towns and villages within easy reach of Cambridge is testament to the amazing changeability of the English landscape. The town of Ely is set in a landscape of flat, empty, and apparently endless fenland, or marsh. Only a few miles south and east into Suffolk, however, all this changes to pastoral landscapes of—if not rolling, then gently undulating—hills, clusters of villages, and towns whose prettiness is easier to appreciate than the sense of eerie romance permeating the fens.

Ely

⑰ *16 mi north of Cambridge.*

Ely is Fenland's "capital," the center of what used to be a separate county called the Isle of Ely (literally "island of eels"). Until the land was drained, Ely was surrounded by treacherous marshland, which inhabitants crossed wearing stilts. Now surrounded by fields of wheat, sugar beet, and carrots, it's a small, dense town dominated by its cathedral. The shopping area and little market square lie to the north and lead down to the attractive riverside, and the well-preserved medieval buildings of the cathedral grounds and the King's School (which trains cathedral choristers) spread out to the south and west.

★ **Ely Cathedral,** known affectionately as the Ship of the Fens, can be seen for miles. It stands on one of the few ridges in the whole of the fens, towering above the flat landscape. The cathedral was begun by the Normans in 1083, on the site of a Benedictine monastery founded by the Anglo-Saxon princess, Etheldreda, in 673. Etheldreda died, legend has it, from a growth in the neck, which she accepted as just punishment for her love of necklaces; she was later venerated as a saint. In the center of the Cathedral you can see a marvel of medieval construction—the octagonal lantern, a sort of stained-glass skylight of colossal proportions, built to replace the central tower after it collapsed in 1322. Much of the decorative carving of the 14th-century Lady Chapel was defaced during the Reformation (mostly by knocking off the heads of the statuary), but enough of the delicate tracery work remains to show its original beauty. The fan-vaulted, carved ceiling remains intact, as it was too high for the iconoclasts to reach. The cathedral's triforium gallery houses a **Stained Glass Museum,** with a wonderful array of exhibits up a flight of 41 steps. ⊠ *Chapter Office, The College,* ☎ *01353/667735,* WEB *www.cathedral.ely.anglican.org.* ⊠ *Cathedral £3.50, free on Sun. (donation requested); stained glass museum £2.50.* ⏱ *Cathedral Mon.–Sat. 7–6, Sun. 7:30–5; free guided tour, daily at 11:15 and 2:15; museum daily 10:30–4.*

Ely's most famous resident was Oliver Cromwell. The half-timber medieval house that was the home of Cromwell and his family stands in the shadows of the cathedral. During the 10 years he lived here, from 1636, Cromwell was leading the rebellious Roundheads in their eventually victorious struggle against King Charles I. **Oliver Cromwell's House** now contains an exhibit on its former occupant and audiovisual presentations about Cromwell and about the draining of the local fens. The house is also the site of Ely's tourist information center. ⊠ *29 St. Mary's St.,* ☎ *01353/662062.* ⊠ *£2.50.* ⏱ *Apr.–Sept., daily 10–5:30; Oct.–Mar., Mon.–Sat. 10–5.*

Housed in the old prison, the compact **Ely Museum** is dedicated to the history of Ely from the Ice Age to the present day. ⊠ *Old Gaol, Market St.,* ☎ *01353/666655.* ⊠ *£2.* ⏱ *Daily 10:30–4:30.*

Dining and Lodging

££ ★ ✕ **Old Fire Engine House.** This restaurant near the cathedral has two dining rooms: the main one, with scrubbed pine tables, opens into the garden; the other, with an open fireplace and a polished wood floor, also serves as an art gallery. Among the English dishes are traditional Fenland recipes, such as pike baked in white wine, as well as eel pie and game in season. ⊠ *25 St. Mary's St.,* ☎ *01353/662582. MC, V. Closed 2 wks at Christmas. No dinner Sun.*

£–££ ✕ **Dominique's.** A delightful little delicatessen-cum-restaurant with stripped pine floors, Dominique's serves brunch, lunch, and dinner in a nonsmoking environment. During the day it sees itself as more of a brasserie, whereas in the evening the specialty is French cuisine with a focus on warm salads, grilled salmon, and terrines. ⊠ *8 St. Mary's St.,* ☎ *01353/665011. No credit cards. No dinner Sun.*

£   🖾 **Old Egremont House.** A five-minute walk from the town center, this 17th-century house has views of the cathedral from its two large rooms. Inside the oak-beam house, everything is immaculate—the family still lives here—and there are books and antiques all around. There's a private garden, where it's a delight to sit in summer. ⊠ *31 Egremont St.,* ☎ 🖾 *01353/663118. 2 rooms. No credit cards. Closed Christmas wk.*

Saffron Walden

⓲   *14 mi south of Cambridge.*

Best known for its many typically East Anglian timber-frame buildings, the town owes its name to the saffron crocus fields that used to be cultivated in medieval times and processed for their dye. Some of the buildings have elaborate pargeting (decorative plasterwork), especially the walls of the former Sun Inn, which was used by Cromwell during his campaigns. In keeping with the long military history of Saffron Walden, the old **Grammar School** here was the World War II headquarters of the U.S. Air Force's 65th Fighter Wing. On the common at the east end of town, there's a 17th-century circular earth maze, created from space left among the crocus beds.

★   Palatial **Audley End House,** a mile or so west of Saffron Walden, is a famous example of Jacobean (early 17th-century) architecture. It was once owned by Charles II, who bought it as a convenient place to break his journey on the way to the Newmarket races. Remodeled in the 18th and 19th centuries, it shows the architectural skill of Sir John Vanbrugh, Robert Adam, and Rebecca Biagio as well as original Jacobean work in the magnificent Great Hall. You can also enjoy a leisurely walk around the park, landscaped by Capability Brown in the 18th century. ☎ *01799/522842,* 🕸 *www.english-heritage.org.uk.* 🎟 *House and park £6.50, park only £4.50.* ⊙ *Apr.–Sept., Wed.–Sun., park noon–5, house 11–6; Oct., park and house Wed.–Sun. 10–3.*

Dining and Lodging

££   ✕🖾 **Saffron Hotel.** This conversion of three houses into one has resulted in a comfortable, modern hotel operating inside a 16th-century building. Three of the bedrooms have splendid bathrooms and four-poster beds. The light and airy conservatory restaurant is very popular locally. ⊠ *10–18 High St., CB10 1AY,* ☎ *01799/522676,* 🖾 *01799/ 513979. 17 rooms. Restaurant, bar, lobby lounge. AE, DC, MC, V.*

Sudbury

⓳   *23 mi east of Saffron Walden, 16 mi south of Bury St. Edmunds, 14 mi northwest of Colchester.*

The prosperity of Sudbury, with its three fine churches and half-timber houses, was founded on the profits of an early silk-weaving industry as well as the wool trade. Its river, the Stour, was once, surprisingly, navigable to the sea, and the town was once filled with quays. Sudbury was Charles Dickens's model for the fictional Eatanswill, where Mr. Pickwick stands for Parliament. Thomas Gainsborough, one of the greatest English portrait and landscape painters, was born here in 1727; a **statue** of the artist holding his palette stands on Market Hill.

Gainsborough's family home is now a museum, containing paintings by the artist and his contemporaries, as well as an arts center. Although

Gainsborough's House presents an elegant Georgian facade, with touches of the 18th-century neo-Gothic style, the building is essentially Tudor. In the walled garden behind the house, a mulberry tree planted in 1620 is still growing. ⊠ *46 Gainsborough St.,* ☎ *01787/372958,* WEB *www.gainsborough.org.* ⌨ *£3, free in Dec.* ۞ *Mar.–Oct., Tues.– Sat. 10–5, Sun. 2–5; Nov.–mid-Apr., Tues.–Sat. 10–4, Sun. 2–4.*

Lodging

£ 🏠 **Old Bull.** This 16th-century inn is furnished with leather chairs and antiques, although the comfortable guest rooms have been modernized. All have TVs and telephones; some also have beams and galleries. The informal restaurant serves Anglo-French dishes, although the hotel is a five-minute walk from the town center, where several other eateries provide good meals. ⊠ *Church St., Ballingdon CO10 2BL,* ☎ *01787/ 374120,* FAX *01787/379044. 10 rooms. Restaurant, bar, lobby lounge. AE, MC, V.*

Long Melford

⓴ *2 mi north of Sudbury, 17 mi south of Bury St. Edmunds.*

It's easy to see how this village got its name, especially if you walk the full length of its 2-mi-long main street, which gradually broadens to include green squares and trees and finally opens into the large triangular green on the hill. Long Melford grew rich on its wool trade in the 15th century and the town's buildings are an attractive mixture— mostly Tudor half-timber or Georgian—and many of them house antiques shops. Utility poles are banned from both Long Melford and Lavenham to preserve the towns' ancient look, although the massed ranks of parked cars down both sides of the street make this a fruitless exercise. Away from the main road, Long Melford returns to its resolutely late-medieval roots.

Holy Trinity Church, founded by the rich clothiers of Long Melford, stands on a hill at the north end of the village. It's unfortunately obscured by Trinity Hospital, thoughtlessly built there in 1573. But close up, the delicate, flint–flush work and huge, 16th-century perpendicular windows that take up most of the church's walls have great impact, especially since the nave is 150 ft long. Much of the original stained glass remains, notably the Lily Crucifix window. The Lady Chapel has an unusual interior cloister. ⊠ *Main St.,* WEB *www.longmelford.co.uk.*

Melford Hall, distinguished from the outside by its turrets and topiaries, is a mid-16th-century house with a fair number of 18th-century additions. Much of the porcelain and many other fine pieces in the house come from the *Santissima Trinidad,* a ship loaded with gifts from the emperor of China and bound for Spain that was captured by one of the house's owners in the 1700s. ⊠ *Long Melford CO10 9AA,* ☎ *01787/ 880286,* WEB *www.nationaltrust.co.uk.* ⌨ *£4.20.* ۞ *May–Sept., Wed.– Sun., 2–5:30 (tours Wed. and Thurs.; call for times); Apr. and Oct., weekends 2–5:30.*

Kentwell Hall, a half mile north of Long Melford Green, is a redbrick Tudor manor house with picturesquely shaped chimneys and domes, surrounded by a wide moat. Built between 1520 and 1550, it was heavily restored inside after a fire in the early 19th century. Today, a restoration program is again under way, and the original gardens are being re-created. On many weekends from mid-April through September, a reenactment of Tudor life is performed here by costumed "servants" and "farmworkers," with great panache and detail. There's also an organic farm, home to rare-breed farm animals. ☎ *01787/310207,* WEB *www.longmelford.co.uk.* ⌨ *House, gardens, and farm £5.50, special*

events £6.70–£11.60. ☉ *Apr.–mid-July, weekends noon–5; mid-July–*
Sept., daily noon–5.

Dining and Lodging

££–£££   ✕⊡ **The Bull.** The public rooms of the Bull—stone-flagged floors,
bowed oak beams, and heavy antique furniture—show its long history.
Throughout, the half-timber Elizabethan building is a joy, and whether
you eat in the restaurant or the bar sporting a huge original fireplace,
you'll be served with efficiency and care. Traditional roasts and grills
are mixed with modern flavors—alongside a local game casserole might
appear mullet in a light Thai curry sauce. Creature comforts and pleasant bathrooms offset the smallish size of the guest rooms, and all retain their original character. ✉ *Hall St. CO10 9JG,* ☎ *01787/378494,*
℻ *01787/880307. 25 rooms. Restaurant, bar. AE, DC, MC, V.*

Lavenham

㉑ *4 mi northeast of Long Melford, 10 mi south of Bury St. Edmunds.*

More like a village than a town, Lavenham seems virtually unchanged
since the height of its wealth in the 15th and 16th centuries. The
weavers' and wool merchants' houses occupy not just one show street
but most of the town. These are timber-frame in black oak, the main
posts looking as if they could last for another 400 years. The **Guildhall of Corpus Christi** (1529) is the most spectacular building in Lavenham. It dominates Market Place, a remarkably preserved square with
barely a foot in the 20th century, and is open to visitors as a museum
of the medieval wool trade. ✉ *Market Pl.,* ☎ *01787/247646,* 🆆🅴🅱
www.nationaltrust.org.uk. 🎫 *£3.50.* ☉ *Apr.–Oct., daily 11–5; Mar.
and Nov., weekends 11–4.*

The **Wool Hall** was torn down in 1913, but it was reassembled immediately at the request of Princess Louise, sister of the then-reigning king,
George V. In 1962, it was joined to the neighboring Swan Hotel. A
splendid Elizabethan building, the **Swan Hotel** had a long history as a
coaching inn and in World War II served as the special pub for the U.S.
Air Force's 48th Bomber Group, whose memorabilia cover the walls
of the tile floor bar.

Lavenham Church is set apart from the village. It was built with wool
money by local cloth merchant Thomas Spring between 1480 and
1520. The height of its tower (141 ft) was meant to surpass those of
the neighboring churches. In this it succeeded, although the rest of the
church is of perfect proportions, with a spacious design.

Dining and Lodging

££–£££   ✕⊡ **Swan Hotel.** This glorious 14th-century lodging has aging timbers,
★   rambling public rooms, open fires, and antique furniture in every con-
ceivable nook and cranny. The downstairs lounges overlook attractive
courtyard gardens, and upstairs, along corridors so low that cushions
are strategically placed on beams, most of the individually styled bedrooms have fine fabrics, rich oak cabinets, and original wood paneling. Double glazing keeps out most of the traffic noise from the street,
and bathrooms have been ingeniously fashioned around ancient timbers and hidden rooms. Traditional English cuisine is served in the restaurant (complete with its own minstrels' gallery). ✉ *High St., CO10 9QA,*
☎ *01787/247477,* ℻ *01787/248286. 46 rooms, 2 suites. Restaurant,
2 bars, lobby lounge. AE, DC, MC, V.*

££   ✕⊡ **The Angel.** This popular spot overlooks Lavenham's picture-book
main square. Modern British cuisine is the draw here, and the specialty
of the house—home-smoked fish—draws rave reviews. Or just sit a
spell at the scrubbed pine tables to enjoy one of the well-kept local beers

on tap. Guest rooms are comfortably furnished, and no-smoking rooms are available. ✉ *Market Sq.,* ☎ *01787/247388. 8 rooms. Restaurant, bar. AE, MC, V.*

Bury St. Edmunds

★ ㉒ *10 mi north of Lavenham, 28 mi east of Cambridge.*

Bury St. Edmunds owes its name, and indeed its existence, to Edmund, the last king of East Anglia and medieval patron saint of England, who was hacked to death by marauding Danes in 869. He was subsequently canonized, and his shrine attracted pilgrims, settlement, and commerce. In the 11th century the erection of a great Norman abbey confirmed the town's importance as a religious center. The town hall was designed by Robert Adam in 1774. The Abbey of Bury St. Edmunds was one of the many that fell during Henry VIII's dissolution of the monasteries. The abbey's enormous scale is evident in the surviving gate tower on Angel Hill. Today, only the Norman Gate Tower, the fortified Abbot's Bridge over the River Lark, and a few ruins remain. These are now the site of the **Abbey Botanical Gardens,** with rare trees, including a Chinese tree of heaven planted in the 1830s.

Originally three churches stood within the walls of the Abbey of St. Edmunds, but only two have survived: St. Mary's and St. James's. **St. Mary's,** built in the 15th century, has a blue-and-gold embossed "wagon" (barrel-shape) roof over the choir. Mary Tudor, Henry VIII's sister and queen of France, is buried here. **St. James's,** like St. Mary's, dates from the 15th century; the brilliant paint on its ceiling and the stained-glass windows gleaming like jewels are the result of restoration in the 19th century by the architect Sir Gilbert Scott. Don't miss the memorial (near the altar) to an event in 1214, when the barons of England gathered here to take a solemn oath to force King John to grant the Magna Carta. The cathedral's original Abbey Gate was destroyed in a riot, and it was rebuilt in the 14th century on clearly defensive lines—you can see the arrow slits. The best way to make sense of the abbey's sprawling grounds is to rent a headset from the **Abbey Visitor Centre** for an audio tour. ✉ *Samsons Tower IP33 1RS,* ☎ *01284/763110.* 🎫 *Free; audio tour £1.50.* ⏲ *Abbey grounds weekdays 7:30 AM–½ hr before dusk, weekends 9 AM–dusk; Visitor Centre mid-Apr.–Oct., daily 10–5.*

A walk along **Angel Hill** is a journey through the history of Bury St. Edmunds. Along one side, the Abbey Gate, cathedral, Norman Gate Tower, and St. Mary's Church make up a continuous display of medieval architecture. Elegant Georgian houses line Angel Hill on the side opposite St. Mary's Church; these include the **Athenaeum,** an 18th-century social and cultural meeting place, which has a fine Adam-style ballroom. The splendid **Angel Hotel** (✉ 3 Angel Hill) was the scene of Sam Weller's meeting with Job Trotter in Dickens's *The Pickwick Papers.* Dickens stayed here while he was giving readings at the Athenaeum.

The **Manor House Museum,** a Georgian mansion facing the abbey's grounds, contains excellent art and horological collections: paintings, clocks, watches, furniture, costumes, and ceramics from the 17th through the 20th centuries. The clocks and watches in particular are extraordinarily beautiful, and there's a café and gift shop, too. ✉ *Honey Hill,* ☎ *01284/757072,* WEB *www.stedmunds.co.uk.* 🎫 *£2.85.* ⏲ *Tues.–Sun. 10–5. Closed Jan.*

At the end of Cornhill is the 12th-century **Moyse's Hall,** probably the oldest building in East Anglia, which houses in the original tiny rooms local archaeological collections. It also has a macabre display relating to the Red Barn murder, a case that gained notoriety in an early 19th-century blood-and-thunder theatrical melodrama, *Maria Marten, or the Murder in the Red Barn;* Maria Marten's murderer was executed in Bury St. Edmunds in 1828. ⊠ *Cornhill,* ☎ *01284/757488,* WEB *www.stedmunds.co.uk.* ☞ *£1.75.* ⊙ *Mon.–Sat. 10–5, Sun. 2–5.*

Dining and Lodging

££–£££   ✕ **Maison Bleu at Mortimer's.** This French restaurant specializes in seafood although it has meat dishes for noncrustacean lovers. The seafood offered depends on the day's catch, but grilled fillets of local trout, salmon, and mussels are always available. ⊠ *30 Churchgate St.,* ☎ *01284/ 760623. Reservations essential. AE, DC, V. Closed Dec. 27–Jan. 25.*

££–£££   ✕⊞ **Angel Hotel.** This is the quintessential ivy-clad, historic, market-
★   town hotel. A former coaching inn, it has spacious and well-furnished rooms. Several have four-poster beds, and one, the Charles Dickens Room, is where the author himself stayed. The bed is fairly small, but the rest of the room is in perfect 19th-century English style. Morning coffee and afternoon tea are served in the cozy lobby, complete with open fireplace. Elegant dining is in the Abbeygate Restaurant. Here, overlooking the abbey's main gate, a classic English menu is impeccably served, with dishes like grilled lemon sole, venison sausages, or roast duck with port sauce. ⊠ *3 Angel Hill, IP33 1LT,* ☎ *01284/753926,* FAX *01284/750092. 43 rooms. 2 restaurants, bar. AE, DC, MC, V.*

££   ⊞ **Ounce House.** This small, friendly, nonsmoking B&B is a three-minute walk from the abbey. It has a great deal of charm, with stylish guest rooms attractively and comfortably furnished. A full breakfast sets you up for the day, and although no other meals are served, the house is very close to Bury's restaurants. ⊠ *Northgate St., IP33 1HP,* ☎ *01284/ 761779,* FAX *01284/768315. 4 rooms. MC, V.*

The Arts

Bury St. Edmunds's splendid **Theatre Royal,** which offers a wide variety of touring shows, was built in 1819 and is a perfect example of Regency theater design. It may be closed during parts of summer, so call ahead. ⊠ *Westgate St.,* ☎ *01284/769505.* ⊙ *Mon.–Sat. 10–8, and for performances. Closed for viewing during rehearsals.*

NORWICH TO NORTH NORFOLK

Norwich, unofficial capital of East Anglia, is the heart of the eastern and northern part of East Anglia's "bump," dominated by the 15th-century spire of its impressive cathedral. It's 63 mi northeast of Cambridge. Norfolk's continuing isolation from the rest of the country, and its unspoiled landscape and architecture—bypassed by the industrial revolution—have proved to be a draw in recent years. Many of the flint-knapped (decorated with broken flint) houses in North Norfolk's pretty villages are, nowadays, weekend or holiday homes. Windmills, churches, and waterways are the area's chief defining characteristics. A few miles inland from the Norfolk coast, the Broads begin, a name that caused much comment among GIs during World War II. In fact, these innocent Broads form a national park, a network of shallow, reed-bordered lakes, many linked by wide rivers. Boating and fishing are great lures here; rent a boat for a day or a week and the local waterside pubs, churches, villages, and nature reserves all fall within easy reach.

Norwich

It used to be said that Norwich had a pub for each day of the week and a church for each week of the year. Although this is no longer true, both types of institutions are still much in evidence in this fine city. Established by the Saxons because of its prime trading position on the rivers Yare and Wensum, the town still has its heart in the triangle between the two waterways, dominated by the castle and cathedral. The inner beltway follows the line of the old city wall, much of which is still visible. It's worth driving around after dark to see the older buildings, which, thanks to skillful floodlighting, stand out from their much newer neighbors. By the time of the Norman Conquest, Norwich was one of the largest towns in England, although much was destroyed by the Normans to create a new town endowed with grand buildings.

★ ㉓ The grandest example of Norman architecture in Norwich is **Norwich Cathedral.** Although its spire, at 315 ft, is visible from everywhere, you cannot see the building itself until you pass through St. Ethelbert's Gate. The cathedral was begun in 1096 by Herbert de Losinga, who had come from Normandy in 1091 to be its first bishop but originally chose Thetford to be the center of his diocese before changing his mind and plumping for Norwich. His splendid tomb is by the high altar. The plain west front and dramatic crossing tower, with its austere, geometrical decoration, are distinctly Norman. The remarkable length of the nave is immediately impressive; unfortunately, the similarly striking height of the vaulted ceiling makes it a strain to study the delightful colored bosses, where Bible stories are illustrated with great vigor and detail. ✉ *The Close,* ☎ *01603/764385,* WEB *www.cathedral.org.uk.* ✉ *Free, but £3 donation requested.* ☉ *Mid-May–mid-Sept., daily 7:30–6; mid-Sept.–mid-May, daily 7:30–7; free guided tours June–Sept., weekdays at 11 and 2:15, Sat. at 11.*

The Cathedral Close (grounds) is one of the most idyllic places in Norwich. Past the attractive mixture of medieval and Georgian houses, a
㉔ path leads down to the ancient water gate, **Pulls Ferry.** The grave of Norfolk-born nurse Edith Cavell, the British World War I heroine shot by the Germans in 1915, is at the east end of the cathedral.

㉕ The decorated stone facing of **Norwich Castle,** high on the hill in the center of the city, makes it look like a children's book illustration. In fact, the castle is Norman (1130), but the wooden bailey (wall) on the castle mound was later replaced with a stone keep (tower). The thick walls and other defense works attest to the castle's military function. For most of its history the castle has been a prison, and executions took place here well into the 19th century, after which it became a museum of natural history. There are daily guided tours of the battlements and dungeons. The castle, which has been closed for redevelopment, is scheduled to reopen in summer 2001; call to confirm. The excellent **Regimental Museum** here has displays on Norfolk's history, including a gallery devoted to the Norwich School of painters who, like the Suffolk artist John Constable, devoted their work to the everyday Norfolk landscape and seascape as revealed in the East Anglian light. ✉ *Norwich Castle,* ☎ *01603/223624.* ✉ *July–Sept. £3.40, Oct.–June £2.40.* ☉ *Mon.–Sat. 10–5, Sun. 2–5.*

West of Norwich Castle is the **marketplace,** with its blanket of brightly striped awnings. It's been the heart of the city for 900 years. Overlooking the marketplace is the imposing—if somewhat severe—early 20th-
㉖ century **City Hall,** whose steps are guarded by bronze Norwich lions. Below
㉗ City Hall and next to the market rises the elaborate church tower of **St. Peter Mancroft.** Narrow lanes and alleys that used to be the main streets
㉘ of medieval Norwich lead away from the market and end at **Tombland** by the cathedral. Neither a graveyard nor a plague pit, Tombland was the site of the Anglo-Saxon trading place, now a busy thoroughfare.
㉙ **Elm Hill,** off Tombland, is a cobbled and pleasing mixture of Tudor and Georgian houses, now mostly given over to gift shops and tearooms.

City Hall . . . **26**
Elm Hill **29**
Norwich
Castle **25**
Norwich
Cathedral . . **23**
Pulls
Ferry **24**
Sainsbury
Centre
for the
Visual Arts . . **32**
St. Peter
Hungate . . . **30**
St. Peter
Mancroft . . . **27**
Tombland . . . **28**
University
of East
Anglia **31**

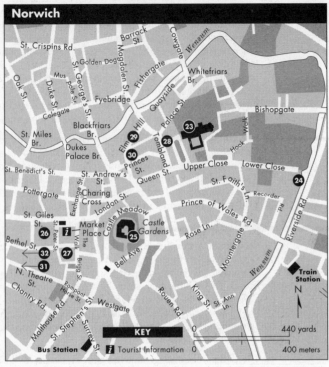

Norwich

③⓪ **St. Peter Hungate** (at the top end of Elm Hill) is a 15th-century former church that displays church art and furnishings. You can try your hand at brass rubbing here. ⊠ *Princes St.,* ☎ *01603/667231.* ☜ *Free; brass rubbing £1.50–£10.* ⊙ *Apr.–Oct., Mon.–Sat. 10–5.*

In complete contrast to Norwich's historical composition is the modern **University of East Anglia** (UEA), built during the great expansion
③① of higher education in the 1960s. Its site on the slopes of the River Yare, 3 mi west of the town center, was used by architect Denys Lasdun to give a dramatic, stepped-pyramid effect. The campus is linked by walkways that center on a fountain courtyard.

③② The award-winning **Sainsbury Centre for the Visual Arts,** a hangarlike building designed by Norman Foster, is on the UEA campus. It holds the extraordinary private art collection of the Sainsbury family, owners of a huge supermarket chain. The collection includes a remarkable quantity of tribal art and 20th-century works, especially Art Nouveau, and includes pieces by Picasso and Giacometti. There's a coffee bar and restaurant on the premises. Buses 4, 5, 26, and 27 run from Norwich Castle Meadow to UEA, providing access to both the university and the Sainsbury Centre. ⊠ *Earlham Rd.,* ☎ *01603/593199,* WEB *www.uea.ac.uk.* ☜ *£2.* ⊙ *Tues.–Sun. 11–5.*

Dining and Lodging

££ ✕ **Marco's.** The Georgian architecture of this building is comple-
★ mented inside by paneled walls, open fires, and pictures, all contributing to a warm, friendly, private atmosphere. Specialties of the Italian cuisine include *salmone al cartoccio* (salmon in parchment); game and local crab are served when available. Portions are generous, and there's a good-value fixed-price menu at lunchtime. ⊠ *17 Pottergate,* ☎ *01603/624044. AE, DC, MC, V. Closed Sun.–Mon.*

££ ✕ **St. Benedict's.** The restaurant is nothing special to look at—homey, and even a little old-fashioned. The food, however, is special, with excellent offerings of robust English dishes in tandem with more-daring creations; for example, crispy duck paired with creamy mash and caramelized apple. ✉ *9 St. Benedict's St.,* ☎ *01603/765377. AE, DC, MC, V. Closed Sun.–Mon., and 1 wk at Christmas.*

£–££ ✕ **Pinocchio's.** Spacious but still intimate, this Italian restaurant in the fashionable St. Benedict's area has been attractively furnished with scatter rugs and colorful murals. There's a wide choice of inventive pasta specials, such as chicken served with saffron noodles in a red pesto sauce, and regional Italian dishes. Meals are accompanied by live jazz or flamenco guitar a couple of times a week. ✉ *11 St. Benedict's St.,* ☎ *01603/ 613318. AE, DC, MC, V. No dinner Sun.*

£ ✕ **Adam and Eve.** Said to be Norwich's oldest pub, the Adam and Eve dates back to 1249—a fine spot for a time-out and conveniently sited between the riverside walk and the cathedral on Bishopsgate. Bar food is served noon–7, with simple dishes like soups, pies, and salads at reasonable prices. ✉ *Bishopsgate,* ☎ *01603/667423. No credit cards.*

£££ ⛢ **Dunston Hall Hotel & Country Club.** Four miles southwest of the city center, this Tudor mansion has undergone extensive renovation and is now a luxurious hotel with good sporting facilities including a golf course. One of its advantages is its peaceful setting in landscaped gardens and woodland, ideal for relaxing after a day's sightseeing. ✉ *Ipswich Rd., NR14 8PQ,* ☎ *01508/470444,* ℻ *01508/471499. 72 rooms. Restaurant, 2 bars, pool, sauna, driving range, golf privileges, 2 tennis courts, recreation room. AE, DC, MC, V.*

££ ⛢ **Beeches Hotel.** About a mile west of the city center, this attractive, family-run, nonsmoking hotel is actually two early Victorian houses, set in an extraordinary park known as the Plantation Gardens. All rooms are simply but pleasantly furnished, and several look out over the gardens, which—with their ornate Gothic fountain and Italianate terrace—are gradually being restored to their original, Victorian splendor. ✉ *2–6 Earlham Rd., NR2 3DB,* ☎ *01603/621167,* ℻ *01603/620151. 25 rooms. Restaurant, bar. AE, DC, MC, V.*

The Arts

The **King of Hearts** (✉ Fye Bridge St., ☎ 01603/766129), a restored medieval merchant's house, is now a small arts center that holds chamber concerts, recitals, and poetry readings and has an exhibition area for art and sculpture. **Norwich Arts Centre** (✉ St. Benedict's St., ☎ 01603/ 660352) has an eclectic program of live music, dance, stand-up comedy, and other cultural events, as well as a good café. **Cinema City** (✉ St. Andrew's St., ☎ 01603/622047) is Norwich's venue for art films. It's situated in a 16th-century building with a terrific associated bistro-bar called *Take 5.*

The **Maddermarket Theatre** (✉ St. John's Alley, ☎ 01603/620917) was patterned after Elizabethan theater design and has been home to the Norwich Players, an amateur repertory company, since 1911. The theater is closed in August. **Norwich Playhouse** (✉ Gun Wharf, St. George's St., ☎ 01603/633635) is a professional repertory group offering everything from Shakespeare to world premieres of new plays and jazz concerts; it also has a bookshop. Norwich's biggest and best-known theater is the **Theatre Royal** (✉ Theatre St., ☎ 01603/630000), which plays host to touring companies staging musicals, ballet, opera, and plays.

Outdoor Activities and Sports

BOATING

The River Yare was once a busy commercial waterway; now most of the traffic is for pleasure. During summer months, a **boat trip** starting from Roaches Court at Elm Hill or from Thorpe Station Quay opposite the train station will give you a fresh perspective on Norwich; longer trips are available down the rivers Wensum and Yare to the nearer Broads. A marked riverside walk follows the Wensum from St. George's Bridge to the city wall at Carrow Bridge. ⊠ *Southern River Steamers, Roaches Court, Elm Hill; and Thorpe Station Quay,* ☎ *01603/624051.* 🖼 *£2.50–£7.50.* ☉ *Apr. 15 and May–Sept., 2–3 departures daily.*

Touring by car isn't really an option if you want to see something of the **Norfolk Broads,** because many are inaccessible by road. Consider a boating holiday instead, where with your own launch you'll be able to cruise at will through 150 mi of waterways. Major operators like **Hoseasons** (☎ 0800/501010) rent boats by the week. Contact **Broads Tours,** based at the quaysides in Wroxham (☎ 01603/782207), 7 mi northeast of Norwich, and Potter Heigham (☎ 01692/670711), 15 mi northeast of Norwich; both offer day cruises in the Broads as well as half-day and full-day launch rental (lessons included). The *Norada, Olive,* and *Hathor* are historic wherry yachts (sailing barges), and all may be chartered from the **Wherry Yacht Centre** (☎ 01603/782470) for luxurious cruises for up to 12 people.

Shopping

The medieval lanes of Norwich, around Elm Hill and Tombland, contain the best antiques, book, and crafts stores. **Peter Crowe** (⊠ 75 Upper St. Giles St., ☎ 01603/624800) specializes in antiquarian books. The **Black Horse Bookshop** (⊠ 8–10 Wensum St., ☎ 01603/626871) sells new books, guides, and maps. Antiques shops abound in Norwich: **James and Ann Tillett** (⊠ 12–13 Tombland, ☎ 01603/624914) specializes in antique jewelry and silver. The **Norwich Antiques Centre** (⊠ in Tombland, opposite the cathedral, ☎ 01603/619129) is an old house whose little rooms are crammed full of shops. **St. Michael-at-Plea** (⊠ Bank Plain, ☎ 01603/618989) is a church converted into an antiques market. The **Elm Hill Craft Shop** (⊠ 12 Elm Hill, ☎ 01603/621076) has interesting stationery and dollhouses.

Great Yarmouth

㉝ *20 mi east of Norwich.*

Once the center of Europe's herring industry, Great Yarmouth is now the busiest seaside resort on the Norfolk coast, with a long (if undistinguished) seafront promenade backed by cafés, guest houses, and amusement arcades. The 14th-century church of St. Nicholas (⊠ Church Plain, ☎ 01493/850666), destroyed in the second world war but since restored, is believed to be the largest parish church in England. Also of interest, but not open to the public are the Hospital for Decayed Fishermen, Church Plain, founded in 1702, and the adjacent Sewell House, the 1820 birthplace of *Black Beauty* author Anna Sewell.

Blickling Hall

★ **㉞** *15 mi north of Norwich, 27 mi northwest of Great Yarmouth, via North Walsham (turn left onto B1354, then right, down a little lane).*

A first sight of Blickling Hall is guaranteed not to disappoint: cars often come to a screeching halt when they spot the house's famous facade, looming in the far distance behind a wrought-iron gate. A grand vista is created by an imposing allée, formed by two mighty yew hedges, making a magnificent frame for this perfectly symmetrical Jacobean masterpiece. The redbrick mansion has towers and chimneys, baroque Dutch gables and, in the center, a three-story timber clock tower. The grounds include a formal flower garden and parkland whose woods conceal a temple, an orangery, a pyramid, and a secret garden. It belonged to a succession of historic figures, including Sir John Fastolf, the model for Shakespeare's Falstaff; Anne Boleyn's family, who owned it until Anne was executed by her husband, Henry VIII; and finally Lord Lothian, an ambassador to the United States. The Long Gallery (127 ft) has an intricate plaster-work ceiling decorated with Jacobean emblems, and the superb 17th-century staircase is also worth examining. Most of the interior is on the austere side, but there's a sumptuous tapestry of Peter the Great at the Battle of Poltawa, which hangs in its own room. Next to the main entrance is the Buckinghamshire Arms, a pub with plenty of atmosphere and a large garden. ⊠ *Blickling,* ☎ *01263/738030,* WEB *www.national-trust.org.uk.* ⊡ *House and gardens £6.70, gardens only £3.80.* ☉ *House and gardens Apr.–Oct. Wed.–Sun; house 1–4:30, gardens 10:15–5:15.*

En Route   The Norfolk coast begins to feel wild and remote near **Blakeney,** 15 mi west of Cromer. If you drive along the coast road, you'll pass marshes, sandbanks, and coves, as well as a string of villages. Blakeney is one of the most attractive, with harbors used for small fishing boats and yachts. From the quay here you can take a boat trip past **Blakeney Point,** a National Trust nature reserve, to see the seals on the sandbanks and the birds on the dunes.

Holkham Hall

★ ㉟   *10 mi west of Blakeney, 37 mi northwest of Norwich.*

Holkham Bay is a huge expanse of sandy beaches, dunes, and salt marsh backed by pine woods. The tide goes out for 2 mi here. Opposite the lane leading down to the beach from the coast road (A149) is the entrance to Holkham Hall. The estate is the seat of the Coke family, the earls of Leicester. In the late 18th century, Thomas Coke went on the fashionable "grand tour" of the Continent, returning with art treasures and determined to build a house according to the new Italian ideas; the result was this Palladian palace, one of the most splendid in Britain. Centered by a grand staircase and modeled after the Baths of Diocletian, the entryway 60-ft-tall Marble Hall may be the most spectacular room in Britain (or, at least, it used to be: an unsightly bannister has defaced the staircase and the room's imperial purple rug has been removed). Beyond this hall lie salons brilliant with gold and alabaster, each filled with Coke's collection of masterpieces, including paintings by Gainsborough, Van Dyck, Rubens, Raphael, and other old masters. This transplant from Neoclassic Italy is set in extensive parkland landscaped by Capability Brown in 1762. The **Bygones Museum,** housed in the stable block, has more than 5,000 items on display, from gramophones to fire engines. You can visit this house using the Norfolk Coach Coastliner bus service from various towns in East Anglia; from London, take the train to Cambridge, then a bus to King's Lynn and the coast. ⊠ *Near Wells-next-the-Sea,* ☎ *01328/710227,* WEB *www.holkham.co.uk.* ⊡ *Hall £4, museum £4, combined ticket £6.* ☉ *Apr. 14–15 and June–Sept., Sun.–Thurs. 1–5; May, Sun. and Mon. 11:30–5.*

Sandringham House

㊱   *15 mi southwest of Holkham, 8 mi northeast of King's Lynn, 43 mi northwest of Norwich.*

Sandringham House, not far from the old-fashioned but still popular seaside resort of Hunstanton, is one of the Queen's country residences—it's where the Royal Family spends Christmas, as well as other vacations. This huge, redbrick Victorian mansion was clearly designed for enormous country-house parties, with a ballroom, billiard room, and bowling alley, as well as a shooting lodge on the grounds—no wonder George V used to write fondly of "dear old Sandringham." The house and gardens are closed when the Queen is in residence, but the woodlands, nature walks, and museum of royal memorabilia (the latter housed in the old stables) remain open, as does the church, medieval but in heavy Victorian disguise. ✉ *Sandringham,* ☎ *01553/772675,* WEB *www.royal.gov.uk.* ☞ *House, gardens, and museum £5.50, gardens and museum £4.50.* ☉ *Mid-Apr.–Sept., house and museum daily 11–5, gardens daily 10:30–5. Closed last 2 wks July.*

King's Lynn

③ *8 mi southwest of Sandringham, 40 mi northwest of Norwich.*

As Bishop's Lynn the town was a thriving port on the River Ouse, growing prosperous in the 15th century through the wool trade with the continent; a Flemish influence is apparent in the church brasses and the style of the town squares. When Bishop's Lynn became royal property the name was changed to King's Lynn and with its Georgian town houses, guildhalls, and ancient quayside warehouses it remains one of the most English of English towns, regularly used by television crews in new productions of Dickens's novels. King's Lynn is now an important container port close to the mouth of the Great Ouse on the Wash.

The enormous **Tuesday Market Place** was big enough to have hosted a sit-down dinner for 600 people to celebrate the end of war with France in 1814. Each Tuesday, it's full of local produce and arts and crafts stalls, forming one of the country's most vibrant weekly markets.

Trinity Guildhall, with its striking checkered stone front, is now the Civic Hall of the Borough Council and is not generally open to the public, although you can visit it during the King's Lynn Festival (☞ The Arts, *below*) and on occasional guided tours in summer. It's possible, however, to explore the **Regalia Rooms,** housed in the Guildhall Undercroft, with the aid of a recorded audio tour, which points out treasures like the 14th-century chalice known as King John's Cup. The rooms are entered through the adjacent **Old Gaol House,** site of the town police station until 1954, whose cells form part of an engaging law and order museum. ✉ *Saturday Market Pl.,* ☎ *01533/774297.* ☞ *£2.30.* ☉ *Apr.–Oct., daily 10–4:15; Nov.–Mar., Fri.–Tues. 10–5.*

St. George's, an early 15th-century guildhall, forms part of the **King's Lynn Arts Centre,** a thriving arts and theater complex administered by the National Trust, and the focal point for the annual King's Lynn Festival. There's also an art gallery and a crafts fair every September. The center's coffee bar serves snacks all day. St. George's Guildhall is the largest surviving English medieval guildhall, and it adjoins a Tudor house and a warehouse used during the Middle Ages. ✉ *29 King St.,* ☎ *01553/764864,* FAX *01553/770591,* WEB *www.kingslynn.org.* ☞ *Free.* ☉ *Apr.–Sept., weekdays 10–4, Sat. 10–1, 2–3:30; Oct.–Mar., Mon.–Sat. 11–4. Gallery closed Mon.*

Dining and Lodging

££ ✗ **Riverside Rooms.** Part of the Arts Centre, this restaurant reflects the style of the original 15th-century warehouse, with its gnarled oak beams and redbrick walls. When the weather is clement, there are tables outside, overlooking the river. Lunches might offer local mussels, fresh salmon, or fisherman's pie; dinner is more elaborate, perhaps broccoli mousse with Stilton sauce followed by halibut steak or venison. There's also an inexpensive coffee shop in the historic undercroft that serves homemade snacks and pastries. ✉ *27 King St.,* ☎ *01553/ 773134. MC, V. Closed Sun.*

££ ✕ **Rococo.** This modern restaurant in an ancient house serves food as
★ stylish as the decor. The cooking is mainly contemporary British, but it has other influences. Fish and vegetarian dishes are particularly imaginative; for example, monkfish with ginger and lemongrass. Traditional English desserts are a specialty. ✉ *11 Saturday Market Pl.,* ☎ *01553/771483. AE, MC, V. Closed Sun. No lunch Mon.*

£££ ⊡ **Duke's Head.** The location can't be better: wake up on Tuesday morning and the front rooms at the pink-washed Duke's Head have prime views of the market in full swing below. In the oldest, 17th-century part of the hotel, where the main staircase is bowed with age, no two of the guest rooms are alike: the floorboards may be creaky, but each room has comfortable beds, and relaxing armchairs. Downstairs, a spacious lounge with open fires delays otherwise keen sightseers, who can fortify themselves with cream teas before venturing outside. ✉ *Tuesday Market Pl., PE30 1JS,* ☎ *01533/774996,* ℻ *01553/763556. 71 rooms. 2 restaurants, 2 bars, brasserie. AE, DC, MC, V.*

£ ⊡ **Russet House Hotel.** With a gentle price, this charming hotel delivers more than a night's worth of comfort and joy. A 10-minute walk from the town center, the Victorian-era house has a garden and bar with a cozy log fire. There is also a restaurant with a menu that includes vegetarian options. ✉ *53 Goodwin Rd., PE30 5PE,* ☎ *01553/ 773098. 11 rooms. Restaurant, bar. AE, DC, MC, V.*

The Arts

Much of the **King's Lynn Festival** (✉ King's Lynn Festival Office, 29 King St., PE30 1HA, ☎ 01553/773578, 🕸 www.lingslynn.org), which takes place in July, is based at the Arts Centre and encompasses concerts, exhibitions, theater, dance, films, literary events, and children's programs. The festival program is available in April or May. The **Corn Exchange** (✉ Tuesday Market Pl., ☎ 01553/764864), housed in a splendidly revamped 19th-century building, hosts a varied program of concerts, theater, comedy, and crafts events.

Shopping

The **Old Granary** antiques center in King's Staithe Lane, off Queen Street, is an Aladdin's cave of china, lamps, silver, jewelry, and other decorative items. There are well-established open markets in the town center, which take place on Tuesday, Friday, and Saturday.

COLCHESTER AND THE ALDEBURGH COAST

Colchester is the oldest town on record in England, dating back to the Iron Age. One of its Roman founders was the emperor Claudius, and the settlement was soon attacked by Queen Boudicca, queen of the Iceni, noted for having carving knives affixed to her chariot wheels—an early instance of road rage. Today the Roman walls still stand, together with a Norman castle, a Victorian town hall, and Dutch-style houses built by refugee weavers from the Low Countries in the late 16th century. Colchester is the traditional base for exploring Constable Country, that quintessentially English rural landscape on the borders of Suffolk and Essex made famous by the early 19th-century painter, John Constable (1776–1837). This area runs north and west of Colchester along the valley of the River Stour. The Suffolk Heritage coast, which wanders northward from Orford up to Lowestoft, is one of the most unspoiled shorelines in the country.

Colchester

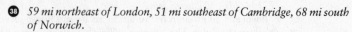 *59 mi northeast of London, 51 mi southeast of Cambridge, 68 mi south of Norwich.*

Recent archaeological research indicates a settlement at the head of the Colne estuary at least as early as 1100 BC. At the time of Christ it was the center of the domain of Cunobelin (Shakespeare's Cymbeline), who was king of the Catuvellauni. On Cunobelin's death, the Romans invaded in AD 43. The emperor Claudius, who was alleged to have entered Colchester on an elephant, built his first stronghold here and made it the first Roman colony in Britain, appropriately renaming the town *Colonia Victricensis* ("Colony of Victory"). Colchester had to wait another millennium, however, before it received its royal charter in 1189 from King Richard Lion-Heart.

Evidence of Colchester's four centuries of Roman history is visible everywhere. Although the Romans prudently relocated their administrative center to London after the Celtic queen Boudicca burned the place in AD 60, Colchester was important enough for them to build massive fortifications around the town. The **Roman Walls,** dating largely from the reign of Emperor Vespasian (AD 69–79), can still be seen, especially along Balkerne Hill (to the west of the town center), with its splendid Balkerne Gate (most of the foundations lie beneath the neighboring Hole-in-the-Wall pub). For further remains, check out Priory and Vineyard streets where there's a Roman drain exposed halfway along. On Maidenburgh Street, near the castle, the remains of a Roman amphitheater have been discovered. The curve of the foundations is outlined in the paving stones of the roadway, and part of the walls and floor have been exposed and preserved in a modern building, where they can be viewed through a window.

Colchester has always had a strategic importance and is still home to a military garrison; a tattoo (military spectacle) is held in even-numbered years. The **castle** was built by William the Conqueror in about 1076. All that remains is the keep (main tower), but it's the largest in Europe. The castle was actually built over the foundations of the huge Roman Temple of Claudius, and in the vaults you can descend through 1,000 years of history. A superb museum inside contains an ever-growing collection of prehistoric and Roman remains. ⊠ *Castle Park,* ☎ *01206/ 282931; 01206/282932 for information on all Colchester museums,* WEB *www.colchester.gov.uk.* ☎ *£3.70, guided tours £1.* ☉ *Mar.–Nov., Mon.– Sat. 10–5, Sun. 2–5; Dec.–Feb., Mon.–Sat. 10–5. Closed Christmas wk.*

The broad High Street follows the line of the main Roman road. Halfway down is the splendid Edwardian **Town Hall,** standing on the site of the original Moot (assembly) Hall. On its tower you can see four figures representing Colchester's main industries: fisheries, agriculture, the military, and engineering. The narrow, medieval streets behind the town hall are called the **Dutch Quarter** because weavers—refugees from the Low Countries—settled here in the 16th century, when Colchester was the center of a thriving cloth trade. The medieval Long Wyre Street, Short Wyre Street, and Sir Isaac's Walk, have many small antiques stores, and are south of High Street, beyond the modern Culver Square pedestrian mall. **Tymperley's Clock Museum,** off Sir Isaac's Walk, displays a unique collection of Colchester-made clocks in the surviving wing of an Elizabethan house. ⊠ *Trinity St.,* ☎ *01206/282932.* ☎ *Free.* ☉ *Mon.–Sat. 10–5, Sun. 11–5.*

Dining and Lodging

££ ✕ **Warehouse Brasserie.** Colchester's most popular eating place has a fairly anonymous exterior and location: it's tucked away in a converted warehouse, down a cul-de-sac off St. John's Street. Inside, though, all is cheerful, with a charming pastel green and rich red split-level dining room, wooden tables, and large wall mirrors. The menu mixes brasserie favorites with classic English dishes. ⊠ *12 Chapel St. N,* ☎ *01206/765656. MC, V. No dinner Sun.*

££ 🖬 **George Hotel.** In downtown Colchester, this 500-year-old inn has been renovated to include a modern extension but has lost none of its age-old charm. Many rooms incorporate original oak beams and are comfortably furnished. The George Bar also retains its historic beams, and in the cellar there's a section of Roman pavement and a 16th-century wall painting on display. The Brasserie restaurant has a good à la carte menu. ⊠ *116 High St., CO1 1TD,* ☎ *01206/578494,* FAX *01206/761732. 48 rooms. Restaurant, bar, grill. AE, DC, MC, V.*

The Arts

The **Mercury Theater** (⊠ Balkerne Gate, ☎ 01206/573948) stages a wide variety of plays, including touring shows, pre–West End runs, and local productions. The **Colchester Arts Centre** (⊠ St. Mary-at-the-Wall, Church St., ☎ 01206/500900) hosts theater, exhibitions, and workshop events.

Dedham

39 *8 mi northeast of Colchester, off A12 on B1029.*

Dedham is the heart of Constable country. Here, rolling hills and the cornfields of Dedham Vale, set under the lovely pale skies that are such a notable and delicate feature of the district, inspired John Constable to paint some of his most celebrated canvases. He went to school in Dedham, a tiny, picture-book kind of place that consists of a single street, a church, and a few timber-frame and brick houses.

From Dedham, on the banks of the River Stour, you can rent a row-boat, which (if you're fit enough) is an idyllic way to travel the 2 mi downriver to **Flatford Mill,** one of the two water mills owned by Constable's father, and the subject of his most famous painting, *The Hay Wain* (1821). Near Flatford Mill is the 16th-century **Willy Lott's House** (not open to the public), which is instantly recognizable from *The Hay Wain.* The National Trust owns Flatford Mill along with the houses around it, including the thatched **Bridge Cottage,** which has a display about Constable's life. *Near East Bergholt,* ☎ *01206/298260,* FAX *01206/299193.* 🖼 *Free.* ☺ *Mar.–Apr. and Oct.–mid Dec., Wed.–Sun. 11–5:30; May–Sept., daily 10–5:30.*

Two miles north of Dedham, off A12, the Constable trail continues in **East Bergholt.** Constable was born here in 1776; only the stables remain of the house that was his birthplace. As well as many other views of East Bergholt, Constable painted the village church, **St. Mary's,** where his parents lie buried. It has one very unusual feature—a freestanding wooden bell house in place of a tower.

Dining and Lodging

£££ ✕ **Le Talbooth.** In a Tudor house idyllically situated beside the River
★ Stour, this famous restaurant has a floodlighted terrace where drinks are served in summer. Inside, original beams, black-lead windows, and a brick fireplace add to the historic atmosphere. Fixed-price menus are offered at lunch and dinner, perhaps including duck breast with braised cabbage or fresh fish. ⊠ *Gun Hill,* ☎ *01206/323150. Jacket and tie. AE, MC, V. No dinner Sun. Nov.–Mar.*

£ ✕ **Marlborough Hotel.** Opposite Constable's school, this early 18th-century pub serves fine lunches from quiche to steak. It gets very busy during the summer, so get there early to ensure a table. ⊠ *Mill La.,* ☎ *01206/323250. AE, MC, V.*

££££   🔲 **Maison Talbooth.** This luxury hotel is a peaceful Victorian house,
★   set in the rich meadowlands painted by Constable. Each of the elegant,
spacious rooms is furnished with period antiques and flowers, with modern amenities such as Jacuzzis. Guests are encouraged to eat in Le Talbooth restaurant, a short walk down the lane and owned by the same
management. ⊠ *Stratford Rd., CO7 6HN,* ☎ *01206/322367,* FAX
01206/322752. 10 rooms. Bar. AE, MC, V.

Woodbridge

40   *8 mi northeast of Ipswich, on B1438 off A12.*

One of the first good ports of call on the Suffolk Heritage Coast,
Woodbridge is a pleasant little town whose upper reaches are centered
on a fine old market square, with two great pubs, the Bull and the King's
Head, vying for your custom. The narrow surrounding streets are
filled with antiques shops, although Woodbridge is at its best down
around its old quayside, where boatbuilding has been carried out since
the 16th century—although these days yachts and pleasure craft are
being built. The most prominent building is a white clapboard mill,
which dates from the 18th century and is powered by the tides. **Boat
trips** from the quay thread their way deftly through the small craft moored
in the harbor and out into the river. 🔳 *Boat trips £2 per person.* ☉
May–Sept., daily 2–5, every 30 mins.

Dining

£–££   ✕ **Spice.** This is just the type of place you *don't* expect to find in rural
East Anglia, and what a pleasant surprise it is. Climb the stairs to this
adventurous restaurant serving Malaysian and Eastern-influenced
dishes. It prides itself on its stir fries and curries with sauces enlivened
by lemongrass, garlic, Southeast Asian spices, and other exotica. ⊠ *17
The Thoroughfare,* ☎ *01394/382557. AE, MC, V. Closed Sun.*

En Route   From Felixstowe northward to Kessingland lies the **Suffolk Heritage
Coast,** a 40-mi stretch including many sections designated by an Act
of Parliament as "Areas of Special Scientific Interest." There are numerous beaches, marshes, and broads, with an abundance of wildflowers
and birds. You can only reach these areas on minor roads running east
off A12 north of Ipswich.

Orford

41   *10 mi east of Woodbridge along B1084, 35 mi northeast of Colchester.*

This small village is split between the quayside and its ancient center.
The small, squat **Orford Castle** surveys the flatlands from atop a green
mound dotted with picnickers in summer. Its splendid triple-tower keep
was built in 1160 as a coastal defense. Climb it for a view over what
was once a thriving medieval port (the 6-mi shingle bank of Orford
Ness eventually cut off direct access to the sea). ☎ *01394/450472.* 🔳
£2.50. ☉ *Mid-Apr.–Oct., daily 10–6; Nov.–mid-Apr., Wed.–Sun. 10–
4.*

Dining and Lodging

£–££   ✕ **Butley-Orford Oysterage.** What started as a little café that sold oysters and cups of tea has become a large, bustling, no-nonsense restaurant. It still specializes in oysters and smoked salmon, as well as smoked
seafood platters and seasonal fresh fish dishes. The actual smoking takes
place in the adjacent smokehouse, and products are also on sale in a
shop around the corner. ⊠ *Market Hill,* ☎ *01394/450277. No credit
cards. No dinner Sun.–Thurs. Nov.–Mar.*

££ ⌂ **Crown and Castle.** Near Orford Castle is this small, well-established hotel in an 18th-century building thought to have had smuggling connections. The tone is set by the timber facade, and the rooms inside are small, cozy, and very quiet. A snug little bar serves lunches and dinners, including fresh fish, but the most attractive aspect is the outdoor terrace, with its grandstand views of the castle. ⊠ *Market Hill, IP12 2LJ*, ☎ *01394/450205*, FAX *01394/450176. 20 rooms. Restaurant, bar, lobby lounge. AE, DC, MC, V.*

Aldeburgh

42 *41 mi northeast of Colchester.*

Aldeburgh is a quiet seaside resort, except in June, when the town fills up with festival goers. Its beach is backed by a long promenade lined with candy-color dwellings, some no bigger than a doll's house. It was Benjamin Britten's home for some time—although he was actually born in the busy seaside resort of Lowestoft, 30 mi to the north. Here the composer grew interested in the story of Aldeburgh's native son, the poet George Crabbe, and ultimately turned the life story of the poet into the celebrated modern opera *Peter Grimes,* a piece that perfectly captures the atmosphere of the Suffolk coasts. Aldeburgh's **Elizabethan Moot Hall,** built of flint and timber, when first erected stood in the center of a thriving 16th-century town; now it's just a few steps from the beach, a mute witness to the erosive powers of the North Sea. ⊠ *Market Cross, Sea Front.* ▦ *60p.* ☼ *Apr.–May, weekends 2:30–5; June and Sept.–Oct., daily 2:30–5; July–Aug., daily 10–12:30 and 2:30–5.*

Dining and Lodging

££–£££ ✕ **The Lighthouse.** This stylish establishment relies exclusively on locally grown or caught produce. Seafood, including oysters and Cromer crabs, is a specialty. It comes simply but imaginatively cooked, usually with an interesting sauce whose origins might just as easily be Asian as English. Desserts, like the creamy bread-and-butter pudding, are particularly good. ⊠ *77 High St.,* ☎ *01728/453377. MC, V. Closed 2 wks in Jan. No dinner Sun. Nov.–Mar.*

£–££ ✕ **Café 152.** Typical of the new breed of fish restaurants sprouting up in the town, Café 152, yards from the beach, is bright and breezy, sporting an inventive, changing menu of daily specials, such as char-grilled squid on a bed of salad leaves, or grilled local sole. Lunch is a particularly good deal. ⊠ *152 High St.,* ☎ *01728/454152. MC, V. Closed Mon.–Tues. Nov.–Mar.*

£££ ✕⌂ **The Brudenell.** Parts of the Brudenell date back to the 16th century, although they're now well hidden beneath a pleasing early 20th-century facade. Some of the attractive, spacious guest rooms face directly across Aldeburgh's shingle beach and are available for a small supplementary charge; the remainder look out over the river and marshes. With its panoramic windows offering uninterrupted vistas of the North Sea, the split-level restaurant has the feel of a luxury cruise ship. ⊠ *The Parade, IP15 5BU,* ☎ *01728/452071,* FAX *01728/454082. 47 rooms. Restaurant, bar, lobby lounge. AE, DC, MC, V.*

£££ ✕⌂ **White Lion.** The hotel, right on the seafront, has been welcoming guests for more than 400 years—since 1563, in fact—and this heritage shines through in the paneled, oak-beam restaurant, the log fires in the lounges, and the other age-old nooks and crannies. The view from the front-facing guest rooms is worth paying the little extra for, and whether it's snacks in the bar or fresh fish in the restaurant, you don't need to move far for affordable, quality meals. ⊠ *Market Cross Pl., IP15 5BJ,* ☎ *01728/452720,* FAX *01728/452986. 38 rooms. Restaurant, 2 bars. AE, MC, V.*

The Arts

The most important arts festival in East Anglia, and one of the best known in Great Britain, is the **Aldeburgh Festival,** held for two weeks in June every year in the small village of Snape, 5 mi west of Aldeburgh, at the Snape Maltings Concert Hall (☎ 01728/453543, box office). Founded by the composer Benjamin Britten, the festival naturally concentrates on music, but there are also related exhibitions, poetry readings, and even walks. Snape Maltings also offers a year-round program of events, such as the two-day Aldeburgh Folk Festival, held each July to celebrate traditional English folk music, and the Britten Festival in October. A festival program is published in March by the Aldeburgh Foundation. ⊠ *High St., Aldeburgh IP15 5AX,* ☎ *01728/687100,* 🕸 *www.aldeburgh.co.uk.*

It's well worth a stop at any time of year to enjoy the peaceful riverside setting of the **Snape Maltings Art Centre** and perhaps pause for a coffee in the friendly cafeteria. There are also crafts shops and an art gallery at the Center. ⊠ *Snape, near Saxmundham,* ☎ *01728/688303.* ☾ *Daily 10–5.*

Southwold

43 *4 mi north of Dunwich, 15 mi north of Aldeburgh, 32 mi southeast of Norwich.*

This attractive seaside town is an idyllic place to spend a day. Old-fashioned beach huts painted in bright colors huddle together against the wind on the shingle beach, which is lined with small pebbles, and up in the town center a pleasing ensemble of old houses lines the main street and surrounds the central green. There aren't many "sights," but since the whole town gives you the sensation of being transported back in time, this doesn't matter very much. George Orwell's parents lived at 3 Queen Street during the 1930s. The **Southwold Museum,** displays works of local archaeology, natural history, and pictures of the Battle of Sole Bay. It's housed in a Dutch-gabled cottage, a style typical of Southwold's domestic architecture. ⊠ *Victoria St.,* ☎ *01502/722375.* 🖾 *Free.* ☾ *Mid-Apr.–Sept., daily 2:30–4:30.*

OFF THE BEATEN PATH **WALBERSWICK** – The charming little village of Walberswick was for many years the haunt of artists, writers, and photographers (including, during 1914–15, the Scottish Art Nouveau architect Charles Rennie Mackintosh, who painted many of his watercolors of plants and flowers here). The village is separated from Southwold by the mouth of the River Blyth, over which there's a footbridge (about 1 mi inland), but no main road bridge. On summer weekends, a boatman ferries foot passengers over the water in a rowboat every few minutes. On the far side, you can see the church tower of Southwold piercing the horizon, a half-hour's walk away through the fields. 🖾 *Ferry 25p.* ☾ *Ferry May–Sept., weekends 9–12:30 and 2–5.*

Dining and Lodging

£££ ✕🏠 **Swan Hotel.** This lovely, 17th-century inn (scenes from the film *David Copperfield* were shot here) has spacious public rooms and decent-size bedrooms decorated in traditional English-country style. Eighteen secluded and quiet garden rooms are set in a superb central position around the old bowling green. In the charming public rooms, you can comfortably sit over tea or something stronger on a winter's day. The hotel staff prides itself on personal service. The restaurant's dishes are mainly traditional English, accompanied by a similarly excellent wine list. ⊠ *Market Pl., IP18 6EG,* ☎ *01502/722186,* 🖷 *01502/724800. 45 rooms. Restaurant, bar. AE, DC, MC, V.*

££ ✗⊡ **Crown Hotel.** Like the Swan, the Crown is owned by the old family firm of Adnam's brewery, the major employer in Southwold. In the simple but tastefully decorated yellow-and-gray bar lounge, faultlessly prepared fish dishes such as Cromer dressed crab or seafood salad and panfried John Dory, cod, and brill are served at shared wooded trestle tables. You can also dine more formally at the adjacent restaurant, The Crown, which has one of the best wine lists in England. The building is 17th century, so although public rooms are spacious enough, some of the guest rooms are on the small side. Antique furniture and a pleasing decorative eye by the management more than compensate, however. ⊠ *90 High St., IP18 6DP,* ☎ *01502/722275,* 𝔽𝔸𝕏 *01502/ 727263. 12 rooms, 9 with bath. Restaurant, bar. AE, DC, MC, V.*

BEYOND THE FENS: LINCOLN, BOSTON, AND STAMFORD

The fens of northern Cambridgeshire pass imperceptibly into the three divisions of Lincolnshire: Holland, Kesteven, and Lindsey are all parts of the great county, divided administratively. Holland borders the Isle of Ely and the delightfully named Soke of Peterborough; this marshland spreads far and wide south of the Wash, the names of the district almost reflecting the squelch of mud the inhabitants of pre-drainage times must have encountered. The chief attractions are two towns: Lincoln, with its magnificent cathedral, and Stamford, to the southwest. En route to Lincoln is the town of Peterborough; well-connected, either by road or rail, it repays a visit to see the glories of its medieval cathedral or to shop in the Queensgate Centre with its boutiques, cafés, and restaurants.

The countryside around Lincoln, especially the Lincolnshire Wolds (chalk hills) to the northeast, consists of rolling hills and copses, with drystone (unmortared) walls dividing well-tended fields. The unspoiled rural area of the Wolds, strikingly evoked in Tennyson's poetry, is particularly worth a visit, whereas the long coastline with its miles of sandy beaches and its North Sea air offers all the usual, if occasionally tacky, seaside facilities for the family. Tulips are the pride and joy of south Lincolnshire, drawing thousands from all parts of Britain to view the Holland and Kesteven bulb fields in springtime.

Peterborough

🏶 *22 mi southwest of King's Lynn, 38 mi north of Cambridge.*

Although Peterborough has become a large commercial city, it is proud of its ancient history and seeks to blend the old with the new. Its main attractions—the cathedral, the Queensgate shopping center, and the Peterborough Museum and Art Gallery—are all in the city center, close to the rail station and 3 mi from the A1, the north–south artery.

Peterborough Cathedral was originally founded in 655 by Peada, a nobleman from the early English kingdom of Mercia in Central Britain. It was destroyed by the Danes in 870 and reconstructed in 972, only to be burnt down again, this time by mistake, in 1116. The next incarnation has been rather luckier: consecrated in 1238 after 120 years of building, the cathedral still towers over Peterborough today. Still, it has seen its fair share of strife, including occupation by Cromwell's forces, who fired muskets into the ceiling and broke most of the statues, stained-glass windows, choir stalls, and high altar. Although the cathedral has been left with few monuments, the result is a startlingly spacious interior into which light streams through the clear glass.

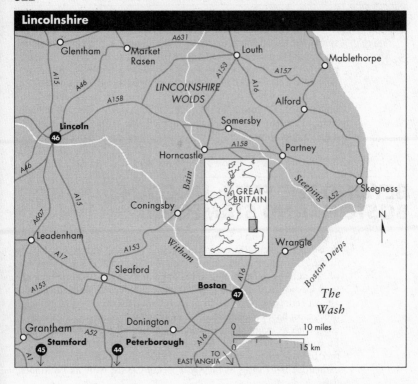

The current nave dates from the early 13th century. The West Front is landmarked by three soaring arches, each 85 ft high. In the peaks of their gables are the three figures of St. Peter, St. Paul, and St. Andrew (the cathedral is consecrated to these three saints), and high up inside the north arch is a modern figure of Queen Elizabeth II. The nave ceiling from 1220 is one of the most significant examples of Romanesque painting in Europe—note the grotesque monsters as well as figures of saints, bishops, and kings. The latter are present for good reason, as many crowned heads have passed through here. Henry VIII buried his first wife here after her death (by natural causes) in 1536, although his choice of Peterborough was less for the splendors of the Abbey than by a desire to save money by having the funeral outside London. In 1541, he conferred cathedral status on the Abbey, and over the tomb of his first, most pious wife now hangs the standard of Henry VIII, given by the present Queen, Elizabeth II. The last addition to the Cathedral is the New Building, actually built between 1496 and 1508. The exquisite vaulting here is probably by the architect John Wastell, who built the famous fan vaulting in King's College Chapel, Cambridge. An exhibition in the north transept depicts the life of the cathedral throughout its long history to the present day. ⊠ *Little Prior's Gate, 12a Minster Precinct,* ☎ *01733/343342,* WEB *www.peterborough-cathedral.org.uk.* ⊡ *Donation requested.* ☉ *Daily 8:30–5:15.*

The **Peterborough Museum and Art Gallery** is a small museum detailing the surprising history of this town. It's a short walk from the cathedral. ⊠ *Priestgate,* ☎ *01733/752451.* ⊡ *Free.* ☉ *Tues.–Sat. 10–5.*

Lodging

££–£££ ⊞ **Bull Hotel.** Formerly a 16th-century coaching inn, this timeless hotel with smartly furnished, comfortable rooms is close enough to the cathedral and Peterborough's shops to be convenient yet still offers decent parking facilities. ⊠ *Westgate, PE1 1RB,* ☎ *01733/561364,* [FAX] *01733/557304. 103 rooms. Restaurant, bar. AE, DC, MC, V.*

££–£££ ▣ **Queensgate Hotel.** Situated five minutes from the center of Peterborough, this hotel takes the sophisticated step of offering allergy-free rooms. Other extras are satellite TV, minibar, and tea- and coffeemaking facilities. ⊠ *5 Fletton Ave., PE2 8AX,* ☎ *01733/562572,* [FAX] *01733/558982. 19 rooms. Restaurant, bar, minibars. AE, DC, MC, V.*

The Arts

The **Key Theatre** (☎ 01733/552439), on the banks of the River Nene, offers plays and concerts almost every night of the year. For a wide variety of live music, cabaret, and other touring shows, check out the **Cresset** venue (⊠ Breton Centre, ☎ 01733/265705). **Peterborough Cathedral** hosts a wide calendar of concert events (contact the Tourist Information Centre, ☎ 01733/452336).

Shopping

The **Queensgate Shopping Centre** (☎ 01733/311666, ☉ Mon.–Wed., Fri.–Sat. 9–5:30, Thurs. 9–8, Sun. 11–5) lies between the railway station and Peterborough Cathedral. From there, follow the pedestrianized boulevards to browse in the traditional family-run shops, which rub shoulders with the high-tech retail chain stores. You can inspect the fresh local produce in the 150 stalls of the **City Market** (⊠ Northminster, ☉ Tues.–Sat. 8:30–4). For antiques, try the **Fitzwilliam Antiques Centre** (⊠ Fitzwilliam St., ☎ 01733/565415), a few minutes from the the Queensgate Centre. Run by the Stafford family, the center was once an ancient smithy. Its cobbled inner courtyard now provides a spacious showroom that houses an extensive range of antique furniture and smaller collectibles.

Stamford

🔴 *14 mi northwest of Peterborough, 47 mi northwest of Cambridge.*

Serene Stamford is set on a hillside overlooking a river and has an extremely well-preserved center, thanks to being designated England's first conservation area in 1967. It's a delightful place to stroll around while admiring the harmonious mixture of Georgian and medieval architecture.

★ Less than a mile outside Stamford is **Burghley House,** an architectural masterpiece acknowledged as "the largest and grandest house of the first Elizabethan age." The mansion, celebrated for its roofscape bristling with pepper-pot chimneys and slate-roof towers, was built in 1587 by William Cecil, first Baron Burghley, when he was Elizabeth I's high treasurer. Set in fine parkland, it has 18 of the most sumptuous state rooms in England, with carvings by Grinling Gibbons and ceiling paintings by Verrio, as well as innumerable paintings and a priceless porcelain collection. A recent chatelain, the sixth marquess of Exeter, was one of the famous Olympic runners whose life story inspired the 1980 film *Chariots of Fire.* ☎ 01780/752451, [WEB] *www.stamford.co.uk.* 🎫 £6.50. ☉ Apr.–Sept., daily 11–4:30.

Lincoln

★ 🔴 *93 mi northwest of Cambridge, 97 mi northwest of Norwich.*

To the Celtic tribesmen who built a settlement on high ground overlooking the River Witham it was Lindon, "the hill fort by a pool"; to the Roman IX legion who arrived in AD 47 it became Lindum, an important settlement at the junction of Ermine Street and Fosse Way, en route between London and York. The Danes made Lincoln the chief of the Five Boroughs of their Danelaw, but it was the Normans who gave Lincoln its medieval stature after William the Conqueror founded Lincoln Castle as a stronghold in 1068. Four years later William appointed Bishop Remigius to run the huge diocese stretching from the Humber to the Thames resulting in the construction of Lincoln Cathedral, the third largest in England after York Minster and St. Paul's. Since medieval times Lincoln's status has declined; however, its somewhat remote location (there are no major motorways or railways nearby) has helped preserve its traditional character.

In the city center you can walk under the 15th-century Stonebow arch on the site of an old Roman gate. Above it is the Guildhall, which houses the city's civic regalia. The River Witham flows unobtrusively under the incongruously named High Bridge, a low, vaulted Norman bridge topped by 16th-century, timber-frame houses. West of High Bridge, the river opens out into Brayford Pool, still busy with river traffic (and, unfortunately, road traffic, as there is a multistory parking lot on one side). Here you can rent various kinds of boats. In addition, from April through September small cruisers tour the River Witham, showing you the city from the water. Contact the Lincoln tourist office.

The aptly named Steep Hill lies at the center of narrow medieval streets that cling to the hillside, south of the cathedral. Jew's House on The Strait, dating from the early 12th century, is one of several well-preserved domestic buildings in this area.

Lincoln's crowning glory is the great **Cathedral of St. Mary.** (Try to see it at night, when it's floodlighted.) Commanding views from the top of the steep limestone escarpment above the River Witham reveal the strategic advantages of the city's site from earliest times.

For hundreds of years, it was the tallest building in Europe, but this magnificent medieval building is now among the least known of the European cathedrals. It was begun in 1072 by the Norman bishop Remigius; the Romanesque church he built was irremediably damaged, first by fire, then by earthquake (in 1185), but you can still see parts of the ancient structure at the west front. The next great phase of building, initiated by Bishop Hugh of Avalon, is mainly 13th century in character. The west front, topped by the two west towers, is a unique structure, giving tremendous breadth to the entrance. It is best seen from the 14th-century Exchequer Gate arch in front of the cathedral, or from the castle battlements beyond.

Inside, a breathtaking impression of space and unity belies the many centuries of building and rebuilding. The stained-glass window at the north end of the transept, known as the Dean's Eye, is one of the earliest (13th-century) traceried windows, whereas its opposite number at the south end shows a 14th-century sophistication in its tracery (i.e., interlaced designs). St. Hugh's Choir, in front of the altar, and the Angel Choir at the east end behind it have remarkable vaulted ceilings and intricate carvings. Look for the famous Lincoln Imp upon the pillar nearest to St. Hugh's shrine; this evil creature was turned to stone by an angel, according to legend. Look even farther up (binoculars or a telephoto lens will help) to see the 30 angels who are playing musical instruments and who give this part of the cathedral its name.

Through a door on the north side is the chapter house, a 10-sided building that sometimes housed the medieval Parliament of England during the reigns of Edward I and Edward II. The chapter house is connected to the 13th-century cloister, notable for its grotesquely amusing ceiling bosses. The cathedral library, a restrained building by Christopher Wren, was built onto the north side of the cloisters after the original library collapsed. ☎ 01522/544544, WEB *www.lincolncathedral.com.* ✉ *£3 donation.* ☉ *Late May–Aug., Mon.–Sat. 7:15 AM–8 PM, Sun. 7:15–6; Sept.–late May, Mon.–Sat. 7:15–6, Sun. 7:15–7.*

In the **Minster Yard,** which surrounds the cathedral on three sides, are buildings of various periods, including graceful examples of Georgian architecture. A statue of Alfred, Lord Tennyson, who was born in Lincolnshire, stands on the green near the chapter house exterior. The **Medieval Bishop's Palace,** on the south side of Minster Yard, is open to the public. ☎ *01522/527468.* ✉ *£1.10.* ☉ *Apr.–Sept., daily 10–6; Mar., weekends 10–5.*

Lincoln Castle, facing the cathedral across Exchequer Gate, was originally built on two great mounds by William the Conqueror in 1068, incorporating part of the remains of the Roman garrison walls. The castle was a military base until the 17th century, after which it was used as a prison. In the extraordinary prison chapel you can see the cage-like stalls in which Victorian convicts listened to sermons. One of the four surviving copies of the Magna Carta, signed by King John at Runnymede in 1215, is on display in the same building. ✉ *Castle Hill,* ☎ *01522/511068.* ✉ *£2.50.* ☉ *Apr.–Oct., Mon.–Sat. 9:30–5:30, Sun. 11:30–5:30; Nov.–Mar., Mon.–Sat. 9:30–4, Sun. 11–4.*

The **Usher Gallery** has an interesting collection of watches and clocks donated by its benefactor, James Ward Usher, a jeweler who invented the legend of the Lincoln Imp. The gallery also contains memorabilia connected with the poet Tennyson, who was born in Lincolnshire. ✉ *Lindum Rd.,* ☎ *01522/527980.* ✉ *£2, free on Fri.* ☉ *Mon.–Sat. 10–5:30, Sun. 2:30–5.*

Dining and Lodging

££–£££ ✕ **Jew's House.** Situated in one of Lincoln's oldest buildings (12th cen-
★ tury), the restaurant has an intimate atmosphere enhanced by antique tables and oil paintings. The cosmopolitan menu, featuring Continental specialties, changes daily, and the restaurant is renowned for its fresh fish and rich desserts, all homemade. ✉ *15 The Strait,* ☎ *01522/524851. AE, DC, MC, V. Closed Sun.–Mon.*

£–££ ✕ **Wig and Mitre.** This interesting downtown pub-café-restaurant stays open all day until 11 PM, offering an extremely wide range of food, from breakfast to full evening meals. Produce comes from the local markets, and dishes may include fresh fish, warming seasonal soups, European specialties, or classic English pies and roasts. ✉ *30 Steep Hill,* ☎ *01522/535190. AE, DC, MC, V.*

£££–££££ 🛏 **D'Isney Place Hotel.** This charming small hotel is a Georgian and Victorian building near the cathedral. If you like privacy, it's ideal: there's no lounge or other communal space. Breakfast is served on Minton china to guests in the beautifully decorated rooms. For a little more style, choose one of the deluxe rooms, which have relaxing Jacuzzi baths. ✉ *Eastgate,* ☎ *01522/538881,* FAX *01522/511321. 17 rooms. AE, DC, MC, V.*

£££ 🛏 **White Hart.** Lincoln's most elegant hotel is luxuriously furnished
★ with a wealth of antiques, including some fine clocks and china. The establishment has been a hotel for 600 years, reflecting a volume of experience that makes the service personal and extremely friendly. Each of the bedrooms is individually decorated; many are outfitted with antiques, and hardwoods such as walnut and mahogany abound. Non-smoking accommodations are available. Dinner, bed, and breakfast rates are a particularly good deal here. ✉ *Bailgate, LN1 3AR,* ☎ *01522/526222,* FAX *01522/531798. 35 rooms, 13 suites. Restaurant, bar, coffee shop. AE, DC, MC, V.*

The Arts

The **Theatre Royal** (⊠ Clasketgate, ☎ 01522/525555) is a fine Victorian theater previewing shows before their London runs and offering tour productions. There are also occasional concerts on Sunday.

Shopping

Lincoln's main shopping area, mostly pedestrianized, is at the bottom of the hill below the cathedral, around the Stonebow gateway and Guildhall, and along High Street. The best stores, however, are on Bailgate, Steep Hill, and the medieval streets leading directly down from the cathedral and castle. The **Cobb Hall Craft Centre** (⊠ St. Paul's La., off Bailgate) is a small mall of crafts shops and workshops, selling clocks, candles, and ornaments. Steep Hill has several good bookstores, antiques shops, and crafts and art galleries, such as the **Harding House Galleries** (⊠ Steep Hill, ☎ 01522/523537). **David Hansord** (⊠ Castle Hill, ☎ 01522/530044) specializes in antiques, especially antique scientific instruments.

Boston

47 *31 mi southeast of Lincoln.*

It was from here that, in 1620, Puritans Isaac Johnson and John Winthrop showed their disapproval of the then-prevailing religious conditions by crossing the Atlantic and helping to found the Massachusetts city of the same name. The Puritans had first tried to set sail for Holland in 1607, but they were arrested, tried, and imprisoned. The town's leading landmark is the Boston Stump, the lantern tower of the 14th-century **Church of St. Botolph.** With a height of 288 ft, it can be seen for 20 mi from both land and sea and once served to house a light that not only guided ships coming to the old port but also directed wayfarers crossing the treacherous marshes; today, it's a directional beacon for aircraft as well. The 15th-century guildhall, now the **Guildhall Museum,** contains the courtroom where the Pilgrims were tried and the cells where they were held. ⊠ *St. Mary's Guildhall, South St.,* ☎ *01205/365954,* WEB *www.boston.gov.uk.* 🖃 *£1.50, includes 45-min personal audio tour; free on Thurs., when audio tour is not available.* ☉ *Apr.–Sept., Mon.–Sat. 10–5, Sun. 1:30–5; Oct.–Mar., Mon.–Sat. 10–5.*

Among several other reminders of Boston's transatlantic links is the early 18th-century **Fydell House,** next to the guildhall, now an adult education center, where a room is graciously set aside for visitors from Boston, Massachusetts. ⊠ *South St.,* ☎ *01205/351520.* 🖃 *Free.* ☉ *Weekdays 9:30–12:30 and 1:30–4:30.*

EAST ANGLIA A TO Z

To research prices, get advice from other travelers, and book travel arrangements, visit www.fodors.com.

BIKE AND MOPED TRAVEL

The Broads Authority maintains a network of cycle paths and bike rental centers throughout the Broads. Rental costs £10 per day, and each rental center can provide local maps and route advice. All centers are within 30–40 minutes' drive of Norwich.

➤ INFORMATION: **Broads Authority** (☎ 01603/782281 mid-Apr.–Oct.; 01603/610734 year-round).

BUS TRAVEL

National Express serves the region from London's Victoria Coach Station. Average travel times: 2½ hours to Bury St. Edmunds, two hours to Cambridge, two hours to Colchester, four hours to Lincoln, and three hours to Norwich. Information about local bus service for Norfolk and parts of the surrounding counties is available from the Norfolk Bus Information Centre. Cambridgeshire's largest bus company is Stagecoach Cambus, which also sells Megarider tickets (£5) for seven days' travel within the city.

CUTTING COSTS

A Ranger ticket (available on board the bus) gives a day's unlimited travel on the whole network for £5.50; a family pass for two parents and two children costs £11.

➤ Bus INFORMATION: **National Express** (☎ 0990/808080). **Norfolk Bus Information Centre** (☎ 0500/626116). **Stagecoach Cambus** (☎ 01223/423554).

CAR RENTAL

➤ LOCAL AGENCIES: **Avis** (✉ 245 Mill Rd., Cambridge, ☎ 0990/900500; ✉ 213 Shrub End Rd., Colchester, ☎ 0990/900500; ✉ Ermine petrol station, Riseholm Rd., Lincoln, ☎ 01522/511200; ✉ Norwich Airport, Cromer Rd., Norwich, ☎ 0990/900500). **Budget Rent-a-Car** (✉ 303–305 Newmarket Rd., Cambridge, ☎ 0541/565656; ✉ Hall Rd., Norwich, ☎ 0541/565656). **Eurodollar** (✉ Newland Rd., Lincoln, ☎ 01522/512233). **Hertz** (✉ Willhire Ltd., Barnwell Rd., Cambridge, ☎ 01223/414600; ✉ Willhire Ltd., Crown Interchange, Old Ipswich Rd., Colchester, ☎ 01206/231801; ✉ Norwich Airport, Cromer Rd., Norwich, ☎ 01603/404010).

CAR TRAVEL

From London, Cambridge (54 mi) is off M11. At Exit 9, M11 connects with A11 to Norwich (114 mi); A14 off A11 goes to Bury St. Edmunds. A12 from London goes through east Suffolk via Colchester, Ipswich, and Great Yarmouth. For Lincoln (131 mi), take A1 via Huntingdon, Peterborough, and Grantham to A46 at Newark-on-Trent. A more scenic alternative is to leave A1 at Grantham and take A607 to Lincoln.

ROAD CONDITIONS

East Anglia has few fast main roads. The principal routes are those mentioned above, but once off the A roads, traveling within the region often means taking country lanes with many twists and turns.

EMERGENCIES

➤ CONTACTS: **Police, fire, ambulance** (☎ 999). **Addenbrooke's Hospital** (✉ Hill's Road, Cambridge, ☎ 01223/245151). **Norfolk and Norwich Hospital** (✉ Brunswick Road, Norwich, ☎ 01603/286286).

TOURS

BUS TOURS

Guide Friday operates open-top bus tours of Cambridge—the Backs (the lawns and gardens between the River Cam and the college buildings), the colleges, and the American war cemetery. The tours start from Cambridge train station, but can be picked up at any of Guide Friday's specially marked bus stops throughout the city. Tickets can be bought from the driver, the Guide Friday office at Cambridge train station, or the Cambridge Tourist Information Centre for £8. Tours run mid-April through September, every 15 minutes, and October through mid-April, every 30 minutes.

➤ FEES AND SCHEDULES: **Guide Friday** (✉ Cambridge train station, ☎ 01223/362444).

Qualified guides for walking tours of the major towns, including Bury St. Edmunds, Cambridge, Ely, Colchester, Ipswich, Norwich, and Lincoln, can be booked through the respective tourist offices. Those in Cambridge are particularly popular and should be booked well in advance. Tours depart at 1:30 throughout the year and more frequently in high summer and cost £6.50. In Lavenham, for £5, you can join the Lavenham Walkabout, a guided historical walk. Tours run year-round, although they're restricted to weekends only from November to mid-April.
➤ FEES AND SCHEDULES: **Cambridge Tourist Office** (☎ 01223/322640). **Lavenham Walkabout** (☎ 01787/247126).

TRAIN TRAVEL

The entire region is served by trains from London's Liverpool Street Station; in addition, there are trains to Cambridge and Lincoln from King's Cross Station. Full information on trains to East Anglia is available from National Rail Enquiries. Average travel times are one hour to Colchester, 50–90 minutes to Cambridge, almost two hours and 50 minutes to Norwich, and two hours to Lincoln.

CUTTING COSTS

A one-day Rover ticket available from any station in either Norfolk or Suffolk for £7.50 lets you disembark to explore any of the little towns en route. Seven-day Regional Rover tickets for unlimited travel in the Anglia Railways region are also available.
➤ TRAIN INFORMATION: **National Rail Enquiries** (☎ 0845/748–4950).

TRAVEL AGENCIES

➤ LOCAL AGENT REFERRALS: **American Express** (⊠ 25 Sidney St., Cambridge, ☎ 01223/461460). **Thomas Cook** (⊠ 18 Market St., Cambridge, ☎ 01223/543100; ⊠ Grafton Centre, Cambridge, ☎ 01223/322611; ⊠ 4 Cornhill Pavement, Lincoln, ☎ 01522/346400; ⊠ 15 St. Stephens St., Norwich, ☎ 01603/241200; ⊠ 14 London St., Norwich, ☎ 01603/241100).

VISITOR INFORMATION

➤ TOURIST INFORMATION: **East of England Tourist Board** (⊠ Toppesfield Hall, Hadleigh, Suffolk IP7 7DN, ☎ 01473/822922, FAX 01473/823063, WEB www.eastofenglandtouristboard.com). **Norfolk Broads Authority** (⊠ 18 Colegate, Norwich, Norfolk NR3 1BQ, ☎ 01603/610734, WEB www.broads-authority.gov.uk). **Boston** (⊠ Blackfriars Arts Centre, Spain La., ☎ 01205/356656, WEB www.boston.gov.uk). **Bury St. Edmunds** (⊠ 6 Angel Hill, ☎ 01284/764667, WEB www.stedmundsbury.gov.uk). **Cambridge** (⊠ Wheeler St., ☎ 01223/322640, WEB www.cambridge.gov.uk). **Colchester** (⊠ 1 Queen St., ☎ 01206/282920, WEB www.colchester.gov.uk). **Ely** (⊠ Oliver Cromwell's House, 29 St. Mary's St., ☎ 01353/662062, WEB www.ely.org.uk). **Great Yarmouth** (⊠ Marine Parade, ☎ 01493/842195, WEB www.great-yarmouth.co.uk). **Lavenham** (⊠ Lady St., ☎ 01787/2482907, WEB www.babergh-south-suffolk.gov.uk). **Lincoln** (⊠ 9 Castle Hill, ☎ 01522/529828, WEB www.lincoln.org.uk). **Norwich** (⊠ Guildhall, Gaol Hill, ☎ 01603/666071, WEB www.norwich.gov.uk). **Peterborough** (⊠ 45 Bridge St., ☎ 01733/452336, WEB www.peterborough.gov.uk). **Stamford** (⊠ Broad St., ☎ 01780/755611, WEB www.stamford.co.uk). **Sudbury** (⊠ Town Hall, Market Hill, ☎ 01787/881320, WEB www.babergh-south-suffolk.gov.uk).

14 YORKSHIRE

LEEDS, BRADFORD, HAWORTH, YORK, WHITBY, CASTLE HOWARD

On a stormy day, it's hard not to imagine Emily Brontë's Heathcliff riding full-gallop out of over the cloud-swept ridges of the Yorkshire Moors. Centered around Haworth, Brontë Country remains a pilgrimage for many. Beyond, however, lie other memories in the making: splendidly elegant Castle Howard, spellbinding Fountains Abbey, and the satisfyingly solid Yorkshire Dales, stomping grounds of James Herriot. Top of the list is York, England's best-preserved medieval city.

Y ORKSHIRE IS ANOTHER COUNTRY, say the locals, and a few days
spent exploring this largest of English regions could well con-
vince you they're right. The famous sights, such as the Minster
at York, the moorland haunts of the Brontës, the ruined monasteries
and stately homes, are justifiably popular but only provide half the picture. Nowhere else in England have industry and the natural world col-
lided with such significant effect, offsetting brisk manufacturing towns
with untamed scenery. Author J. B. Priestley, in his *English Journey* of
1933, noted that "Industrial Man and Nature sing a rum sort of duet"
in Yorkshire, a duet still played out in the hills above Priestley's native
Bradford, or in Leeds, or atop the blustery moors.

Updated by Ed
Glinert

Yorkshire remains an intensely rural region. The most rugged of its landscapes are the Yorkshire Moors, a vast area of lonely moorland, inspiration of Emily Brontë's 1847 *Wuthering Heights* (and if ever a work
of fiction grew out of the landscape in which its author lived, it was
surely this). Brilliant at times with spring flowers and heather, the
moors can change dangerously, often within a few minutes, to stormy
weather, when you'll be lucky to see as far as the next cloud-swept ridge.
Between the bleak areas of moorland and the rocky Pennine hills lie
lush, green valleys known as the Yorkshire Dales, where the high rain-
fall produces luxuriant vegetation, swift rivers, sparkling streams, and
waterfalls. The villages here, immortalized through the books of the
late veterinarian Alf Wight (1916–1995), who wrote under the name
James Herriot, are among the most utterly peaceful in England, although
many burst into life as summer walking bases.

But there's also a gritty, urban aspect to Yorkshire, whose towns have
changed the very course of British history. Two of Britain's major industrial centers are here: Leeds and Bradford, now being rejuvenated
in places following the decline of their industrial base. More aesthet-
ically pleasing is the northern, walled city of York, dominated by the
towers of its great minster; for some, the most noble cathedral in
Britain. Settled originally by Romans and Vikings, York was once England's most important northern city, and it is arguably the best-preserved medieval town in the country.

Outside York, even more medieval marvels await: the ruined monastic remains of Rievaulx Abbey, Whitby Abbey, and Fountains Abbey
are some of the most romantic and picturesque sights in Britain. The
monks of medieval Yorkshire were among the richest in Europe by virtue
of the wool trade that they conducted from their vast religious estates
in the north, and they left a wealth of richly decorated and appointed
monastic buildings, most in ruins since Henry VIII dissolved the monasteries during the 16th century. Thanks to the countless poems written
about these ruins by the great Victorian poets, and the paintings of them
by celebrated 19th-century artists, these sites became world-famous for
their powerful evocation of life in the Middle Ages.

Yorkshire has historically been split into three divisions or "ridings"
(from an old Norse word meaning "third") and although the county
ceased to be run as one administrative entity in 1974, natives still treat
Yorkshire as one homogenous unit and tend to ignore the divisions into
North, South, and West Yorkshire. York, Haworth—the center of
Brontë Country—or the seaside resorts of Scarborough and Whitby
are the best touring bases. Those with very limited time could see
York as a day trip; the fastest trains take just two hours from London
to York, although proper exploration of the region, especially of the

moors and dales, requires time and effort, well rewarded whether you're out to see untamed natural beauty or great medieval art.

Pleasures and Pastimes

Dining

Exploring Yorkshire, with its fresh air and hilltop walks, positively encourages hearty appetites. Happily, locally produced meat (especially lamb) and vegetables are excellent; roast beef dinners come with Yorkshire pudding, the famous popoverlike pastry traditionally cooked under the meat and served with gravy. In the days when meat was a real luxury, it was offered as a first course in hopes of filling you up so you wouldn't want much to eat for the main course. Fish from the coast is a real treat with freshly fried chips (thick french fries); cod or haddock is the main local catch, although sole, crab, and lobster are seasonally available, too. Look for freshly baked bread and homemade cakes, at their best in Yorkshire tearooms. Be sure to try Wensleydale cheese, which has a delicate flavor and honeyed aftertaste. There are fine restaurants here, but pubs are often the best (and in small villages, the only) places to find good, hearty meals for a gentle price.

CATEGORY	COST*
££££	over £22
£££	£16–£22
££	£9–£15
£	under £9

*per person for a main course at dinner

Hiking and Walking

Some of Britain's finest long-distance footpaths cut through the region. The Yorkshire Dales National Park is crisscrossed with trails and long-distance paths. The North York Moors National Park has long, empty swaths of land for tramping, and the dramatic coastline offers a variety of craggy cliff walks. Leading trails include the Cleveland Way (108 mi), from Helmsley to Filey; the hard-going Lyke-Wake Walk (40 mi), from Osmotherley to Ravenscar; and the eastern section of the Coast-to-Coast Walk (190 mi), which starts or finishes in Robin Hood's Bay. In addition, the Dales Way (80 mi) connects Leeds and Bradford with the Lake District. Perhaps the greatest of all English walks, the Pennine Way, which runs from the Peak District to Scotland, has a central section that runs through the Yorkshire Dales.

Lodging

For a high price, you can stay at the stately home of Lady Mary Wortley Montagu and at other Yorkshire luxury hotels, or, to get a real flavor of northern hospitality and cuisine, you can look for farmhouse bed-and-breakfasts in the countryside. Even if you travel by public transportation, you're not necessarily limited to accommodations in town centers (although such places as Skipton and Whitby can make lovely roosts where you can explore the deeper countryside). Many proprietors of places on the outskirts of town will pick you up at the train station or bus depot. Remember that rooms fill very quickly at seaside resorts in July and August, and in winter in the dales and moors, some places close for the season. Always call ahead. Hikers and budgeteers love the region's dozens of youth hostels; along with those in the major dales and moorland villages, there are useful budget bases in York, Whitby, Robin Hood's Bay, and Scarborough. Even more basic accommodation is available in a network of camping barns (rural bunkhouses) in the Yorkshire Dales. Reservation numbers and details on hostels and barns, which can fill up quickly in high season, are available from any local tourist office.

CATEGORY	COST*
££££	over £150
£££	£100–£150
££	£60–£100
£	under £60

All prices are for two people sharing a standard double room, including service, breakfast, and VAT.

Exploring Yorkshire

Yorkshire is the largest English region to explore (its fiercely proud inhabitants would say the only English region *worth* exploring). As such, you need to plan carefully before launching on a tour around the separate geographic regions.

The industrial heartland is West Yorkshire, where the cities of Leeds and Bradford were at the forefront of both the late medieval wool trade and the 19th-century Industrial Revolution. What the tourist office likes to call Brontë Country—basically Haworth, home of the Brontë family—is just to the northwest, and northward spread the hills, valleys, and villages of the Yorkshire Dales, stomping ground of the late James Herriot, the much-loved veterinarian. In the center of the region, York deserves special attention, and there's real interest in its environs, too, in places as diverse as the spa town of Harrogate and the magnificent Fountains Abbey.

Moving east to the coast, Yorkshire reveals itself to be a seaside holiday destination, although never one that will win prizes for summerlike weather. But fine beaches and a fascinating history await you in the resort of Scarborough, the former whaling port of Whitby, Robin Hood's Bay—a cliff-top, one-time smuggler's haunt—and the traditional fishing village of Staithes. Finally, you can strike inland to the North York Moors National Park. Delightful, isolated stone villages, dramatic moorland walks, Rievaulx Abbey, and elegant Castle Howard are all within easy reach.

Numbers in the text correspond to numbers in the margin and on the Yorkshire and York maps.

Great Itineraries

You could drive across Yorkshire in less than a day (as many do, on the way to Scotland), but you would have little quality time to spend anywhere. Three days would give the opportunity for a night in York, followed by a night in rural Yorkshire. However, only with five to seven days does a satisfying itinerary begin to take shape: with this amount of time, you could stop longer in York and visit the coast, as well as allow yourself time to get off the beaten track a bit to seek out the abbeys, castles, and old moorland villages. You'll still have to move quickly, though, if you want to see every region of Yorkshire in a week.

IF YOU HAVE 3 DAYS

Start in 🔲 **York** ⑬–㉔, quintessential city of Yorkshire, where, if you arrive early enough in the day, you'll be able to fit in several of the main medieval city sites, such as York Minster and the Shambles. Then take an excursion bus tour leaving shortly before noon out to spectacular **Castle Howard** ㊵. Return to York about 4:30 in the afternoon, repair to Betty's tearooms, then perhaps go on an evening walking tour. Next morning, continue to see York sights and then travel to Leeds to pick up a bus to 🔲 **Haworth** ④ for a Brontë pilgrimage. (If you have a car, you can go a bit out of the way to make a quick visit to stunning **Studley Royal and Fountains Abbey** ㉗.) Spend your final day in Haworth. Don't forget to take an unforgettable hike over the moors from Top Withins ("Wuthering Heights") to the Hardcastle Crags valley. Return to Leeds.

IF YOU HAVE 7 DAYS

Starting in **Leeds** ①, head for **Bradford** ③ and its museums, and make time for a curry lunch on Morley Street before spending the afternoon at the nearby model factory community of Saltaire. It's then just a short drive to **Haworth** ④ for an overnight stop in Brontë Country, although you'll have to wait until the next morning to see the sights. After this, you can meander up through the Yorkshire Dales, via **Skipton** ⑥ and **Malham** ⑧ before stopping for the night in **Grassington** ⑦. The next day, soak up more remote scenery as you tour the northern dales, Wensleydale and Swaledale, before hitting the main roads and heading south, via **Studley Royal and Fountains Abbey** ㉗, to the spa town of **Harrogate** ㉕. After all this driving, you have only a short journey to York the following day. Stay in **York** ⑬–㉔ for two nights, which will give you time to see everything, and then early on the morning of departure, aim for **Helmsley** ㊳ with a sightseeing stop at either **Rievaulx Abbey** ㊴ or **Castle Howard** ㊵ before driving across the moors to **Danby** ㊱ and on to **Whitby** ㉞ for your overnight stop. The next day, return to York along the coast via **Robin Hood's Bay** ㉝ and **Scarborough** ㉜.

When to Tour Yorkshire

Summer is undoubtedly the best time to visit Yorkshire, especially the coastal areas and moors, when there are festivals and regattas. However, you can expect resorts and walking centers to be overcrowded, and you'll have to book accommodations well in advance. York's city center will also be packed shoulder-to-shoulder with visitors. Spring and fall bring their own rewards: less crowded attractions and crisp, clear days, although there's also the increased risk of rain and fog. Winter is hard to call: with glistening snow and bright, clear days, the coast, moors, and dales are beautiful, but storms and blizzards set in quickly, moorland roads become impassable, and villages can be cut off from the outside world. During winter, stick to York and the main towns if you must keep to a strict timetable.

WEST YORKSHIRE AND BRONTË COUNTRY

Even before the Industrial Revolution, the towns in the hills and river valleys of West Yorkshire were important commercial centers, whose trade in wool made prodigious fortunes for both local merchants and religious foundations. It's still a region synonymous with wool production, and there are a large number of "mill shops" where high-quality knitting wool, sweaters, and woven wool for skirts or suits can be bought at factory prices. Following industrialization, the towns took to new trades such as textiles, chemicals, and engineering, which transformed the urban scene, leaving many places today rather unattractive at first sight. However, ongoing restoration of once-glorious Victorian architecture and the regeneration of inner-city areas is having a beneficial effect, and relief is always close at hand in the region's striking rural and moorland surroundings.

In the gaunt hills north of the Calder Valley and south of the River Aire is the district immortalized by the writings of the Brontë sisters. Haworth, an otherwise gray West Yorkshire village, might have passed unobserved throughout the years but for the magnetism of the family that lived in the old parsonage, now the museum of the Brontë Society. Every summer, thousands toil up the steep main street to visit the hilltop church and the museum, where all too often Brontë enthusi-

Yorkshire

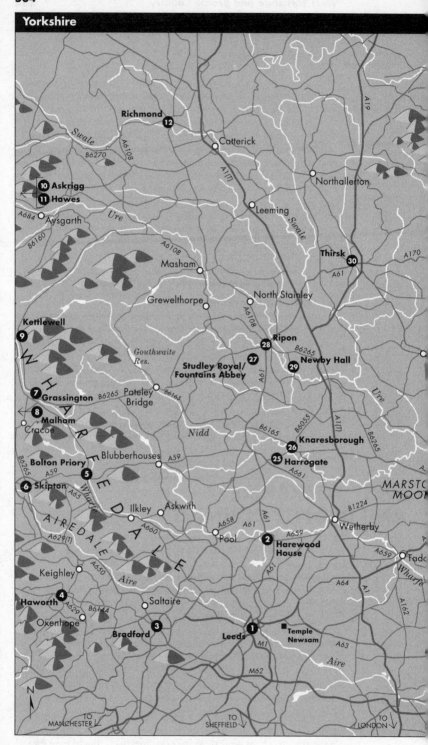

Richmond 12

Catterick

Northallerton

A19

Swale

B6270

A6108

A1(1)

10 Askrigg
11 Hawes

Leeming

Swale

A170

A684

Aysgarth

Ure

Thirsk 30

B6160

A6108

A61

Masham

Grewelthorpe

North Stainley

A6108

Kettlewell

9

Gouthwaite
Res.

Ripon 28

B6265

Newby Hall

27 Studley Royal/
Fountains Abbey

29

W
H
A
R
F
E
D
A
L
E

7 Grassington

B6265 Pateley
Bridge

B6165

Ure

8 Malham

Cracoe

Nidd

B6165

B6055

A1(1)

B6265

Bolton Priory

Blubberhouses

A59

Knaresborough 26

A59

5

25 Harrogate

B1224

MARSTO
MOO

6 Skipton

A65

A661

Ilkley

Askwith

A660

Wetherby

AIREDALE

A629(1)

Wharfe

A658

A61

A659

Tad

Keighley

A650

Aire

Pool

A61

A659

A64

A1

Wharfe

Haworth 4

A629

B6144

Saltaire

2 Harewood
House

A162

Oxenhope

Bradford 3

Leeds 1

■ Temple
Newsam

A63

M1

Aire

M62

N

TO
MANCHESTER

TO
SHEFFIELD

TO
LONDON

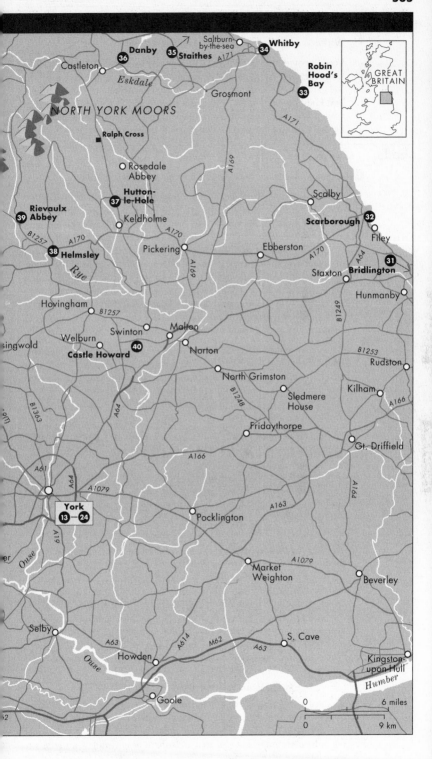

NORTH YORK MOORS

Danby **36**

Castleton

Eskdale

Saltburn-by-the-sea

Staithes **35**

Whitby **34**

A171

Grosmont

Robin Hood's Bay **33**

Ralph Cross

GREAT BRITAIN **31**

Rosedale Abbey

Hutton-le-Hole **37**

Scalby

Keldholme

A169

Rievaulx Abbey **39**

B1257

A170

Pickering

A169

A170

Ebberston

Scarborough **32**

Filey

Helmsley **38**

Rye

Hovingham

B1257

Swinton

Welburn

Malton

Castle Howard **40**

Norton

Staxton

Bridlington **31**

Hunmanby

North Grimston

B1248

Sledmere House

Kilham

A166

Rudston

B1253

Fridaythorpe

Gt. Driffield

A166

A164

York **13** — **24**

A61

A64

A1079

Pocklington

A163

A19

Market Weighton

A1079

Beverley

Ouse

Selby

A63

Howden

A614

M62

S. Cave

A63

Kingston-upon-Hull

Humber

Goole

0   6 miles

0   9 km

asm stops. To understand the real spirit of the Brontë book it is necessary to go farther afield to the moors and the ruined farm of Top Withins, which legend, but not fact, refers to as Wuthering Heights.

Leeds provides an obvious starting point, because it's easily reached from the west by the trans-Pennine M62 and from the south by the M1. Traditional wool towns to the south, like Wakefield, Huddersfield, and Halifax, each have a modicum of interest, but the main thrust of any visit to West Yorkshire is to the west of Leeds, where Bradford and Brontë Country, around Haworth, really begin to repay investigation.

Leeds

❶ *43 mi northeast of Manchester, 25 mi southwest of York.*

The burgeoning city of Leeds has a population of more than 400,000 and a reputation as one of the greenest cities in Europe, although its unkempt industrial outskirts and congested traffic make this difficult for first-time visitors to believe. But there has been real progress in the city during the past decade, and what was formerly an industrial city in severe decline has been given a new lease on life. In addition to the parks, long green routes radiate from the city center; there has been major investment in urban heritage projects and redevelopment such as Millennium Square, and trend-setting restaurants and café-bars with outdoor seating are sprouting all over the city. It's not quite the Mediterranean, but there's a tangible vitality in the air these days.

Leeds had a head start on most comparable cities, since its wealthy, 19th-century days had left it a fine architectural bequest. The city is well known for its superb Victorian Arcades, but the Georgian squares and streets of the West End are just as notable. Tucked away among the streets you'll find old pubs and yards that were originally laid out in the 14th century.

The classical **Town Hall** (✉ The Headrow, ☎ 0113/247–8384, 🌐 www.leeds.gov.uk), built in 1853, sits prominently in the city center, one of the finest of all Victorian public buildings in Britain and the masterpiece of local architect Cuthbert Broderick. It's of most use to visitors as a landmark, because two of the best attractions, the City Art Gallery and the City Museum, lie just across the road. It also hosts an international concert season (October–May), attracting top performers and conductors.

The **City Art Gallery** showcases a fine collection of painting and sculpture, with particularly strong showings of 20th-century British art (including works by Sickert, Hunt, Lowry, and Spencer). The **Craft Centre and Design Gallery,** also in the museum, exhibits fine contemporary crafts. Adjoining the gallery is the **Henry Moore Institute,** named for the famous British sculptor who was a student at Leeds College of Art. The institute displays temporary exhibitions of modern sculpture. To see Moore's own work, step inside the City Art Gallery, which has several examples, or admire his *Reclining Woman* on the steps outside the gallery. ✉ *The Headrow,* ☎ *0113/247–8248.* 🎨 *Free.* ☉ *Mon.–Tues. and Thurs.–Sat. 10–5, Wed. 10–8, Sun. 1–5.*

♻ It's hard to pigeonhole the **City Museum,** whose collections and exhibits of geology, natural history, ethnology, and archaeology run from native flora and fauna and the achievements of prehistoric man to local life in Roman times. But children are sure to be enthralled, and the gift shop has inventive offerings. ✉ *The Headrow,* ☎ *0113/247–8275.* 🎨 *Free.* ☉ *Tues.–Sat. 10–5.*

The **River Aire** was an important trading route in Leeds's early days, although industrial pollution left it in poor shape. In recent years the neglected urban riverside and canalside sites have been revitalized as urban heritage projects. At **Granary Wharf,** in the Canal Basin, reached via the Dark Arches where the River Aire flows under the City Station, there are design and crafts shops, music events, boat trips, and a regular festival market. Farther east at **The Calls,** converted redbrick warehouses hold smart bars, cafés, and restaurants that enliven the cobbled streets and quayside.

Tetley's Brewery Wharf celebrates the history of the English pub through the ages. Since all the main attractions are indoors, including a brewery tour of the Yorkshire company, with free tastings, Tetley's is a useful wet-weather standby. If there are blue skies, take advantage of the riverside venue of the outdoor café-bar. ⊠ *The Waterfront, River Aire,* ☎ *0113/242–0666.* ⊠ *£3.95.* ⊙ *Apr.–Sept., Tues.–Sun. 10:30–5:30; Oct.–Mar., Wed.–Sun. 10–4:30.*

★ ↺ Housing the legendary arms and armor collection from the Tower of London, Leeds's **Royal Armouries** occupies a redeveloped 13-acre dockland site, a 15-minute walk from the city center. The state-of-the-art building was specially built to house much of the vast collection from the Tower of London, which had outgrown its original home long ago. In a series of spirited interactive displays, hands-on exhibits, video presentations, computer simulations, and even live demonstrations, you can trace the history of weaponry in five themed galleries. Shoot a crossbow, direct operations on a battlefield, experience a Wild West gunfight or an Elizabethan joust—it's your own choice. ⊠ *Armouries Dr., off M1 or M621,* ☎ *0113/220–1996,* WEB *www.armouries.org.uk.* ⊠ *£4.90.* ⊙ *Apr.–Oct., daily 10–5:30; Nov.–Mar., weekdays 10:30–4:30, weekends 10:30–5.30.*

Temple Newsam, a huge Elizabethan and Jacobean building that was altered in the 18th century, was the birthplace in 1545 of Lord Darnley, the doomed husband of Mary, Queen of Scots. Surrounded by one of the largest public parks in Western Europe, the house now belongs to Leeds City Council, which uses it to display its rich collections of furniture, paintings, and ceramics. The vast park, with its walled rose gardens, greenhouses, and miles of woodland walks, was originally laid out by Capability Brown in 1762. The house is 4 mi east of Leeds on A63, and there are buses from Leeds Central Bus Station every 30 minutes. ⊠ *Off Selby Rd.,* ☎ *0113/264–7321.* ⊠ *£2.* ⊙ *House Mar.–Oct., Tues.–Sat. 10–5, Sun. 1–5; gardens daily 10–dusk; last entry 1 hr before closing.*

Dining and Lodging

££££ ✕ **Pool Court at 42.** Right in the center of Leeds, in the revitalized warehouse district by the river, Pool Court at 42 is typical of the new wave of fashionable restaurants becoming popular with northern food fanciers. It's a distinctly elegant place serving contemporary French and British food, with Mediterranean influences. Fish is always a good choice. Roast scallops and fresh salmon are favorites, and duck and game are expertly cooked; there are some fine vegetarian dishes, too. The dinner price includes two courses. The adjacent, associated Brasserie 44 (☎ 0113/234–3232) is less formal, and prices are less expensive, although it shares the same cosmopolitan influences. ⊠ *42–44 The Calls,* ☎ *0113/ 244–4242. AE, DC, MC, V. Closed Sun. No lunch Sat.*

££–£££ ✕ **Fourth Floor Café.** If the Harvey Nichols department store has been a roaring success, it's due in part to the lure of its swank Fourth Floor eatery: a café only in name, because this high-design restaurant is a standout for both food and ambience. On summer days, the terrace comes into its own. At other times there's no distraction from the well-crafted modern British menu, which changes several times a week but is sure to include stylish takes on dishes like smoked haddock, char-grilled rib-eye steak, and the freshest lemon sole. ⊠ *Harvey Nichols, 107–111 Briggate,* ☎ *0113/204–8000. MC, V. Closed Sun. No dinner Mon.–Wed.*

£££–££££   🏠 **42 The Calls.** Taking an old grain mill in the once-dilapidated waterfront area of the city and converting it into a high-tech, high-comfort hotel takes some nerve, but the venture has paid off. Each room shows individual flair, while retaining such original features as warehouse skylights, exposed beams, and brickwork. Facilities are up-to-the-minute, with CD players, comfortable bathrooms, and a split-level lobby lounge-bar with eminently cushy armchairs. Weekend rates are softer on the pocket. ⊠ *42 The Calls, LS2 7EW,* ☎ *0113/244–0099,* FAX *0113/234–4100. 41 rooms. Restaurant, bar, breakfast room, lobby lounge. AE, DC, MC, V.*

Nightlife and the Arts

NIGHTLIFE

Fashionable café-bars are sprouting all over Leeds, allowing you to grab a bite or sip cappuccino or designer beer until late into the night. **Bar Norman** (⊠ Call La., ☎ 0113/234–3988) defies description with its weird and wonderful design. The in-crowd can't get enough of it. **Cuban Heels** (⊠ The Arches, 28 Assembly St., ☎ 0113/234–6115) kicks out salsa sounds most nights. Strung-out shoppers take a caffeine fix in Harvey Nichols's graceful arcade **Espresso Bar** (⊠ 107–111 Briggate, ☎ 0113/204–8888). The **Town and Country Club** (⊠ 55 Cookridge St., ☎ 0113/280–0100), a regional offshoot of the famous London live-music venue, hosts regular rock and pop gigs and has theme club nights each weekend.

THE ARTS

Opera North, England's first major provincial opera company, has its home in Leeds at the **Grand Theatre** (⊠ 46 New Briggate, ☎ 0113/245–6014; 0113/222–6222 box office), whose opulent gold-and-plush auditorium is modeled on that of La Scala. It's worth knowing that Opera North also plays for free each summer on the grounds at Temple Newsam.

The ultramodern **West Yorkshire Playhouse** (⊠ Playhouse Sq., Quarry Hill, ☎ 0113/213–7780) was built on the slope of an old quarry. Its interior is designed to be completely adaptable to all kinds of staging.

Shopping

For ethnic clothes, gifts, jewelry, and accessories, visit the shops inside the old **Corn Exchange** (⊠ Call La., ☎ 0113/234–1745). The arrival of **Harvey Nichols** (⊠ 107–111 Briggate, ☎ 0113/204–8804), home-based in London where it is regarded as the crucible of chic, put Leeds firmly on the British shopping map: stop in for an abundance of fashion and a great café-restaurant. The city has some excellent markets, notably **Kirkgate Market** (⊠ Vicar La., ☎ no phone), an Edwardian beauty that's the largest in the north of England. Specialty shops and designer boutiques fill the Victorian shopping arcades, of which the glistening **Victoria Quarter** (⊠ Briggate, ☎ no phone) is the epitome of fin-de-siècle style.

Harewood House

★ ❷   *7 mi north of Leeds.*

Harewood House (pronounced *har*-wood), the home of the earl of Harewood, a cousin of the Queen, is a spectacular Neoclassical mansion, built in 1759 by John Carr of York. It is known for its Robert Adam interiors, important paintings and ceramics, and some of the most ravishing Chippendale furniture extant (Chippendale was born in nearby Otley). On the grounds are gardens, woods, a lake, a bird garden with more than 100 rare and endangered species, an adventure playground, and a butterfly house. ✉ *A61, Harewood,* ☎ *0113/288–6331,* WEB *www. harewood.org.* 🎟 *£8, bird garden and grounds £6.25.* ⊙ *Apr.–Oct., daily 10–5; grounds and bird garden open until 6.*

Bradford

❸ *17 mi southwest of Harewood House, 10 mi west of Leeds, 32 mi northeast of Manchester.*

Bradford was once one of the greatest wool towns in Europe, a trade at which it had excelled since the 16th century. Even as late as the 1960s, wool accounted for a substantial part of its economy, but as with all the other West Yorkshire textile towns, recession and competition from new markets hit hard. It tries hard to be likeable today, and although much of its grandeur has gone, the center still holds the odd Victorian building from its period of greatest prosperity: St. George's Hall on Bridge Street (1851) and the Wool Exchange on Market Street (1864) are two fine examples.

★ ℭ Most people come to Bradford for the museums, particularly the renowned **National Museum of Photography, Film, and Television,** which traces the history of the photographic media. It's a huge, and hugely entertaining, museum, with plenty of interactive models, machines, and related ephemera from early cameras to TV props. A massive makeover in the late 1990s added galleries concentrating on up-to-the-minute topics like digital imaging and computer animation. The museum's popularity with children means you're best advised to come early or late in the day if you want to see the displays in peace. Allow time, too, for a screening at the museum's 50- by 60-ft IMAX screen, which shows stomach-churning movies of flights over the Grand Canyon and other remarkable sequences, including three-dimensional shows. The associated Pictureville cinema has a full repertory program, too. ✉ *Pictureville, Prince's Way,* ☎ *01274/202030,* WEB *www.nmpft.org.uk.* 🎟 *Museum free, IMAX movie £5.80, Pictureville screenings £4.40.* ⊙ *Tues.–Sun. 10–6.*

Bradford's history as a wool-producing town is outlined at the **Industrial Museum and Horses at Work,** housed in a former spinning mill 3 mi northeast of the town center. Exhibits include workers' dwellings dating from the 1870s and a mill owner's house from the 19th century. Children love riding in the Shire horse-drawn tram. Moorside Road is off A658 Harrogate Road; or take Bus 608, 609, or 612 from the city center. ✉ *Moorside Mills, Moorside Rd.,* ☎ *01274/631756.* 🎟 *Free.* ⊙ *Tues.–Sat. 10–5, Sun. noon–5.*

★ Perhaps the most extraordinary attraction in Bradford is the former model factory community of **Saltaire.** Built by textile magnate Sir Titus Salt in the mid-19th century, it exemplifies the enduring trait of philanthropy among certain Victorian industrialists, who erected modern terraced housing for their workers and furnished them with libraries, parks, hospitals, and schools. Saltaire, fashioned in Italianate style, has been remarkably preserved, its former mills and houses turned into shops, restaurants, and galleries. Salt's Mill, built in 1853, resembles a palazzo and was the largest factory in the world when it was built. Today it holds an art gallery and crafts and furniture shops. It's not an official Web site, but WEB http://come.to/saltaire has extensive information.

One-hour guided tours (£2) depart every Saturday and Sunday from the **tourist information center** (✉ 2 Victoria Rd., Saltaire, ☎ 01274/774993). There's a remarkable permanent retrospective exhibition of 400 works by Bradford-born artist David Hockney in the **1853 Gallery** (✉ Salt's Mill, Victoria Rd., ☎ 01274/531163). Admission is free, and the exhibition is open daily 10–6. Saltaire is 4 mi north of Bradford, and there are regular local bus and train services. Drivers should take A650 to Shipley and follow the signs.

Dining and Lodging

£ ✕ **Kashmir.** Morley Street, two minutes from the National Museum of Photography, Film, and Television, is lined with some of Bradford's finest curry houses. The Kashmir is one of the best, a simple, no-frills place dishing out authentically spiced food at extremely low prices. ✉ *27 Morley St.,* ☎ *01274/726513. No credit cards.*

££–£££ ✕🏨 **Quality Victoria Hotel.** This renovated former railway hotel in the center of town, built in 1875, makes a comfortable base if you crave an urban Yorkshire stopover. Public areas are smart and stylish, and guest rooms keep up with appearances, too: armchairs in checked cloth, plump beds, and crisp, cool decor. The standard room rate doesn't include breakfast, although discounted weekend rates do. Vic and Bert's, the stylish and popular attached restaurant (no lunch Sunday), gets rave reviews for its eclectic grill menu. ✉ *Bridge St., BD1 1JX,* ☎ *01274/728706,* 🖷 *01274/736358. 60 rooms. Restaurant, bar, sauna, gym. AE, DC, MC, V.*

Haworth: Heart of Brontë Country

❹ *10 mi northwest of Bradford, 5 mi southwest of Keighley.*

There's not much at first glance that makes the village of Haworth (pronounced *how*-weth) in West Yorkshire special. It's an old, stone-built spot on the edge of the Yorkshire Moors, superficially much like many other craggy Yorkshire settlements. But Haworth has a particular claim to fame; in fact, it's probably the most celebrated literary spot in Britain after Stratford-upon-Avon. It was here, in the middle of the 19th century, that the three Brontë sisters—Emily (author of *Wuthering Heights,* 1847), Charlotte (*Jane Eyre,* 1847), and Anne (*The Tenant of Wildfell Hall,* 1848)—lived. This unlikely trio, daughters of the local vicar, were responsible for some of the most romantic books ever written. "My sister Emily loved the moors," sister Charlotte once wrote. "Flowers brighter than the rose bloomed in the blackest of the heath for her; out of a sullen hollow in a livid hillside her mind could make an Eden. She found in the bleak solitude many and dear delights; and not the least and best loved was liberty. Liberty was the breath of Emily's nostrils; without it she perished." Today, thousands journey to the straggling stone village of Haworth, which lives a little too readily off its associations: visitors in summer, on occasion, threaten to overwhelm the place entirely.

You can access the region by taking a train to Leeds Station or a bus to Leeds's National Express Coach Station. To reach Haworth by bus or train, buy a Metro Day Rover for bus and rail, and take the Metro train from Leeds to Keighley. There are about three hourly. From Keighley, take the Keighley & Worth Valley Railway for the trip to Haworth, or opt instead for Keighley and District Bus 663, 664, or 665 (one leaves every 20 minutes). The same buses make the direct journey from Bradford, also every 20 minutes.

Haworth's steep, cobbled **Main Street** has changed little in outward appearance since the early 19th century, but today acts as a funnel for most of the visitors who crowd into the various points of interest: the **Black Bull** pub, where the reprobate Branwell, the Brontës' only brother, drank himself into an early grave; the **post office** from which Charlotte, Emily, and Anne sent their manuscripts to their London publishers; and the **church,** with its gloomy graveyard (Charlotte and Emily are buried inside the church; Anne, in Scarborough).

The town's **information center** (⊠ 2–4 West La., ☎ 01535/642329) has information about accommodations, maps, and books on the Brontës, and inexpensive leaflets to help you find your way to such outlying *Wuthering Heights* sites as Ponden Hall (Thrushcross Grange) and Ponden Kirk (Penistone Crag).

★ The **Brontë Parsonage Museum,** in the somber Georgian house in which the sisters grew up, displays original furniture (some bought by Charlotte after the success of *Jane Eyre*), portraits, and books. The Brontës first came here in 1820, when the Reverend Patrick Brontë was appointed to the local living, but tragedy soon struck—his wife, Maria, and their two eldest children died within five years (done in, some scholars assert, by water wells tainted by seepage from the neighboring graveyard, a malady that inflicted a tragically high toll on all Haworth at this time). The museum has some enchanting mementos of the four surviving children, including the sisters' spidery, youthful graffiti on the nursery wall, and Charlotte's tiny wedding shoes. Branwell painted several of the portraits on display. ⊠ *Main St.,* ☎ *01535/642323,* WEB *www. bronte.org.uk.* ⊠ *£4.80.* ⊙ *Apr.–Sept., daily 10–5.30; Oct.–Mar., daily 11–4:30. Closed mid-Jan.–early Feb.*

If you know and love the Brontës' works, you'll probably want to walk an hour or so along a field path, a lane, and a moorland track to the **Brontë Waterfall,** described in Emily's and Charlotte's poems and letters. **Top Withins,** 3 mi from Haworth, is the remains of a bleak hilltop farm. Although often taken to be the main inspiration for Heathcliff's gloomy mansion, Wuthering Heights, it probably isn't, as a plaque nearby baldly states. There and back from Haworth is a two-hour walk. Better still is to cross the watershed to Wycollar, over the Lancashire border, or make that fine walk from Withins to the Hardcastle Crags valley. Wherever you chose to head, you'll need sturdy shoes and protective clothing: if you've read *Wuthering Heights,* you'll have a fairly good idea of what weather can be like on the Yorkshire Moors.

☾ Haworth is on the **Keighley & Worth Valley Railway,** a gorgeous 5-mi-long branch line along which steam engines run between Keighley (3 mi north of Haworth) and Oxenhope. Taking the train at least part of the way is exciting enough for everyone, although kids will like it even more on special days when there are family fairs en route. The Museum of Rail Travel, at Ingrow along the line, has a handsome collection of vintage cars. ⊠ *Railway Station, Keighley,* ☎ *01535/645214; 01535/647777 24-hr information,* WEB *www.kwvr.co.uk.* ⊠ *£6 return, £8 day rover ticket.* ⊙ *Sept.–May, weekends; June–Aug., daily; call for schedules and special events.*

Dining and Lodging

££ ✕☐ **Weavers.** You'll have to book well in advance, because there are only three rooms, converted from a series of old cottages, but you'll be glad you did. In a fine village location, Weavers is mainly in business as a restaurant, but the pretty, light rooms are well turned out, and the breakfast is very good. Downstairs, the restaurant serves traditional Yorkshire cuisine, including Yorkshire pudding and local stews. More elaborate dishes include Gressingham duck, or a daily fish special (perhaps in a pie, or baked), and there's a specially priced set dinner (except Saturday) for early arrivals. ✉ *15 West La., BD22 8DU,* ☎ *01535/643822,* 🆁 *01535/644832. 3 rooms. Restaurant, bar. AE, DC, MC, V. Closed 2 wks at Christmas and 1 wk in summer; restaurant and rooms closed Sun.–Mon.*

££ 🏨 **Old White Lion Hotel.** Next door to the church where Patrick Brontë preached and not far from the family parsonage, the Old White Lion is one of the more welcoming hostelries in Haworth. Antique touches and modern conveniences mix happily in the simple rooms. There's a full restaurant on the premises, or you can get bar snacks. ✉ *6 West La., BD22 8DU,* ☎ *01535/642313,* 🆁 *01535/646222,* 🆆🅴🅱 *www. oldlionhotel.com. 14 rooms. Restaurant. AE, DC, MC, V.*

£ 🏨 **Apothecary Guest House.** This 17th-century building at the top of Main Street, near the Parsonage, earns full marks for value and cozy comfort. You can look out on Haworth's historic main street or, at the back, wake up to sweeping views of the bleak moors. And although only breakfast is served, you're close to tearooms and pubs, including Branwell's favorite, the Black Bull, just over the road. ✉ *86 Main St., BB22 8DA,* ☎ 🆁 *01535/643642. 7 rooms. MC, V.*

THE YORKSHIRE DALES

With some of the fairest scenery in England, the Yorkshire Dales stand in complete and startling contrast to the industrial towns of West Yorkshire. These meandering river valleys fall south and east from the hills known as the Pennines and, beyond Skipton, present an almost wholly rural aspect. Most, but not all, of the dales take their name from the rivers that run through them and have a variety of scenery that's quintessentially English: a ruined priory here, a narrow country road there, a babbling river, drystone walls made without mortar, and stone moorland hamlets that were the settings for James Herriot's books. Some of the limestone outcroppings and caves can be explored safely even by those not used to exploring such places. Villages here seem to take on the texture of the fells and fit snugly into little pockets, looking as though they, like the Pennines, have been here from eternity. In places, loveliness of setting goes hand in hand with architectural beauty, such as at Bolton Priory, the monastic ruins that once enchanted Wordsworth and Ruskin. Naturally, the Yorkshire Dales contain prime walking country, and all the villages covered in this section have access to a fine network of paths and trails; they can also provide a full range of accommodations and hiking services. Wharfedale, one of the longest of the Yorkshire Dales, is easily accessible from Bradford. A convenient driving route would take in Bolton Priory, the castle at Skipton, and rural Grassington, Malham, and Kettlewell, before moving farther north to see the towns of Askrigg and Hawes in Wensleydale and the glories of Swaledale. You might finish up at the attractive market town of Richmond, where Henry VII had his family seat and after which he named his palace southwest of London in the now better-known Thames-side district.

Bolton Priory

★ ❺ *12 mi north of Haworth, 6 mi east of Skipton, 18 mi north of Bradford, 24 mi northwest of Leeds.*

Some of the loveliest Wharfedale scenery comes into view around Bolton Priory, the ruins of an Augustinian priory, which sits on a grassy embankment inside a great curve of the River Wharfe itself. The priory is just a short walk or drive from the village of Bolton Abbey (near the junction of A59 and B6160). Once there, you can wander through the 13th-century ruins or visit the priory church, which is still the local parish church; both are open daily, with free access in the daytime (although parking in the estate grounds costs £3). Among the famous visitors enchanted by Bolton Priory were William Wordsworth (who described "Bolton's mouldering Priory" in his poem "The White Doe of Rylstone"), J. M. W. Turner, the 19th-century artist, who painted it, and John Ruskin, the Victorian art critic, who rated it most beautiful of all the English ruins he had seen.

Close to Bolton Priory, surrounded by some of the most romantic woodland scenery in England, the River Wharfe plunges between a narrow chasm in the rocks (a dangerous stretch of white water known as "the Strid") before reaching **Barden Tower,** a medieval hunting lodge. This lodge, where Henry, Lord Clifford, carried out his studies in alchemy in the late 15th century, is now a ruin and can be visited just as easily as Bolton Priory, in whose grounds it stands.

Dining and Lodging

££££ ✕⊞ **Devonshire Arms.** Originally an 18th-century coaching inn, and
★ still belonging to the dukes of Devonshire, this country-house hotel is in a superb setting on the River Wharfe, within easy walking distance of Bolton Priory and the village of Bolton Abbey. Portraits of various dukes hang on the walls, and the bedrooms are tastefully decorated by the duchess of Devonshire with antiques and family memorabilia; many have four-poster beds and carved furniture. The (nonsmoking) Burlington restaurant in the hotel has a fine, traditional menu using homegrown herbs and vegetables, and the good service stands out. ⊠ *Bolton Abbey, Skipton, BD23 6AJ,* ☎ *01756/710441,* 𝔽𝔸𝕏 *01756/ 710564,* 𝚆𝙴𝙱 *www.thedevonshirearms.co.uk. 39 rooms, 2 suites. Restaurant, bar, no-smoking room, pool, sauna, tennis court, gym, health club, fishing, baby-sitting. AE, DC, MC, V.*

Skipton

❻ *6 mi west of Bolton Abbey, 12 mi north of Haworth, 22 mi west of Harrogate.*

Skipton in Airedale, capital of the limestone district of Craven, is a typical Dales market town with as many farmers as tourists milling in the streets. There are markets every day except Tuesday and Sunday, and shops selling local produce predominate.

Skipton Castle, built by the Normans in 1090 and unaltered since the Civil War (17th century), is the town's most prominent attraction and also one of the best-preserved of all English medieval castles, remarkably complete in appearance. After the Battle of Marston Moor during the Civil War, it remained the only Royalist stronghold in the north of England. In the central courtyard, a yew tree, planted 300 years ago by Lady Anne Clifford, still flourishes. The castle is at the top of busy High Street. ⊠ *High St.,* ☎ *01756/792442,* 𝚆𝙴𝙱 *www.skiptoncastle. co.uk.* ⊡ *£4.40.* ⊘ *Mar.–Sept., Mon.–Sat. 10–6, Sun. noon–6; Oct.– Feb., Mon.–Sat. 10–4, Sun. noon–4.*

Dining

£–££ ✕ **Angel Inn.** Diners at the Angel regularly clog the hidden-away hamlet of Hetton with their vehicles, such is the attraction of this locally renowned eatery. You can book in advance for the restaurant, but tables in the various cozy rooms of the bar-brasserie are available on a first-come-first-served basis, and they fill on the dot of opening time most days. Fish is a specialty (especially on Friday), and you might encounter tangy fish soup, cod with an herb crust, or baked sea bass. ⊠ *Hetton, 5 mi north of Skipton, off B6265,* ☎ *01756/730263. AE, MC, V. No dinner Sun.*

Grassington

★ ❼ *10 mi north of Skipton, 14 mi northwest of Ilkley, 25 mi west of Ripon.*

A small, stone village built around an ancient cobbled marketplace, Grassington is well situated for exploring Upper Wharfedale. The Dales Way footpath passes through the village, and there's a surprisingly good range of guest houses, stores, pubs, and cafés, although this is less of a surprise if you visit during summer, when facilities become positively overwhelmed by day-trippers and walkers. Local walks are easily accomplished, however, and if you're prepared to make a day of it, you'll soon find you leave the crowds behind. The **National Park Centre** has a wide choice of guidebooks, maps, and bus schedules to help you enjoy a day in the Yorkshire Dales National Park. ⊠ *Colvend, Hebdon Rd.,* ☎ *01756/752774,* WEB *www.yorkshiredales.org.uk.* ☉ *Apr.–Oct., daily 10–4; Nov.–Mar., weekends 10–4.*

Dining and Lodging

£–££ ✗ **Old Hall Inn.** This stone-flagged, rustic country pub with a small garden on the outskirts of Grassington serves an out-of-the-ordinary menu that attracts people from miles around. Main courses might include salmon with tomato and cilantro sauce, monkfish cooked with white wine and saffron, or local sausages with onion confit. ⊠ *Threshfield, 1 mi west of Grassington,* ☎ *01756/752441. No credit cards. Closed Mon. No dinner Sun.*

£–££ ✗ 🏨 **Black Horse Hotel.** Set back a little from the main square, the good-value rooms at the Black Horse are just the thing if you've walked in from afar, with comfortable beds, TVs, and tea- and coffeemaking facilities; some rooms have four-posters for a touch of luxury. An extensive bar menu is served, although there's more formal dining in the restaurant where an à la carte menu of local and traditional dishes defeats even the heartiest appetites. In winter, open fires keep things cozy; in summer, sit out on the terrace with a drink. ⊠ *Garrs La., BD23 5AT,* ☎ *01756/752770. 15 rooms. Restaurant, bar. MC, V.*

££ 🏨 **Ashfield House.** Three converted 17th-century stone cottages, once home to Grassington lead miners, provide the basis of this amenable, well-run small hotel off the main street. There's a cheery welcome on arrival, modern but pleasing bedrooms with pine furniture that stay warm through fall and spring, and a cozy little brick-and-beam sitting room. Summer afternoons in the walled garden are very pleasant. ⊠ *Summers Fold, BD23 5AE,* ☎ FAX *01756/752584,* WEB *www.ashfieldhouse.co.uk. 7 rooms. Lounge. MC, V. Closed Dec.–Jan.*

Malham

★ ❽ *10 mi west of Grassington, 12 mi northwest of Skipton.*

The keenest hikers descend in their summer droves on Malham to tour some of Britain's most remarkable limestone formations. The tiny hamlet has a population of about 200 yet is visited by a half million people a year. The lesson is to come before June or after August, if at all possible, to avoid the worst of the crowds. It's a magical place at most times of the year, the intensely rural surroundings described glowingly in poems by Wordsworth and Auden, painted by Turner, and photographed by Hockney, proof indeed of Malham's aesthetic potency. To get here from Grassington, take B6265 south 2 mi through Cracoe, then branch west onto the minor road past Hetton and Calton; Malham is also northwest of Skipton, off A65.

Malham's three main destinations—Malham Cove, Gordale Scar, and Malham Tarn—are close enough to see on a circular walk of 8 mi that takes most people four to five hours. Those with less time should cut out the tarn: a circular walk from the village to Malham Cove and Gordale Scar can be completed in just over two hours. **Malham Cove,** a huge, 300-ft-high natural rock amphitheater, is just a mile north of the village and provides the easiest local walk, although following the path *up* to the top is a brutal climb, rewarded by magnificent views. At **Gordale Scar,** a deep natural chasm between overhanging limestone cliffs, the white waters of a moorland stream plunge 300 ft; it's a mile northeast of Malham and can be reached by a lovely riverside path. A longer walk of more than 3 mi leads north from Malham to **Malham Tarn,** an attractive lake set in windswept isolation. There's a nature reserve on the west bank and an easy-to-follow trail on the east bank.

Maps and displays at Malham's **National Park Centre** will give you some more informed ideas of what there is to do and see locally and in Yorkshire Dales National Park. You can get a list of local B&B and pub accommodations here, too; they are relatively plentiful, but highly sought after in summer. ☎ *01729/830363.* ☼ *Mid-Apr.–Oct., daily 9:30–5; Nov.–mid-Apr., weekends 10–4.*

En Route   North of Malham, there's a dramatic moorland drive following the minor road that skirts Malham Tarn, to **Arncliffe** in Littondale, where a superb village inn, the Falcon (☎ 01756/770205) revives flagging spirits and provides accommodations. In winter this road may be impassable: always check local weather forecasts before setting out. At Arncliffe, follow the signs southeast for B6160 and then turn north for Kettlewell.

Kettlewell

⑨   *6 mi north of Grassington, 8 mi northeast of Malham.*

A babbling river runs through the heart of Kettlewell, the main settlement in Upper Wharfedale and a fine base for a couple of days' exploration of the local hills and valleys, with their stone-flagged pubs, riverside walks, and narrow pack bridges constructed from rubble. The Dales Way hiking path passes through the quiet, gray-stone village, and drivers will easily be able to visit Malham and Grassington, returning for a peaceful night away from the crowds.

OFF THE   **HUBBERHOLME –** Drive 4 mi northwest of Kettlewell up B6160 (or walk
BEATEN PATH   along the signposted Dales Way), turning off at Buckden along a very minor road to reach the riverside hamlet of Hubberholme, whose beautiful stone chapel and ancient George Inn were firm favorites of noted Yorkshire-born author J. B. Priestley. There's a plaque inside the chapel recording his burial in the churchyard.

Dining and Lodging

£££   ✕🏠 **Langcliffe Country House.** Tucked up a back road, this charming, flower-filled property is a real home away from home, with fantastic views across Wharfedale. Rooms are neat and tidy, and a log fire crackles away in the lounge in winter. Homemade dinners are served in the conservatory, and the choice might be a hearty stew, a vegetarian specialty, or fish from the local streams. To find the house, look for the King's Head pub; opposite is a road marked FOR ACCESS ONLY: Langcliffe is 500 yards along here. ✉ *Kettlewell, Skipton, BD23 5RJ,* ☎ *01756/760243. 6 rooms. Restaurant, bar. MC, V.*

En Route   From Kettlewell, it's just 4 mi north along B6160 to **Buckden,** the last village in Wharfedale. From here you can go directly through Kidstone Pass (still heading north on B6160) to **Aysgarth** in Wensleydale, where the River Ure plummets over a series of waterfalls. Askrigg is 5 mi farther west.

Askrigg

🔟 *16 mi north of Kettlewell, 25 mi northeast of Malham.*

Askrigg would be just another typical Wensleydale village, were it not for its association with the James Herriot TV series *All Creatures Great and Small*, which was filmed in and around the village. The tourist board pushes "Herriot Country" hard, but although Askrigg—dubbed "Darrowby" in the program—is a pleasing village, there's not a great deal else to keep you here, apart from walks to a couple of local waterfalls. The **King's Arms Hotel** (⊠ Market Pl., ☎ 01969/650258) is a wood-paneled, 18th-century coaching inn in the center of the village. Rechristened the Drover's Arms, this figured in many an episode of the program and is a truly atmospheric building, with nook-and-cranny rooms, good local beer, two restaurants, and guest rooms.

Hawes

⑪ *5 mi west of Askrigg.*

The best time to visit Hawes, reputedly the highest market town in England, is on Tuesday when farmers and locals crowd into town for the weekly market. There's a brisk, businesslike atmosphere at other times, too, since Hawes retains some of Wensleydale's more traditional industries, not least its cheese making: crumbly, white Wensleydale cheese has been made in the valley for centuries. You can buy the cheese at stores in town, and give yourself time to wander the cobbled side streets, too, some of which are filled with antiques shops and tearooms.

At the **Wensleydale Creamery Visitor Centre,** on the outskirts of Hawes, a cheese museum tells the story of how Wensleydale cheese came to be produced. There's a viewing gallery to enable you to watch production (best seen between 10:30 and 3), and then you can repair to the shop, where tasting of the various cheeses is encouraged before you buy. Beside the regular Wensleydale cheese, you can try it smoked, or with ginger, or with apple pie, or even with dried fruit. There's a restaurant on the site. ⊠ *Gayle La.,* ☎ *01969/667664,* ᵂᴱᴮ *www.wensleydale.co.uk/centre.htm.* 🖾 *Museum £2.* 🕙 *Mon.–Sat. 9:30–5.*

Hawes's Yorkshire Dales National Park Information Centre in the old train station contains the **Dales Countryside Museum,** which gives a picture of Dales life in past centuries. A traditional rope-making shop here also welcomes visitors. ⊠ *Station Yard,* ☎ *01969/667450,* ᵂᴱᴮ *www.yorkshiredales.org.uk.* 🖾 *Museum £2.50.* 🕙 *Mid-Apr.–Oct., daily 10–5; Nov.–mid-Apr., Wed., Fri., and weekends 11–4.*

En Route From Hawes, the most direct route to Swaledale is north by minor road over the **Buttertubs Pass,** a 7-mi run to Muker, a lovely village that hosts the annual Swaledale show in September. Many people regard **Swaledale** itself as the finest of all the Yorkshire Dales. From Muker, B6270 and A6108 run down the valley to Richmond.

Richmond

⑫ *22 mi northeast of Hawes, 25 mi northwest of Ripon.*

Richmond tucks itself into a curve above the foaming River Swale, with a network of narrow Georgian streets and terraces opening onto the largest cobbled marketplace in the country. It would be a mistake, however, despite appearances, to date the town's provenance to the 18th century. The Normans first swept in during the late 11th century, determined to subdue the local population and establish Norman rule in the north. This they did by building a mighty castle, around which the town grew, and throughout the Middle Ages Richmond was effectively a garrison town.

The immense keep of Norman **Richmond Castle** towers above the river and grants excellent views over the surroundings. Built around 1071 by Alan Rufus, first earl of Richmond, it was used as a prison for William the Lion of Scotland a hundred years later. When Henry Tudor (son of Edmund Tudor, earl of Richmond) became Henry VII in 1485, he began calling his palace in Shene, southwest London, Richmond (Palace), after his family seat in Richmond. The name gradually came to be used to describe that area of London. Richmond Castle is still one of the best-preserved monuments of this era, retaining its curtain wall and chapel, and a great hall that has been partially restored to its medieval splendor; even the 14th-century graffiti has been preserved. There's a heritage garden, and a path along the river leads to the ruins of golden-stone Easby Abbey. ⊠ *Castle,* ☎ *01748/822493,* WEB *www. english-heritage.co.uk.* ⊠ *£2.70.* ☉ *Apr.–Sept., daily 10–6; Oct., daily 10–5; Nov.–Mar., daily 10–1 and 2–4.*

The tiny Georgian **Theatre Royal,** built in 1788, is unchanged since the days of the 18th-century Shakespearean actor David Garrick. You can watch performances from either gallery boxes or old wooden seats. Try to reserve tickets well in advance. Also, outside performance times, tours take in the backstage areas and finish in the small museum that holds unique painted scenery dating from 1836. ⊠ *Friars Wynd,* ☎ *01748/ 823710; 01748/823021 box office.* ⊠ *Tour and museum £1.50.* ☉ *Apr.– Oct., Mon.–Sat. 10:30–4:30, Sun. 11–2. Box office year-round, Mon.– Sat. 2:30–5:30.*

Dining and Lodging

£ ✕ **The Bistro.** Look for the interior arcade off Finkle Street to find this appealing little café with its own conservatory seating. During the day, there's coffee, croissants, and sandwiches, and lunch and dinner (Wednesday–Saturday only) see the addition of tasty Mediterranean-style dishes. ⊠ *Chantry Wynd, Finkle St.,* ☎ *01748/850792. No credit cards. No dinner Sun.–Tues.*

£ ⊞ **Old Brewery Guest House.** Richmond has a score of guest houses, but few are as striking as this two-story stone building, on the edge of a secluded green in a quiet corner of town below the castle. Interior renovations have highlighted the Victorian character of the compact rooms and there's a lovely little patio garden, as well as a guest lounge. ⊠ *29 The Green, DL10 4RG,* ☎ *01748/822460,* FAX *01748/825561. 5 rooms. No credit cards.*

YORK

It would be unthinkable to visit North Yorkshire without going first to the atmospheric cathedral city of York, and not just because its central location makes it a practical place to start. Named "Eboracum" in Latin, York was the military capital of Roman Britain, and traces of Roman garrison buildings still survive throughout the city. The Vikings also claimed York as their capital and left bountiful evidence of their tenure, and in Norman times the foundations of York Minster, the largest medieval cathedral in England, were laid. During the great industrial age, which caused so much havoc in many northern towns and cities, York was a forgotten backwater—hence the survival of so much medieval and 18th-century architecture. That's not to say that the city exists in a time vacuum: the array of stores that have taken over the heart of the old city can sometimes make the place seem more like an extension of London's Oxford Street than one of the great historical survivals of Europe. The Shambles, a medieval street built between 1350 and 1450, has been particularly altered by overly quaint shops and modern boutiques.

York is 48 mi southeast of Richmond, 25 mi northeast of Leeds, and 82 mi south of Newcastle. By far the most attractive city in the region, it has now become one of the most popular short-stay destinations in Britain (York is only two hours by fast train from London on a good day), and the authorities have cleared up the devastation caused by the severe flooding in fall 2000.

Exploring York

Following the fall of the Roman Empire in the 5th century, a Saxon town grew up over the ruins of the Roman fort at York. On Christmas Eve, AD 627, the Northumbrian King Edwin introduced Christianity to the area by being baptized in a little wooden church here. The city grew in importance during the 9th century, after the Viking conquerors of northern and eastern England made York, which they called "Jorvik," their English capital. You'll notice that many of the city's street names are suffixed with the word "-gate" (Goodramgate, Micklegate, for example). "Gate" was the Viking word for "street."

The old city center of York is a compact, dense web of narrow streets and tiny alleys, "snickleways," in which congestion is so bad that traffic has been banned around the minster. It is, conversely, a fine city for walking, provided you have a map, although try to avoid visiting in July and August when crowds choke the narrow streets and cause long lines at the popular museums. April, May, and October are far better; April is also the time to see the embankments beneath the city walls filled with the pale gold ripple of daffodils. A memorable overview of the city can be had by taking a stroll along these walls.

A Good Walk

York's city center may be compact, but there's so much to see that you'll need an early start and plenty of stamina. At least there's no mistaking your starting point: the towers of **York Minster** ⑬ are visible from virtually every point on the encircling **city walls** ⑭, so once you've got your bearings, make for Duncombe Place and the main entrance to the minster, England's largest Gothic church. After you've ogled the interior (rather cold and barnlike to some), it's time to take off around the narrow streets and alleys of the city. In the area just behind the apse of the minster is one of York's quaintest residential areas. Here along Aldwark, search out medieval Bedern Hall, St. Anthony's Hall, and two picture-perfect half-timbered structures, the Merchant Taylors' Hall and the Black Swan Inn. Heading down either Low Petergate or Goodramgate puts you on the famed **Shambles** ⑮, now a crowded shopping street, at the southern end of which you can head to Fossgate to visit the **Merchant Adventurers' Hall** ⑯, site of one of the best medieval timber-framed halls in Europe. Retrace your steps on Fossgate and turn left on Coppergate, and you're in one of York's oldest areas, where Viking finds were first discovered; the entertaining **Jorvik** ⑰ here has all the details. From Coppergate, Castlegate runs south, passing the former church of St. Mary's and that connoisseur's delight, the superbly elegant Georgian-era **Fairfax House** ⑱ before ending at the historic mound of **Clifford's Tower** ⑲. The **Castle Museum** ⑳, an amazing collection of ephemera, costumes, and vintage machinery, marks the southernmost extent of your explorations.

From the Castle Museum, it's a 20-minute stroll back through the city center, up to the **Guildhall** ㉑ on St. Helen's Square—fainthearts can refuel in Betty's famous tearoom—and nearby **Stonegate** ㉒, another shopping street of considerable historic charm. Doing the walk this way, you've saved two splendid museum collections, both on the outskirts of the historic kernel, until last. From St. Helen's Square it's an easy walk up Lendal and across the main road to the archaeological exhibits of the **Yorkshire Museum** ㉓; enjoy a stroll through the museum's atmospheric gardens, then make your way to Lendal Bridge and cross the River Ouse onto Station Road. Taking a right on Leeman Road brings you to the fascinating **National Railway Museum** ㉔.

TIMING

The walk around York takes about an hour, but you'll need a long day (and perhaps a second, depending on your interests) if you want to spend time at the sights and museums. Try to avoid weekends, when the crowds can be intense.

Sights to See

㉚ **Castle Museum.** A former 18th-century debtors' prison, this museum offers detailed exhibitions and re-creations, including a Victorian street complete with crafts shop, a working water mill, domestic and military displays, and, most important, the Coppergate Helmet, a 1,200-year-old Anglo-Saxon helmet discovered during excavations of the city. You can also visit the cell where Dick Turpin, the 18th-century highwayman and folk hero, spent the night before his execution. ⊠ *Clifford St.,* ☎ *01904/653611.* ☞ *£4.95.* ⊙ *Apr.–Oct., Mon.–Sat. 9:30–5, Sun. 10–5:30; Nov.–Mar., Mon.–Sat. 9:30–4, Sun. 10–4.*

⑭ **City walls.** York's almost 3 mi of ancient stone walls are among the longest and best preserved in England. A walk on the narrow paved path along the top leads you through 1,900 years of history, from the time the earthen ramparts were raised by the Romans and York's Viking kings to repel raiders, to their fortification by the Normans, to their current landscaping by the city council. The path crosses over York's distinctive fortified gates or "bars": the portcullis on Monk's Bar on Goodramgate is still in working order, and Walmgate Bar in the east is the only gate in England to have preserved its barbican. Bottham Bar in Exhibition Square was the defensive bastion for the north road, while Micklegate Bar, in the southwest corner of the city, was traditionally the monarch's entrance. To access the path and the lookout towers, locate a staircase at one of the breaks in the walls. WEB *www.york.gov.uk/walls.* ☞ *Free.* ⊙ *Daily, dawn to dusk.*

⑲ **Clifford's Tower.** Dating from the early 14th century, this forbidding tower stands on the mound originally erected for the keep of York Castle. In 1190 this was the scene of one of the worst instances of anti-Semitism in medieval Europe, when 150 Jews who had sought sanctuary in the castle were massacred. ⊠ *Tower St.,* ☎ *01904/646940.* ☞ *£1.80.* ⊙ *Apr.–Oct., daily 10–6; Nov.–Mar., daily 10–4.*

★ ⑱ **Fairfax House.** In a city known for brutish Norman keeps and cold Gothic towers, it's a delight to find Fairfax House, one of the most elegant Georgian town houses in England and a masterpiece of rococo decoration. Now a museum of decorative arts, this often overlooked treasure was designed by Robin Carr of York and built in 1762. It's furnished with a distinguished collection of Georgian furniture. The marble dining room and the grand salon, all crystal chandeliers and flaming crimson silk walls, are knockouts and rival anything found at Castle Howard, the stately home northeast of York. ⊠ *Castlegate,* ☎ *01904/655543,* WEB *www.fairfaxhouse.co.uk.* ☞ *£3.75.* ⊙ *Mid-Feb.–July and Oct.–Dec., Mon.–Thurs. and Sat. 11–5, Sun. 1:30–5; Aug.–Sept., Mon.–Sat. 11–5, Sun. 1:30–5.*

York

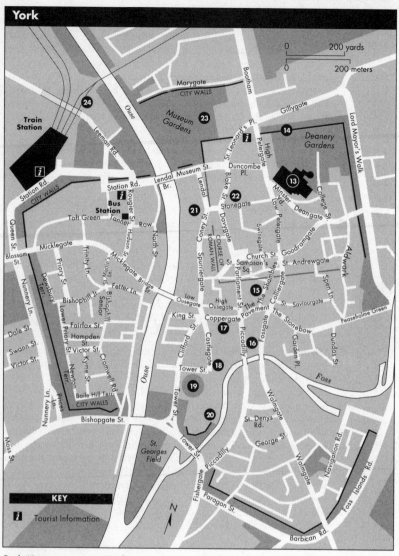

Train Station

i

Bus Station

Museum Gardens

Deanery Gardens

KEY

i Tourist Information

Castle Museum . . .20
City Walls 14
Clifford's Tower . . .19
Fairfax House 18
Guildhall 21
Jorvik 17

Merchant
Adventurers'
Hall 16
National Railway
Museum 24
The Shambles . . .15
Stonegate 22

York Minster 13
Yorkshire
Museum 23

㉑ Guildhall. Right on the river, York's mid-15th-century guildhall was a meeting place for the city's powerful guilds. It was also used for pageants and mystery plays (medieval dramas based on biblical stories and the lives of saints). Although damaged by World War II bombing, it has been restored to something approaching its erstwhile glory, although 14 Victorian stained-glass windows were lost forever—now only one, at the west end, remains as a magnificent, bright reminder. The guildhall is behind the 18th-century Mansion House. ⊠ *St. Helen's Sq.,* ☎ *01904/613161.* ☞ *Free.* ☉ *May–Oct., Mon.–Thurs. 9–5, Fri. 9–4, Sat. 10–5, Sun. 2–5; Nov.–Apr., Mon.–Thurs. 9–5, Fri. 9–4.*

☝ **⑰ Jorvik.** In mid-2001, the popular Jorvik Viking Centre renamed itself and opened redesigned exhibits incorporating the findings of archaeological research since 1984, when the attraction first opened. On an authentic Viking site, Jorvik re-creates a Viking city of the 10th century with astonishing attention to detail. Its time capsules whisk you through the streets to experience the sights, sounds, and smells of Viking England, and excellent displays, using the latest high-tech wizardry, reveal the breadth of the Viking culture and social system. ⊠ *Coppergate,* ☎ *01904/643211; advance booking 01904/543403,* ⓦⒺⒷ *www.jorvik-viking-centre.co.uk.* ☞ *£6.95.* ☉ *Apr.–Oct., daily 9–7:30; Nov.–Mar., daily 9–6:30; last admission 2 hrs before closing.*

⑯ Merchant Adventurers' Hall. Built between 1357 and 1368 and owned by one of the city's richest medieval guilds (its members dealt in wool and lead, which were traded far and wide), this is the largest half-timber hall in York, with a pretty garden in the back. On most Saturdays throughout the year, antiques fairs are held inside the building. ⊠ *Fossgate,* ☎ *01904/654818.* ☞ *£1.90.* ☉ *Mid-Mar.–mid-Nov., daily 8:30–5; mid-Nov.–mid-Mar., Mon.–Sat. 8:30–3:30.*

★ ☝ **㉔ National Railway Museum.** At this train spotters' delight, which began as a northern outpost of the Science Museum in London, you'll find Britain's national collection of locomotives forming part of the world's largest train museum. Among the exhibits are gleaming giants of the steam era, including *Mallard,* holder of the world speed record for a steam engine (126 mph). You can clamber aboard some of the trains, and an interactive exhibit explores working life on board a mail train. Passenger cars used by Queen Victoria are also on display, and hands-on changing exhibits explore the future of the railways. ⊠ *Leeman Rd.,* ☎ *01904/621261,* ⓦⒺⒷ *www.nrm.org.uk.* ☞ *£6.90.* ☉ *Daily 10–6.*

⑮ The Shambles. Ah, that this street remained as picturesque as its name. York's best-preserved medieval street has several half-timber stores and houses with overhangs so massive you could almost reach across the street from one second-floor window to another. It's a little too cute for its own good these days, featuring a line of crafts and souvenir shops—a far cry, certainly, from the days when the Shambles was the city's meat market. Still, aim your camera at rooftop level and see if you can catch York Minster soaring over it all.

㉒ Stonegate. Thanks to being pedestrianized, this narrow street of Tudor and 18th-century storefronts and courtyards retains considerable charm. It has been in daily use for almost 2,000 years, since first being paved in Roman times. A passage just off Stonegate, at 52A, leads to a 12th-century Norman stone house, one of the very few to have survived in England.

★ **⑬ York Minster.** Focal point of the entire city, this vast cathedral is the largest Gothic church in England and attracts almost as many visitors as London's Westminster Abbey. Inside, the effect created by its soaring pillars, lofty vaulted ceilings, and dazzling stained-glass windows—

glowing with deep wine reds and cobalt blues, they are only bested by Chartres Cathedral in France—is almost too overpowering. The church is 534 ft long, 249 ft across its transepts, and 90 ft from floor to roof (so high is the structure, it's best to come with binoculars if you wish to study the stained-glass work); the central towers are 184 ft high. Mere statistics, however, cannot convey the scale of the building. Its soaring columns; the ornamentation of its 14th-century nave; the east window, one of the greatest pieces of medieval glazing in the world; the north transept's **Five Sisters** windows, five tall lancets of frosted 13th-century glass; the enormous choir screen portraying somewhat whimsical images of every king of England from William the Conqueror to Henry VI; the imposing tracery of the **Rose Window** (just one of the minster's 128 stained-glass windows) commemorating the marriage of Henry VII and Elizabeth of York in 1486 (the event that ended the Wars of the Roses and began the Tudor dynasty)—all contribute to its cold, crushing splendor. Don't miss the exquisite 13th-century **Chapter House** and the **Undercroft Museum and Treasury.** After exploring the interior, you might take the 275 winding steps to the roof of the great **Central Tower** (strictly for those with a head for heights), not only for the close-up view of the cathedral's detailed carving but also for a panorama of York and the surrounding Yorkshire Moors. ⊠ *Duncombe Pl.,* ☎ *01904/624426,* W̄E̅B̄ *www.yorkminster.org.* ✆ *Minster free, but £2 donation suggested; foundations (including Treasury) £1.80; Chapter House 70p; Crypt 60p; Central Tower £2.* ☉ *Minster late June–early Sept., daily 7* AM*–8:30* PM*; early Sept.–late-June, daily 7–6. Undercroft, Chapter House, Crypt, and Central Tower late June–early Sept., Mon.–Sat. 10–5:30, Sun. 1–5:30; early Sept.–late-June, Mon.–Sat. 10–4:30, Sun. 1–4:30.*

㉓   Yorkshire Museum. This museum, in a solid, Doric-style building, covers the natural and archaeological history of the county, including material on the Roman, Anglo-Saxon, and Viking aspects of York. Here you can also see the 15th-century Middleham Jewel, a pendant resplendent with a large sapphire. Outdoors in the atmospheric gardens, amid the ruins of St. Mary's Abbey, the city's cycle of medieval mystery plays is performed every four years. The museum lies just outside the walled city, through Bootham Bar, one of York's old gates. ⊠ *Museum Gardens, Museum St.,* ☎ *01904/629745.* ✆ *£3.75.* ☉ *Daily 10–5.*

Dining

££££   ✕ **Melton's.** Once a private house, this unpretentious but excellent restaurant has local art on the walls and an open kitchen. The seasonal fixed-price menus prove to be highly imaginative, a legacy of chef Michael Hjort's former stint at the Roux brothers' establishments in London, and offer modern English, Continental, and fish dishes. Melton's is 10 minutes from the minster. ⊠ *7 Scarcroft Rd.,* ☎ *01904/634341. Reservations essential. MC, V. Closed 3 wks at Christmas and 1 wk in Aug. No dinner Sun., no lunch Mon.*

££–£££   ✕ **19 Grape Lane.** This narrow, slightly cramped restaurant is housed
★   in a typically leaning timbered York building in the heart of town. Hugely popular, it serves modern English food, such as grilled wild boar sausages, from a blackboard of specials. ⊠ *19 Grape La.,* ☎ *01904/ 636366. MC, V. Closed Sun., 1 wk at Christmas, 2 wks in Feb., and 2 wks in Sept.*

£   ✕ **Betty's.** At the opposite end of Stonegate from the minster, Betty's, a York institution since 1912, is arranged elegantly across two large floors in a beautiful Art Nouveau building. Best known for its teas served with mouthwatering cakes (try the "fat rascal," a plump bun bursting with cherries and nuts), Betty's also offers light meals and a splendid selection of exotic coffees. Get a table on the upper floor if you can, next to the floor-to-ceiling windows. ⊠ *6–8 St. Helen's Sq.,* ☎ *01904/ 659142. MC, V.*

£ ✕ **Spurriergate Centre.** Churches are not just for prayers, as this deconsecrated 15th-century church proves. Resurrected as a cafeteria by a community organization, the church of St. Michael's is now a favorite spot for tired tourists and mothers with strollers to refuel spiritually as well as gastronomically. You may end up eating a prawn sandwich on the exact spot where John Wesley prayed in 1768. The decor is magnificently medieval, with religious Gothic shrines all around. Don't pass up the cream scones. ⊠ *Spurriergate,* ☎ *01904/629393. Closed Sun. No dinner.*

Lodging

££££ 🏨 **Middlethorpe Hall.** This splendidly restored 18th-century mansion,
★ about 1½ mi from York's city center, not far from the racetrack, was the sometime home of the traveler and diarist Lady Mary Wortley Montagu (1689–1762). The individually decorated rooms, some in cottage-style accommodations around an 18th-century courtyard, are filled with antiques, paintings, and fresh flowers, and the extensive grounds have a lake and a 17th-century dovecote. At the Anglo-French restaurant, you can eat by candlelight in the wood-paneled dining room. Menus change seasonally but always have more than a hint of luxury in the ingredients used. The fish is a strong point. Breakfast is not included in the room rate. ⊠ *Bishopthorpe Rd., YO23 2GB,* ☎ *01904/641241,* FAX *01904/620176,* WEB *www.middlethorpe.com. 30 rooms. Restaurant, indoor pool, sauna, spa, croquet, health club. AE, MC, V.*

£££–££££ 🏨 **Dean Court Hotel.** This large Victorian house once provided accommodations for the clergy of York Minster, just across the way. It's now a member of the Best Western chain and has comfortably furnished rooms with plenty of print fabrics, plump sofas, and fine views overlooking the minster. Parking is a few minutes from the hotel, but there is valet parking. The restaurant serves good English cuisine, including a hearty Yorkshire breakfast. ⊠ *Duncombe Pl., YO1 2EF,* ☎ *01904/ 625082,* FAX *01904/620305,* WEB *www.deancourt-york.co.uk. 40 rooms. Restaurant, bar, coffee shop. AE, DC, MC, V.*

£££ 🏨 **Judge's Lodgings.** Easily the prettiest hotel in York, this picturesque Georgian mansion used to be a judge's lodging, providing accommodations to justices when they traveled up north from London's Inns of Court. Past the elegant gates and front yard, you mount an imposing staircase. Beyond the lovely, somewhat shabby-genteel lobby is the main salon—a delightful and cozy cocoon of Queen Mum pastels, overstuffed chairs, and gilded mirrors. Upstairs, the decor continues in the same note. One room is called the Queen Mother, another grand suite, named the Prince Albert (he actually stayed here), is a special treat. ⊠ *9 Lendal, YO1 2AQ,* ☎ *01904/638733,* FAX *01904/679947. 12 rooms, 1 suite. Restaurant, bar. AE, DC, MC, V.*

££ 🏨 **Grasmead House.** The comfortable bedrooms in this small, family-run hotel all have antique four-poster beds. Located just beyond the city walls, the lodging is an easy walk from the city center, and the owners are happy to share their local knowledge with guests. There are no meals served other than breakfast, but very good restaurants are only a short walk away. ⊠ *1 Scarcroft Hill, YO2 1DF,* ☎ FAX *01904/629996. 6 rooms. Bar, no-smoking room. AE, DC, MC, V.*

£–££ 🏨 **Savages.** Despite its name, this small hotel on a leafy road near the town center is eminently refined, with a reputation for attentive service. Once a Victorian home, it has a stylish and comfortable interior, and there's a bar in which to relax. ⊠ *15 St. Peter's Grove, Clifton*

YO3 6AQ, ☎ 01904/610818, FAX 01904/627729. *21 rooms. Restaurant, bar. AE, DC, MC, V.*

£ ⊡ **Abbey Guest House.** This charming, nonsmoking, terraced guest house, formerly an artisan's house, is a 10-minute walk from the train station and town center. Although small, it's very clean and friendly, with a peaceful garden right on the river and ducks waddling about outside. Picnic lunches and evening meals can be arranged on request. ⊠ *14 Earlsborough Terr., Marygate YO3 7BQ, ☎ 01904/627782. 7 rooms, 2 with bath. Breakfast room. AE, MC, V.*

Nightlife and the Arts

Festivals

York's annual English **Bonfire Night** celebrations on November 5 have an added piquancy because the notorious 16th-century conspirator Guy Fawkes was a native of the city. Fawkes's failure to blow up the Houses of Parliament is commemorated, and his effigy is burned atop every fire. Ask at the tourist office for the locations of the best fires and fireworks displays.

An **Early Music Festival** is held each summer. For details, call the Festival Office (☎ 01904/658338) or the Tourist Information Centre (☎ 01904/621756). York hosts the annual **Viking Festival** (⊠ Jorvik, Coppergate, ☎ 01904/643211) in February. The celebrations, including a parade and long-ship regatta, end with the Jorvik Viking Combat reenactment, when Norsemen confront their Anglo-Saxon enemies.

The next quadrennial performance of the medieval **York Mystery Plays** (☎ 01904/621756 for information) will take place in summer 2004.

Pubs

York is full of historic pubs, where you can while away an hour over a pint. The **Black Swan** (⊠ Peasholme Green, ☎ 01904/632922) is the city's oldest pub, a 16th-century local of great character. In the cellar bar of the **Judge's Lodgings** (⊠ 9 Lendal, ☎ 01904/638733), the old vaults provide a convivial drinking hole.

Theater

York's **Theatre Royal** (⊠ St. Leonard's Pl., ☎ 01904/623568) is a lively professional theater in a lovely old building. It hosts many other events besides plays: string quartets, choral music, poetry reading, and art exhibitions.

Shopping

The new and secondhand bookstores around Petergate, Stonegate, and the Shambles are excellent. For secondhand books, old maps, and prints, head for the **Minster Gate Bookshop** (⊠ 8 Minster Gate, ☎ 01904/621812). For something high in quality and typically English, **Mulberry Hall** (⊠ Stonegate, ☎ 01904/620736) is a sales center for all the famous names in fine bone china and crystal. It also has a neat café. The **York Antiques Centre** (⊠ 2 Lendal, ☎ No phone) has 34 shops selling antiques, bric-a-brac, books, and jewelry.

YORK ENVIRONS

West and north of York, a number of sights make easy and appealing day trips from the city: the spa town of Harrogate, the castle in Knaresborough, the lovely ruins of Fountain Abbey, the market town of Ripon and nearby Newby Hall, and Thirsk, with its link to James Herriot. If you're heading northwest from York to Harrogate, you may want to take the less direct B1224 across Marston Moor where, in 1644,

Oliver Cromwell won a decisive victory over the Royalists during the Civil War. A few miles beyond, at Wetherby, you can then cut northwest along the A661 to Harrogate.

Harrogate

25 *21 mi west of York, 11 mi south of Ripon, 16 mi north of Leeds.*

During the Regency and early Victorian periods, it became fashionable for the noble and wealthy to retire to a spa to "take the waters" for relaxation. Nowhere else in Yorkshire did this trend reach such grand heights as Harrogate, an elegant town that flourished during the 19th century. When the spas no longer drew crowds, Harrogate shed its old image to become a modern business center and built a huge complex that today attracts international conventions. It has been tactfully located so as not to spoil the town's landscape of poised Regency row houses, pleasant walkways, and sweeping green spaces. Of Harrogate's parks, most appealing is the one in the town center, known as **The Stray,** a 200-acre reach of grassland, which is a riot of color in the spring. The **Valley Gardens** provide varied attractions, including a boating lake, tennis courts, and a little café.

You can still drink the evil-smelling (and nasty-tasting) spa waters at the **Royal Pump Room Museum,** which charts the story of Harrogate from its 17th-century beginnings. The building, built over the original sulfur well that brought such prosperity to the town, dates from 1842. ⊠ *Crown Pl.,* ☎ *01423/556188.* ☞ *£2.* ☼ *Apr.–Oct., Mon.–Sat. 10–5, Sun. 2–5; Nov.–Mar., Mon.–Sat. 10–4, Sun. 2–4.*

In the **Royal Baths Assembly Rooms** (1897), you may take a Turkish bath or a sauna in the exotic, tiled rooms; allow two hours or so for the full treatment. ⊠ *Crescent Rd.,* ☎ *01423/556746.* ☞ *£9 per bath and sauna session, massages additional.* ☼ *Daily; call for men's and women's schedules.*

Dining and Lodging

£ ✕ **Betty's.** The celebrated Yorkshire tearoom began life in Harrogate in the 1920s, when Swiss restaurateur Frederic Belmont brought his Alpine specialties to England. The elegant surroundings have changed little since then, and the same scrumptious cakes and pastries, and hot meals, are on offer every day until 9 PM. A pianist plays nightly. ⊠ *1 Parliament St.,* ☎ *01423/502746. MC, V.*

£££ 🏨 **White House.** This hotel overlooking the Stray resembles an Italianate villa, one that is slightly frayed at the edges. Inside, comfort is king: guest rooms are bright and reasonably large, flowers, mirrors, paintings, artistic bits and pieces, and even the odd antique abound. In the lounge, sugared almonds await guests; the library has games and cards. The restaurant caters to most tastes with its eclectic mix of Continental and British cuisine. ⊠ *10 Park Parade, HG1 5AH,* ☎ *01423/501388,* FAX *01423/527973,* WEB *www.whitehouse-hotel.demon.co.uk. 10 rooms. Restaurant, bar, no-smoking room. AE, MC, V.*

£–££ 🏨 **Cavendish Hotel.** Request a front room at the Cavendish and you wake up with a view of the lovely Valley Gardens. Although the rooms can be cramped, the hotel makes a pleasant and cozy base from which to strike out into Harrogate. Tea shops, cafés, and restaurants are all just a short walk away. ⊠ *3 Valley Dr., HG2 0JJ,* ☎ *01423/509637. 9 rooms. Lounge. MC, V.*

Nightlife and the Arts

Harrogate's **International Festival** (☎ 01423/562303) of ballet, music, contemporary dance, film, comedy, street theater, and more takes place during two weeks at the end of July and beginning of August each year.

Knaresborough

㉖ *3 mi northeast of Harrogate, 17 mi west of York.*

The photogenic old town of Knaresborough is built in a steep, rocky gorge along the River Nidd. Central attractions include its river, lively with pleasure boats, a little marketplace, and a medieval castle, now not much more than the keep where Richard II was once imprisoned (1399). In a historic park site, amid tree-lined riverside walks, **Mother Shipton's Cave** is said to be the birthplace of the 16th-century prophetess. Events supposedly foretold by her include the Great Fire of London and the earlier defeat of the Spanish Armada. It's just a short walk south of Knaresborough town center. ⊠ *Prophesy House, High Bridge,* ☎ *01423/864600,* WEB *www.mothershipton.co.uk.* ⊠ *£4.95.* ☉ *Mid-Apr.–Oct., daily 9:30–5:45; Nov.–mid-Apr., daily 10–4:45.*

Studley Royal and Fountains Abbey

★ **㉗** *9 mi northwest of Knaresborough, 4 mi southwest of Ripon.*

The 18th-century water garden and deer park, Studley Royal, and the ruins of Fountains Abbey blend the glories of English Gothic architecture with a Neoclassical vision of an ordered universe. The gardens include lakes, ponds, and spectacular water terraces, and waterfalls splash around classical temples, statues, and a grotto. The surrounding woods offer long vistas toward the great tower of Ripon Cathedral, some 3 mi north. The majestic ruins of Fountains Abbey, with its own high tower and soaring 13th-century arches, make a striking picture on the banks of the River Skell. Founded in 1132, but not completed until the early 1500s, the abbey still possesses many of its original buildings, and it's one of the best places in England to learn about medieval monastic life. In this isolated valley, the Cistercian community went about its business: the "White Monks" (named for the color of their habits) began a day of silence and prayer with vespers at 2:30 AM, while the lay brothers oversaw operations at the abbey's sheep farms. Of the surviving buildings, the lay brothers' echoing refectory and dormitory in the 300-ft west range impresses most; the landmark Perpendicular tower was a later (early 16th-century) addition, erected by Abbot Huby, most eminent of the abbey's leaders. The whole of this complex, a World Heritage Site, is now owned by the National Trust, which operates free guided tours around abbey and gardens. On your own, buy the pamphlet at the entrance desk to guide you around the 10 buildings. There's a small restaurant (no dinner) and two stores, as well as an exhibition and video display in the 17th-century **Fountains Hall,** one of the earliest Neoclassical buildings in northern England. ⊠ *Off B6265,* ☎ *01765/608888; 01765/601005 weekends,* WEB *www.fountainsabbey. org.uk.* ⊠ *£4.50.* ☉ *Oct.–Mar., daily 10–5; Apr.–Sept., daily 10–7. Free guided tours of abbey and gardens daily Apr.–Oct., usually at 1:30, 2:30, and 3:30.*

Ripon

㉘ *4 mi northeast of Fountains Abbey, 11 mi north of Harrogate, 24 mi northwest of York.*

Ripon was thriving as early as the 9th century as an important market center. A relatively small church has been designated a cathedral since the mid-19th century, which makes Ripon (only about 15,000 inhabitants) technically a city. Market day is Thursday, which is probably the best day to stop by. Successive churches here were destroyed by the Vikings and the Normans, and the present **Ripon Cathedral,** dating from the 12th and 13th centuries, is notable for its finely carved choir stalls and Saxon crypt, now an empty series of chambers, but which housed sacred relics in bygone days. ☒ *Minster Rd.,* ☎ *01765/602072,* WEB *www.riponcathedral.org.uk.* ▨ *£2 donation requested.* ☉ *Daily 8–6:30.*

Lodging

£££–££££   🏨 **Swinton Park.** In 2001, the Cunliffe-Lister family opened part of their ancestral castle—a stately pile rebuilt in the 18th and 19th centuries with turret and battlements—as a hotel. A lovely setting on 200 acres of parkland near Yorkshire Dales National Park guarantees seclusion and abundant opportunities for outdoor pursuits, and the plushly furnished public rooms give you plenty of room to relax. Guest rooms, named and decorated on the theme of Yorkshire castles, abbeys, or dales, vary widely in size and price. Masham is 8 mi north of Ripon and 35 mi north of Leeds and York. ☒ *Off the A1, Masham HG4 4JH,* ☎ *01765/680900,* FAX *01765/680901,* WEB *www.swintonpark.com. 17 rooms, 3 suites. Restaurant, spa, gym, croquet, horseback riding, fishing, mountain bikes, meeting rooms. AE, DC, MC, V.*

Newby Hall

🐚 ㉙   *5 mi southeast of Ripon.*

An early 18th-century house redecorated later in the same century by Robert Adam for his patron William Weddell, Newby Hall contains some of the finest interior decorative art of its period in Western Europe. One room has been designed around a set of priceless Gobelin tapestries, and another was created to show off Roman sculpture. The famous grounds, which extend down to the River Ure, include a collection of old species roses, rare shrubs, and delightful sunken gardens. The children's adventure playground, narrow-gauge steam railroad, river steamers, and garden restaurant make a visit to Newby a full day's outing. ☒ *Skelton-on-Ure,* ☎ *01423/322583,* WEB *www.newbyhall.co.uk.* ▨ *£6.30, gardens only £4.50.* ☉ *Apr.–Oct., Tues.–Sun., grounds 11–5, house noon–5.*

Thirsk

㉚   *15 mi north of Newby Hall, 23 mi north of York.*

This small market town on the western edge of the moors was a thriving place on the main east–west route from the dales to the coast. Lovely Georgian houses abound, and the cobbled medieval Market Place is handsome; Saturday and Monday are market days. Today Thirsk is best known as the place where veterinarian Alf Wight (who wrote under the name James Herriot) had his surgery. The popular **World of James Herriot,** in the author's actual surgery, re-creates the operating room and the living spaces of the 1940s and 1950s; it also has displays of veterinary artifacts. Plenty of Herriot mementos add to the atmosphere. ☒ *23 Kirkgate,* ☎ *01845/524234.* ▨ *£4.50.* ☉ *Nov.–Feb., daily 10–5; Mar.–Oct., daily 10–6; last admission 1 hr before closing.*

THE NORTH YORKSHIRE COAST

Except during the hottest summers, the North Yorkshire coast isn't the warmest place for a beach vacation. That said, there's plenty to make you glad you came, not least the good sandy beaches, rocky coves, and picturesque villages, like Robin Hood's Bay and Staithes, which seem to capture imaginations at first sight. Most coastal towns still support an active fishing industry, and every harbor offers fishing and leisure trips throughout the summer. The east-coast beaches are usually fine for swimming, although you'll find the water cold. Beaches at Scarborough, Whitby, and Filey have patrolled bathing areas: swim between the red-and-yellow flags, and don't swim when a red flag is flying. Major towns also have indoor swimming pools.

From York, the coast is about an hour's drive away, and starting at Bridlington, it's a simple matter to follow the main road north to Scarborough (A165), and on to Robin Hood's Bay and Whitby (A171).

Bridlington

③ *41 mi east of York.*

Bridlington, a fishing port with an ancient harbor, makes a fine introduction to the North Yorkshire coast, with its wide arc of sand that's typical of the beach resorts in the region. Boat trips through the harbor and up the coast depart frequently in summer, or simply join the milling crowds who promenade up and down the seafront, eating fish-and-chips, browsing at the gift shops and stalls, and frequenting the rides at the small amusement park. At **Flamborough Head** a huge bank of chalk cliffs juts out into the North Sea.

A coastal path over the cliff tops ends at **Bempton Cliffs,** one of the finest seabird reserves in England, home to a colony of 7,000 puffins that nest on the impressive 400-ft-high cliffs between March and August. The reserve, off B1229, is open at all times, and the displays at the nearby visitor center can help you get more out of the area. Rent a pair of binoculars for a closer view of the puffins, shags, kittiwakes, gannets, guillemots, and razorbills that make the cliffs their home. ⊠ *Visitor Centre, Cliff La.,* ☎ *01262/851179,* W̅E̅B̅ *www.rspb.org.uk.* ⊠ *Free; £3 parking.* ⊙ *Visitor center Mar.–Nov., daily 10–5; Dec.–Feb., weekends 9:30–4.*

Dining

£ ✕ **Jerome's.** This friendly little seafront café-restaurant keeps up with these multicultural times by featuring a selection of good-value Greek meals, including meze (a sampler of hors d'oeuvres) and vegetarian platters. The outdoor tables see the most use in summer, when Jerome's stays open until 9. This spot closes at 5 in winter. ⊠ *The Floral Pavilion, Royal Prince's Parade,* ☎ *01262/671881. No credit cards.*

Scarborough

③ *17 mi north of Bridlington, 34 mi northeast of York.*

Candy floss and rock candy, Victorian architecture, a great sweep of cliffs above a sandy bay, and a rocky promontory capped by a ruined castle are just some of the elements that make Scarborough a classic English seaside resort. A chance discovery in the early 17th century of a mineral spring on the foreshore led to the establishment of a spa, whose users were encouraged not merely to soak themselves in seawater but even to drink it. By the late 18th century, when sea bathing was firmly in vogue, no beaches were busier than Scarborough's, with its "bathing machines," cumbersome wheeled cabins drawn by donkeys or horses into the surf and anchored there. Scarborough's initial prosperity dates from this period, as evidenced in the handsome Regency and early Victorian residences and hotels in the city.

The contrast between the two distinct faces of Scarborough makes the town all the more appealing. Its older, more genteel side in the southern half of town consists of carefully laid out crescents and squares and cliff-top walks and gardens with views across Cayton Bay. The northern side is a riot of ice cream stands, cafés, stores selling "rock" (luridly colored hard candy), crab hawkers, and bingo halls. In addition, enough survives of the tight huddle of streets, alleyways, and red-roof cottages around the harbor to give an idea of what the town was like before the resort days.

Paths link the harbor with the substantial ruins of **Scarborough Castle** on the promontory; dating from Norman times, it is built on the site of a Roman signal station and near a former Viking settlement. From the castle there are spectacular views across the North Bay, the beaches, and the shore gardens. ⊠ *Castle Rd.,* ☎ *01723/372451,* WEB *www.english-heritage.org.uk.* ⊠ *£2.30.* ☉ *Apr.–Sept., daily 10–6; Oct., daily 10–5; Nov.–Mar., Wed.–Sun. 10–4.*

At Scarborough's little medieval church of **St. Mary** (⊠ Castle Rd., ☎ 01723/500541) you'll find the grave of Anne, the youngest Brontë sister, who died in 1849. She was taken to Scarborough from Haworth in a final desperate effort to save her life in the sea air. The church is near the castle on the way into town.

Wood End was the vacation home of 20th-century writers Edith, Osbert, and Sacheverell Sitwell, and the west wing houses a library of their works as well as portraits and paintings. The rest of the early Victorian house, amid delightful grounds, holds the collections of the **Museum of Natural History.** ⊠ *The Crescent,* ☎ *01723/367326.* ⊠ *£3.20.* ☉ *May–Sept., Tues.–Sun. 10–5; Oct.–Apr., Wed. and weekends 10–4.*

The **Rotunda Museum,** an extraordinary circular building, was originally constructed in 1829 for William Smith of the Scarborough Philosophical Society to display his geological collection; it now houses important archaeological and local history collections. ⊠ *Vernon Rd.,* ☎ *01723/374839.* ⊠ *£3.* ☉ *May–Sept., Tues.–Sun. 10–5; Oct.–Apr., Tues. and weekends 11–4.*

☾ **Scarborough Sea Life Centre** is the best of the cheerful attractions that appeal to kids. Marine life and environmental matters are presented in an entertaining way, with various marine habitats combined under one roof. ⊠ *Scalby Mills, North Bay,* ☎ *01723/376125.* ⊠ *£5.50.* ☉ *June–Sept., daily 10–9; Oct.–May, daily 10–5.*

Dining and Lodging

£–££ ✕ **Lanterna Restaurant.** An intimate atmosphere and a high standard of cuisine make this Italian restaurant a good choice. The classic dishes are all represented, among them tender veal cooked with ham and cheese, but opt for seasonal specials using fresh vegetables and fish. ⊠ *33 Queen St.,* ☎ *01723/363616. MC, V. Closed Sun. No lunch Nov.–Mar.*

£ ✕ **The Golden Grid.** Everyone has to have fish-and-chips at least once in Scarborough, and the harborfront Golden Grid is a classic of its kind. Choose an upstairs window table and tuck into freshly fried cod or haddock, although big spenders (and those flying in the face of British seaside tradition) could also opt for grilled turbot or one of a host of other daily specials. ⊠ *4 Sandside,* ☎ *01723/360922. MC. No dinner Mon.–Thurs. Nov.–Mar.*

££ 🏨 **The Crown.** The centerpiece of Scarborough's Regency Esplanade, this period hotel overlooks South Bay and the castle headland. Originally built to accommodate fashionable 19th-century visitors to Scarborough Spa, it has been considerably refurbished, and the rooms are modern and comfortable. There's a small extra charge for a sea view. The regular room rate doesn't include breakfast, although you might consider the special dinner, bed, and breakfast package. ⊠ *The Esplanade, YO11 2AG,* ☎ *01723/373491,* FAX *01723/362271. 78 rooms. Restaurant, bar, no-smoking rooms. AE, DC, MC, V.*

£ 🏨 **Interludes.** "Theatrical" is the word to describe this Georgian town house in the old town streets behind the harbor. Dedicated to the theme of the performing arts, Interludes' compact rooms are named after famous theaters, and bills, posters, and the owners' own theater photography hang throughout. The ambience is traditional English, with antique and repro furniture, a four-poster in one room, and polished oak, flowers, and heavy drapes. Ask for an upper room with bay views, and consider the "theatre breaks"—room and tickets for productions at the town's Stephen Joseph Theatre. ⊠ *32 Princess St., YO11 1QR,* ☎ *01723/360513,* ℻ *01723/368597. 5 rooms. Dining room. No credit cards.*

Nightlife and the Arts

Scarborough has an internationally known artistic native son in contemporary playwright Alan Ayckbourn. The **Stephen Joseph Theatre** (⊠ Westborough, ☎ 01723/370541), which premieres all of his plays, incorporates two fine stages, a cinema, restaurant, and bar. Stop in at the theater for a program, or contact the tourist office for box office details.

Robin Hood's Bay

★ ㉝ *15 mi northwest of Scarborough.*

Many people's favorite coastal stop is at Robin Hood's Bay, a tiny fishing village squeezed into a ravine near where a stream courses over the cliffs. The perilously steep, narrow roads are fringed with tiny, crazily scattered houses and shops. The name is curious, because the only historical certainty is that there is no connection with the famous English medieval outlaw. The village didn't even come into being until the late 15th century, after which it thrived in a small way as a fishing port and smuggling center. Contraband was passed up the stream bed beneath the cottages, linked to one another by secret passages, often with customs officers in hot pursuit.

It would be hard to find a **beach** anywhere in the British Isles that offers the variety and interest of Robin Hood Bay's. The tide rushes in very quickly, so take care. Provided the tide is out, you can stroll for a couple of hours south from Robin Hood's Bay, along a rough, exposed stone shore full of rock pools, inlets, and sandy strands, where children (and a few adults) can be seen passing hour after hour examining the water for amphibious creatures, and the rocks for tiny fossils. There are also a few stretches of sand suitable for sun bathers. To the south is the curiously named **Boggle Hole**, where a ravine nestles an old water mill, now a youth hostel. Farther south is Ravenscar, a Victorian village that never took off and now consists of little more than a hotel, which can be reached by a hazardous but exhilarating path up the cliff. The walk back, along the cliff-top path, is less tricky but no less energetic.

Dining and Lodging

£ ✕ **Bay Hotel.** The village's most favored pub is this friendly Victorian retreat, perfectly positioned at the bottom of the village and set upon a rocky outcrop lapped by the sea. Its bar is festooned with oak and brass; in winter, a roaring fire warms all comers. Meals are basic but well crafted. ⊠ *The Dock,* ☎ *01947/880278. No credit cards.*

£££ 🏨 **Raven Hall Hotel.** This superb Georgian hotel with landscaped grounds offers unrivaled coastal views from the headland of Ravenscar, 3 mi southeast of Robin Hood's Bay. Try your utmost to secure a room with a bay view; if they're occupied, you can console yourself with the same views from the lounge or restaurant. The hotel is known for its good sports facilities, although you'll have to be polar-bear hardy to use the outdoor pool, despite its enterprising cliff-top location. It's worth noting that the bar marks the traditional end of the punishing, long-distance Lyke-Wake Walk, so on occasion you may share the comfortable lounge (warmed by fire in winter) with exhausted walkers. ✉ *Ravenscar YO13 0ET,* ☎ *01723/870353,* WEB *www.ravenhall. co.uk. 53 rooms. Restaurant, bar, lounge, indoor-outdoor pool, sauna, 9-hole golf course, 2 tennis courts. AE, DC, MC, V.*

Outdoor Activities and Sports

Several superb, long-distance walks start or finish in, or run through, Robin Hood's Bay. The village marks one end of the 190-mi **Coast-to-Coast** walk (the other is at St. Bees Head on the Irish Sea). Coast-to-coast walkers finish at the Bay Hotel, above the harbor. The coastal **Cleveland Way** runs north (to Whitby) and south (to Scarborough) through the village. The trans-moor **Lyke-Wake Walk** finishes 3 mi away at Ravenscar.

Whitby

★ ➌➍ *7 mi northwest of Robin Hood's Bay, 20 mi northeast of Pickering.*

Whitby can claim to be the most splendid town on the English coast, a scenic glory steeped in fishing and whaling lore. It's set around a harbor of great natural beauty formed by the River Esk as it comes down a long glenlike ravine cut through the moors. Above it, on either side, red-roof buildings rise tier upon tier. Fine Georgian houses line some of the central streets on the west side of the river (known as West Cliff), and across the swing bridge in the old town (part of the area known as East Cliff), cobbled Church Street is packed shoulder-to-shoulder in summer with people exploring the dark alleys, enclosed courtyards, and gift shops.

On top of the cliff are the gaunt ruins of Whitby Abbey, a sight that inspired Bram Stoker when he came here to write *Dracula.* Today Whitby is a small, laid-back resort, but it was an important religious center as far back as the 7th century, when Whitby Abbey was first founded, and it later came to prominence as a whaling port. The first ships sailed from here for Greenland in the mid-18th century, captained by local men like William Scoresby, inventor of the crow's nest, to whom Herman Melville paid tribute in his novel *Moby Dick.* At much the same time as whaling made Whitby rich, its shipbuilding made it famous: Captain James Cook (1728–79), explorer and navigator, sailed on his first ship out of the town in 1747, and all four of his subsequent discovery vessels were built in Whitby.

Climb the 199 steps from the end of Church Street and you are at the rather eccentrically designed church of **St. Mary** (✉ Church La., East Cliff, ☎ 01947/603421), with its ship's deck roof, triple-decker pulpit, and enclosed galleries. The church dates originally from the 12th century, although almost everything you see today is the (often less-than-happy) result of 19th- and 20th-century renovations. The spooky, weather-beaten churchyard, filled with the crooked old gravestones of ancient mariners, has superb views of the sea and the town itself. It was here that Bram Stoker's Dracula claimed Lucy as his victim. If you search around the tall grass at the back, you'll find the grave of master mariner William Scoresby.

The romantic, tumbledown ruins of **Whitby Abbey,** set high on the East Cliff, are visible from almost everywhere in town. St. Hilda founded the abbey in AD 657, and Caedmon (died circa 670), the first identifiable poet of the English language, was a monk here; an engraved cross of dubious provenance, which bears his name, stands at the top of the 199 steps near St. Mary's church. Sacked by the Vikings in the 9th century, the monastery was refounded in the 11th century and then enlarged in the 13th century, from which point these ruins date. ⊠ *Abbey La., East Cliff,* ☎ *01947/603568,* WEB *www.english-heritage.org.uk.* 🎟 *£1.80.* ☉ *Apr.–Sept., daily 10–6; Oct.–Mar., daily 10–4.*

Captain Cook is remembered in various places around town, most notably by his bronze statue on top of the West Cliff, near the pair of arched whalebones. However, the most revealing exhibits relating to the man are to be found in the **Captain Cook Memorial Museum,** tucked into the period rooms of the 18th-century house belonging to shipowner John Walker, where Cook lived as an apprentice from 1746 to 1749. Here, you can see mementos of his epic expeditions, including maps, diaries, and drawings, as well as some tracing the privations of his wife and family, left behind to cope with life, loss, and bereavement. ⊠ *Grape La.,* ☎ *01947/601900.* 🎟 *£2.60.* ☉ *Easter–Oct., daily 9:45–5; Mar. and Nov., weekends 11–3.*

Dining and Lodging

£–££   ✕ **Magpie Café.** Whitby is full of fish-and-chip places, but no place serves it with more style than the Magpie, a large old-fashioned restaurant with a well-stocked menu that includes hake and woof along with the perennial plaice, cod, and haddock. Many regulars would argue that the Magpie's non-fish dishes (especially its meat salads) offer even better value. The queues that reach down the street testify to the quality of the food and service; it's worth the wait. ⊠ *14 Pier Rd.,* ☎ *01947/ 602058. No credit cards. Closed mid-Nov.–mid-Mar.*

£   ✕🏠 **Shepherd's Purse.** In the cobbled old town, this splendid little complex comprises boutique-style guest rooms, a vegetarian restaurant that looks as if it has been inserted into a junk shop, and a health-food store. There are two less-expensive bedrooms above the store and five more in the galleried courtyard at the back. Although small, many have bathrooms, with four-poster or brass bedsteads; floors are wooden, the furniture is country style, and the top two rooms even have little balconies. ⊠ *95 Church St., YO22 4BH,* ☎ *01947/820228. 7 rooms, 5 with bath. Restaurant. No credit cards.*

£   ✕🏠 **White Horse and Griffin.** When looking for the perfect inn, you
★   want an old building with character, a roaring fire in the grate, and food to thrill. Step forward to the 18th-century White Horse and Griffin, in which Charles Dickens once slept and railway pioneer George Stephenson lectured. The spruce, renovated rooms are warm and comfortable, and downstairs the cozy bistro-bar serves a fine, changing menu including locally caught fish and game in season. Dinner might be fried calamari or bouillabaisse, followed by grilled Dover sole or salmon in a champagne sauce. ⊠ *Church St., YO22 4BH,* ☎ *01947/604857. 12 rooms. Restaurant, bar. MC, V.*

Nightlife and the Arts

The **Whitby Regatta,** held in August every year, is a three-day jamboree of boat races, fair rides, lifeboat rescue displays, parades, and musical events. Music (but also traditional dance and storytelling) predominates during **Whitby Folk Week,** usually held the week before the late-August bank holiday, when pubs, pavements, and halls become venues for more than 1,000 traditional folk events by performers from all over the country.

Shopping

Whitby is known for its jet, a very hard, black form of natural carbon, which has been used locally for more than a century to make jewelry and ornaments, and was particularly popular as mourning memorabilia during the Victorian era. Several shops in the old town along Church Street and parallel to Sandgate have fine displays.

Staithes

㉟ *9 mi northwest of Whitby.*

Specifically, there's little to see in Staithes, but over the years, many travelers have been seduced by the powerful atmosphere of the town's stepped alleys and courtyards. These, and the surrounding coastal cliffs, were captured on canvas by many members of the so-called Staithes School of artists, who were prominent in the earlier part of the 20th century. Tourists are a vital part of the local economy these days, with perhaps the most surprising visitors being those in wet suits, who know Staithes to have some of the best surfing in the country.

Staithes's few houses huddle below the rocky, seagull-studded outcrop of Cowbar Nab, on either side of the beck (stream) and, having survived storm and flood, present a hoary, weather-beaten aspect. Not all were so lucky. The Cod and Lobster Inn, at the harbor, is in its third incarnation, and the dry-goods shop in which James Cook had his first apprenticeship before moving to Whitby fell into the sea entirely in 1745. The house known as Cook's Cottage, near the pub, is supposedly built out of the salvaged remains of the original building.

Staithes's former Methodist Chapel has been imaginatively converted into the **Captain Cook and Staithes Heritage Centre,** whose central feature is a life-size mid-18th-century street scene of the kind Cook would have recognized. The shop in which the young adventurer worked was re-created, alongside an alehouse, a fisherman's warehouse, and museum displays relating to local industries and, of course, smuggling. ⊠ *High St.,* ☎ *01947/841454.* 🖃 *£2.25.* ☉ *Daily 10–5:30.*

Dining

£–££ ✕ **The Endeavour.** This rather higgledy-piggledy old house on Staithes's
★ main street, near the harbor, is well known for its meals of locally caught fish. Menus change seasonally, but you can count on dishes being presented with care and with Mediterranean or Asian flourishes; soups, salmon, and lobster are strong points. Have a drink in the tiny, low-ceiling bar, choose from the blackboard, and do ask for recommendations from the brisk staff. Three inexpensive guest rooms are available for anyone wishing to stay the night. ⊠ *1 High St.,* ☎ *01947/840825. No credit cards. Closed weekdays in Feb. No dinner Sun. Nov.–Mar.*

THE NORTH YORK MOORS

The North York Moors are a dramatic swath of high moorland starting 25 mi north of the city of York and stretching east to the coast and west to the Cleveland Hills. Once covered in forest, of which a few pockets survive, the landscape changed with the introduction of sheep at the monastic foundations of Rievaulx and Whitby in medieval times. The evidence is clear for all to see today: heather-covered hills that, in late summer and early fall, are a rich blaze of crimson and purple, and a series of isolated, medieval standing stones that once acted as signposts on the paths between the abbeys. For more than four decades, the area has been designated a national park, to protect the moors and grassy valleys that shelter brownstone villages and hamlets. Minor roads and tracks crisscross the moors in all directions, and there's no single, obvious route through the region. Perhaps the most rewarding approach is west from the coast at Whitby, along the Esk Valley to Danby, which is also accessible on the Esk Valley branch train line between Middlesbrough and Whitby. From Danby, minor roads run south over the high moors reaching Hutton-le-Hole, beyond which main roads lead to interesting towns on the moors' edge, such as Helmsley. Completing the route in this direction leaves you with an easy side trip to Castle Howard before returning to nearby York.

Danby

36 *15 mi west of Whitby.*

The straggling old stone village of Danby nestles in a green valley, just a short walk from the tops of the nearby moors. It's been settled since Viking times—Danby means "village where the Danes lived"—and these days it bumbles along contentedly in a semi-touristed way. There's a pub, and a bakery with a tearoom, and if you bring hiking boots with you, within 10 minutes you can be above the village looking down, surrounded by nothing but isolated moorland. To get here from Whitby, take A171 west and turn south for Danby after 12 mi, after which it's a 3-mi drive over Danby Low Moor to the village.

In a converted country house on the eastern outskirts of Danby, the **National Park's Moors Centre** has exhibitions, displays, and a wide range of pamphlets and books about the area. There's a garden out front with picnic tables and superb valley views, and a tearoom. The summer Moorsbus operates from the center for the 30-minute journey south to Hutton-le-Hole. ⊠ *Danby Lodge,* ☎ *01287/660654.* 🔁 *Free.* ☉ *Mid-Apr.–Oct., daily 10–5; Nov.–mid-Apr., weekends 11–4.*

Dining

£ ✕ **Stonehouse Bakery & Tea Shop.** This cozy little place is unusually adventurous for this part of the world, serving sandwiches on sun-dried-tomato or olive bread, herbal teas, local honey, and a heaven-sent peanut brittle. ⊠ *3 Briar Hill,* ☎ *01287/660006. Closed Sun.*

En Route From Danby take the road due west for 2 mi to Castleton, and then turn south over the top of the moors toward Hutton-le-Hole. The narrow road offers magnificent views over North York Moors National Park, especially at the old stone **Ralph Cross** (5 mi), which marks the highest point. Drive carefully: sheep-dodging is something of a necessary art in these parts.

Hutton-le-Hole

★ **37** *13 mi south of Danby.*

Even after seeing the varied splendors of villages throughout North York Moors National Park, it's difficult not to think that Hutton-le-Hole is the pick of the bunch. It's almost too pastoral to be true: a tiny hamlet, based around a wide village green, with sheep wandering about, and a stream babbling in the background. The surroundings are equally attractive, and in summer, the local parking lots fill quickly as people arrive to take to the nearby hills for a day's walking.

The excellent 2-acre, open-air **Ryedale Folk Museum** records life in the Dales from prehistory onward by way of a display of 13 historic buildings: a series of 16th-century cottages, a 19th-century blacksmith's shop, an early photographer's studio, and a medieval kiln. ☎ *01751/417367.* 🔁 *£3.25.* ☉ *Mid-Mar.–Oct., daily 10–5:30*

Helmsley

38 *8 mi southwest of Hutton-le-Hole, 27 mi north of York.*

The pleasant market town of Helmsley, well known as a hiking center, is attractive enough in itself for a day trip and has a castle (partly ruined during the Civil War) and a traditional country marketplace surrounded by fine old inns, cafés, and stores. Market day here is Friday.

The town, on the southern edge of the moors, is the starting point of the long-distance moor-and-coastal footpath, the **Cleveland Way.** Boots are donned at the old cross in the market square, from where it's 50 mi or so across the moors to the coast and then a similar distance south to Filey along the cliff tops; all told, it's 108 mi of walking, which most people aim to complete in nine days. Even nonwalkers will probably find the very early stages of the Cleveland Way irresistible, since the trail passes close to the ruins of Rievaulx Abbey, just outside the town. A leaflet from the tourist information center indicates the route.

Lodging

£££–££££ ⚐ **Black Swan.** This lovely, ivy-covered property sits right on the edge of the market square and makes a splendid, relaxing base. The building is a hybrid—part 16th-century coaching inn, part Georgian house—but careful restoration and renovation have ensured comfort throughout: rooms overlook either the square or the fine walled garden at the back. A restaurant serves traditional British and local dishes; an open fire keeps things cozy in winter. ⊠ *Market Pl., YO6 5BJ,* ☎ *01439/ 770466,* FAX *01439/770174. 44 rooms. Restaurant, bar, croquet. AE, DC, MC, V.*

Rievaulx Abbey

★ ㉟ *2 mi northwest of Helmsley.*

One of the most graceful of all medieval English seats of learning, Rievaulx (pronounced ree-*voh*) Abbey occupies a dramatic setting on the River Rye. The wealth of this Cistercian foundation, which dates from 1132, was derived from the wool trade, and the extensive surviving ruins give some indication of the thriving trade with Europe in which the medieval monks of North Yorkshire engaged. The landscaped grounds have graceful Gothic arches, cloisters, and associated buildings, including the Chapter House, which retains the original shrine of the first abbot, William, by the entrance. The abbey is a 1½-hour walk northwest from Helmsley (there's a signposted footpath), or 2 mi by vehicle, taking B1257. ⊠ *Off B1257,* ☎ *01439/798228,* WEB *www.english-heritage.org.uk.* 🎟 *£3.60.* ☼ *Apr.–Sept., daily 10–6; Oct., daily 10–5; Nov.–Mar., daily 10–4.*

OFF THE   **RIEVAULX TERRACE and TEMPLES –** If you've wandered among the ruins
BEATEN PATH   of Rievaulx Abbey, you might also like to drive up to the Rievaulx Terraces, a long grassy walkway on the hillside above, terminating in the remains of several Tuscan- and Ionic-style classical temples. The views of the abbey from here are magnificent. ⊠ *Off B1257,* ☎ *01439/ 798340,* WEB *www.nationaltrust.org.uk.* 🎟 *£3.60.* ☼ *Apr.–Oct., daily 10:30–5.*

Castle Howard

★ ㊵ *14 mi southeast of Rievaulx Abbey, 12 mi southeast of Helmsley, 15 mi northeast of York.*

Standing serene among the Howardian Hills to the west of Malton, Castle Howard is one of the grandest and most opulent stately homes in Britain, an imposing Baroque building whose magnificent skyline is punctuated by stone chimneys and a graceful central dome. Many people know it best as Brideshead, the home of the Flyte family in Evelyn Waugh's tale of aristocratic woe, *Brideshead Revisited,* as this was where much of the TV series was filmed. The house was designed for the Howard family (who still live here) by Sir John Vanbrugh, who also designed Blenheim Palace, Winston Churchill's birthplace. Remarkably, this was the first building that Vanbrugh designed; until then he was best known as a playwright. The audacity and confidence of the great Baroque house are startling, proclaiming the wealth and importance of the Howards and the utter self-assurance of its architect. Castle Howard took 60 years to build (1699–1759), and it was worth every year. A magnificent central hallway spanned by a hand-painted (and unfortunately, new) ceiling dwarfs all visitors, and there is no shortage of grandeur elsewhere in the building: vast family portraits, delicate marble fireplaces, immense and fading tapestries, huge pieces of Victorian silver on polished tables, and a great many marble busts. Outside, the stately theme continues in one of the most stunning Neoclassical landscapes in England; Horace Walpole, the 18th-century connoisseur, commented that a pheasant at Castle Howard lives better than most dukes elsewhere. Carefully arranged woods, lakes, bridges, and obelisks compose a scene far more like a painting than a natural English landscape. Make sure you see the Temple of the Four Winds and the Mausoleum, whose magnificence caused Walpole to comment that all who view it would wish to be buried alive. ✉ *Coneysthorpe (Off A64 and B1257)*, ☎ *01653/648333*, WEB *www. castlehoward.co.uk.* ✆ *House and gardens £8, gardens only £4.50.* ☺ *Mid-Mar.–Oct., daily 10–4:30.*

YORKSHIRE A TO Z

To research prices, get advice from other travelers, and book travel arrangements, visit www.fodors.com.

AIRPORTS
➤ AIRPORT INFORMATION: **Leeds Bradford International Airport** (✉ A658, Yeadon, ☎ 0113/250–9696, WEB www.lbia.co.uk). **Manchester Airport** (✉ near Junctions 5 and 6 of M56, ☎ 0161/489–3000, WEB www.manairport.co.uk).

BIKE TRAVEL
Although the countryside is too hilly for extensive bicycle touring, except for the most experienced, you can rent bikes locally in several places. In York, where there are special bike paths, contact Cycleworks and pick up a cycling map from the tourist information center.
➤ BIKE RENTALS: **Cycleworks** (✉ 14–16 Lawrence St., York, ☎ 01904/ 626664).

BUS TRAVEL
National Express serves the region from London's Victoria Coach Station. Average travel times are 4½ hours to York, 6½ hours to Scarborough, and 7 hours to Whitby.

Each district now has its own bus company, and you may find you need to call around to discover the full range of services, although local tourist information centers can usually help. Timetable booklets for the Yorkshire Moors and Dales are widely available, and special summer services in both national parks provide useful bus connections. There are local Metro buses from Leeds and Bradford into the more remote parts of the Yorkshire Dales. Other companies are Harrogate & District; Yorkshire Coastliner for services to Castle Howard, Scarborough, Whitby, Malton, and Leeds; United to Ripon, Richmond and the northern Dales, Harrogate, and Leeds; and Tees for Whitby, Scarborough, and Middlesbrough. In York, the main local bus operator is Rider York.

CUTTING COSTS
Many districts have Rover tickets; in York, the Minster Card (£9) gives a week's free travel on all Rider York services. The Moorsbus (information from any National Park office) runs every Sunday and bank

REVISITING BRIDESHEAD: CALLING ON CASTLE HOWARD

EVEN BEFORE YOUR FIRST SIGHT of Castle Howard—that grand birthday cake of a house nestled in North Yorkshire's hills and dales—chances are you are already enamored with it. The quintessential English stately home, its facade is abristle with Baroque sculptures and marble urns, and it's capped with a soaring cupola. Embellished by groves, a twinkling lake, and a preposterously perfect lawn, it's little wonder that Castle Howard became a media celebrity; it co-starred, along with Laurence Olivier and Jeremy Irons, in the popular 1980s TV series *Brideshead Revisited* and in the more recent miniseries *The Buccaneers.* Other British houses may be more treasure-laden or sumptuously decorated, but, clearly, none are as photogenic. Today an image of almost Hollywood splendor, the house attracts thousands of visitors every year, some searching for a sight of faded British aristocrats, but most there just to enjoy the magnificence of it all.

Considering its many theatrical, even flamboyant features, it seems fitting that Castle Howard's designer, Sir John Vanbrugh (1664–1726), was praised more as a playwright than an architect (he also had other careers as a soldier and adventurer). In 18th-century London, his plays were second in popularity only to Congreve's. Even more remarkably, this was Vanbrugh's very first building design. His self-assurance apparently knowing no bounds, this immensely gifted architect went on to create Blenheim Palace, the Versailles of England.

Vanbrugh was smart enough to seek some assistance; he turned to the brilliant but self-effacing Nicholas Hawksmoor (1661–1736), who at 18 was under the tutelage of Christopher Wren. The three architects were the pillars of the English Baroque style. Hawksmoor worked with Vanbrugh at Castle Howard and at Blenheim, providing help with the structural design and supporting Vanbrugh when critics attacked the mismatching of classical orders on Castle Howard. He also encouraged adding bodies of water to the landscape. Hawksmoor alone designed the imposing, original Mausoleum, which was begin in 1729; many consider it a masterpiece equal to his churches in London.

The Baroque grandeur of Castle Howard is without equal in northern England. A neck support would help when viewing the Grand Hall, whose stunning stone pilasters soar 70 ft skyward to the hand-painted cupola. The adjoining marble corridors are populous with classical statues, and the state rooms are resplendent with gleaming paneling, delicate embroideries, and a coterie of Queen Anne sofas. One look at this drop-dead splendor and you'll be thankful for Ikea.

In time-tested English fashion, Lady Annette Howard, the castle's current chatelaine, has made these regal rooms cozy. With bouquets everywhere, intimate spotlights, and Staffordshire spaniels drowsing by the hearth, you almost feel like requesting a revivifying cuppa. Clearly, this grand house is still a home. In fact, the Howards often put up friends in the state bedrooms. If you ever get a weekend invitation—as the delightful tour guides will point out—bring wool pajamas; there's not enough staff now to keep all the fireplaces dancing. And don't plan on sleeping till noon: tourists start coming through the bedrooms at 11.

Many travelers are surprised to learn that, although situated some 200 mi north of London, Castle Howard can be done as a day trip. Catch the 8 AM express train to York from London's King's Cross Station, and link up with a tour bus that leaves York in time to arrive at the estate by noon. After three hours touring the mansion, exploring the gardens, lunching on cucumber sandwiches in the little café (save some tidbits for the resident peacocks), return to York to connect with the 4:30 or 5:30 PM express trains. Back in London, you may feel all tuckered out, but it will have been worth it.

holiday Monday from late May to the end of September, and every Tuesday and Wednesday from late July to the end of August. It connects Danby, Hutton-le-Hole, Helmsley, Rievaulx Abbey, Rosedale Abbey, and Pickering and costs £2 for an all-day ticket.

FARES AND SCHEDULES
➤ Bus Information: **Harrogate & District** (☎ 01423/566061). **Metro** (☎ 0113/2457676). **National Express** (☎ 0990/808080, WEB www.gobycoach.com). **Rider York** (☎ 01904/435600). **Tees** (☎ 01642/210131). **United** (☎ 01325/468771). **Yorkshire Coastliner** (☎ 01653/692556).

CAR RENTAL
➤ Local Agencies: **Avis** (✉ Bowling Bridge Service Station, Wakefield Rd., Bradford, ☎ 01274/306206). **Budget Rent-a-Car** (✉ Station House, Foss Islands Rd., York, ☎ 01904/644919). **Europcar** (✉ 172 Thornton Rd., Bradford, ☎ 01274/733048). **Eurodollar-Rent-a-Car** (✉ Nelson St., Bradford, ☎ 01274/722155). **Hertz** (✉ 20 Laisterdyke, Sticker La., Bradford, ☎ 01274/666666; ✉ York Rail Station, Station Rd., York, ☎ 01904/612586).

CAR TRAVEL
The M1, the principal route north from London, gets you to the region in about two hours, with longer travel times up into north Yorkshire. For York (193 mi) and the Scarborough areas, stay on M1 to Leeds (189 mi), then take A64. For the Yorkshire Dales, take M1 to Leeds, then A660 to A65 north and west to Skipton. For the North York Moors, either take B1363 north from York to Helmsley, or leave A64 at Malton and follow the trans-moor A169 that runs to Whitby. The trans-Pennine motorway, the M62, between Liverpool and Hull, crosses the bottom of this region. North of Leeds, A1 is the major north–south road, although narrow stretches, roadwork, and heavy traffic make this very slow going at times.

ROAD CONDITIONS
Some of the steep, narrow roads in the countryside off the main routes are difficult drives and can be particularly perilous (or closed altogether) in winter. Prime candidates for main roads closed annually by snow drifts are the moorland A169 and the coast-and-moor A171. If you're driving in the dales or moors in winter, listen for the weather forecasts.

EMERGENCIES
➤ Contacts: **Ambulance, fire, police** (☎ 999). **St. Mary's Hospital** (✉ Greenhill Road, Armley, Leeds, ☎ 0113/2790721).

NATIONAL PARKS
For information about local visitor centers, walks, and guided tours, contact Yorkshire Dales National Park and North York Moors National Park.
➤ Contacts: **Yorkshire Dales National Park** (head office, ☎ 01756/752748, WEB www.yorkshiredales.org.uk). **North York Moors National Park** (head office, ☎ 01439/770657, WEB www.northyorkmoors-npa.gov.uk).

TOURS
BUS TOURS
Guide Friday runs frequent city tours of York, including stops at the minster, the Castle Museum, the Shambles, and Jorvik that allow you to get on and off the bus as you please. The bus tours are £7.50, £5.50 if booked in advance. Yorktour offers open-top-bus, riverboat, and walking tours of the city of York and has an excursion bus to Castle

Howard, June–September, Tuesday, Friday, and Sunday, departing around noon.

➤ FEES AND SCHEDULES: **Guide Friday** (✉ De Grey Rooms, Exhibition Sq., ☎ 01904/640896, WEB www.guidefriday.com). **Yorktour** (☎ 01904/641737).

WALKING TOURS

The York Association of Voluntary Guides arranges short walking tours around the city, which depart daily at 10:15; there are additional tours at 2:15 PM April through October, and at 7 PM July through August. The tours are free, but gratuity is appreciated.

➤ FEES AND SCHEDULES: **York Association of Voluntary Guides** (✉ De Grey Rooms, Exhibition Sq., ☎ 01904/640780).

TRAIN TRAVEL

Great Northeastern Railways serves the region from London's King's Cross and Euston stations. Average travel times from King's Cross are 2½ hours to Leeds and two hours to York. It is possible to reach the North Yorkshire coast by train, although service from London to Scarborough (change at York) and, especially, Whitby (change at Darlington and Middlesbrough) can take up to seven hours. It's much less trouble (although not much quicker) to take the direct bus from London.

There is local service from Leeds to Skipton, and from York to Knaresborough and Harrogate and also to Scarborough (which has connections on to the seaside towns of Filey and Bridlington). Whitby can be reached on the minor, and extremely attractive, Esk Valley line from Middlesbrough.

The Embsay & Bolton Abbey Steam Railway runs steam trains every Sunday (and up to five times daily in summer) from Embsay near Skipton. The station at Bolton Abbey is 1½ mi from the abbey ruins, making for a fine approach to this most romantic of spots. For all train travel information in the region, call National Rail Enquiries or any local tourist office.

CUTTING COSTS

Two Regional Rover tickets for seven days' unlimited travel are available: North East and Coast and Peaks.

FARES AND SCHEDULES

➤ TRAIN INFORMATION: **Embsay & Bolton Abbey Steam Railway** (☎ 01756/794727; 01756/795189 recorded timetable). **Great Northeastern Railways** (☎ 0845/484950, WEB www.gner.co.uk). **National Rail Enquiries** (☎ 08457/484950, WEB www.railtrack.co.uk).

TRAVEL AGENCIES

➤ LOCAL AGENT REFERRALS: **Thomas Cook** (✉ Ivebridge House, 67 Market St., Bradford, ☎ 01274/732411; ✉ 51 Boar La., Leeds, ☎ 0113/243–2922; ✉ 47 Westborough, Scarborough, ☎ 01723/364444; ✉ 4 Nessgate, York, ☎ 01904/639928).

VISITOR INFORMATION

The Yorkshire Tourist Board has information about the area. Local tourist information centers have varied opening hours according to their location. Note that many in the North York Moors and Yorkshire Dales are only open during the summer.

➤ TOURIST INFORMATION: **Yorkshire Tourist Board** (✉ 312 Tadcaster Rd., York, YO2 2HF, ☎ 01904/707961, WEB www.ytb.org.uk). **Yorkshire's Coast & Country** (✉ Pickering Tourist Information Center, Eastgate Car Park, Pickering, YO18 7DU, ☎ 01751/473791, WEB www.ycc.org.uk).

Bradford (✉ National Museum of Photography, Film, and TV, Prince's View, BD5 0TR, ☎ 01274/753678, WEB www.bradford.gov.uk). **Bridlington** (✉ 25 Prince St., Humberside YO15 2NP, ☎ 01262/673474). **Harrogate** (✉ Royal Baths Assembly Rooms, Crescent Rd., HG1 2RR, ☎ 01423/537300, WEB www.harrogate.gov.uk). **Haworth** (✉ 2–4 West La., BD22 8EF, ☎ 01535/642329). **Helmsley** (✉ Town Hall, Market Pl., YO6 5BL, ☎ 01439/770173). **Knaresborough** (✉ 35 Market Pl., HG5 8AL, ☎ 01423/866886). **Leeds** (✉ Leeds City Station, LS1 1PL, ☎ 0113/242–5242, WEB www.leeds.gov.uk). **Richmond** (✉ Friary Gardens, Victoria Rd., DL10 4AJ, ☎ 01748/850252). **Scarborough** (✉ Pavilion House, Valley Bridge Rd., YO11 1UZ, ☎ 01723/373333). **Skipton** (✉ 9 Sheep St., BD23 1JH, ☎ 01756/792809). **Whitby** (✉ New Quay Rd., YO21 1YN, ☎ 01947/602674). **York** (✉ De Grey Rooms, Exhibition Sq., YO1 2HB, ☎ 01904/621756, WEB www.york-tourism. co.uk; ✉ York Railway Station, ☎ 01904/621756; ✉ 20 George Hudson St., ☎ 01904/554488).

DURHAM, HADRIAN'S WALL,
LINDISFARNE ISLAND

Ruined castles, holy islands, Roman walls, and the Northumberland Coast— windswept and wild, this is an area for the intrepid adventurer. The region soundly embraces history but refuses to be dwarfed by it. Among the numberless monuments of a vigorous and often warlike past, Hadrian's Wall is the most famous. This northern border of the Roman Empire stretches across prehistoric remains and tractless moorland. Other must-sees include Durham Cathedral—more fortress than church—and magical Lindisfarne Island, a landmark of early Christendom.

Updated by Ed
Glinert

A
LTHOUGH ONE OF THE VILLAGES OF England's northeast corner—Allendale Town, southwest of Hexham—lays claim to being
the geographical center of the British Isles, a decided air of remoteness pervades much of this region. For many Britons the words
"the Northeast" provoke a vision of somewhat bitter, near-Siberian remoteness. The truth is a revelation. For although there are numerous
wind-hammered wide-open spaces and empty roads that thread wild,
high moorland, the Northeast also has simple fishing towns, small villages of remarkable charm, and historic abbeys and castles that are all
the more romantic for their often ruinous state. Even the remoteness
is relative. Suddenly, around the next bend on a lane that seems to lead
nowhere, there stands an imposing church, a tall monastery, or a gorgeous country house built by a Victorian-era millionaire. The value found
in the region's shops and accommodations, the uncrowded beaches ideal
for walking, and the friendliness of the people also add to the appeal
of the area.

Mainly composed of the two large counties of Durham and Northumberland, the Northeast includes among its attractions English villages
adjacent to the Scottish Border area, renowned in ballads and romantic literature for feuds, raids, and battles. Hadrian's Wall, which
served to mark the northern limit of the Roman Empire, runs through
this region; much of it, remarkably, is still intact—so much so that people joke that it now keeps out tourists. Not far north of Hadrian's Wall
are Kielder Forest, the largest planted forest in Europe; Kielder Water,
the largest man-made lake in northern Europe; and some of the most
interesting parts of Northumberland National Park. Steel, coal, railroads, and shipbuilding made prosperous towns such as Newcastle upon
Tyne, Darlington, and Middlesbrough. A number of sights reflect the
area's industrial heritage, including the Beamish Open-Air Museum and
the Darlington Railway Centre and Museum.

On the region's eastern side is a 100-mi-long line of largely undevel-
oped coast, one of the least visited and most dramatic in all Europe.
Several outstanding castles perch on headlands and promontories
along here, including one that legend declares to have been the Joyous
Garde of Sir Lancelot du Lac. Fittingly, Durham Cathedral, the greatest ecclesiastical structure of the region, has memorably been described
as "Half church of God, half castle 'gainst the Scot." For almost 800
years, this great cathedral was the seat of bishops who raised their own
armies and ruled the turbulent northern diocese as prince-bishops with
quasi-royal authority.

Pleasures and Pastimes

Castles

Fought over for centuries by the Scots and the English, and prey to Viking
raiders from across the North Sea, the Northeast is one of the most
heavily fortified regions in Britain. Cities such as Durham and Newcastle—where the "new castle" is 900 years old—still hold impressive
relics, and exploring the stupendous fortresses along the exposed
Northumbrian coastline is among the most memorable experiences the
region has to offer. Dunstanburgh Castle near Craster and Bamburgh
Castle farther north are especially worth seeing.

Dining

The Northeast is one of the best areas in England for fresh local produce. Keep an eye out for restaurants that serve game from the Kielder
Forest, local lamb from the hillsides, and fish both from the streams

threading through the wild valleys and from the fishing fleets along the coast. Don't miss out on the simple fresh seafood sandwiches served in many of the region's local pubs. You might also wish to sample Alnwick Vatted Rum, a blend of Guyanese and Jamaican rum, or Lindisfarne mead, a traditional, highly potent spirit produced on Holy Island and made of honey vatted with grape juice and mineral water.

CATEGORY	COST*
££££	over £22
£££	£16–£22
££	£9–£15
£	under £9

*per person for a main course at dinner

Hiking and Biking

The Northeast offers superb walking almost wherever you go, but to gain an awe-inspiring sense of history with views of stunning scenery nothing beats a hike along the route of ancient Hadrian's Wall. The hilltop section near Housesteads Roman Fort is the best stretch for a short stroll. Long-distance footpaths include the 90-mi Teesdale Way, which follows the course of the River Tees, and St. Cuthbert's Way, an ancient pilgrimage route running the 63 mi from the Scottish border to Holy Island. Otherwise, the russet hills and dales of Northumberland National Park, in the northwest corner of the area, will please any serious walker. Similarly, cyclists relish the wide vistas, quiet roads, and magnificently fresh air of the region. One spot to rent a mountain bike is Kielder Water, north of Hadrian's Wall.

Lodging

The Northeast is not an area where the large hotel chains have much of a presence, outside the few large cities. Rather, this is a region where you can expect to find country houses converted into welcoming hotels, old coaching inns that still greet guests after 300 years, and cozy bed-and-breakfasts conveniently located near hiking trails. You may be pleasantly surprised at the prices of accommodations, with rates often at the low end of the scale. A service charge may be included in the cost or may be added separately; ask in advance.

CATEGORY	COST*
££££	over £150
£££	£100–£150
££	£60–£100
£	under £60

*All prices are for two people sharing a standard double room, including breakfast and VAT.

Exploring the Northeast

Most visitors travel from the south to arrive at the historic cathedral city of Durham, not far east of the picturesque foothill valleys of the Pennines. Farther north, Newcastle, on the region's main river, the Tyne, is a major industrial city with a number of attractions, and nearby the remarkable Roman fortifications of Hadrian's Wall snake through some superb scenery to the west; farther north lies the wilderness of Northumberland National Park. Starting roughly an hour's drive north of Newcastle, the final 40 mi of England's east coast is absolutely stunning, studded with huge castles and scattered with offshore islands such as the Farne Islands and Holy Island, also known as Lindisfarne.

Numbers in the text correspond to numbers in the margin and on the Northeast and Durham maps.

The Northeast

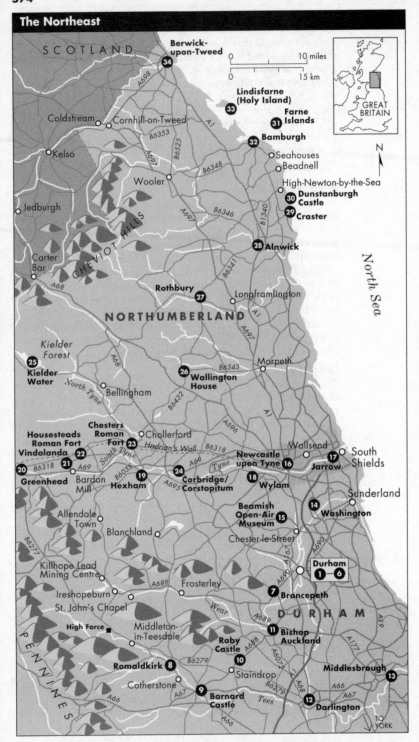

SCOTLAND

Berwick-upon-Tweed **34**

0 ___ 10 miles
0 ___ 15 km

Lindisfarne (Holy Island) **33**

Farne Islands **31**

Coldstream

Cornhill-on-Tweed

Bamburgh **32**

Kelso

Seahouses
Beadnell

Wooler

High-Newton-by-the-Sea

Jedburgh

Dunstanburgh Castle **30**

29 Craster

CHEVIOT HILLS

28 Alnwick

Carter Bar

Rothbury **27**

Longframlington

NORTHUMBERLAND

Kielder Forest

25
Kielder Water

North Tyne

Bellingham

26 Wallington House

Morpeth

Chesters Roman Fort **23**

Chollerford

Wallsend

South Shields

Housesteads Roman Fort
Vindolanda **22**

Hadrian's Wall

Newcastle upon Tyne **16**

17
Jarrow

20
Greenhead

21

Bardon Mill

19
Hexham

24 Corbridge/Corstopitum

18 Wylam

Sunderland

Allendale Town

Blanchland

Beamish Open-Air Museum **15**

14
Washington

Chester-le-Street

Killhope Lead Mining Centre

Ireshopeburn
St. John's Chapel

Frosterley

1 — 6 Durham

7 Brancepeth

DURHAM

High Force

Middleton-in-Teesdale

11 Bishop Auckland

Raby Castle

Romaldkirk **8**

10
Staindrop

Middlesbrough

13

Cotherstone

9 Barnard Castle

12 Darlington

PENNINES

TO YORK

North Sea

GREAT BRITAIN

N

Great Itineraries

Although it's possible to get a sense of the Northeast through an overnight stop en route to or from Scotland, it's worth setting aside four days to explore the region properly. One turn off the A1—the main north–south highway—and you'll soon learn that driving along the meandering backcountry roads can often be slow business, if only because the spectacular scenery encourages long halts.

IF YOU HAVE 2 DAYS

Base yourself at either ⚓ **Durham** ①–⑥, with time to inspect the Norman cathedral and the castle to either side of the central Palace Green, or at smaller, quainter ⚓ **Alnwick** ㉘, with its riverside castle and cobbled square. Drive inland between the two for at least a brief glimpse of **Hadrian's Wall,** ideally at **Housesteads Roman Fort** ㉒, and wind up at the magical monastic settlement on **Lindisfarne** ㉝.

IF YOU HAVE 4 DAYS

Having spent at least a half day exploring ⚓ **Durham** ①–⑥, set aside a full day to follow the course of **Hadrian's Wall.** An overnight stop nearby in ⚓ **Hexham** ⑲ enables you to see the excellent museums of Roman finds at **Vindolanda** ㉑ and **Housesteads Roman Fort** ㉒. Then drive northeast through the countryside to spend the evening in the little market town of ⚓ **Alnwick** ㉘. On the next morning, walk from **Craster** ㉙ to the splendidly bleak ruin of **Dunstanburgh Castle** ㉚; then visit one or two of the huge beaches to the north as you head to ⚓ **Bamburgh** ㉜ for the night. Overlooking the windswept shore, its famous castle conjures up the days of chivalry as few others do. Whether you're heading back to Durham from there, or onward to Scotland, visit wind-battered **Lindisfarne** ㉝, a short distance north, to soak up the saintly atmosphere.

When to Tour the Northeast

Although Hadrian's Wall and the coastal castles are starkly impressive in a blanket of snow, the best time to see the Northeast is in summer. Then you can be sure that the museums—and the roads—will be open, and that you'll be able to enjoy the countryside walks that are one of the region's greatest pleasures. Due to rough seas and inclement weather, there's no question of swimming at any of the magnificent beaches except in the height of summer, July and August. At the end of June, Alnwick hosts its annual fair, featuring a costumed reenactment of a medieval fair, processions, a market, and concerts. Durham Regatta, England's oldest rowing event, also takes place in June.

DURHAM AND ITS ENVIRONS

Durham—the first major northeastern town on the main road up from London—is by far the region's most interesting historic city. Most of the other cities nearby are brash upstarts that made their fortunes during the Industrial Revolution and have since subsided into relative decline. Several cities, such as Darlington, birthplace of the modern railroad, do hold interesting relics of their 19th-century heyday. The land to the west, known as County Durham, toward the Pennine Hills, is far more scenic, and a daylong drive through the valleys of Teesdale and Weardale takes you past ruined castles, industrial heritage sites, isolated moorland villages, and tumbling waterfalls.

Durham

250 mi north of London, 15 mi south of Newcastle.

The great medieval city of Durham, seat of County Durham, is among the most dramatically sited in Britain. Despite the military advantages

Durham
Castle 2

Durham
Cathedral . . .1

Durham Light
Infantry
Museum 5

Framwellgate
Bridge 4

Prebends
Footbridge . . .3

University
of Durham
Oriental
Museum 6

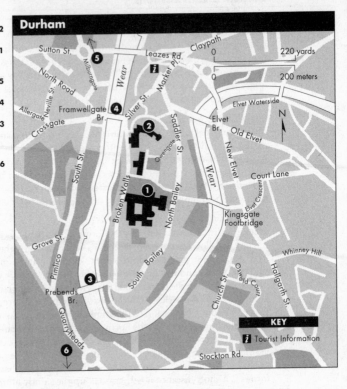

offered by the rocky spur on which it stands, Durham was founded surprisingly late, probably in about the year 1000, growing up around a small Saxon church erected to house the remains of St. Cuthbert. But it was the Normans, under William the Conqueror, who put Durham on the map, building the first defensive castle and beginning work on the cathedral. From here, Durham's prince-bishops, granted almost dictatorial local powers by William the Conqueror in 1072, kept the county on a tight rein, coining their own money, raising their own taxes, and maintaining their own laws and courts; not until 1836 were these rights finally restored to the English Crown. Together, the cathedral and castle stand high on a wooded peninsula almost entirely encircled by the River Wear (rhymes with "beer"). For centuries these two ancient structures have dominated Durham—now a thriving university town, the Northeast's equivalent to Oxford or Cambridge—and the surrounding countryside. Durham is more than its cathedral and castle, however. It's a great place to explore, with steep, narrow streets overlooked by perilously angled medieval houses and 18th-century town houses. The most attractive part of the city is near the Palace Green and along the banks of the river, where families go boating, anglers cast their lines, and strollers walk along the shaded paths.

★ ❶ Architectural historians come from all over the world to admire and study the Norman masterpiece that is **Durham Cathedral,** on the Palace Green in the heart of the city. The cathedral is an amazing vision of solidity and strength, a far cry from the airy lightness of later, Gothic cathedrals. It was begun about 1090, and the main body was finished in about 1150. Durham is the essence of an almost entirely Norman, or Romanesque, edifice: the round arches of the nave and the deep zigzag patterns carved into them are entirely typical of the heavy, gaunt style of Norman building. Yet if the style looks back rather than forward, the technology of Durham was quite revolutionary at the time. This was the first European cathedral to be given a stone, rather than a wooden, roof, and when you consider the means of construction available to its builders—the stones that form the ribs of the roof had to be hoisted up by hand and set on a wooden structure, which was then knocked away—the achievement seems staggering.

The origins of the cathedral go back to the 10th century. Monks fleeing a Viking raid on Lindisfarne Abbey in the year 875 brought the body of St. Cuthbert, a revered bishop of Lindisfarne, to this site in 995, and soon the wealth attracted by Cuthbert's shrine paid for the construction of a cathedral. The bishop's throne here is still the loftiest in medieval Christendom; his miter is the only one to be encircled by a coronet, and his coat of arms is the only one to be crossed with a sword as well as a crosier. **Cuthbert's shrine** lies surrounded by columns of local marble, with the saint's remains buried below a simple slab. A second unobtrusive tomb at the west end of the cathedral, in the so-called Galilee Chapel, is the final resting place of the **Venerable Bede**, the 8th-century Northumbrian monk whose contemporary account of the English people made him the country's first reliable historian. He died in Jarrow in 735, and his remains were placed in the cathedral a quarter century after Cuthbert's.

Upon entering, note the 12th-century bronze **Sanctuary Knocker,** shaped like the head of a ferocious mythological beast, mounted on the massive northwestern entrance door. By grasping the ring clenched in the animal's mouth, medieval felons could claim sanctuary; cathedral records show that 331 criminals (especially murderers) sought this protection between 1464 and 1524. The knocker now in place is, in fact, a replica; the original is kept for security in the cathedral treasury, along with ancient illuminated manuscripts, fragments of St. Cuthbert's oak coffin, and more church treasures. ⊠ *Palace Green,* ☎ *0191/386–4266,* WEB *www.dur.ac.uk/~dla0www/c_tour/cathedral. html.* ⌸ *Cathedral free but £2 donation welcome, treasury £2, tower £2, guided tours £2.50.* ☉ *Cathedral May–Sept., daily 7:15 AM–8 PM; Oct.–Apr., daily 7:15–6. Treasury Mon.–Sat. 10–4:30, Sun. 2–4:30. Choral evensong service Tues.–Fri. at 5:15, Sun. at 3:30. Guided tours June–Aug., Mon.–Sat. at 10:30 and 2.*

❷ **Durham Castle,** which faces the Cathedral across Palace Green, commands a strategic position above the River Wear. For almost 800 years this Norman castle was home to successive prince-bishops; from here, large tracts of northern England were ruled and the Scots kept at bay. Henry VIII first curtailed their independence, although it wasn't until the 19th century that the prince-bishops were finally reined in and had their powers annulled. They abandoned the castle, turning it over to University College, one of several colleges of the University of Durham, the oldest in England after Oxford and Cambridge. You can tour the castle, and during college vacations, very reasonably priced accommodations are available, both in the castle and in other college buildings throughout the city. For a quick and handy bite, head for the Almshouse Café, in a historic almshouse on Palace Green, between the cathedral and castle. ⊠ *Palace Green,* ☎ *0191/374–3800,* WEB *www. dur.ac.uk/~dla0www/c_tour/castle.html.* ⌸ *£3.* ☉ *Guided tours only: Easter wk and July–Sept., Mon.–Sat. 10–noon and 2–4; Oct.–June, Mon., Wed., and weekends 2–4.*

The **River Wear** winds through Durham, curving beneath the cathedral and castle, and playing host in mid-June each year to the Durham Regatta, Britain's oldest rowing event, which attracts 300 racing crews. A short stroll along the Wear's leafy banks is rewarded by delightful
❸ views, especially as you cross **Prebends Footbridge,** reached from

the southern end of Palace Green. J. M. W. Turner reveled in the view from here and painted a celebrated scene of Durham from the bridge. If you follow the far side of the Wear north from Prebends Footbridge, ❹ you can recross the river at **Framwellgate Bridge,** which dates originally from the 12th century. Many of the elegant town houses that line the narrow lanes back up to the cathedral now house departments of the University of Durham.

❺ The **Durham Light Infantry Museum,** ½ mi northwest of Durham city center on A691, is devoted to the history of the county regiment, exhibiting uniforms, weapons, and regalia alongside mementos of British campaigns in India, Iran, the Crimea, and Africa. ⊠ *Aykley Heads,* ☎ *0191/384–2214.* 🎟 *£2.50.* ⏱ *Tues.–Sat. 10–4 (winter), 10–5 (summer), Sun. 2–4 (winter), 2–5 (summer).*

❻ Fine art and craft work from all parts of Asia are on show at the **University of Durham Oriental Museum.** The collection of Chinese ceramics is particularly noted, and don't miss the nearby Botanic Gardens. ⊠ *Elvet Hill, off South Rd. (A1050),* ☎ *0191/374–7911,* 🌐 *www.dur.ac.uk/oriental.museum.* 🎟 *£1.50 (55p).*

Dining and Lodging

££   ✕ **Bistro 21.** Durham's most fashionable restaurant lies a couple of miles out of the center, in a superbly restored farmhouse at Aykley Heads. It's a relaxed spot with a seasonal and eclectic menu with brasserie classics, Asian favorites, and modern British treatments of traditional dishes are all offered at various times. ⊠ *Aykley Heads,* ☎ *0191/384–4354. AE, DC, MC, V. Closed Sun.*

£   ✕ **Vennel's Café.** This welcoming daytime café is named for the local word ("vennel"), which means the very narrowest of thoroughfares. Squeeze up the alley, order at the counter, and then, in good weather, sit outside in the courtyard. Soups, salads, hot dishes, and sandwiches are the mainstay, including several vegetarian options. ⊠ *Saddler's Yard, off Saddler St.,* ☎ *No phone. No credit cards. No dinner.*

£££–££££   ✕🏨 **Durham Marriott Hotel, Royal County.** This comfortable, attractively redecorated Georgian hotel retains many historic details. It's the city's top establishment, with a convenient downtown location and spacious rooms, some with four-poster beds. The oak staircase comes from Loch Leven castle in Scotland, where Mary, Queen of Scots, was imprisoned. The County Restaurant serves wild boar steaks and such traditional fare as Northumbrian broth and roast beef with Yorkshire pudding. ⊠ *Old Elvet, DH1 3JN,* ☎ *0191/386–6821,* FAX *0191/386–0704,* 🌐 *www.marriotthotels.com. 151 rooms. Restaurant, bar, coffee shop, indoor pool, sauna, health club. AE, DC, MC, V.*

££   🏨 **Georgian Town House.** Exactly as the name suggests, this well-sited hotel, at the top of a cobbled street overlooking the cathedral and castle, makes the best of its Georgian exterior and fittings. Some rooms have views of the cathedral; all are comfortable and make a good base for city walks. ⊠ *10 Crossgate, DH1 4PS,* ☎ FAX *0191/386–8070. 6 rooms. No credit cards. Closed last wk Dec.*

Nightlife and the Arts

Durham's nightlife is geared to the university set. The **Coach-and-Eight** (⊠ Bridge House, Framwellgate Bridge, ☎ 0191/386–3284) can get noisy with students, but outdoor seating makes it appealing. The **Hogshead** (⊠ 58 Saddler St., ☎ 0191/386–4134) pub is a true student haunt.

Durham Art Gallery at the Durham Light Infantry Museum is the city's most reliable arts venue, supporting a full program of exhibitions and concerts. ⊠ *Aykley Heads,* ☎ *0191/384–2214.* 🎟 *Charges vary according to event.* ⏱ *Tues.–Sat. 10–5, Sun. 2–5.*

Outdoor Activities and Sports

In Durham, **Brown's Boat House** (✉ Elvet Bridge, ☎ 0191/386–3779) rents rowboats and offers short cruises April–early November.

Shopping

Bramwells Jewellers (✉ 24 Elvet Bridge, ☎ 0191/386–8006) has its own store specialty, a pendant replica of the gold-and-silver cross of St. Cuthbert. **Waterstone's University Bookshop** (✉ 55 Saddler St., ☎ 0191/384–2095) has more than 25,000 volumes in stock.

Brancepeth

❼ *4 mi southwest of Durham on A690.*

Brancepeth was reconstructed early in the 19th century to resemble a traditional Tudor village, and its rows of well-preserved cottages have barely changed since. A flamboyantly restored castle (not open to the public) overlooks the whole ensemble. The real gem of this town was the genuine medieval **church of St. Brandon,** complete with an ornate rood screen. Unfortunately, this was gutted by fire in 1998. Money is being raised, but the church is unlikely to reopen for some time. Tombs in the church held assorted Nevilles, one of the most powerful northern families in feudal times, who owned the castle until 1569. WEB *www.brancepethchurch.org.*

En Route Upper Teesdale's elemental nature shows its most volatile aspect in the sprays of England's highest waterfall, the 72-ft **High Force.** From the roadside parking lot it's a 10-minute walk through woodland to the massive rocks over which the water tumbles; a precarious viewpoint puts you right above the falls, at their best in springtime, after a rain. A welcome pub, on the main road, serves bar meals, something of a boon in this otherwise isolated stretch of moorland road. ✉ *Off the B6277, 22 mi southwest of Brancepeth, 10 mi southeast of Ireshopeburn,* ☎ *01833/640209.* 🎫 *50p; parking £1.* ☉ *Mid-Apr.–Oct., daily 9:30–5; Nov.–mid-Apr., open but unattended.*

Romaldkirk

❽ *20 mi southwest of Durham, 7 mi southeast of High Force.*

Sporadic settlements punctuate the isolation of Teesdale, most notably the pretty village of Romaldkirk, whose extravagantly proportioned church is known as the "Cathedral of the Dale." The stocks for punishing wrongdoers still stand on the village green. The central **Rose and Crown** (☎ 01833/650213) is the very model of comfort—an 18th-century coaching inn with a roaring fire.

Barnard Castle

❾ *7 mi southeast of Romaldkirk, 25 mi southwest of Durham.*

Barnard Castle is a handsome market town. Its unusual butter-market hall (known locally as Market Cross), surmounted by a fire alarm bell, marks the junction of the streets Thorngate, Newgate, and Market Place, which are lined with stores, pubs, and cafés. In 1838 Charles Dickens stayed at the **King's Head Inn** here while researching his novel *Nicholas Nickleby,* which dealt with the abuse of children in local boarding schools. The local tourist office has a *Dickens Drive* leaflet of the places he visited in the area.

The substantial ruins of **Barnard Castle,** which gave its name to the town, cling to an aerie overlooking the River Tees. Inside, you can see parts of the 14th-century Great Hall and the cylindrical, 13th-century tower, built by the castle's original owners, the Anglo-Scottish Balliol family. ✉ *Off Galgate,* ☎ *01833/638212,* WEB *www.english-heritage. org.uk.* ≦ *£2.50.* ✆ *Apr.–Sept., daily 10–6; Oct., daily 10–4; Nov.– Mar., Wed.–Sun. 10–4; call ahead in winter.*

★ The **Bowes Museum,** a vast French-inspired château a little more than a mile west of the town center, was built between 1869 and 1885 to house the outstanding art and artifacts collection of philanthropists John and Josephine Bowes. There are paintings by Canaletto, El Greco, Goya, and Boucher, and one of the greatest collections of 18th-century French furniture in the world. Accessible archaeological displays chart the history of County Durham from the Ice Age to the end of the Roman period, and an entire gallery is taken up by 19th-century dollhouses, games, and models. Most extraordinary of all, though, is an 18th-century mechanical silver swan, which, when activated, catches and swallows a silver fish to the accompaniment of a haunting tune. *Up Newgate, follow signs from Barnard Castle town center,* ☎ *01833/690606,* WEB *www. bowesmuseum.org.uk.* ≦ *£4.* ✆ *Daily 11–5. Closed last wk Dec.*

Raby Castle

🔟 *6 mi northeast of Barnard Castle, 19 mi southwest of Durham.*

The stone battlements of handsome Raby Castle, once the seat of the powerful Nevilles and currently the home of the 11th Baron Barnard, stand amid 200 acres of a landscaped deer park. Charles Neville supported Mary, Queen of Scots, in an uprising against Elizabeth I in 1569; when the uprising failed, the estate was confiscated. Largely dating from the 14th century (and using stone plundered from Barnard Castle), the house displays luxuriously furnished rooms crammed with treasures, in addition to well-preserved medieval kitchens, with original Victorian copperware and other domestic equipment. Stone arcades hold five full-length portraits of Raby personages, including Richard III's mother, who died here. ✉ *A688, 1 mi north of Staindrop,* ☎ *01833/660202,* WEB *www.raby-castle.com.* ≦ *Castle £5; park, gardens, and coach house £3.* ✆ *Castle Apr.–June, Wed., Sun. 1–5; July–Sept., Sun.–Fri. 1–5. Parks and gardens mid-Apr.–June, Wed., Sun. 11–5:30; July–Sept., Sun.–Fri. 11–5:30.*

Bishop Auckland

⓫ *7 mi northeast of Raby Castle, 12 mi southwest of Durham.*

For 700 years, between the 12th and 19th centuries, the prince-bishops of Durham had their country residence in Auckland Castle, in the town of Bishop Auckland. When finally deprived of their powers in 1836, the bishops left Durham and made Bishop Auckland their official home. The grand episcopal palace of **Auckland Castle** that you see today dates mainly from the 16th century, although the limestone and marble chapel, with its dazzling stained-glass windows, was built in 1665 from the ruins of a 12th-century banqueting hall. Among the palace's treasures are paintings by the 17th-century Spanish artist Zurbarán of Jacob and his 12 sons. The unusual 18th-century "deer house" of adjoining Bishops Park testifies to at least one of the bishops' extracurricular interests. ✉ *Off Market Pl.,* ☎ *01388/601627,* WEB *www.auckland-castle.co.uk.* ≦ *£3.50.* ✆ *May–mid-July, Fri. and Sun. 2–5; mid-July–Aug., Sun–Fri. 2–5; Sept., Fri.–Sat. 2–5; park daily 7 AM–sunset.*

Darlington

⓬ *10 mi southeast of Raby Castle, 21 mi south of Durham.*

Still visibly rooted in its 19th-century industrial past, the town of Darlington rocketed to fame in 1825, when George Stephenson piloted his steam-powered *Locomotion* along newly laid tracks the few miles to nearby Stockton, thus kick-starting the railway age. First envisaged as a means of transporting coal from the local pits to the dockside, Stephenson's invention soon attracted paying passengers, and even though it barely traveled faster than 15 mph, the *Locomotion* was a palpable hit. The story of the coming of the railway is well told in the ★ **Darlington Railway Centre and Museum,** housed in the town's original railroad station, built in 1842 and now a (signposted) 20-minute walk outside of the town center. Here, you can inspect historic engines, including Stephenson's *Locomotion,* as well as photographs, documents, models, and all the other paraphernalia associated with a 19th-century station. ⊠ *North Road Station,* ☎ *01325/460532,* WEB *www.drcm. org.uk.* ☜ *£2.50.* ☼ *Feb.–Dec., daily 10–5.*

Dining and Lodging

£££ ✕🏨 **George Hotel.** This sprawling 18th-century coaching inn lies 6 mi west of Darlington in tiny Piercebridge. Beautifully located on the banks of the River Tees, across from the scant remains of a Roman fort, some rooms and the restaurant look out across the gardens and water. Ask for a room with a balcony overlooking the river when booking. Local walks along the river may reveal sightings of kingfishers and herons, and once you've worked up an appetite you can sate it easily. There's a substantial bar menu (with riverside tables for summer dining), or you can order traditional meals and roasts in the more formal restaurant. ⊠ *Piercebridge-on-Tees, Darlington DL2 3SW,* ☎ *01325/374576,* FAX *01325/ 374577. 35 rooms. Restaurant, 2 bars. MC, V.*

Middlesbrough

⑬ *12 mi east of Darlington, 22 mi southeast of Durham.*

In 1802 a mere dozen people lived in Middlesbrough, near the mouth of the River Tees. With the discovery of iron ore, however, it became a boomtown, with steel mills and, later, chemical industries, doing much to boost the economy, although blighting part of the town. The industrial heritage has created a few unique local attractions.

Middlesbrough's unusual **Transporter Bridge,** built in 1911, is the largest of its kind in the world, a vast structure like a giant's Erector-set model, whose gantry system still takes 12 cable cars, holding 200 passengers each, across the river every 20 minutes. A special viewing platform stands on the south bank. Upstream you'll find Newport Bridge, the world's largest lift span bridge, another remarkable sight, but only open if weather permits. ☎ *01642/247563. Crossing time 2 mins.* ☜ *Pedestrians 30p, cars 80p.* ☼ *Mon.–Sat. 5 AM–11 PM, Sun. 2–11.*

The life and times of Captain James Cook (1728–79), the celebrated circumnavigator and explorer, are vividly depicted in the **Captain Cook Birthplace Museum,** in the Middlesbrough suburb of Marton. You can walk through Stewart Park to the modern museum building. Interactive displays, exhibits, and informative films cover Cook's remarkable voyages to Australia, New Zealand, Canada, Antarctica, and Hawaii, where he met an untimely death. On the weekend closest to October 27, Cook's birthday, the museum hosts a celebration. ⊠ *Stewart Park, Marton, Off A174, south of city center,* ☎ *01642/311211.* ☜ *£2.40.* ☼ *June–Sept., Tues.–Sun. 10–5:30; Oct.–May, Tues.–Sun. 9–4.*

Dining

£–££ ✕ **Purple Onion.** An unexpected treat, the Purple Onion is as idiosyncratic as its name, lavishly decorated in a kind of antiques-store style and serving a spirited modern menu. You can have gourmet sandwiches at lunch, and in the evening, fine salads, oven-roasted fish, noodles, and the house specialty, *cioppino di mare*—an American-Italian–inspired fish stew (served for two people), bursting with shellfish, fish, and a rich tomato sauce. ✉ *80 Corporation Rd.*, ☎ *01642/222250. MC, V.*

Washington

⑭ *34 mi northwest of Middlesbrough, 12 mi north of Durham.*

Washington is a planned "new town" divided into numbered districts; it holds a link to the history of the United States. **Washington Old Hall** is the ancestral home of the first U.S. president. George Washington's direct forebears, the de Wessyngtons, lived here between 1183 and 1288. Other members of the family continued to live in the house until 1613, when the present property was rebuilt. Now owned by the National Trust, the mansion retains a decidedly Jacobean (17th-century) appearance, most noticeably in the fine wood paneling of the rooms, the heavy furniture, and the small formal garden that surrounds the house. On the Fourth of July, there are special celebrations and admission is free. ✉ *From A1(M), 5 mi west of Sunderland, follow signs to Washington New Town, District 4, and then on to Washington Village,* ☎ *0191/416–6879,* WEB *www.washington.co.uk/oldhall.* ✑ *£2.75.* ☉ *Mid-Apr.–Oct., Sun.–Wed. 11–5 (last admission 4:30).*

Beamish Open-Air Museum

★ **⑮** *9 mi north of Durham, 3 mi west of Chester-le-Street.*

You'll need to set aside at least a half day to enjoy the 260-acre Beamish Open-Air Museum, which holds historic buildings that have been brought here from throughout the region. A streetcar will take you across a reconstructed 1920s High Street, including a dentist's operating room, a pub, and a grocery. A stableman will talk to you about the Clydesdale workhorses in his care, once used to draw brewery wagons. On the farm you can see such local breeds as Durham Shorthorn cattle and Teeswater sheep. Other attractions include a railroad station, a coal mine, and a transportation collection. The large gift store specializes in period souvenirs and locally made crafts. Winter visits are centered on the reconstructed town only, and admission prices are reduced accordingly. ✉ *Off A693, between Chester-le-Street and Stanley,* ☎ *01207/231811,* WEB *www.beamish.org.uk.* ✑ *£12 or £4 (depending on season).* ☉ *Apr.–mid-July and Sept.–Oct., daily 10–5; mid-July–Aug., daily 10–6; Nov.–Mar., Tues.–Thurs. and weekends 10–4. Closed last 2 wks Dec.*

Dining and Lodging

££££ ✕▤ **Lumley Castle Hotel.** This is a real castle, right down to the dungeons, and a hotel experience not to be missed. Lumley has superb bedrooms in all sizes (some with four-poster beds and/or whirlpool tubs) combined with up-to-date facilities—you'll pay a premium to be inside the castle itself, rather than the courtyard annex. There's plenty of space to wander and an appealing library-bar, with more than 3,000 books and a log fire, for before-dinner drinks. The Black Knight Restaurant serves English specialties such as Northumbrian broth, tournedos of beef (prime roast beef with Stilton cheese, wrapped in bacon), and braised hock of lamb studded with garlic and rosemary. The hotel is east of town via the B1284. ✉ *Chester-le-Street DH3 4NX,* ☎ *0191/389–1111,* FAX *0191/387–1437,* WEB *www.lumleycastle.com. 60 rooms. Restaurant, bar. AE, DC, MC, V.*

Newcastle upon Tyne

16 *16 mi north of Durham.*

Durham may have the glories of its castle, cathedral, and university, but the main and liveliest city of the Northeast is Newcastle. Settled since Roman times, it made its fortune twice, first by exporting coal in the Elizabethan age and then by building ships. As a 19th-century industrial center, it had few equals in Britain, showing off its wealth in a series of grand Victorian buildings lining the sweeping, central Neo-classic streets. Many of these still remain (particularly on Grey Street), and despite years of industrial decline, the city retains a vitality that is hard to ignore. Much of the recent regeneration has been down on the historic quayside, where surviving 17th-century houses stand alongside warehouses converted into restaurants and bars. The new Baltic Contemporary Art Centre is another sign of Newcastle's strength. By the old quayside is the very symbol of the city, the celebrated **Tyne Bridge** (1929), one of a half-dozen bridges spanning the river in the city, whose elegant proportions were later reproduced by the architects responsible for Sydney's Harbour Bridge.

Overlooking the Tyne River, the remains of the **Norman castle** remind you of the city's earlier status as a defensive stronghold. This was the "new castle," originally built in 1080, that gave the city its name. ⊠ *St. Nicholas St.,* ☎ *0191/232-7938.* ⊡ *£1.50.* ☉ *Apr.–Sept., Tues.–Sun. 9:30–5; Oct.–Mar., Tues.–Sun. 9:30–4.*

The finest art gallery in the Northeast, the **Laing Gallery** merits at least an hour's visit. British art is well represented, and some of the most extraordinary paintings are those by 19th-century local artist John Martin, who produced biblical landscapes of dramatic intensity. The Pre-Raphaelites are on show, too, and the gallery offers a display called Art on Tyneside, which traces 400 years of local arts, highlighting glassware, pottery, and engraving. ⊠ *Higham Pl. near John Dobson St.,* ☎ *0191/232-7734.* ⊡ *Free.* ☉ *Mon.–Sat. 10–5, Sun. 2–5.*

The buildings of the **University of Newcastle upon Tyne** house the city's best museums. Here you'll find the **Museum of Antiquities,** showing finds from Hadrian's Wall, as well as the interesting **Shefton Museum of Greek Art and Archaeology** of the Department of Classics, containing ancient arms, ceramics, and terra-cotta pieces, which is open by appointment. ⊠ *The University,* ☎ *0191/222-7966,* WEB *museums.ncl. ac.uk/archive.* ⊡ *Free.* ☉ *Museum of Antiquities Mon.–Sat. 10–5; Shefton Museum weekdays 10–4.*

At Life Interactive World at the ☾ **International Centre for Life,** one of Britain's Millennium Projects, three high-tech shows and 60 exhibits bring science to life, from the latest research on genes to the workings of the brain. There's also a virtual reality arcade. ⊠ *Times Sq.,* ☎ *0870/ 444–3364,* WEB *www.centreforlife.co.uk.* ⊡ *£6.50.* ☉ *Daily 10–5.*

The **Segedunum Archaeological Park and Museum** includes the remains of the substantial Roman fort of Segedunum, built around AD 125 as an eastern extension to Hadrian's Wall; remains of part of the wall as well as a reconstructed section; and a working, reconstructed Roman bath. Site excavations began after Victorian housing was demolished in the 1970s. A museum interprets finds from the area, and an observation tower provides views of the site. ⊠ *Wallsend,* ☎ *0191/295-5757.* ⊡ *£3.* ☉ *Apr.–Aug., daily 10–5; Sept.–Mar., daily 10–3:30.*

Dining and Lodging

£–££ ✕ **Metropolitan.** What was once the city's impressive Bank of England building in the heart of the city now bustles with diners munching on rack of lamb, fish cakes, seared salmon, sausages and mash, and the like. Sandwiches, *moules-frites* (fried mussels), and other light dishes are served all day. If you've never tasted the famous local ale, try the "Newcastle Brown Ale ice cream." ☒ *35 Grey St.,* ☏ *0191/230–2306. AE, DC, MC, V. Closed Sun.*

£ ✕ **Crown Posada.** Adorned with Pre-Raphaelite stained glass, a coffered ceiling, and Victorian lamps, this classic Newcastle pub, near the quayside, wears its 19th-century decor well. ☒ *31 The Side,* ☏ *0191/232–1269. No credit cards.*

££££ 🔛 **Vermont Hotel.** The former County Hall, in the city center next to the castle, is now a luxurious hotel with views of the river and the city's famous bridges. Guest rooms are large and full of amenitites. The Vermont has an all-day brasserie and a more sedate French restaurant, the Blue Room, known for its fish. The railroad station is nearby. ☒ *Castle Garth, NE1 1RQ,* ☏ *0191/233–1010,* 📠 *0191/233–1234. 101 rooms. Restaurant, 5 bars, brasserie, minibars, gym, meeting rooms. AE, DC, MC.*

£££ 🔛 **Malmaison.** One of a glamorous, design-conscious chain, the Malmaison was converted from an old riverside warehouse and takes advantage of some amazing views over the River Tyne and its famous bridges. Rooms are spacious and modern; each contains a CD player. The Brasserie & Bar presents French fare in a setting that overlooks the river through arched windows. At Le Petit Spa you can schedule aromatherapy, relaxation, and beauty treatments. ☒ *Quayside, NE1 3DX,* ☏ *0191/245–5000,* 📠 *0191/245–4545,* 🌐 *www.malmaison. com. 116 rooms. Restaurant, bar, spa, gym. AE, DC, MC, V.*

Nightlife and the Arts

The **Theatre Royal** (☒ Grey St., ☏ 0191/232–2061) is the region's most established theater, with a variety of high-quality productions.

Shopping

Blackfriars Craft Centre (☒ Friars Green, Stowell St., ☏ No phone), in a wonderful medieval friary in the heart of Newcastle's traditional guilds district, is full of little outlets selling local crafts such as textiles and wrought ironwork.

Jarrow

🔟 *4 mi east of Newcastle.*

The name "Jarrow" is to British ears linked to the "Jarrow Crusade," a protest march to London led by unemployed former workers from the town's steelworks and shipyards in the depths of the 1930s. Travelers are attracted here, however, by its much more ancient history.

Bede's World and St. Paul's Church hold substantial monastic ruins, a visitor center–museum, and the church of St. Paul, all reflecting the long tradition of religion and learning that began here in AD 681, when the first Saxon church was established on the site. The Venerable Bede, deemed to be England's earliest historian, was a scholar here and in AD 731 completed his *History of the English Church and People* while ensconced at the monastery. The museum explores the development of Northumbria, using excerpts from Bede's work as well as archaeological finds and reconstructions. You can gain a sense of medieval life from the reconstructed farm buildings erected on the 11-acre Anglo-Saxon farm, and you can get close to rare animals such as Dexter cattle and Iron Age pigs. Still used for regular worship, St. Paul's contains some of the oldest stained glass in Europe and the oldest dedicatory church inscription in Britain (a carved stone inscribed in AD 685). ✉ *Church Bank; from southern exit traffic circle at South Tyne tunnel, take A185 to South Shields, then follow signs to St. Paul's Church and Jarrow Hall.* ☎ *0191/489–2106,* WEB *www.bedesworld.co.uk.* ✄ *£3.* ☉ *Apr.–Oct., Tues.–Sat. 10–5:30, Sun. noon–5; Nov.–Mar., Tues.–Sat. 10–4:30, Sun. 12:30–4:30.*

Wylam

⑱ *8 mi west of Jarrow, 4 mi west of Newcastle.*

Wylam, now a wooded suburb of Newcastle upon Tyne, holds a piece of industrial history. A tiny, red-roof stone cottage, **George Stephenson's Birthplace** is where, in 1781, the "Father of the Railroads" was born. The small house was shared—not unusual for the time—by four families. The Stephensons lived in just one room and it's this room that is open to the public, a modest tribute to an engineer whose invention of the steam locomotive touched every corner of the world. Informative guided tours bring the house to life, and refreshments are served in the garden; you can park your car in the village by the war memorial, a 10-minute walk away. ✉ *Wylam, 1½ mi south of A69,* ☎ *01661/853457.* ✄ *£1.* ☉ *Mid-Apr.–Oct., Thurs. and weekends 1–5.*

HADRIAN'S WALL COUNTRY

A formidable line of Roman fortifications, Hadrian's Wall was constructed in response to repeated barbarian invasions from Scotland. The land through which the wall marches is wild and inhospitable in places, but that seems only to add to the hauntingly powerful sense of history the wall evokes. Sites, museums, and information center along the wall make it possible to learn as much as you want about the Roman era, or you can simply reflect on the evidence of vanished power.

Hadrian's Wall

★ *73 mi from Wallsend, north of Newcastle, to Bowness-on-Solway, beyond Carlisle.*

Dedicated to the Roman god Terminus, the massive span of Hadrian's Wall once marked the northern frontier of the Roman Empire. The most significant reminder of the Roman presence in Britain extends 73 mi from Wallsend ("Wall's End") north of Newcastle, in the east, to Bowness-on-Solway beyond Carlisle, in the west, and was completed in just four years—which gives a pretty good idea of Roman determination. Its construction bears all the hallmarks of Roman efficiency. The wall stretches across the narrowest part of the country and is built following as straight a path as possible.

For more than 250 years the Roman army used the wall to control travel and trade and to fortify Roman Britain against the barbarians to the north. At Emperor Hadrian's command, three legions of soldiers began building the wall in AD 122. Around AD 200 Emperor Severus had the wall repaired and rebuilt. During the Roman era, the wall stood 15 ft high and 9 ft thick; behind it lay the vallum, a ditch about 20 ft wide and 10 ft deep. Spaced at 5-mi intervals along the wall were 3- to 5-acre forts (such as those at Housesteads and Chesters), which could hold 500 to 1,000 soldiers. Every mile was marked by a thick-walled milecastle (a smaller fort that housed about 30 soldiers), and between each milecastle were two smaller turrets, each lodging four men who kept watch from the tower's upper chamber.

During the Jacobite Rebellion of 1745, the English dismantled much of the Roman wall and used its stone to pave the new Military Road (now B6318). The most substantial stretches of the remaining wall are between Housesteads and Birdoswald. Running through the southern edge of Northumberland National Park and along the sheer escarpment of Whin Sill, this section is also an area of dramatic natural beauty. The ancient ruins, rugged cliffs, dramatic vistas, and spreading pastures make it a good area for hiking.

Today, excavating, documenting, interpreting, repairing, displaying, and generally managing the Roman remains is a Northumbrian growth industry. At the forts, notably at Chesters, Housesteads (the best-preserved fort), Vindolanda, and at the Roman Army Museum near Greenhead, you can browse and get a good introduction to the life led by Roman soldiers on the frontier. Special events in summer put more flesh on the archaeological bones: most of the sites sponsor talks, Roman drama, festivals, and even discussions of battle tactics; local tourist offices, or the sites themselves, have details. It is also possible to walk along sections of the wall, but this can be very hard going, and once you are committed to it it's not always possible to get off and step back onto the road (exits and entrances are few and far between). A special Hadrian's Wall Bus between Hexham and Carlisle operates in summer, stopping at all the major sites. For photographers, one spot in particular produces a memorable souvenir: looking east toward the fort of Housesteads from Cuddy's Crag, the wall can be seen snaking up and down across the wild countryside.

Outdoor Activities and Sports

Plans call for completion of a footpath along the entire course of Hadrian's Wall by summer 2002, but before this time only certain sections are accessible to hikers. Best is the 12-mi western stretch between Sewingshields (east of Housesteads) and Greenhead. It's rugged country, unsuited to the inexperienced hiker, and most trekkers choose to walk short stretches in the vicinity of the various visitor centers. There are also riding schools in the region, offering hour-long rides to full-day treks on horseback. For a full list, contact the Hexham tourist information office; advance booking in summer is essential.

Hexham

⑲ *22 mi west of Newcastle, 31 mi northwest of Durham.*

The historic market town of Hexham makes the best base for visiting Hadrian's Wall. It's just a few miles from the most significant remains and retains enough of interest in its medieval streets to warrant a stop in its own right. First settled in the 7th century, around a Benedictine monastery, Hexham later became a byword for monastic learning, famous for its book painting, sculpture, and liturgical singing.

★ Ancient **Hexham Abbey,** a tranquil place of Christian worship for more than 1,300 years, forms one side of the town's main square. Inside, you can climb the 35 worn stone "night stairs," which once led from the main part of the abbey to the canon's dormitory, to overlook the whole ensemble. Most of the present building dates from the 12th century, and much of the stone was taken from the Roman fort at Corstopitum a few miles northeast. ⊠ *Beaumont St.,* ☎ *01434/602031.* ✉ *Free; suggested donation £2.* ☉ *June–Sept., daily 9–7; Oct.–May, daily 9–5. No tours during services.*

Hexham's central **Market Place** has been the site since 1239 of a weekly market, held each Tuesday. Crowded stalls are set out under the long slate roof of the Shambles; other stalls take their chances with the weather, protected only by their bright awnings.

Dating from 1330, Hexham's original jail, the Manor Office across Market Place from the abbey, houses the **Border History Museum.** Photographs, models, a reconstructed blacksmith's shop, a Border house interior, armor, and weapons help tell the story of the "Middle March," the medieval administrative area governed by a warden and centered on Hexham. ⊠ *The Old Gaol, Hallgate,* ☎ *01434/652351.* £2. ☉ *Mid-Apr.–Oct., Mon.–Sat. 10–4:30; Nov. and Feb.–mid-Apr., Sat.–Tues. 10–4:30.*

Dining and Lodging

£ ✕ **Black House.** A mile south of central Hexham, this converted farm building, fitted with lots of old furniture and attractive china, is a great place for morning coffee, lunch, or afternoon tea. Home-cooked dishes are chalked up on the blackboard and allow you to choose anything from a bowl of soup to a three-course meal. And the lovely walk back to town will soon burn off the calories. ⊠ *Dipton Mill Rd.,* ☎ *01434/604744. No credit cards. No dinner. Closed Mon. mid-Apr.–Sept., Mon.–Wed. Oct.–mid-Apr.*

£££ ✕ ⊡ **Langley Castle Hotel.** This 14th-century castle was rescued by its American owner and converted into a luxury hotel and restaurant. Its 7-ft-thick walls are complete with turrets and battlements. All public rooms are grandly furnished, and the bedrooms have luxurious appointments; one has a private sauna, another a four-poster bed, another a fireplace, and so on. There's a premium on rooms actually inside the castle—worth paying—rather than in the "castle view" annex. The restaurant (dinner and Sunday lunch only) has exposed beams and wall tapestries. Sea bass in smoked salmon and duckling with scallops and wild mushrooms are typical main courses. ⊠ *Langley-on-Tyne, 6 mi west of Hexham, NE47 5LU,* ☎ *01434/688888,* 📠 *01434/684019,* 🌐 *www.langleycastle.com. 18 rooms. Restaurant. AE, DC, MC, V.*

£££ ✕ ⊡ **Lord Crewe Arms Hotel.** A historic hotel that once provided guest accommodations for Blanchland Abbey, this unusual place in the tiny stone village of Blanchland has lots of intriguing medieval and Gothic corners, including a priest's hideout and a vault-roofed crypt with its own bar. The bedrooms are solidly furnished with antique wood and oak-beam ceilings; one is said to be haunted by the ghost of a local girl. The restaurant's decor reinforces an atmosphere of cloistered calm. You can try dishes such as roast local pheasant or breast of duck with port wine sauce. ⊠ *Blanchland, off B6306, about 8 mi south of Hexham, DH8 9SP,* ☎ *01434/675251,* 📠 *01434/675337. 19 rooms. Restaurant, bar. AE, DC, MC, V.*

Nightlife and the Arts

Hexham is home to one of the Northeast's most adventurous arts venues, the **Queen's Hall Arts Centre,** which offers drama, dance, and exhibition space for local artists. It also sponsors local events, like the annual Jazz Festival (June), which sees dozens of concerts spread over a single weekend. ⊠ *Beaumont St.,* ☎ *01434/607272.* Free. ☉ *Galleries and box office Mon.–Sat. 9:30–5:30.*

Greenhead

20 *18 mi west of Hexham, 49 mi northwest of Durham.*

Tiny Greenhead has an informative Wall site. The **Roman Army Museum,** at the garrison fort of Carvoran, near the village, makes an excellent introduction to Hadrian's Wall. Full-size models and excavations bring to life this remote outpost of the empire; you can even inspect authentic Roman graffiti on the walls of an excavated barracks. The gift store stocks, among other unusual items, Roman rulers (1 ft = 11.6 inches) and Roman cookbooks. Opposite the museum, at Walltown Crags on the Pennine Way (a long-distance hiking route), are 400 yards of the best-preserved section of the wall. ⊠ *1 mi northeast of Greenhead, off B6318,* ☎ *016977/474857,* [WEB] *www.vindolanda.com.* ▨ *£3, joint admission ticket with Vindolanda £5.60.* ☉ *May–Aug., daily 10–6; Apr. and Sept., daily 10–5:30; Mar. and Oct., daily 10–5; 2nd half Feb. and 1st half Nov., daily 10–4.*

Lodging

£   ⌂ **Holmhead Guest House.** This former farmhouse in open country-side is not only built *on* Hadrian's Wall but also *of* it. It has stone arches, exposed beams, and antique furnishings; there's open countryside in front and a ruined castle almost in the backyard. In addition to "the longest breakfast menu in the world," a set dinner (£18) is served (for guests only) at the farmhouse table in the stone-arched dining room, and ingredients for all three courses are likely to have been growing in the kitchen garden. On call is Mrs. Pauline Staff, a qualified guide who can give talks and slide shows on Hadrian's Wall and the area. ⊠ *Off A69, about 18 mi west of Hexham, CA6 7HY,* ☎ FAX *016977/ 474027. 4 rooms. Dining room. No smoking. MC, V.*

Vindolanda

㉑   *10 mi west of Hexham, 41 mi northwest of Durham.*

The great garrison fort of Vindolanda holds the remains of eight successive Roman forts and civilian settlements, which have provided much information about daily life in a military compound. Most of the visible remains date from the 2nd and 3rd centuries AD, and excavations are always going on here. A section of the wall has been reconstructed, and private houses, the main gate, and administrative buildings are easily made out. Recorded information interprets the site, and the museum contains leather, wood, glass, and pottery exhibits. There's even a reconstructed Roman kitchen. ⊠ *Near Bardon Mill,* ☎ *01434/344277,* [WEB] *www.vindolanda.com.* ▨ *£3.80; joint ticket with Roman Army Museum £5.60.* ☉ *May–Aug., daily 10–6; Apr. and Sept., daily 10–5:30; Mar. and Oct., daily 10–5; 2nd half Feb. and 1st half Nov., daily 10–4; last admission ½ hr before closing.*

Call in at **Once Brewed National Park Visitor Centre,** ½ mi north of Vindolanda, which provides informative displays about the central section of Hadrian's Wall and can advise about local walks. ⊠ *On B6318,* ☎ *01434/344396.* ▨ *Free.* ☉ *Mar. and Apr., daily 10–5; May–Oct., daily 10–6.*

Housesteads Roman Fort

★ ㉒   *7 mi west of Hexham, 38 mi northwest of Durham.*

If you have time to visit only one Hadrian's Wall site, Housesteads Roman Fort is your best bet. It includes an interpretive center, views of long sections of the wall, the excavated 5-acre fort itself, and a museum. It's a steep, 10-minute walk up from the parking lot by B6318 to the site, but it's worth the effort, especially for the view of the wall disappearing over hills and crags into the distance. The excavations reveal granaries, gateways, barracks, and the commandant's house. ⊠ *3 mi northeast of Bardon Mill,* ☎ *01434/344363.* ▨ *£2.80.* ☉ *Apr.– Sept., daily 10–6; Oct.–Mar., daily 10–4.*

Chesters Roman Fort

㉓ *4 mi north of Hexham, 35 mi northwest of Durham.*

Chesters Roman Fort, "Cilurnum," in a wooded valley on the banks of the North Tyne River, protected the point where the wall crossed the river. You approach it directly from the parking lot, and, although the site cannot compete with Housesteads in setting, it does hold a fascinating collection of Roman artifacts, including statues of river and water gods, altars, milestones, iron tools, weapons, and handcuffs. The military bathhouse near the river is the best-preserved example in Britain. ⊠ *B6318, ½ mi southwest of Chollerford,* ☎ *01434/681379.* ☞ *£2.80.* ☉ *Apr.–Sept., daily 10–6; Oct.–Mar., daily 10–4.*

Corbridge and Corstopitum

㉔ *19 mi west of Newcastle, 29 mi northwest of Durham.*

Corbridge is a small town of honey-color stone houses and riverside walks, a prosperous-looking place with an abundance of welcoming pubs and attractive shops. In the churchyard of St. Andrew's Church by Market Place is the **Vicar's Pele.** Nearly 700 years old, this fortified tower was a refuge from Scottish raiders and was built from stones taken from Corstopitum.

The ancient Roman garrison site of **Corstopitum** was occupied longer than any other fort on Hadrian's Wall. In fact, these ruins predate the wall by 40 years. Strategically positioned at the junction of the east–west and north–south Roman routes—Stanegate ran west to Carlisle, Dere Street led north to Scotland and south to London—the fort now contains a museum rich in artifacts. Rent a headset and tape, and stroll past the remains of two giant granaries, as well as temples, houses, and garrison buildings. On a cold day, it's all too easy to agree with Tacitus, who thought it a "wretched climate." The soldiers, who received their pay from a strongbox housed in an underground chamber (still visible today), earned every penny. ⊠ *On a signposted back road ½ mi northwest of Corbridge,* ☎ *01434/632349.* ☞ *£2.80.* ☉ *Apr.–Sept., daily 10–6; Oct., daily 10–5; Nov.–Mar., Wed.–Sun. 10–4.*

Kielder Water

㉕ *22 mi northwest of Hexham, 53 mi northwest of Durham.*

In the rugged hills on the western edge of Northumberland National Park, about 3 mi from the Scottish border, lies Kielder Water, northern Europe's largest man-made lake, surrounded by Europe's largest planted forest. It's a beautiful spot, crisscrossed by hiking paths, a 10-mi riding trail, and mountain-bike trails, and with a host of water-sports possibilities at **Leaplish Waterside Park.** Fishing is popular, too, and the upper part of the reservoir, designated a conservation area, attracts many bird-watchers.

The **Tower Knowe Visitor Centre,** at the southeast corner of Kielder Water, is a springboard from which to explore not only the lake area but also the vast **Kielder Forest.** Exhibits and films illustrate the region's wildlife and natural history, and guided forest walks are offered in summer. A **cruise service** (☎ 01434/240398) operates from the center mid-April–October; the one-hour boat trip costs £4. ☎ *01434/240398,* ☐WEB☐ *www. kielder.org.* ☉ *Apr.–Oct., daily 10–5; Nov.–Mar., daily 10–4.*

Now a Forestry Commission visitor center, complete with exhibitions and a tearoom, **Kielder Castle,** at the northwest corner of Kielder Water, was once a shooting lodge belonging to the duke of Northumberland. It's also the start of a 12-mi toll road that heads deep into the Kielder Forest to the north and meets A68 south of Carter Bar close to the Scottish border. Signposted footpaths provide good forest walks, too. ☎ *01434/250209.* ⊙ *Daily 10–5.*

Outdoor Activities and Sports

You can rent mountain bikes at **Kielder Castle** (☎ 01434/250392). Water sports, including water skiing, and mountain biking are the focus at **Leaplish Waterside Park** (☎ 01434/250312), open all year; you can also use the indoor pool and sauna.

Wallington House

26 *18 mi east of Kielder Water, 15 mi northeast of Hexham, 19 mi northwest of Newcastle.*

Wallington House, a striking 17th-century mansion with Victorian decoration, stands in the midst of an extensive, sparsely populated agricultural region at the village of Cambo. Besides the house, with its fine plasterwork, furniture, porcelain, and dollhouse collection, the walled, terraced garden is a major attraction. In summer, productions of Shakespeare and concerts are held on the grounds, which include 100 acres of woodlands and lakes. ✉ *B6342, Cambo,* ☎ *01670/774283,* WEB *www.nationaltrust.org.uk.* ✒ *House £5.50, garden and grounds only £4.* ⊙ *House Apr.–Oct., Wed.–Mon. 1–5:30; walled garden Apr.–Oct., daily 10:30–dusk; walled garden Nov.–Mar., daily 10–4.*

Rothbury

27 *10 mi north of Wallington House, 25 mi northeast of Hexham, 9 mi southwest of Alnwick.*

The small market town of Rothbury, in the heart of some stunning countryside, developed as a Victorian resort, attracting the gentry who roamed its hills and glades. Buildings from the era survive in the handsome center, although like all such towns, the sheer weight of modern traffic has blunted its appeal. This is still very much a walking destination, and routes through the local Simonside Hills can be discussed with the helpful staff at the **Northumberland National Park Visitor Centre** (✉ Church St., ☎ 01669/620887, WEB www.nnpa.org.uk).

★   The extraordinary Victorian mansion of **Cragside** was built between 1864 and 1895 by the first Lord Armstrong, an early electrical engineer. Designed by Richard Norman Shaw, a well-regarded late Victorian architect, it is a must-see for anyone interested in the glorious age of the Victorian country house. In a forested mountainside, the Tudor-style structure was the first house to be lit by hydroelectricity. In the library you can see antique vases adapted for use as electric lamps; staircase banisters are topped with specially designed lights. In all, 30 rooms of the house, some with Pre-Raphaelite paintings, and one with a mock-Renaissance marble chimneypiece, are open to the public. An energy center, with restored mid-Victorian machinery, including a hydraulic pump and a water turbine, has been established on the grounds. In June, rhododendrons bloom in the 660-acre park surrounding the mansion. ✉ *Off A697 and B6341, 1 mi north of Rothbury,* ☎ *01669/620333,* WEB *www.nationaltrust.org.uk.* ✒ *House £6.70, country park £4.20.* ⊙ *House mid-Apr.–Oct., Tues.–Sun. 1–5:30. Country park and energy center mid-Apr.–Oct., Tues.–Sun. 10:30–7 or dusk.*

Dining and Lodging

££   ✕▤ **Embleton Hall.** The five acres of beautiful grounds are reason enough to stay in this stone country mansion, parts of which date back to 1730. Its individually furnished rooms are decorated with lovely antiques and original paintings. Another reason to visit is the restaurant (open for dinner only); the chintz draperies and cut-glass chandeliers are perfect accompaniments to traditional English dishes such as roast guinea fowl in a game and port wine sauce or Brie-stuffed chicken. A simple bar-meal lunch is available midday. ⊠ *On A697, 5 mi east of Rothbury, Longframlington, NE65 8DT,* ☎ *01665/570249,* ᴀᴋ *01665/ 570056. 13 rooms. Restaurant, bar. AE, DC, MC, V.*

£ ✕⊓ **Queen's Head Hotel.** This cheery inn in the heart of Rothbury has pleasant, straightforward rooms with an old-fashioned touch. The first-floor dining room serves traditional English dishes, with an emphasis on seafood and a number of vegetarian options. ⊠ *Rothbury NE65 7SR,* ☎ *01669/620470. 9 rooms, 3 with bath. Restaurant, bar. MC, V.*

THE FAR NORTHEAST COAST

Before England gives way to Scotland, the final 40 mi of the Northeast coast, lined with extraordinary medieval fortresses and monasteries, is considered by many the best stretch anywhere on the North Sea. Northumbria was an enclave where the flame of learning was kept alive during Europe's "Dark Ages," most notably at Lindisfarne, the "Holy Island of saints and scholars." Castles abound, including the spectacularly sited one at Bamburgh and the desolate ruins of that at Dunstanburgh. The region also has some magnificent broad beaches. Only on rare summer days is swimming at all advisable, but the opportunities for walking are tremendous. The 3-mi walk from Bamburgh to Seahouses gives splendid views over to the Farne Islands, and the 2-mi hike from Craster to Dunstanburgh Castle is unforgettable.

Alnwick

❷❽ *30 mi north of Newcastle, 46 mi north of Durham.*

Alnwick (pronounced *ann*-ick) is the best base from which to explore the dramatic coast and countryside of northern Northumberland. Once a county seat, the town is dominated by its vast castle, but there is plenty more to see. A weekly open-air market (every Saturday) has been held in Alnwick's cobbled **Market Place** for more than 800 years. Note the market cross, built on the base of an older cross; the town crier once made his proclamations from here. Starting on the last Sunday in June, this site is host to the annual weeklong **Alnwick Fair,** a festival noteworthy for the enthusiastic participation of the locals colorfully decked out in medieval costume (⊠ Alnwick Fair, Box 2, Alnwick NE66 1AY, ☎ 01665/605004).

★ **Alnwick Castle,** on the edge of the town center, is still the home of the dukes of Northumberland, whose family (the regal Percys) dominated the Northeast for centuries. Many things about this castle are on a grand scale, earning it the epithet "the Windsor of the North." It has been remodeled on several occasions since the first occupant, Henry de Percy, first adapted the original Norman keep. The 18th century saw its greatest changes, when the grounds were landscaped by Capability Brown; a major garden renovation will be completed in late 2002. In contrast with the cold, formidable exterior, the inside of the building has all the opulence of the palatial home it still is: although you are only permitted to see six of the more than 150 rooms, among the treasures on show are a galleried library, Meissen dinner services, ebony cabinets mounted on gilded wood, tables inlaid with intricate patterns, niches with larger-than-life-size marble statues, and Venetian-mosaic floors. ⊠ *Above the junction of Narrowgate and Bailiffgate,*

☎ *01665/510777,* WEB *www.alnwickcastle.com.* 🖼 *£6.75.* ⊙ *Mid-Apr.–Oct., castle and grounds daily 11–5.*

Dining and Lodging

££ ✕🖼 **White Swan Hotel.** Standing on the site of the Old Swan Inn on the stagecoach route between Newcastle and Edinburgh, this building was restored by one of the greatest Victorian architects, Salvin, who also worked on Alnwick Castle. One of the lounges, the Olympic Suite, reconstructed from the paneling and furnishings of the *Olympic,* sister ship of the ill-fated *Titanic,* is occasionally pressed into service as a dining room. Otherwise, meals are taken in the blue-and-pink restaurant (dinner and Sunday lunch only), which provides a relaxing background for a menu largely drawn from classic Northumbrian cooking. Specialties include Kielder game pie, cooked in rich Guinness sauce, and *cranachan* (a thick cream dessert made with Alnwick rum, raspberries, and oatmeal). ✉ *Bondgate Within, NE66 1TD,* ☎ *01665/ 602109,* FAX *01665/510400,* WEB *www.hotel-selection.co.uk. 58 rooms. Restaurant. AE, MC, V.*

£–££ 🖼 **Bondgate House Hotel.** This small, family-run hotel in a 250-year-old building is close to the medieval town gateway. It's a reasonably priced base for touring the area, and it has parking space for eight cars. ✉ *20 Bondgate Without, NE66 1PN,* ☎ FAX *01665/602025. 8 rooms, 5 with bath. Restaurant. MC, V.*

Shopping

The **House of Hardy** (☎ 01665/602771), just outside Alnwick (from downtown, take A1 south to just beyond traffic circle on left, clearly marked), is one of Britain's finest stores for country sports, especially fishing. It has a worldwide reputation for handcrafted tackle.

Craster

㉙ *6 mi northeast of Alnwick.*

The harbor smokehouses of the tiny fishing village of Craster are known for that great English breakfast delicacy, kippers: herring salted and smoked over smoldering oak shavings. You can visit the tar-blackened smokehouses, eat your fill of fresh and traditionally smoked fish, and even have smoked salmon mailed home to your friends. Opposite the smokehouse, you can savor Craster kippers for lunch or afternoon tea at Craster Fish Restaurant, which is open from mid-April through September, or the Jolly Fisherman pub, where you can feast on its famous fresh crab sandwiches while enjoying the views of crashing waves from the pub's splendid picture window.

Dunstanburgh Castle

㉚ *1 mi north of Craster, 7 mi northeast of Alnwick.*

Perched romantically on a cliff 100 ft above the shore, the ruins of Dunstanburgh Castle can be reached along a windy, mile-long coastal footpath from Craster. Built in 1316 by the Earl of Lancaster as a defense against the Scots, and later enlarged by John of Gaunt (the powerful Duke of Lancaster who virtually ruled England in the late 14th century), the castle is known to many from the popular paintings by 19th-century artist J. M. W. Turner. More recently it appeared in scenes in the 1990 film version of *Hamlet* with Mel Gibson. Several picturesque sandy bays indent the coastline immediately to the north. ☎ *01665/ 576231,* WEB *www.english-heritage.org.uk.* 🖼 *£1.80.* ⊙ *Apr.–Oct., daily 10–6; Nov.–Mar., Wed.–Sun. 10–4.*

Farne Islands

31 *7 mi north of Craster, 13 mi northeast of Alnwick.*

Regular boat trips from the village of Seahouses enable you to sample the attractions of two of the bleak, wind-tossed Farne Islands (owned by the National Trust), which host impressive colonies of seabirds, including puffins, kittiwakes, terns, shags, and guillemots; the islands also attract thriving gray-seal colonies. In addition, Inner Farne, where St. Cuthbert, the great abbot of Lindisfarne, died in AD 687, has a tiny chapel dedicated to his memory. All boat service leaves from Seahouses harbor, from a 2½-hour cruise past the islands to a longer trip, during which you'll make landfall. Landing fees differ depending on season, since there's more wildlife to see at certain times of the year. ☎ *01665/721099 National Trust information center; 01665/720308 boat trips; 01665/720884 Seahouses Tourist Information Centre,* WEB *www.nationaltrust. org.uk.* ☉ *Boat trips Apr.–Sept., daily (weather permitting); access restricted during seal breeding season (May 15–July 15).* 🚢 *Boat trips £7–£14; landing fees £3.20–£4.20 are payable to the wardens.*

Bamburgh

32 *14 mi north of Alnwick.*

Tiny Bamburgh has a splendid castle, and several beaches are a few minutes' walk away. Especially stunning when floodlighted at night, **Bamburgh Castle** dominates the coastal view for miles, set atop a great crag to the north of Seahouses and overlooking a magnificent sweep of sand backed by high dunes. Once regarded as the legendary Joyous Garde of Sir Lancelot du Lac, one of King Arthur's fabled knights, it's one of the most picturesque castles in Britain. Its ramparts have sweeping views of Lindisfarne (Holy Island), the Farne Islands, the stormy coastline, and the Cheviot Hills inland. Much of the castle has been restored, although the great Norman keep (central tower) remains intact, and the present Lady Armstrong lives there now. Exhibits include collections of armor, porcelain, jade, furniture, and paintings. ⊠ *Bamburgh, 3 mi north of Seahouses,* ☎ *01668/214515,* WEB *www.bamburghcastle.com.* 🚢 *£4.50.* ☉ *Apr.–Oct., daily 11–5.*

The **Grace Darling Museum** commemorates a local heroine as well as the Royal National Lifeboat Institute, an organization of volunteers who keep watch at the rescue stations on Britain's coasts. Grace Darling became a folk heroine in 1838, when she and her father rowed out to save the lives of nine shipwrecked sailors from the SS *Forfarshire.* ⊠ *Radcliffe Rd., opposite church near village center,* ☎ *no phone.* 🚢 *Free.* ☉ *Apr.–mid-Oct., Mon.–Sat. 11–7, Sun. 2–6.*

Dining and Lodging

££ ✕🏨 **Lord Crewe Arms.** This is a cozy stone-walled inn with oak beams and open fires, in the heart of the village close to Bamburgh Castle. It's an ideal spot for lunch while you're touring the area. The rooms are fairly simple, but the food, especially the local seafood, is excellent. ⊠ *Front St., NE69 7BL,* ☎ *01668/214243,* FAX *01668/214273. 24 rooms, 22 with bath. Restaurant. MC, V. Closed late Oct.–Mar.*

£££–££££ 🏨 **Waren House Hotel.** The setting for this Georgian hotel is six acres of woodland on a quiet bay between Bamburgh and Holy Island. Bedrooms are decorated in different styles, but most have a Victorian flavor. There are romantic views of Holy Island from the restaurant; five-course dinners might include a smoked goose-and-ham salad, followed by soup, local game or salmon, and a homemade dessert. ⊠ *Waren Mill, Belford NE70 7EE,* ☎ *01668/214581,* FAX *01668/214484,* WEB *www.warenhousehotel.co.uk. 8 rooms, 2 suites. Restaurant, bar, library. AE, DC, MC, V.*

Lindisfarne (Holy Island)

★ ㉝ *6 mi east of A1, north of Bamburgh; 22 mi north of Alnwick; 8 mi southeast of Berwick-upon-Tweed.*

Cradle of northern England's Christianity and home of St. Cuthbert, Lindisfarne (or Holy Island) is reached from the mainland by a long drive along a causeway. The causeway is flooded at high tide, so you *must* check to find out when crossing is safe. The times, which change every day, are displayed at the causeway and printed in local newspapers. As traffic can be heavy, allow at least a half hour for your return trip. The religious history of the island dates from the very origins of Christianity in England, for St. Aidan established a monastery here in AD 635. Under its greatest abbot, the sainted Cuthbert, Lindisfarne became one of the foremost centers of learning in Christendom.

In the year 875, Vikings destroyed the Lindisfarne community; only a few monks managed to escape, carrying with them Cuthbert's bones, which they reburied in Durham. **Lindisfarne Priory** was reestablished in the 11th century by monks from Durham, and the sandstone Norman ruins remain both impressive and beautiful. Anglo-Saxon carvings are displayed in a museum here. ⊠ *Holy Island, 6 mi east of A1, north of Bambrough,* ☎ *01289/389200,* WEB *www.english-heritage.org.uk.* ☒ *£2.80.* ☉ *Apr.–Sept., daily 10–6; Oct.–Mar., daily 10–4.*

Seen from a distance, **Lindisfarne Castle,** reached by a walk around the coast of Holy Island, appears to grow out of the rocky pinnacle on which it was built 400 years ago, looking for all the world like a fairy-tale illustration. In 1903 architect Sir Edwin Lutyens converted the castle into a private home that retains the original's ancient features. Across several fields from the castle is a walled garden, surprisingly sheltered from the storms and winds; its 16th-century plan was discovered in, of all places, California, and the garden has since been replanted, providing again a colorful summer display. ⊠ *Holy Island,* ☎ *01289/ 389244,* WEB *www.nationaltrust.org.uk.* ☒ *£4:20.* ☉ *Apr.–Oct., Sat.– Thurs., call for opening times.*

Berwick-upon-Tweed

㉞ *10 mi northwest of Lindisfarne, 30 mi northwest of Alnwick, 77 mi north of Durham.*

Although Berwick-upon-Tweed now lies just inside the border of England, historians estimate that it has changed hands between the Scots and the English 14 times. The market on Wednesday and Saturday draws plenty of customers from both sides of the border. The town's thick 16th-century walls are among the best-preserved in Europe and completely encircle the old town; a path follows the ramparts, and the views are rewarding. The parish church, Holy Trinity, was built during Cromwell's Puritan Commonwealth with stone from the castle.

In Berwick's **Military Barracks,** built between 1717 and 1721, three accommodation wings surround a square, with the decorated gatehouse forming the fourth side. An exhibition called "By Beat of Drum" depicts the life of the common soldier from the 1660s to the 1880s, and other displays highlight the history of the local regiment, the King's Own Scottish Borderers, and that of the town itself. ⊠ *The Parade, off Church St. in town center,* ☎ *01289/304493,* WEB *www.berwick-online.org.uk/visit.htm.* ☒ *£2.60.* ☉ *Apr.–Oct., daily 10–6; Nov.– Mar., Wed.–Sun. 10–4.*

Dining and Lodging

£ ✕ **Town House.** This spot serves a delicious variety of fresh quiches, pastries, and other snacks. It's tricky to find: cross Buttermarket under the Guildhall and go through the old jail. The café's proprietors say, "Please persevere to find your way in—it's easy when you know how." ✉ *Marygate,* ☎ *01289/307904. No credit cards. Closed Sun.*

££–£££ ✕⌂ **Coach House.** Ten miles southwest of Berwick-upon-Tweed and less than that from the Scottish border, this friendly guest house is part of a cluster of attractive, well-converted farm buildings, including Northumberland's oldest unfortified house. The spacious bedrooms, some of which have exposed wooden beams, share an appealing, homespun atmosphere. There are three pleasant acres of gardens, with miles of stunning scenery on the doorstep. The dining room offers local specialties. ✉ *Crookham, 3 mi north of Milfield on A697, Cornhill-on-Tweed TD12 4TD,* ☎ *01890/820293. 10 rooms, 7 with bath. Restaurant, bar. MC, V. Closed Nov.–Mar.*

£ ⌂ **No. 1 Sallyport.** This bed-and-breakfast set in a 17th-century building in the heart of town, a mere 20 yards from the Elizabethan walls, is a treat. Three pleasantly furnished guest rooms hold pine furniture, books, paintings, dried flowers, and the odd antique; one has its own fireplace. A private kitchen with fresh coffee is available. Breakfast is unbeatable: scrambled egg and smoked salmon, waffles, croissants, porridge, or a traditional full breakfast. Evening meals can be arranged, too. ✉ *1 Sallyport, TD15 1EZ,* ☎ FAX *01289/308827. 3 rooms. Dining room. No credit cards.*

THE NORTHEAST A TO Z

To research prices, get advice from other travelers, and book travel arrangements, visit www.fodors.com.

BUS TRAVEL

National Express serves the region from London's Victoria Coach Station. Average travel times are 4¾ hours to Durham, 5¼ hours to Newcastle, and 8¼ hours to Berwick-upon-Tweed. Connecting services to other parts of the region leave from Durham and Newcastle. In Newcastle and Tyneside, call Nexus for all public transport inquiries. Durham is the hub for buses out to attractions in County Durham, with information available from the County Durham inquiry line.

A special Hadrian's Wall Bus between Hexham and Carlisle operates in summer, stopping at all the major sites. Local tourist offices have timetables; a Day Rover ticket costs £5.

CUTTING COSTS

The Northeast Explorer Pass (£4.75, one-day) allows unlimited travel on most local services and is available from the bus driver or local bus stations.

FARES AND SCHEDULES

For route and fare information in Northumberland, buy the *Northumberland Public Transport Guide* (£1.60) from any tourist office.

➤ BUS INFORMATION: **County Durham Inquiry Line** (☎ 0191/383–3337). **National Express** (☎ 0870/580–8080, WEB www.gobycoach.com). **Nexus** (☎ 0191/232–5325).

CAR RENTAL

➤ LOCAL AGENCIES: **Avis** (✉ 7 George St., Newcastle upon Tyne, ☎ 0191/232–5283). **Hertz** (✉ Newcastle Airport, Newcastle upon Tyne, ☎ 0191/286–6748). **M&S Ford** (✉ A1[M] Carrville, Durham, ☎ 0191/386–1155).

CAR TRAVEL

The most direct north–south route through the Northeast is A1, linking London and Edinburgh via Newcastle (274 mi from London; 5–6 hours) and Berwick-upon-Tweed (338 mi from London; 2 hours past Newcastle). A697, which branches west off A1 north of Morpeth, is a more attractive road, leading past the 16th-century battlefield of Flodden. For Hexham and Hadrian's Wall take the A69 west of Newcastle. For the coast, leave the A1 at Alnwick and follow the minor B1339 and B1340, for Craster, Seahouses, and Bamburgh. Holy Island is reached from a minor exit off the A1. A66 and A69 run east–west.

Many country roads provide quiet and scenic, if slower, alternatives to the main routes. Part of the Cheviot Hills, which run along the Northumbrian side of the Scottish border, is now a military firing range. Don't drive here when the warning flags are flying. The military, though, has restored the Roman road, Dere Street, which crosses this region. Try also B6318, a well-maintained road that runs alongside Hadrian's Wall on the south side.

EMERGENCIES

➤ CONTACTS: **Ambulance, fire, police** (☎ 999). **Berwick Infirmary** (☎ 01289/307484). **Newcastle General Hospital** (✉ Westgate Rd., ☎ 0191/273–8811).

TOURS

Holiday with a Knight is run by Shirley Knight, a guide specializing in general tours of northern England, as well as theme tours based on history, literature, and ghosts and legends.
➤ FEES AND SCHEDULES: **Holiday with a Knight** (☎ 01287/632510).

WALKING TOURS

Durham County Council Environment Department organizes a year-round program of guided walks, from countryside rambles to industrial heritage trails, which cost £1 per person. Guided walks of the region's historic towns and cities are usually available through the local tourist offices—those in Newcastle, Durham, and Berwick-upon-Tweed are particularly recommended.
➤ FEES AND SCHEDULES: **Durham County Council Environment Department** (☎ 0191/383–4144).

TRAIN TRAVEL

Great Northeastern Railways serves the region from London's King's Cross Station, en route to Scotland. Average travel times are 2¾ hours to Darlington, 3 hours to Durham, 3¼ hours to Newcastle, and 3¾ hours to Berwick-upon-Tweed. From Newcastle, there is local service north to Alnmouth (for Alnwick) and to Corbridge and Hexham on the east–west line to Carlisle.

FARES AND SCHEDULES

➤ TRAIN INFORMATION: **Great Northeastern Railways** (☎ 0845/748–4950, WEB www.gner.co.uk).

TRAVEL AGENCIES

➤ LOCAL AGENT REFERRALS: **Thomas Cook** (✉ 24–25 Market Pl., Durham, ☎ 0191/384–8569; 6 Northumberland St., Newcastle, ☎ 0191/261–2163).

VISITOR INFORMATION

Northumbria Regional Tourist Board is open Monday–Thursday 8:30–5, Friday 8:30–4:30. Other tourist information centers are normally open Monday–Saturday 9:30–5:30, but varying by season.

➤ TOURIST INFORMATION: **Northumbria Regional Tourist Board** (✉ Aykley Heads, DH1 5UX, ☎ 0191/375–3000, WEB www.visitnorthumbria. com). **Alnwick** (✉ The Shambles, NE66 1TN, ☎ 01665/510665). **Barnard Castle** (✉ 43 Galgate, DL12 8EL, ☎ 01833/690909). **Berwick-upon-Tweed** (✉ Castlegate Car Park, TD15 1JS, ☎ 01289/330733). **Bishop Auckland** (✉ Town Hall, Market Pl., DL14 7NP, ☎ 01388/604922). **Darlington** (✉ 13 Horsemarket, DL1 5PW, ☎ 01325/388666). **Durham** (✉ Market Pl., DH1 3NJ, ☎ 0191/384–3720, WEB www. durham.gov.uk/tourism). **Hadrian's Wall** (WEB www.hadrians-wall.org). **Hexham** (✉ Manor Office, Hallgate, NE46 1XD, ☎ 01434/605225). **Middlesbrough** (✉ 51 Corporation Rd., Cleveland TS1 1LT, ☎ 01642/243425). **Newcastle upon Tyne** (✉ Central Library, Princess Sq., NE99 1DX, ☎ 0191/261–0610; Main Concourse, Central Station, NE1 5DL, ☎ 0191/230–0030, WEB www.newcastle.gov.uk).

16 SCOTLAND: EDINBURGH TO THE HIGHLANDS

ST. ANDREWS, GLASGOW, ROYAL DEESIDE, INVERNESS

One of the world's stateliest cities and proudest capitals, Edinburgh—built, like Rome, on seven hills—is the perfect setting for the ancient pageant of history. In contrast, Scotland's largest city, Glasgow, is bustling and bionic. Sooner or later, however, all feet march in the direction of mythical Brigadoon—Scotland's shimmering lochs, baronial castles, and those moors that shout pink and purple. Explore the Borders, Sir Walter Scott Country, then call on Royal Deeside and Loch Ness, home to "Nessie," star of the local chamber of commerce.

Updated by
Beth Ingpen,
Morris Paton,
Mark Porter,
and Kenneth
Walton.

S COTLAND IS A SMALL COUNTRY, no bigger than the state of Maine, and it contains barely a tenth of the United Kingdom's population. Yet the idea of Scotland is world-embracing. It has produced some of the world's stormiest history, some of its most romantic heroes and heroines, much of its most admired literature, and many of its most important inventions. Its local products, customs, music, and traditional dress, such as tartan, bagpipes, tweed, travel all over the globe. Scots throughout history, especially those who emigrated to the United States, Canada, Australia, and New Zealand, have been superb propagandists for the land of their ancestors, the land they love. Now, more home-based national pride has been boosted with the reestablishment, after nearly 300 years, of Scotland's own Parliament, albeit one with restricted powers. Its responsibilities include health, education, transport, housing, economic development, agriculture, and the environment; the U.K. Government in London is still responsible for foreign policy, defense, and economic policy.

There are really two Scotlands: the Lowlands (not low at all, but chains of hills along river valleys), where populous cities such as Edinburgh and Glasgow are found; and the Highlands, which contain the highest mountains in the British Isles, the wildest lochs (lakes), and most of the islands. It is often assumed that as you travel north you proceed from Lowlands to Highlands. In fact, it is more of an east–west divide. Most travelers start out with Scotland's greatest cities, Edinburgh and Glasgow. After a while, however, those splendid heather-clad mountain slopes and shimmering lochs exert their pull, as do the fast-flowing streams where salmon leap, and the great castles of baronial pride standing hard among the hills. There are lots of contrasts of landscape, building stone, accent, city size, and you don't have to travel too far to enjoy it all.

Edinburgh (pronounced edin-burra) seems to have been designed as a tourist attraction, but it is very much a capital city, with all the inbuilt dignity that implies. The Scottish Parliament is based here and, until its new building adjacent to the Palace of Holyroodhouse is complete in late 2002, has been using the Assembly Hall of the Church of Scotland, on the Mound. A variety of factors make Edinburgh appealing to visitors: its outstanding geography, like Rome, it is built on seven hills, the Old Town district, with all the evidence of its colorful history, and the New Town, with its large number of elegant, classical buildings conceived in the surge of artistic creativity of the second half of the 18th century.

Glasgow, Scotland's largest city, suffered gravely from the industrial decline of the 1960s and '70s, but efforts at commercial and cultural renewal have restored much of the style and grandeur it possessed in the 19th century when it was at the height of its economic power. It is once again a vibrant metropolitan center with a thriving artistic life. Glasgow is a convenient touring center, too, with excellent transportation links to the rest of the country.

The Borders area comprises the great rolling hills, moors, wooded river valleys, and farmland that stretch south from Lothian, the region crowned by Edinburgh, to England. All the distinctive features of Scotland, such as paper currency, architecture, opening hours of pubs and stores, food and drink, and accent, start right at the border; you won't find the Borders a diluted version of England. Northeast of Edinburgh, on the windswept east coast, stands the ancient town of St. Andrews filled with historic sites and known the world over as the home of golf.

Many a traveler hopes to return home with the tale of a Road Hole birdie on the Old Course.

Beyond the central lowlands, the pleasures and treasures of Aberdeen and Northeast Scotland, Inverness, Loch Ness (with or without its "monster" Nessie), and the Highlands await. Aberdeen is Scotland's third-largest city, and a gateway to the splendor of Royal Deeside and the Grampian Mountains, a wealth of castles, and an unspoiled and, in places, spectacular coastline. Inverness, to the northwest, is the capital of the Highlands, with Loch Ness right on its doorstep. A map of Scotland gives a hint of the grandeur and beauty to be found here: fingers of inland lochs, craggy and steep-sided mountains, rugged promontories, and deep inlets. But the map does not give an inkling of the brilliant purple and emerald moorland, the forests, and the astonishingly varied wildlife: mountain hares, red deer, golden eagles, ospreys, seals, dolphins, the courtesy of the soft-spoken inhabitants, and the depth of ancestral memory and clan mythology. All these are delights that await the visitor who ventures out of the cities.

A car is essential if you want to explore the wildest and most beautiful districts. Roads are always well surfaced though narrow in places. Although the area is large, road distances make it larger: as the eagle flies, one town can be a certain distance from another, but it turns out to be three times that distance by the shortest road! For the short-term visitor, however, a bus excursion from Edinburgh or Aberdeen can possibly give the best value. Whatever the mode of transport, try to spend a couple of days in a small Highland bed-and-breakfast, grand estate hotel, or fishing inn. Only then will you discover the spell of the Highlands, that inexplicable magic that brings people back year after year. Keep in mind that winter touring beyond the central lowlands means you should check weather forecasts: Braemar often records Britain's lowest temperatures and minor roads are occasionally snowbound. Note that if you head north of Aberdeen and Inverness, travel options can be limited on Sunday, perhaps a survival of the otherwise almost vanished Scots Sabbath, and many accommodations and visitor attractions in more isolated areas close during the winter months from November through March.

Pleasures and Pastimes

Arts

There is no escaping a literal sense of theater if you visit Edinburgh from August to early September. As the host for the annual Edinburgh International Festival, the city is quite literally crammed with cultural events in every art form from classic theater and big-name classical concerts to jazz and the most experimental forms of dance and theater. Even more obvious to the casual stroller during this time is the Edinburgh Festival Fringe, the refreshingly irreverent, ever-growing, unruly child of the official festival. During the same time period, that stirring Scottish extravaganza—the Edinburgh Military Tattoo—is also performed. Aberdeen's Alternative Festival in October and the Shetland Folk Festival at Easter are just two of the many other events adding breadth to Scotland's cultural year.

Dining

To sample genuine Scottish cuisine, look out for the TASTE OF SCOTLAND sign in restaurant windows indicating the use of the best Scottish products, including marvelous salmon and venison, and of course the spicy haggis, usually served with "neeps and tatties" (mashed turnip and potato). Culinary delights await, including nouvelle variations on old

Scottish dishes like Partan Bree (a rich crab soup), and Loch Fyne herring. Remember that Scotland is traditionally the "Land o' Cakes," so be sure to enjoy some of those delicious buns, pancakes, scones, and biscuits. In the Highlands, local game and seafood are often presented with great flair; many restaurants deal directly with local boats, so freshness is guaranteed. Oatmeal, local cheeses, and even malt whisky (turning up in any course) amplify the Scottish dimension. And speaking of whisky, try a "wee dram" of a single malt, the pale, unblended spirit, when you visit the Northeast, one of Scotland's major distilling areas.

CATEGORY	COST*
££££	over £22
£££	£16–£22
££	£9–£15
£	under £9

*per person, for a main course at dinner

Golfing

Everyone wants to play just the big names in the British Open—St. Andrews, Turnberry, Troon, and so on. This is a pity because there are more golf courses in Scotland per capita than anywhere else in the world. Out of the 400 or so, there are plenty of gems, from challenging coastal links courses such as Cruden Bay or Royal Dornoch in the north to pinewood parkland delights such as Boat of Garten, near Inverness. In the "East Neuk" of Fife, one of the prettiest Lowland areas of Scotland, the quiet town of St. Andrews beckons with its famous golf course, where the Royal & Ancient, the ruling body of the game worldwide, has its headquarters. But even if St. Andrews is not your headquarters, Scotland remains a golfer's paradise; a round on a municipal course costs very little, while most clubs, apart from a few pretentious places modeled on the English fashion, demand only comparatively modest course fees.

Highland Games

Caber tossing (the caber is a long, heavy pole) and other traditional events figure in the Highland Games, staged throughout the Highlands during summer. All Scottish tourist information centers have full details. It is said that these games, a unique combination of music, dancing, and athletic prowess, grew out of the contests held by clan chiefs to find the strongest men for bodyguards, the fastest runners for messengers, and the best musicians and dancers to entertain guests and increase the chief's prestige.

Hiking and Walking

Walks in the Edinburgh area range from city walkways along the banks of the Water of Leith, to the Pentland Hills, whose breezy but not overdemanding slopes are especially popular with locals on weekends. There is also good East Lothian coastal walking at many points from Aberlady, eastward. As the Borders are essentially rural and hilly, there are a number of walking options. Peebles, within easy reach of Edinburgh, offers excellent, level walking along the banks of the River Tweed, while a visit to Melrose, with its abbey, can be further enhanced by a climb to the top of the Eildon Hills, for wonderful views. The **Southern Upland Way,** a 212-mi official long-distance footpath from Cockburnspath in the east to Portpatrick in the west, also passes through the Borders. Official footpaths in the Highlands include the **West Highland Way,** running 98 mi from the outskirts of Glasgow to Fort William, by Loch Lomond, Rannoch Moor, and Glen Coe, and the **Great Glen Way,** which runs for 70 mi from Fort William to Inverness, via the Caledonian Canal, and Lochs Lochy, Oich, and Ness (for some monster-spotting). Slightly gentler is the Northeast's **Speyside Way**, taking its name from one of Scotland's premier salmon rivers, which offers excellent river valley and some moorland walking for 47 mi, from the Moray Firth coast up to the foothills of the Cairngorms. All four long-distance paths are covered in official guides available from bookshops and tourist information centers.

Lodging

From grand hotel suites done up in tartan fabrics to personal-touch B&Bs, Edinburgh, Glasgow, Aberdeen, and Inverness are splendidly served by a wide variety of guest accommodations. Some of the best are in lovely traditional Georgian or Victorian properties; some are in Edinburgh's New Town, a few minutes from downtown. Because of the removal of much of its indigenous population by forced emigration, many parts of the Highlands became playgrounds for estate owners or Lowland industrialists, who built for themselves shooting lodges, grand mansions, and country estates. Many of these are now fine hotels, or upscale B&B establishments. In rural areas, many farms also offer bed and breakfast, with a breakfast substantial enough to sustain you throughout the whole day.

CATEGORY	COST*
££££	over £150
£££	£100–£150
££	£60–£100
£	under £60

All prices are for two people sharing a double room, including service, breakfast, and VAT.

Shopping

In Scotland, many visitors go for Shetland and Fair Isle woolens, tartan rugs and tweeds, Edinburgh crystal, and Caithness glass. Keep an eye out for craft pottery and for unusual designs in Scottish jewelry, especially when they incorporate local stones. Glasgow has an excellent selection of designer clothing stores. Handmade chocolates, often with whisky or Drambuie fillings, and the traditional "petticoat tail" shortbread in tin boxes are popular. At a more mundane level, try some of the boiled sweets in jars from particular localities, such as Jethart snails, Edinburgh rock, and similar delights. Other edibles that visitors take home include Dundee cake, marmalades, and heather honeys.

Exploring Scotland

Edinburgh and Glasgow, Scotland's two major cities, contrast greatly in style. Both divide easily into two: Edinburgh's Old and New Towns, and Glasgow's medieval-and-merchant heart and culture-rich West End. The Borders lie south of Edinburgh, with their fabled green hillsides, river valleys, ruined abbeys, and stately homes; they can be discovered in one long day, or better still, taken in two bites, returning to Edinburgh overnight. St. Andrews, along the east coast north of Edinburgh, beckons with its golf but also its evocative castle and cathedral ruins.

The Highlands take in a whole range of rugged landscapes: the breathtaking, remote islands of the western seaboard, the silvery granite city of Aberdeen on the east coast, the Grampian Mountains and "Castle Country" of Royal Deeside lying west of Aberdeen, and north, toward Inverness and Loch Ness, and the Northern Highlands, with Scotland's tallest mountains and greatest lochs.

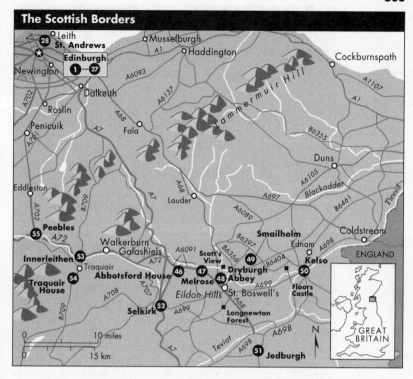

The Scottish Borders

Numbers in the text correspond to numbers in the margin and on the Scottish Borders, Edinburgh, Glasgow, Glasgow Environs, Royal Deeside, and Inverness and Environs maps.

Great Itineraries

Ideally, to get the real flavor of Scotland, visitors need at least a week to take in the diversity of sights and scenery. If you have a shorter period of time, you may have to choose between city or countryside: Edinburgh or Glasgow's main attractions could be seen in two or three days, as could Aberdeen and Royal Deeside. With five or six days, you will be able to base yourself at two centers, perhaps Edinburgh and Aberdeen, or Glasgow and Inverness. Alternatively, you could take day trips to St. Andrews and to the Borders from Edinburgh. To cover all the areas outlined in this chapter, allow at least eight days.

IF YOU HAVE 2-3 DAYS

Spend your time getting to know one area properly. This will be long enough to see most of the major sights described for one of these areas: **Edinburgh** ①–㉗, **Glasgow** ㉙–㊺, **Aberdeen** ㊶, or **Inverness** ㊽ (and Loch Ness)—assuming that you select your own choice among the museums, galleries, or stately homes. Break up your three-day visit to Edinburgh or Glasgow with an overnight excursion to the Borders, staying at 🏠 **Melrose** ㊸ or 🏠 **Peebles** ㊷ to enjoy a rural change of pace; or from Edinburgh, take a day trip to check out the golfers' heaven of **St. Andrews** ㉘—there's actually much more to see in this town than the legendary Royal & Ancient Course.

IF YOU HAVE 5 DAYS

Again, choices have to be made. At least two days and nights should be spent in 🏠 **Edinburgh** ①–㉗ or 🏠 **Glasgow** ㉙–㊺ to allow for visits to all of the most important sights. (If you want to see both cities, you will need the whole five or six days.) For your remaining nights, you

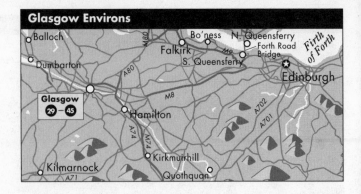

have three options. The first is to head south for the Borders to explore Sir Walter Scott Country. Start out (and spend the night) in ⛾ **Melrose** ㊹, visiting **Abbotsford House** ㊻, Scott's View, and **Dryburgh Abbey** ㊽ as well as sights slightly farther afield, for instance the abbey at **Jedburgh** ㊿. For those interested in grand Scottish residences of the past, a visit to **Floors Castle** is a must. After enjoying the glories of the Scottish countryside on an afternoon walk, stay overnight in ⛾ **Kelso** ㊾ before heading back to the capital.

Your second option, from Edinburgh or Glasgow, is to travel to ⛾ **Aberdeen** ㊶, arriving in the evening. The next morning, follow in the footsteps of Queen Victoria and take a trip among the castles and glens of Royal Deeside. Set out for Crathes Castle and **Banchory** ㊷, with its largely unchanged Victorian High Street. After lunch, follow the river upstream to Aboyne, turning due north on B9094, then left onto B9119 for 6 mi for a panorama (signposted on B9119) known as the Queen's View, a bit north of Dinnet: this is one of the most spectacular vistas in northeast Scotland, stretching across the Howe of Cromar to Lochnagar. Then continue on B9119, dropping gently downhill through the birch woods to A93 to reach ⛾ **Ballater** ㊸ to the west. Here, stop overnight. The next morning, visit Her Majesty's Balmoral Castle if royal residences are high on your list. Take in the royal ballroom and grounds, do a country walk or a pony trek, but note that Balmoral is only open for three months in the summer, then treat yourself to a walk in nearby Glen Muick. Here you'll find the famous climb of Lochnagar, so beloved by Victoria. Head for ⛾ **Braemar** ㊹ for your next overnight stay. The next morning, set off for Castle Country and some serious castle-hopping—**Corgarff Castle** ㊿, **Kildrummy Castle** ㊑, **Craigievar Castle** ㊓, and **Castle Fraser** ㊔, stopping at **Alford** ㊒ to visit the Grampian Transport Museum, then return to Aberdeen, either stopping overnight, or continuing south to Edinburgh or Glasgow.

Your final option, after two days in Edinburgh or Glasgow, is to travel to ⛾ **Inverness** ㊕ for two nights, aiming to arrive in the early evening. Spend the next morning exploring the city, then in the afternoon pay a call on Nessie at Drumnadrochit on the banks of **Loch Ness** ㊖. Return to Inverness for the night, then the next day follow signposts to **Culloden Moor** ㊗, **Fort George** ㊙, **Cawdor Castle** ㊚, or **Brodie Castle** ㊛ for a finale in Macbeth Country. Continue on to spend the night at ⛾ **Nairn** ㊘, before traveling south to Aberdeen and Edinburgh or Glasgow.

IF YOU HAVE 10 DAYS OR LONGER

If, having visited Edinburgh, Glasgow, the Borders, Aberdeen, and Royal Deeside, you wish to continue exploring the Highlands, turn due north, after visiting one or two houses in Castle Country, at **Castle Fraser** ㊔. Take A944 from Castle Fraser west, enjoying the valley of the River

Don as far as Corgarff on A939. The A939 then climbs into the brown hills to Tomintoul, highest village in the Highlands. From there, continue west, dropping into Speyside via the A95 and A938 roads, to pick up the main A9 at Carrbridge and arrive by evening at ⊞ **Inverness** ㉖. Spend your remaining time as described under the five-day option of Inverness and the surrounding area, above.

When to Tour Scotland

August is far and away the most exciting time to visit Edinburgh, largely because of the International Festival. The sheer amount of theater and music going on make the city buzz with cultural activity. However, this is also inevitably the busiest time, and anyone wishing to visit Edinburgh during August and the beginning of September will have to plan and book months in advance. The winters can be cold and wet, but the long summer evenings with sunsets as late as 10:30 from June through September are magical. The Borders are also busiest during festival time with visitors taking a break from city life, but its landscape can be fully appreciated in April and May as well.

Spring in the Highlands can be glorious, when there is still snow on the highest peaks. Those exuberant Highland Games, featuring caber tossing, hammer throwing, and all the rest, are held during summer months: Braemar's Games (September) are often held in the presence of members of the Royal Family. If you wish to drop in on Balmoral, the royal residence on Deeside, keep in mind that it's only open mid-April through July. If the royals are in residence, even the grounds are closed to visitors, so be sure to call in advance. Autumn in Royal Deeside is very colorful.

EDINBURGH

In a skyline of sheer drama, Edinburgh Castle watches over Scotland's capital city, frowning down on Princes Street as if disapproving of its modern razzmatazz. Its ramparts still echo with gunfire when the one o'clock gun booms out each day, startling unwary tourists. But nearly everywhere in the city there are spectacular buildings, whose Doric, Ionic, and Corinthian columns add dignity to the landscape. To this largely Presbyterian gray backcloth, numerous trees and gardens provide lovely color. The top of Calton Hill, to the east, is cluttered with sturdy neoclassic monuments, like an abandoned set for a Greek drama. Also conspicuous from Princes Street is Arthur's Seat, a mountain of bright green and yellow furze rearing up behind the spires of the Old Town. This child-size mountain jutting 800 ft above its surroundings has steep slopes and little crags, like a miniature Highlands set down in the middle of the busy city. These theatrical elements give a unique identity to downtown, but turn a corner, say, off George Street (parallel to Princes Street), and you will see not an endless cityscape, but blue sea and a patchwork of fields. This is the county of Fife, beyond the inlet of the North Sea called the Firth of Forth; a reminder, like the northwest Highlands glimpsed from Edinburgh's highest points, that the rest of Scotland lies within easy reach.

The Old Town

The dark, brooding presence of the castle, the very essence of Scotland's martial past, dominates Edinburgh. The castle is built on a crag of hard, black volcanic rock formed during the Ice Age when an eastbound glacier scoured around this resistant core, creating steep cliffs on three sides. On the fourth side, a "tail" of rock was left, forming a ramp from the top that gradually runs away eastward. This became the street known as the Royal Mile, the backbone of the Old Town, leading from the castle down to the Palace of Holyroodhouse. "The Mile" is actually made up of one thoroughfare that bears, in consecutive sequence, different names: the Esplanade, Castle Hill, Lawnmarket, Parliament Square, High Street, and Canongate. Adjacent to Holyroodhouse is the site of Scotland's Parliament building, under construction to a design by Barcelona architect Enric Miralles; until this is completed (scheduled for late 2002), the Parliament is sitting in the Assembly Hall of the Church of Scotland, at the top of the Mound.

The streets and passages winding into their tenements or "lands" and crammed onto the ridgeback of "the Mile" really *were* Edinburgh until the 18th century saw expansions to the south and north. Everybody lived here, the richer folk on the lower floors of houses, with less well-to-do families on the upper floors: the higher up, the poorer. Time and redevelopment have swept away some of the narrow closes (alleyways) and tall tenements of the Old Town, but enough survive for you to be able to imagine the original profile of Scotland's capital, and there is now refurbishment under way to make many of these surviving closes more inviting to explore. Sir Walter Scott (1771–1832), Robert Louis Stevenson (1850–94), David Hume (1711–76), James Boswell (1740–95), the painter Allan Ramsay (1713–84), and many other well-known names are associated with the Old Town. But perhaps three are more famous than any others: John Knox (1513–72), Mary, Queen of Scots (1542–87), and Prince Charles Edward Stuart (1720–88).

A Good Walk

A perfect place to begin a tour of the Old Town is **Edinburgh Castle** ①. Having absorbed the many attractions within the castle and taken in the marvelous city views, you can begin to stroll down the grand promenade that is the **Royal Mile** ②. To the left of Castlehill, the Outlook Tower offers armchair views of the city with its **Camera Obscura** ③. Opposite, the **Scotch Whisky Heritage Centre** ④ offers an unusual chance to discover Scotland's liquid gold. Stop off for a sample. The six-story tenement known as **Gladstone's Land** ⑤, a survivor of 16th-century domestic life, is on the left walking down. Close by Gladstone's Land, down yet another close, is the **Writers' Museum** ⑥, housed in a good example of 17th-century urban architecture known as Lady Stair's House. Built in 1622, it evokes Scotland's literary past with exhibits on Sir Walter Scott, Robert Louis Stevenson, and Robert Burns.

Farther down on the left, the Tolbooth Kirk (kirk means church) boasts the tallest spire in the city, 240 ft, and is the home of the Edinburgh Festival offices. From Lawnmarket you can start your discovery of the Old Town closes, the alleyways that spread like ribs from the Royal Mile backbone. For a worthwhile shopping diversion, turn right down George IV Bridge, then to the right down Victoria Street, a 19th-century addition to the Old Town. Its shops offer antiques, old prints, clothing, and quality giftware. Down in the **Grassmarket** ⑦, which for centuries was an agricultural market, the shopping continues.

Walk from the Grassmarket back up Victoria Street to George IV Bridge, where you'll see the **National Library of Scotland** ⑧. Farther down George IV Bridge, to the right, is **Greyfriars Kirk** ⑨.

Before returning to Lawnmarket, you might detour down Chambers Street, which leads off from the bottom of George IV Bridge. Here, in a lavish Victorian building, the **Royal Museum of Scotland** ⑩ displays a collection of worldwide scope. Next door, in the magnificent Benson and Forsyth–designed Museum of Scotland, you can explore Scotland's own history. Return to High Street and, near Parliament Square

Edinburgh

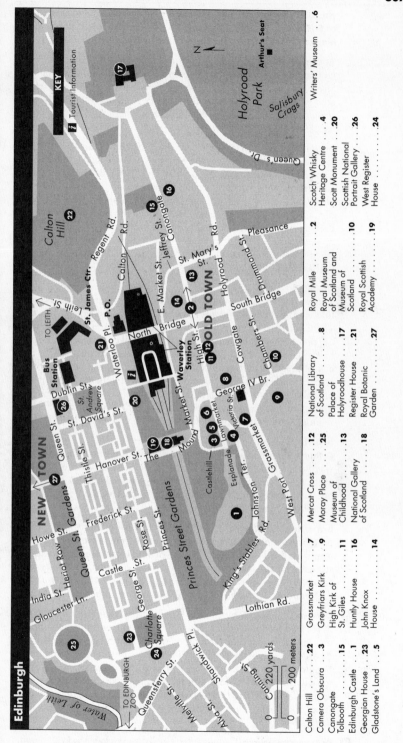

NEW TOWN

OLD TOWN

KEY

i Tourist Information

Water of Leith

TO EDINBURGH ZOO

TO LEITH

Queensferry St.
Melville St.
Alva St.
Shandwick Pl.
Lothian Rd.
King's Stables Rd.
West Port
Grassmarket
Johnston Ter.
Castlehill
Esplanade
Lawnmarket
Victoria St.
George IV Br.
Chambers St.
Cowgate
South Bridge
Pleasance
St. Mary's St.
Canongate
Holyrood Rd.
E. Market St.
Jeffrey St.
E. Market St.
High St.
Market St.
The Mound
Waterloo Pl.
Regent Rd.
Calton Rd.
Leith St.
North Bridge
Princes Street Gardens
Princes St.
Rose St.
George St.
Castle St.
Frederick St.
Hanover St.
Howe St.
Heriot Row
India St.
Gloucester Ln.
Queen St.
Queen St. Gardens
Thistle St.
Dublin St.
St. David's St.
St. Andrew Square
Charlotte Square
St. James Ctr.
Drummond St.

St. Giles
Waverley Station
Bus Station
P.O.

Calton Hill
Holyrood Park
Salisbury Crags
Arthur's Seat
Queen's Dr.

0   220 yards
0   200 meters

Calton Hill 22
Camera Obscura 3
Canongate
Tolbooth 15
Edinburgh Castle 1
Georgian House 23
Gladstone's Land ... 5

Grassmarket 7
Greyfriars Kirk 9
High Kirk of
St. Giles 11
Huntly House 16
John Knox
House 14

Mercat Cross 12
Moray Place 25
Museum of
Childhood 13
National Gallery
of Scotland 18

National Library
of Scotland 8
Palace of
Holyroodhouse ... 17
Register House 21
Royal Botanic
Garden 27

Royal Mile 2
Royal Museum
of Scotland and
Museum of
Scotland 10
Royal Scottish
Academy 19

Scotch Whisky
Heritage Centre ... 4
Scott Monument .. 20
Scottish National
Portrait Gallery .. 26
West Register
House 24

Writers' Museum ... 6

(site of the historic Parliament, not the current one), visit the **High Kirk of St. Giles** ⑪. Just east of St. Giles is another Old Town landmark, the **Mercat Cross** ⑫, which is still the site of royal proclamations.

At the North Bridge and South Bridge junction with High Street, you will find the Tron Kirk. The **Museum of Childhood** ⑬ is nearby on High Street. In contrast, across the street lies **John Knox House** ⑭, associated with Scotland's severe 16th-century religious reformer. Down a close nearby is the **Brass Rubbing Centre,** where you can find an unusual souvenir.

Beyond this point, you would once have passed beyond the safety provided by the town walls, where a plaque outside the Netherbow Arts Centre depicts the former Netherbow Port (gate). Below is the Canongate area, named for the Canons who once ran the abbey at Holyrood. Here you will find the handsome **Canongate Tolbooth** ⑮, the graveyard of Canongate Kirk, and **Huntly House** ⑯, a museum of local history. Facing you at the end of Canongate are the elaborate wrought-iron gates of the **Palace of Holyroodhouse** ⑰, official residence of the Queen when she is in Scotland. Under construction to the right is Scotland's Parliament Building.

TIMING

This walk contains a multitude of historical attractions and its duration is subject entirely to your field of interest. The Royal Mile, from The Castle to The Holyrood Palace (top to bottom) is worth exploring thoroughly on both sides of street and will comfortably take up to half a day. The old Grassmarket is an excellent spot for lunch, from any of the pubs and small restaurants which adorn one side of this ancient market site. Rest those weary legs and look out on what were probably the first "hospitality boxes," (the top windows of the tenements) for many a juicy hanging at the sight of the gallows. The Museum of Scotland building can take up to half a day in itself.

Sights to See

Arthur's Seat. For a grand bird's-eye view of Edinburgh, make your way up the 800 ft of the city's only minimountain, Arthur's Seat, set in the park behind the ☞ **Palace of Holyroodhouse**. It's a steep walk, but well worth it for the views from here and its neighboring eminence, Salisbury Crags.

Brass Rubbing Centre. A delightfully hands-on way to explore the past, brass-rubbing attracts more and more serious tourists every year. You'll find a fascinating selection of replica brasses and inscribed stones, with full instructions and materials supplied. ⊠ *Trinity Apse, Chalmers Close, Royal Mile,* ☎ *0131/556–4364.* ☞ *Free. 90p–£15 for each rubbing.* ☉ *Mon.–Sat. 10–5, Sun. during festival noon–5.*

❸ **Camera Obscura.** Want to view Edinburgh as Victorian travelers once did? Head for the Outlook Tower, where you'll encounter this optical instrument, a sort of projecting telescope, which offers armchair and bird's-eye views of the whole city illuminated onto a concave table. The building was constructed in the 17th century, but was significantly altered in the 1840s and 1850s for the installation of the "magic lantern." ⊠ *Castlehill,* ☎ *0131/226–3709,* WEB *www.explore-edinburgh.com.* ☞ *£3.95.* ☉ *Apr.–Oct., weekdays 9:30–6, weekends 10–6; Nov.–Mar., daily 10–5.*

❶❺ **Canongate Tolbooth.** Canongate originally was an independent "burgh," a Scottish term meaning, essentially, a community with trading rights granted by the monarch. This explains the presence of the Canongate Tolbooth. Nearly every city and town in Scotland once had a tolbooth; originally signifying a customs house where tolls were gathered, the name came to mean the town hall and, later, a prison. Today, the Canongate Tolbooth is the setting for **The People's Story,** an exhibition on the history of the people of Edinburgh. Next door is the graveyard of **Canongate Kirk,** where some notable Scots, including Adam Smith, the economist and author of *The Wealth of Nations,* are buried. ✉ *Canongate,* ☎ *0131/529–4057.* ☞ *Free.* ☉ *Mon.–Sat. 10–5, Sun. during festival 2–5.*

★ ❶ **Edinburgh Castle.** The crowning glory of the Scottish capital, Edinburgh Castle is popular not only because of its symbolic value as the heart of Scotland but also due to the views from its battlements: on a clear day the vistas, stretching to the "kingdom" of Fife, are of breathtaking loveliness. Clear days are frequent now, as Edinburgh is officially smokeless and the nickname "Auld Reekie" no longer applies.

The castle opens the chronicle of Scottish history, which will engulf you from now until you leave the country. You will hear the story of how Randolph, earl of Moray, nephew of freedom-fighter Robert Bruce, scaled the heights one dark night in 1313, surprised the English guard, and recaptured the castle for the Scots. At the same time he destroyed every one of its buildings except for St. Margaret's Chapel, dating from around 1076, so that successive Stuart kings had to rebuild the place bit by bit.

The castle has been held by Scots and Englishmen, Catholics and Protestants, soldiers and royalty. In the 16th century Mary, Queen of Scots, chose to give birth there to the future James VI of Scotland, who was also to rule England as James I. In 1573 it was the last fortress to support Mary's claim as the rightful Catholic queen of Britain, only to be virtually destroyed by English artillery fire.

You enter across the **Esplanade,** the huge forecourt built in the 18th century as a parade ground and now serves as the castle parking lot. It comes alive with color each August when it is used for the Tattoo, a magnificent military display, with the massed pipes and drums of the Scottish regiments beating retreat on the floodlighted heights. Heading over the drawbridge and through the gatehouse, past the guardsmen, you'll find the rough stone walls of the **Half Moon Battery,** where the one o'clock gun is fired every day in an impressively anachronistic ceremony. Climb up through a second gateway and you come to the oldest surviving building in the complex, the tiny 11th-century **St. Margaret's Chapel.** Head up farther still to enter the heart of the mighty complex, the medieval fortress. Here, along the dimly lit, echoing corridors you'll find the **Crown Room,** containing the "Honours of Scotland," the crown, scepter, and sword that once graced the Scottish monarch, and the Stone of Scone, a sacred relic used in Scottish coronations, returned to Scotland from Westminster Abbey in London in 1996. You'll also find the **Great Hall,** under whose 16th-century hammer-beam roof official banquets are still held, and **Queen Mary's apartments,** where the queen gave birth to James. ☎ *0131/225–9846,* 🕸 *www.aboutbritain.com.* ☞ *£7.50.* ☉ *Apr.–Sept., daily 9:30–5:15; Oct.–Mar., daily 9:30–4:15.*

❺ **Gladstone's Land.** A standout for those in search of the authentic atmosphere of old Edinburgh, this is a six-story tenement cared for by the National Trust for Scotland, that dates from the 17th century. Its theatrical setting includes an arcaded ground floor and intricately painted ceilings. The entire edifice is furnished in the style of a 17th-century merchant's house. ✉ *477B Lawnmarket,* ☎ *0131/226–5856.*

WEB *www.nts.org.uk* ⌨ *£3.50.* ☺ *Easter–Oct., Mon.–Sat. 10–5, Sun. 2–5 (last admission 4:30).*

❼ Grassmarket. As its name suggests, this was for centuries an agricultural market. Today, the shopping continues, but the goods have changed: antiques, old prints, clothing, and quality giftware. More boutiques can be found nearby along Victoria Street.

❾ Greyfriars Kirk. Here, on the site of a medieval monastery, the National Covenant was signed in 1638, declaring the Presbyterian Church in Scotland independent of government control, triggering decades of civil war. Be sure to search out the graveyard, one of the most evocative in Europe. Nearby, at the corner of George IV Bridge and Candlemaker Row, stands one of the most photographed sights in Scotland, the statue of **Greyfriars Bobby.** This famous Skye terrier kept vigil beside his master's grave in the churchyard for 14 years, leaving only for a short time each day to be fed at a nearby pub after the one-o'clock salute from Edinburgh Castle. ⌂ *Greyfriars Pl.,* ☎ *0131/225–1900.* ⌨ *Free.* ☺ *Easter–Oct., weekdays 10:30–4:30, Sat. 10:30–2:30; Nov.–Easter, Thurs. 1:30–3:30. Groups by appointment any time.*

⓫ High Kirk of St. Giles. Sometimes called St. Giles's Cathedral (it was briefly a cathedral in the mid-17th century), St. Giles is about one-third of the way along the Royal Mile from Edinburgh Castle. This is one of the city's principal churches, but anyone expecting a rival to Notre Dame or London's Westminster Abbey will be disappointed: St. Giles is more like a large parish church than a great European cathedral. Outside, the building is dominated by a stone crown, towering 161 ft above the ground; inside, the atmosphere is dark and forbidding. At the far end you'll find a life-size bronze statue of the Scot whose spirit still dominates the place, the great religious reformer and preacher John Knox, before whose zeal all Scotland once trembled. The most elaborate feature inside the church is the **Chapel of the Order of the Thistle,** which refers to Scotland's highest order of chivalry and is the counterpart to England's Order of the Garter. ⌂ *High St.,* ☎ *0131/ 225–9442.* ⌨ *Free, suggested donation £1.* ☺ *Mon.–Sat. 9–5 (until 7 in summer), Sun. 1–5; services: Sun. 8 AM, 10 AM, 11:30 AM, 6 PM (music program only), 8 PM; weekdays 8 AM, noon; Sat. noon, 6 PM.*

⓰ Huntly House. This attractive timber-front building houses a fascinating museum of local history, a must for those interested in the details of Old Town life. ⌂ *142 Canongate,* ☎ *0131/529–4143.* ⌨ *Free.* ☺ *Mon.–Sat. 10–5, Sun. during festival 2–5.*

⓮ John Knox House. A typical 16th-century dwelling, this was certainly not the home of Knox (1514–72), Scotland's fiery religious reformer, but it is full of mementos of his life. ⌂ *45 High St.,* ☎ *0131/556–2647.* ⌨ *£2.25.* ☺ *Mon.–Sat. 10–5 (last admission 4:30).*

⓬ Mercat Cross. A great landmark of Old Town life, the Mercat Cross (mercat means market) can be seen just east of the High Kirk of St. Giles. As its name suggests, it was a mercantile center, and, in early days, it also saw executions and was the spot where royal proclamations were—and are still—read. Most of the present cross is comparatively modern, dating from the time of Gladstone, the great Victorian prime minister and rival of Disraeli.

⟲ ⓭ Museum of Childhood. An excellent diversion, this collection is a celebration of toys that even adults will enjoy. ⌂ *42 High St.,* ☎ *0131/ 529–4142.* ⌨ *Free.* ☺ *Mon.–Sat. 10–5, Sun. during festival 2–5.*

❽ National Library of Scotland. Situated on George IV Bridge, this research library is a special magnet for genealogists investigating family trees. Even amateur family sleuths will find the staff helpful in their research. ☎ *0131/226–4531.* WEB *www.nls.uk* ☞ *Free.* ☾ *Mon., Tues., Thurs., Fri. 9:30–8:30, Wed. 10–8:30, Sat. 9:30–1; exhibitions Mon.–Sat. 10–5., 10–8 during festival.*

★ ⑰ **Palace of Holyroodhouse.** Haunt of Mary, Queen of Scots, and the setting for high drama, including at least one notorious murder, a spectacular funeral, several major fires, and centuries of the colorful lifestyles of larger-than-life, power-hungry personalities, this is now the Queen's official residence in Scotland. A doughty and impressive palace standing at the foot of the Royal Mile in a hilly public park, it is built around a graceful, lawned central court. Many monarchs, including Charles II, Queen Victoria, and George V have left their mark on its rooms. Highlights include the **Great Picture Gallery,** 150 ft long and hung with the portraits of 111 Scottish monarchs. These portraits were commissioned by Charles II, eager to demonstrate his Scottish ancestry (some of the royal figures here are fictional, and the likenesses of others imaginary).

Then there's the little chamber in which, in 1566, David Rizzio, secretary to Mary, Queen of Scots, met an unhappy end. Partly because Rizzio was hated at court for his social-climbing ways, Mary's second husband, Lord Darnley, burst into the queen's rooms with his henchmen, dragged Rizzio into an antechamber, and stabbed him more than 50 times (a bronze plaque marks the spot). Darnley himself was murdered in Edinburgh the next year, to make way for the queen's marriage to her lover, Bothwell. When Charles II assumed the British throne in 1660, he ordered Holyrood rebuilt in the architectural style of France's "Sun King," Louis XIV, and that is the palace that visitors see today. When the royal family is not in residence, visitors are free to walk around the palace and to go inside for a conducted tour. Behind the palace lie the open grounds of Holyrood Park, which enclose Edinburgh's own minimountain, **Arthur's Seat,** while just west of the palace, Scotland's new **Parliament building** is under construction. ☎ *0131/556–7371; 0131/556–1096 recorded information.* WEB *www.royal. gov.uk* ☞ *£6.50.* ☾ *Apr.–Oct., daily 9:30–5:15; Nov.–Mar., daily 9:30–3:45. Closed during royal and state visits.*

Parliament House. This was the seat of government until 1707, when the governments of Scotland and England were united, 104 years after the union of the two crowns. It is partially hidden by the bulk of the High Kirk of St. Giles and is now home to the Supreme Law Courts of Scotland. ⊠ *Parliament Sq.,* ☎ *0131/225–2595.* ☞ *Free.* ☾ *Weekdays 10–4.*

❷ **Royal Mile.** The most famous thoroughfare of Edinburgh begins immediately below the Esplanade. It runs roughly west to east, from the castle to the Palace of Holyroodhouse and progressively changes its name from Castlehill to Lawnmarket, High Street, and Canongate. Strolling downhill from the castle, it's easy to imagine and re-create the former life of the city, though you will need sharp eyes to spot the numerous historic plaques and details of ornamentation.

★ ⑩ **Royal Museum of Scotland and Museum of Scotland.** Housed in a lavish Victorian-era building, the Royal Museum displays a wide-ranging collection drawn from natural history, archaeology, the scientific and industrial past, and the history of mankind and civilization. The great galleried Main Hall with its "bird-cage" design is architecturally interesting in its own right. In an adjoining building, the **Museum of Scotland** concentrates on Scotland's own heritage. A state-of-the-art and no-expense-spared, modern museum, it is full of playful models, intricate reconstructions, and paraphernalia from the Bronze Age to the latest Scottish pop stars. ⊠ *Chambers St.,* ☎ *0131/225–7534.* WEB *www.nms.ac.uk* 🖃 *Free (both museums).* ⊙ *Mon.–Sat. 10–5 (Tues. until 8), Sun. noon–5.*

❹ **Scotch Whisky Heritage Centre.** If you've ever been interested in learning about the mysterious process that turns malted barley and spring water into one of Scotland's most important exports, this is the place. ⊠ *354 Castlehill,* ☎ *0131/220–0441.* 🖃 *£6.50.* ⊙ *Daily 10–6 (last tour 5; extended hrs in summer).*

❻ **Writers' Museum.** Close by Gladstone's Land, down yet another close, is the Writers' Museum, housed in a good example of 17th-century urban architecture known as Lady Stair's House. Built in 1622, it evokes Scotland's literary past with exhibits on Sir Walter Scott, Robert Louis Stevenson, and Robert Burns (1759–96). ⊠ *Off Lawnmarket,* ☎ *0131/529–4901.* 🖃 *Free.* ⊙ *Mon.–Sat. 10–5, Sun. during festival 2–5.*

The New Town and Beyond

It was not until the Scottish Enlightenment, a civilizing time of expansion in the 1700s, that the city fathers decided to break away from the Royal Mile's rocky slope and create a new Edinburgh below the castle, a little to the north. This was to become the New Town, with elegant squares, classical facades, wide streets, and harmonious proportions. In 1767 a civic competition to design the new district was won by an unknown young architect, James Craig (1744–95). His plan called for a grid of three main east–west streets, balanced at either end by two grand squares. These streets survive today, though some of the buildings that line them have been altered by later development. Princes Street is the southernmost, with Queen Street to the north and George Street as the axis, punctuated by St. Andrew and Charlotte squares. A look at the map will reveal a geometric symmetry unusual in Britain. Even Princes Street Gardens are balanced by Queen Street Gardens to the north. Princes Street was conceived as an exclusive residential address with an open vista facing the castle. It has since been altered by the demands of business and shopping, but the vista remains.

A Good Walk

Start your walk on The Mound, the sloping street that joins Old and New Towns. Two impressive buildings tucked immediately east of this great linking ramp are the work of W. H. Playfair (1789–1857), an architect whose neoclassic buildings contributed greatly to Edinburgh's earning the title, the "Athens of the North." The **National Gallery of Scotland** ⑱ has a wide-ranging selection of paintings, from the Renaissance to Postimpressionism, and one of the most impressive collections of Scottish art. The **Royal Scottish Academy** ⑲, with its imposing columned facade overlooking Princes Street, holds an annual exhibition of current Academicians' work. It is closed for refurbishment until 2003.

Princes Street is the humming center of Edinburgh; a ceaseless promenade of natives and visitors alike patter along its mile or so of retail establishments. Citizens lament the disappearance of the dignified old shops that once lined this street, now a long sequence of chain stores has replaced most of them. Luckily, the well-kept gardens on the other side of the street act as a wide green moat to the castle. The street is still a grand viewpoint for the dramatic grouping of the castle on its rocky outcrop and the long tail of Royal Mile tenements descending from it. Walk east past the soaring Gothic spire of the 200-ft-high **Scott Monument** ⑳. **Register House** ㉑, on the left, marks the end of Princes

Street. One of the jewels of neoclassic architecture in Scotland, it was designed by Robert Adam (1728–92). Immediately west of Register House is the **Café Royal** (17 W. Register St.), one of the city's most interesting pubs. It has good beer and great character, with ornate tiles and stained glass contributing to the atmosphere.

The monuments on **Calton Hill** ㉒, growing ever more noticeable ahead as you walk east along Princes Street, can be reached by continuing along Waterloo Place, and either climbing steps to the hilltop or taking the road farther on that loops up at a more leisurely pace. On the opposite side of the road, in the Calton Old Burying Ground, is a monument to Abraham Lincoln and the Scottish-American dead of the Civil War.

Cut through the St. James Centre shopping mall and around the building site of the former bus station, which is to make way for a branch of London's trendy Harvey Nichols department store, due to open in 2002, and walk west along George Street, with its variety of shops, to Charlotte Square. Here you will find the **Georgian House** ㉓. Also in the square, the former St. George's Church now fulfills a different role as **West Register House** ㉔, an extension of the original Register House.

To explore further in the New Town, choose your own route northward, down the wide and elegant streets centering on **Moray Place** ㉕, a fine example of an 1820s development, with imposing porticoes and a central, secluded garden. A red sandstone neo-Gothic building on Queen Street houses the **Scottish National Portrait Gallery** ㉖, with fine portraits and also an excellent restaurant. Another attraction within reach of the New Town is the 70-acre **Royal Botanic Garden** ㉗. Walk down Dundas Street, the continuation of Hanover Street, and turn left and across the bridge over the Water of Leith, Edinburgh's small-scale river. You will reach the gardens, still one of the most cherished spots for residents, as well as an important center for scientific research.

TIMING

The first part of this walk into the New Town is a good way of getting your bearings, providing splendid vistas and a clear sense of the architectural differences between The Old and The New Town's. From the top of The Mound along the full length of Princes Street, should take no more than an hour, allowing time for a close inspection of The Scott Monument (known to the locals as Thunder Bird 3) and including a constant, bedrock view of the castle—the jewel in Edinburgh's crown. It is well worth allocating a couple of hours for Calton Hill, which provides a 360 degree view of Edinburgh's magnificent skyline, as far as the Firth of Forth across to The East Neuk of Fife. The early grid system in The New Town provides easy navigation for a wander downhill to the Water of Leith and Stockbridge—a charming part of town with an interesting mix of pubs and shops. It's a 20 minute walk from Princes Street. The Royal Botanic Garden is also a 20 minute walk from Princes Street.

Sights to See

OFF THE
BEATEN PATH

Britannia. Moored on the waterfront at Leith, Edinburgh's port north of the city center, is the former Royal Yacht *Britannia,* launched in Scotland in 1953 and now retired to her home country. You can go aboard to investigate how the Royals lived life on the high seas: Queen Elizabeth said that the ship was the one place where she could truly relax. The Royal Apartments, officers quarters, and the more functional engine room, bridge, galleys and captain's cabin are all open to view. The land-based Visitor Centre has multimedia exhibits that cover *Britannia*'s history. ✉ *Ocean Dr., Leith,* ☎ *0131/555–5566.* WEB *www.royalyachtbritannia.co.uk* 🎫 *£7.75.* ☼ *Daily 9:30–4:30.*

★ ㉒   **Calton Hill.** A marvelous vantage point from which to gain panoramic views, Calton Hill is also address to numerous historic monuments, including the incomplete Parthenon look-alike known as Edinburgh's Disgrace, intended as a National War Memorial in 1822, but contributions fell short, and the **Nelson Monument**, completed in 1814. ⊠ *Off Regent Rd.,* ☎ *0131/556–2716.* ⊡ *£2.50.* ⊙ *Apr.–Sept., Mon. 1–6, Tues.–Sat. 10–6; Oct.–Mar., Mon.–Sat. 10–3.*

OFF THE
BEATEN PATH

EDINBURGH ZOO – In Edinburgh's western suburbs, this zoo offers areas for children to approach or handle animals. It's noted for its penguins, who participate in a delightful parade out of their enclosure every day during summer. Check out the fascinating Darwin Evolutionary Maze. ⊠ *Corstorphine Rd.,* ☎ *0131/334–9171.* ᵂᴱᴮ *www.edinburghzoo. org.uk* ⊡ *£7.* ⊙ *Apr.–Sept., Mon.–Sat. 9–6, Sun. 9:30–6; Mar. and Oct., Mon.–Sat. 9–5, Sun. 9:30–5; Nov.–Feb., Mon.–Sat. 9–4:30, Sun. 9:30–4:30.*

★ ㉓   **Georgian House.** This house stands in Charlotte Square, the elegant urban set piece at the west end of George Street (graced by the palatial facade designed by Robert Adam on the square's north side, considered one of Britain's finest pieces of civic architecture). Thanks to the National Trust for Scotland, the Georgian House has been furnished in period style to show the domestic lifestyle of an affluent late-18th-century family. ⊠ *7 Charlotte Sq.,* ☎ *0131/225–2160,* ᵂᴱᴮ *www.nts. org.uk.* ⊡ *£5.* ⊙ *Mar.–Oct., Mon.–Sat. 10–5, Sun. 2–5; Nov.–Dec., Mon.–Sat. 11–4, Sun. 2–4 (other times by appointment).*

㉕   **Moray Place.** With imposing porticoes and a central, secluded garden, this is an especially fine example of an 1820s development. The area remains primarily residential, in contrast to the area around Princes Street. The Moray Place gardens are still for residents only.

★ ⑱   **National Gallery of Scotland.** This honey-color neoclassic building, midway between the Old and the New Towns, contains just about the best collection of Old Masters in Britain outside the great London museums. Moreover, the gallery has the advantage of being relatively small, so you can easily tour the whole collection in a couple of hours. There are superb works by Carravagio, Titian, Velásquez, El Greco, Rembrandt, Turner, Degas, Monet, and van Gogh, among many others. A headline-making acquisition was Antonio Canova's (1757–1822) famous 19th-century statue, *The Three Graces,* which Scotland managed to snag despite the hopes (and millions) of the United States' Getty Art Museum. Scottish painters are also well to the fore, chief among them the 18th-century portrait painter Sir Henry Raeburn (1756–1823). ⊠ *The Mound,* ☎ *0131/556–8921.* ᵂᴱᴮ *www.natgalscot.ac.uk* ⊡ *Free.* ⊙ *Mon.–Sat. 10–5 (extended during festival), Sun. noon–5; print room, weekdays 10–12:30 and 2–4:30, by appointment.*

㉑   **Register House.** Marking the end of Princes Street, Scotland's first custom-built archives depository was partly funded by the sale of estates forfeited by Jacobite landowners at the close of their last rebellion in Britain (1745–46). Work on the building, designed by Robert Adam, Scotland's most famous neoclassic architect, started in 1774. The statue in front is of the first Duke of Wellington (1769–1852). ⊠ *3 West Register St., east end of Princes St.,* ☎ *0131/535–1314.* ⊡ *Free.* ⊙ *Weekdays 9–4:30.*

㉗   **Royal Botanic Garden.** North of the city center, a 10-minute bus ride from Princes Street, the Royal Botanic Garden is second only to Kew Gardens in London for the variety of the plants it contains, and for the charm of its setting. The 70-acre site presents an immense display of specimens, from tropical to Nordic, including the largest collection of rhododendrons and azaleas in Britain and an impressive Chinese garden. There are also a convenient café, a shop, and a temporary exhibition area. ⊠ *Inverleith Row,* ☎ *0131/552-7171.* 🖭 *Free, donation requested for greenhouses.* ⊙ *Nov.–Jan., daily 9:30–4; Feb., Oct., daily 9:30–5; Mar., Sept., daily 9:30–6; Apr.–Aug., daily 9:30–7. Café, shop, and exhibition areas Mar.–Oct., daily 10–5; Nov.–Feb. daily 10–3:30.*

⑲ Royal Scottish Academy. A fine neoclassic temple complete with grand columns is proudly situated directly in front of The National Gallery of Scotland. It's closed for refurbishment until 2003. ⊠ *Princes St.*

⑳ Scott Monument. The great poems and novels (such as *Ivanhoe* and *Waverley*) of Sir Walter Scott (1771–1832) created a world frenzy for Scotland; the Scots were duly grateful and put up this great Gothic memorial to him in 1844. Under its graceful spire sits Scott himself, his dog, Maida, at his feet. Behind the monument is one of the prettiest city parks in Britain, **Princes Street Gardens.** In the open-air theater, amid the park's trim flower beds, stately trees, and carefully tended lawns, brass bands and classical music ensembles occasionally perform in the summer. ⊠ *Princes St.,* ☎ *0131/529-4068,* 🕸 *www.aboutbritain.com.* 🖭 *Interior of monument £2.50.* ⊙ *Mon.–Sat. 9–4, Sun. 10–4; Summer, Mon.–Sat. 9–8, Sun. 10–6.*

㉖ Scottish National Portrait Gallery. The gallery contains a magnificent Gainsborough and portraits by the Scottish artists Allan Ramsay (1713–84) and Sir Henry Raeburn. The building itself is also of great interest, with richly colored murals in the main hall. ⊠ *Queen St.,* ☎ *0131/556-8921.* 🕸 *www.natgalscot.ac.uk* 🖭 *Free (charge for special exhibitions).* ⊙ *Mon.–Sat. 10–5, Sun. 12–5.*

㉔ West Register House. As an extension of the original Register House, this research facility has records open for public examination, with helpful staff to assist you. ⊠ *Charlotte Sq.,* ☎ *0131/535-1400.* 🖭 *Free.* ⊙ *Weekdays 9–4:30.*

Dining and Lodging

Edinburgh is a diverse, sophisticated city, with its cuisine reflected through an interesting mix of traditional and exotic food, from Scottish dishes to Ethnic variety. Make reservations well in advance, especially at festival time.

£££ ✕ **Martins.** Don't be put off by the look of this restaurant on the out-
★ side. It's tucked away in a little backstreet and has a typically forbidding northern facade. All's well inside, though, and the contemporary food is light and delicious. Fish and game are specialties here, and the cheese board is famous. ⊠ *70 Rose St., North La., between Castle and Frederick Sts.,* ☎ *0131/225-3106. AE, DC, MC, V. Closed Sun.–Mon. Sept.–July. No lunch Sat.*

£££ ✕ **Skippers Bistro.** Don't miss this superb restaurant, tucked away in a corner of Leith. It was once a traditional pub and still retains its cozy and cluttered ambience, with dark wood, shining brass, and lots of pictures and ephemera. As befits its location, this is a seafood restaurant. For a starter, the delectable homemade fish cakes can't be beat. Main dishes change daily but might feature halibut, salmon, or monkfish in delicious and innovative sauces. ⊠ *1A Dock Place, Leith,* ☎ *0131/554-1018. Reservations essential. AE, DC, MC, V.*

££–£££ ✕ **Bann UK.** A thriving restaurant off the Royal Mile, the excellent vegetarian and vegan food at Bann UK is very popular with students and young people. You can come here for breakfast, tapas, and sandwiches, as well as large salads and more substantial dishes including a tasty vegetarian haggis. ⊠ *5 Hunter Sq.,* ☎ *0131/226–1112. AE, MC, V.*

££–£££ ✕ **Café Doc.** This Italian treasure is tucked away on Thistle Street. Don't be deceived by the café front (although you will be assured of a great cappuccino). The restaurant at the back of the café really comes to life in the evening, offering an eclectic menu of authentic north Italian cuisine made with fresh local produce. House specialities include linguine with lobster, and risotto bursting with flavor and character. Given the chance, the Venetian owner Massimo will regale you with lively banter, helped along perhaps by one of the memorable wines. ⊠ *49a Thistle Street,* ☎ *0131/220–6846. Closed Mon. MC, V.*

££–£££ ✕ **The Dome.** The splendid interior of this former bank with its painted plasterwork and central dome provides an elegant backdrop for relaxed dining. Or you could just opt for a drink at the central bar, a favored spot where sophisticates wind down after work. The toasted BLT sandwiches are almost big enough for two, but if you're ravenous the eclectic menu offers many other options: try the penne sautéed in a basil cream with fresh mussels, or the char-grilled chicken salad with nan bread. ⊠ *14 George St.,* ☎ *0131/624–8624. AE, MC, V.*

££–£££ ✕ **Howie's.** This simple neighborhood bistro has four branches and a lively clientele. The steaks are tender Aberdeen beef, and the Loch Fyne herring are sweet-cured to Howie's own recipe. ⊠ *29 Waterloo Place.,* ☎ *0131/556–5766, No lunch Mon.;* ⊠ *63 Dalry Rd.,* ☎ *0131/313–3334, No lunch Mon.;* ⊠ *208 Bruntsfield Pl.,* ☎ *0131/221–1777;* ⊠ *4/6 Glanville Pl.,* ☎ *0131/225–5553. MC, V.*

££ ✕ **A Room in the Town.** This cheerful bistro in one of the most picturesque areas of New Town offers good value for money. Amusing pseudo-classical murals festoon the walls, pop music plays gently, and the service is informal but excellent. The sauces have a sweet edge, to suit the Celtic taste, but the variety of dishes would whet any palate. There's a lively wine list, or you can bring your own bottle. It can sometimes get a bit smoky. ⊠ *16 Howe St., EH3,* ☎ *0131/225–8204. DC, MC, V.*

£–££ ✕ **Indian Cavalry Club.** The menu of this cool and sophisticated Indian restaurant reflects a confident, up-to-date approach. With its steamed specialties, it's almost an Indian nouvelle cuisine. The **Club Tent** in the basement serves light meals. ⊠ *3 Atholl Pl.,* ☎ *0131/228–3282. AE, DC, MC, V.*

£ ✕ **Kalpna.** This Indian eatery has a reputation for outstanding value,
★   especially its lunchtime buffet. Indian art adorns the walls, enhancing your enjoyment of exotic specialties, such as *shahi sabzi* (spinach and nuts in cream sauce) and mushroom curry. All dishes are vegetarian, and skillfully and deliciously prepared. ⊠ *2–3 St. Patrick's Sq.,* ☎ *0131/667–9890. MC, V.*

££££ ✕▥ **Balmoral Hotel.** The attention to detail in the elegant rooms and
★   the sheer élan that has re-created the Edwardian splendor of this former grand railroad hotel make staying at the Balmoral a special introduction to Edinburgh. Here, below the impressive clock tower marking the east end of Princes Street, you get a strong sense of being at the center of Edinburgh life. The main restaurant is the plush and stylish Grill Room (jacket and tie), serving delicacies such as beef carpaccio with warm mushroom salad and grilled salmon steak with hollandaise sauce. ⊠ *Princes St., EH2 2EQ,* ☎ *0131/556–2414,* ℻ *0131/557–3747,* ⓦⓔⓑ *www.rshotels.com. 184 bedrooms, 21 suites. 2 restaurants, bar, indoor pool. AE, DC, MC, V.*

££££ ✕▥ **Caledonian Hilton Hotel.** "The Caley" recalls the days of the great
★   railroad hotels, although its former nearby station is long gone. Its imposing Victorian decor has been faithfully preserved and has lost none of its original dignity and elegance. The main restaurant, La Pompadour, with its elegant plasterwork and rich murals, would please even Louis

XV. The cuisine is *bien sûr,* classic French, using top-quality Scottish produce, sea bass, lobster, and venison. The well-chosen wine list is extensive. Lunchtime tends to be more relaxed. The less formal Chisholms restaurant supplies traditional Scottish roasts, fish, and game. ⊠ *Princes St., EH1 2AB,* ☎ *0131/459–9988,* FAX *0131/225–6632,* WEB *www.caledonianhotel.co.uk. 246 rooms. 2 restaurants. AE, DC, MC, V.*

££££ 🏨 **Channings.** Five Edwardian terraced houses have become an elegant hotel in an upscale neighborhood minutes from Princes Street. Restrained colors, antiques, quiet rooms, and great views toward Fife (from the north-facing rooms) set the tone. The Brasserie offers excellent value, especially at lunchtime. Try the hot-smoked salmon with coriander and saffron risotto. ⊠ *12–16 South Learmonth Gardens, EH4 1EZ,* ☎ *0131/ 315–2226,* FAX *0131/332–9631,* WEB *www.channings.co.uk. 48 rooms. Restaurant. AE, DC, MC, V.*

£££ 🏨 **Malmaison.** Once a seamen's hostel set in the heart of Leith, Edinburgh's seaport, the Malmaison offers good value yet stylish accommodation, featuring king-size beds and CD players in all bedrooms, decorated in a chic, bold modern style. In the public areas a dramatic black, cream, and taupe color scheme prevails. The French theme of the hotel (sister to the Malmaison in Glasgow) is emphasized by the café bar and brasserie. ⊠ *1 Tower Pl., Leith EH6 7DB,* ☎ *0131/468–5000,* FAX *0131/468–5002. 60 rooms. Restaurant, café, bar. AE, DC, MC, V.*

££–£££ 🏨 **Ardmor House.** A 15-minute walk from Princes Street, Ardmor is a restored Victorian house with a comfortable and elegant contemporary style. It is gay owned but very straight friendly, and co-owner Robin is at hand to offer advice on what to see and do during your stay in Edinburgh. ⊠ *74 Pilrig St., EH6 5AS,* ☎ FAX *0131/554–4944,* WEB *www.ardmorhouse.freeserve.co.uk. 5 rooms. MC, V.*

££ 🏨 **Gloria's Place.** This luxurious Georgian B&B is a 10-minute walk from city center. Well-equipped bedrooms (including fridge, direct-dial phone, and socket for your laptop computer) are complemented by the welcoming sitting room, with its wall of books. Smoking is not permitted. ⊠ *20 London St., EH3 6NA,* ☎ *0131/557–0216,* FAX *0131/ 315–3375,* WEB *www.scotland.org. 3 rooms. AE, MC, V.*

££ 🏨 **Kew House and Apartments.** Inside the elegant house, dating from 1860, are six tastefully modernized rooms, each with TV, a tea- and coffeemaker, and a complimentary bottle of sherry. The two apartments have sitting rooms and full kitchens. It's a 15-minute walk from the town center and entirely nonsmoking. ⊠ *1 Kew Terr., EH12 5JE,* ☎ *0131/313–0700,* FAX *0131/313–0747,* WEB *www.kewhouse.com. 6 rooms, 2 apartments. Restaurant, bar. AE, DC, MC, V.*

££ 🏨 **Stuart House.** Within 15 minutes' walk of the city center, this B&B ★ is in a Victorian terraced house with some fine plasterwork. The decor suits the structure: bold colors, floral fabrics, and generously curtained windows combine with antique and traditional-style furniture and chandeliers to create an opulent ambience. Smoking is not permitted. ⊠ *12 E. Claremont St., EH7 4JP,* ☎ *0131/557–9030,* FAX *0131/557– 0563. 7 rooms. AE, DC, MC, V.*

Nightlife and the Arts

Casinos

Stanley Berkeley (⊠ 2 Rutland Pl., ☎ 0131/228–4446) is a private casino that offers free membership on 24 hours' notice. At **Stanley Martell** (⊠ 7 Newington Rd., ☎ 0131/667–7763), a private club, visitors can apply for free membership with a day's notice. **The Stanley Edinburgh** (⊠ 5B York Pl., ☎ 0131/624–2121) offers American roulette, poker, blackjack, and slot machines. It's a private membership casino but you can apply for free membership 24 hours in advance. **Ladbrokes May-**

bury Casino (⊠ 5 South Maybury Rd., ☎ 0131/338–4444) also makes membership available after a 24-hour waiting period. Its restaurant is highly rated.

Cocktail Bars

Tonic. Sip a Cosmopolitan or a Silver Mercedes here before hitting the clubs at the weekend. There's an extensive cocktail list, with unusual vodka and gin drinks, including Jack Daniel fruity mixes. The stylish basement bar is done in pale wood and chrome, with bouncy bar stools and comfy sofas. Tonic draws a mixed crowd in the 20–40 age group with lively music, snacks and tapas. ⊠ *34a Castle St. (off George St.),* ☎ *0131/225–6431.* ☉ *Mon.–Sat. 11 AM–3 AM, Sun. 6:30 PM–3 AM.*

Madogs. This was one of Edinburgh's first all-American cocktail bar-restaurants; it remains popular with professionals after work, with live music most weeknights. ⊠ *38A George St.,* ☎ *0131/225–3408.* ☉ *Mon.–Sat. 11 AM–3 AM, Sun. 6:30 PM–3 AM.*

Concert Halls

The **Festival Theatre** (⊠ Nicolson St., ☎ 0131/529–6000) hosts ballet, opera, and concerts, including performances by the Royal Scottish National Orchestra in season. The **Playhouse** (⊠ Greenside Pl., ☎ 0131/557–2692) leans toward popular artists and musicals. The **Queen's Hall** (⊠ Clerk St., ☎ 0131/668–2019) is intimate in scale and hosts smaller recitals. **Usher Hall** (⊠ Lothian Rd., ☎ 0131/228–1155) is Edinburgh's grandest concert hall, with classical music concerts and opera.

Discos/Nightclubs

L'Attaché Nightclub. The DJs at this club spin '60s, '70s, '80s, and '90s sounds. ⊠ *Beneath the Rutland Hotel, 3 Rutland St.,* ☎ *0131/229–3402.* 🎫 *£3.* ☉ *Fri.–Sat. 10 PM–3 AM.*

Po Na Na Souk Bar. At this North African theme dance club you can hear yourself think. Laid-back yet very slick, it often gets crowded on weekend nights. ⊠ *43B Frederick St.,* ☎ *0131/226–2224.* 🎫 *Varies.* ☉ *Sun.–Tues. 10 PM–3 AM, Wed.–Sat. 8 PM–3 AM.*

The Venue. This is a venue for varying dance sounds, including techno and progressive house; check local press for details. ⊠ *15–21 Calton Rd.,* ☎ *0131/557–3073.* 🎫 *Varies.* ☉ *Tues. and Fri.–Sat. 10:30 PM–3 AM; varied hrs rest of wk.*

Festivals

The flagship arts events in the city is the **Edinburgh International Festival** (August 11–September 31), which for over a half century has attracted performing artists of international caliber in a great celebration of music, dance, and drama. Advance information, programs, tickets, and reservations during the festival are available from Edinburgh Festival Centre, an impressive Victorian gothic church renovated and renamed "The Hub." ⊠ *Castlehill, Edinburgh EH1 1ND,* ☎ *0131/473–2001,* 📠 *0131/473–2003,* 🌐 *www.eif.co.uk.*

The **Edinburgh Festival Fringe** offers a huge range of theatrical and musical events, some by amateur groups (you have been warned), and it's much more of a grab bag than the official festival. The fringe offers a vast choice (a condition of Edinburgh's artistic life found only during the three- or four-week festival season). During festival time, it's possible to arrange your own entertainment program from morning to midnight and beyond. Information, programs, and tickets are available from Edinburgh Festival Fringe. ⊠ *180 High St., Edinburgh EH1 1QS,* ☎ *0131/226–5257; 0131/226–5259 during festival only,* 📠 *0131/220–4205,* 🌐 *www.edfringe.com.*

The **Edinburgh International Film Festival,** held in August around the same time of the Edinburgh International Festival, is yet another aspect of the city's summer festival logjam. Advance information, tickets, and programs are available from Film Festival Office. ✉ *88 Lothian Rd., Edinburgh EH3 9BZ,* ☎ *0131/228–4051,* ₣ₐₓ *0131/229–5501.*

The **Edinburgh Military Tattoo** might not be art, but it is certainly entertainment. It's sometimes confused with the festival itself, partly because the dates overlap (August 2–24). This great celebration of martial music and skills is set on the castle esplanade, and the dramatic backdrop augments the spectacle. Dress warmly for the late-evening performances. Even if it rains, the show most definitely goes on. Tickets and information are available from Edinburgh Military Tattoo Office. (✉ *32 Market St., Edinburgh EH1 1QB,* ☎ *0131/225–1188,* ₣ₐₓ *0131/ 225–8627,* ᵂᴱᴮ *www.edintattoo.co.uk).*

Scottish Entertainments and Ceilidhs
Several hotels present traditional Scottish music evenings in summer season, including the **Carlton Highland Hotel** (✉ North Bridge, ☎ 0131/556–7277). The well-established **Jamie's Scottish Evening** (✉ Thistle Edinburgh Hotel, Leith St., ☎ 0131/556–0111) is another popular evening of traditional entertainment.

Theater
The **Edinburgh Festival Theatre** (✉ Nicolson St., ☎ 0131/529–6000) stages operas, ballet, concerts, and excellent, occasional tours (check with box office for details). You can visit the **King's Theatre** (✉ Leven St., ☎ 0131/ 529–6000) for comedy, musicals, and drama, as well as Christmas pantomime. The **Royal Lyceum Theatre** (✉ Grindlay St., ☎ 0131/248– 4848) offers contemporary and traditional drama. The **Traverse Theatre** (✉ 10 Cambridge St., ☎ 0131/228–1404), housed in a specially designed flexible space, is ideal for the new Scottish plays, which are its specialty.

Outdoor Activities and Sports

Golf
Edinburgh is well endowed with golf courses, with 20 or so near downtown (even before the nearby East Lothian courses are considered). The **Braids United** course, south of the city center, welcomes visitors (☎ 0131/447–6666). **Bruntsfield Links** golf club (☎ 0131/336–4050) permits visitors to play on weekdays by appointment. **Duddingston** (☎ 0131/ 661–4301) is a scenic golf club, with a creek acting as a natural hazard. It's 2 mi from the Edinburgh city center; visitors can play on weekdays by appointment. All the courses have 18 holes.

A quite exceptional destination is the **Gullane Golf Club** (☎ 01620/ 842255), about 20 mi east of Edinburgh on A198, with three courses, all 18 holes. The **Luffness New** (☎ 01620/843114) golf course is open to the public weekdays by advance booking.

Jogging
The most convenient spot downtown for joggers is **West Princes Street Gardens,** which is separated from traffic by a 30-ft embankment, with a half-mile loop on asphalt paths. In **Holyrood Park,** stick to jogging on the road around the volcanic mountain for a 2¼-mi trip. For a real challenge, charge up to the summit of Arthur's Seat, or to the halfway point, the Cat's Nick.

Shopping

Edinburgh features a cross section of Scottish specialties, such as tartans and tweeds. At **Edinburgh Old Town Weaving Company** (✉ 555

Castlehill, ☎ 0131/226–1555), you can chat with and buy from cloth and tapestry weavers as they work. Also along the Royal Mile, you will find several shops selling high-quality tartans and woolen goods. If you are interested in learning the background of your tartan purchases or if you want to see a weaving mill in action, try **Geoffrey (Tailor) Highland Crafts Ltd.** (✉ 57–59 High St., The Royal Mile, ☎ 0131/557–0256, WEB www.geoffreykilts.co.uk). Don't forget to look over the contemporary range, including leather. A popular gift selection is available from **Edinburgh Crystal,** south of the city, in Penicuik (✉ Eastfield, ☎ 01968/675128).

Antiques shops open and close with great rapidity, so it's smart to concentrate on areas with a number of stores close together, for instance, Bruntsfield Place, Causewayside, or St. Stephen Street. **Joseph Bonnar** (✉ 72 Thistle St., ☎ 0131/226–2811) is a specialist in antique jewelry in the heart of the New Town.

Princes Street

The **Edinburgh Woollen Mill** (✉ 62 Princes St., ☎ 0131/225–4966), popular with overseas visitors, sells a wide range of knitwear and tweeds. **Gleneagles of Scotland** (✉ near Princes St. in Waverley Market, ☎ 0131/557–1777) is a mid-range knitwear store. **Jenners** (✉ 48 Princes St., across from the Scott Monument, ☎ 0131/225–2442) is Edinburgh's "mini-Harrods," an independent and top-quality department store.

George Street

George Street features old, established, local names such as **George Waterston** (✉ 35 George St., ☎ 0131/225–5690), which carries stationery and a range of Scottish gifts. The jeweler **Hamilton and Inches** (✉ 87 George St., ☎ 0131/225–4898), established in 1866, is a silver- and goldsmith, worth visiting not only for its modern and antique gift possibilities, but also for its late-Georgian interior. There is a good selection of Scottish titles (and a pleasant upstairs café) in **James Thin** (✉ 57 George St., ☎ 0131/225–4495).

Victoria Street/West Bow/Grassmarket

Where these three streets run together, there are a number of specialty stores in a small area. **Byzantium** (✉ 9A Victoria St., ☎ 0131/225–1768) has an eclectic mix of antiques, crafts, clothes, and an excellent coffee shop on the top level. **Iain Mellis Cheesemonger** (✉ 30A Victoria St., ☎ 0131/226–6215) has about 50–60 varieties of British cheeses; the shop's brochure is an education in itself. The same firm also runs an old-fashioned **grocery store** (✉ 205 Bruntsfield Pl., ☎ 0131/447–8889) with proper dry-cured bacon, hams, freshly roasted coffees, and, of course, more delicious cheeses.

Side Trip to St. Andrews: The Golfer's Heaven

28 *42 mi northeast of Edinburgh.*

It may have a ruined cathedral, ancient castle, and a grand university—the oldest in Scotland—but the modern fame of St. Andrews is mainly as the home of golf. Forget that Scottish kings were crowned here, or that John Knox preached, or Reformation reformers were burned at the stake. Thousands come to St. Andrews to play at the Old Course, home of the Royal & Ancient Club, and to follow in the footsteps of Hagen, Sarazen, Jones, and Hogan.

On the Royal & Ancient's course, golf was perhaps originally played with a piece of driftwood, a shore pebble, and a convenient rabbit hole on the sandy, coastal turf. It has been argued that golf came to Scotland from Holland, but the historical evidence points to Scotland being the cradle, if not the birthplace, of the game. Citizens of St. Andrews were playing golf on the town links (public land) as far back as the 15th century. Rich golfers, instead of gathering on the common links, formed themselves into clubs by the 18th century. Arguably, the world's first golf club was the Honourable Company of Edinburgh golfers (founded in Leith in 1744), which is now at Muirfield in East Lothian. The Society of St. Andrews Golfers, founded in 1754, became the Royal & Ancient Golf Club of St. Andrews in 1834. Find out more at the **British Golf Museum,** where displays recount the growth of golf over the centuries, and golf in Victorian times. ⊠ *Bruce Embankment,* ☎ *01334/460046,* FAX *01334/460064,* WEB *www.britishgolfmuseum.co.uk.* 🎫 *£3.75.* ⊙ *Easter–mid-Oct., daily 9:30–5:30; mid-Oct.–Easter, Thurs.–Mon. 11–3.*

St. Andrews offers a wide range of attractions for nongolfers. The **cathedral,** its ancient university (founded in 1411), and **castle** are poignant reminders that the town was once the ecclesiastical capital of Scotland. The now largely ruined cathedral was one of the largest churches ever built in Scotland. The castle is approached via a visitor center with an audiovisual presentation. ☎ *0131/668–8800,* WEB *www. historic-scotland.gov.uk.* 🎫 *Cathedral museum and St. Rule's Tower £2; castle £2.80; combined ticket £4.* ⊙ *Cathedral museum, castle visitor center, and tower Apr.–Sept., daily 9:30–6; Oct.–Mar., Mon.–Sat. 9:30–4, Sun. 2–4.*

Dining and Lodging

££ ✕ **Balaka.** At this Bangladeshi eatery, with a dusky pink decor, crisp white table cloths, and vases of roses, the Rouf family displays its exceptional cookery skills. Popular dishes include *Mas Bangla* (marinated Scottish salmon fried in mustard oil with garlic, spring onion, and aubergine) and chicken with green herbs, including fresh coriander from the garden. ⊠ *Alexandra Pl.,* ☎ *01334/474825. AE, MC, V. No lunch Sun.*

££££ ✕🏨 **Rufflets Country House Hotel.** This creeper-covered country house just outside St. Andrews is surrounded by 10 acres of formal and informal gardens. All the rooms are attractively decorated and comfortable, with the amenities one would expect of a top-class hotel. Dinner is served in the roomy Garden Restaurant, famous for its use of local produce to create memorable Scottish dishes such as chargrilled fillet of trout with leeks and tarragon butter sauce, or Rannoch venison with a raspberry tea syrup glaze. There is a three-course, fixed-price menu. ⊠ *Strathkinness Low Rd., KY16 9TX,* ☎ *01334/472594,* FAX *01334/ 478703,* WEB *www.rufflets.co.uk. 22 rooms. Restaurant, bar. AE, DC, MC, V.*

Outdoor Activities and Sports

GOLF

The **St. Andrews Links** (☎ 01334/475757, FAX 01334/477036, WEB www.standrews.org.uk) has six seaside courses, all of which welcome visitors. The Old Course, New Course, Jubilee, Eden, and Strathtyrum have 18 holes, although the Balgove Course has nine holes. For information, write to the ⊠ Reservations Department, St. Andrews Links Trust, Pilmour House, St. Andrews, Fife KY16 9SF.

GLASGOW

It has been almost 300 years since Daniel Defoe, author of *Robinson Crusoe,* described Glasgow as the "cleanest and beautifullest and best-built of cities"—20 years ago, many would not have recognized Scotland's largest city from that description. Stretching along both banks of the widening River Clyde, Glasgow was known as a depressed city, and a half century ago, its slums of dockland and the Clyde banks were infamous for their time. Today, however, Glasgow has undergone a full-fledged urban renaissance: trendy downtown stores, a booming and diverse cultural life, stylish restaurants, and above all, a general air of confidence, have given grace and élan to Scotland's most exciting city. If Edinburgh is proud, age-of-elegance, and reserved, Glasgow is aggressive, industrial-revolution, and exuberant.

The city's development over the past two centuries has been unashamedly commercial, tied up with the wealth of its manufacturers and merchants, who constructed a vast number of civic buildings throughout the 19th century. Many of these have been preserved, and Glasgow claims, with some justification, to be Britain's greatest Victorian city. Among those who helped shape Glasgow's unique Victorian cityscape during its greatest period of civic expansion was the local-born architect Alexander "Greek" Thomson (1817–75). But Glasgow, always at the forefront of change, boasts, side by side with the overly Victorian, an architectural vision of the future in the work of Charles Rennie Mackintosh (1868–1928). The amazing Glasgow School of Art, the Willow Tearoom, and the churches and school buildings he designed for Glasgow point clearly to the clarity and simplicity of the best of 20th-century design. Glasgow is 45 mi west of Edinburgh. The journey takes an hour by car on the fast M8/A8 road, or 50 minutes by train.

Medieval Glasgow and the Merchant City

In this central part of the city, alongside the relatively few surviving medieval buildings are some of the best examples of the architectural confidence and exuberance that so characterized the burgeoning Glasgow of late 19th century. Today this area is experiencing a renaissance and a newfound appreciation.

A Good Walk

George Square ㉙, the focal point of Glasgow's business district, is the natural starting point for any walking tour. It's convenient to the Buchanan Street bus and underground stations and parking lot, as well as the two main railway stations, Queen Street and Glasgow Central. After viewing the **City Chambers** ㉚ on the east side of the square, leave George Square by the northeast corner and head eastward along George Street. Turn left at High Street, the spine of the downtown area before Glasgow expanded westward in the 18th century, then go up the hill to **Glasgow Cathedral** ㉛, and the **St. Mungo Museum of Religious Life and Art** ㉜. Opposite the cathedral, across Castle Street, is **Provand's Lordship** ㉝, Glasgow's oldest house.

Retrace your steps down Castle Street and High Street, continuing on to reach the Tolbooth Steeple at **Glasgow Cross** ㉞. Continue southeast along London Road (under the bridge) about a quarter of a mile and you'll come to the Barras (barrows, or pushcarts), Scotland's largest and most colorful market (weekends only). Turn down Greendyke Street from London Road to reach Glasgow Green, Glasgow's oldest park, by the River Clyde, with the **People's Palace** ㉟ museum of social history as its centerpiece.

Take the walkway west through the Green to the towering McLennan Arch, then via Saltmarket northward to Glasgow Cross. Continue westward along Trongate, where the powerful "tobacco lords" who traded with the Americas presided, then turn right into Hutcheson Street. This is Glasgow's Merchant City, with many handsome restored Georgian and Victorian buildings. At the end of the street, just south of George Square, look for **Hutcheson's Hall** ㉟, a visitor center and shop for the National Trust for Scotland. Turn west onto Ingram Street and left down Glassford Street to see the Trades House on the right, which has a facade built in 1791 to designs by Robert Adam. Turn right along Wilson Street to reach Virginia Street. Walk northward up Virginia Street back to Ingram Street. To the left you'll have a good view down to the elegant Royal Exchange Square and the former Royal Exchange building. Once a meeting place for merchants and traders, it is now the **Glasgow Gallery of Modern Art** ㊲. Royal Exchange Square leads, for pedestrians, westward to the pedestrian-zone shopping area of Buchanan Street. The Princes Square shopping mall on the east side has a particularly good selection of specialty shops. To the west of Buchanan Street is **The Lighthouse** ㊳, dedicated to the work of Charles Rennie Mackintosh. From Buchanan Street continue north across St. Vincent Street to reach Nelson Mandela Place. Here is the Scottish Stock Exchange, worthwhile for its ornate French Venetian–style exterior alone. Buchanan Galleries, a shopping mall, dominates the top of Buchanan Street beside the Glasgow Royal Concert Hall and Sauchiehall Street junction, anchored by a branch of John Lewis department store. For an art-filled finale, a short walk along Sauchiehall Street brings you to the restored **Willow Tearoom** ㊴, an Art Nouveau gem designed by native son Charles Rennie Mackintosh, then head over one block to Renfrew Street to see Mackintosh's masterpiece, the **Glasgow School of Art** ㊵. A stop at the **Tenement House** ㊶, a few blocks to the north off Scott Street, shows the simpler side of city life.

TIMING

This walk can be accomplished comfortably in a day, which will allow time to browse in Glasgow Cathedral, the People's Palace and the Gallery of Modern Art. Aim to start after the end of the morning rush hour, say at 10, and to finish before the evening rush starts, at about 4. The Mackintosh sites—the Willow Tearoom and the Glasgow School of Art—are a coda to this walk, but remember the Tearoom closes at 4:30 PM and the City Chambers is open only on weekdays.

Sights to See

★ ㉚ **City Chambers.** Dominating the east side of George Square, this splendidly exuberant expression of Victorian confidence was opened by Queen Victoria herself in 1888. Among the outstanding features of the interior are the vaulted ceiling of the entrance hall, the magnificent banqueting hall and the marble and alabaster staircases. ✉ *George Sq.,* ☎ *0141/287–2000,* WEB *www.glasgow.gov.uk.* ☺ *Free guided tours weekdays at 10:30 and 2:30 (may be closed for occasional civic functions).*

㉙ **George Square.** This is the focal point of Glasgow's business district; the area just south of the square is termed "the Merchant City." On the east side of the square stands the magnificent Italian Renaissance–style **City Chambers,** and the handsome Merchants' House of 1874 fills the northwest corner.

㉛ **Glasgow Cathedral.** On a site sacred since St. Mungo (later known as St. Kentigern) founded a church there in the 6th century, the cathedral is an unusual double church, one above the other. ✉ *Cathedral St.,* ☎ *0131/668–8800.* 🎫 *Free.* ☺ *Apr.–Sept., Mon.–Sat. 9:30–6, Sun. 2–5; Oct.–Mar., Mon.–Sat. 9:30–4, Sun. 2–4 and for services.*

㉞ **Glasgow Cross.** This was the historic commercial center of the medieval city. The Mercat Cross, topped by a unicorn, marks the spot where merchants met, where the market was held, and where criminals were executed. Here, too, was the *tron,* or weigh beam, used to check mer-

Glasgow

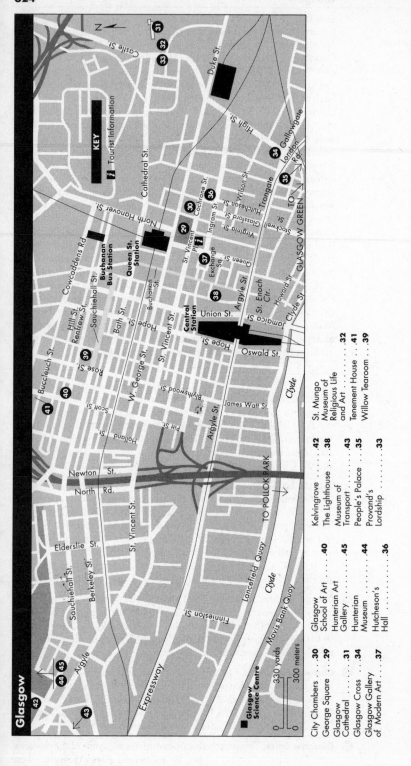

KEY

i Tourist Information

■ Glasgow Science Centre

0 ├─────┤ 330 yards
0 ├─────┤ 300 meters

City Chambers **30**
George Square ...**29**
Glasgow
  Cathedral **31**
Glasgow Cross **34**
Glasgow Gallery
  of Modern Art ...**37**

Glasgow
  School of Art **40**
Hunterian Art
  Gallery **45**
Hunterian
  Museum **44**
Hutcheson's
  Hall **36**

Kelvingrove **42**
The Lighthouse **38**
Museum of
  Transport **43**
People's Palace ...**35**
Provand's
  Lordship **33**

St. Mungo
  Museum of
  Religious Life
  and Art **32**
Tenement House ...**41**
Willow Tearoom ...**39**

chants' weights, installed in 1491. The Tolbooth Steeple dates from 1626 and served as the civic center and place where travelers entering the city paid their tolls.

㊲ Glasgow Gallery of Modern Art. This gallery occupies the former neoclassical Royal Exchange of 1827, originally a tobacco merchant's mansion, which stands to the south of George Square. The display scheme reflects, on each floor, one of the four elements: earth, air, fire, and water, creating some unexpected juxtapositions. The exhibits are eclectic and challenging. ☒ *Queen St.,* ☎ *0141/229–1996.* ☄ *Free.* ⊙ *Mon.– Thurs. and Sat. 10–5, Fri. and Sun. 11–5.*

★ **㊵ Glasgow School of Art.** Charles Rennie Mackintosh's masterpiece, this is a noted monument of 20th-century architecture and decorative arts. The exterior and interior, structure, furnishings, and decoration form a unified whole, reflecting the inventive genius of this man, who was only 28 years old when he won the competition for its design. Conducted tours are available (for limited numbers). There's a shop with a range of Mackintosh gifts: prints, postcards and books, and also a selection of contemporary art by students and graduates of the art school. A block away is Mackintosh's Willow Tearoom. ☒ *167 Renfrew St.,* ☎ *0141/353–4500,* WEB *www.gsa.ac.uk.* ☄ *£5.* ⊙ *Tours weekdays at 11 AM and 2 PM, Sat. at 10:30 AM and 11:30 AM.*

OFF THE BEATEN PATH   **GLASGOW SCIENCE CENTRE –** On the former Glasgow Garden Festival site, the Science Centre consists of an IMAX Film Theatre, the Science Mall, and the 127-meter Glasgow Tower, a unique viewing point for the whole city. The Science Mall focuses its state-of-the-art displays on exploration, discovery, and the environment. ☒ *50 Pacific Quay,* ☎ *0141/ 420–5000,* WEB *www.gsc.org.uk.* ☄ *Admission charge unavailable at press time.* ⊙ *Daily. 10–6.*

㊱ Hutcheson's Hall. Now a visitor center and shop for the National Trust for Scotland, this elegant neoclassic building was designed by David Hamilton in 1802. It was originally a hospice founded by two brothers, George and Thomas Hutcheson. You can see their statues in niches in the facade. ☒ *158 Ingram St.,* ☎ *0141/552–8391.* ☄ *Free.* ⊙ *Mon.–Sat. 10–5 (hall may be closed for occasional functions).*

㊳ The Lighthouse. This former newspaper office, designed by Mackintosh, is Scotland's showcase for design and architecture. It houses the Mackintosh Interpretation Centre, focusing on some of the Glasgow-born designer's most important local buildings. ☒ *11 Mitchell Lane,* ☎ *0141/353–4500,* WEB *www.thelighthouse.co.uk.* ☄ *£1 (additional £2.50 for Interpretation Centre).* ⊙ *Mon. and Wed.–Sat. 10:30–5, Tue. 11–5, Sun. noon–5.*

★ **㉟ People's Palace.** An impressive Victorian red sandstone building houses an intriguing museum dedicated to the city's social history. Behind the museum are the well-restored Winter Gardens, a relatively sheltered spot favored by visitors who want to escape the often chilly winds whistling across the green. ☒ *Glasgow Green,* ☎ *0141/554–0223,* WEB *www.glasgow.gov.uk.* ☄ *Free.* ⊙ *Mon.–Thurs. and Sat. 10–5, Fri. and Sun. 11–5.*

㉝ Provand's Lordship. The oldest building in Glasgow is a 15th-century town house, built as a residence for churchmen. Mary Queen of Scots is said to have plotted the murder of Lord Darnley here. ☒ *Castle St.,* ☎ *0141/ 552–8819.* ☄ *Free.* ⊙ *Mon.–Thurs. and Sat. 10–5, Fri. and Sun. 11–5.*

QUEEN'S CROSS CHURCH – To learn even more about the Glasgow-born designer Mackintosh, head for the Charles Rennie Mackintosh Society Headquarters, housed in a church designed by him. Although one of the leading lights in the Art Nouveau movement, Mackintosh died relatively unknown in 1928. Today, he is widely confirmed as a brilliant innovator. This center provides a further insight into Glasgow's other Mackintosh-designed buildings, which include Scotland Street School, the Glasgow School of Art, and reconstructed interiors in the Hunterian Art Gallery. The church is on the corner of Springbank Street at the junction of Garscube Road with Maryhill Road. A cab ride can get you there or a bus heading toward Queen's Cross can be taken from stops along Hope Street. ⊠ *870 Garscube Rd.,* ☎ *0141/946–6600.* ☞ *Suggested donation £2.* ☉ *Weekdays 10–5, Sun. 2–5 (or by arrangement).*

㉜ St. Mungo Museum of Religious Life and Art. An outstanding collection of artifacts covering the many religious groups that have settled throughout the centuries in Glasgow and the west of Scotland is on display here. The centerpiece is Salvador Dalí's magnificent painting, *Christ of St. John of the Cross.* Inside there's a gift shop and a café. ⊠ *2 Castle St.,* ☎ *0141/553–2557.* ☞ *Free.* ☉ *Mon.–Thurs. and Sat. 10–5, Fri. and Sun. 11–5.*

㊶ Tenement House. This ordinary, simple city-center apartment is anything but ordinary inside: it was occupied from 1911 to 1965 by the same woman, Miss Agnes Toward, who seems never to have thrown anything away. Her legacy is a fascinating time capsule, painstakingly preserved with her everyday furniture and belongings. The red sandstone tenement building itself dates from 1892. ⊠ *145 Buccleuch St.,* ☎ *0141/333–0183.* ☞ *£3.50.* ☉ *Mar.–Oct., daily 2–5 (last admission 4:30).*

㊴ Willow Tearoom. Now restored to its original art deco design by Mackintosh, this tearoom is a lovely place for a time-out. As you enjoy a cup of Earl Grey, drink in all of Mackintosh's marvelous details, right down to the decorated tables and chairs. The tree motifs reflect the street address, as "sauchie" is an old Scots word for "willow." A block away is Mackintosh's masterpiece, the Glasgow School of Art. ⊠ *217 Sauchiehall St.,* ☎ *0141/332–0521.* ☉ *Mon.–Sat. 9:30–4:30, Sun. noon–4:15.*

The West End

Glasgow's West End offers a mix of education, culture, art, and parkland. The neighborhood is dominated by the University of Glasgow, founded in 1451, making it the third-oldest in Scotland after St. Andrews and Aberdeen, and at least 130 years ahead of the University of Edinburgh. It has thrived as a center of educational excellence, particularly in the sciences. The university buildings are set in parkland, reminding the visitor that Glasgow has more green space per citizen than any other city in Europe.

A Good Walk

A good place to start is at the city's main art gallery and museum, **Kelvingrove** ㊷ in Kelvingrove Park, west of the M8 beltway, at the junction of Sauchiehall (pronounced *socky*-hall) and Argyle streets. There are free parking facilities, and plenty of buses go there from downtown. Across Argyle Street next to the Kelvin Hall sports arena is the **Museum of Transport** ㊸.

As you walk up the tree-lined Kelvin Way, the skyline to your left is dominated by the Gilbert Scott building, the University of Glasgow's main edifice. Turn left up University Avenue. On either side of the road are two important galleries, both maintained by the university. On the south side of University Avenue, in the Victorian part of the university, is the **Hunterian Museum** ㊹. Even more interesting is the **Hunterian Art Gallery** ㊺, in an unremarkable building from the 1970s across the road.

TIMING

Although the overall distance involved is not great, a day might not be long enough for this walk, if you want to visit all four museums.

Sights to See

★ ㊺ **Hunterian Art Gallery.** This gallery, part of the University of Glasgow, houses 18th-century Glasgow doctor William Hunter's collection of paintings (his antiquarian collection is housed in the Hunterian Museum nearby), together with an outstanding collection of prints and drawings by Reynolds, Rodin, Rembrandt, and Tintoretto, and a major collection of paintings by James McNeill Whistler. Also in the gallery is a replica of Charles Rennie Mackintosh's town house, which originally stood nearby. ⊠ *Glasgow University, Hillhead St.,* ☎ *0141/ 330–5431,* WEB *www.gla.ac.uk/museum.* 🎟 *Free.* ☉ *Mon.–Sat. 9:30– 5. Mackintosh House closed for lunch 12:30–1:30.*

㊹ **Hunterian Museum.** The city's oldest museum (1807) and part of the University of Glasgow, the Hunterian houses part of the collections of William Hunter, an 18th-century Glasgow doctor who assembled a staggering quantity of extremely valuable material. (The doctor's art treasures are housed in the Hunterian Art Gallery nearby.) The museum displays Hunter's hoards of coins, manuscripts, scientific instruments, and archaeological artifacts in a striking Gothic building. ⊠ *Glasgow University,* ☎ *0141/330–4221.* 🎟 *Free.* ☉ *Mon.–Sat. 9:30–5.*

㊷ **Kelvingrove.** The city's main art gallery and museum looks like a combination of cathedral and castle. It houses a fine collection of British and Continental paintings, 17th-century Dutch art, a selection from the French Barbizon school, French Impressionists, Scottish art from the 17th century to the present, silver, ceramics, European armor, and even Egyptian archaeological finds. ⊠ *Kelvingrove Park,* ☎ *0141/287– 2699.* 🎟 *Free.* ☉ *Mon.–Thurs. and Sat. 10–5, Fri. and Sun. 11–5.*

★ ㊸ **Museum of Transport.** Here Glasgow's history of locomotive building is dramatically displayed with full-size exhibits. The collection of Clyde-built ship models is world famous. Wallow in nostalgia at the re-created street scene from 1938, and enjoy the many handsome Scottish automobiles, spanning the 20th century. ⊠ *Kelvin Hall, 1 Bunhouse Rd.,* ☎ *0141/287–2720.* 🎟 *Free.* ☉ *Mon.–Thurs. and Sat. 10– 5, Fri. and Sun. 11–5.*

OFF THE
BEATEN PATH

POLLOK PARK – A peaceful green oasis off Paisley Road, 3 mi southwest of the city center (you can get there by taxi or car, by city bus, or by a train from Glasgow Central Station to Pollokshaws West Station), Pollok Park is home to two noted sights: the Burrell Collection, one of Scotland's finest art collections, and historic Pollok House.

The Burrell Collection (⊠ Pollok Country Park, Paisley Rd., ☎ 0141/ 287-2550; 🎟 Free; ☉ Mon.–Thurs. and Sat. 10–5, Fri. and Sun. 11–5) is displayed in a modern, glass-walled, and airy building so that its holdings relate to their surroundings: art and nature in perfect harmony. Inside are treasures of all descriptions, from Chinese ceramics, bronzes, and jade to medieval tapestries, stained glass, and 19th-century French paintings, the magpie collection of an eccentric millionaire, Sir William Burrell.

Dating from the mid-1700s, **Pollok House** (✉ Pollok Country Park, Paisley Rd., ☎ 0141/616–6410; 🖅 Apr.–Oct., £4 and Nov.–Mar., free; ⏱ Apr.–Oct., daily 10–5 and Nov.–Mar., daily 11–4), in the care of the National Trust for Scotland, contains the Stirling Maxwell Collection of paintings, including works by El Greco, Murillo, Goya, Signorelli, and William Blake. Fine 18th- and early 19th-century furniture, silver, glass, and porcelain are also on display.

Dining and Lodging

Glasgow has been described as a "café society," which you will never get to know properly unless you spend time drinking coffee in as many cafés as possible. The city also has a sophisticated business and professional population that appreciates the many excellent Glasgow restaurants.

£££–££££ ★ ✕ **Rogano.** The striking black-and-gold art deco design of this restaurant is enough to recommend it. The bonus is that the food at the ground-floor main restaurant, the lively Café Rogano, and the oyster bar near the entrance, is excellent. Contemporary specialties include warm salad of seared scallops with pink ginger and raspberry vinaigrette, and other seafood superbly prepared. Vegetarians are also catered to. Café Rogano is much cheaper and more informal than the main restaurant. ✉ 11 Exchange Pl., ☎ 0141/248–4055. AE, DC, MC, V.

££–£££ ★ ✕ **Buttery.** This restaurant's exquisite Victorian/Edwardian surroundings are echoed by a menu that includes the best of Scottish fish, beef, and game, as well as excellent vegetarian options. Service is friendly and the ambience is relaxed. It is most easily reached by cab. ✉ 652 Argyle St., ☎ 0141/221–8188. AE, DC, MC, V. Closed Sun. No lunch Sat.

££–£££ ✕ **Puppet Theater.** On an unprepossessing side street in the West End is one of Glasgow's most delightful restaurants, a converted Edwardian mews adorned with a striking glass conservatory. Inside are four separate salons, each with its own special ambience. The contemporary Scottish menu, with a French influence, might offer stuffed rabbit leg with langoustine and baby spinach, or brochette of monkfish and panetta. ✉ 11 Ruthven La., ☎ 0141/339–8444. Reservations essential. AE, MC, V. Closed Mon. No lunch Sat.

££–£££ ✕ **Yes.** This stylish restaurant belies its basement location with soigné lighting, grand mirrors, and a high-drama red, purple, and cream palette that even legendary decorator David Hicks might admire. Contemporary Scottish cuisine is featured here. Try the "Surprise Menu": an eclectic four-course selection reflecting the best fresh produce available on the day. ✉ 22 West Nile St., ☎ 0141/221–8044. AE, DC, MC, V. Closed Sun.

££ ✕ **78 St. Vincent.** Originally a bank, with slender interior Doric columns, this is now a stylish place to enjoy contemporary Scottish, French-influenced cuisine. As your eye feasts on the wall-length modern mural by Glasgow artist Donald McLean, your palate can relish the pan-fried venison with gin-scented jus, or seared salmon with brown nut butter. ✉ 78 St. Vincent St., ☎ 0141/248–7878. AE, DC, MC, V.

£££–££££ ★ ✕▥ **Glasgow Hilton.** This is a typical international hotel on first impression, but it's breathtakingly professional. Glasgow friendliness permeates its very upscale image. Three themed restaurants, Cameron's (a Highland shooting lodge), Minsky's (a New York–style deli and carvery), and Shimla Pinks (an Indian restaurant), and Raffles, a colonial-Singapore bar, serve superb food. ✉ 1 William St., G3 8HT, ☎ 0141/204–5555, FAX 0141/204–5004, WEB www.hilton.com. 319 rooms. 3 restaurants, bar, hair salon, health club, meeting rooms. AE, DC, MC, V.

£££ ✕⛫ **One Devonshire Gardens.** This fine town mansion offers luxury
★   accommodations. Elegance is the theme, from the sophisticated drawing room to the sumptuous guest rooms with their rich drapery and
traditional furnishings, including four-poster beds (in 10 rooms). The
restaurant is equally stylish, with a different menu for each meal. Specialties include home-smoked lobster and lime butter sauce, or roast
rack of lamb and polenta and braised shallots. ✉ *1 Devonshire Gardens, G12 0UX,* ☎ *0141/339–2001,* FAX *0141/337–1663,* WEB *www.one-
devonshire-garden.com. 27 rooms. Restaurant. AE, DC, MC, V.*

££ ✕⛫ **Babbity Bowster.** This wonderful old pub, restaurant, and lodging house in the heart of the Merchant City is an atmospheric hangout for musicians and artists. The public café bar and the restaurant
serve a mixture of traditional Scottish and French food, ranging from
bar snacks to venison or salmon with sophisticated sauces in the restaurant. If you want to experience the feisty side of Glasgow this is the
place. Guest rooms feature Victorian reproduction furniture and lacy
bedspreads. ✉ *16–18 Blackfriars St., G1 1PE,* ☎ *0141/552–5055,* FAX
0141/552–7774. 6 rooms. Restaurant, bar. AE, MC, V.

££ ✕⛫ **The Inn on the Green.** Overlooking Glasgow Green, this small highly
individual hotel is a convenient cab ride from downtown. The basement restaurant features live, relaxing jazz and a Scottish-flavored à
la carte menu, which ranges from layered haggis, neeps (turnip), and
mash, to hot Hebridean oak-smoked salmon. ✉ *25 Greenhead St., G40
1ES,* ☎ *0141/554–0165,* FAX *0141/556–4678,* WEB *www.theinnonthe-
green.co.uk. 18 rooms. Restaurant, bar. AE, MC, V.*

££ ⛫ **Kirklee Hotel.** Near the university and in the West End—a particularly quiet, leafy, and genteel district of Glasgow—this B&B is housed
in a small and cozy Edwardian town house, replete with home-away-
from-home comfort. A bay window overlooks the garden, the Victorian morning room is adorned with embroidered settees and silk-wash
wallpapers, while engravings and a large library offer decorative
touches that any university professor would appreciate. The owners
are friendly and helpful. ✉ *11 Kensington Gate, G12 9LG,* ☎ *0141/
334–5555,* FAX *0141/339–3828,* WEB *www.kirkleehotel.co.uk. 9 rooms.
AE, DC, MC, V.*

Nightlife and the Arts

Glasgow is better endowed with functioning theaters than Edinburgh.
One of the most exciting theaters in Britain is the **Citizen's Theatre** (✉
119 Gorbals St., ☎ 0141/429–0022), where productions of often hair-
raising originality are the order of the day. Contemporary works are
staged at **Cottier's Arts Theatre** (✉ 93 Hyndland St., ☎ 0141/287–4000),
in a converted church. The **King's Theatre** (✉ Bath St., ☎ 0141/287–
4000) stages light entertainment and musicals. **Glasgow Royal Concert Hall** (✉ 2 Sauchiehall St., G2 3NY, ☎ 0141/353–8000) offers a
wide-ranging calendar of classical concerts (the Royal Scottish National
Orchestra plays on many Thursdays and Saturdays throughout the year),
pop concerts, jazz, and many international musical events. The **Theatre Royal** (✉ Hope St., ☎ 0141/332–9000) is the elegant home of
Scottish Opera and Scottish Ballet.

Held every January, **Celtic Connections** is Scotland's biggest, most popular Celtic music festival. For details, contact the Royal Concert Hall.

Shopping

Glasgow is preferred by many to Edinburgh as a shopping center and
it offers a lot more shopping fun than its staid rival. Glasgow's main
shopping districts occupy a z-shape area that runs along Sauchiehall

Street from Charing Cross to the Glasgow Royal Concert Hallnad Buchanan Galleries, south down Buchanan Street to St. Enoch's Square, and east along Argyle Street. Many designer boutiques and shopping malls, complete with fountains and glass-walled elevators, can be found on Buchanan Street and along adjacent streets.

The **Argyll Arcade** (✉ Buchanan and Argyle Sts.) is a handsome 19th-century shopping mall with a wide selection of jewelers' shops (don't miss the mosaics over the Buchanan Street entrance). The **Buchanan Galleries** mall (✉ 220 Buchanan St., junction with Sauchiehall St., ☎ 041/333–9898) has major High Street names like John Lewis, Nike, and Virgin. **Princes Square** (✉ 48 Buchanan St., ☎ 0141/221–0324) is a chic, modern mall, with specialty shops on three levels and a café complex above, all under a glittering dome. You'll find Ted Baker, Crabtree and Evelyn, Space NK, Lacoste, and many other top fashion names here, and also the Scottish Craft Centre for unusual, high-quality items, but no tartan dolls. **Stockwell Bazaar** (✉ 67–77 Glassford St., ☎ 0141/552–5781) specializes in fine china and giftware.

Sauchiehall Street has a good selection of shops. **Geoffrey (Tailor) Highland Crafts Ltd.** (✉ 309 Sauchiehall St., ☎ 0141/331–2388) can supply complete Highland dress, right down to the sporran, and it has a wide range of Scottish-made gifts.

Set in a former bank building, **Borders Books, Music and Café** (✉ 98 Buchanan St., ☎ 0141/222–7700) has a particularly friendly Glasgow feel to it. It's has a wide range of Scottish books and a café.

The **Italian Centre** (✉ Ingram St.), a reminder of Glasgow's cosmopolitan image, has one of the only three British branches of Emporio Armani (☎ 0141/552–2277) outside London, as well as Versace Collections (☎ 0141/552–6510) and a choice of Italian restaurants.

On Howard Street is a row of shopping outlets. **Slater Menswear** (✉ 165 Howard St., ☎ 0141/552–7171) stocks traditionally styled high-quality tweeds, woolens, casual wear, and sportswear.

Glasgow's weekend market, the **Barras,** is just north of Glasgow Green. You can find just about anything here, in any condition, from very old model railroads to quality jewelry at bargain prices. Haggling is compulsory. Antiques hunters might make a find, but don't be surprised if you come away empty-handed. ☎ *0141/552–7258.* ☉ *Weekends 9–5.*

THE BORDERS: SIR WALTER SCOTT COUNTRY

The Borders region is the heartland of minstrelsy, ballad, and folklore, much of it arisen from murky deeds of the past. It is the homeland of the tweed suit and cashmere sweater, of medieval abbeys, of the lordly Tweed and its salmon, and of the descendants of the raiders and reivers (cattle thieves) who harried England. It's also the native soil of Sir Walter Scott, the early 19th-century poet, novelist, and creator of *Ivanhoe,* who helped transform Scotland's image from that of a land of brutal savages to one of romantic and stirring deeds and magnificent landscapes. One of the best ways to approach this district is to take as the theme of your tour the life and works of Scott. The novels of Scott are not read much nowadays, but the mystique that he created, the aura of historical romance, has outlasted his books and is much in evidence in the ruined abbeys, historical houses, and grand vistas of the Borders.

Abbotsford House

★ **46**   *Route A7, to Galashiels, 27 mi southeast of Edinburgh, then 1 mi farther on A6091, through the Moorfoot Hills.*

The most visited of Scottish literary landmarks, Abbotsford House, is the modestly sized mansion that Sir Walter Scott made his home in the 1820s. A damp farmhouse called Clartyhole when Scott bought it in 1811, it was soon transformed into what John Ruskin called "the most incongruous pile that gentlemanly modernism ever devised." That was Mr. Ruskin's idiosyncratic take: most people have found this to be one of the most fetching of all Scottish abodes. A pseudo-baronial, pseudo-monastic castle chock-full of Scottish curios, Ramsay portraits, and mounted deer heads, it is an appropriate domicile for a man of such an extraordinarily romantic imagination. To Abbotsford came most of the famous poets and thinkers of Scott's day, including Wordsworth and Washington Irving. Abbotsford is still owned by Scott's descendants. ⊠ *Galashiels B6360,* ☎ *01896/752043.* ⊡ *£4.00.* ⊙ *Mon.–Sat. 9:30–5; also Sun., Mar.–May, Oct. 2–5, June–Sept. 10–5.*

Dining and Lodging

££   ✕⊡ **Woodlands House Hotel.** This Gothic Revival–style hotel with chintz-hung and traditionally furnished interiors has stunning views over Tweeddale. Bar lunches and suppers are served in the **Oakwood** bar and restaurant, while **Alexander's** specializes in fine dining. ⊠ *Windyknowe Rd., Galashiels TD1 1RG,* ☎ FAX *01896/754722 or 01896/754892,* WEB *www.scottishbordershotel.com. 10 rooms. 3 restaurants, golf privileges, horseback riding, fishing. MC, V.*

Melrose

47   *3 mi east of Abbotsford on A6091, 30 mi south of Edinburgh.*

In the peaceful little town of Melrose, you'll find the ruins of the most famous of the great Borders abbeys. All the abbeys were burned in the 1540s in a calculated act of destruction by English invaders acting on the orders of Henry VIII. Scott himself supervised the partial reconstruction
★ of **Melrose Abbey,** one of the most beautiful ruins in Britain. "If thou would'st view fair Melrose aright/Go visit it in the pale moonlight," says Scott in his "The Lay of the Last Minstrel," and so many of his fans took the advice literally that a sleepless custodian begged him to rewrite the lines. ⊠ *Main Sq.,* ☎ *0131/668–8800.* ⊡ *£3.30.* ⊙ *Apr.–Sept., daily 9:30–6:30; Oct.–Mar., Mon.–Sat. 9:30–4:30, Sun. 2–4:30.*

At the Ormiston Institute, the **Trimontium Exhibition** displays artifacts from the largest Roman settlement in Scotland, which was at nearby Newstead. Tools and weapons, a replica Roman horse saddle, a blacksmith's shop, pottery, and scale models of the fort are on display. A guided 5-mi, 4-hour walk to the site takes place each Thursday afternoon. Phone for details. ⊠ *The Square, Melrose,* ☎ *01896/822651.* ⊡ *£1.50.* ⊙ *Apr.–Oct., daily 10:30–4:30. Closed weekends 12:30–1:30.*

A teddy bear museum, **Teddy Melrose,** tells the story of British teddy bears from the early 1900s onward. There is, inevitably, a bear-collectors's shop. ⊠ *High St.* ⊡ *£1.50.* ⊙ *Mon.–Sat. 10–5, Sun. 11–5.*

Dining and Lodging

££–£££   ✕⊡ **Burts Hotel.** This traditional town hostelry dating from the late 18th century offers period charm with modern up-to-date comfort. The elegant dining room features Scottish dishes such as pheasant terrine and venison with a whisky-and-cranberry sauce. Bar food is also offered. ⊠ *Market Sq., Melrose TD6 9PN,* ☎ *01896/822285,* FAX *01896/822870,* WEB *www.burtshotel.co.uk. 20 rooms. Restaurant. AE, DC, MC, V.*

Dryburgh Abbey

48 *5 mi southeast of Melrose, on A6091 then A68, 38 mi south of Edinburgh.*

At Dryburgh, the most peaceful and secluded of the ruined Borders abbeys, set in a bend of the Tweed among strikingly shaped trees, you'll find Scott's burial place. ⊠ *Dryburgh, near St. Boswells,* ☎ *0131/668–8800.* ⊠ *£2.80.* ⊘ *Apr.–Sept., daily 9:30–6:30; Oct.–Mar., Mon.–Sat. 9:30–4:30, Sun. 2–4:30.*

Dining and Lodging

££££   ✕⊡ **Dryburgh Abbey Hotel.** Right next to the abbey ruins, this civilized hotel is surrounded by beautiful scenery and features a restaurant specializing in Scottish fare, which offers a three-course set menu. (Bar snacks are also available at lunch time.) The restrained decor in shades of cream, peach, terra-cotta, green, and gray creates a peaceful atmosphere in keeping with its serene setting. ⊠ *St. Boswells TD6 0RQ,* ☎ *01835/822261,* FAX *01835/823945,* WEB *www.dryburgh.co.uk. 38 rooms. Restaurant, golf privileges. AE, MC, V.*

En Route   Combine a visit to Dryburgh Abbey with a stop at **Scott's View,** 3 mi north on B6356, which provides a magnificent panoramic view of quintessential Borders countryside: the Tweed valley and the Eildon Hills. It is said that the horses pulling Scott's hearse paused automatically at Scott's View, because their master had so often halted them there.

Smailholm

49 *5 mi east of St. Boswells, off B6404, 42 mi south of Edinburgh.*

Another famous Borders lookout point is **Smailholm Tower.** Beloved by Scott as a child, the 16th-century watchtower now houses a museum displaying costumed figures and tapestries relating to Scott's Borders folk ballads. Scott spent his childhood on a nearby farm, where he imbibed his love of Borders traditions and romances. ⊠ *Smailholm,* ☎ *0131/668–8800.* ⊠ *£2.00.* ⊘ *Apr.–Sept., daily 9:30–6. Oct.–Mar., Sat. 9:30–4:30, Sun. 2–4:30.*

Kelso

50 *46 mi from Edinburgh. From Smailholm, take B6397 and then eastward on A6089.*

The Tweedside roads through Kelso and Coldstream sweep with a river through parkland and game preserve and past romantic red-stone gorges. Scott attended grammar school in Kelso. The town has an unusual Continental air, with fine Georgian and early Victorian buildings surrounding a spacious, cobbled marketplace. Only a fragment remains of the once magnificent medieval Kelso Abbey. Rennie's Bridge, on the edge of town, provides good views of **Floors Castle,** seat of the duke of Roxburghe, which was designed by William Adam in 1721 and altered by William Playfair in the 1840s. The largest inhabited castle in Scotland, Floors is an architectural extravagance bristling with pepper-mill turrets and towers that stand on the "floors" or flat terraces of the Tweed bank opposite the barely visible ruins of Roxburghe Castle. A holly tree in the magnificent deer park marks the place where King James II was killed in 1460 by a cannon that "brak in the shooting." ⊠ *A6089,* ☎ *01573/223333,* FAX *01573/226056.* ⊠ *£5.50, £3 grounds only.* ⊘ *Apr.–Oct., daily 10–4:30 (last admission 4).*

Dining and Lodging

£££ ✕🏠 **Edenwater House.** A handsome and restful stone-built house, this former manse overlooks the river Eden, 2 mi north of Kelso in the hamlet of Ednam. It serves some of the best food in the Borders: roast saddle of hare with foie gras, pork fillet with a ginger and honey glaze, or fillet of monkfish crusted with basil and coriander in a beurre blanc typify the refined but simple menu. Open to nonresidents for three meals a week. ✉ *Ednam TD5 7QL, off B6461,* ☎ *01573/224070 or 01573/ 226615,* 🌐 *www.edenwaterhouse.co.uk. 3 rooms. Restaurant, fishing, horseback riding. DC, MC, V. Closed Jan. 1–14, last 2 wks in May.*

££–£££ 🏠 **Ednam House Hotel.** This large, attractive hotel is right on the banks
★ of the River Tweed, close to Kelso's grand abbey and the old Market Square. The majority of guests here are return visitors. The hall, with its open fire, paintings, and cozy armchairs gives the place a homey feel. ✉ *Bridge St., TD5 7HT,* ☎ *01573/224168,* 📠 *01573/226319,* 🌐 *www.ednamhouse.com. 30 rooms. Restaurant, golf privileges, horseback riding, fishing. MC, V. Closed Dec. 25–early Jan.*

Jedburgh

⑤ *12 mi southwest of Kelso on A698, 50 mi south of Edinburgh.*

Jedburgh, a little town 13 mi north of the border, lay in the path of marauding armies for centuries. **Jedburgh Abbey,** although in ruins like so many Borders abbeys, is relatively intact and is a superb example of abbey architecture. It has an informative visitor center that explains the role of the abbeys in the life of the Borders until their destruction, around 1545. ✉ *High St.,* ☎ *0131/668–8800.* 🎫 *£3.30.* ◷ *Apr.–Sept., daily 9:30–6:30; Oct.–Mar., Mon.–Sat. 9:30–4:30, Sun. 2–4:30.*

Mary, Queen of Scots House in Jedburgh is a fortified house highly characteristic of the 16th century, some say contemporaneous with Mary herself. Though historians disagree on whether or not she actually visited here, the house exhibits many displays commemorating Mary. ✉ *Queen St.,* ☎ *01835/863331.* 🎫 *£2.* ◷ *Mar.–Nov., Mon.–Sat. 10–4:45, Sun. 10–4:30.*

Jedburgh Castle Jail re-creates life in a Howard Reform Prison, with prison cells for visitors to inspect, and describes the history of the Royal Burgh of Jedburgh through room settings decorated in period style, costumed figures, and audiovisuals. ✉ *Castlegate,* ☎ *01835/863254.* 🎫 *£1.25.* ◷ *Mid-Mar.–mid-Nov., Mon.–Sat. 10–4:45, Sun. 1–4.*

Lodging

£ 🏠 **Spinney Guest House.** Made up of unpretentiously converted and modernized farm cottages, this is a B&B offering very high standards for the price. For a self-catering option, there are three log cabins. ✉ *Langlee TD8 6PB,* ☎ *01835/863525,* 📠 *01835/864883. 3 rooms, 3 log cabins. MC, V. Closed mid-Nov.–Feb.*

Selkirk

⑤② *40 mi south of Edinburgh.*

From Jedburgh, take A68 7 mi north to the A699 junction, turn left, and follow A699 7 mi. After traveling through miles of attractive river-valley scenery, you'll reach the ancient hilltop town of Selkirk. Scott was sheriff (county judge) of Selkirkshire from 1800 until his death in 1832, and his statue stands in the Market Place. **Sir Walter Scott's Courtroom,** where he presided, contains a display examining Scott's life, his writings, and his time as sheriff. ✉ *Market Pl.,* ☎ *01750/20096.* 🎫 *Free.* ◷ *Apr.– Sept., Mon.–Sat. 10–4, June–Aug., Sun. 2–4; Oct., Mon.–Sat. 1–4.*

Tucked away off the main square in Selkirk, **Halliwell's House Museum** is set in what was once an ironmonger's shop, which has been re-created downstairs; the upstairs exhibit tells the story of the town. ⊠ *Market St.,* ☎ *01750/20096.* 🖼 *Free.* ☉ *Apr.–June and Sept.–Oct., Mon.–Sat. 10–5, Sun. 2–4; July–Aug., Mon.–Sat. 10–6, Sun. 2–6.*

Innerleithen

❸ *11 mi west of Galashiels on A72, 29 mi south of Edinburgh.*

Innerleithen was once famous as a spa, and is the setting of Scott's novel *St. Ronan's Well.* Situated in the picturesque Tweed Valley, Innerleithen is home to **Robert Smail's Printing Works,** a fully restored Victorian print shop with its original machinery in working order and a printer in residence. ⊠ *7–9 High St.,* ☎ *01896/830206.* 🖼 *£2.50.* ☉ *Easter weekend and May–Sept., Mon.–Sat. 10–1 and 2–5, Sun. 2–5; Oct., Sat. 10–1 and 2–5, Sun. 2–5; last admission 45 min before closing, morning and afternoon.*

★ **❺** **Traquair House,** the oldest continually occupied house in Scotland and, many would add, one of the friendliest and most cheerful of the Borders' grand houses with rooms; ale is still brewed in the 18th-century brew house here and it's certainly worth a try. ⊠ *Traquair EH44 6PW, south of Innerleithen on B709,* ☎ *01896/830323.* 🖼 *£5.30.* ☉ *Easter Sat.–Oct. 31, 12:30–5:30 daily; June–Aug., daily 10:30–5:30 (last admission 5).*

Lodging

££££ 🏠 **Traquair House.** Stay in the private quarters at Traquair to experience the unique atmosphere of this ancient house. The Blue Room and the Pink Room, furnished with antiques and with chintz-hung canopied beds, offer a most relaxing environment, as does the 18th-century Lower Drawing Room, where guests can enjoy a glass of the house's own ale. ⊠ *Innerleithen, Peeblesshire EH44 6PW,* ☎ *01896/830323,* FAX *01896/830639. 2 rooms. MC, V. Closed Dec.–Feb.*

££ 🏠 **The Ley.** Here's an exceptional guest house in every way: a country house in its own grounds on the outskirts of Innerleithen, with the expected open fires and comfy sofas, plus antiques and well-appointed bedrooms (named after trees), enhanced by unexpectedly efficient power showers. To top it all off, the kitchen offers superb food. ⊠ *Innerleithen EH44 6NL,* ☎ FAX *01896/830240. 3 rooms. No credit cards.*

Peebles

❺ *7 mi west of Traquair on A72, 24 mi south of Edinburgh.*

Set in a lush and green countryside, with rolling hills deeply cleft by gorges and waterfalls, Peebles is a pleasant town on the banks of the Tweed. **Neidpath Castle,** a 15-minute walk upstream along the banks of the Tweed from Peebles, is perched artistically above a bend in the river, and comes into view through the tall trees. The castle is a medieval structure remodeled in the 17th century, with dungeons hewn from solid rock. You can return on the opposite riverbank after crossing an old, finely skewed railroad viaduct. ⊠ *Near Peebles,* ☎ FAX *01721/720333.* 🖼 *£3.* ☉ *Apr. 20–May 1 and July 1–Sept. 3, Mon.–Sat. 11–6, Sun. 1–5.*

Dining and Lodging

£££–££££ ✕🏠 **Cringletie House Hotel.** A Scottish baronial mansion set amid 28 acres of gardens and woodland, Cringletie has a long tradition of pampering guests with friendly, personalized service. It's decorated in British country-house style. The first-floor drawing room, with views extending up the valley, is particularly restful. Fruit and vegetables from the hotel's own kitchen garden are staples of the traditional Scottish restaurant cuisine. Afternoon tea served in the conservatory is recommended. ⊠ *Eddleston, near Peebles, EH45 8PL,* ☎ *01721/730233,* FAX *01721/730244. 14 rooms. Restaurant, putting green, tennis court, croquet. AE, MC, V.*

ABERDEEN AND ROYAL DEESIDE

Aberdeen, Scotland's third-largest city, is the gateway to a rural hinterland with a wealth of castles and an unspoiled and, in places, spectacular coastline. Deeside, the valley running west from Aberdeen along which the River Dee flows, earned its "Royal" appellation when Queen Victoria and her consort, Albert, built their Scottish fantasy castle, Balmoral, here. To this day, where royalty goes, lesser aristocracy and fast-buck millionaires from around the globe follow. Their yearning to possess an estate here is understandable, since birch woodland, purple moor, and blue river intermingle most tastefully, as you will see from the main road.

Aberdeen

56 *131 mi north of Edinburgh.*

In the 18th century, local granite quarrying produced a durable silver stone that would be used to build the Aberdonian structures of the Victorian era. Thus granite was used boldly, and the downtown Aberdeen seen today remains one of the United Kingdom's most distinctive urban environments, although some would say it depends on the weather and the brightness of the day. The mica chips embedded in the rock act as a million mirrors in sunshine; in rain and heavy clouds, however, their sparkle is snuffed out.

The North Sea has always been an important feature of Aberdeen: in the 1850s, the city was famed for its fast clippers, sleek sailing ships that raced to India for cargoes of tea. In the late 1960s, the course of Aberdeen's history was unequivocally altered when oil and gas were discovered in the North Sea. Aberdeen at first seemed destined to become an oil-rich boomtown, but fortunately, some innate local caution has helped the city to retain a sense of perspective and prevented it from selling out entirely.

★ **Marischal College** was founded in 1593 by the Earl Marischal as a Protestant alternative to the Catholic King's College in Old Aberdeen, though the two combined to form Aberdeen University in 1860. The present facade was built in 1891, and this is still the second-largest granite building in the world; only the Escorial in Madrid is larger. Within the fascinating **Marischal Museum**'s two main galleries are two exhibitions: the Encyclopaedia of the North East, with artifacts and photographs relating to the heritage of the northeast; and Collecting the World, which explores the role of collectors from the northeast on their travels throughout the world and displays Egyptian and 19th-century ethnographic material. ⊠ *Broad St.,* ☎ *01224/274301,* WEB *www.abdn.ac.uk.* ⌖ *Free.* ☉ *Museum weekdays 10–5, Sun. 2–5.*

Beyond the concrete supports of St. Nicholas House (of which the tourist information center is a part) is **Provost Skene's House** (provost is Scottish for mayor). It was once part of a closely packed area of town houses. Steeply gabled and rubble-built, it survives in part from 1545. The house was originally a domestic dwelling and is now a museum portraying civic life, with restored furnished period rooms and a painted chapel. ⊠ *Guestrow off Broad St.,* ☎ *01224/641086.* ⌖ *Free.* ☉ *Mon.–Sat. 10–5, Sun. 1–4.*

Royal Deeside

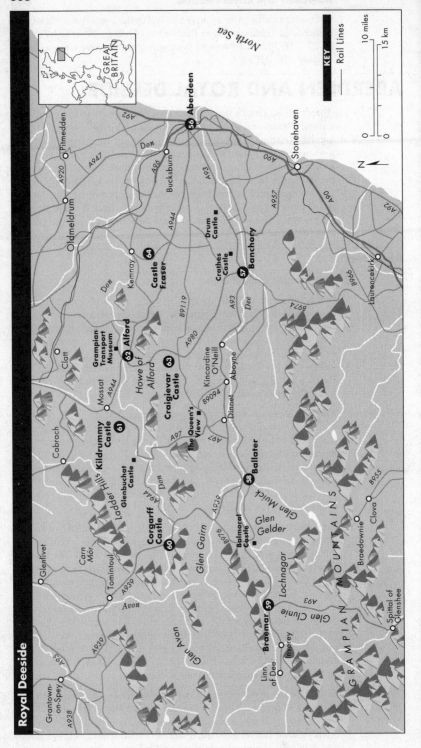

Aberdeen Art Gallery plays an active role in Aberdeen's cultural life and is a popular rendezvous for locals. It houses a wide-ranging collection, from the 18th century to contemporary work. ⊠ *Schoolhill,* ☎ *01224/523700,* WEB *www.aagm.co.uk.* ☐ *Free.* ☺ *Mon.–Sat. 10–5, Sun. 2–5.*

A library, church, and nearby theater on **Rosemount Viaduct** are collectively known by all Aberdonians as Education, Salvation, and Damnation. Silvery and handsome, the **Central Library** and **St. Mark's Church** date from the last decade of the 19th century, while **His Majesty's Theatre** (1904–08) has been restored inside to its full Edwardian splendor.

★ **Provost Ross's House,** dating from 1593, with a striking modern extension, houses **Aberdeen Maritime Museum,** which tells the story of the city's involvement with the sea, from early inshore fisheries by way of tea clippers to the North Sea oil boom. It's a fascinating place for grade-schoolers, with its ship models, paintings, and equipment associated with the fishing, local shipbuilding, and North Sea oil and gas industries. ⊠ *Provost Ross's House, Ship Row,* ☎ *01224/337701,* WEB *www.aagm.co.uk.* ☐ *Free.* ☺ *Mon.–Sat. 10–5, Sun. noon–3.*

Old Aberdeen was once an independent burgh and lies to the north of the city, near the River Don. Although swallowed up by the expanding main city before the end of the 19th century, Old Aberdeen, which lies between **King's College** and **St. Machar's Cathedral,** still retains a certain degree of individual character and integrity. Reach it by taking a bus north from a stop near Marischal College or up King Street, off the Castlegate.

King's College, founded in 1494 and now part of the University of Aberdeen, has an unmistakable flying (or crown) spire to its **Chapel,** which was built around 1500. The tall oak screen that separates nave from choir and the ribbed wooden ceiling and stalls constitute the finest medieval wood carvings to be found anywhere in Scotland.

At the **King's College Centre** you can find out more about one of Britain's oldest universities. ⊠ *High St.,* ☎ *01224/273702,* WEB *www.abdn.ac.uk.* ☺ *Mon.–Sat. 10–5, Sun. noon–5.*

Dining and Lodging

The Northeast is the land of Arbroath "smokies" (smoked haddock) and Cullen Skink (smoked fish soup). With rich pastures supporting the famous Aberdeen-Angus beef cattle, especially high-quality viands are also guaranteed.

££–£££ ✕ **Gerard's Brasserie.** Set on a side street moments away from the West End, Gerard's is a long-established stop on the Aberdeen dining scene. Classic French cuisine meets hearty Scottish appetites, ably supported by local produce, fish, and, in particular, red meat. Seafood thermidor is certainly not nouvelle cuisine, but it's satisfying, and the fixed-price lunch is an especially good value. The relaxed, softly lighted setting includes a flagstone-floor garden room with greenery and tile or marble tables. ⊠ *50 Chapel St.,* ☎ *01224/639500. AE, DC, MC, V.*

££–£££ ✕ **Silver Darling.** Situated right on the quayside, the Silver Darling is one
★ of Aberdeen's most acclaimed restaurants. It specializes, as its name suggests, in fish. The style is French provincial, with an indoor barbecue guaranteeing flavorful grilled fish and shellfish. ⊠ *Pocra Quay, Footdee,* ☎ *01224/576229. AE, DC, MC, V. Closed Sun. No lunch Sat.*

££ ✕▥ **Atholl Hotel.** One of Aberdeen's many splendid silver-granite
★ properties, the Atholl Hotel is turreted and gabled and set within a leafy residential area to the west of the city. Rooms are decorated in a rich

red, green, and cream scheme; the larger rooms are on the first floor. The restaurant prepares traditional dishes such as lamb cutlets and roast rib of beef. ⊠ *54 Kings Gate, Aberdeen AB15 4YN,* ☎ *01224/323505,* FAX *01224/321555,* WEB *www.atholl-aberdeen.com. 35 rooms. Restaurant. AE, DC, MC, V.*

££   ✕🖬 **Craighaar Hotel.** This hotel greets guests with a rustic palette of warm cinnamon and terra-cotta tones, and modern teak furnishings. The comfortable restaurant serves cuisine with a Scottish slant, such as rack of lamb with a herb crust in whisky mint sauce with skirlie tomato; (cheaper) bar meals are also available. Cozy guest rooms continue the rustic-hued theme; the split-level gallery suites are outstanding. ⊠ *Waterton Rd., Bucksburn AB21 9HS,* ☎ *01224/712275,* FAX *01224/716362,* WEB *www.craighaar.co.uk. 55 rooms. Restaurant, bar. AE, DC, MC, V.*

Nightlife and the Arts

Aberdeen Arts Centre (⊠ 33 King St., ☎ 01224/635208) hosts all forms of theater, poetry readings, exhibitions, and many other arts-based presentations. **His Majesty's Theatre** (⊠ Rosemount Viaduct, ☎ 01224/637788) has live shows presented throughout the year. The **Lemon Tree** (⊠ 5 W. North St., ☎ 01224/642230) has an international program of dance, comedians, folk, jazz, rock and roll, and art exhibitions.

Shopping

Aberdeen is a market town, with droves of countryfolk coming to do their major shopping here, lured by big, modern chain stores. However, there are still delightful specialty shops to be found. At the **Aberdeen Family History Shop** (⊠ 164 King St., ☎ 01224/646323, WEB www.anesfhs.org.uk) you can browse through a huge range of publications related to local history and genealogical research. **Colin Wood** (⊠ 25 Rose St., ☎ 01224/643019) is the place to go for antiques, and maps and prints of Scotland. **Nova** (⊠ 20 Chapel St., ☎ 01224/641270) is a treasure-house of gifts ranging from Scottish silver jewelry to Liberty textiles.

Banchory

⑤⑦   *19 mi west of Aberdeen on A93.*

Banchory is an immaculate place with a pinkish tinge to its granite. It's usually bustling with ice cream–licking city strollers, out on a day trip from Aberdeen. If you visit Banchory in autumn and have time to spare, drive out to the **Brig o' Feuch** (pronounced bridge of fyook). Here, salmon leap in season, and the fall colors and foaming waters make for an attractive scene.

OFF THE
BEATEN PATH
CRATHES CASTLE – The castle was once home of the Burnett family. Keepers of the Forest of Drum for generations, the family acquired lands here by marriage and later built a new castle, completed in 1596. Crathes is in the care of the National Trust for Scotland. The Trust also looks after the grand gardens, with their calculated symmetry and clipped yew hedges. ⊠ *Off A93, 3 mi east of Banchory,* ☎ *01330/844525,* WEB *www.nts.org.uk.* 🖾 *Castle or walled garden only £4.50; castle, garden, and grounds £7.* ☉ *Castle Apr.–Sept., daily 10:30–5:30 (last admission 4:45), Oct., daily 10:30–4:30 (last admission 3:45); garden and grounds year-round, daily 9–sunset.*

Dining and Lodging

££££–££££   ✕🖬 **Banchory Lodge.** With the River Dee running past just a few yards away at the bottom of the garden, this fine example of a 17th-century country house is an ideal resting place for anglers. The lodge has retained its period charm and is well-maintained inside and out. Rooms, with bold colors and tartan or floral fabrics, are individually decorated. The restaurant has high standards for its Scottish cuisine with French overtones. Try the fillet of Aberdeen Angus beef with whisky cream sauce, roast duckling, or guinea fowl with wild berries. ⊠ *Banchory, Kincardineshire AB31 5HS,* ☎ *01330/822625,* FAX *01330/ 825019,* WEB *www.banchorylodge.co.uk. 22 rooms. Restaurant, fishing. AE, DC, MC, V.*

Ballater

🔞 *25 mi west of Banchory, 43 mi west of Aberdeen.*

The quaint holiday resort of Ballater, once noted for the curative properties of its local well, has profited from the proximity of the royals at nearby Balmoral Castle. Visitors are amused by the array of BY ROYAL APPOINTMENT signs proudly hanging from many of its shops (even monarchs need bakers and butchers). If you get a chance, take time to stroll around this neat community, which is well laid out in silver-gray masses. Note that the railway station now houses the tourist information center as well as a display on the former glories of this Great North of Scotland branch line, closed in the 1960s, along with many others in this country.

Close to the town, capture the feel of the eastern Highlands in **Glen Muick** (Gaelic for pig, pronounced mick). Cross the River Dee and turn upriver on the south side; shortly after, the road forks into this fine Highland glen. The native red deer are quite common throughout the Scottish Highlands, but Glen Muick is one of the best places to see them in abundance, with herds grazing the flat valley floor. Beyond the lower glen, the prospect opens to reveal not only grazing herds, but also fine views of the battlement of cliffs edging the famed mountain called Lochnagar.

Dining and Lodging

££££ ✕🏨 **Darroch Learg Hotel.** Amid tall trees on a hillside, the Darroch Learg is everything a Scottish country-house hotel should be, with the added bonus that the charming town of Ballater is only moments away. Built in the 1880s as a country residence, the hotel exudes charm. Most guest rooms enjoy a stunning panoramic view south across Royal Deeside. Note that five rooms are in the next-door annex, Oak Hall, another handsome Victorian house, and are slightly cheaper than those in the main hotel. The Scottish food served in the conservatory restaurant is sophisticated, but also substantial, with the rich flavors of local beef and fish; you might find breast of duck, with roast parsnips, haricots blancs, homemade boudin and truffle cream. There is a fixed price menu. The selections on the wine list are great. ⊠ *Braemar Rd., Ballater, Aberdeenshire AB35 5UX,* ☎ *013397/554437,* FAX *013397/552527. 18 rooms. Restaurant. AE, DC, MC, V.*

En Route West from Ballater is **Balmoral Castle,** the Royal Family's Scottish summer residence. Balmoral is a Victorian fantasy, designed, in fact, by Prince Albert himself in 1855. "It seems like a dream to be here in our dear Highland Home again," Queen Victoria wrote. "Every year my heart becomes more fixed in this dear Paradise." Balmoral's visiting hours depend on whether the royals are in residence. In truth, there are more interesting and historic buildings to explore, as the only part of the castle on view is the ballroom, with an exhibition of royal artifacts. The Carriage Hall has an exhibition of commemorative china, carriages, and a native wildlife display. The Queen loved Balmoral more for its setting than its house, so be sure to take in its pleasant gardens.

Around and about Balmoral are some noted beauty spots: Cairn O'-Mount, Cambus O'May, the Cairngorms from the Linn of Dee. Pony trekking is available on the Balmoral stalking-ponies around the grounds and estate. ⊠ *On the A93, 7 mi west of Ballater,* ☎ *013397/ 423347,* WEB *www.royalresidences.com.* ⊒ *£4.50.* ☉ *Mid-Apr.–July, daily 10–5 (last admission 4).*

Braemar

59 *17 mi west of Ballater, 51 mi north of Perth via A93.*

The village of Braemar, surrounded by the Grampian mountains, is a good base from which to explore the mountains and woodlands of Royal Deeside. Braemar is dominated by **Braemar Castle,** dating from the 17th century, with defensive walls later built in the outline of a pointed star. At Braemar (the braes, or slopes, of the district of Mar), the standard, or rebel flag, was first raised at the start of the spectacularly unsuccessful Jacobite rebellion of 1715. Thirty years later, during the last rebellion, Braemar Castle was strengthened and garrisoned by Hanoverian (government) troops. ☎ *013397/41219 for information on opening times and charges.*

Braemar is associated with the **Braemar Highland Gathering** held every September, and distinguished by the presence of members of the Royal Family, owing to the proximity of their summer residence at Balmoral Castle.

A little way north of Braemar is the **Linn of Dee.** *Linn* is a Scots word meaning rocky narrows, and the river's rocky gash here is deep and roaring. Park beyond the bridge and walk back to admire the sylvan setting of the river and woodland, replete with bending larch boughs and deep, tranquil pools with salmon glinting in them.

Dining and Lodging

££–£££ ✕◫ **Invercauld Arms.** This handsome stone-built Victorian hotel is in the center of Braemar. Interiors are traditional in style, with a multitude of interesting prints decorating the walls. The restaurant, with magnificent views overlooking Braemar Castle, serves an international cuisine with Scottish overtones, not least in the use of local fish, game, lamb, and beef. ⊠ *AB35 5YR,* ☎ *013397/416057,* FAX *013397/414287,* WEB *www.peelhotels.com. 68 rooms. Restaurant, bar. AE, DC, MC, V.*

Outdoor Activities and Sports

The **Braemar Golf Club** (⊠ Cluniebank Rd., ☎ 013397/41618) has a tricky golf course laden with foaming waters. Erratic duffers take note: the compassionate course managers have installed, near the water, poles with little nets on the end for those occasional shots that go awry.

Corgarff Castle

60 *23 mi northeast of Braemar, 14 mi northwest of Ballater.*

Eighteenth-century soldiers paved a military highway, now A939, north from Ballater to Corgarff Castle, a lonely tower house with another star-shape defensive wall, a curious replica of Braemar Castle. Corgarff was built as a hunting seat for the earls of Mar in the 16th century. After an eventful history that included the wife of a later laird being burned alive in a family dispute, the castle ended its career as a garrison for Hanoverian troops. ⊠ *Signposted off A939,* ☎ *0131/668-8800,* WEB *www.historic-scotland.gov.uk.* ⊒ *£2.80.* ☉ *Apr.–Sept., daily 9:30–6; Oct.–Mar., Sat. 9:30–4, Sun. 2–4.*

En Route On A944, the excellent castle signposting will tell you that you are on the **Castle Trail.** The A944 meanders along the River Don to the village of Strathdon, where a great mound by the roadside—on the left—turns out to be a *motte,* or the base of a wooden castle, built in the late 12th century. The A944 then joins A97 (go left) and just a few minutes later a sign points to Glenbuchat Castle, a plain Z-plan tower house.

Kildrummy Castle

★ 61 *18 mi northeast of Corgarff, 23 mi north of Ballater.*

Kildrummy Castle is significant because of its age (13th century) and because it has ties to the mainstream medieval traditions of European castle building. It shares features with Harlech and Caernarfon in Wales, as well as with Continental sites, such as Château de Coucy near Laon, France. Kildrummy had undergone several expansions at the hands of English King Edward I when, in 1306, back in Scottish hands, the castle was besieged by King Edward I's son. The defenders were betrayed by a certain Osbarn the Smith, who had been promised a large amount of gold by the English besieging forces. They gave it to him after the castle fell, pouring it molten down his throat, or so the ghoulish story goes. ⊠ *Kildrummy,* ☎ *0131/668–8800,* WEB *www.historic-scotland.gov.uk.* 🎫 *£2.* ☉ *Apr.–Sept., daily 9:30–6.*

Dining and Lodging

££££ ✕🏠 **Kildrummy Castle Hotel.** A grand, late-Victorian country house, this hotel offers an attractive blend of a peaceful setting, attentive service, and sporting opportunities. Oak paneling, beautiful plasterwork, and gentle color schemes create a serene environment, enhanced by the views of Kildrummy Castle Gardens next door. The restaurant's traditional Scottish cuisine features local game and seafood. Fillet of Beef Kildrummy Castle even manages to combine three quintessentially Scottish ingredients, beef, haggis and Drambuie liqueur, in one dish. ⊠ *Kildrummy, near Alford, Aberdeenshire AB33 8RA,* ☎ *019755/712885,* FAX *019755/713455,* WEB *www.kildrummycastlehotel.co.uk. 16 rooms. Restaurant, fishing. AE, MC, V.*

Alford

62 *9 mi east of Kildrummy, 28 mi west of Aberdeen.*

A plain and sturdy settlement in the Howe (Hollow) of Alford, this village on the Castle Trail has the added benefit of offering those visitors who have grown somewhat weary of castle-hopping a break: it has a museum instead. The **Grampian Transport Museum** specializes in road-based means of locomotion and has a library and archive facility. One of its more unusual exhibits is the *Craigievar Express,* a steam-driven creation invented by the local postman to deliver mail more efficiently. ☎ *019755/622925.* 🎫 *£3.80.* ☉ *Apr.–Oct., daily 10–5.*

★ 63 **Craigievar Castle**'s historic structure represents one of the finest traditions of local castle building. It also has the advantage of having survived intact, much as the stonemasons left it in 1626, with its pepper-pot turrets and towers, the whole slender shape covered in a pink-cream pastel. ⊠ *5 mi south of Alford on A980,* ☎ *013398/83635,* WEB *www.nts.org.uk.* 🎫 *£7, grounds only £1 (honesty box).* ☉ *Mid-Apr.–Sept., daily 1:30–5:30 (last admission 4:45); grounds year-round, daily 9:30–sunset.*

64 The massive **Castle Fraser** shows a variety of styles reflecting the taste of owners from the 15th through the 19th centuries. It has the further

advantages of a walled garden, a picnic area, and a tearoom. ✉ *8 mi east of Alford off the A944,* ☎ *01330/833463,* WEB *www.nts.org.uk.* 🎫 *£6.* ⊙ *Mid- Apr.–May and Sept., daily 1:30–5:30; June–Aug., daily 11–5:30; Oct., weekends 1:30–5:30 (last admission 4:45); gardens year-round, daily 9:30–6; grounds daily 9:30–sunset.*

INVERNESS AND LOCH NESS

Inverness is the capital of the Highlands and is the only sizable town in northern Scotland (though it is quite small, nonetheless). It is a clean and compact place, built on both banks of the River Ness, just below Loch Ness. The loch itself is 24 mi long and very deep, passing through scenery that is the match of any in Scotland. Loch Ness is the alleged home of "Nessie," world-famous monster and founding member of the local chamber of commerce. In 1933, during a quiet news week for the local paper, the editor decided to run a story about a strange sighting of something splashing about in Loch Ness. All these years later the story lives on, and the dubious Loch Ness phenomenon continues to keep cameras trained on the deep waters, which have an ominous tendency to create mirages in still conditions. The area sees plenty of tourist traffic, drawn by the well-marketed hokum of the Loch Ness monster. But travelers will be glad to know there is much, much more to see.

Inverness

⑥⑤ *102 mi northwest of Aberdeen, 161 mi northwest of Edinburgh.*

Inverness is a logical touring base, with excellent roads radiating out from it to serve an extensive area. Although popularly called the Capital of the Highlands, Inverness is far from Highland in flavor. Part of its hinterland includes the farmlands of the Moray Firth coastal strip, as well as of the Black Isle. It is open to the sea winds off the Moray Firth, while the high hills, although close at hand, are mainly hidden. Few of Inverness's buildings are of great antiquity, thanks to the Highland clans' careless habit of burning towns to the ground. Even its castle is a Victorian-era replacement on the site of a fort blown up by Bonnie Prince Charlie. Now bypassed by A9, the town doesn't simply bustle in summer, it positively roars. Be careful in its one-way traffic system, whether walking or driving.

Dining and Lodging

££££ ✕🏨 **Dunain Park Hotel.** Guests receive individual attention in a "pri-
★   vate house" atmosphere in this 18th-century mansion 2½ mi southwest on A82. An open fire awaits you in the living room, where you can sip a drink and browse through books and magazines. Antiques and traditional decor make the guest rooms cozy and attractive. You can enjoy French-influenced Scottish dishes in the restaurant, where food is served on bone china and crystal. Shetland salmon baked in sea salt, and medallions of venison rolled in oatmeal with a claret and *crème de cassis* sauce are two of the specialties. ✉ *Dunain IV3 8JN,* ☎ *01463/230512,* FAX *01463/224532,* WEB *www.dunainparkhotel.co.uk. 13 rooms. Restaurant, indoor pool, sauna. AE, MC, V.*

££ 🏨 **Ballifeary House Hotel.** A well-maintained Victorian property, this one serves traditional Scottish breakfasts and offers especially high standards of comfort and service. The hotel is within easy reach of downtown Inverness. This is a nonsmoking hotel and children under 15 are not welcome. ✉ *10 Ballifeary Rd., IV3 5PJ,* ☎ *01463/235572,* FAX *01463/717583. 5 rooms. MC, V. Closed Nov.–Mar.*

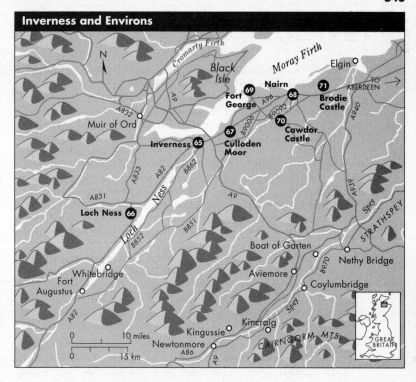

Inverness and Environs

£ 🏠 **Daviot Mains Farm.** This house, decorated in Highland shooting lodge
★ style, provides the perfect setting for home comforts and, for resident
guests only, traditional Scottish cooking. Lucky guests may find wild
salmon on the menu, and the house is licensed so you can enjoy fine
wines with your meal. It is 5 mi south of Inverness on A9. ⊠ *Daviot
Mains, Inverness IV2 5ER,* ☎ *01463/772215,* ℻ *01463/772099,* 🌐
www.daviotmainsfarm.co.uk. 6 rooms. MC, V.

Nightlife and the Arts

Inverness's theater, the **Eden Court** (⊠ Bishops Rd., ☎ 01463/234234,
℻ 01463/713810) is a multipurpose 800-seat theater, cinema, and art
gallery that offers a varied program year-round, including performances by the excellent Scottish Ballet.

Shopping

As you would expect, Inverness has a number of shops with a distinct
Highland flavor. **Duncan Chisholm & Sons** (⊠ 49 Castle St., ☎ 01463/
234599, ℻ 01463/223009) is a fine shop specializing in Highland tartans, woolens, and crafts. Mail-order and made-to-measure services are
available. **Hector Russell Kiltmakers** (⊠ 4–9 Huntly St., ☎ 01463/
222781, ℻ 01463/713414) has a huge selection of kilts, or will run
one up for you made to measure. It can supply by mail order overseas.
James Pringle Weavers (⊠ Holm Woollen Mills, Dores Rd., ☎ 01463/
223311, ℻ 01463/231042) offers self-guided mill tours, a weaving exhibition (where for £2.50 you can have a go on a loom and receive a
certificate), and a restaurant; it sells lovely tweeds, tartans, wool clothing, crystal, and giftware.

Loch Ness

★ ⑥ *9 mi southwest of Inverness.*

Inverness is the northern gateway to the Great Glen, the result of an ancient earth movement that dislocated the entire top half of Scotland. The fault line is filled by three lochs; the most well known, Loch Ness, can be seen from the main A82 road south, though leisurely drivers may prefer the east bank road, B862 and B852, to Fort Augustus, at the loch's southern end (32 mi). If you're in search of the infamous loch beast, Nessie, it's best to stay on the A82 west bank road where, at Drumnadrochit, you will find the **Official Loch Ness Monster Exhibition Centre** midway on the west bank. Loch Ness's huge volume of water has a warming effect on the local weather, making the lake conducive to mirages in still, warm conditions. These are often the circumstances in which the "monster" appears, and you may draw your own conclusions. Whether or not the *bestia aquatilis* lurks in the depths—more than ever in doubt since 1994, when the man who took one of the most convincing photos of Nessie made a deathbed confession that it was a fake—plenty of camera-toting, sonar-wielding, and submarine-traveling scientists and curiosity-seekers haunt the shores, gazing hopefully lochward. ⊠ *Drumnadrochit IV63 6TU,* ☎ *01456/450573 or 01456/450218,* ☒ *01456/450770.* ☒ *£5.95.* ☉ *July–Aug., daily 9–8; June and Sept., daily 9–6; Easter–May, daily 9:30–5; Oct., daily 9:30–5:30; Nov.–Easter, daily 10–3:30; last admission 45 mins before closing.*

Southeast of Drumnadrochit, right on the shores of the loch, stands battered **Urquhart Castle,** which has been guarding the loch since the 13th century. It was largely destroyed by the end of the 17th century, to prevent its use by Jacobite forces, but is still an impressive ruin. ⊠ *2 mi southeast of Drumnadrochit on A82,* ☎ *0131/668–8800,* ☒ *www. historic-scotland.gov.uk.* ☒ *£3.80.* ☉ *Apr.–Sept., daily 9:30–6:30; Oct.–Mar., daily 9:30–4:30 (last admission 45 minutes before closing).*

Dining and Lodging

£££ ✕🏨 **Polmaily House.** This country house offers books, log fires, and
★ a helpful staff, contributing to a warm and personal atmosphere. Families are especially welcome. The restaurant is noted for its traditional British cuisine, which takes advantage of fresh Highland produce. Try salmon in pastry with dill sauce, roast rack of lamb with rosemary, and cold smoked venison with melon, which are some examples of the flavorful Modern British cooking here. ⊠ *Drumnadrochit IV63 6XT,* ☎ *01456/450343,* ☒ *01456/450813,* ☒ *www.polmaily.co.uk. 9 rooms, 5 family suites. Restaurant, indoor pool, tennis court, croquet, horseback riding, boating, fishing, recreation room. MC, V.*

Culloden Moor

⑥ *5 mi east of Inverness on B9006.*

Culloden Moor was the scene of the last battle fought on British soil—to this day considered one of the most infamous and tragic in all of warfare. Here, on a cold April day in 1746, the outnumbered Jacobite forces of Bonnie Prince Charlie were destroyed by the superior firepower of George II's army. The victorious commander, the duke of Cumberland (George II's son), earned the name of "Butcher" Cumberland for the bloody reprisals carried out by his men on Highland families, Jacobite or not, caught in the vicinity. In the battle itself, the duke's army, greatly outnumbering the Scots, decimated more than 1,000 soldiers. The National Trust for Scotland has, slightly eerily, re-created the battlefield as it looked in 1746. The uneasy silence of the open moor almost drowns out the merry clatter from the visitor center's coffee shop and the tinkle of cash registers. ☎ *01463/790607,* WEB *www.nts.org.uk.* 🎫 *Visitor center and audiovisual display £4.* ☾ *Site daily; visitor center Apr.–Oct., daily 9–6; Mid-Jan.–Mar. and Nov.–Dec., daily 10–4 (last entry 30 mins before closing).*

Nairn

68   *17 mi northeast of Inverness, 92 mi northwest of Aberdeen.*

Once an unusual mixture of prosperous fishing port and farming community, Nairn still has a harmonious blend of old buildings in its busy

★ **69** shopping streets. **Fort George,** to the west of the town, was started in 1748 and completed some 20 years later. Today it is perhaps the best-preserved 18th-century military fortification in Europe. Because it is low-lying, its immense scale can be seen only from within. A visitor center and a number of tableaux at the fort portray the 18th-century Scottish soldier's way of life, as does the **Regimental Museum of the Queen's Own Highlanders.** To reach the fort take the B9092 north off A96 west of Nairn. ⊠ *Ardersier,* ☎ *0131/668–8800,* FAX *0131/668–8888,* WEB *www.historic-scotland.gov.uk.* 🎫 *Fort £4.50, museum free.* ☾ *Fort and museum Apr.–Sept., daily 9:30–6; Oct.–Mar., Mon.–Sat. 9:30–4, Sun. 2–4. Last tickets 45 mins before closing.*

70   **Cawdor Castle,** south of Nairn, is a cheerfully idiosyncratic, mellow, and mossy family seat with a 15th-century central tower. Shakespeare's Macbeth was the Thane (or clan chief) of Cawdor, but the sense of history that exists within these turreted walls is more than fictional. Cawdor is a lived-in castle, not an abandoned structure preserved in aspic. The rooms contain family portraits, tapestries, and fine furniture reflecting 600 years of history. The grounds include well-marked nature trails through beautiful and varied woodlands. You will pass ancient oaks and beeches, magnificent waterfalls, and deep river gorges. ⊠ *On B9090,* ☎ *01667/404615.* 🎫 *£5.90; £3 garden and grounds.* ☾ *May–mid-Oct., daily 10–5.*

71   **Brodie Castle,** east of Nairn and in National Trust for Scotland care, is of medieval origin, rebuilt and extended in the 17th and 19th centuries. Fine examples of late 17th-century plasterwork are preserved in the Dining Room and Blue Sitting Room, and the connoisseur collection of pictures extends to works by 20th-century artists. ⊠ *Brodie, by Nairn,* ☎ *01309/641371,* WEB *www.nts.org.uk.* 🎫 *£6.* ☾ *Castle Apr.–Sept., Mon.–Sat. 11–5:30, Sun. 1:30–5:30; Oct., Sat. 11–5:30, Sun. 1:30–5:30 (last admission 4:30); grounds daily 9:30–sunset.*

Dining and Lodging

£££   ✕🏨 **Clifton House.** This Victorian villa, full of antiques, paintings, and
★   open fires, offers excellent seafood on its wide-ranging menu. Most unusually, the hotel is also licensed as a theater, and from September through April each year, you can enjoy live performances, both theatrical and musical, of an excellent standard (send for a program). ⊠ *Viewfield St., IV12 4HW,* ☎ *01667/453119,* FAX *01667/452836,* WEB *www.clifton-hotel.co.uk.* *12 rooms. 2 restaurants. AE, DC, MC, V. Closed Dec.–Jan.*

SCOTLAND A TO Z

To research prices, get advice from other travelers, and book travel arrangements, visit www.fodors.com.

AIR TRAVEL

CARRIERS

Aberdeen is served by British Airways, British European Airways, British Midland, KLM UK, Coastair, easyJet, Eastern Airways, Gama

Aviation, SAS, Brymon, and Gill Air. Airlines serving Glasgow for transatlantic flights include Air Canada, American Airlines and Icelandair (all three are summer only), and Continental (all year). Inverness is served by British Airways (including British Regional Airways/British Airways Express), easyJet, and Servisair.

Ryanair forced its competitors to bring down prices on the Anglo-Scottish routes (between London and Glasgow–Edinburgh) by offering no-frills, rock-bottom airfares between London Stansted and Prestwick. Ryanair also flies to Paris and Dublin direct from Prestwick. For airline telephone numbers *see* Air Travel *in* Smart Travel Tips A to Z.

AIRPORTS

Aberdeen Airport serves both international and domestic flights and is in Dyce, 7 mi west of the city center on the A96 (Inverness). Edinburgh Airport has air links with all the major airports in Britain and many in Europe; the Airport Information Centre answers questions about schedules, tickets, and reservations. Glasgow Airport offers internal Scottish and British services, European and transatlantic scheduled services, and vacation-charter traffic. Inverness Airport, locally known as Dalcross Airport, is central for a wide range of internal flights covering the Highlands and islands region. There are also flights from London, Luton, Edinburgh, and Glasgow.

Prestwick Airport, on the Ayrshire coast about 30 mi southwest of Glasgow, is mainly concerned with package holidays and charter flights, but is also the base for Ryanair's good-value flights, and serves as the main diversion airport in Scotland in bad weather conditions, as it usually stays clear of the worst weather. It has an excellent direct train service to Glasgow.

➤ AIRPORT INFORMATION: **Aberdeen Airport** (☎ 01224/722331). **Edinburgh Airport Information Centre** (☎ 0131/333–1000). **Glasgow Airport** (☎ 0141/887–1111 airport information desk). **Inverness Airport** (☎ 01667/464000). **Prestwick Airport** (☎ 01292/479822).

BUS TRAVEL

Long-distance coach service operates to and from most parts of Scotland, England, and Wales. Edinburgh is approximately eight hours by bus from London, Glasgow approximately 8½–9 hours. The main operator in Scotland is Scottish Citylink. From England and Wales, the main operator is National Express.

Lothian Region Transport, operating dark-red-and-white buses, is the main operator within Edinburgh. First Edinburgh provides much of the service into Edinburgh and also has day tours around and beyond the city and serves the Borders. Getting around the Inverness area and Royal Deeside is best done by car, but there are a number of post-bus services that can help get you to the remote areas. For information contact Royal Mail.

CUTTING COSTS

The LRT Edinburgh Day Saver ticket (£2.20) allows unlimited one-day travel on the city's buses, while the better-value Offpeak Day Saver (£1.50) allows unlimited travel after 9:30 AM Monday to Friday and all day at weekends; both services can be purchased in advance, or on any LRT bus (exact money will be required when purchasing on a bus). Two travel passes are available from First Edinburgh for one day, seven days or four weeks unlimited travel in the Borders: the Reiver Rover for services within the Borders area, and the Waverley Wanderer for services within the Borders and to Edinburgh and Carlisle.

The many different bus companies in Glasgow cooperate with the Underground and ScotRail to produce the Family Day Tripper Ticket (£13), which is an excellent way to get around the whole area from Loch Lomond to Ayrshire. Tickets are a good value and are available from Strathclyde Passenger Transport (SPT) and at main railway and bus stations.

Scottish Citylink sells an Explorer Pass providing three, five, or eight days of unlimited travel on the entire Scottish Citylink network. Aberdeen and Inverness are well served from the central belt of Scotland. ➤ BUS INFORMATION: **First Edinburgh** (☎ 0131/663–9233). **Lothian Region Transport** (☎ 0131/555–6363). **National Express** (☎ 0990/ 808080). **Scottish Citylink** (✉ Buchanan Street Bus Station, Glasgow, ☎ 0990/505050). **Strathclyde Passenger Transport** (✉ Travel Centre, St. Enoch Sq., ☎ 0141/226–4826). **Royal Mail** (✉ 7 Strothers La., Inverness IV1 1AA, ☎ 01463/256273, FAX 01463/256392).

CAR RENTAL

➤ LOCAL AGENCIES: **Avis** (✉ Aberdeen Airport, Aberdeen, ☎ 01224/ 722282; ✉ 5 Westpark Pl., Dalry Rd., Edinburgh, ☎ 0131/337–6363; 0131/333–1866 airport; ✉ 161 North St., Glasgow, ☎ 0141/221–2827; 0141/842–7599 airport; ✉ Inverness Airport, Inverness, ☎ 01667/ 464070). **Budget Rent-a-Car** (✉ Aberdeen Airport, Aberdeen, ☎ 0541/565656; ✉ 394 Ferry Rd., Edinburgh, ☎ 0541/565656; ✉ 101 Waterloo St., Glasgow, ☎ 0541/565656; ✉ Railway Terrace, Inverness, ☎ 0541/565656). **Europcar** (✉ 121 Causewayend, Aberdeen, ☎ 01224/631199; 01224/770770 airport; ✉ 24 E. London St., Edinburgh, ☎ 0131/557–3456; 0131/333–2588 airport; ✉ 38 Anderson Quay, Glasgow, ☎ 0141/248–8788; 0141/887–0414 airport; ✉ Friars Bridge Service Station, Telford St., Inverness, ☎ 01463/235337). **Hertz** (✉ Aberdeen Airport, Aberdeen, ☎ 01224/722373; ✉ 10 Picardy Pl., Edinburgh, ☎ 0131/556–8311; 0131/333–1019 airport; 0131/557–5272 Waverley train station; ✉ 106 Waterloo St., Glasgow, ☎ 0141/248– 7736; ✉ Inverness Airport, Inverness, ☎ 01667/462652). **National Car Rental** (✉ 76 Lancefield Quay, Glasgow, ☎ 0141/204–1051).

CAR TRAVEL

Downtown Edinburgh usually means Princes Street, which runs east-west. Entering from the east coast, drivers will come in on A1, Meadowbank Stadium serving as a good landmark. From the Borders, the approach to Princes Street is by A7/A68 through Newington, an area offering a wide choice of budget accommodations. Approaching from the southwest, drivers will join the west end of Princes Street, via A701 and A702, while those coming east from Glasgow or Stirling will meet Princes Street from A8 on the approach via M90/A90. From Forth Road Bridge, Perth, and the east coast, the key road for getting downtown is Queensferry Road.

Visitors who come to Glasgow from England and the south of Scotland will probably approach the city from M6, M74, and A74. The city center is clearly marked from these roads. From Edinburgh M8 leads to the city center and is the motorway that cuts straight across the city center and into which all other roads feed.

It is now possible to travel from Edinburgh to Aberdeen on a continuous stretch of A90/M90, a fairly scenic route that runs up Strathmore. The coastal route, A92, is a more leisurely alternative. The most scenic route, however, is probably A93 from Perth, north to Blairgowrie and into Glen Shee. The A93 then goes over the Cairnwell Pass, the highest main road in Scotland (not recommended in winter, however).

The direct Edinburgh–Inverness route is M9/A9. From Glasgow to Inverness, the route is M80, then A9. If you are coming from southern Scotland, allow a comfortable 3½ hours from Glasgow or Edinburgh to Inverness via A9, and two hours to Aberdeen via A90.

EMERGENCIES

Dial 999 from any telephone (no coins are needed for emergency calls from public telephones) to obtain assistance from the police, ambulance, fire department, mountain rescue, or coast guard.

LODGING

BED-AND-BREAKFASTS

It is perfectly acceptable to contact individual B&B establishments directly. Tourist information centers offer a same-night local booking service, usually free of charge, although there may occasionally be a small fee. They also operate the national Book-A-Bed Ahead (BABA) service, arranging for accommodation in another locality in Scotland (personal callers only, small booking fee and 10% deposit payable). The Scottish Tourist Board in London will book accommodation for in-person callers; telephone inquiries should be directed to Scottish Information in Edinburgh.

➤ RESERVATION SERVICES: **Scottish Information** (⌧ Edinburgh, ☎ 0131/472–2035). **Scottish Tourist Board in London** (⌧ 19 Cockspur St., London; ⌧ The Scotland Desk, Britain Visitors Centre, No. 1, Regent St., London SW1Y 4XT).

HOTELS

Dial-a-Bed, a free central reservations service, can book rooms in many Edinburgh hotels and guest houses at specially negotiated discount rates.

➤ RESERVATION SERVICES: **Dial-a-Bed** (☎ 0131/556–3955 or 0131/556–0030, FAX 0131/556–2029).

TOURS

BUS TOURS

Lothian Region Transport runs tours in and around Edinburgh departing from Waverley Bridge at regular intervals, from 9:30 to 5:30 daily. Guide Friday also runs tours around Edinburgh in its open-topped buses from Waverley Bridge. This company also runs tours around Glasgow and Inverness. Prestige Tours runs luxury coach tours in small groups to most parts of Scotland. Classique Tours have unusual vehicles: small touring coaches dating from the 1950s and restored to immaculate condition. Specialized tours of Scotland's gardens are operated by Brightwater Holidays.

➤ FEES AND SCHEDULES: **Brightwater Holidays** (☎ 01334/657155). **Classique Tours** (☎ 0141/889–4050). **Guide Friday** (☎ 0131/556–2244). **Prestige Tours** (☎ 0141/886–1000).

CHAUFFEURED TOURS

Ghillie Personal Travel is a very friendly, small operator well experienced in the needs and preferences of visitors from the United States. Little's Chauffeur Drive offers flexible, customized tours in all sizes of cars.

➤ FEES AND SCHEDULES: **Ghillie Personal Travel** (⌧ 64 Silverknowes Rd. E, Edinburgh, ☎ 0131/336–3120, FAX 0131/336–3992). **Little's Chauffeur Drive** (⌧ 5 St. Ninian's Dr., Edinburgh, ☎ 0131/334–2177; ⌧ 1282 Paisley Rd. W, Glasgow G52 1DB, ☎ 0141/883–2111).

WALKING TOURS

The Scottish Tourist Guides Association can recommend fully qualified guides who will arrange walking or driving excursions of varying lengths to suit your interests. The Cadies and Witchery Tours organizes tours of ghost-haunted Edinburgh throughout the year. The Scottish Literary Tour Company takes you on a tour of the wynds, courtyards, and pubs of Edinburgh's Old and New Town, with guides invoking Scottish literary characters.

➤ FEES AND SCHEDULES: **Cadies and Witchery Tours** (☎ 0131/225–6745). **Scottish Literary Tour Company** (✉ Suite 2, 97B West Bow, near Edinburgh Castle, ☎ 0131/226–6657). **Scottish Tourist Guides Association** (☎ FAX 01786/451953).

TRAIN TRAVEL

Edinburgh's main train station, Waverley, is downtown, below Waverley Bridge. Travel time from Edinburgh to London by train is as little as four hours. Glasgow has two main rail stations: Central and Queen Street. Central is the arrival and departure point for trains from London Euston (journey time is approximately five hours), which come via Crewe and Carlisle in England, as well as via Edinburgh from Kings Cross. Travelers can reach Aberdeen directly from Edinburgh (three hours), and Inverness (two and a half hours). There are sleeper connections from London to Inverness, as well as reliable links from Edinburgh. There is also a direct London–Aberdeen service that goes through Edinburgh. For those interested in train service to Aberdeen's airport, Dyce is on ScotRail's Inverness–Aberdeen route. The Borders has no rail service, and the nearest rail station to St. Andrews is Leuchars, on the Edinburgh-Aberdeen main line. For all inquiries, telephone the National Rail Enquiries.

CUTTING COSTS

In Glasgow, the "Go Roundabout Glasgow" discount pass allows unlimited travel on the Underground and trains around Glasgow and out to surrounding towns for one day. Trains depart Edinburgh and Glasgow for Aberdeen, Inverness, and other towns in the north. ScotRail issues discount passes as well: the "Central Scotland Rover" ticket covers Edinburgh, Glasgow, and the Central Belt, while the "Highland Rover" ticket is for travel in the north and west Highlands. For details, contact the National Train Enquiry Line.

➤ TRAIN INFORMATION: **National Rail Enquiries** (☎ 08457/484950).

TRANSPORTATION AROUND SCOTLAND

Edinburgh can be explored easily on foot, so a car is hardly needed. Glasgow, though bigger, has an excellent integrated public transport system, so a car is also unnecessary in this city.

The comprehensive "Freedom of Scotland Travelpass" covers nearly all train and ferry transport and gives discounts on buses in the Highlands and islands for four days out of eight consecutive days (£79) or eight days out of 15 consecutive days (£99). It's available at any main train station in Scotland.

TRAVEL AGENCIES

➤ LOCAL AGENT REFERRALS: **American Express** (✉ 139 Princes St., Edinburgh EH2 4BR, ☎ 0131/718–2501; ✉ 115 Hope St., Glasgow G2 6LX, ☎ 0141/222–1401). **Thomas Cook** (✉ 26–28 Frederick St., Edinburgh EH2 2JR, ☎ 0131/465–7700; ✉ 15–17 Gordon St., Glasgow G1 3PR, ☎ 0141/201–7200).

VISITOR INFORMATION

The "Scottish Explorer Ticket," available from any staffed Historic Scotland (HS) property, allows visits to HS properties over a 7- or 14-day period. The Touring Ticket issued by the National Trust for Scotland (NTS) is also available for 7 or 14 days and allows access to all NTS properties. It is available from the NTS or main tourist information centers.

Edinburgh and Scotland Information Centre is adjacent to Waverley Station in Edinburgh (follow the tourist information center TIC signs in the station and throughout the city) and can make accommodation bookings for you. Greater Glasgow and Clyde Valley Tourist Board offers an excellent tourist information service from its headquarters near Queen Street Station.

The Scottish Tourist Board Central Information Department, for telephone and written inquiries only, will answer any question on any aspect of your Scottish holiday and can supply literature by mail. It cannot, however, make accommodation bookings. The Scottish Tourist Board in London, open weekdays 9:30–6:30 year-round and Saturday 10–5 mid-June–mid-September (rest of year 10–4), can supply information and also has an accommodation and travel booking agency for personal callers only.

Within Scotland, an integrated network of more than 170 tourist information centers is run by a variety of area tourist boards, offering comprehensive information and on-the-spot accommodation bookings. A number of them are listed below by town, under the national and regional tourist information offices.

➤ TOURIST INFORMATION: **Edinburgh and Scotland Information Centre** (✉ 3 Princes St., Edinburgh, ☎ 0131/473–3800, FAX 0131/473–3881). **Greater Glasgow and Clyde Valley Tourist Board** (✉ 11 George Sq., Glasgow, ☎ 0141/204–4400, FAX 0141/221–3524). **National Trust for Scotland** (☎ 0131/243–9300). **Scottish Tourist Board Central Information Department** (✉ 23 Ravelston Terr., Edinburgh EH4 3EU, ☎ 0131/332–2433, FAX 0131/315–4545). **Scottish Tourist Board in London** (✉ 19 Cockspur St., near Trafalgar Sq.; also at The Scotland Desk, ✉ Britain Visitors Centre, No. 1, Regent St., London SW1Y 4XT).

Aberdeen and Grampian (for written inquiries only: ✉ 27 Albyn Pl., Aberdeen AB10 1YL, ☎ 01224/288800, FAX 01224/581367; for walkins: ✉ St. Nicholas House, Broad St.). **Ballater** (✉ Station Sq., Ballater, ☎ 013397/55306). **Banchory** (✉ Bridge St., Banchory, AB31 3SX, ☎ 01330/822000). **Inverness** (✉ Castle Wynd, Inverness IV2 3BJ, ☎ 01463/234353). **Jedburgh** (✉ Murrays Green, Borders TD8 6BE, ☎ 01835/863435). **St. Andrews** (✉ 70 Market St., St. Andrews KY16 9NU, ☎ 01334/472021).

17 BACKGROUND AND ESSENTIALS

Portraits of Great Britain

Books and Videos

Chronology

Map of Great Britain

Smart Travel Tips A to Z

TRUE BRIT

The British are different, and proud of it. They still play cricket and drive on the left. Only reluctantly have they decimalized, turning their cherished pints into liters (except when ordering beer) and inches into centimeters. Until 1971 they had a bizarre, three-tier, nondecimal coinage, whereby a meal check might add up, say, to four pounds six shillings and sevenpence halfpenny. And although the rest of Europe counts distances in kilometers, the British still cling to their miles—though they buy fabric in meters (not yards), groceries are marked in kilograms, and gasoline (petrol) is sold by the liter. Logic is not always a prominent feature of the British character.

These are symptoms of a certain psychological gulf still existing between Britain and the rest of Europe, a gulf not greatly narrowed by its membership in the European Union since 1973. The English Channel, a relatively thin thread of water between Dover and Calais, has played a crucial role in British history, acting as a kind of moat to protect the 'island fortress' from invaders (witness 1940), and preserving a separate mentality. Many Britons had wanted to keep their 'moat' and regarded the project to build the Channel Tunnel, which created a fast weatherproof connection between Britain and France, with wariness, perhaps more emotional than economic. Yet the tunnel has been an increasing success, particularly for businesspeople and bargain-hunting shoppers. Now the latest, and more wide-reaching, assault on the British psyche is the seemingly inevitable scrapping of the pound sterling to join the new euro currency; by the time you read this, the decision may have been made. But this proud and insular nation is not unwelcoming to visitors. On its own terms, it is glad to show them the delights and virtues of what it believes to be one of the most genuinely civilized societies in the world.

There is still some truth in the popular foreign perception that the British are reserved. They are given to the understatement It's not bad, the nearest Britons may get to showing enthusiasm, and they may look a little solemn and stiff-upper-lipped, because they don't easily show their emotions. But they are not on the whole unhappy; the British are easygoing, accepting of nonconformity and eccentricity, and their strong sense of humor and love of the absurd keeps them on an even keel. They have a strange habit of poking good-humored fun at what they love without meaning disrespect, not least at royalty and religion. This kind of humor often disconcerts foreigners.

Britain is a densely populated land. Scotland and Wales have wide open spaces but in England people are crammed 940 to the square mile, more thickly than in any European country save the Netherlands. But it is also a green and fertile land, and because the countryside is a limited commodity, the English tend it with special loving care. Everywhere are trim hedgerows, tidy flower beds, and lawns mown smooth as billiard tables. One Oxford don, asked by an American visitor how the college lawn came to be so perfect, said casually, "Oh, it's been mown every Tuesday for the past 500 years." The English love gardens but are also at ease in untamed surroundings. They relish hiking over moors where the gales blow, or splashing rubber-booted through streams, or bird-watching in a quiet copse. A few people (now, themselves, an increasingly hunted breed), in their black or scarlet coats and riding caps, pursue fox hunting with hounds, "the unspeakable in full pursuit of the uneatable," as Oscar Wilde put it. In 2001 the issue was under hot debate in Parliament, but a ban was defeated.

This smallish island contains great scenic variety. The Midlands and much of eastern England are flat and dull. But the watery fenlands, between Cambridge and the sea, with low horizons broken by rows of poplars, a distant windmill, or a church spire, have a misty, poetic quality, and the sunsets and swirling clouds evoke J.M.W. Turner's skyscapes. Kent, southeast of London, with its cherry and apple orchards, is known as the garden of England; west of here are the wooded hills of Surrey, and to the southwest the bold, bare ridge of the South Downs, beloved of Kipling. Although the east coast of Britain is mainly smooth, with long sandy beaches and occasional chalky cliffs (the Dover ones are celebrated in song, the west coast is far more rugged: here the Atlantic gales set the seas lashing against the rocky headlands of Cornwall and south Wales.

The spine of northern England is a line of high hills, the Pennines, where sheep graze on lonely moors, and just to the west is the beautiful, mountainous Lake District, where Wordsworth lived. Scotland is even more lonely and mountainous. Beyond the urban belt of the lowlands around Edinburgh, you enter the romantic realm of the Highlands, a thinly populated region where heather and gorse cover the hillsides above silent fjordlike lochs and verdant glens. Roads here are few, but they all seem to lead westward to the Isles, blue-gray jewels in a silver Atlantic sea, with their strange Celtic names: Barra, Eigg, Benbecula, Skye.

Western Britain is washed by the warm waters of the Gulf Stream, and therefore its climate is mild and damp. Indeed, Britain's weather is something of a stock joke, and some foreigners imagine the whole country permanently shrouded in fog. This has not been true for years, since the use of smokeless fuel has cleared polluted mists from urban skies. Yet the weather *is* very changeable, by south European standards, with shower and shine often following each other in swift succession. At least it provides the thrill of the unexpected.

Britain is a land where the arts flourish. It is true that the artist, writer, or philosopher is not held in the same public esteem as, say, in France. The average Briton affects a certain philistinism, and intellectual and arty are common terms of reproach. Yet today's London is home to many of the most important, new and cutting-edge artists, designers, and writers in the world. Sales of books and of theater and concert tickets are amazingly high. Helped by the worldwide spread of the English language, the British publishing industry produces around 50,000 new titles a year, perhaps too many for profitability. A passion for classical music developed during World War II and has continued ever since, so that even the smallest town has its choral society performing Bach or Handel. London theater is regarded by many as the best around. In the provinces, hundreds of theaters, some of them small fringe groups in makeshift premises, attract ready audiences.

Culture thrives also in a classical mode; for example, through the Royal Shakespeare Company with its bases in the Bard's hometown of Stratford-upon-Avon and at the Barbican Centre in London. Like Shakespeare, many leading British writers and other creative artists are closely associated with some particular place, in a land where literature and the other arts have always been nourished by strong local roots, by some *genius loci*. A tour around Britain can thus become a series of cultural pilgrimages: to the Dorset that inspired the novels of Thomas Hardy, to the wild Yorkshire moors where the Brontë sisters lived and wrote, to Wordsworth's beloved Lake District, to the Scottish Border landscapes that pervade the novels of Sir Walter Scott, to Laugharne on the south Wales coast that Dylan Thomas's *Under Milk Wood* has immortalized, to Dickensian London, to the Constable country on the Suffolk/Essex border, or to nearby Aldeburgh where composer Benjamin Britten lived.

These personalities belong to British history, a long history that Britons tend to take for granted, though it lies deep in their psyche. Its memorials are on every side. It began in times long before Christ, when huge stone circles were raised at Stonehenge and Avebury, on the Wiltshire downs. Then came the Romans, who left their imprint across the land up to Hadrian's Wall in the north. Great feudal castles survive as reminders of the dark days when barons and kings were in constant conflict, and peaceful fields the length and breadth of the land became nightmarish landscapes of blood and death. Stately redbrick Elizabethan manors bear witness to the more settled and civilized age of Good Queen Bess.

Britain is rich in picturesque towns and villages whose streets are lined with buildings dating from medieval or Elizabethan days, or later with old half-timber houses where black beams crisscross the white plasterwork, or with carefully proportioned facades that bring a measured classical elegance to the townscape. In many areas, buildings are of local stone, most strikingly in the mellow golden-brown Cotswold villages, and often a simple cottage is topped with a neat thatch roof. Above all, British architecture is famed for its cathedrals and abbeys dating mostly from the Middle Ages, with Wells, Ely, Durham, Fountains, and Westminster, among the finest. Local churches, too, are often of great beauty, especially in East Anglia where the wealth of the 15th-century wool trade led to the building of majestic churches on the edge of quite modest villages. Church builders of the past were profligate in their service to God, and modern Britain is deeply in their debt. Unfortunately, the Church is just as deeply in debt, because it has these mammoth edifices to maintain with dwindling congregations to help with its finances.

Despite constant social upheavals, the British maintain many of their special traditions. On a village green in summer, you may see a cricket match in progress between two white-clad teams. It is a slow and stately game that will seem boring to the uninitiated, yet is full of its own skills and subtleties. In village pubs people frequently play darts, or perhaps backgammon, checkers, or chess.

British society, although troubled by doubts and uncertainties, and constantly challenged to resolve key social problems, is certainly not in terminal decline, or even slowly fading away. But it is deeply troubled and seriously questioning many of its traditional, long-accepted institutions. As an American observer remarked during the Falklands War, The British can be relied upon to fall at every hurdle—except the last. When the chips are down, the British come up trumps. This can't be explained rationally. What was it that sank the Spanish Armada or defeated Goering's Luftwaffe? It certainly wasn't superior economic resources or disciplined social organization. Maybe there is more in the souls of a free people united in a common purpose than generations of economists and sociologists could ever hope to understand. The British are such a people; and their quirkiness, their social distance, and their habit of driving on the left are inseparable parts of a greater whole. Without Britain, even a changed Britain, the world would be a poorer place.

THE CURTAIN IS ABOUT TO RISE: THE PERFORMING ARTS IN BRITAIN

One of the main reasons so many people want to visit Britain is its enviable reputation in the performing arts. The country is exactly what Shakespeare described, an isle full of noises, sounds and sweet airs that give delight and hurt not. In music and drama, opera and ballet, there are endless opportunities for people to enjoy themselves to the hilt. Although government subsidies often fall short of spiraling costs, the numerous National Lottery grants have saved, housed, refurbished, and kept many a show on the road, and the performing arts scene is still surprisingly healthy. But there is a fluidity about the performing arts in Britain that helps build their strength and appeal. An actor playing Lear with the Royal Shakespeare Company one day could appear in a television farce the next; an opera that has played to the small exclusive audience at Glyndebourne, who have paid the earth for their evening's performance, reappears the next week at the Albert Hall as part of the BBC's Promenade Concerts, delighting not only the seven thousand there in person, but millions more by radio. The performing arts largely transcend the social barriers that bedevil many aspects of British life to provide cultural nourishment for the widest spectrum of people.

An evening taking in a play is a vital element of any visitor's trip to Britain. Most people head first for London's West End, the city's fabled Theatreland. Here, you might catch Judi Dench and Vanessa Redgrave doing star turns, fabulous musical revivals, such as *Oliver,* more than one Andrew Lloyd Webber extravaganza, and, needless to say, Agatha Christie's *The Mousetrap*. Then, of course, there is that great mainstay, Shakespeare. There was a time when theater managers believed that "Shakespeare spelled ruin." Nowadays he may spell big business; witness *Shakespeare in Love,* winner of the 1999 Best Picture Oscar, plus more filmed versions of the Bard's classics coming out of Hollywood.

Shakespeare provides a touchstone by which actors can measure themselves, and by which other people can measure them. About once a decade the theater-going public in England is sorely tempted to ask for an Act of Parliament to forbid the production of *Hamlet,* so many versions are being staged at the same time. But that protracted procession of princes gives a fascinating lesson in the richness of talent available; indeed, Britain's actors are among the nation's very greatest treasures. However poor the play, the motive power of the performers rarely fails. In the end, all the Hamlets have something to offer that seems to shed a new light on the weary text. Simply put, Spain has its bullfights, Italy its opera, Britain its theater.

The pinnacle of the dramatic scene consists of two great national companies, the Royal National Theatre and the Royal Shakespeare Company (generally known as the RSC). They do have separate identities, though it is not always easy to pin down the way in which they differ. The RSC is more prolific, performing at the Barbican in London and, by late 2002, at theaters in the West End. RSC also has three stages at Stratford-upon-Avon: the large Memorial Theatre, the Swan, and the Other Place. The Swan, constructed on the lines of Shakespeare's Globe, is one of the most exciting acting spaces anywhere in the country. The Other Place is a newer venue used for experimental staging.

The National Theatre plays in the three auditoriums in its concrete fortress on London's South Bank: the Olivier, the Lyttelton, and the Cottesloe, in descending order of size, the

Olivier being huge and the Cottesloe studio-size. Of the two companies, the RSC is the more cohesive, with a very impressive volume of work and a steadily developing style, though it also suffers from serious lapses of taste and concentration in its productions. The great majority of its offerings are works of Shakespeare and the English classics, with occasional ventures into musicals. The National, on the other hand, ransacks world drama, and has had notable successes with Greek classics and French tragedy, as well as mounting some of the best stagings of American musicals anywhere outside Broadway. It also attracts star performers more than the RSC, which relies largely on teamwork, and creates stars from its own ranks. Both companies suffer from serious financial problems, even though some of their best productions have extended runs and often grow into considerable hits.

As for the Bard of Bards, his fabled "Wooden O," the Globe Theatre, the most famous playhouse in the world, and the first venue for many of Master Shakespeare's greatest plays, has risen once again on the banks of the Thames in London, not 200 yards from where the original stood. England has always held special temptations for Shakespeare fans; now the new Globe has added the thrill of seeing his plays performed in the actual neighborhood where he lived and in virtually the same stage set.

Beyond London, there are provincial theaters in most of the cities and large towns up and down the land, and many of them have developed their own national and international reputations. In Scarborough, a seaside town in Yorkshire, for example, the dramatist-director Alan Ayckbourn has run for many years the Stephen Joseph Theatre, where he tries out his own plays, most of which are regularly transferred to London, appearing as often as not at the National Theatre. But the delight of British regional theaters lies in their great diversity and local panache. In the little town of Richmond, in Yorkshire, is the charming little Georgian Theatre Royal, seating about 200 in rows and balconies that still reflect the 18th-century class divisions. Porthcurno, near Penzance, Cornwall, has the Minack Theatre, situated on a cliff top, overlooking the sea. The lovely 1819 Theatre Royal in Bury St. Edmunds is owned and run by the National Trust and is still fully functioning. There are woodland theaters, theaters in barns, and several in grand old country houses.

If you are traveling around the country, it is also worth your time to find out what is on in any spot you may hit, especially in summer. Summer is the time when Britain's acting fraternity take to the open air, and strive to outdo passing planes, vociferous birds, the fading light, and nearby traffic. Notable spots include York, where the famous medieval cycle of mystery plays is performed every four years in surroundings that add incalculable richness to an already moving text; some of the quadrangles of Oxford and Cambridge, which come alive with Oliviers-in-the-bud; and London's Regent's Park, which offers the best of the open-air theaters. There you can watch Shakespeare, after having wandered in Queen Mary's rose garden. To sit in the gathering dusk, as Puck and Oberon plot their magic, and the secret lights gradually create a new world of fantasy, is to take part in an essentially British rite.

Dr. Samuel Johnson, who was a notable grouch, accused opera of being an exotic and irrational entertainment on the British scene. Of course opera *is* irrational. It was born in the royal and ducal courts of Europe, where expense had no meaning. In any event, with the Royal Opera House now rebuilt and reborn, London promises to produce spectacles and productions that vie with those of New York's Metropolitan Opera. London's two main companies are poles apart. The Royal Opera at Covent Garden is socially the most prestigious. But it has suffered from the problems that bedevil all companies that rely largely on international stars: not enough rehearsal time and a wobbly artistic policy. The English National Opera (ENO) was originally a *Volksoper,* based at the small Sadler's Wells Theater in north London. It moved to the Coliseum, beside Trafalgar Square, some 30 years ago. It is still a people's opera, though now housed in a huge theater. For the last decade it has had a brilliantly innovative directorial team that has settled its reputation as the leader of opera fashion. Seat prices for the ENO are generally much gentler than those at the Royal Opera, and the productions are excitingly inventive. The company is a team, mostly of British singers, who act as well as they sing. The one drawback is that the auditorium sometimes dwarfs the voices.

Apart from the two major companies in London, there are two other national companies, the Welsh National at Cardiff, and the Scottish National in Glasgow. They both have adventuresome artistic policies, attacking such blockbusters as Wagner's *Ring* and *The Trojans* of Berlioz. They also tour, the Welsh National especially, appearing in small towns around the principality, even performing in movie houses when no other stage is available. There is also a northern England company, originally a spin-off from the English National, called Opera North, which is based in Leeds and is as venturesome as its begetter.

Opera has always been an extravagant art form, but one company has managed to build itself a new home. Glyndebourne, in deepest Sussex, relies entirely on sponsors and its ticket sales, having no state subsidy. It opened a new theater in 1994, ending 50 years of its let's-do-an-opera-in-the-barn image. A visit there will cost you an arm and a leg, but you'll feel like a guest at a very superior house party.

Ballet is a surprising art to flourish in Britain, and it must be admitted that it only does so with a struggle. The Royal Ballet, the premier company, is entering a new phase, and it couldn't be more well timed. The top job has been passed from the safe hands of Royal Ballet stalwart Sir Anthony Dowell to the Australian ballet su-

premo Ross Stretton. A popular program is promised, much in harmony with the new spirit at the Opera House, where the Royal Ballet now has space to perform. Few other companies present the classics with such seemingly effortless style and accomplishment, and the new element should bring some electrifying performances.

The sibling Birmingham Royal Ballet is a dynamic company to watch. With its zesty director and choreographer David Bintley, it is yet another excellent reason for visiting Birmingham. The English National Ballet (ENB) goes from strength to strength in its mission to give ballet more mass appeal. Matz Skoog, another Australian, became artistic director in 2001 shortly after the company celebrated its 50th anniversary. You can catch the ENB performing its winter season at the London Coliseum, with summer shows at the Royal Albert Hall. Between times, it tours its repertoire of classics countrywide.

Music performance has seen a tremendous surge in popularity in the last 50 years. In London, the three concert halls on the South Bank, together with the Barbican, the Albert Hall, and the Wigmore Hall, provide the capital with venues for a rich and varied musical fare. For example, every night for six weeks in summer, the Albert Hall hosts the BBC-sponsored "Proms," the biggest series of concerts in the world, involving 10 or more orchestras and dozens of other artists. Outside London, cities with fine resident orchestras include Birmingham (home to the noted City of Birmingham Symphony Orchestra), Liverpool, Manchester, and even the seaside town of Bournemouth.

Of course, Britain's amazingly rich musical life fills every hall and theater, church and chapel through the length and breadth of the land. Every week of the year you can attend performances of great choral works in concert halls, recitals of lieder in stately homes by candlelight, provocative modern pieces on remote Scottish islands in the rich Celtic twilight of ancient buildings, lively madrigals from boats on moonlit rivers. It is not just the Welsh who can say, in Dylan Thomas's words, "Thank God we are a musical nation."

Finally, Britain is a land of festivals, mostly, though not exclusively, in summer. Whatever the size of the town, it will have a festival at some time. Some are of international scope, while others are small local wingdings. Leading the parade is the Edinburgh Festival, mid-August–early September, born in the dark days after World War II, when people needed cheering up. Today it is still going strong, with opera, drama, recitals, and ballet by artists from all over the world. The festival now has the added attraction of the Fringe, a concurrent event, with as many as 800 performances crammed into three weeks: small-scale productions from the classic to the bizarre, held in everything from telephone kiosks to church halls.

Smaller than Edinburgh's event, but still notable, are the dozens of festivals up and down the country. In Bath, the International Festival, late May–mid-June, is noted for its music especially. In Aldeburgh, a windswept East Anglian seaside town, the Festival of Music and the Arts, mid–late June, is dedicated to the memory of Benjamin Britten, and again is mainly a music festival. In Cheltenham there are two major festivals, one musical

in July, the other early–mid-October, dedicated to literature, with readings, seminars, and lectures. York has both an early music festival in summer, and a Viking one in February. Llandrindod Wells, in Wales, goes Victorian and dresses up in late August. Worcester, Hereford, and Gloucester take turns mounting the annual Three Choirs Festival in mid-August, the oldest in the world, which has seen premieres of some notable music. Truro stages a Three Spires Festival in June in imitation. Wales has an annual feast of song and poetry late July–early August, called the Royal National Eisteddfod. At Chichester in Sussex there is a summer drama festival that has been so popular that the town has managed to build a theater specially for it. At Ludlow, Shakespeare is performed in summer in the open air, with the dramatic castle as backdrop. All these festivals have the advantage of focusing a visit to a town and helping you to meet the locals, but be sure to book well in advance, as they are extremely popular. As all the above events prove, the British love a festival almost as much as they love a lord. Once the worst of the winter chill seeps out of everyone's bones, festival fever sets in. Year-round, however, Britain's performing arts offer one of the grandest and most unforgettable pageants in the world.

SPLENDID STONES: AN INTRODUCTION TO BRITISH ARCHITECTURE

In Britain you can see structures that go back to the dawn of history, in the hauntingly mysterious circles of monoliths at Stonehenge or Avebury, for example; or the resurrected remains of Roman empire builders preserved in towns such as Cirencester. On the other hand, you can startle your eyes with the very current, very controversial designs of contempo-

rary architects in new developments, including London's Docklands area. Appreciating the wealth of Britain's architectural heritage does not require a degree in art history, but knowing a few hallmarks of various styles can enhance your enjoyment of what you see. Here, then, is a primer of a millennium of various architectural styles.

Norman

The solid Norman style was brought to Britain by Duke William of Normandy, when he invaded and conquered England in 1066, although William's predecessor, King Edward (the Confessor) used the style in the building of Westminster Abbey, a little earlier in 1042. Until around 1200, it was clearly the style of choice for buildings of any importance, and William's castles and churches soon dominated the countryside. Norman towers tended to be hefty and square, arches always round-topped, and the vaulting barrel-shaped. Decoration was mostly geometrical, but within those limits, ornate. Norman motte and bailey castles had two connecting stockaded mounds, with the keep on the higher mound and other buildings on the lower mound. *Best seen in the Tower of London, St. Bartholomew's and Temple Churches, London, and in the cathedrals of St. Albans, Ely, Gloucester, Durham, and Norwich, and at Tewkesbury Abbey.*

Gothic Early English

From 1130 to 1300, pointed arches began to supplant the rounded ones, buttresses became heavier than the Norman variety, and the windows lost their rounded tops to become lancet shaped. Buildings climbed skyward, less squat and heavy, with the soaring effect accentuated by steep roofs and spires. *Best seen in the cathedrals of York, Salisbury, Ely, Worcester, Canterbury (east end), and Westminster Abbey's chapter house.*

DECORATED

From the late 1100s until around 1400, elegance and ornament became fully integrated into architectural design, rather than applied onto the surface of a solid basic form. Windows filled more of the walls and were divided into sections by carved mullions. Vaulting grew increasingly complex, with ribs and ornamented bosses proliferating; spires became even pointier; arches took on the ogee shape, with its unique double curve. This style was one of England's greatest gifts to world architecture. *Best seen at the cathedrals of Wells, Lincoln, Durham (east transept), and Ely (Lady Chapel and Octagon).*

PERPENDICULAR

In later Gothic architecture, the emphasis on the vertical grew even more pronounced, featuring slender pillars, huge expanses of glass, and superb fan vaulting resembling the formalized branches of frozen trees. Walls were divided by panels. One of the chief areas in which to see Perpendicular architecture is East Anglia, where the rich wool towns built magnificent churches in the new style. Houses, too, began to reflect prevailing taste. Perpendicular Gothic lasted for well over two centuries from its advent around 1330. *Best seen at St. George's Chapel, Windsor, the cathedrals of Gloucester (cloister), and Hereford (chapter house), Henry VII's Chapel, Westminster Abbey, Bath Abbey, and King's College Chapel, Cambridge.*

Tudor

With the great period of cathedral building over, from 1500 to 1560 the nation's attention turned to the construction of spacious homes, characterized by this new architectural style. The rapidly expanding nouveau riche class, created by the first two Tudor Henrys (VII and VIII) to challenge the power of the aristocracy, built spacious manor houses, often on the foundations of pillaged monasteries, thus beginning the era of the great stately homes. Brick replaced stone as the most popular medium, with plasterwork and carved wood to carry the elaborate motifs of the age. Another way the new rich could make their mark, and ensure their place in the next world, was by building churches. This was the age of the splendid parish churches built on fortunes made in the wool trade. Some of the most magnificent are in Suffolk, Norfolk, and the Cotswolds. *Domestic architecture is best seen at Hampton Court and St. James's Palace, London, for wool churches, Lavenham, and Long Melford, though its tower is much later, both in Suffolk.*

Renaissance Elizabethan

For a short period under Elizabeth I, 1560–1600, this development of Tudor flourished as Italian influences began to seep into England, seen especially in symmetrical facades. The most notable example was Hardwick Hall in Derbyshire, built in the 1590s by Bess of Hardwick; the jingle that describes it goes "Hardwick Hall, more glass than wall." But, however grand the houses were, they were still on a human scale, warm and livable, built of a mellow amalgam of brick and stone. *Other great Elizabethan houses are Montacute, Somerset, Longleat, Wiltshire, and Burghley House, Cambridgeshire.*

Jacobean

For the first 15 years of the reign of James I (the name Jacobean is taken from the Latin word for James, Jacobus) there was little noticeable change. Windows were still large in proportion to the wall surfaces. Gables, in the style of the Netherlands, were popular. Carved decoration in wood and plaster (especially the geometrical patterning called strapwork, like intertwined leather belts, also of Dutch origin) was still exuberant, now even more so. But a change was on the way. Inigo Jones (1573–1652), the first great modern British architect, was attempting to synthesize the architectural heritage of England with the current Italian theories. Two of his finest remaining buildings—the Banqueting Hall, Whitehall, and the Queen's House at Greenwich—epitomize his genius, which was to introduce the Palladian style that dominated British architecture for centuries. It uses the classical Greek orders: Doric, Ionic, and Corinthian. This was grandeur. But the classical style that was so monumentally effective under a hot Mediterranean sun was somehow transformed in Britain, domesticated and tamed. Columns and pediments were used to decorate the facades, and huge frescoes provided acres of color to interior walls and ceilings, all in the Italian manner. But these architectural elements had not yet been totally naturalized. There were in fact two quite distinct styles running concurrently, the comfortably domestic and the purer classical in public buildings. They were finally fused together by the talent of Christopher Wren. *Jacobean is best seen at the Bodleian Library, Oxford, Audley End, Essex, and Clare College, Cambridge.*

Wren and the English Baroque

The work of Sir Christopher Wren (1632–1723) constituted an era all by itself. Not only was he naturally one of the world's greatest architects, but he was also given an unparalleled opportunity when the disastrous Great Fire of London in 1666 wiped out the center of the capital, destroying no fewer than 89 churches and 13,200 houses. Although Wren's great scheme for a totally new city center was rejected, he did build 51 churches, the greatest of which was St. Paul's, completed in just 35 years. The range of Wren's designs is extremely wide, from simple classical shapes to the extravagantly dramatic baroque. He was also at home with domestic architecture, where his combinations of brick and stone produced a warm, homey effect. The influence of the Italian baroque can be seen in Sir John Vanbrugh's Blenheim Palace, where the facade echoes the piazza of St. Peter's in Rome, and at Vanbrugh's exuberant Castle Howard in Yorkshire. Nicholas Hawksmoor, Wren's pupil, designed the baroque Mausoleum at Castle Howard. The baroque had a brief heyday in England; by 1725 the Palladian style was in favor and the vast pile of Blenheim was being mocked by trendsetters. *Wren's ecclesiastical architecture is best seen at St. Paul's Cathedral (baroque with classical touches) and the other remaining city churches, his domestic style at Hampton Court Palace, Kensington Palace, the Royal Hospital in Chelsea, and the Royal Naval College in Greenwich. English baroque is best seen at Blenheim Palace (Oxfordshire) and Castle Howard (Yorkshire).*

Palladian

This style is often referred to as Georgian, so-called from the Hanoverian kings George I through IV, although it was introduced as early as Inigo Jones's time. Classical inspiration has now been thoroughly acclimatized. Though they were completely at home among the hills, lakes, and trees of the British countryside, Palladian buildings were derived from the Roman-inspired designs of the Italian architectural theorist Andrea Palladio (1508–80), with pillared porticoes, triangular pediments, and strictly balanced windows. In domestic architecture, this large-scale classicism was usually modified to quiet simplicity, preserving mathematical proportions of windows, doors, and the exactly calculated volume of room space, to create a feeling of balance and harmony. There were some outrageous departures from the classical manner at this time, most notably with the Brighton Pavilion, built for the Prince Regent (later George IV). The Regency style comes under the Palladian heading, though strictly speaking it lasted only for the few years of the actual Regency. In Britain, the Palladian style was handled with more freedom than elsewhere in Europe, and America took its cue from the British architects. *Among the best Palladian examples are Regent's Park Terraces (London), the library at Kenwood (London), Royal Crescent and other streets in Bath, Holkham Hall (Norfolk).*

Victorian

Elements of imaginative fantasy, already seen in the Palladian era, came to the fore during the long reign of Victoria. The country's vast profits made from the Industrial Revolution were spent lavishly. Civic building accelerated in all the major cities with town halls modeled after medieval castles or French châteaus. The Victorians plundered the past for styles, with Gothic, about which the scholarly Victorians were very knowledgeable, leading the field. The supreme example here is the Houses of Parliament in London. (To distinguish between the Victorian variety and an earlier version, which flourished in the late 1700s, the earlier one is commonly spelled "Gothick.") But there were many other styles in the running, including the attractively named, and self-explanatory, "Wrenaissance." *Among the most striking examples are Truro Cathedral, the Albert Memorial (London), Manchester Town Hall, Ironbridge, and Cragside (Northumberland).*

Edwardian

Toward the end of the Victorian era, in the late 1800s, architecture calmed down considerably, with a return to a solid sort of classicism, and to even a muted baroque. The Arts and Crafts movement, especially the work and inspiration of William Morris, produced simpler designs, returning often to medieval models. *Best seen in Buckingham Palace and the Admiralty Arch in London.*

Modern

A furious public debate has raged in Britain for many years between traditionalists and the adherents of modernistic architecture. Britons are strongly conservative when it comes to their environment. These arguments have been highlighted and made even more bitter by the intervention of such notable figures as Prince Charles, who derides excessive modernism, and said, for instance, that an advanced design for the new wing of the National Gallery in Trafalgar Square would be like "a carbuncle on a much-loved face." One reason for the strength of the British attitude is that the country suffered from much ill-conceived building development after World War II, when large areas of city centers had to be rebuilt after the devastation of German bombs, and there was a pressing need for housing. Town planners and architects encumbered the country with endless badly built and worse-designed tower blocks and shopping areas.

The situation that was created in the '50s and '60s is slowly being reversed. High-rise apartment blocks are being blown up and replaced by more user-friendly housing. Large-scale commercial areas in a number of cities are being rethought and slowly rebuilt, although so much ill-considered building went on in the past that Britain can never be completely free of it. The emphasis is gradually moving to a type of planning, designing, and construction that pays more attention to the needs of the inhabitants of buildings. At last, the lessons of crime statistics and the sheer human misery caused by unacceptable living conditions are being learned. There is, too, a healthier attitude now to the conservation of old buildings. As part of the postwar building splurge, houses that should have been treasured for posterity were torn down wholesale. Happily, many of those that survived the wreckers' ball are now being restored and put back to use.

The architecture styles employed nowadays are very eclectic. A predominant one, favored incidentally by Prince Charles, draws largely on the past, with nostalgic echoes of the country cottage, and leans heavily on variegated brickwork and on close attention to decorative detail. Supermarkets are going up in every town designed on a debased form of this style. Stark modernism does crop up every now and again. The Lloyd's of London tower in the City of London, by Sir Richard Rogers, designer of the Pompidou Center in Paris, is perhaps a leading, and flamboyantly extreme, example, as is Rogers's *tour de force,* the now-closed Millennium Dome in Greenwich. But England generally is still light years behind the United States in experimentation with design. The skyscrapers of the City of London are the exception in Britain rather than the rule.

However, public buildings are being built on a smaller scale; schools and libraries, designed in a muted modernism, use traditional, natural materials, such as wood, stone, and brick. A slightly special case, though representative of what can be achieved, is the Visitors' Centre at Fountains Abbey in Yorkshire. Designed by Edward Cullinan, it is a fusion of drystone walls, lead and wooden-shingle roofs outside, white-painted steel pillars and flowing ceilings inside. It is perfectly conceived for the needs of such a historically important site. Many cultural institutions, particularly in London, have undergone innovative renovations, in part to embrace space for new technology. The Royal Opera House, the Tate Modern (a power station transformed into art gallery), and the British Museum are among the most noteworthy of the recent projects that have embraced the new, but with a subtle emphasis on regenerating the old. *Among the new buildings to see are the Lloyd's Tower, some of the Docklands development including Canary Wharf, Richmond House (79 Whitehall), and the Clore Building at the Tate Gallery (all in London), the campus of Sussex University (outside Brighton), the Royal Regatta Building (Henley), the Sainsbury Centre for the Visual Arts (Norwich), the Burrell Collection (Glasgow).*

WHAT TO READ AND WATCH BEFORE YOU GO

Books

Many writers' names have become inextricably linked with the regions in which they set their books or plays. Hardy's Wessex, Daphne Du Maurier's Cornwall, Wordsworth's Lake District, Shakespeare's Arden, and Brontë Country are now evocative catch phrases, treasured by local tourist boards. But however hackneyed the tags may now be, you *can* still get a heightened insight to an area through the eyes of authors of genius, even though they may have written a century or more ago. Here are just a few works that may provide you with an understanding of their authors' loved territory.

Thomas Hardy's *Mayor of Casterbridge, Tess of the d'Urbervilles, Far from the Madding Crowd,* and indeed almost everything he wrote is solidly based on his Wessex (Dorset) homeland. Daphne Du Maurier had a deep love of Cornwall from her childhood; *Frenchman's Creek, Jamaica Inn,* and *The King's General* all capture the county's Celtic atmosphere. The Brontë sisters' *Wuthering Heights, The Tennant of Wildfell Hall,* and *Jane Eyre* all breathe the sharp air of the high Fells around their Haworth home. William Wordsworth, who was born at Cockermouth in the Lake District, depicts the area's rugged beauty in many of his poems, especially the *Lyrical Ballads.*

Virginia Woolf's visits to Vita Sackville-West at her ancestral home of Knole, in Sevenoaks, resulted in the novel *Orlando.* The stately home is now a National Trust property. The country around Batemans, near Burwash in East Sussex, the home where Rudyard Kipling lived for more than 30 years, was the inspiration for *Puck of Pook's Hill* and *Rewards and Fairies.* Lamb House in Rye, also in East Sussex, was home to the American writer, Henry James, and after him E. F. Benson, whose delicious Lucia books are set in a thinly disguised version of the town. Both Batemans and Lamb House are National Trust buildings.

A highly irreverent, and very funny, version of academic life, *Porterhouse Blue,* by Tom Sharpe, will guarantee that you look at Oxford and Cambridge with a totally different eye. John Fowles's *The French Lieutenant's Woman,* largely set in Lyme Regis, is full of local color for visitors to Dorset.

James Herriot's successfully televised veterinary surgeon books, among them *All Creatures Great and Small,* give evocative accounts of life in the Yorkshire dales and have been available for years. For a perceptive account of life in the English countryside, try Ronald Blythe's award-winning *Akenfield: Portrait of an English Village.*

Mysteries are almost a way of life in Britain, partly because many of the best English mystery writers set their plots in their home territory. Modern whodunits by P. D. James and Ruth Rendell can be relied on to convey a fine sense of place, while Ellis Peters's Brother Cadfael stories recreate life in medieval Shrewsbury with a wealth of telling detail. Colin Dexter's Inspector Morse mysteries capture the flavor of Oxford's town and gown. There are always, of course, the villages, vicarages, and scandals of Agatha Christie's Miss Marple books.

For the many fans of the Arthurian legends, there are some excellent, imaginative novels, which not only tell the stories, but give fine descriptions of the British countryside. Among them are *Sword at Sunset,* by Rosemary Sutcliffe, *The Once and Future*

King, by T. H. White, and the four Merlin novels by Mary Stewart, *The Crystal Cave, The Hollow Hills, The Last Enchantment,* and *The Wicked Day.*

An animal's close-to-the-earth viewpoint can reveal all kinds of countryside insights about Britain. *Watership Down,* by Richard Adam, was a runaway best-seller about rabbits in the early '70s, and *Wind in the Willows,* by Kenneth Grahame, gives a vivid impression of the Thames Valley almost a hundred years ago, which still holds largely true today.

Those interested in writers and the surroundings that may have influenced their works should look at *A Literary Guide to London,* by Ed Glinert, and *The Oxford Literary Guide to the British Isles,* edited by Dorothy Eagle and Hilary Carnell (now out of print). One author particularly in vogue now is Jane Austen: Janeites will want to read Maggie Lane's *Jane Austen's World* and Nigel Nicolson's wonderful *World of Jane Austen.* For a vast portrait of everyone's favorite English author, weigh in with Peter Ackroyd's *Dickens.*

Some good background books on English history are *The Oxford Illustrated History of Britain,* edited by Kenneth O. Morgan, and *The Story of England,* by Christopher Hibbert. *The English: A Portrait of a People,* by Jeremy Paxman, examines the concept of Englishness in a changing world. *The London Encyclopaedia,* by Ben Weinreb and Christopher Hibbert, now out of print, is invaluable as a source of information on the capital. Simon Schama's *A History of Britain: At the Edge of the World* and *A History of Britain: The Fate of Empire,* with handsome color illustrations, were written to accompany the BBC–History Channel television series. Peter Ackroyd has written historical and contemporary fiction about London, and his latest book, *London: A Biography,* is described as a lifework.

The finest book on the great stately houses of England is Nigel Nicolson's *Great Houses of Britain,* written for the National Trust (now out of print).

More recent are spectacular picture books on *Great Houses of Britain and Wales* and *Great Houses of Scotland,* by Hugh Montgomery-Massingberd. *The Buildings of England* and *The Buildings of Scotland,* originally by Nikolaus Pevsner, but much updated since his death, are a multivolume series, organized by county, which sets out to chronicle every building of any importance. The series contains an astonishing amount of information. In addition, his *Best Buildings of Britain* is a grand anthology with lush photographs. For the golden era of Georgian architecture, check out John Summerson's definitive *Architecture in Britain 1530–1830.* Mark Girouard has written several books that are incomparable for their detailed, behind-the-scenes perspective on art and architecture: *Life in the English Country House* focuses on the 18th century while *The Victorian Country House* is a magnificent account about the lifestyles of the rich and famous of the 19th century. For the ultimate look at that favorite subject, lovely English villages, see *The Most Beautiful Villages of England,* by James Bentley, with ravishing photographs by Hugh Palmer.

Two particularly delightful travel books are those written by Susan Allen Toth, *England for All Seasons* and *My Love Affair with England.* Few of today's authors have managed to top the wit and perception of Henry James's magisterial *English Hours.* As for the flower of cities all, *London Perceived* is a classic text by the noted literary critic V. S. Pritchett, while John Russell's *London* is a superlative text written by a particularly eloquent art historian.

Videos

From *Wuthering Heights* to *Jane Eyre,* many great classics of British literature have been rendered into great classics of film. It's surprising to learn, however, how many of them were creations of Hollywood and not the British film industry (which had its heyday in the 1940s to 1960s). From Laurence Olivier to today's Kenneth Brannagh, noted directors-actors have long cross-pollinated the two centers of cinema. Any survey of British film, of course, begins with the dramas of Shakespeare: Olivier gave us a memorable *Othello* and *Hamlet,* Orson Welles a moody *Macbeth,* Brannagh gave up mod versions of *Hamlet* and *Much Ado About Nothing,* while Leonardo di Caprio graced a contemporary Miami version of *Romeo and Juliet.* Going behind the scenes, so to speak, Tom Stoppard created the 1999 Oscar winner *Shakespeare in Love.* Charles Dickens also provided the foundation for many a film favorite: David Lean's immortal *Great Expectations,* George Cukor's *David Copperfield,* and *A Christmas Carol,* with Alastair Sim as Scrooge, top this list.

Another, more recent, author has provided fodder for many beloved flicks: Agatha Christie. Of the many film versions of her books, one is especially treasured: *Murder, She Said,* which starred the inimitable Margaret Rutherford: with its setting of quaint English village, harpsichord film score, and the dotty Miss Marple of La Rutherford, this must be the most English of all the Christie films.

For lovers of opulence, spectacle, and history, there are many selections to look for. In particular, Robert Bolt's version of Sir Thomas More's life and death, *A Man for All Seasons,* and his *Lady Caroline Lamb,* surely the most beautiful historical film ever made. Richard Harris made a stirring Lord Protector in *Cromwell,* while the miniseries on Queen Elizabeth I, starring Glenda Jackson, is a great BBC addition to videos. Elizabeth's adversary came to breathless life in Vanessa Redgrave's rendition of *Mary, Queen of Scots,* certainly one of her finest performances.

Musicals? Near the top of anyone's list are four films set in England—Hollywood's England—that rank among the greatest musicals of all time, Walt Disney's *Mary Poppins,* George Cukor's *My Fair Lady,* Sir Carol Reed's Oscar-winner *Oliver!,* and—yeah, yeah, yeah!—the Beatles' *A Hard Day's Night.*

If you're seeking a look at contemporary Britain, you might view *My Beautiful Laundrette,* about Asians in London, *Secrets and Lies,* about a dysfunctional London family, or *Trainspotting,* about Edinburgh's dark side. Then you might lighten up with *The Full Monty,* about six former steelworkers in Sheffield who become strippers, or *Notting Hill,* a romantic comedy with Julia Roberts and Hugh Grant. *Harry Potter and the Sorcerer's Stone,* based on the wildly popular children's books by J.K. Rowling, was filmed in London, Gloucester, and the Cotswolds.

Quintessentially British are some comedies of the 1950s and 1960s: Alec Guinness's *Kind Hearts and Coronets,* Peter Sellers's *The Mouse That Roared,* and Tony Richardson's Oscar-winner and cinematic style-setter, *Tom Jones,* starring Albert Finney, are some best bets. Today everyone's visions of turn-of-the-last-century England have been captured by the Merchant and Ivory films, notably their 1992 *Howard's End,* which won innumerable awards. Douglas McGrath's *Emma,* starring Gwyneth Paltrow, and Ang Lee's *Sense and Sensibility,* starring Emma Thompson and Kate Winslet, are two of a spate of recent film versions of Jane Austen's works.

GREAT BRITAIN
AT A GLANCE

3000 BC First building of Stonehenge (later building 2100–1900 BC)

54 BC–AD 43 Julius Caesar's exploratory invasion of England. Romans conquer England, led by Emperor Claudius

60 Boudicca, a native British queen, razes the first Roman London (Londinium) to the ground

122–27 Emperor Hadrian completes the Roman conquest and builds a wall across the north to keep back the Scottish Picts

ca. 490 Possible period for the legendary King Arthur, who may have led resistance to Anglo-Saxon invaders; in 500 the Battle of Badon is fought

563 St. Columba, an Irish monk, founds monastery on the Scottish island of Iona; begins to convert Picts and Scots to Christianity

597 St. Augustine arrives in Canterbury to Christianize Britain

871–99 Alfred the Great, king of Wessex, unifies the English against Viking invaders, who are then confined to the northeast

1040 Edward the Confessor moves his court to Westminster and founds Westminster Abbey

1066 William, duke of Normandy, invades, defeats Harold at the Battle of Hastings, and is crowned at Westminster in December

1086 Domesday Book completed, a survey of all taxpayers in England, drawn up to assist administration of the new realm

1167 Oxford University founded

1170 Thomas à Becket murdered in Canterbury; his shrine becomes center for international pilgrimage

1189 Richard the Lionhearted embarks on the Third Crusade

1209 Cambridge University founded

1215 King John forced to sign Magna Carta at Runnymede; it promulgates basic principles of English law: no taxation except through Parliament, trial by jury, and property guarantees

1272–1307 Edward I, a great legislator; in 1282–83 he conquers Wales and reinforces his rule with a chain of massive castles

1337–1453 Edward III claims the French throne, starting the Hundred Years War. In spite of dramatic English victories—1346 at Crécy, 1356 at Poitiers, 1415 at Agincourt—the long war of attrition ends with the French driving the English out from all but Calais, which finally fell in 1558

1348–49 The Black Death (bubonic plague) reduces the population of Britain to around 2½ million; decades of social unrest follow

1399 Henry Bolingbroke (Henry IV) deposes and murders his cousin Richard II; beginning of the rivalry between houses of York and Lancaster

1402–10 The Welsh, led by Owain Glendŵr, rebel against English rule

1455–85 The Wars of the Roses, the York-Lancaster struggle erupts in civil war

1477 William Caxton prints first book in England

1485 Henry Tudor (Henry VII) defeats Richard III at the Battle of Bosworth, and founds the Tudor dynasty; he suppresses private armies, develops administrative efficiency and royal absolutism

1530s Under Henry VIII the Reformation takes hold; he dissolves the monasteries, finally demolishes medieval England and replaces it with a new society

1555 Protestant Bishops Ridley and Latimer are burned in Oxford; in 1556 Archbishop Cranmer is burned

1558–1603 Reign of Elizabeth I, Protestantism reestablished; Drake, Raleigh, and other freebooters establish English claims in the West Indies and North America

1568 Mary, Queen of Scots, flees to England; in 1587 she is executed

1588 Spanish Armada fails to invade England

1603 James VI of Scotland becomes James I of England

1605 Guy Fawkes and friends plot to blow up Parliament

1611 King James Authorized Version of the Bible published

1620 Pilgrims sail from Plymouth on the *Mayflower* and settle in New England

1629 Charles I dissolves Parliament, decides to rule alone

1642–49 Civil War between the Royalists and Parliamentarians (Cavaliers and Roundheads); the Parliamentarians win

1649 Charles I executed; England is a republic

1653 Oliver Cromwell becomes Lord Protector, England's only dictatorship

1660 Charles II restored to the throne; accepts limits to royal power

1666 The Great Fire of London, accession of William III (of Orange) and his wife, Mary II, as joint monarchs (1689); royal power limited still further

1707 Union of English and Scots parliaments under Queen Anne

1714 The German Hanoverians succeed to the throne; George I's lack of English leads to a council of ministers, the beginning of the Cabinet system of government

1700s Under the first four Georges, the Industrial Revolution develops and with it Britain's domination of world trade

1775–83 Britain loses its American colonies

1795–1815 Britain and its allies defeat French in the Napoleonic Wars; in 1805 Nelson is killed at Trafalgar; in 1815 Battle of Waterloo is fought

Chronology

1801	Union with Ireland
1811–20	Prince Regent rules during his father's (George III) madness, the Regency period
1825	The Stockton to Darlington railway, the world's first passenger line with regular service, is established
1832	The Reform Bill extends the franchise, limiting the power of the great landowners
1834	Parliament outlaws slavery
1837–1901	The long reign of Victoria, Britain becomes the world's richest country, and the British Empire reaches its height; railways, canals, and telegraph lines draw Britain into one vast manufacturing net
1851	The Great Exhibition, Prince Albert's brainchild, is held in Crystal Palace, Hyde Park
1861	Prince Albert dies
1887	Victoria celebrates her Golden Jubilee; in 1901 she dies, marking the end of an era
1914–18	World War I: fighting against Germany, Britain loses a whole generation, with 750,000 men killed in trench warfare alone; enormous debts and inept diplomacy in the postwar years undermine Britain's position as a world power
1919	Ireland declares independence from England; bloody Black-and-Tan struggle was one result
1926	General strike in sympathy with striking coal miners
1936	Edward VIII abdicates to marry American divorcée, Mrs. Wallis Simpson
1939–45	World War II: Britain faces Hitler alone until the bombing of Pearl Harbor; London badly damaged during the Blitz, September '40–May '41; Britain's economy shattered
1945	Labour wins a landslide victory; stays in power for six years, transforming Britain into a welfare state
1952	Queen Elizabeth II accedes to the throne
1973	Britain joins the European Economic Community after referendum
1975	Britain begins to pump North Sea oil
1981	Marriage of Prince Charles and Lady Diana Spencer
1982	Falklands regained
1987	Conservatives under Margaret Thatcher win a third term in office
1990	John Major takes over as prime minister, ending Margaret Thatcher's illustrious, if controversial, term in the office
1991	The Persian Gulf War
1992	Great Britain and the European countries join to form one European Community (EC), whose name was officially changed to European Union in 1993
1994	Official opening of the Channel Tunnel by Queen Elizabeth II and President Mitterand

1996 The Prince and Princess of Wales receive a precedent-breaking divorce. Official opening of the reconstruction of Shakespeare's Globe Theatre in London

1997 Diana, Princess of Wales, dies at 36 in a car crash in Paris on August 31. She is buried at Althorp, the Spencer family estate in Northamptonshire

1999 London welcomes the new century on December 31, 1999, with the gala opening of the Millennium Dome in Greenwich.

2001 The Millennium Dome closes, its future uncertain. Beginning in February, farm animals are slaughtered during an outbreak of foot-and-mouth disease. Some tourist sights and walking paths close, but most reopen by summer. Prime Minister Tony Blair is elected to a second term.

2002 Queen Elizabeth celebrates her Golden Jubilee. The Commonwealth Games are held in Manchester.

Chronology

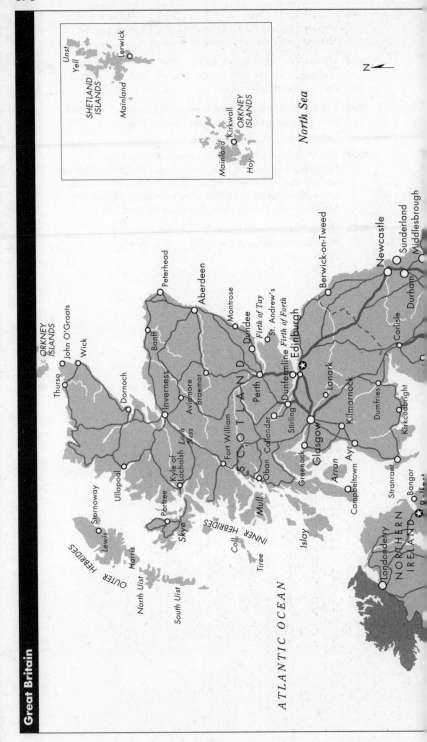

ATLANTIC OCEAN

North Sea

SHETLAND ISLANDS
Unst
Yell
Lerwick
Mainland

ORKNEY ISLANDS
Mainland
Kirkwall
Hoy

ORKNEY ISLANDS
John O'Groats
Thurso
Wick
Dornoch
Ullapool
Inverness
Loch Ness
Aviemore
Braemar
Banff
Peterhead
Aberdeen
Montrose
Dundee
Firth of Tay
St. Andrew's
Firth of Forth
Edinburgh
Berwick-on-Tweed
Perth
Dunfermline
Stirling
Callander
Oban
Fort William
Kyle of Lochalsh
Portree
Skye
Mull
Coll
Tiree
INNER HEBRIDES
Islay
Arran
Campbeltown
Greenock
Glasgow
Lanark
Kilmarnock
Ayr
Dumfries
Kirkcudbright
Stranraer
Bangor
Belfast
Londonderry
NORTHERN IRELAND
Stornoway
Lewis
Harris
North Uist
South Uist
OUTER HEBRIDES
SCOTLAND
Newcastle
Sunderland
Middlesbrough
Durham
Carlisle

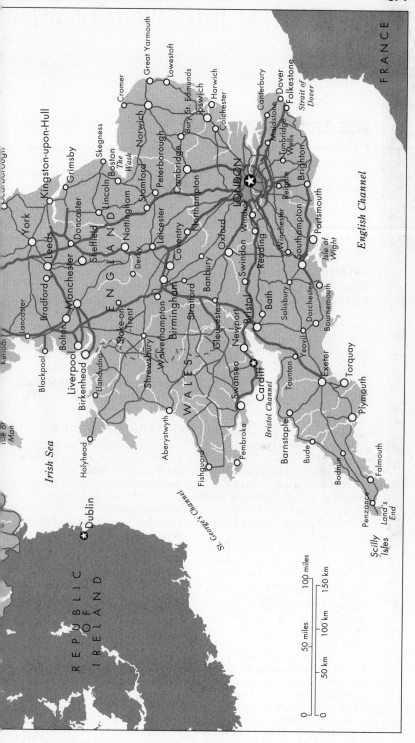

ESSENTIAL INFORMATION

AIR TRAVEL

BOOKING

When you book **look for nonstop flights** and **remember that "direct" flights stop at least once.** Try to avoid connecting flights, which require a change of plane. For more booking tips and to check prices and make online flight reservations, log on to www.fodors.com.

CARRIERS

British Airways is the national flag carrier and offers mostly nonstop flights from 18 U.S. cities to Heathrow and Gatwick airports, along with flights to Manchester, Birmingham, and Glasgow. As the leading British carrier, it offers myriad add-on options, helping to bring down ticket costs. In addition, it has a vast program of discount airfare-hotel packages.

Because Britain is such a small country, internal air travel is much less important there than in the United States. For trips of less than 200 mi, the train is often quicker, with rail stations more centrally located. Flying tends to cost more, but for longer trips—for example, between London and Glasgow or Edinburgh—or where a sea crossing is involved, to places such as the Channel Islands or the Scottish islands, air travel has a considerable time advantage.

British Airways operates shuttle services between London Heathrow and Edinburgh, Glasgow, Belfast, and Manchester. Passengers can simply turn up and get a flight (usually hourly) without booking. There are also shuttle services from Gatwick. British Midland operates from Heathrow to Belfast, Dublin, Glasgow, Leeds, Manchester, and Teesside; it also has service from a number of U.S. cities to Manchester. For services to the Channel Islands, *see* Chapter 5.

➤ MAJOR AIRLINES: **American Airlines** (☎ 800/433–7300; 020/8572–5555 in London) to Heathrow, Gatwick. **British Airways** (☎ 800/247–9297; 0845/7222–1111 in London) to Heathrow, Gatwick. **Continental** (☎ 800/231–0856; 0800/776464 in London) to Gatwick, Stansted. **Delta** (☎ 800/241–4141; 0800/414767 in London) to Gatwick. **Northwest Airlines** (☎ 800/447–4747; 0870/507–4074 in London) to Gatwick. **United** (☎ 800/241–6522; 0845/844–4777 in London) to Heathrow. **US Airways** (☎ 800/622–1015; 0800/783–5556 in London) to Gatwick. **TWA** (☎ 800/892–4141; 0345/333333 in London) to Gatwick. **Virgin Atlantic** (☎ 800/862–8621; 01293/747747 in London) to Heathrow, Gatwick.

➤ SMALLER AIRLINES: **British Midland** (☎ 800/788–0555; 020/8745–7321 in London).

CHECK-IN & BOARDING

Assuming that not everyone with a ticket will show up, airlines routinely overbook planes. When everyone does, airlines ask for volunteers to give up their seats. In return, these volunteers usually get a certificate for a free flight and are rebooked on the next flight out. If there are not enough volunteers, the airline must choose who will be denied boarding. The first to get bumped are passengers who checked in late and those flying on discounted tickets, so **get to the gate and check in as early as possible,** especially during peak periods.

Always **bring a government-issued photo I.D. to the airport;** even when it's not required, a passport is best.

CUTTING COSTS

The least expensive airfares to Great Britain must usually be purchased in advance and are non-refundable. It's smart to **call a number of airlines, and when you are quoted a good price,** book it on the spot—the same fare may not be available the next day. Always **check different routings** and look into using different airports. Travel agents, especially low-fare specialists (☞ Discounts & Deals, *below*), are helpful.

Consolidators are another good source. They buy tickets for scheduled international flights at reduced rates from the airlines, then sell them at prices that beat the best fare available directly from the airlines, usually without restrictions. Sometimes you can even get your money back if you need to return the ticket. Carefully read the fine print detailing penalties for changes and cancellations, and **confirm your consolidator reservation with the airline.**

➤ CONSOLIDATORS: **Cheap Tickets** (☎ 800/377–1000). **Discount Airline Ticket Service** (☎ 800/576–1600). **Unitravel** (☎ 800/325–2222). **Up & Away Travel** (☎ 212/889–2345). **World Travel Network** (☎ 800/409–6753).

ENJOYING THE FLIGHT

For more legroom, **request an emergency-aisle seat.** Don't sit in the row in front of the emergency aisle or in front of a bulkhead, where seats may not recline. If you have dietary concerns, **ask for special meals when booking.** These can be vegetarian, low-cholesterol, or kosher, for example. On long flights, try to maintain a normal routine, to help fight jet lag. At night, **get some sleep.** By day, **eat light meals, drink water** (not alcohol), and **move around the cabin** to stretch your legs. For additional jet-lag tips consult *Fodor's FYI: Travel Fit & Healthy* (available at bookstores everywhere).

FLYING TIMES

Flying time is about 6½ hours from New York, 7½ hours from Chicago, 9½ hours from Dallas, 10 hours from Los Angeles, and 21½ hours from Sydney.

HOW TO COMPLAIN

If your baggage goes astray or your flight goes awry, complain right away. Most carriers require that you **file a claim immediately.**

➤ AIRLINE COMPLAINTS: U.S. Department of Transportation **Aviation Consumer Protection Division** (✉ C-75, Room 4107, Washington, DC 20590, ☎ 202/366–2220, WEB www.dot.gov/airconsumer). **Federal Aviation Administration Consumer Hotline** (☎ 800/322–7873).

AIRPORTS

Most international flights to London arrive at either Heathrow Airport (LHR), 15 mi west of London, or at Gatwick Airport (LGW), 27 mi south of the capital. Most flights from the United States go to Heathrow, which is divided into four terminals, with Terminals 3 and 4 handling transatlantic flights (British Airways uses Terminal 4). Gatwick is London's second gateway. It has grown from a European airport into an airport that serves 21 scheduled U.S. destinations. A third, newer airport, Stansted (STN), is 35 mi northeast of the city. It handles mainly European and domestic traffic, although there is a scheduled service from New York. There are fast connections from all the London airports into the capital. The cost of hotels and car rentals does not vary much between Heathrow and Gatwick.

➤ AIRPORT INFORMATION: **Heathrow Airport** (☎ 0870/000–0123, WEB www.baa.co.uk). **Gatwick Airport** (☎ 01293/535353, WEB www.baa.co.uk). **Stansted Airport** (☎ 0870/000–0303, WEB www.baa.co.uk).

DUTY-FREE SHOPPING

As of July 1999, duty-free shopping allowances between Britain and other European Union member countries were abolished, although there are still numerous merchandise offers for those traveling between E.U. countries by boat, plane, and via the Channel Tunnel. Duty-free sales for travel outside the E.U. remain business as usual (☞ Customs & Duties, *below*).

AIRPORTS & CITY TRANSFERS TO LONDON

See London A to Z *in* Chapter 1 for information on transportation between the airports and London.

BIKE TRAVEL

Bikes are banned from motorways and most dual carriageways or main trunk roads, but on side roads and country lanes, the bike is one of the best ways to explore Britain. Some parts of Britain have bicycle routes in towns and through parts of the countryside; for example, in the Peak District National Parks, bikes can be hired by the day for use on special traffic-free trails. Cyclists can legally use public bridleways—green, unsurfaced tracks reserved for horses, walkers, and cyclists. Some former railway lines have become cycle meccas, such as the Tarka Trail in North Devon, and the Camel Trail in Cornwall. A range of bikes, from racing to mountain, are usually available for rental, and prices vary by area, anywhere from £3–£5 an hour, to £7–£20 for a full day. A deposit of £25 or more is often required. For night cycling, the law requires a full set of reflectors on the wheels and pedals, and lights at the back and front.

For maps, the Landranger by Ordnance Survey series costs £5.50 a map and covers the country in scale 1:50,000 in more than 30 editions. Stanfords bookshop boasts the world's largest selection of maps and has a telephone and Internet ordering service.

Call ahead to the local tourist information office for lists of local bike rental outlets, or contact the Britain Visitor Centre. The Yellow Pages classified telephone directory also lists cycle rentals.

➤ BIKE MAPS: **Landranger** by Ordnance Survey (✉ Order Processing, Romsey Rd., Southampton SO16 4GU, ☎ 02380/792439). **Stanfords** (✉ 12–14 Long Acre, London WC2E 9LP, ☎ 020/7836–1321, WEB www. stanfords.co.uk).

➤ BIKE RENTALS: **Britain Visitor Centre** (✉ 1 Regent St., London SW1Y 4NX, ☎ no phone, WEB www. visitbritain.com). **Yellow Pages** (WEB www.yell.co.uk).

BIKES IN FLIGHT

Most airlines accommodate bikes as luggage, provided they are dismantled and boxed. Airlines sell bike boxes, which are often free at bike shops, for about $5 (it's at least $100 for bike bags). International travelers can sometimes substitute a bike for a piece of checked luggage at no charge; otherwise, the cost is about $100. Domestic and Canadian airlines charge $25–$50.

BOAT & FERRY TRAVEL

Ferries, hovercraft, and seacats travel regular routes to France, Spain, Ireland, and Scandinavia. There are also numerous canal ways through the countryside and to the coast (☞ Outdoor Activities and Sports, *below*).

Hoverspeed provides fast travel to France. P&O runs major ferry routes to France and Spain. Scandinavian Seaways covers Scandinavia, and Stena Line covers routes to Ireland and the Netherlands as well as Scandinavia.

FARES & SCHEDULES

➤ BOAT & FERRY INFORMATION: **Hoverspeed** (☎ 0870/524–0241). **P&O** (☎ 0870/600–0600). **Scandinavian Seaways** (☎ 01255/240240). **Stena Line** (☎ 0870/570–7070).

BUS TRAVEL

Britain has a comprehensive bus (short-haul) and coach (long-distance) network that offers an inexpensive way of seeing the country. National Express is the major coach operator, and Victoria Coach Station in London is the hub of the National Express network, serving around 1,200 destinations. Tickets (payable by most major credit cards, reservations are advisable) and information are available from any of the company's 2,500 agents nationwide, including offices at London's Heathrow and Gatwick airport coach stations. Green Line is the next largest national service; it serves fewer destinations, although airports and major tourist towns are covered. In Scotland, Scottish Citylink runs a similar operation.

The classic double-decker buses make up many of the extensive networks of local bus services, run by separate private companies. Check with the local bus station wherever you're staying, or tourist information center, for bus schedules. Most companies offer day or week "Explorer" or "Rover" unlimited-travel tickets, and those in popular tourist areas invariably operate special scenic tours in summer. The top deck of a stately double-decker bus is a great place from which to view the surrounding countryside. Nearly all bus services have a no-smoking policy.

CUTTING COSTS

National Express's Tourist Trail Pass costs £49 for two days of travel within a three-day period; £85 for five days of travel within 10 days; £120 for seven travel days within 21 days; and £187 for 14 travel days within 30 days. A Discount Coach Card for students, under-25s, and over-50s, which costs £8 and is good for one year, qualifies you for 20%–30% discounts off many standard fares. Tourist Trail Passes, sold by British Travel International, make great savings if you plan to tour Britain, and they can be bought in advance.

FARES & SCHEDULES

➤ BUS INFORMATION: **British Travel International** (✉ Box 299, Elkton, VA 22827, ☎ 540/298–1395).

Green Line (✉ Green Line Travel Office, Bulleid Way, Eccleston Bridge, London, SW1, ☎ 020/8668–7261). **National Express** (☎ 0870/580–8080, WEB www.gobycoach.com). **Scottish Citylink** (☎ 0870/550–5050). **Victoria Coach Station** (✉ Buckingham Palace Rd., London SW1W 9TP).

BUSINESS HOURS

Usual business hours are Monday–Saturday 9–5:30; on Sunday, small grocery stores stay open all day, as do larger food markets, superstores, and shopping malls. Outside the main centers, most shops close at 1 PM once a week, often Wednesday or Thursday. In small villages, many also close for lunch. In large cities—especially London—department stores stay open late (usually until 7:30 or 8) one night a week. On national holidays, most stores are shut, and over the Christmas holidays, most restaurants are closed as well (☞ Holidays, *below*).

BANKS & OFFICES

Most banks are open weekdays 9:30–4:30. Some have Thursday evening hours, and a few are open Saturday morning. Many offices are open 9:30–5:30.

GAS STATIONS

Most gas stations in central London are open seven days, 24 hours. Farther out of London or off the major roads, hours vary considerably but are usually 8–8.

MUSEUMS & SIGHTS

The major national museums and galleries are open daily, including lunchtime, but with shorter hours on Sundays. In London, many museums are open late one evening a week.

PHARMACIES

British pharmacies are called chemists. Independent chemist shops are generally open Monday–Saturday 9:30–5:30, although in larger cities, some stay open until 10 PM; the local newspaper lists which pharmacies are open late. In London, the leading chain drugstore, Boots, is open until 6; the Oxford Street and Piccadilly Circus branches are also open Sundays, and until 8 PM Thursday.

CAMERAS & PHOTOGRAPHY

Don't be surprised if you are asked to refrain from taking pictures during theater, ballet, or opera productions, and in galleries, museums, and stately homes. Locals are generally happy to feature in your photos, but it's polite to ask if they mind before fixing the lens. There are many must-take sights in Britain, but London's Big Ben and the guards on horseback in Whitehall are top of the list. The *Kodak Guide to Shooting Great Travel Pictures* (available at bookstores everywhere) is loaded with tips.

➤ PHOTO HELP: **Kodak Information Center** (☎ 800/242–2424).

EQUIPMENT PRECAUTIONS

Don't pack film and equipment in checked luggage, where it is much more susceptible to damage. X-ray machines used to view checked luggage are becoming much more powerful and therefore are much more likely to ruin your film. Always **keep film and tape out of the sun.** Carry an extra supply of batteries, and **be prepared to turn on your**

camera or camcorder to prove to security personnel that the device is real. Always **ask for hand inspection of film,** which becomes clouded after repeated exposure to airport X-ray machines, and **keep videotapes away from metal detectors.**

FILM & DEVELOPING

Film is available from chemists, newsagents, and supermarkets, as well as photographic stores. Kodak, followed by Agfa, are the most common brands, and prices range from £2–£4 for a roll of 36-exposure color print film. Chain drugstores, such as Boots or Superdrug, and supermarkets run cost-cutting deals. Larger drugstore branches, photo stores, and outlets of Supasnaps in dry cleaners provide 24-hour film developing services.

VIDEOS

Remember that most video cartridges sold in the United Kingdom (marked PAL) do not interface with American video players (NTSC). The top tourist attractions that have videos also market versions specially made for the American and overseas market. If you're bringing your own video camcorder, bring a supply of cassettes as well.

CAR RENTAL

Rental rates vary widely but are generally expensive, beginning at £50 ($80) a day and £200 ($320) a week for a small economy car, usually with manual transmission. Air-conditioning and unlimited mileage generally come with larger automatic transmission cars.

➤ MAJOR AGENCIES: **Alamo** (☎ 800/522–9696; 020/8759–6200 in the U.K., WEB www.alamo.com). **Avis** (☎ 800/331–1084; 800/879–2847 in Canada; 02/9353–9000 in Australia; 09/525–1982 in New Zealand; 0870/606–0100 in the U.K., WEB www.avis.com). **Budget** (☎ 800/527–0700; 0870/156–5656 in the U.K., WEB www.budget.com). **Dollar** (☎ 800/800–6000; 0124/622–0111 in the U.K., where it's affiliated with Sixt; 02/9223–1444 in Australia, WEB www.dollar.com). **Hertz** (☎ 800/654–3001; 800/263–0600 in Canada; 020/8897–2072 in the U.K.; 02/9669–2444 in

Australia; 09/256–8690 in New Zealand, WEB www.hertz.com). **National Car Rental** (☎ 800/227–7368; 020/8680–4800 in the U.K., WEB www.nationalcar.com).

CUTTING COSTS

To get the best deal, **book through a travel agent who will shop around.**

Do **look into wholesalers,** companies that do not own fleets but rent in bulk from those that do and often offer better rates than traditional car-rental operations. Payment must be made before you leave home. Also **check out rates from local agencies,** which are often less expensive and more negotiable than those offered by the major international companies.

➤ LOCAL AGENCIES: **Dimple Car Hire** (✉ Poplar Pl., London W2 4AS, ☎ 020/7243–4400, FAX 020/7243–4408). **Enterprise** (✉ 466–480 Edgeware Rd., London W2 1EL, ☎ 020/7723–4800, FAX 020/7723–4368). **Europcar** (✉ 30 Woburn Pl., London WC1H 0JR, ☎ 020/7255–2339, FAX 020/7255–2347).

➤ WHOLESALERS: **Auto Europe** (☎ 207/842–2000 or 800/223–5555, FAX 207/842–2222, WEB www.autoeurope.com). **Europe by Car** (☎ 212/581–3040 or 800/223–1516, FAX 212/246–1458, WEB www.europebycar.com). **DER Travel Services** (✉ 9501 W. Devon Ave., Rosemont, IL 60018, ☎ 800/782–2424, FAX 800/282–7474 for information; 800/860–9944 for brochures, WEB www.dertravel.com). **Kemwel Holiday Autos** (☎ 800/678–0678, FAX 914/825–3160, WEB www.kemwel.com).

INSURANCE

When driving a rented car you are generally responsible for any damage to or loss of the vehicle. Before you rent, see what coverage your personal auto-insurance policy and credit cards provide.

Before you buy collision coverage, check your existing policies—you may already be covered. However, collision policies that car-rental companies sell for European rentals usually do not include stolen-vehicle coverage.

REQUIREMENTS & RESTRICTIONS

In Great Britain your own driver's license is acceptable. An International Driver's Permit is a good idea; it's available from the American or Canadian automobile association, and, in the United Kingdom, from the Automobile Association or Royal Automobile Club. These international permits are universally recognized, and having one in your wallet may save you a problem with the local authorities. Companies frequently restrict rentals to people over age 23 or under age 75.

SURCHARGES

Before you pick up a car in one city and leave it in another, **ask about drop-off charges or one-way service fees,** which can be substantial. Note, too, that some rental agencies charge extra if you return the car before the time specified in your contract. To avoid a hefty refueling fee, **fill the tank just before you turn in the car,** but be aware that gas stations near the rental outlet may overcharge.

CAR TRAVEL

With well over 55 million inhabitants in a country about the size of California, Britain has some of the most crowded roads in the world. In London, it's best to rely on the excellent public transport network—with the city's tediously slow traffic and restrictive parking rules, a car is a proverbial noose. But away from the towns and cities, you can find miles of little-used roads and lanes where driving can be a real pleasure—and an adventure.

AUTO CLUBS

If you are a member of the American Automobile Association (A.A.A.), check your membership details before you depart for Britain, since under a reciprocal agreement, roadside assistance in the United Kingdom from the British Automobile Association (A.A.) should cost you nothing.

➤ IN THE U.K.: **Automobile Association** (☎ 0870/550–0600). **Royal Automobile Club** (☎ 0870/572–2722).

➤ CONTACTS: **Australian Automobile Association** (☎ 02/6247–7311 in Australia). **Canadian Automobile Association** (☎ 613/247–0117 in Canada). **New Zealand Automobile Association** (☎ 09/377–4660 in New Zealand). **American Automobile Association** (☎ 800/564–6222 in the U.S.).

EMERGENCY SERVICES

If your car breaks down, position the red hazard triangle (which should be in the trunk of the car) a few paces away from the rear of the car. Leave the hazard warning lights on. On major highways, emergency roadside telephone booths are positioned within walking-distance intervals. Contact your car rental company or call the Automobile Association toll-free. You can join and receive roadside assistance from the A.A. on the spot, but the charge is higher—around £75—than a simple membership fee. However, if you are a member of the A.A.A. (American Automobile Association), check your membership details before you depart for Britain.

➤ CONTACTS: **Ambulance, fire, police** (☎ 999). **Automobile Association** (☎ 0800/887766).

GASOLINE

Gasoline is commonly called "petrol" in the United Kingdom and is sold by the liter. Most large stations are open 24 hours a day, seven days a week, except in the rural areas. Service stations generally accept all major credit cards. Service is self-serve; only in small villages are you likely to find a friendly attendant (tips aren't expected). Petrol is becoming increasingly expensive at 85p per liter at press time. Supermarket pumps just outside the city centers frequently offer the best prices. Unleaded petrol is predominant, denoted by green stickers on fuel pumps and pumplines. Premium and Super Premium are the two varieties, and most cars run on regular premium.

ROAD CONDITIONS

There's a very good network of super-highways (motorways) and divided highways (dual carriageways) throughout most of Britain, although in more remote parts, especially Wales and Scotland, where unclassified roads join village to village and are little more than glorified agricultural cart tracks, travel is noticeably slower. Motorways (with the prefix *M*), shown in blue on most maps and road signs, are mainly two or three lanes in each direction, without any right-hand turns. Other fast major roads are shown with the prefix *A*, shown on maps as green and red. Sections of fast dual carriageway have black-edged, thick outlines, have both traffic lights and traffic circles, and right turns are sometimes permitted. Turnoffs are often marked by highway numbers, rather than place names, so it's a good idea to always take note of connecting road numbers.

The vast network of lesser roads, for the most part old coach and turnpike roads, might make your trip take twice the time and show you twice as much. Minor roads drawn in yellow or white, the former prefixed by *B*, the latter unlettered and unnumbered, are the ancient lanes and byways, a superb way of discovering the real Britain. Some of these (the white roads, in the main) are pothole-filled switchbacks, littered with blind corners, and barely wide enough for one car, let alone for two to pass. Be prepared to reverse into a passing place if you meet an oncoming car or truck.

ROAD MAPS

Good planning maps are available from the A.A. and the R.A.C. (☞ Auto Clubs, *above*). Or choose from the excellent Ordnance Survey or Collins road maps, available from newsagents and bookstores; prices run from about £3.95 for a paper fold-out to £5.95 for a spiral-bound paperback.

RULES OF THE ROAD

Always remember to **drive on the left in Britain**; this takes a bit of getting used to, and it's much easier if you're driving a British car where the steering and mirrors are designed for U.K. conditions. Study your map before leaving the airport, and be sure to give yourself plenty of time to adjust. The use of seat belts is obligatory in the front seat and in the back seat where they exist (except for particularly old models, all cars should have both front and rear seat belts).

If you're planning on driving around Britain, **pick up a copy of the official Highway Code** (£1.50) at a service station. Besides driving rules and illustrations of signs and road markings, this useful booklet contains information for pedestrians, cyclists, and motorcyclists.

Speed limits are complicated, and traffic police can be hard on speeders, especially in urban areas. In those areas, the limit (shown on circular red signs) is generally 30 mph, but 40 mph on some main roads. In rural areas the limit is 60 mph on ordinary roads and 70 mph on motorways. At traffic circles ("roundabouts" in Britain), circulation is clockwise, and entering motorists must yield to cars coming from their right. The use of horns is prohibited between 11:30 PM and 7 AM.

Pedestrians have right-of-way on "zebra" crossings (black and white stripes that stretch across the street between two Belisha beacons—orange-flashing globe lights on posts). The curb on each side of the zebra crossing has zigzag markings. It is illegal to park within the zigzag area or to pass another vehicle at a zebra crossing. At other crossings, pedestrians must yield to traffic, but they do have right-of-way over traffic turning left—if they have the nerve.

Parking regulations are very strictly enforced. Meters take 10p, 20p, 50p, and £1 coins. In London, meters have an insatiable hunger—a 20p piece buys just 6 minutes—and some will permit only a two-hour stay. Do not park within 15 yards of a road junction. Within central London parking is not permitted on single yellow lines during restricted hours (check the signs on the sidewalk for these hours). Do not park on double yellow lines or in bus lanes. On "Red Routes"—busy roads with red lines painted in the street—you may not stop even to let out a passenger. At night, you can park in 30-mph zones, but only if you are within 25 yards of a lighted street lamp.

Drunk-driving laws are also strictly enforced. The legal limit is 80 milligrams of alcohol, which means roughly two units of alcohol—two glasses of wine, one pint of beer, or one glass of whisky—but these amounts vary significantly depending on your body weight or on the amount you have eaten that day. It's far safer to avoid alcohol if you're getting behind the wheel.

THE CHANNEL TUNNEL

Short of flying, the "Chunnel" is the fastest way to cross the English Channel: 35 minutes from Folkestone to Calais, 60 minutes from motorway to motorway, or 3 hours from London's Waterloo Station to Paris's Gare du Nord.

➤ CAR TRANSPORT: Le Shuttle (☎ 0870/535–3535 in the U.K.).

➤ PASSENGER SERVICE: In the U.K.: Eurostar (☎ 0870/518–6186), Inter-City Europe (☎ 0870/584–8848 for credit-card bookings). In the U.S.: BritRail Travel (☎ 800/677–8585). Rail Europe (☎ 800/942–4866, WEB www.raileurope.com; ✉ 179 Piccadilly, London, W1, ☎ 0870/584–8848).

CHILDREN IN GREAT BRITAIN

There is a kaleidoscope of activity for children to enjoy throughout Britain. Plan your itinerary to include places and activities that will keep your children happy, and **involve your youngsters** as you outline your trip. Many museums and major attractions now offer special interactive features that appeal to kids; for example, some of the stately homes have added children's "fun trails," where kids can play detective as they explore the property. Cinemas, concert halls, and theaters have plenty of kid-friendly entertainment, particularly during school holidays. And even the more chic restaurants are learning to welcome children (if they are well behaved).

If you are renting a car, don't forget to **arrange for a car seat** when you reserve. For general advice about traveling with children, consult *Fodor's FYI: Travel with Your Baby* (available in bookstores everywhere).

For information on events for kids in and around London, look out for *Kids Out!*, a monthly magazine available from newsagents and bookstores. The London Tourist Board's information line offers two options: What's on for Children and Places for Children to Go, both 60p per minute. Available in the U.K., *Days Out with Kids* is packed with outings, each tried and tested by families for facilities and fun factors. There is a Southeast edition (Janet Bonthron, Bon Bon, £5.99) and separate editions for the West Country, Northeast, Northwest, and Heart of England (£4.99). *Fodor's Around London with Kids* (available in bookstores everywhere) can help you plan your days together.

➤ LOCAL INFORMATION: **London Tourist Board information lines** (☎ 09064/123404).

FLYING

If your children are two or older, **ask about children's airfares.** As a general rule, infants under two not occupying a seat fly at greatly reduced fares or even for free. When booking, **confirm carry-on allowances** if you're traveling with infants. In general, for babies charged 10% of the adult fare you are allowed one carry-on bag and a collapsible stroller; if the flight is full, the stroller may have to be checked or you may be limited to less.

Experts agree that it's a good idea to use safety seats aloft for children weighing less than 40 pounds. Airlines set their own policies: U.S. carriers usually require that the child be ticketed, even if he or she is young enough to ride free, since the seats must be strapped into regular seats. Do **check your airline's policy about using safety seats during takeoff and landing.** And since safety seats are not allowed everywhere in the plane, get your seat assignments early.

When reserving, **request children's meals or a freestanding bassinet** if you need them. But note that bulkhead seats, where you must sit to use the bassinet, may lack an overhead bin or storage space on the floor.

FOOD

You'll find the usual gamut of burger and fast-food chains (Burger King, McDonald's, Kentucky Fried Chicken) in Britain. Pizza chains, such as Pizza Hut and Pizza Express, are family-friendly—with foods to please parents, too; London has one on nearly every corner, and they also crop up in larger cities nationwide. Many families find that ethnic restaurants offer the best combination of moderate prices and interesting food. Most spots in London's colorful Chinatown welcome families, and every town has its share of Asian eateries and Italian pasta joints. If your children have a taste for spice, you'll be warmly received at Indian restaurants, which are particularly common in London and in the northern cities of Birmingham and Manchester. Most pubs and small country hotels are becoming more family-oriented and have family eating rooms (although these can lack character). Unless your children's behavior is impeccable, avoid the high class, terribly British establishments.

LODGING

Most hotels in Great Britain allow children under a certain age to stay in their parents' room at no extra charge, but others charge for them as extra adults; be sure to **find out the cutoff age for children's discounts.**

SIGHTS & ATTRACTIONS

Places that are especially appealing to children are indicated by a rubber-duckie icon (🦆) in the margin.

SUPPLIES & EQUIPMENT

You'll find everything you need for babies and children in supermarkets and in the Boots and Superdrug pharmacies. American brands are widely available.

TRANSPORTATION

For air transportation, *see* Flying, *above*. On trains and buses, children between the ages of five and 15 pay half or reduced fares, and kids under five travel free. When riding in a car, children are required by law to use seat belts; it is the driver's responsibility to ensure that they do. Children under 5 must ride in a child seat. Many car rental companies rent child seats for younger children.

COMPUTERS ON THE ROAD

If you're traveling with a laptop, carry a spare battery and adapter. Never plug your computer into any socket before asking about surge protection. Some hotels do not have built-in current stabilizers, and extreme electrical fluctuations and surges can short your adapter or even destroy your computer. Before connecting your computer to a phone line, you may want to test the line as well. IBM sells an invaluable pen-size modem tester that plugs into a telephone jack to check whether the line is safe to use.

CONSUMER PROTECTION

Whenever shopping or buying travel services in Great Britain, **pay with a major credit card,** if possible, so you can cancel payment or get reimbursed if there's a problem. If you're doing business with a particular company for the first time, **contact your local Better Business Bureau and the attorney general's offices** in your state and (for U.S. businesses) the company's home state as well. Have any complaints been filed? Finally, if you're buying a package or tour, always **consider travel insurance** that includes default coverage (☞ Insurance, *below*).

➤ BBBs: **Council of Better Business Bureaus** (✉ 4200 Wilson Blvd., Suite 800, Arlington, VA 22203, ☎ 703/276–0100, ⨌ 703/525–8277, ⊞ www.bbb.org).

CRUISE TRAVEL

Cunard Line operates four ships that make transatlantic crossings. The *Queen Elizabeth 2* (*QE2*) makes regular crossings April–December, between Southampton, England, and Baltimore, Boston, and New York City. Arrangements for the *QE2* can include one-way airfare. Check the travel pages of your Sunday newspaper for other cruise ships that sail to Britain, or consult a travel agent. To learn how to plan, choose, and book a cruise-ship voyage, check out Cruise How-to's on www.fodors.com and consult *Fodor's FYI: Plan & Enjoy Your Cruise* (available in bookstores everywhere).

➤ CRUISE LINES: **Cunard Line** (☎ 800/221–4770, ⊞ www.cunardline.com).

CUSTOMS & DUTIES

When shopping, **keep receipts** for all purchases. Upon reentering the country, **be ready to show customs officials what you've bought.** If you feel a duty is incorrect or object to the way your clearance was handled, note the inspector's badge number and ask to see a supervisor. If the problem isn't resolved, write to the appropriate authorities, beginning with the port director at your point of entry.

IN AUSTRALIA

Australian residents who are 18 or older may bring home $A400 worth of souvenirs and gifts (including jewelry), 250 cigarettes or 250 grams of tobacco, and 1,125 ml of alcohol (including wine, beer, and spirits). Residents under 18 may bring back $A200 worth of goods. Prohibited items include meat products. Seeds, plants, and fruits need to be declared upon arrival.

➤ INFORMATION: **Australian Customs Service** (Regional Director, ✉ Box 8, Sydney, NSW 2001, Australia, ☎ 02/9213–2000, ℻ 02/9213–4000, ᗯᴇᴮ www.customs.gov.au).

IN CANADA

Canadian residents who have been out of Canada for at least seven days may bring home C$750 worth of goods duty-free. If you've been away fewer than seven days but more than 48 hours, the duty-free allowance drops to C$200; if your trip lasts 24–48 hours, the allowance is C$50. You may not pool allowances with family members. Goods claimed under the C$750 exemption may follow you by mail; those claimed under the lesser exemptions must accompany you. Alcohol and tobacco products may be included in the seven-day and 48-hour exemptions but not in the 24-hour exemption. If you meet the age requirements of the province or territory through which you reenter Canada, you may bring in, duty-free, 1.14 liters (40 imperial ounces) of wine or liquor *or* 24 12-ounce cans or bottles of beer or ale. If you are 19 or older you may bring in, duty-free, 200 cigarettes and 50 cigars. Check ahead of time with the Canada Customs Revenue Agency or the Department of Agriculture for policies regarding meat products, seeds, plants, and fruits.

You may send an unlimited number of gifts worth up to C$60 each duty-free to Canada. Label the package UNSOLICITED GIFT—VALUE UNDER $60. Alcohol and tobacco are excluded.

➤ INFORMATION: **Canada Customs Revenue Agency** (✉ 2265 St. Laurent Blvd. S, Ottawa, Ontario K1G 4K3, Canada, ☎ 204/983–3500 or 506/636–5064; 800/461–9999 in Canada, ᗯᴇᴮ www.ccra-adrc.gc.ca).

IN NEW ZEALAND

Homeward-bound residents 17 or older may bring back $700 worth of souvenirs and gifts. Your duty-free allowance also includes 4.5 liters of wine or beer; one 1,125-ml bottle of spirits; and either 200 cigarettes, 250 grams of tobacco, 50 cigars, or a combination of the three up to 250 grams. Prohibited items include meat products, seeds, plants, and fruits.

➤ INFORMATION: **New Zealand Customs** (Custom House, ✉ 50 Anzac Ave., Box 29, Auckland, New Zealand, ☎ 09/300–5399, ℻ 09/359–6730, ᗯᴇᴮ www.customs.govt.nz).

IN THE U.K.

There are two levels of duty-free allowance for entering Britain: one for goods bought outside the European Union (E.U.) and the other for goods bought within the E.U. (Austria, Belgium, Denmark, Finland, France, Germany, Greece, the Irish Republic, Italy, Luxembourg, the Netherlands, Portugal, Spain, and Sweden).

Of goods bought outside the E.U. you may import duty-free: 200 cigarettes or 100 cigarillos or 50 cigars or 250 grams of tobacco; 2 liters of table wine and, in addition, (a) 1 liter of alcohol over 22% by volume (most spirits), (b) 2 liters of alcohol under 22% by volume (fortified or sparkling wine or liqueurs), or (c) 2 more liters of table wine; 60 milliliters of perfume; ¼ liter (250 ml) of toilet water; and other goods up to a value of £145, but not more than 50 liters of beer or 25 cigarette lighters.

Of goods bought within the E.U., you should not exceed (unless you can prove they are for personal use): 800 cigarettes, 400 cigarillos, 200 cigars, and 1 kilogram of tobacco, plus 10 liters of spirits, 20 liters of fortified wine, 90 liters of wine, and 110 liters of beer.

No animals or pets of any kind can be brought in without a lengthy quarantine. The penalties are severe and are strictly enforced. Similarly, fresh meats, plants and vegetables, controlled drugs, and firearms and ammunition may not be brought into the U.K.

You will face no customs formalities if you enter Scotland or Wales from any other part of the United Kingdom.

➤ INFORMATION: **HM Customs and Excise** (Customer Helpline, ☎ 0345/ 442236).

IN THE U.S.

U.S. residents who have been out of the country for at least 48 hours (and who have not used the $400 allowance or any part of it in the past 30 days) may bring home $400 worth of foreign goods duty-free. U.S. residents 21 and older may bring back 1 liter of alcohol duty-free. In addition, regardless of your age, you are allowed 200 cigarettes and 100 non-Cuban cigars. Antiques, which the U.S. Customs Service defines as objects more than 100 years old, enter duty-free, as do original works of art done entirely by hand, including paintings, drawings, and sculptures.

You may also mail or ship packages home duty-free: up to $200 worth of goods for personal use, with a limit of one parcel per addressee per day (except alcohol or tobacco products or perfume worth more than $5); label the package PERSONAL USE and attach a list of its contents and their retail value. Do not label the package UNSOLICITED GIFT or your duty-free exemption will drop to $100. Mailed items do not affect your duty-free allowance on your return.

➤ INFORMATION: **U.S. Customs Service** (✉ 1300 Pennsylvania Ave. NW, Washington, DC 20229, WEB www. customs.gov; inquiries ☎ 202/354–1000; complaints c/o ✉ 1300 Pennsylvania Ave. NW, Room 5.4D, Washington, DC 20229; registration of equipment c/o Office of Passenger Programs, ☎ 202/927–0530).

DINING

The stereotypical notion of British meals as an unvarying parade of roast beef, overcooked vegetables, and stodgy puddings is gradually being replaced—particularly in London—with a more contemporary picture of Britain as hot "foodie" territory. From the new breed of "gastro-pubs" to the oh-so-hip, see-and-be-seen dining shrines, Britain is shedding its tired image and becoming one of the most global palates on earth.

The restaurants we review in this book are the cream of the crop in each price category. Properties indicated by ✕☰ are lodging establishments whose restaurant warrants a special trip. Price-category information is given in each chapter. In general, restaurant prices are high. If you're watching your budget, **seek out pubs and ethnic restaurants,** which offer excellent food at reasonable prices.

MEALS & SPECIALTIES

Local cafés serving the traditional English breakfast of eggs, bacon, beans, half a grilled tomato, and strong tea are often the cheapest—and best—places for breakfast. For lighter morning fare (or for real brewed coffee), try the Continental-style sandwich bars offering croissants and other pastries.

At lunch, you can grab a burger between sights, pop into the local pub, or sit down in a proper restaurant. Dinner, too, has no set rules, but a three-course meal is standard in most mid-range or high-end restaurants. Pre- or post-theater menus, offering two courses for a set price, are usually a good value.

Note that when "pubbing," most pubs do not have any wait staff and you are expected to go to the bar and order a beverage and your meal—this can be particularly disconcerting when you are seated in a "restaurant" upstairs, but still expected to go downstairs and get your own drinks and food.

These days, especially in London, "local" could mean nearly any global flavor, but for pure Britishness, a traditional roast beef dinner still tops the list. Its typical accompaniment is Yorkshire pudding—a savory soufflé-like batter of eggs, milk, and flour oven-baked until crisp, then topped with a rich dark gravy. Shepherd's pie, a classic pub dish, is made with diced or minced lamb and a mashed potato topping. In the pubs, you'll also find a ploughman's lunch—crusty bread, English cheese (perhaps cheddar, blue Stilton, crumbly Cheshire, or smooth red Leicester), and pickles. And of course, there's also fish and chips, usually made from cod or haddock deep-fried in a crispy batter and served with thick "chips"—what Americans know as French fries. Be sure to take time for tea—whether with scones (with cream and jam) or cucumber sandwiches, it's still a most civilized respite.

You can eat your way around the country seeking out regional food specialties. Every region has its own cheese, beer, cake, and candy—from the crumbly, sharp cheeses of the Yorkshire and Derbyshire dales to the hard cheddars of Somerset, the creamy goats' rounds in Wales, and the nutty Cornish yarg. In Devon and Cornwall, look for tooth-tingling fudge and toffee made with rich clotted cream.

MEALTIMES

Breakfast is generally served between 7:30 and 9 and lunch between noon and 2. Tea—often a meal in itself—is taken between 4 and 5:30, dinner or supper between 7:30 and 9:30, sometimes earlier, seldom later except in large cities. High tea, at about 6, replaces dinner in some areas like the north, where lunch is always called dinner.

Unless otherwise noted, the restaurants listed in this guide are open daily for lunch and dinner.

PAYING

Be sure that you **don't double pay a service charge.** Many restaurants exclude service charges from the printed menu (which the law obliges them to display outside), then add 10%–15% to the check, or else stamp SERVICE NOT INCLUDED along the bottom, in which case you should add the 10%–15% yourself. Just don't

pay twice for service—some restaurateurs have been known to add service, but leave the total on the credit card slip blank. Larger establishments generally accept major credit cards; pubs, small cafés, or ethnic restaurants may be cash-only.

RESERVATIONS & DRESS

Reservations are always a good idea: we mention them only when they're essential or not accepted. Book as far ahead as you can, and reconfirm as soon as you arrive. We mention dress only when men are required to wear a jacket or a jacket and tie.

WINE, BEER & SPIRITS

Traditional beer is not the golden-colored designer stuff in fancy bottles served in trendy cafés. Although there are hundreds of varieties brewed around the country, the traditional brew is known as "bitters." Lighter American-style beer is called "lager" in Britain, and the black brew is called "stout" (with Guinness the major brand). You may also find traditional "hard" cider made from pressed apples, which tastes refreshing but still can pack an alcoholic punch. If you're a wine aficionado, you'll generally find the selection and quality higher in a wine bar or café, rather than in a traditional pub. Pub opening hours are 11–11, with last orders called about 20 minutes before closing time. The legal drinking age is 18; unless there's a special family room or a beer garden, children are not welcome in pubs.

DISABILITIES & ACCESSIBILITY

Compared with the United States, Great Britain has a ways to go in helping people with disabilities, but is making strides in making its major cities more accessible. In London, for instance, most Underground (subway) stations have vast escalators and steps, but contact the London Transport information line for their booklet "Access to the Underground," which gives facts about elevators and ramps at individual tube stations. The grand, regal London Black Cabs are perfectly accommodating in their spacious interiors for people in wheelchairs, and further good news is that many London hotels have wheelchair ramps. The London Tourist Board also produces an updated newsletter, *London for All,* available from Tourist Information Centres. Note that the British Tourist Authority and the London Tourist Board will provide lists of London hotels for people with disabilities; these hotels often post the sign H at their door to welcome such travelers.

Artsline provides information on the accessibility of arts venues (theaters and cinemas) and events. For holiday bookings and special deals on equipped hotel rooms, contact Holiday Care Service. RADAR, or the Royal Association for Disability and Rehabilitation, is command central for travel information and advice on accommodations throughout the British Isles and Europe. Tripscope covers the ground on all transport questions.

➤ LOCAL RESOURCES: **Artsline** (☎ 020/7388–2227). **Holiday Care Service** (✉ Imperial Bldg., Victoria Rd., Horley, Surrey RH6 7PZ, ☎ 01293/774535). **London Transport's Unit for Disabled Passengers** (✉ 172 Buckingham Palace Rd., London SW1W 9TN, ☎ 020/7918–3312, FAX 020/7918–3876, WEB www.londontransport.co.uk). **RADAR** (✉ 12 City Forum, 250 City Rd., London, EC1, ☎ 020/7250–3222). **Tripscope** (☎ 020/8580–7021).

LODGING

If you book directly through Holiday Care, rates at some hotels with special facilities for visitors with disabilities can be discounted.

RESERVATIONS

When discussing accessibility with an operator or reservations agent, **ask hard questions.** Are there any stairs, inside *or* out? Are there grab bars next to the toilet *and* in the shower/tub? How wide is the doorway to the room? To the bathroom? For the most extensive facilities meeting the latest legal specifications, **opt for newer accommodations.**

SIGHTS & ATTRACTIONS

The London Tourist Board can provide information on city attractions with accessible facilities. It is best to phone ahead to check on the details of different venues around Britain. Alternatively, you could put yourself

in the hands of a tour company such as Tour Guides Ltd.; they not only tailor custom tours, but also have a dynamic Blue Badge guide who is a wheelchair user.

➤ LOCAL RESOURCES: **Tour Guides Ltd.** (☎ 020/7495–5504).

TRANSPORTATION

➤ COMPLAINTS: **Aviation Consumer Protection Division** (☞ Air Travel, *above*) for airline-related problems. **Civil Rights Office** (✉ U.S. Department of Transportation, Departmental Office of Civil Rights, S-30, 400 7th St. SW, Room 10215, Washington, DC 20590, ☎ 202/366–4648, FAX 202/366–9371, WEB www.dot.gov/ost/docr/index.htm) for problems with surface transportation. **Disability Rights Section** (✉ U.S. Department of Justice, Civil Rights Division, Box 66738, Washington, DC 20035-6738, ☎ 202/514–0301 or 800/514–0301; 202/514–0383 TTY; 800/514–0383 TTY, FAX 202/307–1198, WEB www.usdoj.gov/crt/ada/adahom1.htm) for general complaints.

TRAVEL AGENCIES

In the United States, the Americans with Disabilities Act requires that travel firms serve the needs of all travelers. Some agencies specialize in working with people with disabilities.

➤ TRAVELERS WITH MOBILITY PROBLEMS: **Access Adventures** (✉ 206 Chestnut Ridge Rd., Scottsville, NY 14624, ☎ 716/889–9096, dltravel@prodigy.net), run by a former physical-rehabilitation counselor. **CareVacations** (✉ No. 5, 5110–50 Ave., Leduc, Alberta T9E 6V4, Canada, ☎ 780/986–6404 or 877/478–7827, FAX 780/986–8332, WEB www.carevacations.com), for group tours and cruise vacations. **Flying Wheels Travel** (✉ 143 W. Bridge St., Box 382, Owatonna, MN 55060, ☎ 507/451–5005 or 800/535–6790, FAX 507/451–1685, WEB www.flyingwheelstravel.com).

➤ TRAVELERS WITH DEVELOPMENTAL DISABILITIES: **New Directions** (✉ 5276 Hollister Ave., Suite 207, Santa Barbara, CA 93111, ☎ 805/967–2841 or 888/967–2841, FAX 805/964–7344, WEB www.newdirectionstravel.com).

DISCOUNTS & DEALS

Be a smart shopper and **compare all your options** before making decisions. A plane ticket bought with a promotional coupon from travel clubs, coupon books, and direct-mail offers or on the Internet may not be cheaper than the least expensive fare from a discount ticket agency. And always keep in mind that what you get is just as important as what you save.

DISCOUNT PASSES

If you plan to visit castles, gardens, and historic houses during your stay in Britain, **look into discount passes or organization memberships** that can provide significant savings. Some passes, including the British Tourist Authority's Great British Heritage pass and English Heritage's Overseas Visitor pass, are for specific amounts of time from a week to a month; memberships in organizations such as the National Trust, English Heritage, and the Historic Houses Association are generally annual. The British Tourist Authority Web site (☞ Visitor Information, *below*) has information about these and other kinds of discounts. In all cases, be sure to **match what the pass or membership offers against your itinerary**; you may or may not be visiting enough places to make it worthwhile. For London Pass information, *see* London A to Z *in* Chapter 1.

DISCOUNT RESERVATIONS

To save money, **look into discount reservations services** with toll-free numbers, which use their buying power to get a better price on hotels, airline tickets, even car rentals. When booking a room, always **call the hotel's local toll-free number** (if one is available) rather than the central reservations number—you'll often get a better price. Always ask about special packages or corporate rates.

When shopping for the best deal on hotels and car rentals, **look for guaranteed exchange rates,** which protect you against a falling dollar. With your rate locked in, you won't pay more, even if the price goes up in the local currency.

➤ AIRLINE TICKETS: ☎ 800/FLY–ASAP.

➤ HOTEL ROOMS: **Hotel Reservations Network** (☎ 800/964–6835, WEB www.hoteldiscount.com). **International Marketing & Travel Concepts** (☎ 800/790–4682, imtc@mindspring.com). **Players Express Vacations** (☎ 800/458–6161, WEB www.playersexpress.com). **Steigenberger Reservation Service** (☎ 800/223–5652, WEB www.srs-worldhotels.com). **Travel Interlink** (☎ 800/888–5898, WEB www.travelinterlink.com). **Turbotrip.com** (☎ 800/473–7829, WEB www.turbotrip.com).

PACKAGE DEALS

Don't confuse packages and guided tours. When you buy a package, you travel on your own, just as though you had planned the trip yourself. Fly/drive packages, which combine airfare and car rental, are often a good deal. If you **buy a rail/drive pass,** you may save on train tickets and car rentals. All Eurail- and Europass holders get a discount on Eurostar fares through the Channel Tunnel.

ELECTRICITY

To use electric-powered equipment purchased in the U.S. or Canada, **bring a converter and adapter.** The electrical current in Great Britain is 230 volts (in line with the rest of Europe), 50 cycles alternating current (AC); wall outlets take three-pin plugs, and shaver sockets take two round, oversize prongs.

If your appliances are dual-voltage, you'll need only an adapter. Don't use 110-volt outlets marked FOR SHAVERS ONLY for high-wattage appliances such as blow-dryers. Most laptops operate equally well on 110 and 220 volts and so require only an adapter. For converters, adapters, and advice, contact the British Airways Travel Shop.

➤ CONTACTS: **British Airways Travel Shop** (✉ 156 Regent St., W1, ☎ 020/7434–4725).

EMBASSIES

➤ AUSTRALIA: **Australia House** (✉ Strand, London WC2, ☎ 020/7379–4334).

➤ CANADA: **MacDonald House** (✉ 1 Grosvenor Sq., London W1, ☎ 020/7258–6600).

➤ NEW ZEALAND: **New Zealand House** (✉ 80 Haymarket, London SW1, ☎ 020/7930–8422).

➤ UNITED STATES: **American Embassy** (✉ 24 Grosvenor Sq., London W1, ☎ 020/7499–9000); for passports, go to the **U.S. Passport Unit** (✉ 55 Upper Brook St., London W1, ☎ 020/7499–9000).

EMERGENCIES

If you need to report a theft or an attack, go to the nearest police station, listed in the Yellow Pages or the local directory. For severe emergencies, dial ☎ 999 for police, fire, or ambulance (be prepared to give the telephone number you're calling from). National Health Service hospitals give free, 24-hour treatment in Accident and Emergency sections, although delays can be an hour or more. Prescriptions are valid only if made out by doctors registered in the U.K. For additional information, *see* the A to Z sections in each regional chapter.

➤ CONTACTS: **Ambulance, fire, police** (☎ 999).

ETIQUETTE & BEHAVIOR

The traditional British reserve is starting to thaw. Particularly with the younger generations, spontaneous displays of delight or displeasure are becoming more commonplace. But in the theater, the opera, and the church, and in other more traditional spots, decorum is still the word. If you're visiting a family home, a simple bouquet of flowers is a welcome gift. If you're invited for a meal, bringing a bottle of wine is appropriate, if you wish, as is some candy for the children—they'll love you for it. Kissing on greeting is still too Continental for most Brits (except among the fashion and media types, who go for two or three air kisses); a warm handshake is just fine. The British can never say please or thank you too often, and to thank a host for hospitality, either a phone call or thank-you card is always appreciated.

BUSINESS ETIQUETTE

Punctuality is of prime importance, so **call ahead if you anticipate a late arrival.** Spouses do not generally attend business dinners, unless specifically invited. If you invite someone to dine, it is usually assumed that you will pick up the tab. However, if you are the visitor, your host may insist on paying.

GAY & LESBIAN TRAVEL

Most major cities (particularly Birmingham, Brighton, Edinburgh, Glasgow, Manchester, and London) have gay communities and social centers. In London, the main gay areas are in the center city—Soho, Old Compton Street, and west to Kensington and Earl's Court. There is a thriving social scene of clubs and cafés; for London event notices, contact Gay's the Word. The *Pink Paper*, available at libraries, large bookstores, and gay bars, and *Time Out* both have comprehensive London listings. The British Tourist Authority has a brochure and Web site for gay and lesbian travelers.

➤ CONTACTS: **British Tourist Authority** (☎ 877/857–2464, WEB www.gaybritain.org). **Gay's the Word** (✉ 66 Marchmont St., WC1, ☎ 020/7278–7654).

➤ GAY- & LESBIAN-FRIENDLY TRAVEL AGENCIES: **Different Roads Travel** (✉ 8383 Wilshire Blvd., Suite 902, Beverly Hills, CA 90211, ☎ 323/651–5557 or 800/429–8747, FAX 323/651–3678, lgernert@tzell.com). **Kennedy Travel** (✉ 314 Jericho Turnpike, Floral Park, NY 11001, ☎ 516/352–4888 or 800/237–7433, FAX 516/354–8849, WEB www.kennedytravel.com). **Now Voyager** (✉ 4406 18th St., San Francisco, CA 94114, ☎ 415/626–1169 or 800/255–6951, FAX 415/626–8626, WEB www.nowvoyager.com). **Skylink Travel and Tour** (✉ 1006 Mendocino Ave., Santa Rosa, CA 95401, ☎ 707/546–9888 or 800/225–5759, FAX 707/546–9891, WEB www.skylinktravel.com), serving lesbian travelers.

GUIDEBOOKS

Plan well and you won't be sorry. Guidebooks are excellent tools—and you can take them with you. You may want to check out the comprehensive *Fodor's London*; color-photo-illustrated *Fodor's Exploring Britain* and *Exploring London,* thorough on